Lecture Notes in Artificial Intelligence 1886

Subseries of Lecture Notes in Computer Science
Edited by J. G. Carbonell and J. Siekmann

Lecture Notes in Computer Science
Edited by G. Goos, J. Hartmanis and J. van Leeuwen

Springer
*Berlin
Heidelberg
New York
Barcelona
Hong Kong
London
Milan
Paris
Singapore
Tokyo*

Riichiro Mizoguchi   John Slaney (Eds.)

PRICAI 2000
Topics in
Artificial Intelligence

6th Pacific Rim International Conference
on Artificial Intelligence
Melbourne, Australia, August 28 – September 1, 2000
Proceedings

 Springer

Series Editors

Jaime G. Carbonell, Carnegie Mellon University, Pittsburgh, PA, USA
Jörg Siekmann, University of Saarland, Saarbrücken, Germany

Volume Editors

Riichiro Mizoguchi
Osaka University, Institute of Scientific and Industrial Research
8-1 Mihogaoka, Ibaraki, Osaka, 567-0047, Japan
E-mail: miz@ei.sanken.osaka-u.ac.jp

John Slaney
Australian National University, Computer Sciences Laboratory
Research School of Information Sciences and Engineering
Canberra, ACT 0200, Australia
E-mail: jks@arp.anu.edu.au

Cataloging-in-Publication Data applied for

Die Deutsche Bibliothek - CIP-Einheitsaufnahme

Topics in artificial intelligence : proceedings / PRICAI 2000, 6th
Pacific Rim International Conference on Artificial Intelligence,
Melbourne, Australia, August 28 - September 1, 2000. Riichiro
Mizoguchi ; John Stanley (ed.). - Berlin ; Heidelberg ; New York ;
Barcelona ; Hong Kong ; London ; Milan ; Paris ; Singapore ; Tokyo :
Springer, 2000
  (Lecture notes in computer science ; Vol. 1886 : Lecture notes in
  artificial intelligence)
  ISBN 3-540-67925-1

CR Subject Classification (1998): I.2

ISSN 0302-9743
ISBN 3-540-67925-1 Springer-Verlag Berlin Heidelberg New York

This work is subject to copyright. All rights are reserved, whether the whole or part of the material is concerned, specifically the rights of translation, reprinting, re-use of illustrations, recitation, broadcasting, reproduction on microfilms or in any other way, and storage in data banks. Duplication of this publication or parts thereof is permitted only under the provisions of the German Copyright Law of September 9, 1965, in its current version, and permission for use must always be obtained from Springer-Verlag. Violations are liable for prosecution under the German Copyright Law.

Springer-Verlag Berlin Heidelberg New York
a member of BertelsmannSpringer Science+Business Media GmbH
© Springer-Verlag Berlin Heidelberg 2000
Printed in Germany

Typesetting: Camera-ready by author, data conversion by Steingräber Satztechnik GmbH, Heidelberg
Printed on acid-free paper   SPIN 10722476   06/3142   5 4 3 2 1 0

Preface

PRICAI 2000, held in Melbourne, Australia, is the sixth Pacific Rim International Conference on Artificial Intelligence and is the successor to the five earlier PRICAIs held in Nagoya (Japan), Seoul (Korea), Beijing (China), Cairns (Australia) and Singapore in the years 1990, 1992, 1994, 1996 and 1998 respectively.

PRICAI is the leading conference in the Pacific Rim region for the presentation of research in Artificial Intelligence, including its applications to problems of social and economic importance. The objectives of PRICAI are:

To provide a forum for the introduction and discussion of new research results, concepts and technologies;
To provide practising engineers with exposure to and an evaluation of evolving research, tools and practices;
To provide the research community with exposure to the problems of practical applications of AI; and
To encourage the exchange of AI technologies and experience within the Pacific Rim countries.

PRICAI 2000 is a memorial event in the sense that it is the last one in the 20th century. It reflects what researchers in this region believe to be promising for their future AI research activities. In fact, some salient features can be seen in the papers accepted. We have 12 papers on agents, while PRICAI 96 and 98 had no more than two or three. This suggests to us one of the directions in which AI research is going in the next century. It is true that agent research provides us with a wide range of research subjects from basic ones to applications. In contrast, the number of papers on knowledge discovery and data mining is not increasing, though this may be because a new conference, PAKDD, was established in 1997. We have a good number of papers on basic AI and see steady activity on that topic in our region. Compared to the theoretical papers, we have had a smaller number of application- or system-oriented papers in the past two conferences. However, we can find a new movement in AI applications to Web technology on which we have 4 papers this year. This also suggests a promising direction to pursue.

The technical program comprised two days of workshops and tutorials, followed by paper and poster sessions and invited plenary lectures. We had five invited speakers: Nick Jennings, Shun-ichi Amari, Randy Goebel, Qiang Yang and Jae Kyu Lee. Their topics included Agents, Brain science, Knowledge representation, Search on the Internet and AI in electronic commerce. These talks nicely reflect the themes of the contributed technical papers and provoked interesting discussion.

There were 207 submissions from 25 countries. The program committee worked hard to ensure that the conference would be of high quality and that every paper was seen by at least two and in most cases three expert reviewers.

The overall standard of submitted papers was high, and owing to space and time constraints several interesting papers could not be accepted for full presentation and publication. As a result, in addition to the 72 full papers in this volume, the conference made a feature of 44 poster presentations, abstracts of which can also be found in these proceedings.

We have many people to thank, starting with the members of the program committee and the many reviewers who worked hard to get more than 200 papers carefully reviewed under quite severe time constraints. The conference chair Geoff Webb, the organising chair Chengqi Zhang and the rest of their committees deserve our grateful thanks and are duly acknowledged below. Finally, we wish to thank administrative assistant Diane Kossatz and program committee member Sylvie Thiébaux without whose help in the practical matter of dealing with the submitted papers, and in the latter case in the process of allocating them to reviewers, the technical program of PRICAI 2000 would not have existed.

August 2000

Riichiro Mizoguchi and John Slaney
Program Co-chairs
PRICAI 2000

Organization

PRICAI 2000 was organized by the department of Computer Science, Deakin Univeristy, and held at the Melbourne Convention Centre from 28 August to 1 September, 2000. It was co-located with RoboCup 2000 and with two other conferences: the Symposium on the Application of Artificial Intelligence in Industry and the Australian Conference on Robotics and Automation (ACRA 2000).

Conference Committee

Conference Chair: Geoff Webb (Deakin University, Australia)
Program Chairs: Riichiro Mizoguchi (Osaka University, Japan)
                  John Slaney (Australian National University)
Organizing Chair: Chengqi Zhang (Deakin University)
Treasurer: Douglas Newlands (Deakin University)
Publicity Chair: Achim Hoffmann (University of New South Wales, Australia)
Workshop Chair: Huan Liu (National University of Singapore)
Tutorial Chair: Eric Tsui (CSC)

Program Committee

Edward Altman
Sung-Bae Cho
John Debenham
Norman Foo
Scott Goodwin
Jieh Hsiang
Mitsuru Ishizuka
David Israel
Shyam Kapur
Shigenobu Kobayashi
Alfred Kobsa
Jae Kyu Lee
Dayou Liu
H Lee-Kwang
Hing Yan Lee
Chee-Kit Looi
Yuji Matsumoto

Satoru Miyano
Riichiro Mizoguchi
Hideyuki Nakashima
Fred Popowich
Ramakoti Sadananda
M Sasikumar
Zhongzhi Shi
John Slaney
Keith Stenning
Leon Sterling
Sylvie Thiébaux
Benjamin Watson
Albert Wu
Takahira Yamaguchi
Wai-kiang Yeap
Alex Zelinsky
Ingrid Zukerman

Referees

Jun Arima
Samer Abdallah
Akinori Abe
Tamas Abraham
Sushil Acharya
Mark Ackerman
Jing-jun Ai
David Albrecht
Ayman Ammoura
Elisabeth Andre
K.S.R. Anjaneyulu
Grigoris Antoniou
Hiroki Arimura
Laura Arns
Minoru Asada
Hideki Asoh
Noboru Babaguchi
Hideo Bannai
Caroline Barriere
Anup Basu
Jonathan Baxter
Bettina Berendt
Jean Berger
Walter F. Bischof
Yngvi Bjornsson
Natashia Boland
Maria Paola Bonacina
Paul Brna
Bhavesh M. Busa
Terry Caelli
Sandra Carberry
Alison Cawsey
Javaan Chahl
François Charpillet
Shiva Chaudhuri
Gordon Cheng
Lee-Feng Chien
Paul Chung
Carolina Cruz-Neira
Jirapun Daengdej
Kerstin Dautenhahn
Arnaud Delhay
Yasuharu Den
Gamini Dissanayake

Alan Dorin
Fadi Dornaika
Norberto Eiji Nawa
Dan Fass
Matthias Fuchs
Xiaoying Gao
Chris Gaskett
Hector Geffner
Ian Gent
David Gerhard
S.B. Goschnick
Simon Goss
R. Greiner
Tom Gross
Yan Guo
Corin Gurr
Eli Hagen
Masateru Harao
Michael Hareries
Clint Heinze
Steve Helmreich
Achim Hoffmann
Eric Horvitz
Guan Shieng Huang
Mitsuru Ikeda
Katsumi Inoue
Kentaro Inui
Alka Irani
Koji Iwanuma
Noriaki Izumi
Anthony Jameson
Ray Jarvis
M.E. Jefferies
Su Jian
Wenpin Jiao
Xu Jinhui
Julia Johnson
Arne Jönsson
Jean-Pierre Jouannaud
Soonchul Jung
Hitoshi Kanoh
Kamran Karimi
S. Karthik
Akihiro Kashihara

Susumu Katayama
Hirofumi Katsuno
Concepcion L. Khan
Philip Kilby
Jonathan Kilgour
Young-il Kim
Hajime Kimura
Hajime Kita
Yasuhiko Kitamura
Les Kitchen
Lindsay Kleeman
Kevin Knight
Alistair Knott
Jürgen Könemann
Sven Koenig
Kevin Korb
Benjamin Korvemaker
Miyuki Koshimura
Sarit Kraus
Frederick Kroon
C. Indira Kumari
Wa Labuschagne
Chris Leckie
Seungsoo Lee
Wee Kheng Leow
Neal Lesh
James C. Lester
Yuefeng Li
Churn-Jung Liau
Tan Chew Lim
Huan Liu
James Liu
Yaxin Liu
John Lloyd
Wong Lung Hsiang
Xudong Luo
Guangwei Ma
Cara MacNish
Raj Madhavan
Victor Marek
Tomoko Matsui
Satoshi Matsumoto
Hiroshi Matsuno
Yutaka Matsuo

Brendan McCane
Jon McCormack
Eric McCreath
Paul McFetridge
Jean McKendree
Vibhu Mittal
Takashi Miyata
Kazuteru Miyazaki
Philippe Mulhem
Shigeru Muraki
Sivakumar Nagarajan
Masaaki Nagata
Akira Namatame
Kanlaya Naruedomkul
Monty Newborn
Katsumi Nitta
Emma Norling
Nasser Noroozi
Kevin Novins
Jon Oberlander
Tsukasa Ogasawara
Miho Ohsaki
Yukio Ohsawa
Takashi Okada
Manabu Okumura
Patrick Olivier
Isao Ono
Mehmet Orgun
Ji-hong OuYang
Dan-tong Ouyang
Mandar Padhye
Maurice Pagnucco
Wanlin Pang
Seihwan Park
Simon Parsons
S.C. Patodi
Adrian Pearce
P. Ravi Prakash
Wanda Pratt
Helmut Prendinger
Wolfgang Prinz
Teodor C. Przymusinski

F. van Raamsdonk
Kanagasabai Rajaraman
Arthur Ramer
Durgesh Rao
M.R.K. Krishna Rao
Bhavani Raskutti
Magnus Rattray
Terry Regier
Fiorella de Rosis
Sebastien Rougeaux
Holly Rushmeier
Michael Rusinowitch
R.A. Russell
Chiaki Sakama
Claude Sammut
K. Samudravijaya
Taisuke Sato
Yoichi Sato
Ken Satoh
Jonathan Schaeffer
Richard Segal
Yeon-Gyu Seo
Shinichi Shimozono
Ayumi Shinohara
Ye Shiwei
Alexander Sigel
Zoltan Somogyi
Liz Sonenberg
Von-Wun Soo
Takahiro Sugiyama
Ji-Gui Sun
Jiping Sun
Erkki Sutinen
Einoshin Suzuki
Hirokazu Taki
Hai-Ying Tang
Tan Boon Tee
Michael Thielscher
Takenobu Tokunaga
Simon Thompson
John Thornton
Qijia Tian

Gordon Tisher
Janine Toole
Eric Tsang
Shusaku Tsumoto
Hsieh-Chang Tu
Cristina Urdiales
Olivier de Vel
Oleg Veryovka
Toby Walsh
Fei Wang
Song-Xin Wang
Xizhao Wang
Takashi Washio
Zhang Wei
Kay C. Wiese
David E. Wilkins
Richard Willgoss
Sartra Wongthanavasu
Vilas Wuwongse
Gordon Wyeth
Toru Yamaguchi
Masayuki Yamamura
Susumu Yamasaki
David Yarowsky
Tralvex Yeap
Naoki Yonezaki
Soe-Tsyr Yuan
Osmar R. Zaiane
Byoung-Tak Zhang
Chengqi Zhang
Dongmo Zhang
Hong Zhang
Jianping Zhang
Wei Zhang
Zili Zhang
Qiangfu Zhao
Jackson Y.S. Zhu
Kenny Zhu
Yanqiu Zhu
Cao Zining

Sponsors

Deakin University, Geelong, Australia

Mindbox Inc., Greenbrae, California, USA

Cooperative Research Centre for Distributed Systems Technology, Brisbane-Sydney-Melbourne, Australia

University of Melbourne, Australia

Griffith University, Brisbane, Australia

Table of Contents

Invited Talks

Automated Haggling: Building Artificial Negotiators 1
   N. Jennings

Information Geometry of Neural Networks 2
   S.-i. Amari

Knowledge Representation, Belief Revision, and the Challenge of Optimality   3
   R. Goebel

Artificial Intelligence Applications in Electronic Commerce 4
   J.K. Lee

Towards a Next-Generation Search Engine 5
   Q. Yang, H.-F. Wang, J.-R. Wen, G. Zhang, Y. Lu, K.-F. Lee,
   H.-J. Zhang

Logic and Foundations of AI

The Gap between Symbol and Non-symbol Processing –
An Attempt to Represent a Database by Predicate Formulae 16
   S. Ohsuga

Argumentation Semantics for Defeasible Logics 27
   G. Governatori, M.J. Maher, G. Antoniou, D. Billington

A Unifying Semantics for Causal Ramifications 38
   M. Prokopenko, M. Pagnucco, P. Peppas, A. Nayak

Inconsistency and Preservation 50
   P. Wong

Induction and Logic Programming

Inductive Inference of Chess Player Strategy 61
   A.R. Jansen, D.L. Dowe, G.E. Farr

Compiling Logical Features into Specialized State-Evaluators
by Partial Evaluation, Boolean Tables and Incremental Calculation 72
   T. Kaneko, K. Yamaguchi, S. Kawai

Using Domain Knowledge in ILP to Discover Protein Functional Models .. 83
   T. Ishikawa, M. Numao, T. Terano

The Hyper System: Knowledge Reformation
for Efficient First-Order Hypothetical Reasoning 93
  H. Prendinger, M. Ishizuka, T. Yamamoto

Determination of General Concept in Learning Default Rules 104
  K. Ohara, H. Taka, N. Babaguchi, T. Kitahashi

Reinforcement Learning

A Theory of Profit Sharing in Dynamic Environment 115
  S. Kato, H. Matsuo

Experience-Based Reinforcement Learning to Acquire Effective Behavior
in a Multi-agent Domain 125
  S. Arai, K. Sycara, T.R. Payne

A Region Selecting Method Which Performs Observation and Action
in the Multi-resolution Environment. 136
  T. Matsui, H. Matsuo, A. Iwata

Machine Learning

RWS (Random Walk Splitting): A Random Walk Based Discretization
of Continuous Attributes 146
  M. Hanaoka, M. Kobayashi, H. Yamazaki

The Lumberjack Algorithm for Learning Linked Decision Forests 156
  W.T.B. Uther, M.M. Veloso

Efficient Iris Recognition System by Optimization
of Feature Vectors and Classifier 167
  S. Lim, K. Lee, O. Byeon, T. Kim

A Classifier Fitness Measure Based on Bayesian Likelihoods:
An Approach to the Problem of Learning from Positives Only 177
  A. Skabar, A. Maeder, B. Pham

Evaluating Noise Correction 188
  C.M. Teng

An Efficient Learning Algorithm Using Natural Gradient
and Second Order Information of Error Surface 199
  H. Park, K. Fukumizu, S.-i. Amari, Y. Lee

Knowledge Discovery

Fast and Robust General Purpose Clustering Algorithms 208
  V. Estivill-Castro, J. Yang

An Algorithm for Checking Dependencies of Attributes in a Table
with Non-deterministic Information: A Rough Sets Based Approach 219
   H. Sakai, A. Okuma

Tropical Cyclone Intensity Forecasting Model:
Balancing Complexity and Goodness of Fit............................ 230
   G.W. Rumantir

Bayesian Networks

Trading Off Granularity against Complexity
in Predictive Models for Complex Domains............................ 241
   I. Zukerman, D.W. Albrecht, A.E. Nicholson, K. Doktor

Recognizing Intentions from Rejoinders
in a Bayesian Interactive Argumentation System 252
   I. Zukerman, N. Jitnah, R. McConachy, S. George

Efficient Inference in Dynamic Belief Networks
with Variable Temporal Resolution 264
   T.A. Wilkin, A.E. Nicholson

Beliefs and Intentions in Agents

Epistemic States Guiding the Rational Dynamics of Information 275
   J. Heidema, I.C. Burger

Merging Epistemic States 286
   T. Meyer

Perceiving Environments for Intelligent Agents 297
   Y. Li, C. Zhang

A Preference-Based Theory of Intention............................... 308
   T. Sugimoto

Autonomous Agents

Autonomy of Autonomous Agents....................................... 318
   D. Zhang, N. Foo

Constructing an Autonomous Agent with an Interdependent Heuristics ... 329
   K. Moriyama, M. Numao

Unified Criterion of State Generalization for Reactive Autonomous Agents 340
   T. Yairi, K. Hori, S. Nakasuka

From Brain Theory to Autonomous Robotic Agents 351
   A. Weitzenfeld

Agent Systems

A Multi-agent Approach for Optical Inspection Technology 362
  T. Buchheim, G. Hetzel, G. Kindermann, P. Levi

The Use of Mobile Agents in Tracing an Intruder in a Local Area Network 373
  M. Asaka, T. Onabuta, T. Inoue, S. Goto

A Framework to Model Multiple Environments in Multiagent Systems 383
  J.-C. Soulié, P. Marcenac

Task Models, Intentions, and Agent Conversation Policies 394
  R. Elio, A. Haddadi, A. Singh

Genetic Algorithms

Genetic Algorithm with Knowledge-Based Encoding
for Interactive Fashion Design 404
  H.-S. Kim, S.-B. Cho

Designing Wastewater Collection Systems Using Genetic Algorithms 415
  L.Y. Liang, R.G. Thompson, D.M. Young

Hybrid Genetic Algorithms Are Better for Spatial Clustering 424
  V. Estivill-Castro

Genetic Programming

Improving Performance of GP by Adaptive Terminal Selection 435
  S. Ok, K. Miyashita, S. Nishihara

Evolving Neural Networks for Decomposable Problems
Using Genetic Programming 446
  B. Talko, L. Stern, L. Kitchen

Constraint Satisfaction

Dual Encoding Using Constraint Coverings 457
  S. Nagarajan, S.D. Goodwin, A. Sattar

Consistency in General CSPs 469
  W. Pang, S.D. Goodwin

Neural Networks

Need for Optimisation Techniques to Select Neural Network Algorithms
for Process Modelling of Reduction Cell 480
  V. Karri, F. Frost

Productivity Improvements through Prediction of Electrolyte
Temperature in Aluminium Reduction Cell Using BP Neural Network 490
    F. Frost, V. Karri

Pruned Neural Networks for Regression 500
    R. Setiono, W.K. Leow

Optimal Design of Neural Nets Using Hybrid Algorithms................ 510
    A. Abraham, B. Nath

Markov Decision Processes

A POMDP Approximation Algorithm
That Anticipates the Need to Observe 521
    V. Bayer Zubeck, T. Dietterich

Generating Hierarchical Structure in Reinforcement Learning
from State Variables... 533
    B. Hengst

Robotics

Humanoid Active Audition System Improved by the Cover Acoustics 544
    K. Nakadai, H.G. Okuno, H. Kitano

Overcoming the Effects of Sensory Delay by Using a Cerebellar Model 555
    D. Collins, G. Wyeth

Layered Specification of Intelligent Agents 566
    P. Scerri, J. Ydrén, N. Reed

Image Processing and Pattern Recognition

Sub-pixel Precise Edge Localization:
A ML Approach Based on Color Distributions 577
    R. Hanek

Efficient Joint Detection Considering Complexity of Contours 588
    M. Kanoh, S. Kato, H. Itoh

Feature-Based Face Recognition:
Neural Network Using Recognition-by-Recall 599
    W. Zhang, Y. Guo

Segmentation of Connected Handwritten Chinese Characters
Based on Stroke Analysis and Background Thinning.................... 608
    S. Zhao, P. Shi

A Framework of Two-Stage Combination of Multiple Recognizers
for Handwritten Numerals 617
    K. Lee, Y. Lee

Natural Language Processing

Aligning Portuguese and Chinese Parallel Texts Using Confidence Bands .. 627
    A. Ribeiro, G. Lopes, J. Mexia

Interactive Japanese-to-Braille Translation
Using Case-Based Knowledge on the Web 638
    S. Ono, Y. Hamada, Y. Takagi, S. Nishihara, K. Mizuno

Speech and Spoken Language

Psychological Effects Derived from Mimicry Voice
Using Inarticualte Sounds 647
    N. Suzuki, Y. Takeuchi, M. Okada

Statistical Model Based Approach to Spoken Language Acquisition 657
    N. Iwahashi

AI in Web Technology

Discovery of Shared Topics Networks among People – A Simple Approach
to Find Community Knowledge from WWW Bookmarks 668
    H. Takeda, T. Matsuzuka, Y. Taniguchi

Collaborative Filtering with the Simple Bayesian Classifier 679
    K. Miyahara, M.J. Pazzani

Supervised and Unsupervised Learning Algorithms
for Thai Web Pages Identification 690
    B. Kijsirikul, P. Sasiphongpairoege, N. Soonthornphisaj, S. Meknavin

Solving the Personal Computer Configuration Problems
as Discrete Optimization Problems : A Preliminary Report 701
    V. Tam, K.T. Ma

Intelligent Systems

Improved Efficiency of Oil Well Drilling through Case Based Reasoning ... 712
    P. Skalle, J. Sveen, A. Aamodt

Functional Understanding Based on an Ontology of Functional Concepts .. 723
    Y. Kitamura, T. Sano, R. Mizoguchi

Probabilistic Modeling of Alarm Observation Delay in Network Diagnosis . 734
    K. Hashimoto, K. Matsumoto, N. Shiratori

A Diagnosis Function of Arithmetical Word Problems
for Learning by Problem Posing 745
  T. Hirashima, A. Nakano, A. Takeuchi

Combining Kalman Filtering and Markov Localization
in Network-Like Environments....................................... 756
  S. Thiébaux, P. Lamb

AI and Music

Microbes and Music... 767
  F. Soddell, J. Soddell

A Lightweight Multi-agent Musical Beat Tracking System 778
  S. Dixon

Posters

Frame-Structure Logic with Extended Attribute Relations.............. 789
  K. Komatsu, N. Nishihara, S. Yokoyama

Fast Hypothetical Reasoning by Parallel Processing 790
  Y. Matsuo, M. Ishizuka

TURAS: A Personalised Route Planning System 791
  L. McGinty, B. Smyth

Analysis of Phase Transitions in Graph-Coloring Problems
Based on Constraint Structures 792
  K. Mizuno, A. Hayashimoto, S. Nishihara

Minimal Model Generation with Factorization and Constrained Search... 793
  M. Koshimura, M. Kita, R. Hasegawa

Method of Ideal Solution in Fuzzy Set Theory
and Multicriteria Decision Making 794
  G. Beliakov

A New Axiomatic Framework for Prioritized Fuzzy Constraint Satisfaction
Problems 795
  X. Luo, H.-f. Leung, J.H.-m. Lee

Constraint Satisfaction over Shared Multi-set Value Domains 796
  M.J. Sanders

Algorithms for Solving the Ship Berthing Problem 797
  K.S. Goh, A. Lim

Temporal Interval Logic in Data Mining 798
  C.P. Rainsford, J.F. Roddick

Data Mining in Disease Management – A Diabetes Case Study 799
   H. He, H. Koesmarno, T. Van, Z. Huang

A Limited Lattice Structure for Incremental Association Mining 800
   Y. Zhao, J. Shi, P. Shi

Markov Modelling of Simple Directional Features
for Effective and Efficient Handwriting Verification 801
   A. McCabe

Texture Analysis and Classification Using Bottom-Up Tree-Structured
Wavelet Transform 802
   Y. Miyamoto, M.N. Shirazi, K. Uehara

A Stereo Matching Algorithm Using Adaptive Window and Search Range . 803
   H.-S. Koo, C.-S. Jeong

A Design of Rescue Agents for RoboCup-Rescue 804
   M. Ohta, N. Ito, S. Tadokoro, H. Kitano

A Cooperative Architecture to Control Multi-agent Based Robots 805
   M. Becht, R. Lafrenz, N. Oswald, M. Schulé, P. Levi

Automatic Development of Robot Behaviour Using Monte Carlo Methods . 806
   J. Brusey

Adapting Behavior by Inductive Prediction in Soccer Agents 807
   T. Matsui, N. Inuzuka, H. Seki

Computing the Local Space of a Mobile Robot........................ 808
   M.E. Jefferies, W.-K. Yeap, L.I. Smith

Learning Situation Dependent Success Rates of Actions
in a RoboCup Scenario 809
   S. Buck, M. Riedmiller

Cooperative Bidding Mechanisms among Agents
in Multiple Online Auctions 810
   T. Ito, N. Fukuta, R. Yamada, T. Shintani, K. Sycara

Framework of Distributed Simulation System for Multi-agent Environment 811
   I. Noda

Dependence Based Coalitions and Contract Net: A Comparative Analysis . 812
   M. Ito, J.S. Sichman

A Tracer for Debugging Multi-agent System Based on P-Q Signal Method 813
   T. Ozono, T. Shintani

A Multi-agent Approach for Simulating Bushfire Spread 814
 W. Magill, X. Li

Multi-agent Cooperative Reasoning Using Common Knowledge
and Implicit Knowledge... 815
 L. He, Y. Chao, K. Yamada, T. Nakamura, H. Itoh

Life-Like Agent Design Based on Social Interaction 816
 Y. Takeuchi, T. Takahashi, Y. Katagiri

Agent-Oriented Programming in Linear Logic: An Example 817
 A. Al Amin, M. Winikoff, J. Harland

Emotional Intelligence for Intuitive Agents 818
 P. Ray, M. Toleman, D. Lukose

Formalization for the Agent Method by Using π-Calculus 819
 K. Iwata, N. Ito, N. Ishii

Utilization of Coreferences for the Translation of Utterances
Containing Anaphoric Expressions 820
 M. Paul, E. Sumita

Word Alignment Using a Matrix 821
 E. Sumita

Deterministic Japanese Word Segmentation by Decision List Method 822
 H. Shinnou

Criteria to Choose Appropriate Graph-Types 823
 H. Yonezawa, M. Matsushita, T. Kato

A Document Classifier Based on Word Semantic Association 824
 X. Li, J. Liu, Z. Shi

Incorporation of Japanese Information Retrieval Method
Using Dependency Relationship into Probabilistic Retrieval 825
 H. Fujitani, T. Mine, M. Amamiya

A Step Towards Integration of Learning Theories
to Form an Effective Collaborative Learning Group 826
 A. Inaba, T. Supnithi, M. Ikeda, R. Mizoguchi, J. Toyoda

Model-Based Software Requirements Design 827
 T. Aida, S. Ohsuga

Acquiring Factual Knowledge through Ontological Instantiation 828
 H. Shin, S. Koehler

Intrusion Detection by Combining Multiple Hidden Markov Models 829
  J. Choy, S.-B. Cho

Conceptual Classification and Browsing of Internet FAQs
Using Self-Organizing Neural Networks 830
  H.-D. Kim, J.-H. Ahn, S.-B. Cho

The Role of Abduction in Internet-Based Applications 831
  A. Abe

FERRET: An Intelligent Assistant for Internet Searching 832
  J. Zhou, J. Baltes

Author Index 833

Automated Haggling: Building Artificial Negotiators

Nick Jennings

Dept of Electronics and Computer Science
University of Southampton
Southampton SO17 1BJ
nrj@ecs.soton.ac.uk

Abstract. Computer systems in which autonomous software agents negotiate with one another in order to come to mutually acceptable agreements are likely to become pervasive in the next generation of networked systems. In such systems, the agents will be required to participate in a range of negotiation scenarios and exhibit a range of negotiation behaviours (depending on the context). To this end, this talk explores the issues involved in designing and implementating a number of automated negotiators for real-world electronic commerce applications.

Information Geometry of Neural Networks

Shun-ichi Amari

Laboratory for Information Synthesis
Brain-Style Information Systems Research Group
RIKEN Brain Science Institute
2-1, Hirosawa, Saitama 351-0198, Japan
amari@brain.riken.go.jp

Abstract. Japan has launched a big Brain Science Program which includes theoretical foundations of neurocomputing. Mathematical foundation of brain-style computation is one of the main targets of our laboratory in the RIKEN Brain Science Institute. The present talk will introduce the Japanese Brain Science Program, and then give a direction toward mathematical foundation of neurocomputing.

A neural network is specified by a number of real free parameters (connection weights or synaptic efficacies) which are modifiable by learning. The set of all such networks forms a multi-dimensional manifold. In order to understand the total capability of such networks, it is useful to study the intrinsic geometrical structure of the neuromanifold.

When a network is disturbed by noise, its behavior is given by a conditional probability distribution. In such a case, Information Geometry gives a fundamental geometrical structure. We apply information geometry to the set of multi-layer perceptrons. Because it is a Riemannian space, we are naturally lead to the Riemannian or natural gradient learning method, which proves to give a strikingly fast and accurate learning algorithm. The geometry also proves that various types of singularities exist in the manifold, which are not peculiar to neural networks but common to all the hierarchical systems. The singularities give severe influence on learning behaviors. All of these aspects are analyzed mathematically.

Knowledge Representation, Belief Revision, and the Challenge of Optimality

Randy Goebel

Department of Computing Science
University of Alberta
Edmonton, Canada, T6G 2H1
goebel@cs.ualberta.ca

Abstract. The fields of KR and BR are closely related, and abstractly circumscribe the two requirements of articulating and consistently accumulating knowledge. The application to particular problem solving tasks provides further constraints on the articulation and accumulation of knowledge, many of which are complex, conflicting, and difficult to formalize.

Beginning with the idea that belief revision provides the most general framework for accumulating knowledge, we review recent experience in optimization problem solving, where the difficulties include specifying the problem, the objective function for solution, and the knowledge of how to search a large search space.

The experience reveals ideas for a general optizmation problem solving framework, in which belief revision, constraint programming, and heuristic optimzation all work together.

Artificial Intelligence Applications in Electronic Commerce

Jae Kyu Lee

Graduate School of Management
Korea Advanced Institute of Science and Technology
207-43 Cheongryang, Seoul, Korea 130-012
jklee@msd.kaist.ac.kr

Abstract. There are various applications of AI on web-based electronic commerce (EC) environment. However, the application of intelligence in EC is confined by the state-of-the-art of the AI although EC has a high potential of AI deployment. In this talk, we will review the status of AI applications in EC, and a research opportunity for future applications

The key AI technologies applied in EC include agents for search, comparison, and negotiations; search by configuration and salesman expert systems; thesaurus of EC terms; knowledge-based processing of workflow; personalized e-catalog directory management; data mining in customer relationship management; natural language conversation, voice recognition and synthesis, and machine translation.

1. **Agent**: Concerning the agents, we will discuss the trend of XML standard such as ebXML for search, communication, and price negotiation. We will also review the status of learning from the seller and buyer agents' point of view.

2. **Search by configuration**: Most searches seek standard commodities, while many products like electronic goods need to add optional parts to fulfill the required specification. This implies that we need to find a most similar template first, and then to adjust the optional parts that offer the minimum cost.

3. **Thesaurus to aid comparison shopping**: The product specification should be comparable each other whether they are represented in numbers, symbols, and words. To comprehend the specifications for comparison, we need a thesaurus of application domain.

4. **Personalized e-catalog directory management**: A buyer site defines a personalized e-catalog directory out of common standard catalog. The anomalies such as unbalanced directory are defined and automatic remedies are developed.

5. **Other issues like data mining in CRM**, natural language, voice recognition, and machine translation on the web will be demonstrated.

The talk will be ended with the AI research opportunities in EC.

Towards a Next-Generation Search Engine

Qiang Yang[1], Hai-Feng Wang, Ji-Rong Wen, Gao Zhang, Ye Lu[1], Kai-Fu Lee, and Hong-Jiang Zhang

Microsoft Research China
5F, Beijing Sigma Center
No. 49 Zhichun Road, Haidian District
Beijing 100080 P.R. China
(qyang,yel)@cs.sfu.ca, (i-haiwan, i-jrwen, i-gzhang, kfl, hjzhang)@microsoft.com

Abstract. As more information becomes available on the World Wide Web, it has become an acute problem to provide effective search tools for information access. Previous generations of search engines are mainly keyword-based and cannot satisfy many informational needs of their users. Search based on simple keywords returns many irrelevant documents that can easily swamp the user. In this paper, we describe the system architecture of a next-generation search engine that we have built with a goal to provide accurate search result on frequently asked concepts. Our key differentiating factors from other search engines are natural language user interface, accurate search results, and interactive user interface and multimedia content retrieval. We describe the architecture, design goals and experience in developing the search engine.

1 Introduction

With the explosive growth of information on the World Wide Web, there is an acute need for search engine technology to keep pace with the users' need for searching speed and precision. Today's popular search engines such as Yahoo! and MSN.com are used by millions of users each day to find information, but the main method of search has been kept the same as when the first search engine appeared years ago, relying mainly on keyword search. This has resulted in unsatisfactory search results, as a simple keyword may not be able to convey complex search semantics a user wishes to express, returning many irrelevant documents and eventually, disappointed users. The purpose of this paper is to sketch a next-generation search engine, which offers several key features that make it more natural and efficient for users to search the web.

---

[1] The research was conducted while the author was visiting Microsoft Research China, on leave from School of Computing Science, Simon Fraser University, Burnaby BC Canada V5A 1S6

Search has so far experienced two main evolutions. The first is keyword based search engines [4, 11], as is currently the case with the majority of search engines on the web (e.g., Yahoo! and MSN.com). These engines accept a keyword-based query from a user and search in one or more index databases. Despite its simplicity, these engines typically return millions of documents in response to a simple keyword query, which often makes it impossible for a user to find the needed information. In response to this problem, a second generation of search engines is aimed at extracting frequently asked questions (FAQ's) and manually indexes these questions and their answers; the result is adding one level of indirection whereby users are asked to confirm one or more rephrased questions in order to find their answer. A prime example of this style of search engines is Askjeeves.com. An advantage of this style of interaction and cataloging is much higher precision: whereas the keyword based search engines return thousands of results, Askjeeves often gives a few very precise results as answers. It is plausible that this style of FAQ-based search engines will enjoy remarkable success in limited domain applications such as web-based technical support.

While the Askjeeves search engine generates impressive results, its design and architecture are not available for other researchers to experiment with due to its proprietary nature. We felt, however, a pressing need in the search-engine research community to exchange ideas in order to move towards newer-generation search engines. We observe that although FAQ-based second-generation search engines have improved search precision, much remains to be desired. A third-generation search engine will be able to deal with concepts that the user intends to query about, by parsing an input natural language query and extracting syntactic as well as semantic information. The parser should be *robust* in the sense that it will be able to return partial parse results whenever possible, and the results will be more accurate when more information is available. It will have the capability to deal with languages other than English, as, for example, the Chinese language poses additional difficulty in word segmentation and semantic processing. When facing ambiguity, it will interact with the user for confirmation in terms of the concept the user is asking. The query logs are recorded processed repeatedly, for providing a powerful language model for the natural language parser as well as for indexing the frequently asked questions and providing relevance-feedback learning capability.

The basis for our approach is that an important hypothesis we call the ***concept-space coverage hypothesis***: A small subset of concepts can cover most user queries. If this hypothesis is true, then we can simply track this small subset and use semi-automated method to index the concepts precisely – this results in a search engine that satisfies most users most of the times. To support our hypothesis, we took a one-day log from MSN.com query log and manually mapped queries to pre-defined concept categories. In Fig. 1, the horizontal axis represents the 27 predefined categories of concepts or keywords, and the vertical axis is the coverage of all queries under consideration by the corresponding subset of concepts or keywords. Examples of the concepts are: "Finding computer and internet related products and services ", "Finding movies and toys on the Internet" and so on. We took the top 3000 distinct user queries that represent 418,248 queries on Sept 4, 1999 (which we chose arbitrarily), and then classified these queries. The keywords are sorted by frequency, such that the *ith* value on the horizontal axis corresponds to the subset of all *i* previous keywords in the sorted list. As can be seen, both the keyword and the concept distribution obey the pattern that the first few popular categories will cover most of the queries. Furthermore, the concept distribution converges much faster than the keyword distribution as we expect. As an example, 30% of the concepts in fact cover about 80% of all queries in the selected query pool. This preliminary result shows that our hypothesis stands at least for MSN.com query log data. We are currently conducting more experiments to further confirm this hypothesis.

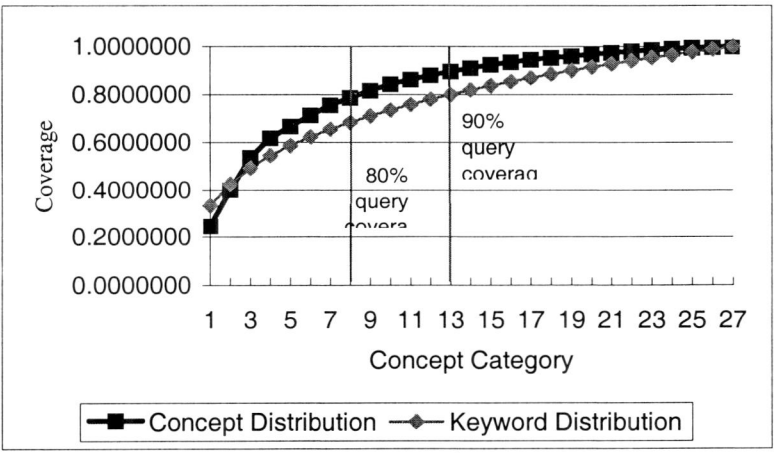

Fig 1. Plotting the query distribution against concept categories

In this paper, we describe our design of a prototype search engine based on FAQ analyses. We show that it is possible to build such search engines based on data mining and natural language processing, as well as well-designed user interfaces. This prototype system, shown in Fig. 2, demonstrates many exciting new opportunities for research in next-generation intelligent computing. We only focus on two main components of the system, the natural language subsystem and the log data mining subsystem, leaving the evaluation of the system to future discussions.

Code-named "***Brilliant***", the search engine has the ability to robustly parse natural languages based on grammatical knowledge obtained through analysis of query log data. In order to assemble answers to questions, it has a methodology to process query logs for the purpose of obtaining new question templates with indexed answers. It also has relevance-feedback capability for improving its indexing and ranking functions. This capability allows the system to record users' actions in browsing and in selecting the search result, so that the ranking of these results and the importance of each selection can be learned over time.

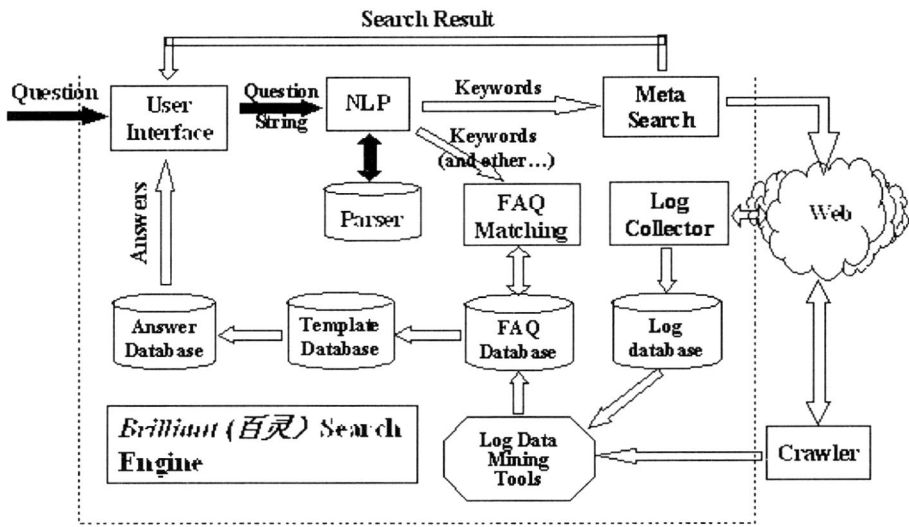

Fig. 2   Brilliant system architecture

2 Natural Language Processing with LEAP

In this section, we first introduce the concept of robust parsing and how to apply it to natural language understanding in search engines. We then describe several challenges of using robust parsing in our search engine design.

2.1 Using Robust Parsing in Search Engine

Spoken language understanding (SLU) researchers have been working on *robust parsing* to handle ill-formed inputs. Usually, a robust parser attempts to overcome the extra-grammaticality by ignoring the un-parsable words and fragments and by conducting a search for the maximal subset of the original input that is covered by the grammar [9, 13]. Natural language understanding share many features with SLU: input sentences are almost always ungrammatical or incomplete. It is difficult to parse such sentences using a traditional natural language parser. One advantage of search engine queries is that they are short – again a feature shared with spoken languages. Therefore we choose a robust parser as our natural language parser in the search engine.

There are several main advantages of robust parsers. First, if an input sentence contains words that are not parsable, a robust parser can skip these words or phrases and still output an incomplete result. In contrast, a traditional parser will either completely break down, or need revision of the grammar rules. Second, if a given sentence is incomplete such that a traditional parser cannot find a suitable rule to match it exactly, robust parsers can provide multiple interpretation of the parsing result and associate with each output a confidence level. In Brilliant™ search engine, this confidence level is built based on statistical training.

LEAP (Language Enabled APplications) is an effort in the speech technology group in Microsoft Research that aims at spoken language understanding [14]. Leap's robust parsing algorithm is an extension of the bottom-up chart-parsing algorithm [1]. The framework of the algorithm is similar to the general chart-parsing algorithm. The differences include: 1) traditional parsers require that a hypothesis h and a partial parse p have to cover adjacent words in the input; in robust parsers this is relaxed. This makes it possible for the parser to omit noisy words in the input. 2) Different hypotheses can result from partial parses by skipping some symbols in parse rules. This allows non-exact matching of a rule.

A LEAP grammar defines *semantic classes*. Each semantic class is defined by a set of rules and productions. For example, we can define a semantic class <Route> for the travel path from one place to another. This class is represented as follows:

```
<Route> TravelPath {
        => @from  <PlaceName:place1> @to  <PlaceName:place2>
    @route;
        @from => from | ...;
        ......
}
<PlaceName> Place {
        Beijing | Shanghai | ...;
}
```

In the semantic classes above, <Route> defines a return class type, and TravelPath is a semantic class that contains a number of rules (the first line) and productions (the second line). In this class, @from must parse a piece of the input sentence according to a production as shown in the second line. The input item after the @from object must match according to <PlaceName> semantic class. If there are input tokens that are not parsable by any parts of the rule, it will be ignored by the parser. In this case, the scoring of the parse result will be correspondingly discounted to reflect a lower level of confidence in the parse result.

Suppose the input query is:

How to go from Beijing to Shanghai?

The LEAP parser will return the following result:

```
<VOID> How to go from place to place
    <Route> How to go from place to place
        <PlaceName:place1> place
        <PlaceName:place2> place
```

Here <VOID> represents the root semantic class. Note that this input query cannot be parsed using the first rule in the semantic class TravelPath completely if we used a traditional parser. In our implementation, we calculated the score of the parsing result by discounting the number of input items and rule items that are skipped during the parsing operation. This value is normalized to give a percentage confidence value.

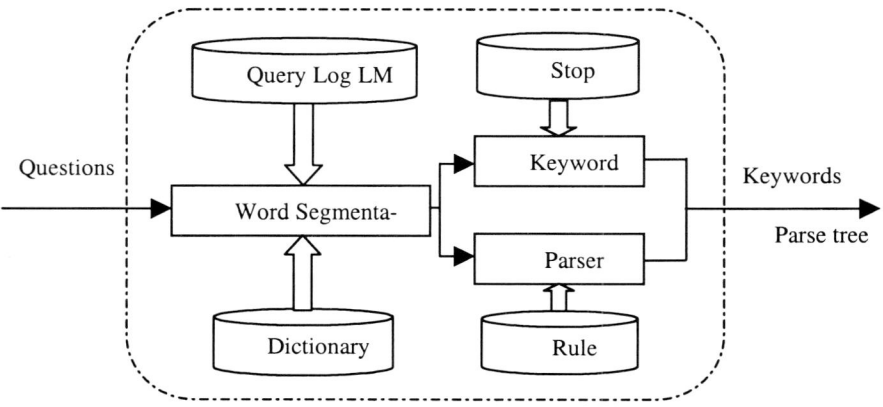

Fig. 3. The flowchart of natural language processing

We have adapted the LEAP system in our search engine using grammar rules trained through query logs. The system architecture is shown in Fig. 3. In this figure, we first perform Chinese word segmentation. The segmented sentence is passed to LEAP next. If LEAP parses the sentence successfully, the module outputs a parse tree. Otherwise keywords will be simply extracted and outputted. The template-matching module of the search engine will be able to use both types of output.

2.2 Evaluate the Parsing Result

In our search engine, we adapt Leap so that it evaluates the output based on the coverage of a rule against the input query. A parsed result will be selected if it covers the most words in the query and the most parts of rules. In order to improve the scoring strategy, we learn probabilities from query logs to include:
   · probabilities of the rules;
   · penalty for robust rule matching (insertion, deletion, substitution);
   · probabilities of "non-matching" words;
   · term probability according to their frequency in query log.

Considering the rule in the semantic class <Route> TravelPath:

                    ☐   @from   <PlaceName:place1>   @to   <PlaceName:place2>
                             @route;

We illustrate how to train the probability values associated with this rule. A rule having a high probability value means that using this rule to parse a query is more reliable. This is similar to PCFG [8]. We can also train the penalty values for robust matching: For an item in either a rule or the query sentence, if the item is skipped during parsing, a penalty will be exacted. In the above rule, if @from is skipped, the penalty can be set relatively low. However, if @route is skipped, the penalty should be high. In the sentence "How to get from Beijing to Shanghai" if "how to go" is skipped, the penalty should be high. In our search engine, penalty and score statistics are gathered using the query log files.

3 Question Matching and Query Log Mining

In this section, we describe the question-matching module. We first describe the question matching process used in the module. We then discuss issues related to obtaining the template and answer databases from the query log data.

3.1 Question Matching Process

The purpose of the question-matching module is to find a set of relevant concepts and their related answers from a given user query. To accomplish this, we set up a collection of FAQ concepts and a mapping from these concepts to answers. These answers can be further compressed by grouping together their similar parameters – the result is what we call templates.

To illustrate this mapping process, we consider a realistic example. Suppose that the user asked "How to go from Beijing to Shanghai?". We store in our FAQ database a collection of concepts indexed on "Route" and "Travel", and possibly other related concepts. We include synonyms to allow a broader coverage of the concepts in the FAQ database in order to increase the recall of matching operation (see the "Concept-FAQ table"). We can achieve a further improvement by including a concept hierarchy to map user queries into a collection of related concepts. The rest of the processing is decomposed into three steps.

Step 1. Mapping from the question space to the concept space

The natural language processing module returns a parse tree that contains a semantic class and its parameters. The LEAP parser returns a concept "Route" as a semantic class. We can use the semantic class "Route" to search the Concept-FAQ table, which can then be used to search the concept-FAQ table. The concept-FAQ table is the core data structure for the whole database. Every FAQ is assigned a FAQ-ID, which is uniquely distinguished from the others. An FAQ is made up of a few concepts that are in fact represented by certain terms such as "Route". Every (*Concept, FAQ ID, Weight*) record denotes that the FAQ is related to the concept with a correlation *Weight* factor, which is learned from a later analysis of the query log file. Every FAQ is related to one or more concepts and every concept is related to one or more FAQ's. Thus there is a many-to-many relationship between FAQ's and concepts. Using the concept-FAQ table, we can compute a correlation factor between a concept set □ (concept$_1$, concept$_2$, …concept$_n$) and a FAQ with ID of x as

$$\sum_{i=1}^{n} Weight(concept_i,\ x).$$

Hence, given a concept set, it is straightforward to obtain the top n best-matched FAQ's.

Step 2. Mapping from the FAQ space to the template space

A template represents a class of *standard* questions. It corresponds to a semantic class in the LEAP module. Every template has one or more parameters with values. Once all the parameters in a template are assigned a value, a standard question is derived from this template. For example, "air flights to *" is a template representing a class of questions about the flight from or to a certain location. Here the wild card "*" denotes that there is a parameter in the template that can be assigned an arbitrary place name. If "Shanghai" is chosen, this template is transformed into a standard question "what are the air flights to Shanghai?". We cannot construct a template for every question since there are many similar questions. We solve this problem by choosing all similar questions and prepare a single template for them. This effectively compresses the FAQ set

Step 3. Mapping from the template space to the answer space

All answers for a template are previously stored in a separate answer table. This answer table is indexed by the parameter values of the template. When a matching is done, the best parameter is calculated and passed to the GUI component to be shown to the user. Every answer is made up of two parts: a URL and its description.

3.2 Query Log Mining

Our system is purely data-driven, where the most important information is derived from the query logs and the World Wide Web. In our current work, we address the following critical questions

a. How to find the frequently asked questions from a large amount of user questions? The challenge here is to address the time-variant nature of the questions, because some questions important today may become unimportant tomorrow.
b. How to find answers for a template automatically or semi-automatically?
c. How to determine the weights between concepts and FAQ's, and between FAQ's and templates?

Our system for query log mining consists of statistical query co-occurrence analysis, clustering and classification analyses. In our experience, we have found these tools to offer the search engine index maintainer very effective help in keeping the FAQ and template databases up to date.

4 User Interface

Fig. 4 and 5 show the process in which users ask natural language queries. Much research has shown that natural language is more powerful in expressing user's intention than keywords. Users usually have difficulty in formulating good searching keywords even when they have clear ideas about what they need [12].

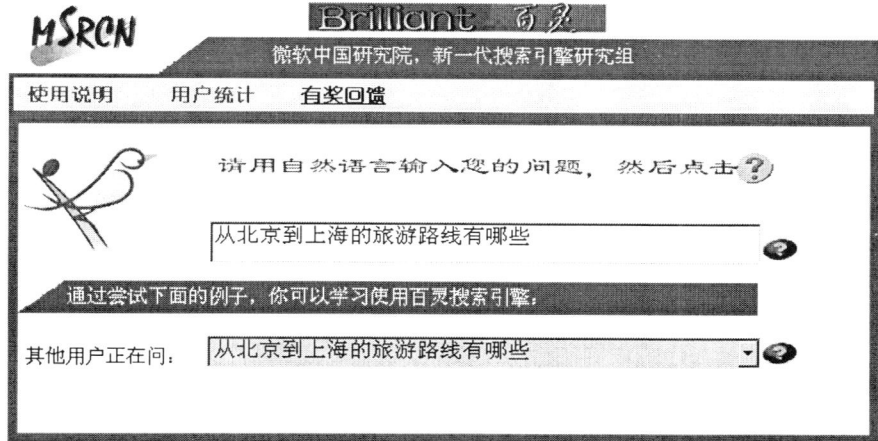

Fig. 4. Using natural language to ask queries in Brilliant ™ search engine.

Research has established that natural language is a powerful tool for expressing the user intention [15], where the most important parts of a query are known as *core phrases*. For example, two typical queries in the traveling domain search are:

How many <u>routes</u> are there <u>from</u> (Beijing) <u>to</u> (Shanghai)?

Please tell me about <u>famous sights</u> to visit in (Beijing)?

In these queries, the underlined words are core phrases, the parenthesized words are keywords, and the remaining words are redundant words. However, sometimes it is impossible to identify users' intention from the original query alone. In this case we can select all possibly relevant concept templates and ask the user to confirm.

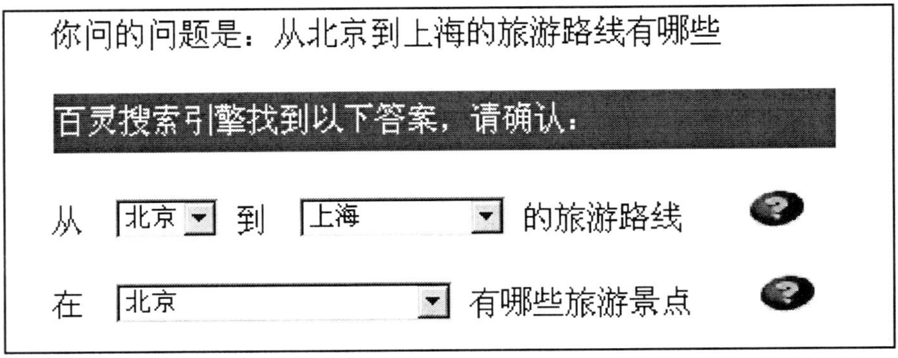

Fig. 5. Use Parameterized search results to asked back

In our user interface design, we clustered related concepts according to their similarity and treated the different parts of the result as parameters. For example, as shown in Fig. 5, the two similar search results ("famous sites in Beijing", and "famous sites in Shanghai") can be combined into one group, where "Beijing" and "Shanghai" can be treated as parameters. The parameterized result can help focus users' attention on the core phrases, which in this case corresponds to famous sites.

5 Conclusions

Search engine technology has gone through several evolutions and has finally reached the point where Artificial Intelligence can offer tremendous help. We have outlined a new architecture of a search engine based on robust parsing of input queries and data mining of query log data. The advantage of the search engine include high precision and efficiency without compromising coverage. In the future, we plan to carry out empirical studies of this type of search engine with data from realistic Internet searches.

References

1. J. Allen, "Natural language understanding". The Benjamin-Cummings Publishing Company, Inc. 1995
2. John B. Best, Cognitive psychology. West Publishing Company, 1995, 4th Edition.
3. Eric Brewer, "Delivering high availability for Inktomi search engines". *Proceedings of ACM SIGMOD international conference on Management of data*, 1998, pp. 538.
4. Cho J., Garcia-Molina H., Page L., "Efficient Crawling Through URL Ordering", *The 7th International WWW Conference* (WWW 98). Brisbane, Australia, April 14-18, 1998.

5. P. R. Cohen, H. J. Levesque. "Intention is choice with commitment". *Artificial Intelligence*, 42, pp. 213-261, 1990.
6. Susan Dumais, John Platt, David Heckerman et al., "Inductive learning algorithms and representations for text categorization". *Proceedings of the 1998 ACM 7th international conference on Information and knowledge management*, 1998, pp. 148-55.
7. Eric Horvitz, "Principles of mixed-initiative user interfaces". *Proceeding of the CHI 99 conference on Human factors in computing systems: the CHI is the limit*, 1999, pp. 159-166.
8. F. Jelinek, J.D. Lafferty, and R.L. Mercer, "Basic Methods of Probabilistic Context Free Grammars", In *Proc. Laface and R. De Mori (eds). Speech Recognition and Understanding--Recent Advances,* Springer-Verlag Berlin Herdelberg, NATO ASI Series, Vol. F75, 1992, 345-360
9. A. Lavie, "GLR*: A Robust Grammar-Focused Parser for Spontaneously Spoken Language". Carnegie Mellon University Ph.D.'s dissertation. 1996.
10. Jakob Nielsen. "User interface directions for the Web". *Commun. ACM* 42(1), pp. 65-72, 1999
11. Page L. and Brin S., "The Anatomy of a Search Engine." *The 7th International WWW Conference* (WWW 98). Brisbane, Australia, April 14-18, 1998.
12. A. Pollock and A. Hockley, "What's wrong with Internet Searching". D-Lib Magazine. http://www.dlib.org/dlib/march97/bt/03pollock.html
13. W. Ward, "Understanding Spontaneous Speech: The Phoenix System". In *Proceedings of IEEE International Conference on Acousitcs, Speech and Signal Processing (ICASSP'91)*, 1991, pp 365-367.
14. Y. Wang. "A robust parser for spoken language understanding". In *Proc. of 6th European conference on speech communication and technology (Eurospeech99)*. Budapest, Hungary, Sept. 1999, pp. Vol.5, 2055-2058.
15. Yen-ju Yang, Lee-feng Chien, Lin-shan Lee. "Speaker intention modeling for large vocabulary mandarin spoken dialogues". *Proc. of Fourth International Conference on Spoken Language,* 1996.
16. Oren Zamir and Oren Etzioni. "Web document clustering: a feasibility demonstration". *Proceedings of the 21st annual international ACM SIGIR conference on Research and development in information retrieval*, 1998, pp46-54.

The Gap between Symbol and Non-symbol Processing

- An Attempt to Represent a Database by Predicate Formulae -

Setsuo Ohsuga

Faculty of Software and Information, Iwate Prefectural University
Phone ; +81 45 972 8692
ohsuga@soft.iwate-pu.ac.jp

Abstract. The gap between symbol processing and non-symbol processing is investigated. Predicate logic and neural network were selected as the typical symbol and non-symbol processing respectively. An intermediate form was introduced to represent both of them in the same framework. Using this intermediate form the characteristics of these two methods of representation and processing are analyzed and compared. Then the syntax of predicate logic is expanded in order to reduce this gap. A way of applying this extended logic to database in order to represent it in a few predicate formulae is discussed.

1. Introduction

Today, various styles of information processing are used such as those based on procedural language, on declarative language, on neural network mechanism, etc. Every style has its own processing objective and object to which the processing style is best suited. It also has its own problem representation scheme and processing method that are defined based on the scheme. A specific information-processing engine (IPE in the sequel) can be implemented in each style based on the representation scheme and processing method. A computer program for a specific problem, for example, is an IPE of the procedural processing style. A specific neural network is also an IPE. A scope of problem that each IPE can deal with is limited however and often is very narrow. It is desirable from user's point of view that these different styles can be integrated easily for solving their problems with the scope that goes beyond the scope of each single IPE. The larger the problems become, the stronger such desire becomes. In general, however, it is not easy to integrate different styles.

In order to integrate two different IPEs a special method is necessary for transforming one representation to the other. It is not easy however to find such a transformation as a general method but in many cases it has been done manually by persons in an ad hoc way for each specific pairs of IPEs to be integrated. The author has discussed in [2] a framework of integration from the possibility of transforming different representation schemes. The capability depends on the flexibility to expand the scope of information processing of each IPE as well as the expressive power of representation scheme of one or both of IPE to be integrated. The expandability depends on representation scheme. Some scheme has a large expandability but the others have not. It is discussed in Section 2 that if one or both of IPEs has such a large expandability, the possibility of integrating these IPEs increases. Thus it is desirable to let a representation scheme that has the largest expandability as well as the enough expressive power a central scheme of future information processing style. Then, a transformation method is defined between representations of the different schemes. Among all schemes that are used today, only purely declarative representation scheme has such expandability. A typical example is predicate logic. In the following therefore classic first order logic is considered as such a central scheme.

Knowledge discovery from database is considered as a case of transformation in this general framework. Objective of discovery is to obtain knowledge on an object through observation. Every object has a structure or a behavioral principle based on which an observable data is generated. In many cases however these structure /behavioral-principle are not visible directly. The objective of discovery is to let them explicit and represent it in some formal representation scheme. If a database represents a record of an operation of an IPE, it must be translated into a finite set of predicate formulae by means of integration technique discussed above trough learning. Such a kind of discovering predicate logic to represent whole observations is an objective of this paper. It is shown that it is difficult as a general discussion because of the difficulty of integrating non-symbol IPE and predicate logic in general.

First, the relation between non-symbolic processing and symbolic processing is discussed in Section 2. Then a transformation from the former to the latter, are discussed. A mathematical representation is introduced as an intermediate form for bridging them in Section 3. In Section 4, the framework of predicate is extended and a quantitative measure is introduced there. The results are used for representing a database by predicate formulae in Section 5. Section 6 is the conclusion.

2. Symbol and Non-symbol Processing

Both symbolic and non-symbolic forms are the formal way of information representation. These are used to refer some object in the universe of discourse, such as entity, relation between entities, behavior/activity of entity and so on. This is a general and common framework of information-and-object relation. Non-symbolic and symbolic representations are different within this common framework. A non-symbolic expression has a direct and rigid connection with the object. Observation in non-symbolic form is strictly dependent on a hardware devise for measurement that is designed specifically for the object to be observed. On the other hand, symbolic form is defined independently from any object. It is not restricted to any hardware device. The connection between symbolic information and object to be referred by it is indirect and is made by means of a (conceptual) mapping table. This mapping table can be changed and the same symbolic system can represent the different universes of discourse.

The different symbolic systems have been defined in this basic scheme. Some has a fixed universe of discourse and accordingly the mapping table is fixed. This example is seen in procedural language for computers with the universe of discourse being fixed to a computer. Some others have the mapping tables that can be rewritten and the universe of discourse is not fixed but the same representation can apply to the different universes of discourse by changing the mapping table. This example is seen in predicate logic. Thanks to this flexibility of mapping and its modularized representation scheme it gets a capability to accept new additional expressions any time. Therefore when new objects are added in the universe, the scope of this type of symbol processing can expand by adding new representations corresponding to these new objects. This is called expandability of predicate logic in this paper that give predicate logic a large potentiality of integrating various IPEs.

For example, let a case of integrating predicate logic system as a symbolic IPE with another IPE of the different style be considered. Let these IPEs have the separate worlds of objects. That is, the description systems of the different IPEs have no common object. Then the universe of discourse of the symbolic IPE is expanded to include the objects of non-symbolic IPE. At the same time symbolic representations for the new objects are added to the information world of the symbolic IPE. Then these two IPEs share the common objects and these objects have different representations in the different styles. If a formal method of converting these different representations is developed, then these two IPEs can be integrated. This is possible if predicate logic is able to represent the added objects with its representation scheme. This expansion is possible by predicate logic but not by non-symbolic IPE.

It is also possible to find unknown relation between objects in the universe of discourse by the relation between expressions in the corresponding information world by using logical inference. At the time completeness of inference is assured to predicate logic. These are the characteristics that give predicate logic a large potentiality of integrating various IPEs [2].

That two IPEs have the same objects in common is a necessary condition of an IPE for being transformed formally to the other IPE. In general however it is difficult to represent non-symbolic objects by predicate logic because the granularity of expression by predicate logic is too course to represent non-symbolic expressions. Some method to expand the framework of predicate logic to make the granularity finer while preserving its advantages is necessary. This is an approach taken in this paper. A quantitative measure is introduced in classical predicate logic and a symbol processing system that represents approximately non-symbol processing is obtained.

There is another approach to merge symbol and non-symbol processing. It is to represent a neural network by means of special intuitive logic. Some attempts have been made so far and some kinds of intuitive logic have been proved equivalent to neural network [3]. But these approaches lose some advantages of classic logic such as expandability and completeness of inference. As the consequence these systems cannot have large usability as the classic logic system. This approach merely shifts the location of the gap from between symbolic processing and non-symbolic processing to between the classic logic and the special intuitive logic. Because of this reason, this paper does not take the latter approach but take an approach to approximate neural network by extended classical logic.

3. An Intermediate Form

An implicative typed-formula $(\forall x/D)[F(x) \rightarrow G(x)]$ is considered. Here D is a set of elements, $D = (a,b,c,--z)$, and x/D means $D \ni x$. Let the predicates F (and $\Box$) be interpreted as a property of x in D, that is, `F(x) ; an element x in D has a property F'. Then the following quantities are defined.

First a state of D is defined as a combination of F(x) for all x/D. For example, `F(a):True`, `F(b):False`, `F(c):False`,--, `F(z):True` forms a state, say SF_I, of D with respect to F. Namely, $SF_I = (F(a), -F(b), -F(c), --, F(z))$. There is $N=2^n$ different states.

Let `F(x):True` and `F(x):False` be represented by 1 and 0 respectively. Then SF_I as above is represented $(1, 0,0,--,1)$. Let the sequence is identified by a binary number $I = 100--1$ obtained by concatenating 0 or 1 in the order of arrangement. Also let SF_I be I-th state in N states. By arranging all states in the increasing order of I, a state vector **Sf** is defined. That is, $\mathbf{Sf} = (SF_0, SF_1, --, SF_{N-1})$. Among them, $\mathbf{Sf}_\Box = \{(1,1,--,1)\} = (\forall x/D)F(x)$ and $\mathbf{Sf}_\Box = \Box \mathbf{Sf}$ $\Box(0,0,--0)\Box = (\exists x/D)F(x)$ are the only vectors that the ordinary predicate can represent.

If the truth or false of F for one of the elements in D changes, then the state of D changes accordingly. Let this change occur probabilistically. Then a state probability $Pf_\Box$ is defined to a state SF_I and a probability vector **Pf** are also defined as follows.

$\mathbf{Pf} = (Pf_0, Pf_1, --, Pf_{N-1})$ where $Pf_\Box$; probability of D being in the state SF_I.

Then it is shown that a logical inference $F\Box [F \rightarrow G] \Rightarrow G$ can be represented in the similar manner as a stochastic process, $\mathbf{Pg} = \mathbf{Pf} \times \mathbf{T}$, if a transition matrix $\Box = \Box t_{IJ} \Box$ satisfies a special condition as is shown in Figure 1 as an example. This matrix is made as follows. Since $F \rightarrow G =- F \vee G$ by definition, if `F(x);True` for some x in D, then G(x) for corresponding x must be true. That is, there is no transition from a state SF_I including `F(x);True` to a state SG_J of D in regard to G including `G(x); False` and t_{IJ} for this pair is put zero. The other elements of the transition matrix can be any positive values under a condition of their row sum equal one for every row. Many elements in this matrix are zero [1].

This method is extended to $(\forall x/D)[F1(x) \Box F2(x) \rightarrow G(x)]$, $(Ax/D)(Ay/E)[F1(x) \Box F2(x, y) \rightarrow G(y)]$ and to the more general cases. If the premise of an implicative formula includes two predicates with the same variable like $(\forall x/D)[F1(x) \Box F2(x) \rightarrow G(x)]$, then two independent states **Sf1** and **Sf 2** of D are made corresponding to F1(x) and F2(x) respectively. Then a compound state **Sf** such as **Sf** = **Sf1** x **Sf 2** is made as the Cartesian product. From its compound probability vector **Pf** a probability vector **Pg** for the state **Sg** is derived in the same way as above. In this case the number of states in **Sf** is 2^{2n} and transition matrix T becomes $2^{2n} \Box 2^n$ matrix. Or it can be represented in a three-dimensional space by a $2^n \Box 2^n \Box 2^n$ matrix and is called a Cubic Matrix. Each of three axes represents a predicate in the formula, that is, either F1 or F2 or G. It is a convenient way for a visual understanding and making the matrix consistent with logical definition. (I, J)-th element in each plane is made in such a way that it represents a consistent relation with the definition of logical imply when the states of D with respect to F1 and also to F2 are I and J respectively. For example, in a plane of the state vector **Sg** including G(a) =0, (I,J)-th element corresponding to the states I and J of **Sf1** and **Sf 2** including $\Box 1(a)=1$, F2(a)=1 must be zero. It is to prevents a contradictory case of □1(a)=1, F2(a)=1 and G(a) =0 to occur.

There can be cases in which more than two predicates are included in the premise. But in principle, these cases are decomposed to the case of two predicates. For example, F1(x)□F2(x)□F3(x)→ G(x) can be decomposed into F1(x)□F2(x) → K(x) and K(x)□F3(x)→ G(x).

	p0	p1	p2	p3	p4	p5	p6	p7	p8	p9	p10	p11	p12	p13	p14	p15
p0	x	x	x	x	x	x	x	x	x	x	x	x	x	x	x	x
p1	0	x	0	x	0	x	0	x	0	x	0	x	0	x	0	x
p2	0	0	x	x	0	0	x	x	0	0	x	x	0	0	x	x
p3	0	0	0	x	0	0	0	x	0	0	0	x	0	0	0	x
p4	0	0	0	0	x	x	x	x	0	0	0	0	x	x	x	x
p5	0	0	0	0	0	x	0	x	0	0	0	0	0	x	0	x
p6	0	0	0	0	0	0	x	x	0	0	0	0	0	0	x	x
p7	0	0	0	0	0	0	0	x	0	0	0	0	0	0	0	x
p8	0	0	0	0	0	0	0	0	x	x	x	x	x	x	x	x
p9	0	0	0	0	0	0	0	0	0	x	0	x	0	x	0	x
p10	0	0	0	0	0	0	0	0	0	0	x	x	0	0	x	x
p11	0	0	0	0	0	0	0	0	0	0	0	x	0	0	0	x
p12	0	0	0	0	0	0	0	0	0	0	0	0	x	x	x	x
p13	0	0	0	0	0	0	0	0	0	0	0	0	0	x	0	x
p14	0	0	0	0	0	0	0	0	0	0	0	0	0	0	x	x
p15	0	0	0	0	0	0	0	0	0	0	0	0	0	0	0	1

x; non-negative value with row sum =1

Fig. 1. Transition matrix to represent logical expression (Ax/d)[F(x)•G(x)]
D = (a1, a2, a3, a4)

Further extension is necessary for more than two variables, for example, (Ax/D)(Ay/E)[F1(x)□F2(x, y) → G(y)]. In this case a new variable z defined over the set D x E is introduced and a cubic matrix can be made. The following treaty is similar to the above case. In this way the set of logical implicative forms with the corresponding transition matrices is extended to include very practical expressions.

The computation $Pg_J = \Sigma_\square Pf_\square \times t_{IJ}$ for $\mathbf{Pg} = \mathbf{Pf} \times T$ is formally the same as that included in a neural network of which the input and output vectors are $Pf_\square$ and Pg_J respectively and the weight of an arc between nodes I and J is t_{IJ}. A neural network includes a non-linear transformation after this linear operation. Usually a function called Sigmoid Function is used. At the moment this part is ignored.

A transition matrix for representing predicate logic has many restrictions comparing with a matrix to represent a neural network. First, since the former represents a probabilistic process, every element in this matrix must be zero or a positive finite number less than or equal one while any weight value of neural network is not restricted to an interval [0,1]. But this is to some extent the matter of measurement. By preprocessing the input values the different neural network of which the range of every input value becomes similar to probability may be obtained with substantially the same functionality as original one. Thus the first difference is not substantial one.

Second, in order for a matrix to keep the same relation as logical implication, it has to fulfil a further restriction as shown in Figure 1, while the matrix to represent neural network is free from such a restriction. A neural network can represent an object at the very fine level and in many cases to continuous level. In other words, granularity of representation is very fine in the framework of neural network. But the framework is rigid and to expand its scope is difficult. Therefore integration of two or more neural networks, or a neural network with the other non-symbol processing, is not easy. Persons must define an ad hoc method for integration for every specific case. The granularity of logical predicate on the other hand is very course. Predicate logic can expand the scope with the sacrifice of granularity of representation at the fine level. Therefore predicate logic cannot represent neural network correctly. In general, it is difficult for symbolic systems to represent non-symbolic processing precisely.

For the purpose of discovering knowledge automatically, a new style of information processing with a new representation scheme and its processing method must be defined. It is desirable to have advantages of both non-symbolic and symbolic processing systems. An approach to expand the syntax of an orthodox predicate logic toward to include probabilistic measure is taken in the sequel.

One of the problems included in this method is the rapid increase of computational complexity by combination. It is discussed in section 5 that it is possible to reduce the number of computations in some cases of discovery in databases.

4. Extending Syntax of Logical Expression

Predicate logic is lacking a quantitative measure for representing non-symbolic processing. In this section therefore the syntax of predicate logic is expanded to include probability of truth of a logical expression while preserving its advantages of expandability.

In the representation of matrix form a probability vector **Pf** of the state vector **Sf** represented an occurrence probability of logical states. In the formal syntax of classical first order logic however only two cases of **Pf** actually appear. These are $(0,0,0,---,1)$ and $(0, *, *,---,*)$ that correspond to $(Ax/D)F(x)$ and $(Ex/D)F(x)$ respectively. Here $*$ denotes any value in [0, 1]. Since a set $\Box = \{a, b, c, --, z\}$ is assumed finite, $(Ax/D)F(x) = F(a) \wedge F(b) \wedge -- \wedge F(z)$. Even if the probability of `F(x); True` is different for every element, that is, for $x = a$ or $x = b$ or $--$ or $x = z$, ordinary first order logic cannot represent it. In order to improve it a probability measure is introduced there. Let a probability of `F(x):True` be $p(x)$ for $D \ni x$. Then the syntax of logical fact expressions $(\forall x/\Box)F(x)$ is expanded to $(\forall x/\Box)\{F(x), p(x)\}$ meaning `for every x of $\Box$, F(x) is true with probability p(x)`.

Since $p(x)$ is a distribution over the set D, it is different from **Pf** that is a distribution over the set of states **Sf** . It is possible to obtain **Pf** from $p(x)$ and vice versa. Every state in **Sf** is defined as the combination of `F(x); True` or `F(x); False` for all elements in D. I-th element of **Sf** is SF_I. An element in **Pf** corresponding to SF_I is $Pf_\Box$. Let `F(x); True` for the element x; i, j, -- and `F(y); False` for y; k, l, - - in SF_I. Then $Pf_\Box$ = p(i) $\Box$p(j) $\Box$- - $\Box$(1-p(k)) $\Box$(1-p(l)) $\Box$- -.

On the other hand, let an operation to sum up all positive components with respect to i in **Pf** be$\Sigma_{*i\Box I}$ **Pf** $_I$. Here the `positive component with respect to i` is $Pf_\Box$ corresponding to SF_I in which `F(i);True`. This represents a probability that i -th element x in D is in the state `F(x); True`. That is,$\Sigma_{*i\Box I} Pf_I$ = p(x).

Implicative formula is also expanded. Let an extension of an implicative formula $(\forall x/D)[F(x) \rightarrow G(x)]$ be considered as an example. The detail of the quantitative measure is discussed later. Whatever it may be it generates from $(\forall x/\Box)\{F(x), p(x)\}$ a conclusion in the same form as the premise with its own probability distribution, i.e. $(\forall x/\Box)\{G(x), r(x)\}$. In general r(x) must be different from p(x) because an implicative formula may also have some probabilistic uncertainty and it affects the probability distribution of the consequence.

The matrix introduced in section 3 gives a basis for extension of implicative formula. Figure 1 showed an example of transition matrix that generated a logical formula as conclusion for logical premise. If one intends to introduce a probabilistic measure in the inference, the restriction imposed to the matrix is released in such a way that any positive value in [0, 1] is allowed to every element under only the constraint that row sum is one for every row. With this matrix and an extended fact representation as above, it is possible to represent extended logical inference as follows.

(1) Generate **Pf** from p(x) of $(\forall x/\Box)\{F(x), p(x)\}$.
(2) Obtain **Pg** as the product of **Pf** and the expanded transition matrix.
(3) Obtain r(x) of $(\forall x/\Box)\{G(x), r(x)\}$ from **Pg**.

This is a process to obtain a conclusion given $(\forall x/\Box)\{F(x), p(x)\}$ and the transition matrix. Thus if matrix representation is available in predicate logic, it seems a good extension of predicate logic because it includes continuous values and appears to represent the same process as non-symbolic operation. But it has drawback in two aspects. First, it needs to keep a large matrix to every implicative representation and second, and the more important, it loses modularity that was the largest advantage of predicate logic for expanding the scope autonomously. Modularity comes from the mutual independence of elements in D in a logical expression. The mutual independence between elements in D is lost in the operation **Pg** = **Pf** × T and it causes the loss of modularity. This is an operation to derive Pg_J by $Pg_J = \Sigma_\Box Pf_\Box \times t_{IJ}$ = $Pf_1 \times t_{1J}$ + $Pf_2 \times t_{2J}$ + -- + $Pf_N \times t_{NJ}$. That is, J-th element of **Pg** is affected by the other elements of **Pf** than J-th element. If this occurs, any logical predicate is affected by the other predicates. There is no modularity any more.

In order to keep modularity it is desirable to represent logical implication in the same form as the fact representation like $(\forall x/D)\{[F(x) \rightarrow G(x)], q(x)\}$. It is read `for every x of $\Box$, F(x) $\rightarrow$ G(x) with probability q(x)`. In this expression q(x) is defined to each element in D independently. Then logical inference is represented as follows.

$(\forall x/D) \{F(x), p(x)\} \wedge (\forall x/D)\{[F(x) \rightarrow G(x)], q(x)\} \Box\Box (\forall x/D)\{G(x), r(x)\}$, r(x) = f(p(x), q(x)).

If it is possible to represent logical inference in this form, the actual inference operation can be divided into two parts. The first part is the ordinary logical inference such as, $(\forall x/D)\ F(x) \wedge (\forall x/D)\{F(x) \rightarrow G(x)\}\ \Box\ (\forall x/D)G(x)$

The second part is the probability computation $r(x) = f(p(x), q(x))$. This is the operation to obtain $r(x)$ as the function only of $p(x)$ and $q(x)$ with the same variable and is performed in parallel with the first part. Thus logical operation is possible only by adding the second part to the ordinary inference operation.

This is the possible largest extension of predicate logic to include a quantitative evaluation meeting the condition for preserving the modularity. This extension reduces the gap between non-symbolic and symbolic expression to a large extent. But it can not reduce the gap to zero but leaves a distance between them. If this distance can be made small enough, then predicate logic can approximate non-symbolic processing. Here arises a problem of evaluating the distance between non-symbolic processing and this expanded predicate logic.

Coming back to the matrix operation, the probability of the consequence of inference is obtained for i-th element as

$r(x_i) = \Sigma_{*i \Box I}\ Pg_I = \Sigma_{*i \Box I}(\Sigma_I\ Pf_I \times t_{IJ}), \Box x_i$ is i-th element of $D \Box$

This expression belongs to non-symbolic processing. Then an approximation is made that produces an expression like the expression (*).

First the following quantities are defined.

$q(x_k) = \Sigma_{*k \Box I}\ t_{NJ},\ r'(x_k) = (\Sigma_{*k \Box J}\ t_{NJ})(\Sigma_{*i \Box I}\ Pf_I), \Box x_k$ is k-th element in $D \Box$

$r'(x)$ is obtained by replacing every IJ-th element by NJ-th element, that is, by the replacement $\Box t_{IJ} \leftarrow t_{NJ}$. Since only last row is effective, this is the result obtained by a matrix operation when input vector is $\mathbf{Pf} = (0,0,--,1)$, that is, $(\forall x/D)\ F(x)$ holds true with certainty. If some uncertainty is included in $(\forall x/D)\ F(x)$, then there is some finite difference between the true value $r(x_k)$ and its approximation $r'(x_k)$. It is:

$r(x_k) - r'(x_k) = \Sigma_{*k \Box J}\ [\ (\Sigma_I Pf_I \times t_{IJ}) - t_{NJ} \times (\Sigma_I Pf_I)\ ]$
$= \Sigma_{*k \Box J}(\Sigma_I Pf_I \times (t_{IJ} - t_{NJ})) = \Sigma_J(\Sigma_{*k \Box J} Pf_I \times (t_{IJ} - t_{NJ}))$
$= \Sigma_I Pf_I \times (\Sigma_{*k \Box J}(t_{IJ} - t_{NJ}))$

This is not always small enough for a general non-symbolic processing. In order to represent logical inference as a stochastic process, many elements must be zero in the transition matrix as has been seen in Figure 1. If there are large quantities coming to these elements in a non-symbolic system, above approximation is no longer good but the error as the difference between $r(x_k)$ and its approximation $r'(x_k)$ increases. This error however becomes small for a logical implicative formula when the stochastic process is very close to the formula.

One of the objectives of this paper is to discover knowledge from databases and use this extended logic for discovery. A hypothetical predicate is created that is assumed to represent the given databases. A probability distribution is obtained by learning and used for evaluating the correctness of hypothesis. If the hypothesis is not suited for representing the databases, above error becomes large. In this case the absolute value of probability $q(x)$ included in the hypothetical implicative formula become lows. It shows that this hypothesis must be rejected. On the contrary, if $q(x)$ is over the pre-defined threshold and is thought to represent the database with high probability, then the above error becomes small. For this reason, this approximation can be used. At this time the probability distribution $r(x)$ of the conclusion of inference is obtained as an inner product of $p(x)$ and $q(x)$, $r(x) = p(x) \Box q(x)$.

24   S. Ohsuga

Even though this discussion has been made based on a very simple implicative formula, this discussion holds true for the more general cases. The importance of this approximation is that, first of all, predicate logic can be expanded without destroying the basic framework of logical inference but by simply adding a part to evaluate quantitatively the probability. In general non-symbolic processing includes computation for coupling different elements in a set. On the other hand predicate logic stands on the premise that every element is independent to each other. This is the substantial difference between symbolic and non-symbolic representation / processing. In the above approximation this coupling terms are ignored. It brought the above advantage of this approach.

This is one of the conclusions of this paper. With this result, the matrix form representation is no more necessary but an extended logical expression including probability distribution can be used as its approximation. It simplifies its application, for example, to discovery in databases.

5. To Discover Logical Expression in Databases

Database is not an IPE but merely a collection of data. Therefore above discussion is not applicable directly to databases. If the data are observations of an object, then a predicate formula or a set of formulae to represent the structure/behavioral-principle of the object that is hidden behind the data is created as hypothesis. Thus the database is used as the learning data for obtaining the probability distribution of the hypothetical predicate. If it is proved that the predicate formula represent the databases well, then it represents a discovered knowledge and has the larger applicability for wider class of problems than the database itself. This is the objective of discovery in this paper.

5.1 Use of Transition Matrix

There can be two approaches for evaluating the hypothesis. One is to use the transition matrix method directly. A predicate is created as a hypothesis and the framework of the corresponding matrix is generated. Then IJ-th element is modified by data in the database by a learning procedure. In an ordinary learning, if there is a datum to show the positive evidence the corresponding terms are increased by the small amount while for the negative data these are decreased. In this case an initial value must be decided in advance for every element. If there is no prior knowledge to decide it, the initial value of every element is made the same. In the case being discussed, there are some elements that correspond to every positive data satisfying the formula, i.e. those that are increased by the small amount. In the matrix, these are at the cross points of those rows corresponding to the states SF_I of premise and the columns corresponding to the states SG_J of consequence meeting the condition as hypothetical predicate. The other elements are decreased by some amount such that the row sum keeps one for every row. There are many such cross points corresponding to SF_I and SG_J including the data. For example, in the case of the simplest example $(\forall x/D)\{F(x){\rightarrow}G(x)\}$, if there are a pair of F(a) and G(a) in the database, all states in **Sf** and **Sg** including 'F(a); True' and `G(a);True' make up such cross points. This approach needs a huge amount of computation.

5.2 Use of Extended Predicate

Using an extended inference,
  $(\forall x/D)$ $(F(x), p(x)) \land (\forall x/D)\{F(x) \to G(x), q(x)\}$ $\Box((\forall x/D)(G(x), r(x)),$ $r(x)=p(x)\Box q(x)$, $q(x)$ is obtained directly by learning from the data in a database.

Assuming that every datum is error-free, there can be three cases such as (1) the data verify the implicative logical formula, (2) the data deny the logical formula and (3) some datum does not exist. The way of coping with the data is different by a view to the database. There are two views for databases. In one view, it is assumed that a database represents every object in the universe of discourse exhaustively or, in other words, a closed world assumption holds to this database. In this case if some data to prove the hypothesis does not exists in the database the database denies the hypothesis. On the other hand, it is possible to assume that a database is always incomplete but is open. In this case, even if data to prove a predicate do not exist, it does not necessarily mean that the hypothesis should be rejected.

In this paper the latter approach is taken. Different from business databases in which every individual datum has its own meaning, the scope of data to be used for knowledge discovery cannot be defined beforehand but is augmented by adding new data. A way of obtaining the probability distribution for a hypothesis is shown by an example.

Example: A couple of databases, DB1(F1,G) and DB2 (A,B), be given that includes DB1 = (--,(a1, b1), (a1, b2), (a1,b4), (a2,b2),--) and DB2 = (--, (a1,b1), (a1,b2), (a1,b3),(a2,b2),--). Assume that a logical implicative formula $(Ax/D)(Ay/E)\{[F1(x)\Box F2(x, y) \to G(y)]\ q(x)\}$ is made as a hypothesis. Every initial value in the probability distribution $q(x)$ is made equal to 0.5. Then since F1(a1) holds true for an element a1 and F2(a1, b1), F2(a1,b2), F2(a1,b3) hold true in the database, G(b1),G(b2),G(b3) must hold true with this hypothesis. But there is no datum to prove G(b3) in the databases. Thus for 2 cases out of 3 required cases the hypothesis is proved true actuary by data. The probability distribution $q(x)$ of the logical formula is obtained as a posterior probability starting from the prior probability 0.5 and evaluating the contribution of the existing data to modify the effective probability like $q(a1) = 0.5 + 0.5 \times 2\Box 3 = 5\Box 6$

By calculating the probability for every data in this way, a probability distribution, $q(x)$, is obtained. If for every element of D the probability is over the pre-specified threshold value, this hypothetical formula is accepted.

6. Conclusion

This paper has discussed first a relation between symbolic processing and non-symbolic processing. Predicate logic and neural network were selected as the typical symbolic and non-symbolic processing respectively. An intermediate form was introduced to represent both of them in the same framework. Using this intermediate form the characteristics of these two methods of representation and processing are analyzed and compared. Predicate logic has capability to expand its scope. This expandability brings the predicate logic a large potential capability to integrate different information processing schemes. On the other hand the granularity of representation is course. These characteristics are brought into predicate logic by elimination of quantitative representation caused by symbolization and also by inhibition of mutual dependency between elements. Non-symbolic processing has opposite characteristics. Therefore there is a gap between them and it is difficult to reduce it to null. In this paper the syntax of predicate was extended so that some quantitative representation became possible. It reduces the gap to a large extent. Even though this gap cannot be eliminated completely, this extension is useful for some application including knowledge discovery from database when this gap has small effect on the result. Then this paper discussed a way to discover one or more implicative predicate in databases using the above results.

References

[1] S. Ohsuga; Symbol Processing by Non-Symbol Processor, Proc. PRICAI'96
[2] S.Ohsuga; Integration of Different Information Processing Methods, (to appear in) DeepFusion of Computational and Symbolic Processing, (eds. F.Furuhashi, S.Tano, and H.A. Jacobsen), Springer, 2000
[3] Hiroshi Tsukimoto: Symbol pattern integration using multi-linear functions, (to appear in) Deep Fusion of Computational and Symbolic Processing, T. Furuhashi, S.Tano, and H.A. Jacobsen), Springer, 2000

Argumentation Semantics for Defeasible Logics

G. Governatori[1], M.J. Maher[2], G. Antoniou[2], and D. Billington[2]

[1] School of Information Systems, Queensland University of Technology,
GPO Box 2434 Brisbane, QLD 4001, Australia
[2] School of Computing and Information Technology, Griffith University,
Nathan, QLD 4111, Australia
{guido,mjm,ga,db}@cit.gu.edu.au

Abstract. Defeasible logic is a simple but efficient rule-based non-monotonic logic. It has powerful implementations and shows promise to be applied in the areas of legal reasoning and the modelling of business rules. So far defeasible logic has been defined only proof-theoretically. Argumentation-based semantics have become popular in the area of logic programming. In this paper we give an argumentation-based semantics for defeasible logic.

Recently it has been shown that a family of approaches can be built around defeasible logic, in which different intuitions can be followed. In this paper we present an argumentation-based semantics for an ambiguity propagating logic, too. Further defeasible logics can be characterised in a similar way.

1 Introduction

Defeasible logic is a practical nonmonotonic logic. This logic, and similar logics, have been proposed as the appropriate language for executable regulations [3], contracts [22], and business rules [13]. Unlike other nonmonotonic approaches, defeasible logic was designed to be easily implementable. In fact, recently very powerful implementations of defeasible logic became available, capable of handling 100,000s of defeasible rules [4]. Moreover, in [2] we have shown how to "tune" defeasible logic in order to deal with several nonmonotonic phenomena described in the literature.

Dung [9, 10] presented an abstract argumentation framework, and [7] shown that several well-known nonmonotonic reasoning systems are concrete instances of the abstract framework. Although defeasible logic can be described informally in terms of arguments, the logic has been formalized in a proof-theoretic setting in which arguments play no role. In this paper we will provide an argumentation-theoretic semantics for defeasible logic.

In addition to innovations we make in argumentation theory, the resulting argumentation-theoretic semantics will be advantageous for defeasible logic. The logic currently has no model theory, and the proof theory is clumsy. The semantics we provide is considerably more elegant. It will prove useful in the intended applications of defeasible logic mentioned above, where arguments are a natural feature of the problem domain.

This work is part of our ongoing effort to establish close connections between defeasible reasoning and theories of argumentation. Such connections usually lead to better understanding, and cross-fertilisation. Also it is worth noting that usually argumentation is studied theoretically, while not so much emphasis is placed on implementation. On the other hand, there are already very powerful systems of defeasible reasoning. Thus our research may lead to the implementation of abstract argumentation systems on the basis of defeasible reasoning.

This paper is structured as follows. In the next section we provide a brief introduction to defeasible logic. In this short paper there is no room for full details; for those we refer the reader to [17, 2]. We then provide our argumentation-theoretic semantics for defeasible logic and an ambiguity propagating variant in Section 3.

2 Overview of Defeasible Logics

We begin by presenting the basic ingredients of defeasible logic. A defeasible theory contains five different kinds of knowledge: facts, strict rules, defeasible rules, defeaters, and a superiority relation. We consider only essentially propositional rules. Rules containing free variables are interpreted as the set of their variable-free instances.

Facts are indisputable statements, for example, "Tweety is an emu". In the logic, this might be expressed as $emu(tweety)$.

Strict rules are rules in the classical sense: whenever the premises are indisputable (e.g. facts) then so is the conclusion. An example of a strict rule is "Emus are birds". Written formally: $emu(X) \rightarrow bird(X)$.

Defeasible rules are rules that can be defeated by contrary evidence. An example of such a rule is "Birds typically fly"; written formally: $bird(X) \Rightarrow flies(X)$. The idea is that if we know that something is a bird, then we may conclude that it flies, *unless there is other evidence suggesting that it may not fly*.

Defeaters are rules that cannot be used to draw any conclusions. Their only use is to prevent some conclusions. In other words, they are used to defeat some defeasible rules by producing evidence to the contrary. An example is "If an animal is heavy then it might not be able to fly". Formally: $heavy(X) \leadsto \neg flies(X)$. The main point is that the information that an animal is heavy is not sufficient evidence to conclude that it doesn't fly. It is only evidence that the animal *may* not be able to fly. In other words, we don't wish to conclude $\neg flies$ if $heavy$, we simply want to prevent a conclusion $flies$.

The *superiority relation* among rules is used to define priorities among rules, that is, where one rule may override the conclusion of another rule. For example, given the defeasible rules

$$r : \quad bird \Rightarrow flies$$
$$r' : brokenWing \Rightarrow \neg flies$$

which contradict one another, no conclusive decision can be made about whether a bird with a broken wing can fly. But if we introduce a superiority relation $>$ with $r' > r$, then we can indeed conclude that the bird cannot fly. The superiority relation is required to be acyclic.

It is not possible in this short paper to give a complete formal description of the logic. However, we hope to give enough information about the logic to make the discussion intelligible. We refer the reader to [19, 6, 17, 2] for more thorough treatments.

A *rule* r consists of its *antecedent* (or *body*) $A(r)$ which is a finite set of literals, an arrow, and its *consequent* (or *head*) $C(r)$ which is a literal. Given a set R of rules, we denote the set of all strict rules in R by R_s, the set of strict and defeasible rules in R by R_{sd}, the set of defeasible rules in R by R_d, and the set of defeaters in R by R_{dft}. $R[q]$ denotes the set of rules in R with consequent q. If q is a literal, $\sim q$ denotes the complementary literal (if q is a positive literal p then $\sim q$ is $\neg p$; and if q is $\neg p$, then $\sim q$ is p).

A *defeasible theory* D is a triple $(F, R, >)$ where F is a finite set of facts, R a finite set of rules, and $>$ a superiority relation on R.

A *conclusion* of D is a tagged literal; in our original defeasible logic there are two tags, ∂ and Δ, that may have positive or negative polarity (further tags for defeasible logic variants will be introduced shortly):

$+\Delta q$ which is intended to mean that q is definitely provable in D (i.e., using only facts and strict rules).

$-\Delta q$ which is intended to mean that we have proved that q is not definitely provable in D.

$+\partial q$ which is intended to mean that q is defeasibly provable in D.

$-\partial q$ which is intended to mean that we have proved that q is not defeasibly provable in D.

Provability is based on the concept of a *derivation* (or *proof*) in $D = (F, R, >)$. A derivation is a finite sequence $P = (P(1), \ldots P(n))$ of tagged literals satisfying four conditions (which correspond to inference rules for each of the four kinds of conclusion). Here we briefly state the conditions for positive defeasible conclusions [6]. The structure of the inference rules for negative literals is the same as that for the corresponding positive one, but the conditions are negated in some sense. The purpose of the $-\Delta$ and $-\partial$ inference rules is to establish that it is not possible to prove a corresponding positive tagged literal. These rules are defined in such a way that all the possibilities for proving $+\partial q$ (for example) are explored and shown to fail before $-\partial q$ can be concluded. Thus conclusions with these tags are the outcome of a constructive proof that the corresponding positive conclusion cannot be obtained.

In this paper we present the inference rules in a simplified form instead of the general one. In particular we do not consider the superiority relation. In fact, in [1], we proved that the superiority relation can be simulated in terms of the other elements of defeasible logic, and we provide an effective translation to transform a defeasible theory in an equivalent one with an empty superiority relation. The use of the simplified conditions will make our formal considerations much simpler.

In the following $P(1..i)$ denotes the initial part of the sequence P of length i.

$+\partial$:
If $P(i+1) = +\partial q$ then either
(1) $+\Delta q \in P(1..i)$ or
   (2.1) $\exists r \in R_{sd}[q] \forall a \in A(r)$
      $+\partial a \in P(1..i)$ and
   (2.2) $-\Delta \sim q \in P(1..i)$ and
   (2.3) $\forall s \in R[\sim q]$
      $\exists a \in A(s) : -\partial a \in P(1..i)$

$-\partial$:
If $P(i+1) = -\partial q$ then
(1) $-\Delta q \in P(1..i)$ and
   (2.1) $\forall r \in R_{sd}[q] \exists a \in A(r) :$
      $-\partial a \in P(1..i)$ or
   (2.2) $+\Delta \sim q \in P(1..i)$ or
   (2.3) $\exists s \in R[\sim q]$ such that
      $\forall a \in A(s) : +\partial a \in P(1..i)$

Let us work through the condition for $+\partial$. To show that q is provable defeasibly we have two choices: (1) We show that q is already definitely provable; or (2) we need to argue using the defeasible part of D as well. In particular, we require that there must be a strict or defeasible rule with head q which can be applied (2.1). But now we need to consider possible "attacks", that is, reasoning chains in support of $\sim q$. To be more specific: to prove q defeasibly we must show that $\sim q$ is not definitely provable (2.2). And finally (2.3), we need to show that all rules with head $\sim q$ are inapplicable.

In [2] we presented a framework for defeasible logic, where we showed how to tune defeasible logic in order to define variants able to deal with different nonmonotonic phenomena. In particular, we proposed different ways in which conclusions can be obtained. One of the properties most discussed in the literature is whether ambiguities should be propagated or blocked. In the logic above ambiguities are blocked. In the following we introduce an ambiguity propagating variant. The result of [1] can be easily extended to this variant; thus the appropriate inference rules will be presented in simplified form without reference to the superiority relation.

The first step is to determine when a literal is "supported" in a defeasible theory D. Support for a literal p ($+\Sigma p$) consists of a chain of reasoning that would lead us to conclude p in the absence of conflicts. This leads to the following inference conditions:

$+\Sigma$:
If $P(1+1) = +\Sigma p$ then
(1) $p \in F$, or
(2) $\exists r \in R_{sd}[p]$:
$\forall a \in A(r) + \Sigma a \in P(1..i)$

$-\Sigma$:
If $P(1+1) = -\Sigma p$ then
(1) $p \notin F$, and either
(2) $\forall r \in R_{sd}[p]$:
$\exists a \in A(r) - \Sigma a \in P(1..i)$

A literal that is defeasibly provable is supported, but a literal may be supported even though it is not defeasibly provable. Thus support is a weaker notion than defeasible provability.

A literal is *ambiguous* if there is a chain of reasoning that supports a conclusion that p is true, and another that supports that $\neg p$ is true.

We can achieve ambiguity propagation behaviour by making a minor change to the inference condition for $+\partial$: instead or requiring that every attack on p be inapplicable in the sense of $-\partial$, now we require that the rule for $\sim p$ be inapplicable because one of its antecedents cannot be *supported*. Thus we are imposing a stronger condition for proving a literal defeasibly. Here is the formal definition:

$+\partial_{ap}$:
If $P(i+1) = +\partial_{ap} q$ then either
(1) $+\Delta q \in P(1..i)$ or
(2.1) $\exists r \in R_{sd}[q] \forall a \in A(r)$:
$+\partial_{ap} a \in P(1..i)$ and
(2.2) $-\Delta \sim q \in P(1..i)$ and
(2.3) $\forall s \in R[\sim q]$
$\exists a \in A(s) : -\Sigma a \in P(1..i)$

$-\partial_{ap}$:
If $P(i+1) = -\partial q$ then
(1) $-\Delta q \in P(1..i)$ and
(2.1) $\forall r \in R_{sd}[q] \exists a \in A(r)$:
$-\partial_{ap} a \in P(1..i)$ or
(2.2) $+\Delta \sim q \in P(1..i)$ or
(2.3) $\exists s \in R[\sim q]$ such that
$\forall a \in A(s) : +\Sigma a \in P(1..i)$

3 Argumentation for Defeasible Logic

Arumentation systems usually contain the following basic elements: an underlying logical language, and the definitions of: argument, conflict between arguments, and the status of arguments. The latter elements are often used to define a consequence relation. In what follows we present an argumentation system containing the above elements in a way appropriate for defeasible logic.

Obviously, the underlying logical language we use is the language of defeasible logic; however, we consider facts to be strict rules with empty bodies.

As usual arguments are defined to be proof trees (or monotonic derivations). However, defeasible logic requires a more general notion of proof tree that admits infinite trees, so that the distinction is kept between an unrefuted, but infinite, chain of reasoning and a refuted chain.

A *proof tree* for a literal p based on a set of rules R is a (possibly infinite) tree with nodes labelled by literals such that the root is labelled by p and for every node h:

- If $b_1, \ldots, b_n$ label the children of h then there is a ground instance of a rule in R with body $b_1, \ldots, b_n$ and head h.
- If, in addition, h is not the root of the tree then the rule must be a strict or defeasible rule.

If the rule at the root of a proof tree is strict or defeasible and the proof tree is finite we say it is a *supportive proof tree*. If all the rules in a proof tree are strict then we say that it is a *strict proof tree*.

An *argument* for a literal p is a proof tree for p. We say that an argument A is *finite* if the proof tree associated to A is finite. An argument A is *strict* if the proof tree associated to A is strict. If an argument is not strict it is *defeasible*. An argument A for p is a *supportive argument* if the proof tree for p associated to A is supportive.

Given a defeasible theory D, the set of arguments that can be generated from D is denoted by $Args_D$.

Defeasible logic has three kinds of rules and only two of them can be used to support the derivation of a conclusion. Defeaters can only block derivations. Intuitively a supportive argument is an argument from which a conclusion can be drawn.

At this stage we can characterize the definite conclusions of defeasible logic in argumentation-theoretic terms.

Proposition 1. *Let D be a defeasible theory and p be a literal.*

- *$D \vdash +\Delta p$ iff there is a strict supportive argument for p in $Args_D$*
- *$D \vdash -\Delta p$ iff there is no (finite or infinite) strict argument for p in $Args_D$*

This characterization is straightforward, since strict rules are the monotonic subset of defeasible logic.

At the same time we are ready to characterize the connection between the notion of support in defeasible logic and the existence of arguments.

Proposition 2. *Let D be a defeasible theory and p a literal.*

- $D \vdash +\Sigma p$ iff there is a supportive argument for p in $Args_D$.
- $D \vdash -\Sigma p$ iff there is no (finite or infinite) strict or defeasible argument for p in $Args_D$.

On the hand, characterizing defeasible provability requires more definitions.

A *(proper) subargument* of an argument A is a subtree of the proof tree associated to A.

An argument A *attacks* an argument B if a conclusion of A is the complement of a conclusion of B. A set of arguments S attacks a defeasible argument B if there is an argument A in S that attacks B.

An argument A is *supported* by a set of arguments S if every proper subargument of A is in S.

Despite the similarity of name, this concept is not directly related to support in defeasible logic, nor to supportive arguments/proof trees. Essentially the notion of supported argument is meant to indicate when an argument may have an active role in proving or preventing the derivation of a conclusion. The main difference between the above notions is that infinite arguments and arguments ending with defeaters can be supported (and thus preventing some conclusions), while supportive proof trees are finite and do not contain defeaters (cf. Proposition 2).

An argument A is *undercut* by a set of arguments S if S supports an argument B attacking a proper subargument of A.

It is worth noting that the above definitions concern only defeasible arguments; for strict arguments we stipulate that they cannot be undercut or attacked.

Example 1. We consider the defeasible theory D consisting of the following rules:

$$a \Rightarrow p \qquad b \Rightarrow \neg p \qquad p \Rightarrow q$$

Let $S = \{a, b\}$ be a set of arguments. The argument

$$A: \quad a \Rightarrow p \Rightarrow q$$

is undercut by S since the argument $B : b \Rightarrow \neg p$ attacks a subargument of A, and it is supported by S.

That an argument A is undercut by S means that we can show that some premises of A cannot be proved if we accept the arguments in S.

The heart of argumentation semantics is the notion of acceptable argument. However, different definitions are possible and they characterise different variants of defeasible logic. Such a notion is used as a basis to define recursively the set of justified arguments. For the moment we leave it undefined (we shall propose later two different definitions: the first characterises the ambiguity propagating variant of defeasible logic – Definition 3 in Section 3.1–, and the second the ambiguity blocking variant – Definition 5 in Section 3.2), and we proceed to define the set of justified arguments.

Definition 1. *Let D be a defeasible theory. We define J_i^D as follows.*

- $J_0^D = \emptyset$

- $J_{i+1}^D = \{a \in Args_D \mid a \text{ is acceptable w.r.t. } J_i^D\}$

The set of justified arguments *in a defeasible theory* D *is* $JArgs^D = \cup_{i=1}^{\infty} J_i^D$.

A literal p is *justified* if it is the conclusion of a supportive argument in $JArg^D$.

That an argument A is justified means that it resists every reasonable refutation. However, defeasible logic is more expressive since it is able to say when a conclusion is demonstrably non provable ($-\partial, -\partial_{ap}$). Briefly, that a conclusion is demonstrably non provable means that every possible conclusive argument has been refuted. In the following we show how to capture this notion in our argumentation system by assigning the status rejected to arguments that are refuted. Roughly speaking, an argument is rejected if it has a rejected subargument or it cannot overcome an attack from a justified argument.

Again there are several possible definitions for the notion of rejected argument. Similarly to what we have done for the notion of acceptable argument we leave it temporarily undefined (the appropriate definitions will be given in Section 3.1 and Section 3.2).

Even in the case of rejected argument we need a recursive construction (see example 2 below for an explanation).

Definition 2. *We define R_i^D as follows.*

- $R_0^D = \emptyset$
- $R_{i+1}^D = \{a \in Args_D \mid a \text{ is rejected by } R_i^D\}$

The set of rejected arguments *in a defeasible theory* D *is* $RArgs^D = \cup_{i=1}^{\infty} R_i^D$.

A literal p is *rejected* if there is no argument in $Args_D - RArgs^D$ that ends with a supportive rule for p.

3.1 Grounded Semantics and Ambiguity Propagation

Dung [9, 10] proposed an abstract argumentation framework giving rise to several argumentation semantics, in particular to a skeptical semantics (called grounded semantics) which has been widely used to characterize several defeasible reasoning systems [10, 7].

In this section we show how to modify Dung's definition of acceptable argument in order to suit defeasible logic.

Definition 3. *An argument A for p is acceptable w.r.t a set of arguments S if A is finite, and*

1. *A is strict, or*
2. *every argument attacking A is attacked by S.*

As we have seen defeasible logic is more expressive, insofar as it is able to determine when a conclusion is demonstrably non provable; thus, before proving that grounded semantics characterises the ambiguity propagating variant of defeasible logic, we have to define the appropriate notion of rejected argument.

Definition 4. *An argument A is* rejected *by a set of arguments S when A is not strict, and either*

1. *a proper subargument of A is in S, or*
2. *it is attacked by a supportive argument.*

Using the notions of acceptable and rejected argument in definitions 1 and 2 enables us to prove the following theorem.

Theorem 1. *Let D be a defeasible theory and p be a literal.*

- $D \vdash +\partial_{ap} p$ *iff p is justified.*
- $D \vdash -\partial_{ap} p$ *iff p is rejected.*

This theorem provides a characterization of defeasible provability in defeasible logic with ambiguity propagation.

3.2 Defeasible Semantics and Ambiguity Blocking

In the previous section we gave an argumentation theoretic characterization of defeasible logic with ambiguity propagation. In this section we see how to modify the notions of acceptable and rejected argument in order to capture defeasible provability in defeasible logic with ambiguity blocking (our original defeasible logic).

Definition 5. *An argument A for p is* acceptable *w.r.t to a set of argument S if A is finite, and*

1. *A is strict, or*
2. *every argument attacking A is undercut by S.*

The simple existence of a competing argument is not enough to state that an argument is rejected. The attacking argument must be supported by the set of justified arguments.

Definition 6. *An argument A is* rejected *by sets of arguments S and T when A is not strict and*

1. *a proper subargument of A is in S, or*
2. *it is attacked by an argument supported by T.*

To accommodate with the slightly different notion of rejected argument we have to modify the second point of Definition 2 as follow

- $R_{i+1}^D = \{a \in Args_D \mid a \text{ is rejected by } R_i^D \text{ and } JArgs^D\}$

Theorem 2. *Let D be a defeasible theory and p be a literal.*

- $D \vdash +\partial p$ *iff p is justified.*
- $D \vdash -\partial p$ *iff p is rejected.*

This theorem provides a characterization of defeasible conclusions in ambiguity blocking defeasible logic in terms of justified and rejected argument in defeasible argumentation semantics.

Governatori and Maher [11] have developed an argumentation theoretic semantics for ambiguity blocking defeasible logic with superiority relation. It is easy to see that the semantics presented here is a special case of that of [11] when the superiority relation is empty. However, as we have already alluded to, the superiority relation does not add anything to the expressive power of the variants of defeasible logic presented in this paper. Therefore we believe that the present semantics enables a better understanding of the basic mechanisms of defeasible reasoning.

Example 2. The following defeasible logic theory illustrates why $RArgs^D$ needs to be constructed iteratively, even after all the justified literals have been identified.

There are the following rules, for $i = 1, \ldots, n$:

$$true \Rightarrow b_i$$
$$a_i \Rightarrow \neg b_i$$
$$b_{i-1} \Rightarrow a_i$$
$$true \Rightarrow \neg a_i$$

and the fact b_0.

This theory produces the following conclusions: $-\partial a_i, -\partial \neg a_i, +\partial b_i, -\partial \neg b_i$, for $i = 0, \ldots, n$.

For each i, consider the following arguments:

$$A_i : \qquad\qquad true \Rightarrow \neg a_i$$
$$B_i : true \Rightarrow b_{i-1} \Rightarrow a_i \quad \Rightarrow \neg b_i$$

and their subarguments. Notice that

- each argument A_i is attacked by B_i at a_i.
- each argument B_i is attacked by B_{i-1} at b_{i-1}.

Eventually, both A_i and B_i will be rejected, since neither can defeat the other, but this cannot be done until the status of b_{i-1} is determined. As noted above, this depends on B_{i-1}. Thus the situation incorporates some sequentiality, where B_{i-1} must be resolved before resolving B_i, and this suggests that a characterization of $RArgs^D$ must be iterative, even after all the justified literals have been identified.

4 Related Work

[16] proposes an abstract defeasible reasoning framework that is achieved by mapping elements of defeasible reasoning into the default reasoning framework of [7]. While this framework is suitable for developing new defeasible reasoning languages, it is not appropriate for characterizing defeasible logic because:

- [7] does not address Kunen's semantics of logic programs which provides a characterization of failure-to-prove in defeasible logic [18].

- The correctness of the mapping needs to be established if [16] is to be applied to an existing language like defeasible logic. In fact the representation of priorities is inappropriate for defeasible logic.

Two more systems characterized by Dung's grounded semantics, even if developed with different design choices and motivations, are those proposed by Simari and Loui [23] and Prakken and Sartor [21, 20]. Both are similar to the ambiguity blocking variant of defeasible logic, but their superiority relations are different: the first is argument based instead of rule based, while the second does not deal with teams of rules.

The abstract argumentation framework of [24] addresses both strict and defeasible rules, but not defeaters. However, the treatment of strict rules in defeasible arguments is different from that of defeasible logic, and there is no concept of team defeat. There are structural similarities between the definitions of inductive warrant and warrant in [24] and J_i^D and $JArgs_D$, but they differ in that acceptability is monotonic in S whereas the corresponding definitions in [24] are antitone. The semantics that results is not sceptical, and more related to stable semantics than Kunen semantics. The framework does have a notion of *ultimately defeated argument* similar to our rejected arguments, but the definition is not iterative, possibly because the framework does not have a directly sceptical semantics.

Among other contributions, [8] provides a sceptical argumentation theoretic semantics and shows that LPwNF – which is weaker, but very similar to defeasible logic [5] – is sound with respect to this semantics. However, both LPwNF and defeasible logic are not complete with respect to this semantics.

5 Conclusion

Defeasible logic is a simple but efficient rule-based nonmonotonic logic. So far defeasible logic has been defined only proof-theoretically. In this paper we presented an argumentation-theoretic semantics for defeasible logic and an ambiguity propagating variant. This paper is part of our ongoing effort to establish close connections between defeasible reasoning and theories of argumentation.

Acknowledgments

We thank Alejandro Garcia for fruitful discussions on defeasible logic and argumentation. This research was supported by the Australia Research Council under Large Grant No. A49803544.

References

1. G. Antoniou, D. Billington, G. Governatori and M.J. Maher. Representation Results for Defeasible Logic. Technical Report, CIT, Griffith University, 2000.
2. G. Antoniou, D. Billington, G. Governatori and M.J. Maher. A Flexible Framework for Defeasible Logic. *Proc. American National Conference on Artificial Intelligence (AAAI-2000)*.

3. G. Antoniou, D. Billington and M.J. Maher. On the analysis of regulations using defeasible rules. In R.H. Sprague (Ed.) *Proc. of the 32nd Annual Hawaii International Conference on System Sciences.* IEEE Press, 1999.
4. G. Antoniou, D. Billington, M.J. Maher, A. Rock, Efficient Defeasible Reasoning Systems, *Proc. Australian Workshop on Computational Logic*, 2000.
5. G. Antoniou, M. Maher and D. Billington, Defeasible Logic versus Logic Programming without Negation as Failure, *Journal of Logic Programming*, 42, 47–57, 2000.
6. D. Billington. Defeasible Logic is Stable. *Journal of Logic and Computation* 3 (1993): 370–400.
7. A. Bondarenko, P.M. Dung, R. Kowalski, and F. Toni. An Abstract, Argumentation-Theoretic Framework for Default Reasoning. *Artificial Intelligence*, 93 (1997): 63–101.
8. Y. Dimopoulos and A. Kakas. Logic Programming without Negation as Failure. In *Proc. ICLP-95*, MIT Press 1995.
9. P.M. Dung. An Argumentation Semantics for Logic Programming with Explicit Negation. *Proceedings of the Tenth Logic Programming Conference.* MIT Press, Cambridge: 616–630.
10. P.M. Dung. On The acceptability of Arguments and Its Fundamental Role in Non-monotonic Reasoning, Logic Programming, and n-person games. *Artificial Intelligence*, 77 (1995): 321–357.
11. G. Governatori and M.J. Maher. An Argumentation-Theoretic Characterization of Defeasible Logic. In W. Horn (ed.) *ECAI 2000. Proceedings of the 14th European Conference on Artificial Intelligence*, IOS Press, Amsterdam, 2000.
12. B.N. Grosof. Prioritized Conflict Handling for Logic Programs. In *Proc. Int. Logic Programming Symposium*, J. Maluszynski (Ed.), 197–211. MIT Press, 1997.
13. B.N. Grosof, Y. Labrou, and H.Y. Chan. A Declarative Approach to Business Rules in Contracts: Courteous Logic Programs in XML, *Proceedings of the 1st ACM Conference on Electronic Commerce (EC-99)*, ACM Press, 1999.
14. J.F. Horty. Some Direct Theories of Nonmonotonic Inheritance. In D.M. Gabbay, C.J. Hogger and J.A. Robinson (eds.): *Handbook of Logic in Artificial Intelligence and Logic Programming Vol. 3*, 111–187, Oxford University Press, 1994,
15. H. Jakobovits and D. Vermeir. Robust Semantics for Argumentation Frameworks. *Journal of Logic and Computation*, Vol. 9, No. 2, 215-261, 1999.
16. R. Kowalski and F. Toni. Abstract Argumentation. *Artificial Intelligence and Law* 4 (1996): 275–296.
17. M. Maher, G. Antoniou and D. Billington. A Study of Provability in Defeasible Logic. In *Proc. Australian Joint Conference on Artificial Intelligence*, 215–226, LNAI 1502, Springer, 1998.
18. M. Maher and G. Governatori. A Semantic Decomposition of Defeasible Logics. *Proc. American National Conference on Artificial Intelligence (AAAI-99)*, 299–305.
19. D. Nute. Defeasible Logic. In D.M. Gabbay, C.J. Hogger and J.A. Robinson (eds.): *Handbook of Logic in Artificial Intelligence and Logic Programming Vol. 3*, Oxford University Press 1994, 353–395.
20. H. Prakken. *Logical Tools for Modelling Legal Argument: A Study of Defeasible Reasoning in Law.* Kluwer Academic Publishers, 1997.
21. H. Prakken and G. Sartor. Argument-based Extended Logic Programming with Defeasible Priorities. *Journal of Applied and Non-Classical Logics* 7 (1997): 25–75.
22. D.M. Reeves, B.N. Grosof, M.P. Wellman, and H.Y. Chan. Towards a Declarative Language for Negotiating Executable Contracts, *Proceedings of the AAAI-99 Workshop on Artificial Intelligence in Electronic Commerce (AIEC-99)*, AAAI Press / MIT Press, 1999.
23. G.R. Simari and R.P. Loui. A Mathematical Treatment of Argumentation and Its Implementation. *Artificial Intelligence*, 53 (1992): 125–157.
24. G. Vreeswijk. Abstract Argumentation Systems. *Artificial Intelligence*, 90 (1997): 225–279.

A Unifying Semantics for Causal Ramifications

Mikhail Prokopenko[1], Maurice Pagnucco[1], Pavlos Peppas[2], and Abhaya Nayak[1]

[1] Computational Reasoning Group
Department of Computing, Macquarie University, NSW 2109, Australia
[2] Sisifou 27, Korinthos 20100, Greece

Abstract. A unifying semantic framework for different reasoning approaches provides an ideal tool to compare these competing alternatives. However, it has been shown recently that a pure preferential semantics alone is not capable of providing such a unifying framework. On the other hand, variants of preferential semantics augmented by additional structures on the state space have been successfully used to characterise some influential approaches to reasoning about action and causality. The primary aim of this paper is to provide an augmented preferential semantics that is general enough to unify two prominent frameworks for reasoning about action and causality — Sandewall's causal propagation semantics [4] and Thielscher's causal relationships approach [5]. There are indications that these and other different augmented preferential semantical approaches can by unified into a general framework, and provide the unified semantics that is lacking so far.

1 Introduction

Preferential style semantics have always been seen as a critical step on the way towards a concise solution to the frame and ramification problems. However, it has been argued in recent literature that an explicit representation of causal information is required to solve these problems in a concise manner. It has been shown that some approaches demand a more complex semantics than a pure preferential semantics. For example, McCain and Turner's causal theory of action [1] was recently characterised by an augmented preferential semantics, using an appropriately constructed binary relation on states in addition to a preference relation [2]. This additional relation captured causal context of action systems by translating individual causal laws into state transitions. Another causal theory of action — that of Thielscher [5] — has been characterised by a variant of an augmented preferential semantics [3]. Here the minimality component was complemented by a binary relation on states of higher dimension. The standard state-space of possible worlds was extended to a hyper-space, and action effects (including indirect ones) were traced in the hyper-space. Again, the purpose of these hyper-states was to supply extra context to the process of causal propagation. The hyper-space semantics [3] can be clearly seen to employ a component of minimal change coupled with causality. On the other hand, another rather general semantical approach — the *causal propagation semantics* proposed by Sandewall [4] — deals with causal ramifications without explicitly relying on the principle of minimal change.

This work introduces a preferential style semantics augmented with a causal transition relation on states, that is general enough to unify two of the above-mentioned frameworks to reasoning about action and causality — Sandewall's causal propagation semantics [4] and Thielscher's causal relationships approach [5]. This is achieved by observing that the principle of minimal change is hidden behind action invocation and causal propagation in both proposals.

2 Causal Propagation Semantics

The causal propagation semantics introduced by Sandewall [4], uses the following basic concepts. The set of possible states of the world, formed as a Cartesian product of the finite sets of a finite number of state variables, is denoted as $\mathcal{R}$. E is the set of possible actions. The causal propagation semantics extends a basic state transition semantics with a *causal transition relation*. The causal transition relation C is a non-reflexive relation on states in $\mathcal{R}$. A state r is called *stable* if it does not have any successor s such that $C(r, s)$; we will denote the set of stable states $\{r \in \mathcal{R} : \neg \exists s \in \mathcal{R}, C(r, s)\}$ as $\mathcal{S}_c$. Another component, $\mathcal{R}_c \subseteq \mathcal{S}_c$, is a set of admitted states. Another important concept, introduced by Sandewall, is an *action invocation relation* $G(e, r, r')$, where $e \in E$ is an action, r is the state where the action e is invoked, and r' is "the new state where the instrumental part of the action has been executed" [4]. In other words, the state r' satisfies direct effects of the action e. It is required that every action is always invokable, that is, for every $e \in E$ and $r \in \mathcal{R}$ there must be at least one r' such that $G(e, r, r')$ holds. Of course, this requirement does not mean to guarantee that every action results in an admitted state—on the contrary, the intention is to trace the indirect effects of the action, possibly reaching an admitted (and, therefore, stable) state.

A finite (the infinite case is omitted) transition chain for a state $w \in \mathcal{R}_c$ and an action $e \in E$ is a finite sequence of states $r_1, r_2, ..., (r_k)$, where $G(e, w, r_1), C(r_i, r_{i+1})$ for every $i, 1 \leq i < k$, and where r_k is a stable state. The last element of a finite transition chain is called a result state of action e performed in state w.

These basic concepts define an *action system* as a tuple $\langle \mathcal{R}, E, C, \mathcal{R}_c, G \rangle$. The following definition strengthens action systems based on the causal propagation semantics.

Definition 1. *If three states w, p, q are given, we say that the pair p, q respects w, denoted as $\lhd_w(p, q)$, if and only if $p(f) \neq q(f) \rightarrow p(f) = w(f)$ for every state variable f that is defined in $\mathcal{R}$, where $r(f)$ is a valuation of variable f in state r.*

An action system $\langle \mathcal{R}, E, C, \mathcal{R}_c, G \rangle$ is called respectful if and only if, for every $w \in \mathcal{R}_c$, every $e \in E$, w is respected by every pair r_i, r_{i+1} in every transition chain for the state w, and the last element of the chain is a member of $\mathcal{R}_c$.

According to Sandewall [4], respectful action systems are intended to ensure that in each transition there cannot be changes in state variables which have changed previously upon invocation or in the causal propagation sequence. This requirement, of course, guarantees that a resultant state is always consistent with the direct effects of the action (which cannot be cancelled by indirect ones), and that there are no cycles in transition chains. As with many other state transition action systems, the intention is to characterise a result state in terms of an initial state w and action e, without "referring explicitly to the details of the intermediate states" [4]. In other words, it is desirable to define a selection function $Res(w, a)$. For a respectful action system $\langle \mathcal{R}, E, C, \mathcal{R}_c, G \rangle$, a selection function can be given as

$$Res_{C\mathcal{R}_c G}(w, e) = \{r_k \in \mathcal{R}_c : G(w, e, r_1), C(r_i, r_{i+1}), \lhd_w(r_i, r_{i+1}), 1 \leq i < k\}.$$

3 Causal Relationships Approach

Let $\mathcal{F}$ be a finite set of symbols from a fixed language $\mathcal{B}$, called fluent names. A fluent literal is either a fluent name $f \in \mathcal{F}$ or its negation, denoted by $\neg f$. Let $L_\mathcal{F}$ be the set of all fluent literals defined over the set of fluent names $\mathcal{F}$. We will adopt from Thielscher [5] the following notation. If $\epsilon \in L_\mathcal{F}$, then $|\epsilon|$ denotes its affirmative component, that is, $|f| = |\neg f| = f$, where $f \in \mathcal{F}$. This notation can be extended to sets of fluent literals as follows: $|S| = \{|f| : f \in S\}$. By the term *state* we intend a maximal consistent set of fluent literals. We will denote the set of all states as W, and call the number m of fluent names in $\mathcal{F}$ the dimension of W. By $[\phi]$ we denote all states consistent with the sentence $\phi \in \mathcal{B}$ (i.e., $[\phi] = \{w \in W : w \vdash \phi\}$). Domain constraints are sentences which have to be satisfied in all states.

Thielscher's [5] causal theory of action consists of two main components: *action laws* which describe direct effects of action performed in a given state, and *causal relationships* which determine indirect effects of action. Every action law contains a condition C, which is a set of fluent literals, all of which must be contained in an initial state where the action is intended to be applied; and a (direct) effect E, which is also a set of fluent literals, all of which must hold in the resulting state after having applied the action. An action may result in a number of state transitions.

Definition 2. *Let $\mathcal{F}$ be the set of fluent names and let $\mathcal{A}$ be a finite set of symbols called action names, such that $\mathcal{F} \cap \mathcal{A} = \emptyset$. An action law is a triple $\langle C, a, E \rangle$ where C, called* condition, *and E, called* effect, *are individually consistent sets of fluent literals, composed of the very same set of fluent names (i.e., $|C| = |E|$) and $a \in \mathcal{A}$. If w is a state then an action law $\alpha = \langle C, a, E \rangle$ is applicable in w iff $C \subseteq w$. The application of α to w yields the state $(w \setminus C) \cup E$ (where $\setminus$ denotes set subtraction).*

Causal relationships are specified as ϵ causes ρ if Φ, where ϵ and ρ are fluent literals and Φ is a fluent formula based on the set of fluent names $\mathcal{F}$.

Definition 3. *Let (s, E) be a pair consisting of a state s and a set of fluent literals E. Then a causal relationship ϵ causes ρ if Φ is applicable to (s, E) iff $\Phi \wedge \neg \rho$ is true in s, and $\epsilon \in E$. Its application yields the pair (s', E'), denoted as $(s, E) \leadsto (s', E')$, where $s' = (s \setminus \{\neg \rho\}) \cup \{\rho\}$ and $E' = (E \setminus \{\neg \rho\}) \cup \{\rho\}$.*

In other words, a causal relationship is applicable if Φ holds, the indirect effect ρ is false and the cause ϵ is among the current effects. A possible *successor state* is determined through repeated application of causal relationships. Specifically, given an initial state w and action a, the set of successor states $Res_{RDL}(w, a)$ is determined as follows.

Definition 4. *Let $\mathcal{F}$ be the set of fluent names, $\mathcal{A}$ a set of action names, $\mathcal{L}$ a set of action laws, $\mathcal{D}$ a set of domain constraints, and R a set of causal relationships. Furthermore, let w be a state satisfying $\mathcal{D}$ and let $a \in \mathcal{A}$ be an action name.*

A state r is a successor state of w and a, denoted $r \in Res_{RDL}(w, a)$, iff there exists an applicable (with respect to w) action law $\alpha = \langle C, a, E \rangle \in \mathcal{L}$ such that $((w \setminus C) \cup E, E) \stackrel{*}{\leadsto} (r, E')$ for some E', r satisfies $\mathcal{D}$, and $E \subseteq r$, where $\stackrel{*}{\leadsto}$ denotes the transitive closure of $\leadsto$.

The last requirement ($E \subseteq r$) ensures that a (conservative) successor state does not violate action direct effects [3]. As mentioned before, an occurrence of a literal ϵ in a state s does not guarantee that a causal relationship ϵ *causes* ρ *if* Φ is applicable to a pair (s, E) — to ensure applicability, the literal ϵ has to belong to the current effects E. That is why, in order to trace causal propagation with causal relationships, one needs to keep an explicit (and changing) account of context-dependent action effects.

4 General Augmented Preferential Semantics

Let us now consider a general augmented preferential semantics, in terms of state transition systems. This system may be viewed as a tuple $\langle \mathcal{W}, \Gamma, \mathcal{E}, \mathcal{M}, \mathcal{W}', \mathcal{O} \rangle$, where $\mathcal{W}$ is a set of states; Γ is a set whose elements are referred to as power-states (and Γ itself is referred to as power-space); $\mathcal{E}$ is a set of actions; $\mathcal{M}$ is a binary relation on Γ; $\mathcal{W}' \subseteq \mathcal{W}$ is the set of legitimate (admitted) states, and $\mathcal{O}$ is a set of orderings $<_\gamma$, each with respect to some $\gamma \in \Gamma$.

Some distinguishing features of this system are worth noting. The preference orderings in $\mathcal{O}$ capture minimality whereas the binary relation $\mathcal{M}$ captures causality, thus minimality and causality play distinct roles. In order to provide a concise solution for the frame and ramification problems, both $\mathcal{O}$ and $\mathcal{M}$ are defined over the power-space Γ instead of the normal state-space $\mathcal{W}$. In particular, use of the power space allows us to encode causal contextual information in the power-states themselves, thereby providing a means to avoid encoding of contextual information in (state, history) pairs as in Thielscher [5]. Intuitively, a successor state is an admitted state which is reachable (by means of some transition relation) from states nearest (to the initial one) among states satisfying post-conditions of the performed action. In the current framework, when an action e takes place, instead of using the minimal normal states that satisfy the post-conditions of e as the starting point, we start from the minimal elements (with respect to some $<_\gamma \in \mathcal{O}$) among the power-states whose projections in the normal space $\mathcal{W}$ satisfy the post-conditions of e. The relation $\mathcal{M}$ is then used for causal propagation in the power-space, and the "final" power-states are ultimately projected back to the normal state space in order to determine the successor states resulting from action e.

Let $[e]$ denote a set of states satisfying the post-conditions of an action e, and $\mathcal{P}$ a projection function from Γ to $\mathcal{W}$. A set of power-states $[e]^\Gamma$ is defined as $\{\gamma \in \Gamma : \mathcal{P}(\gamma) \in [e]\}$. In other words, $[e]^\Gamma$ denotes the set of power-states whose normal-space projections make up the set $[e]$. We also define a set $min(<_\gamma, [e]^\Gamma)$ as a subset of $[e]^\Gamma$ containing states nearest to the state γ in terms of the ordering $<_\gamma$. In other words, $min(<_\gamma, [e]^\Gamma) = \{\beta \in [e]^\Gamma, \neg \exists \alpha \in [e]^\Gamma, \alpha \neq \beta, \alpha <_\gamma \beta\}$. Sometimes, we will refer to an element of $min(<_\gamma, [e]^\Gamma)$ as a $<_\gamma$-minimal state in $[e]^\Gamma$.

Let $\mathcal{M}^*$ be a transitive closure of the relation $\mathcal{M}$. We shall say that a power-state β is $\mathcal{M}$-reachable from a power-state α, if $\mathcal{M}^*(\alpha, \beta)$. Finally, let us denote by $\mathcal{K}_\mathcal{M}$ the set $\{p \in \Gamma : \neg \exists q \in \Gamma, \mathcal{M}(p, q)\}$—an obvious counterpart of the set of stable states in the causal propagation semantics. In spirit of the latter we require that any admitted state is a projection of some stable power-state: if $r \in \mathcal{W}'$ then $r = \mathcal{P}(\beta)$ for some $\beta \in \mathcal{K}_\mathcal{M}$. Also, for simplicity, we denote by γ_w any power-state such that $\mathcal{P}(\gamma_w) = w$.

We say that an admitted state r satisfying direct action effects is a successor state, $r \in Res(w, e)$, if and only if r is a projection of some stable power-state β, which is $\mathcal{M}$-reachable from a power-state nearest to γ_w[1] among power-states in $[e]^\Gamma$. More precisely, a selection function of the action system $\langle \mathcal{W}, \Gamma, \mathcal{E}, \mathcal{M}, \mathcal{W}', \mathcal{O} \rangle$ is given as

$$Res_{\mathcal{M}\mathcal{W}'\mathcal{O}}(w,e) = \{r \in \mathcal{W}' \cap [e] : \; r = \mathcal{P}(\beta), \; \mathcal{M}^*(\alpha, \beta), \; \text{where} \\ \alpha \in min(<_{\gamma_w}, [e]^\Gamma) \; \text{and} \; \beta \in \mathcal{K}_\mathcal{M} \}.$$

The power-space concept is not always necessary. Sometimes, we may choose $\Gamma = \mathcal{W}$ and set the projection function as $\mathcal{P}(\lambda) = \lambda$. Then the set $[e]^\Gamma$ becomes $[e]$, $\gamma_w = w$, and $\mathcal{W}' \subseteq \mathcal{K}_\mathcal{M}$. This essentially specifies an action system $\langle \mathcal{W}, \mathcal{E}, \mathcal{M}, \mathcal{W}', \mathcal{O} \rangle$, with the following selection function

$$Res_{\mathcal{M}\mathcal{W}'\mathcal{O}}(w,e) = \{r \in \mathcal{W}' \cap [e] : \mathcal{M}^*(\alpha, r), \alpha \in min(<_w, [e])\}.$$

Following [2], we say that an action system with a function Res_1 is *selection-equivalent* to an action system with a function Res_2 if and only if $Res_1(w,e) = Res_2(w,e)$, for every action e and state w. Now, our goal becomes clear: we intend to find under what conditions it is possible to achieve a selection-equivalence between a generalised action system and action systems based on the causal propagation semantics and the causal relationships approach. More precisely, we wish to identify conditions when $Res_{\mathcal{M}\mathcal{W}'\mathcal{O}}(w,e) = Res_{\mathcal{CR}_cG}(w,e)$ and $Res_{\mathcal{M}\mathcal{W}'\mathcal{O}}(w,e) = Res_{RDL}(w,e)$.

4.1 Invoking Minimal Change

In this section, we intend to analyse under what conditions it is possible to represent the Sandewall's causal propagation semantics as an instance $\langle \mathcal{W}, \mathcal{E}, \mathcal{M}, \mathcal{W}', \mathcal{O} \rangle$ of the general augmented preferential semantics, where $\Gamma = \mathcal{W}$. This reduction will be carried out while staying within the same sets of states and actions ($\mathcal{W} = \mathcal{R}$, $\mathcal{W}' = \mathcal{R}_c$, and $\mathcal{E} = E$) and transforming the causal transition relation C into the binary relation $\mathcal{M}$. In other words, our primary focus will be discovering the nature of minimality hidden, as we believe, in the invocation relation G. Motivated by a preferential-style semantics, one may be tempted to suggest an ordering on states such that the invocation relation can be simply realised by selecting nearest states satisfying action post-condition. However, this does not appear to be possible without restricting relation G.

Lemma 1. *There is no ordering $<_w$ such that for every action e and state r, $G(e, w, r)$ if and only if $r \in min(<_w, [e])$.*

Consequently, our intention at this stage is to restrict the invocation relation G in such a way that, given an initial state and an action, the invoked states can be characterised precisely as states nearest to the initial one in terms of some appropriate minimality ordering. Before we identify required restrictions on the invocation relation G, we introduce some more abbreviations. If $S \subseteq [a]$, for a set of states S and an action $a \in E$, we call the action a an *S-covering* action. Furthermore, if there exists an S-covering action a such that $G(a, w, x)$ for states $w, x \in \mathcal{R}$, we say that the state x is *S-cover accessible* from state w. Also, we say that a state x is *not S-cover accessible* from state w, if there is no S-covering actions a such that $G(a, w, x)$.

---
[1] It does not matter which of the power-states γ_w such that $\mathcal{P}(\gamma_w) = w$ is chosen.

Importantly, it follows that all states in a set S satisfy post-conditions of an S-covering action. It is worth pointing out that, given two states p and q satisfying post-conditions of some action a (that is, the action a is a $\{p,q\}$-covering action), the state p may be $\{p,q\}$-cover accessible from some state w, while state q is not $\{p,q\}$-cover accessible from w. The first restriction on invocation relation is given as

(G_1)   if p is $\{p,q\}$-cover accessible from w but q is not, and
   q is $\{q,x\}$-cover accessible from w but x is not
   then p is $\{p,x\}$-cover accessible from w and x is not,
   for arbitrary states w,p,q,x.

The premise of the implication is that, considering all actions whose post-conditions are satisfied by two states p and q, state p is chosen at least once by the invocation relation and state q is never chosen; and considering all actions whose post-conditions are satisfied by two states q and x, state q is chosen at least once, while state x is never chosen. This then necessitates that, considering all actions whose post-conditions are satisfied by states p and x, invocation of the state p must eventuate at least once, but state x cannot be invoked at all. Undoubtedly and not surprisingly, the condition (G_1) has a transitive flavour. Another condition is given as

(G_2)   Given any two $\{p,q\}$-covering actions e' and e'',
   if $G(e',w,p)$ and $G(e'',w,q)$ then $G(e',w,q)$.

This condition simply requires that if neither of two states p and q is chosen over the other in terms of the criterion implicitly used in the condition (G_1), then selection of either of them necessitates selection of the other. Finally, we reinforce the requirement that any action is invokable in principle.

(G_3) $\forall e \in E, w \in \mathcal{R}, \exists p \in [e], G(e,w,p)$

As noted above, this condition does not guarantee that the invoked action will succeed—it may possibly be qualified by causal propagation ending in a non-admitted state. Now, we are ready to describe a set of orderings $\mathcal{O}$ corresponding to the invocation relation. Ideally, any ordering $<_w$ should satisfy only the transitivity property:

(M_1)   if $p <_w q$ and $q <_w x$ then $p <_w x$.

However, it turns out that, given an action system, the related ordering has to satisfy, in addition, two other properties.

(M_2)   if p is $<_w$-minimal in $[a]$ for some $\{p,q\}$-covering action a and
   q is not $<_w$-minimal in $[e]$ for any $\{p,q\}$-covering action e then $p <_w q$.

(M_3)   if $p <_w q$ then p is $<_w$-minimal in $[e]$ for some $\{p,q\}$-covering action e.

Basically, the second property (M_2) requires that any state p which is $<_w$-minimal in some set $[a]$ is preferred to any state q, where q belongs to the set $[a]$ as well, and which is not $<_w$-minimal in any set $[e]$ where post-conditions of e are satisfied by both p and q. The third property (M_3) posits that if a state p is preferred to a state q by a preference relation $<_w$, then there must exist an action e, whose post-conditions are satisfied by these two states, such that state p is $<_w$-minimal in $[e]$.

We intend to prove at this stage that there is a way to define the invocation relation in terms of a preference relation and vice versa, while preserving respective selections of states, satisfying direct action effects. The following two definitions will be shown to ensure such an equivalence.

Definition 5. *A new invocation relation $G_<$ is defined as follows: $G_<(e, w, r)$ if and only if r is $<_w$-minimal in $[e]$, where $w, r \in \mathcal{R}, e \in E$.*

Put simply, the new relation $G_<(e, w, r)$ specifies states r that are nearest among all states in $[e]$ to the initial state w, where the action e was invoked.

Definition 6. *Given an invocation relation G, for each $w \in \mathcal{R}$ we define an ordering $<_{w,G}$ on states in $\mathcal{R}$ as follows: $p <_{w,G} q$ if and only if state p is $\{p, q\}$-cover accessible from w and state q is not $\{p, q\}$-cover accessible from w.*

This definition specifies a preference relation on states driven by a given invocation relation—state p is nearer to an initial state w than state q if and only if for all actions whose direct effects are satisfied by both states p and q, the state q is never selected by the invocation relation G, while state p is selected at least once. The following lemma establishes the sought-after equivalence between invocation and preference relations.

Lemma 2. *If the relation G satisfies the conditions $(G_1) - (G_3)$, then for each $w \in \mathcal{R}$, the ordering $<_{w,G}$ satisfies conditions $(M_1) - (M_3)$.*
If each ordering $<_w$ for $w \in \mathcal{R}$ satisfies conditions $(M_1) - (M_3)$, then the relation $G_<$ satisfies the conditions $(G_1) - (G_3)$.

Having established the role of minimality in the process of action invocation, we shall analyse actual propagation in the state-space. First of all, it is interesting to observe that the respectfulness requirement in terms of states, is related to the notion of minimality as well. More precisely, the former can be achieved by a preference relation on states. We shall say that a state x is preferred to a state y in terms of the PMA ordering [6], denoted $x \prec_w y$, if and only if $Diff(x, w) \subset Diff(y, w)$, where $Diff(p, q)$ represents the symmetric difference of p and q, i.e., $(p \backslash q) \cup (q \backslash p)$. Formally, the following observation holds.

Lemma 3. *The pair p, q respects w, $\triangleleft_w(p, q)$, if and only if $p \prec_w q$ in the PMA ordering $\prec_w$ associated with w.*

This connection indicates a way to capture $respectful$ action systems, given a system based on general augmented preferential semantics. The following two conditions further constrain orderings in $\mathcal{O}$.

(M_4) if $p \prec_w q$ then $p <_w q$.

The additional condition (M_4) ensures that an ordering $<_w$ incorporates the PMA ordering, or, in other words, includes all pairs p, q such that $p \prec_w q$. Our next condition relates to a connectivity of the set $[e]$ in terms of an ordering $\prec_w$.

(M_5) For every action e and state w, the set $min(\prec_w, [e])$ is a singleton.

Now we are ready to specify conditions ensuring desired selection-equivalence.

Theorem 1. *For every respectful action system $\langle \mathcal{R}, E, C, \mathcal{R}_c, G \rangle$ there exists a selection-equivalent action system $\langle \mathcal{W}, \mathcal{E}, \mathcal{M}, \mathcal{W}', \mathcal{O} \rangle$, if the relation G satisfies conditions $(G_1) - (G_3)$. Conversely, for every action system $\langle \mathcal{W}, \mathcal{E}, \mathcal{M}, \mathcal{W}', \mathcal{O} \rangle$ there exists a selection-equivalent respectful action system $\langle \mathcal{R}, E, C, \mathcal{R}_c, G \rangle$, if the orderings in $\mathcal{O}$ satisfy conditions $(M_1) - (M_5)$.*

Basically, this observation establishes that, under considered conditions, we obtain
$$Res_{C\mathcal{R}_cG}(w,e) = Res_{\mathcal{MW'O}}(w,e)$$
for any action e and state w. The observed selection-equivalence has been achieved without extending the state-space, action domain, or causal transition relation—indicating that minimal change is present in the causal propagation semantics masked by the invocation relation.

4.2 Propagating Minimal Change with Causal Relationships

While the hyper-state space, proposed in [3], is a powerful concept that would allow us to completely characterise Thielscher's approach, we shall now introduce another novel concept that abstracts away certain elements of the hyper-state space semantics. It is this *power-state space* proposal that we believe can be unified with Sandewall's causal propagation semantics under the general augmented preferential semantics.

First of all, we need to re-iterate the main idea behind the hyper-state space semantics. This proposal augmented the underlying language by adding to the set of fluent names $\mathcal{F}$, and constructing the set of *justifier fluents* $\mathring{\mathcal{F}}$ which has the same cardinality as $\mathcal{F}$. The justifier fluents maintain contextual information that becomes important during causal propagation. The set of *justifier literals* $\mathring{L}_{\mathcal{F}} = \mathring{\mathcal{F}} \cup \{\neg q : q \in \mathring{\mathcal{F}}\}$ is mapped from $L_{\mathcal{F}}$ by the function $l : L_{\mathcal{F}} \to \mathring{L}_{\mathcal{F}}$ which intuitively provides an added space-dimension corresponding to each fluent $f \in \mathcal{F}$. We will use the abbreviation $\mathring{f}$ instead of $l(f)$ for simplicity. In addition, a justifier set $\mathring{J}$ for any set of fluent literals $J \subseteq L_{\mathcal{F}}$ is defined as $\mathring{J} = \cup_{f \in J}\{l(f)\} = \cup_{f \in J}\{\mathring{f}\}$. These constructions allow us to state more precisely what is meant by a hyper-state.

Definition 7. *Given a set of fluents $\mathcal{F}$, a* hyper-state *is a maximal consistent set of literals from $L_{\mathcal{F}} \cup \mathring{L}_{\mathcal{F}}$.*

That is, we produce "clones" or copies of all the fluent names in our language and use this expanded language in forming (hyper-)states. We will denote the set of all hyper-states as Ω, where the dimension of Ω is $2m$, m being the dimension of W. The following two functions map hyper-state space Ω to normal space W and vice versa.

Definition 8. *A* projection *from Ω to W, $p : \Omega \to W$, is the function mapping a hyper-state $s = \{f_1, ..., f_m, \mathring{f}_1, ..., \mathring{f}_m\} \in \Omega$ to a state $r = \{f_1, ..., f_m\} \in W$.*

Definition 9. *A* hyper-neighbourhood *of a state $r \in W$, $N : W \to 2^{\Omega}$, is the function mapping a state r to a set of hyper-states: $N(r) = \{s \in \Omega : r = p(s)\}$.*

Intuitively, justifier literals represent explicit causes for a state $r \in W$, and the set $N(r)$ contains states where all possible causes (i.e., justifier literals) vary, while the (proper) literals defined on $\mathcal{F}$ are fixed. We denote the hyper-part of a hyper-state $s \in \Omega$ as $h(s) = s \setminus p(s)$. Before we formally introduce the required notion of a binary causal relation on hyper-states, let us illustrate its purpose.

Suppose we have an action system with $\mathcal{F} = \{a, b, c\}$, $\mathcal{D} = \{\neg b \to \neg a\}$, $R = \{\neg b \text{ causes } \neg a \text{ if } \top\}$, and $\mathcal{L} = \{\langle\{b\}, x, \{\neg b\}\rangle\}$. Let us consider action x executed at initial state $w = \{a, b, c\}$. The action's direct effect is $\{\neg b\}$, yielding the intermediate state $\{a, \neg b, c\} = (w \setminus \{b\}) \cup \{\neg b\}$. This state contradicts the given domain constraint. However, the system's sole causal law applies: $(\{a, \neg b, c\}, \{\neg b\}) \rightsquigarrow (\{\neg a, \neg b, c\}, \{\neg a, \neg b\})$. The state component of the resultant pair obeys the domain constraint and satisfies direct effect. Therefore it is an element of $Res_{RDL}(w, a)$. It can be verified that $Res_{RDL}(w, a)$ is a singleton. We now indicate how this propagation can be traced in the hyper-state space. The hyper-neighbourhood $N(r)$ of the intermediate state $r = \{a, \neg b, c\}$ contains eight hyper-states (see Figure 1). Some of these represent the initial history component $\{\neg b\}$ — these hyper-states are exactly those in $N(r) \cap [\overset{\circ}{\neg b}]$. The hyper-neighbourhood of the successor state $r' = \{\neg a, \neg b, c\}$ contains some hyper-states accountable for the final history component $\{\neg a, \neg b\}$. These states are exactly those in $N(r') \cap [\overset{\circ}{\neg a} \wedge \overset{\circ}{\neg b}]$ The idea, then, is to construct just such a binary relation on hyper-states for an action system so that transitions in hyper-state space correspond to causal propagation.

Definition 10. *A binary relation $\mathcal{C}$ is defined on $\Omega \times \Omega$. We say that $\mathcal{C}(s, s')$ if and only if there exists a causal relationship ϵ causes ρ if Φ such that*

$$p(s) \vdash \epsilon \wedge \Phi \wedge \neg \rho \quad \text{and} \quad p(s') = (p(s) \setminus \{\neg \rho\}) \cup \{\rho\}$$
$$h(s) \vdash \overset{\circ}{\epsilon} \quad \quad \quad \text{and} \quad h(s') = (h(s) \setminus \{\overset{\circ}{\neg \rho}\}) \cup \{\overset{\circ}{\rho}\}.$$

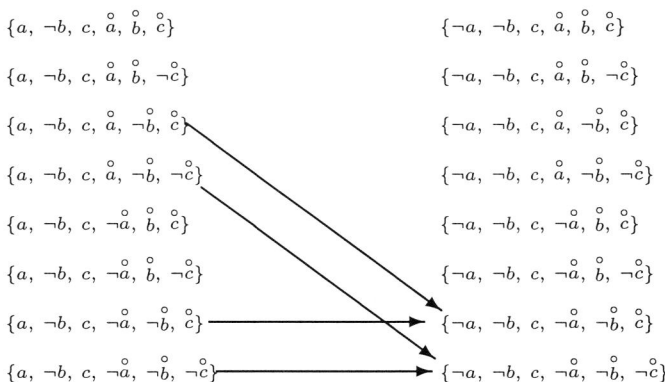

Fig. 1. The $\mathcal{C}$-links between hyper-neighbourhoods of the states $r = \{a, \neg b, c\}$ and $r' = \{\neg a, \neg b, c\}$, generated by a causal relationship $\neg b$ causes $\neg a$ if $\top$.

The fact that all the states in $N(r) \cap [\overset{\circ}{\neg b}]$ have $\mathcal{C}(s, s')$-links to the states in $N(r') \cap [\overset{\circ}{\neg a} \wedge \overset{\circ}{\neg b}]$ is not a coincidence, and is formally captured by a so-called *power-state space* semantics which allows us to concentrate more on the actual causal propagations occurring between one hyper-neighbourhood and another. First, however, the following definition will prove convenient.

Definition 11. *For a state $q \in W$ and a set $z \subseteq N(q)$, a partial state $\gamma_q(z)$ is defined as* $\cap_{s \in z} s$.

For example, $r = \{a, \neg b, c\}$ and $z = N(r) \cap [\neg \overset{\circ}{b}]$ yield a partial state $\gamma_r(z) = \{a, \neg b, c, \neg \overset{\circ}{b}\}$. Now let us consider a set Γ of cardinality equal to that of 2^Ω. We define a mapping $\gamma : 2^\Omega \to \Gamma$, such that $\gamma(z) = \gamma_q(z)$ if $z \subseteq N(q)$ for some $q \in W$, and $\gamma(z) = \emptyset$ otherwise. This set Γ will be referred to as *power-state space*, being isomorphic to the power set of the hyper-state space Ω. Having defined the function $\gamma(z)$ for every subset of the hyper-state space Ω, we construct a binary relation on elements of Γ.

Definition 12. *A binary relation $\rightharpoonup$ is defined on $\Gamma \times \Gamma$. Given two elements $x_1, x_2 \in \Gamma$ such that $x_1 \neq \emptyset$ and $x_2 \neq \emptyset$, we say that $x_1 \rightharpoonup x_2$ if and only if $x_1 = \gamma(z_1)$ and $x_2 = \gamma(z_2)$ for some $z_1, z_2 \in 2^\Omega$ such that*

$$\forall s \in z_1, \exists s' \in z_2, \text{ such that } \mathcal{C}(s, s') \quad \text{and} \quad \forall s' \in z_2, \exists s \in z_1, \text{ such that } \mathcal{C}(s, s').$$

We will abbreviate $x_1 \rightharpoonup x_2$, where $x_1 = \gamma(z_1)$ and $x_2 = \gamma(z_2)$, as $\gamma(z_1) \rightharpoonup \gamma(z_2)$. Intuitively, $\gamma(z_1) \rightharpoonup \gamma(z_2)$ means that there are no hyper-states in z_1 without an outcoming $\mathcal{C}$−link to some hyper-state in z_2, and there are no hyper-states in z_2 without an incoming $\mathcal{C}$−link from some hyper-state in z_1. Figure 1 exemplifies that $\gamma(N(r) \cap [\neg \overset{\circ}{b}]) \rightharpoonup \gamma(N(r') \cap [\neg \overset{\circ}{a} \wedge \neg \overset{\circ}{b}])$. It is easy to verify that the defined relation $\rightharpoonup$ is transitive. It is precisely the binary relation $\rightharpoonup$ that captures causal propagation in Thielscher's system. We begin by introducing a few notions that will be useful in analysing causal links $\mathcal{C}(s, s')$ and $x \rightharpoonup x'$.

Definition 13. *A trigger set of states, denoted $\|E\|_w$, is defined for an initial state $w \in W$ and an action a, where $\langle C, a, E \rangle$ is the action law, as*

$$\{s \in N(q) : q \in W, q \in min(\prec_w, [a]), h(s) \vdash \overset{\circ}{E}\}$$

where $\prec_w$ is the PMA ordering, and $[a]$ stands for a set of states consistent with $\wedge E$ (a conjunction of all literals in E).

That is, in terms of the PMA ordering, $\|E\|_w$ is the set contained in the hyperneighbourhood $N(q)$ of state q nearest to the initial state w, and the states $s \in \|E\|_w$ represent the initial causal context, i.e., initial causally justified changes triggered by effects E. For instance, if an action law $\langle \{b\}, x, \{\neg b\} \rangle$, is applied to the initial state $\{a, b, c\}$, then the trigger set $\|\{\neg b\}\|_{\{a,b,c\}}$ contains exactly those states which happen to have out-coming $\mathcal{C}$-links in Figure 1. We can view changes triggered by the set $\|E\|_w$ as propagating in hyper-state space towards a hyper-neighbourhood of a possible successor state. The point where this propagation ends can now be defined explicitly.

Definition 14. *A state $s \in \Omega$ is final iff $\{s' : \mathcal{C}(s, s')\} = \emptyset$.*
A state $x \in \Gamma$ is final iff $\{x' : x \rightharpoonup x'\} = \emptyset$.

We are now in a position to define a selection function for power-space semantics specifying the set of possible successor states $Res_\Gamma(w, a)$. We shall see that this completely characterises Thielscher's resultant state set $Res_{RDL}(w, a)$.

Definition 15. *Let $\mathcal{F}, A, \mathcal{L}, w, \langle C, a, E \rangle$ be the same as in definition 4, Γ the set of power-states, and $\rightharpoonup$ binary relation defined by Definition 12. A state $r \in W$ is a successor state of w and a, that is, $r \in Res_\Gamma(w, a)$, if and only if $\gamma(\|E\|_w) \rightharpoonup \gamma(z)$, where $\gamma(z)$ is final and $p(z) = r$.*

Intuitively, the causal propagation in power-state space starts in a power-state which corresponds to a trigger set of hyper-states and ends in a final power-state corresponding to a set transitively reachable from *all* initial justifier literals. In other words, this process propagates "minimal change" within a set of possible states of higher dimensions, instead of keeping an explicit (and changing) account of context-dependent action effects. The second central result of this study can now be obtained.

Theorem 2. $Res_{RDL}(w, e) = Res_{\Gamma}(w, e)$.

It is quite clear that the power-space semantics is an instance of the general augmented preferential semantics. Specifically, we just need to construct an action system $\langle \mathcal{W}, \Gamma, \mathcal{E}, \mathcal{M}, \mathcal{W}', \mathcal{O} \rangle$, where $\mathcal{E} = A$, $\mathcal{M} = \rightarrow$, and $\mathcal{W}'$ is a subset of $\mathcal{W}$ such that its elements satisfy constraints $\mathcal{D}$. The projection function $\mathcal{P}$ is defined via the hyper-space projection function p as $\mathcal{P}(\gamma(z)) = p(s)$, where $s \in z$. The set $\mathcal{O}$ is a set of orderings $\ll$ defined on power-states in such a way that respective projections satisfy the PMA ordering while preferring maximal subsets within each hyper-neighbourhood — more precisely, $\gamma(z_1) \ll_{\gamma(x)} \gamma(z_2)$ if and only if $p(z_1) \prec_{p(x)} p(z_2)$ and $z_1 \supseteq z_2$. This tiered preference relation ensures that, given an initial state w and an action law $\langle C, a, E \rangle$, the power-state $\gamma(\|E\|_w)$ is $\ll_{\gamma(N(w))}$-minimal state among all power-states in $[a]^{\Gamma}$.

5 Discussion and Conclusions

In this paper we considered a general augmented preferential semantics for reasoning about action and causality. This semantics appears to be intuitively simple and involves, as the only components, a state-space, its admitted subset of legitimates states, a power-space, an action domain, a (causal) binary relation on states, and a uniform set of orderings. Varying all these components allows us to specify different instances of the framework. For example, a pure preferential semantics can be obtained by requesting that the causal relation is an empty set. The nature of the distinction between Sandewall's and Thielscher's approaches to propagation-oriented ramification is uncovered and reduced to the variance in transition space dimensions and an employment of different preference metrics when identifying states nearest to the initial one. In light of the general semantics, both of these cases can be found to be very similar to McCain and Turner's causal theory of action using causal fix-points [1]. This was also characterised by an augmented preferential semantics relying on the PMA ordering and an appropriate binary relation on normal state-space [2]. The main difference is that the treatment in [2] requires a *Hamiltonian* path through certain states in a state transition system leading to a McCain and Turner causal fix-point. Essentially, such a Hamiltonian path serves as a context-oriented mechanism: the effects of causality are allowed to contribute in certain situations and not in others. Formal capture of such additional contextual requirements will be the subject of future research.

References

1. Norman McCain and Hudson Turner. A causal theory of ramifications and qualifications. In *Proceedings of the 14th Int. Joint Conf. on Artificial Intelligence*, pages 1978–1984. 1995.
2. Pavlos Peppas, Maurice Pagnucco, Mikhail Prokopenko, Abhaya Nayak and Norman Foo. Preferential Semantics for Causal Systems. In *Proceedings of the Sixteenth International Joint Conference on Artificial Intelligence*, pages 118–123. Stockholm, 1999.
3. Mikhail Prokopenko, Maurice Pagnucco, Pavlos Peppas, Abhaya Nayak. Causal Propagation Semantics — A Study. In *Proceedings of the 12th Australian Joint Conference on Artificial Intelligence*, pages 378–392. Sydney, 1999.
4. Erik Sandewall. Assessments of ramification methods that use static domain constraints. In L. Aiello, J. Doyle, and S. Shapiro, editors, *Proceedings of the Fifth International Conference on Knowledge Representation and Reasoning*. Morgan-Kaufmann, 1996.
5. Michael Thielscher. Ramification and Causality. Artificial Intelligence 89: 317–364, 1997.
6. Marianne Winslett. Reasoning about actions using a possible models approach. In *Proceedings of the Seventh National Artificial Intelligence Conference*, San Mateo, CA, 1988.

Inconsistency and Preservation

Paul Wong

Automated Reasoning Group
Computer Science Laboratory
Research School of Information Sciences and Engineering
Australian National University
wongas@arp.anu.edu.au

Abstract. One of the main goals of paraconsistent logics is to develop a theory of reasoning that can tolerate inconsistencies. In this paper we present a novel way to analyze and compare several paraconsistent reasoning mechanisms in terms of their *preservational* properties. The main idea is that although an inconsistent set of data cannot all be true, such a set may nevertheless carry useful properties that are worthy of preservation. One of these properties provides a theoretically interesting way to measure the relative incoherence of a data set; another one provides a way to measure the quantity of *empirical information* in an inconsistent set.

1 Introduction

Correct reasoning is usually characterized as patterns of inference which preserve truth. According to the standard view an inference is valid if it is impossible for its premises to be true but its conclusion false. While not incorrect, the standard view is unhelpful when we are confronted with inconsistent data. Since all inconsistent sets are unsatisfiable in the standard two-valued semantics, inferences licensed by classical logics become unprincipled in the presence of inconsistencies.

Many proposals and remedies are available to achieve inconsistency tolerant reasoning. They include both semantic and syntactic approaches:

1. introduce additional truth values to alter the semantics [2, 4, 8, 16]
2. introduce additional semantic parameters such as nonstandard possible worlds, setups or situations to evaluate formulae [10, 17, 19]
3. introduce labels or annotations into formulae to represent inconsistencies [9, 13, 15]

Undoubtedly, many semantic and syntactic innovations are involved in these approaches; nonetheless, they are in agreement with the standard account of reasoning in terms of truth preservation. In contrast, Jennings *et al* [12] have proposed a more general and pragmatic account of reasoning according to which the aim of logic is to provide a theory of reasoning which specifies the procedures for preserving important metalinguistic properties of premiss sets. Accordingly, a practical reasoning system provides procedures by which a set of sentences having some metalinguistic properties can be unfailingly extended to a larger set with the same properties.

¿From this preservation-theoretic framework we can articulate two strategies for studying reasoning: the first is the identification of important metalinguistic properties of premises, and the second is the discovery of mechanisms that preserve these properties. Provisionally, no restriction is imposed on the kind of properties to be studied, except the properties in question must be nonmonotonic, i.e. not closed under supersets. Our main objective and contribution here is to carry out a program of research which takes the notion of preservation seriously and to give an analysis of various inconsistency tolerant reasoning therein.

In this paper we assume that Φ is a set of propositional formulae constructed from propositional atoms, $\{p_1, p_2, \ldots, q_1, q_2, \ldots\}$, with the usual boolean connectives, $\neg, \wedge, \vee, \rightarrow, \leftrightarrow$. We use $A, B, C, \ldots$, to denote formulae, $\top$ for any tautology, $\bot$ for any contradiction, $\Gamma, \Sigma, \Delta, \ldots$, to denote sets of formulae, and $\mathcal{A}, \mathcal{B}, \ldots$, to denote subsets of a set of formulae. We use $\vdash$ to denote the classical provability relation and $Cn(\Gamma)$ to denote $\{A \in \Phi : \Gamma \vdash A\}$. A set of formulae Γ is inconsistent if $\Gamma \vdash \bot$, otherwise Γ is consistent.

2 Paraconsistent Inferences

One common approach to handle inconsistencies resulting from data fusion of multiple sources is to fragment an inconsistent set into consistent subsets and then extract conclusions by applying classical inference to these subsets. This approach was first introduced by Rescher and Manor [18] and more recently extended by Benferhat et al [5–7].

In this section we present similar but slightly more general inference mechanisms to extract conclusions from an inconsistent set based on ideas presented in [22]. We take an inference to be a triple consisting of a premiss set Γ, a consistent *constraint* set Σ and a conclusion A. The main role of Σ is to rule out premises that are *bad* relative to Σ. Intuitively, we may take Σ to be a set of secured or prioritized data, a set of intuitions, background beliefs, or even defaults an agent has at a given time.

Definition 1. *Let Γ be a premiss set and Σ be an arbitrary but fixed consistent set which we call a constraint set on Γ. Then a subset $\mathcal{A}$ of Γ is Σ-inconsistent iff $\mathcal{A} \cup \Sigma$ is inconsistent, else $\mathcal{A}$ is Σ-consistent. A maximal Σ-consistent subset of Γ is a subset of Γ which has no proper Σ-consistent extension.*

¿From now on, we assume that Σ is an arbitrary but fixed constraint set. The set of all maximal Σ-consistent subsets of Γ is denoted by $M_\Sigma(\Gamma)$. Given a Σ-inconsistent premiss set Γ, an element $A \in \Gamma$ is a Σ-witness if $\{A\}$ is Σ-consistent, otherwise A is a Σ-villain. We define the safe part of Γ as, $S(\Gamma) = \bigcap M_\Sigma(\Gamma)$. We say that a subset $\mathcal{A} \in M_\Sigma(\Gamma)$ is large iff for each $\mathcal{B} \in M_\Sigma(\Gamma)$, $|\mathcal{B}| \leq |\mathcal{A}|$. We use $L(\Gamma)$ to denote the set of all large subsets of Γ. We now define the following notions of consequence:

Definition 2.

Σ-**universal-consequence** $A \in C_{U\Sigma}(\Gamma)$ iff for each $\mathcal{A} \in M_\Sigma(\Gamma)$, $\mathcal{A} \vdash A$
Σ-**existential-consequence** $A \in C_{E\Sigma}(\Gamma)$ iff for some $\mathcal{A} \in M_\Sigma(\Gamma)$, $\mathcal{A} \vdash A$
Σ-**argued-consequence** $A \in C_{A\Sigma}(\Gamma)$ iff there exists some $\mathcal{A}_i \in M_\Sigma(\Gamma)$ with
$\mathcal{A}_i \vdash A$ and for every $\mathcal{A}_j \in M_\Sigma(\Gamma)$, $\mathcal{A}_j \not\vdash \neg A$.
Σ-**safe-consequence** $A \in C_{S\Sigma}(\Gamma)$ iff $S(\Gamma) \vdash A$
Σ-**large-consequence** $A \in C_{L\Sigma}(\Gamma)$ iff $\mathcal{A} \vdash A$ for each $\mathcal{A} \in L(\Gamma)$.

The relative (set inclusion) ordering of Σ-consequences is summarized in the following figure. Downward arrows indicate proper set inclusions. We note that

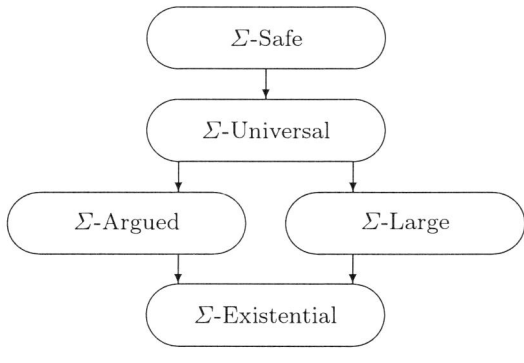

Fig. 1.

by setting $\Sigma = \emptyset$, we recover the paraconsistent consequences defined in [7]. We also note that in our definitions Σ only provides side constraints on premises. We can in fact allow Σ to be used directly to derive conclusions. We have the following stronger notions of consequence:

Definition 3.

Σ-**universal-consequence*** $A \in C^*_{U\Sigma}(\Gamma)$ iff for each $\mathcal{A} \in M_\Sigma(\Gamma)$, $\mathcal{A} \cup \Sigma \vdash A$
Σ-**existential-consequence*** $A \in C^*_{E\Sigma}(\Gamma)$ iff for some $\mathcal{A} \in M_\Sigma(\Gamma)$, $\mathcal{A} \cup \Sigma \vdash A$
Σ-**argued-consequence*** $A \in C^*_{A\Sigma}(\Gamma)$ iff there exists some $\mathcal{A}_i \in M_\Sigma(\Gamma)$ with
$\mathcal{A}_i \cup \Sigma \vdash A$ and for every $\mathcal{A}_j \in M_\Sigma(\Gamma)$, $\mathcal{A}_j \not\vdash \neg A$.
Σ-**safe-consequence*** $A \in C^*_{S\Sigma}(\Gamma)$ iff $S(\Gamma) \cup \Sigma \vdash A$
Σ-**large-consequence*** $A \in C^*_{L\Sigma}(\Gamma)$ iff $\mathcal{A} \cup \Sigma \vdash A$ for each $\mathcal{A} \in L(\Gamma)$.

It is easy to verify the following proposition:

Proposition 21 For $x \in \{U\Sigma,\ E\Sigma,\ A\Sigma,\ S\Sigma,\ L\Sigma\}$, $C_x(\Gamma) \subseteq C^*_x(\Gamma)$.

Moreover, the relative set inclusion ordering of the Σ-consequences* is analogous to figure 1.

3 Properties of Sets

In this section, we introduce two different properties of inconsistent sets. The first allows us to measure the relative *level of incoherence* of a premise set. The second provides a measurement of the relative *quantity of empirical information* of a premise set.

3.1 Level of Incoherence

Some inconsistent sets are clearly more unstable or incoherent then others. Consider, for instance,

Example 1. $\Gamma = \{p \wedge q,\ \neg p \wedge q,\ \neg q\}$ $\Delta = \{p,\ \neg p,\ q\}$

Clearly, there is a sense in which Γ is less stable, i.e. more incoherent, then Δ. More specifically, we can define a function to measure the relative *level of incoherence* of a set. By an n-covering of a set Γ, we mean a collection, $\mathcal{C} = \{\mathcal{A}_1, \ldots, \mathcal{A}_n\}$, of non-empty subsets of Γ such that $\Gamma = \bigcup \mathcal{C}$ (where $n \leq \omega$). Elements of an n-covering are called *clusters*. An n-covering is Σ-consistent iff each of its clusters is Σ-consistent.

Definition 4. *The ℓ_Σ-value of a set Γ is defined as:*

$$\ell_\Sigma(\Gamma) = \begin{cases} 0 & \text{if } \Gamma = \emptyset \text{ or } \Gamma \subseteq \{A : \vdash A\} \\ \text{the cardinality of the least} & \\ \Sigma\text{-consistent covering of } \Gamma & \text{if such a covering exists} \\ \text{up to and including } \omega & \\ \infty & \text{otherwise} \end{cases}$$

We use $\mathfrak{C}_{\ell_\Sigma}(\Gamma)$ to denote the set of all $\ell_\Sigma(\Gamma)$-fold coverings of Γ. The sentence '$\ell_\Sigma(\Gamma) = \infty$' does not say that Γ has infinite Σ-level; rather it says that Γ has no Σ-level at all. So we must distinguish between $\ell_\Sigma(\Gamma) = \infty$ and $\ell_\Sigma(\Gamma) = \omega$. More specifically if Γ contains a Σ-villain, then $\ell_\Sigma(\Gamma) = \infty$. Also observe that if $\ell_\Sigma(\Gamma) = n \neq \infty$, then there must be a Σ-consistent n-covering of Γ.

Though the ℓ_Σ function offers us a natural way to classify inconsistent sets, it is sensitive to the syntax of the premises. Consider for instance,

Example 2. $\Sigma = \{q\}$ $\Gamma = \{p \wedge \neg p\}$ $\Delta = \{p, \neg p\}$

According to our definition, the Σ-level of Γ and the Σ-level of Δ are distinct – $\ell_\Sigma(\Gamma) = \infty$ but $\ell_\Sigma(\Delta) = 2$. However, other less syntax-sensitive means to classify inconsistent sets are available. In [11], Grant proposes three model theoretic means to classify inconsistent first order theories. To our knowledge, Grant is the first to offer such systematic classifications of inconsistent theories.

3.2 Quantity of Empirical Information

Some inconsistent data are less informative then others. For instance, $\Gamma = \{p, \neg p, q, \neg q\}$ intuitively contains no information since the atoms p and q and their negation are all in Γ. While we agree that it is difficult to come up with a useful definition of value of information, we do not agree with Aisbett and Gibbon in [1] that inconsistent data provides no information to a decision maker. What is and what isn't informative seems to depend, at least partly, on the goal of the agent in possession of the data. For a tax auditor, inconsistencies in a taxpayer's records are useful information for detecting possible fraud. Inconsistencies may also be useful in cases where they are deployed as directives to guide learning or as indicators for faulty components in a complex system. Hence we need to develop a theoretical framework to distinguish different sorts of inconsistent data. In [14], a definition for measuring the amount of *semantic information* of an inconsistent set is given. In this section we give a definition for measuring the amount of *empirical information* in an inconsistent set.

By a quasi-model of Γ, we mean any two-valued model of any $\mathcal{A} \in M_\Sigma(\Gamma)$. Taking Γ to be a set of empirical data, i.e. data about the state of the world, we may intuitively interpret each quasi-model as representing a possible state of the world according to Γ. To define the relative quantity of empirical information of an inconsistent set, we first define the following function:

Definition 5. *The λ_Σ-value of a set Γ is defined as:*

$$\lambda_\Sigma(\Gamma) = \begin{cases} 0 & \text{if } \Gamma = \emptyset \text{ or } \Gamma \subseteq \{A : \vdash A\} \\ |M_\Sigma(\Gamma)| & \text{if } M_\Sigma(\Gamma) \neq \emptyset \\ \infty & \text{otherwise} \end{cases}$$

In effect, the λ_Σ-value is just the number of maximal Σ-consistent subsets of Γ. In terms of the relation between ℓ_Σ and λ_Σ, it is straightforward to show the following:

Proposition 31 *For any $\Gamma \subseteq \Phi$,*
$\ell_\Sigma(\Gamma) = n \Rightarrow \lambda_\Sigma(\Gamma) \geq n$, *for $1 \leq n < \omega$*

Since Σ-villains are Σ-inconsistent and tautologies do not contribute any information about the world, we may disregard them when we are considering the amount of empirical information of a set. We let the root of Γ, $R(\Gamma)$, be the set of propositional atoms occurring in the set $\bigcup M_\Sigma(\Gamma) - \{A \in \Gamma : \vdash A\}$, i.e., $R(\Gamma)$ is the set the propositional atoms occurring in Σ-witnesses that are not tautologies. In counting the number of quasi-models of Γ, we are only concerned with the number of *equivalence classes* of quasi-models with respect to $R(\Gamma)$. So the the maximum possible number of such equivalence classes is $2^{|R(\Gamma)|}$. We use $Q_{R(\Gamma)}(\Gamma)$ to denote the collection of such equivalence classes of quasi-models. We note that $|Q_{R(\Gamma)}(\Gamma)| \leq 2^{|R(\Gamma)|}$.

Definition 6. *The quantity of empirical information of Γ is given by:*

$$I_\Sigma(\Gamma) = \begin{cases} |R(\Gamma)| - \log_2 |Q_{R(\Gamma)}(\Gamma)| & \text{if } \lambda_\Sigma(\Gamma) = 1 \\ |R(\Gamma)| - \log_2 \lambda_\Sigma(\Gamma) & \text{if } \lambda_\Sigma(\Gamma) > 1 \\ 0 & \text{otherwise} \end{cases}$$

When $\lambda_\Sigma(\Gamma) = 1$, $I_\Sigma(\Gamma)$ is based on the ratio between $2^{|R(\Gamma)|}$ and $|Q_{R(\Gamma)}(\Gamma)|$. When $\lambda_\Sigma(\Gamma) > 1$, $I_\Sigma(\Gamma)$ is defined by a decreasing function of the λ_Σ-value of Γ. Intuitively, the λ_Σ-value of Γ provides a way to measure the amount of conflict amongst the Σ-witnesses. When $\lambda_\Sigma(\Gamma) = 1$, there is no conflict and when $\lambda_\Sigma(\Gamma) > 1$ it means that there are conflicts amongst the Σ-witnesses. Moreover, the higher the λ_Σ-value of Γ, the more Σ-inconsistent subsets reside amongst the Σ-witnesses. If $\lambda_\Sigma(\Gamma) = k > 1$, then by taking the union of each distinct pair $\mathcal{A}, \mathcal{B} \in M_\Sigma(\Gamma)$ there are at least $\frac{k(k-1)}{2}$ many ways to generate Σ-inconsistent subsets amongst the Σ-witnesses. Consider the following example:

Example 3. Let $\Sigma = \{s\}$.

$\Gamma_1 =$	$\{p \wedge q,\ \neg p \wedge r,\ \neg s\}$	$\Gamma_2 =$	$\{p \wedge q \wedge r,\ \neg p \wedge q \wedge r,\ p \wedge \neg q \wedge r,\ \neg s\}$
$R(\Gamma_1)$	$\{p,q,r\}$	$R(\Gamma_2)$	$\{p,q,r\}$
$|R(\Gamma_1)|$	3	$|R(\Gamma_2)|$	3
$\lambda_\Sigma(\Gamma_1)$	2	$\lambda_\Sigma(\Gamma_2)$	3
$I_\Sigma(\Gamma_1)$	2.00	$I_\Sigma(\Gamma_2)$	1.42

In our example, $R(\Gamma_1)$ and $R(\Gamma_2)$ are identical. Moreover, since $\neg s$ is a Σ-villain s is not in $R(\Gamma_i)$, $i = 1, 2$. The λ_Σ-value of Γ_1 is lower and so the amount of conflicts in the set of Σ-witnesses in Γ_1 is also lower. Consequently, $I_\Sigma(\Gamma_1) > I_\Sigma(\Gamma_2)$.

4 Σ-Forced Consequence

In this section we introduce a new paraconsistent consequence, called Σ-forced consequence, based on the notion of Σ-level. Σ-forced consequence is a generalization of a paraconsistent consequence operator introduced in [20, 21].

Definition 7.

Σ**-forced consequence** $A \in C_{F\Sigma}(\Gamma)$ iff for each $\mathcal{C} \in \mathfrak{C}_{\ell_\Sigma}(\Gamma)$, there exists some $\mathcal{A} \in \mathcal{C} : \mathcal{A} \vdash A$.

Σ**-forced consequence*** $A \in C^*_{F\Sigma}(\Gamma)$ iff for each $\mathcal{C} \in \mathfrak{C}_{\ell_\Sigma}(\Gamma)$, there exists some $\mathcal{A} \in \mathcal{C} : \mathcal{A} \cup \Sigma \vdash A$.

In other words, A is a Σ-forced consequence of Γ iff for every $\ell_\Sigma(\Gamma)$-fold covering of Γ, there is a cluster which classically implies A. Again, the main difference between $C_{F\Sigma}$ and $C^*_{F\Sigma}$ is the role Σ plays in deriving conclusions. Similar to the previous result, any Σ-forced consequence is a Σ-forced consequence*, i.e. for any $\Gamma \subseteq \Phi$, $C_{F\Sigma}(\Gamma) \subseteq C^*_{F\Sigma}(\Gamma)$.

We also note that $C_{F\Sigma}$ and $C^*_{F\Sigma}$ are defined relative to the Σ-level of a set. Since the Σ-level of a set is not closed under supersets in general, $C_{F\Sigma}$ and $C^*_{F\Sigma}$ are both non-monotonic with respect to Γ. However, if we define Σ-forced consequence and consequence* relative to a fixed n, for $n \in \mathbb{N}$, (i.e., replace 'every $\ell_\Sigma(\Gamma)$-fold covering' with 'every n-covering' in the definition), then the resulting notions of consequence are monotonic with respect to Γ. Nonetheless, these consequences are unprincipled when $\ell_\Sigma(\Gamma) > n$. ¿From a nonmonotonic reasoning perspective, it would be of some theoretical interest to study a varying-Σ approach to Σ-consequence. For instance, it is easy to see that for a fixed premiss set Γ, if Σ' contains Σ, then $C_{x\Sigma}(\Gamma)$ contains $C_{x\Sigma'}(\Gamma)$, where $x \in \{E, A, F, L, U, S\}$. In effect, we need to distinguish between two kinds of nonmonotonicity – those with respect to the premiss set and those with respect to the constraint set. This is particularly interesting in modeling agents who are endowed with meta-beliefs that govern and provide constraints on lower level beliefs. Intriguing as it may be, however, we will not work out the details of the varying-Σ approach here.

On the assumption that a premise set Γ does not contain any Σ-villain, the relationship between Σ-forced consequence and other Σ-consequences (of Γ) is summarized in figure 2. Downward arrows indicate set inclusions.

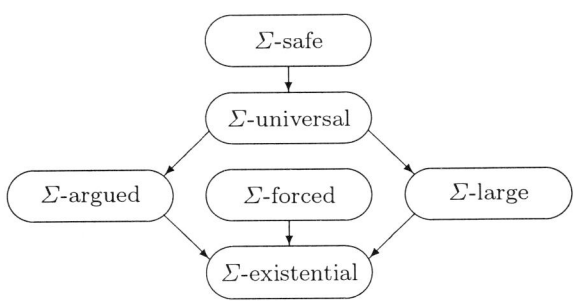

Fig. 2.

5 Preservation

In this section we will focus on the preservational properties of our inference mechanisms in terms of the ℓ_Σ, λ_Σ and I_Σ values of premiss sets. We can characterize the preservational property of a consequence operator C both weakly and strongly. The weak characterization specifies the effect of extending the premiss set with a single consequence; whereas the strong characterization specifies the effect of extending the premiss set with the entire consequence set. These notions are explicated formally in the following definitions:

Definition 8. *Let C be a consequence operator defined over the language Φ, i.e., $C : \wp(\Phi) \longrightarrow \wp(\Phi)$. We say that C is*

weak ℓ_Σ-preserving iff for any $\Gamma \subseteq \Phi$ and any $A \in C(\Gamma)$,
$\ell_\Sigma(\Gamma) = n \Rightarrow \ell_\Sigma(\Gamma \cup \{A\}) = n$
strong ℓ_Σ-preserving iff for any $\Gamma \subseteq \Phi$,
$\ell_\Sigma(\Gamma) = n \Rightarrow \ell_\Sigma(\Gamma \cup C(\Gamma)) = n$
weak λ_Σ-preserving iff for any $\Gamma \subseteq \Phi$ and any $A \in C(\Gamma)$,
$\lambda_\Sigma(\Gamma) = n \Rightarrow \lambda_\Sigma(\Gamma \cup \{A\}) = n$
strong λ_Σ-preserving iff for any $\Gamma \subseteq \Phi$,
$\lambda_\Sigma(\Gamma) = n \Rightarrow \lambda_\Sigma(\Gamma \cup C(\Gamma)) = n$
weak I_Σ-preserving iff for any $\Gamma \subseteq \Phi$ any $A \in C(\Gamma)$ with $R(\{A\}) \subseteq R(\Gamma)$,
$I_\Sigma(\Gamma) = n \Rightarrow I_\Sigma(\Gamma \cup \{A\}) = n$
strong I_Σ-preserving iff for any $\Gamma \subseteq \Phi$,
  1. $R(C(\Gamma)) \subseteq R(\Gamma)$ and
  2. $I_\Sigma(\Gamma) = n \Rightarrow I_\Sigma(\Gamma \cup C(\Gamma)) = n$

We note that strong preservation is a much stronger property than weak preservation. To show that a consequence operator is not strong x-preserving, it suffices to show that it is not weak x-preserving.

Proposition 51

1. For $x \in \{\ell_\Sigma, \lambda_\Sigma, I_\Sigma\}$, any strong x-preserving consequence operator is also weak x-preserving.
2. Let C_1 and C_2 be two consequence operators such that for any $\Gamma \subseteq \Phi$, $C_1(\Gamma) \subseteq C_2(\Gamma)$. If $C_2(\Gamma)$ is weak (or strong) x-preserving, then $C_1(\Gamma)$ is weak (or strong) x-preserving for $x \in \{\ell_\Sigma, \lambda_\Sigma, I_\Sigma\}$.

Thus to show that a Σ-consequence is x-preserving it suffices, to show that its Σ-consequence* counterpart is x-preserving. In terms of the classical consequence operator Cn however, it is clear that for $x \in \{\ell_\emptyset, \lambda_\emptyset, I_\emptyset\}$ Cn is neither weak nor strong x-preserving (since for an inconsistent Γ, $Cn(\Gamma) = \Phi$).

The preservational properties of our Σ-consequences and Σ-consequences* are summarized in figure 3. '+' ('−') indicates that the relevant property is (is not) preserved.

	weak			strong				weak			strong		
	ℓ_Σ	λ_Σ	I_Σ	ℓ_Σ	λ_Σ	I_Σ		ℓ_Σ	λ_Σ	I_Σ	ℓ_Σ	λ_Σ	I_Σ
$C_{E\Sigma}$	−	−	−	−	−	−	$C^*_{E\Sigma}$	−	−	−	−	−	−
$C_{A\Sigma}$	+	+	+	−	−	−	$C^*_{A\Sigma}$	+	+	+	−	−	−
$C_{F\Sigma}$	+	−	−	+	−	−	$C^*_{F\Sigma}$	+	−	−	+	−	−
$C_{L\Sigma}$	−	−	−	−	−	−	$C^*_{L\Sigma}$	−	−	−	−	−	−
$C_{U\Sigma}$	+	+	+	+	+	−	$C^*_{U\Sigma}$	+	+	+	+	+	−
$C_{S\Sigma}$	+	+	+	+	+	−	$C^*_{S\Sigma}$	+	+	+	+	+	−

Fig. 3.

5.1 Maximality

Since for each consequence operator C we can define a consequence relation $\mathrel{\vert\!\sim}_C$ such that $\langle \Gamma, A\rangle \in \mathrel{\vert\!\sim}_C$ iff $A \in C(\Gamma)$, we may speak of the consequence relation $\mathrel{\vert\!\sim}_C$ as being induced by C. Furthermore we say that $\mathrel{\vert\!\sim}_C$ is (weakly or strongly) x-preserving iff C is. One important fact is that strictly speaking there is no smallest (weakly or strongly) x-preserving consequence relation, $x \in \{\ell_\Sigma, \lambda_\Sigma, I_\Sigma\}$. By this we mean that for a fixed x the intersection of all x-preserving consequence relations (induced by their respective consequence operators) is in fact empty. However, it is possible that two consequence operators C_1 and C_2 may be related in such a way that (1) C_1 is (weakly or strongly) x-preserving but C_2 is not, and (2) for any Γ, $C_1(\Gamma)$ is contained in $C_2(\Gamma)$. In such a case it is natural to ask whether $\mathrel{\vert\!\sim}_{C_1}$ can be extended maximally within $\mathrel{\vert\!\sim}_{C_2}$ to a (weakly or strongly) x-preserving consequence relation. In fact, this is exactly the situation at hand. For instance, $C_{U\Sigma}$ is strongly ℓ_Σ-preserving but $C_{L\Sigma}$ is not (moreover for any Γ, $C_{U\Sigma}(\Gamma) \subseteq C_{L\Sigma}(\Gamma)$). So a natural question is whether $\mathrel{\vert\!\sim}_{C_{U\Sigma}}$ can be extended maximally to a ℓ_Σ-preserving extension within $\mathrel{\vert\!\sim}_{C_{L\Sigma}}$. Such maximal extensions are theoretically interesting since they allow us to deduce more conclusions while still preserving the relevant property in question.

5.2 Special Conditions

Another theoretically interesting question is whether there are special conditions under which a particular inference mechanism can preserve a property even though the mechanism does not preserve the property in general. We may think of these special conditions as *application* conditions which allow us to use certain inference mechanisms to preserve certain properties. For instance, if each maximal Σ-consistent subset of a premise set Γ has the same cardinality, then $C_{L\Sigma}(\Gamma)$ is identical to $C_{U\Sigma}(\Gamma)$. So the λ_Σ value of Γ is preserved by $C_{L\Sigma}$ in this case even though $C_{L\Sigma}$ is neither weakly nor strongly λ_Σ-preserving in general. For instance, the following fact allows us to use $C_{A\Sigma}$ to locally preserve the ℓ_Σ value of Γ when $\ell_\Sigma(\Gamma) = \lambda_\Sigma(\Gamma) = n$.

Proposition 52 *For any $\Gamma \subseteq \Phi$,*
$\ell_\Sigma(\Gamma) = \lambda_\Sigma(\Gamma) = n < \omega \Rightarrow \ell_\Sigma(\Gamma \cup C_{A\Sigma}(\Gamma)) = n$.

5.3 Combining Inference Mechanisms

Finally, we have not considered the effect of combining different inference mechanisms. For instance by taking the union and intersection of $\mathrel{\vert\!\sim}_{C_{F\Sigma}}$ and $\mathrel{\vert\!\sim}_{C_{U\Sigma}}$, we can obtain two new consequence relations. Clearly, $\mathrel{\vert\!\sim}_{C_{F\Sigma}} \cap \mathrel{\vert\!\sim}_{C_{U\Sigma}}$ is both non-empty and ℓ_Σ-preserving (since $C_{F\Sigma}$ and $C_{U\Sigma}$ are both ℓ_Σ-preserving). Again from the point of view of section 5.1, $\mathrel{\vert\!\sim}_{C_{F\Sigma}} \cup \mathrel{\vert\!\sim}_{C_{U\Sigma}}$ is a more interesting option since it extends both $\mathrel{\vert\!\sim}_{C_{F\Sigma}}$ and $\mathrel{\vert\!\sim}_{C_{U\Sigma}}$.

6 Conclusion

In this paper we have applied the preservation-theoretic approach to analyze and compare six different inconsistency tolerant inference mechanisms. The crux of our motivation is to demonstrate that *truth is not the only property worthy of preservation*. What properties are to be preserved in an inference can depend on our interests and goals. As the late Jon Barwise puts it:

> ... the study of valid inference as a situated activity shifts attention from *truth preservation to information extraction* and *information processing*. Valid inference is seen not as a relation between sentences that simply preserves truth, but rather as a situated, purposeful activity whose aim is the extraction of information from a situation, information relevant to the agent. ([3], p.xiv)

In a broader context, the notion of preservation can provide a theoretically rich framework for understanding a variety of formalisms. In future work, we hope to extend our approach to analyze belief revision mechanisms, nonmonotonic reasoning systems and other practical reasoning systems.

References

1. J. Aisbett and G. Gibbon. A practical measure of the information in a logic theory. *Journal of Experiment and Theoretical Artificial Intelligence*, 11:201–217, 1999.
2. O. Arieli and A. Avron. Reasoning with logical bilattices. *Journal of Logic, Language, and Information*, 5:25–63, 1996.
3. J. Barwise. *The Situation in Logic*. CSLI, 1989.
4. N. D. Belnap. A useful four-valued logic. In J. M. Dunn and G. Epstein, editors, *Modern Uses of Multiple-Valued Logic*, pages 8–37. D. Reidel Pub., 1975.
5. S. Benferhat, C. Cayrol, D. Dubois, J. Lang, and H. Prade. Inconsistency management and prioritized syntax-based entailment. In *Proceedings of the Thirteenth International Joint Conferences on Artificial Intelligence*, volume 1, pages 640–645, 1993.
6. S. Benferhat, D. Dubois, and H. Prade. How to infer from inconsistent beliefs without revising? In *Proceedings of the Fourteenth International Joint Conferences on Artificial Intelligence*, pages 1449–1455, 1995.
7. S. Benferhat, D. Dubois, and H. Prade. Some syntactic approaches to the handling of inconsistent knowledge bases: A comparative study, part i: The flat case. *Studia Logica*, 58 (1):17–45, 1997.
8. P. Besnard and T. H. Schaub. Circumscribing inconsistency. In *Proceedings of the Fifteenth International Joint Conferences on Artificial Intelligence*, volume 1, pages 150–155, 1997.
9. H. A. Blair and V. S. Subrahmanian. Paraconsistent logic programming. *Theoretical Computer Science*, 68 (2):135, 1989.
10. R. Fagin, J. Y. Halpern, and M. Y. Vardi. A nonstandard approach to the logical omniscience problem. *Artificial Intelligence*, 79:203–240, 1995.
11. J. Grant. Classifications for inconsistent theories. *Notre Dame Journal of Formal Logic*, 19 (3):435–444, 1978.

12. R. E. Jennings, C. W. Chan, and M. J. Dowad. Generalised inference and inference modelling. In *Proceedings of the Twelfth International Joint Conferences on Artificial Intelligence*, volume 2, pages 1046–1051, 1991.
13. M. Kifer and E. L. Lozinskii. A logic for reasoning with inconsistency. *Journal of Automated Reasoning*, 9:179–215, 1992.
14. E. L. Lozinskii. Resolving contradictions: A plausible semantics for inconsistent systems. *Journal of Automated Reasoning*, 12:1–31, 1994.
15. J. J. Lu and E. Rosenthal. Annotations, signs, and generally paraconsistent logics. In E. A. Yfantis, editor, *Intelligent Systems: Third Golden West International Conference, Edited and Selected Papers Volume 1 and 2*, pages 143–157. Kluwer Academic Pub., 1995.
16. G. Priest. Minimally inconsistent LP. *Studia Logica*, 50 (2):321, 1991.
17. N. Rescher and R. Brandom. *The Logic of Inconsistency: A Study in Non-Standard Possible World Semantics and Ontology*. American Philosophical Quarterly, 1979.
18. N. Rescher and R. Manor. On inference from inconsistent premisses. *Theory and Decision*, 1:179–217, 1970.
19. R. Routley and R. K. Meyer. The semantics of entailment. In H. Leblanc, editor, *Truth, Syntax and Modality: Proceedings of the Temple University Conference on Alternative Semantics*, pages 199–243. North-Holland Pub., 1973.
20. P. K. Schotch and R. E. Jennings. Inference and necessity. *Journal of Philosophical Logic*, 9:327–340, 1980.
21. P. K. Schotch and R. E. Jennings. On detonating. In G. Priest, R. Routley, and J. Norman, editors, *Paraconsistent Logic: Essays on the Inconsistent*, pages 306–327. Philosophia Verlag, 1989.
22. P. Wong. Paraconsistent inference and preservation. Workshop on Logic in Computing Science, University of Technology, Sydney, 1998.

Inductive Inference of Chess Player Strategy

Anthony R. Jansen, David L. Dowe, and Graham E. Farr

School of Computer Science and Software Engineering,
Monash University,
Clayton, Victoria 3800
Australia
{tonyj, dld, gfarr}@csse.monash.edu.au

Abstract. We investigate the problem of inferring, from records of chess games, some aspects of the strategy used to play the games. Initially, game records are generated from self-play by two simple chess programs, one of which does a one-ply search while the other does a four-ply quiescent search. In each case, we are able to infer, from just the game records, good estimates of the weights used in the evaluation function. The approach is then applied to grandmaster games. Our one-ply and quiescent four-ply programs are now drastic simplifications of the true strategy used. Nonetheless, using inferred weights for these hypothetical models, we are still able to achieve some success (as measured by compression rates for the games) in predicting moves made by the players.

1 Introduction

Most research on Computer Game Playing has concentrated on getting programs to play games as well as possible. This is usually achieved by the use of appropriate search algorithms together with some explicit coding of human knowledge about strategies for the game (Shannon, 1950), although learning methods have also been used (Samuel, 1959, draughts/checkers; recent chess examples include Thrun, 1995, Morales, 1996).

In this paper we go in an opposite direction. Starting from records of games played, we wish to infer something about the strategy used. This is clearly a machine learning problem, but different to problems of improving play by learning from experience. We approach the problem in two steps. First, we attempt to infer a strategy from records of chess games generated by a simple chess program. Here the actual algorithm is known, so this provides an important test of the feasibility of our approach.

We then attempt to infer aspects of the strategy used by human chess players, based on the success of the first step. This is the primary motivation behind this research. There is much unknown about the algorithms humans use, although there have been attempts by psychologists and others to understand how humans play the game (for example, Newell and Simon, 1972). The works of de Groot (1978), Frey (1977), and Levy and Newborn (1991) reveal the contrast between current game playing strategies used in computer programs, and the techniques that humans use.

Despite the amount of research exploring computer chess playing, little work appears to have been done along the lines reported here. The approach of Carmel and Markovitch (1993) tries to learn the strategy used by the opponent during play, but does not use records of games. Muggleton (1988) takes expert descriptions of how to play some specific chess endgame positions and does 'sequence induction'. The aim there is to infer a finite automaton which encodes a more general strategy for that phase of that particular type of endgame. Our approach is to begin with the result of a strategy, in the form of records of games played, and then to infer aspects of that strategy. Work in a similar vein has been done by Walczak (1992), in which an Inductive Adversary Modeler was developed that can infer the perceptual chunks used by a chess player based on game records.

In the next Section we introduce a simple game player model, its implementation, and the results obtained by doing inference with it. The work done there provides evidence of the validity of our approach. We then introduce a more advanced game player model, and discuss the results of our attempts at inference. Finally, we discuss the conclusions and future directions.

2 Simple One-Ply Player Model

2.1 Description of the Model

The simple player model is based on a 1-ply search. Positions at this depth are evaluated in the following manner. The player uses an *evaluation function* $v(\_)$ of the form

$$v(P) = \sum_{k=1}^{n} \lambda_k a_k(P), \qquad (1)$$

where

- the $a_k(\_)$ are *attributes* (or *advisors*), i.e. functions which report on some specific aspect of a position. The total number of attributes is n. Typical attributes for chess would be
  - $a_1(P)$ = the *material balance* of the position (where here, Queen = 9, Rook = 5, Bishop = Knight = 3, Pawn = 1), being the difference between the player's and opponent's total material;
  - $a_2(P)$ = the *mobility balance*, i.e. the difference between the numbers of moves available to the player and the opponent.
- the λ_k are the *weights* attached to the attributes.

The two attributes described here are the only ones used for the simple model. For each (and hence for the evaluation function as a whole), a positive value is good for the player, while a negative value is good for the opponent, and reversal of roles negates the values.

A key feature of the model is that the player chooses *probabilistically* from the moves available. This random element serves several purposes. Firstly, people do not always choose the same move from the same position, and may err. Also, the model can never account for all possible considerations a player uses to determine what move will be played. This will naturally result in uncertainty when choosing a move. Probabilistic choice of moves also allows statistical inference to be used. A consequence of probabilistic move choice is that we are not attempting to develop a model that selects the correct move in every position. Rather, we wish the correct move to have a high probability of being played. While it is desirable that the correct move be the most probable, the model will still be successful if the correct move tends to have a high probability.

The model also assumes that the player strategy is consistent – and so variation in strategy based on things like the playing style of the opponent, or whether the game is in the opening, middle or end phase, is ignored.

We now describe how the player moves under this model.

1. Input: position P.
2. Generate all positions $P_1, P_2, \ldots, P_m$, to which the player can move from position P. (We can think here of the positions $P_1, P_2, \ldots, P_m$ as corresponding to the possible **moves**, numbered $1, 2, \ldots, m$ respectively, which the player can make from the position P.)
3. Compute the evaluation $v(P_i)$ of each position P_i, $i = 1, \ldots, m$.
4. Choose a move probabilistically from $\{1, \ldots, m\}$ according to

$$\Pr(\text{move } i) = e^{v(P_i)} / (e^{v(P_1)} + \ldots + e^{v(P_m)}). \tag{2}$$

This multivariate logistic function maps position values, which range over $(-\infty, \infty)$, to the interval $[0, 1]$ in a natural and elegant way.

Let the chosen move be i^*.

5. Make the necessary move to the chosen position, P_{i^*}.

From our database of game records, we have a large set $\mathcal{P}$ of positions and for each position we are given the move that was made. It is these choices of move which are the data from which we seek to infer a model. We regard the positions themselves as prior information and do not seek to explain them.

Likelihood Function. Consider for simplicity a single position P, from which one can move to any of $(P_i : i = 1, \ldots, m)$. The observed data is the index i^* of the position P_{i^*} to which the player chose to move. Our model is $\theta = (\lambda_1, \ldots, \lambda_n)$. The likelihood function for this single data item i^* is

$$f_P(i^* | \theta) = \frac{e^{v(P_{i^*})}}{\sum_{i=1}^m e^{v(P_i)}}.$$

The actual data we have is a whole set of moves, one for each position in $\mathcal{P}$. For each $P \in \mathcal{P}$, denote the move chosen by $i^*(P)$. Then our likelihood function is

$$\prod_{P \in \mathcal{P}} f_P(i^*(P) \mid \theta) = \prod_{P \in \mathcal{P}} \frac{e^{v(P_{i^*(P)})}}{\Sigma_i e^{v(P_i)}} \tag{3}$$

The simple game player model described determines the probability of each move being played based on the weights of the attributes that are being considered. To infer the weights, a Maximum Likelihood approach was used with a simple and robust hill climbing algorithm.

2.2 Inference Results

Generated Data. To test the validity of the inference technique, a simple chess program was written which, in each position, essentially did a 1-ply search, and pseudorandomly chose a move based on the λ values that the program was given, according to Equation 2. To keep things simple, the player model only considers two attributes ($n = 2$): material balance and mobility balance. Using several sets of λ values (from Equation 1), databases of up to 1000 games were generated by the chess program playing against itself.

A question of initial interest was how large a database needs to be to allow successful inference to take place. Databases of various sizes were created considering the single attribute, material balance. The attribute weight was set at $\lambda_{MAT} = 3.0$. Inference was then conducted on the different sized databases. For a database containing only one game, the inferred λ_{MAT} value was 4.11; for a 10 game database, 3.28; for 100 games, 3.20; for 1000 games, 3.09 was inferred.

The inference results show that as the size of the database increases, the inferred value of λ_{MAT} gets closer to the correct value. For the database of 1000 games the inference performs well, although it still overestimates slightly.

To test our approach further, inference was tried on other databases of generated data, each consisting of 1000 games, with two attributes (material balance and mobility balance). In Table 1, the weights that were used to generate the games for the databases are given (as Actual Values), as are the inferred weights.

Table 1. Inference results from 1000 game databases using the simple model.

Attribute Weights	Data Set 1		Data Set 2	
	λ_{MAT}	λ_{MOB}	λ_{MAT}	λ_{MOB}
Actual Values	5.0	0.5	10.0	1.0
Inferred Values	5.15	0.51	10.23	1.02

The results show that the inference method performs well on both of these databases. Note that the inference method again slightly overfits the data, with no parameter values being underestimated.

Grandmaster Databases. Since the inference results from the generated data indicate that accurate inference is possible, it seemed worth trying our approach on grandmaster data. Although such players do not conform to our simple model, it may still be interesting to see what attribute weights are inferred for them. The same two attributes (material and mobility) are used.

The two grandmasters selected are Robert J. Fischer and Garry Kasparov. Since inference seems to perform better with larger amounts of data, the entire available database for each player is used. The results can be seen in Table 2, which shows the number of games in each grandmaster database and the inferred weights.

Table 2. Inference results from grandmaster databases using the simple model.

Player	No. Games	λ_{MAT}	λ_{MOB}	I-Random	I-Inferred	Comp (%)
Fischer	732	0.510	0.021	146047	138383	94.8
Kasparov	1030	0.458	0.025	191936	183021	95.4

These weights, however, give no indication of how well the model can predict the move made in a given position. Probabilistic prediction of information corresponds to compression of data. This fact has been exploited in the work of Althöfer (1991), where chess databases have been compressed by using a chess program to predict the most likely move to be played by a grandmaster in a given position. Here we also use data compression as a measure of predictive accuracy. The information content (in bits) of a move can be readily calculated from the probability of that move being played, using

$$I(\text{move } i) = -\log_2 Pr(\text{move } i)$$

The last three columns in Table 2 give details of the information content of the two grandmaster databases. The first value, I-Random, gives the amount of data (in bits) when the move choice is completely random, with no strategy assumed and each move equally likely. This is just uncompressed data. The next value, I-Inferred, indicates the size of the data (in bits) when compressed using the results of the Maximum Likelihood inference. The inferred weights will mean that all moves are no longer equally likely in a given position, and thus the information content will be different. The final column, Comp (%), indicates the compression achieved by giving the size of the post-compression data as a percentage of the original random information. For both grandmasters, the inferred values compress the data to about 95% of its original size. Considering the simplicity of the player model being used, this is an encouraging result.

The successful implementation and inference of the simple game player strategy in this Section has shown that even a simple model can be applied to grandmaster games with positive results. The next Section looks at a more advanced game player model that uses more aspects of the strategies that humans use.

3 A More Advanced Player Model

3.1 Description of the Model

In the previous Section we introduced a very simple player model which we used primarily to confirm the validity of our approach. The success with this model leads us to consider a more advanced model. The advanced player model takes into account more aspects used by human chess players, such as considering more position attributes, searching deeper than 1-ply, and searching some lines deeper than others. There are still many aspects missing in our advanced model, such as adjusting attribute weights depending on whether the game is in the opening, middle or end phase. However, it is a significant improvement on the simple player model.

The advanced player model is based on a quiescent 4-ply search, which works as follows. All positions at depth 1-ply are generated. Further search is done only if a capture is possible, a promotion is possible, a check can be played, or the player is already in check. Maximum search depth is 4-ply, but of course not all lines are explored to this depth.

As with the simple model, the player chooses the move probabilistically. Since the number of dimensions in the search space depends on the number of attributes, we use just four attributes ($n = 4$). We realize that both humans and computer programs generally examine many more attributes, but we have chosen this constraint in order to make the search space for our inference more tractable. The attributes used are the balance of *material*, *mobility*, *control of the centre 16 squares* and *number of attacks* (see, for example, Levy and Newborn, 1991). Attacks against pieces of equal or lesser value are considered to be worth only one tenth of an attack against a more valuable piece.

Likelihood Function. The evaluation of a single position in this model is the same as the evaluation used for the simple game player model. Each attribute is given a weighting, i.e. a λ value. The multiple ply search is also probabilistic, again just as the simple 1-ply model was. The probability of each move from the root position is calculated in the same manner as was used in Section 2. However, the evaluation for each of the 1-ply positions is now determined by considering positions at deeper levels in the search tree.

A probabilistic variation of the minimax algorithm is applied to determine the probabilities of each move available from the root position. This is similar to the way that the minimax algorithm is applied to games such as backgammon, which involve both strategy and chance. The full likelihood function for the 4-ply quiescent search is quite complex, and is contained in the Appendix.

For the inference, a Maximum Likelihood approach is again used along with a simple and robust hill climbing algorithm. It should be noted that for our 4-ply quiescent model, a typical search to determine the probabilities of the available moves needs to evaluate over 2000 positions, with the evaluation of each position depending on the four weights that need to be inferred. Rather than repeatedly searching and evaluating all of the positions on each iteration of the hill climbing algorithm, this is done only once initially with the resulting attribute values from each position stored in a search tree database. This data requires additional information about where in a given search tree each position arose. As a result, the inference programs have very large memory requirments, especially when all the moves from several games are being considered. For example, encoding all of the information from five games requires over 150 megabytes of memory. This memory expense is justified by the speed increase obtained as a result of only generating the search tree data once.

3.2 Inference Results

Generated Data. As with the simple player model, we first try inferring weights from databases created using the player model.

A chess program based on this player model was used to create databases of games that used the four attributes defined by the model with a 4-ply quiescent search. The game records were generated by the program playing against itself. Again, a pseudo-random choice between possible moves was made, based on probabilities obtained from the likelihood function. The coefficients were selected to try and make the program play as well as possible, given that it is still much simpler than human play. The level of play achieved by this model is quite weak, but it is competitive against a human beginner.

The results using the generated data showed that the Maximum Likelihood inference method worked very well, and are given in Table 3. The λ weights (from Equation 1) used to generate the data are also given (as Actual Values). Each inference is from the data of a single player in a single game, with five games being considered. The Table also gives the information content (in bits) of the data both when the move choice is random (the data is uncompressed), I-Random, and after the Maximum Likelihood inference, I-Inferred. The amount of compression of the data, Comp (%), as defined previously in Section 2.2, is also given. It can be seen that most of the games have been compressed to less than 50% or their original size. The second last row of the table shows the inference result when both the white and black moves from five games are used for inference.

Table 3. Inference results from generated data using the advanced model.

Colour	No. Moves	λ_{MAT}	λ_{MOB}	λ_{CEN}	λ_{ATT}	I-Random	I-Inferred	Comp (%)
White	126	7.11	0.25	0.49	3.65	464.7	208.5	44.9
Black	126	7.89	0.22	0.62	3.45	598.6	265.2	44.3
White	94	7.49	0.22	0.51	3.56	404.1	160.3	39.7
Black	94	8.13	0.24	0.51	3.89	458.8	169.9	37.0
White	147	7.14	0.25	0.50	3.34	662.6	299.4	45.2
Black	147	7.74	0.25	0.53	3.88	579.0	244.7	42.3
White	30	6.12	0.25	0.50	2.84	160.3	92.8	57.9
Black	30	6.49	0.19	0.29	8.36	147.0	80.5	54.8
White	99	7.75	0.17	0.47	2.98	498.3	190.4	38.2
Black	99	8.09	0.24	0.69	4.10	479.5	107.5	22.4
W & B	5 Games	7.53	0.21	0.52	3.31	3879.4	1442.1	37.2
Actual Values		7.0	0.2	0.5	3.0			

An interesting result about the inference with the advanced player model is that very good results are obtained using the data from a single game. This appears to be because each position in the search tree contributes to the data available, and the inference for a single move has such a large search tree that accurate inference is possible without needing to consider too many database positions.

This is a welcome result, because the memory requirement for a single chess game is already very large. However, the inference on five games also gave an excellent result, and the compression achieved over five games is superior to the average compression achieved for a single game. As a final point, unlike with the simple game player model, not all inferred weights overfit the correct values.

Grandmaster Databases. After successful inference on the generated data, the next step was to apply the advanced player model to do inference from grandmaster games. Again we used games by Fischer and Kasparov.

Table 4 shows the results of the inferences on two games by Fischer and two games by Kasparov. For each player, we chose the longest game the player won with both white (W) and black (B). The games were: Fischer–Taimanov, Vancouver, 1971, 89 moves; Sherwin–Fischer, USA Championship, 1966, 100 moves; Kasparov-Karpov, 1990, 102 moves; Kamsky–Kasparov, New York, 1989, 107 moves. The inferred weights are given, as is the information in the data before and after inference, and the compression achieved. The last row gives an inference using as data the 11 games played by Fischer in the 1963 USA Championships.

Table 4. Inference results from grandmaster games using the advanced model.

Player	No. Moves	λ_{MAT}	λ_{MOB}	λ_{CEN}	λ_{ATT}	I-Random	I-Inferred	Comp (%)
Kasparov	102 (W)	1.20	0.09	0.10	3.19	481.4	370.8	77.0
Kasparov	107 (B)	0.82	0.18	0.09	1.81	443.7	328.7	74.1
Fischer	89 (W)	1.31	0.00	0.06	0.89	385.5	307.6	79.8
Fischer	100 (B)	1.61	-0.06	0.09	2.82	416.7	339.1	81.4
Fischer	11 Games	1.24	0.04	0.09	1.15	1995.3	1555.3	77.9

Where the simple 1-ply model was used, we managed to compress the grandmaster data to about 95% of its original size (see Table 2). The results in Table 4 show significant improvement, with compression ranging from approximately 81% to only 74% of the original data. This demonstrates that the advanced player model certainly helps in the inference of aspects of the strategy used by these players. It is also interesting to note that Kasparov's games compressed better than those of Fischer. This could indicate that the attributes considered by the model are more in keeping with Kasparov's evaluation of a position than that of Fischer.

The final results examine compression using different training and test data. Table 5 shows the results of taking λ values inferred from one set of data taken from grandmaster games, and using it to compress other grandmaster games.

The training data used was Fischer's 11 games played in the 1963 USA Championships. This has been used to compress the same games that were used in Table 4, whose original Maximum Likelihood compression results are listed again for comparison. The final two columns in Table 5 are the information content of the games after the strategy inferred from the training data is applied to them, I-Training, and the subsequent compression achieved.

Table 5. Inference results using the advanced model with different training data.

Player	No. Moves	I-Random	I-Inferred	Comp (%)	I-Training	Comp (%)
Kasparov	102 (W)	481.1	370.8	77.0	380.2	79.0
Kasparov	107 (B)	443.7	328.7	74.1	345.0	77.8
Fischer	89 (W)	385.5	307.6	79.8	312.1	81.0
Fischer	100 (B)	416.7	339.1	81.4	348.1	83.5

The results show that the compression achieved using strategies obtained from training data that are different to the test data, is nearly as good as when strategies inferred directly from the test data are used. This is expected, since all grandmasters try to play the best possible move in a given chess position. This result shows that general strategies can be inferred from large databases, and then successfully be applied to specific instances.

4 Conclusions and Future Work

The goal of this research was to infer something about the strategies used by chess programs and, ultimately, humans based on the records of games played. Initially, a simple 1-ply model was developed to confirm the validity of the concept. The results indicated that successful inference was possible over both data generated using the simple 1-ply model, and grandmaster databases. The amount by which the data was compressed was used throughout as a measure of the modelling accuracy of the inferred strategy.

This led to the development of a more advanced player model that used a 4-ply quiescent search. The results show that excellent compression was achieved for data generated using the advanced 4-ply quiescent model (on average, data was compressed to less than 50% of its original size), and that grandmaster games could also be significantly compressed. It was also possible to compress grandmaster games using a strategy inferred from a different grandmaster.

The results indicate that it is possible to infer something about the strategies used by chess players, and that the more advanced the model is, the better is the predictive accuracy of the inferred strategy. Inductive inference of strategies based solely on information contained in databases can thus allow successful learning and prediction.

There are several directions for future work. These include developing more advanced game player models that better mimic the way humans really play chess and looking at different inference methods, such as Minimum Message Length (MML). Also, the power of the inference could be investigated further by going beyond data compression as a performance measure and determining if specific questions about game records can be answered. For example, given that strategies have been inferred for several grandmasters, can this information be used to predict who the players are in a particular chess game? Finally, these techniques can also be applied to domains other than chess and game playing.

References

Althöfer, I. (1991). Data compression using an intelligent generator: the storage of chess games as an example, *Artificial Intelligence, 52*, 109–113.

Carmel, D. and Markovitch, S. (1993). *Learning models of opponent's strategy in game playing*, (CIS Report #9318), Israel Institute of Technology.

de Groot, A.D. (1978). *Thought and Choice in Chess*, (2nd ed.), The Hague: Mouton.

Frey, P.W. (1977). *Chess Skill in Man and Machine*, New York: Springer-Verlag.

Levy, D. and Newborn, M. (1991). *How Computers Play Chess*, New York: W.H Freeman & Company.

Morales, E.M. (1996). Learning playing strategies in chess, *Computational Intelligence, 12*(1), 65–87.

Muggleton, S.H. (1988). Inductive acquisition of chess strategies. In J.E. Hayes, D. Michie & J. Richards (Eds.), *Machine Intelligence 11: Logic and the Acquisition of Knowledge* (pp. 375–389). Oxford.

Newell, A. and Simon, H. A. (1972). *Human Problem Solving*, Englewood Cliffs, N.J.: Prentice-Hall.

Samuel, A.L. (1959). Some studies in machine learning using the game of checkers, *IBM Journal*, July.

Shannon, C.E. (1950). Programming a computer for playing chess, *Philosophical Magazine, 41*, 256–275.

Thrun, S. (1995). Learning to play the game of chess. In Tesauro, G., Touretzky, D. and Leen, T. (Eds.), *Advances in Neural Information Processing Systems 7*, Massachusetts: MIT Press.

Walczak, S. (1992). Pattern-Based Tactical Planning. *International Journal of Pattern Recognition and Artificial Intelligence, 6*, 955–988.

Appendix. Quiescent 4-ply Search Likelihood Function

Some definitions:

$P_{i_1 i_2 \ldots i_d}$ = position resulting from P after sequence of moves $i_1, i_2, \ldots, i_d$.

$$\sigma_h = \sigma_h(P) = \begin{cases} +1, \text{ if Black is to move in a position } h \text{ ply distant from } P; \\ -1, \text{ if White is to move in a position } h \text{ ply distant from } P. \end{cases}$$

So, if White is to move in position P, then $\sigma_1 = +1$, $\sigma_2 = -1$, $\sigma_3 = +1$, ...

k_h = absolute value of won position at depth h from P
     = $600 - 10h$
     (a little arbitrarily, but so as to make early checkmates better than late ones);

For $h \geq 1$, define

$$v_h(P_{i_1 i_2 \ldots i_h}) = \begin{cases} 0, & \text{if } P_{i_1 i_2 \ldots i_h} \text{ is a Draw of some kind, e.g. Stalemate;} \\ k_h, & \text{if } P_{i_1 i_2 \ldots i_h} \text{ is a won position (i.e. checkmate) for White;} \\ -k_h, & \text{if } P_{i_1 i_2 \ldots i_h} \text{ is a won position for Black;} \\ \sigma_h(P) v(P_{i_1 i_2 \ldots i_h}), \\ \quad \text{if } \textit{either } P_{i_1 i_2 \ldots i_h} \text{ is quiescent } \textit{or} \text{ it is a terminal non-} \\ \quad \text{won position, i.e. } h = d; \\ \dfrac{\sum_{i_{h+1}} v_{h+1}(P_{i_1 i_2 \ldots i_{h+1}}) \exp\left(\sigma_{h+1}(P) v_{h+1}(P_{i_1 i_2 \ldots i_{h+1}})\right)}{\sum_{i_{h+1}} \exp\left(\sigma_{h+1}(P) v_{h+1}(P_{i_1 i_2 \ldots i_{h+1}})\right)}, \\ \quad \text{if } h < d \text{ and } P_{i_1 i_2 \ldots i_h} \text{ is neither won nor quiescent.} \end{cases}$$

Thus $v_h(\_)$ assigns values to positions which are h-ply distant from P. Recall that $v(\_)$ is the ordinary evaluation function. The summations are over all moves i_{h+1} that can be made in position $P_{i_1 i_2 \ldots i_h}$. Note that $v_d(\_)$ never equals the last of the possibilities listed above, since all non-won non-quiescent positions at d-ply are evaluated using $v(\_)$.

The move from position P is chosen probabilistically according to

$$\Pr(\text{move } i^*(P)) = \frac{\exp\left(\sigma_1(P) v_1(P_{i^*})\right)}{\sum_{i=1}^{m} \exp\left(\sigma_1(P) v_1(P_i)\right)}.$$

In the implementation reported in Section 3 of this paper, we use $d = 4$, and P itself is always fully searched to at least depth 1 (so is treated as non-quiescent).

This gives our likelihood for a single position P. For a set of positions, $\mathcal{P}$, we use the likelihood

$$\prod_{P \in \mathcal{P}} \Pr(\text{move } i^*(P)).$$

Compiling Logical Features into Specialized State-Evaluators by Partial Evaluation, Boolean Tables and Incremental Calculation

Tomoyuki Kaneko, Kazunori Yamaguchi, and Satoru Kawai

Graduate School of Arts and Sciences
The University of Tokyo
3-8-1 Komaba, Meguro-ku, Tokyo, 153-8902, JAPAN
{kaneko, yamaguch, kawai}@graco.c.u-tokyo.ac.jp

Abstract. A good evaluation function is needed for a good game program, and good features, which are primitive metrics of a state, are needed for a good evaluation function. In order to obtain good features, automatic generation of features by machine learning is promising. However, the generated features are usually written in logic programs, whose evaluation is much slower than that of other native expressions due to the interpretive evaluation of the logic programs. In order to solve this problem, we propose a method which constructs a specialized evaluator using a combination of techniques: partial evaluation, Boolean tables, and incremental calculation. It exhaustively unfolds logical programs until they can be represented as simple Boolean tables. The constructed specialized evaluator is efficient since it consults only these compiled tables. Experiments with Othello showed that speed can be increased approximately 2,000 times.

1 Introduction

1.1 Evaluation Function and Features

In order to make computer players of games strong, an *evaluation function* of possible states in a match plays a crucial role, and the automatic construction of a good evaluation function is a challenging research goal. The popular way to construct an evaluation function automatically is to make it a linear combination[1] of evaluation primitives called features, and to adjust the parameters of the combination[10] [3]. In most of this research, the features have been provided by human experts of the game, and the automatic generation of features remains an ambitious research goal.[2]

---
[1] More complex mechanisms such as neural networks are often used as well.
[2] Although we use two-player games as an example of search problems in this paper, the proposed method can be directly applied to single- (and multi-) agent search problems as well.

1.2 Logical Features

Among few works on the automatic generation of features, we found Fawcett[4][5] most promising. In the work, a feature is represented by Horn Clause in the first-order logic. We call the clause in such use *logical feature*.[3]

Because the first-order logic is a logically well-founded language and rules of a game can be described in it, the adoption of the first-order logic as the description of features is quite natural. This is an example of a logical feature.[4]

```
f(A):-owns(black,A).    % PIECES FOR BLACK
```

We call the bindings of constants to variables which make the clause true *solutions* of the logical feature and the number of the bindings *value* of the logical feature. In the above example, A is a variable, owns is a predicate which means that the black player owns square A. So, the value of this feature f(A) emits the number of squares currently owned by black.

A logical feature allows a uniform description of rules, a goal, and states of a game, and is suitable for automatic construction. However, its universality makes the evaluation quite costly. We solved this problem by a new combination of techniques: partial evaluation, Boolean tables with index, and incremental calculation with counters. The effectiveness of the solution is demonstrated by experiments.

This paper is organized as follows. The next section briefly reviews the problem and previous works and presents the main idea of our approach. Sect. 3 details our method. Sect. 4 shows the experimental results. Sect. 5 concludes this paper.

2 Logical Feature Evaluation Problem

2.1 A Domain Theory and Dynamic Facts

Features consist of two types of predicates: those of a domain theory and those defined for a state.

A *domain theory* is the specification of a game, which is described by a set of Horn Clauses that specify the rules of the game and the goal conditions. The domain theory is independent of matches.

A *state* is an intermediate status of a game, which is described by a set of facts. A fact is a clause without body. A state changes according to the progress of a match. Such facts are called *dynamic facts*.

2.2 State Change and Logical Feature Evaluation

As a state changes according to the progress of a match, solutions of predicates which depend on dynamic facts change. We call such predicates *dynamic rules*.

---

[3] It is also used in Metagame[8].
[4] It is written as f2(Num):-count([A],(owns(black,A)),Num) in the work by [4]. In this paper, we assume counting as the default semantics of logical features and omit the predicate "count".

An example of domain theory for Othello-4x4 is shown in Appendix A. In the example, `neighbor/3` and `square/1` represent the board topology and never change throughout matches. So, they are non-dynamic facts. `Owns/2` and `blank/1` represent the stones in squares in a state. Since they change according to the progress of matches, they are dynamic facts. `Legal_move/2` is a predicate which depends on a state. So, it is a dynamic rule.

Because a logical feature often includes a component of dynamic rules, it is required to efficiently calculate their solutions in order to evaluate the logical feature.

2.3 Related Works

The evaluation of predicates is studied in a few fields under slightly different contexts:

Logic Programming In the field of logic programming, the emphasis is on the flexibility and the SLD-resolution is still the most popular way to find a solution. For the complete enumeration of solutions, a technique called tabling (or often called memorization) [9] is used.

Deductive Databases In the field of deductive databases[11], the emphasis is on the complete enumeration of the solutions. Also, an incremental update has been studied and is called materialized view maintenance[6].

Production Systems In the field of production systems[1], the emphasis is on detecting a change in the truth values of rules in order to trigger events. For such change propagation, the discrimination network has been studied (RETE[7].)

2.4 Our Approach

For logical feature evaluation, we have to find out the number of solutions of rules, and a complete enumeration is required. Therefore, we use the techniques of the materialized view maintenance as a reference. The rules of a game often depend on a state. For example, in the game of Othello, the rule `span` depends on the `owns` where truth values depend on a state. The evaluation of such rules cannot be accelerated by just materializing intentional databases. Since state changes are usually not drastic for popular games, the true dynamic facts in two different states tend to only slightly vary. In such cases, the incremental maintenance technique of such materialized views can be useful.

In our approach, we use the partial evaluation technique[2] for speeding up the evaluation of such rules. By repeatedly applying unfolding and pruning, we can make each rule fully expanded until the body of the rule consists of dynamic facts only. Theoretically, the unfolding and pruning process may continue infinitely, but, for the rules of popular games which have finite boards, it terminates and produces fully expanded rules.

The RETE network[7] represents the dependency of rules on dynamic facts, and it is often used for propagating a change in the truth values of dynamic facts to changes in those of rules. The unfolding and pruning process is a symbolic way to calculate this propagation process in advance in order to speed up the evaluation.

Once we have a direct relation between rules and dynamic facts, we can encode the relation in Boolean tables. Then, the incremental evaluation on the tables can be sped up further by associating the tables with counters in order to detect the crossing of marginal numbers of trues and falses and proper indexing.

In summary, our approach is a combination of techniques: partial evaluation, Boolean tables with indices, and incremental calculation with counters. We applied this approach to the game of Othello, and see that this combination generates a specialized evaluator which is approximately 2,000-times faster than the reference. So, we believe that this is the right combination of techniques and is therefore worth further study.

3 Generation of Specialized Evaluator

In this section, we explain how we generate a specialized evaluator by the combination of the techniques of the partial evaluation, Boolean tables, and incremental calculation.

3.1 Partial Evaluation

First, given features are transformed into the equivalent set of ground clauses (i.e., clauses without variables). Two operations, *unfolding* and *pruning* in partial evaluation of logic programming[2] are used.

Unfolding Unfolding is an operation to replace a clause A :- $A_1, ..., A_i, .., A_n$ with clauses $(A$:- $A_1, ..., A_{i-1}, B_1, ..., B_h, A_{i+1}, ..., A_n)\theta_j$ for B :- $B_1, ..., B_h$ such that $B\theta_j = A_i\theta_j$ for some substitution θ_j. In this paper, we apply the unfolding from the left term to the right term in the depth first order.

Pruning Pruning eliminates a clause whose body has no chance to be true. Such type of clauses can be detected by the fact that

1. its body has an unsatisfiable term, or
2. its body has a term not unifiable to any head of clauses, or
3. its body has terms unifiable to the body of some integrity constraint.

In general, it is difficult to know that a given clause is unsatisfiable. In order to simplify the task to prove that a clause is unsatisfiable, we introduce integrity constraints so that we can say explicitly that some combination of terms is unsatisfiable.

Appendix B shows an example of integrity constraints of the game of Othello. ic1 means that a square (Square) cannot be blank and owned by some player at the same time. ic2 means that a square (Square) cannot be owned by both black and white players. These are some of the specifications of Othello, although they have not been utilized in previous works.

Exhaustive Partial Evaluation Algorithm Our method performs unfolding and pruning repeatedly until all the remaining clauses are grounded so that they have no variables in their head or body.

Appendix A shows a sample predicate span which represents a consecutive line of stones in Othello. In our strategy, terms are unfolded from left to right: i.e., terms square(S1) and neighbor(S1,Dir,S3) are unfolded before span(S3,S2,Dir,Owner) when the first definition of span is unfolded. Since all variables in the term span(S3,S2,Dir,Owner) are bound in the prior process, the partial evaluation of the term will stop after the unfolding operation is applied four times in this case, which is the size of the board. Finally, the exhaustive partial evaluation on span produces the following clauses:

– span(a1,a2,s,black) :- owns(black,a1),owns(black,a2).
– span(a1,a3,s,black) :- owns(black,a1),owns(black,a2),owns(black,a3).
  ...
– span(a1,a1,s,black) :- owns(black,a1).
– span(a2,a2,s,black) :- owns(black,a2).
  ...

Generally speaking, this process of unfolding and pruning may continue forever due to some recursively defined clauses. In the case of conventional games with reasonable rules, however, it is easy to write features and a domain theory so that this process stops, due to the finiteness of the number of squares and satisfiable terms.

Property 1. The exhaustive partial evaluation terminates under the following assumption.

1. The number of solutions of each dynamic fact is finite. Also, it is assumed that they are bound by other terms which are placed to the left of dynamic facts in each clause. For example, square(S1), player(Owner) bind the solutions of owns(Owner, S1) in the first definition of span.
2. For each predicate, the solutions are finite and can be enumerated by the SLD-resolution at any state. The leftmost term is selected in the SLD-resolution.

Proof. First, it should be noted that the unfolding operation preserves solutions. When one unfolding operation replaces a clause c in a program with a set of clauses $c_1, ...c_n$, the original program and the new program with replaced clauses have the same solutions for all goals. The pruning operation preserves solutions as well.

Under the assumption (1), exhaustive unfolding of a clause c totally produces clauses equivalent to nodes in the SLD-tree whose goal is the body of c.

Because of the assumption (2), such nodes are finite, the exhaustive partial evaluation of a clause terminates after a finite number of clauses are produced. □

Therefore, this method cannot be applied to such games in which the number of the solutions of some dynamic fact is infinite. However, the board and pieces are finite and the solutions of dynamic facts are also likely to be finite in conventional games.

3.2 Boolean Tables

Each clause in the final set of clauses after successful exhaustive partial evaluation has a ground head (span(a1,a2,s,black),) and a body which is a conjunction of dynamic facts (owns(black,a1)-owns(black,a2).) We decompose this relationship into two tables: an and-table and or-table. The and-table represents the relationship between the conjunction of dynamic facts and a dynamic fact, and the or-table represents the relationship between a set of the conjunctions of dynamic facts and a set of ground heads.

Table 1 shows a part of the and-table for exhaustively partially evaluated clauses in Sect. 3.1. The and-table shows that a conjunction in the left column becomes true if and only if all the dynamic facts with ◯ in the same row are true.

Table 1. A part of an and-table

conjunction of dynamic facts	dynamic facts		
	owns(b,a1)	owns(b,a2)	owns(b,a3)
owns(b,a1)-owns(b,a2)	◯	◯	
owns(b,a2)-owns(b,a3)		◯	◯
owns(b,a1)-owns(b,a2)-owns(b,a3)	◯	◯	◯

*'b' stands for black.

Table 2 shows a part of the or-table for exhaustively partially evaluated clauses in Sect. 3.1. The or-table shows that all the ground heads in the right column are true if and only if any one of the conjunctions of dynamic facts in the left column is true. Ground heads with the same set of conjunctions are gathered and placed in a single row of the or-table.

Table 2. A part of an or-table

the set of conjunction	the set of ground heads
{owns(b,a1)-owns(b,a2)}	{span(a1,a2,s,b),span(a2,a1,n,b)}
{owns(b,a2)-owns(b,a3)}	{span(a2,a3,s,b),span(a3,a2,n,b)}
{owns(b,a1)-owns(b,a2)-owns(b,a3)}	{span(a1,a3,s,b),span(a3,a1,n,b)}

*'b' stands for black.

3.3 Incremental Calculation

Counting In order to speed up the detection of conjunctions which change their truth values, we associate each row in an and-table with a counter. The counter represents a number of true dynamic facts in the row, and it is incremented or decremented when the related dynamic facts change their truth values. A conjunction is true if and only if its associated counter has the same value as the number of related dynamic facts. So, the change in the truth values of conjunctions is promptly detected by adjusting their counters.

Similarly, a counter is associated with the set of ground heads in each row. The counter represents a number of true conjunctions in the left column of the row. Since a ground head is true if and only if any one of the related conjunctions is true, the truth value of the head is promptly determined by checking whether its associated counter is zero or not.

The standard indexing technique is employed to find out the related rows in the and-table and or-table.

Difference Propagation Changes in the truth values of dynamic facts cause changes in those of the ground heads. We compute them by the following incremental algorithm. Suppose that dynamic fact P changes its value.

```
For each row in the and-table which is related to the dynamic fact P.
    adjust the counter associated with the row.
    if the conjunction becomes true ... (1)
        find the rows in which the conjunction is included using the index.
        then adjust the counters associated with the rows and
        report the ground heads in the rows with counters
        changing their value from zero to nonzero. ...(2)
    if the conjunction becomes false ... (3)
        find the rows in which the conjunction is included using the index.
        then adjust the counters associated with the rows and
        report the ground heads in the rows with counters
        changing their value from nonzero to zero. ...(4)
```

We show an example. Suppose that dynamic facts {owns-a1-black, owns-a2-black} are true in Table 1 and Table 2, and we delete {owns(black,a1)} (makes owns(black,a1) false) and insert {owns(black,a3)} (makes owns(black,a3) true). First, it is reported that owns(black,a1)-owns(black,a2) becomes false at (3), and span(a1,a2,s,black) and span(a2,a1,n,black) become false at (4). Then, it is reported that owns(black,a2)-owns(black,a3) becomes true at (1), and span(a2,a3,s,black) and span(a3,a2,n,black) become true at (2).

4 Experimental Results

4.1 Time Efficiency

Experiments are performed on the game of Othello. We used a domain theory which is a slightly simpler version than that which was used in the Zenith system([4]).[5]

Table 3. Comparison of three methods in evaluation time

Method	average (sec.)	standard deviation	states/sec
Our method (incremental)	0.027	0.0048	2186.7
Our method (from scratch)	0.13	0.0072	459.7
Deductive DB	114.4	4.98	0.536

Table 3 shows the relation between the evaluation methods and the evaluation time. We applied three evaluation methods over 300 matches using 127 features. The first evaluation method is the one proposed in this paper. The second evaluation method is identical to our method except that it is without incremental calculation, i.e, for each state, all dynamic facts in the state are evaluated from scratch. The last evaluation method is a bottom-up evaluation technique used in the deductive databases[11]. 300 matches are extracted from the game records of IOS[6] consisting of 17931 states. Relatively simple 127 features are selected manually from the ones generated automatically by the Zenith's method. The purpose of the selection is to perform slow evaluation by deductive databases so as to finish in a reasonable time. For the experiment, a computer with 200-MHz CPU Pentium Pro. running FreeBSD is used and the program is implemented in GNU C++. As seen in the table, our method is about 2,000-times faster than that used in the deductive databases. The merit of the incremental calculation is in the factor of five. This efficiency is partly thanks to the efficient implementation language suitable for low-level operations such as counter adjustments.

It is said that top-level Shogi programs with relatively heavy evaluation functions can examine more than 3,000 states in a second. It seems that this method achieved almost the same efficiency. It is, however, difficult to compare them directly, because the efficiency of evaluation functions strongly depend on what they evaluate (what features they have).

Fig. 1 shows the dependency of the evaluation time on the number of features. A point on the graph shows the mean evaluation time of a match and its error-bar shows its standard deviation. The figure suggests that the evaluation time increases almost linearly as the number of features increases, although it actually depends on the methods for generating features. In this experiment, we

---
[5] The original version is available at ftp://ftp.ics.uci.edu/pub/machine-learning-databases/othello/.
[6] They are available at ftp://external.nj.nec.com/pub/igord/othello/ios/

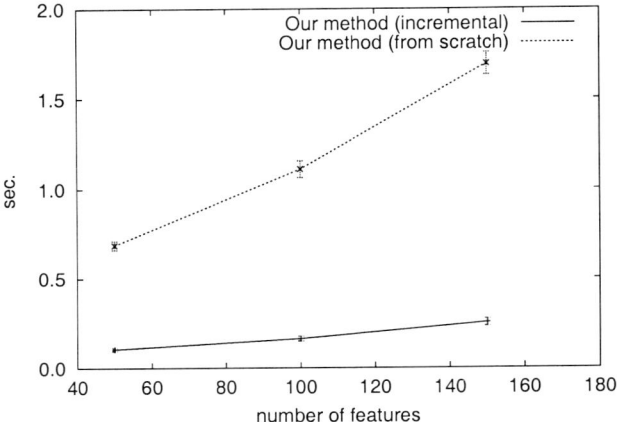

Fig. 1. Dependency of the evaluation time on the number of features

employed the features selected randomly from automatically generated ones and used a computer with 600-MHz CPU Pentium III running Linux. The matches employed are the ones we used in the previous experiment.

4.2 Space Efficiency

Experiments are performed for the game of Othello with varying board sizes in order to find out the space complexity of our approach. Table 4 and Fig. 2 show the number of clauses in the original domain theory, ground clauses after exhaustive partial evaluation, and the size, that is the number of the rows of the and-table and or-table. They show that the number of the clauses and the size of the tables increase almost exponentially with respect to the number of features.

Table 4 also shows the time required for exhaustive partial evaluation.

Table 4. Comparison of unfolded domain theories for various sizes of Othello

	Othello 4x4	Othello 8x8	Othello 16x16
no. of clauses	129	513	2345
no. of unfolded clauses	6653	211101	6217082
no. of counters in and-table	2100	116940	4559737
no. of counters in or-table	773	8459	82570
time for unfolding	24.4 sec	2556.4 sec	(about a week)

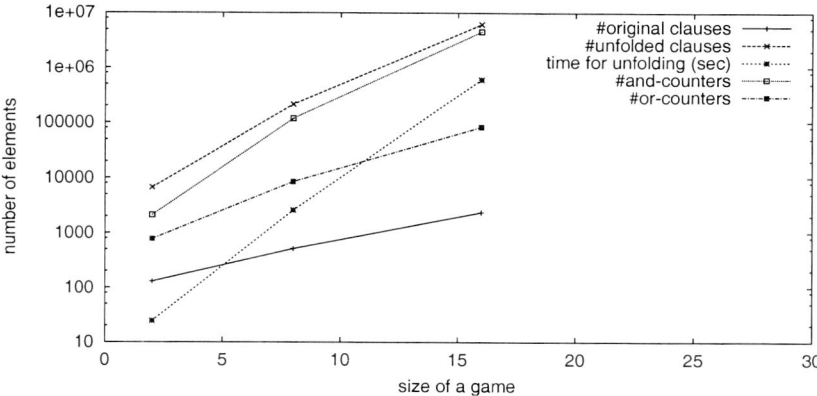

Fig. 2. Comparison of unfolded domain theories for various sizes of Othello

5 Conclusion

In this paper, we proposed an evaluation method of logical features by combing exhaustive partial evaluation, Boolean tables, and incremental calculation.

Experiments on features and a domain theory for the game of Othello showed that the proposed method was 2000-times faster than the naive bottom-up evaluation method used in the deductive databases.

There is room for improvement in our method. The efficiency of the exhaustive partial evaluation depends on the order of terms to which unfolding is applied. The automatic selection of the appropriate term to unfold is important in order to reduce users' efforts. For a more powerful description of features, we would like to incorporate aggregation predicates such as maximum or minimum in our method. These are our future works.

References

1. N. Bassiliades and I. Vlahavas. DEVICE: Compiling production rules into event-driven rules using complex events. *Information and Software Technology*, 39(5):331–342, 1997.
2. A. Bossi, N. Cocco, and S. Dulli. A method for specializing logic programs. *ACM Transactions on Programming Languages and Systems*, 12(2):253–302, 1990.
3. M. Buro. From simple features to sophisticated evaluation functions. In *Proceedings of the First International Conference on Computers and Games*, pages 126–145. Springer-Verlag, 1998.
4. T. E. Fawcett. *Feature Discovery for Problem Solving Systems*. PhD thesis, Department of Computer Science, University of Massachusetts, Amherst, 1993.
5. T. E. Fawcett and P. E. Utgoff. Automatic feature generation for problem solving systems. In D. Sleeman and P. Edwards, editors, *Proceedings of the 9th International Conference on Machine Learning*, pages 144–153. Morgan Kaufmann, 1992.

6. Ashish Gupta, Inderpal Singh Mumick, and V. S. Subrahmanian. Maintaining views incrementally. *SIGMOD Record (ACM Special Interest Group on Management of Data)*, 22(2):157–166, June 1993.
7. H. S. Lee and M. I. Schor. Match algorithms for generalized rete networks. *Artificial Intelligence*, 54:249–274, 1992.
8. Barney Darryl Pell. *Strategy Generation and Evaluation for Meta-Game Playing*. PhD thesis, University of Cambridge, 1993.
9. Konstantinos Sagonas, Terrance Swift, and David S. Warren. Xsb as an efficient deductive database engine. *ACM SIGMOD*, 5:442–453, 1994.
10. A. L. Samuel. Some studies in machine learning using the game of checkers. ii - recent progress. *IBM Journal of Research and Development*, 11(6):601–617, 1967.
11. Jeffrey D. Ullman. *Prinsiples of Database and Knowledge-Base Systems, Volume II:The New Technologies*. Computer Science Press, Maryland, 1989.

A   A Simple Domain Theory of 4x4 Othello

```
%%% Rules
legal_move(Square, Player) :- square(Square), bs(Square, _FlipEnd, Player).
bs(S1,S3,P) :- blank(S1), opponent(P,Opp), neighbor(S1,Dir,S2),
               span(S2,S3,Dir,Opp), neighbor(S3,Dir,S4), owns(P,S4).
span(S1, S2, Dir, Owner) :- square(S1), square(S2), player(Owner),
       owns(Owner, S1), neighbor(S1, Dir, S3), span(S3, S2, Dir, Owner).
span(S, S, Dir, Owner) :-
       square(S), player(Owner), owns(Owner,S), direction(Dir).
%%% Dynamic Facts defined upon states.
% owns(Player, Square).
% blank(Square).
%%% Static Rules
line(From, From, Dir) :- square(From), direction(Dir).
line(From, To, Dir) :- neighbor(From, Dir, Next), line(Next, To, Dir).
%%% Static Facts
opponent(x, o). opponent(o, x).
direction(n). direction(ne). direction(e). direction(se).
direction(s). direction(sw). direction(w). direction(nw).

square(a1). square(a2). square(a3). square(a4).
...
square(d1). square(d2). square(d3). square(d4).

neighbor(a1, s, a2). neighbor(a2, n, a1). neighbor(a2, s, a3).
...
neighbor(d4, nw, c3). neighbor(c4, ne, d3). neighbor(d3, sw, c4).
```

B   Integrity Constraints of Othello

```
ic1(Square) :- blank(Square), owns(_Player,Square).
ic2(Square) :- owns(black,Square), owns(white,Square).
```

Using Domain Knowledge in ILP to Discover Protein Functional Models

Takashi Ishikawa[1], Masayuki Numao[2], and Takao Terano[3]

[1] Dept. of Computer and Information Eng., Nippon Institute of Technology,
Saitama 345-8501, Japan,
tisikawa@ci.nit.ac.jp,
WWW home page: http://www.nit.ac.jp/~tisikawa/
[2] Dept. of Computer Sci., Faculty of Eng., Tokyo Institute of Technology,
Tokyo 152-8552, Japan,
numao@cs.titech.ac.jp,
WWW home page: http://www.nm.cs.titech.ac.jp/
[3] Graduate School of Systems Management, The University of Tsukuba,
Tokyo 112-0012, Japan,
terano@gssm.otsuka.tsukuba.ac.jp,
WWW home page: http://www.gssm.otsuka.tsukuba.ac.jp/staff/~terano/

Abstract. The paper describes a method for machine discovery of *protein functional models* from protein databases using *Inductive Logic Programming* (ILP). The method uses *domain knowledge* in ILP to generate appropriate hypotheses to predict functions of a protein from its amino acid sequence. The method is based on top-down search for *relative least general generalization* and uses domain knowledge defining *the conceptual hierarchy* of protein functions and *search biases*. The method discovers effectively protein function models that explain the relationship between functions of proteins and their amino acid sequences described in protein databases. The method succeeds in discovering protein functional models for forty membrane proteins, which coincide with conjectured models in literature of molecular biology.

1 Introduction

Inductive Logic Programming (ILP) [13] has succeeded in applications to molecular biology including secondary structure prediction of protein [12] and other problems [4]. However, ILP has not been applied to the central problem that is to explain the relationship between protein functions and their amino acid sequences. The paper aims at solving the problem of *protein function prediction* by discovering *protein functional models* [6] using ILP.

A lot of information about proteins is stored in databases shown in Table 1 and is used for biological researches. Among information types, amino acid sequence, 3D-structure and enzyme reaction are primary information as fact data obtained by experiments, whereas sequence motif and literature are secondary information obtained by some information processing. Specifically sequence motifs

Table 1. Protein Databases

type of information	name of database
amino acid sequence	SWISS-PROT, PIR, MIPS, TrEMBL, PRF etc
sequence motif	PROSITE, Profiles, PRINTS, Pfam, BLOCKS etc
3D structure	PDB, NRL-3D etc
enzyme reaction	LIGAND etc
literature	Medline etc

are knowledge discovered with computer processing, which represent relationship between function of proteins and their amino acid sequences [1].

Traditional methods for protein function prediction use *homology search* and *sequence motif*. Homology search uses global similarities of amino acid sequences to find proteins of similar functions. On the other hand, sequence motifs are local patterns of amino acid sequences that are unique to certain functions of proteins and are stored in the database for some protein functions [3]. Protein function prediction by sequence motifs is based on matching the target amino acid sequence with sequence motifs in the database. These methods use global or local similarities among amino acid sequences to find protein of similar functions. Therefore these methods are limited to proteins with almost same amino acid sequences in global or local regions from their fundamental principles. An another method for protein function prediction uses 3D structures of proteins, but 3D structures are difficult to predict from amino acid sequences.

2 Protein Functional Models

The approach of the paper to protein function prediction is based on the assumption that combinations of functional sites, which are sequence patterns of amino acid sequences, characterize a protein function. Functional sites are associated with secondary structures of proteins in order to specify their position in the 3D structures. Figure 1 depicts the concept of protein functional model for *ion pump* as an example protein function. In our protein functional models, functional sites are represented by strings of characters that code amino acids and combination of functional sites are used to discriminate narrow functional difference. Furthermore, using protein functional models allows us to predict protein functions from only amino acid sequences instead of requiring geometrical information representing 3D structures. We apply inductive logic programming to discover protein functional models.

A protein functional model is represented by the following clause in a logical framework [9].

$$protein(ID, FUNCTION) \leftarrow subseq(ID, PATTERN, POS/STD), ...$$

The head of the clause is a literal representing that the protein *ID* has *FUNCTION* using predicate *protein*. The body of the clause is a conjunction of lit-

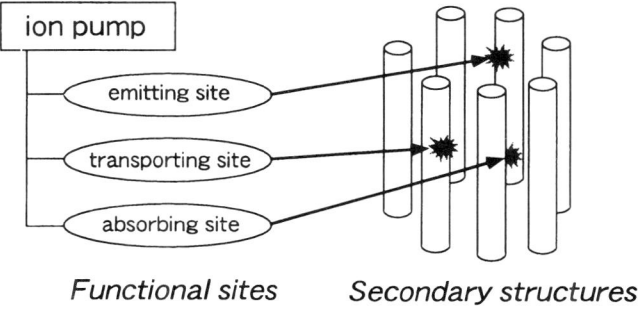

Fig. 1. Concept of Protein Functional Model

erals representing that the protein ID has subsequence pattern $PATTERN$ at POS/STD using predicate $subseq$. Here POS stands for *secondary structure position* of the pattern and STD stands for standard protein's ID for which POS is given. The secondary structure position is determined by finding the most similar subsequence in the amino acid sequence of the protein STD in the corresponding secondary structure.

Here subsequence patterns are defined by the following syntax rules.

$<$ subsequence pattern $>$::=
    $<$ character $>$ | $<$ character $><$ subsequence pattern $>$
$<$ character $>$::=$<$ character symbol $>$ | $<$ class symbol $>$
$<$ character symbol $>$::= A | B | C | .... | Y
$<$ class symbol $>$::= a | b | c | .... | x

In the above rules, a character symbol is a letter representing one of twenty amino acids. A class symbol is a character representing a group of amino acids with certain physicochemical properties.

The generaliation relation between amino acid sequences is defined in the following way. First, a proposition stating that *an amino acid sequence S of a protein has a subsequence pattern p* is defined as follows.

(1) The sequence S includes a subsequence pattern p_0.
(2) The subsequence pattern p_0 is subsumed by a subsequence pattern p.

Here we define that a subsequence pattern p_0 is subsumed by subsequence pattern p as that both subsequence patterns have same length and each character $c_0[i]$ at position i in p_0 is subsumed by the character $c[i]$ at position i in p. The subsumption relation between characters is defined as the same characters subsuming each other and a class symbol subsumes characters belonging to the class. The subsumption relation between subsequence patterns determines generalization relation required in inductive logic programming.

3 A Method for Discovery

The approach of the paper to protein function prediction employs inductive logic programming to discover protein functional models. Inductive logic programming is a machine learning technique suitable for generating hypotheses represented by first order predicate logic allowing to describe elements of objects and relation among elements like protein functional models. Unfortunately, traditional inductive logic programming systems such as Progol [14] and FOIL [16] are difficult to be applied to discovering of protein functional models because of their restriction for hypothesis language. Therefore we had to develop an ILP method satisfying the following requirements:

(1) the method does not restrict determinacy of literals in the body of hypothesis,
(2) allows function terms in arguments of predicate without using auxiliary predicate,
(3) and does not require mode declaration for variables in the hypothesis clause.

We have developed an ILP method [7] that satisfies the above requirements, which integrates a top-down method and a bottom-up method of inductive logic programming. The method is based on the top-down search utilizing an information theoretic heuristic used in FOIL [16] and generates literals in the hypothesis clause using *relative least general generalization* (*rlgg*) [15] used in GOLEM [11] in a bottom-up manner. The information theoretic heuristic makes the method efficient without using mode declaration. The use of *rlgg* enables the method to generate hypotheses involving literals with function terms in order to describe subsequence patterns as a list of characters.

The algorithm generates hypothesis by the procedure shown in Figure 2. In the top-down search for hypothesis clauses, the method *selectively* generates literals satisfying the following conditions

(a) having common variable(s) with existing literals in the hypothesis clause;
(b) being *lgg* of two ground unit clauses in the background knowledge; and
(c) giving information gain (i.e., $I < I_0$ in Figure 2) when the literal is added to the body of the clause

in order to generate clauses with less redundant literals. Hence the condition (a) means that a literal that does not satisfy the condition would not alter the coverage of the hypothesis clause when the literal is added to the body of the clause. The condition (b) comes from the fact that the body literals are generated by *lgg* according to the definition of the *rlgg*. The condition (c) is a heuristic used in the top-down search for literals.

Here *information amount* I of a clause C is computed with the following approximation formula, where $coverage(C, E, B)$ stands for the number of examples in E implied by the clause $\{C\} \cup B$.

$$c^+ = coverage(C, E^+, B)$$
$$c^- = coverage(C, E^-, B)$$
$$I = -\ln(c^+/(c^+ + c^-))$$

Hypothesis Generation:
Input: positive examples E^+, negative examples E^-, background knowledge B,
   a set of predicates P including target function t, sample size s
Output: a set hypothesis clauses H
Process:
   $H \leftarrow \phi$
   forall $p \in P$ **do**
      for the predicate p, get positives E_p^+ and negatives E_p^-
      maximum coverage $max \leftarrow 0$, previous maximum coverage $max_0 \leftarrow max$
      while $max \geq max_0$ **do**
         $max_0 \leftarrow max$
         make a set of sample pairs S of size s from E_p^+
         for all sample pair $(e_1, e_2) \in S$ **do**
            head of a hypothesis clause $h \leftarrow lgg(e_1, e_2)$, body $L \leftarrow \phi$
            compute information amount I of the hypothesis clause $(h\text{:-}L)$,
            previous information amount $I_0 \leftarrow I$
            while the hypothesis clause implies a negative $e^- \in E^-$ **do**
               if be able to select a ground atom pair (l_1, l_2) from B **then**
                  compute the lgg literal $l = lgg(l_1, l_2)$
                  if $(h\text{:-}L \cup \{l\})$ implies E_t^+ **then**
                     compute information amount I of $(h\text{:-}L \cup \{l\})$
                     if $I < I_0$ **then** $L \leftarrow L \cup \{l\}$, $I_0 \leftarrow I$
               else the body of the hypothesis clause $L \leftarrow fail$, **break**
            compute the positive coverage c of the hypothesis clause $(h\text{:-}L)$
            if $c > max$ **then** $C \leftarrow (h\text{:-}L)$, $max \leftarrow c$
         if $max > max_0$ **then** $H \leftarrow \{C\}$, $max_0 \leftarrow max$
         else if $max = max_0$ **then** $H \leftarrow H \cup \{C\}$
   return H

Fig. 2. The Algorithm of Hypothesis Generation

4 Using Domain Knowledge in ILP

In general, a protein functional model involves elements being common to the super functions of the target function as well as elements specific to the target function. When applying an ILP method to discovering protein functional models, a problem that elements common to super functions may not be included in the model will arise. The cause of the problem is that negative examples of the target function may include positive examples of the super functions.

Protein functions are described in protein databases often as keywords as well as annotations. The keywords are prepared by biologists to denote the conceptual hierarchy of protein functions. In our experiment, protein functions are obtained from these keywords in the database.

In order to generate hypotheses describing the super functions of a target function, it only needs to use an ILP method for the examples of the super functions. However the generated hypotheses may not imply all positive examples of the target function. We solve this problem by adding the following requirements in the hypothesis generation.

- hypotheses for super functions must imply all positive examples of the target function.

The problem of hypothesis generation using conceptual hierarchy of protein functions is formalized as follows:

- **Given:**
    - a target function and its super functions (*conceptual hierarchy*)
    - sets of positive examples E^+ and negative examples E^- for the target and super functions and background knowledge B
- **Find:**
    - a set of hypothesis clauses H that implies all positives and no negative for the target function and super functions in conjunction with background knowledge B
    - *hypothesis clauses for the super functions must imply all positives of the target function*

In the following, we describe the discovering method using the improved ILP method [8]. Note that a conceptual hierarchy can be introduced without modifying an employing ILP method.

Search biases are the domain knowledge used in the top-down search for hypothesis. The reason why search bias is needed in discovering protein functional models is that it requires selection of body literals among many candidates that can reduce information amount using appropriate criteria. The search biases used in the paper are to select literals by the preferential order in the following tendencies in the amino acid sequences of proteins.

(1) functional sites exist in corresponding structural elements
(2) functional sites include charged amino acids
(3) functional sites continues to the neighboring functional sites
(4) important functional sites exist in the center of contiguous sites
(5) important functional sites exist in the middle of trans membrane domain.

5 Discovering Experiments

We have conducted learning experiments in which the discovered results are compared to the known functional models to evaluate the effectiveness of the proposed method. The materials are forty membrane proteins with similar amino acid sequences in the protein database SWISS-PROT [2] listed below, for which several protein functional models are known in the literature of molecular biology.

A1AB_MESAU, A2AA_HUMAN, A2AC_HUMAN, ACM1_HUMAN,
ACM2_HUMAN, ACM3_HUMAN, ACM4_HUMAN, B1AR_HUMAN,
B1AR_MELGA, B2AR_HUMAN, B2AR_MESAU, BACA_HALS1,
BACH_HALSP, BACH_NATPH, BACR_HALHA, BACS_HALHA,
CAR1_DICDI, NK2R_HUMAN, OPS1_CALVI, OPS1_DROME,
OPS2_DROME, OPS3_DROME, OPS4_DROME, OPSB_HUMAN,
OPSD_BOVIN, OPSD_CHICK, OPSD_HUMAN, OPSD_LAMJA,
OPSD_LOLFO, OPSD_MOUSE, OPSD_OCTDO, OPSD_SHEEP,
OPSG_ASTFA, OPSG_HUMAN, OPSH_ASTFA, OPSR_ASTFA,
OPSR_CHICK, OPSR_HUMAN, REIS_TODPA, TMAS_HUMAN

The protein group listed above is called *rhodopsin family* that is characterized by the structural similarity to the photo sensor protein *rhodopsin*. In the following, we describe the experiment by selecting *bacteriorhodopsin* as a target function among them, since its functional model is already known. The super functions of *bacteriorhodopsin* are *ion transport* that transports ions such as proton across cell membrane and *retinal protein* characterized by the existence of *retinal* in the protein.

The objective of the experiments is to re-discover the protein functional models of the target functions using developed ILP method. The input and output of the experiments are follows:

- **Input:**
    - target protein functions and the super protein functions (*conceptual hierarchy*)
    - amino acid sequences and position of trans membrane domain from a protein database
    - physicochemical classification of amino acids
- **Output:**
    - a set of hypothesis clauses that implies all positive examples and no negatives in conjunction with the given background knowledge

Input data and the discovering program are described by MacProlog32 [10] and the computation is performed on Power Macintosh 8100/100AV. The sum of positives and negatives is forty and the number of background unit clauses is about 16000.

Bacteriorhodopsin is a protein that exist in cell membrane of a special bacteria and has protein function of *proton pump* which transports proton (i.e., hydrogen ion) using photo energy (Figure 3). The functional sites of *bacteriorhodopsin* are considered to be three amino acids D, K, D in the amino acid sequences at the position shown in Figure 4.

Figure 5 shows the result of the discovering experiment on *bacteriorhodopsin* given super functions as RETINAL_PROTEIN, BACTERIAL_OPSIN and ION_TRANSPORT. These clauses conform a protein functional model of *bacteriorhodopsin*. This result includes all of the functional sites known in the literature of molecular biology [5].

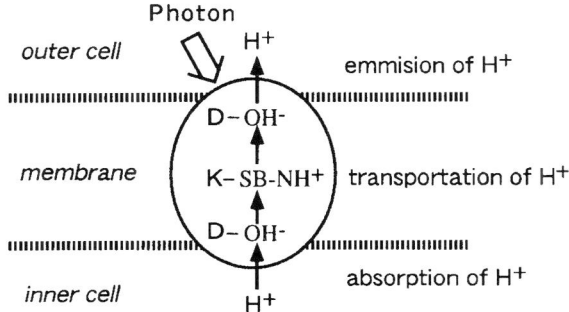

Fig. 3. A Conceptual Model of Proton Pump

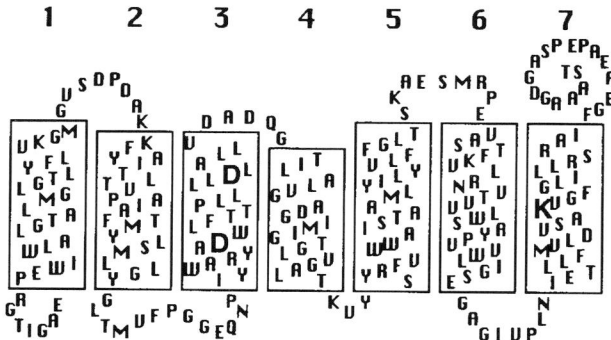

Fig. 4. Amino Acid Sequence of *bacteriorhodopsin*

```
protein(X, 'RETINAL_PROTEIN') :-
    subseq(X, ['A', 'K', _, _, _], 227/'BACA_HALS1').
protein('OPS3_DROME', 'RETINAL_PROTEIN').
protein('OPS4_DROME', 'RETINAL_PROTEIN').
protein('OPSB_HUMAN', 'RETINAL_PROTEIN').
protein('REIS_TODPA', 'RETINAL_PROTEIN').
protein(X, 'BACTERIAL_OPSIN') :-
    subseq(X, ['R', 'Y', _, _, 'W'], 94/'BACA_HALS1').
protein(X, 'BACTERIAL_OPSIN') :-
    subseq(X, ['L', 'D', _, _, 'A'], 223/'BACA_HALS1').
protein(X, 'BACTERIAL_OPSIN') :-
    subseq(X, ['Y', 'P', _, _, 'W'], 197/'BACA_HALS1').
protein(X, 'ION_TRANSPORT') :-
    subseq(X, [_, 'G', _, 'E', 'G'], 203/'BACA_HALS1').
protein(X, 'ION_TRANSPORT') :-
    subseq(X, [_, 'L', 'L', _, 'L'], 103/'BACA_HALS1').
protein(X, proton_pump) :-
    subseq(X, ['L', 'L', 'D', 'L', 'A'], 106/'BACA_HALS1').
```

Fig. 5. Results of Discovering Experiment on *Bacteriorhodopsin*

Figure 6 shows the correspondence between the experimental results and the known functional sites in the amino acid sequence of *bacteriorhodopsin*. The numbers above amino acid in Figure 6 indicate the number of trans membrane domain and symbols '+' and '-' denote specific amino acids in the discovered functional sites and any amino acids respectively. The correspondence indicates that the method re-discovered all the functional sites of *bacteriorhodopsin*.

6 Discussion

The experiments described above show the following effectiveness of the proposed method.

(1) Functional sites of discovered protein functional models include most of important functional sites conjectured in the literature of molecular biology. The following are the functional motifs of *bacteriorhodopsin* and its super classes [3].

```
                         11111111 1111111111
            MDPIALTAAV GADLLGDGRP ETLWLGIGTL LMLIGTFYFI

            1111          22222 2222222222 2222222222
            VKGWGVTDKE AREYYSITIL VPGIASAAYL SMFFGIGLTE

            2             3*333 3333333*33 333         4
            VQVGSEMLDI YYARYADWLF TTPLLLLDLA LLAKVDRVSI
                       ++--+        -+++++++

            4444444444 444444444            5 5555555555
            GTLVGVDALM IVTGLVGALS HTPLARYTWW LFSTICMIVV

            5555555555              66666 6666666666
            LYFLATSLRA AAKERGPEVA STFNTLTALV LVLWTAYPIL
                                                   ++--

            66666       77777777 7777777*77 777777
            WIIGTEGAGV VGLGIETLLF MVLDVTAKVG FGFILLRSRA
            +  -+-++                ++--++-- -

            ILGDTEAPEP SAGAEASAAD
```

Fig. 6. Functional Sites of *bacteriorhodopsin*

(a) *bacteriorhodopsin* (proton_pump)
    R-**Y**-x-[DT]-**W**-x-[LIVMF]-[ST]-T-P-[LIVM]
(b) BACTERIAL_OPSIN
    [FYIV]-x-[FYVG]-[LIVM]-**D**-[LIVMF]-x(2)-[STA]-**K**-x-[FY]
(c) OPSIN (retinal binding)
    [LIVMWAC]-[PGAC]-x(3)-[SAC]-**K**-[STALIMR]-[GSACPNV] -
    [STACP]-x(2)- [DENF]-[AP]-x(2)-[IY]

(2) the method has discovered another functional sites not conjectured yet.

The point (1) is considered to be the effect of using conceptual hierarchy and search biases. Furthermore, the point (2) suggests latent ability of the proposed method to discover unknown functional sites.

7 Related Work

The top-down and bottom-up feature of the proposed method is similar to the approach of CHILLIN [17]. But CHILLIN applies *lgg* only to head literals on the contrary to the method in the paper applies *lgg* also to body literals. The use of *range constraint* to arguments of predicates is performed implicitly in the ILP system Progol [14]. Progol uses type information to search body literals, while the proposed method prepares range information by extensional enumeration automatically.

8 Conclusion

The paper described a method to discover *protein functional models* from protein databases using *Inductive Logic Programming* utilizing *conceptual hierarchy* and *search biases*. The protein function models explain the relationship between protein functions and their amino acid sequences described in protein databases. The method succeeded in discovering protein functional models for forty membrane proteins, which coincide with conjectured functional models in the literature of molecular biology.

References

1. Attwood, T. K. and Parry-Smith, D. J.: *Introduction to bioinformatics.* Longman (1999)
2. Bairoch, A and Boechmann, B.: *Nucl. Acids Res.*, Vol.22, pp.3578–3580 (1994)
3. Bairoch, A., Bucher, P., and Hofmann, K.: The PROSITE database, its status in 1997, *Nucl. Acids Res.*, Vol.24, pp.217–221 (1997)
4. Fayyad, U. M., Piatetsky-Shapiro, G., Smyth, P., and Uthurusamy, R. (eds.).: *Advances in Knowledge Discovery and Data Mining*, AAAI Press/The MIT Press (1996)
5. Futai, M. (ed.): *Biomembrane Engineering* (in Japanese), Maruzen (1991)
6. Ishikawa, T., Mitaku, S., Terano, T., Hirokawa, T., Suwa, M., and Seah, B-C.: Building A Knowledge-Base for Protein Function Prediction using Multistrategy Learning, In *Proceedings of Genome Informatics Workshop 1995*, pp.39–48 (1995)
7. Ishikawa, T., Terano, T., and Numao, M.: A Computation Method of Relative Least General Generalization Using Literal Association and MDL Criteria, *Journal of Japanese Society for Artificial Intelligence* (in Japanese), Vol.14, No. 2, pp.326–333 (1999)
8. Ishikawa, T., Mitaku, S., and Terano, T.: Discovery of Protein Functional Models with an ILP Method Using Conceptual Hierarchy and Search Biases, *Journal of Japanese Society for Artificial Intelligence* (in Japanese), Vol.15, No.1, pp.169–176 (2000)
9. Lloyd, J.: *Foundations of Logic Programming*, Springer Verlag (1984)
10. *LPA-PROLOG References*, Logic Programming Associates Ltd. (1994)
11. Muggleton, S. and Feng, C.: Efficient Induction of Logic Programs, In *Proceedings of the 1st Conference on Algorithmic Learning Theory*, Ohmsha (1990)
12. Muggleton, S., King, R., and Sternberg, M.: Protein Secondary Structure Prediction using Logic., *Protein Engineering*, Vol.5, pp.647–657 (1992)
13. Muggleton, S. and De Raedt, L.: Inductive Logic Programming: Theory and Methods, *The Journal of Logic Programming*, Vol.19, pp.629–679 (1994)
14. Muggleton, S.: Inverse Entailment and Progol. *New Generation Computing*, Vol.13, pp.245–286 (1995)
15. Plotkin, G. D.: A Note on Inductive Generalization. *Machine Intelligence*, Vol. 5, pp.153–163 (1970)
16. Quinlan, R.: Learning Logical Definition from Relations, *Machine Learning*, Vol.5, pp.239–266 (1990)
17. Zelle, J. M., Mooney, R. J. and Konvisser, J. B.: Combining Top-down and Bottom-up Techniques in Inductive Logic Programming. In *Proceedings of the Eleventh International Workshop on Machine Learning*, pp.343–351 (1994)

The Hyper System: Knowledge Reformation for Efficient First-Order Hypothetical Reasoning

Helmut Prendinger, Mitsuru Ishizuka, and Tetsu Yamamoto

Department of Information and Communication Engineering
School of Engineering, University of Tokyo
7-3-1 Hongo, Bunkyo-ku, Tokyo 113-8656, Japan
{helmut,ishizuka,tetsu}@miv.t.u-tokyo.ac.jp

Abstract. We present the HYPER system that implements a new approach to knowledge compilation, where function-free first-order acyclic Horn theories are transformed to propositional logic. The compilation method integrates techniques from deductive databases (relevance reasoning) and theory transformation via unfold/fold transformations, to obtain a compact propositional representation. The transformed theory is more compact than the ground version of the original theory in terms of significantly less and mostly shorter clauses. This form of compilation, called *knowledge (base) reformation*, is important since the most efficient reasoning methods are defined for propositional theories, while knowledge is most naturally expressed in a first-order language. In particular, we will show that knowledge reformation allows low-order polynomial time inference to find a near-optimal solution in cost-based first-order hypothetical reasoning (or 'abduction') problems. We will also present experimental results that confirm the effectiveness of our compilation method.

1 Introduction and Motivation

The need for knowledge reformation derives from two facts about declarative representations of knowledge. First, representations are designed for a variety of queries; hence, they will contain information that is not relevant to answering some particular query or query type (Levy *et al.* [8], see also the literature on semantic query optimization [2]). Second, many interesting problems in artificial intelligence require the representational power of first-order theories, but it is well-known that reasoning with such theories is computationally expensive (Levesque [7]). On the other hand, considerable progress has been made in developing efficient mechanisms for *propositional* reasoning. For instance, GSAT is an efficient procedure for solving propositional satisfiability problems (Selman and Kautz [14]), and the NBP and SL methods are fast mechanisms for solving propositional hypothetical (or 'abductive') reasoning problems (Ishizuka and co-workers [9,5]). Recall that hypothetical reasoning is NP-hard, even for very basic forms of propositional problems (Eiter and Gottlob [4]). The aim of knowledge reformation is to preserve the generality and compactness of *representing* knowledge in first-order Horn logic, while at the same time allow for *processing* a highly efficient propositional knowledge base (KB). Knowledge reformation extends existing work on *knowledge compilation* (Cadoli and Donini [1]) to the first-order case. Compilation methods preprocess a propositional KB off-line such that the result can be used to speed up on-line query answering. By contrast, we start with a first-order KB and generate a propositional KB of manageable size.

In principle, the idea of knowledge reformation can be implemented by a transformation that instantiates variables in first-order theories by constants ('grounding'). If no non-zero function symbols are allowed, a finite set of essentially propositional clauses is obtained. This simple-minded approach is obviously impractical since a huge number of propositional clauses will be produced (Levesque [7]). Therefore, we suggest to apply theory transformation (Tamaki and Sato [16]) before actually instantiating the theory. Specifically, the principled application of unfold—definition—fold transformation steps eliminates 'unnecessary' variables, i.e., variables that occur in the body B but not in the head H of a clause $H \leftarrow B$. Since the instantiation of a clause C is exponential in the number of different variables occurring in C, the clauses resulting from transforming C allow for significantly less ground clauses than instantiating C. Let the original clause (with four different variables) be

$$C_0: \ q(X,Y) \leftarrow p1(X,Z1) \wedge p2(Z1,Z2) \wedge p3(Z2,Y)$$

that yields $\mathcal{O}(n^4)$ clauses upon instantiation. Transformation replaces C_0 by

$$C_1: \ q(X,Y) \leftarrow newp(X,Z2) \wedge p3(Z2,Y)$$
$$C_2: \ newp(X,Z2) \leftarrow p1(X,Z1) \wedge p2(Z1,Z2)$$

that result in $\mathcal{O}(2n^3)$ instantiated clauses since both C_1 and C_2 have three different variables each. The reformation procedure is combined with the *Slide-down and Lift-up* (SL) method, an efficient hypothetical reasoning method (Ishizuka and Matsuo [5]).

The main contribution of knowledge reformation for the KR community is twofold. First, propositional theories can be derived *automatically* from their first-order pendants. Consequently, researchers interested in propositional algorithms may approach problems traditionally formulated in function-free first-order Horn logic without extra effort. Second, the resulting propositional theories have attractive computational properties in terms of small size and shorter clauses, and can thus be processed very efficiently. Interestingly, our transformation procedures may serve a similar function to *knowledge object decomposition* described by Debenham [3], who uses decomposition for KB maintenance. Our reformation procedure can also be used as a translator from first-order to propositional form, which is planned for the TPTP Problem Library (Sutcliffe and Suttner [15]).

The paper is organized as follows. Section 2 describes the configuration of the HYPER system. In Section 3, we show how techniques from relevance reasoning can be used to rule out parts of a KB that are not related to a set of queries. Section 4 introduces the transformation procedures by example. In Section 5, we

> **Off-line phase.**
> **Input:** first-order hypothetical reasoning problem.
>
> - *Relevance reasoning.* Isolate part of KB relevant to query type $p(\bar{X})$.
> - *Theory transformation.* Apply unfold/fold transformation steps.
> - *Instantiation.* Generate ground theory by constructing query-tree.

> **On-line phase.**
> **Input:** propositional hypothetical reasoning problem.
>
> - *Relevance reasoning.* Isolate part of KB$'$ relevant to query $p(\bar{c}_i)$.
> - *Hypothetical reasoning.* Apply the SL method to generate a near-optimal solution to the hypothetical reasoning problem.

Fig. 1. Configuration of the HYPER system.

describe how clauses are actually instantiated, as a by-product of constructing the so-called query-tree for a query type. Section 5 reports on our experimental results. In Section 6, we briefly discuss and summarize the paper.

2 System Configuration

Computational efforts in the HYPER system are divided into an *off-line* and an *on-line* phase, as illustrated in Fig. 1. HYPER is an acronym for "Hypothetical reasoning employing reformation". In the off-line (preprocessing) phase we first isolate the portion of the first-order KB that is relevant to answering some query *type* [8, 13]. A query type $p(\bar{X})$ is like a ground query such as $p(a,b)$, but with all constants replaced by variables. Next, the KB is transformed via unfold/fold transformation steps [16, 12]. Finally, the transformed theory is instantiated as a by-product of constructing the query-tree [8]. The output of the off-line phase is the ground (i.e., propositional) knowledge base KB$'$ relevant to all instantiations $p(\bar{c}_1), ..., p(\bar{c}_n)$ of the query type that may have a solution with respect to the hypothetical reasoning problem.

The on-line phase assumes a ground query such as $p(\bar{c}_i)$ and computes all propositional clauses relevant to the ground query. Then, the SL method is applied to actually generate a solution to some (cost-based) hypothetical reasoning problem.

3 Relevance Reasoning

In this section we will introduce procedures that (i) partition a Horn theory into (independent) subtheories, and (ii) remove clauses from a subtheory that cannot contribute to the solution of any query, also called *strongly (proof-based) irrelevant* clauses (Levy et al. [8], Schurz [13]).

We consider first-order Horn theories T, i.e., sets of clauses C of the form "$q(\bar{X}_{n+1}) \leftarrow p_1(\bar{X}_1) \wedge ... \wedge p_n(\bar{X}_n)$" where $q(\bar{X}_{n+1}), p_1(\bar{X}_1), ..., p_n(\bar{X}_n)$ are atomic formulas, and $\bar{X}_i$ denotes the sequence of variables $X_{i,1}, ..., X_{i,m_i}$. The atom $q(\bar{X}_{n+1})$ is called the *head* of the clause, denoted by $hd(C)$, the conjunction $p_1(\bar{X}_1) \wedge ... \wedge p_n(\bar{X}_n)$ is called the *body* of the clause, denoted by $bd(C)$. The variables occurring in a clause are implicitly universally quantified. A clause (theory) containing no variables is called *ground* (or simply propositional). A clause C is called function-free if it does not contain non-zero function symbols (i.e., constants are allowed). Let $\mathcal{V}(hd(C))$ denote the set of variables occurring in the head of a clause C, and $\mathcal{V}(bd(C))$ the set of variables occurring in the clause body. A clause C is range-restricted if $\mathcal{V}(hd(C)) \subseteq \mathcal{V}(bd(C))$. All clauses considered here are Horn, function-free, and range-restricted. Moreover, we impose the restriction that theories are *acyclic*, i.e., the corresponding directed graph contains no cycles. Observe that if all clauses in T are function-free and acyclic, then there cannot be recursive definitions in T. A theory T is called *tree-structured* if the directed graph corresponding to T consists of subtrees $T_1, ..., T_n$, i.e., each T_i has only one top node and there exists only one (directed) path from every node in T_i to the top node.

In the first phase of the reformation process, the first-order theory T is factorized as follows: (i) if T is tree-structured, it can be partitioned into independent subtheories; (ii) if T is acyclic, a subtheory is generated for each query type $p(\bar{X})$. A tree-structured theory T is split into disjoint subtheories $T_1, ..., T_n$ such that no clause C in a given subtheory T_i resolves with some clause D from a different subtheory T_j. This means that the search space for a given atomic query type $p(\bar{X})$ can be restricted to a single subtheory T_i. In the more general case of acyclic theories, factorizing is performed by means of an algorithm that computes all clauses that are 'reachable' from a query type. Informally, a clause C is *reachable* from a query type $p(\bar{X})$ if there exists some path from $p(\bar{X})$ to the head of C. Observe that theory factorizing can be done in polynomial time.

This concludes the first reformation phase. It is important to note that for acyclic T, factorizing can be done by only considering the query types $p(\bar{X})$, and with tree-structured T, even independent of a query type. The procedures introduced so far already significantly reduce the number of clauses that have to be considered when answering a ground query. Since this claim is not experimentally supported in this paper, we have to refer the interested reader to the results in [8, 11].

4 Theory Transformation via Variable Elimination

The motivation for applying unfold/fold transformations [16, 12] is to reduce the complexity of a theory *as measured by the number of possible ground instantiations* of clauses. Since a clause C is exponential in the number n of different variables occurring in C, we try to minimize n. Theory transformation is an equivalence-preserving form of transformation [16].

Theory transformation proceeds by successively applying unfold (optional), definition, and fold rules, in that order, to the theory. More specifically, the application of transformation rules eliminates *unnecessary* variables, i.e., variables that occur in the body $bd(C)$ but not in the head $hd(C)$ of a clause C. One algorithm described in Proietti and Pettorossi [12] eliminates all unnecessary variables, but the algorithm is not guaranteed to halt. We will suggest terminating procedures that eliminate a sufficient number of unnecessary variables. In particular, we introduce a novel set of procedures that automatize the definition rule for a broad class of clause bodies. There is a lot of technical detail involved in describing the procedures (see Prendinger and Ishizuka [10]). For brevity, we only show the result of performing definition and folding steps. For definitions of unfolding, definition and folding rules, see Tamaki and Sato [16].

We start with some terminology to distinguish different kinds of clause bodies. The distinction is intended to cover a broad range of possible clause bodies. The most central notion is that of a *block* of a clause body [12].

Block. Given a clause C and a set B of atoms in $bd(C)$. We define a binary relation R over B such that: given two atoms B_1 and B_2 in B, $R(B_1, B_2)$ if and only if $\mathcal{V}(B_1) \cap \mathcal{V}(B_2) \neq \emptyset$. We let R^* denote the reflexive and transitive closure of R over $bd(C)$. By $partbd(C)$ we denote the partition of the body of C into blocks w.r.t. R^*. Note that each variable occurs in at most one block of $partbd(C)$. For instance, let C be the clause

$$q(X, Y, Z) \leftarrow p1(X, X1) \wedge p2(Y, Y1) \wedge p3(X1, Z)$$

Here $partbd(C)$ has two blocks, $\{p1(X, X1), p3(X1, Z)\}$ and $\{p2(Y, Y1)\}$. Consider a clause

$$C_0: \quad q(X, Y) \leftarrow p1(X, Z1, Z2) \wedge p2(Z1) \wedge p3(Z2, Y)$$

where the clause body forms a single block. The new clause

$$C_1: \quad newp(X, Z2) \leftarrow p1(X, Z1, Z2) \wedge p2(Z1)$$

is generated by the definition rule ($newp/2$ a fresh predicate symbol), and then folded with C_0. By folding C_1 with C_0, we obtain

$$C_2: \quad q(X, Y) \leftarrow newp(X, Z2) \wedge p3(Z2, Y)$$

The transformed theory consists of the two clauses C_1 and C_2, that allow for significantly less instantiations than the originial theory (C_0).

A block can have a variety of syntactical forms.

Chain. An example for a chain was given in the introductory section. We will revisit a chain example in the section on experiments.

Isolated blockpart. Consider the clause

$$C_0: \quad q(X, Y) \leftarrow p1(X, Z) \wedge p2(Z, Y) \wedge p3(Z, Z1)$$

The variable $Z1$ in $bd(C)$ is called 'isolated' (occurs only once in C_0), and $p3(Z, Z1)$ is thus an isolated blockpart. The definition rule for isolated blockparts generates the clause

$$C_1: \quad newp(Z) \leftarrow p3(Z, Z1)$$

which is folded with C_0 to produce

$$C_2: \quad q(X,Y) \leftarrow p1(X,Z) \wedge p2(Z,Y) \wedge newp(Z)$$

The theory transformation procedure is described in Prendinger and Ishizuka [10] (see also Proietti and Pettorossi [12]). The transformation procedure performs unfolding—definition—folding cycles until none of the procedures is applicable. The procedure significantly extends the algorithm in [12]. Except for a special instance of clause bodies with isolated blockparts, their algorithm did not eliminate any unnecessary variables. Observe that after applying theory transformation, we obtain slightly more first-order clauses, but they yield significantly fewer instantiations.

5 Theory Instantiation

In the last phase of the reformation process, the theory is instantiated. By employing the query-tree method (Levy *et al.* [8]), we obtain exactly the set of ground clauses relevant to a query type. A *query-tree* (QT) is a compact representation of a search tree for first-order Horn theories in the form of an AND-OR tree with goal-nodes and rule-nodes. Since we do not allow recursion in clauses, our construction of the QT is simpler than the original one in [8]. On the other hand, we allow that some leaves of the query-tree are uninstantiated. Those are typically *hypotheses* that may be assumed in order to prove a query.

The query-tree algorithm consists of two successive phases. In the *bottom-up* phase, the instantiations of the base atoms (denoting facts and hypotheses) are propagated upwards to the query type. Instantiations are conceived as constraints on the arguments of predicates. Then, in the *top-down* phase, the constraint generated for the query type is 'pushed down' along the branches of the QT. Thereby, the constraints of nodes (of predicates) in the QT might be further constrained, which possibly leads to pruning parts of the tree constructed bottom-up. In effect, we obtain exactly the set of ground clauses relevant to a query type together with all instantiations of the query type that have a solution with respect to the theory if certain hypotheses can be consistently assumed (Prendinger and Ishizuka [11]). The complexity of building the QT is linear in the number of rules and possibly exponential in the arity of predicates.

6 Empirical Evaluation

The impact of the savings gained by knowledge reformation is tested by means of the *Slide-down and Lift-up* (SL) mechanism (Ishizuka and Matsuo [5]), an efficient propositional hypothetical reasoning method for computing a near-optimal solution (e.g., diagnosis). In short, the SL method uses a linear programming technique (the simplex method) to determine an initial search point, and a non-linear programming technique to find a near-optimal 0-1 solution. The inference speed of the SL method is low-order polynomial, approximately $\mathcal{O}(n^{1.85})$, where

n is the number of propositional variables in the problem formulation. The SL method runs on a SGI ONYX workstation (200 MHz CPU × 2, 512 MB memory). The theory factorizing, variable elimination, and instantiation procedures are implemented in C and run on the same machine.

In hypothetical reasoning (or 'abduction'), we are given a knowledge base T, hypotheses (or 'assumables') $\mathcal{H}$, and a query q. Sometimes the problem formulation contains inconsistency constraints $I \subset T$ of the form "$inc \leftarrow h_1(\bar{c}_1) \wedge ... \wedge h_n(\bar{c}_n)$" where $h_i \in \mathcal{H}$, $\bar{c}_n$ a sequence of constant symbols, and the symbol "inc" denotes the impossible state (*falsum*). The hypothetical reasoning task consists in finding minimal sets $H_1, ..., H_n$ ($H_i \subseteq \mathcal{H}$) such that (i) $T \cup H_i \vdash q$, and (ii) $T \cup H_i \not\vdash inc$.

Since the SL method generates a near-optimal solution, it is natural to ask how 'near' the solution is to the optimal solution. For theories including inconsistency constraints, it can be shown experimentally that in 92.6% of the cases, the near-optimal solution is among the three best solutions. Here, solutions with the same cost are not distinguished, even if they contain different hypotheses.

The experiments are intended to show the speedup effect due to knowledge reformation (except for factorizing which is not needed here but has been shown elsewhere [8]). They involve simple theories that are not very interesting in themselves but allow us to make easy comparisons by varying relevant parameters, such as the number of unnecessary variables, and the number of constants in the problem formulations. We expect the efficiency gain to be the more significant the more unnecessary variables are eliminated.

As an example for a *chain*, let the theory T consist of the clauses

(r_1) $path(X, Y) \leftarrow link1(X, Z1) \wedge link2(Z1, Z2) \wedge$
$\quad\quad link3(Z2, Z3) \wedge link4(Z3, Y)$
(r_2) $inc \leftarrow link1(X, Y) \wedge link3(Y, X)$

As the set of element hypotheses we take $\mathcal{H} = \bigcup_{k=1}^{4}\{link_k(a_i, a_j)/w : i, j \in \{1, ..., n\}\}$. By varying the number of constants n, we obtain theories of different size. We may also look at theories with a greater (smaller) number of links in the definition of $path/2$, by varying the number k.

In our experiment, we assume $n \leq 12$ and $k = 4$ and call this instance *4-path example*. For simplicity, we assume a default value w as the cost (or weight) for all element hypotheses $h \in \mathcal{H}$, i.e., we are essentially looking for a subset-minimal solution to the hypothetical reasoning problem [4]. After applying the reformation procedure, r_1 is replaced by

(r_1') $path(X, Y) \leftarrow newp1(X, Z3) \wedge link4(Z3, Y)$
(r_1'') $newp1(X, Z3) \leftarrow newp2(X, Z2) \wedge link3(Z2, Z3)$
(r_1''') $newp2(X, Z2) \leftarrow link1(X, Z1) \wedge link2(Z1, Z2)$

The inconsistency constraint (r_2) and $\mathcal{H}$ remain unchanged.

The impact of knowledge base reformation on problem size and processing time for the 4-path example is summarized in Fig. 2. Here, '# consts' is the number of constants occurring in the problem formulation. '# rules' refers to the

# consts	# rules		# atoms		inst.-time (sec)		sol.-time (sec)	
	unref.	ref.	unref.	ref.	unref.	ref.	unref.	ref.
3	243	81	1278	306	0.24	0.18	0.75	0.71
4	1024	192	5232	688	0.57	0.33	1.04	0.70
5	3125	375	15800	1300	2.30	0.50	2.60	0.80
6	7776	648	39132	2196	9.23	0.78	7.41	0.89
7	16807	1029	84378	3430	34.08	1.02	26.62	1.04
8	32768	1536	164288	5056	119.83	1.41	98.67	1.28
9	59049	2187	295812	7128	393.22	1.91	148.48	1.62
10	100000	3000	500700	9700	1327.55	2.70	–	2.08
11	161051	3993	806102	12826	6611.00	3.58	–	2.69
12	248832	5184	1245168	16560	–	4.81	–	3.45

Fig. 2. Results for the 4-*path* example.

number of instantiated (propositional) rules before and after reformation. The numbers do not include the number of instantiated inconsistency constraints which is the same for both unreformed and reformed theories. '# atoms' is the number of atoms (propositional variables) in the problem formulation (including hypotheses atoms and atoms occurring in inconsistency constraints). The two columns under 'inst.-time (sec)' show the CPU times needed to instantiate the original and reformed theories, respectively, and the two columns under 'sol.-time (sec)' give the CPU times to find a near-optimal solution for an instantiated goal $path(a, b)$, for the original and reformed theories, respectively. The CPU time needed to reform the theory via the variable elimination procedures is 0.015 seconds. The relevance reasoning part of the on-line phase is integrated into the SL method.

Instantiating a clause in the original theory effectively means to create a lookup table with m^n entries, where m is the number of constants in the problem formulation, and n is the number of different variables in the clause. In the 4-path example, for instance, if there are ten constants, we obtain $10^5 = 100000$ propositional clauses corresponding to the first-order definition of a path (r_1), that has five different variables. The space-reducing effect of knowledge reformation can be seen as decreasing the exponent n. In the given example, the original clause r_1 is transformed to three clauses with three different variables in each clause, which allow for $3 \times 10^3 = 3000$ propositional clauses. Another property of the reformed part of the output theory is that the transformed clauses are *shorter*, which has a direct effect on the number of atoms in the problem formulation. The total number of atoms in the respective theories is given in Fig. 2.

It is interesting to see how the instantiated reformed theory mimics the behavior of a first-order reasoning method (minus unification). Assume the path example is run with a Prolog-style reasoner on the goal $path(a, b)$. For simplicity, we assume that there are no inconsistency constraints contained in the problem formulation. First, the $link1$-atom is solved with X bound to a, and $Z1$ bound

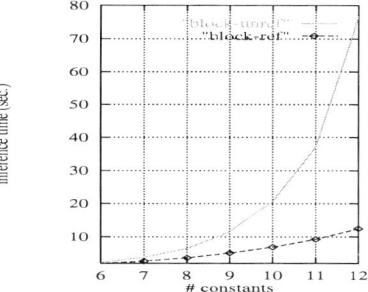
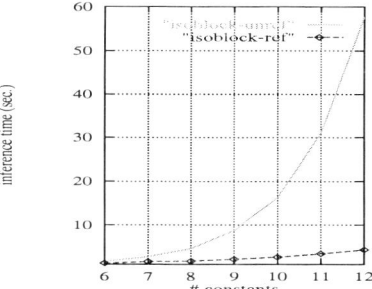

Fig. 3. Block example.   **Fig. 4.** Isolated blockpart example.

to, say, c. Then the solution to solve $link1(X, Z1)$ will be kept for all the different values of $Z2$ and $Z3$. However, grounding of the unreformed theory will effectively produce all other instantiations for $link1(X, Z1)$, even though this is not required. The reformed ground theory, on the other hand, will first find a solution for $newp1(X, Z3)$ and $link4(Z3, Y)$ and then use that solution for all other variables. Since there are no inconsistency constraints, the instantiation of $link4(Z3, Y)$ is guaranteed to be contained in the solution hypotheses set. In general, however, it is difficult to compare such radically different approaches as integer linear programming and search-style oriented reasoning methods.

Regarding the time needed to instantiate the first-order theories (which is done off-line), note that the query-tree method produces a ground theory that can be used for *all* instantiations of a particular query type that may have a solution. So, if all possible ground queries are posed, the actual time needed for each query is $\frac{t}{m^k}$, where t is the instantiation time, m is the number of constants in the problem formulation, and k is the arity of the query predicate. In the case of ten constants, for instance, the actual cost for the reformed theory is $\frac{2.7}{100} = 0.027$ seconds for each individual query (if all ground queries are posed). Although it is unrealistic to assume that all possible queries are posed, we nevertheless expect that compiled theories are *reused* a sufficiently large number of times to amortize the cost to instantiate the theory. The last two columns in Fig. 2 summarize the efficiency gain resulting from knowledge reformation in CPU seconds. The *total* speedup is up to a factor of 153 for nine constants. The total speedup considers both instantiation time and the time needed to find a solution, e.g., for nine constants, the unreformed theory requires 393.22 + 148.48 = 541.7 (sec), whereas the reformed theory only needs 1.91 + 1.62 = 3.53 (sec).

To support our hypothesis that performance is crucially dependent on how many unnecessary variables are eliminated, we performed another experiment that is analogous to the 4-path example, but has three body atoms in the definition of $path/2$ instead of four. For this example (where less variables are eliminated) we measured speedups up to a factor of 14 (for twelve constants). Figures 3 and 4 summarize the speedup effect of the transformation procedures for blocks and isolated blockparts (using the examples of Section 4). Inference time here refers to the total time needed to solve a problem, i.e., off-line and on-line reasoning for a specific goal. For less than six constants, the speedup effect was negligible. For realistic theories, we expect (i) that our reformation procedures can be applied to a significantly large portion of the KB, and (ii) that all of our three transformation procedures are used to a varying extent.

7 Conclusion

In this paper, we address the following problem: given a problem formulation in first-order acyclic Horn logic without function symbols, how can we arrive at a compact propositional representation? In particular, we have presented the HYPER system, an effective method for cost-based first-order hypothetical reasoning problems, where a KB in the language of function-free first-order Horn logic is first compiled into a propositional KB and then an efficient propositional method is applied to compute a near-optimal solution. We have shown that off-line knowledge reformation of first-order rules is very effective in reducing the number and length of generated propositional rules. Consequently, the total inference time for solving cost-based first-order hypothetical reasoning problems can be significantly reduced.

The idea to preprocess some part of the input off-line to improve on-line efficiency is employed by many others (Williams and Nayak [17], Cadoli and Donini [1]). However, those compilation methods are restricted to the propositional case, i.e., the original KB is expressed in propositional logic. By contrast, we introduce an effective way to produce a compact propositional theory from a given *first-order* theory. In this respect, our approach shares intuitions with the 'first-order planning as (propositional) satisfiability' framework of Kautz and Selman [6]. One problem, however, applies to both approaches: the presence of too many constants makes the translation (first-order to propositional) infeasible. This problem was pointed out by Levesque [7] who imagines a knowledge base with 10^5 constants.

Although the focus of the present paper is more foundational, a subset of our compilation techniques has already been shown to be practical for diagnostic tasks (Prendinger and Ishizuka [11]). In the near future, the HYPER system will be available as free software.

Acknowledgements

We would like to thank the anonymous referees for their very helpful and detailed comments. Special thanks go to our colleague Yutaka Matsuo who provided the hypothetical reasoning engine for our experiments and many insightful comments. The first author was supported by a grant from the Japan Society for the Promotion of Science (JSPS).

References

1. Marco Cadoli and Francesco M. Donini. A survey on knowledge compilation. *AI Communications*, 10:137–150, 1997.
2. U. S. Charkravarthy, John Grant, and Jack Minker. Foundations of semantic query optimization for deductive databases. In Jack Minker, editor, *Foundations of Deductive Databases and Logic Programming*, pages 243–273. Morgan Kaufmann Publishers, 1988.
3. John Debenham. Knowledge object decomposition. In *Proceedings 12th International FLAIRS Conference (FLAIRS-99)*, pages 203–207, 1999.
4. Thomas Eiter and Georg Gottlob. The complexity of logic-based abduction. *Journal of the ACM*, 42(1–2):3–42, 1995.
5. Mitsuru Ishizuka and Yutaka Matsuo. SL method for computing a near-optimal solution using linear and non-linear programming in cost-based hypothetical reasoning. In *Proceedings 5th Pacific Rim Conference on Artificial Intelligence (PRICAI-98)*, pages 611–625, 1998.
6. Henry Kautz and Bart Selman. Pushing the envelope: Planning, propositional logic, and stochastic search. In *Proceedings 13th National Conference on Artificial Intelligence (AAAI-96)*, 1996.
7. Hector J. Levesque. A completeness result for reasoning with incomplete first-order knowledge bases. In *Proceedings 6th Conference on Principles of Knowledge Representation and Reasoning (KR-98)*, pages 14–23, 1998.
8. Alon Y. Levy, Richard E. Fikes, and Yehoshua Sagiv. Speeding up inferences using relevance reasoning: a formalism and algorithms. *Artificial Intelligence*, 97:83–136, 1997.
9. Yukio Ohsawa and Mitsuru Ishizuka. Networked bubble propagation: a polynomial-time hypothetical reasoning method for computing near-optimal solutions. *Artificial Intelligence*, 91:131–154, 1997.
10. Helmut Prendinger and Mitsuru Ishizuka. Preparing a first-order knowledge base for fast inference. In *Proceedings 12th International FLAIRS Conference (FLAIRS-99)*, pages 208–121, 1999.
11. Helmut Prendinger and Mitsuru Ishizuka. Qualifying the expressivity/efficiency tradeoff: Reformation-based diagnosis. In *Proceedings 16th National Conference on Artificial Intelligence (AAAI-99)*, pages 416–421, 1999.
12. Maurizio Proietti and Alberto Pettorossi. Unfolding—definition—folding, in this order, for avoiding unnecessary variables in logic programs. *Theoretical Computer Science*, 142:89–124, 1995.
13. Gerhard Schurz. Relevance in deductive reasoning: A critical overview. In G. Schurz and M. Ursic, editors, *Beyond Classical Logic*. Academia Press, St. Augustin, 1999.
14. Bart Selman and Henry Kautz. Domain-independent extensions to GSAT: Solving large structured satisfiability problems. In *Proceedings 13th International Conference on Artificial Intelligence (IJCAI-93)*, pages 290–295, 1993.
15. G. Sutcliffe and C. B. Suttner. The TPTP Problem Library: CNF Release v1.2.1. *Journal of Automated Reasoning*, 21(2):177–203, 1998.
16. Hisao Tamaki and Taisuke Sato. Unfold/fold transformation of logic programs. In *Proceedings 2nd International Logic Programming Conference*, pages 127–138, 1984.
17. Brian C. Williams and P. Pandurang Nayak. A model-based approach to reactive self-configuring systems. In *Proceedings 13th National Conference on Artificial Intelligence (AAAI-96)*, pages 971–978, 1996.

Determination of General Concept in Learning Default Rules*

Kouzou Ohara, Hideyuki Taka, Noboru Babaguchi, and Tadahiro Kitahashi

I.S.I.R., Osaka University,
8-1 Mihogaoka, Ibaraki, Osaka 567-0047, JAPAN
{ohara,taka,babaguchi,kitahashi}@am.sanken.osaka-u.ac.jp

Abstract. In this paper, we discuss a method to determine which concept, the target concept or its opposite, is more general in given examples when learning rules with exceptions, or *default rules* in the Inductive Logic Programming (ILP) framework. The ILP system learning default rules has to learn both the concepts in a three valued setting which clearly distinguishes what is true, what is false, and what is unknown. In order to learn hypotheses which holds as generally as possible in the domain, we should give a higher priority to the concept which is more general, or covers more examples than does the other. For this purpose, our method dynamically determines the general concept according to the ratio of positive examples covered by the hypothesis which is correct and most general in the hypothesis space.

1 Introduction

Recently some researchers have introduced non-monotonic formalism to Inductive Logic Programming (ILP) in order to acquire the rules with exceptions, which is called the *default rules*[1, 2, 5, 7, 8]. ILP aims at generating logic programs describing a target concept, when given are the positive and negative examples of the target concept and background knowledge[3, 9]. Each rule in the logic programs is called the *hypothesis*. Learning default rules as hypotheses is important in the sense that it could improve both coverage and understandability of learned descriptions, as well as improve their expressive power. Furthermore learning the definitions of the exceptions to default rules could improve accuracy of the defaults since we can predict future exceptions with the definitions.

One of the important results in the recent work on learning default rules is it had been shown that a three valued setting is essential in inductive concept learning, especially in learning default rules[7, 8]. In a three valued setting, what is true, what is false, and what is unknown are clearly distinguished, while the distinction between what is false and what is unknown is not clear in the two valued setting which automatically applies *negation as failure* (NAF) to unknown instances. The exceptions to the learned default rules should appear in negative examples under a three valued setting.

---
* This research was partly supported by a Grant-in-Aid for Encouragement of Young Scientists of Japan Society for the Promotion of Science.

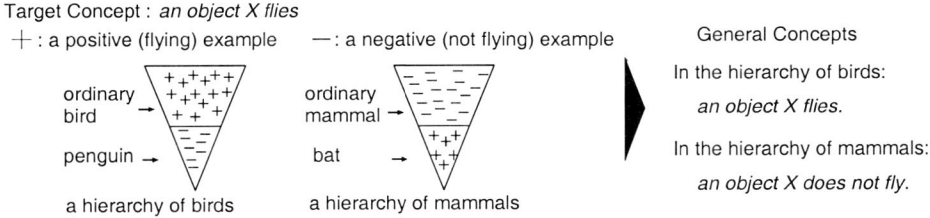

Fig. 1. Existence of multiple taxonomic hierarchies in the given examples

On the other hand, the ILP system is required to learn both the target concept and its opposite in a three valued setting, because we have already *known* positive and negative examples are instances of either of the two concepts. This means that the target concept is not always given any higher priority than its opposite in learning under a three valued setting. The opposite concept should be given a higher priority if it is more *general*, or covers more examples than does the target one. Namely we have to determine which of the two concepts is more general in order to learn the description holding as generally as possible in the domain.

In the literature[7] on learning default rules in a three valued setting, Inoue and Kudoh used the ratio of given positive examples to all examples as the criterion to determine which concept is general. However the generality of the concept is not always corresponding to the ratio. It may be impossible to *uniquely* determine it. Fig.1 illustrates such a situation, in which the target concept "*an object X flies*" is more general than its opposite in the taxonomic hierarchy of birds, while its opposite is more general in mammals. Practically it is impossible to know how many hierarchies exist in given examples and which concept is more general in each of them before learning; if we know that, we would not have to learn anything any more.

The main purpose of this paper is to provide an algorithm, called *GREX*, which is capable of learning default rules and determining the *general concept* for each taxonomic hierarchy even if there exist multiple hierarchies in given examples like Fig.1. The basic idea of our method is to change the head of a general hypothesis, or the concept to be defined by the hypothesis. Our method first finds out a correct hypothesis which is more general, or covers more examples than does any other one, independently of the concept it defines. Next the general concept is determined according to the ratio of the positive examples the hypothesis covers to all of examples it covers. After that, the general hypothesis is specialized, or converted into a default rule if it covers negative examples of the concept it defines. The exceptions to the resulting default rule are also generalized in the same way, except that the determination of the general concept is omitted. As a result, the most general default rule in the learned hierarchical defaults defines the general concept in the taxonomic hierarchy.

2 Knowledge Representation

In this paper, we employ the *exc-representation* (ER)[11] as the knowledge representation to express the default rules. ER does not require the default cancellation rules which are necessary if we employ Extended Logic Programs (ELPs)[6]. This simplifies the learning algorithms and improves readability of the hypotheses learned. In this section, we will explain some notations and the interpretations of rules in ER we need here, and may leave the formal definitions to [11].

ER is an extension of definite Horn clauses. The default rule is represented as the rule with the symbol $\Leftarrow$ which means implication allowing exceptions, while the ordinary rule is a Horn clause with the logical implication symbol $\leftarrow$. For example, the knowledge "birds normally fly" which has exceptions like penguins is represented as follows:

$$fly(X) \Leftarrow bird(X) . \tag{1}$$

The exceptions to a default rule are specified by the *exc-literal* in the form of $exc^d\text{-}P$, where d is a non-negative integer called the *degree* and P is the head of the default rule. The degree expresses the hierarchical relation among exceptions, and the degree 1 is omitted. For example, the exc-literal $exc\text{-}fly(X)$ represents the exceptions to the rule(1), while $exc^2\text{-}fly(X)$ ($= exc\text{-}exc\text{-}fly(X)$) represents the exceptions of exceptions. The exc-literals appear only in the front of the rules or ground atoms as labels to identify exceptions. The knowledge "penguins cannot fly" is represented by the following rule.

$$[exc\text{-}fly(X)]\overline{fly}(X) \leftarrow penguin(X), \tag{2}$$

where $\overline{fly}(X)$ is a positive literal expressing the negation of $fly(X)$. The inconsistency $\bot$ is defined by the rule such as $\bot \leftarrow fly(X), \overline{fly}(X)$ since ER does not permit any occurrence of the negative literal. And the rule which defines the inconsistency is tacitly assumed between any pair of *complementary literals* such as $fly(X)$ and $\overline{fly}(X)$. In this paper, we use $comp(P)$ to denote the complementary literal of a literal P. In addition, $head(r)$ and $body(r)$ denote the head and body of the rule r, respectively.

In ER, modus ponens holds for ordinary rules. On the other hand, the default rule(1) can be read as: "if $bird(X)$ is true then $fly(X)$ is true unless $exc\text{-}fly(X)$ is true". Note that the semantics of the default rule in ER implicitly involves the idea of NAF. When given are the *facts*, or ground literals $penguin(tweety)$ and $bird(tweety)$, $fly(tweety)$ cannot be derived from the rule(1) because $exc\text{-}fly(tweety)$ is derived from the rule(2). If a default rule r has an exc-literal $exc^d\text{-}P$, then $head(r)$ is true unless either $exc\text{-}head(r)$ or $exc^{d+1}\text{-}P$ are true. The *answer set* in ER is a set of ground literals derivable from a set of rules in ER. A literal P is true if it appear in an answer set, and P is false if its complementary literal is in the answer set; P is unknown if neither P nor its complementary literal is in the answer set.

Here we mention the ILP setting in this paper. Suppose that positive examples E^+, negative ones E^- and background knowledge BK are given to the ILP system, which are described as Horn clauses. Then the ILP system outputs a set of rules H in the form of ER. We say the ILP system is *complete* and *sound* if and only if its output H satisfies the following conditions:

$$BK \cup H \vdash_{exc} E^+, Comp(E^-) \quad (completeness), \tag{3}$$
$$BK \cup H \not\vdash_{exc} Comp(E^+), E^- \quad (soundness), \tag{4}$$

where $Comp(E^-)$ ($Comp(E^+)$) stands for a set of complementary literals of elements of E^- (E^+). The first condition means any ground atom in $E^+ \cup Comp(E^-)$ is derivable from $BK \cup H$ in the semantics of ER, while the second one means any ground atom in $Comp(E^+) \cup E^-$ is *not* derivable from $BK \cup H$.

3 Learning Algorithm with Determination of General Concept

In this section, we present the algorithm called $GREX$ (Generating Rules with EXceptions) and its components. The outline of $GREX$ is summarized as follows:

Algorithm 1 $GREX(E^+, E^-, BK, H)$
INPUT : positive examples E^+, negative examples E^-, and background knowledge BK
OUTPUT : hypotheses H
until all examples in $E^+ \cup E^-$ have been marked **do**
 1. select a non-marked example $e_1 \in E^+ \cup E^-$;
 2. $Generate\_Rule(e_1, E^+, E^-, BK, h_1)$;
 3. $E_p := \{e | e \in E^+, BK \cup \{h_1\} \vdash e\}$;
 4. $E_n := \{e | e \in E^-, BK \cup \{h_1\} \vdash e\}$;
 5. mark $e \in E^+ \cup E^-$ such that $e \in E_p \cup E_n$;
 6. $Determine\_Concept(h_1, |E_p|, |E_n|, h_2)$;
 7. **if** $|E_n| < |E_p|$ **then** $GEX(E_n, E_p, BK, h_1, Negative, 1, head(h_2), T)$;
   else $GEX(E_p, E_n, BK, h_1, Positive, 1, head(h_2), T)$;
 8. $H := H \cup \{h_2\} \cup T$, □

where $|E|$ means the number of examples in the set E.

$GREX$ generates a set of hypotheses H in the form of ER, when are given positive examples E^+, negative examples E^- and background knowledge BK. The internal procedure $Generate\_Rule$ generates a general hypothesis h_1 from the selected positive example e_1. Then the procedure $Determine\_Concept$ determines the general concept of the taxonomic hierarchy e_1 belongs to, according to the ratio of positive examples h_1 covers. And the procedure GEX generalizes the exceptions to the default rule resulting from the specialization of h_1. In the following subsections, we explain the details of these internal procedures, as well as discuss the relation between the hypothesis space and the general concept.

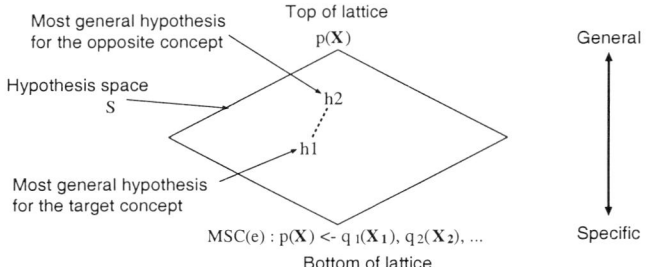

Fig. 2. The relation among hypotheses and concepts in a hypothesis space

3.1 Determination of General Concept

Learning a hypothesis in ILP is equivalent to searching for the hypothesis with the highest evaluation value from a set of hypotheses called the *hypothesis space*, which is a lattice whose partial order is defined by subsumption: a hypothesis h is more general than another hypothesis h' if h is an ancestor of h' in the lattice, because h subsumes h'. The root of the lattice is the most general hypothesis, or a literal $p(\boldsymbol{X})$ where p stands for the target concept and $\boldsymbol{X}$ is a set of variables needed to describe it. On the other hand, we use as the bottom of the space the *Most Specific Clause* (MSC), which is produced by *Inverse Entailment*[10] from an example and background knowledge. The MSC is the most specific one to describe the example under the background knowledge. We use $MSC(e)$ to express the MSC generated from an example e.

Now let us consider the relation between the hypothesis space and the general concept. Suppose that h_1 is a hypothesis which covers more positive examples than does any other one in the hypothesis space S whose bottom is $MSC(e)$. Then if the general concept in the taxonomic hierarchy e belongs to is the opposite one, there must exit a hypothesis h_2 in S such that it is an ancestor of h_1 and covers more negative examples than positive ones h_1 covers as shown in Fig.2. This is because any definition of all classes containing e appears in S as the body of a hypothesis and this means that any definition of all classes in the hierarchy also appears in S. The general concept is the standard one in the most general class in the hierarchy.

Therefore the first step to determine the general concept in a taxonomic hierarchy is to find the hypothesis h_{best} which is *correct* and *most general*, or has the greatest coverage of either positive or negative examples. After that, we have only to determine the general concept according to the ratio of positive examples h_{best} covers to all of examples it covers: if it covers more positive examples than negative ones, then the general concept is the target concept; otherwise it is the opposite one.

Here it is necessary to evaluate both the *generality* and *correctness* of the hypothesis to find h_{best}. Intuitively the more the number of positive examples a hypothesis covers is, the higher its generality is, while the lower the ratio of negative ones it covers is, the higher its correctness is. Thus we use the following heuristic function f to evaluate the generality and correctness of a hypothesis h:

$$f(p,n,b) = (p-n-b) \times (1 - H(\frac{p}{p+n})), \tag{5}$$

where p, n, b are the number of positive and negative examples h covers, and the number of literals in $body(h)$, respectively, and $H(x) = -x\log(x) - (1-x)\log(1-x)$. The first term $p-n-b$ is based on minimal description length principle like the function in Progol[10]. On the other hand, $H(\frac{p}{p+n})$ is the entropy of h, or its uncertainty, which reflects the risk of covering negative examples in the evaluation value. For example, if the hypothesis h_1 with 5 literals in its body covers 100 positive examples and 10 negative ones, and the other hypothesis h_2 with the same length as h_1 covers 1,000 positive ones and 910 negative ones, then f_1, the evaluation value of h_1, is higher than f_2, that of h_2, while $f_1 = f_2 = 85$ if we use only the first term in the equation(5).

Let us now return to the finding h_{best}. We focus on the fact that we can evaluate the hypothesis as a definition of the opposite concept only if we reverse the roles of positive and negative examples in the heuristic function. Practically we use the function $\max(f(p,n,b), f(n,p,b))$ to evaluate a hypotheses to find h_{best}. Then we replace $head(h_{best})$ by $comp(head(h_{best}))$ if $p < n$.

The above discussion is formalized as the following algorithms *Generate_Rule* and *Determine_Concept*. *Generate_Rule* generates the best hypothesis h_{best} from an example e using the evaluation function $\max(f(p,n,b), f(n,p,b))$. The head of h_{best} is determined based on the number of positive and negative examples h_{best} covers in *Determine_Concept*. In addition, if h_{best} covers the negative examples of the concept it defines, h_{best} is converted into the default rule: this conversion is regarded as a kind of specialization.

Algorithm 2 $Generate\_Rule(e, E^+, E^-, BK, h_{best})$
INPUT : an example e, positive examples E^+, negative examples E^-, and background knowledge BK
OUTPUT : a hypothesis h_{best}
Let $F(r)$ be $\max(f(p,n,b), f(n,p,b))$ where f is defined by the equation(5);
1. search the hypothesis space whose bottom is $MSC(e)$ for a hypothesis h_{best} such that $F(h') \leq F(h_{best})$ for any hypothesis h' ($\neq h_{best}$);
2. if the hypothesis h_{best} exists, then return h_{best}; otherwise return e. □

Algorithm 3 $Determine\_Concept(h, p, n, h')$
INPUT : a hypothesis h, the number of positive examples h covers, p, and the number of negative examples h covers, n
OUTPUT : a hypothesis h' in ER
if $n < p$ then
    if $n \neq 0$ then $h_2 := head(h_1) \Leftarrow body(h_1)$;
    else $h_2 := h_1$;
else
    if $p \neq 0$ then $h_2 := comp(head(h_1)) \Leftarrow body(h_1)$;
    else $h_2 := comp(head(h_1)) \leftarrow body(h_1)$. □

3.2 Generalization of Exceptions

Once we have determined the general concept and generated the default rule, we have only to generalize its exceptions, similarly to existing methods: we regard the exceptions to the default rule as positive examples and regard the examples of the concept defined by the default as negative ones. But note that the concept to be learned in this turn has already been definite. Therefore *Determine_Concept* is not necessary any more. In addition, we evaluate the hypothesis with the heuristic function $f(p, n, b)$, but not $\max(f(p, n, b), f(n, p, b))$. On the other hand, the hypothesis which defines the exceptions should be more specific than the default rule.

From this discussion, to learn the definitions of exceptions, the following procedures GEX (Generalizing EXceptions) generalizes only the positive examples with *Generate_Rule2* involving the function $f(p, n, c)$. In fact, the negative examples have already been generalized in the precedent procedure which calls GEX: $GREX$ or itself. GEX may generate hierarchical default rules by calling itself recursively. The hypotheses GEX generates are more specific than the hypothesis h_{pre} which has been generated in the precedent procedure, and they have the exc-literals consisting of a literal P and the degree d: P is the head of the most general default rule learned in $GREX$, and d means the depth of the hierarchy of exceptions. The argument C of GEX is either *Positive* or *Negative*, which means the concept to be defined in that turn.

Algorithm 4 $GEX(E^+, E^-, BK, h_{pre}, C, d, P, T)$
INPUT : positive examples E^+, negative examples E^-, background knowledge BK, a hypothesis in the previous layer h_{pre}, a flag expressing learning concept C, a non-negative integer for the degree d, and the head of the default rule generated in $GREX$ P
OUTPUT : hypotheses in ER T
until all examples in E^+ have been marked **do**

1. select a non-marked example $e_1 \in E^+$;
2. $Generate\_Rule2(e_1, E^+, E^-, BK, h_{pre}, h_1)$;
3. $E_p := \{e | e \in E^+, BK \cup \{h_1\} \vdash e\}$;
4. $E_n := \{e | e \in E^-, BK \cup \{h_1\} \vdash e\}$;
5. mark $e \in E^+$ such that $e \in E_p$;
6. **if** $E_n = \phi$ **then**
    if $C = Positive$ **then** $h_2 := [exc^d\text{-}P]h_1$;
    else $h_2 := [exc^d\text{-}P]comp(head(h_1)) \leftarrow body(h_1)$;
   else
    if $C = Positive$ **then**
        $h_2 := [exc^d\text{-}P]head(h_1) \Leftarrow body(h_1)$;
        $GEX(E_n, E_p, BK, h_1, Negative, d+1, P, T')$;
    else
        $h_2 := [exc^d\text{-}P]comp(head(h_1)) \Leftarrow body(h_1)$;
        $GEX(E_n, E_p, BK, h_1, Positive, d+1, P, T')$;
7. $T := T \cup \{h_2\} \cup T'$. □

Algorithm5 $Generate\_Rule2(e, E^+, E^-, BK, h_{pre}, h_{best})$
INPUT : an example e, positive examples E^+, negative examples E^-, background knowledge BK, and a hypothesis in the previous layer h_{pre}
OUTPUT : a hypothesis h_{best}
Let $F(r)$ be $f(p, n, b)$ where f is defined by the equation(5);

1. search the hypothesis space whose bottom is $MSC(e)$ for a hypothesis h_{best} such that h_{best} is subsumed by h_{pre} and $F(h') \leq F(h_{best})$ for any hypothesis $h' (\neq h_{best})$;
2. if the hypothesis h_{best} exists, then return h_{best}; otherwise return e. □

Furthermore $GREX$ satisfies the following property.

Theorem 1. *When given are a finite set of positive examples E^+, a finite set of negative ones E^-, and the finite background knowledge BK, $GREX$ H is complete and sound.* □

Proof. $<Completeness>$ We prove only $BK \cup H \vdash_{exc} e \in E^+$, since we can prove also $BK \cup H \vdash_{exc} e \in E^-$ in the same way. First of all, the output of $Generate\_Rule$ h_1 in $GREX$ is either e itself or a clause h. And $\{h\} \cup BK \vdash_{exc} e$ since h subsumes $MSC(e)$. Then if $|E_n| < |E_p|$, $BK \cup h_2(\in H) \vdash_{exc} e$ from the definition of *Determine_Concept*. On the other hand, let us consider the case of $|E_p| < |E_n|$. Now the output of $Generate\_Rule2$ in GEX is either e itself or a clause h'_1, and $\{h'_2\} \cup BK \vdash_{exc} e$ where h'_2 is the rule generated in the step6 in GEX. Since for the output of GEX T, $h'_2 \in T$ and $T \subseteq H$, $BK \cup H \vdash_{exc} e \in E^+$.
$<Soundness>$ We have to prove that $exc\text{-}e$ is derivable from $BK \cup H$ for $e \in Comp(E^+)$. Now we assume $BK \cup H \vdash_{exc} e$. Then there is a rule $h \in H$ which defines the opposite concept and $BK \cup \{h\} \vdash_{exc} e$. However since $comp(e) \in E^+$, $comp(e) \in E_p$ in the step3 of $GREX$ and there must be a generalization h' of $comp(e)$ which is generated in GEX. Here the termination of GEX is guaranteed both from the finite examples and background knowledge and from the limitation that the output of $Generate\_Rule2$ is subsumed by h_{pre}. And from the definition of GEX, h' has the exc-literal $exc\text{-}P$ where P is the head of h. Thus for T which is the output of GEX, $BK \cup T \vdash_{exc} exc\text{-}e$, and then $BK \cup H \vdash_{exc} exc\text{-}e$ since $T \subseteq H$. It is contradiction. Thus $BK \cup H \not\vdash_{exc} e \in Comp(H^+)$. □

4 Example and Discussion

Here let us consider the following example concretely describing the situation shown in Fig.1.

Example 1. Consider the following examples and background knowledge E^+, E^-, BK are given to $GREX$ to learn the target concept fly.

$E^+ = \{fly(a), fly(b), fly(c), fly(d), fly(o), fly(p)\}$,
$E^- = \{fly(e), fly(f), fly(g), fly(h), fly(i), fly(j), fly(k), fly(l),$
$\qquad fly(m), fly(n)\}$,

$BK = \{bird(a), bird(b), bird(c), bird(d), penguin(e), penguin(f),$
$bird(X) \leftarrow penguin(X), mammal(g), mammal(h), mammal(i),$
$mammal(j), mammal(k), mammal(l), mammal(m), mammal(n),$
$bat(o), bat(p), mammal(X) \leftarrow bat(X)\}$.

First $Generate\_Rule$ generates $fly(X) \leftarrow bird(X)$ from the example $fly(a)$ in $GREX$, which is converted into the following default rule in $Determine\_Concept$ since it covers four positive examples and two negative ones: $p = 4$ and $n = 2$.

$$fly(X) \Leftarrow bird(X) . \tag{6}$$

Next since the rule(6) covers two negative examples as its exceptions, GEX is called by $GREX$, and it generates the following rule from the negative example $fly(e)$ which is an exception to the default rule(6).

$$[exc\text{-}fly(X)]\overline{fly}(X) \leftarrow penguin(X) . \tag{7}$$

After that, again $Generate\_Rule$ generates $fly(X) \leftarrow mammal(X)$ from a positive example $fly(o)$, which is converted into the following default rule in $Determine\_Concept$ because it covers more negative examples than positive ones: $p = 2$ and $n = 8$.

$$\overline{fly}(X) \Leftarrow mammal(X) . \tag{8}$$

Finally GEX generates the following rule from $fly(o)$, an exception to the rule(8), and GREX terminates since all examples have been marked.

$$[exc\text{-}\overline{fly}(X)]fly(X) \leftarrow bat(X) . \tag{9}$$

□

Now we use this example to discuss the difference between GREX and exiting systems, LELP[7] and LearnELP[8], which can learn hierarchical defaults in a three valued setting. LELP is the first system adopting ELPs as the form of generated rules, in which NAF and classical negation freely appear in the body of the rule. LELP determined the general concept according to the ratio of the *given* positive examples to all given examples. This means that LELP can not always learn the hypotheses holding as generally as possible. For Example 1, LELP generates the following rules as well as the ground atoms, $fly(a), fly(b), fly(c),$ and $fly(d)$:

$$\neg fly(X) \leftarrow mammal(X), not\ ab_1(X), \tag{10}$$
$$ab_1(X) \leftarrow bat(X), \tag{11}$$
$$fly(X) \leftarrow bat(X), \tag{12}$$
$$\neg fly(X) \leftarrow penguin(X), \tag{13}$$

where the symbol "¬" stands for classical negation, while the symbol "*not*" stands for NAF. Clearly the rule "birds normally fly" lacks in contrast with the results of GREX. In this case, LELP leans the opposite concept of the target one, "$\neg fly(X)$", because the negative examples are more than the positive ones. To obtain the same results as GREX, LELP has to learn both the concepts. However the criterion to learn both the concepts is not clarified in LELP.

LearnELP is an algorithm very close to LELP and it also can generate hierarchical defaults in the form of ELPs. In [8], the concept defined by the most general default was not mentioned. Instead LearnELP always intends to learn both the target concept and its opposite. In the result, it can generate all possible hierarchical rules. This approach is very simple to obtain the same result as GREX, but it is not always efficient because LearnELP regenerates the subset of hierarchical default rules generated in the other turn. For example, LearnELP generates the rules(12) and (13) twice, both in learning the target concept and in learning the opposite one, although GREX generates them only once as mentioned above.

Another systems to learn hierarchical default rules[1, 2, 5] are not based on a three valued setting. In such a system, we do not have to determine the general concept, because they always begin with generalization of the *target concept*. Therefore we do not discuss the difference between GREX and them here.

5 Conclusions

In this paper, we proposed a method of determining the general concept in a taxonomic hierarchy in the domain in order to learn default rules with ILP. Our method is a novel approach in ILP in the sense that it can change the head of hypothesis dynamically according to its coverage. This flexibility makes our method tolerant to the existence of one or more taxonomic hierarchies in given examples. The user will not have to consider how many hierarchies exist and which of the concepts, the target one or its opposite, is more general in each of them before learning. Consequently our method would greatly contribute to applying the technique of learning defaults to the domain in the real world. In addition, our method can provide the criterion to determine when we should learn the rules called the *non-deterministic defaults*[7, 8]. We will discuss its details on another occasion.

As the future work, we have to extend the generalization, or rule induction method so as to deal with the background knowledge including default rules. The ordinary ILP method such as Inverse Entailment is a theory in monotonic logic. Thus we could not obtain one of the advantages ILP provides, or reuse of learned hypotheses in the succeeding learning, as long as employing such the ordinary method, because it can not use default rules to construct hypotheses. This problem should be solved to establish learning from the incomplete information.

References

1. Bain, M.: Experiments in non-monotonic first-order induction. In: S. Muggleton (ed.): Inductive logic programming. Academic Press, London (1992) 423–436
2. Bergadano, F., Gunetti, D., Nicosia, M., & Ruffo, G.: Learning logic programs with negation as failure. In: De Raedt, L. (ed.): Advances in inductive logic programming. IOS Press, Amsterdam (1996) 107–123
3. De Raedt, L. (ed.): Advances in inductive logic programming. IOS Press, Amsterdam (1996)
4. De Raedt, L., & Bruynooghe, M.: On negation and three-valued logic in interactive concept-learning. Proceedings of the 9th European Conference on Artificial Intelligence. Pitman (1990) 207–212
5. Dimopoulos, Y., & Kakas, A.: Learning non-monotonic logic programs: learning exceptions. Proceedings of the 8th European Conference on Machine Learning, Lecture Notes in Artificial Intelligence, Vol. 912. Springer, Berlin Heidelberg New York (1995) 122–137
6. Gelfond, M., & Lifschitz, V.: Classical negation in logic programs and disjunctive databases. New Generation Computing. **9** (1991) 365–385
7. Inoue, K., & Kudoh, Y.: Learning extended logic programs. Proceedings of Fifteenth International Joint Conference on Artificial Intelligence. Morgan Kaufmann, San Francisco (1997) 176 – 181
8. Lamma, E., Riguzzi, F., & Pereira, L. M.: Strategies in combined learning via logic programs. Machine Learning. **38** (2000) 63–87
9. Lavrač, N., & Džeroski, S.: Inductive logic programming: Techniques and applications. Ellis Horwood (1994)
10. Muggleton, S.: Inverse entailment and progol. New Generation Computing. **13** (1995) 245–286.
11. Ohara, K., Babaguchi, N., & Kitahashi, T.: Non-monotonic inference system handling knowledge allowing classified exceptions. Proceedings of 1998 IEEE International Conference on Systems, Man, and Cybernetics (1998) 1558 – 1563

A Theory of Profit Sharing in Dynamic Environment

Shingo Kato and Hiroshi Matsuo

Department of Electrical & Computer Engineering, Nagoya Institute of Technology,
Gokiso-cho, Showa-ku, Nagoya, 466-8555, Japan
{katosin@mars., matsuo@}elcom.nitech.ac.jp

Abstract. Reinforcement learning is one of the most popular learning method for machine learning. Some reinforcement learning algorithms for adapting to the dynamic environment are proposed. In this paper, the number of episode to suppress the ineffective rule after the change of the environment was examined analytically. Afterwards, the forgettable profit sharing method to suppress the ineffective rule quickly is proposed, and the effectiveness was experimentally confirmed comparing the proposed method with conventional method.

Keywords: reinforcement learning, profit sharing, dynamic environment

1 Introduction

Reinforcement learning[1–3] is one of the most popular learning methods for machine learning. It aims to adapt a system to a given environment according to rewards. The application in a robot system is expected in order to realize the autonomous action in unknown environment and dynamically changing actual environment [4, 5]. The use of the routing in dynamic networks is proposed in [6, 7]. Reinforcement learning in the multi-agent system is recently advanced[8–10]. For example, the research for the speedup of the learning by transmitting the learning result between agents, and imitating other agent is proposed in [11]. At other, the theoretical consideration of reward allocation in profit sharing in the multi-agent reinforcement learning is also proposed in [12].

In the conventional reinforcement learning algorithm, static environment is assumed. However, it is important to consider changes in the environment (dynamics of the environment). Yamamoto proposed the detection algorithm to recognize environment changes using stochastic gradient method [13, 14]. However, learning method after environment changes is important.

In this paper, the number of episodes which needs to suppress the ineffective rule as the environment changes was examined analytically. And, the forgettable profit sharing which quickly suppresses the ineffective rule is proposed.

The paper is organized as follows: In Section 2, the rationality theorem of profit sharing is discussed as a preparation. Number of episodes necessary for suppression of the ineffective rule as the environment changes is also discussed. In Section 3, the proposal technique is discussed. In Section 4, the experimental

2 Profit Sharing in the Environmental Change

2.1 Preparation

Profit Sharing memorizes rule series, which consists of the pair of state x and action a in the episode, and the rule on the series are reinforced in the following equation when the reward was obtained.

$$w(x_i, a_i) \leftarrow w(x_i, a_i) + f(r, i) \qquad (1)$$

where $w(x_i, a_i)$ is the weight of the rule of i on the episode series, r is reward value, and f is the reinforcement function. Afterwards, we describe the learning machine as an agent.

The rule "if x then a" which chooses action a of state x is described as $\overrightarrow{xa}$. Rule series of the interval is called detour, when the rule differs in some episode for the identical state has been chosen. For example, the detour $(\overrightarrow{xb} \cdot \overrightarrow{zb} \cdot \overrightarrow{yb})$ exists(Fig.2) for the episode $(\overrightarrow{yb} \cdot \overrightarrow{xb} \cdot \overrightarrow{zb} \cdot \overrightarrow{yb} \cdot \overrightarrow{xa})$ in the environment of Fig.1. The rule on the detour may not contribute to the acquisition of the reward. The rule in detour always is called ineffective rule in the episode, and the rule except for it is called effective rule. When an ineffective rule competes with an effective rule, it should reinforce clearly the effective rule.

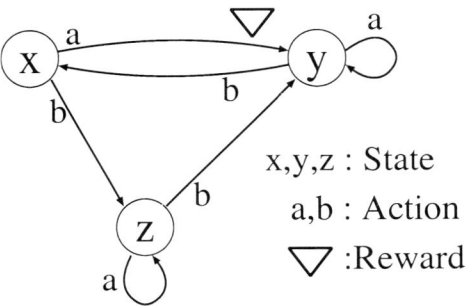

Fig. 1. Environment

The condition described in (2) which effective rule always suppresses the ineffective rule was derived in [15].

$$L \sum_{j=i}^{W} f_j < f_{i-1}, (\forall i = 1, 2, \cdots, W.) \qquad (2)$$

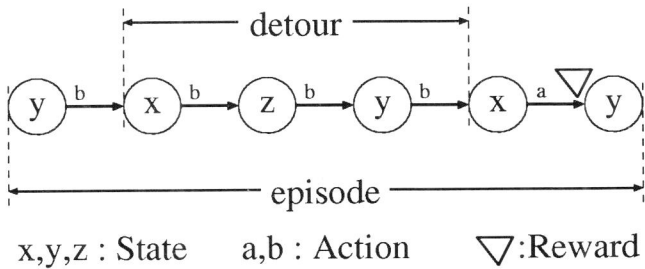

Fig. 2. Example of episode and detour

where W is the largest length of episode, and L is the maximum number of effective rules which exists under an identical state. Equal ratio decrease function shown next, is considered as the simplest reinforcement function which satisfies the equation (2),

$$f_n = \frac{1}{S} f_{n-1}, \ n = 1, 2, \ldots, W - 1.(S \geq L + 1) \quad (3)$$

The ratio of weight of effective rule and weight of the ineffective rule which acquired the maximum reward is shown in (4).

$$P \times f_{i-1} = L \sum_{j=i}^{W} f_j, (P < 1) \quad (4)$$

For example, P is shown by the following equation, when the reinforcement function presented in equation (3) with $W = \infty$.

$$P = \frac{L}{S - 1} \quad (5)$$

2.2 The Environment Changes

The change of the environment is considered. The reward, which gives the effective rule of identical state, is considered to be constant for the simplification.

The most difficult condition in which the ineffective rule is suppressed in the new environment is considered. It is clear that to suppress only recursive and ineffective rule is the most difficult task in the static environment [15]. Recursive rule is the rule in which the state does not change as a result of action. According to the amount of the ineffective rule, the suppression of the ineffective rule becomes hard. Therefore, the most difficult condition is the case in which the only recursive and ineffective rule has got all reward of the effective rule in previous environment.

In such conditions, the reward after X episode learning step becomes $Rw \cdot \frac{X}{L}$, because the effective rule gets the reward in the every L episode. The initial value of the ineffective rule is the value obtained multiplying the number of episodes from previous environment by the reward which the effective rule gets before environment changing. And, the ineffective rule gets the reward obtained multiplying P by the reward which the effective rule gets in the new environment. Therefore, the weight of the ineffective rule is calculated as $G \cdot Rw + P \cdot Rw \cdot \frac{X}{L}$.

The necessary condition for suppression of the ineffective rule is shown by following equation.

$$G \cdot Rw + P \cdot Rw \cdot \frac{X}{L} < Rw \cdot \frac{X}{L} \qquad (6)$$

$$\frac{L}{1-P} \cdot G < X \qquad (7)$$

where G is the number of episodes of previous environment and Rw is the value of the reward in which the effective rule gets.

A lot of episodes X shown in equation (7) is needed to suppress ineffective rule in the most difficult condition. For example, number of episodes which needs to certainly suppression of the ineffective rule is 12th times as much as number of episode in the previous environmental change in $L = 3$ and $P = 0.75$.

3 Forgettable Profit Sharing

The reason why the conventional method could not quickly adapt for environmental changes is that the previous information is kept permanently. For adapting to the new environment, the adapting method which forget the disadvantageously rule in the new environment quickly is suitable. However, to recognize the environmental change and disadvantageous rule in the new environment is difficult. The forgettable profit sharing in which the weight of rule gradually decreases is proposed.

3.1 Profit Sharing with Queue

Adding queue with an agent was considered in order to eliminate gradually previous information. The agent puts the reward got in each episode in the queue(Fig.4).

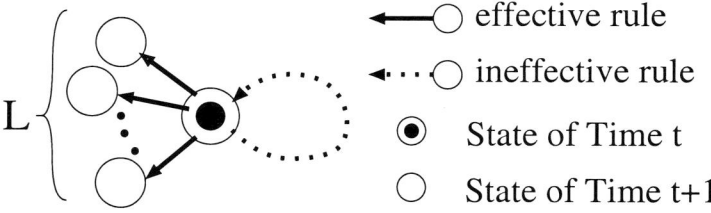

Fig. 3. Example of state with only recursive and ineffective rule.

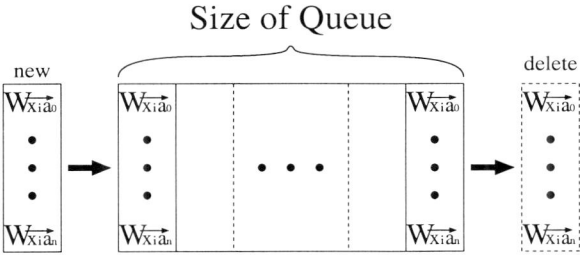

Fig. 4. Queue

Let's assume that the number of the episode from previous environment is larger than the length of the queue. The weight of the effective rule is $Rw \cdot \frac{X}{L}$, which is equal to the conventional method. The initial value of the ineffective rule is $(Q_{size} - X) \cdot Rw$, because to store the reward over the size of the queue is not possible. Therefore, the necessary condition for suppression of the ineffective rule is shown by following equation.

$$(Q_{size} - X) \cdot Rw + P \cdot Rw \cdot \frac{X}{L} < Rw \cdot \frac{X}{L} \tag{8}$$

$$\frac{Q_{size} \cdot L}{1 + L - P} < X \tag{9}$$

where Q_{size} is the size of queue.

3.2 Profit Sharing with Weighted Virtual Queue

The propose method in 3.1 adding queue with agent is surely effective. But to apply this method, a lot of queue(memory) is needed. Therefore it is impracticable to use generally. The new method named "weighted virtual queue" is proposed. This method decreases previous reward virtually. Therefore, "weighted virtual queue" is expressed in the following equation.

$$w(x,a) \leftarrow w(x,a) \times \tau + \sum_{k=0}^{W} g(x,a,k) \tag{10}$$

$$g(x,a,k) = \begin{cases} f(r,k) & (\text{if } x = x_k \text{ and } a = a_k) \\ 0 & (\text{else}) \end{cases} \tag{11}$$

where τ is the forgetting rate.

The number of episodes in previous environment G is set to infinity, because the suppression of the ineffective rule becomes difficult, as the initial value of the ineffective rule is larger. The weight of the effective rule is $\frac{1}{L}\sum_{i=1}^{X} Rw \cdot \tau^{i-1}$ which can be derived from equation (10). And, the initial value of the ineffective rule is $\sum_{i=X+1}^{\infty} Rw \cdot \tau^{i-1}$. Hence, the necessary condition for suppression of the ineffective rule is shown by following equation.

$$\sum_{i=X+1}^{\infty} Rw \cdot \tau^{i-1} + \frac{P}{L}\sum_{i=1}^{X} Rw \cdot \tau^{i-1} < \frac{1}{L}\sum_{i=1}^{X} Rw \cdot \tau^{i-1} \quad (12)$$

$$\frac{Rw \cdot \tau^X}{1-\tau} < \frac{Rw(1-P)(1-\tau^X)}{L(1-\tau)} \quad (13)$$

$$\tau^X < \frac{1-P}{1+L-P} \quad (14)$$

4 Experiment

4.1 The Experimental Method

The grid world in which the discrimination of effective rule and ineffective rule is easy is used for the experiment. Fig.5 shows a grid world in which each cell the agent has four actions(N,S,E,W) and transitions are made deterministically to an adjacent cell, unless there is a block, in which case no movement occurs. The agent gets the reward when it arrives at the goal from the start.

We take w, the initial weight, to be 0.1, and Rw, the reward, to be 1, and S, a parameter of reinforcement function in equation (3), to be 5. In the proposed method described in 3.1, the Q_{size} set at 5.0×10^5. Every 1.0×10^3 episodes were assigned to the same element of the queue. As a result each queue has 500 elements.

In the proposed method which use weighted virtual queue, we set τ to 0.999996.

S : Start Point
G_i : Goal Point
■ : Block

Fig. 5. Grid World for experiment.

As a result of the preliminary experiment, it is desirable that the environment was changed after 5.0×10^7 episodes, because 3.0×10^7 episodes are necessary for the convergence using conventional method. But due to the limitation of the accuracy of the floating point calculation, the environment changes after 5.0×10^5 episodes. The goal is located at G_1 in Fig.5, in the case of the environment was not changed. The artificiality environment changes are generated to move the goal from G_1 to G_2.

The experiment performed 10 times as changing seeds of random value, and the obtained mean value is used as final result.

4.2 Experimental Result and Consideration

No Artificial Environment Change. The learning curve (the relationship between number of episodes and number of steps in which agent get reward) is shown in Fig.6. Converged numerical value of proposed method "weighted virtual queue" becomes worse compare with other methods. This is because the value of τ was set by adjusting as the environment is changed at 5.0×10^5 episodes. However, the same converged numerical value can be taken by substituting an appropriate value to τ (for example, $\tau = 0.99999993$).

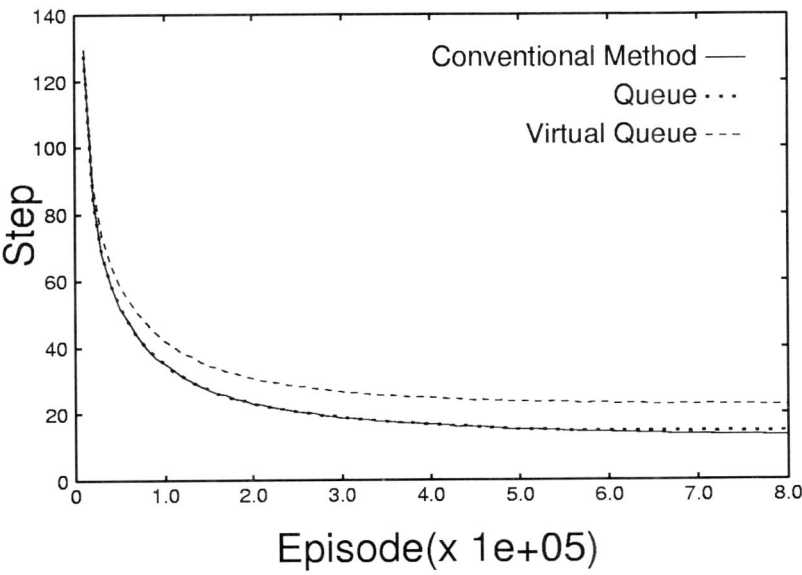

Fig. 6. Learning curve on static environment.

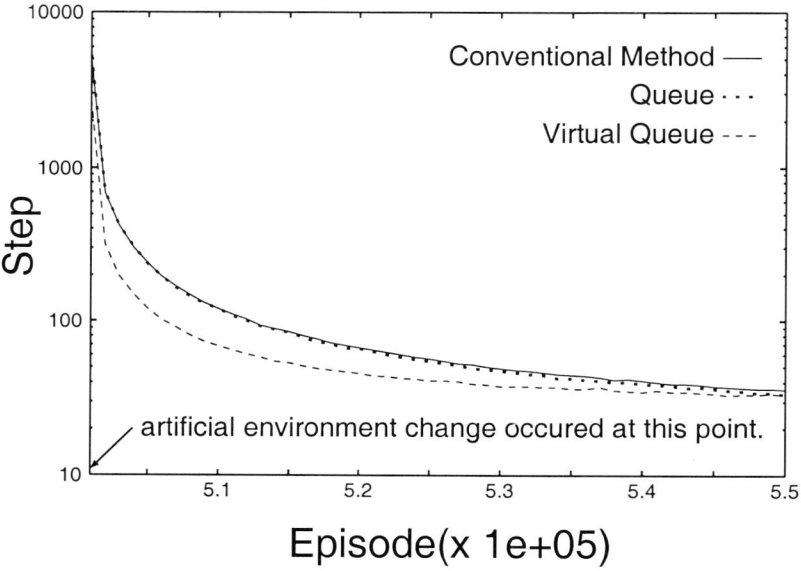

Fig. 7. Learning curve after artificial environment changes.

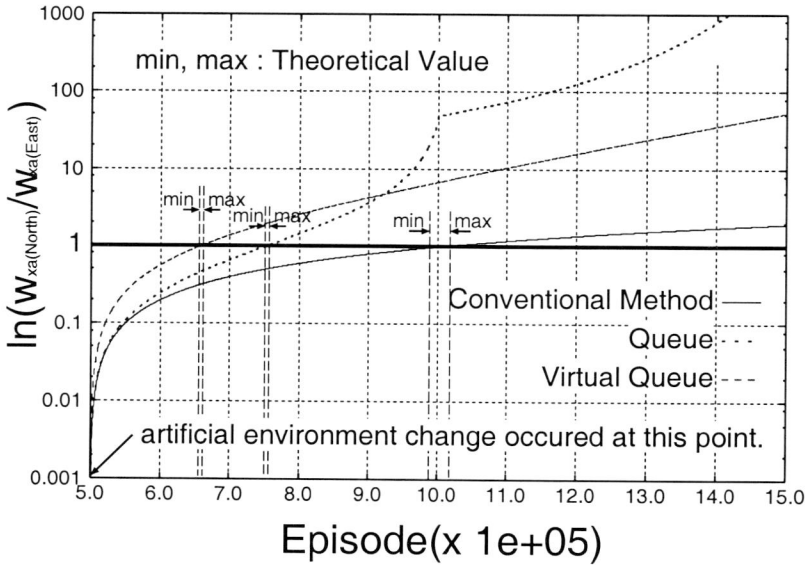

Fig. 8. Rate between weight of effective rule and weight of ineffective rule.

Add Artificial Environment Change. The learning curve after artificial environmental change is shown in Fig.7. Fig.8 shows the transition of the weight in the position Z on Fig.5. The horizontal axis shows number of episodes (artificial environment change occurred at 5.0×10^5). The vertical axis shows the rate between weight of rule which moves to North and weight of rule which moves to East. When the rate exceed 1.0, the ineffective rule is suppressed. Fig.8 shows also the theoretical number of episodes necessary to suppress the ineffective rule.

Table.1 shows experimental and theoretical maximum and minimum[1] results which suppress the ineffective rule. This theoretical value of proposal methods in Table.1 is very small, because τ and Q_{size} were decided on the assumption of the most difficult condition. It is appropriate to set these value τ and Q_{size} at most difficult condition, because the knowledge of the largest number of the effective rule can not be informed in advance.

Table 1. Number of episodes in which the ineffective rule is suppressed.

Learning method	Experimental value	Theoretical maximum value(L=1)	Theoretical minimum value(L=1)
Conventional Method	5.12×10^5	5.21×10^5	4.80×10^5
Queue	2.54×10^5	2.55×10^5	2.45×10^5
Virtual Queue	1.60×10^5	1.61×10^5	1.51×10^5

5 Conclusions

In this paper, the analytical consideration of the number of the necessary episode which suppresses the ineffective rule using profit sharing as the environment changes was performed, and the relation between number of episode before the environment changes and number of episode necessary for suppressing the ineffective rule was carried out. Forgettable profit sharing which suppress the ineffective rule after the environment change within the constant episodes was proposed, and the effectiveness of the proposed algorithm was confirmed by the experiment.

The proposed method needs the knowledge of the convergence, but generally this knowledge can not be informed in advance. Future research will address the development of this algorithm to apply it in various practical cases.

References

1. Leslie Pack Kealbling, Michael L. Littman, and Andrew W. Moore: Reinforcement Learning: A Survey, Journal of Artificial Intelligence Research 4, pp237-285(1996)
2. Miyazaki, K., and Kobayashi, S.: Reinforcement Learning Systems for Discrete Markov Decision Processes, JJSAI,Vol.12,No.6,pp811-821(1997)

---
[1] the derivation procedure is eliminated because of page limitations

3. Miyazaki, K., Yamamura, M., and Kobayashi, S.: MarcoPolo : A Reinforcement Learning System Considering Tradeoff Exploitation and Exploration under Markovian Environments, JSSAI, Vol.12, No.1, pp78-88(1997)
4. Yamaguchi, T., Masubuchi, M., Fujihara, K., and Yachida, M.: Accelerating Reinforcement Learning for a Real Robot with Automated Abstract Sub-Rewards Generation, JSSAI, Vol.12, No.5, pp712-723(1997)
5. Minoru A.: Research Issues on Real Robot Reinforcement Learning, JSSAI, Vol.12, No.6, pp.831-836(1997)
6. Devika Subramanian, Peter Druschel, and Johnny Chen: Ants and reinforcement learning: A case study in routing in dynamic networks, In Proceedings of IJCAI-97, 1997.
7. Justin A. Boyan and Michael L. Littman. Packet routing in dynamically changing networks: A reinforcement learning approach. In Jack D. Cowan, Gerald Tesauro, and Joshua Alspector, editors, Advances in Neural Information Processing Systems, volume 6, pages 671–678. Morgan Kaufmann, San Francisco CA, 1993
8. Arai, S., Miyazaki, K., and Kobayashi, S.: Methodology in Multi-Agent Reinforcement Learning –Approaches by Q-learning and Profit Sharing–, JJSAI, Vol.13, No.4, pp609-617(1998)
9. Unemi, T.: Collective Behavior of Reinforcement Learning Agents, MACC, pp137-150(1993)
10. Yamamura, M., Miyazaki, K., and Kobayashi, S.: A Survey on Learning for Agents, JSSAI, Vol.10, No.5, pp683-689(1995)
11. Yamaguchi, T., Miura, M., and Yachida, M.: Multi-Agent Reinforcement Learning with Adaptive Mimetism, JSSAI, Vol.12, No.2, pp323-330(1997)
12. Miyazaki, K., Arai, S., and Kobayashi, S.: A Theory of Profit Sharing in Multi-Agent Reinforcement Learning, JSSAI, Vol.14, No.6, pp1156-1164(1999)
13. Kimura, H., Yamamura, M., and Kobayashi, S.: Reinforcement Learning in Partially Observable Markov Decision Processes: A Stochastic Gradient Method, JSSAI, Vol.11, No.5, pp761-768(1996)
14. Yamamoto, S., Yamaguchi, F., Saito, H., and Nakanishi, M.: A recognition method of environmental change on reinforcement learning, TECHNICAL REPORT OF Institute of Electronics Information and Communication Engineers, AI99-81, pp31-36(2000-01)
15. Miyazaki, K., Yamamura, M., and Kobayashi, S.: A Theory of Profit Sharing in Reinforcement Learning,JJSAI, Vol.9, No.4, pp.580-587(1994)

Experience-Based Reinforcement Learning to Acquire Effective Behavior in a Multi-agent Domain

Sachiyo Arai[1], Katia Sycara[1], and Terry R. Payne[1]

The Robotics Institute, Carnegie Mellon University
5000 Forbes Avenue, Pittsburgh, PA 15213 USA
Phone +1 (412) 268 7019
{sachiyo, katia, terryp}@cs.cmu.edu

Abstract. In this paper, we discuss *Profit-sharing*, an experience-based reinforcement learning approach (which is similar to a Monte-Carlo based reinforcement learning method) that can be used to learn robust and effective actions within uncertain, dynamic, multi-agent systems. We introduce the *cut-loop* routine that discards looping behavior, and demonstrate its effectiveness empirically within a simplified *NEO (non-combatant evacuation operation)* domain. This domain consists of several agents which ferry groups of evacuees to one of several shelters. We demonstrate that the *cut-loop* routine makes the Profit-sharing approach adaptive and robust within a dynamic and uncertain domain, without the need for pre-defined knowledge or subgoals. We also compare it empirically with the popular Q-learning approach.

1 Introduction

Many existing approaches that reason about agent interaction have used a symbolic representation within multi-agent planning domains [5], and within the context of dynamic domains [4]. These approaches normally adopt a top-down strategy, and hence require an explicit model of the environment and a definition of the communication protocol used for multi-agent cooperation. Although the corresponding agents work successfully in complex, dynamic domains, it can be difficult to design whole parts of the agent's knowledge. As the number of agents within these multi-agent communities rises, it is becoming increasingly difficult to design static knowledge.

For dynamic domains (such as the one presented in this paper), it is not unreasonable to design agents that use local *condition-action rules* to react to each world state [4], as it can be very difficult to model the whole domain. The problem therefore becomes that of determining how these rules should be designed for dynamic environments. In recent years, bottom-up approaches such as reinforcement learning have become increasingly popular for determining these condition-action, or state-action rules, without having a priori models of the environment. However, there are still several important issues that arise when applying these bottom-up approaches to multi-agent domains.

In this paper, we present an approach known as *Profit-sharing* that allows agents to learn effective behaviors from their experiences within dynamic environments, where the agents are competitive and may have to face resource conflicts. A dynamic domain based on a *NEO (non-combatant evacuation operation)* is described, which presents the agents with limited resources and introduces uncertainty. Thus it can be very difficult to plan the different agent's activities, such as path planning and resolving resource conflicts. We demonstrate empirically that our Profit-sharing approach is effective within this domain and clarify some of the requirements that face multi-agent reinforcement learning problems.

In Section 2, we describe a simplified NEO domain from the perspective of a reinforcement learning approach, and present our agent model. Section 3 introduces the principles of Profit-sharing, the *Rationality Theorem*, which makes Profit-sharing powerful, and its advantage over other learning algorithms which are usually found within multi-agent domains. An empirical comparison of the performance of multiple agents using two learning approaches: Profit-sharing and Q-learning, is presented via several experiments in Section 4. Finally, we discuss the applicability and effectiveness of the Profit-sharing based method for real-world dynamic domains, and summarize our future work.

2 Problem Domain

Non-combatant evacuation operations, or *NEOs*, have been used to test a variety of coordination strategies. Though real-world NEOs have many constraint and resource conflicts, the domain used in this study models multiple transportation vehicles which transfer groups of evacuees to safe shelters. Each transport is operated asynchronously by an autonomous agent, which makes its own decision based on locally available information.

This NEO domain is an example of one that exhibits the following characteristics. First, there are several agents which are all "self-interested"; i.e. they pursue their own goals competitively rather than cooperatively. Second, the agents must resolve conflicts due to shared resources. Third, the agents should behave rationally, even though the domain is uncertain. By "rational", we mean that each agent should reach one of the safe shelters in a finite time period. Fourth, the domain is both uncertain and dynamic. Fifth, the agent should learn "on-line", i.e. it should learn while executing some action. Because of these characteristics, it is very difficult to design rules through mathematical analysis, as the information required by each agent is not only distributed but also changes over time.

2.1 The NEO Domain

The NEO domain consists of a grid world with multiple transporter agents, each of which carries a group of evacuees. The goal of a transporter agent is to ferry its group to one of the shelters as quickly as possible. However, there may be conflicts, as transporters cannot co-exist in the same location at the same time

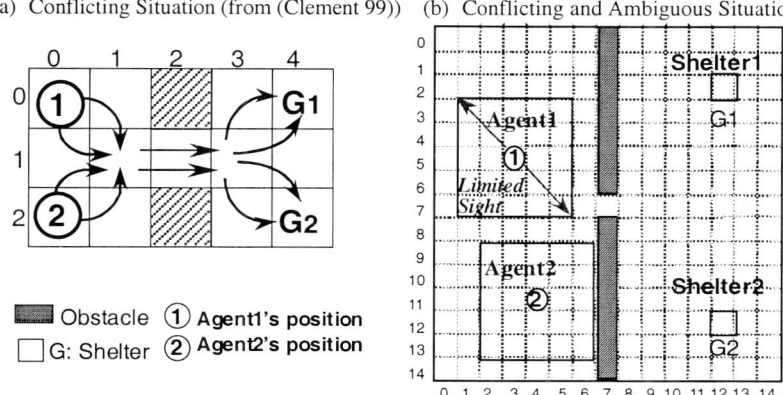

Fig. 1. Two Agents move within the grid world. Fig.(a) has been reproduced from [2]

(Figure 1a). In addition, the location of the shelters changes over the time. In dynamic domains such as this, agents should exhibit reactive behaviors rather than deliberative ones. We claim that the only effective approach is to learn reactive behaviors through trial and error experiences, since it is very difficult to know in advance what effective action should be taken at each possible state of the environment.

2.2 Modelling

Each transporter agent is modeled as a reinforcement learning entity in an unknown environment, where there is no communication with the other agents, and there are no intermediate subgoals for which intermediate rewards can be given. Thus, no reward is generated until the agent reaches its target shelter. It should be noted that there are other agents within the environment that are also learning independently of each other, without sharing sensory inputs or policies. As a result, the other agents appear as additional components within the environment, whose behavior is dynamic and unpredictable.

Each agent consists of five modules (Figure 2); a *State Recognizer*, a *LookUp Table*, an *Action Selector*, an *Episodic Memory* and the *Learner*, which includes the Profit-sharing algorithm. Initially, the agent observes O_t, the partially available state of its environment at time t. An action is then selected (using a *Roulette Selection* method) from the action set A_t, which contains all the available actions at time t. After the action is selected, the agent determines if a reward has been generated. If there is no reward after action a_t, the agent stores the state-action pair, (O_t, a_t), in its *Episodic Memory*, and repeats this cycle until a reward is generated. The terms "state-action pair" and "rule" are used interchangably in this paper. The process of moving from a start state to the

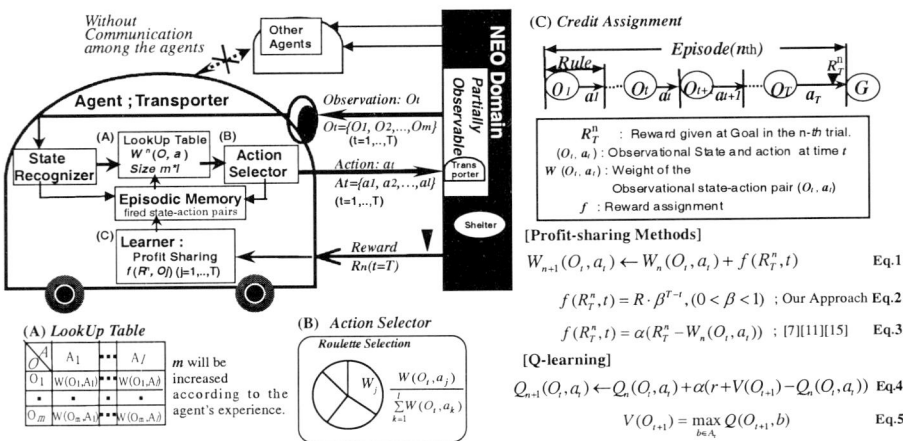

Fig. 2. Model of a Profit-sharing Agent and Credit Assignment Functions

final reward state is known as an *episode*. Once the agent receives the reward R, it reinforces the rules stored in its episodic memory by modifying the lookup table using the credit assignment function $f(R,t) = R \cdot \beta^{T-t}$ (Figure 2, Eq.2), in which $\beta(0 < \beta < 1)$ is a *discount rate*, to acquire an effective policy.

2.3 Requirements of Multi-agent Reinforcement Learning

There are three problems which have previously been encountered when reinforcement learning approaches are applied to domains with the same characteristic as our NEO domain. The first is due to the "agent's sensory limitation", in which the agent is fooled into perceiving two or more different states as the same state. This is known as *perceptual aliasing* [17]. If all these different states require the same action, then perceptual aliasing is desirable, as it results in a generalization of the state space. However, if each state requires a different action, then this can lead to the agent becoming "confused", and hence performing the wrong action. The second problem is due to *concurrent learning* [12,1], in which the dynamics of the environment vary unpredictably as, due to learning, each agent modifies its own policies and behaviors asynchronously. Thus, midway though the learning process, an agent cannot estimate the model of state transitional probabilities for its environment. These two problems can result in non-Markovian properties within state transitions. The third problem is that the approach should minimize the amount of memory required to make an agent behave effectively.

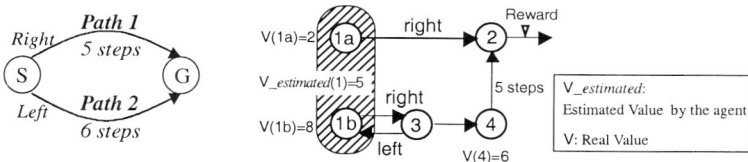

Fig. 3. Examples: (a) explains the effectiveness of β and (b) illustrates confusion in the perceptual aliasing area

3 Approach

3.1 Profit-Sharing with Cut-Loop Routine

Our multi-agent reinforcement learning approach is based on *Profit-sharing*, a type of reinforcement learning originally proposed by [6]. The original version used Profit-sharing as a credit assignment method based on trial-and-error experiences, without utilizing any form of value estimation. However, this approach does not take the infinite loops in the agent's episode into consideration. These loops may result in the agent exhibiting irrational behavior with respect to achieving its goal. Although in general, the acquired policy need not be optimal for multi-agent situations, it is important that this policy is rational. A rational policy is one that is guaranteed to converge on a solution; i.e. the agent should not become trapped within infinite loops in the state machine. To guarantee convergence to a rational policy in a non-Markovian domain, we introduce the *cut-loop* routine and credit assignment function, with the *discount rate* $(0 < \beta < 1)$, and describe how these augment the Profit-sharing method.

Though the *Rationality Theorem*[11] can be used to design a credit assignment function that excludes the loops without our *cut-loop* routine, applying this theorem becomes problematic when the length of the episode is long. In addition, though the *Rationality Theorem* guarantees that the ineffective rules, which make up the loop, are always given smaller rewards than the effective rules, these smaller rewards decrease the efficiency of the convergence. On the other hand, our *cut-loop* routine prohibits the agent from reinforcing the weight of the rules which make up the loop, and can shorten the length of the episode.

The function that assigns a reward among rules in the episode is called a *credit assignment function*, $f(R_t, t)$ (Figure 2, Eq.1) which denotes a reinforcement value for the rule which is fired at time t. In our Profit-sharing algorithm, the weight of each rule is reinforced according to its distance from the goal. For example, at time t, an agent enters state o_t and selects action a_t, and continues this cycle until it receives a reward R at time T. At this point, the episode consists of the rules $((o_t, a_t), (o_{t+1}, a_{t+1}), \cdots\cdots, (o_T, a_T))$, as shown in Figure 2. Each rule is then assigned some credit, according to the function $f = R \cdot \beta^{T-t} (0 < \beta < 1)$. Thus, the last rule, (o_T, a_T) is assigned credit R; the penultimate state,

(o_{T-1}, a_{T-1}), is assigned credit $R \cdot \beta$, and so on. The weight of each rule within the episode is modified by Eq.1 in Figure 2. There are two important points to note here: the weight of o_{t+1} is not required when modifying the weight of o_t; and the discount rate β assigns a greater individual reward to the most effective action than to other alternative actions. For example, consider the state diagram illustrated in Figure 3(a). If the agent's 1st(*Path 1*) and 2nd(*Path 2*) episodes required 5 and 6 steps (respectively) to achieve the goal, the weight of action *Right* at the initial state S gets a larger credit, $R \cdot \beta^5 (0 < \beta < 1)$, than the action *Left*(which gets $R \cdot \beta^6$). Therefore, the agent could choose the effective action which selects the shortest path within its experience.

The Profit-sharing algorithm is different from other methods, such as Q-learning [16] and Temporal Difference Learning [15], which make the assumption that an environment can be modeled by a Markov Decision Process(MDP). Under the Markovian assumption, the agent can perceive a set S of distinct states of its environment, and has a set A of actions that it can perform. At each discrete time step t, the agent senses the current state o_t, chooses a current action a_t, and performs it. The environment responds by giving the agent a reward $r_t = r(o_t, a_t)$ and by producing the succeeding state $o_{t+1} = \delta(o_t, a_t)$. These functions δ and r are part of the environment and are not necessarily known by the agent. Domains that obey the Markovian assumption are called MDP as the functions $\delta(o_t, a_t)$ and $r(o_t, a_t)$ depend only on the current state and action.

An agent that learns using Q-learning modifies the value of the current rule, $Q(o_t, a_t)$, using a value of sequential state $V(o_{t+1})$ to estimate the current value $V(o_t)$, as shown in Figure 2, Eq.4. At each time step, the agent updates $Q(o_t, a_t)$ by recursively discounting future utilities and weighting them by a positive learning rate α. Thus, $Q_n(o_t, a_t)$ corresponds to the nth modification of Q's components, o_t and a_t. The parameter $\gamma(0 < \gamma < 1)$ is a discount parameter, and $V(o_{t+1})$ is the value of the consecutive state (as given in Figure 2 Eq.5). Therefore, if o_{t+1} is an aliasing state, the agent fails to estimate not only the value of the current rule o_t, but also the values of the following states o_{t+1} and corresponding actions. This failed estimation will then be propagated through the learning process. To illustrate this, consider the example in Figure 3(b). The state value, V, represents the minimum number of steps to a reward. In this example, the highest value of V is 1. The values of states 1a and 1b, V(1a), and V(1b) are 2 and 8, respectively. Although these two states are different, they are perceived by the agent as being the same state (i.e. state 1). If the agent moves to state 1a and 1b with equal weight, $V(1) = \frac{2+8}{2} = 5$. Therefore the value of state 1 is equal to the value of state 3, i.e. $V(3) = 5$. If the agent uses these state values, it will move *left* into state 3. Otherwise, the agent moves *right* into state 1. This means that the agent learns the irrational policy where it only transits between states 1b and 3.

3.2 Cut-Loop Routine in Profit-Sharing

Consider the state diagram illustrated in Figure 3(b). At time t, an agent starts in state 3. If it moves left, it enters state 1. It can then return to state 3 by moving right. Thus, the agent could cycle between these two states indefinitely, before moving onto another state (e.g. state 4) which will lead to the goal (state 2). If the agent's episode consists of the rules: $(3, Left)$, $(1, Right)$, $(3, Left)$, $(1, Right)$, ..., $(3, Right)$, $(4, Up)$, $(2, Right)$, $(Goal)$, and function f(such as the constant or simple geometrical decreasing function) does not satisfy the *Rationality Theorem*[11], then the weight of $(3, left)$ will be larger than that of $(3, right)$, as the agent will have visited $(3, left)$ several times. If the *Rationality Theorem*[11] is used to design a credit assignment function that excludes these loops, then it will fail when the length of the episode is very long.

Our solution to this problem is very simple. If the current state is the re-visited one, the agent "cuts off" the rules which make up the cyclic loop from the current *Episodic Memory*. This routine does not require any knowledge other than that used by the current framework of the Profit-sharing algorithm, because this algorithm uses an *Episodic Memory* to accumulate rules until the goal is achieved. Therefore, the agent is able to tell whether the current state is the first-visited one or the re-visited one. In the case of the above example, the original sequence of the rules becomes $(3, Right)$, $(4, Up)$, $(2, Right)$, $(Goal)$ after the *cut-loop* routine is applied. Profit-sharing uses trial and error experiences, and reinforces effective rules instead of estimating values for the different state. Therefore, it uses this policy to escape states susceptible to perceptual aliasing. This property also makes the agent robust within uncertain domains, and reduces memory requirement as it only stores rules which are essential for navigating the state space. Since the NEO domain cannot be assumed to be an MDP, and since it has a very large state space which results in very long episodes before the goal is reached, an approach that combines Profit-sharing with the *cut-loop* routine is more suitable than other reinforcement learning method(such as Q-learning).

3.3 Related Work

The perceptual aliasing problem has been addressed by a number of studies, and to date, two solutions have been proposed. The first is *memory-based* [3, 9], which maintains a history of rules for each episode. The second adopts a *stochastic policy* [8] where the agent selects a random action to escape from partially observable states. The first solution requires additional memory to store the tuple history. The approach adopted by our Profit-sharing algorithm is based on the later solution, which includes TD(1) and the Monte-Carlo methods [13] in that they do not use the values of consecutive states. Our approach differs from TD(1) and Monte-Carlo in that our method does not use the values of state (or state-action pairs) which require very large memory space to keep eligibility traces to manage the delayed reward. In the tabular version of TD(1) and Sarsa(1) algorithms, the required memory space is twice as large as that which is required by our Profit-sharing method.

A number of studies have recently explored the concurrent learning problem. Sub-goals were used by [10, 14] to find effective rules using Eq.3 (Figure 2), but there is no theoretical background for this approach. This problem has also been discussed theoretically for the Q-learning approach [7].

Comparison: PS(*with-Cut-loop*) v.s. **PS**(*with-Rationality Theorem*) v.s. **QL**

Algorithm	Environment Size	Average and Standard Deviation of 10 Trials				Av.(S.D.)
		After 1,000 Episodes	After 5,000 Episodes	After 10,000 Episodes	After 50,000 Episodes	After 100,000 Episodes
PS1 Cut-Loop	7 x 7	43.4(4.9)	25.1(4.1)	20.2(3.4)	16.4(1.8)	13.8(2.0)
	15 x 15	239.3(234.8)	76.7(19.9)	70.6(21.9)	56.2(18.5)	45.5(5.7)
PS2 with Rational f	7 x 7	119.6(33.1)	50.8(15.5)	36.9(11.7)	21.6(4.7)	16.6(2.6)
	15 x 15	642.9(297.6)	367.6(399.2)	192.4(194.8)	72.3(40.5)	69.6(40.8)
Q learning	7 x 7	347.7(102.1)	289.7(94.9)	297.0(90.4)	255.7(80.8)	190.6(50.7)
	15 x 15	2135.1(665.9)	1898.4(482.8)	1716.9(453.1)	1582.5(342.9)	1260.0(306.1)

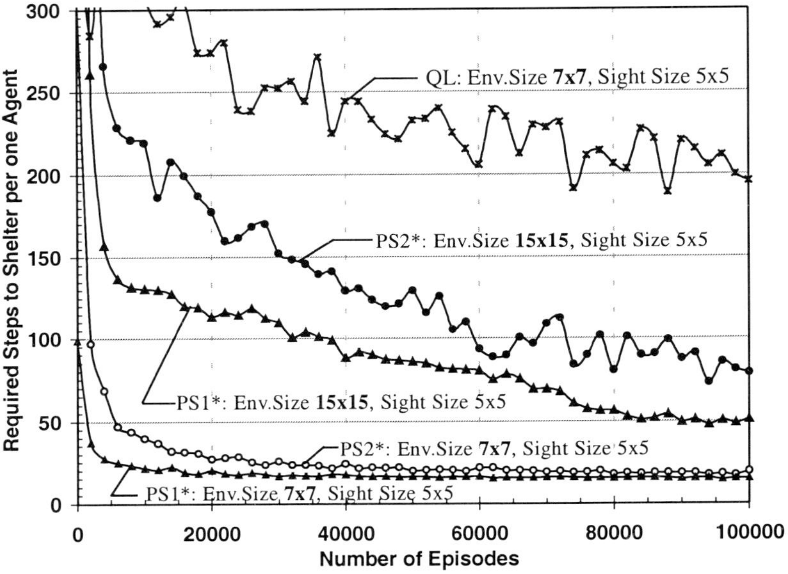

PS1* : Using Cut-loop routine and f=(0.8)$^{T-t}$
PS2* : Using Rationality Theorem and f=(0.3)$^{T-t}$, without cut-loop routine.

Fig. 4. Performance in the Dynamic and Uncertain Domain

4 Experimental Results

To demonstrate the effectiveness of our Profit-sharing approach (presented in the previous Section), we compared its performance with that of Q-learning[16] on the two NEO grid worlds, as shown in Figure 1. The comparison with Q-learning is a reasonable comparison in that the memory requirements and time complexity of both algorithms are the same. (Note: Sarsa(λ) and Q(λ) need larger memory space, as mentioned in the previous Section.)

In the case of both Figure 1(a) and (b), two agents started from different locations, and their task was to learn policies for finding one of two shelters as quickly as possible. There are five actions within the action set, $A_t = \{Stay, Up, Right, Down, Left\}$. However, both agents cannot occupy the same position at the same time, nor may they pass through obstacles. In the first world (Figure 1(a); this world also appeared in [2]), the number of locations is small (5×3 locations), and the agents can see the whole environment. However, the second grid world is larger (15×15 locations), and in this case the perceptual distance of each agent is only a 5×5 region, as shown in Figure 1(b); i.e. each agent can only see a shelter or the other agent when they are no more than two moves away.

In each episode, the order in which the two agents move is determined randomly. Agents always start in the same location (i.e. $(0,0)$ & $(0,2)$ in the smaller grid world, and $(0,0)$ & $(0,14)$ in the larger one). The location of the shelters varies within the right half of the grid world in each episode. Although the first experiment may appear easier to learn, the agent will require different actions for when it occupies the left or the right half of the world. Therefore, the problem of perceptual aliasing may be greater with this than with the second experiment. When one agent reaches its target shelter, its episode terminates, and the agent remains in the shelter until the second agent reaches its goal. The evaluation metric is determined by averaging the number of states required by both agents to reach the shelters. Experiments consist of 10 trials, each of which consists of 100,000 episodes. The lookup table is reset for each trial. The learning parameters were selected as follows:

Profit-sharing: In Profit-sharing(Miya) and Profit-sharing(Ours), a geometrically decreasing function (*common ratio* = 0.3) and (*common ratio* = 0.9) was used to assign a credit to each rule, respectively. The former one satisfies the *Rationality Theorem* described above. Although the latter one does not satisfies this theorem, loops may still be removed by the *cut-loop* routine because the common ratio succeeds as the discount rate β achieves effective rules. Conflicting actions are resolved using a weighted roulette selection.

Q-learning: We used the parameters *learning rate* = 0.05 and *discounting factor* = 0.9, as these were found to be the best parameters in our experiments. When the agent reaches the goal state (i.e. the shelter), it receives a reward of 1.0. The Q-learning agent uses the Boltzmann distribution $p(a_i|s) = \frac{e^{Q(s,a_i)/T}}{\sum_{k \in actions} e^{Q(s,a_i)/T}}$ ($T = 0.2$) to select its action.

Environment 5×3 (*without Perceptual Aliasing*)

These experiments demonstrate the effectiveness of Profit-sharing for resolving conflicts under the concurrent learning context. The average steps-per-episode for Profit-sharing with the *cut-loop* routine, (Ours), Profit-sharing with the *Rationality Theorem*, (Miya), and Q-learning are 6.78, 6.80 and 8.98, respectively after 100,000 episodes. Initially, the difference is large, as Q-learning takes a long time to propagate the reinforcement throughout all of the rules. In contrast, Profit-sharing reinforces the successful rules immediately after one episode. Specifically, Profit-sharing(Ours) with the *cut-loop* routine converges to the optimal policy with a smaller number of episodes(i.e. experience) than Profit-sharing with the credit assignment function which satisfies the *Rationality Theorem*. For example, the average steps per episode after 1,000 episodes for Profit-sharing(Ours) and Profit-sharing(Miya) are 14.21 and 26.70, respectively. There are some differences between the Profit-sharing methods and Q-learning towards the final stage of the experiments. This is because this environment changes in every episode and due to the concurrent learning of the agents when seeking higher rewards, and hence it is more difficult to estimate the value of the rule. Because Profit-sharing exploits successful actions in each state, its emerged plan is very closed to the optimal one. These differences are due to the concurrent learning of the agents when seeking higher rewards.

Environment $15 \times 15, 7 \times 7$ (*with Perceptual Aliasing*)

In these experiments, two grid worlds were used; the 15×15 world illustrated in Figure 1(b), and a similar but smaller 7×7 world. The results illustrated in Figure 4 indicate that Q-learning fails to converge for either world (only the results for the 7×7 world are shown) even after 100,000 episodes. This is not surprising, as Q-learning learns deterministic policies for MDPs, and hence is unsuited for dynamic domains. In addition, due to the perceptual limitation of the agent, the environment seems to be the non-MDPs from the agent point of view. However, Profit-sharing, which collects stochastic data and reinforces only useful rules using the *cut-loop* routine or *Rationality Theorem* could acquire an effective policy. Also in these experiments, Profit-sharing(Ours) converges to the optimal policy with smaller experience than Profit-sharing with the credit assignment function which satisfies the *Rationality Theorem*. Because the *cut-loop* routine prohibits the agent from reinforcing the weight of the rule which makes up the loop, the agent's stochastic policy becomes accurate even in the earlier stages of learning.

5 Conclusion and Future Work

In this paper, we introduce the *cut-loop* routine, and present a variant of the Profit-sharing algorithm that guarantees convergence, and demonstrate its effectiveness within a multi-agent domain characterized by conflicting situation and uncertainty. Profit-sharing solves the problems of perceptual aliasing and concurrent learning whilst minimizing memory requirements. In addition, the *cut-loop* routine makes Profit-sharing more amenable for multi-agent domains that require a stochastic policy and in which episodes become long.

While Profit-sharing is appropriate for an episodic task where the reward is only given at the end of the goal, it is less suited for domains that include intermediate rewards. We plan to combine Profit-sharing with other bottom-up approaches, such as genetic algorithms, and with top-down approaches for real world applications.

References

1. Arai,S.,Miyazaki,K., Kobayashi,S.: Generating Cooperative Behavior by Multi-Agent Reinforcement Learning, *Proceedings of 6th European Workshop on Learning Robots* p111-120 (1997).
2. Clement, J.Bradley and Durfee, H.Edmund: Top-Down Search for Coordinating the Hierarchical Plans of Multiple Agents. *Proceedings of the 3rd International Conference on Autonomous Agents,* pp252-259 (1999).
3. Chrisman, L.: Reinforcement learning with perceptual aliasing: The Perceptual Distinctions Approach, *Proceedings of the 10th National Conference on Artificial Intelligence*, pp.183-188 (1992).
4. Firby, R.J., An Investigation into Reactive Planning in complex Domains, *Proceedings of 10th National Conference on Artificial Intelligence '87*, 202-206 (1987).
5. Georgeff, M.P.: Communication and interaction in Multi-agent Planning, *Proceedings of the 3rd National Conference on Artificial Intelligence*, pp.125-129 (1983).
6. Grefenstette, J. J.: Credit Assignment in Rule Discovery Systems Based on Genetic Algorithms, *Machine Learning Vol.3*, pp.225-245(1988).
7. Hu, Junling and Wellman, Michael P.: Multiagent Reinforcement Learning: Theoretical Framework and an Algorithm, *Proceedings of the 15th International Conference on Machine Learning*, pp.242-250(1998).
8. Jaakkola, T., Singh,S.P. and Jordan, M.I.: Reinforcement Learning Algorithm for Partially Observable Markov decision Problems, *Advances in Neural Information Processing Systems 7* (NIPS-94), pp.345-352 (1994).
9. MacCallum, R. A.: Instance-Based Utile Distinctions for Reinforcement Learning with Hidden State, *Proceedings of 12th International Conference on Machine Learning*, pp387-395(1993).
10. Mataric, J.M.: Reinforcement Learning in the Multi-Robot Domain, *Autonomous Robots 4(1)*, pp.77-83(1997).
11. Miyazaki, K., Yamamura, M. and Kobayashi, S. : On the Rationality of Profit Sharing in Reinforcement Learning, *Proceedings of the 3rd International Conference on Fuzzy Logic, Neural Nets and Soft Computing*, pp.285-288 (1994).
12. Sen, S. and Sekaran, M. : Multiagent Coordination with Learning Classifier Systems, in Weiss, G. and Sen, S.(eds.), *Adaption and Learning in Multi-agent systems*, Berlin, Heidelberg. Springer Verlag, pp.218-233(1995).
13. Singh, S.P. and Sutton, R.S.: Reinforcement Learning with Replacing Eligibility Traces, *Machine Learning Vol.22*, pp.1-37(1996).
14. Stone, P. and Veloso, M.: Team Partitioned, Opaque Transition Reinforcement Learning, *Proceedings of the 3rd International Conference on Autonomous Agents*, pp.206-212(1999).
15. Sutton, R.S.: Learning to Predict by the Methods of Temporal Differences, *Machine Learning, Vol. 3*, pp.9-44(1988).
16. Watkins, C. J. H., and Dayan, P.: Technical note: Q-learning, *Machine Learning Vol.8*, pp.55-68(1992).
17. Whitehead, S. D. and Balland, D. H.: Active perception and Reinforcement Learning, *Proceedings of the 7th International Conference on Machine Learning*, pp.162-169(1990).

A Region Selecting Method Which Performs Observation and Action in the Multi-resolution Environment

Toshihiro Matsui, Hiroshi Matsuo and Akira Iwata

Department of Electrical & Computer Engineering, Nagoya Institute of Technology, Gokiso-cho, Showa-ku, Nagoya, 466-8555, Japan

Abstract. We propose a method for selecting the characteristic region in the environment based on the occurrence probability of the pattern. If the occurrence probability of the pattern is unknown in initial stage, estimation of the distribution of the pattern and selection of the characteristic region must be done simultaneously. We noticed that a method for exploration of the state-space in reinforcement learning was similar to such task. Then, we propose a method for selecting the characteristic region by repeating observation and action in the environment. In the observation using only one resolution, the position in the environment can not be decided. The multi-resolution concept is introduced in order to solve this problem. The experimental result shows that the characteristic region is selected from the environment.

1 Introduction

In the tasks such as pattern recognition, the part of information observed for the environment is selected as a important region at one time. A criteria to select such region is the occurrence probability of the partial pattern. Because the characteristic area is correspondent to the pattern of which the occurrence probability is small, it is appropriate to select mainly such pattern in order to decide the important region. If the region is selected in proportion to the occurrence probability of the pattern, the frequency of the observation for each pattern becomes equal. When the occurrence probability of the pattern is unknown in the initial condition, it is reasonable to correct the polarization of the observation frequency for each pattern by each point of time in the selection of the region. It requires large calculation cost to select next region from all regions. And, when it is selected in the absolute position, the error of the position becomes a problem. Therefore, it is efficient to relatively select the region from the neighborhood defined for the current position.

In reinforcement learning [1] which is one of the unsupervised learning methods, the agent starts the learning from the condition without knowledge on the environment, and it acquires the rule. The rule reflects the series of the action which obtains the reward from the environment. The agent repeats observation and action in the environment, and it constitutes the state-space. In the environment identification type learning, it is necessary to select the action that explores all states in order to constitute the state-space which reflects the environment. Miyazaki et al. proposed the algorithm for exploring all state-space[2]. In this algorithm, the agent explores environments by selecting all actions at least $k = 1$ time. Next, the agent repeats the similar action, after the value of k is increased for 1. This method is the selection of the action which averages the trial frequency of all actions in all known states. In the environment, the distribution of the pattern observed as an identical state will influence the distribution of the position of the agent. In reinforcement learning, if an identical state is observed at different positions in the environment, it causes a mismatching between the state-space of the agent and the environment. However, we discuss how the position in the environment of the agent is distributed in the repetition of action and observation. It is not possible to classify the identical pattern observed in the different position, if the agent has no information about the position in the environment. In such case, the agent will explore around local area. For the solution of this problem, the multi-resolution is introduced into the environment. We define the multi-resolution for observation and action in the environment. Then, we propose a framework which aim to equalize frequency of each action on each state. By this method the agent mainly exists at the characteristic position in the environment.

The concept of peripheral vision and multi-resolution is used for visual attention in the computer vision. The multi-resolution concept is used in the modeling of the saccade phenomenon[6]. B. Takacs et al. proposed a method using a dynamic and multi-resolution model[7]. C. Bandera et al. applies reinforcement learning for the visual attention. Its purpose is the model based target recognition[5]. The visual field of the multi-resolution is used even in this method.

In the following, we describe our technique, and it is evaluated by the experiment.

2 The Modeling of the Problem

We describe environment, observation and action in order to simplify the problem. We assume that the environment is a n-dimensional torus. Reasons for assuming the n-dimensional torus are as follows: (1) It is possible to limit the whole of the space in the observation. (2) There is no contradiction in our definition on the neighborhood.

The function $f(x) = \{0, 1\}$ is defined for the all position $\{x\}$ in the environment. For the observation, the whole of $\{x\}$ is equally divided into the unit interval $u_i (i = 0, \cdots, n)$ in proportion to the resolution(Fig.1(a)). In the observation, the unit interval u_i is selected, and $\max_{u_i} f(x)$ is obtained as the value by the observation. In the observation, the values of the unit intervals, which are selected as the center and adjoining it, are obtained.

There is no constraint on the movement in the environment. However, the unit in the transfer is supposed to be identical with the unit interval in the observation. In addition, the moving range in each iteration is limited to unit intervals selected as the center and adjoining it.

By the above, the state-space is constituted. The agent repeats observation and action using this state-space. This framework is similar to general reinforcement learning. However, our purpose is that the distribution of the position of the agent is made to adapt to the distribution of the pattern in the environment. For this purpose, we combine two approaches. One approach aims to equalize the frequency of the observation of all states. Another approach is to introduce the multi-resolution into the state-space.

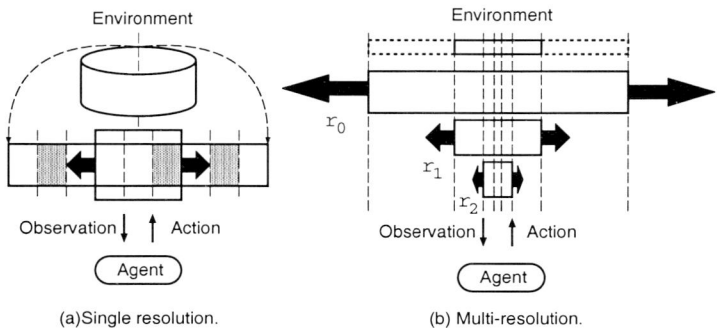

Fig. 1. Resolution for the action and the observation.

3   An Algorithm Which Equalize the Number of Trials of All Action on All Observed State

In our framework, the agent repeats observation and action as well as general reinforcement learning. In this framework, each state does not have information of the position in the environment. Therefore, the agent can fail to local exploration. We describe this problem in the next section.

The observation frequency of the pattern follows the occurrence probability, if the agent equally scans the environment. Reversely, the distribution of the position of the agent is dependent on the occurrence probability of the pattern, if the frequency of the observation of all states is equalized. Since each state does not have information about the position, it is impossible to decide the action which equalizes the frequency of the observation of each state directly. Then, we use the method for equalizing the frequency of the selection of each action instead of each state. In reinforcement learning, it is not desirable that the agent detects the different position in the environment as an identical state. But, our purpose is not the acquisition of the rule by reinforcement learning.

Miyazaki et al. proposed the k-Certainty Exploration Method as an algorithm for the environment identification type learning. The purpose of this method is that the agent explores all state-space. In this algorithm, the agent explores all environments by selecting all actions to over $k = 1$ time. Next, the agent repeats the similar action, after the value of k is increased for 1. The algorithm is as follows (We arranged the notation).

procedure k-Certainty Exploration Method
begin

if the k-Uncertainty rule exists for current state **then** k:=1.
else if all known rules are k-Certainty **then** k:=k+1;

if the k-Uncertainty rule exists for current state **then**
One of the such state is randomly selected.
else
begin

    set flags for all known states.
for all known states except for present condition **do**

    if the k-Uncertainty rule exists **or**
the rule which makes transition to the state
that the flag is off, is exist **then**
reset flag of the state.

    while the state that the flag was newly reset exists;

    One of the rules which can make transition
to the state that the flag is off from present state,is randomly selected.

    end;

end.

In this method, only the action which does not satisfy the k value becomes a candidate for the selection. This is a very simple method. However, it is appropriate as the constraint which brings the distribution close to the desired value, because it can be understood as a weighting based on upper part accumulation probability of normal distribution $(k,0)$. And, the calculation cost is small, since it does not need to calculate the distribution. In this algorithm, the exceptional processing is executed when all action in present state has already been selected over k time. Such mechanisms are necessary in order to prevent the local exploration.

4 The Region Selecting Method Using Multi-resolution to Correct the Scale Mismatch between the Environment and the State Space

We have assumed the state-space based on the single resolution. However, an identical pattern in different positions can not be distinguished. In such case, the frequency of the action on each state is equalized, while the agent explore around local area. Then, we introduce multi-resolution $r_j(j = 0 \cdots n)$ in order to solve this problem(Fig.1(b)). The whole of $\{x\}$ is equally divided into the unit interval $u_i^n(i = 0, \cdots, 3^n)$ in proportion to the highest resolution r_n. At the resolution r_n, any of the unit interval u_i^n is selected. In the observation, the values of the unit intervals which are selected as the center and adjoining it, are obtained. At other resolution r_j, the visual field at the resolution r_{j+1} is selected as a center. In the observation, the values of the unit intervals, which are selected as the center u_i^j and adjoining it, are obtained. The whole environment is fixed, because the lowest resolution wraps the environment.

At each resolution, the algorithm similar to the k-Certainty Exploration Method is prepared. It is necessary to select one action at a time, because the agent has only one body. It means that only one resolution must be selected to decide the action. For this selection, we use the method which is similar to the k-Certainty Exploration Method. The m value is introduced for k_j value at each resolution r_j. One of the resolution with k_j value under the m value is selected. However, the resolution in which the frequency of each action in present state has achieved k_j is removed from the selection candidate. This expansion is based on the assumption that the increase of k_j value at each resolution reflects the number of the observed state. Our algorithms using the multi-resolution are as follows.

> **procedure**
> **begin**
>
> **for** all resolution $r_j(j = 0, \cdots, n)$
> **begin**
> **if** the unknown state is detected **then**
> **begin**
> All $k_j:=1$.
> $m:=1$.
> **end**
> **else if** all known rules are executed over k_j times **then** $k_j:=k_j+1$;
> **end**;
>
> **if** all $k_j > m$ **then** $m:=m+1$;
>
> **if** some of $k_j \leq m$ **and** one of rules of current state are not executed more than k_j times **then**
> select one of such resolution randomly.

else select a resolution randomly from all resolutions;

if for selected resolution, rules of current state are not executed more than k_j times
then select one of such rule randomly.
else select a rule randomly form all rules of selected resolution;

execute the rule.

end.

5 Experiment

We show the experimental result using proposed method. We apply our method in a 1-dimensional torus environment including the characteristic pattern. And, we also show the example in a two-dimensional torus environment.

5.1 The Result in 1-Dimensional Torus

The result in the 1-dimensional torus environment is shown. In this example, the number of resolutions is 5. Therefore, the environment is divided into $3^{5-1} = 81$ in the highest resolution. The accumulation of the agent of the position in the environment where the characteristic pattern exists is shown in the figure 2. The m value is 1000. It takes 411520 iterations. In the result, the characteristic pattern has mainly been selected. The change of the accumulation from start point of time is shown in the figure 3.

The result as the pattern contains the simple texture is shown in the figure 4. The distribution increases, while the characteristic pattern occurrence probability is reflected.

5.2 The Result in 2-Dimensional Torus

The result in the 2-dimensional torus environment is shown(Fig.5). In this example, the number of resolutions is 4, and the environment is divided into 27×27. The m value is also 1000,but it takes 10837593 iterations. This result reflects that the occurrence probability of the pattern of the vertices are small.

6 Summary

In the proposed method, the agent repeats observation and action in the environment using the multi-resolution. The agent equalizes the trial frequency of each action, and as the result, the characteristic region in the environment is mainly explored. It is indicated that the exploration which adapted to the environment is a filter processing for the spatial characteristic of the environment.

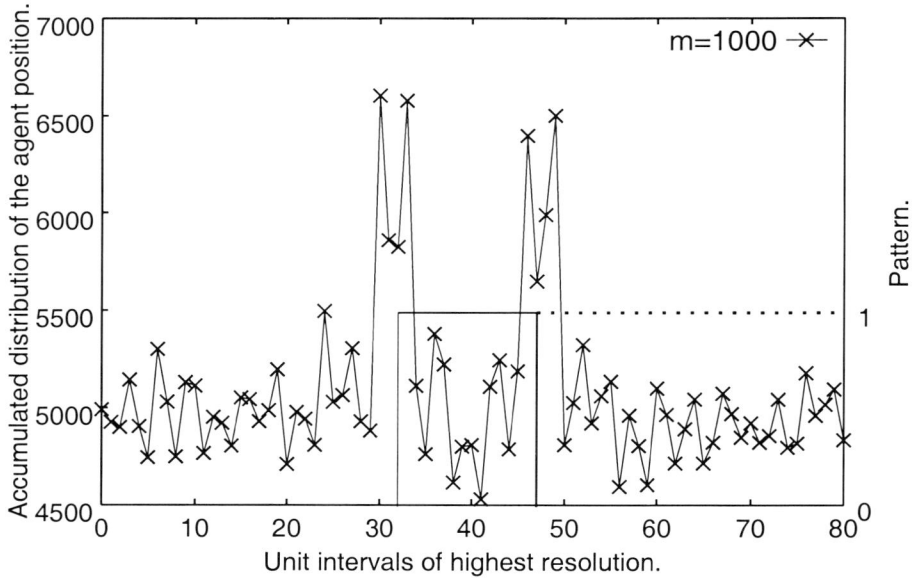

Fig. 2. The accumulation of the agent position (m=1000).

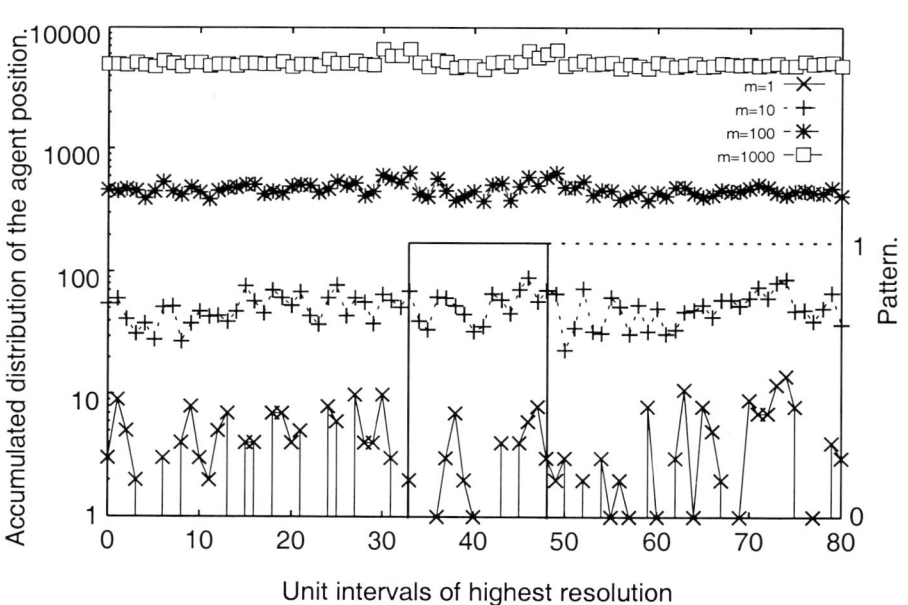

Fig. 3. The accumulation of the agent position (m=1,10,100 and 1000).

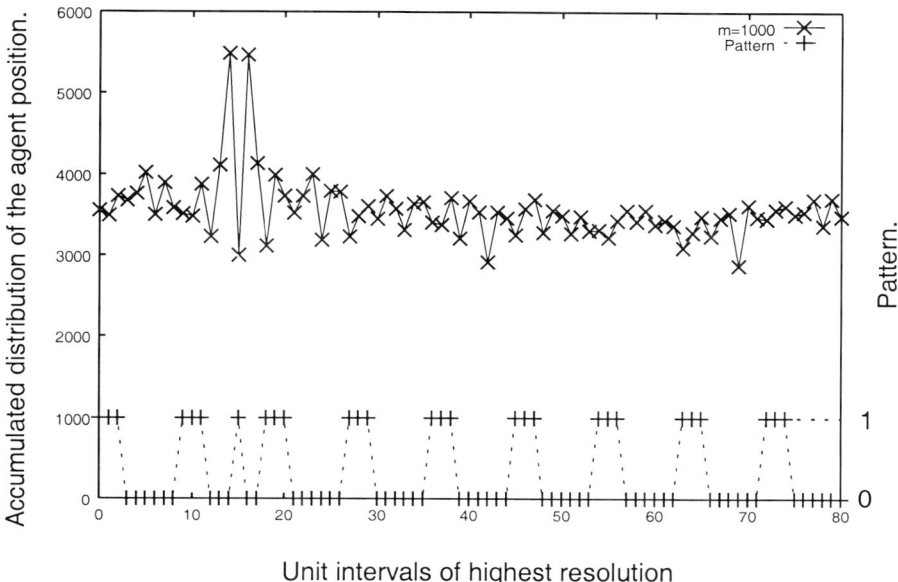

Fig. 4. The accumulation of the agent position in the texture.($m=1000$).

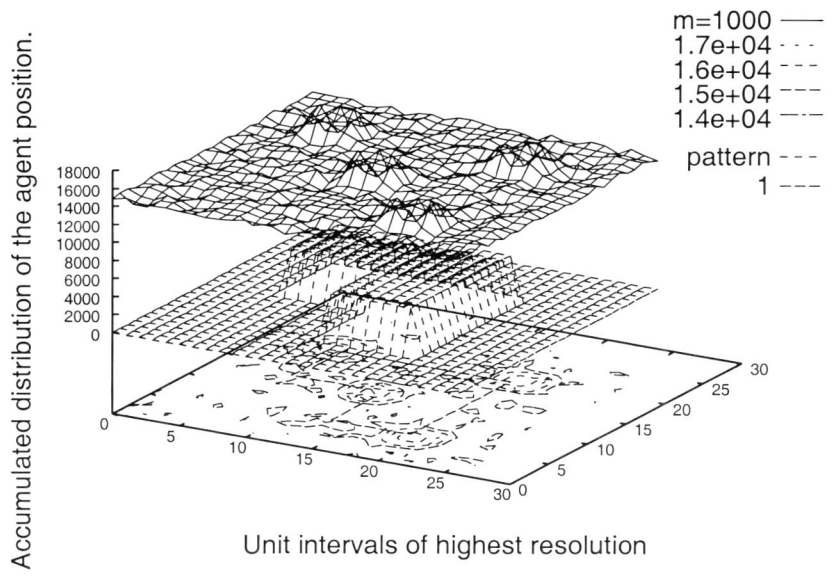

Fig. 5. The accumulation of the agent position in 2d torus.($m=1000$).

Information about the position in the environment is necessary so that this distribution may be correspondent to the whole environment. The introduction of the multi-resolution enables the decision of the relative positional relation. In the experiment using this method, the distribution in proportion to the characteristic region in the environment was obtained.

There is another type of implementation the multi-resolution, that places the visual field of the logarithm scale in the single layer. This implementation seems to be essentially equivalent to the proposed method. However, the dimension of observed vector increases. The state-space exponentially increases for the dimension of the state vector observed. Therefore, we currently divided the state-space at each resolution.

The agent view whole environment in the lowest resolution. Observed pattern in the lowest resolution environment is not changed while the agent explores. However, the visual field can be limited in the practical environment. In such case, the agent will fail to local exploration.

How to abstract the environment for multi-resolution is also important problem. To classify the observed pattern with high accuracy, another multi-resolution model is needed.

The serious problem of this method is to require many trials. In this method, the frequency of the selection of all actions is equalized. Therefore, many trials are necessary for the case in which there are many types of patterns in the environment in order to try all actions. And, the global perturbation by the low resolution does not supplement the local perturbation at the high resolution, because the weight of the selection of each resolution is simply equalized. Exploration of the whole environment and selection of the specific region are trade-off. Both balance must be set in proportion to actual purpose.

It is a future problem to introduce some pattern recognition mechanism in order to apply it to the incremental feature extraction processing. Some theoretical consideration on this problem is also necessary.

References

1. L. P. Kaelbling, M. L. Littman, Andrew W. Moore: Reinforcement Learning: A Survey; Journal of Artificial Intelligence Research 4, pp.237-285 (1996).
2. K. Miyazaki, M. Yamamura and S. Kobayashi: k-Certainty Exploration Method: An Action Selector on Reinforcement Learning to Identify the Environment; Journal of Artificial Intelligence, Vol.91, pp.155-171 (1997).
3. K. Miyazaki, M. Yamamura and S. Kobayashi: l-Certainty Exploration Method: An Action Selector to Identify the Identify the Environment – An Extension of k-Certainty Exploration Method to Stochastic MDPs –; Journal of Japanese Society for Artificial Intelligence, Vol.11, pp.804-808 (1996).
4. K.Miyazaki, M. Yamamura and S. Kobayashi: MarcoPolo-A Reinforcement Learning System Considering Tradeoff Exploration and Exploitation under Markovian Environment; Proc. of 4th Int. Conf. on Soft Computing, pp.561-564 (1996).
5. Bandera, C., Vico, F. J., Bravo, J. M., Harmon, M. E., and Baird, L. C.: Residual Q-learning applied to visual attention; Proceedings of the Thirteenth International Conference on Machine Learning, Bari, Italy, 3-6 July, pp. 20-27. (1996).

6. Moddeling Saccadic Targeting in Visual Search; R. P. N. Rao, G. J. Zelinsky, M. M. Hayhoe, D. H. Ballard.: Advances in Neural Information Processing Systems 8, D. S. Touretzky, M. C. Mozer, M. E. Hasselmo, eds., MIT Press (1996).
7. B. Takacs, H. Wechsler: A Dynamic and Multiresolution Model of Visual Attention and Its Application to Facial Landmark Detection; Computer Vision and Image Understanding Vol.70, pp.63-73 (1998).
8. I. Marsic: Data-Driven Shifts of Attention in Wavelet Scale Space; CAIP-TR-166, CAIP Center, Rutgers University, September (1993).

RWS (Random Walk Splitting): A Random Walk Based Discretization of Continuous Attributes

Masaaki Hanaoka, Masaki Kobayashi, and Haruaki Yamazaki

Faculty of Engineering, Yamanashi University,
4-3-11 Takeda, Kofu, Yamanashi, Japan

Abstract. The discretization of continuous attributes in a given training set is an important issue, which significantly affects the performance of decision trees. This paper proposes a method to discretize the continuous attributes based on a random walk modeled statistical test. In this method, the algorithm tries to find the point which divides the training set T into two groups T_1 and T_2 such that $T = T_1 \cup T_2$ with possibly many instances from a majority class included in T_1. In other words, the algorithm detects the splitting point, which gives the maximum discrepancy between the two empirical distributions, the majority class and the rest. The algorithm recursively executes this procedure until some statistical criterion is satisfied. Further, we report the effectiveness of the algorithm over ChiMerge and MDLPC based on an experiment with UCI repository.

1 Introduction

The discretization of the continuous attributes of a given training set significantly affects the classification capability of a decision tree as well as the selection of the attribute and decision tree pruning. So far, many discretization methods have been reported [2][4][6][8]. These methods are classified into two categories. One is called dynamic discretization, which discretizes the attribute values while constructing a decision tree, and the other is called the static method, which discretizes before decision tree construction [3].

The typical dynamic method is the binary discretization in C4.5 [8] which is a modified version of a well-known algorithm ID3 [7]. The typical static method includes D-2 [2], ChiMerge [6], and MDLPC [4]. Some experiments based on UCI repository [1] show the advantage of MDLPC [3].

However, MDLPC does not necessarily dominate over other methods on all of the repository data. In real world data, like UCI repository, many classes are overlapped in training data. Therefore, it is quite difficult to obtain the most advantageous method on arbitrary types of data. In order to construct the decision tree with high capability of classification, the discretization method applicable to as many types of data as possible is an important issue.

This paper proposes a new discretization method, which can be applicable to various types of data. Here, we define that the appropriate discretizing point gives the maximum discrepancy between two empirical distributions. And the terminating condition of the algorithm is reduced to the statistical test. We employ a random walk model [5] in statistical testing. Further, we compared this method with ChiMerge and MDLPC by experiments based on UCI repository data.

In Sect.2, we discuss ChiMerge and MDLPC, and in Sect.3, we discuss our discretization method RWS (Random Walk Splitting). In Sect.4, for these three methods, RWS, ChiMerge, and MDLPC, the experimental results and the comparison based on UCI repository data are reported. Finally, we summarize our discussion in Sect.5.

2 Existing Methods

Here, we outline two typical discretization methods, ChiMerge and MDLPC.

2.1 ChiMerge

For a given training data set sorted in order of the values of a continuous attribute, ChiMerge [6] repeats the following processes: 1) compute differences in class distributions of adjacent intervals, 2) merge two of the least different or the most similar intervals into a single new interval. And finally several intervals remain.

The algorithm of ChiMerge tests the hypothesis that *the class distributions at the two adjacent intervals are different*. And if it is rejected, the merge process continues until the hypothesis is accepted in all adjacent intervals.

2.2 MDLPC

In MDLP (Minimum Description Length Principle) [9], the best probability model is defined as the one that gives the shortest encoding for given data, including the description of the model itself. In MDLPC [4], the discretization of continuous attributes is modeled as a communication between sender and receiver where a sender transfers class information with the least number of bits to a receiver who has training data but does not know those classes. In this communication model, a sender splits a training data set into two subsets, and encodes class and split information to send them.

When the code length with splitting, MLength(HT), and the code length without splitting, MLength(NT) are given, the algorithm of MDLPC decides whether to split or not, as follows:
(a) If MLength(HT) < MLength(NT), then split.
(b) Otherwise, terminate the split.

These conditions are applied on the candidate of the splitting point at which MLength(HT) is minimized. The continuous attributes are discretized by repeating the splitting processes until Condition (b) is satisfied in all intervals.

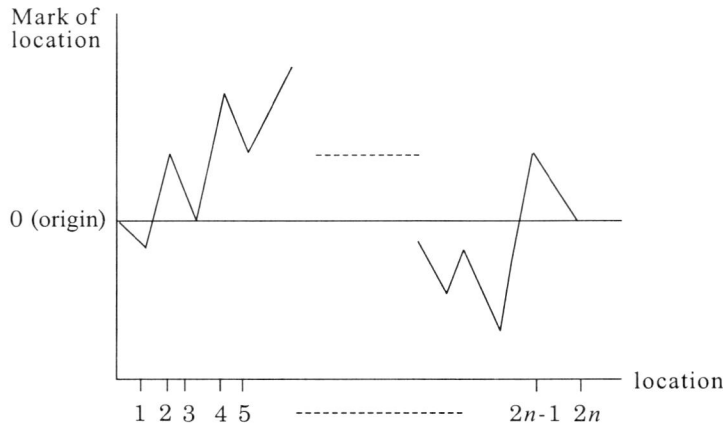

Fig. 1. The example of random walk

3 RWS: Proposed Method

3.1 Model

In the RWS model, we suppose that the training set is a group of training instances and each instance consists of a number of attribute values and is labeled by a class (category) in which the instance is included. For a given training set T, there exists a class such that the number of instances of that class is maximum in T, we call this class a majority class, and the instance in majority class a majority member. Since each training instance has its own class label, a given training set T can be divided into two subsets T_1 and T_2, where T_1 consists only of majority members, and T_2 consists of all the rest. First, we randomly choose n instances from T_1 and T_2 respectively. Then, we can derive the empirical distributions of T_1 and T_2. We denote these empirical distributions F_1, F_2. Here, the empirical distribution is the step function with jumps $1/n$ at each point on the line. ($F_i(\infty) = 1$, $F_i(-\infty) = 0$). Let D denote a random variable of maximum discrepancy between these two empirical distributions.

Intuitively, we model this as follows: Suppose the instances from T_1 and T_2 stand for red balls and white balls. Then, we locate the balls on the line according to the instance's attribute value. Therefore, $2n$ balls are arranged on the line. Here, we put the score $+1$ to the red ball, and -1 to the white ball.

Suppose that j red balls exist before the location where i th ball is, then the number of the white balls is $i-j$, so we can define the mark of the i th location as $2j-i$. Let R_i denotes the mark of i th location, then $\{R_i\}$ forms a random walk with length $2n$, starting at and returning to the origin. At each step, it increments or decrements 1 as shown in Fig.1.

If these red and white balls are from the same population, that is, the distributions based on F_1 and F_2 are the same, then every arrangement of the $2n$

Table 1. RWS algorithm

Procedure 1 For given training set T, find the majority class and divided T into T_1 and T_2 where T_1 consists of majority instances and T_2 consists of other instances. Then, extract the same number n of instances from T_1 and T_2, resulting in a new set S.

Procedure 2 Sort the instances in S according to the underlying attribute values, forming one initial interval.

Procedure 3 For the newly generated interval, find the two empirical distributions of T_1 instances and T_2 instances in S. Solve for the attribute value v which gives the maximum discrepancy d of two empirical distributions. Based on (1), compute the probability p that the maximum discrepancy is d, and then compare p with the given level of significance.
  (a) If p is under the level of significance, choose v as a splitting point. This results in creating two new training sets and intervals. For each interval, apply Procedure 1 through 3.
  (b) If p exceeds the level of significance, then reject v.

Procedure 4 If the number of generated intervals does not exceed the predetermined upper bound, select all splitting points. Otherwise select highly ranked splitting points.

---

balls have equal probability. Therefore, the distribution of D is independent of the distribution of the population.

According to Gnedenko and Koroljuk [5], the probability that D exceeds a certain value d is given as follows:

$$P\{D \geqq d\} = \binom{2n}{n-d} \bigg/ \binom{2n}{n}. \qquad (1)$$

In the RWS algorithm, the statistical test to determine whether T_1 and T_2 are from the same population or not is made based on this probability. In other words, the RWS algorithm first selects the location, which gives the maximum discrepancy between two empirical distributions F_1 and F_2 as the candidate for the splitting point. Then, at that candidate point, the algorithm tests the hypothesis: "*the instances from two groups are originally from the same population*" using the probability given in (1) as the level of significance. If the hypothesis is rejected, the candidate is chosen as the splitting point, resulting in two new intervals. Then, the procedure operates on these two new intervals and the procedure continues recursively. The splitting process is terminated if the hypothesis is accepted. The algorithm terminates if all recursive procedures operating on the intervals are terminated.

3.2 Discretization Algorithm Based on Random Walk

Table 1 describes the detailed algorithm of RWS.
In Procedure 1, the training set T is divided into two classes: the majority class, T_1 and the rest, T_2. Here, we suppose $|T_1| = m$, $|T_2| = n$ and without loosing

Table 2. Data sets used for the evaluation experiment

Data sets	Num. of continuous attributes	Num. of discrete attributes	Num. of instances	Num. of classes
1 iris	4	0	150	3
2 wine	13	0	178	3
3 glass	9	0	214	7
4 new-thyroid	5	0	215	3
5 cleveland	6	7	303	5
6 australian	6	8	690	2
7 crx	6	9	690	2
8 vehicle	18	0	846	4
9 waveform	21	0	5000	3
10 page-blocks	10	0	5473	5

generality, we further suppose $m \geqq n$. Then, n instances are randomly extracted from T_1 and T_2 respectively. Therefore, the sample training set consisting of $2n$ instances is created.

In Procedure 2, sorting of $2n$ training instances is executed:
$$v_1 \leqq v_2 \leqq ... \leqq v_{2n}$$
In Procedure 3, the algorithm calculates the maximum discrepancy d and the value v_i which gives d. The statistical test based on (1) is then executed to determine whether $(v_i+v_{i+1})/2$ is the splitting point or not. Since the procedure is executed recursively, the depth of recursion ranks each splitting point (the deeper the recursion, the lower the rank).

In Procedure 4, in order to avoid generating too many intervals, checks are performed to determine whether the number of intervals exceeds the predetermined upper bound. If they exceed the upper bound, highly ranked splitting points are selected.

4 Evaluation Experiment

4.1 Data for Experiment

In the experiments, we used 10 data sets from UCI repository [1] as shown in Table 2. These data sets are ordered according to the number of instances. Data sets are selected not only on the basis of the continuous attributes, but discrete ones, the number of attributes, instances, and classes, so that the whole data sets include various patterns.

4.2 Method for Experiment

In this experiment, to evaluate the effectiveness of RWS, RWS software is loaded on DELL DIMENSION XPS-M233s (CPU: 233MHz MMX Pentium, Memory: 64MB) operating with Windows 95 installed.

Table 3. The algorithm for decision tree generation

Procedure 1 If no data exist in a training data set, generate a leaf that makes the largest class of the upper node as the label. Then return.
Procedure 2 If all data in a training data set have the same class, generate a leaf that makes the class the same as the label. Then return.
Procedure 3 If there exist no attributes to be selected, generate a leaf that makes the largest class of a training data set as the label. Then return.
Procedure 4 Compute an evaluation index for each attribute and select the attribute with the highest evaluation. Generate a node that splits training data into subsets using the value of the selected attribute.
Procedure 5 Make each subset split at the node in Procedure 4 to be a training data set, and apply Procedure 1 through 5 recursively. However, the attribute selected at the node in Procedure 4 is excluded.
Procedure 6 Generate a decision tree using the nodes and leaves and terminate the procedure.

First, for each continuous attributes of the data sets in Table 2, the splitting points are selected by three methods: RWS, ChiMerge, and MDLPC. For RWS, the level of the significance and the maximum number of intervals are set to 5% and 6 respectively. For ChiMerge, the significance level and the maximum number of intervals are set to 95% and 6 respectively, and the increment of threshold is 0.1%.

Next, the cross-validation test is carried out on the data discretized by these three methods, and the results are compared. In cross-validation, data sets are divided into arbitrary subsets each of which are an equal number of instances, then subsets are used as test data and the others used as training data. Then, a decision tree is generated using these training sets and the capabilities of these trees are evaluated. These procedures are applied to all subsets repeatedly [11].

In this experiment, each data set is divided into five equal subsets, and the cross-validations are executed. Therefore, 80% of the data are the training data and 20% are the test data. The decision tree generation and decision evaluation is repeated five times. Table 3 describes the algorithm [10] used for decision tree generation. In Procedure 4, the gain ratio of information entropy [8] is used as an evaluation index for the attributes. In decision tree evaluation, the classification accuracy of a decision tree is defined as the ratio of the number of properly classified data to the number of all data in the test (the percentage of correct answers). The complexity of a decision tree is defined as the number of generated nodes. The average accuracy and complexity on five-time executions are computed, and the performances of these three methods are compared.

4.3 Experiment Results and Considerations

First, the continuous attributes from UCI repository have been discretized by three methods: as shown in Table 2.

Table 4. The number of splitting points for continuous attributes

Data sets	RWS	Chi-Merge	MDLPC
1 iris	10	10	8
2 wine	23	48	25
3 glass	17	35	13
4 new-thyroid	15	19	13
5 cleveland	5	17	3
6 australian	14	29	7
7 crx	16	29	6
8 vehicle	55	81	54
9 waveform	87	100	85
10 page-blocks	48	42	60

Table 4 shows the number of splitting points for the continuous attributes. RWS and MDLPC have almost the same number of splitting points. However, ChiMerge gives a larger number of points except for page-blocks. In particular, for wine, glass, cleveland, australian, and crx, the number of splitting points in ChiMerge increases to more than twice that for RWS's and MDLPC's. In RWS, the fewer the training instances the smaller the value of maximum discrepancy, resulting in accepting the hypothesis. Therefore, the splitting process terminates. In MDLPC, the splitting information as well as the split class information are considered, so the code length gap between splitting class and no splitting class information is small, which results in the rare occurrence of splitting. One of the reasons why the number of the splitting points is equally small for RWS and MDLPC may be because the features mentioned above suppress splitting in these two methods. On the other hand, in the case of ChiMerge, an expected frequency less than 1.0 produces a very large χ^2-value. Two adjacent intervals, which should be merged, would be split due to this very large χ^2-value, thus ChiMerge generates excessive splitting points.

Next, for each of the data sets in Table 2, of which continuous values are discretized, the decision trees have been generated, and the cross-validation has been carried out. Then for these decision trees, we obtained the percentage of correct answers and the number of generated nodes.

Table 5 shows the percentage of correct answers for each decision tree. The values on the right column of each method are the ratio of the percentage of correct answers for ChiMerge and MDLPC to that of RWS. A value greater than 1.0 means a higher percentage than RWS, and a value less than 1.0 means a lower. For the data sets that have a large number of splitting points, ChiMerge tends to have a lower percentage than the other methods. Only in iris and wine, does ChiMerge show a higher percentage. Though the values are almost the same for RWS and MDLPC, RWS shows a higher percentage than MDLPC on six out of ten data sets. For the data sets with a relatively large number of data, such as cleveland to page-block, RWS tends to dominate other methods

Table 5. The percentage of correct answers for the decision trees

Data sets	RWS		ChiMerge		MDLP	
1 iris	94.7 ± 2.67	1.000	96.0 ± 3.90	1.014	94.0 ± 3.90	0.993
2 wine	91.6 ± 3.54	1.000	94.9 ± 2.79	1.036	97.2 ± 3.13	1.061
3 glass	75.2 ± 6.06	1.000	75.2 ± 8.83	1.000	76.6 ± 7.57	1.019
4 new-thyroid	95.3 ± 2.94	1.000	93.5 ± 1.74	0.981	96.7 ± 2.37	1.015
5 cleveland	51.0 ± 3.71	1.000	48.6 ± 1.02	0.953	50.7 ± 4.69	0.994
6 australian	81.4 ± 2.70	1.000	80.9 ± 2.73	0.994	80.3 ± 3.90	0.986
7 crx	82.8 ± 6.07	1.000	80.9 ± 6.04	0.977	80.2 ± 2.92	0.969
8 vehicle	67.1 ± 1.29	1.000	64.4 ± 2.11	0.960	63.2 ± 4.43	0.942
9 waveform	71.3 ± 0.76	1.000	71.1 ± 0.77	0.997	71.4 ± 1.19	1.001
10 page-blocks	96.7 ± 0.57	1.000	96.2 ± 0.71	0.995	96.5 ± 0.66	0.998
Average	80.7 ± 3.03	1.000	80.2 ± 3.06	0.991	80.7 ± 3.48	0.998

The values on the left are the average percentages of correct answers with the standard deviations on five-time executions, and the values on the right are the ratios of the percentage for each method to the percentage for RWS.

in the percentage of correct answers. On the other hand, for the data sets that have a smaller number of data, the percentage of correct answers for MDLPC is higher. Also, in general, the deviation of the percentage is in the order of RWS, ChiMerge, and MDLPC.

From these results, the following facts can be inferred: when excessive splitting occurs, fewer instances are included in the interval, which decreases the classification accuracy. On the other hand, the rare occurrence of splitting makes for fewer patterns of attributes used for a decision tree. Therefore, the number of training instances from various classes increases, resulting in a high error ratio. Thus, the number of splitting points significantly affects the correct answer. The reason why the percentage of correct answers of ChiMerge is low is due to too many splitting points, and the correct answers of MDLPC, on cleveland, australian, and crx, is lower than RWS due to too few splitting points. In RWS, the more instances, the more accurate the probability given in (1). Therefore, the percentage of correct answers is higher in the data set containing more instances.

Table 6 shows the number of nodes for the decision trees. The right columns of each method describe the ratio of the number of nodes for ChiMerge and MDLPC to that of RWS. A value less than 1.0 means that the number of decision trees is less than for RWS, and a value greater than 1.0 vice versa. The number of nodes is extremely large for cleveland with RWS, and for cleveland, australian, crx, and vehicle with MDLPC. In general, fewer splitting points makes a large size subset, with a large number of training instances from various classes. Therefore, in the decision trees of cleveland with RWS, or of cleveland, australian, crx, and vehicle with MDLPC, the number of nodes gets large, since the algorithms try to generate a pure leaf that consists only of a single class.

Table 6. The number of nodes for the decision trees

Data sets	RWS		ChiMerge		MDLP	
1 iris	8.0	1.000	9.0	1.125	9.6	1.200
2 wine	10.4	1.000	7.4	0.712	8.6	0.827
3 glass	31.6	1.000	42.0	1.329	44.8	1.418
4 new-thyroid	13.4	1.000	11.6	0.866	11.0	0.821
5 cleveland	117.8	1.000	86.2	0.732	122.0	1.036
6 australian	83.2	1.000	71.0	0.853	129.4	1.555
7 crx	70.4	1.000	56.2	0.798	120.6	1.713
8 vehicle	235.0	1.000	224.6	0.956	327.6	1.394
9 waveform	562.4	1.000	559.4	0.995	552.2	0.982
10 page-blocks	248.6	1.000	297.6	1.197	241.6	0.972
Average	138.1	1.000	136.5	0.956	156.7	1.192

The values on the left indicate the average number of nodes on five-time executions, and the values on the right indicate the ratios of the number for each method to the number for RWS.

5 Conclusion

Based on random walk, we proposed a new discretization method called RWS. With regard to RWS and two typical discretization methods, ChiMerge and MDLPC, we examined the numbers of splitting points, the percentage of correct answers, and the number of nodes in the decision trees. In the evaluation experiment with ten data sets from UCI repository, RWS generated simpler and more accurate decision trees, compared with ChiMerge and MDLPC. This tendency was observed particularly on the data sets with a larger number of training instances. So, we have confirmed that RWS is a promising method for discretization of continuous attributes.

As for further study, in order to improve classification capability of the decision tree, we are planning to study better attribute selection in the pre-processing of discretization and discretization taking account of the relationship among the attributes. Moreover, we plan to apply RWS to automatic classification of sleep EEG patterns that deal with a large amount of data and thereby evaluate the effectiveness of RWS.

References

1. Blake, C., Keogh, E., and Merz, C.J.: UCI Repository of Machine Learning Databases, http://www.ics.uci.edu/~mlearn/MLRepository.html, Irvine, CA: University of California, Department of Information and Computer Science (1998)
2. Catlett, J.: On Changing Continuous Attributes into Ordered Discrete Attributes, Proceedings of the European Working Session on Learning (1991) 164–178
3. Dougherty, J., Kohavi, R., and Sahami, M.: Supervised and Unsupervised Discretization of Continuous Features, Proceedings of the 12th International Conference on Machine Learning (1995) 194–202

4. Fayyad, U.M. and Irani, K.B.: Multi-Interval Discretization of Continuous-Valued Attributes for Classification Learning, Proceedings of the 13th International Joint Conference on Artificial Intelligence (1993) 1022–1027
5. Feller, W.: An Introduction to Probability Theory and Its Applications Vol.2, First Edition, John Wiley & Sons, New York (1966)
6. Kerber, R.: ChiMerge: Discretization of Numeric Attributes, Proceedings of the 10th National Conference on Artificial Intelligence (1992) 123–128
7. Quinlan, J.R.: Induction of Decision Trees, Machine Learning, Vol.1 (1986) 81–106
8. Quinlan, J.R.: C4.5: Programs for Machine Learning, Morgan Kaufmann, San Mateo, CA (1993)
9. Rissanen, J.: Modeling by Shortest Data Description, Automatica, Vol.14 (1978) 465–471
10. Russell, S.J. and Norvig, P.: Artificial Intelligence A Modern Approach, Prentice-Hall (1995)
11. Schaffer, C.: Selecting a Classification Method by Cross-Validation, Machine Learning, Vol.13, No.1 (1993) 135–143

The Lumberjack Algorithm for Learning Linked Decision Forests

William T.B. Uther and Manuela M. Veloso*

Department of Computer Science, Carnegie Mellon University, Pittsburgh, PA, U.S.A.
{uther,veloso}@cs.cmu.edu

Abstract. While the decision tree is an effective representation that has been used in many domains, a tree can often encode a concept inefficiently. This happens when the tree has to represent a subconcept multiple times in different parts of the tree. In this paper we introduce a new representation based on trees, the *linked decision forest*, that does not need to repeat internal structure. We also introduce a supervised learning algorithm, Lumberjack, that uses the new representation. We then show empirically that Lumberjack improves generalization accuracy on hierarchically decomposable concepts.

1 Introduction

Trees have been used for the representation of induced concepts in numerous areas of AI, including supervised learning with decision trees Breiman *et al.* (1984); Quinlan (1992) and reinforcement learning (RL) with tree based representations Chapman and Kaelbling (1991); McCallum (1995); Uther and Veloso (1998). Trees are a powerful representation. However, to represent some concepts they may need to represent some subconcepts multiple times. For example, to represent the boolean concept $AB \vee CD$ a decision tree has to repeat the representation of either AB or CD (see Fig. 1a where CD is repeated).

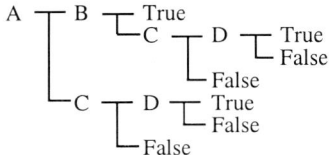 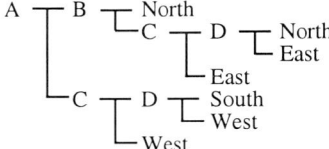

a) A tree representing the boolean concept $AB \vee CD$

b) A concept with repeated internal structure

Fig. 1. Trees with repeated structure

This repetition of entire subtrees is well known and has been studied by several researchers (see Section 2). In addition, we have found many RL domains in

---

* Prof. Veloso is currently visiting faculty at the MIT AI Laboratory, Cambridge, MA.

which the tree repeats *internal* structure. For example, consider a concept mapping boolean inputs, $\{A, B, C, D\}$, to action outputs, {North,South,East,West} as shown in Fig. 1b. The internal structure of the CD subtree is repeated even though the leaves are not. It chooses between either North and East, or South and West depending upon the value of A.

In most inductive systems work must be performed to learn each part of the tree. If a subconcept is represented twice then it must be learnt twice. Moreover, each individual representation of a sub-concept will be learnt using only part of the available data. For example, in Fig. 1a the representation of CD when A is true is learned separately from the representation of CD when A is false. In an RL domain, these repeated structures can be viewed as subtasks or macros.

In this paper we present a new representation, the *linked decision forest*,[1] which, while similar to a tree, does not have to repeatedly represent, and so repeatedly relearn, sub-concepts. We also introduce an algorithm, Lumberjack, for growing these linked forests. Through this representation we can give Lumberjack a bias towards learning abstract decompositions of the target concept. We show empirically that Lumberjack generalizes more effectively than a simple tree based approach on hierarchically decomposable concepts.

2 Related Work

Duplicated subtrees, as in Fig. 1a, are a well known problem. Two decision tree-like systems that attempt to factor out repeated substructure are Pagallo and Haussler's (1990) FRINGE system and Oliver and Wallace's (1992) decision graph induction system. Kohavi's (1995) read once oblivious decision graphs are also related, though less closely as they use a significantly different method to generate the graph.

The FRINGE system works by first growing a normal decision tree. Once this tree is fully grown, the last two decisions above each leaf in the tree (the fringe of the tree) are processed to form new attributes. The original tree is discarded and a new tree is grown using both the original attributes and the new attributes. The whole process is repeated, with the number of attributes constantly growing, until accuracy on a separate dataset starts dropping. The fact that attributes are not removed if they turn out not to be useful is an efficiency concern, as is the repeated re-growing of the tree.

In Oliver and Wallace's (1992) system, decision graphs are inferred directly using the Minimum Message Length Principle (MML) Wallace and Boulton (1968); Quinlan and Rivest (1989); Wallace and Patrick (1993). The system proceeds much as would a decision tree learner, except for two changes. Firstly, instead of a depth first approach to recursively splitting the dataset, the splits are

---

[1] The term 'decision forest' has been used previously in the machine learning literature to refer to a collection of different decision trees, each separately representing the same concept Murphy and Pazzani (1994). We introduce the term 'linked decision forest' to refer to a collection of decision trees with references between the trees so the forest as a whole, not just the individual trees, represents a concept.

introduced in a best first manner. The location and decision in the next decision node to be introduced are chosen using MML. Secondly, instead of introducing a new decision node, the system can join two leaves together.

Kohavi's (1995) HOODG system is very closely related to Ordered Binary Decision Diagrams Bryant (1992). These have a number of differences from arbitrary decision graphs. They both require an ordering among the variables and will only generate a graph that tests the variables in that order. As discussed by Kohavi, this limits the representation so that it is less efficient than an arbitrary decision graph. However, it allows a canonical representation to be found that is often compact. Most imp ortantly as far as the authors are concerned, the algorithm is not incremental and so cannot be transferred to RL using the techniques of Chapman and Kaelbling (1991); McCallum (1995); Uther and Veloso (1998) (see Hoey et al. (1999) for the application of OBDDs to RL).

Both Oliver and Wallace (1992) and Kohavi (1995) use a decision graph representation. A decision graph is not capable of factoring out structure which is only repeated internally, like the repeated CD structure in Fig. 1b. Additionally, Oliver and Wallace's (1992) decision graph algorithm chooses when to factor out repeated structure (join two leaves) using MML. The algorithm is choosing subtrees to 'join' based on comparison of their outputs, without any comparison of the structures required t o represent the correct subconcepts (which haven't been grown at the time the decision to join is made).

In addition to the related work on decision graphs, our work is based on Nevill-Manning's (1996) work on the automatic decomposition of strings. Given a linear sequence of symbols with no prior structure, his SEQUITUR algorithm forms a simple grammar where repeated substrings are factored out. For example, given the string $S \rightarrow abcdababcd$, SEQUITUR produces the grammar: $A \rightarrow ab, B \rightarrow Acd, S \rightarrow BAB$. This grammar re-represents the original string in a compact form.

3 The Linked Forest Representation

For linear strings the grammar is a well known representation for a hierarchical decomposition. We introduce the linked forest representation which allows hierarchical decomposition of trees. A linked forest is composed of trees with references between them in the same way a grammar is composed of rewrite rules with references between them. One tree in the linked forest is marked as the root tree. The root node of this tree is the starting point for classification by the forest. Figure 2 shows an example of a boolean linked decision forest.

The inter-tree references take two forms. When a node makes a *value reference* to another tree the semantics are similar to a jump instruction; processing simply continues in the new tree. When a node makes an *attribute reference* to another tree the semantics are similar to a function call. The referencing node has children which are in one-to-one correspondence with the leaves of the referenced tree. Control is passed across to the referenced tree until a leaf is reached, then passed back to the corresponding child of the referencing node.

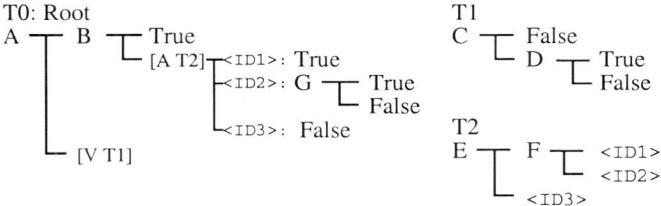

Fig. 2. A linked decision forest showing the root tree T0, and the trees T1 and T2; T0 includes a value reference to T1, [V T1], and an attribute reference to T2, [A T2]

If a tree is only referenced by attribute references, an *attribute tree*, then it does not require class labels or other data in its leaves. It simply has ID values that allow the corresponding children to be found. Lumberjack does not yet form value trees. They are mentioned for comparison purposes. One can view FRINGE as forming attribute trees, like Lumberjack, and the Decision Graph induction algorithm as forming value trees.

4 The Lumberjack Algorithm

Nevill-Manning's (1996) SEQUITUR algorithm detects common subsequences in strings by tracking digrams. For our algorithm we define a structure similar to a digram for trees, a *di-node*, that can be hashed for fast duplicate detection.

A di-node is defined as a pair of internal nodes in the forest such that one node is a child of the other. Two di-nodes are defined to be equal if the parent nodes are equal, the child nodes are equal, and the child is in the same location in both di-nodes (i.e. child ordering is important). For example, in Fig. 1a the two nodes labelled A and B form a di-node. The two nodes labelled A and B in Fig. 2 also form a di-node. These di-nodes are equal; the difference in nearby nodes is irrelevant. There are also two di-nodes made up of nodes labelled C and D in Fig. 1a. Those di-nodes are equal, but they are not equal to the di-node made up of nodes labelled C and D in Fig. 2; the D node is not in the same location relative to its parent.

Note that either, or both, of the nodes in a di-node could be a reference to another tree, and so a di-node can represent an arbitrarily large set of nodes. Also note that two di-nodes will be equal if and only if they represent equivalent sets of nodes that have been decomposed in the same way.

We are now in a position to give an overview of the Lumberjack algorithm. Table 1 shows the algorithm in detail. Initially the forest starts as a single tree with a single leaf node. Leaves are then split and a new decision nodes added, one at a time. As the forest is updated a hash table records all di-nodes currently in the forest. We use the Minimum Description Length (MDL) principle to choose the next decision node and to decide when to stop growing the forest (the details of the MDL selection are discussed later). Once an internal node has been added the forest is checked for duplicate di-nodes using the di-node hash. Any non-overlapping duplicates are extracted to form a new attribute tree and the original di-nodes are replaced with references to the new tree. Any trivial attribute trees (trees referenced only once or having less than two internal nodes) are removed and their structure reinserted into the referencing tree(s).

This extraction and reinsertion of di-nodes removes all duplicated substructure from the forest. Because duplicate di-nodes are detected in all trees, it is common for the structure to be more than two levels deep.

Note that we only ever form attribute trees from internal nodes. In SEQUITUR it is possible to form a rewrite rule containing the last character of a string because the end of the string is unique. If we merge leaves in Lumberjack then we lose the ability to differentiate the positions where we might wish to add further nodes. While this might sometimes be useful for linked decision forests, as shown by Oliver and Wallace (1992), it is difficult to find a suitable criterion for doing this while retaining the ability to form attribute references.

4.1 Altering the Inductive Bias

In the previous text we didn't supply all the details of the algorithm. If the decision criteria for new nodes are chosen from only the original attributes, and only leaves of the root tree are extended, then the concept learned will be the same as that learned by a normal tree induction algorithm; there will be no change in inductive bias. The representation will have all repeated structure separated into other trees, but this is only a change in representation, not concept. We can change the inductive bias of the algorithm, and hence the concept learned, by extending the ways the forest is grown.

The first change is to allow the induction algorithm to split not only on the original attributes, but also to introduce an attribute reference to any tree in the forest. This can be viewed as a form of macro replay. The one restriction is that the use of this tree not introduce a cycle in the forest. Lumberjack records which trees reference which other trees in a directed acyclic graph (DAG). No split that would introduce a cycle in this graph is allowed.

The second change is to allow the algorithm to grow the forest not only at leaves of the root tree, but at the leaves of any tree in the forest. This can be viewed as a form of macro refinement. Again there is a restriction. Recall that leaves of attribute trees correspond with the children of the nodes that reference them. If you split a leaf of an attribute tree, then you must split the corresponding children of the referencing node(s). If any of the corresponding children is not a leaf then we do not allow the split.

Growing attribute trees changes the number of outcomes of decision nodes elsewhere in the forest. That in turn changes the number of outcomes of other decision nodes, etc. Because the trees form a DAG, it is possible to update the trees in reverse topological order and know that all trees being referenced by the tree currently being updated are themselves up to date.

Finally, the correspondence between the leaves of an attribute tree and the children of a node that references that tree is important for the hashing of di-

Table 1. The Lumberjack algorithm

- Begin with a single leaf, empty di-node hash and empty tree DAG
- Record this forest as the best forest so far
- Repeat until no further splits are possible
  - Set best description length this iteration to ∞
  - For each leaf in the root tree or other trees:
    * Check if splitting this leaf would mean splitting a non-leaf elsewhere
    * If so, continue with next leaf
    * For each possible split criterion
      · If this split causes a cycle in the tree DAG then continue with next split
      · Introduce new decision node with this split
      · Update forest structure (see part b)
      · Calculate description length
      · If length is less than the best length this iteration, remember this split
      · Remove new decision node from forest
      · Update forest structure (see part b)
  - Reintroduce node with best split
  - Update forest structure (see part b)
  - Add new di-node to hash
  - While there are duplicate di-nodes, single use trees or degenerate trees
    * Use non-overlapping duplicate di-nodes to form a new attribute tree and replace original di-nodes
    * Reinsert any trees used only once
    * Reinsert any degenerate trees (less than two internal nodes)
    * (all while maintaining the di-node hash and tree DAG)
  - If forest has a shorter code length than current best forest, remember it
- Return best forest

a) The main linked forest learning algorithm

- For each tree in reverse topological order of the tree DAG
  - For each node in a post-order traversal of the tree
    * If this node is not a reference to an attribute tree then continue to next node
    * Delete each child which corresponds to a leaf no longer in the referenced tree
    * Insert a new child (leaf) for each new leaf in the referenced tree

b) The subroutine to update forest structure

Table 2. Costs to encode a non-root node

Node Type	Bits
Leaf	$\log_2(\frac{b}{b-1})$
decision node	$\log_2(b) + \log_2(N_A + N_{PT})$

nodes. The hash table should use that correspondence rather than child numbering for generating hash codes and testing equality. By avoiding the use of child numbering the algorithm does not have to re-hash di-nodes when an attribute tree grows or shrinks.

4.2 MDL Coding of Linked Decision Forests

The Minimum Description Length Rissanen (1983), or Minimum Message Length Wallace and Boulton (1968), Principle is a way of finding an inductive bias. It uses Bayes' Rule, $P(T|D) \propto P(T)P(D|T)$, and Shannon's information theory, the optimal code length of a symbol that has probability p is $-\log_2(p)$, to choose between competing models for data. The model and data are both encoded according to a coding scheme. The model which has the shortest total code length is chosen.

The Lumberjack algorithm could also be used with other decision node selection criteria. MDL was chosen for ease of implementation and because it supplies a stopping criterion.

Our coding scheme for MDL comparisons is a minor change from the Wallace and Patrick (1993) scheme for decision trees. Let N_T be the number of trees, N_A the number of attributes, N_{PT} the number of trees after the current tree in the topological ordering and b be the branching factor of our parent node. First, the number of trees in the forest is encoded using $L^*(N_T)$ bits.[2] Then the trees are encoded in reverse topological order. Each tree is encoded by performing a pre-order traversal of the tree and encoding each node using the number of bits shown in Table 2.

The one cost not yet specified is the cost to encode the root nodes of the trees. These have no parent node; b is undefined. When there is only one tree, a leaf at the root is encoded using $\log_2(N_A)$ bits and a decision node is encoded using $\log_2(\frac{N_A}{N_A-1}) + \log_2(N_A)$ bits, as in Wallace and Patrick (1993). When there is more than one tree, we know that none of the root nodes are leaves. The root decision nodes can be encoded using only $\log_2(N_A + N_{PT})$ bits. Finally, the examples are encoded using the costs in Table 3.

---

[2] $L^*(X) = \log_2^*(X) + \log_2(c)$, where $c \simeq 2.865064$, is a code length for an arbitrary integer. $\log_2^*(X) = \log_2(X) + \log_2(\log_2(X)) + \ldots$ summing only positive terms Rissanen (1983).

Table 3. Costs of MDL example coding

- For each value leaf in the forest
  - Encode each example using $-\log_2(p_{i,j})$ bits

where,

- i is the number of examples of this class we've seen so far in this leaf
- j is the total number of examples seen so far in this leaf
- M is the number of classes
- $p_{i,j} = \frac{i+1}{j+M}$

5 Experiments

We tested Lumberjack using standard supervised learning experiments. We compared the generalization accuracy of a decision tree learner and Lumberjack, each using the same MDL coding. The results are shown in Figs. 3 and 4. The graphs show the averages over 10 trials. We tested for significance using a paired Wilcoxon rank-sum test ($p = 0.05$).

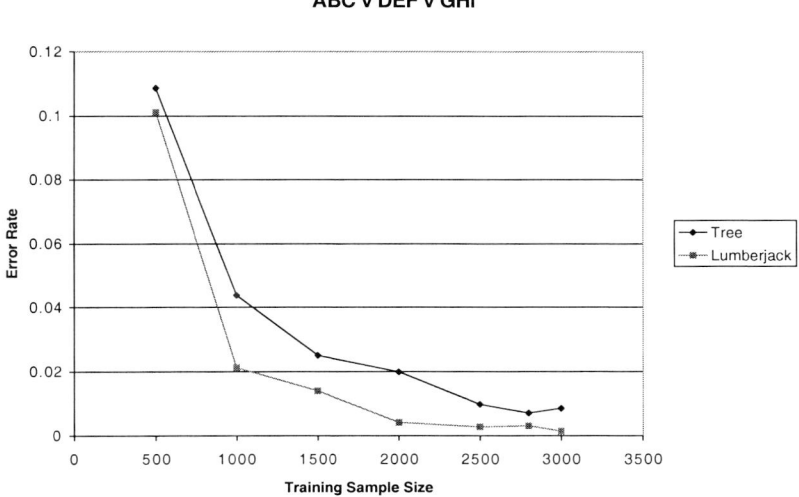

Fig. 3. Experimental results learning the concept $ABC \vee DEF \vee GHI$

The first set of results are for the boolean function $ABC \vee DEF \vee GHI$. Training samples were sampled with replacement from the concept, then the output was flipped in 10% of the samples. The testing dataset was a complete dataset without noise. Results are shown in Fig. 3. The difference in error rate between the tree and forest algorithms is significant for sample sizes 1000 through 2500 inclusive, and also for the 3000 sample dataset.[3]

The second set of results uses a dataset generated by mapping a reinforcement learning problem back into a supervised learning problem. In this domain a two legged robot learns to walk about a simple 10×10 maze. The Robot cannot slide its feet along the ground, nor can it hover with two feet in the air - it requires a sequence of movements to walk. The robot knows its X, Y location and the ΔX, ΔY and ΔHeight differences between its legs. There are eight actions; the robot can raise or lower either foot or it can move the raised foot, if any, in any of the compass directions. This problem was fed into a traditional Markov Decision Problem algorithm, and the resulting policy was used as a dataset for our supervised learning experiment. The domain is discrete - the Δ's each have only 3 possible values, and the X, Y location was encoded using a series of variables $\{X < 1, X < 2, \ldots, X < 9, Y < 1, Y < 2, \ldots, Y < 9\}$. This coding is similar to the one implicitly used by C4.5 for continuous variables. Training datasets were generated by randomly sampling, with replacement, from this true dataset. The testing dataset was the full true dataset.

Again the results, in Fig. 4, are the averages over 10 trials. There is a significant difference between the two algorithms for sample sizes of 2000 or more. While the results at sample size 4000 are still significant, it is clear that both al-

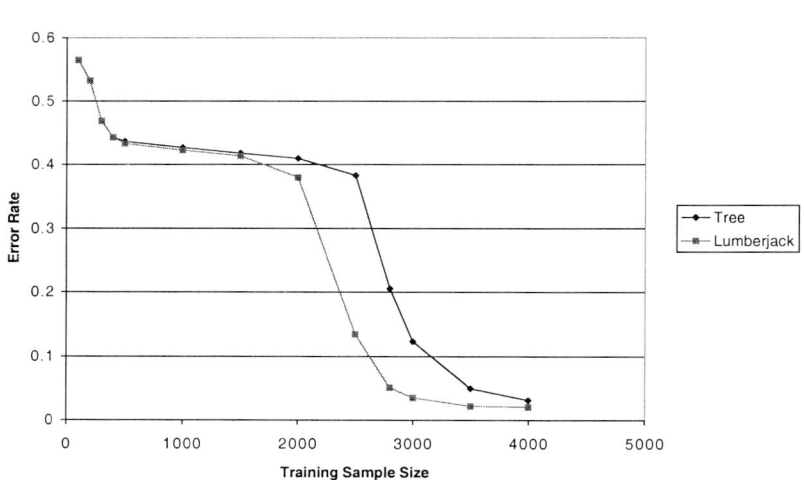

Fig. 4. Experimental results learning a policy to walk through a maze

---

[3] We also compared with C4.5. C4.5 is always significantly better than the MDL tree learning system. This is a well known deficiency of MDL vs. C4.5 and is orthogonal to the use of Lumberjack style decomposition. With 1000 or more datapoints, C4.5 and Lumberjack perform similarly.

gorithms are converging again as sample size increases; the tree has enough data to grow the repeated structure. Looking at the forest for large sample sizes it is possible to see the separation of structure representing the maze from structure representing the ability to walk.

6 Conclusion

We have introduced a new tree-based representation, the linked decision forest, and a learning algorithm, Lumberjack that can use the linked forest representation. This representation doesn't need to repeat substructure leading to more efficient use of data.

The Lumberjack algorithm combines SEQUITUR style decomposition with decision tree learning. Unlike decision graph generation algorithms, Lumberjack only decomposes internal nodes in the forest. This improves the representational power of Lumberjack over decision graph algorithms, but this comes at a price: Lumberjack currently does not join leaves even when this would be useful. We have empirically shown improved generalization accuracy over a simple tree.

References

Leo Breiman, Jerome H. Friedman, Richard A. Olshen, and Charles J. Stone. *Classification And Regression Trees*. Wadsworth and Brooks/Cole Advanced Books and Software, Monterey, CA, 1984.

Randal E. Bryant. Symbolic boolean manipulation with ordered binary decision diagrams. *ACM Computing Surveys*, 24(3):293–318, 1992.

David Chapman and Leslie Pack Kaelbling. Input generalization in delayed reinforcement learning: An algorithm and performance comparisons. In *Proceedings of the Twelfth International Joint Conference on Artificial Intelligence (IJCAI-91)*, pages 726–731, Sydney, Australia, 1991.

Jesse Hoey, Robert St-Aubin, Alan Hu, and Craig Boutilier. Spudd: Stochastic planning using decision diagrams. In *Fifteenth Conference on Uncertainty in Artificial Intelligence (UAI-99)*, Stockholm, Sweden, 1999. Morgan Kaufmann.

Ron Kohavi. *Wrappers for Performance Enhancement and Oblivious Decision Graphs*. Ph. d. thesis, Department of Computer Science, Stanford University, 1995.

Andrew Kachites McCallum. *Reinforcement Learning with Selective Perception and Hidden State*. PhD thesis, Department of Computer Science, University of Rochester, 1995.

Patrick M. Murphy and Michael J. Pazzani. Exploring the decision forest: An empirical invesitgation of occam's razor in decision tree induction. *Journal of Artificial Intelligence Research*, 1:257–275, 1994.

Craig G. Nevill-Manning and Ian H. Witten. Identifying hierarchical structures in sequences: A linear-time algorithm. *Journal of Artificial Intelligence Research*, 7:67–82, 1997.

Craig G. Nevill-Manning. *Inferring Sequential Structure*. Ph. d. thesis, Computer Science, University of Waikato, Hamilton, New Zealand, 1996.

J. Oliver and C. S. Wallace. Inferring decision graphs. Technical Report 91/170, Department of Computer Science, Monash University, November 1992.

Giulia Pagallo and David Haussler. Boolean feature discovery in empirical learning. *Machine Learning*, 5:71–99, 1990.

J. R. Quinlan and R. L. Rivest. Inferring decision trees using the minimum description length principle. *Information and Computation*, 80(3):227–248, 1989.

J. Ross Quinlan. *C4.5: Programs for Machine Learning*. Morgan Kaufmann, San Mateo, CA, 1992.

Jorma Rissanen. A universal prior for integers and estimation by minimum description length. *The Annals of Statistics*, 11(2):416–431, 1983.

William T. B. Uther and Manuela M. Veloso. Tree based discretization for continuous state space reinforcement learning. In *Proceedings of the Fifteenth National Conference on Artificial Intelligence (AAAI-98)*, pages 769–774, Madison, WI, 1998.

William T. B. Uther and Manuela M. Veloso. The lumberjack algorithm for learning linked decision forests. In *Symposium on Abstraction, Reformulation and Approximation (SARA-2000)*, volume 1864 of *Lecture Notes in Artificial Intelligence*. Springer Verlag, 2000.

C. S. Wallace and D. M. Boulton. An information measure for classification. *Computer Journal*, 11(2):185–194, 1968.

C. S. Wallace and J. D. Patrick. Coding decision trees. *Machine Learning*, 11:7–22, 1993.

Efficient Iris Recognition System by Optimization of Feature Vectors and Classifier

Shinyoung Lim[1], Kwanyong Lee[1], Okhwan Byeon[2], Taiyun Kim[3]

[1]Electronic Commerce Team, Electronics and Telecommunications Research Institute,
Gajong-dong, Yusong-gu, Taejon, 305-600, Korea
{sylim, kylee}@econos.etri.re.kr
[2]KORDIC, # 1, Uheun-dong, Yusong-gu, Taejon, 305-333, Korea
ohbyeon@garam.kreonet.re.kr
[3]Department of Computer Science, Korea University, Seoul, Korea
tykim@netlab.korea.ac.kr

Abstract. This paper presents an efficient system for recognizing the identity of a living person on the basis of iris patterns that are one of the physiological and biological features with high reliability. After various preprocessing are conducted for the iris data acquired by a CCD camera and an image grabber, feature vectors are extracted using Wavelet transform. A competitive learning neural network is used to classify the patterns. To represent the iris pattern efficiently, a new method for optimizing the dimension of feature vectors is proposed without any influence to the system performance. In order to increase the recognition accuracy of competitive learning algorithm, an efficient initialization of the weight vectors and a new method to determine the winner are also proposed. With all of these novel mechanisms, the experimental results showed that the proposed system could be used for personal identification in an efficient and effective manner.

1. Introduction

To control access to secured areas or materials, reliable personal identification infrastructure is required. Conventional methods of recognizing the identity of person by using a password or cards are not altogether reliable. The reason is they can be forgotten or stolen. Biometric technology, which is based on biological and physiological features of human such as face, fingerprints, hand shape, signature and eyes, has now been considered as an alternative to extant systems in a great deal of application domains. The automated human recognition systems can be applied to such application domains as the alternative of passwords or ID cards, entrance management for a specified areas, and airport security checking system.

Iris patterns have been focused for the last few decades in biometric technology in which human features should be stable and distinctive in order to be a good feature for personal identification. That is because every iris has a fine and unique pattern and doesn't change over time since 2 or 3 years after the birth, so it might be called as a kind of optical fingerprint[1][2]. Compared with the fingerprint recognition, the human iris recognition can obtain the images at a distance from a camera without any physical contact since the iris is an overt body. Fig. 1 shows an image of human iris patterns.

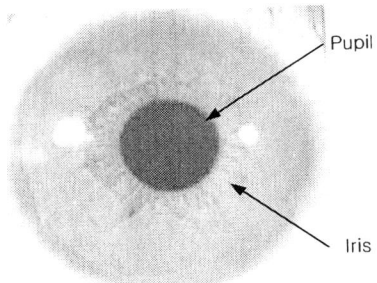

Fig. 1. Image of human iris

Most of works on personal identification and verification by iris patterns have been done in the 1990s [3-7]. Some works have limited capabilities in recognizing the identity of a person accurately and efficiently, so there is much room for improvement of some technologies affecting performance in a practical light.

In this paper, we propose some efficient and robust methods for improving the performance from the practical viewpoint. To achieve the efficiency of the proposed system, we conduct the related works: the performance evaluation of the popular feature extraction methods - Gabor transform and Haar wavelet transform - to select a good method suitable for iris patterns, the optimization of the dimension of feature vectors by using the selected feature extraction method, and the performance improvement of a competitive learning neural network by some novel mechanisms.

2. Analysis and Recognition of Iris Image

The overall structure of the proposed system is illustrated in Fig. 2, and its processing flow is as follows. At first, an image surrounding human eye region is obtained at a distance from a CCD camera without any physical contact to the device. In the preprocessing phase, the following steps are taken. First, we detect eyelids and exclude them if they intrude, and eliminate the reflected light caused by the environmental illumination. Second, we should localize an iris, the portion of the image to be processed actually. Last, the normal coordination system of the image is converted into the polar coordination system so as to facilitate the feature extraction process. In the feature extraction phase, 2-D wavelet transform is used to extract a feature vector from the iris image. In the final phase, the identification and verification phase, a revised competitive learning method is exploited to classify the feature vectors and recognize the identity of a person. In order to improve the efficiency of the system, some novel methods are applied to the feature extraction phase and the identification phase.

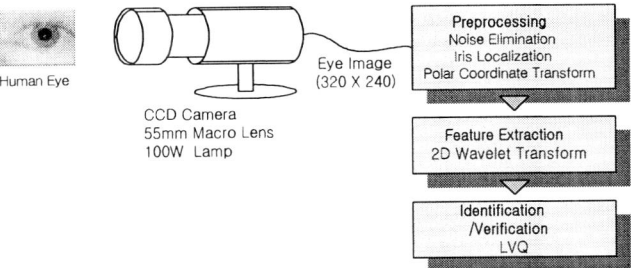

Fig. 2. The proposed iris recognition system

2.1. Preprocessing Phase

We should first check whether eyelids intrude the image, and then exclude them if they are. The reflected light resulted from the environmental illumination is eliminated by blurring and enhancing the image with a threshold (see Fig. 3). After eliminating noises, we determine an iris part of the image by localizing the portion of the image derived from inside the limbus (outer boundary) and outside the pupil (inner boundary). To localize an iris, it is required to find the center of the pupil and it is also used to convert the iris into polar coordination system. When the center of the pupil is found, we find the inner boundary and the outer boundary by extending the radius of a circle from the center of pupil and checking the intensity of the background. Fig. 4 shows the two boundaries for the image of Fig. 3.

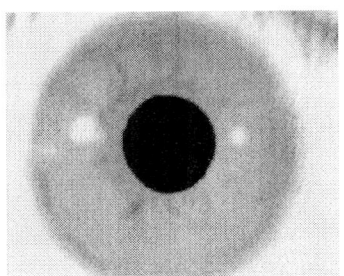
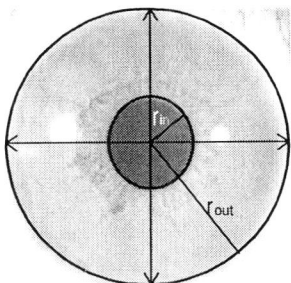

Fig. 3. Blurred and enhanced iris image

Fig. 4. Process of finding the inner and outer boundaries from the center of the pupil

The localized iris part of the image is transformed into polar coordination system to extract features in an efficient way. The portion of the pupil is excluded from the conversion process because it has no biological characteristics at all. Fig. 5 shows the process of converting the orthogonal coordination system into the polar coordination system for the iris image. By increasing the angle θ by $0.8°$ for an arbitrary radius r, we obtain 450 values. We can get a 450×60 iris image for the plane (θ, r) by repeating this process until the radius is increased to 60.

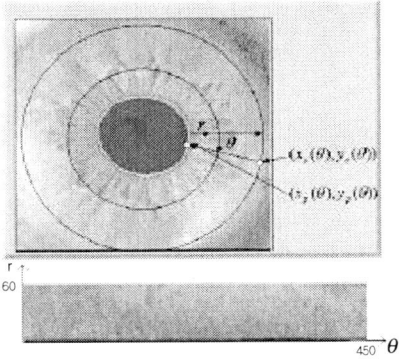

Fig. 5. Representation of iris image by polar coordination system

2.2. Feature Extraction Phase

Gabor transform is generally used for extracting feature vector from human iris patterns[3]. In this paper, Wavelet transform [8-10], which is widely used for many applications in signal processing nowadays, is used to extract features vector from human iris image. Among the six mother wavelets, we use Harr wavelet illustrated in Fig. 6 as a basis function.

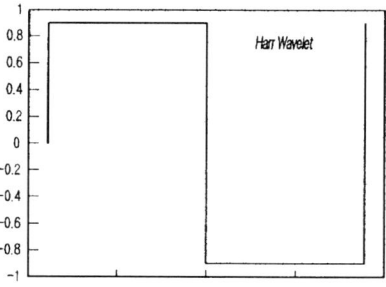

Fig. 6. Harr Mother Wavelet

After finishing the preprocessing, we apply Haar wavelet transform to the image represented by the polar coordination system to obtain a feature vectors.

For the iris image with the size of 450×60 obtained from the preprocessing, we apply wavelet transform four times in order to get a 28×3 subimage with the same properties of the original iris image. Finally, we organize the feature vector by combining 84 features of the highpass filter of the fourth transform and the average values of three remaining parts. The dimension of the resulting feature vector is 87, which means that we can represent an iris pattern with only 87 bits. Fig. 7 shows the conceptual process of obtaining the feature vector with the optimized dimension.

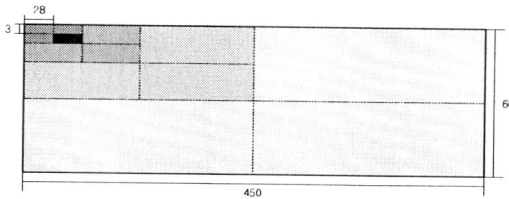

Fig. 7. Conceptual diagram of Wavelet transform of human iris image

2.3. Identification and Verification Phase

In general, the competitive learning neural network like LVQ has the faster learning mechanism than error backpropagation algorithm but its performance is easily affected by initial weight vectors[11][12].

To solve such a problem for at least iris patterns, a new method for initializing the initial weight vectors in an effective manner is proposed. This method generates the initial vectors that can be located around the boundary of each class. In the learning process, the usual learning process for LVQ is accomplished after initializing the weight vectors by the proposed method. In the recognition process, we set the acceptance level and use it to determine whether the final result is accepted or rejected.

The process of the proposed initialization algorithm, what we called the uniform distribution of initial weight vectors is as follows. (see Fig. 8)

Step 1 Set initial weight vectors with the vector of the first training data of each class and other weight vectors to be zero.

$$W_1^k = X_1^k \quad for \quad k = 1,2,...M$$

, where

X_1^k : the vector of the first input data of the k - th class.

W_1^k : the first weight vector of the k - th class

M : the number of class.

Step 2 Select another data of each class as a new training data

Step 3 Calculate the distance d_j between the training data and the weight vector by the following equation.

$$d_j^2 = \sum_{i=0}^{N-1}(X_{ip}^k - W_{ij}^k)^2$$

, where

X_{ip}^{k} : the i - th component of the p - th learning data of k - th class

W_{ij}^{k} : the i - th component of the j - th weight vector of k - th class

N : the dimension of a training data

Step 4 Determine whether the class of the weight vector with the minimum distance among all d_j is equal to the class of the training data. If the class of the weight vector is not equal to the class of the training data, then add the vector of the training data as a new weight vector.

Step 5 Goto step 2 until all of the training data are used in the learning process.

The winner selection method based on Euclidean distance that is generally used in competitive learning neural networks has no problem in determining the minimum distance of each class. However, if the dimension of feature vectors is increased, it has high possibility of selecting a wrong winner because of the failure of obtaining the information on each dimension. To solve such a problem, a new algorithm of winner selection called multidimensional winner selection method is proposed. The proposed algorithm is to determine the winner of each dimension, count the frequency of becoming the winner according to each class, and then select a class with the largest value as the final winner. Fig. 9 shows the conceptual diagram of the proposed winner selection method. In the figure, a plate in a neuron indicates a feature dimension.

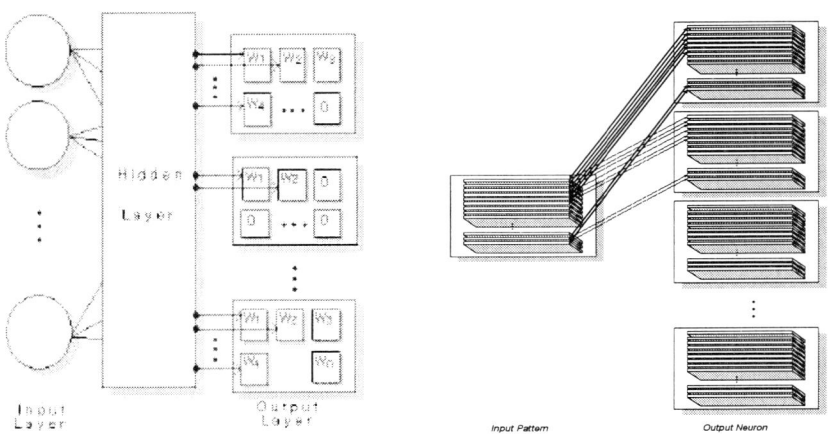

Fig. 8. Concept of the uniform distribution of initial weight vectors

Fig. 9. Conceptual Diagram of Multi-dimensional Winner Selection Algorithm

3. Experimental Results

To evaluate the performance of the proposed human iris recognition system, we used the image set contained 2000 iris images consisting of 100 subjects at each of twenty images. A half of them is used as the training data for LVQ and the remaining half as the test data. The parameters used in LVQ such as the learning rate and the iteration number are shown in Table 1.

Table 1. Parameters for LVQ

Initial learning rate	0.1
Update of learning rate	$\alpha(t) = \alpha(0)(1 - \dfrac{t}{\text{total number of iteration}})$
Total iteration	300

Under the experimental environments above, the following subsections describe the results on each phase or the proposed methods.

3.1. Feature Extraction Method

Table 2 shows the recognition rate on two different feature extraction methods, Gabor transform and Haar wavelet transform, under the same classifier. The difference of recognition rate on the training data is hard to find, but in case of the test data, the recognition rate of wavelet transform is better than that of Gabor transform by 2.1%.

Table 2. Comparison of two feature extraction methods

	Gabor Transform	Wavelet Transform
Training data	95.8 %	96.2 %
Test data	92.3 %	94.4 %

3.2. Weight Vector Initialization Method

On the basis of the result of Table 2, Haar wavelet transform is chosen as a method for extracting feature vectors. Table 3 shows the results on the accuracy comparison of two initialization methods under the same experimental environments. In the case of the proposed method called the uniform distribution of initial weight vectors, the experimental results on both the training data and the test data show better performance than that of the initialization with random values which is regarded as a common initialization method.

Table 3. Comparison of weight vector initialization methods

	Initialization with random values	Proposed method
Training data	96.2 %	96.8 %
Test data	94.4 %	97.0 %

3.3. Winner Selection Method

Table 4 shows the experimental results on two winner selection methods when we use Haar wavelet transform for feature extraction and LVQ with the proposed initialization method. You can see that the proposed method, the multidimensional method showed a good result for human iris features.

Table 4. Comparison of winner selection methods

	Euclidian distance method	Multi-dimensional method
Training Data	96.8 %	98.1 %
Test Data	97.0 %	97.6 %

3.4. Size of Feature Vector

From the three experimental results of 3.1, 3.2, and 3.3, we selected each method with high accuracy to configure a good system for personal identification based on iris patterns. The selected methods for each phase are as follows; Haar wavelet transform for feature extraction, uniform distribution method for initializing weight vectors, and multidimensional method for winner selection.

Under the iris recognition system with these methods, we try to minimize or optimize the dimension of feature vector without any influence to the recognition accuracy. Our current size of a feature vector is 93 dimensions, each of which takes 4 bytes. However, we proposed a new feature extraction process as mentioned in 2.2. This method can efficiently represent a feature vector with 87 dimensions and it requires only one bit per dimension. Table 5 shows the performance evaluation according to the size of a feature vector.

Table 5. Performance evaluation according to the size of feature vectors

	93 dimension (4 bytes/dimension)	87 dimension (1 bit/dimension)
Training Data	98.1 %	98.1 %
Test Data	97.6 %	97.7 %

All of the experimental results on the proposed methods are summarized in Table 6.

Table 6. Performance evaluation on the propsed methods

Comparison Factors	Feature Extraction	Gabor transform	Wavelet transform			
	Recognition	Initializaiton with random values	Uniform distribution of initial weight			
		Eucledian distance-based winner selection			Multi-dimensional Winner Selection	
	Size of Feature Vector	93 dimension (4 bytes/dimension : 2976 bits)				87 dimension (1bit/dimension) 87 bits
Performance	Success Ratio of Training Data	95.8 %	96.2 %	96.8 %	98.1 %	98.1 %
	Success Ratio of Test Data	92.3 %	94.4 %	97.0 %	97.6 %	97.7 %

4. Conclusions

In this paper, an efficient method for personal identification and verification by means of human iris patterns is presented. To process the iris patterns in an efficient and effective way against existing methods, the following works are conducted; First, two methods - Gabor transform and Haar wavelet transform which are widely used for extracting features - are evaluated. Haar wavelet transform had better performance than Gabor transform. Second, Harr wavelet transform is used for optimizing the dimension of feature vectors in order to reduce processing time and space. With only 87 bits, we could represent an iris pattern without any influence to the system performance. Last, we improved the accuracy of a classifier, a competitive learning neural network, by proposing an initialization method of the weight vectors and a new winner selection method. Thanks to these methods, we could increase the recognition performance to 97.7% for the test data. From the experimental results, we convince that the proposed system can be applied to the various real applications.

References

[1] Adler F. H., *Physiology of the Eye: Clinical Application*, The C. V. Mosby Company, 1965.
[2] Hallinan P. W., "Recognizing Human Eyes", *SPIE Proc. Geometric Methods in Computer Vision*, 1570, pp. 214-226, 1991.
[3] John G. D., "High Confidence Visual Recognition of Persons by a Test of Statistical Independence", *IEEE Trans. on Pattern Analysis and Machine Intelligence*, 15(11), pp. 1148-1161, 1993.
[4] Wildes, R.P., "Iris Recognition: An Emerging Biometric Technology", *Proc. of the IEEE*, 85(9), pp.1348-1363, 1997
[5] Boles, W.W. and Boashash, B., "A Human Identification Technique Using Images of the Iris and Wavelet Transform", *IEEE Trans. on Signal Processing*, 46(4), pp.1185-1188, 1998

[6] Williams, G.O., "Iris Recognition Technology", *IEEE Aerospace and Electronics Systems Magazine*, 12(4), pp.23-29, 1997
[7] Wildes, R.P., et.al, "A System for Automated Iris Recognition", *Proc. of the Second IEEE Workshop on Applications of Computer Vision*, pp.121-128, 1994
[8] Randy K. Y., *Wavelet Theory and Its Application*, Kluwer Academic Publisher, 1992.
[9] Rioul O. and Vetterli M., "Wavelet and Signal Processing", *IEEE Signal Processing Magazine*, pp. 14-38, October 1981.
[10] Gilbert S. and Truong N., *Wavelets and Filter Banks*, Wellesley-Cambridge Press, 1996.
[11] Fausset L., *Fundamentals of Neural Networks*, Prentice Hall, 1994.
[12] Kohonen T., *The Self-organization and Associate Memory*, Springer-Verlag, 1985

A Classifier Fitness Measure Based on Bayesian Likelihoods: An Approach to the Problem of Learning from Positives Only

Andrew Skabar[1], Anthony Maeder[1], and Binh Pham[2]

[1]School of Electrical & Electronic Systems Engineering, [2]Faculty of Information Technology
Queensland University of Technology
GPO Box 2434, Brisbane QLD 4001, Australia
{a.skabar, a.maeder, b.pham}@qut.edu.au

Abstract. A classifier evaluation function based on Bayesian likelihoods of necessity and sufficiency is defined. This function can be used to measure the performance of an arbitrary classifier on a set of examples consisting of labeled positives together with a corpus of unlabeled data. A neural network system has been implemented in which the evaluation function is used as a heuristic to guide search through the space of network weight configurations. Results are presented from testing the system on three artificial datasets. The results are comparable to those that can be obtained using back-propagation, despite the fact that the latter method requires labeled counter-examples.

1 Introduction

Inductive learning techniques attempt to derive knowledge from a set of training examples contained in a database. Each *example* or *instance* in the database can be thought of as representing a point in an *attribute-based space* in which each field corresponds to a single *attribute* or *feature*, and the set of legal values for a given field constitutes the *domain* for that attribute. The aim of inductive learning is to discover a set of rules, or some other representational structure, which can be used to predict the class membership of novel examples. If the class membership of the training examples is utilised by the learning algorithm the learning is said to be *supervised*, otherwise it is *unsupervised*.

Algorithms commonly used for supervised learning include decision tree induction algorithms such as C4.5 [1] and CART [2], sequential covering algorithms such as the AQ family of algorithms [3], and the back-propagation algorithm for training feed-forward artificial neural networks [4]. Each of these algorithms requires that the training set used for learning contains sufficient examples representative of each of the classes in the learning domain. In the case of learning a single class description only, we say that the algorithm requires examples of the class to be learned, as well as known (i.e. labeled) *counter-examples*.

Our research into this area is motivated by the existence of a class of problems in which it is impossible to supply known counter-examples of the class whose description is to be learned. For example, consider the problem of using sightings of a rare animal species to identify its probable habitat. The attributes in this case are the environmental conditions that can be used to describe habitat; the class description we wish to discover is the combination of these attribute values that describes the habitat of the species. Sightings correspond to positive examples as they associate the presence of the animal species with a particular set of conditions. However because sightings are a rare event, we would be reluctant to assume that failure to observe the animal over a particular set of environmental conditions indicates conclusively that this combination of attribute values is not part of the animal's normal habitat. That is, we cannot conclusively claim that any particular combination of conditions constitutes a counter-example of the class that we wish to describe.

In previous work [5], we have presented a symbolic approach to this problem. Genetic search [6, 7] through the space of class descriptions (expressed in the VL1 concept description language [3]) was guided by a heuristic which evaluates competing descriptions according to (i) the proportion of labeled positives correctly predicted, and (ii) a clustering bias factor that favours class descriptions that result in high interclass separation between positively and negatively classified instances. The use of a symbolic knowledge representation allowed for efficient calculation of clustering quality, because the distance of a negatively classified instance from the positive membership boundary could be computed simply by summing the number of unmatched attributes. However, there is no equivalent means of efficiently computing the clustering quality in the case of sub-symbolic representations (i.e. neural networks).

In this paper we describe how Bayesian likelihoods of necessity and sufficiency can be used to define an evaluation function for measuring the performance of an arbitrary classifier in classification tasks in which only positive examples appear with training labels. The function favours classifiers that represent decision boundaries for which the odds of labeled positive examples and unlabeled examples being contained within the decision boundary are respectively high and low. Intuitively, this can be thought of a search for a classification boundary, such that containment within this boundary is both a sufficient and necessary condition for predicting positive class membership. Because the function is based on overall classification statistics acquired using a generate-and-test procedure, it can be applied to sub-symbolic, as well as symbolic, knowledge representations.

In Section 2 we derive the evaluation function based on Bayesian likelihoods of necessity and sufficiency. Section 3 describes how this evaluation function can be implemented as a fitness function in an evolutionary search through the space of network weights configurations. Section 4 describes three datasets constructed for testing this approach, and provides results comparing performance with that of a standard supervised learning technique. The results are discussed in Section 5, and are followed by a concluding section.

2 Measuring Classifier Performances Using Bayesian Likelihoods

Classifier learning can be viewed as the problem of discovering a decision boundary in attribute space that can be used to discriminate between objects belonging to a target class and objects not belonging to the target class. The decision boundary could be described symbolically in terms of rules or a decision tree, or else it could be represented sub-symbolically in the weights of a neural network. In this section we show how Bayesian likelihoods of necessity and sufficiency can be used to define an evaluation function for measuring the performance of an arbitrary classifier on a set of examples consisting of labeled positives together with a corpus of unlabeled positive and negative examples.

Let $Pr(P)$ represent the *prior* probability that an example belongs to the target class (i.e. the positive class), and let $Pr(P|C)$ represent the *posterior* probability of an example belonging to the target class given that the example falls within some decision boundary describing positive class membership. A link between the posterior and prior probabilities is provided by Bayes' Theorem:

$$Pr(P|C) = \frac{Pr(P) \times Pr(C|P)}{Pr(C)} \quad (1)$$

Similarly, the posterior probability of NOT belonging to the positive class is given by

$$Pr(\overline{P}|C) = \frac{Pr(\overline{P}) \times Pr(C|\overline{P})}{Pr(C)} \quad (2)$$

Dividing (1) by (2) gives

$$\frac{Pr(P|C)}{Pr(\overline{P}|C)} = \frac{Pr(P)}{Pr(\overline{P})} \times \frac{Pr(C|P)}{Pr(C|\overline{P})} \quad (3)$$

Defining the *prior odds* as $O(P) = Pr(P)/Pr(\overline{P})$ and the *posterior odds* as $O(P|C) = Pr(P|C)/Pr(\overline{P}|C)$, Equation 3 can be written as

$$O(P|C) = O(P) \times \frac{Pr(C|P)}{Pr(C|\overline{P})} \quad (4)$$

The odds of an example being a positive, given that it is not contained within the class boundary can be expressed similarly

$$O(P|\overline{C}) = O(P) \times \frac{Pr(\overline{C}|P)}{Pr(\overline{C}|\overline{P})} \quad (5)$$

The ratio $P(C|P)/P(C|\overline{P})$ in Equation (4) is often called the *likelihood of sufficiency* (*LS*). As the value of this ratio approaches ∞, the posterior odds of an example being positive given that it is contained within the decision boundary also approaches ∞. That is, the higher the value of LS, the greater is the sufficiency of containment within the decision boundary for determining positive class membership. Similarly, the ratio $Pr(\overline{C} \mid P) / Pr(\overline{C} \mid \overline{P})$ in Equation (5) is called the *likelihood of necessity* (LN). As the value of this ratio approaches 0, so too does the posterior odds of an example not being positive, given that it is not contained within the decision boundary. LN thus provides a measure of the *necessity* of containment within the class boundary for determining positive class membership.

Intuitively we would like the *likelihood of sufficiency* (LS) due to a particular decision boundary to be high (i.e. $LS >> 1$) and the *likelihood of necessity* (LN) to be small ($0 < LN << 1$). This is equivalent to stating that we wish containment within the decision boundary to significantly increase our confidence that an example is positive, and non-containment within the decision boundary to significantly decrease our confidence that an example is positive. This suggests that a measure of a class boundary's capacity for discriminating between classes be defined as the ratio of LS to LN. The fitness of a class boundary corresponding to a classifier Φ can thus be expressed as

$$f(\Phi) = \frac{LS}{LN} \tag{6}$$

which is equivalent to

$$f(\Phi) = \frac{O(C \mid P)}{O(C \mid \overline{P})} \tag{7}$$

Evaluation of this function still requires that we have labeled positives (P) as well as labeled negatives, ($\overline{P}$). We now derive an expression involving L (the set of *labeled* positive examples) and $\overline{L}$ (the set of *unlabeled* positive and negative examples) which can be shown to be a lower bound on $f(\Phi)$.

If we make the assumption that the set of labeled positives is representative of the set of all positives (which is the assumption made by all machine learning techniques), then $O(C \mid P) \approx O(C \mid L)$. Also, since the set of unlabeled examples, ($\overline{L}$), includes positive examples as well as negative examples, the odds of a negative example being contained within the decision boundary will in general be less than the odds of an example which is not a labeled positive being contained within the boundary; that is, $O(C \mid \overline{P}) \leq O(C \mid \overline{L})$. This means that $O(C \mid P) / O(C \mid \overline{P})$ is greater than or equal to $O(C \mid L) / O(C \mid \overline{L})$. Therefore, because $O(C \mid L) / O(C \mid \overline{L})$ is a lower bound on $O(C \mid P) / O(C \mid \overline{P})$ it is sufficient to maximise $O(C \mid L) / O(C \mid \overline{L})$.

This leads to the following expression for the fitness of a class decision boundary corresponding to a classifier Φ:

$$f(\Phi) = \frac{\sum_{x \in L} \delta(x, \Phi)}{\left(n(L) - \sum_{x \in L} \delta(x, \Phi)\right)} \times \frac{\left(n(U) - \sum_{x \in U} \delta(x, \Phi)\right)}{\sum_{x \in U} \delta(x, \Phi)} \quad (8)$$

where

$$\delta(x, \Phi) = \begin{cases} 1 & \text{if } x \text{ is contained within class boundary } \Phi \\ 0 & \text{if } x \text{ is not contained within class boundary } \Phi \end{cases}$$

L is the set of labeled (positive) examples
U is the set of unlabeled (positive and negative) examples
$n(L)$ is the number of labeled examples
$n(U)$ is the number of unlabeled examples

Note that the fitness function in Equation 8 is undefined if the denominator in either of the factors is equal to 0. To avoid this problem, if a denominator evaluates to 0 we assign it a value of 0.5. This enables the same functional form to be maintained, while preventing the asymptotic behaviour.

In principle, this evaluation function can be implemented in either a rule based or neural network based system. The only restriction is that the search method used to explore the space of classifiers must be based on a generate-and-test procedure. That is, a classifier must be generated in its entirety before its measure of performance can be measured using the evaluation function. In the next section we describe the implementation of this evaluation function within a neural network system.

3 Neural Networks

A neural network consists of many self-adjusting processing elements called neurons co-operating in a densely interconnected network. The basic function of a single neuron is to perform a weighted sum of its inputs, x_1 to x_n, and to produce an output if this weighted sum is greater than a *threshold* value. This threshold can be thought of as a *bias* on the neuron, and can be implemented by defining an extra input, x_0, which is always set to one. The weight on this input represents the bias applied to the neuron. Each neuron generates a single output signal that is transmitted to other neurons.

Neural networks typically contain three or more layers: an input layer consisting of fanning units that receive input signals and distribute them to a hidden layer; one or more hidden layers which sum the weighted inputs and perform non-linear transformations; and an output layer that sums the weighted results of the non-linear transformations and produces outputs. Each unit in the output is representative of one class. After presenting an input pattern to the neural network, classification is performed by assigning the example to the class with the strongest response in the output layer. In the case of learning a single class boundary, only one node is required in the output layer.

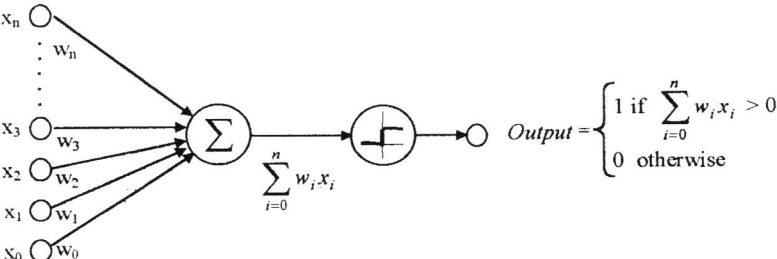

Fig. 1. A single neuron receives a set of weighted inputs and produces an output. Note that if back-propagation is not being used for training the network, it is not necessary that the activation function be differentiable (e.g. sigmoidal)

Neural networks are capable of describing arbitrarily complex decision boundaries in n-dimensional space, where n is the number of inputs to the network. In general, a neural network with one hidden layer is capable of representing a convex hull; that is, an open or closed region in which any point can be connected to any other point by a straight line that does not cross the boundary of the region. In the case of a network with two hidden layers, each neuron in the second hidden layer receives an input that describes a convex hull. This means that the output of the network will be a combination of the convex regions received as input at the second hidden layer.

The most widely used algorithm for discovering the neural network weights is the back-propagation algorithm [4]. This algorithm calculates the error at each output node for a particular input, and this error is back-propagated from one layer to the previous one. The weights for a particular unit are then adjusted proportionally to the error in the units to which it is connected.

3.1 Discovering Network Weights Using Genetic Algorithms

The absence of labeled counter-examples to include in a training set directly prohibits the use of back-propagation. Because the error at the output can only be calculated for positive examples, back-propagation will simply proceed unhindered until all of the training examples have been classified as positive. This will clearly lead to overgeneralisation as there is no specialization process to oppose the thrust toward generalization. An alternative to back-propagation is to use some type of parameter optimization technique to discover an optimal set of neural network weights.

Genetic algorithms [6] are robust search and optimisation techniques based on the mechanics of natural selection. They combine survival of the fittest with mechanisms for the generation of new candidates to form search algorithms. Unlike gradient descent methods such as back-propagation in which search is biased towards a locally optimal solution, the robustness of genetic algorithms is due to their capacity to locate a global optimum in a multi-modal landscape.

Representation of a set of weights as a binary string is relatively straightforward. An individual in the genetic search population consists of n by l bits, where n is the number of weights required from the topology of the network, and l is the number of bits used in the representation of a single weight. Individual weights are represented by mapping an unsigned integer encoding linearly from $[0, 2^l]$ to a specified interval $[E_{min}, E_{max}]$. Thus E_{min} is mapped to the binary representation of 0, E_{max} maps to the binary representation of the integer $2^l - 1$, and other values map linearly in between.

Search is performed as per standard genetic search. An initial population of individuals is generated. These individuals are then decoded and evaluated according to a fitness metric based on the evaluation function defined above. The fitter individuals are then chosen to undergo reproduction, crossover, and mutation operations in order to produce a population of children for the next generation. This procedure is continued until either convergence is achieved, or a sufficiently fit individual has been discovered. Further information on genetic algorithms can be found in [6] and [7].

4 Experiments

The technique has been applied to three two-dimensional datasets that we have assembled for testing purposes. Each dataset contains 600 examples over two continuous variables which each take a value between 0.0 and 1.0. Of the 600 examples in each dataset, 100 are labeled positives, 250 are unlabeled positives and 250 are unlabeled negatives[1]. All examples were generated using a random procedure. Figure 2 illustrates the three datasets. The dashed line in each diagram represents the region corresponding to positive class membership.

For comparison purposes, back-propagation was also used to discover a classification boundary for each of the datasets. In this case, the training set consisted of the same labeled positives as for the Bayesian case with an additional 100 labeled negatives also being used for training. The test set consisted of the 500 examples that appeared unlabeled in the Bayesian case.

The Bayesian approach does not require the tuning of any parameters other than those associated with the genetic search. These parameters were set as follows: population size = 200; crossover rate = 0.5; and mutation rate = 0.005. The number of bits used to represent weights was 8. Accuracy is taken to be the performance of the best individual found after 1000 generations. In the case of back-propagation, the target error was set at 0.5. This means that an output value greater than 0.5 was classified as a positive, and an output less than 0.5 was classified as a negative. Training proceeded until 100% accuracy had been achieved on training examples.

---

[1] All 600 examples were generated with class labels, but 500 of these had their class label hidden from the learning algorithm.

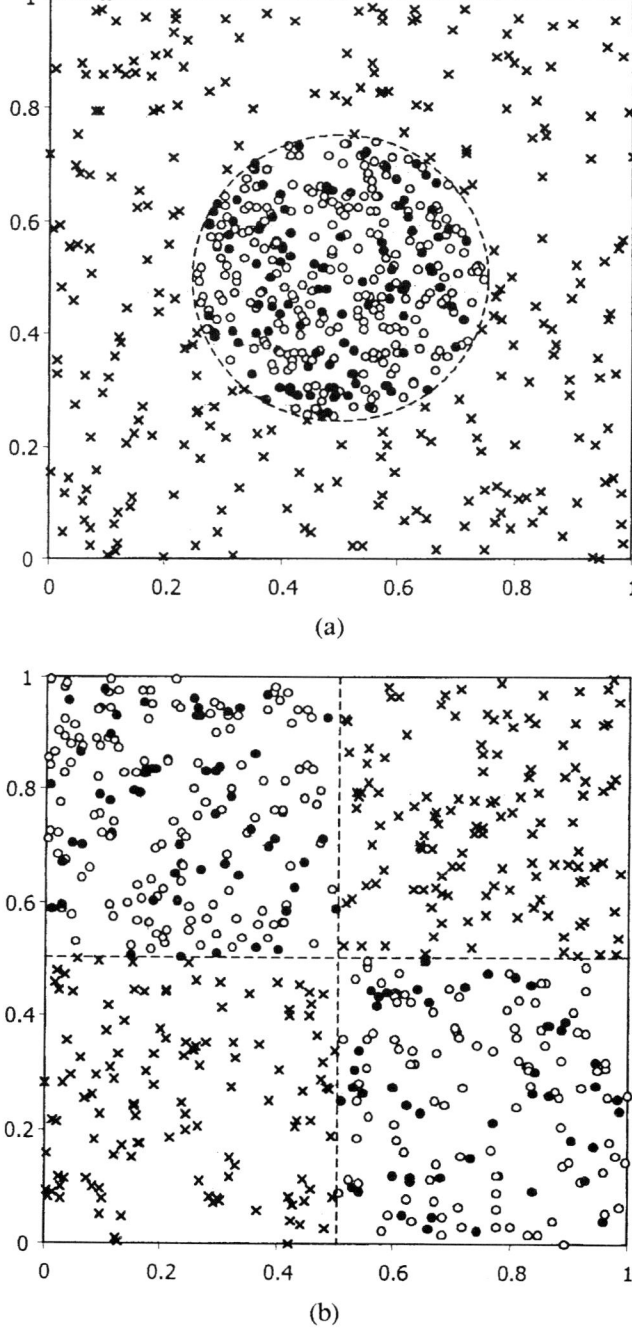

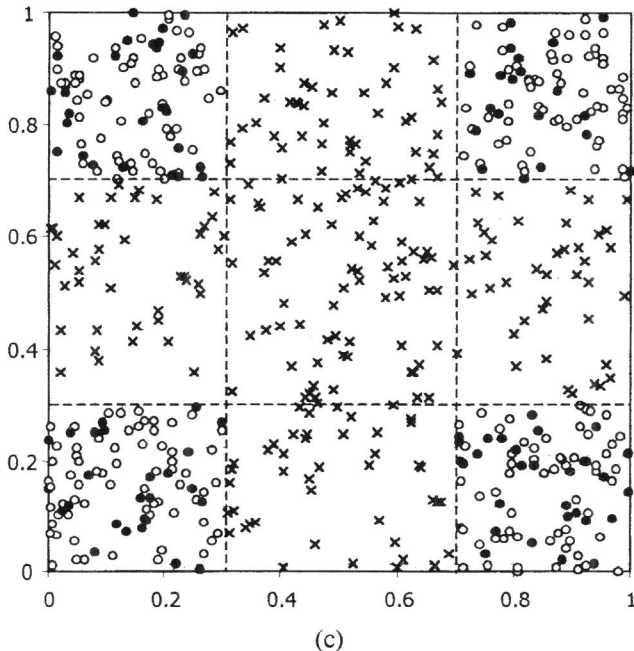

(c)

Fig. 2. Test datasets: closed circles represent labeled positives, open circles represent unlabeled positives, and crosses represent unlabeled negatives (a) positive subspace is a circle of radius 0.25 centered at (0.5, 0.5); (b) positive subspace is the combination of the upper left and lower right quadrants; (c) positive subspace is the combination of each of the four corner regions

Table 1 compares the classification performance of the Bayesian approach with that of back-propagation. Each of the results reports the best classification accuracy obtained out of three random starts. All results refer to accuracy on the same set of examples (i.e. unlabeled examples in the Bayesian case, test set in back-propagation). The numbers in the *network topology* column indicate the number of units in each layer of the network (i.e. input layer - 1st hidden layer - 2nd hidden layer - output layer).

Table 1. Classification performance on three test datasets

	Network Topology	*GA with Bayesian Likelihoods*	*Back-Propagation with labeled counter-examples*
Dataset 1	(2-8-1)	97.0%	98.6%
Dataset 2	(2-4-2-1)	99.6%	97.2%
Dataset 3	(2-16-4-1)	94.4%	97.6%

5 Discussion

As can be seen from the results in Table 1, the classification accuracy achieved using the Bayesian likelihoods approach is comparable to that achieved using back-propagation. The difference in overall classification performance between the two approaches is less than 3.2% for each dataset, and in the case of dataset 2, the technique based on Bayesian likelihoods outperformed back-propagation. This suggests that the evaluation function based on Bayesian likelihoods is capable of providing an adequate measure of classifier performance on these types of classification tasks.

With regard to efficiency, the time taken to find a near-optimal solution using the Bayesian likelihoods approach was comparable to that required for back-propagation in the case of the first and second datasets, but considerably longer for the third. Whilst it may be expected that the Bayesian method would require considerably more computation because of the large number of networks that must be evaluated at each generation, the expense of evaluating a large number of networks is largely compensated for by the fast evaluation of the networks. That is, the cost of applying a network to the *classification* of test examples is very small in comparison with the expense of calculating and back-propagating errors. However, as the number of neural network weights increases, the space of weight configurations increases dramatically; thus the long genetic search time for the third dataset (121 weights) compared with that using back-propagation. We emphasize that these inefficiencies in the case of large numbers of weights are due to the nature of the search itself, and not the evaluation function. It may be possible to increase performance by fine tuning the genetic learning parameters, or by using some alternative technique to discover an optimal set of network weights.

The datasets used for testing did not contain noise. That is, all of the labeled positives were contained within the boundaries depicted in Figure 2. Suppose that the dataset did contain negative examples mislabeled as positives. How would this affect the performance of search using this evaluation function? The first factor in Equation 8 represents the odds, $O(C|L)$, of a labeled positive being contained within the decision boundary. As the number of labeled positives contained within the boundary approaches $n(L)$, $O(C|L) \to \infty$. This means that the first factor in Equation 8 will heavily favour decision boundaries that correctly classify all of the labeled positives. Now consider the situation in which a negative has been mislabeled as positive. The value of the first factor will increase if the classification boundary is extended to include this example. However, extending the boundary in this way will result in additional (unlabeled) negatives also being contained within the boundary. This will have the effect of increasing the denominator of the second factor in Equation 8, thereby decreasing the overall value of this factor. But because the proportional change in the value of the first factor (resulting from extending the decision boundary) will be much greater then the proportional change in the value of the second factor, the first factor will dominate, and therefore the extended boundary will be favoured over the initial boundary. From this argument, it can be concluded that the technique based on Bayesian likelihoods is very sensitive to the presence of noise amongst the labeled positives, and should not be used in such circumstances.

Although we have applied the evaluation function in a neural network implementation, in principle it can also be applied in rule-based systems. However, as stated above, the procedure used for learning must be based on generating classifiers in their entirety before their performance can be evaluated. This directly rules out decision tree induction algorithms such as C4.5, which use a greedy search to generate trees incrementally. De Jong *et al* (1993) have shown how genetic algorithms can be used to discover symbolic rules in disjunctive normal form [8]. The evaluation function that we have proposed can easily be incorporated into their model.

6 Conclusions

A classifier evaluation function based on Bayesian likelihoods of necessity and sufficiency has been defined. This function can be used to measure the performance of an arbitrary classifier on a set of examples consisting of labeled positives together with a corpus of unlabeled data. A neural network system has been implemented in which the evaluation function is used as a heuristic to guide search through the space of network weight configurations. Results from applying the system to three artificial datasets show that the performance is comparable to that of back-propagation, despite the fact that the latter method requires labeled counter-examples. The technique is applicable to a broad range of classification and pattern recognition problems in which the provision of counter-examples is problematic.

References

1. Quinlan, J.R., *C4.5 Programs for Machine Learning*, Morgan Kaufmann Publishers, San Francisco, 1993.
2. Brieman, L., Friedman, J.H., Olshen, R.A. & Stone, C.J., *Classification and Regression Trees*, Wadsworth International Group, Belmont, California, 1984.
3. Michalski, R.S., Mozetic, I, Hong, J. and Lavrac, N., *The AQ15 Inductive Learning System: An Overview and Experiments*, University of Illinois, Urbana-Champaign, 1986.
4. Rumelhart, D.E. & McClelland, J.L.: *Parallel distributed processing: exploration in the microstructure of cognition* (Vols. 1 & 2). Cambridge, MA: MIT Press, 1986.
5. Skabar, A., Biswas, K., Pham, B. and Maeder, A. (1999) "Learning a Concept in the Absence of Labeled Counter-Examples" In *Proceedings of the 4th International Conference on Pattern Recognition and Digital Techniques ICAPRDT '99* ISBN-81-7319-247-9, December 27-29, Calcutta, India, pp.32-36.
6. Holland, J., *Adaptation in Natural and Artificial Systems*, University of Michigan Press, Ann Arbor, 1983.
7. Goldberg, D., *Genetic algorithms in search, optimization, and machine learning*, Addison-Wesley, Reading, Massachusetts, 1989.
8. De Jong, K.A., Spears, W.M., and Gordon, D.F.: "Using genetic algorithms for concept learning", *Machine Learning*, 13, 1993, pp.161-188.

Evaluating Noise Correction

Choh Man Teng

School of Computer Science and Engineering
University of New South Wales, Sydney NSW 2052 Australia

Abstract. Data quality is a prime concern for many tasks in learning and induction. We proposed in a previous paper a noise correction mechanism called polishing, which exploits the interdependence between the different components of a data set, to identify the noisy values and their appropriate replacements. The design of a sound and informative metric for evaluating the effectiveness of a noise correction scheme turned out to be non-trivial. We motivate here a number of classifier dependent measures and proximity measures, each focusing on a different aspect of the corrected data and the associated classifier. We report on some extended experimentation with polishing, as measured by the proposed metrics. The results suggested that polishing is able to repair a corrupted data set to some extent, and the metrics we devised appear to be reasonable.

1 Introduction

Data quality is a prime concern for many tasks in learning and induction. The utility of a procedure is limited by the quality of the data we have access to. For a classification task, for example, a classifier built from a noisy training set might be less accurate than one built from the noise-free version of the same data set using an identical algorithm. Noise stems from many sources, such as clerical errors, faulty instruments, and transmission failures. Thus, noise handling is a major issue in machine learning systems.

There are several approaches to coping with noise. The standard approach is to avoid overfitting, so that the robust classifier does not build overly complicated structures just to fit the noise [Quinlan, 1987; Clark and Niblett, 1989]. This noise tolerance however may interfere with the quality of the classifier, whose accuracy might suffer and the representation might be less compact.

Another approach tackles the problem at the input end, and eliminates from the data set instances that are suspect of noise according to certain evaluation mechanisms [John, 1995; Brodley and Friedl, 1996; Gamberger *et al.*, 1996]. A classifier is then built using the cleaner but smaller data set. Similar ideas can be found in robust regression and outlier detection techniques in statistics [Rousseeuw and Leroy, 1987].

In removing noisy instances, there is a tradeoff between the amount of noise removed from the data set and the amount of data retained for training. We investigate a third approach, namely, correcting the noisy instances rather than eliminating them. Ideally the repaired data set would preserve the maximal information available, approximating the noise-free case. A classifier built from this corrected data should have a higher predictive power.

Noise correction has been shown to give better results than simply removing the noise from the data set in some cases [Drastal, 1991]. It is quite possible that noise correction cannot always be accomplished, as complexity or atypicality in a data set might not be easily distinguishable from noise. However, this approach is still worth pursuing, especially in situations where re-collecting the data is costly or even impossible, as in the case of historical data.

In [Teng, 1999] we proposed a noise correction mechanism called *polishing*, and presented some preliminary results. We found that polishing seemed to work quite well in improving the classifier accuracy and size; the unanswered questions was, *why*? When we tried to quantify the amount of noise we have repaired, the results were not quite what we expected. Some data sets showed an increase in noise despite a large improvement in classification accuracy.

This paper is an expository discussion on the evaluation of noise correction. We try to understand some of the factors affecting classification and the measurement of proximity, as a basis for developing a germane indicator of the effectiveness of a noise correction mechanism. We extended the experimentation on polishing with some more data sets, and applied the proposed metrics to the results.

The rest of the paper is organized as follows. We give a brief summary of polishing in Section 2. The experimental evaluation setup is described in Section 3. In Section 4, we report the results using the classifier dependent metrics. Section 5 concerns the factors affecting proximity measures, and the results using a relevant nearest neighbor model follow in Sections 6 and 7. We conclude the discussion in Section 8.

2 Polishing

Polishing tries to locate the noisy attributes and class in an instance, and guess the correct values for them. The procedure of polishing and some preliminary experimental results were reported in [Teng, 1999]. In this section we give a brief summary of the basic methodology.

Polishing exploits the interdependence between the different components in a data set. Just as we can predict the target concept by examining the attribute values, we can turn the process around and use the target class value together with some attributes to predict the value of another attribute. Note that except for totally irrelevant attributes, each attribute would at least be related to some extent to the target class even if not to another attribute. This idea is related to structured induction [Shapiro, 1987], where classifiers for individual attributes are built from a set of other attributes.

There are two stages in polishing. In the *prediction* stage, we swap each attribute with the original class in the data, and try to predict the values for the target attribute using classifiers built from this transformed data. The misclassified attribute-value pairs are collected and passed on to the *adjustment* phase.

```
Polishing(OldData, NewData, votes, changes, cutoff)
Input OldData: (possibly) noisy data
      votes: #classifiers that need to agree
      changes: max #changes per instance
      cutoff: size of attribute subset considered
Output NewData: polished data

    for each attribute a_i
        AttList_i ← ∅;
        tmpData ← swap a_i and class c in OldData;
        10-fold cross-validation of tmpData;
        for each instance x_j misclassified
            new ← value of a_i predicted for x_j;
            AttList_i ← AttList_i ∪ {⟨j, new⟩};
        end
    end

    NewData ← ∅;
    AttSorted ← attributes sorted
                in ascending order of |AttList_i|;
    Classifiers ← classifiers from 10-fold
                  cross-validation of OldData;
    for each instance x_j
        for k from 0 to changes
            adjusted ← flip(j, votes, k, cutoff);
            if adjusted then break;
        end
        if (not adjusted) and (∃class c s.t.
            classify(Classifiers, x_j, c) ≥ votes)
        then
            class of x_j ← c;
            NewData ← NewData ∪ {x_j};
        end
    end

flip(j, votes, k, cutoff)
Input j: index of the instance to be adjusted
      votes: #classifiers that need to agree
      k: #changes yet to be made
      cutoff: size of attribute subset considered
Output true/false: whether a change has been made
      (also modifies NewData)

    if k = 0 then
        if classify(Classifiers, x_j, class of x_j) ≥ votes
        then
            NewData ← NewData ∪ {x_j};
            return true;
        end
        else return false;
    else for i from 0 to cutoff
        a_{i'} ← AttSorted[i];
        if ⟨j, new⟩ ∈ AttList_{i'} then
            attribute a_{i'} of x_j ← new;
            adjusted ← flip(j, votes, k − 1, i − 1);
            if adjusted then return true;
            reset a_{i'} of x_j;
        end
    end
    return false;
```

Fig. 1. Polishing

We selectively replace some of the attribute values in a misclassified instance with the ones nominated during the prediction phase, so that the polished instance could be classified correctly. A number of heuristics have been adopted to keep the task manageable and the adjustment conservative. The class value may also be replaced with the value predicted by the majority of the classifiers if we cannot find a combination of acceptable attribute changes.

The barebones description of polishing is given in Figure 1. `Polishing` makes use of a procedure `flip` to recursively try out different combinations of attribute changes. The function `classify`($Classifiers, x_j, c$) returns the number of classifiers in the set $Classifiers$ which assign the instance x_j to class c.

3 Experimental Setup

We evaluated experimentally the effectiveness of polishing as a noise correction mechanism. Decision trees generated using c4.5 [Quinlan, 1993] with pruning served as the basic classifiers. Twelve data sets from the UCI repository of machine learning databases [Murphy and Aha, 1998], shown in Table 1, were used. Where separate training and test sets exist for a data set at the repository, we combined the two into a single data set. All the attributes are nominal (or ordered), and attributes for identification purposes only were ignored.

Table 1. Noise characteristics of data sets at various noise levels. For the columns under "Original", an attribute or class is considered noisy if its value is different from that of the instance it was derived from. The columns under "Revised" are computed with respect to each instance's relevant nearest neighbor (see Section 6).

Data Set	Noise Level	Original		Revised		Data Set	Noise Level	Original		Revised	
		Actual Noise	Instances with Noise	Actual Noise	Instances with Noise			Actual Noise	Instances with Noise	Actual Noise	Instances with Noise
audiology	0%	0.0%	0.0%	0.0%	0.0%	nursery	0%	0.0%	0.0%	0.0%	0.0%
	10%	5.2%	96.0%	4.9%	52.2%		10%	6.9%	47.4%	2.0%	17.6%
	20%	10.6%	100.0%	10.7%	81.9%		20%	13.9%	74.2%	3.6%	32.2%
	30%	15.5%	100.0%	14.8%	92.5%		30%	20.8%	87.7%	4.9%	44.0%
	40%	21.4%	100.0%	19.3%	96.0%		40%	27.9%	94.7%	6.1%	54.5%
car	0%	0.0%	0.0%	0.0%	0.0%	promoters	0%	0.0%	0.0%	0.0%	0.0%
	10%	6.8%	39.4%	2.2%	15.5%		10%	7.6%	97.2%	5.3%	24.5%
	20%	14.6%	66.8%	4.2%	29.5%		20%	14.3%	100.0%	7.7%	38.7%
	30%	21.4%	82.9%	5.7%	39.7%		30%	22.0%	100.0%	12.1%	54.7%
	40%	28.4%	90.5%	6.9%	48.1%		40%	29.9%	100.0%	14.7%	62.3%
LED-24	0%	0.0%	0.0%	0.0%	0.0%	soybean	0%	0.0%	0.0%	0.0%	0.0%
	10%	5.3%	74.8%	5.4%	33.2%		10%	5.6%	85.7%	5.5%	76.6%
	20%	10.3%	94.2%	10.2%	56.7%		20%	11.5%	96.2%	11.1%	92.2%
	30%	15.4%	98.3%	14.4%	71.6%		30%	17.0%	99.6%	16.2%	98.1%
	40%	20.9%	99.9%	18.7%	84.0%		40%	22.9%	100.0%	20.9%	99.4%
lenses	0%	0.0%	0.0%	0.0%	0.0%	splice	0%	0.0%	0.0%	0.0%	0.0%
	10%	5.8%	29.2%	2.1%	8.3%		10%	7.4%	98.9%	6.2%	48.9%
	20%	13.3%	50.0%	6.2%	25.0%		20%	15.0%	100.0%	11.4%	76.1%
	30%	15.6%	45.8%	5.2%	20.8%		30%	22.5%	100.0%	15.3%	88.6%
	40%	23.3%	75.0%	8.3%	33.3%		40%	30.1%	100.0%	18.0%	94.2%
lung cancer	0%	0.0%	0.0%	0.0%	0.0%	vote	0%	0.0%	0.0%	0.0%	0.0%
	10%	7.3%	100.0%	7.5%	53.1%		10%	6.4%	66.2%	4.6%	38.9%
	20%	14.8%	100.0%	12.5%	81.2%		20%	12.9%	89.2%	7.9%	58.6%
	30%	21.9%	100.0%	20.9%	90.6%		30%	19.8%	97.7%	12.0%	75.4%
	40%	27.5%	100.0%	22.2%	90.6%		40%	26.0%	99.8%	15.6%	86.9%
mushroom	0%	0.0%	0.0%	0.0%	0.0%	zoo	0%	0.0%	0.0%	0.0%	0.0%
	10%	7.3%	82.5%	6.4%	49.1%		10%	5.4%	63.4%	4.5%	42.6%
	20%	14.8%	97.4%	12.7%	75.8%		20%	11.8%	87.1%	9.9%	68.3%
	30%	22.1%	99.8%	18.4%	88.8%		30%	15.6%	98.0%	13.1%	85.1%
	40%	29.5%	100.0%	23.7%	95.5%		40%	20.0%	100.0%	14.9%	82.2%

We performed a 10-fold cross validation on each data set. For each run, approximately 90% of the data was injected with noise and used for training, while the remaining 10% was held for testing. The training data was artificially corrupted by introducing random noise into both the attributes and the class. A noise level of $x\%$ means that the value of each attribute and the target class is assigned a random value $x\%$ of the time, with each alternative value being equally likely to be selected.

The actual percentages of noise in the data sets are given in the columns under "Original" in Table 1. These values are never higher, and in almost all cases lower, than the advertised $x\%$ since the original noise-free value could be selected as the random replacement as well. Also shown in Table 1 are the percentages of instances with at least one corrupted value. Note that even at fairly low noise levels, the majority of instances contained some amount of noise.

There are two main aspects of noise correction we would like to look at. Operationally, we would like to improve our classification performance. We can look at the classification accuracy and confidence, together with the structure of the classifiers built using the polished data, compared to those built using the unpolished data as the training set. Another aspect is to obtain a classifier-independent measure of how close two data sets are. We would like to see whether the polished data is any closer than the unpolished data to the original noise free set. This would give us a more informative measure than, for example, classification accuracy when we want to put the polished data to uses other than building classifiers. Let us start with the more standard measures, the classifier characteristics.

4 Metrics: Classifier Characteristics

We looked at the classification accuracy and confidence as well as the pruned tree size of the decision trees built from the unpolished and polished data. The results are summarized in Table 2. Differences that are significant at the 0.05 level using a one-tailed paired t-test are marked with an $*$.

There are two aspects regarding classification quality. The classification *accuracy* is the percentage of instances in the test set that were classified correctly. The classification *confidence* measures the strength of the correct classification. Consider an instance x_i whose correct class is c_i. Suppose it is predicted to be of class c'_i by the decision tree, and at the leaf where this instance is classified, the proportion of instances of class c_i in the training set is $P_i(c_i)$. The classification accuracy is then the percentage of instances where $c_i = c'_i$, and the confidence is the sum of the "weights" of the correct classifications: $\sum_i P_i(c_i)$.

Thus, the classification accuracy counts the number of categorically correct predictions, while the confidence gives a measure of how strong these predictions are. From Table 2, in terms of classification accuracy, the decision trees built from polished data performed at least as well as those built from unpolished data in most cases, but the improvement was significant only in about half of the cases.

The gain was much more evident when we considered the classification confidence. In most cases the polished data gave rise to a significant improvement over the unpolished data. This seems to indicate that even though the *number* of instances that were classified correctly might not have increased significantly, the *confidence* given to a correct prediction was substantially higher after polishing. In other words, the margin of error was improved by polishing: $P_i(c_i)$ increased, even if the correct class c_i might still not be the dominant class at the leaf for the classification.

Note also for the classification confidence, there was significant improvement for some of the data sets at the 0% noise level. At first glance, this might seem like a mistake: no noise has been added to the data sets. However, the thesis for noise correction is that noise occurs naturally in real data; thus it is safe to assume that the data sets as given are not all noise-free. The improvement we obtained at the 0% noise level may very well be due to the correction of some of this inherent noise, although there is no easy way to verify this claim.

The average pruned tree size is also shown in Table 2. Except for the data sets car and lenses, for all others the polished data gave rise to trees at least as small as the ones built from the unpolished data at most noise levels, sometimes with a fairly substantial reduction in size. Note that this reduction is in addition to any achieved by pruning, which is applied to all trees. Polishing seems to be able to remove some of the irregularities in the data, allowing a more compact tree to be built from the more uniform data.

We would expect the tree size to increase with the amount of noise present in the data, as the tree would grow more branches and leaves to fit some of the noise as well. However, for the car and nursery data sets, the average tree size decreased clearly as the noise level increased. This curious phenomenon

Table 2. Accuracy and confidence of classification (with standard deviation) and pruned tree size, before and after polishing. Classification accuracy reports the percentage of correct classification, and confidence measures the strength of the correct predictions. An ∗ indicates a significant difference in classification accuracy and confidence at the 0.05 level.

Data Set	Noise Level	Classification Accuracy ± Standard Deviation unpolished	polished		Confidence ± Standard Deviation unpolished	polished		Tree Size unpolished	polished
audiology	0%	78.0 ± 7.7%	80.2 ± 7.0%		71.6 ± 6.6%	79.0 ± 7.0%	∗	50.5	47.0
	10%	73.0 ± 7.9%	73.0 ± 5.8%		58.2 ± 6.2%	66.1 ± 4.2%	∗	66.6	56.2
	20%	67.8 ± 8.0%	70.9 ± 5.2%	∗	54.0 ± 6.0%	59.3 ± 4.7%	∗	90.3	90.9
	30%	54.8 ± 11.5%	61.6 ± 7.8%	∗	42.2 ± 8.6%	50.0 ± 5.1%	∗	125.0	121.6
	40%	33.6 ± 11.7%	48.2 ± 5.7%	∗	30.4 ± 8.4%	39.1 ± 5.7%	∗	143.3	130.1
car	0%	93.2 ± 1.7%	92.9 ± 1.6%		92.4 ± 1.6%	92.8 ± 1.6%		173.4	169.1
	10%	86.3 ± 2.6%	86.7 ± 2.9%		76.5 ± 1.6%	86.0 ± 2.8%	∗	108.5	102.1
	20%	83.6 ± 3.3%	84.3 ± 2.7%		65.8 ± 1.4%	84.2 ± 2.7%	∗	103.7	102.7
	30%	76.5 ± 2.3%	80.6 ± 2.5%	∗	56.0 ± 1.1%	77.2 ± 1.9%	∗	88.8	104.0
	40%	74.5 ± 2.1%	77.1 ± 2.0%	∗	46.9 ± 1.8%	73.9 ± 1.3%	∗	41.6	61.2
LED-24	0%	100.0 ± 0.0%	100.0 ± 0.0%		100.0 ± 0.0%	100.0 ± 0.0%		19.0	19.0
	10%	100.0 ± 0.0%	100.0 ± 0.0%		83.2 ± 0.6%	99.4 ± 0.3%	∗	78.2	34.8
	20%	92.3 ± 4.3%	97.2 ± 2.2%	∗	66.9 ± 2.3%	94.2 ± 2.3%	∗	193.4	85.6
	30%	76.2 ± 4.7%	90.0 ± 3.3%	∗	54.8 ± 3.4%	80.6 ± 3.4%	∗	335.8	162.4
	40%	49.4 ± 5.9%	68.1 ± 5.3%	∗	39.9 ± 4.0%	59.2 ± 4.8%	∗	490.8	317.8
lenses	0%	83.3 ± 30.7%	86.7 ± 30.5%		74.0 ± 27.2%	86.7 ± 30.5%	∗	6.4	5.0
	10%	50.0 ± 24.7%	78.3 ± 31.7%	∗	47.2 ± 15.8%	73.1 ± 30.1%	∗	4.2	6.7
	20%	55.0 ± 28.9%	73.3 ± 32.7%	∗	52.0 ± 22.0%	70.6 ± 28.1%	∗	3.5	3.4
	30%	48.3 ± 32.9%	56.7 ± 41.6%		43.7 ± 21.7%	56.3 ± 35.5%		3.8	7.3
	40%	58.3 ± 38.2%	60.0 ± 30.9%		41.9 ± 14.4%	47.0 ± 16.0%		3.9	4.5
lung cancer	0%	50.0 ± 23.9%	54.2 ± 31.0%		47.8 ± 18.4%	50.1 ± 26.4%		19.0	14.2
	10%	30.8 ± 24.2%	46.7 ± 23.6%	∗	35.2 ± 25.0%	49.8 ± 22.0%	∗	20.6	23.0
	20%	45.8 ± 37.5%	54.2 ± 37.1%		46.7 ± 34.7%	53.8 ± 35.6%		15.8	15.4
	30%	57.5 ± 26.0%	55.0 ± 27.7%		52.9 ± 20.0%	51.4 ± 21.0%		12.2	11.8
	40%	50.8 ± 16.9%	63.3 ± 24.8%	∗	52.3 ± 11.9%	64.4 ± 20.7%	∗	16.6	16.2
mushroom	0%	100.0 ± 0.0%	100.0 ± 0.0%		100.0 ± 0.0%	100.0 ± 0.0%		30.6	30.6
	10%	99.9 ± 0.1%	100.0 ± 0.1%		94.1 ± 0.3%	99.9 ± 0.1%	∗	214.3	109.9
	20%	99.7 ± 0.4%	100.0 ± 0.1%		86.2 ± 0.7%	99.5 ± 0.2%	∗	268.3	124.6
	30%	98.9 ± 0.6%	99.3 ± 0.6%		80.7 ± 0.6%	98.7 ± 0.5%	∗	345.0	129.3
	40%	98.6 ± 0.5%	98.8 ± 0.5%		75.3 ± 0.7%	98.4 ± 0.6%	∗	535.2	286.4
nursery	0%	97.0 ± 0.4%	96.8 ± 0.3%		96.2 ± 0.4%	96.8 ± 0.3%	∗	508.4	464.1
	10%	94.4 ± 0.4%	94.5 ± 0.4%		78.1 ± 0.2%	94.4 ± 0.4%	∗	315.3	286.4
	20%	90.9 ± 0.6%	91.2 ± 0.8%		63.7 ± 0.3%	91.2 ± 0.8%	∗	177.0	149.5
	30%	90.0 ± 0.7%	90.3 ± 1.0%		53.3 ± 0.4%	90.2 ± 1.0%	∗	174.8	133.6
	40%	87.4 ± 1.1%	88.1 ± 0.7%	∗	44.2 ± 0.4%	87.9 ± 0.7%	∗	258.0	212.6
promoters	0%	75.6 ± 13.5%	77.5 ± 16.7%		74.9 ± 11.8%	75.6 ± 14.9%		21.4	12.2
	10%	73.0 ± 12.5%	80.4 ± 10.4%	∗	67.7 ± 10.4%	77.2 ± 9.5%	∗	21.8	12.2
	20%	65.9 ± 9.0%	78.5 ± 12.7%	∗	61.3 ± 7.6%	75.8 ± 11.1%	∗	28.2	15.0
	30%	55.6 ± 10.3%	67.9 ± 15.0%	∗	51.4 ± 9.7%	65.2 ± 13.8%	∗	32.2	17.4
	40%	55.6 ± 14.7%	58.5 ± 14.8%	∗	52.2 ± 11.2%	55.3 ± 13.8%		34.6	34.2
soybean	0%	92.1 ± 2.0%	92.1 ± 1.8%		87.1 ± 1.9%	88.4 ± 2.1%	∗	94.1	91.2
	10%	86.2 ± 4.9%	88.7 ± 2.3%		69.6 ± 3.5%	77.8 ± 1.7%	∗	157.9	162.7
	20%	83.0 ± 3.3%	85.8 ± 3.6%		63.3 ± 3.3%	75.5 ± 4.8%	∗	202.5	189.2
	30%	72.2 ± 6.1%	76.7 ± 4.4%	∗	51.7 ± 5.5%	66.1 ± 3.7%	∗	278.5	218.7
	40%	50.7 ± 8.4%	55.4 ± 3.7%	∗	33.6 ± 4.8%	40.6 ± 3.1%	∗	328.7	289.4
splice	0%	94.0 ± 1.3%	94.2 ± 1.4%		91.0 ± 1.2%	93.9 ± 1.2%	∗	171.8	156.2
	10%	89.3 ± 1.8%	91.8 ± 1.5%	∗	79.1 ± 1.7%	91.0 ± 1.5%	∗	318.2	120.6
	20%	83.1 ± 2.1%	88.3 ± 1.5%	∗	69.1 ± 1.8%	85.4 ± 1.2%	∗	537.4	233.4
	30%	73.1 ± 4.0%	83.8 ± 2.6%	∗	60.9 ± 1.9%	77.6 ± 2.8%	∗	836.2	335.4
	40%	61.6 ± 2.9%	72.3 ± 3.0%	∗	53.9 ± 2.2%	65.4 ± 2.7%	∗	1143.0	680.2
vote	0%	94.7 ± 2.0%	94.7 ± 2.5%		93.1 ± 2.6%	94.7 ± 2.5%	∗	14.5	5.8
	10%	94.7 ± 2.5%	95.2 ± 3.0%		86.9 ± 1.8%	95.1 ± 3.1%	∗	17.8	13.6
	20%	94.0 ± 2.1%	95.4 ± 2.3%	∗	81.1 ± 2.4%	94.6 ± 2.4%	∗	20.8	11.8
	30%	92.9 ± 3.2%	90.6 ± 5.5%		78.1 ± 1.9%	89.6 ± 5.7%	∗	43.3	24.7
	40%	92.4 ± 3.1%	92.8 ± 3.9%		74.5 ± 1.6%	90.7 ± 5.8%	∗	27.1	19.6
zoo	0%	92.2 ± 7.2%	93.1 ± 6.4%		92.7 ± 6.4%	93.3 ± 5.6%		17.8	16.2
	10%	91.2 ± 8.3%	95.2 ± 7.7%		84.8 ± 7.3%	90.1 ± 8.1%		24.2	21.2
	20%	83.2 ± 7.8%	85.2 ± 9.1%		72.4 ± 8.5%	80.3 ± 7.8%	∗	20.6	22.2
	30%	77.4 ± 11.4%	86.2 ± 4.7%	∗	59.4 ± 8.6%	76.8 ± 3.5%	∗	30.2	30.0
	40%	78.3 ± 11.5%	87.1 ± 7.8%	∗	58.4 ± 7.8%	76.1 ± 5.8%	∗	35.4	30.0

warrants further study, but for the time being, let us turn to the measurement of proximity.

5 Proximity Considerations

The performance measures discussed in the previous section are classifier-specific. We judge how well the noise correction mechanism fares by looking at the quality of the classifiers built. In the following sections we study a couple of more general proximity metrics. These metrics would be more relevant than classifier characteristics when the corrected data is intended for purposes other than classification. They would also provide more direct evidence as to whether the noise in the data is indeed being successfully repaired.

Consider the i-th instance in a data set. Let us call this instance in the original noise-free data set the *root instance* x_i; the (possibly) corrupted version of it in the noisy data set the *noisy instance* y_i; and the version in the polished data set the *polished instance* z_i. The question we want to answer is whether the polished instance z_i is less noisy than the noisy instance y_i.

One simple (but not quite satisfactory, as we will see) interpretation of this question is: is z_i any better than y_i in approximating the root instance x_i? We might count the differences between z_i and x_i, and compare that to the number of differences between y_i and x_i. However, there are a number of problems associated with quantifying proximity this way, making it a non-trivial task. We will illustrate these difficulties with examples from the LED-24 domain. This data set has the advantage of being synthetic: we have complete knowledge of its structure and underlying concept, making it well suited for analytical exercises.

5.1 Irrelevant Attributes

LED-24 contains 7 "real" attributes, and another 17 with randomly generated values. The 7 real attributes correspond to the 7 LED units that make up the display of a digit. They can be on or off depending on the class, which is one of the ten digits (0...9) being displayed.

A little thought would convince one that it is unreasonable to expect a noise correction mechanism to be able to handle the "noise" in an attribute with random values.[1] In a not as extreme case, some attributes may not be totally random, but they may not be very relevant to the classification task either. To get a clearer picture of how much noise we have corrected, we should exclude these irrelevant attributes from the tally.

To accomplish this we need to identify the (ir)relevant attributes. The approach we have adopted is to consider as relevant only those attributes used in building the original classifiers from the noisy data. If an attribute is not part of a classifier, it is irrelevant at least with respect to this classifier and the classification task at hand, regardless of whether it can be important in other aspects. This gives us an operational definition of relevance which is simple to use.

Note that the irrelevant attributes do not have to be removed from the data set before polishing; they are just skipped over when we perform a count.

5.2 Adjustment towards an Alternative

Another difficulty with measuring proximity is that the noise added and the adjustments we made may move an instance towards an alternative instance (that is not the root instance) in the original noise-free data set. Consider the case in Figure 2(a) for example. An instance representing the digit "5" has

---

[1] In fact, one should be very concerned if the mechanism can indeed locate the "correct" random value...

Fig. 2. (a) Adjustment towards an alternative (b) Different nearest neighbors

been corrupted to the noisy display in the middle column. To revert to the root instance, in this case "5", three LED units need to be reversed. However, to change the noisy instance to either a digit "3" or a digit "2" would require only one switch (or two switches if the class needs to be changed as well).

Two points are illustrated here. First, the root instance may not be the noise-free instance in the original data set that is closest to the noisy instance. Fewer changes may be required of the corrupted instance to match an alternative than to revert back to the root instance. Second, there can be multiple alternatives that are equally close, each requiring a minimal number of changes to match.

These adjustments towards an alternative instance should be considered correct with respect to the alternative, yet they would be counted as incorrect with respect to the root instance, as the polished instance is moved (usually) even further away from the root instance in these cases. Thus, a straightforward comparison between the root, noisy, and polished versions of an instance would miscount these adjustments as undesirable, and penalize any deviation away from the root instance towards an alternative.

6 Relevant Nearest Neighbor

We propose a relevant nearest neighbor metric to circumvent the problems discussed in the previous section. The relevant attributes are taken to be the ones that have been used to build the original classifiers. The distance $d(z, x)$ between two instances z and x is measured by the number of differences between their relevant attributes plus the class. A *relevant nearest neighbor* of an instance z is then an instance z^* in the original noise-free data set, where $d(z, z^*)$ is minimal.

We have already noted that there can be more than one nearest neighbor for an instance. For the time being, we just pick a random instance off the list of multiple relevant nearest neighbors for the proximity counts. We should also note that a noisy instance and its polished version might not have the same nearest neighbor, as illustrated in Figure 2(b).

The root instance "5" was corrupted and then partially repaired. The nearest neighbor of the noisy instance is "6", but after (imperfect) noise correction, the nearest neighbor has become "8". To obtain a fair comparison, we need to take this into account. Rather than utilizing a single fixed nearest neighbor for both the noisy and polished versions of an instance, we determine the amount of noise present by the distances relative to their respective (relevant) nearest neighbors.

We formulated two proximity metrics based on the idea of a relevant nearest neighbor: the net percentage reduction in overall noise, and the percentage of correct adjustment. But first let us note that the estimate of the amount of noise present in the training data should also reflect this change. The columns under "Revised" in Table 1 show the figures computed using a relevant nearest neighbor instead of the root instance as the basis for comparison. Most of these numbers are lower than the corresponding ones in the columns under "Original", as a noisy instance is usually closer to a relevant nearest neighbor than to its root instance. The amount of reduction depends on, among other factors, how many relevant attributes we are considering in each data set. The slight increase in some of the categories can be attributed to the extra "irrelevant" attributes included in the original counts.

7 Proximity Metrics

The two proximity metrics are formulated as follows. Let y_i and z_i be the noisy and polished versions of the i-th instance in the data set, and y_i^* and z_i^* be their respective relevant nearest neighbors. The distance $d(y_i, y_i^*)$ denotes the number of differences between the two instances. Let n_i and m_i be the number of correct and incorrect adjustments made to the i-th instance (with respect to a relevant nearest neighbor). We then have

$$\text{Net Reduction:} \frac{\sum_i [d(y_i, y_i^*) - d(z_i, z_i^*)]}{\sum_i d(y_i, y_i^*)} \ ;$$

$$\text{Correct Adjustment:} \frac{\sum_i n_i}{\sum_i (n_i + m_i)} \ .$$

Net Reduction indicates how much less (or more) noise exists in a data set after polishing, and Correct Adjustment reports what proportion of the adjustments made is considered correct. The results for the data sets after we ran them through polishing are shown in Table 3. Entries that are not well defined are marked with an ∗.

The scores for Net Reduction extended over a fairly large range, but for most categories, the reduction in overall noise was positive though small. One exception was the lung cancer data set, which showed an increase in noise (negative reduction) after polishing. The scores for Correct Adjustment were more consistent across the data sets, with a fairly high percentage of adjustments being correct for most categories. Again, the lung cancer data set was an exception, with more incorrect than correct adjustments (less than 50% correct).

The non-zero scores for Correct Adjustment at the 0% noise level are an artifact of our relevant nearest neighbor model. Even though no noise has been added, an instance might be adjusted so that after polishing it is closer to an alternative instance than to the root instance. Note that this occurs only when the classifier fails to classify the root instance correctly—either the classifier is not powerful enough, or the root instance contains intrinsic noise—as we would not attempt to adjust a correctly classified instance.

Table 3. Proximity to the original data, with respect to a relevant nearest neighbor model

Data Set	Noise Level	Net Reduction	Correct Adjustment	Data Set	Noise Level	Net Reduction	Correct Adjustment
audiology	0%	*	79.3%	nursery	0%	*	99.9%
	10%	11.6%	95.5%		10%	89.1%	99.8%
	20%	0.9%	94.4%		20%	81.9%	99.6%
	30%	0.7%	83.8%		30%	82.8%	99.4%
	40%	1.4%	91.2%		40%	80.0%	99.5%
car	0%	*	91.5%	promoters	0%	*	86.8%
	10%	70.9%	99.1%		10%	-3.8%	93.0%
	20%	64.8%	99.3%		20%	7.9%	95.3%
	30%	62.3%	99.1%		30%	6.9%	96.8%
	40%	58.7%	98.4%		40%	0.2%	83.2%
LED-24	0%	*	*	soybean	0%	*	35.8%
	10%	59.3%	99.9%		10%	2.6%	80.4%
	20%	45.8%	99.5%		20%	2.7%	77.9%
	30%	29.9%	96.0%		30%	3.1%	76.9%
	40%	17.0%	91.6%		40%	1.2%	76.8%
lenses	0%	*	100.0%	splice	0%	*	32.4%
	10%	40.0%	98.2%		10%	4.7%	84.6%
	20%	49.2%	100.0%		20%	8.8%	92.0%
	30%	5.6%	93.3%		30%	7.1%	92.4%
	40%	13.3%	88.2%		40%	4.5%	92.5%
lung cancer	0%	*	44.0%	vote	0%	*	69.1%
	10%	-0.4%	0.0%		10%	6.9%	86.4%
	20%	0.0%	80.0%		20%	11.3%	93.8%
	30%	-0.5%	33.3%		30%	10.2%	94.0%
	40%	-1.9%	56.0%		40%	9.7%	97.0%
mushroom	0%	*	*	zoo	0%	*	88.9%
	10%	9.2%	95.4%		10%	8.4%	100.0%
	20%	9.9%	96.3%		20%	6.0%	96.6%
	30%	7.7%	93.1%		30%	6.6%	92.9%
	40%	5.6%	93.6%		40%	4.9%	100.0%

8 Concluding Remarks

In this paper we follow up on the work on polishing. We experimented with some more data sets and developed a number of metrics for evaluating the performance of a noise correction mechanism. At one end we have the classifier specific measures: classification accuracy, confidence of classification, and classifier size. These measures reflect the utility of noise repair in terms of its effect on the classification task. The experimental results indicated that polished data gave rise to higher classification accuracy and confidence, as well as smaller decision trees in many cases.

At the other end, we tried to develop metrics that are more classifier independent. Noise correction is relevant not just for classification, but for any task that is sensitive to the quality of the data. For these other purposes, a more general measure that compares the actual amount of noise in the data sets would be more informative than, say, classification accuracy. A number of issues make simple counting a not so desirable metric. We instead developed revised metrics in a relevant nearest neighbor setting.[2] The results given by these proximity measures suggested that polishing is able to repair a corrupted data set to some extent.

One notable exception was the lung cancer data set, which fared pretty poorly with respect to most metrics we applied. This points to an important issue we

---

[2] Note however that the metrics are still not entirely independent of the classifier. Although the general idea of relevance need not be dependent on classification, for the time being the relevant attributes are defined with respect to the classifiers used.

need to resolve: we need to determine what characterizes the data sets that lend themselves to polishing, so that we can know in advance whether a target data set would respond well to polishing. To understand the factors involved in polishing would require systematic experimentation with a wider range of (most likely synthetic) data sets of different properties, as well as with various perturbations of the polishing procedure to determine its flexibility and limits.

Another direction is to explore the connection between the two kinds of metrics. There is no obvious correlation between the figures in Tables 2 and 3. The question we set out to answer has only been partially examined. We have identified some of the confounding factors we need to take into account when evaluating noise correction mechanisms. Further study would help to fine tune the metrics to achieve a truly sound and realistic measure.

Acknowledgement

I would like to thank Ross Quinlan for enlightenment and tolerance during a hectic year. This work was supported by the Australian Research Council Grant A49801208 and the travelling salesman.

References

[Brodley and Friedl, 1996] Carla E. Brodley and Mark A. Friedl. Identifying and eliminating mislabeled training instances. In *Proceedings of the Thirteenth National Conference on Artificial Intelligence*, 1996.
[Clark and Niblett, 1989] P. Clark and T. Niblett. The CN2 induction algorithm. *Machine Learning*, 3(4):261–283, 1989.
[Drastal, 1991] George Drastal. Informed pruning in constructive induction. In *Proceedings of the Eighth International Workshop on Machine Learning*, pages 132–136, 1991.
[Gamberger et al., 1996] Dragan Gamberger, Nada Lavrač, and Sašo Džeroski. Noise elimination in inductive concept learning: A case study in medical diagnosis. In *Proceedings of the Seventh International Workshop on Algorithmic Learning Theory*, pages 199–212, 1996.
[John, 1995] George H. John. Robust decision trees: Removing outliers from databases. In *Proceedings of the First International Conference on Knowledge Discovery and Data Mining*, pages 174–179, 1995.
[Murphy and Aha, 1998] P. M. Murphy and D. W. Aha. UCI repository of machine learning databases. University of California, Irvine, Department of Information and Computer Science, 1998. `http://www.ics.uci.edu/~mlearn/MLRepository.html`.
[Quinlan, 1987] J. Ross Quinlan. Simplifying decision trees. *International Journal of Man-Machine Studies*, 27(3):221–234, 1987.
[Quinlan, 1993] J. Ross Quinlan. *C4.5: Programs for Machine Learning*. Morgan Kaufmann, 1993.
[Rousseeuw and Leroy, 1987] Peter J. Rousseeuw and Annick M. Leroy. *Robust Regression and Outlier Detection*. John Wiley & Sons, 1987.
[Shapiro, 1987] Alen D. Shapiro. *Structured Induction in Expert Systems*. Addison-Wesley, 1987.
[Teng, 1999] Choh Man Teng. Correcting noisy data. In *Proceedings of the Sixteenth International Conference on Machine Learning*, pages 239–248, 1999.

An Efficient Learning Algorithm Using Natural Gradient and Second Order Information of Error Surface

Hyeyoung Park[1], Kenji Fukumizu[2], Shun-ichi Amari[3], and Yillbyung Lee[1]

[1] Dept. of Computer Science, Yonsei University, Seoul, Korea
{hypark,yblee}@csai.yonsei.ac.kr
[2] Institute of Statistical Mathematics, Tokyo, Japan
fukumizu@ism.ac.jp
[3] Institute of Physical and Chemical Research, Saitama, Japan
amari@brain.riken.go.jp

Abstract. Natural gradient learning algorithm, which originated from information geometry, is known to provide a good solution for the problem of slow learning speed of gradient descent learning methods. Whereas the natural gradient learning algorithm is inspired from the geometric structure of the space of learning systems, there have been other approaches to acceleration of learning by using the second order information of error surface. Although the second order methods cannot give as successful solutions as the natural gradient learning method, their results showed the usefulness of the second order information of error surface in the learning process. In this paper, we develop a method of combining these two different approaches to propose a more efficient learning algorithm. At each learning step, we calculate a search direction by means of the natural gradient. When we apply the search direction to parameter-updating process, the second order information of error surface is applied to determine an efficient learning rate. Through a simple experiment on a real world problem, we confirmed that the proposed learning algorithm show faster convergence than the pure natural gradient learning algorithm.

1 Introduction

The natural gradient learning algorithm, which is a kind of stochastic gradient descent learning algorithms, originated from information geometry[2]. By considering the geometric structure of the space of learning systems such as neural networks, the information geometrical approach gives a more appropriate metric, Fisher information metric, than the Euclidean metric. Using this metric, we can calculate a gradient of any differentiable error function defined on the space, and the gradient gives the steepest descent direction of the error surface at any point on the space. This gradient is called the *natural gradient*, and the natural gradient learning algorithm can directly be obtained by using the natural gradient instead of the ordinary gradient defined on the Euclidean space. There have been several researches showing the ideal performances of the natural gradient learning method[1, 8, 9] and the practical advantages of its adaptive version[3, 7]. These researches showed that the natural gradient learning can be successfully applied to practical problems and solve the plateau problem in the learning of neural networks. The plateaus are the main causes of the problem of slow learning speed of neural networks.

On the other hand, there have been quite different approaches to solve the slow convergence of the ordinary gradient descent learning, which come from the optimization theory[4]. In addition to the first derivative of error function, they tried to use the second order information represented by the Hessian matrix of the error function in the learning process. Newton method and its variations, Conjugate gradient method, and Gauss-Newton method are representative ones, and they have shown faster convergence than the standard gradient descent learning method in many cases. Since these methods are based on the quadratic approximations, however, they cannot give rigorous theoretical justification of using them in the real problems, and can guarantee satisfying performance only when the learning parameter is near by the optimal parameter. Despite the theoretical weakness, their superiority over the standard gradient descent learning algorithm is enough to show the importance of the second order information of error function in the learning process.

In this paper, we propose a new learning algorithm which combines two concepts; the natural gradient and the second order information. While the first derivative of the error function gives the information of search direction, the second derivative of error function gives the curvature information so as to give some hints about how much the parameter need to move along the search direction. Even though the natural gradient is known to give a good search direction using the information of the first derivativ e of error function, it does not consider any other characteristics of the error surface. By adding the curvature information of the error surface to the natural gradient learning method, we expect to get a more efficient learning method than the pure natural gradient learning.

In the next section, we briefly describe the second order methods and the natural gradient learning method. The proposed learning method combining the two concepts is introduced in section 3. We conduct a simple experiment in order to check the performance of the proposed method, and show the results in section 4. Conclusions and discussions on future works are made in section 5.

2 Natural Gradient and Second Order Method

Since the slow learning speed of the gradient descent methods is a serious problem for practical applications, there have been a lot of techniques for accelerating convergence[5, 6]. While many of them depend on heuristics, the natural gradient learning method and the second order method have their own theoretical background. Before going into the descriptions of the two methods on which the proposed method is based, let us explain stages of learning process briefly with our notations.

Given a learning data set $\{(\boldsymbol{x}_n, \boldsymbol{y}_n^*)\}_{n=1,...,N}$, the goal of learning is to find an optimal parameter $\boldsymbol{\theta}^*$ which minimizes the value of error function $E(\boldsymbol{\theta})$ defined appropriately for the purpose of applications. The learning process thus can be written by

$$\boldsymbol{\theta}_{t+1} = \boldsymbol{\theta}_t + \Delta\boldsymbol{\theta}_t \tag{1}$$
$$\Delta\boldsymbol{\theta}_t = \eta_t \boldsymbol{d}_t \tag{2}$$
$$\boldsymbol{\theta}^* = \arg\min_{\boldsymbol{\theta}} \{E(\boldsymbol{\theta})\} \tag{3}$$

where $\boldsymbol{d}_t$ is a search direction at step t. In the gradient descent learning, the gradient of error function ∇E plays main role to determine $\boldsymbol{d}_t$. Note that $E(\boldsymbol{\theta})$ is not only the function of $\boldsymbol{\theta}$, but also the function of learning data. If E is the function of the whole learning data set, we call the learning process by batch learning. On the contrary, if it depends only on a current data $(\boldsymbol{x}_t, \boldsymbol{y}_t^*)$, we call it by on-line learning. Even though the on-line learning is generally known to provide better performances in practical problems and the natural gradient learning is mainly developed for on-line learning, we focus on batch learning in this paper as the first step for developing a new algorithm.

2.1 Second Order Method

There have been many researches which use the second order information of error surface, such as Newton method, Quasi-Newton methods, Conjugate Gradient method, and Gauss-Newton method. Even though these methods are slightly different from each other in the explicit learning algorithms, all of them use the Hessian matrix for the second order information of error surface in common. In this section, we briefly describe the Newton method, the basic second order method.

The main characteristic of the Newton method is that it uses the second order information of error surface represented by the Hessian matrix H. It also uses the local quadratic approximation to obtain an expression for the location of the minimum of the error function. Let us consider the Taylor expansion of error function $E(\boldsymbol{\theta})$ around the optimal point $\boldsymbol{\theta}^*$ in the parameter space,

$$E(\boldsymbol{\theta}) = E(\boldsymbol{\theta}^*) + (\boldsymbol{\theta} - \boldsymbol{\theta}^*)^T \nabla E(\boldsymbol{\theta}^*) + \frac{1}{2}(\boldsymbol{\theta} - \boldsymbol{\theta}^*)^T H^*(\boldsymbol{\theta} - \boldsymbol{\theta}^*) \tag{4}$$

$$H^* = \left[\left\{\frac{\partial^2 E}{\partial \theta_i^* \partial \theta_j^*}\right\}_{ij}\right], \tag{5}$$

where H^* is the Hessian matrix at the optimal point $\boldsymbol{\theta}^*$. By differentiating Eq. 4, we can get the gradient at a point $\boldsymbol{\theta}$ near by the optimal parameter $\boldsymbol{\theta}^*$ of the form

$$\nabla E(\boldsymbol{\theta}) = H^*(\boldsymbol{\theta} - \boldsymbol{\theta}^*), \tag{6}$$

and the parameter vector $\boldsymbol{\theta}^*$ can be given as

$$\boldsymbol{\theta}^* = \boldsymbol{\theta} - (H^*)^{-1} \nabla E(\boldsymbol{\theta}). \tag{7}$$

The vector $-(H^*)^{-1}\nabla E(\boldsymbol{\theta})$ is known as the Newton direction and it can directly give the minimum of a quadratic error surface. In most practical problems, however, the error surface is hardly quadratic, so the Newton method is regarded as a local approximation. In other words, at each learning step t, we assume the error function to be locally quadratic, and try to find the local solution by the parameter updating rule,

$$\boldsymbol{\theta}_{t+1} = \boldsymbol{\theta}_t - \eta_t H(\boldsymbol{\theta}_t)^{-1} \nabla E(\boldsymbol{\theta}_t), \tag{8}$$

where η_t is a learning rate and $H(\boldsymbol{\theta}_t)$ is the Hessian matrix at point $\boldsymbol{\theta}_t$.

Due to the limitation of quadratic approximation, the Newton method is efficient only near by the optimal point. Moreover, since the Hessian matrix is not always positive definite, it can not guarantee the convergence of the algorithm. From the practical point of view, the calculation of the Hessian matrix and its inverse is very time-consuming, as well. Other second order methods, such as Quasi-Newton method and Gauss-Newton method have been developed to solve these problems. However, all of them commonly use the Hessian matrix implicitly or explicitly, for the curvature information of error surface.

2.2 Natural Gradient Learning Method

Since the natural gradient learning is a kind of the stochastic gradient descent learning methods, we have to consider a system to be trained as a stochastic system so that it can be represented by a probability density function. Then we can consider a space of the probability density functions $\{p(\boldsymbol{x}, \boldsymbol{y}; \boldsymbol{\theta}) | \boldsymbol{\theta} \in \Re^M\}$, and define an appropriate error function $E(\boldsymbol{\theta})$ on the space. The typical error function is the loss function defined by the negative logarithm of the likelihood function which is of the form,

$$E(\boldsymbol{\theta}) = -\log p(\boldsymbol{x}, \boldsymbol{y}^*; \boldsymbol{\theta}) \tag{9}$$
$$= -\log p(\boldsymbol{y}^*|\boldsymbol{x}; \boldsymbol{\theta})q(\boldsymbol{x}) = -\log p(\boldsymbol{y}^*|\boldsymbol{x}; \boldsymbol{\theta}) - \log q(\boldsymbol{x}) \tag{10}$$

where $q(\boldsymbol{x})$ is the pdf of the input $\boldsymbol{x}$ and $p(\boldsymbol{y}|\boldsymbol{x}; \boldsymbol{\theta})$ is the conditional pdf of $\boldsymbol{y}$ conditioned on $\boldsymbol{x}$. The learning is a process of finding an optimal point in the space of the probability density functions, which minimizes the value of the error function. Although the stochastic learning methods assume a true probability distribution from which the training data are generated, the derived learning rule from this assumption can be applied for conventional learning systems such as neural networks. We shall show an example in section 4.

The natural gradient learning method is based on the fact that the space of $p(\boldsymbol{x}, \boldsymbol{y}; \boldsymbol{\theta})$ is a Riemannian space in which the metric tensor is given by the Fisher information matrix $G(\boldsymbol{\theta})$ defined by

$$G(\boldsymbol{\theta}) = \iint \frac{\partial \log p}{\partial \boldsymbol{\theta}} (\frac{\partial \log p}{\partial \boldsymbol{\theta}})^T p(\boldsymbol{y}|\boldsymbol{x}, \boldsymbol{\theta}) q(\boldsymbol{x}) \, d\boldsymbol{y} \, d\boldsymbol{x} \tag{11}$$

$$= E\boldsymbol{x} \left[E_{\boldsymbol{y}|\boldsymbol{x};\boldsymbol{\theta}} \left[\frac{\partial \log p(\boldsymbol{y}|\boldsymbol{x}; \boldsymbol{\theta})}{\partial \boldsymbol{\theta}} (\frac{\partial \log p(\boldsymbol{y}|\boldsymbol{x}; \boldsymbol{\theta})}{\partial \boldsymbol{\theta}})^T \right] \right] \tag{12}$$

where $E_{\boldsymbol{x}}[\cdot]$ and $E_{\boldsymbol{y}|\boldsymbol{x};\boldsymbol{\theta}}[\cdot]$ denote the expectation with respect to $q(\boldsymbol{x})$ and $p(\boldsymbol{y}|\boldsymbol{x};\boldsymbol{\theta})$, respectively, and T denotes the transposition. Using the Fisher information matrix of Eq. 12, we can obtain the natural gradient $\tilde{\nabla}E$ and its learning algorithm for the stochastic systems;

$$\tilde{\nabla}E(\boldsymbol{\theta}) = G^{-1}(\boldsymbol{\theta})\nabla E(\boldsymbol{\theta}), \tag{13}$$

$$\boldsymbol{\theta}_{t+1} = \boldsymbol{\theta}_t - \eta_t \tilde{\nabla}E(\boldsymbol{\theta}_t) = \boldsymbol{\theta}_t - \eta_t G^{-1}(\boldsymbol{\theta}_t)\nabla E(\boldsymbol{\theta}_t). \tag{14}$$

As shown in Eq. 14, the formula is similar to that of the Newton method of Eq. 8 except that the Hessian matrix of the Newton method is replaced with the Fisher information matrix. This difference has some important meanings. Since the Fisher information matrix is semi-positive definite, it can guarantee the convergence provided that we prevent it from approaching to the singular conditions using some constraints. In addition, the Fisher Information matrix can give the steepest descent at each point in the space of the stochastic learning system, whereas the Newton method uses quadratic approximation around the optimal point. Moreover, the Fisher information matrix does not depend on the learning data, whereas the Hessian matrix is obtained from the whole learning data set in order to the curvature information of the error surface.

3 Proposed Learning Algorithm

Whereas the natural gradient considers the geometric structure of the space of learning systems and gives the steepest descent direction at any point of the space, the second order method exploits the curvature information of the error surface in order to decide where and how much the parameter should move. The purpose of this paper is to combine the two different approaches to obtain a more efficient learning algorithm. To this end, we take the natural gradient to decide a search direction at each learning step, and use the curvature information in order to decide the size of update of the parameter.

At each learning step, let us assume that a search direction $\boldsymbol{d}$ is given by the natural gradient of the form,

$$\boldsymbol{d} = -G^{-1}(\boldsymbol{\theta})\nabla E(\boldsymbol{\theta}). \tag{15}$$

With the pure natural gradient learning, the parameter is then udapted to be $\boldsymbol{\theta} + \alpha\boldsymbol{d}$ using $\boldsymbol{d}$ and a learning rate α. To determine an efficient learning rate by means of the second order information of the error surface, we start from the Taylor expansion around $\boldsymbol{\theta}$ of the form

$$E(\boldsymbol{\theta} + \alpha\boldsymbol{d}) = E(\boldsymbol{\theta}) + \alpha\boldsymbol{d}^T\nabla E(\boldsymbol{\theta}) + \frac{1}{2}\alpha^2\boldsymbol{d}^T H\boldsymbol{d}. \tag{16}$$

Here, we try to minimize $E(\boldsymbol{\theta} + \alpha\boldsymbol{d}) - E(\boldsymbol{\theta})$ with respect to the learning rate α. By differentiating Eq. 16 with respect to α, we can get the equation

$$\boldsymbol{d}^T\nabla E(\boldsymbol{\theta}) + \alpha\boldsymbol{d}^T H\boldsymbol{d} = 0, \tag{17}$$

and then we obtain an equation for the learning rate α of the form

$$\alpha = -\frac{d^T \nabla E(\boldsymbol{\theta})}{d^T H(\boldsymbol{\theta}) d}. \tag{18}$$

Applying this α to the pure natural gradient learning, we can get a new learning algorithm of the form

$$\boldsymbol{\theta}_{t+1} = \boldsymbol{\theta}_t - \frac{d_t^T \nabla E(\boldsymbol{\theta}_t)}{d_t^T H(\boldsymbol{\theta}_t) d_t} d_t \tag{19}$$

$$d_t = -G^{-1}(\boldsymbol{\theta}_t) \nabla E(\boldsymbol{\theta}_t). \tag{20}$$

From the updating rule of Eq. 19, we can see that the learning rule includes the curvature information which is represented by Hessian matrix.

We should note here that the problem of the calculation of the Hessian matrix H. Considering the computational cost, we calculate $H(\boldsymbol{\theta})d$ directly instead of pure $H(\boldsymbol{\theta})$ using a well known approximation technique of the form,

$$H(\boldsymbol{\theta})d = \frac{1}{\delta}(\nabla E(\boldsymbol{\theta} + \delta d) - \nabla E(\boldsymbol{\theta})) \tag{21}$$

where δ is a small constant.

The proposed learning rule can be applied for general learning systems for probability estimation problems. A representative learning system is a feedforward neural network model, and we use the model for checking the performance of the proposed learning algorithm in the next section.

4 Experimental Results

To check the efficiency of the proposed learning algorithms we conducted a computational experiment using a feedforward neural network model of the form,

$$y = \sum_{\alpha=1}^{m} v_\alpha \varphi(\boldsymbol{w}_\alpha \cdot \boldsymbol{x}) + \xi, \tag{22}$$

where $\boldsymbol{x}$ is an n-dimensional input; y is an output from a linear output unit; $\boldsymbol{w}_\alpha$ is an n-dimensional connection weight vector from the input to the α-th hidden unit($\alpha = 1, \cdots, m$); v_α is the connection weight from the α-th hidden unit to the output unit; and ξ is a random noise subject to $N(0, \sigma^2)$. The function φ is a sigmoidal activation function. Using this stochastic form of feedforward neural networks, we can get the corresponding probability distribution of output y conditioned on input $\boldsymbol{x}$,

$$p(y|\boldsymbol{x}, \boldsymbol{\theta}) = \frac{1}{\sqrt{2\pi}\sigma} \exp\left[-\frac{1}{2\sigma^2}\{y - f(\boldsymbol{x}, \boldsymbol{\theta})\}^2\right], \tag{23}$$

where

$$f(\boldsymbol{x}, \boldsymbol{\theta}) = \sum_{\alpha=1}^{m} v_\alpha \varphi(\boldsymbol{w}_\alpha \cdot \boldsymbol{x}) \tag{24}$$

is the mean value of y given input $\boldsymbol{x}$.

For this model, the error function for the pure natural gradient learning of Eq. 10 has the same form as the sum of squared error function,

$$E(\boldsymbol{\theta}_t) = \frac{1}{2}\sum_{n=1}^{N}\{y_n^* - f(\boldsymbol{x}_n;\boldsymbol{\theta}_t)\}^2, \qquad (25)$$

if we ignore the parameter-independent term in Eq. 10.

Using the model and the error function of Eq. 25, the explicit form of the pure natural gradient learning algorithm and the proposed learning algorithm can be easily obtained, and we compared two algorithms using a well known benchmark problem. The application problem used for our experiment is the Mackey-Glass chaotic time series prediction which is widely used to check the performances of learning systems. The time series data were generated from the equation

$$x(t+1) = (1-b)x(t) + a\frac{x(t-\tau)}{1+x(t-\tau)^{10}}, \qquad (26)$$

where $a = 0.2$, $b = 0.1$, and $\tau = 17$. The input values of the network are given from four previous time series data, i.e., $x(t), x(t-6), x(t-12)$, and $x(t-18)$, and the output value of the network is given from 1 future time series datum, $x(t+6)$. We used 500 data which were generated at $t = 200, \ldots, 700$, for training, and other 500 data at $t = 5000, \ldots, 5500$ were used for test. The time series for training at $t = 200, \ldots, 700$ is shown in Fig. 1.

We conducted 10 independent runs with different initial values of parameter for each algorithm, respectively. We stopped the learning process when the mean square error (MSE) for the training data became to be smaller than 2×10^{-5} or the number of learning step exceeds a sufficiently large number. We regarded a learning task failed if MSE remains larger than 2×10^{-5} through the whole learning process. The initial values of parameters were randomly chosen from the interval $[-0.1, 0.1]$, and we chose the learning rate for the pure natural gradient learning method empirically so as to give fast convergences and high success rate.

Table 1. Average results on the Mackey-Glass time series prediction problem (NGL: the pure natural gradient learning, PL : the proposed learning)

	NGL	PL
Learning rate	0.001	-
Num. of hidden nodes	10	10
Rate of success	7/10	7/10
Learning cycle for MSE $< 2 \times 10^{-5}$	426	238
MSE for test data	2.5×10^{-5}	2.5×10^{-5}

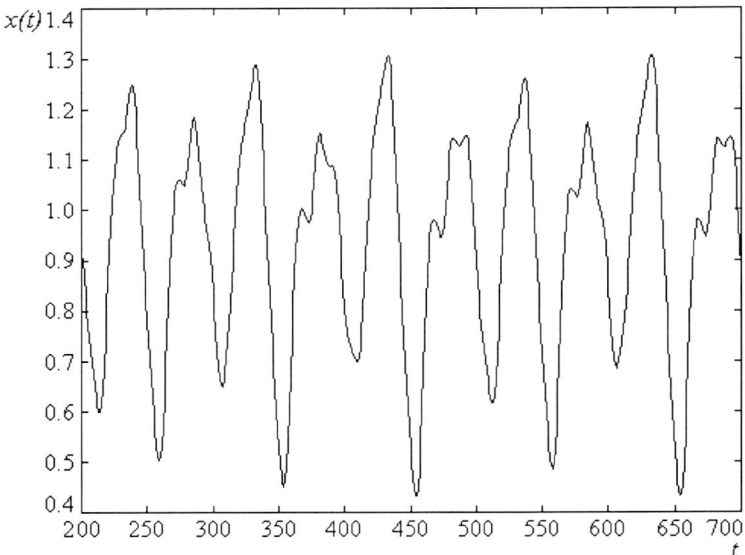

Fig. 1. Mackey-Glass time series

The average results over 10 independent runs are shown in Table 1. For this problem, the proposed learning method showed about two times faster convergence than the pure natural gradient learning method in the sense of the learning cycle.

5 Conclusions and Discussions

Even though there have been many learning algorithms using the second order information, they could not provide satisfying solutions to the problem of then slow learning speed of the conventional gradient descent learning algorithms. On the contrary, the natural gradient learning method has been recently shown to provide a good solution to the problem and to be successfully applied to practical problems. In this paper, we proposed a new learning algorithm based on the natural gradient learning algorithm and the second order information of the error surface. By adding the curvature information of error surface to the pure natural gradient leaning, we expect to get a more efficient learning algorithm. We confirmed from an experiment that the proposed learning algorithm gives faster convergence than the pure natural gradient learning. For future works, it is required to revise the proposed learning algorithm in order to apply to on-line learning. Further consideration about the computational cost of the proposed learning method would also be necessary.

References

1. S. Amari, Natural Gradient Works Efficiently in Learning, *Neural Computation,* 10, 251-276, 1998.
2. S. Amari and H. Nagaoka, *Information Geometry*, AMS and Oxford University Press, 1999.
3. Amari, S., Park, H., and Fukumizu, F., Adaptive method of realizing natural gradient learning for multilayer perceptrons, *Neural Computation*, 12, xx-xx, 2000.
4. D. P. Bertsekas, *Nonlinear Programming*, Athena Scientific, Belmout, Massachusetts, 1995.
5. C. Bishop, *Neural Networks for Pattern Recognition*, Oxford University Press, 1995.
6. Y. LeCun, L. Bottou, G. B. Orr, and K. -R. Müller, *Neural Networks: Tricks of the Trade*, ed. G. B. Orr and K. R.Müller, (pp. 5-50), Springer Lecture Notes in Computer Sciences, 1524, Springer Heidelberg, 1998
7. H. Park, Efficient On-line Learning Algorithms Based on Information Geometry for Stochastic Neural Networks, Ph.D. Thesis, Dept. of CS, Yonsei University, 2000.
8. M. Rattray and D. Saad, Transient and Asymptotics of Natural Gradient Learning, *Proceedings of the 8th International Conference on Artificial Neural Networks*, 165-170, 1998.
9. M. Rattray, D. Saad, and S. Amari, Natural Gradient Descent for On-line Learning, *Physical Review Letters*, 81, 5461-5464, 1998.

Fast and Robust General Purpose Clustering Algorithms

Vladimir Estivill-Castro and Jianhua Yang

Department of Computer Science & Software Engineering,
The University of Newcastle, Callaghan, NSW 2308, Australia.

Abstract. General purpose and highly applicable clustering methods are required for knowledge discovery. k-MEANS has been adopted as the prototype of iterative model-based clustering because of its speed, simplicity and capability to work within the format of very large databases. However, k-MEANS has several disadvantages derived from its statistical simplicity. We propose algorithms that remain very efficient, generally applicable, multidimensional but are more robust to noise and outliers. We achieve this by using medians rather than means as estimators of centers of clusters. Comparison with k-MEANS, EM and GIBBS sampling demonstrates the advantages of our algorithms.

1 Introduction

Efficient clustering is fundamental for data mining where the goal is to discover patterns in large data sets that are also high dimensional. Many clustering methods exist to partition a data set by some natural measure of similarity. While no definition of cluster is widely accepted, many algorithms have been recently developed to suit specific domains. However, general purpose and highly applicable clustering methods are required during early stages of knowledge discovery exercises to investigate potential for data mining. k-MEANS has been widely adopted as such general purpose algorithm because of its simplicity and speed. It offers practically no limitation on the size of data sets because it typically requires linear time. It also does not explicitly restrict the dimensionality of the data. General purpose clustering methods should be stoppable and resumable [4,9], with the capacity to obtain a solution at any time, and to be able to improve on the quality of the solution given more time. They should also work within the window or access methods of databases and data-warehouses.

However, a closer look at k-MEANS reveals that it is probably a poor choice for a clustering task unless very specific conditions on the data are met. For example, k-MEANS typically requires that the clusters be spherical, that the data be free of noise and that its operation be properly initialized. This conditions hardly occur in practical knowledge discovery situations. The weaknesses of k-MEANS result in poor quality clustering, and thus, more statistically sophisticated alternatives have been proposed. Representatives of these alternatives are Expectation Maximization (EM) (and model-based clustering [10]), Data

Augmentation and Gibbs sampling Markov chain Monte Carlo algorithms [22]. While these alternatives offer more statistical accuracy, robustness and less bias, they trade this for substantially more computational requirements.

This paper describes fast and robust general purpose algorithms. While equally or just slightly slower than k-MEANS, they offer robustness to additive and multiplicative noise. Our methods are faster that the next level of sophistication (namely, EM) and remain conceptually simple. For example, our methods do not demand the selection of a family of models for a mixture, the provision of good estimates of variance, the use of bilinear programming, or the provision of prior probabilities; thus, they are simple to use. We achieve this by minimizing different loss functions in the learning of representatives of clusters. Since our algorithms derive from the basic structure of iterative methods, Section 2 reviews k-MEANS and EM. Section 3 presents our two algorithms in detail. Section 4 describes a series of experiments that illustrate the efficiency of our algorithms and compare them with k-MEANS, EM and GIBBS sampling. This section also includes experiments that demonstrate the robustness of our methods and the quality of results. We conclude with some final remarks in Section 5.

2 General Purpose Clustering Algorithms

The attractiveness of k-MEANS is due to its program-code simplicity and its computational efficiency. It requires only $O(tDkn)$ time, where t is the number of iterations over the entire data set, D is the dimension, k is the number of clusters, and n is the number of data items. As $t, D, k \ll n$ for data mining applications, k-MEANS takes $O(n)$ time. The fascination with k-MEANS's speed has motivated researchers to adapt the method to both numeric and categorical data. By iteratively improving an initial clustering, the k-MEANS method produces an approximate solution to the minimization of:

$$M(C) = \sum_{i=1}^{n} w_i \, \text{EUCLID}^2(\boldsymbol{x}_i, \text{REP}[\boldsymbol{x}_i, C]), \tag{1}$$

where
1.- $S = \{\boldsymbol{x}_1, \boldsymbol{x}_2, \ldots, \boldsymbol{x}_n\}$ is a set of n points in D-dimensional real space $\Re^D$;
2.- the weight $w_i > 0$ may reflect relevance of the observation $\boldsymbol{x}_i$;
3.- the Euclidean metric $\text{EUCLID}(\boldsymbol{x}, \boldsymbol{y}) = (\sum_{d=1}^{D} |x_d - y_d|^2)^{1/2}$ measures distances;
4.- $C = \{\boldsymbol{c}_1, \ldots, \boldsymbol{c}_k\}$ is a set of k *centers*, or representative points of $\Re^D$; and
5.- REP$[\boldsymbol{x}_i, C]$ is the closest point in C to $\boldsymbol{x}_i$.

Clusters are defined by assigning each $\boldsymbol{x}_i$ to its representative REP$[\boldsymbol{x}_i, C]$. Those data items assigned to the same representative are deemed to be in the same cluster; thus, the k centers encode the partition $S = C_1 | \ldots | C_k$ of the data. That is, $C_j = \{\boldsymbol{x}_i \in S | \text{EUCLID}(\boldsymbol{x}_i, \boldsymbol{c}_j) \leq \text{EUCLID}(\boldsymbol{x}_i, \boldsymbol{c}_q) \forall \boldsymbol{c}_q \in C \setminus \{\boldsymbol{c}_j\}\}$.

k-MEANS iteratively refines a partition alternating a minimization step and a classification step. In the minimization step, for each cluster in the partition, a new representative is computed. In k-MEANS, the *weighted arithmetic mean* of the cluster's points is a "center" that minimizes the sum of squared errors between the center and the points in the cluster. Next, using the new representatives, a classification step obtains new clusters. There are a number of variants of k-MEANS. These may (1) use random or other methods to obtain an initial partition; (2) recompute the clustering each time a new representative is computed (the so-called 'combinatorial' reclassification [1]), rather than waiting until the new representatives of all clusters have been determined ('non-combinatorial' reclassification). Basic ISO-data [1] is one variant of k-MEANS that uses random initialization and non-combinatorial reclassification. It was the procedure inside the software package CLUSTAN. Combinatorial reclassification has been favored in Data Mining applications. Commercial software typically includes some version of k-MEANS, (for example, DBMiner^{TM}), Clementine^{TM} and MineSet^{TM}. A third popular variant of k-MEANS is a combinatorial version in which the update of a representative takes place only if that update decreases $M(C)$. This variant goes by several names: hill-climber [1], basic minimum squared error [7], and cluster-swapping [19]. Other variants of k-MEANS also appear in the literature of vector quantization [6]. k-MEANS variants have several drawbacks:

1.- They often converge to a local optimum of poor quality [5, 10].

2.- k-MEANS is very sensitive to the presence of noise and outliers, as well as to the initial random clustering [12, page 277]. In particular, much effort has been focused on the sensitivity of k-MEANS on the set of representatives used to initialize the search [1, 4, 9].

3.- The method is statistically biased. For parametric statisticians, this implies that even if provided with the exact number of distributions in a uniform family mixture (for example, all multivariate normal distributions), and large volumes of noiseless data, k-MEANS converges to the wrong parameter values. This has favored other statistical methods such as EM. k-MEANS is also statistically inconsistent. This has favored Bayesian methods.

The most popular alternative to k-MEANS for learning with mixtures is EM. This adds to k-MEANS a probabilistic assignment treating class labels as hidden variables. Its formal analysis is much more complex than k-MEANS, but EM is asymptotically unbiased. Convergence is slow near local maxima so some implementations switch to conjugate gradient methods or other methods near a solution.The foundations of this approach were originally developed for the exponential family of distributions. There is also concern for EM's sensitivity to initialization [9]. Attempts to accelerate its performance on large data sets via summarization indicate that the tails of distributions are critical [17]. Different EM methods update their parameters at each iteration slightly differently. In order to have analytical solutions, it is assumed that each cluster is a multivariate Gaussian density $N(\boldsymbol{\mu}_j, \Sigma_j)$ [10]. Further simplifications assume that all components have the same known covariance Σ, and thus, the only unknowns are the means $\boldsymbol{\mu}_j$. Only the simplest EM versions compete in speed with k-MEANS.

k-MEANS is not only measuring dissimilarity by the Euclidean distance, but more importantly, it is a least squares approach. This is usually unnoticed because the pseudo-code or the descriptions of k-MEANS and its variants do not make it explicit. Nowhere are distances squared, but when k-MEANS finds a representative for a cluster by computing the arithmetic mean, k-MEANS finds the minimum of a strictly convex function. More precisely, let $C_j = \{\boldsymbol{x}_1, \ldots, \boldsymbol{x}_{n_j}\}$ be the points in cluster C_j. Consider the objective function

$$\text{GRAVITY}(\boldsymbol{x}) = \sum_{i=1}^{n_j} w_i \text{EUCLID}^2(\boldsymbol{x}, \boldsymbol{x}_i) = \sum_{i=1}^{n_j} w_i (\boldsymbol{x} - \boldsymbol{x}_i)^T \cdot (\boldsymbol{x} - \boldsymbol{x}_i). \quad (2)$$

Because the function is strictly convex, it has a unique minimum. Denote by $\nabla G(\boldsymbol{x})$ the gradient of $G(\boldsymbol{x})$, so $\nabla G(\boldsymbol{x}) = (\partial G/\partial x_1, \cdots, \partial G/\partial x_D)$. Then, the unique minimum can be found by solving $\nabla G(\boldsymbol{x}) = \boldsymbol{0}$. So, for the d-th coordinate, $0 = \partial G/\partial x_d \sum_{i=1}^{n_j} w_i (\boldsymbol{x} - \boldsymbol{x}_i)^T \cdot (\boldsymbol{x} - \boldsymbol{x}_i) = 2 \sum_{i=1}^{n_j} w_i (x_d - x_{i_d})$. Letting $W_j = \sum_{i=1}^{n_j} w_i$, this implies $\hat{x}_d = \sum_{i=1}^{n_j} w_i x_{i_d} / W_j$. That is, the minimum is the arithmetic mean $\hat{\boldsymbol{x}}^T = (\hat{x}_1, \ldots, \hat{x}_D)$ of cluster C_j. It can be computed, as is typical in k-MEANS, in $O(n)$ time as $\hat{\boldsymbol{x}} = \sum_{i=1}^{n_j} w_i \boldsymbol{x}_i / W_j$.

All variants of k-MEANS minimize $\text{GRAVITY}(\boldsymbol{x})$ for each cluster in their minimization step. Thus, k-MEANS is a EM method where after each classification step, the maximization step maximizes the likelihood by minimizing $\text{GRAVITY}(\boldsymbol{x})$ within each cluster. Because of this, k-MEANS is a least squares error method where the sum of the squared discrepancies between the representative and each data point is minimized. Another view is that the error incurred by choosing the arithmetic mean $\hat{\boldsymbol{x}}$ as a representative for C_j is proportional to the total sum of squared discrepancies within cluster C_j. That is,

$$2W \text{GRAVITY}(\hat{\boldsymbol{x}}) = \sum_{i=1}^{n_j} \sum_{m=1}^{n_j} w_i w_m \text{EUCLID}^2(\boldsymbol{x}_i, \boldsymbol{x}_m). \quad (3)$$

The arithmetic mean may have no valid interpretation, so one step towards robustness is to find the point in the data that minimizes $\text{GRAVITY}(\boldsymbol{x})$. This is called the discrete center optimization and it is simple to compute. For any convex function F, the set $L(c) = \{\boldsymbol{x} \in \Re^d | F(\boldsymbol{x}) \leq c\}$ is a convex set, for all $c \geq 0$. However, for $\text{GRAVITY}(\boldsymbol{x})$, it is not hard to show that $L(c)$ is a solid sphere. Thus, the data point that minimizes $\text{GRAVITY}(\boldsymbol{x})$ can be found in $O(n)$ time simply by finding the center of all these spheres (the arithmetic mean $\hat{\boldsymbol{x}}$) in $O(n)$ time as before, and then, finding the nearest data point to the arithmetic mean in $O(n)$ time. Unfortunately, this variant is only slightly more robust.

3 Medians Are Better

The problem with means is that they are not robust estimators of central tendency in the statistical sense [18]. Means are very sensitive to noise and outliers. Medians represent better a typical value in skew distributions and are invariant under monotonic transformations of the random variable. Means are invariant only under linear transformations. The median of a distribution is much less tractable from the mathematical point of view than the mean. In clustering, as in vector quantization, the mean is to be a representative of the data points x_i that are nearest to it. The mean and the median are both measures of location. Equation (1) represents what statisticians call a L_2 loss functional [18]. Thus, an immediate alternative is to use a error evaluation that measures the sum of absolute errors rather than the sum of squared of errors. This L_1 criterion results in the Fermat-Weber clustering criterion [13]:

$$\text{minimize } FW(C) = \sum_{i=1}^{n} w_i \text{ EUCLID}(s_i, \text{REP}[s_i, C]). \tag{4}$$

Solving Equation (4) with $\text{REP}[s_i, C] \in S$ has been named medoids clustering [12], but obtaining optimal solutions is an NP-complete problem because medoids clustering is equivalent to the p-medians problem (the optimization literature uses p rather than k for the number of representatives). However, several heuristics have been suggested to obtain medoids-based clustering [8,14]. Medoids based clustering is much more robust than k-MEANS with respect to multiplicative or additive noise, thus resulting in clustering of much better quality. However, the heuristics are still slower than k-MEANS and fundamentally applicable only for spatial data, in particular, the bidimensional case.

k-D-MEDIANS: Our approach here uses medoids based clustering but in the maximization phase of an iterative algorithm of the EM or k-MEANS family. Our first proposal, is to use the L_1 function. Thus, we are using the same inductive principle, but different loss function. Therefore, when we find the representative for cluster $C_j = \{x_1, \ldots, x_{n_j}\}$ we find the minimum for the function

$$\text{FW}(x) = \sum_{i=1}^{n_j} w_i \text{EUCLID}(x, x_i) = \sum_{i=1}^{n_j} w_i \sqrt{(x - x_i)^T \cdot (x - x_i)}. \tag{5}$$

Because the function is strictly convex, it has a unique minimum. However, there is no algorithm to compute the exact coordinates of this point [3]. The *gradient* of $\text{FW}(x)$ is not defined for data points $x = s_i$. Setting this gradient to zero only results in an iterative algorithm whose convergence or divergence depends on initialization [13], and when converging, it is slow [16].

Our first proposal is to find the data point in each cluster that minimizes $\text{FW}(x)$. That is, we solve a discrete 1-median problem for each cluster. In a nutshell, our algorithm has the same structure as k-MEANS. But, the new center of each cluster C_j is the discrete 1-median of the points in C_j. This can trivially be solved in $O(n_j^2)$ time by evaluating $\text{FW}(x_i)$ (for $i = 1, \ldots, n_j$) and returning the data point that has minimum FW value. However, this results in quadratic time requirements. In what follows we present our strategy to obtain the discrete 1-median problem for each cluster in $O(n_j \log n_j)$ time. Our strategy uses the extended gradient [13] and imposes no restrictions on the dimension of the data.

Lemma 1. *For* $m = 1, \ldots, n_j$, *let* $\text{FW}_{\neg m}(x) \sum_{i=1, i \neq m}^{n} \text{EUCLID}(x, x_i)$ *be an objective function where the m-th point in C_j is excluded from consideration.*

Let $\nabla \mathrm{FW}(\boldsymbol{x})$ be the gradient of $\mathrm{FW}(\boldsymbol{x})$ defined in $\Re^D \setminus C_j$. Let the extended gradient of $\mathrm{FW}(\boldsymbol{x})$ be denoted by $\nabla_E \mathrm{FW}(\boldsymbol{x})$ and defined by

$$\nabla_E \mathrm{FW}(\boldsymbol{x}) = \begin{cases} \nabla \mathrm{FW}(\boldsymbol{x}) & \text{if } \boldsymbol{x} \notin C_j \\ \max\left\{1 - \frac{1}{\|\nabla \mathrm{FW}_{\neg m}(\boldsymbol{x})\|}, 0\right\} \nabla \mathrm{FW}_{\neg m}(\boldsymbol{x}_m) & \text{if } \boldsymbol{x} = \boldsymbol{x}_m \in C_j \end{cases}$$

Then, $\nabla_E \mathrm{FW}(\boldsymbol{x})$ is defined in $\Re^D$ and the point f minimizes $\mathrm{FW}(\boldsymbol{x})$ if and only if $\nabla_E \mathrm{FW}(\mathsf{f}) = \mathbf{0}$.

The extended gradient has the properties of the gradient with respect to the level curves. For our purposes the following is most important.

Property 1. For all $\boldsymbol{x} \in \Re^D$, the extended gradient vector $\nabla \mathrm{FW}_E(\boldsymbol{x})$ is normal to the tangent hyper-plane at $\boldsymbol{x}$ to $L(\mathrm{FW}(\boldsymbol{x})) = \{\boldsymbol{y} \in \Re^D | \mathrm{FW}(\boldsymbol{y}) \leq \mathrm{FW}(\boldsymbol{x})\}$.

Thus, the extended gradient can be used as a filtering mechanism to eliminate data points than cannot possibly be the discrete 1-median. Consider a point $\boldsymbol{x}$ on a level curve bounding $L(c)$; thus, $c = \mathrm{FW}(\boldsymbol{x})$. The tangent hyper-plane of $L(c)$ at $\boldsymbol{x}$ will divide the space $\Re^D$ into two parts. One half-space contains the set $L(c)$. We call this half space the *keeping zone*. For any point $\boldsymbol{y}$ in the other half space, $\mathrm{FW}(\boldsymbol{y}) > c = \mathrm{FW}(\boldsymbol{x})$. We call the other half space the *filtering zone*. Thus, any point in the filtering zone can be discarded from being the discrete 1-median if there is a data point $\boldsymbol{x}_i \in C_j$ in the keeping zone with $\mathrm{FW}(\boldsymbol{x}_i) \leq c = \mathrm{FW}(\boldsymbol{x})$. In addition, we call the dividing hyper-plane between the keeping zone and the filtering zone the *judge hyper-plane*. In particular, the point $\boldsymbol{x}$ is called the *judge point*. Note also that after computation of the extended gradient we have the judge hyper-plane encoded by its normal vector $\boldsymbol{n}_x$. Moreover, testing if a point is in the filtering zone can be done in constant time with respect to n_j. Namely, for any point $\boldsymbol{y}$ in $\Re^D$, if the dot product between the normal $\boldsymbol{n}_x$ and $\boldsymbol{y} - \boldsymbol{x}$ is not negative, $\boldsymbol{y}$ is in the filtering zone.

Our algorithm for 1-medoid repeatedly finds a hyper-plane and filters the points. In order for our algorithm to be effective, we need a data point $\boldsymbol{x}_i$ in the keeping zone with $\mathrm{FW}(\boldsymbol{x}_i) \leq c = \mathrm{FW}(\boldsymbol{x})$. This is easily achieved if we select $\boldsymbol{x}$ to be some data point $\boldsymbol{x}_i$. Note the importance of the extended gradient (selecting $\boldsymbol{x} = \boldsymbol{x}_i$ is impossible with the standard gradient). However, we also need computational efficiency.

We now describe how the hyper-planes remove half of the candidates in each filtering step, thus reducing the n_j candidates in $\log n_j$ steps to a very small number where the discrete 1-median can be found in $O(n_j)$ time. The halving strategy will result in a total of $O(n_j \log n_j)$ time to compute the discrete 1-median. Since the arithmetic mean corresponds to the center of mass and its level curves are spheres, any hyper-plane on the arithmetic mean, independently of direction, divides the mass in half. Thus, by Equation (3), a procedure that repeatedly uses the center of mass as the judge point will require $O(n_j \log \sum_{i=1}^{n_j} \sum_{m=1}^{n_j} \mathrm{EUCLID}^2(\boldsymbol{x}_i, \boldsymbol{x}_m)/2W)$ time in the worst case to reduce the number of candidates to a small constant. Since with $O(n_j)$ time we can make sure that $\sum_{i=1}^{n_j} \sum_{m=1}^{n_j} \mathrm{EUCLID}^2(\boldsymbol{x}_i, \boldsymbol{x}_m)/2) = O(n_j^l)$ with l a small constant, we have a total of $O(n_j \log n_j)$ time to filter n_j items.

The only problem with this procedure is that the arithmetic mean may be very close to the Fermat-Weber point and the discrete 1-median may actually be on the filtering zone. We need to select a point $\boldsymbol{x} = \boldsymbol{x}_i \in C_j$. We select the u nearest neighbors in C_j to the arithmetic mean of C_j as judge points ($u \geq 1$ a small integer constant). We also ensure that the hyper-planes cut a large proportion of the mass. There are very constrained configurations where this strategy will fail to remove a fraction of the candidates (for example, when the data points are bidimensional and constitute the vertices of a regular polygon). We monitor the number of candidates filtered, if the u judging hyper-planes filter less than a fourth of the candidates, we just pick the discrete center (the nearest neighbor to the arithmetic mean) as the center of this cluster. This maintains the $O(n_j \log n_j)$ time bound. Convergence of the overall clustering method results from its maximization/classification structure [21].

k-C-L1-MEDIANS: Our second proposal uses a strategy suggested by Bradley et al [5]. In order to avoid the Fermat-Weber problem, they use the L1 metric in $\Re^D$ (rectilinear or Manhatan). Thus, we find the L1 median of each cluster and we also use L1 in the classification step. That is, for the minimization step we find the representative for cluster $C_j = \{\boldsymbol{x}_1, \ldots, \boldsymbol{x}_{n_j}\}$ minimizing

$$\text{L1}(\boldsymbol{x}) = \sum_{i=1}^{n_j} w_i \text{L1}(\boldsymbol{x}, \boldsymbol{x}_i) = \sum_{i=1}^{n_j} w_i \sum_{d=1}^{D} \|x_d - x_{i_d}\|, \tag{6}$$

without the restriction $\boldsymbol{x} \in C_j$. For the classification, we let REP$[\boldsymbol{x}_i, C_j]$ be the closes point in C_j to x_i by the L1-metric. However, in contrast with Bradley et al [5] we do not solve the minimization of Equation (6) by bilinear programming, but since L1$(\boldsymbol{x})$ is separable per coordinate [2, 11], we find the Euclidean median for each coordinate (unidimensional data) in $\Theta(n_j)$ expected time [20]. Thus, we optimize Equation (6) to a global optimum in optimal $\Theta(Dn)$ time. Thus, we obtain a clustering algorithm that has the same time complexity as k-MEANS; that is, it takes $O(tDkn)$ time.

4 Performance

We first compare the efficiency of our algorithms. We refer to our first algorithm as k-D-MEDIANS for short (k-Discrete-Medians), while we refer to our second algorithm as k-C-L1-MEDIANS for short (k-Continuous-L1-medians). Our C implementation of our algorithms are compared with our C implementation of k-MEANS and EM. For EM we used the assumption that the covariance matrix Σ_j of each component, although unknown, is diagonal [15]. This is the most flexible EM with efficiency comparable with k-MEANS. We also compared with GIBBS sampling. Thus we used the 1999 release (also in C) of the *fbm-software* by R. N. Neal[1] for the GIBBS sampling.

We used the *fbm-software* to generate datasets from 500 to 100,000 points and measured the CPU time of the algorithms (refer to Fig. 1). The first example is a

---
[1] http://www.cs.toronto.edu/~radford/

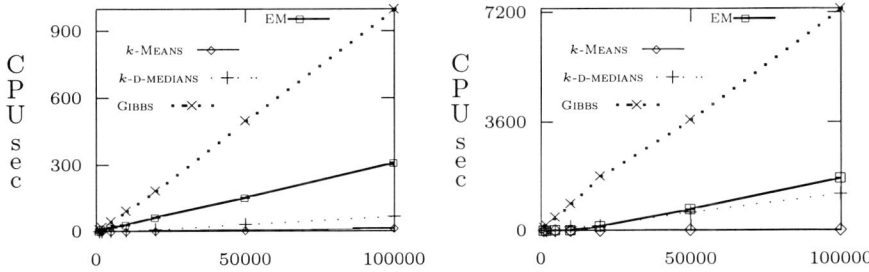

Fig. 1. Comparison of CPU times for R. N. Neal examples for Bayesian mixture models.

bivariate density estimation problem. The second example by R. N. Neal consist of 10 dimensional data where all attributes are categorical (and Boolean). In both experiments, all methods were essentially equivalent in clustering quality. Thus, the only difference for these datasets was speed. However, k-C-L1-MEDIANS and k-MEANS had equivalent time measurements and so only one is shown in Fig. 1. The Bayesian GIBBS sampling was slowest. It requires several meta-parameters and prior probabilities but provides much more information on termination. In fact, for most numerical data, specially from mixtures of Gaussians with noise, k-D-MEDIANS was significantly faster than EM and just slightly slower than k-MEANS. However, Neal's second dataset is the most difficult for our type of methods, because, when data items are regarded as vectors in $\Re^{10}$, they all are placed in the vertices of the Hilbert cube. For these datasets quality of clustering was not an issue. However, k-D-MEDIANS becomes slower for Neal's Boolean set, about the same of EM, while k-MEANS and k-C-L1-MEDIANS remain extremely fast. This type of dataset constitutes the worst case for k-D-MEDIANS, and we are pleased to see that it remains comparable to EM. We should remark that if the categorical domain of attributes is enlarged, k-MEANS's performance deteriorates and k-D-MEDIANS's performance improves.

Table 1. Missclasification with 95% confidence intervals.

$n=300$ $k=10$ $u=1$		One data set (10 runs per set)				10 data sets (10 runs per set)				
		\multicolumn{9}{c	}{Algorithm}
		k-MEANS		k-D-MEDIANS	k-C-L1-MEDIANS	EM	k-MEANS		k-D-MEDIANS	k-C-L1-MEDIANS	EM
Noise	Start	Random	MST	Random	Random	Random	Random	MST	Random	Random	Random
ψ	ϕ										
0	0	39%±7	8%	16%±4	17%±4	25%±5	31%±4	7%±2	16%±5	17%±5	24%±6
	0.1	30%±4	27%	16%±4	16%±4	30%±4	30%±4	23%±5	18%±5	17%±5	42%±6
	0.2	30%±5	30%	22%±5	22%±5	39%±3	30%±5	30%±3	20%±4	18%±3	40 %±6
0.5	0	29%±5	12%±4	14%±4	15%±4	24%±4	30%±4	12%±4	19%±7	20%±6	24%±4
	0.1	30%±4	30%±6	14%±4	14%±4	38%±4	30%±4	30%±4	19%±7	18%±7	37%±6
	0.2	30%±5	31%±3	18%±5	17%±5	38%±4	30%±5	30%±4	18%±6	16%±6	39%±7
1.0	0	33%±5	19%±4	18%±4	20%±4	22%±3	31%±5	20%±4	22%±6	22%±6	22%±4
	0.1	26%±6	36%±9	17%±4	17%±4	39%±4	30%±4	32%±4	20%±4	20%±3	38%±7
	0.2	35%±6	30%±5	15%±5	14%±4	38%±4	31%±6	30%±5	19%±5	18%±5	40%±8
1.5	0	34%±4	22%±3	18%±4	18%±3	30%±5	33%±4	22%±4	18%±5	19%±4	31%±6
	0.1	30%±4	31%±6	14%±5	14%±5	37%±10	32%±4	31%±4	20%±4	18%±4	38%±9
	0.2	34%±4	30%±5	20%±5	19%±5	34%±4	32%±4	31%±5	20%±5	20%±5	36%±8

To contrast the quality of clustering in the presence of noise, we present an experimental illustration contrasting k-MEANS, EM, and our algorithms k-D-MEDIANS and k-C-L1-MEDIANS. We used a simple GENERATOR of bidimensional data sets and mechanisms to regulate noise[2]. We have modeled noise as the additive term in the finite mixture model corresponding to uniform distribution on the unit square. Additive noise are points that do not belong to any cluster. Our experiments compare clustering algorithms with different levels of additive noise. Also, for the same data set and level of additive noise we compare with different levels of multiplicative noise – the term for it would appear multiplying in the finite mixture model. Namely, a second program takes each data point and perturbs it slightly. The idea here is to test the numerical robustness (or robustness to multiplicative noise) of the algorithms. The levels of additive and multiplicative noise are regulated by the parameters ϕ and ψ. As these parameters grow, the more noise. Table 1 shows comparisons of the algorithms for data sets of 300; but extremely similar results were obtained also for $n = 1000$. The algorithms compared are k-MEANS, k-MEANS initialized by single linkage clustering (found in $O(n \log n)$ time by Minimum Spanning Tree computation) our k-D-MEDIANS and k-C-L1-MEDIANS and EM (with diagonal covariance matrices). The results show robustness of our algorithms to both types of noise.

A second experiment consisted of generating data with respect to a mixture of 3-dimensional (multivariate) normal distributions with noise. Thus, data was generated with the form $p(\boldsymbol{x}) = \pi_1 N_{\boldsymbol{\mu}_1, \Sigma_1}(\boldsymbol{x}) + \ldots + \pi_k N_{\boldsymbol{\mu}_k, \Sigma_k}(\boldsymbol{x}) + \pi_{k+1} U(\boldsymbol{x})$ where each component $N_{\boldsymbol{\mu}_j, \Sigma_j}(\boldsymbol{x})$ is a multivariate normal distributions with mean $\boldsymbol{\mu}_j$ and the covariance matrix Σ_j. Again we compared k-MEANS, EM, and our algorithms k-D-MEDIANS and k-C-L1-MEDIANS. We used 20% noise, $k = 3$ and $\pi_j = .8/k$ for $j = 1, \ldots, k = 3$. Moreover, the three covariance matrices Σ_j were set to the identity in order to create data sets as favorable as possible to k-MEANS and EM.

We evaluated the quality of the clustering results by the sum of the norms between the original $\boldsymbol{\mu}_j$ and the approximations $\hat{\boldsymbol{\mu}}_j$ obtained for the algorithms. Data sets with $n = 2,000$ were generated by selecting three points $\boldsymbol{\mu}_j$ at random in $[0, 20.0] \times [0, 20.0] \times [0, 20.0]$. For example, a typical data set had $\boldsymbol{\mu}_1^T = (13.1, 7.6, 6.9)$, $\boldsymbol{\mu}_2^T = (2.6, 7.1, 14.5)$ and $\boldsymbol{\mu}_3^T = (16.6, 9.3, 14.9)$. Table 2 shows the results for one data set. Typically, the sum of discrepancies between norms was twice as large for k-MEANS than for k-D-MEDIANS. k-D-MEDIANS consistently outperformed the others with respect to quality. On average, EM is closer than the results in Table 2 but still surpassed by k-D-MEDIANS. k-C-L1-MEDIANS is the fastest, followed by k-D-MEDIANS. k-MEANS has problems detecting convergence and sometimes is the slowest. Both EM and k-MEANS end up being several times slower that k-D-MEDIANS and k-C-L1-MEDIANS. k-C-L1-MEDIANS can produce some poor results, as illustrated by Table 2.

k-C-L1-MEDIANS is faster than k-D-MEDIANS, but one should be aware that k-C-L1-MEDIANS performs poorly when the clusters are the synergy (interaction) of the attributes. For example, Fig. 2 shows two 2D clusters. They have the very

---

[2] See http://www.cs.newcastle.edu.au/Dept/techrep.html (tr-99-03)

Table 2. Results for 3-D mixture of normals with 20% noise.

Algorithm	$\hat{\boldsymbol{\mu}}_j^T$	$\sum_{j=1}^3 \|\hat{\boldsymbol{\mu}}_j - \boldsymbol{\mu}_j\|$	CPU time
k-Means	$\boldsymbol{\mu}_1^T = (12.7, 8.4, 6.3)$ $\boldsymbol{\mu}_2^T = (3.1, 7.8, 13.5)$ $\boldsymbol{\mu}_3^T = (16.3, 9.6, 14.8)$	2.83	96 sec
EM	$\boldsymbol{\mu}_1^T = (10.1, 9.7, 9.4)$ $\boldsymbol{\mu}_2^T = (2.7, 7.1, 14.4)$ $\boldsymbol{\mu}_3^T = (15.1, 8.6, 11.3)$	7.77	5 sec
k-D-Medians	$\boldsymbol{\mu}_1^T = (12.8, 8.0, 6.9)$ $\boldsymbol{\mu}_2^T = (2.8, 7.1, 14.4)$ $\boldsymbol{\mu}_3^T = (16.6, 9.6, 14.8)$	0.97	0.7 sec
k-C-L1-Medians	$\boldsymbol{\mu}_1^T = (7.8, 16.0, 6.0)$ $\boldsymbol{\mu}_2^T = (3.8, 7.1, 14.4)$ $\boldsymbol{\mu}_3^T = (15.0, 8.5, 9.8)$	16.8	0.4 sec

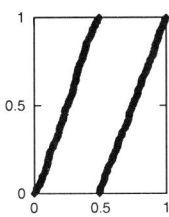

Fig. 2. Data is uniform if projected to either axis, but has a clear pattern in the plane.

distinctive pattern that they are lines. However, for each coordinate, the data is a uniform distribution. k-C-L1-Medians finds cluster with over 40% error 90% of the time and 10% of the time is totally wrong providing two clusters separated by the line $Y = 0.5$. By contrast, k-D-Medians performs very well in this data set, 90% of the time the misclassification is only 10%.

The statistical literature has rejected the L1-metric optimization because the estimator of location can be outside the convex hull of the cloud of points for which it is estimating a center [18].

5 Final Remarks

The algorithms presented here are suitable for exploratory data analysis. They do not depend on the order of the data (some variants of k-Means do) and they do not demand detailed initialization. Their use brings insight into the structure of a large multidimensional data set. Because faster than EM, they can be applied in combination with criteria for determining the number k of clusters. Recall that the most robust criteria find robust estimates of the value of k by repeated clustering with different values of k [15].

References

1. M.S. Aldenderfer and R.K. Blashfield. *Cluster Analysis*. Sage, USA, 1984.
2. C. Bajaj. *Geometric Optimization and Computational Complexity*. PhD thesis, D. Computer Science, Cornell University, NY, 1984.
3. C. Bajaj. Proving geometric algorithm non-solvability: An application of factoring polynomials. *J. Symbolic Computation*, 2:99–102, 1986.
4. P.S. Bradley, U. Fayyad, and C. Reina. Scaling clustering algorithms to large databases. R. Agrawal and P. Stolorz, eds, *Fourth Int. Conf. on Knowledge Discovery and Data Mining*, pages 9–15. AAAI Press, 1998.
5. P.S. Bradley, O.L. Mangasarian, and W.N. Street. Clustering via concave minimization. *Advances in neural information processing systems*, 9:368–, 1997.

6. V. Cherkassky and F. Muller. *Learning from Data — Concept, Theory and Methods.* Wiley, NY, 1998.
7. R. Duda and P. Hart. *Pattern Classification and Scene Analysis.* Wiley, NY, 1973.
8. V. Estivill-Castro and M.E. Houle. Robust clustering of large geo-referenced data sets. *3rd Pacific-Asia Conf. on Knowledge Discovery and Data Mining (PAKDD-99)*, 327–337. Springer-Verlag LNAI 1574, 1999.
9. U. Fayyad, C. Reina, and P.S. Bradley. Initialization of iterative refinement clustering algorithms. R. Agrawal and P. Stolorz, eds., *Fourth Int. Conf. on Knowledge Discovery and Data Mining*, 194–198. AAAI Press, 1998.
10. C. Fraley and A.E. Raftery. How many clusters? which clustering method? answers via model-based cluster analysis. *Computer J.*, 41(8):578–588, 1998.
11. R.L. Francis. *Facility layout and location: An analytical approach.* Prentice-Hall, NJ, 1974.
12. L. Kaufman and P.J. Rousseeuw. *Finding Groups in Data: An Introduction to Cluster Analysis.* Wiley, NY, 1990.
13. H.W. Kuhn. A note on Fermat's problem. *Mathematical Programming*, 4(1):98–107, 1973.
14. R.T. Ng and J. Han. Efficient and effective clustering methods for spatial data mining. J. Bocca, M. Jarke, and C. Zaniolo, eds., *20th Conf. on Very Large Data Bases (VLDB)*, 144–155, 1994. Santiago, Chile, Morgan Kaufmann.
15. J.J. Oliver, R.A. Baxter, and C.S. Wallace. Unsupervised learning using MML. *13th Machine Learning Conf.*, 364–372, CA, 1996. Morgan Kaufmann.
16. M.L. Overton. A quadratically convergent method for minimizing a sum of Euclidean norms. *Mathematical Programming*, 27:34–63, 1983.
17. G.W. Rogers, B.C. Wallet, and E.J. Wegman. A mixed measure formulation of the EM algorithm for huge data set applications. L. Billard and N.I. Fisher, eds., *28th Symposium on the Interface between Computer Science and Statistics*, 492–497, Sydney, 1997.
18. P.J. Rousseeuw and A.M. Leroy. *Robust regression and outlier detection.* Wiley, NY, 1987.
19. R.J. Schalkoff. *Pattern Recognition — Statistical, Structural and Neural Approaches.* Wiley, NY, 1992.
20. R. Sedgewick. *Algorithms.* Addison-Wesley, MA, 1988.
21. S.Z. Selim and M.A. Ismail. k-means-type algorithms: A generalized convergence theorem and characterization of local optimality. *IEEE T. Pattern Analysis and Machine Intelligence*, PAMI-6(1):81–86, 1984.
22. A.F.M. Smith and G.O. Roberts. Bayesian computation via the Gibbs sampler and reated Markov chain Monte Carlo methods. *J. Royal Statistical Society B*, 55(1):2–23, 1993.

An Algorithm for Checking Dependencies of Attributes in a Table with Non-deterministic Information: A Rough Sets Based Approach

Hiroshi Sakai and Akimichi Okuma

Department of Computer Engineering, Kyushu Institute of Technology,
Tobata, Kitakyushu 804, Japan
Tel(Fax) +81-93-884-3258, e-mail:sakai@comp.kyutech.ac.jp

Abstract. Rough sets theory depending upon deterministic information has recently been applied to machine learning, knowledge discovery and knowledge acquisition. For handling some incomplete information, we are now discussing rough sets on non-deterministic information and we have developed some tool programs. In this paper, we propose a definition for dependencies of attributes on non-deterministic information and an algorithm for checking it. According to this algorithm, we have realized a program. To clarify the dependency on non-deterministic information will be useful for extraction of rules from non-deterministic information.

1 Introduction

Rough sets theory is seen as a mathematical foundation of soft computing, which covers some areas of research in AI, i.e., knowledge, imprecision, vagueness, learning, induction[1,2,3,4]. We recently see many applications of this theory to machine learning and knowledge discovery[5,6,7,8,9].

The original rough sets theory is basically on a table with deterministic information which we call $DIS(Deterministic\ Information\ System)$. Therefore, we think that rough sets on non-deterministic information will be important issue. We need a framework where we can handle not only deterministic information but also non-deterministic information. Of course, we know there are several works, but the almost works seem to depend upon the way of probability and numerical values. On the other hand, our work depends upon the way of constraint satisfaction. We think here is the big difference between previous works and our approach.

According to such motivation, we are now discussing rough sets theory on a table with non-deterministic information which we call $NIS(Non-deterministic\ Information\ System)$. In [10,11], we have already shown some algorithms and programs. In such background, here we propose a definition for the dependencies of attributes in NIS and an algorithm for checking it. This proposal comes from as an application of [10,11]. After discussing the dependencies of attributes, we will go to the next step, namely the extraction of rules from NIS.

2 Preliminary

In this section, we simply survey the rough sets theory according to [1]. We define every $DIS = (OB, AT, \{VAL_a | a \in AT\}, f)$, where OB is a finite set whose element we call *object*, AT is a finite set whose element we call *attribute*, VAL_a for $a \in AT$ is a finite set whose element we call *attribute value* and f is a mapping such that $f : OB * AT \rightarrow \cup_{a \in AT} VAL_a$ which we call *classification function*. For every $x, y (x \neq y) \in OB$, if $f(x,a) = f(y,a)$ for every $a \in AT$ then we see there is a relation for x and y, which becomes an equivalence relation on OB. If a set $X (\subset OB)$ is the union of some equivalence classes, then we say X is *definable* in DIS. Otherwise we say X is *rough*.

Suppose two sets $CON (\subset AT)$ which we call *condition attributes* and $DEC (\subset AT)$ which we do *decision attributes*. We say *there is a dependency from* CON *to* DEC in the following case. For every $x, y (x \neq y) \in OB$, if $f(x,a) = f(y,a)$ for every $a \in CON$ then $f(x,a) = f(y,a)$ for every $a \in DEC$. In case there is not any dependency, we think a value $m/|OB|$. Here the m is the number of objects which satisfy the above condition. We call this value the *degree of dependency from* CON *to* DEC in DIS. If degree of dependency is 1, then we may say DIS is *consistent* for CON and DEC. If there is a dependency from CON to DEC in DIS, then we see every tuple restricted to CON and DEC shows a rule. We may call such rule an *association rule*. For very large databases with deterministic information, we can see another method *apriori*[12] to get association rules. In [12], we can see some algorithms for getting *large item sets* with *minimal support* and *minimal confidence*. The ID3[13] is also an important algorithm for getting more simple decision trees from databases with deterministic information.

Here, we show an important proposition connecting the dependency in DIS with equivalence relations on OB. Suppose two equivalence relations EQ_1 and EQ_2 on OB. If there exists equivalence class $M \in EQ_2$ such that $L \subset M$ for every equivalence class $L \in EQ_1$, then we express it as $EQ_1 \subset EQ_2$.

Proposition 1[1]. For DIS, suppose $eq(CON)$ be an equivalence relation by condition attributes and $eq(DEC)$ be an equivalence relation by decision attributes. In this case, the following (1) and (2) are equivalent.
(1) There is a dependency from CON to DEC.
(2) $eq(CON) \subset eq(DEC)$.
We discuss this proposition by using the following example DIS_1.

OB	age	weight(kg)	height(cm)
tom	20	65	170
john	30	70	165
mary	20	60	165

Here, $eq(\{age\}) = \{\{tom, mary\}, \{john\}\}$, $eq(\{age, weight\}) = \{\{tom\}, \{john\}, \{mary\}\}$ and $eq(\{height\}) = \{\{tom\}, \{john, mary\}\}$. Because $eq(\{age, weight\}) \subset eq(\{height\})$, we know there is a dependency from $\{age, weight\}$ to $\{height\}$. The degree of dependency is 1. On the other hand, $eq(\{age\}) \not\subset eq(\{height\})$ and we know only *john* satisfies condition. Therefore, the degree of dependency from $\{age\}$ to $\{height\}$ is 0.33(=1/3). We make use of this property in the subsequent discussion.

Now we define $NIS = (OB, AT, \{VAL_a | a \in AT\}, g)$, where g is a mapping such that $g : OB * AT \to P(\cup_{a \in AT} VAL_a)$(Power set for $\cup_{a \in AT} VAL_a$)[3,14]. According to this definition, if we do not know Tom's age well in DIS_1 then we express it like $\{18, 19, 20, 21, 22, 23\}$ instead of null value. We can see such concept in [15], too. There are some interpretations for every set $M(\in P(\cup_{a \in AT} VAL_a))$ and we see it $\vee_{m \in M} m$. We usually see $\vee_{m \in M} m$ such that there exists a real value in the set M but we do not know it. We may see $\vee_{m \in M} m$ such that we have to select a value from M.

3 An Example of NIS and Issues

Now, we give an example of NIS and we clarify issues.

Example 1. Suppose the next NIS_1 such that $OB = \{1, 2, \cdots, 10\}$, $AT = \{1, 2, 3, 4\}$, $VAL_1 = \{0, 1, 2\}$, $VAL_2 = \{0, 1, 2, 3\}$, $VAL_3 = VAL_4 = \{0, 1, 2, 3, 4, 5\}$ and g is given by the following table. This table was automatically made by using random number programs. In this table, if we select an element for every

OB	1	2	3	4
1	0	2 ∨ 3	5	3
2	0	0 ∨ 1 ∨ 3	4	5
3	2	3	5	0 ∨ 4 ∨ 5
4	0 ∨ 1 ∨ 2	3	1	1
5	1	0 ∨ 1	5	0
6	2	1	3 ∨ 5	4
7	1	0	2	2
8	1	3	1 ∨ 2 ∨ 4	4
9	0	1	5	4
10	2	1	0	1

disjunction then we get a DIS. There are $648(=3^4*2^3)$ $DISs$ for this NIS_1. In this NIS_1, is there a dependency from $\{1,2,3\}$ to $\{4\}$?

To solve the above question, we need to clarify the next issues.

(Issue 1) We know the dependency in DIS, but we do not know it in NIS. How do we think the dependency in NIS?

(Issue 2) Is there an effective algorithm for checking the dependency in NIS?

(**Issue 3**) If we can find a dependency in NIS, then how can we get rules ?
In the subsequent sections, we mainly discuss Issue 1 and Issue 2.

4 A Proposal of Dependency in NIS

Now in this section, we propose a definition of the dependency in NIS. We first give some definitions.

Definition 1. Suppose $NIS = (OB, AT, \{VAL_a | a \in AT\}, g)$. In a $DIS = (OB, AT, \{VAL_a | a \in AT\}, f)$, if $f(x, a) \in g(x, a)$ for every $x \in OB$, $a \in AT$ then we say this DIS is *derived* from NIS.

We know how to check the dependency in DIS and we can extend this concept to the following new concept in NIS.

Definition 2. There is *a strict dependency from CON to DEC in NIS*, if there is a dependency from CON to DEC in all derived $DISs$ from NIS.

However this definition seems strict, so we loosen the condition and propose the next definition.

Definition 3(A Proposal of Dependency in NIS).
Suppose NIS, all derived $DIS_1, \cdots, DIS_m$, condition attributes CON, decision attributes DEC, two threshold values val_1, $val_2 (0 \leq val_1, val_2 \leq 1)$. If the (1) and (2) hold, then we see *there is a dependency from CON to DEC in NIS*.
(1) Suppose n be the number of derived consistent $DISs$ for CON and DEC. Then a ratio satisfies $n/m > val_1$. We especially call this ratio *degree of consistent $DISs$* in NIS.
(2) $min\{\text{degree of dependency in } DIS_i | 1 \leq i \leq m\} > val_2$. We especially call this value *minimum degree of dependency* in NIS.

This proposal clearly contains the definition of the strict dependency. In the strict dependency, both degree of consistent $DISs$ and minimum degree of dependency must be 1, respectively.

In order to clarify the contents, here we show the real execution of implemented program. We discuss the above proposal by using Example 1.

```
?-dependency.
Dependency Check [1,2,3] => [4]
CRITERION 1(Num_of_Consistent_DISs/Num_of_All_DISs)
   Number of Derived DISs: 648
   Number of Derived Consistent DISs: 576
   Degree of Consistent DISs: 0.8888888889
CRITERION 2(Total_Min_and_Max_Degree)
   Minimum Degree of Dependency: 0.8
   Maximum Degree of Dependency: 1.0
EXEC_TIME = 0.07570397854 (sec)
```

For the program of *dependency*, we got the above result. In the criterion 1, 576 derived $DISs$ from NIS_1 are consistent for $\{1, 2, 3\}$ and $\{4\}$. Namely, we know 89% of derived $DISs$ from NIS_1 have dependency. In the criterion 2, the minimum degree of dependency in $72(=648-576)$ derived $DISs$ is 0.8. Therefore in NIS_1, there seems to exist a dependency from $\{1, 2, 3\}$ to $\{4\}$. In another point of view, if we select some appropriate values from non-deterministic information, then we can get $DISs$ where there is dependency from $\{1,2,3\}$ to $\{4\}$.

Through the above discussion, we gave a way to deal with a dependency from CON to DEC in NIS. If we can find a dependency in NIS, then we will be able to discuss the extraction of rules from NIS. Namely for every object x, we generally see $x(CON) \Rightarrow x(DEC)$ ($x(A)$ denotes a tuple of x restricted to attributes set A) shows a rule from CON to DEC in NIS. We soon think the next sequential check algorithm for dependencies.

A Sequential Check Algorithm for Dependencies
For NIS, we first prepare every derived DIS and we sequentially repeat to check the dependency for every derived DIS.
If we depend upon the sequential check algorithm in Example 1, then we need 648 different files for every derived DIS and we have to execute the same program for 648 times. However, we do not depend upon the sequential heck algorithm. We realized the program of *dependency* by another algorithm.

5 An Algorithm for Checking Dependencies in NIS

Now in this section, we discuss an algorithm of implementation. According to Proposition 1, we can check the dependency from CON to DEC by the relation between $eq(CON)$ and $eq(DEC)$. The degree of dependency can also be calculated by $eq(CON)$ and $eq(DEC)$. We use this property and propose the next algorithm.

Overview of An Algorithm for Checking Dependency
(1) Pick up equivalence relations $eq(CON)_i$ and $eq(DEC)_i$ from derived DIS_i.
(2) If $eq(CON)_i = eq(CON)_j (i < j)$ then we remove $eq(CON)_j$ and make a
    pointer from $eq(CON)_i$ to j.
(3) For every $eq(DEC)_i$, make the same procedure as in (2).
(4) For every rest $eq(CON)_i$ and $eq(DEC)_j$, calculate the degree of depen-
    dency. According to every calculated value, we can get two criterion values.
This algorithm mainly consists of two parts. The first part (1), (2) and (3) is to pick up every equivalence relation from NIS. The second part (4) is to get two criterion values from equivalence relations. The second part seems easy for implementation, because we can sequentially check the dependency for all combinations of $eq(CON)_i$ and $eq(DEC)_j$. But the first part is pretty difficult. We will show the details of it in the subsequent sections.

The second part of this algorithm does not directly depend upon the number of derived $DISs$. In Example 1, there are only two equivalence relations by condition attributes CON and three equivalence relations by decision attributes DEC. We are enough to calculate two criterion values for only six cases instead of 648 $DISs$. The real execution of *dependency* shows the results according to these six cases. According to our experience, the number of all combinations for $eq(CON)_i$ and $eq(DEC)_j$ is usually much smaller than the number of derived $DISs$.

6 Equivalence Relations in Derived DISs from NIS

In order to accomplish the algorithm for checking dependencies in NIS, we discuss the equivalence relations in derived $DISs$.

6.1 Some Definitions in NIS

We first show some definitions according to [10,11].
Definition 4. Suppose $NIS = (OB, AT, \{VAL_a | a \in AT\}, g)$ and a set $CON(\subset AT)$. For every derived DIS from NIS, we call the equivalence relation by CON in DIS a *possible equivalence relation* by CON in NIS. We call every element in this relation a *possible equivalence class* by CON in NIS.
Definition 5. Suppose $NIS = (OB, AT, \{VAL_a | a \in AT\}, g)$ and a set $CON(\subset AT)$. If $g(x, a)$ is a singleton set for every $a \in CON$ then we say that object x is $fixed$ in CON. Furthermore, $OB_{fixed}(CON) = \{x \in OB |$ object x is fixed in $CON\}$.
Definition 6. Suppose $NIS = (OB, AT, \{VAL_a | a \in AT\}, g)$, a set $CON(\subset AT)$ and $g(x, a)$ be not a singleton set for some $a \in CON$. By picking up an element in such $g(x, a)$, we can make object x fixed in CON. Here, we call a set of pairs $\{[a, picked\_element] | a \in CON\}$ *selection* in x. For a selection θ, $x_\theta(CON)$ denotes the fixed tuple in CON for x.
Definition 7. Suppose $NIS = (OB, AT, \{VAL_a | a \in AT\}, g)$ and a set $CON(\subset AT)$. For every $x(\in OB)$ and selection θ in x, we give the following definitions.
(1) $inf(x, \theta, CON) = \{x\} \cup \{y \in OB_{fixed}(CON) | y(CON) = x_\theta(CON)\}$.
(2) $sup(x, \theta, CON) = \{y \in OB | y_{\theta'}(CON) = x_\theta(CON)$ for some $\theta'\}$.
According to these definitions, we get the following proposition.
Proposition 2[11].
(1) The $inf(x, \theta, CON)$ is the minimal possible equivalence class including object x for the selection θ.
(2) For every $y \in (sup(x, \theta, CON) - inf(x, \theta, CON))$, there are selections θ' and θ'' such that $y_{\theta'}(CON) = x_\theta(CON)$ and $y_{\theta''}(CON) \neq x_\theta(CON)$.
(3) A subset $X(\subset OB)$ which satisfies $inf(x, \theta, CON) \subset X \subset sup(x, \theta, CON)$ for some x and θ can be a possible equivalence class by CON.
We make use of Proposition 2, especially (3) in Proposition 2, for finding possible equivalence relations in NIS. Here, we show an example which clarifies the application of Proposition 2.
Example 2. Let's consider the following NIS_2 and suppose $CON = \{1, 2\}$.

OB	1	2	3
1	1 ∨ 2	2	1 ∨ 2 ∨ 3
2	1	2	1 ∨ 2 ∨ 3
3	1	1 ∨ 2	2
4	1	2	2 ∨ 3

In this case, we get the next inf and sup.
  (A) $inf(1, [[1,1]], \{1,2\}) = \{1,2,4\}$, $sup(1, [[1,1]], \{1,2\}) = \{1,2,3,4\}$.
  (B) $inf(1, [[1,2]], \{1,2\}) = \{1\}$, $sup(1, [[1,2]], \{1,2\}) = \{1\}$.
  (C) $inf(2, [], \{1,2\}) = \{2,4\}$, $sup(2, [], \{1,2\}) = \{1,2,3,4\}$.
  (D) $inf(3, [[2,1]], \{1,2\}) = \{3\}$, $sup(3, [[2,1]], \{1,2\}) = \{3\}$.
  (E) $inf(3, [[2,2]], \{1,2\}) = \{3,2,4\}$, $sup(3, [[2,2]], \{1,2\}) = \{1,2,3,4\}$.
  (F) $inf(4, [], \{1,2\}) = \{4,2\}$, $sup(4, [], \{1,2\}) = \{1,2,3,4\}$.
As for object 1, we can use either (A) or (B). If we select (A), then we can get two possible equivalence classes $\{1,2,4\}$ and $\{1,2,3,4\}$ by (3) in Proposition 2. If we select $\{1,2,4\}$ then we implicitly decided that the tuples of object 1, 2 and 4 are (1,2) but the tuple of object $3(\in sup - inf)$ is not (1,2). In this case, we say objects 2 and 4 are *positively used*. On the other hand object 3 is *negatively used*. As for object 3, we can take another selection (D) and we get a possible equivalence relation $\{\{1,2,4\},\{3\}\}$. If we select $\{1,2,3,4\}$ in (A), then we implicitly decided every tuple is (1,2) and we get a possible equivalence relation $\{\{1,2,3,4\}\}$. In this way, we can pick up every possible equivalence relation in NIS. However, we need to manage the previous selections in a sequence of getting a possible equivalence relation. For example, when we get a possible equivalence class $\{1,2,4\}$ we can not use (E) any more.

6.2 An Algorithm for Getting All Possible Equivalence Relations

Now in this subsection, we first show an algorithm for checking the definability of every set in NIS.

Overview of An Algorithm: Sup-Inf Method

Suppose we are given $inf(x, \theta, CON)$ and $sup(x, \theta, CON)$ for every $x(\in OB)$.
Input: A set $X(\subset OB)$.
Output: X is definable in $NIS(CON)$ or not.
(1) Set $X^* = X$ and $EQUIV = \{\}$.
(2) For the first element $x(\in X^*)$, find $X'(\subset X^*)$ such that
  • $inf(x, \theta, CON) \subset X' \subset sup(x, \theta, CON)$ for some θ,
  • The selections θs for X' makes no contradiction for every inf and sup.
  (2-1) If we can find X' in (2), then set $[x] = X'$, $EQUIV = EQUIV \cup \{[x]\}$ and $X^* = X^* - X'$. If $X^* \neq \emptyset$ then go to (2). If $X^* = \emptyset$ then the set X is definable in $NIS(CON)$.
  (2-2) If we can not find X', then backtrack this branch. If there is no branch for backtrack, then the set X is not definable in $NIS(CON)$.

By extending Sup-Inf method, we have an algorithm for getting all possible equivalence relations in NIS. Namely, we replace X in Sup-Inf method with OB, then we can get a possible equivalence relation $EQUIV$ as a side effect. In order to get all relations, we use backtrack of search. In this way, we can get all possible equivalence relations in NIS. This algorithm seems simple and natural, but it is pretty difficult to keep the constraints for every inf and sup. In order to solve this problem, we introduced two lists $PLIST$ and $NLIST$. The $PLIST$ keeps the selection θs for positively used objects like in Example 2. The $NLIST$ does the selection θs for negatively used objects. If we check some conditions for $PLIST$ and $NLIST$, then we can get X' which makes no contradiction for every inf and $sup[11]$.

7 A Real Execution of Checking Dependency

We have to do the next steps for checking dependency in NIS.
(Step1) Make a *table data file* and an *attributes file* specifying CON and DEC.
(Step2) Execute the program of translation and get the *internal expression*, like inf and sup.
(Step3) Execute the program of getting all possible equivalence relations.
(Step4) Execute the program of getting dependency.
The syntax of data file is very simple. We show the real data file in Example 1.
```
object(10,4). % numbers of objects and attributes
data(1,[0,[2,3],5,3]). data(2,[0,[0,1,3],4,5]).
         :              :              :
data(9,[0,1,5,4]). data(10,[2,1,0,1]).
total_cases(648).
```
We show the contents of real attributes file in Example 1.
```
condition([1,2,3]). decision([4]).
```
The following is the real execution of Step2.
```
?- consult(tf.pl). % translation program
yes
?- go.
File Name for Read Open : 'data8.pl'.
Attribute Definition File( No use =0 ) : 'attrib3.pl'.
File Name for Write Open : 'data8-3.rs'.
EXEC_TIME = 0.1358059645 (sec)
yes
```
The file data8-3.rs contains inf, sup and other information. In Step3, we first specify the name of file with internal expression.
```
?- relall(con).
[1] [[1],[2],[3],[4,8],[5],[6],[7],[9],[10]] 24
[2] [[1],[2],[3],[4],[5],[6],[7],[8],[9],[10]] 192
POSSIBLE CASES 216
EXEC_TIME = 0.5357359648 (sec)
SAVE TO FILE (y/n): y.
yes
?- relall(dec).
[1] [[1],[2,3],[4,10],[5],[6,8,9],[7]] 1
[2] [[1],[2],[3,5],[4,10],[6,8,9],[7]] 1
[3] [[1],[2],[3,6,8,9],[4,10],[5],[7]] 1
POSSIBLE CASES 3
EXEC_TIME = 0.0147550106 (sec)
SAVE TO FILE (y/n): y.
```
In the Step3, we have got two kinds of possible equivalence relations by condition

attributes CON in NIS and we know there are 24 and 192 same relations. After this step, we can execute the program of *dependency* which we have shown in section 4.

We can pik up every derived DIS from NIS by specifying the possible equivalence relation. Namely, if we solve the definability of a possible equivalence relation, then as a side effect we can get $DISs$ which cause this possible equivalence relation. For example, if we execute $relex(dec, [[1], [2, 3], [4, 10], [5], [6, 8, 9], [7]])$, then as a side effect we can get a derived DIS by $DEC(= \{4\})$.

```
?- relex(dec,[[1],[2,3],[4,10],[5],[6,8,9],[7]]).
[1] RELATION: [[1],[2,3],[4,10],[5],[6,8,9],[7]] on Decision Attributes
POSITIVE SELECTION
CONDITION OF 1: [3]
CONDITION OF 2: [5]
CONDITION OF 3: [5] *
CONDITION OF 4: [1]
      :    :    :
CONDITION OF 10: [1]
NEGATIVE SELECTION
CONDITION OF 3: [0] *
CONDITION OF 3: [4] *
EXEC_TIME = 0.01420497894 (sec)
yes
```

In the above execution, the positive selection shows the selected values for decision attribute $\{4\}$. The $*$ implies a selection from non-deterministic information.

8 Complexity of Algorithm and Execution Time

Now in this section, we discuss the complexity. As for the program of *dependency*, the complexity depends upon the kinds of possible equivalence relations by CON and DEC. In Example 1, 216 possible equivalence relations are reduced to 2 kinds of relations. In such case, our proposing algorithm seems more effective than sequential check algorithm in Section 4. However, the computational complexity of Sup-Inf method will be NP-complete or exponential order in worst case. Because, to get a possible equivalence relation is to pick up some possible equivalence classes $CL_1, \cdots, CL_m$ which satisfy $\cup_{i=1}^{m} CL_i = OB$ and the condition of inf and sup. Namely, to get a possible equivalence relation is a kind of *constraint satisfaction problem*[16], whose complexity is NP-complete[17]. Therefore, we think that the proposing algorithm is not appropriate for very large databases. But it will be useful for small size databases with much non-deterministic information.

Here, we show the results of execution time for some examples. We have not survey other programs which calculate the dependency of attributes in NIS completely yet, so we show the execution time of only our programs. The purpose is to show the overview of applicable size for NIS.

(**CASE 1**) Number of objects is 100, number of attributes is 4, number of derived $DISs$ is 1944, $CON = \{1,2,3\}$ and $DEC = \{4\}$. We got the internal expression in 1.434 (sec). We got 2 kinds of possible equivalence relations by CON in 6.715 (sec) and 9 kinds of possible equivalence relations by DEC in 0.803 (sec). We could get dependency in 3.438 (sec).

(**CASE 2**) In the CASE 1, we examined a case without non-deterministic information, namely number of derived DIS is 1. We got the internal expression in 1.288 (sec). We got a possible equivalence relation by CON in 0.521 (sec) and a possible equivalence relation by DEC in 0.323 (sec). We could get dependency in 0.423 (sec).

(**CASE 3**) In the CASE 1, we examined a case with much non-deterministic information. The number of derived $DISs$ is 62208. We got the internal expression in 1.520 (sec). We got 16 kinds of possible equivalence relations by CON in 220.971 (sec) and 8 kinds of possible equivalence relations by DEC in 0.689 (sec). We could get dependency in 21.841 (sec). The minimum dependency was 0.89 and the maximum dependency was 0.95.

(**CASE 4**) In CASE 1, we changed the number of objects to 300. The number of derived $DISs$ is 3888. We got the internal expression in 16.735 (sec). We got 4 kinds of possible equivalence relations by CON in 108.157 (sec) and 4 kinds of possible equivalence relations by DEC in 6.133 (sec). We could get dependency in 5.944 (sec).

In every CASE, the kinds of possible equivalence relations are so small that we can effectively get the dependency. If the kinds of possible equivalence relations are almost the same number of derived $DISs$, then proposing algorithm will be the same as sequential check algorithm. However in this case, we do not need all files for derived $DISs$. We can manage all derived $DISs$ by using the internal expression.

9 Concluding Remarks and Perspective

We proposed a definition of dependency in NIS and an algorithm for checking it. We have already realized some tool programs, too. We will apply this framework to a machine learning from NIS, especially the extraction of association rules from NIS. For example in NIS_1, if we see there is a dependency from $\{1,2,3\}$ to $\{4\}$, then we will get a rule $(0, 2 \vee 3, 5) \Rightarrow 3$ from tuple 1. There is no tuple $(0,2,5,\_)$ nor $(0,3,5,\_)$, therefore the accuracy and cover value[4,5,12] of this rule will be 1, respectively. We will get a rule $(2,3,5) \Rightarrow 0 \vee 4 \vee 5$ from tuple 3.

As for programs, we are going to revise them for handling more large number of objects. In real, we changed the format of internal expression and we could reduced the size of this file. In the better cases, the size was reduced to 1/4 of the former file. We revised the subcommand $dependency$ in prolog to C language, too. In (CASE 3) of previous section, we could get the same dependency in 0.0(sec) by C program. We will use C language for implementation except algorithm depending upon Sup-Inf method.

We think that our framework will be applicable to automated hypothesis generator from vague and uncertain information, too.

References

[1] Z.Pawlak: Rough Sets, Kluwer Academic Publisher, 1991.

[2] Z.Pawlak: Data versus Logic A Rough Set View, Proc. 4th Int'l. Workshop on Rough Set, Fuzzy Sets and Machine Discovery, pp.1-8, 1996.

[3] E.Orlowska and Z.Pawlak: Logical Foundations of Knowledge Representation, Pas Reports, 537, 1984.

[4] A.Nakamura, S.Tsumoto, H.Tanaka and S.Kobayashi: Rough Set Theory and Its Applications, Journal of Japanese Society for AI, Vol.11, No.2, pp.209-215, 1996.

[5] J.Grzymala-Busse: A New Version of the Rule Induction System LERS, Fundamenta Informaticae, Vol.31, pp.27-39, 1997.

[6] J.Komorowski and J.Zytkow(Eds.): Principles of Data Mining and Knowledge Discovery, Lecture Notes in AI, Vol.1263, 1997.

[7] Z.Ras and S.Joshi: Query Approximate Answering System for an Incomplete DKBS, Fundamenta Informaticae, Vol.30, pp.313-324, 1997.

[8] S.Tsumoto: PRIMEROSE, Bulletin of Int'l. Rough Set Society, Vol.2, No.1, pp.42-43, 1998.

[9] N.Zhong, J.Dong, S.Fujitsu and S.Ohsuga: Soft Techniques to Rule Discovery in Data, Transactions of Information Processing Society of Japan, Vol.39, No.9, pp.2581-2592, 1998.

[10] H.Sakai: Some Issues on Nondeterministic Knowledge Bases with Incomplete and Selective Information, Proc. 1st Int'l. Conf. on Rough Sets and Current Trend of Computing, Lecture Notes in AI, Vol.1424, pp.424-431, 1998.

[11] Sakai and A.Okuma: An Algorithm for Finding Equivalence Relations from Tables with Non-deterministic Information, Proc. 7th Int'l. Conf. on Rough Sets, Fuzzy Sets, Data Mining and Granular-Soft Computing, Lecture Notes in AI, Springer-Verlag, Vol.1711, pp.64-72, 1999.

[12] A.Agrawal, T.Imielinski and A.Swami: A Database Mining, IEEE Trans. on Knowledge and Data Engineering, Vol.5, No.6, pp.914-925, 1993.

[13] J.Quinlan: Introduction of Decision Trees, Machine Learning, Vol.1, pp.81-106, 1986.

[14] W.Lipski: On Semantic Issues Connected with Incomplete Information Data base, ACM Transaction on Database Systems, Vol.4, pp.269-296, 1979.

[15] A.Skowron and J.Grzymala-Busse: From Rough Sets Theory to Evidence Theory, Advances in the Dempster-Shafer Theory of Evidence, John Wiley, pp.193-236, 1994.

[16] R.Haralick: The Constraint Labeling Problems, IEEE Trans. PAMI, Vol.1, No.2, pp.173-184, 1979.

[17] S.Nishihara: Fundamentals and Perspectives of Constraint Satisfaction Problems, Journal of Japanese Society for AI, Vol.12, No.3, pp.351-358, 1997.

Tropical Cyclone Intensity Forecasting Model: Balancing Complexity and Goodness of Fit

Grace W. Rumantir

School of Computer Science and Software Engineering
Monash University – Clayton Vic 3168 Australia
gwr@csse.monash.edu.au

Abstract. Building forecasting models for tropical cyclone intensity is one of the most challenging area in tropical cyclone research. Most, if not all, of the existing models have been built using variants of Maximum Likelihood (ML) approach. The need to partition data into two sets for model development is seen to be one of the drawbacks of ML approach in the face of limited available data. This paper proposes a way to build forecasting model using a number of model selection criteria which take the penalized-likelihood approach, namely MML, MDL, CAICF, SRM. These criteria claim to have the mechanism to balance between model complexity and goodness of fit. The models selected are then compared with the benchmark models being used in operation.

Keywords: industrial applications of Artificial Intelligence, tropical cyclone intensity forecasting, knowledge discovery and data mining

1 Introduction

Tropical cyclone, also known as typhoon or hurricane, is a severe weather system in the form of intense circular vortices which accounts for the strongest sustained winds observed anywhere in the earth's atmosphere. For the Atlantic basin which covers the areas of North Atlantic Ocean, Caribbean Sea and Gulf of Mexico, tropical cyclone (TC) intensity is defined as the near-surface sustained wind speed (1 minute averaged speed) around its eye (center).

As explained in [8], numerical models have not been able to demostrate real-time improvement over no-skill predictions (i.e. simple extrapolation of the trend in TC intensity data, known as *presistence*) because of the strong interactions between mesoscale and synoptic features in the atmosphere leading to TC intensity change. TC intensity data are recorded in sparse intervals of 5 knots prompting the common use of intensity change (strengthening or weakening) within a specified amount of time into the future, e.g. 12, 24, 48, 60, or 72 hours, as the dependent variable of TC forecasting models.

For Atlantic basin, there are three statistical TC forecasting models being used in operation: SHIFOR [7]), SHIFOR94 [8] and SHIPS [3]. All of the three statistical TC forecasting models have been built using variants of Maximum

Likelihood (ML) approach. This means that separate 'test' (i.e. 'semi' independent) data sets are needed to guide the search for a set of independent variables to form an optimum forecasting model. This implies that the predictive performance reported on the test data sets should not be seen as reflections of the performance of a completely independent data sets. The need to partition data into two sets for model development is seen to be one of the drawbacks of ML approach in the face of limited available data.

This paper proposes a way to build forecasting models using a set of methods proven in the experimental survey in [12] to be the most robust amongst most of the commonly cited penalized-likehood model selection criteria. In contrast to a maximum likelihood method, a penalized-likehood method claims to have the mechanism to balance between model complexity and goodness of fit. This enables optimum models to be developed purely using training data sets. Test data sets are used solely for the purpose of giving an indication of the performance of the selected models on unseen data. The models are then compared with the benchmark models, namely SHIFOR and SHIFOR94.

2 Building Forecasting Models

The forecasting models to be built typically take the form of a polynomial regression model to the second-order by considering products of two basic variables as well as the basic variables. The following is the representation of the model with the values of the target variable y_n shifted to zero mean:

$$y_n = \sum_{p=1}^{P} \gamma_p u_{np} + \sum_{p=1}^{P}\sum_{q \geq p}^{P} \gamma_{pq} u_{np} u_{nq} + \epsilon_n \Leftrightarrow y_n = \sum_{k=1}^{K} \beta_k x_{nk} + \epsilon_n \quad (1)$$

where for each data item n:

y_n	: target variable	x_{nk}	: regressor k;
		$x_{nk} = u_{np}$ or $x_{nk} = u_{np}u_{nq}$; $q \geq p$	
u_{np}	: regressor p	β_k	: coeff. for regressor k
γ_p	: coeff. for single regressor	K	$= 2P + P!/2!(P-2)!$
γ_{pq}	: coeff. for compound regressor	ϵ_n	: noise/residual/error term

The values of the error term ϵ is assumed to be uncorrelated, normally and independently distributed $\epsilon_n \sim NID(0, \sigma^2)$.

Table 1 summarizes the set of methods used in this paper. The non-backtracking search method explained in [12] is used for all of the methods. The performance criteria for model comparison are:

1. Parsimony, reflected in the model cost calculated using the cost functions in Table 1 (on training data)
2. Model predictive performance (on test data), quantified by
   (a) Root of the mean of the sum of squared deviations: $RMSE = \sqrt{\frac{1}{n}\sum_{i=1}^{n} e_i^2}$
   (b) Coefficient of determination: $R^2 = 1 - (\sum_{i=1}^{n} e_i^2)/\sum_{i=1}^{n}(y_i - \bar{y})^2$

The proposed procedure for building forecasting models using a specified set of methods is as follows:

1. Using random subsampling, create m pairs of training and test data sets. As explained in Section 3.1, temporal relationships between values of a variable over a period of time have been taken into account in the form of a set of related variables.
   The test data sets are needed not for model development but to see whether or not the performance of a method on unseen data is much different from that on training data.
2. For each of the method in Table 1, search for forecasting models on each pair of data sets.
3. For each independent variable, count its frequency of being chosen in any of the forecasting models discovered in the previous point. Create a set of new models, each as a collection of variables with at least a certain frequency. Calculate the set of coefficients for each model using all of the available data.
4. Compare the models with increasing complexity based on all of the performance criteria

Table 1. Summary of the model selection criteria used. i is index for sample item ranging from 1 to n and k is the number of variables in a model

Method		Ref.	Objective Function
Minimum Message Length	MML	[14]	$-\log f(x\|\theta) + \frac{1}{2}log\|I(\theta)\| - \log h(\theta) -$ $-\frac{k+1}{2}\log 2\pi + \frac{1}{2}\log(k+1)\pi - 1 - \log h(\nu, \xi, j, l, J, L)$
Minimum Description Length	MDL	[10]	$-\log f(x\|\theta) + \frac{k}{2}\log n + (\frac{k}{2}+1) + \log k(k+2)$
Corrected AIC	CAICF	[1]	$-\log f(x\|\theta) + \frac{1}{2}log\|I(\theta)\| + k + \frac{1}{k}\log n$
Structured Risk Minimisation	SRM	[13]	$\frac{1}{n}\sum_{i=1}^{n} e_i^2 / (1 - \sqrt{\frac{(k+1)(\log \frac{n}{k+1}+1) - \log \eta}{n}})$
Stochastic Complexity	SC	[11]	$\frac{n}{2}\log \sum_{i=1}^{n} e_i^2 + \frac{1}{2}\log \|X'X\|$

3 Experimental Design

For the task of building hurricane intensity change forecasting models, it is actually possible to considerably reduce the search space by using only the combinations of variables that would likely be influential to the target variable and removing the combinations that are implausible after consultations with meteorologists. This in fact has been the common approach in hurricane research due to the limitations of the multiple linear regression method used.

Based on the results of their experiments, most atmospheric scientists have come to the conclusion that search space should be limited to potentially significant variables only because it is believed that even random numbers will inadvertently be selected as significant predictors, e.g. [7, 4, 3]. This approach however is not taken in this paper for two reasons:

- It has been proven using artificial data sets in [12] that the methods used in this paper managed to parsimoniously choose a handful of significant regressors amongst a large pool of variables
- Part of the goal of these experiments is to test whether or not the above conclusion applies to real and more complex problem domains like the tropical cyclone systems

3.1 Potential Predictors

The task of building TC intensity change forecasting models is difficult due to the following reasons:

- the fact that exact relationships amongst the variables are not known
- each independent variable is highly preprocessed, either using a thermodynamic formulae chosen from a number of possibilities (e.g. Potential Intensity as a function of sea surface temperature, see [3] or a completely stochastic procedure)
- noise inherent in observational data

Table 2 gives the summary of the independent variables used to build the TC intensity change forecasting models which can be categorized into three groups:

1. *Persistence:* the TC intensity in knots (5,6)
2. *Climatology:* Julian data (1,2), global position (3,4) and motion in knots (7,8,9)
3. *Synoptic* environmental features: sea sub/surface temperature (12,13–15), shear(16–18), distance from land (25–26), etc.

In this paper, the target variable is the intensity change 72 hours into the future. The TC track forecasting model CLIPER [9] is used to provide future forecast positions for which the climatological independent variables are calculated.

3.2 Sample Sets

There are in total 4347 data items available. The experiments are conducted on data sets built using two types of sampling method. Ten training–test data sets are built using 2 : 1 random sampling method. One data set is built so that the training data is taken from the years 1950–1987 and the test data from the years 1988–1994. Convenient separation of data based on consecutiveness is common practice in hurricane intensity change forecasting. SHIFOR (modified by Pike from [7]) and SHIFOR94 [8] have both been built using training data from 1950 to 1987 and test data from 1988 to 1994. The purpose of using these two categories of data sets in this paper is to see whether or not the possible changes in atmospheric dynamics from year to year should be taken into account in experimental design.

The author has been unable to come up with exactly the same parameter coefficients for the variables in SHIFOR and SHIFOR94 as reported in [7] and [8]

Table 2. Basic regressors used to build the Atlantic TC intensity change forecasting models. The target variable is the change of intensity (wind speed) 72 hour into the future. To get the *average*, *at end* and *change* values of a variable, the TC track/location (longitude and latitude) forecast out to 72 hours is required: *average* means the average of the values at the location forecast at 0, 24, 48 and 72 hours, *at end* means the value at 72 hours and *change* means the difference between the current value and the value at 72 hours. Figure 1 illustrates the location of the seasonal variables, i.e. variable 30 to 36

No	Basic Regressor: acronym and explanation
1,2	Julian, JulOff – date: Julian, |Julian - 253|
3,4	LatData, LonData – position: latitude (deg N), longitude (deg W)
5,6	Vmax, Del12V – intensity (in knots): initial, previous 12 hour change
7,8,9	UCurr, VCurr, Speed – motion (in knots): eastward, northward, resultant
10,11	POT, POTEnd – potential intensity: initial, at end
12	DelSST – change of sea surface temperature
13,14,15	SSST, SSSTend, DSSST – sea sub-surface temperature: average, at end, change
16,17,18	UppSpd, Uppend, DUppSpd – windspeed at 200mb: average, at end, change
19,20,21	Stabil, Stabend, DelStab – moist stability 1000mb to 200mb: average, at end, change
22,23,24	200mbT, 200Tend, Del200T – temperature at 200mb: average, at end, change
25,26	DisLand, Closest – distance from land: initial, closest approach
27,28,29	200mbU, 200Uend, Del200U – eastward motion at 200mb: average, at end, change
30	U50 – 50mb Quasi-Biennial Oscillation (QBO) zonal winds
31	RainS – African Western Sahel rainfall index (5W-15W, 10N-20N)
32	RainG – African Gulf of Guinea rainfall index (0W-10W, 5N-10N)
33	SLPA – April-May Caribbean basin Sea Surface Pressure Anomaly
34	ZWA – April-May Caribbean basin Zonal Wind Anomaly at 200mb (12 km)
35	ElNino – Sea surface temperature anomaly in the eastern equatorial pacific
36	SOI – Surface pressure gradient between Darwin and Tahiti

despite the fact that the same data sets and least squares method have been used. Therefore, with respect to the benchmark models, it is decided to run 2 types of experiment. First, to find new coefficients for the variables on each training data set and test the new model on the corresponding test set. The benchmark models with the new coefficients are named SHIFOR' and SHIFOR94'. Second, to use the models SHIFOR and SHIFOR94 as reported in the papers and simply test the same models on the test data sets.

The fact that the models were built using maximum likelihood method (with the test data being used to guide the search for model) implies that SHIFOR and SHIFOR94 have 'seen' all of the data items available. This means that the resulting predictive performance should be less conservative than if the models have been tested on completely independent data sets.

4 Results and Discussions

Table 3 show the models chosen by each method for each of the 10 data sets. Although Stochastic Complexity (SC) has been proven to be a good candidate for automated model discovery using artificial data in [12], it failed to converge into an optimum model before the maximum number of variables set for a model has been reached. Therefore, it is decided not to use nor show the results of SC.

For each of the first 10 data set, there is not too much difference between the predictive performance of MML, MDL, CAICF and SRM on the training

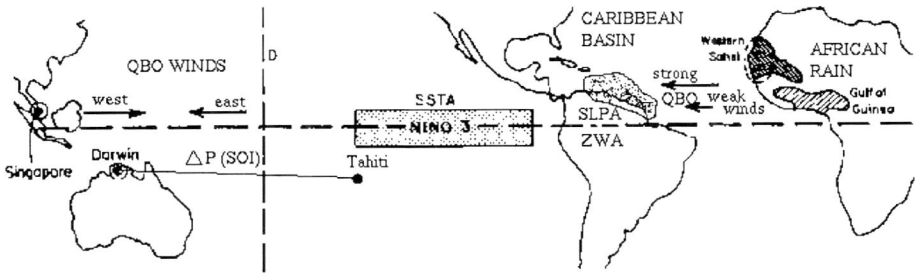

Fig. 1. Locations of the seasonal meteorological variables explained in Table 2 (variable 30 to 36). *Source:* [2]

data and on the test data. This confirms the findings in [12] and strengthen the believe that all of the available data can be used as training data since overfitting is not a problem for these methods.

The consistent performance of SHIFOR and SHIFOR94 across all of the data sets including the last data set (where the training and test data sets are taken from consecutive years) should be taken with caution because of the way the models were built as discussed in Section ??. This is proven by the substantially worse performance of all of the penalized-likelihood methods for the last data set. This phenomenon can be observed both by comparing the predictive performance between the training and test data for the last data set and by comparing the level of model parsimony and predictive performance on test data across the 11 data sets.

It is clear from the observations, that partitioning training and test data based on consecutiveness has resulted in two non-homogeneous data sets; a lot of the regularities learned by a model from the training data set are not present in the test data set resulting in much reduced performance.

Following the second item in the procedure in Section 2, Table 4 shows the models built by categorizing variables based on the minimum frequency of being chosen in all of the 10 data sets in Table 3. It is no surprise that Potential Intensity (variable 10 - POT) and intensity change during the previous 12 hours (variable 6 - Del12V) have been chosen by all of the methods for the 10 data sets. Potential Intensity as a function of sea surface temperature indicates the maximum wind speed a TC can intensify should the system not be perturbed by dampening factors in the environment.

Table 5 shows the performance of the models built in Table 4. The fact that all of the cost values calculated using MML, MDL, CAICF and SRM do not monotonically decrease in models less complex than the 'best model' Model 18 demonstrates how selection bias introduced by using a non-exhaustive search strategy plays a part in determining which path chosen in the search space.

Since both SHIFOR and SHIFOR94 comprise 9 variables, Table 6 compares them with the best 9 variables chosen using the procedure implemented in this paper. All of the three models only agree on one compound intensity variable (Del12V*Vmax). Among the independent variables explained in Section 3.1, SHIFOR was built using persistence and climatology. However SHIFOR94 was built using all of the variables in Table 2.

As explained above, it is not a surprise that POT and Del12V are included in both SHIFOR94 and the new model. It is interesting to note, however, that in contrast of the prevalence of the seasonal predictors in the new model, none of them is chosen for SHIFOR94 despite the fact that they have successfully been used as predictors of Atlantic cyclone activity (in terms of named storms, named storm days, hurricanes, hurricane days, intense hurricanes, intense hurricane days, etc) [2, 5].

For example, it has been reported that the effect of moderate or strong El-Nino (warm water) and low SOI values reduces Atlantic basin hurricane activity. This is because during ElNino seasons, ZWA and SLPA are enhanced creating strong vertical shear over the Atlantic. By contrast, cold water and high SOI values (i.e. La Nina) enhances Atlantic basin hurricane activity. The negative correlation between SOI and intensity is correctly reflected in the inclusion of variable (SOI*SOI) with coefficient -0.123373 in the new model.

Another example is, that according to Gray [6], Gulf of Guinea rainfall during the prior autumn season (Aug-Nov) is likely related to the strength of the West African monsoon (Jun-Jul) in the following year through positive feedbacks of evapotranspiration and soil moisture. RainS and RainG combined (known as "early season combination rainfall index") is very good predictor of intense hurricane activity during Aug-Oct. When the western Sahel region has above-average rainfall, Atlantic hurricane activity is greatly enhanced. The inclusion of RainG with coefficient 0.067429 in the new model is consistent with this finding.

5 Conclusion

A procedure for building forecasting models for tropical cyclone intensity using a set of penalized-likelihood methods is proposed. The experiments highlight three things. First, the importance of having homogeneous data (i.e. those coming from the same probability distribution) for training and test data sets for a model selection method to pick up regularities in the training data that can be extrapolated into the test data set and beyond. Second, that the unavoidable practice of using non-exhaustive search strategy on large search space pronounces the influence of selection bias in determining to which local minimum a model selection method would converge. Third, that in contrast to SHIFOR94, there is strong presence of the seasonal predictors in the new model discovered using the proposed procedure. These predictors have been proven in the literature to have strong influence to the Atlantic cyclone activity.

Tropical Cyclone Intensity Forecasting Model   237

Table 3. Models selected for Atlantic hurricane intensity change forecasting. SHIFOR and SHIFOR94 are the original benchmark models. SHIFOR' and SHIFOR94' are models with the same variables as those of the original models but with coefficients recalculated to fit the training data of each data set. The last set has training data from the year 1950 to 1987 and test data from the year 1988 to 1994.

Data set	Method	Tot Reg	Message Length	training data RMSE	training data R^2	test data RMSE	test data R^2
1	MML	14	3568.3599	21.5337	0.4451	21.9360	0.4578
	MDL	22	3571.9245	21.0042	0.4734	21.7157	0.4719
	CAICF	14	3568.3599	21.5337	0.4451	21.9360	0.4578
	SRM	14	3568.3599	21.5337	0.4451	21.9360	0.4578
	SHIFOR'	9	4146.1623	26.3637	0.1668	27.0951	0.1695
	SHIFOR94'	9	3675.8142	22.9202	0.3703	23.1839	0.3920
	SHIFOR	9	n/a	24.64	n/a	25.08	n/a
	SHIFOR94	9	n/a	22.50	n/a	22.97	n/a
2	MML	17	3470.3483	21.1317	0.4874	22.0990	0.3960
	MDL	17	3494.2895	21.1978	0.4842	22.2196	0.3894
	CAICF	17	3494.2895	21.1978	0.4842	22.2196	0.3894
	SRM	17	3494.2895	21.1978	0.4842	22.2196	0.3894
	SHIFOR'	9	4121.8865	26.6905	0.1800	26.3002	0.1392
	SHIFOR94'	9	3609.8455	22.8881	0.3970	23.2677	0.3263
	SHIFOR	9	n/a	25.15	n/a	25.24	n/a
	SHIFOR94	9	n/a	22.58	n/a	22.78	n/a
3	MML	16	3501.8237	21.3013	0.4741	21.7768	0.4272
	MDL	22	3525.6188	21.0137	0.4892	21.9255	0.4220
	CAICF	22	3526.8604	21.0067	0.4896	21.9845	0.4189
	SRM	14	3541.3063	21.6404	0.4569	22.1669	0.4055
	SHIFOR'	9	4113.0345	26.4903	0.1848	26.7255	0.1326
	SHIFOR94'	9	3631.5392	22.9458	0.3883	23.1232	0.3506
	SHIFOR	9	n/a	24.78	n/a	25.17	n/a
	SHIFOR94	9	n/a	22.59	n/a	22.76	n/a
4	MML	15	3544.6713	21.5543	0.4585	21.3028	0.4581
	MDL	22	3527.0303	20.9527	0.4895	21.4421	0.4539
	CAICF	22	3527.0303	20.9527	0.4895	21.4421	0.4539
	SRM	34	3529.3299	20.2208	0.5264	21.2702	0.4677
	SHIFOR'	9	4160.5295	26.8368	0.1589	25.9770	0.1904
	SHIFOR94'	9	3670.4534	23.1806	0.3725	22.5890	0.3878
	SHIFOR	9	n/a	24.95	n/a	25.39	n/a
	SHIFOR94	9	n/a	22.85	n/a	22.13	n/a
5	MML	16	3517.5771	21.0877	0.4698	22.4091	0.4321
	MDL	22	3526.3994	20.7077	0.4897	23.2168	0.4394
	CAICF	22	3515.7079	20.7330	0.4883	22.2483	0.4424
	SRM	29	3534.6611	20.3360	0.5090	21.6955	0.4731
	SHIFOR'	9	4137.0499	26.3244	0.1718	27.1136	0.1642
	SHIFOR94'	9	3649.0758	22.7536	0.3812	23.5696	0.3684
	SHIFOR	9	n/a	24.41	n/a	24.88	n/a
	SHIFOR94	9	n/a	22.39	n/a	23.20	n/a
6	MML	19	3541.8138	21.1563	0.4723	21.9039	0.4460
	MDL	22	3551.1410	21.0008	0.4806	21.9859	0.4431
	CAICF	22	3551.1410	21.0008	0.4806	21.9859	0.4431
	SRM	28	3548.9379	20.6145	0.5005	21.4804	0.4709
	SHIFOR'	9	4144.5904	26.5266	0.1677	26.6490	0.1736
	SHIFOR94'	9	3658.2100	22.9404	0.3775	23.2089	0.3732
	SHIFOR	9	n/a	25.60	n/a	25.10	n/a
	SHIFOR94	9	n/a	22.68	n/a	22.53	n/a
7	MML	16	3550.5365	21.4161	0.4570	21.6605	0.4609
	MDL	20	3555.6959	21.1497	0.4711	21.4657	0.4722
	CAICF	20	3555.6959	21.1497	0.4711	21.4657	0.4722
	SRM	20	3555.6959	21.1497	0.4711	21.4657	0.4722
	SHIFOR'	9	4129.8202	26.3546	0.1757	27.0755	0.1531
	SHIFOR94'	9	3664.3147	22.9488	0.3750	23.1047	0.3833
	SHIFOR	9	n/a	25.10	n/a	25.01	n/a
	SHIFOR94	9	n/a	22.64	n/a	22.64	n/a
8	MML	18	3547.1234	21.4495	0.4593	21.3224	0.4683
	MDL	18	3557.4183	21.3424	0.4651	21.3072	0.4699
	CAICF	18	3557.4183	21.3424	0.4651	21.3072	0.4699
	SRM	18	3557.4183	21.3424	0.4651	21.3072	0.4699
	SHIFOR'	9	4150.8674	26.6377	0.1642	26.3814	0.1816
	SHIFOR94'	9	3670.8837	23.0851	0.3723	22.8126	0.3880
	SHIFOR	9	n/a	25.31	n/a	24.99	n/a
	SHIFOR94	9	n/a	22.73	n/a	22.42	n/a
9	MML	17	3516.6721	21.3600	0.4738	21.3381	0.4442
	MDL	22	3522.0461	21.0540	0.4896	21.0350	0.4620
	CAICF	17	3513.9074	21.3405	0.4747	21.2465	0.4489
	SRM	27	3525.8268	20.7391	0.5056	20.8957	0.4711
	SHIFOR'	9	4122.9112	26.6371	0.1795	26.4400	0.1413
	SHIFOR94'	9	3637.2253	23.0412	0.3860	22.9308	0.3541
	SHIFOR	9	n/a	25.37	n/a	25.17	n/a
	SHIFOR94	9	n/a	22.42	n/a	22.42	n/a
10	MML	14	3545.9281	21.7222	0.4507	21.7164	0.4333
	MDL	22	3542.4352	21.4043	0.4674	21.3084	0.4561
	CAICF	18	3542.4352	21.4043	0.4674	21.3084	0.4561
	SRM	18	3545.8094	21.4065	0.4673	21.3807	0.4524
	SHIFOR'	9	4155.6197	26.8147	0.1616	26.0096	0.1839
	SHIFOR94'	9	3645.6768	23.0106	0.3826	22.9506	0.3646
	SHIFOR	9	n/a	25.97	n/a	25.24	n/a
	SHIFOR94	9	n/a	22.73	n/a	22.42	n/a
years: 1950-87 1988-94	MML	23	4131.9872	20.1489	0.5162	26.6464	0.2345
	MDL	26	4127.9430	19.9376	0.5267	27.7543	0.1735
	CAICF	26	4127.9430	19.9376	0.5267	27.7543	0.1735
	SRM	26	4127.9430	19.9376	0.5267	27.7543	0.1735
	SHIFOR'	9	5036.0730	26.6455	0.1507	26.3322	0.2361
	SHIFOR94'	9	4432.1653	22.8928	0.3731	23.7897	0.3765
	SHIFOR	9	n/a	25.18	n/a	24.64	n/a
	SHIFOR94	9	n/a	22.44	n/a	23.74	n/a

Table 4. Models as collections of variables with the same minimum frequency of being chosen to form a model by MML, MDL, CAIF, or SRM for the 10 data sets in Table 3

Model	Size	Freq. (of 40)	Commonly chosen regressors in models
1	2	40	6 10
2	3	38	6 10 (36,36)
3	4	36	6 10 (36,36) (28,5)
4	5	33	6 10 (36,36) (28,5) (33,32)
5	7	30	6 10 (36,36) (28,5) (33,32) (6,5) 29
6	8	28	6 10 (36,36) (28,5) (33,32) (6,5) 29 32
7	9	25	6 10 (36,36) (28,5) (33,32) (6,5) 29 32 (35,29)
8	10	24	6 10 (36,36) (28,5) (33,32) (6,5) 29 32 (35,29) 31
9	11	23	6 10 (36,36) (28,5) (33,32) (6,5) 29 32 (35,29) 31 (3,2)
10	12	19	6 10 (36,36) (28,5) (33,32) (6,5) 29 32 (35,29) 31 (3,2) (32,11)
11	13	18	6 10 (36,36) (28,5) (33,32) (6,5) 29 32 (35,29) 31 (3,2) (32,11) (34,11)
12	15	17	6 10 (36,36) (28,5) (33,32) (6,5) 29 32 (35,29) 31 (3,2) (32,11) (34,11) 7 (32,15)
13	16	16	6 10 (36,36) (28,5) (33,32) (6,5) 29 32 (35,29) 31 (3,2) (32,11) (34,11) 7 (32,15) (9,3)
14	17	15	6 10 (36,36) (28,5) (33,32) (6,5) 29 32 (35,29) 31 (3,2) (32,11) (34,11) 7 (32,15) (9,3) 2
15	18	12	6 10 (36,36) (28,5) (33,32) (6,5) 29 32 (35,29) 31 (3,2) (32,11) (34,11) 7 (32,15) (9,3) 2 4
16	19	11	6 10 (36,36) (28,5) (33,32) (6,5) 29 32 (35,29) 31 (3,2) (32,11) (34,11) 7 (32,15) (9,3) 2 4 (30,22)
17	25	10	6 10 (36,36) (28,5) (33,32) (6,5) 29 32 (35,29) 31 (3,2) (32,11) (34,11) 7 (32,15) (9,3) 2 4 (30,22) 3 9 (9,4) 13 25 (29,29)
18	27	9	6 10 (36,36) (28,5) (33,32) (6,5) 29 32 (35,29) 31 (3,2) (32,11) (34,11) 7 (32,15) (9,3) 2 4 (30,22) 3 9 (9,4) 13 25 (29,29) 15 (32,31)
19	30	8	6 10 (36,36) (28,5) (33,32) (6,5) 29 32 (35,29) 31 (3,2) (32,11) (34,11) 7 (32,15) (9,3) 2 4 (30,22) 3 9 (9,4) 13 25 (29,29) 15 (32,31) (4,4) (8,6) 35
20	35	7	6 10 (36,36) (28,5) (33,32) (6,5) 29 32 (35,29) 31 (3,2) (32,11) (34,11) 7 (32,15) (9,3) 2 4 (30,22) 3 9 (9,4) 13 25 (29,29) 15 (32,31) (4,4) (8,6) 35 5 (5,5) (9,1) (22,9) (35,33)
21	42	6	6 10 (36,36) (28,5) (33,32) (6,5) 29 32 (35,29) 31 (3,2) (32,11) (34,11) 7 (32,15) (9,3) 2 4 (30,22) 3 9 (9,4) 13 25 (29,29) 15 (32,31) (4,4) (8,6) 35 5 (5,5) (9,1) (22,9) (35,33) (4,1) (11,5) 30 (34,17) (34,21) (34,28) (35,28)
22	43	5	6 10 (36,36) (28,5) (33,32) (6,5) 29 32 (35,29) 31 (3,2) (32,11) (34,11) 7 (32,15) (9,3) 2 4 (30,22) 3 9 (9,4) 13 25 (29,29) 15 (32,31) (4,4) (8,6) 35 5 (5,5) (9,1) (22,9) (35,33) (4,1) (11,5) 30 (34,17) (34,21) (34,28) (35,28) 18
23	50	4	6 10 (36,36) (28,5) (33,32) (6,5) 29 32 (35,29) 31 (3,2) (32,11) (34,11) 7 (32,15) (9,3) 2 4 (30,22) 3 9 (9,4) 13 25 (29,29) 15 (32,31) (4,4) (8,6) 35 5 (5,5) (9,1) (22,9) (35,33) (4,1) (11,5) 30 (34,17) (34,21)(34,28) (35,28) 18 (7,2) (13,2) (13,13) (27,14) (31,3) (32,21) (36,35)
SHIFOR	9	n/a	7 (3,1) (5,1) (6,1) (4,3) (5,3) (7,5) (5,5) (6,5)
SHIFOR94	9	n/a	10 11 5 16 (16/4) 25 (10,10) (4,5) (6,3)

6 Future Work

Although it is impossible to explain all of the interactions between the variables stochastically chosen for TC intensity change forecasting models, one would hope that, to a certain extent, the reasons why some variables were chosen and some were not could be explained. The total absence of the seasonal predictors, which have been proven to be influential to Atlantic TC systems, from the TC intensity

Table 5. Performance of each model in Table 4

Model	Size	MML	MDL	CAICF	SRM	RMSE	R^2
1	2	5227.1275	5215.0073	5225.0946	0.6944	23.2945	0.3588
2	3	5213.8092	5195.3430	5207.7612	0.6937	23.1557	0.3666
3	4	5202.4689	5178.5372	5193.1246	0.6929	23.0321	0.3735
4	5	5183.3942	5154.5672	5171.1571	0.6891	22.8707	0.3823
5	7	5144.7799	5109.8437	5130.0198	0.6810	22.5659	0.3990
6	8	5137.7611	5101.6132	5123.4250	0.6808	22.4872	0.4033
7	9	5128.5315	5088.4975	5111.8294	0.6788	22.3830	0.4089
8	10	5116.4937	5075.6970	5100.4513	0.6767	22.2806	0.4145
9	11	5095.5560	5051.2319	5077.2850	0.6707	22.1187	0.4231
10	12	5069.3557	5021.7370	5048.9831	0.6630	21.9322	0.4329
11	13	5060.4083	5009.7104	5038.1178	0.6606	21.8345	0.4381
12	15	5070.1827	5016.4281	5047.0496	0.6646	21.7933	0.4405
13	16	5063.9349	5007.5211	5039.1089	0.6627	21.7109	0.4448
14	17	5058.9406	5002.6561	5035.1638	0.6619	21.6487	0.4481
15	18	5040.9346	4984.9951	5018.3082	0.6571	21.5229	0.4546
16	19	5045.0687	4986.7331	5020.8790	0.6581	21.4933	0.4563
17	25	5001.3226	4942.4237	4980.2451	0.6460	21.0455	0.4794
18	27	4996.8836	4937.5439	4976.2822	0.6444	20.9444	0.4846
19	30	5000.6515	4939.6237	4979.5095	0.6444	20.8375	0.4902
20	35	5031.1451	4966.6092	5007.9117	0.6505	20.7698	0.4941
21	42	5070.0102	5002.0126	5044.0818	0.6569	20.6588	0.5003
22	43	5069.8073	5004.1261	5046.1716	0.6567	20.6285	0.5019
23	50	5111.5253	5042.4039	5083.8683	0.6625	20.5259	0.5077
SHIFOR'	9	5871.9392	5825.8890	5850.9167	0.9529	26.5225	0.1701
SHIFOR94'	9	5179.8152	5178.5030	5202.0420	0.7075	22.8515	0.3840

Table 6. The new model (Model 7, consisting the best 9 variables), SHIFOR94 and SHIFOR: variable names and their respective coefficients

Chosen Variable		Normalized Coefficient		
No.	Acronym	New Model	SHIFOR94'	SHIFOR'
(6,5)	(Del12V,Vmax)	-0.099445	-0.085522	0.900026
10	POT	0.649806	0.644563	
6	Del12V	0.165545	0.180562	
(36,36)	(SOI,SOI)	-0.123373		
(28,5)	(200Uend,Vmax)	-0.119977		
29	Del200U	0.109351		
(33,32)	(SLPA,RainG)	0.108001		
(35,29)	(ElNino,Del200U)	0.075820		
32	RainG	0.067429		
12	DSSST		-0.105468	
(10,10)	(POT,POT)		-0.101357	
26	Closest		0.074916	
17	Uppend		0.023286	
(4,7)	(LonData,UCurr)		0.013477	
(17/6)	(Uppend/Vmax)		-0.006972	
(5,5)	(Vmax,Vmax)			-0.314015
7	UCurr			-0.294385
(5,3)	(Vmax,LatData)			-0.069982
(3,1)	(LatData,Julian)			-0.069132
(4,3)	(LonData,LatData)			0.069030
(7,5)	(UCurr,Vmax)			-0.054350
(5,1)	(Vmax,Julian)			-0.017290
(6,1)	(Del12V,Julian)			0.012620

forecasting models being used in operation begs a closer look into the way the models have been built. New models built using scientifically better methods like the ones proposed in this paper should be tested in operation over a period of time.

Acknowledgments

The atmospheric data discussed in this paper has been generously supplied by Chris Landsea of the Hurricane Research Centre NOAA, Miami Florida. The author is grateful to Chris Wallace for ideas and guidance in the development of the MML method.

References

1. H. Bozdogan. Model selection and akaike's information criterion (AIC): the general theory and its analytical extensions. *Psychometrika*, 52(3):345–370, 1987.
2. C.W. Landsea, W.M. Gray, P.W. Mielke Jr. and K.J. Berry. Seasonal forecasting of atlantic hurricane activity. *Weather*, 49(8):273–284, August 1994.
3. M. DeMaria and J. Kaplan. A statistical hurricane intensity prediction scheme (SHIPS) for the Atlantic basin. *Weather and Forecasting*, 9(2):209–220, June 1994.
4. P.J. Fitzpatrick. Forecasting cyclone intensity change in the West Pacific. In *Proceedings of the 21st Conference on Hurricanes and Tropical Meteorology*, pages 94–96, Miami, Florida, 1995. American Meteorological Society.
5. W.M. Gray. Seasonal forecasing. In G.J. Holland, editor, *Global Guide to Tropical Cyclone Forecasting*, chapter 5. World Meteorological Organization (in press), Geneva - Switzerland, 1999. available: http://www.bom.gov.au/bmrc/meso/New/wmocas_pubs/global_guide/globa_guide_intro.htm.
6. W.M. Gray and C.W. Landsea. African rainfall as a precursor of hurricane-related destruction on the us east coast. *Bulletin of American Meteorological Society*, 73(9):1352–1364, September 1992.
7. B.R. Jarvinen and C.J. Neumann. Statistical forecasts of tropical cyclone intensity. Technical Report Tech. Memo. NWS NHC-10, National Oceanic and Atmospheric Administration (NOAA), Miami, Florida, 1979.
8. C.W. Landsea. SHIFOR94 - atlantic tropical cyclone intensity forecasting. In *Proceedings of the 21st Conference on Hurricanes and Tropical Meteorology*, pages 365–367, Miami, Florida, 1995. American Meteorological Society.
9. C.J. Neumann. An alternate to the HURRAN tropical cyclone forecasting system. Technical Memo NWS-62, NOAA, 1972.
10. J. Rissanen. Modeling by shortest data description. *Automatica*, 14:465–471, 1978.
11. J. Rissanen. Stochastic complexity. *Journal of the Royal Statistical Society B*, 49(1):223–239, 1987.
12. G.W. Rumantir. Minimum Message Length criterion for second-order polynomial model discovery. In T. Terano, H. Liu, A.L.P. Chen, editor, *Knowledge Discovery and Data Mining: Current Issues and New Applications, PAKDD 2000, LNAI 1805*, pages 40–48. Springer–Verlag, Berlin Heidelberg, 2000.
13. V. Vapnik. *The Nature of Statistical Learning Theory*. Springer, New York, 1995.
14. C.S. Wallace and P.R. Freeman. Estimation and inference by compact coding. *Journal of the Royal Statistical Society B*, 49(1):240–252, 1987.

Trading Off Granularity against Complexity in Predictive Models for Complex Domains

Ingrid Zukerman, David W. Albrecht, Ann E. Nicholson, and Krystyna Doktor

School of Computer Science and Software Engineering
Monash University, Clayton, Victoria 3800, Australia
{ingrid,dwa,annn,krys}@csse.monash.edu.au

Abstract. The automated prediction of a user's interests and requirements is an area of interest to the Artificial Intelligence community. However, current predictive statistical approaches are subject to theoretical and practical limitations which restrict their ability to make useful predictions in domains such as the WWW and computer games that have vast numbers of values for variables of interest. In this paper, we describe an automated abstraction technique which addresses this problem in the context of Dynamic Bayesian Networks. We compare the performance and computational requirements of fine-grained models built with precise variable values with the performance and requirements of a coarse-grained model built with abstracted values. Our results indicate that complex, coarse-grained models offer performance and computational advantages compared to simpler, fine-grained models.

1 Introduction

It has long been recognized in the Artificial Intelligence community that problem reformulations are central to the ability of systems to reason effectively in complex domains. A commonly used type of reformulation is abstraction, which involves ignoring or combining parts of the state space to overcome computational intractability. Of course, this reduction in complexity comes at a cost; using an abstraction, rather than the complete state-space, usually means that the computed solution is less accurate than the solution obtained with the complete state space. However, good abstractions achieve a state space reduction without significantly compromising the quality of the solution. Abstraction techniques have been used in a variety of problem-solving settings, such as automatic programming, design, diagnosis, planning and theorem proving [6].

In this paper, we focus on the use of abstraction techniques in Bayesian Networks (BNs) [11]. In particular, we utilize BNs in predictive statistical models for plan recognition – the area of user modeling which endeavours to predict a user's plans and goals from observations of the user's state. The recent application of predictive statistical models to realistic application domains, such as the WWW, computer games or interactive systems, has placed increased demands on these models to handle vast numbers of values for the variables of interest.

For instance, the WWW has millions of locations, and computer games may have thousands of possible actions and locations. However, BNs cannot handle efficiently such application domains. This may be due to theoretical boundaries or restrictions imposed by currently available systems and operating conditions. For instance, a theoretical limitation of statistical prediction models in general and BNs in particular pertains to the amount of data that needs to be collected in order to perform meaningful predictions when there is a large number of variables or variable values. Further, the belief-update algorithms of BNs are exponential in their state space (Section 2). Current BN software packages, such a Netica [10] and Hugin [8], are subject to memory restrictions that limit the number of variables and variable values they can handle. This problem is exacerbated in Java-based WWW applications, where executing programs must reside in the client's site.

In this paper, we describe an automated abstraction technique to address the "large state space" problem in the context of Dynamic Bayesian Networks (DBNs) [4] – a variant of BNs used in a variety of applications, e.g., [7, 12]. We use DBNs to predict a user's quest (goal) in a Multi-User Dungeon (MUD) adventure game with 2140 locations where 1311 actions were performed by players when attempting to achieve 24 different quests (Section 3). In our previous work, we addressed the large state space problem by removing low-probability values from the state space and taking advantage of domain features [1]. This involved deleting from the state space events that were not found during training, ignoring commands that contain typographical errors, and taking advantage of the hierarchical structure of the domain to merge specific locations into regions. While these approaches to abstraction often yield good results, they frequently do not generalize across domains with different features. In this paper, we offer a general clustering approach to abstraction which uses automatically learned categories, instead of precise variable values, to reduce the size of the state space (Section 5).

In the next section, we review abstraction methods applied to prediction models similar to ours. We then describe the features of our domain, our basic (fine-grained) prediction models and our abstraction process. In Section 6, we compare the performance and computational requirements of a coarse-grained prediction model with the performance and requirements of our fine-grained models. We then present concluding remarks and outline our plans for future work.

2 Related Research

DBNs have been used for knowledge representation and reasoning in domains where the world changes and the focus is reasoning over time. In these domains, the DBN grows over time, and the state of each domain variable at different times is represented by a series of nodes. In addition to having the same computational problems as those experienced by ordinary BNs during belief updating (both exact and approximate inference are NP-hard [2, 3]), DBNs incur additional complexity as the number of time-slices increases. In order to constrain the state space, the DBN connections over time are typically Markovian, and a temporal 'window' is imposed. For example, our DBN for predicting a user's goals in the MUD is limited to a two-time-slice window [1].

In this paper, we focus on the use of abstraction to reduce the size of the state space when the DBN nodes represent domain variables that have vast numbers of values. Abstraction encompasses a number of techniques: (1) ignoring variables of low relevance; (2) ignoring some of the less relevant values a variable may take; and (3) modulating the precision (or granularity) of the variables by combining values.

In a BN framework, ignoring a variable of low relevance is equivalent to pruning it from the network. An example of this is the work of Jitnah [9], who uses a relevance measure based on mutual information to prune past nodes from a DBN. In the related area of decision-theoretic planning using Markov Decision Processes, Dearden and Boutilier [5] remove completely variables of low relevance in terms of their impact on utilities of actions. Merging or ignoring individual values, as proposed in this paper, is not an option for the problems considered by these researchers, as the variables are either Boolean propositions or have very few values.

An example of the second form of abstraction – ignoring some of the less relevant values a variable may take – is the removal of low-probability values from the action state space, as described in [1].

An example of the third approach is Wellman and Liu's use of abstraction for the approximate evaluation of BNs when the state space is prohibitive or when a real-time response is required [14]. They trade off accuracy in the result for computational efficiency by varying the granularity of the variable state spaces. This is done by merging values that are adjacent in the enumeration of the variable's state space. This approach can be effective when such values are "similar", but is not suitable for many domains. Jitnah [9] investigates measures for choosing which values to merge based on similarities of their entries in the network's Conditional Probability Tables (CPTs). Another example of this clustering form of abstraction is our previous exploitation of hierarchical aspects of the domain to merge individual locations into regions [1]. As mentioned in the previous section, although this method gives reasonable results, it is not generalizable across domains with different features. In this paper, we describe a machine learning classification method for abstraction that automatically groups values that have similar features.

3 Domain

Our application domain is the "Shattered Worlds" Multi-User Dungeon (MUD) – a text-based virtual reality game where players compete for limited resources in an attempt to achieve various quests. As stated in Section 1, the MUD has 24 different quests, and 2140 locations where 1311 actions were observed. As shown in [1], the MUD is a complex domain whose features challenge traditional plan recognition systems. This motivated our use of DBNs to develop models that predict users' actions, locations and goals. In this paper, we extend our previous

Table 1. Sample data for the Avatar quest.

Action No.	Time	Player	Location	Action
1	773335156	spillage	room/city/inn	ENTERS
12	773335264	spillage	players/paladin/room/trading_post	buy
17	773335291	spillage	players/paladin/room/western_gate	bribe
28	773335343	spillage	players/paladin/room/abbey/guardhouse	kill
37	773335435	spillage	players/paladin/room/abbey/stores	search
40	773335451	spillage	players/paladin/room/shrine/Billy	worship
54	773335558	spillage	players/paladin/room/brooksmith	give
60	773335593	spillage	players/paladin/room/shrine/Dredd	avenger
62	773335596	spillage	players/paladin/room/abbey/chamber	*Avatar quest*

results by providing a generally applicable abstraction method that supports the development of DBNs in complex domains.

The MUD software collects information about the *runs* performed by each player. Each run is composed of a sequence of data points collected from the time a player enters the MUD or completes a quest until s/he achieves a new quest. Each data point contains information regarding the state of the player when an event happens (either an action is performed or a quest is achieved). Table 1 shows the following information for a subset of the data points collected during a sample run: a time stamp, the name of the player, the location where the action was executed, and the name of the action (or quest achieved). This is the information used to build our DBNs (Section 4).

4 Knowledge Representation

In this section, we discuss briefly three simple DBNs developed for the MUD domain [1]. These models, whose predictive power was investigated in our previous research, were selected since they enable us to compare the predictive performance and computational requirements of our fine- and coarse-grained modeling techniques under otherwise equivalent conditions.

The domain variables represented as DBN nodes are actions, locations and quests.

Action (A) – represents the possible actions a player may perform in the MUD while trying to achieve a quest ($|A|$=1311 actions in our current trials), plus the special `other` action, which includes all previously unseen actions. In our current implementation, we take an action to be the first string of non-blank characters entered by a user.

Location (L) – represents the possible locations visited by a quest-achieving player ($|L|$=2140 locations), plus the special `other` location, which includes all previously unseen locations.

Quest (Q) – represents the 24 different quests a player may undertake.

Figure 1 shows our three DBNs: (a) `actionModel`, (b) `locationModel`, and (c) `indepModel`. `actionModel` infers a user's quest from his/her observed ac-

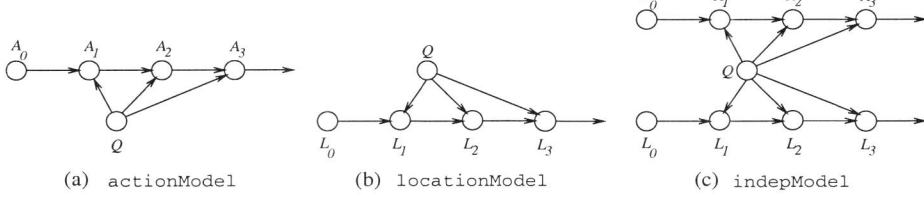

Fig. 1. Dynamic Belief Networks for the MUD: (a) `actionModel`; (b) `locationModel`; (c) `indepModel`.

tions only; `locationModel` infers a user's quest from observed locations only; and `indepModel` considers both actions and locations. The arcs in the DBNs reflect the different influences between the domain variables. For example, the next action in `actionModel` depends on the previous action and the quest being undertaken. Each node in a DBN is associated with a CPT that quantifies its relationship with its parents. For example, the CPT associated with node A_{i+1} in `actionModel` represents the conditional probability $\Pr(A_{i+1}|A_i, Q)$.

The main CPT used by `actionModel` has $(|A|+1)^2 \times Q$ entries ($= (1311+1)^2 \times 24 \cong 41 \times 10^6$); the main CPT used by `locationModel` has $(|L|+1)^2 \times Q$ entries ($= (2140+1)^2 \times 24 \cong 110 \times 10^6$); and `indepModel` requires both of these CPTs, which have a total size of $\cong 41 \times 10^6 + 110 \times 10^6$ (151×10^6). In our previous work, the size of the CPTs was substantially reduced by not storing zero-probability events, e.g., for `indepModel`, this yielded CPTs whose total size was 1.1×10^6 on average [1]. As a result, the real-time belief updating process was computationally feasible. However, this approach is effective only if the CPTs are sparse.

5 Automated Abstraction

The primary purpose of the models considered in this paper is to predict which quest a user is doing. Consequently the abstractions we considered involve using features of the state space which are quest related. These abstractions are based on the observation that the locations/actions which are more frequently visited/performed in the process of doing a quest are more important for that quest.

The abstraction of the locations involves clustering the locations into regions. To do this we first calculated for each location L_i 24 attributes, a_{ij} for $j = 1, \ldots, 24$, one attribute for each quest, where each attribute counts the number of times location L_i was visited by all users while trying to accomplish quest Q_j. For each location L_i:[1]

$$a_{ij} = \sum_{\text{all users}} \sum_{L_k} [\text{\# of times each user moved from } L_k \text{ to } L_i \ (L_k \neq L_i) \text{ while doing } Q_j]$$

---

[1] Note that the attribute value is not incremented when a user stays in the same location over several actions.

Once all the attributes were calculated, we applied the classifier Snob [13] to these attributes in order to automatically determine the regions. The classifier identified 116 regions consisting of locations with similar attributes. One region consisted of all the locations which were never visited and hence were not important for the prediction of any quest. The other regions consisted of groups of locations, such that each group comprised locations with similar hierarchical descriptions. However, not all locations with a similar hierarchical description were found in the same region.

The abstraction of actions into action classes was learned in a manner similar to the learning of regions for locations:[2] 24 attributes were calculated for each action, one for each quest, representing how often an action was performed by all users doing a particular quest. Once all the attributes were calculated, we used the Snob classifier to automatically cluster the actions into classes. Snob found 85 actions classes, including one with all the unused actions.

Having obtained the abstractions of the locations and actions, we investigated abstractModel – a DBN which has the same structure as indepModel, but with regions instead of locations, and action classes instead of actions. The total size of the main CPTs in abstractModel is $(116+1)^2 \times 24 + (85+1)^2 \times 24$ ($\cong 50 \times 10^4$), compared with 151×10^6 for indepModel. This corresponds to a reduction by 99.7% in the size of the models. Further, the size of abstractModel is 99.6% smaller than that of locationModel and 98.8% smaller than that of actionModel.

In the future, we intend to investigate using other attributes to classify locations and actions, such as the number of users who visited a location or performed an action. This would enable the classifier to distinguish between locations/actions which are visited/performed often by one user and those which are visited/performed only a few times by many different users.

6 Results

In this section, we present empirical results showing how the predictive performance of the DBN models described in Section 4 compares with that of abstractModel (Section 5). The measure of performance used to compare these models is *average prediction*, which assesses how well a model predicts the actual quest [1]. This measure computes the average across all test runs of the predicted probability of the actual quest at a particular point t during the performance of a quest:

$$average\ prediction_t = \frac{1}{n}\sum_{i=1}^{n} \Pr(\text{actual value of } quest \text{ at point } t \text{ in the } i\text{-th test run}),$$

where n is the number of test runs. Our results were obtained by training each model on 80% of the data and testing on 20% with cross-validation using 5 different splits of the data.

---

[2] However, repeated action occurrences were counted, since several actions may be performed in the same location.

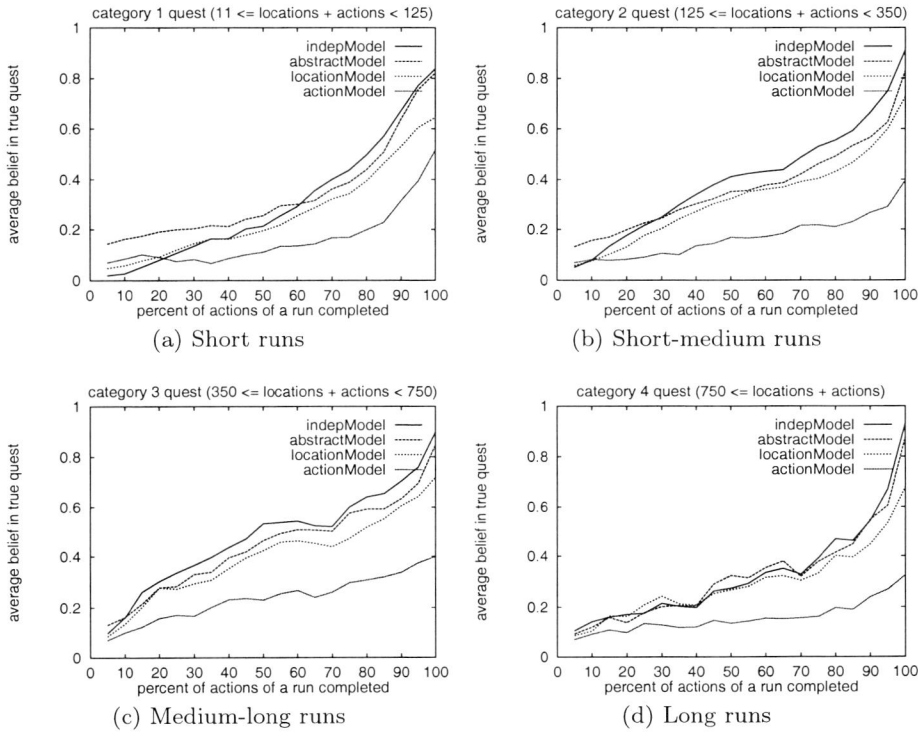

Fig. 2. Predictive performance of precise versus abstracted models.

In order to determine whether the length of a run (in terms of number of actions performed and locations visited) affects the relative performance of the different models, we divided the test runs into four categories as follows: *short* – between 11 and 124 locations and actions; *short-medium* – between 125 and 349 locations and actions; *medium-long* – between 350 and 749 locations and actions; and *long* – more than 750 locations and actions. Each of these categories contained approximately 300 runs.

Figure 2 shows the average predicted probability of the actual quest for each of the four DBNs considered in this paper (actionModel, locationModel, indepModel and abstractModel) for each of the four categories of runs. In order to compare the performance of the different models across runs where the number of recorded actions varies, the x-axis was chosen to represent the percentage of the actions in a run that have been performed. Specifically, the plots in Figure 2 show the average prediction after 5%, 10%, 15%, ..., 100% of the actions in a run have been performed.

The general trends emerging from the results shown in Figure 2 are: (1) the performance of all the models improves as quest completion draws near; (2) indepModel has the best performance overall, followed by abstractModel, locationModel and actionModel; (3) abstractModel outperforms the other models during some time span (often at the beginning of a quest); and (4) the performance of actionModel is substantially worse than that of the other models.[3] This last (seemingly counter-intuitive) result may be explained by the observation that MUD players often interleave quest-related actions with other actions that do not contribute to quest achievement. We now consider the first three of these trends in turn.

The performance of all the models improves as quest completion draws near. At first glance, it appears that in the initial stages of a run, the predictive accuracy of all the models is low in absolute terms. However, even after only 10% of the actions in a run have been performed, the average predictive accuracy of the best performing model (which is either indepModel or abstractModel) is approximately 16%. This is significantly better than randomly selecting a quest from 24 uniformly distributed quests (which has an average predictive accuracy of 4%). When 70% of the actions in a run have been performed, the average predictive accuracy of indepModel, which has the best performance at that stage, is 40% for short runs, 49% for short-medium runs, 53% for medium-long runs and 33% for long runs. These probabilities indicate that the actual quest is often assigned the highest probability mass among the candidate quests (indeed, at this point in a run indepModel assigns the highest probability to the actual quest 35% of the time for short runs, 51% for short-medium runs, 48% for medium-long runs and 32% for long runs). The predictive accuracy of the three best models, indepModel, abstractModel and locationModel, climbs sharply from that point, with indepModel reaching an average predictive accuracy of approximately 90% upon quest completion for all run categories.

indepModel *has the best performance overall, followed by* abstractModel, locationModel *and* actionModel. The superior overall performance of indepModel is expected, as it is both complex and precise. The fact that abstractModel outperforms locationModel and actionModel indicates that it is worth trading off simple but fine-grained DBN models against more complex but coarse-grained DBN models. This trade off yields both substantial computational savings as well as improved performance.

abstractModel *outperforms the other models during some time span.* As seen in Figure 2, for the three shorter run categories this time span occurs at the beginning of a run: the first 60% of a run for short runs, the first 25% for short-medium runs, and the first 10% for medium-long runs. In contrast, for the long runs, abstractModel has the best performance between 45% and 65% of the actions in a run (while locationModel outperforms the other models between 25% and 40% of the actions in a run).

The superior performance of abstractModel during the initial stages of the shorter runs may be attributed to the following factors.

---

[3] T-tests performed for each set of predictions and each pair of models confirmed these results at the 5% significance level.

Vague predictions are better at ruling out unlikely quests. This is a result of the relative sparseness of the CPTs for the fine-grained DBNs. Many entries in the $L \times L \times Q$ CPT or the $A \times A \times Q$ CPT contain a rather low probability or 0. Thus, the distinction between events seen in training and those not seen in training is quite low, resulting in a low discrimination between likely and unlikely quests. In contrast, each entry in the CPTs of the coarse-grained model collates information from several locations (which are grouped according to the quests achieved while visiting these locations) or several actions (which are also grouped in this manner). Thus, the differences between the various entries in these CPTs are more pronounced than the differences between the entries of the fine-grained CPTs, leading to a greater ability to rule out unlikely quests, and assigning a higher probability mass to the remaining quests.

Precise predictions may be misleading at the beginning, but are useful at the end. This follows from the observation that the precise information with the most discriminatory power is often collected close to quest completion. In the MUD, as in many other domains, a particular event (e.g., action or location) observed at the beginning of a quest may not be particularly indicative of the quest being attempted, but the same event observed later on may be a powerful indicator of the quest under consideration. Since the frequency counts for the CPTs are collected throughout the performance of a quest (without distinguishing between its beginning or its end), the information in CPT entries with higher conditional probabilities may be more representative of the later stages of a run, rather than its earlier stages. Nonetheless, these CPTs are used to make predictions at all stages of a run, thereby yielding lower quality predictions at the beginning of a run.

The superior performance of `abstractModel` around the middle of the long runs may be explained by the observation that initially players may not be attempting the quest they end up doing. Thus, one could argue that they are actually starting this quest only later in a run. Further, in long runs players perform more actions that do not contribute to quest completion than in shorter runs. These two observations account for the lower predictive accuracy of all the DBNs for the long runs, compared to their performance in the shorter runs (as indicated above, after 70% of the actions have been performed, `indepModel` – the best performing model – predicts the actual quest with an average probability of 0.35 for the long runs, compared 0.4, 0.48 and 0.53 for the other run categories).

7 Conclusions and Future Work

We have offered an automated abstraction technique which addresses the large state space problem in the context of DBNs. The comparison of the predictive performance and computational requirements of fine-grained models with the performance and requirements of the coarse-grained model built with our abstraction technique leads to the following conclusions: (1) fine-grained DBN models generally have a higher predictive accuracy than coarse-grained models with the same structure (this is corroborated by our experiments with coarse-grained versions of actionModel and locationModel); (2) coarse-grained DBN models perform better than fine-grained models with a simpler structure; (3) coarse-grained DBN models generally perform better than fine-grained models with the same structure during the initial stages of a task; (4) the space requirements of the coarse-grained DBN model built with our abstraction technique are approximately 1/100 of the space requirements of the fine-grained models; and (5) the space savings achieved by coarse-grained DBN models are twice as large as the savings achieved by ignoring zero-probability events.

These conclusions clearly point towards complex, coarse-grained models as a viable alternative to fine-grained, simpler models for domains with large data spaces. The coarse-grained complex models not only perform better than their simpler fine-grained counterparts, but also incur very large savings in space. In the future, we intend to extend this idea to include additional variables, e.g., MUD players, who may be classified according to the length of their sessions and their quest completions. This will enable us to determine whether the insights obtained from this research regarding the granularity-complexity trade-off extend to models of a higher complexity than those investigated here.

As indicated in Section 5, the results presented in this paper were obtained by performing abstractions with respect to one type of variable, i.e., quests. In the future, we intend to investigate using other attributes to classify locations and actions, such as the number of users who visited a location or performed an action. In addition, we propose to study the computational and performance implications of an abstract DBN that relies on the joint classification of actions and locations (rather than their separate classification, as done in this paper), and the computational implications of combining coarse-grained models with sparse CPTs that do not represent zero-probability events.

Finally, an interesting result of our work pertains to the good performance of the coarse-grained DBN during the initial stages of a quest. This points to the need to investigate a dynamic model selection policy, which can change from a coarse-grained model to a fine-grained model at some point during task performance.

References

1. D.W. Albrecht, I. Zukerman, and A.E. Nicholson. Bayesian models for keyhole plan recognition in an adventure game. *User Modeling and User-Adapted Interaction*, 8(1-2):5–47, 1998.
2. G.F. Cooper. The computational complexity of probabilistic inference using Bayesian belief networks. *Artificial Intelligence*, 42:393–405, 1990.
3. P. Dagum and M. Luby. Approximating probabilistic inference in belief networks is NP-hard. *Artificial Intelligence*, 60:141–153, 1993.
4. T. Dean and M.P. Wellman. *Planning and control*. Morgan Kaufmann Publishers, San Mateo, California, 1991.
5. R. Dearden and C. Boutilier. Abstraction and approximate decision theoretic planning. *Artificial Intelligence*, 89(1):219–283, 1997.

6. T. Ellman. Symposium on abstraction, reformulation and approximation. *http://www.cs.vassar.edu/~ellman/sara98/sara98.html*, 1998.
7. J. Forbes, T. Huang, K. Kanazawa, and S. Russell. The BATmobile: Towards a Bayesian automated taxi. In *IJCAI95 – Proceedings of the Fourteenth International Joint Conference on Artificial Intelligence*, pages 1878–1885, Montreal, Canada, 1995.
8. Hugin. HUGIN: Expert. *http://www.hugin.dk*, 2000.
9. N. Jitnah. *Using Mutual Information for Approximate Evaluation of Bayesian Networks*. PhD thesis, Monash University, School of Computer Science and Software Engineering, 1999.
10. Netica. Norsys: Software corp. *http://www.norsys.com/netica.html*, 2000.
11. J. Pearl. *Probabilistic Reasoning in Intelligent Systems*. Morgan Kaufmann Publishers, San Mateo, California, 1988.
12. D.V. Pynadath and M.P. Wellman. Accounting for context in plan recognition with application to traffic monitoring. In *UAI95 – Proceedings of the Eleventh Conference on Uncertainty in Artificial Intelligence*, pages 472–481, Montreal, Canada, 1995.
13. C.S. Wallace. Classification by minimum-message-length inference. In G. Goos and J. Hartmanis, editors, *ICCI '90 – Advances in Computing and Information*, pages 72–81. Springer-Verlag, Berlin, 1990.
14. M.P. Wellman and C.L. Liu. State-space abstraction for anytime evaluation of probabilistic networks. In *UAI94 – Proceedings of the Tenth Conference on Uncertainty in Artificial Intelligence*, pages 567–574, Seattle, Washington, 1994.

Recognizing Intentions from Rejoinders in a Bayesian Interactive Argumentation System

Ingrid Zukerman, Nathalie Jitnah, Richard McConachy, and Sarah George

School of Computer Science and Software Engineering
Monash University, Clayton, Victoria 3800, AUSTRALIA
{ingrid,njitnah,ricky,sarahg}@csse.monash.edu.au

Abstract. We describe a mechanism which recognizes a user's intentions from short-form rejoinders to arguments generated from Bayesian networks. The mechanism builds candidate reasoning paths that link the user's rejoinder with a previously presented argument, and considers the following factors to select a path: linguistic clues, the impact of the user's rejoinder on the system's argument along the different paths, the user's attentional focus, and the system's confidence in its representation of the user's beliefs. The results of our preliminary evaluation indicate that the interpretations produced by our mechanism are generally appropriate.

1 Introduction

Ideally, an interactive argumentation system would allow a user to respond to an argument with a counterargument, and it would allow the argumentation process to go on indefinitely, producing a series of arguments and counterarguments. During argumentation, conversational partners often use expressions of doubt, such as "*But the victim was stabbed*", and requests for the consideration of additional facts, such as "*What about the fingerprints on the gun?*". In this paper, we describe a mechanism which interprets such rejoinders to arguments generated from Bayesian networks (BNs) [8]. This mechanism is implemented in a system called BIAS (*Bayesian Interactive Argumentation System*).

Given an argument produced by BIAS followed by a rejoinder posed by a user, our mechanism identifies the user's likely line of reasoning and the proposition(s) in BIAS' argument the user intends to affect. This is done by taking into account the following factors: the linguistic clues in the rejoinder, the impact of the rejoinder on BIAS' argument, the user's attentional focus, and BIAS' confidence regarding its representation of the user's beliefs. Once a line of reasoning has been postulated, BIAS generates a rebuttal to the user's rejoinder [6].

In Section 2, we introduce BIAS' current scenario and show a sample interaction with BIAS. Next, we describe our knowledge representation formalism, followed by the algorithm which identifies the user's line of reasoning. We then discuss results of a preliminary evaluation of BIAS' performance, review related research and present concluding remarks.

2 Scenario

BIAS and the user are partners in solving a crime. They have access to information about the world, e.g., the crime scene, witnesses and forensic reports. At the beginning

Preamble:
Mr Body was found dead in his bedroom, which is in the second story of his house. Bullet wounds were found in Mr Body's body. The bedroom window was broken, and broken glass was found inside the window. A gun was found at the premises, and some fingerprints were found on the gun. In addition, inspection of the grounds revealed footprints in the garden and circular indentations in the ground outside the bedroom window.
Initial argument:
Bullets being found in Mr Body's body implies Mr Body was almost certainly shot. This implies Mr Body was murdered. *Forensics matching the bullets with the found gun implies the gun is almost certainly the murder weapon. Forensics matching the fingerprints with Mr Green implies Mr Green probably fired the gun, which together with the gun almost certainly being the murder weapon implies Mr Green probably fired the murder weapon. This implies he very probably had the means to murder Mr Body.* *The Bayesian Times reporting Mr Body took Mr Green's girlfriend implies Mr Green and Mr Body very probably were enemies, which implies Mr Green probably had a motive to murder Mr Body.* *A witness reporting Mr Green being at the football at 10:30 implies Mr Green almost certainly wasn't in the garden at 11.* *Forensics reporting the time of death being 11 implies the time of death was very probably 11. This together with Mr Green almost certainly not being in the garden at 11 implies he almost certainly wasn't in the garden at the time of death, which implies he almost certainly didn't have the opportunity to murder Mr Body.* *Even though Mr Green very probably had the means to murder Mr Body and he probably had a motive to murder Mr Body, Mr Green almost certainly not having the opportunity to murder Mr Body implies he probably didn't murder Mr Body.*
Rejoinder: *But Mr Green was in the garden at 11.*
Interpretation:
Mr Green being in the garden at 11 implies he was more probably in the garden at the time of death. This implies he more probably had the opportunity to murder Mr Body, which implies he more probably murdered Mr Body.

Fig. 1. Preamble, initial argument, sample rejoinder and BIAS' interpretation

of the interaction, BIAS and the user receive a preamble that describes the preliminaries of the case (Figure 1). After receiving the preamble, the user can use BIAS' WWW interface to obtain additional information about the world, e.g., from witnesses or the crime scene, and to post his/her beliefs about selected propositions (this is done by clicking a belief value for these propositions). BIAS has access to these beliefs and to the obtained information, but it does not necessarily share the user's beliefs. Further, BIAS can investigate the world directly to obtain additional information that will enable it to formulate an argument.

When the user asks for BIAS' opinion about the case, BIAS calls a Bayesian argument generator [11] to produce a preliminary argument in support of a goal proposition. In our scenario, this proposition is either *Mr Green is guilty* or *Mr Green is innocent*, whichever is most likely. If possible, our argument generator produces an argument that is compatible with both BIAS' beliefs about the world and the user's presumed beliefs. Otherwise, BIAS' beliefs take precedence. Figure 1 shows the argument generated by BIAS for Mr Body's innocence in light of the preamble and information gathered from the world.

After receiving BIAS' argument, the user can formulate a rejoinder or continue investigating the world. At present we consider two types of rejoinders (which are formulated by making selections from a dynamic menu in our WWW interface).

- Expressions of doubt ("But **R**", where **R** is a proposition). We focus on one type of expression of doubt where the user asserts or negates a proposition to undermine a proposition stated or implied in the system's argument [2].
- Requests for the consideration of a proposition ("Consider **R**"). Unlike expressions of doubt, which have negative implications, this type of rejoinder just implies that BIAS has omitted a factor that could be relevant.

For example, after receiving the rejoinder in Figure 1, BIAS postulates the line of reasoning shown at the end of Figure 1.[1] This line of reasoning takes into account the user's beliefs in other nodes that were mentioned in BIAS' argument, e.g., *the time of death was 11*, and the user's belief in nodes s/he investigated through the WWW interface. BIAS then generates a rebuttal which addresses the user's rejoinder [6] or produces an updated argument which acknowledges the impact of the rejoinder proposition. The user can now continue inspecting the world or pose another rejoinder, and so on.[2]

3 Knowledge Representation

We have chosen BNs as our main representational formalism owing to their ability to represent normatively correct reasoning under uncertainty. The information about the world and the models of belief consulted by BIAS during the argumentation process are represented as BNs. These models are a normative model and a user model. The normative model contains information that is presumed to be correct according to the world, i.e., observable facts obtained from the world or beliefs inferred by means of Bayesian propagation from the observable facts. The user model stores propositions that are presumed believed by the user, where the probability values of these propositions represent the user's beliefs. These propositions are obtained from a variety of sources, such as BIAS' arguments or the beliefs entered by the user through the interface, and are labelled according to their source(s). For example, a proposition is labelled `accepted` if a belief in it has been entered by the user (either through the interface or by confirming BIAS' interpretation of the user's rejoinder), while it is labelled `seenObservation` or `seenIntuition` if it has been shown to the user, but the user has not indicated a belief in it (`Observations` represent observable events, while `Intuitions` represent inferable propositions). The labels are ranked according to the trustworthiness of the source from which the user's belief was obtained. For instance, `accepted` propositions rank higher than `seenObservations`, which in turn rank higher than `seenIntuitions`. In addition, in order to support a numerical process for rating the candidate reasoning paths (Section 4), these labels are associated with a numerical score according to their ranking.

---

[1] The implications in this line of reasoning may be causal or evidential.
[2] At present, we assume that a user's rejoinder addresses BIAS' initial argument. The dialogue features that determine whether a rebuttal is being addressed are yet to be implemented.

The interpretation process, which is the focus of this paper, is performed in the context of the user model, since the rejoinder should "make sense" in light of the user's beliefs. In contrast, the processes for generating the initial argument and the rebuttals consult the user model and the normative model in order to produce arguments that rely on beliefs held by both BIAS and the user if possible [11]. These arguments are represented by means of a sub-network of the normative model BN, called an *Argument Graph*, which ideally also contains nodes from the user model BN.

During the generation of arguments and rebuttals and the interpretation of a user's rejoinders, we model the user's attentional focus. The use of attentional focus during argument generation is described in [11]. In this paper, we focus on its impact on the interpretation process. We postulate that the interpretation intended by a user is likely to contain propositions in his/her focus of attention. In order to determine whether a proposition is in the user's focus of attention, we use a model of attention which follows associative links (rather than causal or evidential links) and invoke a process called *spreading activation* [1]. This process passes activation from active propositions, e.g., recently seen propositions, to propositions and concepts that have an associative relation to the active propositions. For instance, after reading the fragments "Bayesian Times" and "Mr Body is dead", the concepts "time" and "death" get activated, in turn activating propositions pertaining to the "time of death". Our model of attention is implemented by incorporating in the user model an associative semantic network which includes the propositions in the user model BN (such a network is also incorporated in the normative model).

4 Path Identification

Algorithm *IdentifyPath* proposes paths in the user model BN that represent possible lines of reasoning from the user's rejoinder. The algorithm receives two inputs: a linguistic clue ("but" or "consider") and the rejoinder proposition (**R**).

Algorithm *IdentifyPath(linguisticClue,* **R***)*

1. **Path construction** – Find paths that connect the rejoinder node **R** to the goal proposition in the Argument Graph generated by BIAS.
2. **Path evaluation** – Compute a score for each path based on its effect on the argument according to the user model, its presence in the user's focus of attention and BIAS' confidence in it.
3. **Path selection** – Select one path if possible. Otherwise, present the candidate path(s) to the user for confirmation.

4.1 Path Construction

The user may select a rejoinder node **R** that is not in the user model BN. In this case, **R** is added to the user model (and to the normative model if necessary). When trying to connect **R** to the Argument Graph, BIAS iteratively expands the user model BN from **R** and from the Argument Graph. In each iteration, BIAS adds to the user model nodes and links from the world BN that connect with **R**, and nodes and links from the world BN that connect with the Argument Graph (the corresponding conditional probability tables

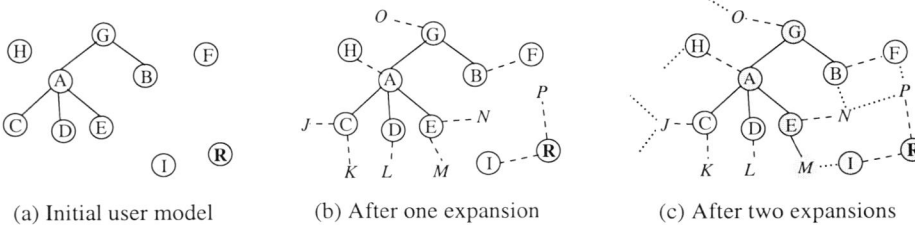

Fig. 2. Path construction in a sample Argument Graph

are also copied from the world BN).[3] If this process is successful, upon its completion **R** will be connected to the Argument Graph by one or more paths. These paths may contain causal links (from the rejoinder node towards the goal) or evidential links (in the opposite direction). This process is performed in a *temporary user model*, since at most one of the paths found by BIAS is intended by the user. This path will be incorporated in the user model after performing path selection (Section 4.3).

To illustrate the path construction process, consider the user model in Figure 2(a), which contains the Argument Graph corresponding to an argument presented by BIAS (the tree whose root is the goal node G), the nodes investigated by the user in the interface (F, H, I), and the user's rejoinder proposition **R**. After one expansion, propositions F, H and I become connected to **R** or to the Argument Graph, and additional propositions, *J, K, L, M, N, O* and *P* (shown in italics in Figure 2(b)), are added to the temporary user model and also linked to **R** or the Argument Graph (these links are drawn with dashed lines). After the second expansion (drawn with dotted lines), **R** becomes connected to the original Argument Graph and the goal through several paths in the temporary user model: **R**-I-*M*-E-A-G (composed of grey nodes in Figure 2(c)), **R**-*P*-*N*-E-A-G, **R**-*P*-F-B-G and **R**-*P*-F-B-*N*-E-A-G.

We assume that the user intends a straightforward interpretation of his/her rejoinder, and that s/he has bounded inferential capacity. BIAS implements these assumptions during path construction by looking for *direct* paths that represent *small inferential leaps*. A direct path represents a simple line of reasoning between the rejoinder node and the goal. A direct path is not necessarily the shortest path to the goal. Rather, it is a path that does not meander unnecessarily, i.e., if there are several routes between two neighbouring nodes, a direct path takes the link between these nodes. An inferential leap occurs when a user intends to affect a proposition in the argument that is different from the rejoinder proposition. For instance, if the user says *"But Mr Green was near the house at 11:15"* after the argument in Figure 1, s/he licenses an implication regarding Mr Green's opportunity to kill Mr Body (through a small inferential leap). However, if the user had said *"But Mr Green owns a blue car"*, a system should not be expected to find an interpretation that connects this rejoinder to the goal, since the inferential leap is too large.

---

[3] During this process, BIAS drops from consideration d-separated paths [8]. A path is d-separated when the presence or absence of some evidence in the user model prevents the rejoinder node from affecting the goal proposition.

BIAS also copes with two types of inaccuracies in its user model: incompleteness (when BIAS is not aware of some of the user's beliefs) and granularity discrepancies (when the user makes a 'complex' inference that connects non-adjacent nodes in the user model BN). During path construction, these inaccuracies show up as *reasoning gaps* in the user's presumed line of reasoning, i.e., the line of reasoning includes propositions that are not in the user model. BIAS considers only paths with *small and easily inferable reasoning gaps*. A gap should be small in order to avoid attributing to a user overly complex inferences (across a large gap); the inference across a gap should be "easy", meaning that is plausible that the user is engaged in this reasoning activity. We adopt the "ease of inference" definition from [7], which requires that the node at the tail of the gap have a strong effect on the node at the head of the gap, and that the nodes at both ends of the gap be in the user's focus of attention. This last requirement approximates the idea that thinking of the antecedent of an inference will make one think of its consequent (across the gap).

BIAS finds reasoning paths which represent small inferential leaps by performing only three iterations to connect **R** to the Argument Graph, and by restricting the length of the paths being built. The small size of the reasoning gaps is ensured by allowing an inferred path to contain at most two consecutive nodes that are not in the user model. For instance, path **R**-I-*M*-E-A-G in Figure 2(c) has a gap of length 1 between I and E. The ease of inference across a reasoning gap is implemented by requiring that (1) the nodes at both ends of the gap, e.g., I and E, have a high activation level; and (2) some value of the node at the 'head' of the gap have a high level of belief given the value of the node at the 'tail' of the gap (inferred from the user's rejoinder).

4.2 Path Evaluation

The path evaluation process produces a score for each path returned by the path construction process. This score, called *pathValue*, incorporates the following factors: (1) the impact of **R** along this path on BIAS' argument, (2) the linguistic clue of the rejoinder, (3) whether the nodes in this path are in the user's focus of attention, and (4) BIAS' confidence regarding its representation of the user's beliefs in the nodes along this path. These factors are assessed in the context of the user model, since BIAS is trying to determine what the user means by the rejoinder. The calculation of *pathValue* is performed by means of heuristics which combine Bayesian principles (Factor 1) with dialogue-related and user modeling aspects (Factors 2, 3 and 4).

Impact of R along a path on BIAS' argument. The impact of a rejoinder **R** along $path_j$ on a proposition $\mathcal{X}$, denoted $Impact_j(\mathbf{R}, \mathcal{X})$, represents the change in belief in proposition $\mathcal{X}$ in light of the value of **R** stated in the rejoinder (denoted *userVal*). This change is relative to the previous belief in $\mathcal{X}$ (in light of a different value of **R** or no information about **R**). The impact of **R** on $\mathcal{X}$ is calculated using the following formula.

$$Impact_j(\mathbf{R}, \mathcal{X}) = \log \frac{\Pr_j(\mathcal{X}=x|\mathbf{R}=userVal)}{\Pr(\mathcal{X}=x)} \qquad (1)$$

$\Pr_j(\mathcal{X}=x|\mathbf{R}=userVal)$, the probability of node $\mathcal{X}$ along $path_j$ given the user's value of **R**, is calculated by propagating the user's value of **R** over a temporary BN consisting of the current user model BN plus the nodes in $path_j$ (the conditional probability tables are marginalized to take into account nodes that are absent from the user model).

We assume that the user's rejoinder was generated to affect at least one node in the Argument Graph and possibly the goal proposition, e.g., in path R-I-*M*-E-A-G in Figure 2(c), the propositions of interest are E, A and G. The effect of the rejoinder depends on its linguistic clue. A request for consideration implies that the rejoinder affects some propositions in the argument (without indicating whether it supports or contradicts these propositions), while an expression of doubt implies that the rejoinder contradicts a proposition in the argument. These considerations are combined with $Impact_j(\mathbf{R}, \mathcal{X})$ to yield the *effective impact* of **R** along $path_j$ on a node $\mathcal{X}_{AG}$ in the Argument Graph.

$$EffImpact_j(\mathbf{R}, \mathcal{X}_{AG}) = \begin{cases} |Impact_j(\mathbf{R}, \mathcal{X}_{AG})| & \text{if request for consideration} \\ Impact_j(\mathbf{R}, \mathcal{X}_{AG}) & \text{if } \Pr(\mathcal{X}_{AG} = argBIAS) < 0.5 \\ -Impact_j(\mathbf{R}, \mathcal{X}_{AG}) & \text{otherwise} \end{cases} \quad (2)$$

where *argBias* is the value of node $\mathcal{X}_{AG}$ resulting from BIAS' argument. According to this formula, if BIAS argued for a high/low degree of belief in node $\mathcal{X}_{AG}$, then a felicitous expression of doubt should reduce/increase the belief in this node. For example, if BIAS argued for $\mathcal{X}_{AG}$=True, yielding $\Pr(\mathcal{X}_{AG} = \text{True}) = 0.8$ in the user model, and the user's expression of doubt reduced this belief to $\Pr_j(\mathcal{X}_{AG} = \text{True}|\mathbf{R}) = 0.6$ when propagated along $path_j$, then the effective impact of this rejoinder on node $\mathcal{X}_{AG}$ would be positive.

BIAS uses the effective impact of a rejoinder along a path to suggest a node in the Argument Graph that the user intended to affect. We submit that this is the *highest-impact* node, i.e., the node with the highest value for *EffImpact* along this path (the goal may also be the highest-impact node). Thus, when considering the effective impact of a rejoinder to assess a proposed path, we focus on two target propositions: the goal (G) and the *highest-impact* proposition (*HI*). For example, assume that the user said "But **R**", and consider path R-I-*M*-E-A-G in Figure 2(c). Further, assume that Pr(E=True)=0.3, Pr(A=True)=0.6 and Pr(G=True)=0.7 after BIAS' argument, and that Pr(E=True)=0.55, Pr(A=True)=0.2 and Pr(G=True)=0.5 due to the user's rejoinder. Thus, all three propositions have been contradicted, but A is the highest-impact proposition.

The presence of the nodes along a path in the user's focus of attention. When presenting a rejoinder proposition, the user has in mind a line of reasoning that links this proposition to the system's argument. We postulate that it is more likely that the user will perform this inferential leap if the nodes along his/her intended line of reasoning are in his/her focus of attention. That is, they have a high level of activation.

BIAS' confidence regarding its representation of the user's beliefs in the nodes along a path. The more trustworthy are the sources from which BIAS obtained the user's beliefs in the nodes along a path, the more confident BIAS should be regarding the plausibility of this path. This confidence is a function of the numerical score associated with the label of each node (Section 3).

Determining the overall value of a path. The factors discussed above have the following contribution to the value of a path.
- **Linguistic clue and impact along a path** – Paths with a high combined effective impact on the goal and the highest-impact node are preferred, since it is more likely that the user intended to have a large effect on BIAS' argument.

- **Focus of attention** – Paths with highly activated nodes are preferred, since these nodes are likely to be in the user's mind. We compute the average level of activation over a path (rather than total activation) so shorter paths are not disadvantaged.
- **BIAS' confidence** – Paths whose nodes have labels with high scores are preferred, since the system is more certain about these nodes. As above, we compute the average label score over a path.

These considerations are incorporated into the following formula, which represents the overall value of a path.

$$pathValue_j(\mathbf{R}) = N_G \times \textit{EffImpact}_j(\mathbf{R}, G) + N_{HI} \times \textit{EffImpact}_j(\mathbf{R}, HI) + \\ N_A \times \log\left(1 + \frac{\sum_{node_i \in path_j} Activation(node_i)}{Length(path_j)}\right) + \\ N_L \times \log \frac{\sum_{node_i \in path_j} LabelScore(node_i)}{Length(path_j)} \quad (3)$$

where the weights N_G, N_{HI}, N_A and N_L determine the contribution of the above factors to the value of a path: effective impact of the rejoinder on the goal (N_G) and on the highest-impact proposition (N_{HI}), level of activation of the nodes in the path (N_A), and scores of the labels of these nodes (N_L).[4] In Section 5, we consider the effect of these weights on the performance of the system.

4.3 Path Selection

As indicated in Section 4.2, the value of a path reflects the likelihood that this is the path intended by the user. Thus, when there is a single path with a high *pathValue* or the *pathValue* of a path is significantly higher than that of the other candidate paths, this path is selected and passed to the rebuttal generation procedure [6]. However, when several paths with similar *pathValues* are generated, BIAS cannot discriminate between them, and lets the user choose; a single path with a low *pathValue* is also presented to the user for confirmation.

The recognition process fails if BIAS could not find a path between the rejoinder proposition and the Argument Graph during path construction, or too many paths with similar *pathValues* were found (so they could not be presented for confirmation), or the user does not select any of the presented paths. In the future, our interface will ask the user to further specify his/her rejoinder in these situations.

5 Preliminary Evaluation

Our preliminary evaluation assesses the overall performance of our system and the influence of the factors considered in Equation 3 on this performance.

The overall performance of the system was evaluated by means of the following experiment. Twelve subjects were shown the preamble and argument from Figure 1, and

---
[4] We compute the log of the last two factors so that their contribution to the value of a path is compatible with that of *EffImpact*.

Interpretation for Rejoinder₁ (*But Mr Green and Mr Body had an argument*):
Mr Green arguing with Mr Body implies Mr Green and Mr Body more probably were enemies. This implies Mr Green more probably had a motive to murder Mr Body, which implies he more probably murdered Mr Body.

Interpretation for Rejoinder₂ (*But the forensic analysis of the found fingerprints is reliable*):
The forensic analysis of the found fingerprints being reliable and forensics matching the fingerprints with Mr Green imply the found fingerprints more probably belong to Mr Green. This implies Mr Green more probably fired the found gun, which implies he more probably fired the murder weapon. This implies he more probably had the means to murder Mr Body, which implies he more probably murdered Mr Body.

Fig. 3. Sample rejoinders with BIAS' interpretations

Table 1. Scores given by subjects to BIAS' interpretations for five rejoinders

Interpretation for	Number of people who gave a score of					Average score
	1	2	3	4	5	
Rejoinder₁	0	2	0	8	2	3.83
Rejoinder₂	0	0	0	8	4	4.33
Rejoinder₃	0	3	3	3	3	3.50
Rejoinder₅	0	2	0	4	6	4.17

Interpretation for Rejoinder₄	Number of people who gave a score of					Average score
	1	2	3	4	5	
Interpretation₁	0	3	2	4	3	3.58
Interpretation₂	1	3	3	4	1	3.08
Interpretation₃	2	3	4	2	1	2.75

were shown the following rejoinders, each accompanied by the candidate interpretation(s) proposed by BIAS: (1) *But Mr Green and Mr Body had an argument*, (2) *But the forensic analysis of the found fingerprints is reliable*, (3) *Consider that the found gun was not registered to Mr Green*, (4) *But Mr Green's ladder was at Mr Body's window*, and (5) *But Mr Green was in the garden at 11*. Rejoinders 1, 2, 3 and 5 had a single interpretation, while Rejoinder 4 had three interpretations (the interpretations for Rejoinders 1 and 2 are shown in Figure 3, and that for Rejoinder 5 appears in Figure 1). These interpretations were generated in light of the user model which results from the presentation of the preamble and BIAS' argument (the values for the weights in Equation 3 were $N_G = 2, N_{HI} = 3$ and $N_A, N_L = 1$, i.e., the effective impact of the rejoinder on the highest-impact proposition is the most important factor). The subjects were then asked to give each interpretation a score between 1 (very UNreasonable) and 5 (very reasonable), and to propose their own interpretations if they found BIAS' inappropriate. The number of people who gave each score is shown in Table 1 together with the average score for each interpretation. These results indicate that the interpretations proposed by BIAS were considered generally appropriate. In addition, the single interpretations generally had more support than the multiple ones, indicating that users split their support when several plausible interpretations are available. For Rejoinder 4, all the interpretations had support from some subjects (scores of 4 and 5), indicating that all the generated interpretations were worth presenting. It is also worth noting that the ranking produced by the scores of the interpretations of Rejoinder 4 (3.58>3.08>2.75) matches BIAS' ranking for these interpretations according to their *pathValues*.

The influence of the factors considered in Equation 3 on BIAS' performance was assessed by means of three experiments. In the first experiment, we activated BIAS with two settings: (1) EqualWeights, where $N_G = N_{HI} = N_A = N_L = 1$; and (2) ImpactOnly, where $N_G = N_{HI} = 1$ and $N_A = N_L = 0$. The objective of this experiment was to determine whether attentional focus and BIAS' confidence in a path affect the relative ranking of the paths. Each setting was tested on five rejoinder nodes for which BIAS generated multiple paths. In three of the five cases, the ImpactOnly setting yielded different rankings to those produced by the EqualWeights setting. This indicates that the weights assigned to attentional focus and the system's confidence in a path affect BIAS' results.

The second experiment was performed with the same five rejoinder nodes as the first experiment. Here we activated BIAS with the EqualWeights setting, and simulated user clicks of nodes in lower-ranked paths, thereby increasing their activation and changing their labels. This caused the lower-ranked paths to move up in rank in all the runs. The results of this experiment indicate that by taking into account a user's attentional focus and the system's confidence in a path, BIAS can react appropriately to the user's input.

The third experiment was conducted on four rejoinders, such as "*But a blue car was here*", for which BIAS returned no paths, because the paths found during path construction had reasoning gaps that were too large. We then simulated user clicks to relevant nodes, which resulted in the addition of these nodes to the user model BN (and also affected their activation and labels). This in turn enabled BIAS to propose interpretations for the problematic rejoinders. The results of this experiment show that additional contextual information enables BIAS to propose interpretations which would otherwise be considered far fetched.

6 Related Research

In this section, we focus on related research that specifically pertains to the topic of this paper, viz computational mechanisms for intention recognition during argumentation and applications of BNs to argumentation and plan recognition.

Our research builds on the system described in [11], which generates arguments from BNs, and the system described in [12], which allows a user to explore an argument by performing certain modifications, such as excluding a proposition. However, these systems did not interpret a user's utterances.

Several researchers have dealt with different aspects of intention recognition during argumentation, e.g., [2, 4, 9, 10]. Flowers *et al.* [4] focused on recognizing episodic justifications to historical events, Quilici [9] considered plan-related arguments, and Carberry and Lambert [2] and Restificar *et al.* [10] modeled expert-consultation dialogues.

Our system is closest to Carberry and Lambert's [2] in its focus on rejoinders and its combination of linguistic, contextual and world knowledge to recognize a user's intentions. However, there are significant differences between our models. Carberry and Lambert covered a wider range of linguistic phenomena than those considered in this paper. However, they considered short exchanges where each participant utters a few propositions in each conversational turn, and they used a plan-based inference mechanism to recognize a user's intention. Restificar *et al.* [10] also modeled short exchanges, using simple argument schemata combined with inference rules to detect whether an utterance attacks or supports an argument. The interpretation of rejoinders to complex, probabilistic arguments calls for techniques such as Bayesian propagation and spreading activation to determine the impact of a proposition and to model attentional focus respectively.

BNs have been used in a variety of plan recognition tasks. For example, Heckerman and Horvitz [5] used a BN applied to features extracted from users' queries to infer their software assistance requirements. Charniak and Goldman [3] used BNs and marker passing (a form of spreading activation) for plan recognition during story understanding. They automatically built and incrementally extended a BN from propositions read in a story, so that the BN represented hypotheses that became plausible as the story unfolded. During this process, they used marker passing to restrict the nodes included in the BN. In contrast, we use BNs as a formalism for argument representation, apply Bayesian propagation to recognize a user's intention when posing a rejoinder to an argument, and use spreading activation to model the user's attentional focus. In the future, we intend to investigate the use of spreading activation during path construction (as well as path evaluation).

7 Conclusion

We have described a mechanism for interpreting expressions of doubt and requests for the consideration of information in the context of arguments generated by a Bayesian argumentation system. The interpretation process, which is performed on a BN that represents a model of a user's beliefs, takes into consideration linguistic clues, the impact of the user's rejoinder on the system's argument, the user's attentional focus, and the system's confidence in the candidate interpretations. Our evaluation suggests that the interpretations generated by BIAS are generally appropriate, and shows how the last two factors can improve the relative rankings of multiple interpretations.

In the future, we intend to perform a full system evaluation where users read arguments, pose rejoinders and receive rebuttals to these rejoinders. In addition, we propose to build upon our results to implement more complex types of rejoinders, such as *what about* questions (e.g., "*What about the murder weapon?*") and explicit inferences (e.g., "*Mr Green being in the garden implies he had opportunity*"), as further stepping stones towards a full argumentation capability.

Acknowledgments

This work was supported in part by Australian Research Council grant A49927212. The authors also thank the three anonymous reviewers for the insightful comments.

References

1. J. R. Anderson. *The Architecture of Cognition*. Harvard University Press, Cambridge, Massachusetts, 1983.
2. Sandra Carberry and Lynn Lambert. A process model for recognizing communicative acts and modeling negotiation subdialogues. *Computational Linguistics*, 25(1):1–53, 1999.

3. Eugene Charniak and Robert P. Goldman. A Bayesian model of plan recognition. *Artificial Intelligence*, 64(1):50–56, 1993.
4. Margot Flowers, Rod McGuire, and Lawrence Birnbaum. Adversary arguments and the logic of personal attack. In *Strategies for Natural Language Processing*, pages 275–294. Lawrence Erlbaum Associates, Hillsdale, New Jersey, 1982.
5. David Heckerman and Eric Horvitz. Inferring informational goals from free-text queries: A Bayesian approach. In *Proceedings of the Fourteenth Conference on Uncertainty in Artificial Intelligence*, pages 230–237, Madison, Wisconsin, 1998.
6. Nathalie Jitnah, Ingrid Zukerman, Richard McConachy, and Sarah George. Towards the generation of rebuttals in a Bayesian argumentation system. In *Proceedings of the International Natural Language Generation Conference*, Mitzpe Ramon, Israel, 2000.
7. R. McConachy, K. B. Korb, and I. Zukerman. Deciding what not to say: An attentional-probabilistic approach to argument presentation. In *Proceedings of the Twentieth Annual Conference of the Cognitive Science Society*, pages 669–674, Madison, Wisconsin, 1998.
8. Judea Pearl. *Probabilistic Reasoning in Intelligent Systems*. Morgan Kaufmann Publishers, San Mateo, California, 1988.
9. Alex Quilici. Arguing about planning alternatives. In *COLING-92 – Proceedings of the Fourteenth International Conference on Computational Linguistics*, pages 906–910, Nantes, France, 1992.
10. A. Restificar, A. Syed, and S. McRoy. Arguer: Using argument schemas for argument detection and rebuttal in dialogs. In *UM99 – Proceedings of the Seventh International Conference on User Modeling*, pages 315–317, Banff, Canada, 1999.
11. Ingrid Zukerman, Richard McConachy, and Kevin B. Korb. Bayesian reasoning in an abductive mechanism for argument generation and analysis. In *AAAI98 – Proceedings of the Fifteenth National Conference on Artificial Intelligence*, pages 833–838, Madison, Wisconsin, 1998.
12. Ingrid Zukerman, Richard McConachy, Kevin B. Korb, and Deborah A. Pickett. Exploratory interaction with a Bayesian argumentation system. In *IJCAI99 – Proceedings of the Sixteenth International Joint Conference on Artificial Intelligence*, pages 1294–1299, Stockholm, Sweden, 1999.

Efficient Inference in Dynamic Belief Networks with Variable Temporal Resolution

Tim A. Wilkin[1,2] and Ann E. Nicholson[2]

[1] Department of Mathematics and Statistics
[2] School of Computer Science and Software Eng., Monash University
Clayton, Victoria, 3800 Australia. {taw,annn}@csse.monash.edu.au

Abstract. Dynamic Belief Networks (DBNs) have been used for the monitoring and control of stochastic dynamical processes where it is crucial to provide a response in real-time. DBN transition functions are typically specified as conditional probability distributions over a constant time interval. When these functions are used to model dynamic systems with observations that occur at irregular intervals, both exact and approximate DBN inference algorithms are inefficient. This is because the computation of the posterior distribution at an arbitrary time in the future involves repeated application of the fixed time transition model. We draw on research from mathematics and theoretical physics that shows the dynamics inherent to a Markov model can be described as a diffusion process. These systems can be modelled using the Fokker-Planck equation, the solutions of which are the transition functions of the system for arbitrary length time intervals. We show that using these transition functions in a DBN inference algorithm gives significant computational savings compared to the traditional constant time-step model.

1 Introduction

One of the more difficult tasks for knowledge representation schemes has been to model complex, dynamic systems efficiently. The correlations that exist between variables in dynamic systems make it a non-trivial task to keep track of the state of the system at any time. This system complexity can also make it difficult to accurately predict future states. Probabilistic models have become popular in recent times, primarily because they permit a quantitative assessment of the possible states of the system at a given time. Within the artificial intelligence community, one popular method of probabilistic knowledge representation has been the Belief Network (BN) [9]. BNs admit a compact representation of a static domain by taking advantage of the fact that many systems have only a limited set of causal dependencies between variables.

Dynamic Belief Networks (DBNs) [3] are an extension to BNs that allow the representation of temporal correlations between variables over time. Traditionally, to simplify the representation of the domain, the transition functions of the DBN – which embody the temporal correlations between variables – have been specified as conditional probability distributions over a fixed, predetermined interval. When observations are received at irregular time intervals, current inference algorithms waste time computing intermediary posterior distributions without evidence. To overcome the loss of speed induced by this extra computation and the intractability of inference, some researchers [6, 2, 8] have developed approximation methods for inference in DBNs which trade-off accuracy with speed. Our need for fast, accurate inference is driven by the requirements of a real time flight planner and replanner to be used by an autonomous aircraft performing meteorological data measurement [5]. We use a DBN to model the aircraft and its local environment. The DBN is required to model accurately the present state of the domain and to make accurate predictions about possible future states, given its present beliefs and its current plan. Evidence, coming from various sources, is not available at regular intervals. Given that current DBN inference procedures are inefficient in this situation, we are motivated to develop an alternative to the constant time-step transition models.

In this paper we present such an alternative. Mathematicians, theoretical physicists, economists and engineers have long used the Fokker-Planck equation to model diffusive processes. By imposing the Markov assumption upon a stochastic, dynamic system, we enforce certain properties on the temporal evolution of the system. These properties are modelled by the Fokker-Planck equation. We find that solutions of this differential equation can be used as arbitrary time-step transition functions for DBNs that model Markov processes. For a class of processes characterised by constant diffusion and linear potentials we provide an analytic transition function suitable for arbitrary time-step inference. We implement this function for a simple process and compare the results with those obtained using a traditional constant time-step function. We show that with a minor alteration to the inference algorithm, we obtain the same inferred distributions with significantly less computation than the constant time-step method.

Section 2 outlines DBNs and a common inference technique for updating the model. In Section 3 we look at the dynamics inherent to Markov processes and find that these lead to the Fokker-Planck equation for diffusion processes. In Section 4 we use this knowledge to improve the efficiency of inference in a simple system. In Section 5 we discuss the results obtained from this model and compare them to results obtained using the corresponding standard inference technique. We also discuss the applicability of arbitrary time interval transition functions in more general models.

2 Inference in Dynamic Belief Networks

A Dynamic Belief Network (DBN) (also called a Dynamic Bayesian Network) is a directed, acyclic graph used to model stochastic systems that exhibit temporal correlations between the system variables. The set of nodes, $\mathbf{X}^t = \{X_1^t, ..., X_n^t\}$, have a 1-1 correspondence with the system variables at time t. Each directed link represents a direct influence between two nodes. We denote X_i^t as a parent of X_j^t and denote the set of all parents of X_j^t as $\mathbf{Pa}(X_j^t)$. A node may have parent nodes at times other than the current time, meaning a temporal correlation exists between the two variables.

Each node has associated with it a conditional probability distribution, $p(X_i^t|\mathbf{Pa}(X_i^t))$, that quantifies the correlations between the node and its parents. A node that has no parents is represented as a prior distribution, $p(X_i^t)$. We can also define a joint probability distribution at time t as $p(\mathbf{X}^t) = p(X_1^t, X_2^t, ...X_n^t)$.

A particular assignment to this distribution, $p(\mathbf{X}^t = \mathbf{x}) = p(X_1^t = x_1, X_2^t = x_2, ... X_n^t = x_n)$ will be denoted by $p(\mathbf{x}^t)$. This represents the probability of the occurrence of the composite state $\mathbf{x}$ at time t.

In order to represent arbitrary systems efficiently, DBNs traditionally make use of two assumptions. The *Markov assumption* holds that the future and past states are conditionally independent given the present state: $\forall t, p(\mathbf{x}^{t+1} \mid \mathbf{x}^t, \mathbf{x}^{t-1}, ..., \mathbf{x}^0) = p(\mathbf{x}^{t+1} \mid \mathbf{x}^t)$. Assuming *time invariance* means that the transition model $p(\mathbf{x}^{t+1} \mid \mathbf{x}^t)$ does not depend on t.

For many real world processes we have no direct knowledge of state values at any given time, but may have access to observations of these variables, which we donote by $\mathbf{y}^t$. In general these observations are distorted by noise, created by the observation method. Therefore, $\mathbf{y}^t$ depends stochastically on $\mathbf{x}^t$ and is conditionally independent of all other variables given $\mathbf{x}^t$. We can therefore write $p(\mathbf{y}^{t+1} \mid \mathbf{x}^{t+1}, \mathbf{x}^t, \mathbf{y}^t) = p(\mathbf{y}^{t+1} \mid \mathbf{x}^{t+1})$, which is known as the sensor model for the system. Given these distributions, a generic DBN model can be specified by two 'time-slices', as in Figure 1(a).

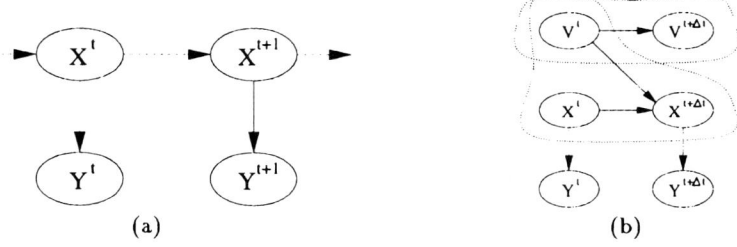

Fig. 1. (a) Generic DBN structure. (b) DBN modelling motion of an object in 1-D

One important inference task for the DBN model is to maintain a probability distribution over the possible states at the present time, given a prior state and some current evidence (observations). This can be achieved using the following two step process [10, pp508-516], where the current knowledge is held in the distribution $p(\mathbf{X}^t)$ and a unit of time has since elapsed.

Step 1) *Prediction*: predict the present distribution using the last known state as the prior distribution. For all $\mathbf{x}^{t+1}$ compute:

$$\widehat{p}(\mathbf{x}^{t+1}) = \int p(\mathbf{x}^{t+1} \mid \mathbf{x}^t) p(\mathbf{x}^t) d\mathbf{x}^t \qquad (1)$$

Step 2) *Estimation*: incorporate any evidence, if available. For all $\mathbf{x}^{t+1}$ compute:

$$p(\mathbf{x}^{t+1}) = \alpha p(\mathbf{y}^{t+1} \mid \mathbf{x}^{t+1}) \widehat{p}(\mathbf{x}^{t+1}) \qquad (2)$$

where α is a normalising constant for $p(\mathbf{X}^{t+1})$. If evidence is not available, then Step 2 is simply omitted from the inference procedure until an observation is made. In the situation where evidence arrives at irregular times, the above procedure can be very inefficient. Assuming that the next observation is made at time $t + n$, then equation (1) is applied iteratively n times to compute:

$$\hat{p}(\mathbf{x}^{t+n}) = \int p(\mathbf{x}^{t+n}|\mathbf{x}^t)p(\mathbf{x}^t)d\mathbf{x}^t \quad (3)$$

$$p(\mathbf{x}^{t+n}|\mathbf{x}^t) = \int ... \int p(\mathbf{x}^{t+n}|\mathbf{x}^{t+n-1})...p(\mathbf{x}^{t+1}|\mathbf{x}^t)d\mathbf{x}^{t+1}...d\mathbf{x}^{t+n-1} \quad (4)$$

Since we have assumed time invariance, $p(\mathbf{x}^{t+i}|\mathbf{x}^{t+i-1}) = p(\mathbf{x}^{t+1}|\mathbf{x}^t)$ for all $i = 2...n$. $p(\mathbf{x}^{t+n}|\mathbf{x}^t)$ therefore represents n convolutions of the constant interval transition function $p(\mathbf{x}^{t+1}|\mathbf{x}^t)$ with itself. Clearly this is a very inefficient method for obtaining $p(\mathbf{x}^{t+n})$. It would be preferable to represent $p(\mathbf{x}^{t+n}|\mathbf{x}^t)$ directly, for an arbitrary time interval.

The above inference procedure, called 'roll-up', computes approximate distributions at $t + 1$ due to the practice of using the posterior distributions at time t as the prior distributions in the iteration $(t) \rightarrow (t + 1)$ and discarding all information from times prior to t. To perform exact inference in a DBN, each node, including all nodes from earlier time-steps, would need to be conditioned on all evidence up to the current time. This can be achieved by maintaining a static network which represents the 'rolled out' dynamic network. At each new time-step after t_0 a DBN 'slice' is added to the static network along with any available evidence. This computation very quickly becomes intractable. Kjaerulff [8] investigated the effects of keeping only a limited number of network slices and pruning irrelevant nodes from the network while Jitnah and Nicholson [6] use a different measure of relevance to determine which arcs to remove in order to simplify the inference task. Each of these methods produce errors that are bounded over time. Regardless of which of these techniques is applied for inference, they utilise a fixed interval transition function to compute a posterior distribution. In situations where evidence does not arrive at regular times, the computational speed of all of these techniques can be improved by the use of a transition function that can represent arbitrary time steps. In the next section we will derive such a function by investigating the dynamics of diffusion processes.

3 Diffusion Processes

3.1 Chapman-Kolmogorov Equation

Equation (3) can be reduced – by integrating over all other times – to a simpler function relating three separate times. That is:

$$p(\mathbf{x}^{t+\tau_1}|\mathbf{x}^{t+\tau_3}) = \int p(\mathbf{x}^{t+\tau_1}|\mathbf{x}^{t+\tau_2})p(\mathbf{x}^{t+\tau_2}|\mathbf{x}^{t+\tau_3})d\mathbf{x}^{t+\tau_2} \quad (5)$$

for $\tau_1 > \tau_2 > \tau_3$. This equation is known as the *Chapman-Kolmogorov equation*. It is a statement about consistency that results from marginalising out intermediary time-steps. Consistency is actually a statement about the dynamics of Markov processes, so it is here that we will focus our investigation.

To understand the special dynamics of a Markov process, we need to look at the differential form of the Chapman-Kolmogorov equation. A derivation of the *differential Chapman-Kolmogorov equation* can be found in various texts on stochastic methods (for example [4]). The result is, using primes to denote a later time-step[1]. and i,j to index the state vector:

$$\partial_t p(\mathbf{x}'|\mathbf{x}) = -\sum_i \partial_{x'_i}[A_i(\mathbf{x}',t')p(\mathbf{x}'|\mathbf{x})] + \sum_{i,j} \frac{1}{2}\partial^2_{x'_i x'_j}[B_{ij}(\mathbf{x}',t')p(\mathbf{x}'|\mathbf{x})]$$
$$+ \int [W(\mathbf{x}'|\mathbf{z}')p(\mathbf{z}'|\mathbf{x}) - W(\mathbf{z}'|\mathbf{x}')\mathbf{p}(\mathbf{x}'|\mathbf{x})]\mathbf{dz}' \quad (6)$$

where we require that $\lim_{\Delta t \to 0} \frac{1}{\Delta t}p(\mathbf{z},t+\Delta t|\mathbf{x},t) = W(\mathbf{z}|\mathbf{x},t)$ and W is only defined for $\mathbf{z} \neq \mathbf{x}$. This differential equation describes the evolution of the conditional distribution that represents the transition model of the Markov process. The various terms represent the possible methods of a state change of $\mathbf{X}$. The first term on the right hand side describes deterministic motion, as in classical mechanics. The second is a diffusive term, induced by stochastic forcing[2], while the integral represents instantaneous jumps in the system state. The functions $A_i(\mathbf{x}',\mathbf{t}')$ describe the system *potential*. The tensor $\mathbf{B}$ is the diffusion matrix of the system. It is symmetric and positive semidefinite as a result of its definition.

In this paper we are only concerned with Markov processes with continuous sample paths, which is to say that there are no instantaneous jumps in the system state. As such we will assume that $W(\mathbf{x}'|\mathbf{z}') = W(\mathbf{z}'|\mathbf{x}') = 0$. The resulting differential equation is known as the *Fokker-Planck equation*.

$$\partial_t p(\mathbf{x}'|\mathbf{x}) = -\sum_i \partial_{x'_i}[A_i(\mathbf{x}',t')p(\mathbf{x}'|\mathbf{x})] + \frac{1}{2}\sum_{i,j}\partial^2_{x'_i x'_j}[B_{ij}(\mathbf{x}',t')p(\mathbf{x}'|\mathbf{x})] \quad (7)$$

The solution of this system, $p(\mathbf{x}^{t+\Delta t}|\mathbf{x}^t, \Delta t)$, can be obtained using various methods which will, in general, depend on $\mathbf{A}$ and $\mathbf{B}$. For certain choices of these quantities, exact solutions of (7) may not exist. In these circumstances there are several approaches that may lead to a solution. Outlining the various solution methods of Equation 7 is beyond the scope of this paper.

We now wish to demonstrate the usefulness of a transition function derived from the *Fokker-Planck equation*. We have chosen the example problem of inferring the state of a moving object. Such tracking problems have been covered extensively in the literature and well established filtering techniques exist to perform this inference task. See [1] for a good coverage of the problem. This particular problem was chosen merely for the clarity with which it highlights the inefficiencies generated by irregular observations when using an inference technique such as that described in Section 2. In tracking a moving object we are interested in inferring both the position, $\mathbf{x}$, and velocity, $\mathbf{v}$, of the body over time. If the position and velocity are each subject to stochastic forcing then we can use the following equations to model the process.

$$\mathbf{s}^{t+\Delta t} = \mathbf{s}^t + \mathbf{A}^t \mathbf{s}^t \Delta t + \omega_\mathbf{s}^t \qquad \omega_\mathbf{s}^t \sim N(0, \Gamma^t) \quad (8)$$
$$\mathbf{s} = \begin{bmatrix} x \\ v \end{bmatrix} \qquad \mathbf{A} = \begin{bmatrix} 0 & 1 \\ 0 & 0 \end{bmatrix}$$

$\omega_\mathbf{s}^t$ is a Gaussian process with covariance structure Γ^t.

---
[1] Hence, $p(\mathbf{x}'|\mathbf{x})$ means $p(\mathbf{x}', t'|\mathbf{x}, t)$ and $t' > t$
[2] A randomly fluctuating force that generates perturbations (noise) in the state of a variable over time.

However, these equations do not model the continuous Markov process of a moving object precisely. They are only a local linear approximation and therefore only accurate at modelling the actual process over small time-steps. Although, in the limit as $\Delta t \to 0$ these equations do correctly model the continuous Markov process. Considering (7) again, we note that for arbitrarily small time-steps, $p(\mathbf{x}'|\mathbf{x})$ will still be sharply peaked. Hence, the derivatives of the functions A_i and B_{ij} will be negligible compared with those of $p(\mathbf{x}'|\mathbf{x})$. We can therefore ignore these terms and we can also ignore the time dependency of each A_i and B_{ij}. This leads to the differential equation that is a local approximation of a continuous Markov process.

$$\partial_t p(\mathbf{x}'|\mathbf{x}) = -\sum_i A_i(\mathbf{x},t) \partial_{x'_i} p(\mathbf{x}'|\mathbf{x}) + \frac{1}{2} \sum_{i,j} B_{ij}(\mathbf{x},t) \partial^2_{x'_i x'_j} p(\mathbf{x}'|\mathbf{x}) \quad (9)$$

Subject to the initial condition, $p(\mathbf{x}^{t_0})$, the solution of this equation is:

$$p(\mathbf{x}^{t+\Delta t}|\mathbf{x}^t, \Delta t) = (2\pi)^{-1} \{\det[\mathbf{B}]\}^{\frac{1}{2}} [\Delta t]^{-\frac{1}{2}} \times \exp\left\{\frac{-1}{2\Delta t} \mathbf{z}^T [\mathbf{B}]^{-1} \mathbf{z}\right\} \quad (10)$$

$$\mathbf{z} = [\mathbf{x}^{t+\Delta t} - \mathbf{x}^t - \mathbf{A}(\mathbf{x}^t, t)\Delta t]$$

The physical representation of (10) is a system moving with velocity $\mathbf{A}(\mathbf{x}^t, t)$ onto which a Gaussian distributed fluctuation, with covariance $\mathbf{B}\Delta t$, is imposed. The DBN model for this process is given in Figure 1(b) where the distributions for each node are Gaussian. With a suitable choice of $\mathbf{A}$ and $\mathbf{B}$ the function, (10), separates to give two multivariate Gaussian distributions that represent the transition processes outlined in Figure 1(b). In the next section we will see that these distributions permit more efficient execution of the two step inference procedure described in Section 2.

4 Application to DBN Inference

4.1 An Example for Linear Filtering

The 'roll-up' method described in Section 2 is a classic inference algorithm used for DBNs. When the system model is a Linear Dynamical System, as in the moving object model (8), then the Kalman filter [7] is a fast and efficient implementation of 'roll-up'. The Kalman filter equations also provide an easy implementation of the arbitrary time step transition function given by equation 10. The system model (8) is extended to include an observation process, $\mathbf{y}^t$, and thus the system equations are:

$$\mathbf{s}^{t+\Delta t} = \mathbf{F}^t \mathbf{s}^t + \omega^t_s \quad \omega^t_s \sim N(0, \Gamma^t) \quad (11)$$
$$\mathbf{y}^t = \mathbf{H}\mathbf{s}^t + \upsilon^t \quad \upsilon^t \sim N(0, \Sigma) \quad (12)$$

$$\mathbf{F}^t = (\mathbf{I} + \mathbf{A}\Delta t) = \begin{bmatrix} 1 & \Delta t \\ 0 & 1 \end{bmatrix} \quad \mathbf{H} = \begin{bmatrix} 1 & 0 \\ 0 & 0 \end{bmatrix}$$

$$\Sigma = \begin{bmatrix} \sigma & 0 \\ 0 & 0 \end{bmatrix} \quad \Gamma^t = \begin{bmatrix} B_{11}\Delta t & 0 \\ 0 & B_{22}\Delta t \end{bmatrix}$$

$\mathbf{F}^t$ is the transition matrix and $\mathbf{I}$ is the identity matrix. $\mathbf{H}$ is the observation matrix that identifies the variables on which observations are made. Σ and Γ are the noise covariance matrices. The Kalman filter equations are now given by:

$$\mathbf{m}^{t+\Delta t} = \mathbf{F}^t \mathbf{m}^t + \mathbf{K}^{t+\Delta t}(\mathbf{y}^{t+\Delta t} - \mathbf{HF}^t \mathbf{m}^t) \qquad \mathbf{m}^t = E[\mathbf{s}^t]$$
$$\mathbf{V}^{t+\Delta t} = (\mathbf{I} - \mathbf{K}^{t+\Delta t}\mathbf{H})\mathbf{P}^t \qquad \mathbf{V}^t = E[(\mathbf{s}^t)(\mathbf{s}^t)^T]$$
$$\mathbf{K}^{t+\Delta t} = \mathbf{P}^t \mathbf{H}^T (\mathbf{HP}^t \mathbf{H}^T + \Sigma)^{-1} \qquad \mathbf{P}^t = \mathbf{F}^t \mathbf{V}^t (\mathbf{F}^t)^T + \Gamma^t$$

E is the expectation operator and the model is initialised with $\mathbf{s}^0 \sim N(\mathbf{m}^0, \mathbf{V}^0)$.

4.2 Experimental Results

To initialise the inference problem we set $\Delta t = 1$ for all time and sampled the model (8) to obtain a time series of 40 position coordinates, as well as observations of these positions. We performed this sampling in 2 dimensions. All but 10 observations were discarded. The first observation was kept as well as those at times $t_i + \Delta t_i$, where the Δt_i were sampled randomly from a Poisson distribution. Next we filtered these observations using the standard filtering technique of

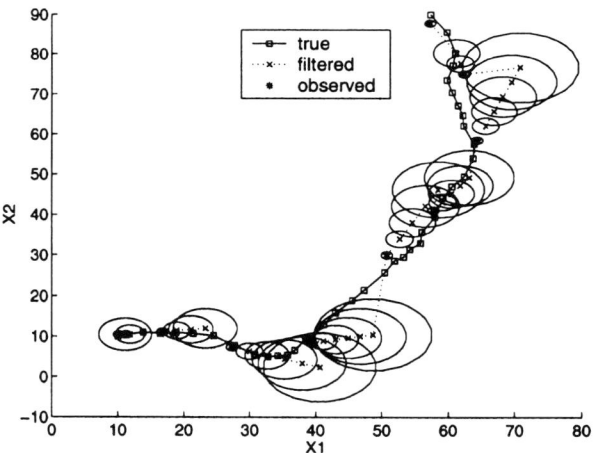

Fig. 2. Actual and inferred object position in the 2-D plane using a constant interval transition function.

a constant time interval transition function. We set $\Delta t = 1$ and at each time that an observation was not available the *Kalman gain* matrix $\mathbf{K}$ was set to zero. This is in accordance with the standard procedure for dealing with absent observations with this filter. The results of this inference process are given in Figure 2 for position and Figure 3 for velocity. Figure 2 shows the actual path of the object in two dimensions, denoted by the squares. The inferred path, marked by triangles, is a series of linear approximations to the true path, which is exactly what we expect from our linear system model. The relatively poor inference of the path at various times is caused by the fact that the period between observations is far greater than the time scale of the variability of the underlying process. At times when observations become available, we see a sudden jump in the position of the object which closely reflects the new observation. In Figure 3 we see a corresponding sudden change in the inferred value of velocity of the object. The velocity then remains constant, as is the assumption made by the system model (8). Figure 2 also shows a set of ellipses. Each is centred on an inferred value and

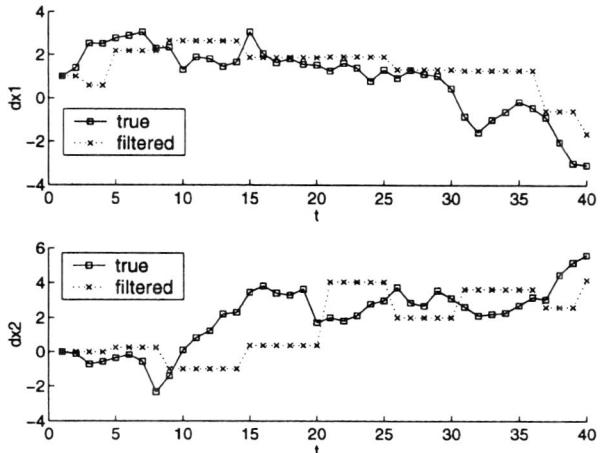

Fig. 3. Actual and inferred velocities of object in each coordinate dimension, plotted against time. Obtained using a constant interval transition function.

is representative of the uncertainty in the position at that time. It can be clearly seen that the uncertainty grows as the time since the last observation increases. This is to be expected since the 'older' our information, the less confident we are that it correctly describes the state of the process we are monitoring. Any inference of positions and velocities at times between observations provides no new information for the model. New information only comes from making observations and as such, the intermediary inference steps are wasteful of computation time. Next we filtered the observations using the arbitrary time interval transition function given by (10). At each time after $t = 0$ the elapsed time since the last observation was used as the time-step, Δt. This value was applied to $\mathbf{F}^t$ and Γ^t and then we ran the system through one iteration of the same code as used in the standard technique. This produced the filtered value at time $t + \Delta t$. We performed this procedure once for each observation. The results for inferred position and velocity are given in Figures 4 and 5, respectively. Both of these figures contain the same information as Figures 2 and 3 respectively. The inferred positions and velocities agree exactly with those obtained using the standard filter at the times when observations were available. This indicates that no errors

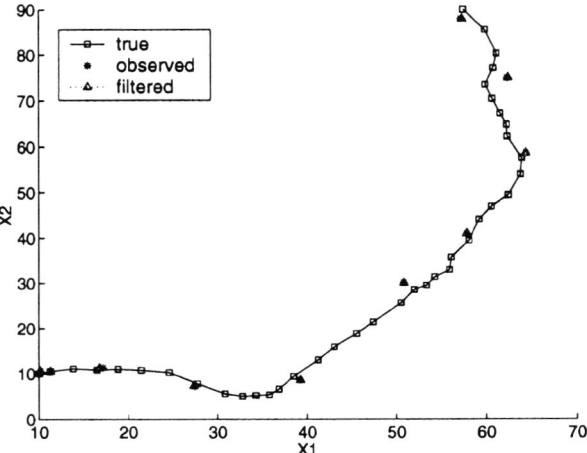

Fig. 4. Actual and inferred object position in the 2-D plane using an arbitrary interval transition function.

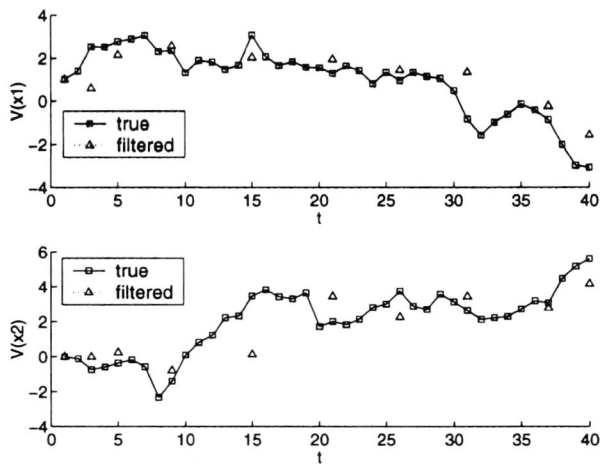

Fig. 5. Actual and inferred velocities of object in each coordinate dimension, plotted against time. Obtained using an arbitrary interval transition function.

were introduced by omitting computations between observations. In Figures 3 and 5 the deviation of inferred velocity from actual velocity is the result of the inference procedure.

The system model states that the velocity at the current time depends only on the value at the previous time, plus noise. As such, any errors in the inferred velocity will be propagated through the system. The errors do not grow unbounded though, as can be seen in Figure 3. Boyen and Koller [2] proved that such errors remain bounded over time and in fact contract at an exponential rate.

We conclude this section with a brief look at the computational saving provided by using an arbitrary time interval transition model. We ran 32 experiments varying the sample path, the number of observations and the variability of time intervals, recording the ratio of the number of floating point operations (flops) performed by each method. The average of the ratio of modified method flops to standard method flops was 0.49, indicating a significant computational saving was made when using the arbitrary time step transition function in these experiments.

5 Discussion

Although we implemented the 'roll-up' inference procedure using a Kalman filter, this does not limit the applicability of arbitrary time-step transition functions to just this inference tool. The inefficencies observed are indicative of the inference techniques described in Section 2, rather than any particular method of implimenting them. In addition, the fact that we chose a linear approximation model and transition function does not reduce the applicability of solutions of the Fokker-Planck equation to general DBN models or inference techniques. In fact it increases this applicability, showing that models that only approximate a continuous Markov process can be described locally as a linear diffusion process and be expressed as a DBN.

The use of arbitrary time interval transition functions is not limited to linear models either. If the system dynamics can be represented by an *Ito stochastic differential equation* [4] of the form:

$$d\mathbf{x} = \mathbf{A}(\mathbf{x},t)dt + \sqrt{\mathbf{B}(\mathbf{x},t)}d\mathbf{W}^t \qquad (13)$$

then the process is a continuous Markov process that can be modelled by a Fokker-Planck equation. Here $d\mathbf{W}$ is an n-dimensional *Weiner process*.

There exists a further benefit of arbitrary time interval transition functions. In the event that predictions are required at an arbitrary time in the future, previous models using fixed interval transition functions required lengthy computations to obtain the posterior distribution at the future time step. With an arbitrary time interval function, these distributions can be obtained with only one iteration of the inference code. In our DBN model for the Aerosonde, fast and accurate prediction of future states of the domain given current knowledge is vital for efficient real-time planning and replanning of missions.

6 Conclusions

Probabilistic inference is computationally expensive, more so as the complexity of the model increases. We have provided a method for eliminating the unnecessary computation of intermediary posterior distributions in models where observations arrive at irregular time intervals. We have tested an example of an arbitrary time interval transition function, which we derived using the Fokker-Planck equation, and found that the computational saving averaged 50% over many different experiments. We produced a transition function from a differential equation that locally approximated the Fokker-Planck equation, as a result of the system model we had implemented. In general, solutions of the Fokker-Planck equation can be used in DBN models that describe a continuous Markov process. When observations are obtained at irregular times, we have shown that using these arbitrary time interval transition functions gives significant computational savings when compared to the use of traditional constant time interval functions.

Acknowledgements We would like to thank Kevin Korb for his helpful discussions; and Kevin Murphy for his Bayes Net and Kalman Toolboxes for MatLab.

References

1. K. Bar-Shalom and T. E. Fortmann. *Tracking and data association*. Mathematics in Science and Engineering Series. Academic Press, 1988.
2. X. Boyen and D. Koller. Tractable inference for complex stochastic processes. In *Proceedings of the Fourteenth Conference on Uncertainty in AI*, pages 33–42, 1998.
3. Thomas Dean and Keiji Kanazawa. A model for reasoning about persistence and causation. *Computational Intelligence*, 5:142–150, 1989.
4. C. W. Gardiner. *Handbook of Stochastic Methods*. Springer-Verlag, 1990.
5. T. Holland, G.J. McGeer and H. Youngren. Autonomous Aerosondes for economical atmospheric soundings anywhere on the globe. *Bulletin of the American Meteorological Society*, 73(12):1987–1998, 1992.
6. Nathalie Jitnah and Ann E. Nicholson. Arc weights for approximate evaluation of Dynamic Belief Networks. In *Proceedings of the 12th Australian Joint Conference on Artificial Intelligence, AI'99*, pages 393–404, Sydney, 1999.
7. R.E. Kalman. A new approach to linear filtering and prediction problems. *Trans. ASME, J. Basic Engineering*, 82:34–45, March 1960.
8. Uffe Kjaerulff. Reduction of computation complexity in Bayesian networks through removal of weak dependencies. In *Proceedings of the 10th Conference on Uncertainty in Artificial Intelligence*, pages 374–382, 1994.
9. Judea Pearl. *Probabilistic Reasoning in Intelligent Systems*. Morgan Kaufmann, San Mateo, Ca., 1988.
10. Stuart Russell and Peter Norvig. *Artificial Intelligence: A Modern Approach*. Prentice-Hall, 1995.

Epistemic States Guiding the Rational Dynamics of Information

Johannes Heidema[1] and Isabella C Burger[2]

[1] Department of Mathematics, University of South Africa
P.O. Box 392, Pretoria 0003, South Africa
heidej@unisa.ac.za

[2] Department of Mathematics, Rand Afrikaans University
P.O. Box 524, Auckland Park (Johannesburg), 2006, South Africa
icb@na.rau.ac.za

Abstract. An epistemic state here means a total preorder on the set of possible worlds. Simple epistemic states, with one or two equivalence classes, correspond to belief sets. Relative to a fixed belief set t, we define a comparative order on belief sets, expressing that 'y sorts the worlds closer to the way in which t sorts them than x does'. This induces a Boolean algebra, ordered very differently from, but isomorphic to the Lindenbaum-Tarski algebra under the isomorphism which sends x to $x \leftrightarrow t$. The isomorphism allows us to classify each inferential or conjectural step as being either in concord or in discord with the beliefs t. So t may now guide the logical dynamics of inference and conjecture, and hence of corroboration, refutation, diagnosis, abduction, etc. Going from belief sets to more general epistemic states, we show how similar constructions may guide AGM belief change.

Key words: epistemic states; total preorders; abduction; belief revision

1 Introduction

Information, in the context of Computational Intelligence, can be represented and employed rationally in various ways. We consider information representable as an *epistemic state* of an agent, which here means a total preorder (i.e. a connected, transitive and reflexive relation) on the set of possible worlds – or possible states of some system – under consideration. The relation may compare the worlds with respect to, e.g., having a certain structural property (to a certain degree); being normal; being likely; being safe; being costly; or being preferred.

An epistemic state partitions the set of possible worlds into equivalence classes (where 'equivalent' means 'comparable both ways') on which a linear order is induced. The simplest epistemic state would have only one partition class – that of all possible worlds, a totally undifferentiated 'cloud of unknowing', which carries no information. An epistemic state with two classes dichotomizes the worlds: 'has the property' versus 'does not have the property'; 'normal' versus 'abnormal'; 'good' versus 'bad'; 'accepted' versus 'rejected'. An epistemic state with more partition classes realizes finer discriminations, and hence carries more information of a certain nature. (One could consider richer epistemic states, consisting not just of a single total preorder on worlds, but of a list of such orders, representing comparisons of worlds on different criteria. For the purposes of this paper we stay with a single preorder.)

When we have a language available which is suitable for expressing the distinguishing properties of worlds sorted by an epistemic state into two classes, we may be able to axiomatize one of the classes – say the 'good' one – by a *belief set*, this being a sentence, or set of sentences, or theory (i.e. deductively closed set of sentences) in the language, of which the relevant equivalence class is the set of models. (The epistemic state with a single class corresponds of course to a tautologous, or logically true belief set.) In this sense a belief set is a special case of an epistemic state.

When we are going to investigate how the information captured in an epistemic state may be used rationally to guide some of the transformations to which we subject (other) information, we shall focus on three such processes: *inference*, whether strictly deductive or plausible; the inverse of inference – call it *conjecture*, or abduction, or diagnosis; and *belief change*. In section 2 we set the scene with a general discussion of information semantically represented by an epistemic state, information syntactically represented by a belief set, and relations between the two types of information.

In section 3 we explain how a simple epistemic state, that is a belief set t, allows us to categorize inferential steps as well as conjectural steps as either conforming to or conflicting with t. This implies that t can guide the dynamics of inference for corroboration or refutation, and also the dynamics of conjecture for diagnosis or explanatory hypothesis formulation. The crucial notion here, which is formalized in the framework of Boolean algebras, can be expressed informally as follows. Any belief set t *sorts* the worlds into 'accepted' (models of t) and 'rejected' (non-models of t). When t is a fixed belief set, we compare any two belief sets x and y with respect to t by defining a binary relation 'the x-sorting is at most as *close* to the t-sorting as the y-sorting is'. This ordering makes a Boolean algebra of the set of all belief sets, which gives the classification of inferences and conjectures as being either in concord (upward) or in discord (downward in the Boolean algebra) with t.

In section 4 general epistemic states give rise to generalizations of the Boolean algebras of section 3 and to (philosophically and mathematically uncomplicated) notions of knowledge and belief. Distinguishing logically weaker – and hence more secure – knowledge from logically stronger – and hence bolder – beliefs, leads to more sophistication in the classification of inferential and conjectural steps as being either compliant with or adverse to particular beliefs or knowledge. In section 5 we utilize all of the machinery developed in previous sections to demonstrate how the information available in epistemic states may be employed to make rational choices in the AGM framework for belief change (Alchourrón, Gärdenfors and Makinson [1]).

2 Epistemic States, Semantic Information, Language and Logic

To grasp how an epistemic state (total preorder on worlds) embodies information, it helps to see the link with the theory of semantic information of Bar-Hillel and Carnap [2]. (This theory must be distinguished from the 'information theory' of the communications engineer, i.e. Shannon's mathematical theory of communication, which is about the statistics of message strings – not primarily about their meaning.) Simply put, Carnap and Bar-Hillel tell us that the smallest atom of information that we can have – a *content-element* of semantic information – is the information that one particular possible world is *excluded*. We may think of this bit of semantic information as syntactically represented by the negation of the state description of the excluded world. To illustrate, consider the propositional logic generated by the two atomic symbols p and q. The four state descriptions $p \wedge q$, $p \wedge \neg q$, $\neg p \wedge q$ and $\neg p \wedge \neg q$ correspond to the four possible worlds (truth valuations) 11, 10, 01 and 00 for p,q (where 1 means 'true' and 0 means 'false'). The four content-elements of this language are $\neg p \vee \neg q$, $\neg p \vee q$, $p \vee \neg q$ and $p \vee q$, which are the four co-atoms of the Lindenbaum-Tarski algebra of this language – i.e. the four logically weakest non-tautological propositions of the language (Figure 1). They state the exclusion of, respectively, the worlds 11, 10, 01 and 00. Every proposition is the conjunction of the content-elements entailed by it.

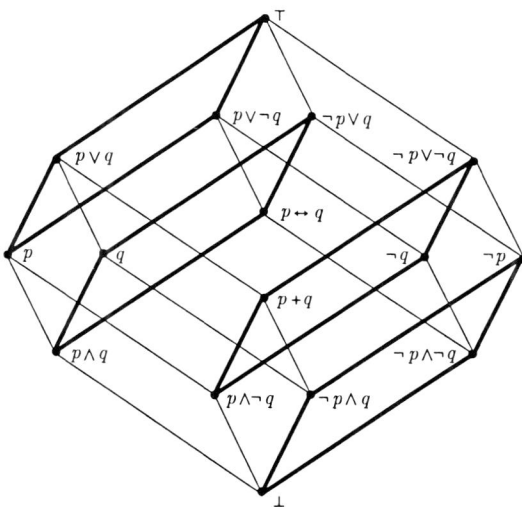

Fig. 1. The Lindenbaum-Tarski algebra $\mathcal{B}$ generated by $\{p,q\}$

The semantic information expressed by the belief set p (or $\{p\}$, or $Cn\{p\}$) with its two content-elements, $p = (p \vee q) \wedge (p \vee \neg q)$, is equivalently captured by the epistemic state of Figure 2. (The reader will know that it has become conventional when using total preorders, e.g. in minimal model semantics for nonmonotonic logics, to represent 'good', 'normal' etc. by 'small', 'down', 'minimal' etc. We use the opposite convention in order not to have a clash between the epistemic order on worlds and the Boolean order induced on propositions in the next section as pictured according to the standard conventions of Hasse diagrams and as exemplified in Figure 4. And it is, after all, a universal of human culture that 'better' is signified by 'upward'.)

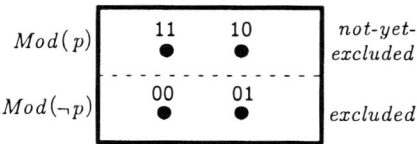

Fig. 2. Simple epistemic state, corresponding to belief set p

When the quest for more information has the aim of targeting the one actual world among the possible worlds, then obtaining information can be seen as shoving worlds down into the 'excluded' class and at each such step gaining one content-element of information. The quest ends with what in this context may be called complete information, when one world is left and all the others are excluded. Of course, epistemic states may not be about finding the actual world at all, but about, say, the relative cost of realizing the different possibilities. Nevertheless, whenever the top equivalence class of an epistemic state $\leq$ is axiomatisable by a belief set t, we call t the belief set *corresponding* to $\leq$. In the case that $\leq$ has at most two classes, t contains all the information in $\leq$, since it sorts just like $\leq$. If $\leq$ has more than two classes, t cannot discriminate between the non-models of t. In the next section we study simple epistemic states, with at most two classes, and which correspond to belief sets.

3 Belief Sets and Boolean Algebras

The mathematical constructions that we want to expound now can be done in any Boolean algebra, but for present purposes we limit our exposition to the Lindenbaum-Tarski (LT) algebra of a finitely generated classical propositional language, of which Figure 1 gives an example. We highlight, without complete proofs, just some relevant aspects of the transformation to which we shall subject the LT algebra and some uses of the transformed algebra in guiding the processes of inference and conjecture.

So we have a finitely generated propositional language suitable for expressing information about the set of possible worlds, or possible states of some system that interests us – the latter being represented by the set $\mathbf{W}$ of all truth valuations of the language. We pick one fixed element $t \in B$ from the LT algebra $\mathcal{B} := (B, \models, \wedge, \vee, \neg, \bot, \top)$ of propositions (logical equivalence classes of sentences). Think of t as a belief set that remains a fixed bench-mark throughout this section, against which other beliefs are compared. It may represent background information, or the (part of the) truth that is available to us now, or a hypothesis or theory that is under investigation and that we are trying to corroborate or refute by testing some of its consequences or even some conjectures that it may suggest.

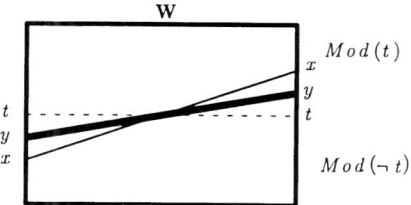

Fig. 3. y sorts closer to t than x

The belief t sorts the worlds in $\mathbf{W}$ into the accepted set $Mod(t)$ (above the dotted sorting line in Figure 3) and the rejected set $\mathbf{W} - Mod(t) = Mod(\neg t)$ (below the dotted line). If now $x, y \in B$ are any two beliefs, we want to compare them as to how well they sort, given the t-sorting as norm. Looking at Figure 3, it seems natural to say that 'x sorts at best as well as y does (relative to the t-sorting as norm)' if and only if the following equivalent conditions hold:

- $Mod(x) \cap Mod(t) \subseteq Mod(y) \cap Mod(t)$ and
  $Mod(y) \cap Mod(\neg t) \subseteq Mod(x) \cap Mod(\neg t)$;
- $x \wedge t \models y \wedge t$ and $y \wedge \neg t \models x \wedge \neg t$;
- $(x \leftrightarrow t) \models (y \leftrightarrow t)$.

(For any sorting-line $u \in B$, $Mod(u)$ lies above and $Mod(\neg u)$ below the line.) Let us give this relation on B a formal name:

Definition 1. $x \sqsubseteq_t y :\Leftrightarrow (x \leftrightarrow t) \models (y \leftrightarrow t)$

This definition has previously been proposed (Miller [9] and Kuipers [6]) in the context of the study of verisimilitude (Brink [3], Niiniluoto [12], Zwart [13]), but is unsatisfactory from that point of view, since it has some properties which are contrary to our intuitions about truthlikeness. What we suggest is that the relation is very useful, but should not be read as 'x is at best as *close to the (part of the) truth* expressed by t as y is' nor something similar in terms of *being true*. Nor has the relation primarily to do with logical strength of belief sets. It compares the *similarity of the x-sorting to the t-sorting* (expressed syntactically by $x \leftrightarrow t$ and semantically by $[Mod(x) \cap Mod(t)] \cup [Mod(\neg x) \cap Mod(\neg t)]$) with the *similarity of the y-sorting to the t-sorting* (expressed correspondingly in y). It says that the *sorting-information* in y is equal to or better than that in x, given that in t as the norm. It seems that the mathematics of $\sqsubseteq_t$ and its relationship to $\models$ have not previously been studied in great detail – at least not in the present context – but it is very elegant. We encapsulate what we need here in a theorem.

Theorem 1. *The relation $\sqsubseteq_t$ is a Boolean ordering on the set of propositions B, and hence induces a Boolean algebra $\mathcal{B}_t := (B, \sqsubseteq_t, \sqcap_t, \sqcup_t, \neg, \neg t, t)$, which has t as its top, $\neg t$ as its bottom, the same complementation $\neg$ (negation) as $\mathcal{B}$, and meet and join operations which are related to those in $\mathcal{B}$ ($\wedge$ and $\vee$) as follows:*
$x \sqcap_t y = (x \wedge y) \vee [(x \vee y) \wedge \neg t]$,
$x \sqcup_t y = (x \vee y) \wedge [(x \wedge y) \vee t]$.

*The original LT algebra $\mathcal{B}$ and the new t-**modulated** Boolean algebra $\mathcal{B}_t$ are isomorphic under the isomorphism $m_t : B \to B$, $m_t(x) := (x \leftrightarrow t)$, which is its own inverse, and hence also establishes an isomorphism in the opposite direction.*

We note that under m_t $\top$ goes to t, $\bot$ goes to $\neg t$, t goes to $\top$, and $\neg t$ goes to $\bot$. To illustrate, we show $\mathcal{B}_p$ for the p, q language in Figure 4.

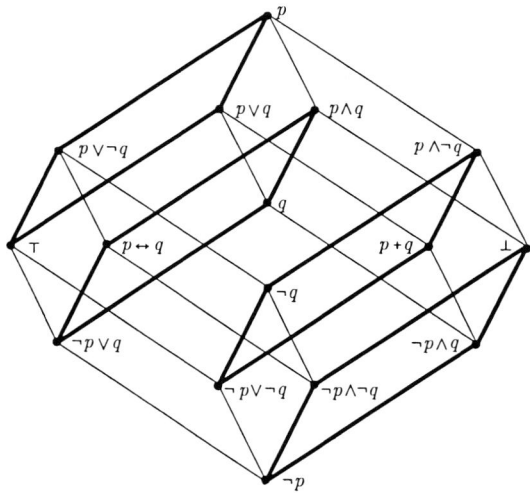

Fig. 4. The p-modulated Boolean algebra $\mathcal{B}_p$ generated by $\{p, q\}$

Note that in $\mathcal{B}_p$ the state descriptions of the four possible worlds sit ordered in a way which obviously contains the same information as the p-sorting of Figure 2. Hence one may see the ordering $\sqsubseteq_t$ on propositions (sets of worlds) as a natural extension of the original epistemic ordering on the worlds. The general idea of letting a proposition t induce an ordering on worlds finds a related expression in the theory of ATMS's, assumption-based truth maintenance systems, (Dubois, Lang & Prade [4] and Forbus & de Kleer [5], Chapter 12), where a given proposition orders "environments". The relationship with our approach deserves further clarification, but is not pursued in this paper.

We now explain how the ordering $\sqsubseteq_t$ classifies each inferential and each conjectural step that we can take as being either t-positive (t-enhancing, in concord with t) or t-negative (t-diminishing, in discord with t). To illustrate simultaneously what we explain, we treat the special case of the p, q language and $t = p$, and ask the reader to follow what we say in the diagram of Figure 1 for $\models$ and the diagram of Figure 4 for $\sqsubseteq_p$.

When, for a pair of propositions (x, y), $x, y \in B$, $Mod(x)$ and $Mod(y)$ differ by a single world, we say that there is a *step* from x to y or that (x, y) is a step. When there is a step from x to y and $x \models y$, i.e. y has one model more than x, then we say that there is an *inferential step* from x to y, while in the opposite case, $y \models x$, we say that there is a *conjectural step* from x to y. The 32 (pairs of) steps of the p, q language are represented by the 32 lines in Figure 1 and by the same 32 lines in Figure 4, although now arranged differently. Note that in Figure 1 every step upward is an inferential step (the diagram depicts $\models$), while each step downward is conjectural. In Figure 4, depicting $\sqsubseteq_p$, we call a step upward *p-positive*, since it goes from a sorting to another one which is (by the changed sorting of one world) more similar to the p-sorting. A step downward in $\sqsubseteq_p$ is *p-negative*. Some p-positive steps are inferential, i.e. they go up in both $\models$ and $\sqsubseteq_p$. These are represented by the *thin* lines going in the same direction in $\models$ and $\sqsubseteq_p$. The other p-positive steps are conjectural, i.e. they go up in $\sqsubseteq_p$, but down in $\models$. They are represented by the *thick* lines, which go in opposite directions in $\models$ and $\sqsubseteq_p$.

Much more can be said about the mathematical relations between $\models$ and $\sqsubseteq_t$, but here we just mention one other property of $\sqsubseteq_t$. Whenever $x \sqsubseteq_t y$, $x \wedge y$ and $x \vee y$ both lie between x and y in $\sqsubseteq_t$.

What have we achieved? Suppose that t is any truth, theory, belief, hypothesis, conjecture, diagnosis, etc. that interests us in the course of the rational dynamics of information. We may want to use t as an assumption; we may want to corroborate it; refute it; test it; weaken it; strengthen it; etc. However we want to employ it, the logical processes of inference and conjecture, the relation $\models$ and its inverse, are likely to play some role. The relation $\sqsubseteq_t$ now classifies each inferential or conjectural step that we may take from anywhere as either t-positive or t-negative. This may guide, illuminate and facilitate the logical dynamics in many ways. One example: Suppose you want to corroborate t by testing and verifying logical consequences of $t \wedge b$, where b is background information. One surmises that t-positive verified consequences of $t \wedge b$ represent stronger corroboration of t than t-negative verified consequences of $t \wedge b$. Similarly, one may use $\sqsubseteq_t$ in processes around *another* proposition. We just mention the possibility of generalizing the role of $\models$ to plausible entailment $\mid\sim$.

4 Epistemic States, Knowledge and Belief

We now consider not just belief sets, but general epistemic states (Figure 5).

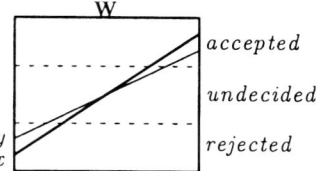

Fig. 5. General epistemic state

The setting is still a finitely generated classical propositional logic with its truth valuations. We call the (non-empty) top equivalence class the set of *accepted* worlds, and the bottom class the set of *rejected* worlds. (In the degenerate case of the top class being **W**, we postulate an empty rejected class.) The union of the classes between the top and the bottom classes will be the set of *undecided* worlds. Given an epistemic state, the proposition b corresponding to its accepted class of worlds is called its *belief (set)*: $b := Th(accepted\ class)$, while the proposition k corresponding to the set **W**$-$ *(rejected class)* of worlds is called its *knowledge (set)*: $k := Th(union\ of\ the\ non\text{-}rejected\ classes)$. Note that $b \models k$, belief is logically bolder than knowledge. (For general background on knowledge and belief, see e.g. Laux and Wansing [8]. Kuipers [7] studied the relation of a weaker to a stronger theory in the context of verisimilitude.)

More generally, for any $x \in B$ we may define the *belief generated from* x by the epistemic state as $b(x) := Th(\mathbf{max}Mod(x))$, and the *knowledge generated from* x by the epistemic state as $k(x) := Th(Mod(x) - \mathbf{min}Mod(x))$, unless $Mod(x) = \mathbf{min}Mod(x)$, in which case $k(x) := x$. While it is customary to represent x by its 'best' models, i.e. by $b(x)$, the dual notion of representing x by all its models except the 'worst' ones, i.e. by $k(x)$, has received some attention in the literature. Recently Nayak and Foo ([10] and [11]) have explored belief revision and abduction from this second point of view.

Note that for simple epistemic states (with at most two partition classes) $b = k$ and $b(x) = k(x)$. We can now generalize the construction and results of the previous section by replacing the role of $t \in B$ by a similar role, but this time played by the interval $[b, k] = \{u \in B \mid b \models u \text{ and } u \models k\}$ in $\mathcal{B}$ between belief and knowledge.

Propositions whose model sets differ only on the set of undecided worlds are equivalent in the new ordering. The equivalence classes are also intervals in $\mathcal{B}$ and they become the elements of the new Boolean algebra, say $\mathcal{B}_{[b,k]}$, which has $[b, k]$ as top and $[\neg k, \neg b]$ as bottom. To come again to a classification of (at least some) inferential and conjectural steps as being either positive or negative, we define a lexicographical ordering on the set of propositions B as follows: Construct $\mathcal{B}_{[b,k]}$ and then pick some $t \in [b, k]$ which interests you. Now 'blow up' each element of $\mathcal{B}_{[b,k]}$ to the class of elements of B that it is, and order them by $\sqsubseteq_t$, but retain the $[b, k]$-ordering between the classes. We call B with the resulting order $\mathcal{B}_{[b,t,k]}$. This is of course no longer a Boolean algebra. Rather than give all the

Epistemic States Guiding the Rational Dynamics of Information   283

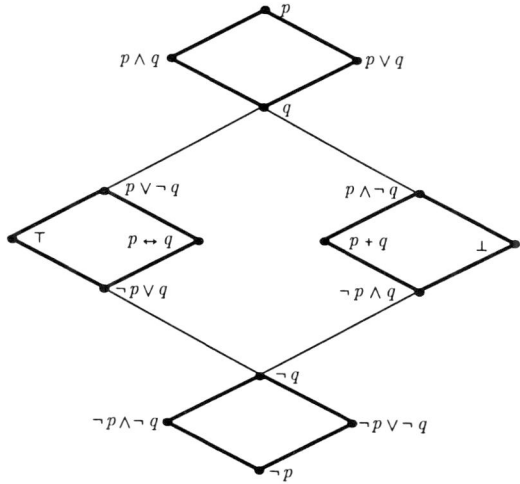

Fig. 6. $\mathcal{B}_{[b,t,k]}$ with $b = p \wedge q$, $t = p$, $k = p \vee q$

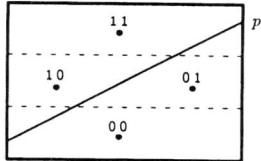

Fig. 7. Epistemic state with $b = p \wedge q$, $t = p$, $k = p \vee q$

mathematical details, we illustrate in Figure 6 the results for the p, q language with $[b, k] = [p \wedge q, p \vee q]$ and $t = p$.

The ordering of the 16 propositions of the p, q language in Figure 6 may be interpreted as follows. If you consider the belief $b = p \wedge q$ and the knowledge $k = p \vee q$ corresponding to the epistemic state of, say, Figure 7, then the Boolean algebra $\mathcal{B}_{[b,k]}$ is the one obtained by collapsing the four classes drawn with thick lines in Figure 6 to four single elements. The four propositions within each of the classes are ordered amongst themselves by $\sqsubseteq_p$ (as in Figure 4).

If in the total (lexicographic) picture y lies higher than x, then this says that y sorts better than x given a norm, which now consists of

i) the general background of an epistemic state which accepts 11, rejects 00, and is undecided about 10 and 01; and

ii) superimposed on (but not replacing) that, the more specific state p, which decides to accept 10 (with 11) and reject 01 (with 00).

Those inferential and conjectural steps which give a comparable pair in $\mathcal{B}_{[b,t,k]}$ may now be classified as $[b, t, k]$-*positive* or $[b, t, k]$-*negative*.

5 Belief Change

In this final section we briefly indicate how the construction of the previous section may help to guide AGM belief contraction (and hence also belief revision) by available information. In the usual AGM notation we have the following: K is a belief set, $\phi \in K$ (or $K \models \phi$), and we want to remove ϕ from K to obtain a logically weaker belief set $K - \phi$, which no longer entails ϕ, but which still comprises as much as possible of the other information in K. In terms of semantic information this means that we must remove at least one of the content-elements of ϕ from those in K, i.e. we must add at least one model of $\neg\phi$ to those of K. The model(s) to be added are typically taken from the best models of $\neg\phi$ according to some epistemic state with K as beliefs.

We translate the problem to the notation of section 4. We have two propositions, $b, k \in B$, with $b \models k$, and we want to construct a proposition $b - k$, logically weaker than b, from which k does not follow, but which in some sense preserves as much of the information in b as is compatible with the stipulations on $b - k$. Note that we have to remove the interval $[b, k]$ from the filter $Cn(b)$ above b in $\mathcal{B}$. Here is a construction to do this. Form the Boolean algebra $\mathcal{B}_{[b,k]}$ as in the previous section. (For the case $b = p \wedge q$, $k = p \vee q$, look at Figure 6, but with the four classes collapsed to single elements.) Its top element is precisely the interval $[b, k]$ of which we want to get rid. Decapitate the Boolean algebra – simply delete its top element. In the next level down (i.e. among the classes which are *as close as possible* to $[b, k]$, the sacrificed information) there is guaranteed to be at least one class with a proposition in it which has the models of b plus precisely one model of $\neg k$, and hence qualifies to be $b - k$. (In Figure 6 the only candidate is $p \leftrightarrow q$, adding the model 00 of $\neg(p \vee q)$ to the model 11 of $p \wedge q$. If however, when making your choice, you do not mind adding more than one world to $Mod(b)$ and in addition you have trust in the p-sorting (which plays a role in Figure 6) you may prefer to take $(p \wedge q) - (p \vee q) = p \vee \neg q$ rather than the logically stronger $p \leftrightarrow q$.) In the ordering of $\mathcal{B}_{[b,k]}$ with the top removed the candidates for $b - k$ are displayed for your inspection, ordered by closeness to $[b, k]$, and, maybe, within the classes ordered by any other considerations which may guide your choice.

References

1. Alchourrón, C., Gärdenfors, P., Makinson, D. (1985) "On the logic of theory change: Partial meet contraction and revision functions", *Journal of Symbolic Logic* **50,** 510-530.
2. Bar-Hillel, Y., Carnap, R. (1953) "Semantic information", *The British Journal for the Philosophy of Science* **4**, 147-157.
3. Brink, C. (1989) "Verisimilitude: Views and reviews", *History and Philosophy of Logic* **10**, 181-201.
4. Dubois, D., Lang, J., Prade, H. (1991) "A possibilistic assumption-based truth maintenance system with uncertainty justifications, and its application to belief revision" pp. 87-106 in Martins, J.P., Reinfrank, M. (eds.) (1991) *Truth maintenance systems* (LNAI, Vol. 515), Springer-Verlag, Berlin.

5. Forbus, K.D., de Kleer, J. (1993) *Building Problem Solvers*, MIT Press, Cambridge MA.
6. Kuipers, T.A.F. (1987) "A structural approach to truthlikeness", pp. 79-99 in Kuipers, T.A.F. (ed.) (1987) *What is Closer-to-the-truth?* (Poznan Studies in the Philosophy of Science, Vol.10), Editions Rodopi, Amsterdam.
7. Kuipers, T.A.F. (1992) "Naive and refined truth approximation", *Synthese* **93**, 299-341.
8. Laux, A., Wansing, H. (eds.) (1995) *Knowledge and Belief in Philosophy and Artificial Intelligence* (Series Logica Nova), Akademie Verlag, Berlin.
9. Miller, D. (1978) "On distance from the truth as a true distance", pp. 415-435 in Hintikka, J., Niiniluoto, I., Saarinen, E. (eds.) (1978) *Essays in Mathematical and Philosophical Logic*, D.Reidel, Dordrecht.
10. Nayak, A., Foo, N. (1998) "Reasoning without minimality", pp. 122-133 in Lee, H., Motoda, H. (eds.) (1998) *PRICAI'98: Topics in Artificial Intelligence. Proceedings of the Fifth Pacific Rim International Conference on Artificial Intelligence* (LNAI, Vol. 1531), Springer-Verlag, Berlin.
11. Nayak, A., Foo, N. (1999) "Abduction without minimality", pp. 365-377 in Foo, N. (ed.) (1999) *Advanced Topics in Artificial Intelligence. Proceedings of the 12th Australian Joint Conference on Artificial Intelligence (AI'99)* (LNAI, Vol. 1747), Springer-Verlag, Berlin.
12. Niiniluoto, I. (1998) "Verisimilitude: The third period", *The British Journal for the Philosophy of Science* **49**, 1-29.
13. Zwart, S.D. (1998) *Approach to the Truth: Verisimilitude and Truthlikeness* (ILLC Dissertation Series 1998-02), Institute for Logic, Language and Computation, Amsterdam.

Merging Epistemic States

Thomas Meyer

Department of Computer Science,
School of Information Technology,
University of Pretoria, Pretoria, 0002, South Africa
tmeyer@cs.up.ac.za
http://www.cs.up.ac.za/~tmeyer

Abstract. Intelligent agents are often faced with the problem of trying to merge possibly conflicting pieces of information obtained from different sources into a consistent view of the world. We propose a framework for the modelling of such merging operations with roots in the work of Spohn [14]. Unlike most approaches we focus on the merging of epistemic states, not knowledge bases. We construct a number of plausible merging operations and measure them against various properties that merging operations ought to satisfy. Finally, we discuss the connection between merging and the use of infobases [9], [10].

1 Introduction

[1]To be able to operate in its environment it is necessary for an intelligent agent to have a consistent view of the world. This demand is often complicated by the fact that such agents receive conflicting pieces of information from different sources. The process of combining possibly inconsistent pieces of information, known as *merging*, has started to receive more attention recently [7, 1, 2, 5, 6, 13, 12, 15]. In this paper we propose a framework for the modelling of merging operations. The proposal has its roots in the work of Spohn [14]. Unlike most approaches we adopt a description of merging on the level of *epistemic states* instead of *knowledge bases*. In section 2 we give a brief introduction to the merging of knowledge bases, focussing on the work of Konieczny and Pino-Pérez [5]. This is followed, in section 3, by a description of our framework for the merging of epistemic states. In section 4 we construct a number of merging operations and show how they measure up to proposed properties of merging. Section 5 discusses links between merging and the *infobases* of Meyer [9]. We assume a finitely generated propositional language L closed under the usual propositional connectives, and with a classical model-theoretic semantics. U is the set of interpretations of L and $M(\alpha)$ is the set of models of $\alpha \in L$. Classical entailment is denoted by $\models$. We use $\sqcup$ to denote the concatenation of lists. We let x^n denote the list consisting of n versions of x. The length of a list l is denoted by $|l|$.

---

[1] Currently a Post-Doctoral Research Fellow in the Department of Information Systems, University of Wollongong, Wollongong, Australia.

2 Merging Knowledge Bases

In the spirit of the work of Katsuno and Mendelzon [4], approaches to the merging of knowledge bases usually represent the beliefs of an agent as a single wff ϕ of L, known as a *knowledge base*, where ϕ represents the set of all wffs entailed by ϕ. The goal is to construct, from a finite list of such knowledge bases, an appropriate consistent knowledge base in some rational fashion. Konieczny and Pino-Pérez [5] have proposed a general framework for the merging of knowledge bases. A *knowledge list* e is a finite list of consistent knowledge bases $[\phi_1, \ldots, \phi_{|e|}]$. Two knowledge lists e_1 and e_2 are *element-equivalent*, written as $e_1 \approx e_2$, iff for every element ϕ_1 of e_1 there is a unique element ϕ_2 (position-wise) of e_2 such that $\phi_1 \equiv \phi_2$ and for every element ϕ_2 of e_2 there is a unique element ϕ_1 (position-wise) of e_1 such that $\phi_2 \equiv \phi_1$. A *KP-merging operation* δ is a function from the set of all knowledge lists to the set of all knowledge bases satisfying the following postulates (the KP-postulates):

(KP1) $\delta(e) \not\models \bot$
(KP2) If $\bigwedge_{i=1}^{|e|} \phi_i \not\models \bot$ then $\delta(e) \equiv \bigwedge_{i=1}^{|e|} \phi_i$
(KP3) If $e_1 \approx e_2$ then $\delta(e_1) \equiv \delta(e_2)$
(KP4) If $\phi_1 \wedge \phi_2 \models \bot$ then $\delta([\phi_1] \sqcup [\phi_2]) \not\models \phi_1$
(KP5) $\delta(e_1) \wedge \delta(e_2) \models \delta(e_1 \sqcup e_2)$
(KP6) If $\delta(e_1) \wedge \delta(e_2) \not\models \bot$ then $\delta(e_1 \sqcup e_2) \models \delta(e_1) \wedge \delta(e_2)$

Konieczny and Pino-Pérez also distinguish between two subclasses of merging operations. An *arbitration* operation tries to take as many differing opinions as possible into account, while the intuition associated with *majority* operations is that the opinion of the majority should prevail. They initially propose the following postulates for arbitration and majority operations.

(arb) $\forall n \; \delta(e \sqcup \phi^n) = \delta(e \sqcup [\phi])$
(maj) $\exists n \; \delta(e \sqcup \phi^n) \models \phi$

It turns out that no KP-merging operation satisfies (arb). Unlike Konieczny and Pino-Pérez we are of the opinion that it is not (arb) that is at fault, but some of the KP-postulates. Below we argue against the inclusion of (KP4) and (KP6) as postulates that need to be satisfied by all merging operations.

3 Merging Epistemic States

In this section we discuss merging on the level of epistemic states. We see an epistemic state as providing a plausibility ranking of the interpretations of L; the lower the number assigned to an interpretation, the more plausible it is deemed to be.

Definition 1. *An epistemic state Φ is a function from U to the set of natural numbers. Given an epistemic state Φ, the knowledge base associated with Φ, denoted by ϕ_Φ, is some $\alpha \in L$ such that $M(\alpha) = \{u \mid \Phi(u) = 0\}$.*

This representation of an epistemic state and its associated knowledge base can be traced back to the work of Spohn [14]. It should be clear that an epistemic state with an inconsistent associated knowledge base still contains useful information. An *epistemic list* $E = [\Phi_1^E, \ldots, \Phi_{|E|}^E]$ is a finite list of epistemic states. It

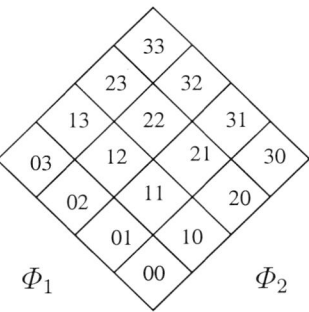

Fig. 1. A pictorial representation of an epistemic list containing two epistemic states Φ_1 and Φ_2. The sequence of two digits in each cell above indicates the natural numbers associated with interpretations by the two epistemic states. A cell containing the sequence ij indicates the placement of those interpretations assigned the value i by Φ_1 and assigned the value j by Φ_2.

is instructive to view an epistemic list pictorially as in figure 1. While such a pictorial view is only useful in representing epistemic lists containing two elements, it serves as a good foundation for understanding the principles underlying the merging of epistemic states in general.

For any epistemic state Φ, let $\min(\Phi) = \min\{\Phi(u) \mid u \in U\}$, let $\max(\Phi) = \max\{\Phi(u) \mid u \in U\}$, and for an epistemic list E, let $\max(E) = \max\{\max(\Phi_i^E) \mid 1 \leq i \leq |E|\}$. For an epistemic list E and $u \in U$ we let $\min^E(u) = \min\{\Phi_i^E(u) \mid 1 \leq i \leq |E|\}$ and $\max^E(u) = \max\{\Phi_i^E(u) \mid 1 \leq i \leq |E|\}$. We denote by $seq(E)$ the set of all sequences of length $|E|$ of natural numbers, ranging from 0 to $\max(E)$. We denote by $seq_\leq(E)$ the subset of $seq(E)$ of all sequences that are ordered non-decreasingly, and by $seq_\geq(E)$ the subset of $seq(E)$ of all sequences that are ordered non-increasingly. For $u \in U$, we let $s^E(u)$ be the sequence containing the natural numbers $\Phi_1^E(u), \ldots, \Phi_{|E|}^E(u)$ in that order, we let $s_\leq^E(u)$ be the sequence $s^E(u)$ ordered non-decreasingly, and we let $s_\geq^E(u)$ be the sequence $s^E(u)$ ordered non-increasingly. Clearly $s^E(u) \in seq(E)$, $s_\leq^E(u) \in seq_\leq(E)$ and $s_\geq^E(u) \in seq_\geq(E)$. Given any set seq of finite sequences of natural numbers and a total preorder $\sqsubseteq$ on seq, we define the function $\Omega_\sqsubseteq^{seq} : seq \to \{0, \ldots, |seq|-1\}$ by assigning natural numbers to the elements of seq in the order imposed by $\sqsubseteq$, starting by assigning 0 to the elements lowest down in $\sqsubseteq$. We denote the *lexicographic* ordering on seq by $\sqsubseteq_{lex}$.

A *merging operation on epistemic states* Δ is a function from the set of all non-empty epistemic lists to the set of all epistemic states. We propose the following basic properties for the merging of epistemic states:

(E1) $\exists u$ s.t. $\Delta(E)(u) = 0$
(E2) $\Phi_i^E(u) = \Phi_j^E(u)$ $\forall 1 \leq i, j \leq |E|$ and $s_{\leq}^E(u) \sqsubset_{lex} s_{\leq}^E(v)$ implies $\Delta(E)(u) < \Delta(E)(v)$
(E3) $\Phi_i^E(u) \leq \Phi_i^E(v)$ $\forall 1 \leq i \leq |E|$ implies $\Delta(E)(u) \leq \Delta(E)(v)$
(E4) $\Delta(E)(u) \leq \Delta(E)(v)$ implies $\Phi_i^E(u) \leq \Phi_i^E(v)$ for some $1 \leq i \leq |E|$

(E1) is a restatement of (KP1) and (E2) generalises (KP2). (E3) states that if all epistemic states in E agree that u is at least as plausible as v, then so should the resulting epistemic state. (E4) expects justification for regarding an interpretation u as at least as plausible as v: there has to be at least one epistemic state in E which regards u as at least as plausible as v. The following fundamental principle for the merging of epistemic states follows easily from (E3):

(Unit) If $\Phi_i^E(u) = \Phi_i^E(v)$ $\forall 1 \leq i \leq |E|$ then $\Delta(E)(u) = \Delta(E)(v)$

(Unit) requires interpretations that are treated identically by all epistemic states in an epistemic list to be treated identically in the epistemic state resulting from a merging operation.

Two epistemic lists E_1 and E_2 are *element-equivalent*, written as $E_1 \approx E_2$, iff for every element Φ_1 of E_1 there is a unique element Φ_2 (position-wise) of E_2 such that $\Phi_1 = \Phi_2$ and for every element Φ_2 of E_2 there is a unique element Φ_1 (position-wise) of E_1 such that $\Phi_2 = \Phi_1$. The following property is a generalisation of (KP3). It requires merging to be commutative.

(Comm) $E_1 \approx E_2$ implies $\Delta(E_1) = \Delta(E_2)$

We do not think that (Comm) should hold for all merging operations. Instead, (Comm) should be seen as a postulate picking out an interesting subclass of merging operations.

For a finite list of epistemic lists $\mathcal{E} = [E_1, \ldots, E_{|\mathcal{E}|}]$, let $\Delta(\mathcal{E})$ denote the epistemic list $[\Delta(E_1), \ldots, \Delta(E_{|\mathcal{E}|})]$. We consider the following properties:

(E5) If $\Delta(E_i)(u) \leq \Delta(E_i)(v)$ $\forall 1 \leq i \leq |\mathcal{E}|$ then
$\Delta(\bigsqcup_{i=1}^{|\mathcal{E}|} E_i)(u) \leq \Delta(\bigsqcup_{i=1}^{|\mathcal{E}|} E_i)(v)$
(E6) If $\Delta(\bigsqcup_{i=1}^{|\mathcal{E}|} E_i)(u) \leq \Delta(\bigsqcup_{i=1}^{|\mathcal{E}|} E_i)(v)$ then $\Delta(E_i)(u) \leq \Delta(E_i)(v)$ for some $1 \leq i \leq |\mathcal{E}|$

(E5) generalises (E3) and (E6) generalises (E4). In fact, (E5) also implies (KP5). We generalise (arb) and (maj) as follows:

(Arb) $\forall n$ $\Delta(E \sqcup [\Phi])(u) = \Delta(E \sqcup \Phi^n)(u)$
(Maj) $\exists n$ s.t. $\forall u, v \in U$, $\Phi(u) \leq \Phi(v)$ if $\Delta(E \sqcup \Phi^n)(u) \leq \Delta(E \sqcup \Phi^n)(v)$

We have not provided a generalised version of (KP4) since we do not regard it as a suitable postulate for merging. Our basic argument is that the models of a knowledge base associated with an epistemic state Φ_1 may sometimes be given such an implausible ranking by an epistemic state Φ_2 that it would seem reasonable to exclude all these models from the models of $\phi_{\Delta([\Phi_1]\sqcup[\Phi_2])}$. None of the merging operations we consider in section 4 satisfies (KP4). Similarly, we have not provided a generalised version of (KP6) since we regard it as too strong a condition to impose on all merging operations.[2] In section 4 we encounter a number of reasonable merging operations which do not satisy (KP6).

4 Constructing Merging Operations

Konieczny and Pino-Pérez [5] discuss several merging operations on knowledge bases using Dalal's measure of distance between interpretations [3]. For any two interpretations u and v, let $dist(u,v)$ denote the number of propositional atoms on which u and v differ. The distance $Dist(\phi, u)$ between a knowledge base ϕ and an interpretation u is defined as follows: $Dist(\phi, u) = \min\{dist(u,v) \mid v \in M(\phi)\}$. It is clear that this distance measure can be used to define an epistemic state Φ as follows: $\forall u \in U$, $\Phi(u) = Dist(\phi, u)$. It is easily seen that $\Phi(u) = 0$ iff $u \in M(\phi)$ and therefore $\phi_\Phi \equiv \phi$. Many of the merging operations on epistemic states that we propose below are appropriate generalisations of these merging operations on knowledge bases.

Throughout the remainder of this section the reader should observe that the construction of every merging operation consists of two steps. In the first step natural numbers are assigned to interpretations. Now it may well be the case that *none* of the interpretations have been assigned the value 0. To ensure compliance with (E1) the second step performs an appropriate uniform subtraction of values which we shall refer to as *normalisation*.

4.1 Arbitration

Inspired by an arbitration operation proposed by Liberatore and Schaerf [6] we propose the following two merging operations on epistemic states.

Definition 2. *1. Let* $\Phi_{ls}^E(u) = 2\min^E(u)$ *if* $\Phi_i^E(u) = \Phi_j^E(u)$ *for* $1 \leq i,j \leq |E|$, *and* $\Phi_{ls}^E(u) = 2\min^E(u) + 1$ *otherwise.* $\Delta_{ls}(E)(u) = \Phi_{ls}^E(u) - \min(\Phi_{ls}^E)$.
2. Let $\Phi_{Rls}^E(u) = \Omega_{\sqsubseteq_{lex}}^{seq_\leq(E)}(s_\leq^E(u))$. *Then* $\Delta_{Rls}(E)(u) = \Phi_{Rls}^E(u) - \min(\Phi_{Rls}^E)$.

Figure 2 contains pictorial representations of both these merging operations. It can easily be shown that Δ_{Rls} is a refined version of Δ_{ls}. Both satisfy (E1)-(E6) and (Comm), neither satisfies (Maj), and only Δ_{Rls} satisfies (KP6). Moreover, Δ_{ls} satisfies (Arb) but Δ_{Rls} does not. So, while both are valid merging operations, Δ_{Rls} should not be seen as an arbitation operation.

Next we consider two merging operations that are generalisations of the $\delta_{\max}$ and δ_{Gmax} operations of Konieczny and Pino-Pérez. The former was inspired by an example of Revesz's model-fitting operations [12].

---
[2] (E6) can be regarded as a generalised version of a weaker form of (KP6), but (KP6) does not follow from (E6).

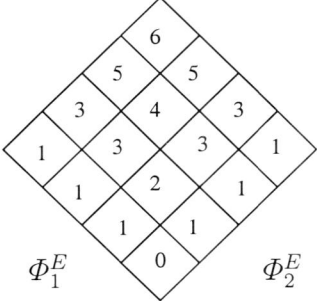 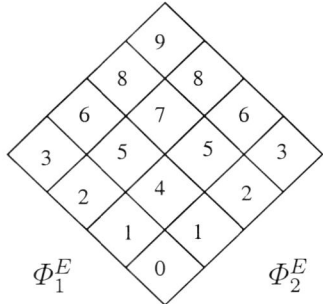

Fig. 2. The figure on the left represents the merging operation Δ_{ls} and the one on the right the merging operation Δ_{Rls}. The number in a cell represents the numbers that the appropriate merging operation assigns to the interpretations contained in that cell before normalisation.

Definition 3. 1. Let $\Phi_{\max}^E(u) = \max^E(u)$. Then let $\Delta_{\max}(E)(u) = \Phi_{\max}^E(u) - \min(\Phi_{\max}^E)$.
2. Let $\Phi_{Gmax}^E(u) = \Omega_{\sqsubseteq_{lex}}^{seq_\geq(E)}(s_\geq^E(u))$. Then we let $\Delta_{Gmax}(E)(u) = \Phi_{Gmax}^E(u) - \min(\Phi_{Gmax}^E)$.

Figure 3 contains pictorial representations of $\Delta_{\max}$ and Δ_{Gmax}. Both satisfy (E1)-(E6), neither satisfies (Maj), and only Δ_{Gmax} satisfies (KP6). Moreover, $\Delta_{\max}$ satisfies (Arb), but Δ_{Gmax} does not. So, analogous to the case above, both are valid merging operations but Δ_{Gmax} should not be seen as an arbitation operation. The fact that we do not regard Δ_{Gmax} as an arbitration operation is in conflict with the view of Konieczny and Pino-Pérez who regard δ_{Gmax} as an arbitration operation on knowledge bases even though it does not satisfy (arb). Conversely, Konieczny and Pino-Pérez do not regard $\delta_{\max}$ as a merging

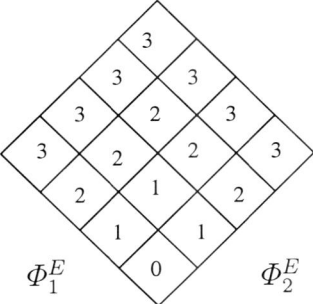 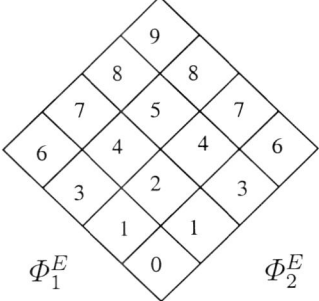

Fig. 3. The figure on the left represents the merging operation $\Delta_{\max}$ and the one on the right the merging operation Δ_{Gmax}. The number in a cell represents the numbers that the appropriate merging operation assigns to the interpretations contained in that cell before normalisation.

operation on knowledge bases since it fails to satisfy (KP6). But we regard it as a valid arbitration operation since it satisfies (E1)-(E6), (Comm) and (Arb).

4.2 Consensus

In this section we consider *consensus* operation, where agreement on the ranking of interprerations, instead of the ranking itself, is of overriding importance.

Definition 4. *For $s \in seq(E)$, let $d^E(s) = \sum_{i=1}^{|E|} \sum_{j=i+1}^{|E|} |s_i - s_j|$, where s_i denotes the ith element of s.*

1. *Now, define the total preorder $\sqsubseteq$ on $seq(E)$ as follows: $s \sqsubseteq t$ iff $d^E(s) \leq d^E(t)$. Let $\Phi^E_{cons}(u) = \Omega^{seq(E)}_{\sqsubseteq}(s^E(u))$. Then $\Delta_{cons}(E)(u) = \Phi^E_{cons}(u) - \min(\Phi^E_{cons})$.*
2. *Define the total preorder $\sqsubseteq$ on $seq_\leq(E)$ as follows: $s \sqsubseteq t$ iff $d^E(s) < d^E(t)$ or $(d^E(s) = d^E(t)$ and $s \sqsubseteq_{lex} t)$. Now, let $\Phi^E_{Rcons}(u) = \Omega^{seq_\leq(E)}_{\sqsubseteq}(s^E_\leq(u))$. Then $\Delta_{Rcons}(E)(u) = \Phi^E_{Rcons}(u) - \min(\Phi^E_{Rcons})$.*

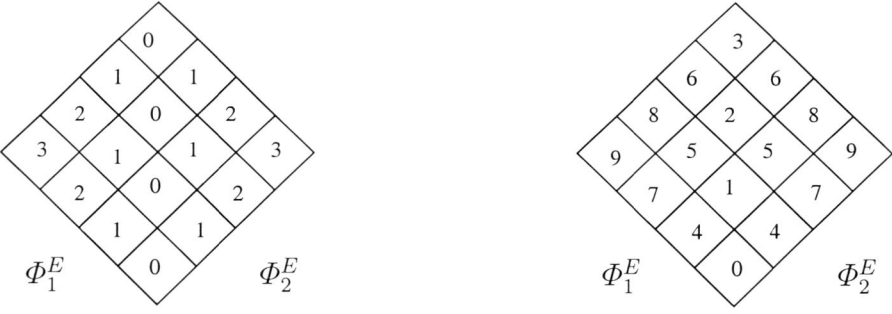

Fig. 4. The figure on the left represents the merging operation Δ_{cons}. The figure on the right represents the merging operation Δ_{Rcons}. As usual, the number in a cell represents the numbers that the appropriate merging operation assigns to the interpretations contained in that cell before normalisation.

Figure 4 contains pictorial representations of Δ_{cons} and Δ_{Rcons}. Both fail to satisfy (E3) and (E4). Both satisfy (Unit), though. We do not regard these two operations as suitable candidates for merging. The problem with these consensus operations seems to be that they place too strong an emphasis on agreement and do not take the ranking of interpretations seriously enough.

4.3 Majority

We consider the following two majority operations.

Definition 5. For $s \in seq(E)$, let $sum^E(s) = \sum_{i=1}^{|E|} s_i$, where s_i is the ith element of s.

1. Let $\Phi_\Sigma^E(u) = sum^E(s^E(u))$. Then $\Delta_\Sigma(E)(u) = \Phi_\Sigma^E(u) - \min(\Phi_\Sigma^E)$.
2. Define the total preorder $\sqsubseteq$ on $seq(E)$ as follows: $s \sqsubseteq t$ iff $sum^E(s) < sum^E(t)$ or ($sum^E(s) = sum^E(t)$ and $d^E(s) \leq d^E(t)$). Now, let $\Phi_{R\Sigma}^E(u) = \Omega_\sqsubseteq^{seq(E)}(s^E(u))$. Then $\Delta_{R\Sigma}(E)(u) = \Phi_{R\Sigma}^E(u) - \min(\Phi_{R\Sigma}^E)$.

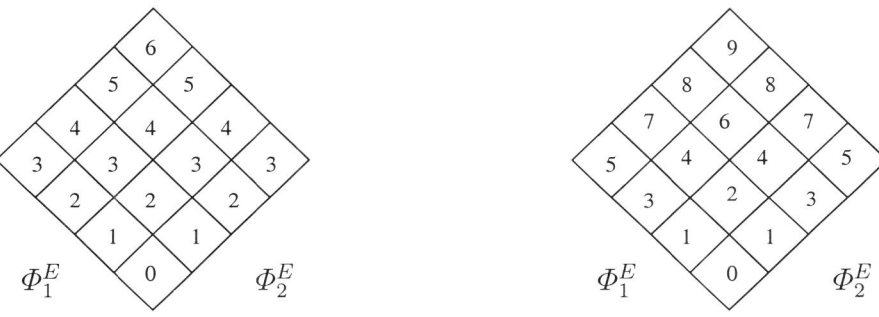

Fig. 5. The figure on the left represents the merging operation Δ_Σ. The figure on the right represents the merging operation $\Delta_{R\Sigma}$. As usual, the number in a cell represents the numbers that the appropriate merging operation assigns to the interpretations contained in that cell before normalisation.

Figure 5 contains pictorial representations of these two majority operations. Δ_Σ is an appropriate generalisation of an example by Lin and Mendelzon [8]. The latter was independently proposed by Revesz [13] as an example of weighted model fitting. The idea is simply to obtain the new plausibility ranking of an interpretation by summing the plausibility rankings given by the different epistemic states. $\Delta_{R\Sigma}$ is Δ_Σ refined by using consensus. Both Δ_Σ and $\Delta_{R\Sigma}$ satisfy (E1)-(E4), (Comm) and (Maj), and neither satisfies (Arb). But while Δ_Σ satisfies (E5)-(E6) and (KP5)-(KP6) as well, $\Delta_{R\Sigma}$ does not.

4.4 Non-commutative Merging

Thus far we have restricted ourselves to the construction of *commutative* merging operations – i.e., satisfying (Comm) – but a complete description of merging ought to take into account constructions such as that of Nayak [11], in which the merging of two epistemic states is obtained by a lexicographic refinement of one by the other. We present here a generalised version of Nayak's proposal. For this case the epistemic states in an epistemic list are assumed to be ranked according to reliability. That is, given an epistemic list $E = [\Phi_1^E, \ldots, \Phi_{|E|}^E]$, Φ_i^E is at least as reliable as Φ_j^E iff $i \leq j$.

Definition 6. Let $\Phi^E_{lex}(u) = \Omega^{seq(E)}_{\sqsubseteq_{lex}}(s^E(u))$. Then $\Delta_{lex}(E)(u) = \Phi^E_{lex}(u) - \min(\Phi^E_{lex})$.

Δ_{lex} does not satisfy (Comm), but it satisfies (E1)-(E6), as well as (KP5)-(KP6). By exploiting the non-commutativity of Δ_{lex}, both (Arb) and (Maj) can be phrased in a way to ensure that Δ_{lex} fails to satisfy them.

5 Merging and Infobases

Our description of merging uses a representation of epistemic states as functions assigning a plausibility ranking to the interpretations of L, but where do these plausibility rankings come from? One way in which to generate them is by using the *infobases* of Meyer [9]. An infobase is a finite list of wffs. Intuitively it is a structured representation of the beliefs of an agent with a foundational flavour. It is assumed that every wff in an infobase is obtained independently. Meyer uses an infobase to define a total preorder on U, which is then used to perform belief change. However, we can also use an infobase to define an epistemic state. The idea is to consider the number of times that an interpretation occurs as a model of one of the wffs in an infobase: the more it occurs, the higher its plausibility ranking.

Definition 7. *For $u \in U$, define the IB-number u_{IB} of u as the number of elements α in an infobase IB such that $\not\vdash \alpha$ and $u \in M(\alpha)$, and let $\max(IB) = \max\{u_{IB} \mid u \in U\}$. Now we define the epistemic state associated with IB as follows: for $u \in U, \Phi^{IB}(u) = \max(IB) - u_{IB}$.*

Observe that the knowledge base associated with an epistemic state Φ^{IB} is always consistent, regardless of whether the wffs in IB are jointly consistent. We show that infobases seem to provide a natural setting in which to apply merging.

Firstly, define an *infobase list* $EB = [IB_1, \ldots, IB_{|EB|}]$ as a finite non-empty list of infobases and let E^{EB} denote the epistemic list $[\Phi^{IB_1}, \ldots, \Phi^{IB_{|E|}}]$ of epistemic states associated with the infobases occurring in EB. Then it can be verified that $\Delta_\Sigma(E^{EB}) = \Phi^{IB}$ where $IB = \bigsqcup_{i=1}^{|EB|} IB_i$.

Secondly, Konieczny and Pino-Pérez [5] give a convincing example to show that we may sometimes want to include, as models of $\delta(e)$, interpretations other than the models of the knowledge bases in e. Below is a scaled down version of their example.

Example 1. We want to speculate on the stock exchange and we ask two equally reliable financial experts about two shares. Let the atom p denote the fact that share 1 will rise and q the fact that share 2 will rise. The first expert says that both shares will rise: $\phi_1 = p \wedge q$, while the second one believes that both shares will fall: $\phi_2 = \neg p \wedge \neg q$. Intuitively it seems reasonable to conclude that both experts are right (and wrong) about exactly one share, although we don't know which share in either case. That is, we require the result of the merging of these two knowledge bases to be such that $M(\delta([\phi_1] \sqcup [\phi_2])) = \{10, 01\}$.[3] Observe that $M(\delta([\phi_1] \sqcup [\phi_2])) \nsubseteq M(\phi_1) \cup M(\phi_2)$.

An analysis of this example shows that both experts are assumed to make an implicit assumption of independence of the performance of the shares. Thus the beliefs of the first expert is best expressed as the infobase $IB_1 = [p, q]$ and the beliefs of the second expert as the infobase $IB_2 = [\neg p, \neg q]$. The epistemic states obtained from these two infobases are: $\Phi^{IB_1}(11) = 0, \Phi^{IB_1}(10) = \Phi^{IB_1}(01) = 1, \Phi^{IB_1}(00) = 2$, and $\Phi^{IB_2}(00) = 0, \Phi^{IB_2}(10) = \Phi^{IB_2}(01) = 1, \Phi^{IB_2}(11) = 2$. It can be verified that $\Delta_{\max}(E^{EB}) = \Delta_{Gmax}(E^{EB}) = \Delta_{R\Sigma}(E^{EB}) = \Phi$, where $EB = [IB_1, IB_2]$, $\Phi(10) = \Phi(01) = 0$ and $\Phi(11) = \Phi(00) = 1$. So $\Delta_{R\Sigma}$, $\Delta_{\max}$ and Δ_{Gmax} yield the results corresponding to our intuition for this example.

6 Conclusion

The merging operations we have constructed provide evidence that (E1)-(E4) may be regarded as basic postulates for merging operations on epistemic states. Two of the operations constructed, the two consensus operations, do not satisfy (E3) and (E4), but this seems to be because consensus strays too far from the basic assumption of a plausibility ranking of interpretations. Furthermore, we regard (Arb) as an appropriate postulate for the subclass of arbitration operations, (Maj) for the subclass of majority operations, and (Comm) for the subclass of commutative merging operations. The status of (E5) and (E6) is less clear. While all but one of the valid merging operations we have considered satisfy both, the fact that $\Delta_{R\Sigma}$ does not, suggests that they are not as universally applicable as (E1)-(E4). Perhaps they should be seen as picking out particular subclasses of merging operations in the way that (Arb), (Maj) and (Comm) do.

References

1. C. Baral, S. Kraus, and J. Minker. Combining multiple knowledge bases. *IEEE Transactions on Knowledge and Data Engineering*, 3(2):208–220, 1991.
2. C. Baral, S. Kraus, J. Minker, and V.S. Subrahmanian. Combining multiple knowledge bases consisting of first-order theories. *Computational Intelligence*, 8(1):45–71, 1992.
3. Mukesh Dalal. Investigations into a theory of knowledge base revision. In *Proceedings of the 7th National Conference of the American Association for Artificial Intelligence, Saint Paul, Minnesota*, pages 475–479, 1988.
4. H. Katsuno and A.O. Mendelzon. Propositional knowledge base revision and minimal change. *Artificial Intelligence*, 52:263–294, 1991.
5. Sébastien Konieczny and Ramón Pino-Pérez. On the logic of merging. In A. G. Cohn, L. Schubert, and S. C. Shapiro, editors, *Principles of Knowledge Representation and Reasoning: Proceedings of the Sixth International Conference (KR '98)*, pages 488–498, San Francisco, California, 1998. Morgan Kaufmann.

---

[3] We represent interpretations as sequences consisting of 0s (representing falsity) and 1s (representing truth), where the first digit in a sequence represents the truth value of p and the second one the truth value of q.

6. Paolo Liberatore and Marco Schaerf. Arbitration (or How to Merge Knowledge Bases). *IEEE Transactions on Knowledge and Engineering*, 10(1):76–90, January/February 1998.
7. J. Lin. Integration of weighted knowledge bases. *Artificial Intelligence*, 83(2):363–378, 1996.
8. J. Lin and A. O. Mendelzon. Knowledge base merging by majority. In R. Pareschi and B. Fronhoefer, editors, *Dynamic Worlds: From the Frame Problem to Knowledge Management*. Kluwer Academic Publishers, Dordrecht, 1999.
9. Thomas Meyer. Basic Infobase Change. In Norman Foo, editor, *Advanced Topics in Artificial Intelligence*, volume 1747 of *Lecture Notes In Artificial Intelligence*, pages 156–167, Berlin, 1999. Springer-Verlag.
10. Thomas A. Meyer, Willem A. Labuschagne, and Johannes Heidema. Infobase Change: A First Approximation. *Journal of Logic, Language and Information (to appear)*, 2000.
11. Abhaya C. Nayak. Iterated belief change based on epistemic entrenchment. *Erkenntnis*, 41:353–390, 1994.
12. P. Z. Revesz. On the semantics of arbitration. *International Journal of Algebra and Computation*, 7(2):133–160, 1987.
13. P. Z. Revesz. On the Semantics of Theory Change: Arbitration between Old and New Information. In *Proceedings PODS '93, 12th ACM SIGACT SIGMOD SIGART Symposium on the Principles of Database Systems*, pages 71–82, 1993.
14. Wolfgang Spohn. Ordinal conditional functions: A dynamic theory of epistemic states. In William L. Harper and Brian Skyrms, editors, *Causation in Decision: Belief, Change and Statistics: Proceedings of the Irvine Conference on Probability and Causation: Volume II*, volume 42 of *The University of Western Ontario Series in Philosophy of Science*, pages 105–134, Dordrecht, 1988. Kluwer Academic Publishers.
15. V.S. Subrahmanian. Amalgamating knowledge bases. *ACM Transactions on Database Systems*, 19(2):291–331, 1994.

Perceiving Environments for Intelligent Agents

Yuefeng Li and Chengqi Zhang

School of Computing and Mathematics
Deakin University, Geelong VIC 3217, Australia
{yuefeng, chengqi}@deakin.edu.au

Abstract. One of the important characteristics for intelligent agents is to be able to assess their environments in order to decide on the correct action to take. It is always difficult to do so because many factors including uncertain information, knowledge and bounded time will affect intelligent agent to perceive their environments. In this paper, we propose a procedure descriptive framework to perceive the environments for intelligent agents. The process of belief updating in this framework remains to be constantly changing, until the point of decision making is reached. During the dynamic change of beliefs, the intelligent agents will incorporate their knowledge about other agents, and the possible uncertain information they received from their local sensors and other agents.

1 Introduction

Many mental-level models have been proposed to represent and reason about agents' environments (including other agents). The initial idea of mental-level models came from McCarthy [16] and Newell [17]. Rao and Georgeff [19] used three mental components: belief, intentions and desires in their paper. Rosenschein and Kaelbing [21] developed an interpreter that can implement behavior that is specified using notions such as knowledge and goals. Shoham [23] presented an agent oriented programming language according to the notions of belief and commitment.

What the above structures lack is the notion of decision criterion, which embodies the agent's approach to action choice under uncertainty [2]. Some attentions have been given for this research topic. Thomason [25] incorporated some type of common-sense deliberation about conflicting goals. Rao and Georgeff [18] incorporated expected payoff calculations for decision making, and recently Brafman and Tennenholtz incorporated qualitative decision criteria [1] [2].

Generally, an intelligent agent (IA) describes its beliefs in terms of the knowledge, plausibility and time about its environment [7] [5]. In applications, an IA's beliefs are not known a priori and has to be estimated on-line based on its knowledge and some information (such as the message it receives from other potential agents, and the observation it gets from its local sensors). The above researchers emphasize more what the beliefs are than how the beliefs are formed.

Our motivation in this paper is to develop a procedure descriptive framework rather than a logical framework, in which we would like to gain a sound understanding of how an IA can form its beliefs in multi-agent environments. This framework will provide an approach for an IA to solve conflicts between messages through a global overlooking. To execute the correct actions, this framework could also capture many notions of beliefs before and after changes in the current environment. The process of belief updating in this framework remains to be constantly changing, until the point of decision making is reached. During the dynamic change of its belief, an IA will incorporate its knowledge about other agents (such as trustworthy degrees and similarities of problem solving approaches) and the possible uncertain information.

The organization of this paper is as follows. Section 2 shows a picture of how an IA evaluates its environment. Section 3 specifies how an IA forms its belief about the current state. Section 4 addresses how the beliefs are interpreted, and how the IA uses these beliefs when it makes decisions. In Section 5 we review related works and compare our framework with other research work. Section 6 closes this paper and gives some outlook of our contributions.

2 How IAs Perceive Their Environments

The possible information for an IA includes events it observes and messages it receives [8]. An IA could observe events about the current world by using its local sensors. In this paper, we use $PW_{\mathcal{A}}(l)$ to abstract the event that an IA observes, which depends on the local state l appearing in its local sensors. We call $PW_{\mathcal{A}}(l)$ the observation made by an IA itself, where the observation is driven by the states of the possible worlds. In this paper, we assume that the current state does not change during one loop of the process of perceiving environments, and thus we do not attach a time factor to $PW_{\mathcal{A}}(l)$. The observation, however, is generally vague, and the IA hopes to rely on other agents' messages about the current state.

The messages come from users and other potential agents. The messages which come from the user are called requests in this paper. After a supervisor IA (the agent of main discussion) sends its user's request to other potential agents, it expects their replies. In most cases, however, the supervisor IA cannot predict when the information will arrive, or indeed insure that every potential agent will send back information in reply to its requests. For this situation, the supervisor IA could use a set Θ_t to describe the agents who have sent back the information at a time point t. We call the set Θ_t the group of cooperating agents at time t. The group of cooperating agents is also variable, however, cease to change at the point of decision making.

The supervisor IA will consider two kinds of factors when it uses its observation and the messages provided by the group of cooperating agents: the uncertainties contained in the information, and the conflicts between the observation and messages; where, a message (or an agent) is said to be a conflict message (or a conflict agent) if the intersection between the massage and the observation is empty.

The observation and messages usually are subsets of the set of possible worlds, i.e., the agents believe that the true world state is in the subset, but they do not know which world state it is. For the research in the uncertainty world, people always assume that the true world state absolutely belongs to the observation, so they usually cast away all of the conflict agents' contributions.

In the agent world, however, the observation is just a local observation. Figure 1(a) shows a possible example for the case of the agent world. In this example, the supervisor agent receives 8 messages from 8 cooperating agents in order to decide which state in its observation is mostly like the true state. If the supervisor agent discards all of the conflict messages (see Figure 1(b)), the supervisor agent will believe that the true state is likely at the left side of the observation. On the other hand, because there are many messages occur at the right side of the observation, if the supervisor agent could overlook the global picture, it would have a belief that the true state would be at the right side of the observation.

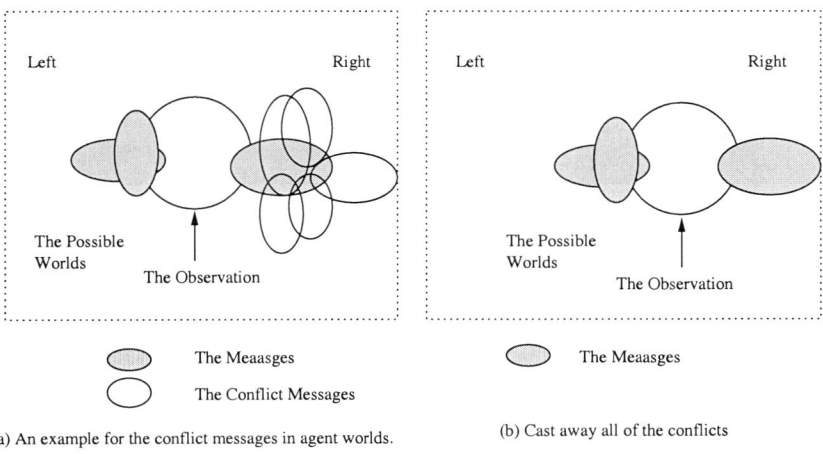

(a) An example for the conflict messages in agent worlds.

(b) Cast away all of the conflicts

Fig. 1. An Example for Conflicts

In this paper, the supervisor agent will not cast away all of the conflicts, and we expect it to have the ability of overlooking the global picture. It is difficult to do so, because the conflict messages cannot be described by local knowledge. Instead of describing the conflict messages, in this paper we re-evaluate agents by transferring trustworthy degrees from conflict agents to the related non-conflict agents. We use an interval structure (one kind of Pawlak rough set on two distinct but related universes [27]) to describe the uncertainties contained in the information. To solve the conflicts, we use trustworthy degrees to describe how the supervisor IA trusts other agents' messages, and an equivalence relation to characterize the dependencies among other agents. The equivalence relation reveals the fact that agents with similarities of problem solving approaches are related, and must be put into the same equivalence class.

More formally, we use a finite set $\mathcal{W}$ to illustrate the possible worlds (states), and a finite set Θ to represent other potential agents. A prior probability distribution $Pr_\mathcal{A}$ on Θ is used to characterize trustworthy degrees of the other agents, and an equivalence relation R on Θ to describe the knowledge about the similarities of problem solving approaches. The equivalence relation R would determine a partition of Θ, i.e., Θ would be divided into some equivalence classes (the agents in the same equivalence class have similar problem solving approaches). The equivalence class of $\theta \in \Theta$ could be defined as follows:

$$C_\theta = \{\theta' \mid \theta' \in \Theta, \theta' R \theta\}$$

Based on the above assumptions, the supervisor IA's belief about the possible information and the knowledge of the group of cooperating agents at time t will be represented by a pair (see Section 3 for details)

$$BIK_t = <Pr_\mathcal{A}^t, B_\mathcal{A}^t>,$$

in which

- $Pr_\mathcal{A}^t$ is a posterior probability on Θ_t, which could be induced by transfer prior probability ($Pr_\mathcal{A}$) from some cooperating conflict agents to its related agents[1],
- Multi-set valued mapping $B_\mathcal{A}^t$ from $2^\mathcal{W}$ to 2^{Θ_t} is an interval structure, which synthesizes all of the possible information at time t, and
- $\Theta_t \subseteq \Theta$ is the group of cooperating agents at time t.

The belief is changeable with the passage of time, up until the point of decision making. At this time, the supervisor IA would give a number function m_t from $2^\mathcal{W}$ to $[0,1]$, which satisfies

$$m_t(S) = Pr_\mathcal{A}^t(B_\mathcal{A}^t(S))$$

by combining $Pr_\mathcal{A}^t$ and $B_\mathcal{A}^t$. This number function is a Dempster-Shafer mass function [22] (see Section 4).

By combining this mass function and the number utility function, the supervisor IA could estimate the expected utilities and select the suitable action whose expected utility is maximum (the appropriate decision approaches can be found in [15]).

3 Modelling Agent Beliefs

In this section, we firstly present an approach for information synthesizing, then we introduce a method to evaluate the posterior probabilities.

---

[1] An agent is said to be a related agent of a conflict agent if they both belong to a same equivalence class, and their messages are joined

3.1 Information Synthesizing

An agent in mental level states is described as a state machine, a triplet $\mathcal{A} = <\mathcal{L}_\mathcal{A}, \mathcal{A}_\mathcal{A}, \mathcal{P}_\mathcal{A}>$, which has a set of possible (local) states, $\mathcal{L}_\mathcal{A}$, a set of possible actions, $\mathcal{A}_\mathcal{A}$, and a map $\mathcal{P}_\mathcal{A} : \mathcal{L}_\mathcal{A} \to \mathcal{A}_\mathcal{A}$ [3] [2]. The agent's observation at $l \in \mathcal{L}_\mathcal{A}$, $PW_\mathcal{A}(l)$, is defined as

$$\{w \in \mathcal{W} \mid \text{the agent's local state in } w \text{ is } l\},$$

when agent's local state is l. $PW_\mathcal{A}(l)$ is a set of possible worlds, which is consistent with the agent's information of local states. This definition is used to describe knowledge to an agent at a local state [8] [20].

The observation tells some facts at a possible world w_0 if its local state l in w_0 is such that these facts hold in all the worlds in $PW_\mathcal{A}(l)$. The knowledge implied here is that the agent believes the current world state $w_0 \in PW_\mathcal{A}(l)$, however, it cannot be sure which world in $PW_\mathcal{A}(l)$ is the current world state w_0. So agent $\mathcal{A}$ hopes other agents' messages in order to do the correct actions.

All of the messages can be represented by a random set [12]. This representation approach requires a multi-set valued mapping from the set of the other potential agents to the power set of the possible worlds, and a prior probability distribution on the set of the other potential agents.

We call $(Pr_\mathcal{A}, \Gamma_\mathcal{A})$ a random set, if $\Gamma_\mathcal{A}$ is a multi-set valued mapping:

$$\Gamma_\mathcal{A} : \Theta \to 2^\mathcal{W}$$

and $Pr_\mathcal{A}$ is a probability distribution over Θ.

In a random set, the multi-set valued mapping represents the messages provided to agent $\mathcal{A}$ at time t by the other agents, and the probability is a prior probability which characterizes the trustworthy degrees of agent $\mathcal{A}$ trusting other agents. The group of cooperating agents is the set Θ_t, which satisfies

$$\Theta_t = \{\theta \mid \theta \in \Theta, \; \Gamma_\mathcal{A}(\theta) \neq \emptyset\}.$$

A pair $BIK_t = <Pr_\mathcal{A}^t, B_\mathcal{A}^t>$ is called a belief of agent $\mathcal{A}$ at time t, if $Pr_\mathcal{A}^t$ is a posterior probability distribution over Θ_t (in the next subsection we will see how to induce it); and $B_\mathcal{A}^t$ is a function that maps subsets of $\mathcal{W}$ onto subsets of Θ_t, which satisfies

$$B_\mathcal{A}^l : 2^\mathcal{W} \to 2^{\Theta_t}, \text{ such that}$$

$$B_\mathcal{A}^t(S) = \begin{cases} \{\theta \in \Theta_t \mid \Gamma_\mathcal{A}(\theta) \cap PW_\mathcal{A}(l) = S\} & \text{if } S \neq \emptyset \\ \emptyset & otherwise \end{cases} \quad (1)$$

We can prove that $B_\mathcal{A}^l$ is an interval structure [14]. In the above definition, the set $\{\theta \in \Theta_t \mid \Gamma_\mathcal{A}(\theta) \cap PW_\mathcal{A}(l) = S\}$ contains all cooperating agents at time t, whose messages do not completely conflict with agent $\mathcal{A}$'s observation, and the intersections of the messages and the observation all equal $S \subseteq \mathcal{W}$. We call $B_\mathcal{A}^t$ the belief about uncertain information at time t. Each subset S such that $B_\mathcal{A}^t(S) \neq \emptyset$ is called the focal element of $B_\mathcal{A}^t$, and the set of all focal elements of

Table 1. Algorithm for belief updating.

Input   The group of cooperating agents Θ_t at time t, belief $B_\mathcal{A}^t$ at time t, and a message S_1 provided by agent θ_1 at time $t+1$.
Output   The group of cooperating agents Θ_{t+1} at time $t+1$, and belief $B_\mathcal{A}^{t+1}$ at time $t+1$.
Step 1. $\Theta_{t+1} = \Theta_t \cup \{\theta_1\}$;
Step 2. $S_1' = PW_\mathcal{A}(l) \cap S_1$; $newfocal = true$;
Step 3.   for $S \in G_B(t)$ if $(S == S_1')$ { $newfocal = false$; $exit$; }
Step 4.   if $newfocal$ {   for $\forall S \in G_B^t$ $B_\mathcal{A}^{t+1}(S) = B_\mathcal{A}^t(S)$; $B_\mathcal{A}^{t+1}(S_1') = \{\theta_1\}$; }   else   for $\forall S \in G_B^t$ if $(S == S_1')$ $B_\mathcal{A}^{t+1}(S) = B_\mathcal{A}^t(S) \cup \{\theta_1\}$;   else $B_\mathcal{A}^{t+1}(S) = B_\mathcal{A}^t(S)$;
Step 5.   return $(\Theta_{t+1}, B_\mathcal{A}^{t+1})$;

$B_\mathcal{A}^t$ is called the granule collection at time t, indicated as G_B^t. We call $Pr_\mathcal{A}^t$ the knowledge about cooperating agents at time t.

The algorithm in Table 1 is used to update the belief about uncertain information at time t when the supervisor IA receives a new message from a potential agent at time $t+1$. In this algorithm, the group of cooperating agents is increased at time $t+1$ (see Step 1). Because of the new message S_1, the supervisor IA may get a new focal element. Step 2 and Step 3 are used to decide whether a new focal element will occur. If the IA gets a new focal element the boolean variable $newfocal$ is $true$, otherwise $newfocal$ is $false$. In Step 4 the belief about uncertain information at time $t+1$ is derived. If there is a new focal element, the belief at time $t+1$ can be derived by duplicating the belief at time t to the belief at time $t+1$ and adding a new focal element; otherwise the belief at time $t+1$ could be obtained by modifying one focal element's belief value.

3.2 The Posterior Probabilities

As mentioned in Section 2, a prior probability distribution $Pr_\mathcal{A}$ on Θ could be used to characterize the supervisor IA's trustworthy degrees towards other agents. This can be learned in an on-line setting based on long term observations (notice: the agents in a same equivalence class may have the different trustworthiness, because some agents may refuse to cooperate). However, we will not discuss the on-line setting here.

Considering there may be some dependencies between agents, we can transfer the prior probability from some conflict agents to other agents to obtain the posterior probability. An equivalence relation R on Θ is used to describe the dependencies in this paper. Let agent θ_i and agent θ_j both belong to equivalence class C_{θ_j}, and they both provide messages to the supervisor IA at time t. We assume there is a conflict between θ_j's message and the observation, and the intersection between θ_j's message and θ_i's message is not empty, i.e., θ_i is a related agent with θ_j. At this situation, we can imagine that θ_j will partially support θ_i's result.

The evaluation process for the posterior probability is to:

(1) Identify the agents occurring in the group of cooperating agents Θ_t at time t.

(2) Determine a conflict agent (e.g., θ_j).

(3) Find the equivalence class C_{θ_j} in Θ_t for the conflict agent.

(4) Determine the set of related agents with θ_j, denoting as $C^j \subseteq C_{\theta_j}$.

(5) Evaluate the posterior probability $Pr_{\mathcal{A}}^t$ by transferring θ_j's probability to each agent θ' of C^j:

$$Pr_{\mathcal{A}}^t(\theta') = \frac{1}{K} \sum_{\theta \in C^j \cup \{\theta_j\}} Pr_{\mathcal{A}}(\theta) Pr_{\mathcal{A}}(\theta') \qquad (2)$$

where $K = \sum_{\theta \in C^j} Pr_{\mathcal{A}}(\theta)$.

A graphical interpretation of this process is depicted in Figure 2. In Figure 2(a) each agent is represented by a circle with its prior probability. The agents that are shaded belong to the group of cooperating agents Θ_t, where θ_6 is a conflict agent. The equivalence classes are in three curved surfaces. Figure 2(b) shows the process of transferring the probabilities from the conflict agents to the related agents.

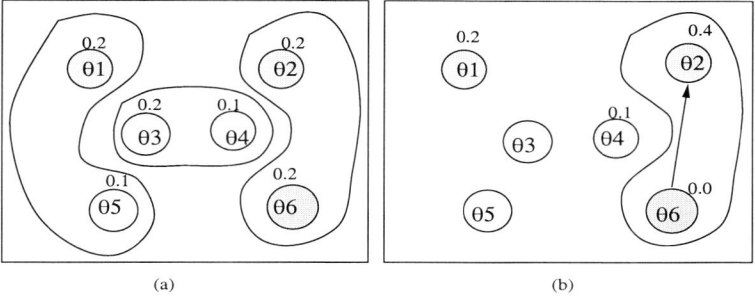

Fig. 2. The process of transferring

4 The Interpretations of Beliefs

In this section we first explain the probabilities over Θ and Θ_t, then interpret the belief about uncertain information at time t.

We assume that there is a prior probability distribution $Pr_{\mathcal{A}}$ over Θ. Given a sentence y, by using the technique called *Logical Imaging* [24], we can derive a new probability distribution $Pr'_{\mathcal{A}}$ over Θ_t from the prior probability distribution $Pr_{\mathcal{A}}$:

$$Pr'_{\mathcal{A}}(\theta') = \sum_{\theta \in \Theta} Pr_{\mathcal{A}}(\theta) \sigma(\theta', \theta, y)$$

where

$$\sigma(\theta', \theta, y) = \begin{cases} 1 \text{ if } \theta \text{ is most similar to } \theta' \text{ where } y \text{ is true} \\ 0 \text{ } otherwise \end{cases}$$

This *Logical Imaging* [13] implies a restrictive assumption that is related to the "uniqueness" problem. That is, an agent θ is only most similar to one agent. In 1988, a generalization of the logical imagine process was proposed [6]. The generalization can overcome the "uniqueness" problem. By using the generalization, we can derive a new probability distribution $Pr''_{\mathcal{A}}$ over Θ_t from the prior probability distribution $Pr_{\mathcal{A}}$:

$$Pr''_{\mathcal{A}}(\theta') = \sum_{\theta \in \Theta} Pr_{\mathcal{A}}(\theta) Pr^{\theta}_{\mathcal{A}}(\theta') \sigma(\theta', \theta, y)$$

where

$$\sigma(\theta', \theta, y) = \begin{cases} 1 \text{ if } \theta' \in C_\theta \\ 0 \text{ } otherwise \end{cases}$$

$Pr^{\theta}_{\mathcal{A}}(\theta')$ is a probability function to represent the degree that agent θ supports agent θ', and C_θ is all the agents to which θ are most similar where y is true.

Let y be the imagination that we used in section 3.2, $Pr^{\theta}_{\mathcal{A}}(\theta') = \frac{1}{K} Pr_{\mathcal{A}}(\theta')$, and C_θ be the sets of related agents for θ. One can easily observe that the posterior probability defined by equation (2) is one kind of the generalization of *Logical Imaging*.

As mentioned before the IA's belief is constantly updating with the passage of time, and ceases to update at the point of decision making. At this time t, the supervisor IA would derive a number function $m_t : 2^{\mathcal{W}} \to [0, 1]$ based on its belief $< Pr^t_{\mathcal{A}}, B^t_{\mathcal{A}} >$. It is not difficult to prove that function $m_t : 2^{\mathcal{W}} \to [0, 1]$ is a Dempster-Shafer mass function, if it satisfies

$$m_t(S) = \begin{cases} Pr^t_{\mathcal{A}}(B^t_{\mathcal{A}}(S)) \text{ if } S \in G^t_B \\ 0 \quad\quad\quad\quad\quad otherwise \end{cases}$$

Given this, we can only understand that the IA can synthesize all of the information into a number function based on its belief at time t. However, it is still not clear what synthesis approach is used here. The following analysis will answer this question.

The messages provided by the group of cooperating agents can be captured by a random set $(Pr_\mathcal{A}, \Gamma_\mathcal{A})$ as mentioned in Section 3.1. This random set can derive a Dempster-Shafer mass function [12] at time t, which satisfies

$$m : 2^\mathcal{W} \to [0,1],\ m(S) = \begin{cases} Pr^t_\mathcal{A}(\{\theta \in \Theta_t \mid \Gamma_\mathcal{A}(\theta) = S\}) & \text{if } S \neq \emptyset \\ 0 & otherwise \end{cases}$$

The observation that the IA makes is $PW_\mathcal{A}(l)$, a subset of $\mathcal{W}$. For the mass function m and the observation $PW_\mathcal{A}(l)$, the Dempster rule of conditioning can be used to synthesize the two kinds of information. The following is the synthesis formula:

$$m_\mathcal{A} : 2^\mathcal{W} \to [0,1],\ m_\mathcal{A}(S) = \begin{cases} \dfrac{\sum_{T \cap PW_\mathcal{A}(l)=S} m(T)}{1 - \sum_{T \cap PW_\mathcal{A}(l)=\emptyset} m(T)} & \text{if } S \neq \emptyset \\ 0 & otherwise \end{cases}$$

In above equation the function $m_\mathcal{A}$ is still a Dempster-Shafer mass function, and it is easy to prove that $m_t = m_\mathcal{A}$.

5 Related Work

The principle implied in our framework is the approach of synthesizing all of information at a time point. This kind of research is related to two topics: how to model the process of belief change and how to synthesize the possible information.

In the process of uncertainty management, Khan and Jain believed that the outputs are based on not only the mean value of corresponding inputs but also the uniformity about corresponding inputs [10]. A synthesis strategy for heterogeneous distributed expert systems was developed by C. Zhang et al [28] [29]. What the above approaches lack is the concept of belief updating. Our framework in this paper implies a dynamic strategy for information synthesis under uncertainties. In this dynamic strategy, a probability is used to describe the factors of authorities from other agents, and the influence among agents is completed by the *Logical Imaging* technique.

In our framework, the synthesis result at time t is a mass function. This result is quite different from the conditions made by Kreps [11] and Brafman and Tennenholtz [1] [2] in their decision models. Kreps assumed that the agent can use a numerical probability to model its belief. In opposite, Brafman and Tennenholtz used the complete ignorance condition to describe the current state.

The study of belief change has been an active area in philosophy and artificial intelligence [6]. The standard frameworks for beliefs can be given by means of *Kripke structures* used in modal logics of knowledge and belief [9]. A *Kripke* structure for belief is a tuple $(\mathcal{W}, \pi, K_1, \ldots, K_n)$, where $\mathcal{W}$ is a set of possible worlds, $\pi(w)$ is a truth assignment to the primitive proposition at world $w \in \mathcal{W}$, and the K_is are accessibility relations on the worlds in $\mathcal{W}$. If we define $K_i(w) = \{w' \mid (w, w') \in K_i\}$, then $K_i(w)$ describes the set of worlds that agent i considers possible in w. In this modal logical framework, the knowledge (also including common knowledge, and distributed knowledge) encoded by the standard *Kripke structures* is discussed. This modal logical framework has also been extended by Friedman and Halpern [5], in which they discuss knowledge, plausibility (a plausibility measure [4] to each agent at each world), and time.

In applications, it is always difficult for an IA to recognize the exact knowledge as described within the *Kripke structures* (e.g., conflict messages). So we cannot make sure that the logical frameworks are most successful although they take long times to get the knowledge.

6 Summary

In this paper we have formalized a framework for IAs to perceive their environments. In this framework, the descriptions about belief and belief updating are given by the procedure descriptive approach rather than the logical approach. The contributions of this research include:

(1) A dynamic strategy to model agents' knowledge about a group of cooperating agents is proposed in our framework. In this dynamic strategy, a probability is used to describe the factors of trustworthy degrees from agents, and the dependencies among agents is described by the technique of *Logical Imaging*.

(2) A new dynamic strategy to solve the conflicts in multi-agent environments is presented in this framework.

(3) Our framework provides a technique for on-line agents to form beliefs based on the knowledge an IA has and the information it receives.

References

[1] R. I. Brafman and M. Tennenholtz, On the foundations of qualitative decision theory, in: *Proceedings of AAAI, 1996*, 1291-1296.
[2] R. I. Brafman and M. Tennenholtz, Modeling agents as qualitative decision makers, *Artificial Intelligence, 1997,* **94**: 217-268.
[3] R. Fagin, J. Y. Halpern, Y. Moses and M. Y. Vardi, *Reasoning about knowledge*, MIT Press, 1995.
[4] N. Friedman and J. Y. Halpern, Plausibility measures: a user's manual, in: *Proceedings of 11th Conference on Uncertainty in Artificial Intelligence, San Francisco, CA, 1995, 175-184.*
[5] N. Friedman and J. Y. Halpern, Modeling belief in dynamic systems, part I: foundations, *Artificial Intelligence, 1997,* **95(2)**: 257-316.
[6] P. Gardenfors, *Knowledge in Flux: modelling the dynamics of epistemic states,* MIT Press, Cambridge, MA, 1988.
[7] J.Y. Halpern and R. Fagin, Modelling knowledge and action in distributed systems, *Distributed Comput., 1989,* **3(4)**: 159-179.
[8] J. Y. Halpern and Y. Moses, Knowledge and common knowledge in a distributed environment, *J. of ACM, 1990,* **37**: 549-587.
[9] J. Y. Halpern and Y. Moses, A guide to completeness and complexity for modal logics of knowledge and belief, *Artificial Intelligence, 1992,* **54**: 319-379.

[10] N. A. Khan and R. Jain, Uncertainty management in a distributed knowledge based system, *in: Proceedings of IJCAI, Los Angeles, CA, 1985*, 318-320.

[11] D. M. Kreps, *Notes on the theory of choice*, Boulder: Westview Press, 1988.

[12] R. Kruse, E. Schwecke and J. Heinsoln, *Uncertainty and vagueness in knowledge based systems (Numerical Methods)*, Springer-Verlag, New York, 1991.

[13] D. Lewis, Probability of conditionals and conditionals probabilities, in: Ifs, Harper, W. L., Stalnaker, R., and Pearce G. Eds, *University of Western Ontario Series in Philosophy of Science*, D. Reidel Publishing Co., Inc., New York, NY, 1981, 129-147.

[14] Y. Li and C. Zhang, A method for combining interval structures, *in: Proceedings of 7th International Conference on Intelligence Systems, Paris France, 1998*, 9-13.

[15] Y. Li and C. Zhang, Information fusion and decision making for utility-based agents, *in: Proceedings of 5th International Conference on Information Systems Analysis and Synthesis, Orlando, USA, 1999, Volume 3*, 377-384.

[16] J. McCarthy, Ascribing mental qualities to machines, in: M. Ringle, ed., *Philosophical Perspectives in Artificial Intelligence*, Humanities Press, Atlantic Highlands, NJ, 1979.

[17] A. Newell, The knowledge level, *AI Mag., 1981*, **2(2)**: 1-20.

[18] A. S. Rao and M. P. Georgeff, Deliberation and its role in the formation of intentions, *in: Proceedings 7th Annual Conference on Uncertainty Artificial Intelligence, Los Angeles, CA, 1991*.

[19] A. S. Rao and M. P. Georgeff, An abstract architecture for rational agents, in: *Principle of Knowledge Representation and Reasoning: Proceedings 3rd International Conference*, Cambridge, Ma, 1992, 439-449.

[20] S. J. Rosenschein, Formal theories of knowledge in AI and robotics, *New Generation Comput., 1985*, **3**: 345-357.

[21] S. J. Rosenschein and L. P. Kaelbling, A situated view of representation and control, *Artificial Intelligence, 1995*, **73**: 149-174.

[22] G. Shafer, *A mathematical theory of evidence*, Princeton University Press, Princeton,NJ, 1976.

[23] Y. Shoham, Agent-oriented programming, *Artificial Intelligence, 1993*, **60**: 51-92.

[24] R. Stalnaker, Probability and conditionals, in: Ifs, Harper, W. L., Stalnaker, R., and Pearce G. Eds, *University of Western Ontario Series in Philosophy of Science*, D. Reidel Publishing Co., Inc., New York, NY, 1981, 107-128.

[25] R. H. Thomason, Towards a logical theory of practical reasoning, *in: AAAI Spring Symposium on Reasoning About Mental States: Formal Theories and Applications, 1993*.

[26] S. K. M. Wong, L.S. Wang and Y.Y. Yao, Interval structure: a framework for representing uncertain information, *in: Proceedings of the Eighth Conference on Uncertainty in Artificial Intelligence, California, 1992*, 336-343.

[27] Y. Y. Yao, S. K. M. Wong and T.Y. Lin, A review of rough set models, in: *Rough sets and data mining*, edited by T.Y. Lin and N. Cercone, Kluwer Academic Publishers, Boston, 1997, 47-75.

[28] C. Zhang, Cooperation under uncertainty in distributed expert systems, *Artificial Intelligence, 1992*, **56(1)**: 21-69.

[29] M. Zhang and C. Zhang, Potential cases, methodologies and strategies of synthesis in distributed expert systems, *IEEE Transactions on Knowledge and Data Engineering, 1999*, **11(3)**: 498-503.

A Preference-Based Theory of Intention

Toru Sugimoto

Department of Information Sciences, Science University of Tokyo
2641 Yamazaki, Noda-City, Chiba 278-8510, Japan
sugimoto@is.noda.sut.ac.jp

Abstract. Although there has been much work on the logical formulation of intention, only little attention has been paid on the close relationship between intentions and preferences of an agent. As a result, the previous work cannot properly treat reasoning with information about preferences. In this paper, we investigate a preference-based approach to the logic of intention. Based on an intuition that intentions are desirable choices of an agent, we define a notion of intention in terms of the preference order of an agent. The definition is a simple and intuitive one, and intentions satisfy good and interesting properties. Then we apply our logic to the intention recognition problem. Based on our preference-based definition of intention, we give several sufficient conditions on preferences of an agent under which the action-effect heuristic rule is valid. In this way, we demonstrate that our formalism can give a good basis for designing and understanding heuristics and control strategies for them in the intention recognition domain.

1 Introduction

In recent years, it has become increasingly obvious that intention, a kind of mental attitudes of an agent, plays an important role in communications in multi-agent environment [5,7], and thus better understanding of the concept is required. Various properties that intentions should satisfy are proposed in the literature [11,12]. Among them, the following property is important: intentions are *not* closed under logical consequence, that is, an agent need not intend all consequences of his intentions. In fact, it is not only incorrect but also harmful to assume consequential closure of intentions, since it distracts an agent's (and his observer's) attention.

The first attempt to formalize intention is made by Cohen and Levesque [4]. They begin with the notion of *choice*[1] of an agent. Intuitively speaking, a choice is a consequence of the scenario which an agent chooses to pursue. Choices are closed under logical consequence, and may be either desirable or undesirable for the agent though the chosen scenario is the most preferred one which he could choose. Intentions are considered to be choices, but not all choices are intentions.

---
[1] They use the term "goal" instead of "choice" for this notion. But we prefer to use "choice" following Bratman [2] and Sadek [12] rather than to use "goal" which is somewhat misleading.

In order to extract intentions from other simple choices, they formalized a dynamic property of intentions called *persistency*. That is, an intention is identified with a special kind of choice which will not be dropped until the agent thinks it has been satisfied or he thinks it will never be true.

Though this formulation of intention provides many significant properties of intentions, it has a counterintuitive aspect: their definition of persistency is too strong. For instance, if an agent comes to know that his intentions ϕ and ψ are mutually exclusive, he must give up at least one of these intentions, while each of them may be still achievable. In fact, since an agent may drop his intentions for various reasons, it is not easy to give an adequate definition of persistency.

Konolige and Pollack [10] took another approach, a representationalist approach to intention. They represent intentions directly in a cognitive structure of an agent. Restricting admissible structures, they show that intentions satisfy a number of desirable properties without suffering from the consequential closure. However, the dynamics of intention must be provided from outside the model, therefore we cannot at all examine such properties as persistency in their formalism.

Moreover, neither of these theories deals with information about *preferences* of an agent. Preferences are closely related to intentions. If two intentions of an agent become inconsistent, the agent gives up the intention which he does not prefer to the other intention. If an agent knows two plans for achieving an intention and he prefers one plan to the other, he usually intends to perform the preferred plan. Conversely, if an agent intends to perform a plan, we can infer under certain conditions that he intends the result of the plan and that he prefers that plan to the other plans. This close relation between intention and preference stems from the fact that intentions reflect certain features of an agent's preferences. Roughly speaking, an agent intends propositions which is desirable for him. The previous theories of intention cannot deal with preferences not only because they have no means to express information about preferences but also because they ignore preferential aspects of intention.

In this paper, we present a preference-based characterization of intention. We represent an agent's preferences by a partial order over models (possible worlds), and define intention in terms of the preference order and belief. We give a new preference-based account for the consequential closure problem, and then we apply our theory to intention recognition. Incorporating knowledge about preferences of an agent into a model, we can examine conditions under which heuristics for recognition are valid.

In Sect. 2, we introduce our logic of belief, choice, preference and intention. Choice and intention are defined in terms of the preference order of an agent. We show that intentions satisfy several desirable properties without suffering from the consequential closure, and demonstrate by an example that our definition agrees with our intuitions. In Sect. 3, we apply our logic to the intention recognition problem. Based on our preference-based definition of intention, we give several sufficient conditions on preferences of an agent under which the action-effect inference rule [1], a heuristic for intention/plan recognition, is valid. In this way, we demonstrate that our formalism can give a good basis for designing and understanding heuristics and control strategies for them in the intention recognition domain.

2 Defining Intention via Preference

2.1 Belief and Choice

In order to describe states of affairs and events in the world, we use a standard propositional language L with a set of atoms $\text{atom}(L)$. Each element of $\text{atom}(L)$ is assumed to express a time-independent fact such as "an agent is hungry at 1 p. m." and "an agent eats lunch from 1 p. m. to 2 p. m." In this way, we develop our logic independently of specific theories of time and action. We characterize an agent's mental state by a *structure*, a pair $\langle W, \prec \rangle$. The set of *epistemic alternatives* W is a nonempty set of models of L. $M \in W$ means that M is consistent with the agent's belief. The *preference order* $\prec$ is a strict partial order (i.e., an irreflexive and transitive relation) over models of L. $M_1 \prec M_2$ means that M_2 is preferred to M_1 by the agent. To simplify our definitions and resulting properties, we assume in this paper that for every nonempty set of models W', both of the following sets are nonempty:

$$\text{Max}(W', \prec) = \{M \in W' \mid \text{ there exists no } M' \in W' \text{ such that } M \prec M'\}$$
$$\text{Min}(W', \prec) = \{M \in W' \mid \text{ there exists no } M' \in W' \text{ such that } M' \prec M\} \ .$$

An element of these sets is called a *maximally/minimally preferred model* in W', respectively.

In order to describe mental attitudes of an agent, we define from L another language L^{att}, whose sentence takes one of the following forms (we denote sentences of L by $\phi, \psi, \ldots$, and sentences of L^{att} by $\Phi, \Psi, \ldots$): $\text{BEL}(\phi)$ (belief), $\text{CHO}(\phi)$ (choice), $\text{INT}(\phi)$ (intention), $\text{PREF}^T(\phi, \psi)$ (preference), $\Phi \wedge \Psi$, and $\neg \Psi$ where T is a subset of $\text{atom}(L)$.[2] Satisfaction of these sentences (except $\text{INT}(\phi)$ and $\text{PREF}^T(\phi, \psi)$) is defined as follows:

Definition 1.

1. $\langle W, \prec \rangle \models \text{BEL}(\phi)$ iff $M \models \phi$ for all $M \in W$
2. $\langle W, \prec \rangle \models \text{CHO}(\phi)$ iff $M \models \phi$ for all $M \in \text{Max}(W, \prec)$
3. $\langle W, \prec \rangle \models \Phi \wedge \Psi$ iff $\langle W, \prec \rangle \models \Phi$ and $\langle W, \prec \rangle \models \Psi$
4. $\langle W, \prec \rangle \models \neg \Phi$ iff $\langle W, \prec \rangle \not\models \Phi$.

If $\langle W, \prec \rangle \models \Phi$ holds for all structures $\langle W, \prec \rangle$, we write $\models \Phi$.

An agent chooses ϕ only if ϕ is satisfied in every chosen model, that is, a maximally preferred model which is consistent with his belief. It obviously follows from the definition that both beliefs and choices are consistent and closed under logical consequence. Every valid sentence is believed and every belief is chosen.

---
[2] We only consider mental attitudes of one agent, and omit the agent argument in attitudinal operators. We also use $\Phi \vee \Psi, \Phi \supset \Psi$ and $\Phi \equiv \Psi$, which are introduced by definition in a usual fashion.

2.2 Preference

Reduction of preferences between sentences to preferences between models is investigated by several authors (e.g., [6, 13]), and we take an essentially similar approach here. Namely, we say that an agent prefers ϕ to ψ if he prefers models of $\phi \wedge \neg\psi$ to models of $\neg\phi \wedge \psi$. According to the parts of the world which should be fixed through the comparison, we can define preference of various strength. Here we take a general approach and use a parameter $T \subset \text{atom}(L)$ to specify which atoms must be fixed.

Definition 2. $\langle W, \prec \rangle \models \text{PREF}^T(\phi, \psi)$ iff $M_1 \prec M_2$ for all pairs $M_1, M_2 \in W$ such that

1. $M_1 \models \neg\phi \wedge \psi$,
2. $M_2 \models \phi \wedge \neg\psi$, and
3. $M_1 \models p$ iff $M_2 \models p$ for all $p \in T$.

The following is a direct consequence of the definition:

Proposition 1.

1. If $\phi \supset \psi$ is a tautology, $\models \text{PREF}^T(\phi, \psi) \wedge \text{PREF}^T(\psi, \phi)$.
2. $\models \text{PREF}^T(\phi, \psi) \equiv \text{PREF}^T(\neg\psi, \neg\phi)$.
3. If $T \subset T'$, $\models \text{PREF}^T(\phi, \psi) \supset \text{PREF}^{T'}(\phi, \psi)$.

Item 1 of the proposition says that for two sentences one of which is a logical consequence of the other, preference relations always hold. 2 says that preferring ϕ to ψ is equal to preferring $\neg\psi$ to $\neg\phi$. 3 says that if a parameter set T is the smaller, the preference PREF^T is the stronger.

Although we allow T to be any set of atoms, we frequently use two extreme cases for T, for which we introduce the following notations:

(1) $\text{PREF}^0(\phi, \psi) = \text{PREF}^T(\phi, \psi)$ where T is an empty set.
(2) $\text{PREF}^{\text{eq}}(\phi, \psi) = \text{PREF}^T(\phi, \psi)$ where $T = \text{atom}(L) \setminus (\text{atom}(\phi) \cup \text{atom}(\psi))$.

(1) expresses the strongest preference, that every model of $\phi \wedge \neg\psi$ is preferred to every model of $\neg\phi \wedge \psi$. For example, a sentence $\text{PREF}^0(\neg hungry, hungry)$ means that an agent prefers to be not hungry even if he must spend much money and time to satisfy his hunger.

On the other hand, (2) expresses the weakest preference, that ϕ is preferred to ψ if *all else are equal*. If ϕ and ψ cause different effects on other parts of the world, they are not compared. For example, a sentence $\text{PREF}^{\text{eq}}(\neg hungry, hungry)$ means that an agent prefers to be not hungry if the other conditions are equal. In this case, he may not want to spend money and time to satisfy his hunger.

Preference between sentences has a close relationship with other attitudes. In particular, for the strongest type of preferences PREF^0 we get the following interesting results:

Proposition 2.
1. $\models \mathrm{PREF}^0(\phi, \neg\phi) \wedge \neg\mathrm{BEL}(\neg\phi) \supset \mathrm{CHO}(\phi)$.
2. $\models \mathrm{PREF}^0(\phi, \psi) \wedge \neg\mathrm{BEL}(\phi \supset \psi) \supset \mathrm{CHO}(\psi \supset \phi)$.

If an agent strongly prefers ϕ to $\neg\phi$ and ϕ is consistent with his belief, he chooses ϕ.

2.3 Intention

Intuitively speaking, an agent's intentions are *desirable* parts of his choice. But how can we define a notion of desirability of sentences here? First, we might define desirable sentences as those sentences ϕ which satisfy $\mathrm{PREF}^T(\phi, \neg\phi)$, specifying some T. But, whatever we take for T, this definition does not agree with our intuitions, since an intention is generally *not* preferred to its negation in *all* possible situations, though it is certainly preferred in most of them. For example, consider an agent who intends to satisfy his hunger and intends to eat lunch at his office. If we restrict our attention to situations where the hunger is satisfied (e.g., situations where he attends a lunch party), his eating lunch at his office may not be preferred to its negation.

Examining the above example, we can classify intentions into two kinds: first, there exist intentions which are strongly preferred to their negations (e.g., satisfying the hunger). Second, there exist intentions which is believed to imply another intention of the first kind (e.g., eating lunch in the office). Therefore, desirable sentences can be defined as those sentences ϕ which are believed to imply another (non-tautological) sentence ψ which is strongly preferred to its negation, that is, $\mathrm{PREF}^0(\psi, \neg\psi)$ holds. Paraphrasing this condition, we have the following definition of intention:

Definition 3. $\langle W, \prec \rangle \models \mathrm{INT}(\phi)$ *iff*
1. $M \models \phi$ *for all* $M \in \mathrm{Max}(W, \prec)$, *and*
2. $M \not\models \phi$ *for all* $M \in \mathrm{Min}(W, \prec)$

Condition 1 says that ϕ is a choice, and Condition 2 says that ϕ is desirable in the above sense. The latter condition is reasonable, since if there exists a model of ϕ which is minimally preferred, attempting to satisfy ϕ may result in that minimally preferred model, that is, may not make the things better, and thus there is no reason for the agent to pursue ϕ.

We can easily show the following properties of intentions:

Proposition 3. 1. $\models \mathrm{INT}(\phi) \supset \mathrm{CHO}(\phi)$
2. $\models \mathrm{INT}(\phi) \supset \neg\mathrm{BEL}(\phi) \wedge \neg\mathrm{BEL}(\neg\phi)$
3. $\models \mathrm{INT}(\phi) \wedge \mathrm{BEL}(\phi \equiv \psi) \supset \mathrm{INT}(\psi)$
4. $\models \mathrm{INT}(\phi) \wedge \mathrm{INT}(\psi) \supset \mathrm{INT}(\phi \wedge \psi)$
5. $\models \mathrm{INT}(\phi) \wedge \mathrm{INT}(\psi) \supset \mathrm{INT}(\phi \vee \psi)$.

An agent does not intend sentences which he believes to be satisfied already. Intentions must be consistent with beliefs and with each other, and they are closed under conjunction and disjunction. The converse of 4 and 5 does not hold in general. Namely, intending a conjunction does not imply intending its conjuncts. It is not surprising, because we can easily see that the converse of 4 is logically equivalent to the consequential closure of INT. However, if one conjunct is preferred to the other, we can conclude that at least the preferred conjunct is intended:

Proposition 4.
1. $\models \text{INT}(\phi \wedge \psi) \wedge \text{PREF}^0(\phi, \psi) \wedge \neg \text{BEL}(\psi \supset \phi) \supset \text{INT}(\phi)$.
2. $\models \text{INT}(\phi \vee \psi) \wedge \text{PREF}^0(\phi, \psi) \wedge \neg \text{BEL}(\phi \supset \psi) \supset \text{INT}(\phi)$.

2.4 Example

Imagine a student who goes to a bookstore intending to buy a paperback and also intending to buy a magazine, because he likes to buy them. This situation is described by a propositional language L whose atoms are p (the student buys the paperback at some time t) and m (the student buys the magazine at t). The set of epistemic alternatives

$$W = \{\{p, m\}, \{p, \neg m\}, \{\neg p, m\}, \{\neg p, \neg m\}\}^3$$

and the preference order $\prec$ is depicted as follows:

$$\{\neg p, \neg m\} \prec \{p, \neg m\} \prec \{p, m\}$$
$$\{\neg p, \neg m\} \prec \{\neg p, m\} \prec \{p, m\} \ .$$

Then we can conclude

$$\langle W, \prec \rangle \models \text{INT}(p) \wedge \text{INT}(m) \ .$$

Consider a sentence $p \equiv m$ which means buying both or neither. Although it is a tautological consequence of an intention $p \wedge m$ and hence it is a choice, it is *not* an intention because it is satisfied in a minimally preferred model $\{\neg p, \neg m\}$. This shows that intentions are not closed under tautological consequence in our logic:

$$\langle W, \prec \rangle \models \text{INT}(p \wedge m) \wedge (p \wedge m \supset p \equiv m) \wedge \neg \text{INT}(p \equiv m) \ .$$

At a bookstore, the student happens to know that he has not enough money to buy both of them. If he has no preference between buying the paperback and buying the magazine, he drops intentions to buy each of them, and now only intends to buy one of them:

$$\langle W', \prec \rangle \models \text{INT}(p \vee m) \wedge \neg \text{INT}(p) \wedge \neg \text{INT}(m)$$

where $W' = W \setminus \{\{p, m\}\}$. On the other hand, if he prefers the paperback to the magazine, he continues intending to buy the paperback, while he gives up the intention to buy the magazine:

$$\langle W', \prec' \rangle \models \text{INT}(p \vee m) \wedge \text{INT}(p) \wedge \neg \text{INT}(m)$$

---
[3] We denote a model of a propositional language by the set of atoms and negations of atoms which are true in it.

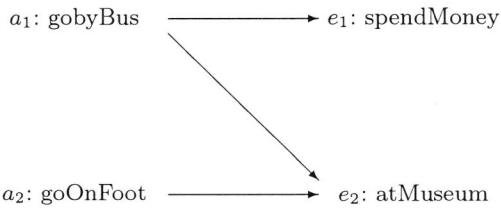

Fig. 1. Actions and their effects

where $\prec'$ is depicted as follows:

$$\{\neg p, \neg m\} \prec' \{\neg p, m\} \prec' \{p, \neg m\} \prec' \{p, m\} \ .$$

In this way, we can explain the dynamics of intentions in an intuitive example situation mentioned earlier where the strong assumption of persistency [4] fails.

3 Intention Recognition and Reasoning about Preferences

In multi-agent environments, an agent must reason about other agents' intentions and plans in order to behave cooperatively. For example, if an agent observes another agent's intending to go to a museum by bus (for example, by hearing the utterance like "I want to take a bus for the museum"), he should infer the agent's intention of being at the museum. This type of inference is explained in traditional plan recognition models (e.g., [1]) by using the action-effect inference rule: from an intention of performing an action infer an intention of achieving its effects. Since this rule is not valid in general, its application must be controlled by various heuristic strategies.

To make the problem clearer, let us consider two actions: going to a museum by bus (a_1), and going there on foot (a_2). Action a_1 has two effects, spending money on the bill (e_1) and his being at the museum (e_2), while Action a_2 has only one effect e_2 (see Fig. 1).

Suppose that we observe the agent's intention to perform Action a_1, and then what should we infer? There are at least four possibilities:

I_1. do not use the rule and infer no intentions;
I_2. use the rule and infer an intention e_1;
I_3. use the rule and infer an intention e_2; and
I_4. use the rule twice and infer intentions e_1 and e_2.

Although I_3 is appropriate in most cases, all of these inferences can be appropriate, according to the agent's preferences. For example, if the agent likes to take a bus, I_1 may be appropriate. Otherwise, it is inappropriate. Similarly, if the agent likes to spend money, I_2 and I_4 may be appropriate. Otherwise, they are inappropriate. In previous models of intention/plan recognition [1, 8, 9], it is difficult to distinguish these possibilities, since they lack sufficient facilities for representing an agent's preferences. On the other hand, our logic can be used to examine which inference is valid under which condition in a purely formal manner. Below we give several sufficient conditions under which Inference I_3 is valid.

Let L be a propositional language with atoms a_1, a_2, e_1 and e_2, which express the facts "the agent goes to a museum by bus", "the agent goes there on foot", "he spends money" and "he is at the museum", respectively. First, we assume $\text{PREF}^{eq}(\neg a_1, a_1)$, $\text{PREF}^{eq}(\neg a_2, a_2)$ and $\text{PREF}^{eq}(\neg a_1 \wedge \neg a_2, a_1 \wedge a_2)$. It means that the agent does not like the going actions *in themselves*, and he does not want to perform them if unnecessary. We think that this type of preference is common in our daily life, since most actions are done at some cost. Now from $\text{INT}(a_1)$ we can infer $\text{INT}(e_1 \wedge e_2)$, an intention of achieving both effects of a_1, provided that a_1 and a_2 are not believed to be mutually exclusive:

Proposition 5.

$$\models (\text{BEL}(a_1 \supset e_1 \wedge e_2) \wedge \tag{1}$$
$$\text{BEL}(a_2 \supset e_2) \wedge \tag{2}$$
$$\text{INT}(a_1) \wedge \tag{3}$$
$$\text{PREF}^{eq}(\neg a_1, a_1) \wedge \tag{4}$$
$$\text{PREF}^{eq}(\neg a_2, a_2) \wedge \tag{5}$$
$$\text{PREF}^{eq}(\neg a_1 \wedge \neg a_2, a_1 \wedge a_2)) \tag{6}$$
$$\supset (\text{BEL}(e_1 \wedge e_2 \supset a_1 \vee a_2) \wedge \tag{7}$$
$$(\neg \text{BEL}(a_1 \supset \neg a_2) \supset \text{INT}(e_1 \wedge e_2)) \wedge \tag{8}$$
$$\text{PREF}^{eq}(a_1, a_2)) . \tag{9}$$

Proof. Let $\langle W, \prec \rangle$ be a structure that satisfies (1)–(6). For (7). We wish to show W does not include a model of $\neg a_1 \wedge \neg a_2 \wedge e_1 \wedge e_2$. If it includes such a model, that model is preferred to all models of a_1 by (4) and (6), but this conflicts with (3).

For (8). Suppose $\langle W, \prec \rangle \models \neg \text{BEL}(a_1 \supset \neg a_2)$. This means that there exist a model M_1 of $a_1 \wedge a_2$. Since M_1 is a model of an intention a_1 and by (4)–(6) all the other models of $e_1 \wedge e_2$ are preferred to M_1, M_1 must be preferred to some model of $\neg(e_1 \wedge e_2)$. It follows that $\langle W, \prec \rangle \models \text{INT}(e_1 \wedge e_2)$.

For (9). by (3) and (5), all models of $a_1 \wedge \neg a_2$ are preferred to all models of $\neg a_1 \wedge a_2$, and thus $\langle W, \prec \rangle \models \text{PREF}^{eq}(a_1, a_2)$. □

Note that we can infer not only intention (8) of the agent but also his belief (7) (performing one of the going action is a necessary condition for achieving both effects) and preference (9) (going by bus is preferred to going on foot) in this example. Inferred beliefs and preferences will be used for recognition in the future.

Next, we give conditions under which $\text{INT}(e_2)$ (an intention of being at the museum) is inferred. The first such condition is $\text{PREF}^0(e_2, e_1) \wedge \neg \text{BEL}(e_1 \supset e_2)$. It directly follows from Propositions 4 and 5 that $\text{INT}(e_2)$ is inferred under this condition, though the first half of this condition, $\mathrm{PREF}^0(e_2, e_1)$, seems to be too strong and not very realistic.

The second condition under which $\mathrm{INT}(e_2)$ is inferred is $\mathrm{PREF}^{eq}(\neg a_1 \wedge \neg e_1, a_1) \wedge \mathrm{PREF}^{eq}(\neg a_1 \wedge \neg a_2 \wedge \neg e_1, a_1 \wedge a_2)$. It means that the agent does not like the "go and spend money" scenarios in themselves. In the similar way to the previous proposition, we can easily prove the following:

Proposition 6.

$$\begin{align}
\models \big(\mathrm{BEL}(a_1 \supset e_1 \wedge e_2) \wedge & \tag{10}\\
\mathrm{BEL}(a_2 \supset e_2) \wedge & \tag{11}\\
\mathrm{INT}(a_1) \wedge & \tag{12}\\
\mathrm{PREF}^{eq}(\neg a_1, a_1) \wedge & \tag{13}\\
\mathrm{PREF}^{eq}(\neg a_2, a_2) \wedge & \tag{14}\\
\mathrm{PREF}^{eq}(\neg a_1 \wedge \neg a_2, a_1 \wedge a_2) \wedge & \tag{15}\\
\mathrm{PREF}^{eq}(\neg a_1 \wedge \neg e_1, a_1) \wedge & \tag{16}\\
\mathrm{PREF}^{eq}(\neg a_1 \wedge \neg a_2 \wedge \neg e_1, a_1 \wedge a_2)\big) & \tag{17}\\
\supset \big(\mathrm{BEL}(e_2 \supset a_1 \vee a_2) \wedge & \tag{18}\\
(\neg \mathrm{BEL}(a_1 \supset \neg a_2) \supset \mathrm{INT}(e_2)) \wedge & \tag{19}\\
\mathrm{PREF}^{eq}(a_1, a_2)\big) \, . & \tag{20}
\end{align}$$

It is often the case that preferences like (16) and (17) are not available to the observer. Even in such cases, if the observer knows that an agent's intending e_2 is more plausible than his intending e_1, the observer can infer $\mathrm{INT}(e_2)$. So, the third condition under which $\mathrm{INT}(e_2)$ is inferred is not a condition on the agent's preference but a condition on the observer's knowledge about plausibility. Such a condition can be formulated in our logic by specifying a plausibility ordering over structures. Namely, for all pairs S_1, S_2 of structures such that

1. $S_1 \models \neg \mathrm{INT}(e_1) \wedge \mathrm{INT}(e_2)$ and
2. $S_2 \models \mathrm{INT}(e_1) \wedge \neg \mathrm{INT}(e_2)$,

the observer is assumed to think that S_1 is more plausible than S_2. Then, for all maximally plausible structures S that satisfy (10)–(15), $S \models \mathrm{INT}(e_2)$. In this way, we can deal with most of heuristics proposed, for example, in [8,9] in our framework.

4 Conclusion

Most of practical planning systems have some kind of representation of agent's intentional states (e.g., goals) and preferences (e.g., evaluation functions and heuristic decision rules) which control his behavior. An interesting aspect of our approach is that we can explain various interactions between those two components in a systematic way: information about preferences of an agent is used to identify his intentions, and observed intentions constrain preferences which the agent may have.

Treatment of the dynamics of mental attitudes, that is, their change over time, is also important for planning systems as well as foundational theories of them. Although the notion of time is implicit in our logic, we can deal with the dynamics of mental attitudes such as give up and recovery of intentions, as demonstrated in Sect. 2.4. Here, the progress of time is modeled by elimination of epistemic alternatives of an agent, that is, incorporation of new beliefs.

Finally, though we use an extremely simple language to present our logic of intention, extension of our logic to richer languages is not difficult in most cases. In particular, we can easily extend the syntax of our language L^{att} to permit *nesting* of mental attitudes, whose satisfaction is defined by using an ordered accessibility relation [3] over epistemic alternatives.

References

1. J. F. Allen. Recognizing intentions from natural language utterances. In Michael Brady and Robert C. Berwick, editors, *Computational Models of Discourse*, pages 107–166. MIT Press, 1983.
2. Michael E. Bratman. *Intention, Plans and Practical Reason*. Harvard University Press, 1987.
3. Brian F. Chellas. *Modal Logic: An Introduction*. Cambridge University Press, 1980.
4. Philip R. Cohen and Hector J. Levesque. Intention is choice with commitment. *Artificial Intelligence*, 42:213–261, 1990.
5. Philip R. Cohen and Hector J. Levesque. Rational interaction as the basis for communication. In Philip R. Cohen, Jerry L. Morgan, and Martha E. Pollack, editors, *Intentions in Communication*, pages 221–255. MIT Press, 1990.
6. Jon Doyle, Yoav Shoham, and Michael P. Wellman. A logic of relative desire. In Z. W. Ras and M. Zemankova, editors, *Methodologies for Intelligent Systems: Proceedings of ISMIS '91, Lecture Notes in Artificial Intelligence 542*, pages 16–31. Springer-Verlag, 1991.
7. Barbara J. Grosz and Sarit Kraus. Collaborative plans for complex group action. *Artificial Intelligence*, 86:269–357, 1996.
8. Henry A. Kautz. A circumscriptive theory of plan recognition. In Philip R. Cohen, Jerry L. Morgan, and Martha E. Pollack, editors, *Intentions in Communication*, pages 105–133. MIT Press, 1990.
9. Kurt Konolige and Martha E. Pollack. Ascribing plans to agents: preliminary report. In *Proceedings of IJCAI–89*, pages 924–930, 1989.
10. Kurt Konolige and Martha E. Pollack. A representationalist theory of intention. In *Proceedings of IJCAI–93*, pages 390–395, 1993.
11. Anand S. Rao and Michael P. Georgeff. Asymmetry thesis and side-effect problems in linear-time and branching-time intention logics. In *Proceedings of IJCAI–91*, pages 498–504, 1991.
12. M. D. Sadek. A study in the logic of intention. In *Proceedings of the 3rd International Conference on Principles of Knowledge Representation and Reasoning*, pages 462–473, 1992.
13. Ken Satoh. Relative plausibility based on model ordering: preliminary report. In Z. W. Ras, editor, *Methodologies for Intelligent Systems*, volume 4, pages 17–24. North-Holland, 1989.

Autonomy of Autonomous Agents

Dongmo Zhang and Norman Foo

Knowledge Systems Group
School of Computer Science and Engineering
University of New South Wales, Australia
{dongmo,norman}@cse.unsw.edu.au

Abstract. Autonomy is one of the most notable attributes of agency, and this paper presents a formal framework for modelling it. By representing the mental states of agents, we provide an analysis of some attributes of autonomy. In particular, we define three sorts of autonomous agents and examine their structure. We also outline features of higher autonomy. Our framework can be a basis for classifying hierarchies of autonomy of agency.

1 Introduction

There is a great deal of interest in developing intelligent agents in recent years and numerous products of intelligent agents came to the fore. However, there are some to which one might hesitate to attribute intelligence. Although there are various formal or informal definitions of intelligent agent in the literature ([3][4][9][15]) which may help us to judge whether a software or hardware system is an intelligent agent, most of them involve *autonomy* as one of the essential attributes of an intelligent agent, a concept which looks very clear but has not had a general agreed formalization.

Autonomy of agency was defined in [1] as operating without the direct intervention of human or others, and having some kind of control over its actions and internal state. In other words, an autonomous agent has two kinds of control power: one determines its action choice and the other controls its internal state transition. Let $\mathcal{M}$ be the set of all the possible internal states of an agent and $\mathcal{A}$ the set of all actions it can do. Then a tentative definition of autonomy would be: *there exists an action choice function $H : \mathcal{M} \to \mathcal{A}$ and a state transition function $T : \mathcal{M} \times \mathcal{A} \to \mathcal{M}$ which control the run of the agent.*

According to this definition, however, there are many programs such as operation systems, infinite loops and computer viruses, that would qualify for autonomy, but may not generally be viewed as intelligent agents.

This paper offers a formal analysis of autonomy by using action theory, mainly the situation calculus introduced in [8] and [11], in the spirit of BDI models ([2][4]). We propose a potential multiple-dimensional classification of autonomous agency by constructing in detail three sorts of agents with different levels of action decision and adumbrating another sort of agents with different levels of mental state updating.

2 Representation of Agent

In this section, we extend the many-sorted first-order language with action connectives to represent mental states of agency and the agent itself.

2.1 Action Description Language $\mathcal{L}_a$

We start with a 2-sorted first-order language $\mathcal{L}_a$ with equality and action connectives $;, \cup, \star, \pi, ||, \gg$, where $;, \cup, \star$ are the standard program connectives in dynamic logic, denoting sequence, non-deterministic choice, non-deterministic iteration, respectively; and $\pi, ||, \gg$ denoting non-deterministic argument choice, concurrent execution, concurrency with different priorities of actions, respectively (see [8] and [5])[1]. The sorts are *action* and *object*, similar to the ones in situation calculus ([11]). The alphabet of $\mathcal{L}_a$ consists of countable individual constant, variable, predicate and function symbols, and countable action symbols (including two special action symbols ε and Θ, called *empty* and *stall*, respectively). The notions of *first-order term, formula* and *sentence* are as same as ones in first-order logic.

An *action term*, denoted by α, β, is generated by primitive actions through action connectives:

$$\alpha ::= a(x_1, \cdots, x_n) \mid \varphi? \mid \alpha;\beta \mid \alpha \cup \beta \mid \alpha^* \mid \pi x \alpha(x) \mid \alpha||\beta \mid \alpha \gg \beta$$

where $a(x_1, \cdots, x_n)$ is a primitive action, φ? a test action. $\pi x \alpha(x)$ means an action α with a non-deterministic assignment to argument x. $\alpha || \beta$ means doing α and β concurrently. $\alpha \gg \beta$ means doing α and β concurrently with α having higher priority than β.

2.2 Representation of Mental State

It has been well recognized in the AI community that an agent's behavior is determined by its mental state, but there is no agreement about the composition of mental state. The most influential doctrine is the so-called *BDI-model*, which views beliefs, goals or desires, and intentions as the main components of agent's mental state (see [4]). However, such selection and classification seem not to be enough to explain the autonomy of autonomous agents. For the purpose of this paper, we will adopt a slightly different selection from the mental attitudes, viz.: *beliefs* about the outside world and its state, knowledge about *action effects*, knowledge about *feasibility of actions*, *intention* for the future actions and *strategies* for performing complex actions. Therefore t*he mental state of an agent* can be represented by a five-tuple $M = (B, E, Q, I, S)$, one component for each attitude respectively, where B is a set of first-order sentences; E is a finite set of effect rules; Q is a finite set of feasibility rules; I is a finite set of intention rules; S is a finite set of strategy rules. Let's explain these items in more detail.

---

[1] We will not give a fully formal specification of such action connectives because it requires more sophisticated logic, such as dynamic logic or high-order logic.

Effect rules: express effect of actions or effect axioms. We write the effect axioms in the following three forms of rule and deal with the frame problem by relying on Pednault's solution for its simplicity ([10]).

A *positive effect rule* for a fluent[2] R and a primitive action a is:
$(R(\mathbf{x}), \bot \Rightarrow \top, a(\mathbf{y}), \gamma(\mathbf{x}, \mathbf{y}))$
where $\mathbf{x}, \mathbf{y}$ may be vectors. This rule says that the value of $R(\mathbf{x})$ changes from false to true after performing the action $a(\mathbf{y})$ provided $\gamma(\mathbf{x}, \mathbf{y})$ holds in the current belief state[3].

Similarly, a *negative effect rule* for R and a is: $(R(\mathbf{x}), \top \Rightarrow \bot, a(\mathbf{y}), \gamma(\mathbf{x}, \mathbf{y}))$
An *effect rule* for function F and primitive action a is the form:
$(F(\mathbf{x}), z_1 \Rightarrow z_2, a(\mathbf{y}), \gamma(\mathbf{x}, \mathbf{y}, z_1, z_2))$,
meaning that the value of function $F(x)$ changes from z_1 to z_2 after performing the action $a(\mathbf{y})$ provided $\gamma(\mathbf{x}, \mathbf{y}, z_1, z_2)$ holds in the current belief state.

Feasibility rules: state the conditions of feasibility of actions. The form of *feasibility rule* is: $(a(\mathbf{x}), \gamma(\mathbf{x}))$, meaning that the agent believes that the action $a(\mathbf{x})$ is feasible provided $\gamma(\mathbf{x})$ holds in the current belief state.

Intention rules: express which action the agent wants to do for which goal under which condition. More precisely, an intention consists of four components:

- *action* the agent intends to do, represented by a closed action term;
- *goal* for which the agent takes this action, expressed by a first-order sentence;
- *prerequisite* specifying when the intention is valid, represented by a first-order sentence;
- *rating* indicating the priority among the agent's intentions, represented by a real number between 0 and 1.

Therefore the general form of an *intention* is:
$(\alpha(\mathbf{t}), g(\mathbf{t}), p(\mathbf{t}), r)$
which means performing the action $\alpha(\mathbf{t})$ provided the goal $g(\mathbf{t})$ is not achieved, the prerequisite $p(\mathbf{t})$ holds and the rating r is currently maximal among all the intentions with this condition. For example, the intention $(pickup(a); stack(a, b), on(a, b), on(b, c), 1)$ means that to achieve a on b, the block-move robot intends to pickup a first and then stack it onto b provided $on(b, c)$ has been achieved.

We use a special action ε, called *empty action*, to denote the absence of action in an intention. For instance, if we have a goal $on(a, b)$ but have no idea how to achieve it, this intention can be expressed by $(\varepsilon, on(a, b), \top, 1)$.

Some more examples of intention:
1. "Fight till you drop": $(fight^*, victory, alive, 1)$.
2. "Try it three times": $((\alpha; n ::= n + 1)^*, goal \vee n = 3, \top, 1)$
3. Interrupt process:
$(\alpha_1, goal_1, \neg interrupt\_condition, r_1)$
...

---

[2] We do not distinguish fluent from predicate or function in the syntax. We simply assume that those predicates or functions which have effect rules are fluents, the others are the ordinary predicates or functions.
[3] In the situation calculus language, this rule means
$\gamma(\mathbf{x}, \mathbf{y}, s) \rightarrow (\neg R(\mathbf{x}, s) \rightarrow R(\mathbf{x}, do(a(\mathbf{y}, s))))$

$(\alpha_n, goal_n, \neg interrupt\_condition, r_n)$
$(interrupt\_process\_program, \bot, interrupt\_condition, 0)$

We remark that our representation and treatment are quite different from the BDI-model. In fact, we think intention is one of the most complex mental attitudes of agency, which involves reasoning about causation and commitment. In the other words, (α, g, p, r) is an intention of an agent only if the agent thinks the action α can achieve its goal g (or α can cause g) under the prerequisite p and commits itself to do α in the priority of r. We will see that the intention of agency is the real impetus of autonomy.

Strategy rules: summarize the *experience* of agent in complex actions. A strategy is a rule in the form: $(a(\mathbf{x}), \alpha(\mathbf{x}))$, where a is an action symbol, called a strategy, $\alpha(\mathbf{x})$ is an action term whose free variables are among $\mathbf{x}$, being like a "canned" plan.

For instance, a block-move robot could have the following experience:
- $clearing(x)$: make the block x clear by moving away all the blocks on it.
- $move(x, y)$: stack x on y after clearing them.

Let's show a snapshot of mental state of a block-move robot.

Example 1 Consider a block-move robot. Suppose that we have three block a, b, c which are put on the table d. There are two primitive actions ($pickup(x)$ and $stack(x, y)$) and two strategies ($clearing(x)$ and $move(x, y)$). The current intention is

1. Pickup a and stack it onto c in order to achieve a on c.
2. Move b onto c by performing $move(b, c)$.
3. Make a tower in the order a, b, c from top to bottom.

Then the following is the mental state of this robot at the moment:
$M = (B, E, Q, I, S)$, where
$B = \{block(a), block(b), block(c), table(d), on(a,b), on(b,d), on(c,d), clear(a),$
$\quad \neg clear(b), clear(c), \forall x \neg(block(x) \land table(x)), \forall x(table(x) \to clear(x))\}$
$E = \{(clear(x), \bot \Rightarrow \top, pickup(y), on(y,x)), (clear(x), \top \Rightarrow \bot, stack(y,x), \neg table(x)),$
$\quad (on(x,y), \bot \Rightarrow \top, stack(x,y), \top), (on(x,y), \top \Rightarrow \bot, pickup(x), \top),$
$\quad (inhand(x), \bot \Rightarrow \top, pickup(x), \top), (inhand(x), \top \Rightarrow \bot, stack(x,y), \top)\}$
$Q = \{(pickup(x), block(x) \land clear(x),$
$\quad (stack(x,y), block(x) \land inhand(x) \land clear(y) \land x \neq y)\}$
$I = \{(pickup(a); stack(a,c), on(a,c), \top, 1), (move(b,c), on(b,c), \top, 0.8),$
$\quad (\varepsilon, on(a,b) \land on(b,c), \top, 0.6)\}$
$S = \{(clearing(x), clear(x)? \cup (; \pi y \pi z((on(y,x) \land table(z))?; move(y,z))),$
$\quad (move(x,y), clearing(x); clearing(y); pickup(x); stack(x,y))\}$

It is not hard to see that a mental state determines an action theory. In fact, for any mental state $M = (B, E, Q, I, S)$, we add situation variables to each fluent symbol and view B as the set of initial state axioms, E as the set of effect axioms and Q as the set of precondition axioms, then we can exactly get an action theory, denoted by M_{SC}, in situation calculus by attaching the basic axioms of the situation calculus and the associated unique names axioms for actions[4]([11]).

2.3 Representation of Autonomous Agent

As we mentioned before, the behaviors of an autonomous agent are determined by its mental state. On the other hand, an autonomous agent should also be able to manipulate its mental state. In the other words, operating on and being controlled by its mental state is a feature of an autonomous agent. Such characteristic of self-government comes from the abilities of agency as follows:

Ability to reason: estimate its current state, evaluate feasibility of actions and etc. We use a consequence operator C, which could be monotonic or nonmonotonic, consistent or inconsistent, to express agent's reasoning ability. $\varphi \in C(B)$ means that the agent thinks that φ is true according to its current belief state B.

Ability to decide future actions: make a decision for its future action. We use an action choice function H to specify such an ability.

Ability to update mental state: When an agent takes an action, its mental state may change with the action. We represent such a procedure by a mental state updating function T.

With the above analysis, we can define autonomous agents as follows:

Definition 1 Let $\mathcal{M}$ be a non-empty set of mental states and $\mathcal{A}_h$ a set of ground primitive actions. An *autonomous agent* is a four-tuple $(\mathcal{M}, C, H, T)$, where C is a consequence operator, $H : \mathcal{M} \rightarrow \mathcal{A}_h$ and $T : \mathcal{M} \times \mathcal{A}_h \rightarrow \mathcal{M}$.

Paraphrasing this definition, an autonomous agent acts in this manner: it reasons by means of consequence operator C, chooses its next action in terms of H, and updates its mental state by T. Therefore, an autonomous agent can be described by the following *main procedure of automonous agent*.

```
procedure agent(M)      /* M = (B, E, Q, I, S)
    while I ≠ φ do
    a ::= H(M)          /* Choose the next action.
    execute a
    M ::= T(M, a)       /* Update mental state.
    endwhile
endpro
```

3 Construction of Autonomous Agents

According to Definition 1, the main problem in building an autonomous agent is how to construct the functions: C, H and T. In fact, different designs of these functions may reveal different degrees of autonomy and elicit quite different

---

[4] Due to the space limitation, we omit the treatment of the frame problem.

complexity of implementation. In this section, we illustrate how to build an autonomous agent by defining these functions and how to classify autonomous agents by varying the construction of such functions.

Before we start, we need some terminology to describe some basic attributes of action and agent.

A primitive action $a(\mathbf{t})$ is *feasible* w.r.t a mental state M if there exists a feasibility rule $(a(\mathbf{t}), \gamma(\mathbf{t})) \in Q$ such that $\gamma(\mathbf{t}) \in C(B)$. An intention set I of a mental state M is *achieved* w.r.t M if for any intention $(\alpha, g, p, r) \in I$, $g \in C(B)$.

For any given agent $(\mathcal{M}, C, H, T)$ and $M_0 \in \mathcal{M}$, a sequence $(a_1, M_1) \circ \cdots \circ (a_n, M_n)$ is a *run of the agent from M_0* if for any k $(1 \leq k \leq n)$, i). $M_k \in \mathcal{M}$; ii). $H(M_{k-1}) = a_k$; iii). $T(M_{k-1}, a_k) = M_k$.

Such a run is *feasible* if a_k is feasible w.r.t M_{k-1} for every k $(1 \leq k \leq n)$. It is *successful* if the intention of the last mental state M_n is achieved.

A mental state M is *achievable* if there exists a successful run from it.

3.1 Simple Autonomous Agents

Let us start with a kind of autonomous agents which have relatively simple structure. This sort of agents can reason with classical logic, decide their future actions and update their mental state autonomously, but have limited foresight.

To construct such an agent, we firstly assume that the consequence function C is the one of classical first-order logic. So we will use Cn instead of C.

Next, we consider the construction of function H. Let α be a closed action term. We call (a, α') a *single step decomposition* (SSD for short) of α if (i). a is the first primitive actions of one of the possible execution paths of α and (ii). α' is the rest part of the associated path (A more precise definition can be given by induction). Then the action choice function in the main procedure is the following:

    function $H(M)$ /* $M = (B, E, Q, I, S)$
        if there exists an intention $(\alpha, g, p, r) \in I$ such that
            1) $\neg g \wedge p \in Cn(B)$
            2) there is a SSD (a, α') of α such that a is feasible;
            3) r is maximal among the intentions in I which satisfy 1) and 2).
        return a
        /* replace the action term of the intention with the rest part.
        $I ::= I \cup \{(\alpha', g, p, r)\} \setminus \{(\alpha, g, p, r)\}$
        else
            return Θ /* Θ is a special primitive action means *stalling*.
        endif
    endfun

Finally, we give the definition of function T. For any belief set B and action a, let $B \diamond a$ be the updating operator which is defined in the spirit of Winslett's possible model approach (PMA) (see [14] and [6], due to the limitation of space, we omit its definition). Then the mental state updating function is:

```
function T(M, a)       /* M = (B, E, Q, I, S)
    B ::= B◇a
    I ::= I ∪ \{i ∈ I : i.goal ∈ Cn(B)}      /* delete all the achieved intentions.
    return (B, E, Q, I, S)
endfun
```

We call the resultant agent a *simple autonomous agent*. According to the construction of action choice function, the following claim is obviously true:

Claim 1 *Any run of a simple autonomous agent is feasible.*

We say a run $(a_1, M_1) \circ \cdots \circ (a_n, M_n)$ is *ended* if $I_n = \phi$ or $a_n = \Theta$. It is easy to see that any successful run of a simple autonomous agent is ended. Unfortunately, the reverse is not true. The following example shows us that a simple autonomous agent may only look forward one feasible step. If there are several feasible choices, it does not have the ability to estimate which one can eventually reach its goals.

Example 2 Consider an intention set $I = \{(pickup(a); (stack(a,c) \cup stack(a,d)); pickup(b); stack(b,c), on(b,c), \top, 1)\}$. Let M_0 is a mental state in which the intention set is I and the other components are as same as the ones in Example 1. Then a simple autonomous agent could have two possible runs from this mental state:

$(pickup(a), M_1) \circ (stack(a,c), M_2) \circ (pickup(b), M_3) \circ (\Theta, M_4)$
$(pickup(a), M_1) \circ (stack(a,d), M_2) \circ (pickup(b), M_3) \circ (stack(b,c), M_4)$

Only the second one is successful, but it could be ignored by a simple autonomous agent.

3.2 Deliberative Agents

A natural question is how to construct an autonomous agent so that it can always achieve its goals if they are achievable.

To construct such an agent, we first reduce an intention set into a singleton. This can be done by the following two steps:

Step 1. *Elimination of Prerequisites*

For any intention $(\alpha, g, q, r) \in I$, let $q(\alpha)$ be an action generated inductively as follows:

$q(a) = q?; a$, where a is a primitive action;
$q(B?) = B?$
$q(\alpha \# \beta) = q(\alpha) \# q(\beta)$, where $\#$ can be $;, \cup, ||, \gg$;
$q(\alpha^*) = (q(\alpha))^*$

Then replace (α, g, q, r) with $(q(\alpha), g, \top, r)$ in I.

Step 2. *Reduction of Intention Set*

Let $i^1, \cdots, i^n$ be a permutation of the elements in I in the decreasing order of ratings. We write $\alpha_I = \alpha_{i^1} \gg (\text{or } ||) \cdots \gg (\text{or } ||) \alpha_{i^n}$, where α_{i^j} means the action term of intention i^j and $\gg (\text{or } ||)$ means if the ratings of two intention rules are equal, then we use $||$, otherwise use $\gg$. Let $g_I = \bigwedge_{i \in I} g_i$.

With this two steps, we can reduce any intention set I into a singleton $(\alpha_I, g_I, \top, 1)$.

Now we extend the definition of predicate Do in [8] by the one of $Tran$ in [5], and redefine it as follows: for any action α,

1. if α is a primitive action, then $Do(\alpha, s, s') \stackrel{def}{=} \exists (a, \gamma) \in Q(a = \alpha \wedge \gamma[s] \wedge s' = [s; \alpha]$.
2. if $\alpha = \phi?, \alpha_1; \alpha_2, \alpha_1 \cup \alpha_2, \pi x \alpha_1(x)$ and α_1^*, $Do(\alpha, s, s')$ is defined as same as in [8].
3. if $\alpha = \alpha_1 || \alpha_2$ and $\alpha_1 \gg \alpha_2$, $Do(\alpha, s, s')$ is defined as same as $Tran$ in [5].
4. if α is a strategy, $Do(\alpha, s, s') \stackrel{def}{=} \exists (a, \beta) \in S(\alpha = a \wedge Do(\beta, s, s'))$.

We say that an intention set I is *workable* in the mental state M if $M_{SC} \models \exists s (Do(\alpha_I, [\,], s) \wedge g_I[s])$, where α_I and g_I are defined as above.

A mental state is *workable* if its intention is workable in M.

Then we a call simple autonomous agent *deliberative* if we lift up the condition 2) in the function $H(M)$ with the following extra item:

$I' = I \cup \{(\alpha_1', g, p, r)\} \setminus \{(\alpha, g, p, r)\}$ *is workable in the current mental state.*

Then we have

Claim 2 *Any ended run of a deliberative agent from a workable mental state is successful.*

It is easy to see that for the intention in Example 2, a deliberative agent can only have the second run.

3.3 Planning Agents

Even though a deliberative agent may be much more "foresighted" than a simple autonomous agents, it works only when its intention contains a *right* action plan for its goals. In fact, that a mental state is not workable does not mean it is not achievable. An intention set can be unworkable when an intention in it has an empty action ε, or when a run results in an empty action without the goal being achieved. In this case, we need to generate proper actions for unachieved goals. This requires an autonomous agent to have the ability to plan.

It is well-known that there is no practical solution to all-purpose planning. Theoretically, however, if a goal is achievable with respect to an action theory, there must be a program or an action to achieve it ([7]). Now suppose we have had a planner $planning(g, M)$. For any input of goal g and mental state M, it can always return a feasible action if this goal is achievable with respect to M, otherwise, returns ε. With this planner, we rewrite the action choice function $H(M)$ by replacing the sentence "**return** Θ" with following sentence:

    if there is $(\varepsilon, g, p, r) \in I$ such that $\neg g \wedge p \in Cn(B)$ and r is maximal
        $\alpha ::= Planning(g, M)$ /*invoke planner
        $I ::= (I \setminus \{(\varepsilon, g, p, r)\}) \cup \{(\alpha, g, p, r)\}$
    endif

We call a deliberative agent with the above modification a *planning agent*. Then we have

Claim 3 *Any run of a planning agent from an achievable mental state is successful.*

It is easy to see that if a planning agent starts with an achievable mental state, it can always end and only need to invoke planner once.

3.4 Autonomous Agents with Communication

The previous subsections defined autonomy by varying the ability of action decision and keeping the other components constant. We note that in the above construction, the mental state updating function can only update two components of its mental state: belief and intention. In fact, if an agent can autonomously change the other components, it could display higher autonomy and flexibility. Moreover, if these agents are endowed with the ability of communication, which is generally viewed as one of essential attributes of agency, they could reach higher levels of autonomy. We outline the nature of these more autonomous agents.

Communicative agents: a kind of autonomous agents which can communicate with other agents or people and as a result changes their belief with new information([3]). Because the belief set may dynamically change, none of the claims we have made about the previous constructed agents are necessarily true. Another difficulty in realizing such an agent is when and how an agent revises its belief. In the other words, an agent needs to evaluate the information from different sources and reconstruct its belief set. In this case, the belief updating function should be replaced by some kind of belief revision function in order to deal with possible inconsistency.

Learning agents: a kind of communicative agents which can learn from the environment and other agents in order to obtain more and newer knowledge and strategies([3]). The difficulty about this kind of agent lies in the fusion of knowledge. Knowledge or strategies from other agents or public resources may not be applicable for their intention.

Adaptive agents: a kind of learning agent which can change its behavior for the better achievement of its goals with its previous or other agent's experience(strategies) ([9]). For instance, such an agent can add or delete intentions according to external requests or its own strategies, and as a result, its goals, intentions and focus could change dynamically.

4 Conclusion

In this paper, we have presented a framework for describing autonomous agent and its mental state. This framework provides us with a coordinate system of four dimensions: representation of mental state, ability of reasoning, ability of action decision and ability of mental state revision. We have illustrated how it can be used to classify autonomous agents by constructing three different kinds of agent, varying the ability of action decision and keeping the other components constant. We also glanced at higher autonomy in which the ability of mental state revision is variable.

With this coordinate system, people can specify their criteria of autonomous agency by setting thresholds for each dimensions or their combinations and judge whether a program is an autonomous agent based on these criteria. For instance, an infinite loop is not an autonomous agent because of poor internal state representation and communication ability with outside. An operation system may not qualify as an autonomous agent because of the lack of goal-orientation or its low level of action decision. A computer virus could be viewed as an autonomous agent provided it can cross each threshold of each dimension.

We would like to remark that the agents described in this paper are only the theoretical models of autonomous agents, which may not be suitable for implementation. In fact, what we highlighted is the difficulty of the realization of autonomy. For instance, as far as action decision is concerned, a simple autonomous agent needs linear time whereas a deliberative agent requires second-order reasoning and a planning agent even more. Therefore we think that it should be a great challenge for AI researchers to realize high level autonomous agents.

References

1. C. Castelfranchi, Guarantees for autonomy in cognitive agent architecture, In: *M. Wooldridge and N. R. Jennings, eds., Intelligence Agents: Theories, Architectures, and Languages,* Springer, 1995, 56-70.
2. P. Cohn and H. Levesque, Intention is choice with commitment, A*rtificial Intelligence* 42(1990), 213-261, 1990.
3. S. Franklin and A. Graesser, Is it an agent, or just a program?: a taxonomy for autonomous agents,In:*Proceedings of the Third International Workshop on Agent Theories, Architectures, and Languages, Intelligent Agent III*, Springer, 21-35,1997.
4. M. Georgeff, B. Pell, M. Pollack, M. Tambe and M. Wooldridge, The belief-desire-intention model of agency, *Proceedings of the 5th International Workshop on Intelligent Agents V : Agent Theories, Architectures and Languages (ATAL-98)*, 1-10, Springer, 1999.
5. G. De Giacomo, Y. Lespérance and Hector J. Levesque, Reasoning about concurrent execution, prioritized interrupts, and exogenous actions in the situation calculus, In: *IJCAI-97*, 1221-1226, 1997.
6. H. Katsuno and A. O. Mendelzo, On the difference between updating a knowledge base and revising it, In: *KR'91*, 387-395,1991.
7. H.J. Levesque. What is planning in the presence of sensing?, *AAAI-96*, 1139–1146,1996.
8. H. J. Levesque, R. Reiter, Yves Lespérance, Fangzhan Lin, and Richard B. Scherl, GOLOG: a logic programming language for dynamic domanins, *Journal of Logic Programming*, 31:59-84, 1997.
9. P. Maes, Modeling adaptive autonomous agents, *Artificial Life*, Vol. 1, No.1&2, 135-162, 1994.
10. E. Pednault, ADL: exploring the middle ground between STRIPS and the situation calculus, In: *KR'89*, 324-332, 1989.
11. F. Pirri and R. Reiter, Some contributions to the metatheory of the situation calculus. *J.ACM,* 3(46), 325-361, 1999.

12. S. Shapiro, Y. Lespérance, and H.J. Levesque. Specifying Communicative Multi-Agent Systems with ConGolog. In: W. Wobcke *et. al.* eds. *Agents and Multi-Agent Systems - Formalisms, Methodologies, and Applications*, 1-14, Springer-Verlag, 1998.
13. A. Sloman, What sort of architecture is required for a human-like agent? *Cognitive Modeling Workshop, AAAI-96*, Protland Oregon, Aug 1996.
14. M. Winslett, Reasoning about action using a possible models approach,In: *AAAI-88*, 89-93,1988.
15. M. Wooldridge and N.R. Jennings, Intelligent agent: theory and practice, *The Knowledge Engineering Review*, 10 (2), 115-152,1995.

Constructing an Autonomous Agent with an Interdependent Heuristics

Koichi Moriyama and Masayuki Numao

Department of Computer Science,
Graduate School of Information Science and Engineering,
Tokyo Institute of Technology.
2–12–1, Ookayama, Meguro, Tokyo, 152–8552, Japan.
koichi@nm.cs.titech.ac.jp, numao@cs.titech.ac.jp

Abstract. When we construct an agent by integrating modules, there appear troubles concerning the autonomy of the agent if we introduce a heuristics that dominates the whole agent. Thus, we design an agent that has an interdependent heuristics influenced by a module controlled by the heuristics, and we apply these agents into a problem of obtaining cooperation of Multi-Agents. We enable a present method that can solve the problem in a reinforcement learning context to be applied into a dynamic environment, and the improved method is embodied into the agent as the interdependent heuristics. We conduct experiments comparing the proposed agents with agents such as those ones each of which has a heuristics controlled by a supervisor, then we empirically confirm that the proposed agent having the interdependent heuristics is the most flexible of all the tested agent.

1 Introduction

Many researchers want to construct autonomous agents that do not need to be controlled directly by a human during execution time. It might seem easy to construct the autonomous agent by introducing in advance some heuristics into the agent. If these heuristics are *absolute* for the whole agent, however, there appear troubles concerning the autonomy of the agent. Therefore, in this paper, we design an agent that does *not* have any absolute heuristics, but has an *interdependent* heuristics that is influenced by a module controlled by the heuristics.

We apply the agents to a problem of obtaining cooperation of Multi-Agents (MA) as an example of auto-adaptation of the agent to a changing environment. To solve this problem in a reinforcement learning context, Mikami et al. [4, 5] proposed the reward filtering method that uses a *filtered* reward instead of a reward itself in a reinforcement learning process. This method can be regarded as a kind of heuristics of the problem. However, since their method uses several fixed filtering functions only one of which is selected in advance by a designer, it is useless in a problem whose class we do not know in advance or whose conditions are variable. Therefore, we propose a parameterized filtering function called *General Filter*. Since General Filter can work as one of all the original filtering functions by changing its parameters, it is important for the agent to get a way of controlling the parameters. Thus, in this paper, we embody General Filter into the agent with providing a learning mechanism for the parameters. To learn the parameters, however, the evaluation of the parameters is needed. So we introduce two evaluation methods: an *interdependent* one described above and a *subordinate* one that is subject to an absolute factor introduced by a designer. We also introduce another type of General Filter whose parameters are *controlled by a supervisor* that can check up on all the agents in the problem. We conduct experiments comparing several fixed filters and these three General Filters in a problem of obtaining cooperation of MA in order to determine the comparative performance of our proposed General Filter *with the interdependent evaluation*.

This paper is organized as follows. In Section 2, we describe troubles caused by an absolute heuristics and give an outline of an agent having an interdependent heuristics. In Section 3, we introduce the reward filtering method and propose General Filter. Then we embody General Filter into the agent outlined in Section 2 with the interdependent evaluation. In Section 4, we conduct experiments in a problem of obtaining cooperation of MA in order to compare the proposed agents embodied in Section 3 with agents such as those ones each of which has General Filter controlled by a supervisor. In Section 5, we discuss the result of the experiments and the social role of filters. In Section 6, we conclude this paper and mention several future works.

2 Outline of an Agent

We suppose that an agent has a learning module and a heuristic module for the learning module, perceives the outside environment through a sensor, acts to it through an actuator, and receives rewards from it. When we introduce a heuristics into the agent in advance, we usually tend to give *absolute power* for it. The structure of an agent having an absolute heuristics is shown in Fig. 1.

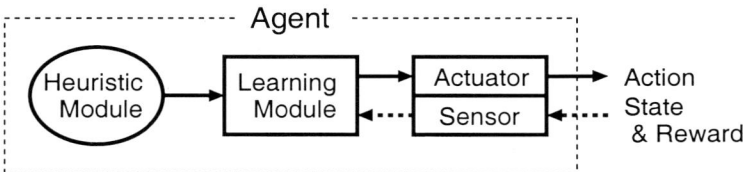

Fig. 1. Outline of an agent having an absolute heuristic module: solid arrows mean controls and dotted arrows mean data flows.

When an agent has a heuristic module that has absolute power, there appear troubles concerning the autonomy of the agent. If the absolute heuristics is fixed, it should be effective for all inputs of the agent. This might be feasible in a very simple environment, but, in a complex environment, a fixed heuristics causes troubles like the frame problem [6]. On the other hand, if the absolute heuristics is variable, the problem switches to determining who changes the heuristics. If the heuristics directly controls actions of the agent, we are able to avoid these troubles because we can give the agent a learning mechanism that learns the actions from the *outside information*. However, in this paper, since the heuristic module controls the learning module in the agent, the heuristics can only control actions of the agent indirectly. Then, if a human is needed to change the heuristics, the agent is not autonomous anymore, and if it is supposed that a meta heuristics changes the heuristics, on the other hand, similar troubles described in this paragraph occur to the meta heuristics again.

In order to avoid the troubles, by extending the *interdependency* between the agent and the environment described above, we design an agent that does *not* have any absolute heuristics, but has an *interdependent* heuristics that is influenced by the learning module controlled by the heuristics. The structure of the agent having an interdependent heuristics is shown in Fig. 2. The arrow labeled by an asterisk (∗) in Fig. 2 represents the interdependency between the learning module and the heuristic module.

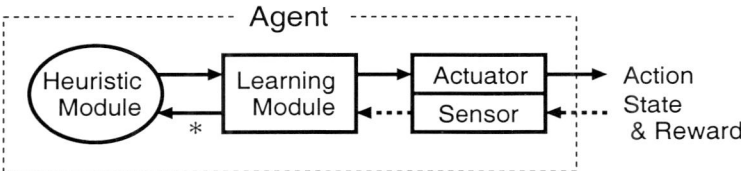

Fig. 2. Outline of an agent having an interdependent heuristic module: the arrow labeled by an asterisk (∗) represents the interdependency between the learning module and the heuristic module.

3 Obtaining Cooperation of Multi-agents

3.1 Classification of Multi-agent Problems

In [2], problems for obtaining cooperation of Multi-Agents (MA) are classified into two classes[1].

- Cooperative Problem Solving
  Achieving common purposes among agents.
- Negotiation and Balancing
  Dealing with competition among agents.

---
[1] In fact, in [2], this classification is given for Distributed Artificial Intelligence (DAI). At first, the studies of MA were formulated as a part of the studies of DAI, but the difference between MA and the rest of DAI is fading away now [2].

Agents engaged in a problem belonging to the former class have common purposes, so their motives for cooperation, if they have, are to solve the problem faster, more effectively, and so on. Agents in a problem in the latter class, on the other hand, have independent purposes, so their motives for cooperation are to avoid deadlocks caused by shared resources.

3.2 Reward Filtering Method

To solve problems in the two classes described above in a reinforcement learning context, Mikami et al. [4,5] proposed a method using a *filtered* reward instead of a reward itself in a reinforcement learning process. In their proposal, in order to filter its own reward, an agent uses a fixed filter constructed as a function of the mean reward of agents in the neighborhood of the agent, including the agent itself. These agents are called *neighbors* of the agent. Mikami et al. defined two types of filtering functions: Average Filter and Enhancement Filter. Average Filter flattens a reward that is over/under the mean reward of neighbors. Enhancement Filter, on the other hand, exaggerates a reward that is under the mean reward of neighbors. It has been shown in [4] that Average Filter and Enhancement Filter are effective for a problem in Cooperative Problem Solving and for a problem in the class called Deadlock Avoidance Problem similar to Negotiation and Balancing, respectively. Therefore, these filters can be regarded as a kind of heuristics for learning.

3.3 General Filter

Since the filters defined by Mikami et al. are fixed, they are useless in a problem whose class we do not know in advance and/or whose conditions are variable. So we propose a parameterized filter defined as follows:

$$r' = \begin{cases} M + \alpha(r - M) & \text{if } r < M \\ M + \beta(r - M) & \text{otherwise.} \end{cases}$$

In this definition, for a particular agent, r means a reward of the agent, r' means a filtered reward of the agent, M means the mean reward of neighbors of the agent, and α and β are parameters. This filter can represent all the original filters defined in [4] and other filters through a proper setting of the parameters. So we call this parameterized filter *General Filter*.

In the following, we use the term "the parameters" to refer to the parameters α and β of General Filter defined above. If an agent can adjust the parameters appropriately according to the changes in the environment, then the agent is able to make a heuristics that is effective for the problem whose class we do not know in advance and/or whose conditions are variable. Therefore, it is important for the agent to get a way of controlling the parameters. In this paper, we consider that the agent *learns* proper modifications of the parameters.

3.4 Embodying General Filter into an Agent

In this subsection, we discuss how to embody General Filter into an agent having an interdependent heuristics. On the agent structure shown in Fig. 2, the following modifications should be done:

- Divide the learning module into two components, one with Reinforcement Learning Module (RLM), and the other one with General Filter.
- Change the heuristic module to Parameters Learning Module (PLM), which is in charge of controlling General Filter.

By these modifications alone, however, there are two issues: the agent has no arrow labeled by an asterisk in Fig. 2, and, in order to learn the parameters in PLM, PLM needs the evaluation of the parameters. To solve these issues, we propose that the parameters are evaluated by RLM.

As a result of the modifications, the structure of the agent having General Filter with the interdependent evaluation takes the form shown in Fig. 3.

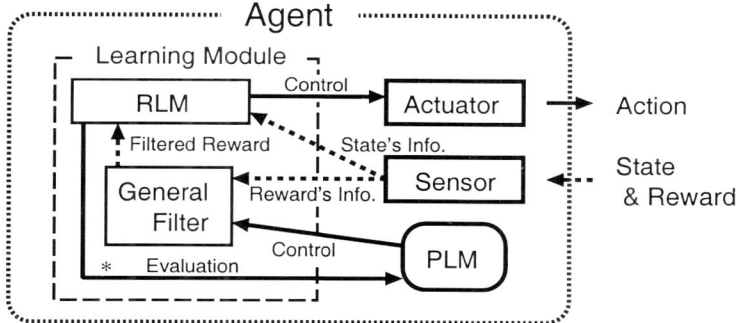

Fig. 3. The agent having General Filter with the interdependent evaluation

4 Experiments

In order to determine the comparative performance of our proposal, we conduct two experiments comparing the agent shown in Fig. 3 with several variants of the agent in a problem of obtaining cooperation of Multi-Agents (MA). Due to space limitations, we only show here the result applying the agents to a problem in the class Cooperative Problem Solving.

4.1 Preparation

As the experimental problem, owing to [4], we use a game similar to the *tragedy of the commons* [1] for the experiment. This problem is famous in the domain of game theory [7]. The tragedy of the commons means that if each player acts according to his/her *individual* rationality, it is happened that certain *common* property among the players is decreased and, in consequence, his/her own payoff is also decreased. Since the players must cooperate with one another to get more payoffs, this problem is an example in the class Cooperative Problem Solving.

An agent in our game has three actions: selfish, cooperative, and altruistic. In every cycle, each agent in the game shows an action simultaneously and gets a reward calculated by the actions of *all* the agents in the cycle. It is defined that the reward given for a particular agent in a particular situation is maximum when the agent acts selfishly, and minimum when the agent acts altruistically. However, it is also defined that negative common property (common cost) among the agents is increased when an agent acts selfishly and decreased when an agent acts altruistically, so the reward of each agent is small when all the agents act selfishly. If the variation of the common cost r_c is represented to Δr_c, the common cost r_c, initialized to zero at every cycle beginning, is added by Δr_c if an agent acts selfishly, is not changed if an agent acts cooperatively, and is subtracted by Δr_c if an agent acts altruistically. Once the common cost r_c has been calculated by the actions of all the agents, each agent gets a reward of $3 - r_c$ if the agent acts selfishly, $1 - r_c$ if the agent acts cooperatively, and $-3 - r_c$ if the agent acts altruistically.

We conduct two experiments: one is in a *static* environment, the other is in a *dynamic* environment. The static environment is the one where all factors except for agents are static. The dynamic environment is, on the other hand, the one where some factors besides agents are also variable. In this paper, in order to realize these environments, we make the parameter Δr_c fixed in the static environment and make it variable according to the number of cycles in the dynamic environment.

We use ten agents each of which has an unique ID in the experiments. Neighbors N_i of an agent a_i ($0 \leq i \leq 9$) are defined as follows:

$$N_i \triangleq \{a_k \mid k = (i+j) \bmod 10, \ j = 0, 1, 2, 3\}.$$

Note that the neighbors include the agent itself.

In order to determine the comparative performance of our proposal, we have conducted the experiments comparing the following six types of agent. These types are divided into two groups: having a fixed filter or having General Filter. We describe three fixed filters first, then describe three General Filters. The three fixed filters are No Filter (NF), Full Average Filter (FAF), and Full Enhancement Filter (FEF). The agent having NF uses rewards themselves in learning. FAF is a filter into which the original two Average Filters defined in [4] are merged. FEF is a filter into which the original Enhancement Filter defined in [4] and an opposite Enhancement Filter are merged[2]. NF, FAF, and FEF are represented

---

[2] Since the original Enhancement Filter exaggerates a reward *under* the mean reward of neighbors, we introduce an opposite Enhancement Filter that exaggerates a reward *over* the mean reward of neighbors. The original Enhancement Filter has a parameter determining the degree of exaggeration of rewards, and we set this parameter to 1.

as $r' = r$, $r' = M$, and $r' = 2r - M$, respectively. Symbols in the equations are identical with the ones described in Section 3.3.

The three General Filters are distinguished according to the way of evaluation of the parameters. The first type is that the parameters in an agent are evaluated by the *interdependent* method described so far (GF-Int). As the interdependent evaluation, the filtered reward, which is used in Reinforcement Learning Module (RLM), is *sign-inversed* in RLM and this sign-inversed filtered reward is sent to Parameters Learning Module (PLM). The second type is that the parameters in an agent are evaluated by a *subordinate* method using the sum of rewards the agent gets in a certain time interval fixed in advance (GF-Sub). As the fixed interval, we use ten cycles. The third type is that we introduce a *supervisor* that can check up on rewards of all the agents, and the parameters in the agents are controlled by the supervisor directly (GF-Sv).

In RLM, for an agent, states used for learning are defined as the combination of the actions of neighbors of the agent. This means that the agent can get only the local information about the environment. The mean reward of the neighbors, necessary for filtering a reward of the agent, is calculated by filtered rewards of them. The reinforcement signal used for learning suitable actions is a reward filtered by the filter the agent has inside.

For General Filter, initial values of the parameters are both set to 1, then the filter is identical with No Filter. We set upper and lower bounds of the parameters to 0 and 2, respectively. The parameters are modified, in a particular cycle, *before* a reward got by the agent is filtered.

When the parameters are changed in an agent itself, PLM learns three modifications, namely increasing, maintaining, and decreasing *each* parameter, through a reinforcement learning method. States used for learning the parameters are the modification itself of each parameter, and the range of this modification is determined randomly after considering the frequency of learning and modifying the parameters in PLM. This frequency is identical with the frequency of evaluating the parameters. Therefore, in this paper, when PLM is evaluated by the interdependent method, PLM modifies the parameters at every cycle, or when PLM is evaluated by the subordinate method, on the other hand, PLM modifies the parameters at every ten cycles.

When the parameters are changed by a supervisor, on the other hand, the supervisor learns the same three modifications of each parameter described above through reinforcement signals each of which is the sum of rewards got by all agents in a cycle. The supervisor directly modifies the parameters in all the agents at every cycle.

As the reinforcement learning method, we use Q-learning [8] with the learning rate and the discount factor both set to 0.5. Action selections using Q-values follow the probability calculated by Boltzman distribution [3] with the temperature set to 1.

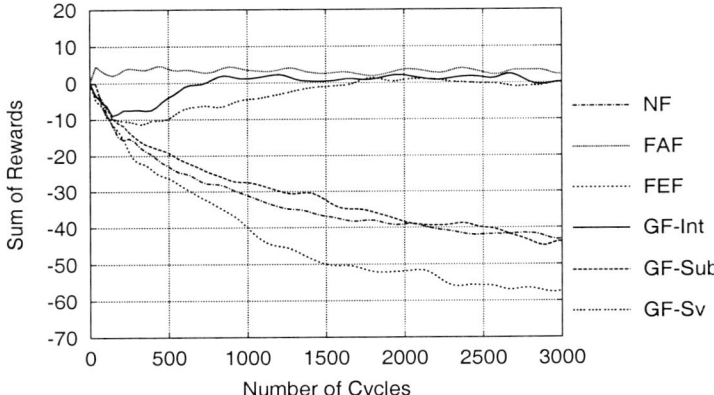

Fig. 4. Result in a static environment: each line in the plot shows the sum of rewards of the agents when applying the filter whose label is printed in the right part of the figure. NF stands for No Filter. FAF stands for Full Average Filter. FEF stands for Full Enhancement Filter. GF-Int stands for General Filter evaluated interdependently. GF-Sub stands for General Filter evaluated subordinately. GF-Sv stands for General Filter controlled by a supervisor.

4.2 Result in a Static Environment

Here we show the result of a experiment in a static environment. In this paper, to make the environment static, we set the parameter Δr_c to the constant value 1.

Figure 4 shows the result of this experiment. The horizontal axis designates the cycles of the game, and the vertical axis represents the sum of rewards got by all the agents. Each line is plotted every five cycles and approximated with a Bézier curve.

This figure shows that

- When using whether NF, FEF, or GF-Sub, the sum of rewards decreases as the number of cycles increases. This means that the tragedy of the commons is occurring.
- When using FAF, the line in the plot is almost horizontal. This indicates that FAF manages to keep a high value of the sum of rewards, thereby avoiding the occurrence of the tragedy of the commons.
- When using whether GF-Int or GF-Sv, although the sum of rewards decreases at the beginning, it stops decreasing halfway and starts increasing until it sets close to the sum of rewards of FAF. This means that both evaluations of General Filter are able to learn the proper parameters that can avoid the tragedy of the commons.

4.3 Result in a Dynamic Environment

On the other hand, we show here a result of a experiment in a dynamic environment. To make the environment dynamic, we make the parameter Δr_c variable

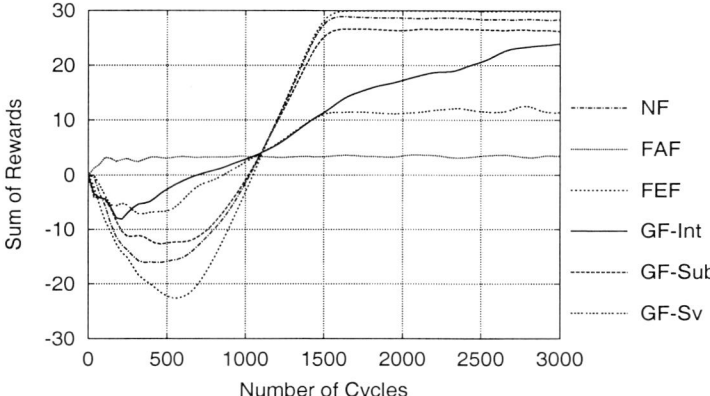

Fig. 5. Result in a dynamic environment: the label of each line is identical with the one in Fig. 4.

according to the number of cycles as follows:

$$\Delta r_c = \begin{cases} 1 - \dfrac{cycles}{1500} & \text{if } cycles < 1500 \\ 0 & \text{otherwise.} \end{cases}$$

This definition of the parameter Δr_c implies that the agents should be cooperative at the beginning and do not have to be at the end.

Figure 5 shows the result of this experiment. The plot in the figure was constructed in a similar way to the one shown in Fig. 4.

This figure shows that

- When using whether NF, FEF, or GF-Sub, the sum of rewards decreases at the beginning, and it increases at the end. This means that the performance of these filters is simply influenced by the change of Δr_c.
- When using FAF, the line in the plot is almost horizontal. This means that FAF can not adapt to the changes in the environment.
- When using whether GF-Int or GF-Sv, at the beginning, the filter tries to be like FAF, but it tries to be like NF and others at the end. This means that GF-Int and GF-Sv can learn the proper parameters to be the best filter for the conditions of the environment. Note that although the sum of rewards of GF-Sv stopped increasing halfway, that of GF-Int continues to increase to that of NF and others. This means that the adaptability of GF-Int is superior to that of GF-Sv.

5 Discussion

In the experiment, although it is natural that General Filters were more adaptable than the fixed filters, General Filter with the interdependent evaluation, in particular, was the most flexible of all the tested filters. We used the sign-inversed filtered reward got in a cycle as the interdependent evaluation of General Filter. Here we consider the reason why the operation of sign-inversion is good for learning the proper modifications of the parameters in a changing environment first.

It is true that, in a cycle, the parameters of General Filter are changed *before* the filter controls a reward, but we must consider that there is a time gap between the cycle in which the parameters are modified by Parameters Learning Module (PLM) and the cycle in which the agent performs an action influenced by these modified parameters. Since the parameters have an immediate effect on the learning module and not on the actuator of the agent, the influence of modification of the parameters is lately appeared in the action of the agent. Thus, for a particular cycle, an action of the agent producing a reward is the result of learning from filtered rewards that were calculated using the parameters *before modified*. Therefore, although the parameters have been renewed by PLM before the agent learns its behavior through Reinforcement Learning Module, the filtered reward is mainly influenced by the *former* values of the parameters. If the filtered reward is small, that is, the reward of the agent is also small, the former values of the parameters should be modified because they are not suitable for the environment. This means that the modification of the parameters is laudable, so the modification should receive a big reward. Similarly, if the filtered reward is big, the modification of the parameters should receive a small reward. These relations between the filtered reward and the evaluation of the parameters may be represented in the operation of sign-inversion. Thus, General Filter with the interdependent evaluation was the most flexible of all.

Next, we argue about the social role of filters. In the experiment, Full Average Filter (FAF) produced good results when cooperation among agents was needed. FAF cut a reward of an agent over and under the mean reward of neighbors of the agent, and the agent learns its behavior using this cut reward. Note that this cutting is executed in the agent itself, namely, is executed *not* out of the agent, even if the agent has General Filter controlled by a supervisor. Thus, since the filter can change the *internal* evaluation, which the agent has inside, of the environment, the filter might be regarded as a kind of characteristic or emotional parameter of the agent. Now we can consider that the character of an agent having FAF is reformed not to pursue rewards by the filter. This agent was not rational anymore in the sense used in game theory, so Multi-Agents in which each agent has FAF were able to avoid the tragedy of the commons.

6 Conclusion

In this paper, we have designed an agent that has two interdependent modules, the learning module and the heuristic module, which both influence each other. Then we applied the agent to a problem of obtaining cooperation of Multi-Agents. We introduced the reward filtering method to solve this problem, and constructed General Filter that could adapt to the changes in the environment. In the proposed agent having General Filter with the interdependent evaluation, the parameters of General Filter were evaluated by Reinforcement Learning Module in order to realize the interdependency between the modules. From the result of the experiment with several alternatives for the structure of the agent, it was confirmed that the agent whose modules were interdependent, proposed in this paper, was the most flexible of all the tested agent for the changes in the environment. In the discussion, we considered that the filter was like a kind of characteristic or emotional parameter of the agent.

We point out the future works as follows. First, we must formulate the mathematical properties of the interdependent evaluation used in this paper. We might be able to use knowledge from the mathematical analyses done in system theory and game theory. Second, we must realize the interdependency without sign-inversion that is a kind of heuristics. In other words, the learning module in the agent must automatically obtain how to evaluate the heuristic module.

References

1. Garrett Hardin. The Tragedy of the Commons. *Science*, 162:1243–1248, 1968.
2. Toru Ishida and Kazuhiro Kuwabara. Distributed Artificial Intelligence (1): Cooperative Problem Solving. *Journal of Japanese Society for Artificial Intelligence*, 7(6):945–954, 1992. (in Japanese).
3. Leslie P. Kaelbling, Michael L. Littman, and Andrew W. Moore. Reinforcement Learning: A Survey. *Journal of Artificial Intelligence Research*, 4:237–285, 1996.
4. Sadayoshi Mikami and Yukinori Kakazu. Co-operation of Multiple Agents Through Filtering Payoff. In *1st European Workshop for Reinforcement Learning*, 1994.
5. Sadayoshi Mikami, Yukinori Kakazu, and Terence C. Fogarty. Co-operative Reinforcement Learning By Payoff Filters. In *Proc. 8th European Conference on Machine Learning, ECML-95*, (Lecture Notes in Artificial Intelligence 912), pages 319–322, Heraclion, Crete, Greece, 1995.
6. Stuart J. Russell and Peter Norwig. *Artificial Intelligence: A Modern Approach*. Englewood Cliffs, NJ: Prentice-Hall, 1995.
7. Mitsuo Suzuki. *Shin Gehmu Riron* (New Game Theory). Tokyo: Keiso Shobo, 1994. (in Japanese).
8. Christopher J. C. H. Watkins and Peter Dayan. Technical Note: Q-learning. *Machine Learning*, 8:279–292, 1992.

Unified Criterion of State Generalization for Reactive Autonomous Agents

Takehisa Yairi, Koichi Hori and Shinichi Nakasuka

Research Center for Advanced Science and Technology, University of Tokyo
4-6-1 Komaba, Meguro-ku, Tokyo 153-8904, Japan
{yairi, hori, nakasuka}@ai.rcast.u-tokyo.ac.jp

Abstract. Autonomous state generalization problem is a key issue in the research field of behavior learning of reactive agents, and many approaches have been proposed in recent years. However, those existing methods have a diversity in their *criteria of state generalization* or "how to define the similarity or distance between different sensor inputs", while it is not yet clear how this difference in the criteria would affect the entire learning process. In this paper, we first classify and examine those conventional heuristic criteria of state generalization, and then propose a new general framework for unifying all of them. This novel general criterion is based on minimization of weighted sum of entropies in multiple behavior outcomes of agents. An experimental study in the latter part suggests that this state generalization criterion enables a reactive agent to construct or reconstruct its state space in a more efficient and flexible way.

1 Introduction

In recent years, a variety of behavior learning methods have been proposed for autonomous reactive systems. Generally speaking, "behavior learning" of a reactive agent can be viewed as a process of acquiring appropriate mappings or reaction rules between the primitive sensor input and motor output spaces (Fig.1). In most of the existing behavior learning systems, however, primitive sensor and motor spaces are manually abstracted into discrete state and action spaces beforehand, and only the mapping rules between these abstract spaces are supposed to be learned. This is problematic because it is not always easy for the system designers to define such appropriate state and action spaces in advance. Especially, it is possible that an inappropriately defined state space will cause serious problems such as *symbol grounding problem* and *frame problem*.

To deal with this problem, there are two main approaches. One way is to use the continuous sensor spaces *as they are*, i.e., without discretization [4][9]. The other way is to construct discrete state spaces autonomously by generalizing similar sensor inputs [1][2][3][5][8][10][11]. We employ the latter approach in this paper, because it can use the theoretical basis such as convergence guarantees which have been developed for the conventional reinforcement learning research field [7].

The state generalization problem is different from ordinary supervised concept learning problems in that the names (labels) of state classes to which examples (or sensor input vectors) belong are not given in advance. Therefore, another criterion for state generalization or "how to define the similarity or distance between different states (or sensor input vectors)" is required. The existing state generalization methods have employed their own heuristic criteria as to this issue, but it has not been made clear what kind of effects this difference would make on the entire learning processes of agents.

From this background, in this paper we first classify and examine the conventional heuristic criteria for state generalization, and then propose a new general framework for unifying them. This method is based on minimization of weighted sum of entropies in multiple behavior outcomes of agents, and it enables reactive agents to construct or reconstruct their state spaces in a more efficient and flexible way.

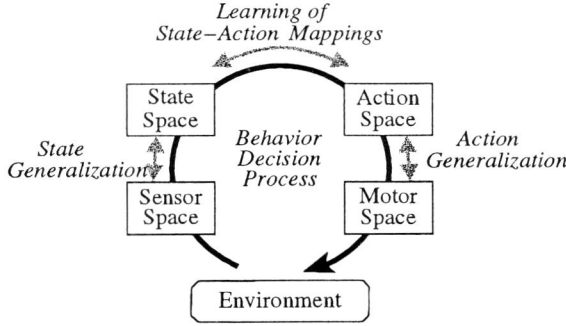

Fig. 1. Behavior decision process of a reactive agent

2 Survey on Conventional Criteria for State Generalization

Existing state generalization methods share a basic idea which can be expressed as: "Generalize a set of sensor inputs which lead to equivalent (or similar) outcomes by equivalent actions into one state class". For example, if we have a series of experiences of "bumping against a door by stepping forward", we can generalize the preconditions of the experiences into a state class of "standing in front of door". While this heuristics seems to be almost reasonable, there is a fundamental question - "how to define the similarity among the different behavior outcomes before generalizing states ?". As to this issue, we found that those previous works can be generally classified into three types as follows.

2.1 State Generalization Based on Goal/Subgoal Achievement

The first one is the state generalization based on *goal/subgoal state achievement*, in which sensor inputs are generalized into a new subgoal state when an agent reaches the goal state by equivalent actions, and then more subgoals are generated repeatedly in the same way when the agent reaches the subgoal states previously generated. This state generalization strategy is employed in [1][2][11].

Although an agent with this strategy obtains *optimal* behavior policy in which it can reach the final goal state from any initial state, application of this state generalization method is limited to very simple tasks which have the one and only goal state. Moreover, this strategy becomes very inefficient for the tasks in which the goal state is rarely encountered, because the agent requires more trials and errors to accumulate positive examples of reaching the goal. Re-use of acquired knowledge to other tasks is also difficult, because it heavily depends on a specific task environment.

2.2 State Generalization Based on Reward Acquisition

The second one is the state generalization based on *similar reward acquisition*, in which sensor inputs of the behavior experiences obtaining identical (or similar) rewards from the environment are generalized into one state class. While [5] considers only direct rewards, [3] and [10] take also discounted rewards obtained by some state transition into account. This state generalization criterion is more general than the first one in that it can be applied to a wide variety of tasks which have more than one positive and negative reward sources. However, state generalization methods with this criterion have the same problem as the first one that they tend to be very inefficient in such environments that rewards are rarely encountered.

2.3 State Generalization Based on Similar Sensor Input Change

The last one is state generalization based on *similar sensor input change or identical state transition*, in which the sensor inputs of the behavior experiences resulting in similar sensor input change[8] or similar state transition[6] are categorized into a state class. What is important is that this strategy is generally efficient in data use, compared with the other two policies, because it does not necessarily require the experiences of reaching goal state or acquiring some rewards to generalize a new state class. This property of independence from goal state and rewards also means that it is comparatively easy to reuse of the state space once acquired. On the other hand, it also has a disadvantage that the constructed state space (set of generalized states) is not necessarily optimal in terms of learning to reach a certain goal or obtain certain positive rewards, because there is a possibility that the sensor space is divided into small pieces meaninglessly based on the behavior experiences unrelated to the goal or reward.

From the above comparison, we can conclude that any of these three generalization criteria has its merits and demerits (Table 1), and it is desirable to combine them. In other words, all of the goal achievement, reward acquisition and sensor input change should be taken into account as agents' behavior outcomes. In the next section, we explain the way of integrating these different criteria.

Table 1. Comparison of state generalization criteria

based on	goal/subgoal	reward	sensor change
Character	Goal-oriented	Reward-oriented	Data-driven
Behavior policy	Obtained	Partially obtained	Learning required
Task dependence	high	high	low
Data usage rate	low	middle	high
Reuse of result	difficult	difficult	easy

3 State Generalization Based on Entropy Minimization of Bahavior Outcomes

In this section, we explain a state generalization method based on entropy minimization of agent's multiple behavior outcomes. Basic idea in this method is to divide a primitive sensor space into a set of discretized states which minimizes the "non-uniformity" (defined by weighted sum of information entropy) of the behavior experiences about the multiple behavior outcomes.

3.1 Problem Definition

First we denote a behavior experience of an agent by $beh = <s, a, r>$ which is a triplet of s (sensor input before action), a (applied action) and r (multiple behavior outcomes). s is a vector in the primitive sensor inputs space $\mathcal{S}$, and a takes a value of the elements of the action set $\mathcal{A} = \{A_1, A_2, \cdots A_{n_a}\}$ (for example, A_1 is "moving forward", A_2 is "rotate right", and so on). It is assumed in this paper that the *behavior outcome vector* $r = [s_{post}, rwd, c_{post}]$ is composed of three elements, s_{post} - sensor input vector after the action, rwd - acquired reward in that behavior, and c_{post} - state class the agent reached by the action. We also assume that $\mathcal{B} = \{beh_1, beh_2, \cdots, beh_{n_b}\}$ is a set of behavior experiences collected by the agent during a certain period and that $\mathcal{C} = \{C_1, C_2, \cdots C_{n_c}\}$ is a set of state classes which should be evaluated. $\mathcal{C}$ partitions the primitive and continuous sensor input space into non-overlapping subspaces.

Now we consider dividing the whole experience set $\mathcal{B}$ into subsets by classifying s and a of each experience into C_j and A_k respectively. For example, $\mathcal{B}_{j,k}$ is a set of behavior experiences whose s's belong to state class C_j and a's belong to action A_k. At this point we define $J_{\mathcal{B}_{j,k}} = \sum_l w_l \cdot H_{\mathcal{B}_{j,k}}(r_l)$ as *non-uniformity of behavior outcomes* in $\mathcal{B}_{j,k}$, where $H_{\mathcal{B}_{j,k}}(r_l)$ is information entropy about the l-th element of behavior outcome vector r in $\mathcal{B}_{j,k}$, and w_l is the weight coefficient for the element. By averaging $J_{\mathcal{B}_{j,k}}$ over all the subsets $\{\mathcal{B}_{j,k}\}$, we obtain

$$J_{\mathcal{B},\mathcal{C}} = \frac{1}{|\mathcal{B}|} \sum_{j,k} |\mathcal{B}_{j,k}| \cdot J_{\mathcal{B}_{j,k}} \quad (1)$$

where, $|\mathcal{B}_{j,k}|$ is the number of elements in $\mathcal{B}_{j,k}$ and $|\mathcal{B}|$ is that of all behavior elements.

Intuitively, $J_{\mathcal{B},\mathcal{C}}$ measures the degree of *non-uniformity* as to the behavior outcome of the agent, when the experiences $\mathcal{B}$ are classified by the state set $\mathcal{C}$ and the action set $\mathcal{A}$. So it can be said that a state class set with less value of $J_{\mathcal{B},\mathcal{C}}$ is likely to describe the causal relationship of the agent's behavior with *less uncertainty*. Now, we can define the state generalization problem based on entropy minimization of behavior outcomes as follows:

Definition : [*State Generalization based on Entropy Minimization of Multiple Behavior Outcomes*]
Find a set of state classes $\mathcal{C}_{opt}$ which minimizes $J_{\mathcal{B},\mathcal{C}}$, when the maximum number of state classes ($n_{s,max}$) is specified.

The most important point is that this framework combines the three different generalization criteria described in the former section, since the objective function $J_{\mathcal{B},\mathcal{C}}$ is the form of weighted sum of entropy about different kinds of behavior outcomes – s_{post} (sensor input after action), rwd (acquired reward), and c_{post} (reached state class).

As to the actual calculation of $H_{\mathcal{B}_{j,k}}(r_l)$ - the entropy of each behavior outcome property, it can be easily computed using the fundamental definition $H_{\mathcal{B}_{j,k}}(r_l) = -\sum_m P(r_{l,m}) \log_2 P(r_{l,m})$ if r_l is a discrete variable. For the continuous properties, on the other hand, it is approximately computed by $H_{\mathcal{B}_{j,k}}(r_l) = \log_2(\sqrt{2\pi e}\sigma_{r_l})$ because strict calculation is difficult. σ_{r_l} is the standard deviation of r_l in $\mathcal{B}_{j,k}$.

3.2 Entropy Minimization with Classification Tree

Though various approaches can be considered for the actual optimization of $J_{\mathcal{B},\mathcal{C}}$, this time we propose a relatively simple method which decreases the value of $J_{\mathcal{B},\mathcal{C}}$ incrementally by dividing the sensor input space using a classification tree. In this method, a set of state classes is represented in the form of tree which is depicted with respect to the primitive sensor inputs. The construction algorithm of a state classification tree is described as follows:

Algorithm : [*State Space Construction with Classification Tree*]
 (*Given* : $\mathcal{A}$, $\mathcal{B}$, w, $n_{s,max}$ *Find* : $\mathcal{C}$)

1. Initialize the state class set $\mathcal{C}$ with only one class which contains all sensor input vectors ($\mathcal{C} = \{C_1\}$).
2. Classify each element of behavior experiences in $\mathcal{B}$ into any of subset $\{\mathcal{B}_{j,k}\}$ based on $\mathcal{A}$ and current $\mathcal{C}$. Then compute the value of $J_{\mathcal{B}_{j,k}}$ for each $\mathcal{B}_{j,k}$.
3. Compare the value of $\sum_k |\mathcal{B}_{j,k}| \cdot J_{\mathcal{B}_{j,k}}$ for each state class C_j, and choose the one with the largest value as the state to be divided next.
4. Find the optimum partition which decreases the value of $J_{\mathcal{B}_{j,k}}$ most greatly as to the state class selected in the previous step, and divide it into two.
5. Stop and return $\mathcal{C}$ if the total number of state classes reaches $n_{c,max}$, otherwise go to 2.

The main point of this algorithm is that the primitive sensor input space is *incrementally* divided by selecting the region with the highest entropy, which reduces the exploration cost drastically compared with the case of optimizing $\mathcal{C}$ directly with the number of state classes fixed from the beginning. This method has a limitation, however, that it may be trapped in a local optimum.

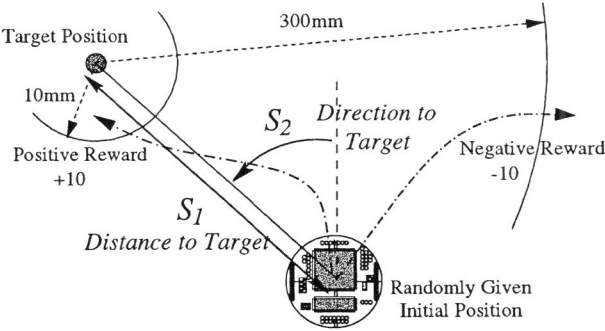

Fig. 2. Assumed task and available sensors

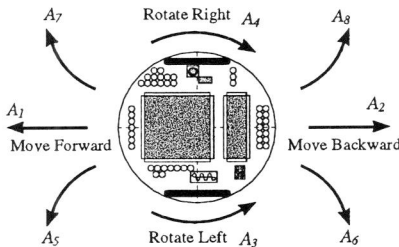

Fig. 3. Available actions

4 Simulation Studies

4.1 Task and Environment

Simulated mobile robot environment which models the well-known desktop robot Khepera is used as a test-bed here. This robot agent involves the task of reaching a specific target position in a obstacle-free area (Fig. 2). The agent obtains a positive reward of $+10$ when it reaches within a certain distance from the goal position, and a negative reward of -10 on the other hand when it goes outside the specified area.

This robot can use 8 actions (A_1 - A_8) illustrated in Fig. 3 by specifying the rotation of the two wheels in the right and left sides. As to the sensors, it is assumed that two kinds of information are available for the agent, i.e., *distance between the center of the robot and the goal position* (S_1), and *relative angle between the robot axis and the direction to the goal* (S_2).

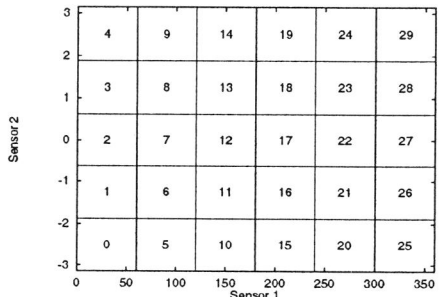

Fig. 4. Grid-like state space in *Case A* (also used as initial space in *Case C*)

4.2 Comparison among Manual Definition, Contruction and Reconstruction

To investigate the effectiveness of the state generalization method with the unified criterion, we compared the following three cases of the agent's behavior learning process.

[Case A]: **Learning with a grid-like fixed state space**
   The robot performs ordinary Q-learning with a manually defined state space. It is a grid-like one (Fig. 4) and is fixed during the learning process. The number of states is 30.

[Case B]: **Learning with state space construction from scratch**
   The robot collects behavior experiences by random actions in the first 600 steps. Then it constructs state space based on the state classification tree

method in 3.2. After next 600 steps, it reconstructs the space again. The number of the states is limited to 30. Fig. 5 and Fig. 6 illustrates the state spaces constructed and reconstructed in this case. Each rectangle region represents a generated state class. It should be noticed that *state IDs* (the numbers in the regions) do not necessarily coincide with the order of the generation or split of the states. As seen from these figures, in the first construction the state classes are defined mainly based on the similarity of sensor input changes and acquisition of negative rewards. In the reconstruction of state space, on the other hand, they are divided into smaller regions near the positive reward, which means that the state space becomes more *goal-oriented*.

[Case C]: **Reconstruction of initial space**

The robot firstly performs Q-learning with the grid-like initial state space (Fig. 4). Then it reconstructs the space. At this point, the agent converts the Q values for the grid-like state space into those for the new state space by a similar technique described in [8], and use them as initial values. The number of the states is limited to 30.

In the state space construction / reconstruction processes in *Case B* and *Case C*, the weight vector w is set as: $w = [1.0, 2.0, 20.0, 0.1]$. Four elements in w are coefficients for s_1, s_2, rwd and c_{post} respectively. These weight values were selected by trial and error in a preliminary simulation.

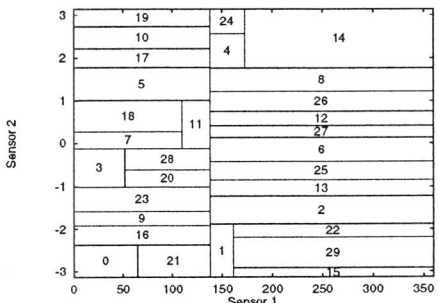

Fig. 5. Constructed state space in *Case B*

Fig. 7 shows the performance changes in those 3 cases. *Performance* is defined here by the average number of required steps to reach the target position. In *Case A* (dotted line), it converges at the very early stage, and there is little improvement after that. In *Case B* (dashed line), it becomes better than in *Case A* after the reconstruction of the state space (at 1200 steps). But it takes a lot of training data and time. In *Case C* (solid line), the number of training data necessary for reaching a certain level of performance is drastically reduced, com-

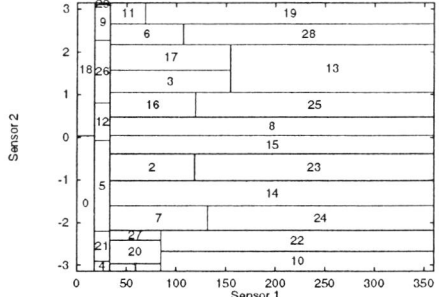

Fig. 6. Reconstructed state space in *Case B*

pared with *Case B*. This result indicates that our state generalization method with reconstruction strategy has a great effect on the reduction of learning cost and the final performance.

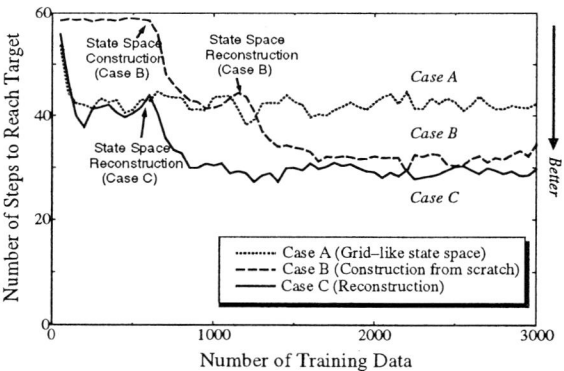

Fig. 7. Performance Changes in Case A,B,C

4.3 Comparison among Different Weight Values

Next we investigated the influence of the difference in the weight coefficients on the three types of behavior outcome properties - s_{post}, rwd, c_{post}. In this experiment, three cases with different values of weight vector are compared. The overall learning strategy in them is same to that in *Case C*, i.e., the state space is re-constructed after the Q-learning process with the initial grid-like state space.

(**Case D-1**) only rwd and c_{post} are considered
($\boldsymbol{w} = [0.0, 0.0, 20.0, 0.5]$)
(**Case D-2**) only s_{post} and c_{post} are considered
($\boldsymbol{w} = [1.0, 2.0, 0.0, 0.1]$)
(**Case D-3**) only s_{post} and rwd are considered
($\boldsymbol{w} = [1.0, 2.0, 20.0, 0.0]$)

Fig. 8 shows the performance change of the agent in these three cases. In this figure, *Case A* (fixed grid-like state space) and *Case C* (reconstruction with all of s_{post}, rwd and c_{post} considered) are also shown for comparison. From this, we can see that any of the tree cases (*Case D-1,D-2,D-3*) outperforms *Case A* in the long run, but does not exceed *Case C*. This result indicates the meaning of taking the different kinds of behavior outcomes into consideration in state abstraction. In other words, advantage of unified state generalization criterion is proved.

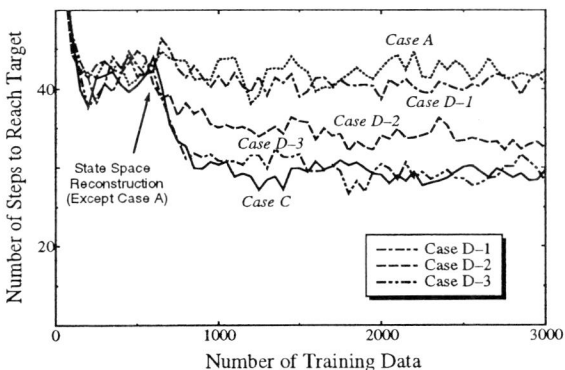

Fig. 8. Performance Changes in Case D-1,2,3

5 Conclusion and Future Work

This paper proposed a new state generalization framework based on entropy minimization of multiple behavior outcomes. It unifies the various heuristic state generalization criteria conventionally used in the earlier works. We also proposed a space (re-)construction algorithm using a classification tree based on this framework. This enables reactive agents to obtain optimum state spaces in more efficient and flexible way.

Though our results have been encouraging so far, there are still important problems to be solved. Firstly, a general theory for finding an optimum weight vector w is required, because it is considered to be dependent on environments and tasks. A method for deciding the granularity or the number of state classes is also important. We are expecting some information criteria such as MDL and AIC can be applied to this issue. In addition, it is desirable to enhance the algorithm in 3.2 to the *online* state space construction process, whereas it is currently a *offline* or *batch* learning process.

References

1. Albus, J., Lacaze, A., Meystel,A.: Multiresolutional intelligent controller for baby robot. Proceedings of the 10th International Symposium on Intelligent Control (1995)
2. Asada, M., Noda, S., Hosoda, K.: Action-based sensor space categorization for robot learning. Proc. of IEEE/RSJ International Conference on Intelligent Robots and Systems (1996) 1502–1509
3. Chapman, D., Kaelbling, L.P.: Input generalization in delayed reinforcement learning: An algorithm and performance comparisons. Proceedings of Twelfth International Joint Conference on Artificial Intelligence (1991) 726–731
4. Gaskett, C., Wettergreen, D., Zelinsky, A.: Q-learning in continuous state and action spaces. Proceedings of 12th Australian Joint Conference on Artificial Intelligence (1999)
5. Ishiguro, H., Sato, R., Ishida, T.: Robot oriented state space construction. Proc. of IEEE/RSJ International Conference on Intelligent Robots and Systems (1996) 1496–1501
6. Moore, A. W., Atkeson, C. G.: The parti-game algorithm for variable resolution reinforcement learning in multidimensional state-spaces. Machine Learning, Vol. 21. (1995) 199–233
7. Sutton, R. S., Barto, A. G.: Reinforcement Learning. MIT Press (1998)
8. Takahashi, Y., Asada, M., Hosoda,K.: Reasonable performance in less learning time by real robot based on incremental state space segmentation. Proc. of IEEE/RSJ International Conference on Intelligent Robots and Systems (1996) 1518–1524
9. Takahashi, Y., Takeda, M., Asada, M.: Continuous valued q-learning for vision-guided behavior acquisition. Proceedings of 1999 IEEE International Conference on Multisensor Fusion and Integration for Intelligent Systems (MFI'99) (1999)
10. Ueno, A., Hori, K., Nakasuka, S.: Simultaneous learning of situation classification based on rewards and behavior selection based on the situation. Proc. of IEEE/RSJ International Conference on Intelligent Robots and Systems (1996) 1510–1517
11. Yairi, T., Nakasuka, S., Hori, K.: State abstraction from heterogeneous and redundant sensor information. Proceedings of International Conference on Intelligent Autonomous Systems 5 (IAS-5) (1998) 234–241

From Brain Theory to Autonomous Robotic Agents

Alfredo Weitzenfeld[1]

[1]Departamento Académico de Computación
Instituto Tecnológico Autónomo de México (ITAM)
Río Hondo #1, San Angel Tizapán, CP 01000
México DF, MEXICO
alfredo@itam.mx

Abstract. The study of biological systems has inspired the development of a large number of neural network architectures and robotic implementations. Through both experimentation and simulation biological systems provides a means to understand the underlying mechanisms in living organisms while inspiring the development of robotic applications. Experimentation, in the form of data gathering (ethological physiological and anatomical), provides the underlying data for simulation generating predictions to be validated by theoretical models. These models provide the understanding for the underlying neural dynamics, and serve as basis for simulation and robotic experimentation. Due to the inherent complexity of these systems, a multi-level analysis approach is required where biological, theoretic and robotic systems are studied at different levels of granularity. The work presented here overviews our existing modeling approach and describes current simulation results.

1 Introduction

The study of biological systems comprises a cycle of biological experimentation, computational modeling and robotics experimentation, as depicted in Figure 1. This cycle serves as framework for the study of the underlying neural mechanisms responsible for behavior in animals and serving as inspiration in designing autonomous robotic agents.

To address the underlying complexity in building biologically inspired robotic systems we have developed a multi-level analysis approach integrating across different modeling and simulation levels studied primarily with respect to four different ones: (1) autonomous robotic agents, (2) behavior, (3) neural networks, and (4) detailed neurons.

1. At the highest level, autonomous robotic agents are designed to interact with the world via sensors and actuators. These agents are simulated in virtual autonomous agents and implemented in real robots. Autonomous robotic agents are exemplified by biologically inspired systems, such as the computational frog (*rana*

---

[1] We thank the NSF-CONACyT collaboration grant (#IRI-9522999 in the US and #546500-5-C018-A in Mexico), the CONACyT REDII grant in Mexico, as well as the "Asociación Mexicana de Cultura, A.C.".

computatrix) [1], the computational praying mantis [5], the computational cockroach [6], and the computational hoverfly [11].
2. At the behavior level, neuroethological data from living animals is gathered to generate single and multi-agent systems to study the relationship between an agent and its environment, giving emphasis to aspects such as cooperation and competition between agents. We describe agent behavior in terms of perceptual and motor *schemas* [3] decomposed and refined in a recursive fashion. Behaviors, and their corresponding schemas, are simulated via the Abstract Simulation Language ASL [22]. Examples of behavioral models include the praying mantis *Chantlitlaxia* ("search for a proper habitat") [9] and the frog and toad prey acquisition and predator avoidance models [12].
3. At the neural network level, neuroanatomical and neuronphysiological data are used to generate perceptual and motor neural network models corresponding to schemas developed at the behavioral level. These models try to explain the underlying mechanisms for sensorimotor integration. Neural networks are simulated via the Neural Simulation Language NSL [24][25]. Neural network models are exemplified by the prey acquisition and predator avoidance neural models [10] and the toad prey acquisition with detour behavior model involving adaptation and learning [13].
4. At the detailed neural level, electrochemical neural mechanisms are studied to understand different neural phenomena such as synaptic plasticity and presynaptic inhibition. A number of models are used depending of the mechanisms simulated, such as the compartmental model, where a single axon is divided in compartments [19], and the ion kinetics model, where chemical concentration responsible for electric current is simulated [18]. These models are simulated with systems such as GENESIS [7] and NEURON [17].

2 Modeling Levels

In the following sections we overview the different modeling levels using as an example *rana computatrix* [Arbib 1987] behaviors inspired on biological studies of frogs and its application to different robotic experiments.

2.1 Autonomous Robotic Agents

Autonomous robotic agents can be either simulated in a virtual world or executed in the real world. In particular, frogs (and toads) and the corresponding *rana computatrix* use vision and tact as their primary sensors with legs and tongue as their primary actuators, both virtual and real. In Figure 2 we show an illustration of a frog in a setup involving a prey (worm) interposed by a fencepost.

2.2 Behaviors

Behaviors are described by ethograms, as the one shown in Figure 3 defining *rana computatrix* behaviors. The particular behavior we will describe in more detail is the frog's prey acquisition with detour shown in Figure 2. The setup involves a frog and a barrier in front of a prey, where fencepost gaps have the same width, with a number of experiments carried out [13] as shown in Figure 4.

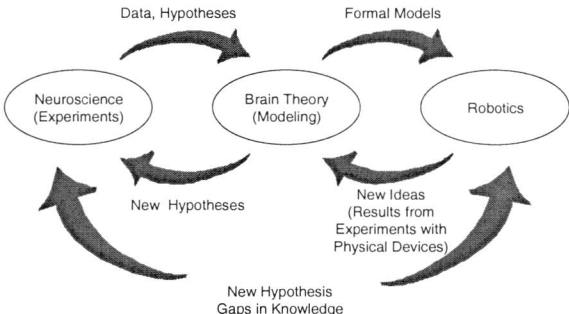

Fig. 1. Framework for the study of living organisms through cycles of biological experimentation, computational modeling, and robotics experimentation.

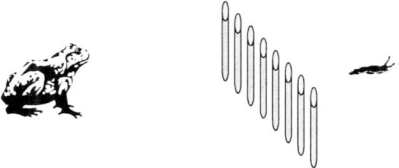

Fig. 2. Computational frog in a prey and barrier setup.

- **Experiment I**: Barrier 10cm Wide. Frogs that started from a long enough distance (15-25cm) in front of a 10cm wide barrier (and with the worm 10cm behind the barrier) showed (in 95% of the trials) reliable detour behaviors from the first interaction with the 10cm barrier. They produced an immediate approach movement towards one of the edges of the barrier.
- **Experiment II**: Barrier 20 cm wide. The "naive" frog (a frog that has not been yet exposed to the barrier) tends to go for a fencepost gap in the direction of the prey (this was the case for 88% of the trials). The frog starts out approaching the fence trying to make its way through the gaps. During the first trials the frog goes straight towards the prey thus bumping into the barrier. Since the frog is not able to go through a gap it backs-up about 2cm and then reorients towards one of the neighboring gaps. After 2 (43%) or 3 (57%) trials, the "trained" frog is already detouring around the barrier without bumping into the barrier. The behavior involves a synergy of both forward and lateral body (sidestep) movements in a very smooth and continuous single movement.

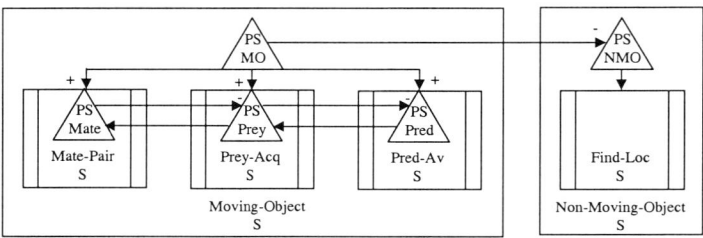

Fig. 3. *Rana Computatrix* ethogram: Mating, Prey Acquisition and Predator Avoidance schemas (moving and non-moving objects) [8]. The diagram shows feedback between perceptual schemas (triangles) and regular schemas (rectangles). Note the hierarchical schema organization. (Acronyms are as follows: PS - Perceptual Schema, MO - Moving Object, NMO - Non-Moving Object, S -Schemas.)

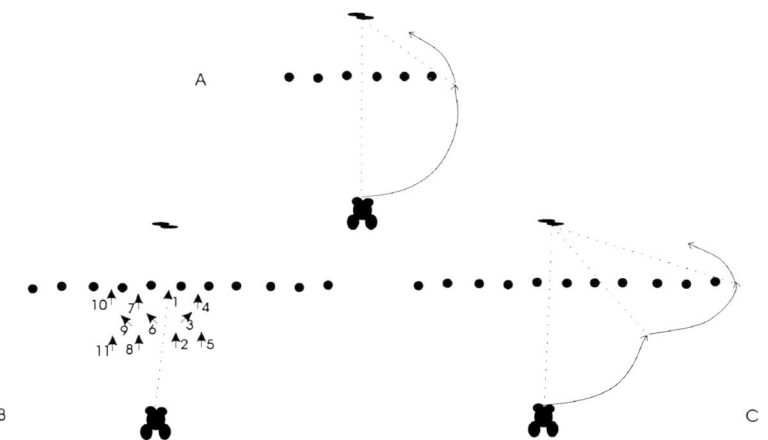

Fig. 4. A. Approach to prey with single 10cm barrier with immediate detour. **B.** Approach to prey with single 20 cm barrier: first trial with frog in front of 20cm barrier (numbers indicate the succession of the movements). The toad directly approaches de center of the barrier requiring successive trials to manage the detour around it. **C.** Approach to prey with single 20cm barrier. After 3 trials the frog detours directly around the 20cm barrier. Arrowheads indicate the position and orientation of the frog following a single continuous movement after which the frog pauses.

In Figure 5 we show in more detail a typical prey acquisition behavior for the frog. In order to model such behaviors we introduce the schema computational model. Schemas define a hierarchical distributed model for action-perception control, where each schema incorporates its own structure and control mechanisms. At the higher abstraction levels, the detailed schema implementation is left unspecified, only specifying what is to be achieved. At a lower level, schemas are implemented with neural networks or other processes. The schema computational model follows a tree-like structure as shown in Figure 6 (schemas may also be shared making the structure a directed graph). At the top, a high level schema is decomposed into two lower level schemas where the three schemas together are known as schema *aggregates*, or *assemblages*. When at the same level, schemas are interconnected (solid arrows), or when at different levels, schemas are relabeled having their task delegated (dashed arrows).

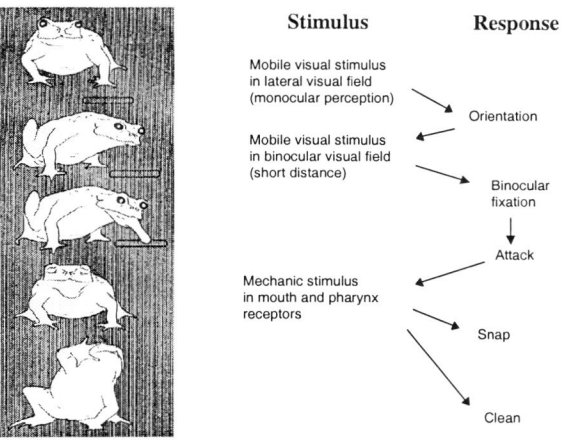

Fig. 5. Frog's prey acquisition behavior involving a worm as shown on the left-hand side. The right-hand side describes the frog's response in relation to the stimulus [16].

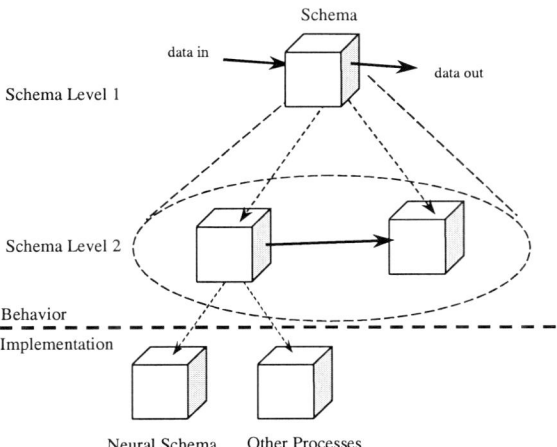

Fig. 6. The ASL/NSL computational model is based on hierarchical interconnected schemas. A schema at a higher level (level 1) is decomposed (dashed lines) into additional interconnected (solid arrow) subschemas (level 2). At the lowest level schemas are implemented by neural networks or other processes.

The schema interface consists of multiple unidirectional control/data, input and output ports having a body where schema behavior is specified, as shown in Figure 7.

Communication is in the form of asynchronous message passing, hierarchically managed, internally, through anonymous port reading and writing, and externally, through dynamic port *connections* and *relabelings*.

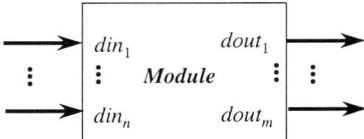

Fig. 7. Each schema may contain multiple input, $din_1,...,din_n$, and output, $dout_1,...,dout_m$, ports for unidirectional communication.

Figure 8 shows the schema model hierarchy corresponding to the toad's prey acquisitions with detour model [14]. We show a single schema level (level 1) describing the different behaviors being modeled, primarily *prey approach* and *static object avoid*. Additional schemas include visual and tactile input, moving stimulus selector (when more than one prey exists), prey and static object recognizers together with the four types of motor actions: forward, orient, sidestep and backward. Tasks at this level are delegated to the next level down, the neural level, where schemas perform more refined tasks. In this model, both the prey approach and the static object avoid schemas are implemented by neural schemas: a *Retina* [21], *Maximum Selector* [15], *Tectum* and *PreTectum-Thalamus* [8], together with neural motor heading maps.

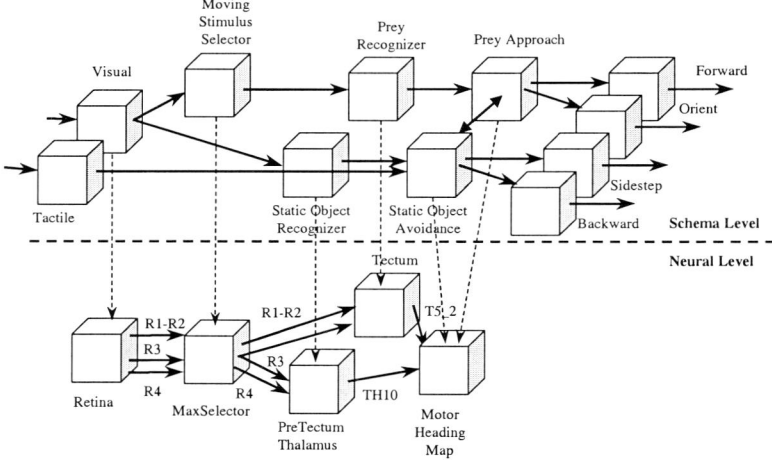

Fig. 8. Schema model hierarchy for the toad's prey acquisition and static object avoidance model previously described.

Complexity is much more significant when considering more behaviors and other brain regions [4].

2.3 Neural Networks

Biologically inspired neural networks are based on physiological and anatomical neural mappings. For example, Figure 9 shows a diagram of different neural areas involved in the frog's prey acquisition and detour model.

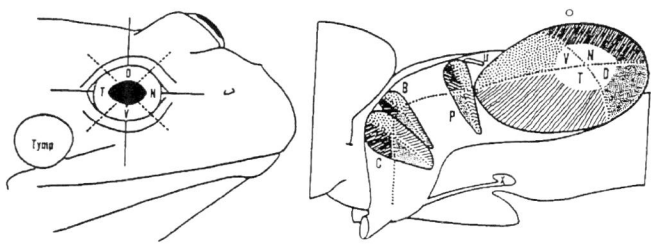

Fig. 9. The two illustrations show the most important areas in the frog's prey acquisition model. These are the Optic Tectum (O) (divided in four regions: Temporal (T), Dorsal (D), Nasal (N) and Ventral (V)), the Thalamic Pretectal Neuropil (P), together with other regions: Nucleus of Belonci (B), Lateral Geniculate Nucleus (C) and Basal Optic Root (X) [20].

Neural schemas provide their implementation in terms of neural networks processing, as shown in Figure 10.

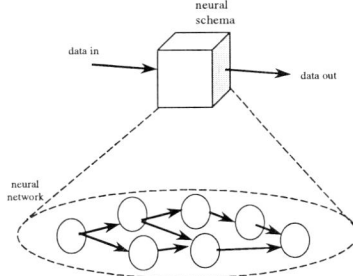

Fig. 10. Neural schema hierarchy showing task delegation to neural networks processing.

At this level, neural networks are simple processing units interconnected among each other to provide large-scale computation. Each neuron is defined by its membrane potential value m depending on its previous history and current input s_m while its output value M is defined by a non-linear threshold function over its membrane potential, as shown in Figure 11. For example, the leaky integrator model [2] is used to simulate such neurons.

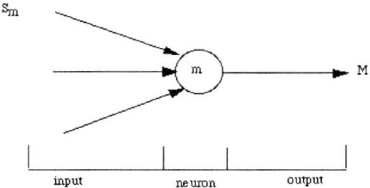

Fig. 11. Simple neural element as basic component at the neural network level.

For example, at this level of granularity the MaxSelector [15] neural schema is implemented by the neural network shown in Figure 12.

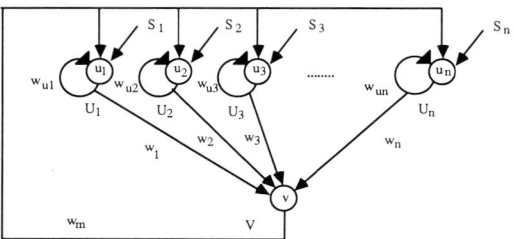

Fig. 12. The neural network shown corresponds to the architecture of the Maximum Selector model, where u_i and v represent neural membrane potentials, U_i and V represent neural firing rates, S_i represent inputs to the network, and w_i represent connection weights. The network is initialized with a number of positive inputs assigned to different cells. After many iterations the network stabilizes producing a single "winner", i.e. a single active cell.

The neural schema model also provides an extended model where neurons themselves may have their task delegated by neural implementations of different levels of detail, from the very simple neuron models to very detailed ones [23].

2.4 Neurons

Neuron models vary in their detail, depending on the particular simulated mechanisms, involving at the top level of a soma (nucleus of the neuron), an axon (output of the neuron), and dendrites (input to the neuron). Connections between neurons take place in the synapses at the axon terminals of one neuron connected to the dendrites of another neuron. Synapses are the main mechanism for plasticity in neurons and can be further refined into much more detail, as shown in Figure 13.

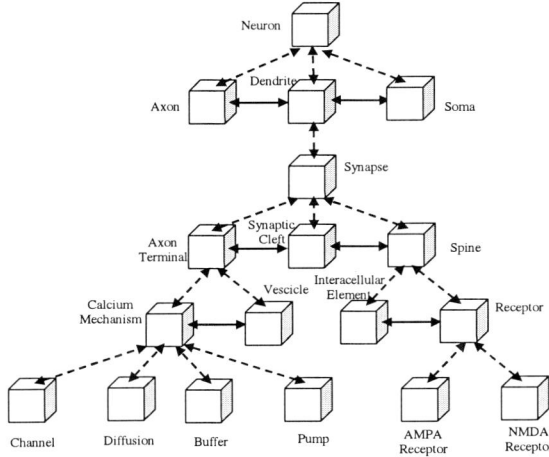

Fig. 13. Neural modeling at different levels of details.

3 Simulation Results

Due to space limitations in this paper we only show the resulting path motion seen at the top level for the previous basic experiments, as shown in Figure 14. Additional graphs (not shown here) display neural network states for the different neural schemas.

4 Discussion

The work presented here overviews the inherent complexity in modeling biological systems. This complexity can be managed by taking a multi-level approach emphasizing both top-town and bottom-up designs through different granularity levels. At the top level agents are defined in terms of sensors and actuators and may involve interaction with other agents, such as in competition and cooperation. Next level down, each agent is described in terms of its behaviors such as in the frog's prey acquisitions with detour model. Once basic behaviors are defined additional ones may be added taking advantage of the underlying schema architecture. Next level down, behaviors are implemented by different (or common) neural schemas representing neural network processing. The detailed neuron bottom level is required only when simple neural models do not provide sufficient processing capabilities such as those requiring synaptic plasticity or presynaptic inhibition. Current work involves experimentation with these and other models and applying them to robots to provide the feedback in experimentation as described in Figure 1.

Fig. 14. The above diagrams display the *Rana Computatrix* basic experiments for the prey acquisition and detour model. The different dots correspond to the frog's trajectory from its initial location as it finally reaches the prey. The left-hand side shows the resulting motion path for the 10cm barrier. Note how the frog heads directly towards the side of the barrier. The middle diagram displays the resulting motion path for the 20cm barrier experiment before learning. We have added numbers corresponding to the frog's position in time. In this particular experiment the frog hits the barrier three times before perceiving the side of the barrier and moving towards the prey. The right-hand side diagram shows the resulting motion path for the 20cm wide barrier after learning.

References

[1] Arbib, M.A., Levels of Modelling of Mechanisms of Visually Guided Behavior, *Behavior Brain Science* 10:407-465, 1987.
[2] Arbib, M.A., *The Metaphorical Brain 2*, Wiley, 1989.
[3] Arbib, M.A., Schema Theory, in the *Encyclopedia of Artificial Intelligence*, 2nd Edition, Editor Stuart Shapiro, 2:1427-1443, Wiley, 1992.
[4] Arbib, M.A., Erdi, P. and Szentagothai, J., *Neural Organization: Structure, Function and Dynamics*, MIT Press, 1998.
[5] Arkin, R.C., Ali, K., Weitzenfeld, A., and Cervantes-Perez, F., Behavior Models of the Praying Matis as a Basis for Robotic Behavior, in *Jouranl of Robotics and Autonomous Systems*, 2000 (to be published).
[6] Beer, R. D., *Intelligence as Adaptive Behavior: An Eperiment in Computational Neuroethology*, San Diego, Academic Press, 1990.
[7] Bower, J.M., and Beeman, D., *The Book of GENESIS, Exploring Realistic Neural Models with the GEneral NEural SImulation System*, Telos, Springer-Verlag, 2nd Edition, 1998.
[8] Cervantes-Perez, F., Lara, R., and Arbib, M.A., A neural model of interactions subserving prey-predator discrimination and size preference in anuran amphibia, Journal of Theoretical Biology, 113, 117-152, 1985.
[9] Cervantes-Perez, F., Franco, A., Velazquez, S., Lara, N., 1993, A Schema Theoretic Approach to Study the 'Chantitlaxia' Behavior in the Praying Mantis, *Proceeding of the First Workshop on Neural Architectures and Distributed AI: From Schema Assemblages to Neural Networks*, USC, October 19-20, 1993.
[10] Cervantes-Perez, F., Herrera, A., and García, M., Modulatory effects on prey-recognition in amphibia: a theoretical 'experimental study', in *Neuroscience: from neural networks to artificial intelligence*, Editors P. Rudoman, M.A. Arbib, F. Cervantes-Perez, and R. Romo, Springer Verlag Research Notes in Neural Computing vol 4, pp. 426-449, 1993.

[11] Cliff, D., Neural Networks for Visual Tracking in an Artificial Fly, in *Towards a Practice of Autonomous Systems: Proc. of the First European Conference on Artifical Life (ECAL 91)*, Editors, F.J., Varela and P. Bourgine, MIT Press, pp 78-87, 1992.
[12] Cobas, A., and Arbib, M.A., Prey-catching and Predator-avoidance in Frog and Toad: Defining the Schemas, *J. theor. Biol* 157, 271-304, 1992.
[13] Corbacho, F., and Arbib M. Learning to Detour, *Adaptive Behavior*, Volume 3, Number 4, pp 419-468, 1995.
[14] Corbacho, F., and Weitzenfeld, Learning to Detour, in *The Neural Simulation Language NSL, System and Applications*, MIT Press, 2000 (to be published).
[15] Didday, R.L., A model of visuomotor mechanisms in the frog optic tectum, *Math. Biosci.* 30:169-180, 1976.
[16] Ewert, J.P, *Neuroethology, an introduction to the neurophysiological fundamentals of behavior*, Springer-Verlag, 1980.
[17] Hines, M., and Carnevale, T., The NEURON Simulation Environment, *Neural Computation*, 9:1179-1209, 1997.
[18] Hodgkin, A.L. and Huxley, A.F., A quantitative description of membrane current and its application to conduction and excitation in nerve, *Journal of Physiology*, 117, 500-544, 1952.
[19] Rall, W., Branching dendritic trees and motoneuron membrane resistivity, *Exp. Neurol.*, 2:503-532, 1959.
[20] Scalia, F., and Fite., K.V., A retinotopic analysis of the central connections of the optic nerve in the frog, J. Comp. Neurol., 158:455-478.
[21] Teeters, J.L., and Arbib, M.A., A model of the anuran retina relating interneurons to ganglion cell responses, *Biological Cybernetics*, 64, 197-207, 1991.
[22] Weitzenfeld, A., ASL: Hierarchy, Composition, Heterogeneity, and Multi-Granularity in Concurrent Object-Oriented Programming, *Proceedings of the Workshop on Neural Architectures and Distributed AI: From Schema Assemblages to Neural Networks*, USC, October 19-20, 1993.
[23] Weitzenfeld, A., Arbib, M., A Concurrent Object-Oriented Framework for the Simulation of Neural Networks, *Proceedings of ECOOP/OOPSLA '90 Workshop on Object-Based Concurrent Programming*, OOPS Messenger, 2(2):120-124, April 1991.
[24] Weitzenfeld, A., Arbib, M.A., NSL,Neural Simulation Language, in *Neural Networks Simulation Environments*, Editor J. Skrzypek, Kluwer, 1994.
[25] Weitzenfeld, A., Arbib, M., Alexander, A., *NSL - Neural Simulation Language: System and Applications*, MIT Press, 2000 (to be published).

A Multi-agent Approach for Optical Inspection Technology

T. Buchheim, G. Hetzel, G. Kindermann, and P. Levi

University of Stuttgart, IPVR
Breitwiesenstr. 20-22, D-70565 Stuttgart, Germany
thorsten.buchheim@informatik.uni-stuttgart.de
http://www.sfb514.uni-stuttgart.de

Abstract. Today's approaches in quality-measurement and inspection-technology are merely based on highly specialized mechanisms and fixed measurement schedules lacking adaptability for differing measuring conditions (e.g. illumination). Especially for non-mass-products the consequences are expensive, non-economical solutions. Our approach tries to combine diverse partial results towards a global solution of a given problem. In a self-organizational manner those partial results adapt themselves to the given inspection tasks and thus optimize the final results. This strategy we denominate active exploration. In our work we present a hierarchical multi-agent-approach for optical quality-measurement. On a flexible inspection-platform different products shall be examined on quality-deficiencies by using different optical sensors and illumation techniques. Through a coordinated interaction of mechanical actuators the measurement procedure can be adapted flexibly to the current situation. As a result the area of application of optical sensors is expanded and the verification of optical and visual features (glossiness, color) is enabled. The procedure how to apply and coordinate the sensors and actuators shall not be given explicitly in the system but follows from negotiation and cooperation strategies on a higher level of abstraction.

1 Introduction

Quality-Measurement today is based on certain quality-features defined for a specific product which are tested by specialized sensors according to a given inspection-schedule. To obtain reasonable results, especially with optical sensors, it is necessary that for each tested product exactly the same conditions hold (type of sensor, illumination, sensor calibration, position and orientation of the product).

The aim of the collaborative research centre (SFB) "Active Exploration by Sensor-Actuator-Feedback for Adaptive Measurement and Inspection Technology" [HL97] is to overcome these limitations by developing new adaptive concepts for industrial measuring and inspection technology. This research project is a collaboration of various institutes of the University of Stuttgart concerned with different aspects of the project involving

- evaluation of relevant quality-features,
- coarse and fine grained planning of inspection-tasks,
- image-processing and
- mechanical sensor-control.

By iteratively optimizing the measuring conditions a flexible means for quality-measurement which adapts itself to a given inspection task is achieved. The quality-measurement is done at a inspection-platform named MEGA having the following types of optical sensors

- stereo-camera,
- structured-light-sensor,
- digital-micromirror-device-sensor,
- multi-parametric camera.

The sensors are independently maneuverable by actuators with up to 5 degrees of freedom for appropriate positioning inside the measuring space. Additionally a mesh of light sources is attached around the measurement-apparatus allowing a flexible lighting of the inspection-scene by variably controlling the intensity of each light source. Figure 1 shows the measuring construction without the lighting construction.

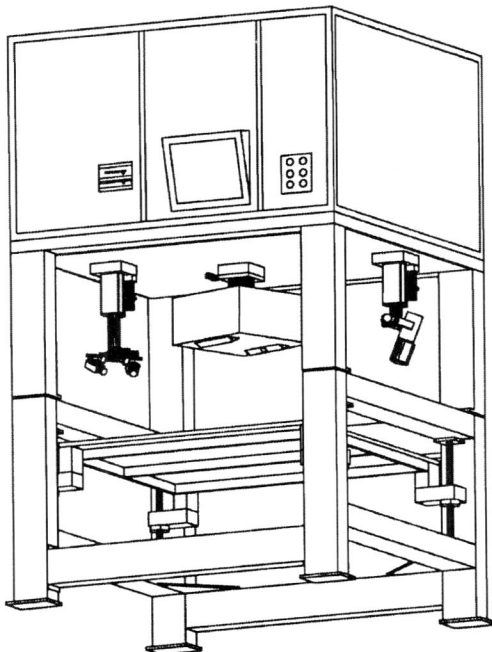

Fig. 1. The inspection platform MEGA

Through a coordinated interaction of sensors, actuators and image processing algorithms the measurement of additional visual features (glossiness, color-patterns) is facilitated. Furthermore the spectrum of application of optical sensors is expanded by innovative concepts and methods for self-optimizing measuring systems. The primary task of our institute in the context of this research project is the development of a multi-agent-software architecture which enables an easy integration of the software developed by each of the institutes involved.

By choosing a multi-agent approach each group is provided the possibility of developing its own agents on a system and in a programming language of choice as long as the required communication facilities are met. Furthermore the choice of the used sensorics is still subject to changes requiring a flexible software-architecture as it is offered by the multi-agent programming paradigm. Not only sensors but also different quality-features or types of products may require different measuring strategies which, if modeled as agents, can easily be added to the system.

To perform an inspection-task generally various sensors and the lighting have to be controlled in accordance with each other to gather the necessary data for evaluating whether certain quality features are fulfilled or not. In most cases the data supplied by a single sensor measurement is insufficient or incomplete so that various measurements have to be taken and unified to a single result. In some cases a specific sensor may only be capable of perceiving one aspect of a given quality-feature while a second sensor may merely sense the missing second part of the feature. This requires distributed planning to achieve the global goal by defining and coordinating subtasks which lead to the desired result.

2 Multi-agent-systems

The most cited advantages of Multi-Agent-Systems (MAS) are parallelism, scalability, robustness and an easier methodology for software-development [Wei95], [Nwa96].

Complex tasks can generally be split easily into various subtasks. By solving all of these subtasks a solution for the primary problem is found. However these approaches are not recommendable in all domains as the main problem consists in finding a reasonable task-decomposition of the primary problem.

An optimal decomposition is usually characterized by few dependencies among the various subtasks to enable an autonomous processing of each task. As those ideal decompositions rarely are possible, subtasks have to be coordinated and partial results or status-information have to be exchanged at processing time. Which information has to be exchanged at a certain time is normally defined by a rigid global plan causing the side-effect that a failure of a single subtask processing unit can lead to a complete stop or a global failure of the whole system.

Multi-Agent-Systems on the contrary don't possess any global problem solving plan but define a multitude of agents having own interests, capabilities and goals. To achieve a global goal each subtask is assigned to a single agent having the relevant capabilities to cope with the given problem. Each agent has a particular plan for solving certain tasks also including collaboration strategies or information exchange with other agents. In contrast to a fixed global plan it is not predefined which agents cooperate with each other. The personal plan of an agent does not specify which agent to collaborate with, but only the capabilities needed to fulfill its personal goals. These needed capabilities are resumed and described by the role-concept [BKM99].

For an agent being able to assume a requested role it has to possess all functionalities demanded by the role, reducing therefore the number of potential applicants. In a negotiation process one of these agents capable and willing to perform the role is chosen for the needed cooperation. As there are no restrictions on the number of agents nor their capabilities it is permitted to have agents with partially or entirely equal capabilities within the system.

Thus in case of a single agent failing in performing a certain task there are other agents at hand to undertake its job granting a greater robustness of the whole system.

Also from a software-development perspective this approach embodies several advantages:

- In domains where various different groups with particular interests are involved each group designs its own agents whereby interaction is controlled by the MAS-framework.
- It is of no interest which operation-systems, programming languages or computer-hardware are involved, as long as a common communication-channel is provided.
- Rapid prototyping is easily done as agents with reduced capabilities can also be added to the system. Prototypes even may remain in the system competing with later developed agent versions.
- MAS are easily extensible to a greater functionality by adding agents with new capabilities to the system.

3 The Multi-agent-architecture

In contrast to many multi-agent approaches, where homogeneous or heterogeneous agents normally negotiate and cooperate as equal partners, for the underlying problem a hierarchical multi-agent approach seemed more appropriate. Here, only agents of the same hierarchical layer cooperate or compete as entities of equal rank to perform subtasks which were subcontracted to them by agents of the next higher layer. After completing a certain task the committed agent delivers the result back to the agent from which it received the task-request. The software-architecture can be be visualized in a three-dimensional way consisting of five layers and three planes, as shown in figure 2. The planes separate the agents responsible for the following functions:

- **explorative execution:** All Agents involved in the inspection process are located at this plane. Here planning and execution of measurements tasks,

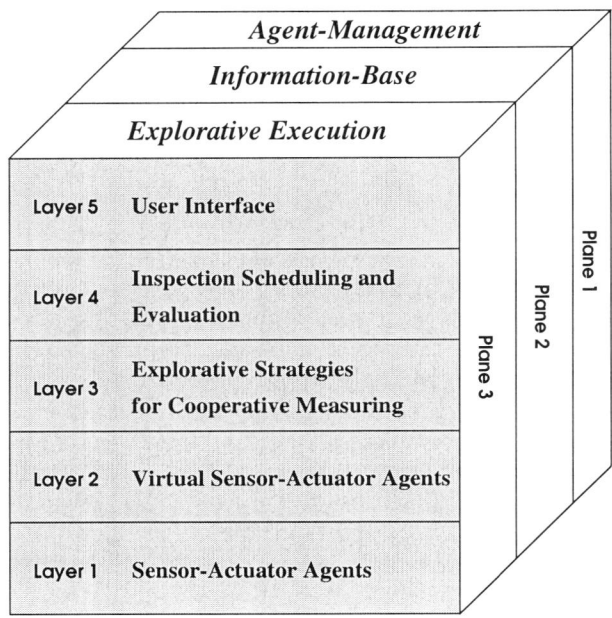

Fig. 2. Agent-Hierarchy

as well as the processing and evaluation of measured data is done at different levels of abstraction. The additional information to perform those tasks, e.g. CAD-model of a specific product, are provided by the information base.
- **information base:** The main function of this plane is the provision of necessary information to the agents at the executional plane. This embodies data about the products to inspect, like quality-features or geometrical data, as well as information about specific agents at the executional plane or former successful cooperations of agents on different tasks. Agents at this plane act generally as information-brokers supplying necessary information to the agents of plane 3 according to their degree of abstraction. However, they may also participate in cooperation processes of the executional plane contributing useful information to speed up processing time.
- **agent management:** This plane forms the infrastructure of the multi-agent system. Here methods for locating and communication between agents are provided, along with a supervising and administrational functionality allowing the detection of system-faults and the insertion and deletion of agents.

Generally at plane 3 the agents have two different functionalities. First they perform a task-decomposition, where accepted tasks are subdivided into various subtasks which are again subcontracted to agents of the next lower layer. Secondly, after the subcontracted tasks are accomplished, the partial-results are merged into one common result which is then passed to the requesting higher-

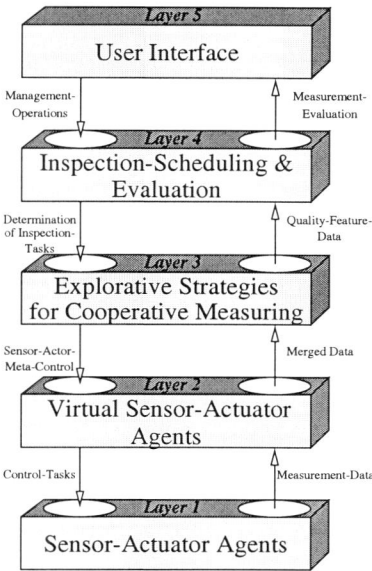

Fig. 3. Inspection-Cycle

layer-agent. An inspection-task therefore is processed in a cyclic manner, consisting in a forward-pass, where the global goal is gradually decomposed into partial, more elementary, goals and a backward pass where the partial results are gathered, merged and delivered back upwards until the global result is constructed. Figure 3 depicts the information-flow within the agent-hierarchy. At the highest layer (layer 5) the user-interface is situated which enables the user to add, delete and supervise agents as well as interfere into their actions.

In the fourth layer a coarse planning of the necessary measurements is done determining relevant quality-features for a given product. This can be done by a single agent having a universal functionality but also various agents with specific plans for different product-classes are thinkable.

At layer 3 so called feature-agents are defined for diverse quality-features, e.g. color, geometry, size, reflexive or micro-structural product properties. Each agent has specific knowledge about explorative measuring strategies for the respective feature, which it uses to generate plans involving subtask-requests for the agents at layer 2. As there is no knowledge about the agents at the layers below, those plans have to base on suppositions and may have to be revised from time to time. For instance if there is no sensor to take a picture of width X with resolution Y, alternatively n pictures of width X/n and resolution Y may be taken and merged afterwards, given that an agent for the necessary merge-operation exists within the system.

Virtual sensor/actuator-agents (layer 2) have mainly the functionality of providing a higher level of abstraction by hiding (physical) details from the higher level agents. Adaptive feedback-based sensor control takes in a primary position at this level as measuring conditions are continually adapted until acceptable results are obtained or seem to be unreachable. This also includes cooperative strategies for example to minimize shadow-effects or reflexion on objects. At this layer also the transition from iconical to symbolical information is done by additional tool agents.

Finally at layer 1 reside physical agents representing the sensors, actuators and illumination. These agents interact directly with the environment and try to optimize their parameters autonomously and/or in accordance with other agents (e.g. lighting and camera) in order to achieve optimal results. However, they only have a local view on their environment and their partial goal, so their capabilities to achieve good results are limited to their view.

Before an agent commits to a task, it has to assure that all consequent subtasks can be performed by the agents of the next lower layer. Thus, with a user specifying a certain inspection-task, first of all there is a forward-pass of subtask-requests from layer 5 down to layer 1. In this forward-pass however, no commitment of any agent to perform a certain subtask is involved, it is solely a feasibility-request for the given task. After verifying the feasibility, the task is either rejected or the real processing is initiated.

After performing a measurement at layer 1 the sensor-information is passed backwards. At each layer the agents gather the partial results of their sub-contracted agents and try to merge them to a common result passing it to the upper-layer-agent from which it received the subtasks-request. Grave data-inconsistencies are locally detected and analyzed and lead instantaneously to a new modified measurement-request to the agent-layer below.

This process is repeated until a sufficient degree of data-consistence is achieved or a certain number of measurement-loops was performed without major improvements. At layer 4 the obtained inspection-results are finally analyzed and evaluated whether the predefined quality criteria were matched or the measurements didn't provide reliable results.

4 Communication and Cooperation

In our model a communication and cooperation process involves 3 different stages of interaction. Figure 4 depicts these stages for a cooperation-process outlining the communication and the results of the negotiation.

The **strategical stage** deals with cooperation aspects about how to solve a task which is to be subcontracted to the next layer (inter-layer communication). This implies in particular the selection of the agents which seem to be best suitable to perform the task within possible boundary conditions of the problem (quality criteria, time restrictions, ...) as well as the determination of an appropriate cooperation pattern for them.

The **tactical stage** incorporates information exchange between agents of the same layer (intra-layer communication) concerning the cooperation process itself. Depending on the degree of autonomy of the task to perform, this may

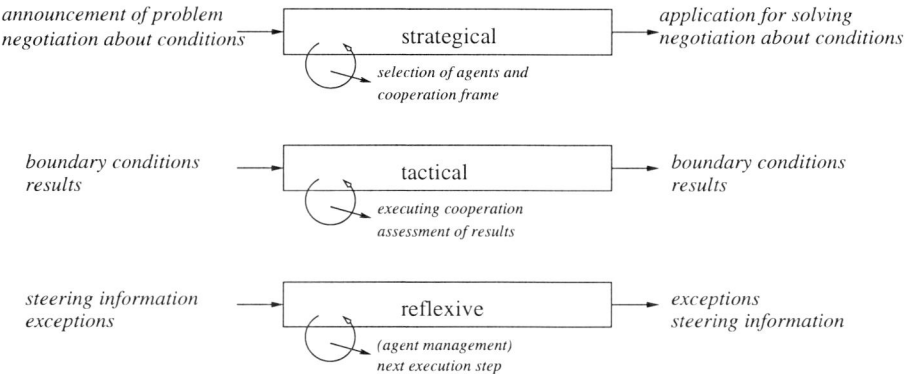

Fig. 4. Communication levels of an applying agent

include negotiation about parameters (constraints) or other information as well as evaluation whether a task could be performed or not. In the latter case a new negotiation process at the strategic level has to be initiated.

The **reflexive level** is needed for instantaneous or direct interaction. This may include interaction with the agent-management (e.g. STOP-signal) or exchange of status-information (e.g. exceptions). In some cases it may become necessary that the control of an agent is taken over by a second agent bypassing its decision-unit. As this requires a great amount of knowledge about the first agent and means a significant intervention in its autonomy, this should only be used in exceptional situations.

The three stages of communication are inherent in the planning structure of an agent. The strategic plans of an agent determine when and how to take part in specific negotiations for a task requested by a higher-level-agent. This also may require additional intra-layer communication to acquire necessary knowledge about other agents of the same layer for a cooperation on a specific task. How to negotiate and communicate within a cooperation process to perform a task is described by the tactical plan. Finally the reflexive plans only imply autonomous actions of an agent in order to achieve locally optimal results. For physical agents this is done through an optimization of their local parameters, while the autonomy of agents at higher levels consists in the determination of an optimal task decomposition.

Figure 5 shows the structure of an agent. The knowledge-base contains model skeletons e.g. for the environment and cooperation. The **Decision Unit (DU)** represents the central part of the agent controlling all actions of an agent. Depending on the situation (partial states, information) the decision unit instantiates new models from the knowledge-base (model-instances). In an evaluation process the decision unit selects the most appropriate model-instance which forms the plan for further actions.

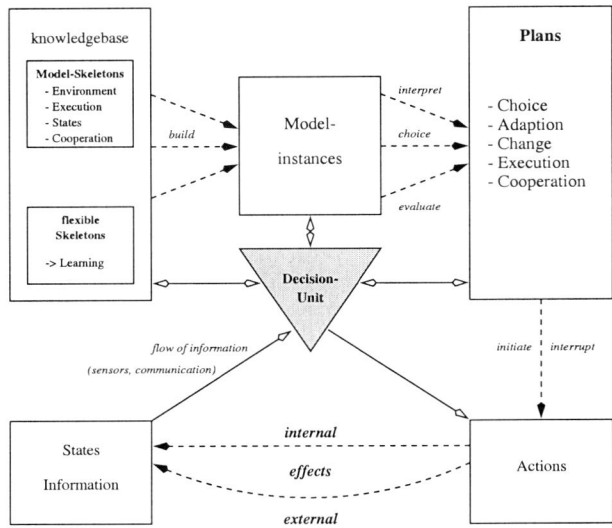

Fig. 5. Agent structure

The actions can be divided into communicational acts (negotiation, cooperation, information-exchange, ...) and executional acts (sensor positioning, calculating, model creation/adaption). Each action causes internal and/or external effects. The observations of these effects form the basis for future learning.

Learning takes place at two different levels. On one hand each agent can learn by causal effects of certain actions it performed which requires also observation evaluation of other agent's actions, while on the other hand there may exist special learning agents within the system. Their functionality merely consists in gathering and evaluating actions of agents, cooperations, etc. thus learning useful patterns of interaction or additional information regarding specific tasks. They contribute to cooperations by either supplying information on demand to requesting agents or by directly participating in a cooperation process.

During the realization of our system, we must consider harmful side-effects often inherent in multi-agent systems which have a great impact on the efficiency of the system. Chaotic behavior [LSA98] in particular must be avoided. This should be achieved by restrictions and a limitation of communication.

5 Current Work

Up to now our work predominantly concentrated on the development of a multi-agent framework which meets the requirements of the different institutes involved. We are developing the communicational fundamentals using and extending the functionality of CORBA [Obj98] providing the infrastructure for communication. This embodies the provision of locating and enabling communication between agents (situated at the agent-management plane in our architecture-model).

An elementary agent was designed having all necessary functionalities for interaction with other agents. This elementary agent is intended to serve as a prototype for future agent designs. It includes the following capabilities:

- reacting on incoming messages at any time,
- participation in negotiations,
- communication with the agent-management and the visualization component,
- self-monitoring and assessing of own performance.

The language for communication is based on KQML-primitives [FLM97] to privide the different institutes a flexible means for information exchange.

A formalization of negotiation and cooperation processes using decision-networks [BML98] is currently investigated to develop and compare different models which fit the system requirements.

To verify the compatibility of an agent's interface we are also developing a tool which will be integrated into the agent management allowing to check new agents for system compliance.

Our first prototype has already been successfully tested in a inspection-scenario involving simple communication and subcontracting techniques.

6 Conclusion and Outlook

By improving the adaptability of optical measuring techniques to different problems and situations we aspire to enhance the general acceptance of those technologies. We hope to achieve this by combining different sensors which are coordinated by an intelligent application planning-methodology. The here introduced hierarchical multi-agent architecture provides the necessary premises for the realization of the measuring and inspection system which will be developed within this research project.

For the future we intend to extend this multi-agent system based on our experiences with the first prototype. Additional features will later be added to the agent-management to facilitate the inter-agent communication. Later also a graphical interface is planned to provide an easier interaction with the agent-management.

The following phases of our project are especially concerned with learning aspects in MAS as well as a continuous extension of the capabilities of the system. This includes

- incorporating learning functionality into the agents,
- adding additional agents with similar capabilities to the system enhancing the aspect of concurrency,
- developing special learning-agents which participate in cooperation processes or provide additional information to agents.

Acknowledgments

This project is funded by the "Sonderforschungsbereich Aktive Exploration mittels Sensor/Aktor-Kopplung für adaptive Meß- und Prüftechnik" (Collaborative research centre Active Exploration by Sensor-Actuator-Feedback for Adaptive Measurement and Inspection Technology) of the "Deutsche Forschungsgemeinschaft (DFG)".

References

[BKM99] M. Becht, J. Klarmann, and M. Muscholl. Software demo of rope: Role oriented programming environment for multiagent systems. In *Proceedings of the Agent 99*, Seattle, Washington, USA, May 1999.

[BML98] M. Becht, M. Muscholl, and P. Levi. Transformable multi-agent systems: A specification language for cooperation processes. In *Proceedings of the World Automation Congress (WAC), Sixth International Symposium on Manufacturing with Applications (ISOMA)*, 1998.

[FLM97] T. Finin, Y. Labrou, and J. Mayfield. KQML as an agent communication language. *in Jeff Bradshaw (Ed.)*, 1997.

[HL97] G. Hetzel and P. Levi. Sensor-Aktor-Kopplung zur explorativen Bildauswertung. In R.-J. Ahlers, editor, *Bildverarbeitung '97, 5. Symposium*, Ostfildern, Germany, November 1997.

[LSA98] P. Levi, M. Schanz, and V. Avrutin. Chaos-theory-based analysis of manufacturing robot-teams. In *Proceedings of the 5nd International Conference on Intelligent Autonomous Systems IAS-5*. IOS-Press, 1998.

[Nwa96] H. S. Nwana. Software agents: An overview. *Knowledge Engineering Review*, 11(3):1–40, 1996. Cambridge University Press.

[Obj98] Object Management Group (OMG). *The Common Object Request Broker: Architecure and Specification, Revision 2.2*, February 1998.

[Wei95] G. Weiß. Adaption and learning in multi-agent systems: Some remarks and a bibliography. In G. Weiß and S. Sen, editors, *Proceedings of the IJCAI '95 Workshop*, pages 1–21, Montreal, Canada, August 1995. Springer-Verlag.

The Use of Mobile Agents in Tracing an Intruder in a Local Area Network

Midori Asaka[1], T. Onabuta[1], T. Inoue[1], and S. Goto[2]

[1] Information-technology Promotion Agency,
Honkomagome 2-28-8-16F,
Bunkyo-ku, Tokyo, Japan
{asaka,t-onabu,t-inoue}@ipa.go.jp
[2] Waseda University,
3-4-1 Shin-Ohkubo, Tokyo, Japan
goto@goto.info.waseda.ac.jp

Abstract. We are developing an intrusion detection agent system called IDA. Not only can the IDA detect an intrusion, it can also trace the route of the intrusion in a local area network. It is very important for administrators to know where an intruder is coming from and which machines the intruder hopped and compromised in the LAN because the administrators must restore the compromised systems, especially the system attacked first, in order to help prevent intrusions again. When a mark is detected indicating that an intruder might leave, the IDA starts collecting information related to the mark as it traces the candidate. The system analyzes the information and decides whether an intrusion has occurred. In the IDA, mobile agents collect information from the target systems across the network and trace the intruder. The mobile agents collect information only related to the intrusion. Therefore, the IDA can reduce analyzing overhead and network bandwidth loss.

1 Introduction

At the Information-technology Promotion Agency (IPA) we are developing an intrusion detection system (IDS) that we call the IDA (Intrusion Detection Agent system). The IDA is a multihost-based intrusion detection system that analyzes system logs obtained from hosts on a network and detects intrusions. The IDA can not only detect an intrusion but also trace the route of intrusion in a local area network. In many cases, especially if an attacker evades a firewall protecting a site, it is very important for administrators to know where an intruder is coming from and which machines the intruder has hopped and compromised in the LAN. That information is necessary to the administrators who must restore the compromised systems and eliminate backdoors to their network, which will help prevent future intrusions. When a mark that an intruder might leave is detected, the IDA starts collecting information related to the mark as it traces the candidate, and analyzes the information and decides whether an intrusion has occurred. In the IDA, mobile agents collect information from the target systems across the network and trace the intruder. The mobile agents collect information only related to the mark of intrusion. Therefore, the IDA can reduce analyzing overhead and network bandwidth loss and, as a result, the IDA can reside in large-scale networks.

This paper describes how the mobile agents in the IDA trace intrusions and collect information. We propose a method of information exchange and intrusion tracing by means of mobile agents. Section 2 describes the structure and basic action of the IDA . Section 3 describes how mobile agents act when an attacker's route is complicated, and how mobile agents exchange information through the use of bulletin boards and message boards. Section 4 gives our evaluation of the IDA and related discussion. Section 5 outlines our conclusions and indicates the direction of our future work.

2 Intrusion Detection System IDA

2.1 IDA Structure

In developing the IDA, we planned that it would concomitantly reduce the overhead of the system and detect new or unknown forms of attack. The system's goal is not to precisely detect all intrusions but to detect many intrusions efficiently. To accomplish this goal the IDA works by watching events that may relate to intrusions –Marks Left by Suspected Intruders (MLSI)– instead of analyzing all of the users' activities. If an MLSI is found, the IDA will collect information related to the MLSI, analyze the information, and decide whether or not an intrusion has occurred. For example, the IDA monitors whether or not password files have been modified because in many cases, intruders tamper with them. However, since legitimate users may also change password files, the system cannot conclude solely on the basis of file modifications that an intrusion has occurred. The IDA therefore collects further information related to the modification of the file before deciding if an intrusion has occurred. In [1], we described MLSI's in more detail.

Intrusion detection systems (IDSs) can be divided into two types, one that is network-based and another that is host-based[2]. A network-based IDS analyzes network packets and decides whether an intrusion has occurred. In contrast, a host-based IDS analyzes system logs in hosts on a network. It is very important for the designer of a host-based IDS to decide where the IDS analyzes information. The IDS can analyze information on each target system in a distributive manner, or centrally on a server. When we planned the IDA, which is a host-based IDS, we aimed at reducing the analysis-overhead of a server and at preventing wastes of network bandwidth. We did not, however, design the target systems of the IDA to analyze system logs. If the target systems did analyze system logs, the analyzing overhead and management-cost of the target systems would have actually increased. In order to avoid these problems, the IDA employs mobile agents to retrieve only the information related to the intrusion, which is contained in system logs in target systems, to the server. Therefore, the IDA can reduce the volume of data analysis on the server and network bandwidth loss, and need not deploy analyzing functions on the target systems because the mobile agents clip information from system logs on the target systems.

We can deploy the IDA on a local area network with a TCP/IP protocol. The IDA consists of a manager, sensors, bulletin boards, message boards, tracing agents, and information-gathering agents in each network segment. If an intrusion-route is included in one network segment, a manager in the segment is responsible for analyzing. If an intruder roams some systems included in more than two network segments, the managers of those segments collaborate with each other, and a master manager puts together the results and provides a user interface. We outline the structure of the IDA in the following (Fig. 1).

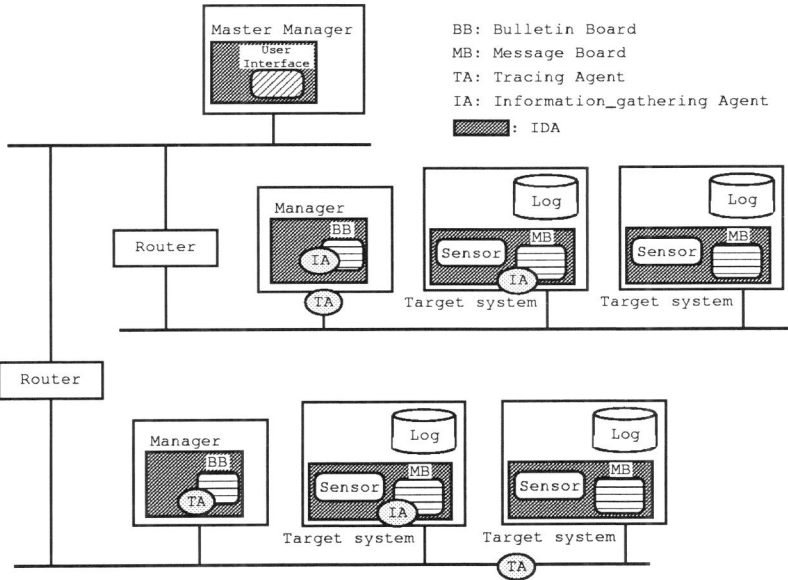

Fig. 1. IDA Structure

The details of the components are as follows.

- Manager
  The manager analyzes information collected by information-gathering agents (which are described below.) One manager resides on each network segment, managing the mobile agents and bulletin boards (also described below.) In the IDA, we set the "weight" of the information collected by the mobile agents. The manager accumulates the weight of the information, and if that weights exceeds a specified threshold, the manager concludes that an intrusion has occurred.

- Sensors
  The sensors, which are present on each target system, monitor system logs in search of MLSIs. If a sensor finds an MLSI, it reports it to the manager, along with the type of MLSI.
- Tracing Agent
  The intrusion-route tracing agent, simply called the tracing agent, traces the path of an intrusion and identifies its point of origin, the place from which the user leaving an MLSI has remotely logged onto the target host. En route to finding the origin, a tracing agent can find any intermediate nodes that may have been compromised.
- Information-gathering Agent
  An information-gathering agent, which is mobile, gleans information related to an MLSI from a target system. Each time a tracing agent in pursuit of an intruder is dispatched into a target system, it activates an information-gathering agent in that system. The information-gathering agent gleans information dependent on the type of MLSI, returns to the manager, and then reports (enters information onto the bulletin board). If the tracing agent migrates to another target system, it will activate another information-gathering agent, which will gather information on the next target system.
- Bulletin Board and Message Board
  The bulletin boards and message boards are common-use areas that can be accessed by tracing agents and information-gathering agents, and provide a means of information exchange. There is a message board on each target system used by tracing agents to exchange information; any tracing agent can determine whether a track under its scrutiny has already been traced by other agents, and can use that information in deciding where to go. The bulletin board is on the manager-machine and is used for recording information gathered from target systems by information-gathering agents as well as for integrating the information gathered about every tracing route.
- Master Manager
  The master manager puts together the resulting analysis of each manager and provides a user interface.

A manager and a master manager can reside together on the same machine.

2.2 Basic Action of IDA

Here we outline how the IDA works after a sensor detects an MLSI on a target system. The IDA consistently records the data required in intrusion-route tracing (i.e., about network connection, the various processes running on the system, etc.) on each target system. We describe the basic action of the IDA below. A basic action consists of an attack by an intruder to more than one host, included in only one network segment, with the intruder leaving only one MLSI on his or her way to a destination.

1. Each sensor on the target system seeks an MLSI from the system log.
2. If the sensor detects an MLSI, it reports this finding to the manager.

3. The manager dispatches a tracing agent to the target system where the MLSI was detected.
4. The tracing agent arrives at the target system and activates an information-gathering agent.
5. The information-gathering agent collects information related to the MLSI on the target system.
6. After activating the information-gathering agent, the tracing agent investigates the point of origin of the MLSI in an effort to identify the user's remote site. The tracing agent can derive this from the accumulated data regarding network connections and the processes running on the system.
7. After collecting information, the information-gathering agent, independent of the tracing agent, returns to the manager and enters the information on the bulletin board.
8. The tracing agent moves to the next target system on the tracing route and activates a new information-gathering agent.
9. If the tracing agent arrives at the origin of the route, cannot move anywhere, or if other tracing agents have chased the route it could follow, it returns to the manager.
10. The manager accumulates the weight of the information entered into the bulletin board and reports the value to the master manager. The master manager then provides an interface to the administrators.

2.3 Basic Function of the Bulletin Board and Manager

The bulletin board on the manager-machine contains information brought to the manager by the information-gathering agents that have been activated by the tracing agents. Each information-gathering agent brings information to the manager independently, and, as a result, the information concentrated in the manager is not arranged by intrusion-route. The bulletin board on the manager-machine functions as a clearing-house where this unorganized mass of information can be arranged by intrusion-route for the manager's analysis.

The manager judges whether or not an intrusion has occurred with the information obtained by the information-gathering agents. The manager does this by evaluating the information entered onto the bulletin board on the manager-machine. It evaluates not only each bit of information but also the information on each intrusion-route as a whole. The manager derives the intrusion route by examining the information provided by the tracing agents and information-gathering agents.

3 The Case of a Complicated Intrusion-Route

We described the basic action of the IDA in the preceding section. In this section we will explain a complicated case such that an intruder attacks several machines, including more than two network segments and / or leaves more than two MLSIs on his or her way to the destination.

3.1 The Case of More than Two MLSIs on an Intrusion-Route

If the IDA detects more than two MLSIs on an intruder's way to the destination, as many tracing agents as the MLSIs are activated and dispatched to each target system by the manager. However, before tracing the intruder, the manager and the tracing agents do not know whether these MLSIs are on the same intrusion route. As a result, more than two agents trace a certain range of the same intrusion route and collect the same information if the IDA does not have any mechanism that controls the activities of the tracing agents.

For example, suppose user X remotely logs onto target systems A, B, C, and D in this order: A → B → C → D. User X compromises the systems, and MLSIs are detected on targets D and B, respectively. The sensors of D and B report to the manager independently, and the manager dispatches tracing agents to both D and B. The tracing agent on target system D (Dag) traces intrusions in the following order: D → C → B → A. The tracing agent on target system B (Bag), on the other hand, traces in the following order: B → A. The two agents' tracings therefore overlap on B → A (Fig. 2).

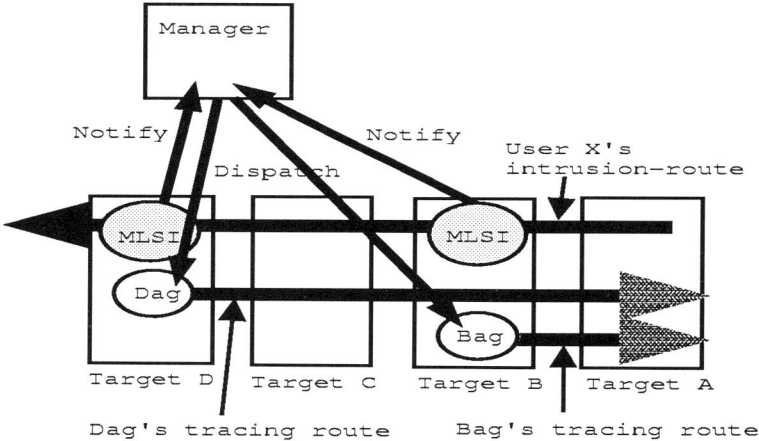

Fig. 2. Overlap Trace

To avoid this overlapping, tracing agents employ a message board, which is a common-use area to exchange trace information on a target system. Through the use of the message board, more than two tracing agents can take charge of the trace without overlapping. Tracing agents trace an intruder as below.

1. A tracing agent, which is dispatched to the target system, uses the process ID and user ID to trace a process that has left an MLSI.
2. If the tracing agent detects that the user who has left MLSIs logs onto the target system remotely, then the agent determines its destination from information about the user's login session.

3. The tracing agent refers to the message board on the target system.
4. If there is no information on the message board pertaining to the login session that the agent intends to trace, the tracing agent then enters such information and moves on to the target system from which the user logged on.
5. If there is already information on the message board relating to that session, meaning that another agent has already traced that particular user, then the tracing agent enters its reference on the message board and returns to the manager.
6. If step 4 (rather than step 5) has been followed, and it turns out that the target system being traced is the origin of the intrusion, the tracing agent returns to the manager. If not, the agent repeats steps 1 – 6.

If it turns out that another agent is tracing or has traced the intrusion, the tracing agent in question also brings the agent's ID and the name of the system to the manager.

3.2 Cases Where an Intrusion-Route Included in More than Two Network Segments

In cases where an intrusion-route consists of more than two network segments, the IDA follows the steps below (Fig. 3) in addition to the basic actions.

1. Tracing agent TA1 dispatched from manager Ma traces intruder X and arrives at target system A in network segment SA. If it detects that intruder

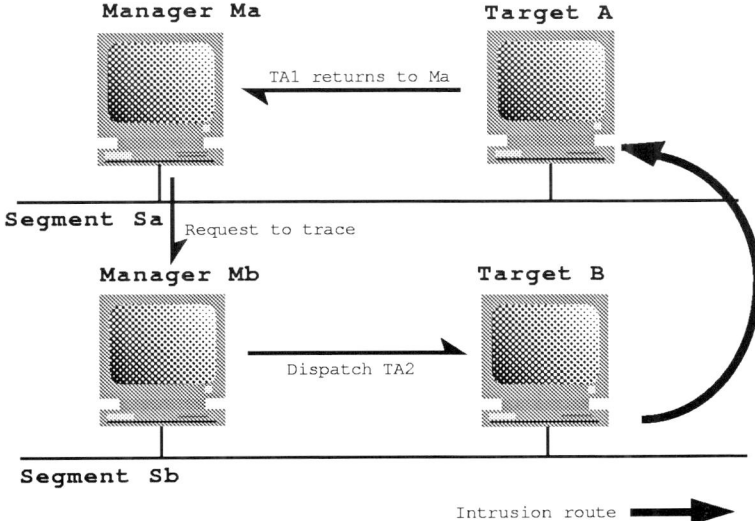

Fig. 3. Chase Across Two Segments

X comes from target system B, which exists in a different network segment (Sb), agent TA1 returns to manager Ma.
2. After the tracing agent TA1 returns to the manager Ma, it reports the information related to user X's network connection between A and B.
3. The manager Ma requests that manager Mb trace the intruder X.
4. The manager Mb in the network segment Sb dispatches a tracing agent TA2 to the target system B, and the tracing agent TA2 traces the intruder X.

As described in the preceding section, each tracing agent reports information regarding its tracing route to the manager in the same network segment. If an intrusion route included in more than two network segments, more than two managers analyze the intrusion. In such cases, each manager analyzes the information collected by its mobile agents and reports the results to the master manager. At that time, each manager transfers the information regarding their requests to other managers to the master manager. The master manager then integrates that information and makes the final decision as to whether an intrusion has occurred in the site. The method of integration is the same as that used by the managers.

4 Evaluation and Discussion

4.1 Definition of MLSIs and Information-Gathering

We implemented the IDA based on the design described previously. Currently, the IDA can detect local attacks.[1] We implemented the IDA on Sun Solaris 2.5.1 and Redhat Linux 5.2. We wrote the IDA's mobile agents in D'Agents 2.0[3] and the other part in C. We employed the BSM (Basic Security Module)[4] as the audit mechanism for the Solaris and developed original auditing tools for Linux.

We define MLSIs as below,

1. start up of root shell and
2. modification of critical files such as /etc/passwd, /etc/shadow, /etc/hosts.equiv, or /.rhosts

in local-attack detection, and the sensors monitor these marks on each target system. Information-gathering on the target system where the MLSI was left is based on the definition of MLSIs. Information-gathering for the first MLSI includes whether or not the user who caused the MLSI issued the su command, and for the second MLSI it includes the following.

- issues the suid command
- links the symbolic link to the target file

An information-gathering agent collects this information on the target system and reports to the manager.

---
[1] local attacks that are initiated against a machine to which the attacker already has access but in which the attacker is attempting to exceed his or her authority.

4.2 Evaluation

- Local-Attack Detection
  Because many Internet intrusions are enabled by cracking tools available on the Internet, it would be appropriate to evaluate the efficacy of the IDA against these cracking tools. We obtained a number of cracking tools aimed at local attacks on the Internet and simulated IDA attacks through the use of these tools that could run on a Sun Solaris 2.5.1 or Redhat 5.2, and found that within limits, the IDA could detect a local attack with the tools tested 92.3% of the time (12/13 simulations). The IDA cannot yet detect intrusions that involve password sniffing.
- Occurrence Rate of MLSIs
  To establish system performance, it is important for the IDA to determine how many MLSI triggers occur because the number of MLSIs should be the same as the number of tracing agents activated on the manager. We investigated the rate of MLSIs in our developing environment and found that the MLSIs triggered at a rate of 0.024% of all system events (22/88742) per day. The machine investigated is a mail server in an IDA project also used in developing the IDA, and has six users.
- Size of Mobile Agents
  The average size of a tracing agent is 2.2K bytes; the size of information-gathering agents without information is 0.8K bytes; and that of information-gathering agents with information is 0.8K bytes.
- Round-Trip Time of Mobile Agents
  We measured the time period from when a sensor triggers to when the tracing agent related to that MLSI returns to the manager. It takes less than one second for a tracing agent to process its work on a target system and to then migrate to the next target system, depending on the volume of the system log, the network's condition, and so on. This time includes the authenticating and encrypting of mobile agents.
- Volume of Log
  It is important for multihost-based IDS to reduce the volume of the system log transferred to the manager in order to avoid scalability problems. The volume of the log depends on the number of users and their respective activities. The average size of a log transferred to the manager in the IDA is 24K bytes per day on each target system. The whole log on each target is 7M bytes per day in the IDA . If BSM allows the target system an all-events log, it will be 70M bytes per day.

4.3 Discussion

The IDA has distinctive features and advantages that many conventional IDSs do not have, as described below.

- In the IDA, each target system seeks MLSIs. If it finds an MLSI, then only information related to that MLSI is centered on the manager. That is, not

all system log entries for each target system are transferred to the manager. Consequently, the volume of information the manager must analyze is lower than that gathered by current IDSs. Therefore, network traffic between the target systems and the manager will be reduced, as will the processing overhead of the manager.
- The IDA can trace intrusions through the use of mobile agents, and these agents can detect the location and the intermediate hosts of the intrusion. The mobile agents collect only information related to the MLSI while they are engaged in tracing the intrusion.
- In the IDA, information-gathering agents clip the information related only to the intrusion from the system log on the target, and return it to the manager. This means that information-gathering agents stand proxy for the manager and execute the task on the target system. Therefore, the analyzing overhead of the manager will be reduced.

5 Conclusion and the Direction of Future Work

We have described how the IDA detects intrusions by detecting MLSIs and tracing intrusions through the use of mobile agents. We have also described how the IDA detects local attacks. The IDA project is currently in the prototype phase. In the IDA, mobile agents are written by D'Agent, which is presently under development at Dartmouth College and offers PGP, which is able to authenticate and encrypt the mobile agents[5]. Thus far, the local attack-detection mechanism and the intrusion-route tracing are ready for use on a LAN. Our future work includes the following:

- Teach the IDA to detect remote attacks
- Run the IDA on large-scale networks and the Internet

The IDA 's alpha version is now available on the Internet[6].

References

1. M. Asaka, A. Taguchi, and S. Goto, "The Implementation of IDA: An Intrusion Detection Agent System," in Proceedings of the 11th FIRST Conference 1999, Brisbane, Australia, June 1999.
2. http://www.cs.purdue.edu/coast/intrusion-detection/ids.html
3. R. Gray, D. Rus, and D. Kotz, "Transportable Information Agents," Technical Report TR96-278, Department of Computer Science, Dartmouth College, 1996. http://www.cs.dartmouth.edu/ agent/
4. "SunSHIELD Basic Security Module Guide" Part No:802-1965-10, Revision A, Sun Microsystems,Inc.
5. R.Gray, David Kotz, George Cybenko and Daniela Rus. "Security in a multiple-language mobile-agent system," In Giovanni Vigna, editor, Lecture Notes in Computer Science: Mobile Agents and Security, 1998. http://actcomm.dartmouth.edu/ rgray/#papers
6. http://www.ipa.go.jp/STC/IDA

A Framework to Model Multiple Environments in Multiagent Systems

Jean-Christophe Soulié and Pierre Marcenac

IREMIA – Université de La Réunion
15, av. René Cassin – BP. 7151
F – 97715 Saint Denis Messag Cedex
email: [soulie][marcenac]@univ-reunion.fr

Abstract. Nowadays, multiagent systems are very often used to run environmental simulations. Thanks to the fact than multiagents focus more on interactions rather than on the system in its globality, scientists and researchers are now able to represent complex systems and they can simulate them. Consequently, a large number of multiagents platforms allows to perform such kind of simulations. But there is no work on the fact that an agent can evolve simultaneously in multiple environments. This is why, in this paper, we present a very innovative architecture that allow to model multiple environment for a single agent in a multiagent system. But as this multiplicity of environments raises new problems with regard to classic architecture, we explain how, by adding new entities, we obtain a coherent and viable model. These new entities are notably the virtual environmental instance and the virtual environment. This new model is explained and detailed due to concrete examples and more particularly with an example on the movement of shoals of fish in Indian Ocean.

1 Introduction

Nowadays the last progress of artificial intelligence allowed numerous overhangs in several domains, more particularly in the simulation of natural phenomena, social behavior or robotic, ethology, ecology. It is notably the case of the multiagent systems that allows to simulate very complex phenomena without having to describe all this complexity because they concentrate more on the interactions which exist within the system rather than on the global vision which we could have of the system. This is why a lot of research teams have developed more or less generic multiagent platforms that allow to build simulations based on multiagent systems. For instance, let us quote MADKIT [4] from J. Ferber, SWARM [9] from N. Minar, R. Burkhart, C. Langton and M. Askenazi, CORMAS [1] from F. Bousquet, the platform from H. Gimblett [6].

During the last five years, our team has been involved in the development of a generic multiagent architecture called GEAMAS[1] [8] [11]. Because of the local specificities of the Reunion Island, our team concentrates more particularly on the modelling and the simulation of complex natural phenomena such as volcano eruptions, earthquakes, cyclones, ...

---

[1] acronym of GEneric Architecture for MultiAgent Simulations

The work presented in this paper fits in with this problematic. Indeed, for the last year we stated a new survey concerning the modelling and the simulation of movement of benches of swordfishes. In order to do that, we have a set of satellites images. These images are shooted periodically by the satellites NOAA[2] and ERS1-2[3]. Their colours describe certain type of parameter bound in the Ocean. For instance, we have images describing the surface temperature of the ocean or we have also images describing the vorticity of the ocean. Obviously, the aim of this work is not to increase the volumes of fishing by the professional fishermen, but to come to a better renewable resources management for the Indian Ocean.

By considering these data, it is easy to notice that it is necessary that the agent must evolve at the same time in each satellite image in order to take into account these data. Consequently we studied multiagent platforms listed above and we noticed that none of them was able to simulate multiple environments and GEAMAS either.

This is why, with the aim of filling this lack, we present in this paper a very interesting architecture which allows an agent to evolve in different environments. Furthermore, this architecture allows to take into account the possible influences of an environment and to inform the other environments of these influences. Finally, this architecture insures us that the integrity of data is maintained on the set of environments thanks to two new entities: a virtual environmental instance and a virtual environment.

In this paper, section 2 shows and explains what is our architecture for an agent. Section 3 explains how, from the definition givent in the section 2, an extension is made in order to be able to build an agent who can take into account these new features.

2 Definitions and Backgrounds

Although a great number of scientists and researchers work in the field of the multiagent systems, there is no common definitions for an agent. Indeed, according to the considered research area, we can find definition for Software Agents [7], Reactive Agents [2] or Cognitive Agents [12], ... This is why, in order to remove all possible confusion, in this section explains what is our agent model and how we represent a multiagent system.

According to the J. Ferber's definition provided in [3], an agent is defined as follow:

Definition 1. *An agent is a physical or a virtual entity that:*

- *is able to act on its environment,*
- *is able to directly communicate with other agents,*
- *is prompted by a set of tendencies,*
- *holds some resources,*
- *is able to perceive its local environment,*
- *holds a local representation of its environment,*
- *and can eventually reproduce itself.*

And, a multiagent system is defined as follow:

---

[2] National Oceanic and Atmospheric Administration – American Satellite
[3] Launched and operated by the European Space Agency

Definition 2. *A multiagent system is composed of the following elements:*

- *an environment E,*
- *a set O of objects,*
- *a set A of agents, which are particular objects ($A \subseteq O$),*
- *a set of relation R, that link objects (and agents) together,*
- *a set of processes P, that enable agents to perceive, create, destroy, alter and manipulate some objects of O.*

Finally, J. Ferber isolates two main kinds a multiagent systems:

Definition 3. *A purely communicating multiagent system.*
This is when $A = O$ and $E = \emptyset$, then the relations R define a network: each agent is directly in relation with other agents (these agents are called acquaintances). And in this case, the environment is defined by the underlying network of acquaintances.

and

Definition 4. *A situated multiagent system.*
This is when all agents are situated in the environment. In this case, E is generally provided with a metric (e.g the Euclidean distance defines a geometric distances space).

But unfortunately, these definitions are not satisfactory for us. Indeed, they are too restrictive for our problem because environments defined in definition 3 and definition 4 do not allow to represent and manage the interactions between the environment and the agent. Furthermore, they do not take into account the fact that an agent evolves in the environment and that it must be able to perform a reasoning process. This is why, according to these definitions, we enrich them by adding the following features.
The agent is divided in three distinct entities:

- The first entity called *conative system* is the reasoning entity of the agent. It is composed of two sub-entities, the *autonomous* entity and the *environmental representation* entity. The autonomous entity is responsible for all the reasoning and the processing of information coming from the agent's environment. Obviously, this entity will be more complex if the designed agent is cognitive and conversely, if the designed agent is reactive, this entity will be "less intelligent".
- The second entity called *environmental instance* is the physical representation of the conative system in the environment. In other words, the environmental instance is plugged in the environment and is responsible for the actions and the perceptions on the environment; on the contrary, the conative system has no "physical" contact with the environment. This is the conative system that will request the physical instance to perform actions on the environment. In order to perceive the environment, the physical instance is equipped with a set of dedicated *captors*. These captors are application dependent and they can collect symbolic or numeric value, low-level or high-level information, for instance we can use captor of luminosity in order to perceive a light or a captor temperature in order to perceive a temperature gradient [10]. On the same way, the physical instance is equipped with a set of *effectors*. These effectors are application dependent too and they should perform some dedicated actions on the environment. For instance we can use an effector of motion

in order to perform a movement in the environment, or we can use an effector of rotation in order to perform a rotation.
– The third entity called *bidirectional dependency link* is the communication medium between the conative system and the environmental instance. When the environmental instance collects information in the environment, this information will be transferred to the conative system; and on the contrary, when the conative system make a decision that affects the environment, the associated command will be transferred to the physical instance thanks to this medium.

Moreover, we can observe that this decomposition is viable in both cases: a situated multiagent system or a purely communicating multiagent system. Indeed, the action of communication along the acquaintance network can be considered as an action and a perception: when the agent emits a message for another, the associated action is the emission; and on the other side, the associated perception is the detection of a new message. Then we can use this model in every case of multiagent system.

More precisely, the Figure 1 illustrates our agent architecture.

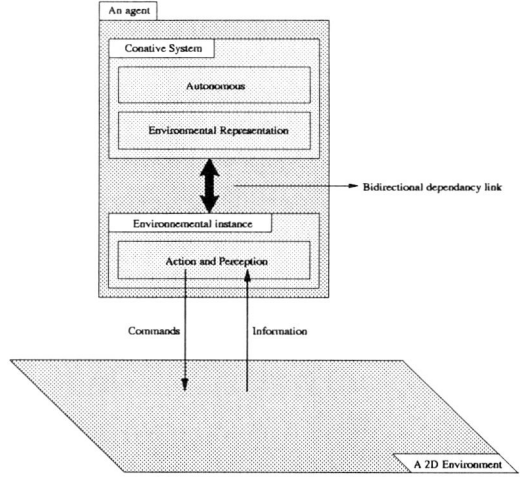

Fig. 1. Our agent model

In the next section we will show how, according to the definitions above, we build our model so that it can manage multiple environments.

3 Building a Multiple Environment Multiagent System

In order to do this, we isolate two main tasks to do: the first one consists in identifying what we will do with the agent's effectors and captors, and the second on consists in managing the integrity of data over these environments.

3.1 How to Keep all the Effectors and Captors in These Environment?

As defined above, the effectors and the captors are dedicated to a certain kind of perception or action. Indeed, when the designer of the multiagent system gives some effectors or captors to an environmental representations these captors and effectors can just perform simple and unique operations. For instance, we can use a captor of luminosity, heat or humidity and an effector or motion or rotation. But we can observe that these equipments could be dedicated to a precise kind of environment. Indeed, when an effector acts on the environment, it just acts on data which it relates to. Similarly, when a captor senses something in the environment, they are right only data which it relates to.

Then, according to these observations, it is evident that only solution to take into account these characteristics is to split data concerning a certain type of effector and sensor in as many environments. For instance, in our case, we have data concerning certain values of parameters in the environment: temperature, wind, vorticity, ...Then, we can isolate captors that will sense the temperature, the wind and the vorticity; and effectors that will act eventually on the temperature, the wind and the vorticity. Obviously, this decomposition is very basic because we can find other captors or effectors that could correspond with these three kinds of environments, but these equipments come in addition to the minimal set presented below. By this way, we have three environments and each environment contains a set of captors and effectors. These three environments define the *global environment* of the simulation. Then by a generalization, we can express the global environment as follow:
Let n ($n \in \mathbb{N}^*$) the number of environment, we have:

$$global\ environment = \bigcup_{i=1}^{n} environment_i$$

And in each $environment_i$ of the global environment, we have a set of effectors $E_i = \{e_{1_i}, e_{2_i}, \ldots, e_{n_i}\}$ where n is the number of effectors used in $environment_i$, and a set of captors $C_i = \{c_{1_i}, c_{2_i}, \ldots, c_{m_i}\}$ where m is the number of captors used in $environment_i$.

With this definition, we can manage environment with different size and even with different type. For instance, we can use two dimensions environment with a given width and a given height, another two dimensions environment with another given width and height, a three dimensions environment and a graph of acquaintances environment simultaneously.

Moreover, we can have at our disposal two kinds of data for the environments:

- Just a set of data at the initial state t_0. And after the evolution of these data are given by mathematical formulas that are time dependent or even there is no mathematical formulas and then we should use just the initial set of data during all the simulation. In this case, there is no change in our first definition of the global environment.
- We have at our disposal a set of data that are clearly defined over the time. Consequently we can isolate for each $environment_i$, the data used at each time step. And then, we can define an environment noted $environment_{i_t}$ that will change over the time. And consequently, our first definition of the global environment is

not valid any more because it does not take into account this feature. This is why we extend our definition as follow:

$$global\ environment = \bigcup_{i=1}^{n} \left(\bigcup_{t=t_0}^{T} environment_{(t,i)} \right)$$

where n is the number of environment attached to the conative system of the agent, t_0 is the first simulation step and T is the number of simulation steps used. For example, this case could be encountered when we use the set of satellite images presented in 1 as support. In this case, we can have images describing temperature or vorticity and then these two parameters will seen as two environments for the agent (e.g we have $n = 2$). Similarly, the satellite images are shooted periodically (e.g each 12 hours or 24 hours) by these satellites and then we have a set describing the same area, but with different values for it. This example agrees with the definition above.

But with this definition appears another problem: how can we define adequate environmental representations of the agent for these environments? Our assumption here is to create a dedicated environmental representation for each $environment_i$ of the global environment. By this way, as in our first definition given in 2 on page 2 the agent is composed of one conative system and one environmental instance, we extend this definition by adding a *type* in the environmental instance. Then each environmental instance is typed according to the type of the environment in which they are plugged. And then, for a single conative system we can have multiple environmental instances that are plugged in their dedicated environment. Finally, with all these new features added below, we can define an agent as follow:
An agent is a physical or a virtual entity that is composed of:

- A *conative system* that has in charge the reasoning process of the agent. This reasoning is more or less sophisticated in function that the agent has a profile more reactive than cognitive or conversely.
- A *bidirectional dependency link* that connects the environmental instances with their own conative system. This is on this link that the information will pass in order to inform the conative system of perceptions and conversely, in order send commands for the environmental instance.
- A *set of environmental instances* noted $\mathcal{SEI}$ that contains all the environmental instances used by the agent. Each environmental instance in $\mathcal{SEI}$ noted ei_i is typed with a type t_i. This type t_i is the same than the environment: $environment_{k,(t_o,T)}$ for a given k.
- Each ei_i in $\mathcal{SEI}$ contains two distinct sets: a *set of effectors* noted $\mathcal{EFF}$ that contains all the effectors that are compliant with t_i; and a *set of captors* noted $\mathcal{CAP}$ that contains all the captors that are compliant with t_i.

And we finally define a multiagent system as follow:
A multiagent system contains the following elements:

- A global environment that is defined as above.

- Each $environment_i$, for a given i, embeds a register called *register of environmental instances* and noted $\mathcal{REI}$ that contains all the environmental instances with the same type than $environment_i$ (e.g $\mathcal{SEI}$).
- A *timer* that gives rhythm to all the $environment_i$. This timer can express just a simulated time or a real time.
- A set of *situated objects* that are the environmental passive objects that are used during the simulation. For instance, with the example of the motion of fish in the Indian Ocean, the situated objects could be an island or a submarine crest, ...
- A set of *phenomena* for the $environment_i$. For instance, it could be physical phenomena such as the gravity law or the fact that the rain is going to fall in such place or in such hour.

More precisely, the Figure 2 illustrates our architecture for multiple environments with the example of the motion of fish in the Indian Ocean.

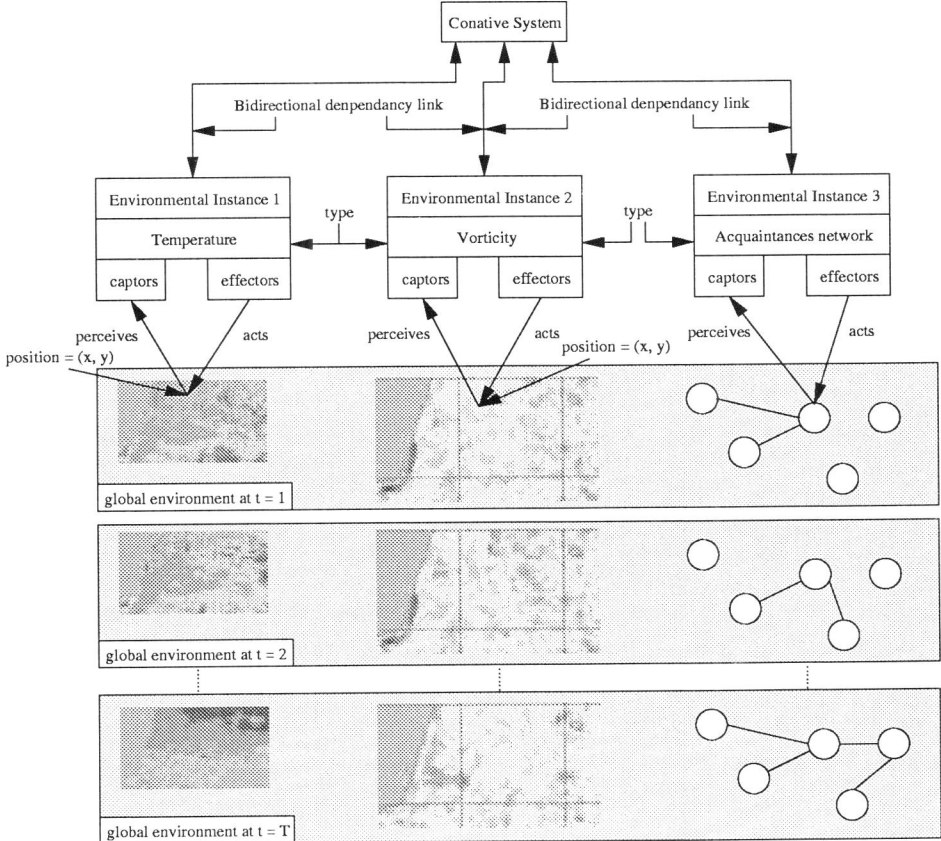

Fig. 2. Our architecture

In the next section we will show how to maintain the integrity of data on all of these environment by adding some new features.

3.2 How to Mantain the Integrity of Data on the Environment?

In the previous section we have seen how we can build multiple environments for a single agent, but our architecture, at present, suffers from a major problem: it can not manage the integrity of data on the set of environments. For example, if the conative system makes the decision to move, it should send this information in all the environments that could understand this command. Because if it does not make it, a same agent will be able to have its environmental instances in different positions. And in this case, we will lose the integrity of our data and motion in our environments. Similarly, if an action on an $environment_i$ implies other actions in the other environments, we can not manage this fact with the definitions supplied in the previous section.

Concretely, It is missing in our model the presence of one or several entities which can manage and control the integrity of data and the consequences of actions on one or several environments. This is why, in order to fill this lack, two new features have been added to our architecture: the first one is called the *virtual environmental instance* and the second one is called the *virtual environment*.

The virtual environmental instance

In the same way as for not virtual environmental instances, the virtual environmental instance is connected with the conative system of the agent. Moreover, it embeds a set of effectors and a set of captors. But this instance is called "virtual" because it is not connected with a "real" environment but it is connected with the virtual environment.

Concretely, the virtual environmental instance embeds the effectors which can have an influence on all or a part of environments (an effector of motion for instance), the effectors which are present in all the environmental instances of the other environments (*e.g,* when $\bigcap_{i=1}^{n} \mathcal{EFF}_i \neq \emptyset \ \forall i$) and finally the effectors which are necessary for the simulation, but which are not attached to a particular environment. In a similar way, the virtual environmental instance embeds the captors which are present in all the environmental instances if the other environments (*e.g,* when $\bigcap_{i=1}^{n} \mathcal{CAP}_i \neq \emptyset \ \forall i$) and the captors which are necessary for the simulation, but which are not attached to a particular environment.

Consequently, the virtual environmental instance allows to reduce the number of repeated effectors and captors in the system because according to the presentation above they delete redundant captors and effectors.

The virtual environment

The virtual environment is necessary because it is connected with all the virtual environmental instances. Consequently, all the effectors and captors defined in these environmental instances are plugged in this virtual environment. Moreover, the virtual environment is connected with all the "real" environment, this link called *integrity link* is a bidirectional communication link. For instance, when an effector requests the execution of a command on the virtual environment, this one will execute the appropriate command and then it will echo the effect of this command on all the environments thanks to the integrity link. And consequently, the integrity will be maintain on all the environments.

Moreover, the virtual environment contains the timer for all the environments, then when the virtual environment changes the time (*e.g* from $t = t_k$ to $t = t_{k+1}$) at its level and then it sends a special message on the integrity link that informs the environments that the simulation time has changed. More, the environments used for the simulation can cover different areas and have different types (2 dimensions, graphs, ...) and this is the virtual environment that will manage this diversity. For instance, let us imagine that there is two environments in our simulation: as explain above, one environment for the temperature of the ocean called env_t and another one for the vorticity of the ocean called env_v. The size of env_t is ($width \times height$) and the size of env_v is ($width' \times height'$) with $width < width'$ and $height < height'$ because this is not the same satellite that shoots these images. Then if the conative request a motion from a point $P(x,y)$ to a point $P'(x',y')$, the probability that $x' > width$ or that $y' > height$ is not null. Consequently, in this case, the virtual environment will execute effectively the motion on env_v and not on env_t and it sends a special message to env_t thanks to the integrity link that inform env_t that until a certain message, it does not put information in the captors of the environmental instance connected to it. Conversely, let us imagine that an action on env_t implies a change in data of env_v (a rise of the temperature for instance), then env_v will send a special message to the virtual environment that will forward this message to env_v. Then env_v will takes into account this feature and make the appropriate change.

Finally, in order to summarize, the figure 3 on the next page illustrates the final organization of our architecture.

4 Conclusion

In this paper we presented an architecture that aims to provide a framework to model and represent multiple environments in multiagent systems. This framework is composed of an agent model and an environmental model. The agent model relies on a strict separation between a conative system and its environmental instance. Between these two entities, the bidirectional dependency link allows them to communicate. This feature allows us to build a multiple environmental model. We are able to connect multiple environments on a single conative system. More, the integrity of data and evolution of the agents on these environments is ensured thanks to the virtual environmental instance and the virtual environment.

The contribution of this paper is very interesting because this architecture allows us to take into the fact that an agent can evolve in multiple environments simultaneously and that the evolution on an agent in one environment can have consequences on the other environments. And this approach opens new fields of simulation, in particular case of natural simulation and social simulation.

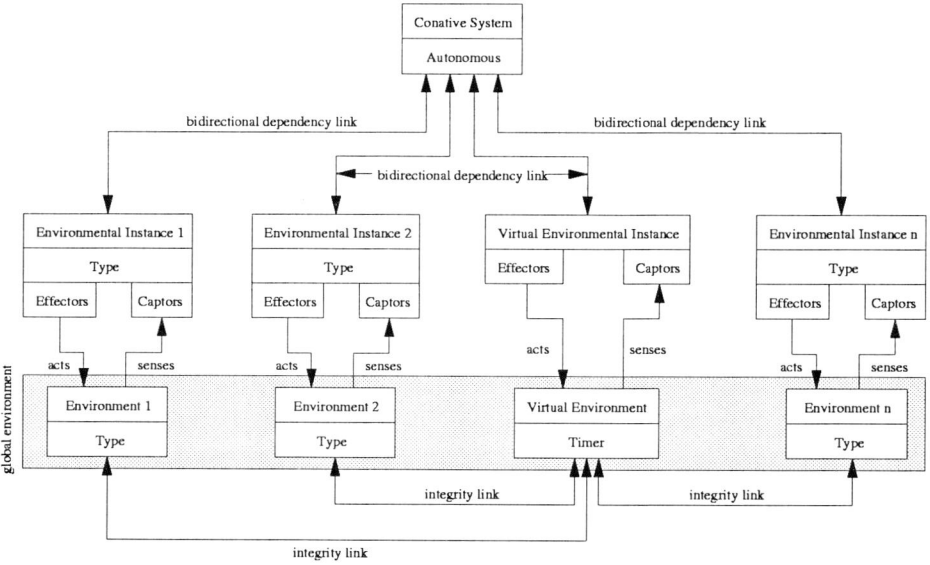

Fig. 3. Our final architecture

At present, this framework is ready to use. We use the Java language [5] to develop it, and we conform our code with de 100% Pure Java style. This fact ensure us that our code is entirely portable on other operating systems. It will be added to the GEAMAS project soon and thanks to Java, it will be soon available on our web pages. Finally, a new version is currently under development. This last version will be able to manage networked environment. By this way, we will be soon ready to perform networked simulations without the necessity of having the set of data on our local network.

The figure 4 on the facing page is a screenshot of our simulator.

Acknowledgments

It is a pleasure to acknowledge the Institut de Recherche en Mathématiques et Informatique Appliquées (IREMIA) for the stimulating intellectual environment it provided to us, as well as financial support for this project.

References

1. François Bousquet, Innocent Bakam, Hubert Proton, and Christophe Le Page. Cormas: Common-pool ressources and multi-agents system. In A.P del Pobil and M. Ali, editors, *Proceedings of the 11th IEA–AIE'98*, volume 1416 of *LNAI*, pages 826–838. Springer Verlag, June 1998.
2. Jacques Ferber. Reactive distributed artificial intelligence: Principles and applications. In G.M.P O'Hare and N.R. Jennings, editors, *Sixth Generation Computer Technology*, pages 287–314, New York, USA, 1994. Waley-Interscience Publication.

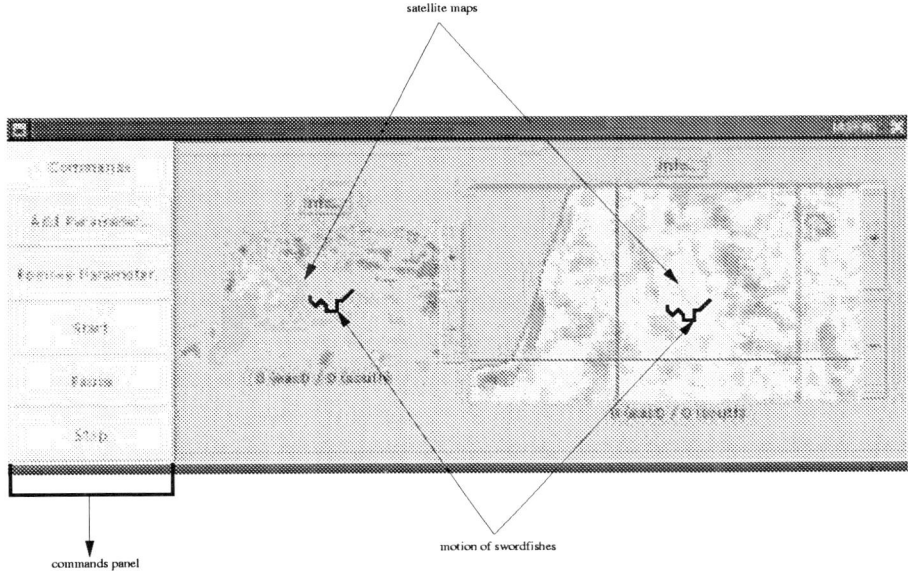

Fig. 4. A screenshot of our simulator

3. Jacques Ferber. *Les Systèmes Multi-Agents – Vers une intelligence collective.* iia – InterEditions, 1995.
4. Jacques Ferber and Olivier Gutknecht. A meta-model for the analysis and design of organizations in multi-agents systems. In *Proceedings of ICMAS'98*, pages 128–135, Paris, France, July 1998. IEEE Computer Society Press.
5. David Flanagan. *Java in a nutshell (version 1.1)*. O'Reilly, 2nd edition, 1997.
6. H. Randy Gimblett and Robert M. Itami. Modelling the Spatial Dynamics and Social Interaction of Human Recreators Using GIS and Intelligent Agent. In *Proceedings of the International Congress on Modelling and Simulation*, Hobart, Tasmania, December 1997.
7. Björn Hermans. *Intelligent Software Agents on The Internet: An Inventory of Currently Offered Functionality in the Information Society and a Prediction of (N ear) Future Developments.* First Monday – Peer-Reviewed Journal On The Internet, 1997.
8. Pierre Marcenac and Sylvain Giroux. *GEAMAS: A Generic Architecture for Agent-Oriented Simulations of Complex Processes.* International Journal of Applied Intelligence, Kluwer Academic Publishers, 1998.
9. N. Minar, R. Burkhart, C. Langton, and M. Askenazi. The swarm simulation system: A toolkit for building multi-agent simulations. Technical report, Santa Fe Institute, 1996.
10. Jean-Christophe Soulié and Pierre Marcenac. Environmental simulations using multiagent systems. In *Proceedings of ICIIS'99*, Washington, DC, USA, November 1999. IEEE Computer Society Press.
11. Jean-Christophe Soulié, Pierre Marcenac, Stéphane Calderoni, and Rémy Courdier. GEAMAS v2.0: An object oriented platform for complex systems simulations. In M. Singh, B. Meyer, J. Gil, and R. Mitchell, editors, *Proceedings of TOOLS USA'98*, pages 230–242, Santa Barbara, California, USA, August 1998. IEEE Computer Society Press.
12. M. Wooldridge and N.R Jennings. *Intelligent Agents: Theory and Practice.* Knowledge Engineering Review, 1995.

Task Models, Intentions, and Agent Conversation Policies

Renée Elio[1], Afsaneh Haddadi[2], and Ajit Singh[1]

[1] Department of Computing Science, University of Alberta,
Edmonton, Alberta Canada, T6G 2H1
ree@cs.ualberta.ca ajit@cs.ualberta.ca
[2] DaimlerChrysler, AG Alt-Moabit 96A,
10559 Berlin, Germany
afsaneh.haddadi@daimlerchrysler.com

Abstract. It is possible to define conversation policies, such as communication or dialogue protocols, that are based strictly on what messages and, respectively, what performatives may follow each other. While such an approach has many practical applications, such protocols support only "local coherence" in a conversation. Lengthy message exchanges require some infrastructure to lend them "global coherence." Recognition of agent intentions about the joint task is essential for this global coherence, but there are further mechanisms needed to ensure that both local and global coherence are jointly maintained. This paper presents a general yet practical approach to designing, managing, and engineering agents that can do simple run-time intention recognition without creating complex multi-state protocols. In this approach we promote developing abstract task models and designing conversation policies in terms of such models. An implemented agent assistant based on these ideas is briefly described.

1 Introduction

Recently, there has been considerable interest in specifying agent *conversation policies* [4], which speak to a range of matters in managing lengthy message exchange, from turn-taking and message time-out conventions to responding to dynamic constraints imposed by the environment. Our concern here is with what some researchers [3] claim is a crucial function of a broadly-defined conversation policy, namely constraining "the messages that appear on the wire." It is argued that this need arises from the many-to-many mapping between an agent's intention and the specific agent communication language (ACL) primitive used to convey that intention. The call for conversation policies stems from a belief that the solution to these matters will not be found at the level of individual message primitives or performatives within an agent communication language, such as KQML or FIPA's ACL [5,7]. However well-specified the semantics for a performative might be, they are under constrained with respect to the full illocutionary force of the communicative act. For example, an "inform" ought sometimes to be interpreted as a "suggestion" but in another context, as a "command." This in turn has given rise to a more *protocol* oriented view of ACL semantics, i.e., the specification of semantics for conversational sub-units [5,6,11,13].

Elevating the level of analysis from the individual performative to protocols (which we think is a crucial step) only moves the set of problems back a level. There is no consensus here either on what the primitive protocols are, let alone their semantics [3]. Although this matter is in principle resolvable, protocols can only maintain what we call *local coherence*—some unity between very short sequences of messages. In general, a protocol at best specifies all the possible courses of dialogue (alternative sequences of messages) that we, as designers, can predict as being possible and sufficient with respect to a specific goal or a task. When a dialogue expands beyond 2-3 message sequences, there must be some way to ensure *global coherence*, i.e., a coherence to how short message sequences are, crudely put, patched together.

While we fully believe that precise semantics are crucial for individual performatives and protocols, the full illocutionary force of a message sequence will be under constrained without some appeal to what we call an abstract task model. As one component of a publicly posted conversation policy, an abstract task model addresses two elements of a broadly-defined conversation policy [9]: specific goal achievement policies and conversation management policies. This paper is primarily an explication of this position and its pragmatic import. We have realized the ideas presented here in an implementation of a simple agent assistant using a BDI architecture [12].

2 Abstract Task Types and Intentions

For us, an abstract task type is something like "scheduling," "negotiation", "database search", or "diagnosis." Similar notions of generic tasks have supported domain-independent methodologies and architectures for developing knowledge-based problem-solving systems [1]. It seems useful to explore the notion that two agents begin a communication exchange with 'knowing' that their joint (abstract) task is one of negotiation, diagnosis, database search, or whatever. To do this, the agents must explicitly share an ontology for the abstract task they are jointly solving, and this ontology is different from the ontology for the actual domain (e.g., medical diagnosis vs. fault diagnosis). It is this meta-level ontology for the abstract task that defines initial, intermediate, and solution states and also defines how movement through those states can be accomplished. Without such a model, it seems that two agents cannot recognize when to begin exchanging messages, what protocol to initiate next, whether progress on the task is being made, or even when message exchange can stop.

We adopt a pragmatic perspective of intention as a commitment to goal, with a specification of when and how the goal is to be pursued and when the goal is abandoned [6]. Intentions move an agent to act and in multi-agent systems, they can be the impetus to engage in dialogue with a collaborating agent in order to act. Thus, intentions drive the conversation and it is these intentions that make multi-message sequences about some task globally coherent.

An abstract task model supports coherence beyond a single protocol by defining intentions as goals to achieve, a general strategy for goal-ordering, and methods for achieving those goals. By defining intentions, an abstract task model also serves to specify and constrain the content of individual messages by defining (i) what the messages can be about, or what we call message objects or "objects of discourse," (ii) what legal intentions (computational actions) an agent can have towards those objects, and (iii) how to progress on the task and when the task is completed. We address what we call local coherence as many others have, namely by specifying protocols for conversational sub-units. Unlike most protocols, our protocols are restricted to message-type *pairs* whose definition includes an option for a "violation" or "unexpected message." While a message type may be "unexpected" in the context of some protocol, its underlying intention cannot be unexpected in the context of the abstract task model that is jointly held by the two agents. Thus, an agent must be designed with (i) the notion that protocols *can* be violated, (ii) a mechanism for recognizing the intended new context, and (iii) the ability to evaluate the implication of the new context for the resumption of the current protocol (and its associated intention). That these notions are crucial to multi-agent cooperation has been argued from a theoretical perspective (e.g., [2]), but solutions implied by that work require systems with sophisticated reasoning engines. Our implementation illustrates that these can be handled flexibly and pragmatically with limited "reasoning" enabled by an abstract task model methodology.

3   Motivating Application: Successive Refinement Search

Our motivating application called for an agent that would assist a human (e.g., a driver in an automobile) in a variety of tasks, which include location and retrieval of information from various databases. The database entities are defined by feature-value tuples. This application is sufficiently challenging under the assumptions that: (a) the database is so large that the human agent cannot specify a single, simple database query for which there is one single answer; (b) the human agent may not necessarily have a definitive set of constraints in mind when starting the search task, or may change constraints during the message exchange, (c) there may be multiple search goals, and (d) the interface cannot be visual or require direct manipulation. Although we present our distinctions terms of human-agent communication, the general issues of intention recognition, resolving unexpected messages, and shifting initiative are generally relevant to agent-agent communication as well. In the following example dialogue (with English gloss), DBA designates the database agent and U designates the user.

U-2:	I want inexpensive food in San Francisco.
DBA-3:	O.K.. There are several hundred inexpensive restaurants in San Francisco.
DBA-4:	What type of food do you want?
U-5:	What do you mean?
DB-6:	I mean ethnic type such as Hungarian or French.
U-7:	Italian.
DBA-8:	O.K. Do you want a take out or sit-down place?
U-9:	What about on the Peninsula?
DBA-10:	O.K.-- we'll leave San Francisco for a moment.
DBA-11:	There are 35 Italian restaurants on the Peninsula.

Our concern here is the analysis of the task at a level of abstraction and generality that supports the specification of a jointly held abstract task model. We include the above dialogue for illustrative purposes only: the task model is not derived from dialogue analysis (which might serve as a starting point) but from task analysis. Our pragmatic specification of task semantics flow directly from the traditional view of a problem-solving as movement through a state space, where each state has a direct or indirect correspondence to a problem state. Such a formulation requires (a) a goal test that indicates whether a state (or path to a state) constitutes a problem solution, (b) a specification of an initial state, and (c) the specification of operators as functions performed on one state to produce a successor state. Task actions or operators are realized as inspectable preconditions that must match features in state s and inspectable post-conditions that define the transformation of state s into some successor state.

From this perspective, an abstract task model for successive refinement search may be formulated as follows. The message objects (which define different task state) are (i) a *domain*: a particular domain database in which entities are defined by features and values; (ii) a *constraint*: any feature that has a particular value assigned to it; (iii) a *search space*: a set of database entities that satisfy a set of constraints; (iv) *search-space members*: particular entities within a particular search space. What can be said about these objects is restricted to the computational actions that can be taken with them, and these are the intentions an agent can have about them. In our analysis these actions are limited to: (i) *loading* a database to be searched, which defines the initial search space, (ii) *contracting*, or reducing the search space by specifying additional constraints that members must satisfy, (iii) *expanding* that search space by relaxing one or more constraints, and (iv) *describing* information about a particular member of the search space, about a particular constraint, or about the search space as a set. These traditional database operations may be augmented with other capabilities that are unique to each agent (e.g., an agent might also compute the most-discriminating feature for a given search space). Generally speaking, these operators are the *only* that are legal actions for an agent. As such, they define the complete set of task actions about which either agent can be committed to take and hence, they correspond to the complete set of *task intentions*. The satisfaction of these intentions causes a movement to another state in the space, though some computation that changes the problem. Contextual features of the current task state impose some partial order on the next necessary or plausible intention to have, which in turn implicate some particular task operator. But the crucial point is that task intentions are defined by task operators that are executed on objects that comprise task states.

In the above message exchange, U-9 does not provide an answer to the question posed in message DBA-8, and instead shifts the direction of the task. Handling this case could be done with protocols with additional transition arcs. But taken to the extreme, this solution must anticipate every such possible adjacency and represent those possible adjacencies with conditional arcs. Defining semantics for a completed protocol becomes difficult, since many alternative paths might be traversed before the protocol exit state is reached. As we present below, we use two-state protocols and shift part of the burden away from anticipation (by the designer) and onto recognition (by the agent). *Intentions that an agent can have about the task (and presumably express during the message exchange) are limited by the objects of discourse, what can be done with them, and therefore what can be said about them.* This is crucial to having a pragmatic but somewhat flexible approach to posting and recognizing intentions, for these objects of discourse serve to circumscribe the set of task intentions.

The abstract task specification may also define *discourse intentions* —the commitment to perform a communication act*s*. These arise in service of task intentions. The simplest example is when one agent is known to have information necessary that another agent recognizes is necessary to advance the task (i.e., to satisfy a task intention). Thus, task operator preconditions delimit one set of objects for discourse intentions. A second set of discourse intentions is defined by a task operator's post-conditions, which define a new successor state. An agent must form discourse intentions to communicate these post-conditions, if another agent without direct access to these post-conditions must know about them to fulfill its role in the joint tasks. Conversely, there are tasks in which the post-conditions of a task action ought not to be shared. Such specifications (which participating agent must, or must not, know what) are rightly part of an abstract task model as well. In essence, the abstract task model defines a protocol at the level of intentions that must, may, or may not be held by each agent. This too can be part of a shared conversation policy.

4 Message Types, Objects, and Content

The semantics underlying the language primitives are based on a number of pragmatic principles discussed in [6]. Our primary concern is not with the syntactic form of the message but with specifying its content. We use the schematic format *(performative $agent-name1 $agent-name2 $object-of-discourse $content)*, although any ACL message syntax with additional necessary parameters might be employed.

The outermost performative, or message type, represents the general class of a message. In ATS, we make use of the classes *request, query,* and *inform* (see Table 1). The *$agent-name1* parameter refers to the speaker, sender or generally the actor of the performative, while *$agent-name2* refers to the hearer, receiver or generally the agent that would be effected by the performative. We discuss *$object-of-discourse*, which is constrained for each performative class, below. The *$conten*t of a message can be another ("inner") performative, which further specializes the class by supplying information related to the result of the task action that has been performed, the task itself or the action the speaker intends/expects the hearer to perform.

The second column of Table 1—the immediately expected reply—designates the performative that would "complete" the dialogue initiated by the performative in column 1. Put another way, the information in Table 1 defines a basic state-transition definition for sub-dialogues.

Request. Following [6], we view a request as having an associated level of commitment. A request performative is tightly coupled with advancing the task. The objects of discourse associated with request are (i) a system *action* that enables a search task to begin or terminate, such as loading a particular database for searching and (ii) a *constraint*, which specifies a feature-value vector according to which database entities can be identified. Most request performatives concern constraints. When a request is made by the database agent, the agent is making a pre-commitment to how the progress on the search task might be accomplished and it prompts the user agent for information in order to do this. Requests from the database agent thus take *suggest* as an inner performative. A suggestion refers to a possible task strategy and it must be *accepted* or *rejected* by the other agent. By supplying the information asked for, the user is committing to this computation. When a request is made by the user agent, the user is simultaneously committing to a computation on the search space and delivering the information necessary to execute it. User requests thus take *provide* as an inner performative. The objects-of-discourse that may accompany suggest and provide are (i) the *domain* (e.g., restaurants, hospitals); (ii) the *value* of one or more specified features that comprise a constraint; and (iii) the search space *(i.e., the set of database entities described by the current set of constraints)*. Table 2 provides some examples of agent and database agent requests (with English gloss).

Table 1: Performatives and their combination

Outer Performative	Inner Performative	Immediately Expected Reply
Request	Provide	(Acknowledge) + Inform
	Suggest	(Acknowledge)+Inform+ Accept/Reject
Query	Provide	Inform
	Confirm	Inform + Confirm/Deny
	Suggest	Inform + Accept/Reject
Inform	Provide, Confirm	
	Deny, Accept, Reject	

Table 2: Example request and query messages

Req-U: Let's look for a restaurant in Mid-Peninsula.
(request U DBA :action (initiate :task search :domain restaurants))
(request U DBA :constraint (provide DBA U :value (fv-pairs :feature location :value Mid-peninsula)))
Req-DBA: How about French?
(request DBA U :constraint (suggest DBA U :value (fv-pairs :feature rest-type :value French)))
Que-U: What do you mean by restaurant type?
(query U DBA :knowl-base (provide DBA U :domain (describe-feature :domain $domain-id feature-list :feature rest-type :attribute range))
Que-U: What are the opening hours for this restaurant?
(query U DBA :database (provide DBA U :member (describe-member :member $member :feature hours)))

Query. A query is not about advancing a task but about exchanging information. Its objects of discourse are (i) agent *capabilities*, (ii) the domain *knowledge base*, which includes domain-specific information, such as the range of values on a particular feature, (iii) the *database*, which includes queries about the availability of information about particular entities in the database, and (iv) *task-information*, information relevant to the current state of the task. Queries may take either *provide, suggest*, or *confirm* as an inner performative. A *confirm* expresses the truth or falseness with respect to a property of some object-of-discourse and it must be confirmed or denied.

When a query is sent by the user agent, the database agent must respond with an *inform* followed by an appropriate inner performative. The objects-of-discourse that may accompany the inner performatives associated with queries can be (i) the *domain* (e.g., restaurants, hospitals); (ii) the current search *space*; and (iii) a particular *member* in the current search space or database.

Inform. Inform messages take on the outer and inner objects-of-discourse, and a content specification, that occur in the request or query dialogue that they complete.

The crucial aspect of this analysis is not its realization in these particular message objects. Rather, it is that message objects and content are defined by some commitment to an abstract task model, which can be part of a conversation policy.

5 Protocols as Operators

A task intention concerns advancement of a task-related goal or sub-goal and a discourse intention concerns advancement of information exchange, in support of a task intention. We believe it is important to model the task intentions and discourse intentions as characterizing two distinct state spaces. Whenever an agent cannot proceed in the task space, it adopts a discourse intention (e.g., sends a query message to gather information). This transfers control to discourse space until sufficient information has been gathered from the other agent to proceed in the task space. Similarly, whenever an agent cannot proceed further in the discourse space (e.g., answer a received query), a task intention is formed to compute the necessary information (causing a state transition in task space) in order to satisfy a discourse intention and allow a transition to a new state of shared information.

In our view, *protocols are the realizations of operators in each of these two spaces*. A protocol defines a structured exchange of information between two agents. Task protocols correspond to task operators for computing task successor states. A task protocol is defined as a set of input parameters, that include a given state, and a set of output parameters, which fully define the successor state. Discourse protocols are similarly defined, while additionally representing the temporal and contextual conditions on what message performatives may follow each other, as per Table 1.

This discourse vs. task space distinction has, we believe, both theoretical and practical import agent design. It supports a clean separation of semantics associated with agent knowledge (modeled in discourse space as satisfied discourse intentions) from semantics associated with progress on the task (modeled as progress in task space through satisfied task intentions).

6 Implementation of a Database Assistant

We have built the agent-assistant for successive refinement search based on abstract task model and the distinctions outlined above using PRS-CL [10], a BDI style architecture. We have put forward our groundwork for these distinctions, at the expense of having the opportunity to provide many implementation details. Here, we emphasize how the abstract task specification supports a pragmatic and flexible handling of "unexpected" messages—those not sanctioned as immediately expected responses for a running discourse protocol.

Generally put, a BDI architecture consists of a dynamic (working) memory that holds current goals and beliefs (symbolic patterns), a plan library for holding representations of methods and actions to achieve goals, and intention structures that correspond to plans that are in some state of execution or activity. Due to space constraints, we assume the reader is familiar with the execution cycle of these architectures [12].

Within this architecture, we functionally partition dynamic memory into a task space and discourse space. Task and discourse intentions, as well as task and discourse protocols for message exchange, are implemented as different plan types the plan library, and their invocation and resumption is influenced by a priority scheme defined for those types. Conceptually, a plan has an invocation condition, resumption conditions, and satisfaction conditions. Invocation conditions are those conditions that trigger the plan and form an instance of an intention, i.e., constitute a goal that has been adopted. Plans that represent task intentions either trigger discourse intentions (if they cannot be immediately satisfied) or pass control to task protocols (if their satisfaction conditions are satisfied and information can be sent to the foreign agent for some computation). Similarly, discourse intentions may give rise to task intentions or pass control to discourse protocols to initiate message exchange with the user. The plan bodies for all discourse protocols are the same: the protocol formulates the message, sends the message out, posts its expected reply to dynamic memory with an appropriate protocol ID tag, and then suspends.

When a message arrives, a message handler plan determines which protocol is waiting for it (there might be many suspended threads of conversation). The most recently suspended protocol expecting that message type receives it. This resumes execution of the discourse protocol, whose successful completion causes updates to discourse space. Resumption of the discourse intention ensues, and its completion causes transfer of information from the new discourse space-state into the current task-space state. The task intention then resumes to check whether all its satisfaction conditions are met. If not, its plan body may set another discourse intention.

If an incoming message is not recognized as an expected message by a waiting protocol, the message handler releases it to dynamic memory. That is, the arrival of a message that is unexpected in the local context of an executing discourse protocol is resolved at the global level of possible discourse intentions or task intentions: a plan from the plan library is triggered.

Our database agent handles the conversation flow illustrated by the sample dialogue, as well as others in which there are several changes of direction, multiple sub dialogues embedded within sub-dialogues that in turn shift the task direction, and so forth. This application domain is admittedly simple: there are 24 intentions in the plan library corresponding to task and discourse intentions, and discourse protocols.

7 Related Work and Discussion

Several researchers have specified semantics at protocol-level, realized as pre-, post- and completion conditions [2, 7, 13]. There is a correspondence to these ideas to the semantics we have for our abstract task intentions and protocols, except that our task intentions concern how to advance the task, given the agent's beliefs about the current task state, and discourse protocols are then called in service of the intention. Thus, we separate our communication semantics from our task semantics. We have argued for a clean separation between discourse and task spaces, believing that it clarifies what the "local" and "extended" effects of a successfully-completed message exchange are [9]. For us, local effects of completing a message exchange via a protocol are effects on the discourse space. Many proposals for ACL semantics based on joint intention or mutual belief theory specify axioms for what intentions or beliefs are jointly held, given a particular message exchange [13, 14]. By our model and in our implementation, these are post conditions associated with satisfied discourse intentions (plans), that were accomplished via completed discourse protocols (also plans). The extended perlocutionary effects of a successfully executed discourse protocol, in our framework, are specified as changes first to the discourse space and then possibly, through an associated task intention, as changes to the task space.

Pitt and Mamdani [9] present protocol-level semantics that includes what they call an "add function"—an agent's procedure for computing the change in its information state from the content of an incoming message using a particular performative uttered in the context of a particular protocol. We have pragmatically realized many aspects of their protocol-based semantics in our current implementation via the abstract task specification, which designates the relationship between task intentions, discourse intentions, and ultimately, well-structured communication acts.

We are considering a suitable representation for presenting an abstract task specification as a downloadable conversation policy. We particularly need to examine the matter of agent roles and functionality within the abstract task specification. Further, in our implementation, there were numerous control difficulties that resulted from representing both intentions and protocols as plans, allowing reactive recognition of new intentions where appropriate, and balancing sequential and reactive elements of the system. We are considering architectures like SOAR [8], in which an "impasse" in one problem space spawns a new problem space with associated operators. This architecture would support a clean separation of task and discourse semantics (as different problem solving spaces), but at the expense of a plan-based approach to intention representation. In sum, we advocate a pragmatic approach to determining intentions based on task specifications that agents may jointly share. In doing so, this approach serves as a way of constraining what messages agents send to each other at the task level and reduces the burden of imposing all such constraints at just the individual performative or at just the protocol level. This is one step towards coherent message exchange, based on "intentional states" that can be directly traced to a representation of the global task that may be part of a public conversation policy specification.

Acknowledgements

This work was supported in part by NSERC research grant A0089 to R. Elio.

References

1. Bylander, T., Chandrasekaren, B.: Generic tasks for knowledge-based reasoning: The "right" level of abstraction for knowledge engineering. Int. J. Man-Machine Studies **26** (1987) 231-243
2. Cohen, P. R., Levesque, H. J.: Communicative actions for artificial agents. In J. M. Bradshaw (ed.), Software Agents, AAAI Press, Menlo Park CA, (1997) 419-436
3. Greaves, M., Holmback, H., Bradshaw, J. What is a conversation policy? In M. Greaves & J. Bradshaw (eds). Specifying and implementing conversation policies. Autonomous Agents '99 Workshop (Seattle WA, May 1999), 1-10
4. Greaves, M, Bradshaw, J. (eds.): Specifying and Implementing Conversation Policies, Autonomous Agents '99 Workshop, (Seattle, WA, May 1999)
5. FIPA-99 specifications, see www.fipa.org/spec
6. Haddadi, A.: Communication and cooperation in agent systems: A pragmatic theory. Lecture Notes in Computer Science, Vol.1056 Springer-Verlag, Berlin New York (1996)
7. Labrou, Y., Finin, T.: Semantics and conversations for an agent communication language. In Huhn, M. N., Singh, M. P. (eds.): Readings in Agents. Morgan Kaufmann, San Francisco, (1998) 235-242
8. Laird, J.E., Newell, A., and Rosenbloom, P.S. SOAR: An architecture for general intelligence. Artificial Intelligence **33** (1987) 1-64
9. Moore, S.: On conversation policies and the need for exceptions. In M. Greaves and J. Bradshaw (eds). Specifying and implementing conversation policies. Autonomous Agents '99 Workshop (Seattle WA, May 1999), 19-29
10. Myers, K.: A procedural approach to task-level control knowledge, Proc. Third Int. Conf. on AI Planning Systems, AAAI Press, Menlo Park CA, (1996), 166-173
11. Pitt, J., Mamdani, A.: Communication protocols in multi-agent systems. In M. Greaves and J. Bradshaw (eds): Specifying and implementing conversation policies. Autonomous Agents '99 Workshop (Seattle WA, May 1999), 39-48
12. Rao, A.S., Georgeff, M.P.: BDI agents: From theory to practice. Tech. Rep. 56, Australian Artificial Intelligence Institute, Melbourne, Australia, (1995)
13. Smith, I. A., Cohen, P.R., Bradshaw, J. M., Greaves, M.,Holmback, H: Designing conversation policies using joint intention theory. In Proc. Third Int. Conf. on Multi-agent Systems, (Paris, France 1998) IEEE Press, 269-276
14. Sidner, C. L.: An artificial discourse language for collaborative negotiation, Proc. of 12th. Int. Conf. on Art. Intell (AAAI), AAAI Press, Menlo Park CA, (1994) 814-819.

Genetic Algorithm with Knowledge-Based Encoding for Interactive Fashion Design

Hee-Su Kim and Sung-Bae Cho

Department of Computer Science, Yonsei University
134 Shinchon-dong, Sudaemoon-ku, Seoul 120-749, Korea
[madoka, sbcho]@candy.yonsei.ac.kr

Abstract. Evolutionary computation gives a great potential in several real-world problems as a powerful tool for optimization and classification, but there still remain a lot of obstacles to be applied to artistic domains. To overcome the shortcoming a variety of techniques have been proposed, and among them interactive genetic algorithm (IGA) is extensively studied in these days. IGA exploits the interaction with human in the course of evolution by taking his evaluation as fitness. In this paper, we propose an effective knowledge-based encoding scheme for IGA in a real-world application. This method has been applied to a fashion design aid system, which can reflect user's preference or emotion that is usually difficult to be expressed explicitly. To show that the proposed encoding scheme produces more realistic and practical design, an experimental study as well as a theoretical investigation with schema theorem has been conducted.

1 Introduction

Evolutionary computation (EC) provides efficient method of machine learning, optimization and classification that is based on evolution mechanisms such as biological genetics and natural selection. EC operates with a set of points called population, and improves the population by generation. There has been extensive research on EC, making it a major stream of artificial intelligence. However, EC techniques themselves have been seldom applied to artistic domains such as music or design, because of the difficulty of deriving formal fitness functions to evaluate the individuals in a population. Interactive genetic algorithm (IGA) can solve this problem, for it takes user's evaluation as fitness function directly to evaluate each individual.

As an application of IGA to artistic domain, we have proposed a fashion design aid system. It can capture user's preference, support him to find out his favorite design within huge search space effectively, and be operated even by non-professional designers. A casual manufacturer, for example, may collect consumer's preferred designs instead of ambiguous adjectives from common survey and marketing research, using proposed fashion design aid system. In this paper we attempt to justify the encoding scheme with both the theoretical support of schema theorem, and empirical data.

2 Background

2.1 Interactive Genetic Algorithm

GA was proposed by John Holland in early 1970s. It applies some of natural evolution mechanisms like crossover, mutation, and survival of the fittest to optimization and machine learning. GA provides very efficient search method working on population, and has been applied to many problems of optimization and classification [2, 6]. General GA process is as follows [5]:
- Step 1 : Initialize the population of chromosomes.
- Step 2 : Calculate the fitness for each individual in the population using fitness function.
- Step 3 : Reproduce individuals to form a new population according to each individual's fitness.
- Step 4 : Perform crossover and mutation on the population.
- Step 5 : Go to step 2 until some condition is satisfied.

IGA is the same as GA except fitness function. In IGA user gives fitness to each individual instead of explicit fitness function. In this way IGA can 'interact' with user, and also can perceive user's emotion or preference in the course of evolution. For this reason IGA can be used to solve problems that cannot be easily solved by GA, such as design and art [11, 14, 15, 17]. Fig. 1 compares the processes of GA and IGA.

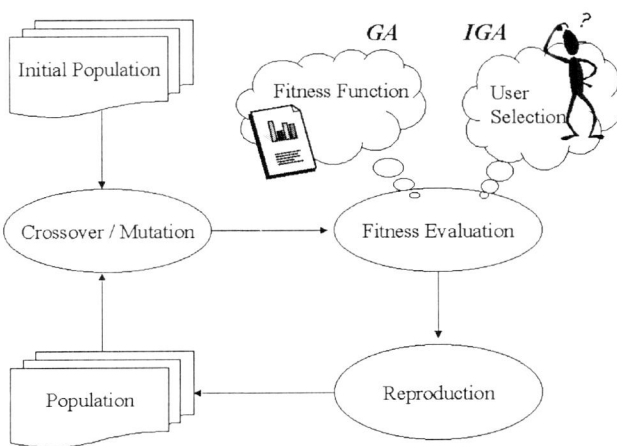

Fig. 1. GA and IGA processes

The advantage of using IGA instead of GA is clear. The goal of fashion design is to make some 'good design' of clothes. We can apply GA for fashion design by initializing the population of individuals encoded from design characteristics, setting and evolving the fitness as 'how good the design of dress is.' However, there is no standard of 'goodness of design,' and it is almost impossible to organize fitness function. Granting it to be possible, it will become useless after being behind the fashion. IGA might be a solution for this. IGA can reflect personal preference or changing fashion, because it perceives fitness directly from user instead of using some function [11].

2.2 Fashion Design Aid System Using IGA

Though the meaning of design has changed by time, the works that designers do has not changed much when they design dress. They start with a sketch and flesh it out into an illustration. With clippings from magazines, journals and photographs of similar or rival designs from fashion shows, they make these concepts into some sample pieces. These samples are tested for quality, feel and aesthetics very rigorously [1]. Recently, computer has begun to aid these works. AutoCAD from Autodesk along with ApparelCAD [13] and Creative Designer System from Gerber [10] are some good examples. Virtual Reality (VR), which is achieved by some computer system, can also reduce time and cost to design a dress [3, 7]. These fashion design aid systems work well, but they are usually for professionals only, and it is hard for non-professionals to use. Some design-aid systems such as one developed by Nakanishi have been developed using interactive EC [14]. It may be used by non-professionals, because it evolves individuals according to interaction with user, but most of its productions are somewhat impractical because encoded individuals do not contain realistic knowledge on the domain of fashion.

To solve this problem, we have proposed a fashion design aid system using IGA with domain specific knowledge. The proposed fashion design aid system uses IGA to get a preferred design by user. Fig. 2 shows the overview of entire system. There is a database of partial design elements. Each design is stored as 3D models. System selects the models of each part according to the decoding from individual chromosome, and combines them into a number of individual designs. The population is displayed on screen and user gives fitness to each design. Then, the system reproduces the population proportional to the fitness value of each design, and applies crossover and mutation to make the next generation. The results are displayed again in the screen with 3D graphics. Iteration of these processes can produce the population of higher fitness value, namely better designs. He gives fitness values according to his emotions 'felt' from seeing and imagining each design. As the result, selected characteristics that are encouraged more by user's emotion will appear at the next generation with large possibility.

We have used 3D Studio MAX R2.5 to create each design part as 3D model (see Fig. 3), and the models are converted into OpenGL lists [18]. We have used GLUT library, an advanced OpenGL library developed by Mark Kilgard and ported to

Win32 by Nate Robins [8], with original OpenGL library from SGI to reduce program burden without any loss of its execution speed. Converted models are inserted into C program, written in Visual Studio 6.0 of Microsoft. The system can show combined 3D models through OpenGL operation, according to decoding from individual genotype. Fig. 4 shows the user interface of our system. It shows current population composed of 8 individual models in one screen. There are slider bars for each individual design to obtain user's feedback or preference. The rightmost part of screen shows the current status of evolution, and provides the controls 'to generate next population' and 'to restore previous population.' One can find out their favorite design from the large search space by interacting with the system.

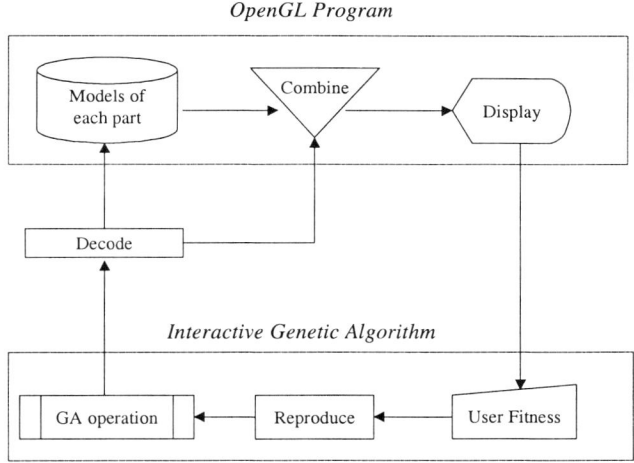

Fig. 2. System overiew

3 Knowledge-Based Encoding

3.1 Method

As mentioned earlier, previous design aid systems using evolutionary computation produce impractical designs because they do not consider domain-specific knowledge. To solve this problem, we have encoded the detail model based on the knowledge of the fashion design [16]. First, we have reclassified general detail factors into three parts: neck and body, arm and sleeve, skirt and waistline. Next, we have encoded them with extra 3 bits for each, which determines the color of each part. A design is made from combining them, and with IGA some combination that produces the design preferred by user is found out, resulting in more realistic and reasonable design. Encoded detail parts are described as follows [12], and Fig. 5 shows some of them with chromosome design. Fig. 6 gives an example of combining models from genotype bit string.

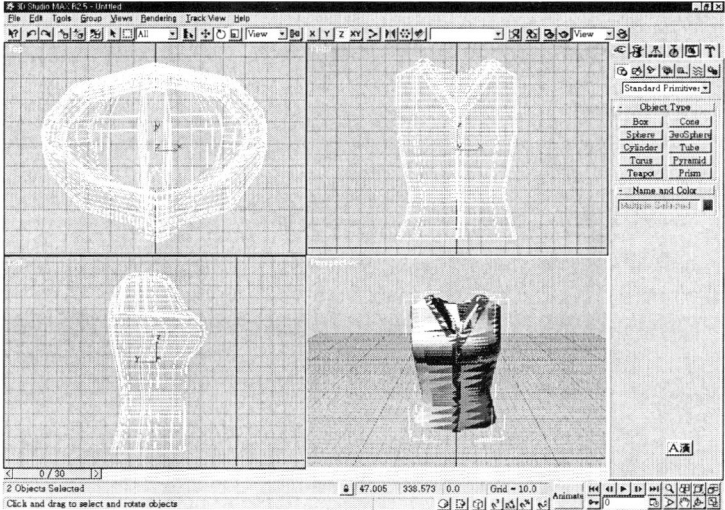

Fig. 3. 3D modeling with 3D Studio MAX.

Fig. 4. User interface of the system.

- Arm and sleeve part contains sleeve and cuffs detail. There are 12 models including armless design, and encoded into 4 bits.
- Neck and body part includes neckline, collar, and body shape. We have collected and encoded 34 models into 6 bits.
- Skirt and waistline part includes waistline and skirt below it. We have collected and encoded 9 models into 4 bits.

Genetic Algorithm with Knowledge-Based Encoding for Interactive Fashion Design   409

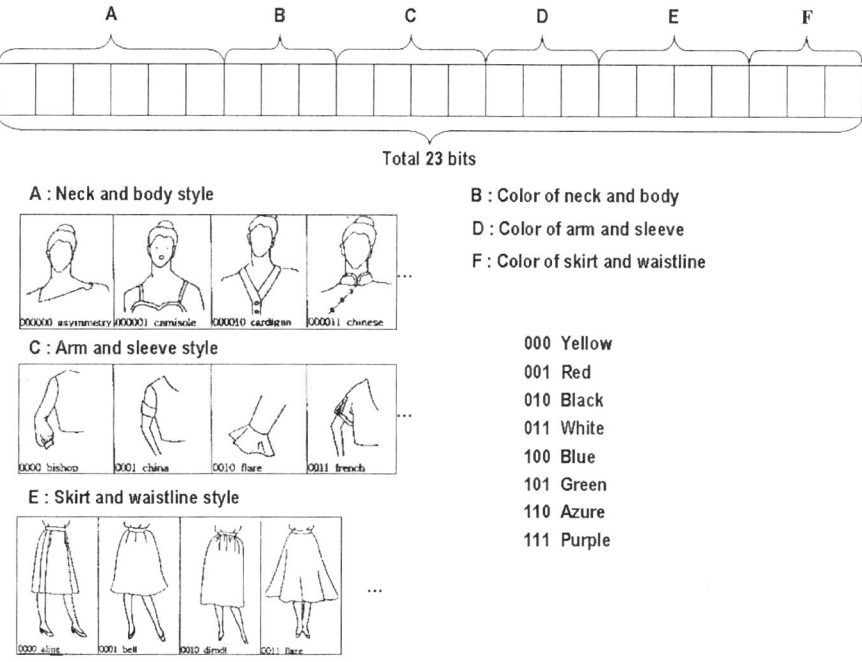

Fig. 5. Chromosome structure

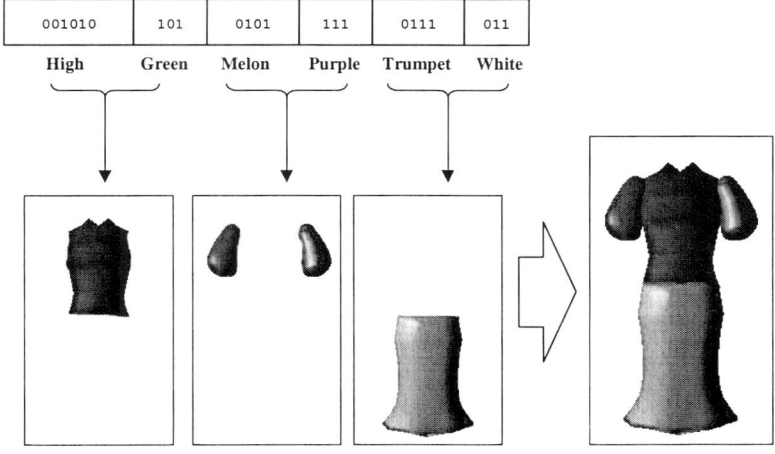

Fig. 6. Decoding from an example genotype

3.2 Theoretical Analysis

John Holland introduced the concept of schema to explain how each individual 'evolves' in GA. He explained how similarities among highly fit strings can help direct the search in GAs. According to it, the number of strings contained by some schema in the next generation can be predicted in terms of those in the current generation [6]. In other words, the instances of schema H in particular generation $t+1$, $m(H, t+1)$, can be expressed in terms of $m(H, t)$. With the traditional genetic operations of reproduction (propotional selection and generational replacement), recombination (one-point crossover) and mutation (binary mutation), the number of strings contained by a schema in generation $t+1$ can be predicted by the following equation, which we call the schema equation :

$$m(H,t+1) \geq m(H,t) \cdot \frac{f(H)}{\overline{f}} \left[1 - p_c \cdot \frac{\delta(H)}{l-1} \right] \left[1 - p_m \right]^{o(H)}$$

$$\cong m(H,t+1) \geq m(H,t) \cdot \frac{f(H)}{\overline{f}} \left[1 - p_c \cdot \frac{\delta(H)}{l-1} - o(H) \cdot p_m \right]$$

(1)

- l is the string length
- $\delta(H)$ is a defining length of a schema H, which denotes the distance between the first and last positions of fixed values in schema H
- $o(H)$ denotes an order of schema H, which is the number of fixed values of the schema H
- $f(H)$ is the average fitness of the strings representing schema H at time t, which we call schema average
- $\overline{f}$ is the average fitness of the entire population, which we call population average
- p_c is the probability for crossover, called crossover rate
- p_m is the probability for mutation, called mutation rate

With the schema equation, we can conclude that schemata with short defining length, low order and above-average fitness receive exponentially increasing trials in subsequent generations. We can expect the increase of survived building blocks containing useful information assuming that an individual genotype contains n meaningful building blocks.

With common 1-point crossover, one or no building block would be destroyed. Therefore, the increase of survived building blocks that are informative after crossover is computed as follows :

$$((n-1) \sum_{k=1}^{n} p_c \cdot \frac{\delta(H_k)}{l-1} + n \cdot p_c \cdot \frac{n-1}{l-1}) + n(1-p_c)$$

$$= p_c \cdot \frac{n-1}{l-1} (\sum_{k=1}^{n} \delta(H_k) + n) + n(1-p_c)$$

(2)

In our concern, the total sum of every schema's defining length is equal to $(l-n)$ and the equation comes to :

$$p_c \cdot \frac{n-l}{l-1} + n$$

(3)

For mutation, the effect is clearer. From the equation (1), we know that the probability of survival for a schema H is $(1-p_m)^{o(H)}$. Therefore, the probability at which a schema H will be destroyed after mutation is equal to $1-(1-p_m)^{o(H)}$. Therefore, the number of building blocks which would be destroyed is computed as follows:

$$\sum_{k=1}^{n}(1-(1-p_m)^{o(H_k)})$$
$$= n - \sum_{k=1}^{n}(1-p_m)^{o(H_k)} \quad (4)$$

Regarding the results (3) and (4), the number of survived building blocks after crossover and mutation can be computed as:

$$(p_c \cdot \frac{n-l}{l-1}+n)-(n-\sum_{k=1}^{n}(1-p_m)^{o(H_k)})$$
$$= p_c \cdot \frac{n-l}{l-1}+\sum_{k=1}^{n}(1-p_m)^{o(H_k)} \quad (5)$$

Finally, we should concern about fitness values, and (5) must be rewritten as follows:

$$\frac{f(I)}{\bar{f}}(p_c \cdot \frac{n-l}{l-1}+\sum_{k=1}^{n}(1-p_m)^{o(H_k)}) \quad (6)$$

where $f(I)$ is the fitness value for an individual I.

Notice that the proposed knowledge-based encoding re-classifies nearby detail elements into the three of each design cluster and encodes them into corresponding block within chromosome. Because each short 'building block' contains useful information about each dress design corresponding to current individual's chromosome encoding, we can expect that our encoding method takes advantages in the evolution process as described above.

4 Experimental Results

The system runs on Pentium PC. The population is composed of 8 individuals. We have used one-point crossover of 0.5 and mutation of 0.05. As a strategy of evolution, we have preserved one elitist individual in each generation for the next generation. It is difficult to show the convergence of IGA with quantitative analysis and there is no standard method to do so, because it is operated based on human's evaluation different from standard GA. To show the convergence, we have obtained the fitness values from each user. We have chosen 10 subjects who are 5 male and 5 female graduate and undergraduate students. They are all twenties and have no background of fashion design. We have requested them to find cool-looking design using the system.

Generation number is limited to 10, due to the characteristics of interactive evolutionary computation. In IGA, user should evaluate each individual himself, and therefore we should limit the number of generations and the population size. Fig. 7 shows the changes of fitness on average and the best, while subjects are searching cool-looking design. Though the search space is large, it shows steady improvement of the result over generations.

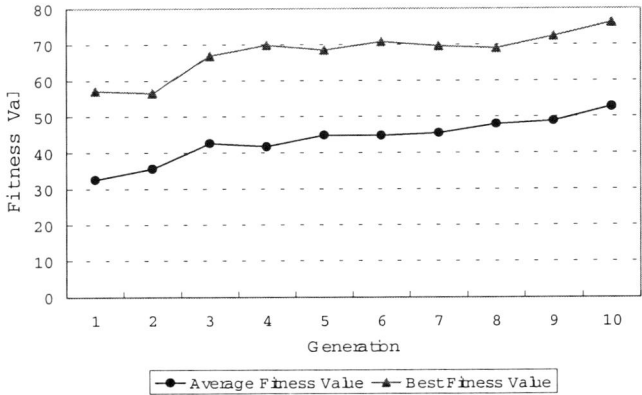

Fig. 7. Fitness changes on searching for cool-looking design.

To show that the number of preferred schemata is increasing, we have presumed the best individual from the last generation as the nearest solution, and chosen some meaningful building blocks contained in it. One process of searching for cool-looking design is selected randomly, and the frequency of chosen building blocks is calculated in each generation. Fig. 8 shows the result. The nearest solution selected is an individual with slit body design with white color, sleeveless arm design, and scooter skirt design with blue color. We can see that each building block corresponding to the solution's characteristic increases independently. In other words, preferred schemata have been tried more generation by generation. Another important point is that the number of solution schema is near 0 at the initial population. It indicates that though the number of generations is limited by 10, the evolution process does not depend upon its initial population, and searches for ideal solution.

We have conducted another test to show the usefulness of the encoding method. We have developed a system identical to the original one, except that it makes use of different encoding method : sequential encoding. This encodes all the possible design combinations sequentially without any knowledge. In this scheme a genotype represents a design as a whole, while the proposed knowledge-based modular encoding scheme has 6 separated parts on the genotype representing 6 design characteristics. With this sequential encoding system, we have requested the same 10 subjects to find their own designs that give cool-feeling in 10 generations, using those two systems without notice of the differences between them. Fig. 9 shows the result and we can easily see that sequential encoding method does not show steady convergence, different from the knowledge-based one. After getting resulted designs of each method we have requested the subjects to compare and give scores from −3 to 3, positive value if he or she prefers the result of knowledge-based encoding and negative value otherwise. This pair-to-pair comparison [4] is a kind of subjective test, and the result is described in Fig. 10. We can assert that subjects are significantly more satisfied with the designs from knowledge-based encoding than those from sequential one.

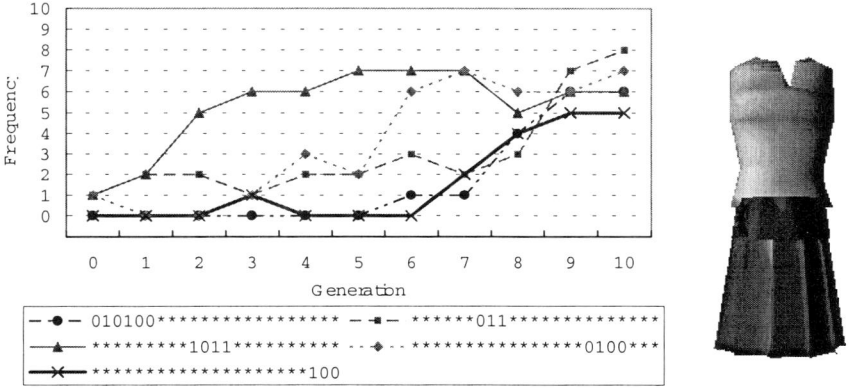

Fig. 8. Example solution design and frequency of each solution schema.

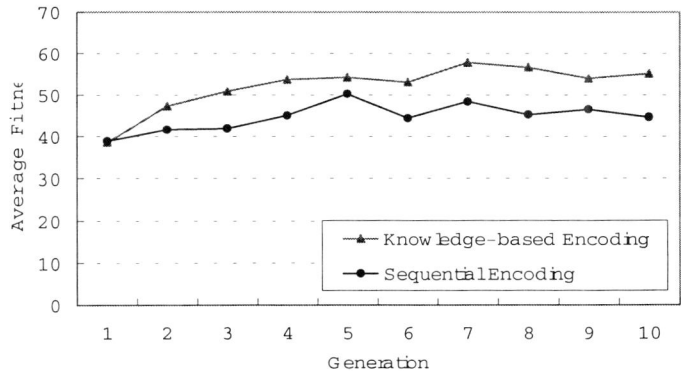

Fig. 9. Fitness changes on searching for cool-looking design, using knowledge-based encoding method and sequential encoding method.

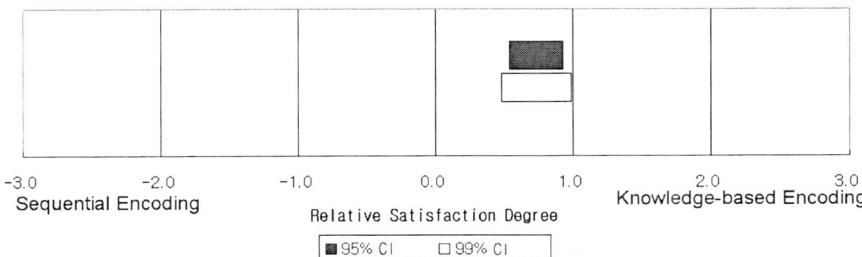

Fig. 10. Mean of satisfaction degrees between the result of knowledge-based encoding and sequential encoding

5 Concluding Remarks

We have proposed and developed an IGA-based fashion design aid system, for an application of IGA to artistic domains. Unlike simple GA that cannot be applied to artistic domains, our system using IGA shows successful performance. Experimental results indicate that preferred schemata appear more frequently within each generation to evolve the population. Though the search space is relatively large, the system has shown steady convergence, and the proposed encoding provides more satisfiable design than sequential encoding. There still remain some problems caused by the small size of population, and we are under way to solve them.

Acknowledgement

This research was supported by Brain Science and Engineering Research Program sponsored by Korean Ministry of Science and Technology.

References

1. Brockman, H.L., *The Theory of Fashion Design*, John Wiley & Sons, Inc., 1965.
2. Chamber, L., *Practical Handbook of Genetic Algorithms*, CRC Press, 1995.
3. Cyberware Inc., http://ghiberti.cyberware.com.
4. David, H.A., *The Method of Paired Comparison*, Charles Griffin and Co. Ltd., 1969.
5. Eberhart, R., Simpson, P. and Dobbins, R., *Computational Intelligence PC Tools*, Waite Group Press, 1996.
6. Goldberg, D.E., *Genetic Algorithms in Search, Optimization, and Machine Learning*, Addison-Wesley Publishing Co. Inc., 1989.
7. Gray, S., "In virtual fashion," *IEEE Spectrum*, pp. 19-25, Feb. 1998.
8. Kilgard, M.J., *The OpenGL Utility Toolkit (GLUT) Programming Interface API Version 3*, Silicon Graphics, Inc., http://reality.sgi.com/mjk_asd/spec3/spec3.html.
9. Kim, H.-S. and Cho. S.-B., "Development of an IGA-based fashion design aid system with domain specific knowledge," *Proc. of IEEE Int. Conf. On Systems, Man, and Cybernetics*, 1999.
10. Ku, I.-S., *Computer-Aided Fashion Design, Kyomunsa*, 1994. (In Korean)
11. Lee, J.-Y. and Cho, S.-B., "Interactive genetic algorithm for content-based image retrieval," *Proc. of Asia Fuzzy Systems Symposium*, pp. 479-484, 1998.
12. McKelvey, K., *Fashion Source Book*, Blackwell Science, 1996.
13. Miller, P. B., *AutoCAD for the Apparel Industry*, Delmar Publishers Inc., 1994.
14. Nakanishi, Y., "Applying evolutionary systems to design aid system," *Proc. of Artificial Life V (Poster Presentation)*, pp.147-154, 1996.
15. Ohsaki, M., Takagi, H. and Ingu, T., "Methods to reduce the human burden of interactive evolutionary computation," *Proc. of Asia Fuzzy Systems Symposium*, 495-500, 1998.
16. Sharon, L. T., *Inside Fashion Design*, Harper & Row, Publishers, Inc., 1984.
17. Takagi, H., "Interactive evolutionary computation – Cooperation of computational intelligence and human KANSEI," *Proc. of Int. Conf. on Soft Computing*, pp. 41-50, 1998.
18. Wright, R.S. and Sweet, M., *OpenGL Superbible*, Waite Group Press, 1996.

Designing Wastewater Collection Systems Using Genetic Algorithms

Lou Y. Liang, Russell G. Thompson, and David M. Young

Department of Civil and Environmental Engineering,
The University of Melbourne, Victoria, 3052 Australia
{l.liang, r.thompson}@civag.unimelb.edu.au
d.young@eng.unimelb.edu.au

Abstract. This paper presents procedures that automate the design of wastewater collection systems. The application of these procedures in determining the optimal configuration of pipeline networks design is described. Genetic algorithms (GA) are used to identify good feasible pipeline networks. GA use a number of operators including, reproduction, crossover and mutation to solve complex search and optimization problems. A number of hydraulic criteria are incorporated as constraints within the modeling procedures. The purpose of these procedures is to automatically generate construction cost information and related pipe data for designing pipeline networks. The objective of the model is to minimize the overall cost of constructing a wastewater collection system.

1 Introduction

Traditional design of gravity wastewater collection systems is a time-consuming task based on trial-and-error. Designers use charts and specialized rules to determine the slopes, diameters and materials of pipes when designing wastewater collection networks. They select suitable pipe diameter and slope combinations for every pipeline between manholes, so the wastewater can be transported without violating any hydraulic constraints. Since there is a large diversity of pipe slopes, diameters and coefficients in the hydraulic relationships, designers can only analyze a few combinations that do not violate any of the criteria. However, the cost function and constraints are not linearly related and there are no simple formulas to find the least-cost design for pipeline networks.

An optimization-based approach using linear programming methods to minimize the total cost of sewers subject to the constraints was presented [5]. Dynamic programming has also been applied to optimize wastewater collection networks [8],[10]. Since these optimization methods were based on discretional procedures to determine the nearest standard diameters to optimal solutions, they cannot guarantee optimality for standard commercial pipe diameters. Several network design programs have been developed to operate on personal computer [4],[11]. However, these systems are limited to small networks.

GA are a meta-heuristic technique based on the concepts of genetic evolution that were introduced by Holland [9]. They have greater global orientation than many methods encountered in engineering optimization practice [7]. Recently, there has been a number of applications of GA in pipeline systems optimization. The mechanics and energy consumption of a pipeline system were examined using a simple GA. Computer results in the pipeline problem show that the GA obtain near-exact solutions after generating a very small number of solutions. Computer programs were presented to provide detailed insight into the working of this important technique [6]. The aim of this work is to develop a GA for designing a large gravity wastewater collection system.

2 Hydraulic Analysis for Large Gravity Wastewater Collection Systems

Gravity wastewater collection pipelines are usually designed using the Colebrook-White equation. Colebrook published the equation for turbulent flow in circular pipes flowing full in 1939. It followed from the smooth and rough turbulent logarithmic resistance laws for circular tubes. These had been evaluated experimentally by Nikuradse, after theoretical work by Prandtl and Karman [12].

2.1 Hydraulic Formulation

The equations describing smooth and rough turbulent flow are:
smooth turbulent flow:

$$\frac{1}{\sqrt{\lambda}} = 2\log\left(\frac{R\sqrt{\lambda}}{2.51}\right) \qquad (1)$$

rough turbulent flow:

$$\frac{1}{\sqrt{\lambda}} = 2\log\left(\frac{3.71D}{K_s}\right) \qquad (2)$$

The following combination provides a transition between the individual laws.

$$\frac{1}{\sqrt{\lambda}} = -2\log\left(\frac{K_s}{3.71D} + \frac{2.51}{R\sqrt{\lambda}}\right) \qquad (3)$$

friction factor, $\lambda = 2SgD/V^2 = 1.2337SgD^5/Q^2$ (4)

Reynold number, $R = VD/\nu = 4Q/\pi\nu D$ (5)

Mean velocity, $V = 4Q/\pi D^2$ (6)

Where D, K_s, Q, S, g and ν are diameter, roughness size, discharge, pipeline slope, acceleration due to gravity and kinematic viscosity respectively.

When equations (4),(5) and (6) are substituted into equation (3), one obtains:

$$\frac{V}{\sqrt{2SgD}} = \frac{0.9003Q}{D^{2.5}\sqrt{Sg}} = -2\log\left(\frac{K_s}{3.71D} + \frac{1.775v}{D^{1.5}\sqrt{Sg}}\right) \quad (7)$$

[1] defined the transitioning parameter θ in calculation of depth in part-full circular pipes.

$$\theta = \left(\frac{K_s}{D} + \frac{1}{3600DS^{\frac{1}{3}}}\right)^{-1} \quad (8)$$

The value of θ determines the pattern of proportional flow variation in circular tubes of widely varying degrees of roughness.

2.2 Hydraulic Constraints

In order to find the optimal cost, the following constraints must be satisfied in large gravity wastewater collection systems:

1. Diameter progression constraints:
   $D_{i+1} \geq D_i$
   Where D_i is the diameter of pipeline i^{th} link
2. Minimum velocity constraints:
   $V \geq V_{min}$
   The minimum self-cleaning velocity (0.6m/s) has to reach in flow
3. Maximum velocity constraints:
   $V_{max} \geq V$
   The excessive velocity of flow would cause erosion of the pipe materials by the grit-laden sewage. In this research, the maximum velocity is 2m/s.
4. Minimum cover constraints GC_{min}
   In this research, the minimum ground cover is 1.2 m
5. Maximum cover constraints GC_{max}
   GC_{max} is taken as 6m in this work
6. Invert level constraints
   $INV_i \geq INV_{i+1}$
   The downstream invert level must be lower or equal to the upstream level
   Where INV_i is the ith link of invert level of pipeline

3 Project of the Changbin Wastewater Collection Systems

A traditional GA for optimizing the combined, sizing and cost problem for a typical industrial wastewater collection system was developed. The application of this model using the Changbin Coastal Industrial Park in Taiwan as a case study is presented in this paper. This system consists of five piping layout sections that cover a length of

6,345m in Hsien-Si Zone East I in Figure 1. Vitrified Clay Pipes (VCP) and Resin Reinforced Concrete Pipes (RRCP) have been installed in general to collect industrial wastewater in coastal sewerage systems [3]. Eight discrete commercial diameters of the collection pipes are represented for each option in the piping layout using the binary codes shown in Table 1.

Table 1. Binary coding for the Eight Commercial Pipes

Diameter (m)	Pipe Type	Binary Coding
0.3	VCP	000
0.35	VCP	001
0.375	VCP	010
0.4	RRCP	011
0.425	RRCP	100
0.45	RRCP	101
0.475	RRCP	110
0.5	RRCP	111

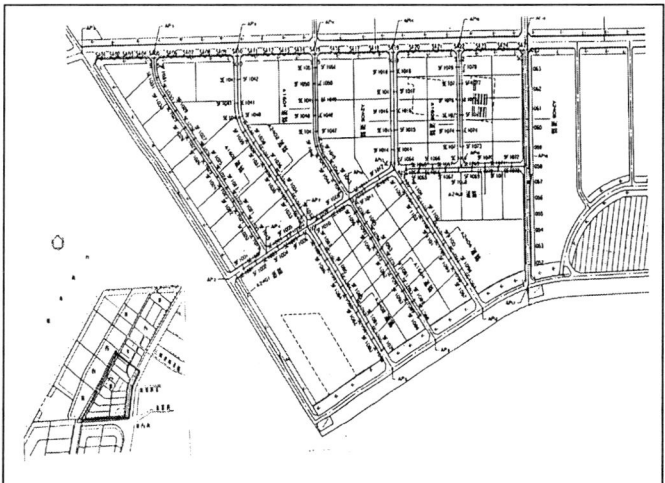

Fig. 1. Hsien-Si East I Wastewater Collection System Layout, Changbin, Taiwan

4 Methodology Description

4.1 Search Method

The initial population was randomly generated. From this population, offspring were produced using three distinct operators: reproduction, crossover and mutation. Strong chromosomes (good solutions) have a high probability of being selected to produce the next generation (set of solutions), while weak chromosomes (poor solutions) have little chance of influencing future generations (subsequent solutions).

Assuming that the required precision is 2 cm for the elevation of the pipeline, the precision required implied that the range [0.0008,0.0038] should be divided into at least 15 equal size intervals, requiring 4 bits to represent the slope of the pipeline within the chromosome:

$2^3 \leq 15 \leq 2^4$

GA usually requires the decision variables to be represented as binary digits and concatenated together as a binary string to form a chromosome. An algorithm is used to convert the decision variables to binary digits consisting of a specific number of bits. For the pipeline problem, each chromosome has its own binary digits corresponding to the minimum and maximum values of the parameters. For example, consider the piping network represented by the following 21-bit string:

000- 001- 010- 0010- 0011- 0100

Referring to Table 1. and the pipeline sloping decoding rule, this piping network solution is comprised of three diameters pipes 0.3m, 0.35m and 0.375m and slope gradients are 0.04%, 0.06% and 0.08%, respectively. The chromosomes were decoded to identify the discrete pipe diameters and different pipe slopes. Another binary code was selected to adjust the ground cover design variables of the problem.

The first population consisted of chromosomes that were randomly generated using a random seed. GA searches the solution space by generating new populations (sets of solutions) from existing populations (solution set). In this research, the population size was varied between 20 and 50. The single point crossover operation involves taking two members of population and cutting their chromosome strings at some randomly chosen position. The trailing parts of chromosomes are exchanged. After this operation two new chromosomes are produced that contain some of the genes from each parent chromosome. To avoid premature convergence to a local optimum, a random mutation of genes is usually performed after crossover. This involves changing the binary bit for each gene selected. After crossover and mutation, the offspring will generate a different fitness value. The fitness value is directly related to the value of the objective function. Convergence is often measured using the concept of bias, which is defined as a measure of agreement among the population. The convergence rate is largely influenced by the selection procedure. If selection procedure allocates a high probability to good solutions (ie. it is heavy handed), then the population will converge quickly [2].

4.2 The Penalty Function in GA

A penalty function was used for every search pipeline layout that violated the diameter progression constraints on every link. The penalty cost is the penalty factor multiplied by difference of the ith link of diameter and the $(i+1)^{th}$ link of diameter. The penalty function is given as:

Penalty cost = $pf \times (Diameter_i - Diameter_{i+1})$
$pf = 200$
cost unit: NT$ 1,000

4.3 The Fitness Function in Cost Optimization

The objective function is comprised of three types of costs:
1. pipe materials
2. excavation, backfilling and dumping of earthwork
3. penalty cost, if the network does not satisfy the diameter progress constraints of the pipeline.

5 Results and Discussion

For the Changbin Coastal Industrial Park wastewater collection systems, a section (2401) consisting of 18 links was selected. The total cost for this section using a design based on traditional methods was NT$ 3,386,195 dollars, i.e. the cost for pipe layout (pipe layout NT$ 2,417,495 dollars; earthwork is NT$ 968,700 dollars). Using the above model with a GA with a population size of 50, a crossover probability (Pc) of 0.3 and a probability of mutation (Pm) of 0.5%, the best solution's total costs was NT$ 3,075,091 dollars.

Using other GA parameters, a solution was found whose total cost was 97% that of the best cost. Similar results were obtained for other sections. The GA optimal and conventional design profiles for section 2401 are shown in Fig. 2. This illustrates that the performance of the algorithm is very good for an engineering application such as the design of large gravity wastewater collection systems. A detailed design of the optimal design layout section 2401 is shown in Table 2.

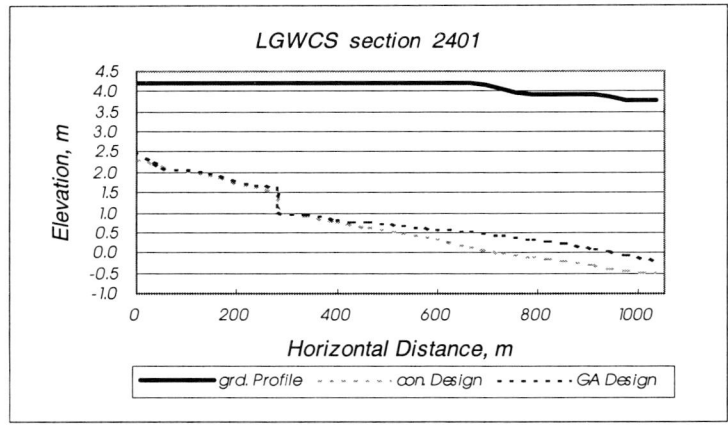

Fig 2. Optimal and Conventional Design Profile for LGWCS

To test the efficiency of the method and establish good estimates for the parameters of the GA, the values of several parameters were varied. The effect of the population size on the convergence of the process is presented in Fig. 3. The curves correspond to the population size of 20, 30 and 50, Pc = 0.3 and Pm = 0.005. The best performance was with a population size of 50. The results of different probabilities of crossover on the convergence of the process are presented in Fig. 4. It is observed that GA significantly reduces the costs and the probability of crossover had little effect on convergence.

Table 2. Comparing the conventional design with the GA optimal design

LWCS Hsien-Si East I section 2401, Changbin Coastal Industrial Park, Taiwan					
Link No.	Length m	Conventional Design		GA Optimal Design	
		Diameter, m	Slope	Diameter, m	Slope
SE1001	50	0.3	0.0025	0.3	0.0014
SE1002	50	0.3	0.0024	0.3	0.0012
SE1003	45	0.3	0.0024	0.3	0.0014
SE1004	45	0.3	0.0024	0.35	0.0016
SE1005	45	0.3	0.0024	0.375	0.0010
SE1006	39.58	0.3	0.0023	0.375	0.0014
SE1007	62.1	0.4	0.0019	0.375	0.0010
SE1008	62.1	0.4	0.0018	0.375	0.0020
SE1009	61.2	0.4	0.0018	0.375	0.0012
SE1010	69	0.4	0.0017	0.4	0.0012
SE1011	69	0.4	0.0017	0.425	0.0010
SE1012	66.4	0.4	0.0018	0.425	0.0032
SE1013	62.1	0.5	0.0016	0.45	0.0014
SE1014	62.1	0.5	0.0018	0.45	0.0014
SE1015	62.1	0.5	0.0016	0.45	0.0018
SE1016	62.1	0.5	0.0014	0.45	0.0016
SE1017	62.1	0.5	0.0013	0.45	0.0016
SE1018	59.15	0.5	0.0013	0.45	0.0026
Total Cost, (NT$m)		3.38		3.08	

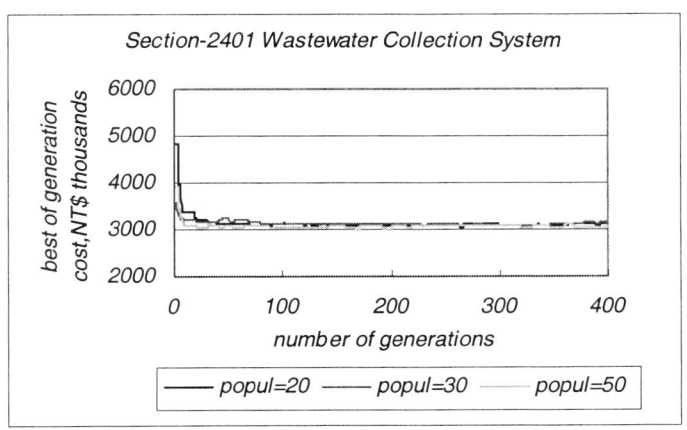

Fig 3. Comparison of Cost in Population: 20, 30 and 50

The effects of the probability of mutation on the convergence of the process are presented in Fig. 5. It is observed that for high probabilities of mutation the problem becomes fairly unstable. The best performance was found with near zero probability of mutation.

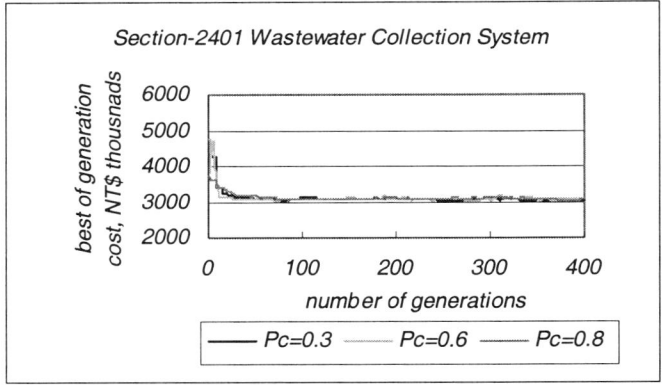

Fig 4. Comparison of Cost in Probability of Crossover: 0.3, 0.6 and 0.8

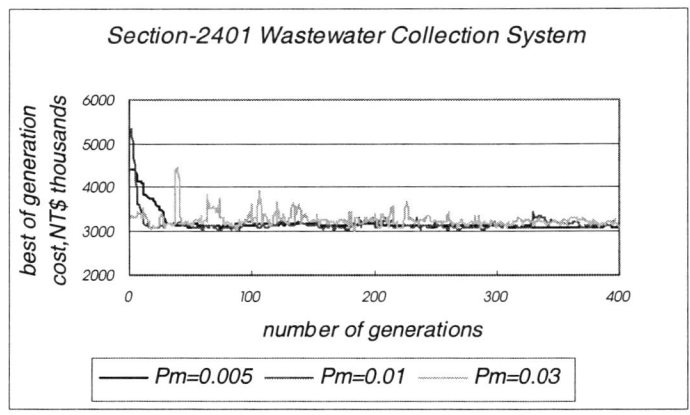

Fig 5. Comparison of Cost in Probability of Mutation: 0.005, 0.01 and 0.03

6 Conclusions

This paper presented the application of GA for designing wastewater collection systems. The capabilities of GA for large gravity wastewater collection systems are summarized below:
1. For the discrete problem of pipe diameters, the GA heuristic technique proved to be an effective solution procedure. GA can be used for large gravity wastewater collection systems and can incorporate hydraulic constraints.

2. Designers can use different pipe data and design criteria to obtain a revised design of wastewater collection systems.
3. GA provide an effective approach for minimizing earthwork costs and can help designers select the best possible design in a short time. The overall cost saving for a network designed using the optimization procedures was estimated to be 9%.

Acknowledgements

The authors would like to thank the Department of Changbin Coastal Construction, SEC for their valuable comments and helpful suggestions regarding this paper.

References

1. Ackers, P.: Charts for the hydraulic design of channels and pipes. Thomas Telford, London. (1983)
2. Bauer, R. J.: Genetic algorithms and investments strategies. Wiley Finance Editions, New York. (1994)
3. Changbin Coastal Industrial Park Hsien-Si Zone East I Wastewater Collection System Engineering Design, in Chinese, SEC, Taiwan. (1992)
4. Desher, D. P., Davis, P. K.: Designing sanitary sewers with microcomputers. *J. of Envir. Engrg.*, ASCE, 112(6), (1986) 993-1007.
5. Elimam, A. A., Charalambous, C. and Ghobrial, F. H.: Optimum design of large sewer networks. *J. of Envir. Engrg.*, ASCE, 115(6), (1989) 1171-1190.
6. Goldberg, D. E., Kuo, C. H.: Genetic algorithms in pipeline optimization. *J. of Comp. in Civ. Engrg.*, ASCE, 1(2), (1987) 128-141.
7. Goldberg, D. E.: Genetic algorithms in search optimization and machine learning. Addison-Wesley, Reading, Mass., USA. (1989)
8. Gupta, A., Mehndiratta, S. L. and Khanna, P.: Gravity wastewater collection systems optimization. *J. of Envir. Engrg.*, ASCE, 109(5), (1983) 1195-1209.
9. Holland, J. H.: Adaptation in natural and artificial systems. *University of Michigan Press*, Ann Arbor, Mich., USA. (1975)
10. Kulkarni, V. S., Khanna, P.: Pumped wastewater collection systems optimization. *J. of Envir. Engrg.*, ASCE, 111(5), (1985) 589-601.
11. Tekeli, S., Belkaya, H.: Computerized layout generation for sanitary sewers. *J. of Water Resources Planning and Management.*, ASCE, 112(4), (1986) 550-515.
12. Wallingford, H., Barr, D.I.H.: Tables for the hydraulic design of pipes, sewers and channels. Thomas Telford, London. (1998)

Hybrid Genetic Algorithms Are Better for Spatial Clustering

Vladimir Estivill-Castro

Department of Computer Science & Software Engineering,
The University of Newcastle, Callaghan, NSW 2308, Australia.
vlad@cs.newcastle.edu.au

Abstract. Iterative methods and genetic algorithms have been used separately to minimize the loss function of representative-based clustering formulations. Neither of them alone seems to be significantly better. Moreover, the trade-off of effort versus quality slightly favors gradient descent. We present a unifying view for the three most popular loss functions: least sum of squares, its fuzzy version and the log likelihood function. We identify commonalities in gradient descent algorithms for the three loss functions and the evaluation of the loss function itself. We can then construct hybrids (genetic algorithms with a mutation operation that performs few gradient descent steps) for all three clustering approaches. We demonstrate that these hybrids are much efficient and effective (significantly render better performance as normalized by the number of function evaluations or CPU time).

1 Introduction

Clustering partitions an heterogeneous data sets into groups of more homogeneous characteristics. It is so central to data analysis that has origins in statistics as learning mixture models, but has also emerged in vector quantization. In machine learning, clustering is more commonly known as unsupervised learning. Clustering is a central task in knowledge discovery and data mining. Here we consider clustering in the context of spatial databases and spatial data mining [8]. In spatial settings, the clustering almost invariably makes use of the Euclidean metric to capture proximity, as it reflects the essence of spatial association.

There seems to be a large diversity of clustering methods, but we show that indeed they attack equivalent problem statements, and with very similar methods. The diversity emerges from the inductive principle that formulates a loss function [3]. For example, some statisticians may be motivated by inference with the Maximum Likelihood principle, while those motivated by fuzzy systems generalize the squared loss cost function. However, once the loss function is specified, the clustering problem is an optimization problem. Namely, the task is to find the model that minimizes the loss. Finding global optima belongs to a complexity class beyond polynomial algorithms. Thus, heuristics are used to search and obtain approximately optimal solutions. Iterative methods for representative-based clustering are essentially gradient descent derived from the mathematical structure defined in the minimization of the loss function. Recently, genetic algorithms (GAs) have been proposed to carry out this search because they can avoid being trapped in local optima. Because the simple iterative methods for representative-based clustering are significantly much faster, genetic algorithms (and similarly simulated annealing) are unconvincingly more adequate. While coding GAs is simple, we show that the effort for the iterative methods is less. Once coded, GAs demand vast experimentation to satisfactorily determine many parameters like population size, crossover rate and mutation rate. Variations on the programming are gray encoding, binary or floating point representation and the different variants of selection, elitism and so on; however, they only provide minor improvements in the context of clustering. Determining the most suitable set up consumes valuable time. Similarly, simulated annealing demands determination of the temperature management scheme. The disappointing aspect for representative-based clustering is that once the GAs and its parameterization are completed, they are not much more effective than iterative methods for the same number of function evaluations. For example, Hall *et al* report that their GA was two orders of magnitude slower than fuzzy-c-clustering [6]. GAs demand almost as many function evaluations as the product of the number of generations and the population size. Because iterative methods resemble gradient descent, they revise a current solution with the effort of only one function evaluation.

We show that GAs by themselves will rarely outperform the iterative methods for the same cost (measured as number of function evaluations or CPU time). Our efficient and effective alternative is to combine both optimization methods into hybrids. We describe the hybrids for three very common and popular representative-based clustering approaches, the least sum of squares loss function (whose iterative methods is k-MEANS and its variants), the fuzzy loss function for representative-based clustering (whose iterative methods is fuzzy-c-means), and for the minimization of the log likelihood function of an exponential family in a finite mixture (whose iterative method is *Expectation Maximization*(EM)). A unifying framework of these loss functions underlines many commonalities that have remained unnoticed. Our experiments confirm that the hybrids are more efficient and effective than the iterative methods by themselves, or than the GAs by themselves, as normalized by function evaluations or by CPU time.

We let $X = \{x_1, \ldots, x_n\}$ denote the set of n objects to be clustered into k groups. Each object $x_i \in \Re^D$ is already a vector of D numerical attributes. Our experimental results will concentrate in the case when n is large and k and D are small, as it is the context of spatial data mining. However, our complexity analysis indicates that our assertions will hold in situations where k and D are large since this will only make loss function evaluations even more costly.

2 Iterative Methods Alternate a Classification Step and a Reconstruction Step

Because we are to partition a set into more homogeneous clusters, we need to asses homogeneity. The statistical theory of multivariate analysis of variance suggests a starting point for evaluating homogeneity. This starting point is the structure of total scatter matrix T. A traditional measure of the size of this matrix is the *trace*. The trace of a square and symmetric matrix is just the sum of its diagonal elements, and thus minimizing $trace[T]$ is exactly the least sum of squares loss function (known in the statistics literature as L_2 [13]):

$$\text{minimize } L_2(C) = \sum_{i=1}^{n} \text{EUCLID}^2(\boldsymbol{x}_i, \text{REP}[\boldsymbol{x}_i, C]), \tag{1}$$

where $\text{EUCLID}(\boldsymbol{x}, \boldsymbol{y}) = [(\boldsymbol{x}-\boldsymbol{y})(\boldsymbol{x}-\boldsymbol{y})^T]^{1/2} = [\sum_{j=1}^{D} |x_j - y_j|^2]^{1/2}$ is the Euclidean metric; $C = \{\boldsymbol{c}_1, \ldots, \boldsymbol{c}_k\}$ is a set of k *centers*, or representative points of $\Re^D$; and for $i = 1, \ldots, n$, the point $\text{REP}[\boldsymbol{x}_i, C]$ is the closest point in C to $\boldsymbol{x}_i$. Note that Equation (1) is the search for a set C of k representatives. This is illustrative of representative-based clustering: the partition into clusters is defined by assigning each $\boldsymbol{x}_i$ to its representative $\text{REP}[\boldsymbol{x}_i, C]$.

The k-MEANS method produces an approximate solution to Equation (1) by iteratively refining the partition encoded by the representatives. It alternates a classification step with a reconstruction step. For classification, the representatives $C^t = \{\boldsymbol{c}_1^t, \ldots, \boldsymbol{c}_k^t\}$ at iteration t are used to obtain new clusters. Thus, the new j-th cluster is revised by the rule

$$C_j^{t+1} \leftarrow \{\,\boldsymbol{x}_i \mid \text{REP}[\boldsymbol{x}_i, C^t] = \boldsymbol{c}_j^t\,\}. \tag{2}$$

In the reconstruction step, for each cluster, a new representative is computed. In k-MEANS, the *arithmetic mean* of the cluster's points is a "center" that minimizes the sum of squared errors between the center and the points in the cluster. That is, at iteration t, the j-th representative is revised by the rule

$$\boldsymbol{c}_j^{t+1} \leftarrow \sum_{\boldsymbol{x}_i \in C_j^{t+1}} \boldsymbol{x}_i / \|C_j^{t+1}\|. \tag{3}$$

Despite its efficiency, k-MEANS variants have many drawbacks [1]. For example, on convergence, the class label for each point and the vectors $\boldsymbol{c}_j^{(t+1)}$ are at a joint maximum. If $\boldsymbol{c}_j^{(t+1)}$ are taken as centers of distributions or prototypes of the clusters (as in mixture models or vector quantization), they are known to be biased for almost all probabilistic models. Intuitively, this is because assigning a single class to a case is creating the bias.

Fuzzy methods provide a formalization for describing the degree of membership of a point in a fuzzy set. Thus, allowing for points to have degrees of membership to the groups in a partition. Fuzzy clustering methods seek to find this fuzzy partition by minimizing a generalization of the loss function in Equation (1). This is still a representative-based approach that will seek to find k centers $\boldsymbol{c}_j$ for the fuzzy clusters (the literature on fuzzy clustering uses c instead of k for the number of groups). It replaces the rule of assigning a point to its nearest representative by assigning fuzzy membership values to each point. Thus, $\text{MEM}_j(\boldsymbol{x}_i) \in [0, 1]$ is the degree of membership of point $\boldsymbol{x}_i$ to cluster j. Then, the fuzzy-clustering results in the following optimization problem:

$$\text{minimize } Fuzzy_b(C) = \sum_{j=1}^{k} \sum_{i=1}^{n} [\text{MEM}_j(\boldsymbol{x}_i)]^b \text{ EUCLID}^2(\boldsymbol{x}_i, \boldsymbol{c}_j), \quad (4)$$

restricted to $\sum_{j=1}^{k} \text{MEM}_j(\boldsymbol{x}_i) = 1$ (for $i = 1, \ldots, n$) where the parameter $b \geq 1$ regulates the degree of fuzziness. As $b \to \infty$ all clusters become very fuzzy, all items belong to all clusters with equal degree and all representatives $\boldsymbol{c}_j$ become the observed mean in the data. Crisper partitions are obtained if $b \to 1$, so typically $b = 2$ is used. Also note that if we add the restriction $\text{MEM}_j(\boldsymbol{x}_i) \in \{0, 1\}$ (for $j = 1, \ldots, k$ and $i = 1, \ldots, n$), $Fuzzy_b(C)$ defines the same optimization problem as Equation (1).

The FUZZY-c-MEANS method produces an approximate solution to Equation (4) by iteratively refining the centers of clusters. It alternates a fuzzy classification step with a minimization step. In the fuzzy classification step the current set of representatives $C^t = \{\boldsymbol{c}_1^t, \ldots, \boldsymbol{c}_k^t\}$ is used to compute the $(t+1)$-th version of the matrix $\text{MEM}_j(\boldsymbol{x}_i)$, for $j = 1, \ldots, k$ and $i = 1, \ldots, n$ by the rule

$$\text{MEM}_j^{t+1}(\boldsymbol{x}_i) \leftarrow \frac{(1/\text{EUCLID}(\boldsymbol{x}_i, \boldsymbol{c}_j^t)^2)^{1/(b-1)}}{\sum_{r=1}^{k}(1/\text{EUCLID}(\boldsymbol{x}_i, \boldsymbol{c}_r^t)^2)^{1/(b-1)}}. \quad (5)$$

In the minimization step, for each cluster in the partition, a new representative is computed. That is, at iteration t, the j-th representative is revised by the rule

$$\boldsymbol{c}_j^{t+1} \leftarrow \frac{\sum_i^n \left[\text{MEM}_j^{t+1}(\boldsymbol{x}_i)\right]^b \boldsymbol{x}_i}{\sum_i^n \left[\text{MEM}_j^{t+1}(\boldsymbol{x}_i)\right]^b}. \quad (6)$$

The fundamental steps of k-MEANS (detailed in Equations (2) and (3)) and FUZZY-c-MEANS (detailed in Equations (5) and (6)) are obtained using multivariate calculus to derive the gradient of the loss, equate it to zero and formulate necessary conditions for an optimal solution. This ensures convergence of each variant of k-MEANS or FUZZY-c-MEANS to stable clusters. In particular, it is not hard to see that converge is to a local optimum of the optimization criteria. They simply stop when the necessary conditions hold.

Statistical inference with finite mixtures offer a third representative-based clustering approach. Inference using the principle of Maximum Likelihood selects a family of probabilistic models indexed by unknown parameters. The statistical inference exercise is then to use the data to estimate the values of parameters that maximize the log likelihood function.

$$\text{maximize } l(\boldsymbol{\theta}_1, \ldots, \boldsymbol{\theta}_k, \boldsymbol{\pi}) = \sum_{i=1}^{n} \log \left[\sum_{j=1}^{k} \pi_j f(\boldsymbol{x}_i|\boldsymbol{\theta}_j)\right]. \quad (7)$$

This parametric estimation also has an iterative algorithm derived from differentiating the objective function and finding necessary conditions for the optimum.

EM corresponds to a variety of iterative methods [14] for approximating a solution to Equation (7). Simplifications are made for computational efficiency and for the loss $l(C)$ to depend only on the representatives. Each component $f(\bm{x}|\bm{\theta}_j)$ is assumed a multivariate normal distribution. It is also commonly assumed that the covariance matrix Σ_j of each component f_j, although unknown, is diagonal. Denoting by $\bm{c}_j^t$ the representatives at time t (for $j = 1, \ldots, k$), Σ_j^t the covariance matrices (for $j = 1, \ldots, k$), and $\bm{\sigma}_j^t$ the k diagonal entries of Σ_j^t, the EM updating rule for estimating w_{ij} at the t-th iteration is:

$$w_{ij}^{t+1} \leftarrow \frac{\pi_j^{(t)} f_j(\bm{x}_i|\bm{\theta}_j^{(t)})}{p(\bm{x}_i|\bm{\theta}_1^t \ldots \bm{\theta}_k^t, \bm{\pi}^t)} = \frac{\left(\frac{1}{n}\sum_{q=1}^n w_{qj}^t\right) N_{\bm{c}_j^t, \Sigma_j^t}(\bm{x}_i)}{\sum_{r=1}^k \left(\frac{1}{n}\sum_{q=1}^n w_{qr}^t\right) N_{\bm{c}_r^t, \Sigma_r^t}(\bm{x}_i)} \quad (8)$$

for $j = 1, \ldots, k$ and $i = 1, \ldots, n$. Once this fuzzy-classification (or *data completion* as referred by the statisticians) step is completed, the new representatives and the covariance of their groups is obtained by the rules:

$$\bm{c}_j^{t+1} \leftarrow \frac{\sum_{i=1}^n w_{ij}^{t+1} \bm{x}_i}{\sum_{i=1}^n w_{ij}^{t+1}}, \quad \sigma_{js}^{t+1} \leftarrow \sqrt{\frac{\sum_{i=1}^n w_{ij}^{t+1}(\bm{x}_{is} - \bm{c}_{js}^{t+1})^2}{\sum_{i=1}^n w_{ij}^{t+1}}}. \quad (9)$$

for $j, s = 1, \ldots, k$. A further simplification is that all components have the same known covariance Σ, and thus, the only unknown parameter of each component f_j in the mixture is the mean $\bm{c}_j$ (the representative). In this special case, the rule for σ_{js}^{t+1} is no loner needed, and in the estimation of w_{ij} the assumed covariance Σ is used in $N_{\bm{m}_j^t,\Sigma}(\bm{x}_i)$ (Rule (8)). Note that in this case EM is extremely similar to FUZZY-c-MEANS (w_{ij} corresponds to MEM$_j(\bm{x}_i)$). Moreover, if the w_{ij} are forced to be crisp, (i.e, $w_{ij} \in \{0,1\}$), then EM reduces to k-MEANS.

3 The Hybrid GAs

Using GAs for representative-based clustering means that each chromosome will be an encoding of a set C of k representatives. That is, each feasible solution is an encoding of k vectors $\bm{c}_1, \ldots, \bm{c}_k$. The objective function corresponds to $L_2(C)$ in Equation (1) for the analysis of variance approach, to $Fuzzy_b(C)$ in Equation (4) for fuzzy clustering, and to $l(C)$ in Equation (7) for Maximum likelihood. Whatever variant of genetic program is used, it requires the evaluation of the objective function on chromosome C. We underline that evaluating the objective function demands carrying out the classification step. For $L_2(C)$, we need to compute Equation (2), for $Fuzzy_b(C)$, we need to compute Equation (5), and for $l(C)$, we need to find w_{ij} as in Equation (8). This requires $\Theta(Dkn)$ time and corresponds to the classification step of the body of the iteration. Once the classification step is completed, any of the 3 objective functions demands the sum of kn terms and the computation of dot products of vectors of dimension D. Thus, again, requiring $\Theta(Dnk)$ time.

Iterative Step(C)
  Classification step(C)
    [Equation (2) for k-MEANS, Equation (5)
    for FUZZY-c-MEANS and Equation (8) for EM]
  return $C \leftarrow$ reconstruction step
    [Equation (3) for k-MEANS, Equation (6)
    for FUZZY-c-MEANS and Equations (9) for EM]
	Function Evaluation(C)
	  Classification step(C)
	    [Equation (2) for $L_2(C)$, Equation (5)
	    for $Fuzzy_b(C)$ Equation (8) for $l(C)$]
	  return(Sum of terms)
	    [Equation (1) for $L_2(C)$, Equation (4)
	    for $Fuzzy_b(C)$ Equation (7) for $l(C)$]

Fig. 1. For representative-base clustering, the iterative step (in iterative methods) and the function evaluation (in genetic algorithms) share a classification step.

We make 3 observations from this analysis. 1.- Evaluating the objective function cost $\Theta(Dkn)$ time and consists of a classification step costing $\Theta(Dkn)$ time and a sum-of-terms step costing $\Theta(Dkn)$ time. 2.- The classification step in the corresponding iterative method is the same as the one required for function evaluation. 3.- The reconstruction step of iterative methods costs $\Theta(Dkn)$ time.

Observation 2 is important because it shows that implementation of iterative methods is easier than their respective GA. It also shows that we can identify a common module to iterative methods and the respective genetic algorithms (refer to Fig. 1). We strongly recommend modular implementation of the classification step so it is re-used in the iterative step and in the function evaluation.

Observation 3 above is important because it says that a function evaluation or an iteration of the corresponding iterative method have the same computational cost, and thus, require comparable CPU time and have the same scalability with respect to D, k and n. Thus, given a sufficiently large budget of f function evaluations, a genetically-based optimization of any of the 3 clustering approaches will be the selection of the best solution in $\lfloor f/sg \rfloor$ independent executions of the GA (where s is the population size and g is the number of generations). Alternatively, using the iterative method, we would select the best of approximately $\lfloor f/t \rfloor$ independent executions of the iterative methods (randomly initialized), where t is the expected number of iterations for convergence.

Our proposal for representative-based clustering is a modular construction where many parts of the developing effort can be re-used. Implement the iterative methods first, encapsulating the classification step as a routine that can be used for both, objective function evaluation and the body of the iteration. Make sure that the number of iterations to convergence is measured by the code. If the selection of the best of several randomly independent executions of the iterative method does not give a satisfactory result, implement a simple genetic algorithm reusing the module for classification in the function evaluation. Experiment to see if the GA can easily (small population size and few generations) find much better solutions that iterative methods. Estimate the potential improvements of GAs with respect to fixed budget of function evaluations. Construct a simple serial hybrid, where the solution of the GA is improved to local optima by the

```
Gradient Descent                    Multi-start(f:budget,A:algorithm)
  C^0 ← Random                        repeat
  repeat                                (C, units) ← A; f ← f − units − 1;
    C^{t+1} ← Iterative Step(C^t)      value ← Function Evaluation(C)
    t++                                (B, best) ← (value < best)? (C, value):(B, best);
  until C^t == C^{t−1}                until f < 0
  return (C^t, t)                     return(B, best)
```

Fig. 2. Generic iterative method and generic multi-start.

iterative method. Estimate the potential improvements of **hybrid GAs** with respect to fixed budget of function evaluations. Construct an integrated hybrid where the iteration step is applied to a chromosome as a mutation operator. Determine the mutation rate of this hybrid by optimizing with respect to a fixed budget f of function evaluations.

We advocate [5] (as others [6]) it is ineffective to investigate sophisticated alternatives to the GAs (like designing sophisticated crossover operators). Their overhead rarely pays in much improved solutions. Note that rich mathematical structure of the optimization problems leads to very fast iterative methods. Note that all our claims are independent of the domain where the clustering is to be performed. Moreover, the unifying framework presented here allows to consider hybrids across approaches where genetic operators may mix an iterative step of k-MEANS with an iterative step of FUZZY-c-MEANS, for example [4].

4 FUZZY-c-MEANS as Case Study 1

Our first a case study demonstrates that hybrids are much better than standard GAs and that hybrids also improve upon the multi-start local search. FUZZY-c-MEANS has been most recently approximated with GAs [6]. We used computer generated two-dimensional data sets. We exclude the details of the generator except that it generates circular disjoint clusters in the plane with a distribution peaking at the center of the clusters. It is possible to generate a certain percentage of uniform noise; that is, points that do not belong to any cluster.

We compare three methods. The standard FUZZY-c-MEANS. The recently proposed GA [6], using exactly the suggested settings (that is, tournament selection, simple crossover in each entry of the set of representatives, elitism, and the same values for crossover-rate and mutation rate; we refer to our implementation as SIMPLE-GA). Our HYBRID-GA, is the SIMPLE-GA but with population size 25 (and not 50), running for 50 generations (and not 300), a new mutation operator that is applied with probability 1/3 to each new chromosome, and if applied, it performs two standard FUZZY-c-MEANS iteration steps (more on this choice of parameters later), when the 50 generations are up, the best chromosome is used to initialize a standard FUZZY-c-MEANS and obtain the final result.

For a fair comparison, we fix a budget of *unitary operations*. Methods are independently and randomly re-started within their budget of unitary operations. The best solution out of all independent restarts is the bid of the method. The unitary operations are those in Fig. 1; namely, we say that an *iterative step* or a *function evaluation step* are unitary operations. The three methods have an asymptotic cost of $\Theta(Dkn)$ times the number of unitary operations performed. We performed experiments to assess the ratio of CPU time of an iterative step versus a function evaluation step. They clearly show (refer to tech-report of same title) that the differences in CPU time between the two unary operations are minimal. Mainly because the ratio (CPU time for evaluation step)/ (CPU time for iteration step) remains constant independently of k and n for all methods.

A comparison for a fixed budget of 4166 unitary operations was set where the multi-start FUZZY-c-MEANS gives the best answer of 595 independent starts of the standard FUZZY-c-MEANS. It uses 595 of the unitary operations as function evaluation steps to find which of the independent runs resulted in the best answer. The remaining 3570 unitary operations are iterative steps spread over the 595 starts that on average require 6 iterations to converge. One run of our HYBRID-GA uses approximately 1250 unitary operations as function evaluation steps, (because on average 25 new individuals appear in each of the 50 generations). On average 883 iterative steps are made in one run because the mutation rate of 1/3 makes 417 of the new individuals to have a mutation of two iterative steps. Thus, the budget of 4166 is just enough for 2 independent runs of our HYBRID-GA; the best solution of the two is the contestant solution for the method. This budget forces SIMPLE-GA to halt after 83 generations. The best chromosome then is the contestant of the method.

Table 1 shows results of 12 independent competitions on data with 30% noise ($n = 300$ and $n = 3,000$). Both data sets had 10 clusters, so the correct value of k is 10. However, we tested smaller and larger values of k because typically k is unknown and several k are evaluated [10] to decide on the value of k. Thus, it is of up-most importance that the optimization method gives good solutions even when the value of k is not the natural value for the dataset. As k grows, the number of partitions of n items into k subsets grows. Thus, the number of local optima grows. More multi-starts within the same budget will improve. This explains why FUZZY-c-MEANS performance improves for $k = 15$.

The HYBRID-GA is the best alternative within a fixed budget. Moreover, the best solutions found by HYBRID-GA were never found by multi-start FUZZY-c-MEANS. The SIMPLE-GA solution was extremely poor with budget = 4166 because the method could not even finish properly. We extended the budget to 29,162 unitary operations for a competition. The results of 3 independent competitions are shown in the last 3 columns of Table 1. While SIMPLE-GA was able to complete two runs with this budget and the quality of the solution was much improved, it could not surpass the other two methods. Moreover, the extended budget favors HYBRID-GA, which now was always the one that found the best solution. HYBRID-GA produces the highest quality. With 30% noise

Table 1. Ratio of times the best solution was provided by a method (fixed budget of unitary operations in each competition). The percentage of noise in the data is 30%.

Provider of best solution (noise =30%)							
Method	12 competitions each with a budget=4,166 unitary operations				3 competitions each with a budget=29,162		
		number k of clusters				number k of clusters	
$n = 300$	Best of	5	10	15	Best of	5 10	15
Hybrid-GA	2 runs	12/12	10/12	6/12	14 runs	3/3 3/3	3/3
Fuzzy-c-Means	595 runs	0/12	2/12	6/12	4195 runs	0/3 0/3	0/3
Simple-GA	0.28 runs	0/12	0/12	0/12	2 runs	0/3 0/3	0/3
$n = 3,000$	Best of				Best of		
Hybrid-GA	2 runs	12/12	10/12	7/12	14 runs	3/3 3/3	3/3
Fuzzy-c-Means	595 runs	0/12	2/12	5/12	4195 runs	0/3 0/3	0/3
Simple-GA	0.28 runs	0/12	0/12	0/12	2 runs	0/3 0/3	0/3

(30% of the data does not belong to any cluster), the objective function exhibits more local optima but Hybrid-GA is a 14-fold multi-start.

The experiment was repeated but with only 10% noise. Here, the Fuzzy-c-Means method and Hybrid-GA remain much better than Simple-GA. However, the superiority of Hybrid-GA fades. This confirms one of our points: iterative methods are efficient and effective. Thus, with less noise, the more evident the clustering and the less local optima. If the data consists of noiseless well-separated clusters, multi-start iterative methods are the best. However, as the clusters are more obscure because of noise, different densities or proportions, or ore elliptical shape not aligned with the axis, the more benefit of introducing GAs. Our results here stress that GAs alone will be too slow even on those situations and that hybrids should be applied then. Thus, only if multi-start iterative methods reveal that the data is hard to cluster we progress to hybrid GAs.

5 k-Means as Case Study 2

We use k-Means as a second case study to demonstrate that hybrids are much better than standard GAs and that hybrids also improve upon the multi-start local search. After these two case studies, it should be clear that our claims also extend to the third loss function (EM). We used the same computer generated two-dimensional data. We compare three methods. The standard k-Means. The recently proposed GA [6], using exactly the suggested settings but the objective function is now Equation (1). Our Hybrid-GA is as in the previous section but the objective function is now Equation (1) and the new mutation operator that is applied with probability 1/3 to each new chromosome consists of two standard k-Means iteration steps. Again, we fix a budget of unitary operations. Similar results hold for the k-Means clustering approach as in Case Study 1. However, because k-Means is more sensitive to noise, the contrast with hybrids is apparent with even less noise. (refer to Table. 2).

Table 2. Ratio of times the best solution was provided by a method (fixed budget of unitary operations in each competition). The percentage of noise in the data is 10%.

	Provider of best solution (noise=10%)						
Method	12 competitions each with a budget=4,166 unitary operations				3 competitions each with a budget=29,162		
$n = 300$		number k of clusters				number k of clusters	
	Best of	5	10	15	Best of	5 10	15
HYBRID-GA	2 runs	11/12	8/12	6/12	14 runs	3/3 2/3	2/3
k-MEANS	595 runs	1/12	4/12	6/12	4195 runs	0/3 1/3	1/3
SIMPLE-GA	83 generations	0/12	0/12	0/12	2 runs	0/3 0/3	0/3

6 The Design of Hybrids

Hybrids require smaller population sizes. The settings for HYBRID-GA's mutation parameter is derived as follows. We calculated A the average number of iterations that gradient descent requires on a problem. Then we tested HYBRID-GA for the most effective integer value $p \in \{2, \ldots, 9\}$ such that the mutation rate for applying iterative steps is $1/p$ and the number of iterative steps per mutation is $\lceil A/p \rceil$. In our experiments, we quickly found $p = 3$. The population size is then adjusted in consideration to the convergence obtained with this mutation and with regard to the variance and effectiveness of a multi-start iterative method (which should have been implemented and used first).

We also confirmed the scalability of gradient descent and HYBRID-GA by recording the CPU time required for a budget of 4166 unitary operations. The linear CPU time requirements for varying n with fixed k and varying k with fixed n were confirmed (refer to tech report). Results to a fixed budget of CPU time are similar, because CPU time to a fixed budget of unitary operations is within by 20% independently of n and k.

We also confirmed experimentally that chromosome encoding as binary strings or real-codes [11] does not have but the slightest impact on the performance of GA in the context of the numerical optimization of the clustering we have discussed. We stress that for these problems, either variant of GA still requires essentially s function evaluations at each generation (recall s is the population size). These unitary operations cost $\Theta(Dkn)$ time for either variant and the decoding/encoding effort is of the same order of magnitude.

7 Final Remarks

Representative-based clustering results in optimization problems. These optimization problems have been investigated independently. By identifying commonalities, this paper presents a package of hybrid GAs. Our hybrids obtain much more cost-effective optimization without complex and slow crossover operators. Our approach to hybrid algorithms is a tightly coupled approach rather than a serialization of iterative methods with GAs. This involves a careful analysis of the time requirements of several subtasks.

Progress on hybrids of GAs with local search has concentrated on combinatorial optimization [2, 7, 12, 15]. While in some cases, numerical optimization has been studied [9], those problems do not offer the challenge that we have seen here. In particular, that the iterative method is the result of necessary conditions for optimality derived by equating the gradient of the loss to zero. Thus, the iterative method is extremely fast in finding local optima. It is then hard for a GA to compete with multi-start versions of these iterative methods. The best alternative is hybridization: it achieves better quality for the same CPU time.

References

1. M.S. Aldenderfer and R.K. Blashfield. *Cluster Analysis*. Sage, Beverly Hills, 1984.
2. C.K. Chak and Feng G. Accelerated genetic algorithms: combined with local search for fast and accurate global search. In *1995 IEEE Int. Conf. Evolutionary Computation*, 378–383, NY, 1995. IEEE Neural Network Council.
3. V. Cherkassky and F. Muller. *Learning from Data — Concept, Theory and Methods*. Wiley, NY, 1998.
4. V. Estivill-Castro and A.T. Murray. Clustering and capacitated facility location via hybrid optimisation. *Proc. Int. ICSC Symp. on Intelligent Systems and Applications ISA-2000*, Wollongong, Australia, Dec. 12-15 2000.
5. V Estivill-Castro and R. Torres-Velázquez. Hybrid genetic algorithm for solving the p-median problem. A Yao, et al eds., *Proc. SEAL-98*, 18–25. Springer Verlag LNAI 1585, 1999.
6. I.B. Hall, L.O. Özyurt and J.C. Bezdek. Clustering with a genetically optimized approach. *IEEE T. Evolutionary Computation*, 3(2):103–112, 1999.
7. C.L. Huntley and Brown D.E. Parallel genetic algorithms with local search. *Computer Ops Res*, 26(6):559–571, 1996.
8. K. Koperski, J. Han, and J. Adhikari. Mining knowledge in geographical data. *Communications of the ACM*. to appear.
9. A.C. Kwong, S. abd Ng and K.F. Man. Improving local search in genetic algorithms for numerical global optimization using modified grid-point search technique. In *Proc. GALESIA*, 419–423, London, UK, 1995. IEE.
10. J.J. Oliver, R.A. Baxter, and C.S. Wallace. Unsupervised learning using MML. *Proc. 13th Machine Learning Conf.*, 364–372, 1996. Morgan Kaufmann.
11. I. Ono and S. Kobayashi. A real coded genetic algorithm for function optimization using unimodal normal distributed crossover. T. Back, ed., *Proc. 7th Int. Conf. on Genetic Algorithms*, 246–253, 1997.
12. C. Reeves. Hybrid genetic algorithms for bin-packing and related problems. *Annals of Operations Research*, 63:371–396, May 1996.
13. P.J. Rousseeuw and A.M. Leroy. *Robust regression and outlier detection*. Wiley, NY, 1987.
14. M.A. Tanner. *Tools for Statistical Inference*. Springer-Verlag, NY, US., 1993.
15. N.L.J. Ulder, E.H.L. Aarts, H.-J. Bandelt, P.J.M. van Laarhoven, and E. Pesch. Genetic local search algorithms for the travelling salesman problem. H.-P. Schwefel et al, eds. *Proc. 1st Workshop on Parallel Problem Solving from Nature*, 109–116, Berlin, Germany, 1991. IEEE, Springer Verlag.

Improving Performance of GP by Adaptive Terminal Selection

Sooyol Ok[1,2], Kazuo Miyashita[1,2], and Seiichi Nishihara[2]

[1] Electrotechnical Laboratory(ETL)
{sooyol, miyasita}@etl.go.jp
http://www.etl.go.jp/~sooyol
1-1-4,Umezono,Tsukuba,Ibaraki,305–8568 Japan
[2] Institute of Information Sciences and Electronics(IISE),
University of Tsukuba
{sooyol,nishihara}@algor.is.tsukuba.ac.jp
http://www.npal.is.tsukuba.ac.jp/
1-1-1, Tennodai, Tsukuba City, Ibraki,305–8577 Japan

Abstract. Genetic Programming (GP) is an evolutionary search algorithm which searches a computer program capable of producing the desired solution for a given problem. For the purpose, it is necessary that GP system has access to a set of features that are at least a superset of the features necessary to solve the problem. However, when the feature set given to GP is redundant, GP suffers substantial loss of its efficiency. This paper presents a new approach in GP to acquire relevant terminals from a redundant set of terminals. We propose the adaptive mutation based on terminal weighting mechanism for eliminating irrelevant terminals from the redundant terminal set. We show empirically that the proposed method is effective for finding relevant terminals and improving performance of GP in the experiments on symbolic regression problems.

1 Introduction

Genetic Programming(GP) [3] is an evolutionary algorithm that handles an artificial chromosome structured as a tree, which represents a hierarchical computer program of a dynamically changing shape and size. In GP, the process of problem solving is search for a highly fit individual program in the space of *possible* computer programs. In the standard architecture of GP, a "chromosome" is composed of *function nodes* and *terminal nodes*. These nodes typically consist of fixed sets of symbols selected to be appropriate for a solution in the domain of interest. For successful application of GP, it is important to determine the useful nodes for solving the target problem, and the domain dependent knowledge is required for the purpose. This is one of the major difficulties for applying GP to realistic problems where domain knowledge is unavailable.

The performance of GP is directly dependent on the design of the set of functions and terminals. If the terminal set and function set are not together sufficient to express a solution of the problem, GP cannot solve the problem. On the other hand, if extraneous terminals and functions are included in the sets, the performance of GP is degraded by a fruitless search in the extended hypothesis space. In many problem solving situations, since a sufficient set of terminals and functions are not known in advance, terminals and functions are chosen from a large presumably sufficient superset and thus the chosen set may contain extraneous terminals and functions. For improving efficiency of GP process, it is desirable to exclude the extraneous terminals and functions and choose only relevant ones.

The process of determining the repertoire of relevant terminals and functions in GP is analogous to similar required steps in other machine learning paradigms. This step is called *feature selection* or *feature subset selection* [1, 2, 4]. When many irrelevant features are present, most learning methods require an exponentially growing number of training samples to induce an accurate concept, independent of the target concept. This phenomenon is referred to as the *curse of dimensionality* and it makes learning from data containing large amount of irrelevant information intractable. One of the simplest techniques for overcoming this problem is to reduce dimensionality by selecting a subset of features that are useful for representing a target concept. Thus, feature selection is one of the central issues in machine learning research.

In GP, the problem of irrelevant functions and terminals has not gained enough attention by researchers. Koza wrote in his first book on GP that "it will generally just reduce the efficiency" [3]. In the evolution of GP, the normal mutation process gradually eliminates the redundant nodes contained in the population of trees. Nonetheless, inefficiency caused by the redundant nodes is critical when GP is applied to real world problems with large amount of irrelevant information. In this paper, we present a new approach to accelerate selection of relevant terminals and functions in GP. In the paper, we focus our attention to the problem of extraneous terminals since it is a prevailing problem in many GP applications, but the proposed approach can be equally applied to eliminating extraneous functions. First, we describe the details of our approach to eliminating irrelevant terminals during a run of the GP's evolution process and relate it to the past research on feature selection in machine learning. Then, we explain the experiments of two types of symbolic regression problems with redundant terminals. Lastly, the results of applying our method to those experiments are presented and fully analyzed.

2 Terminal Selection in GP

In machine learning, two approaches have been proposed for feature selection: one is a explicit heuristic search of the feature subset. The other is feature weighting [1]. In the heuristic search approach, each state in the search space specifies a subset of the possible features, and search proceeds in the way of either *forward selection* or *backward elimination* and the feature subset is selected either before learning (*filter methods*) or during learning (*wrapper methods*). In the feature weighting approach, features are assigned a measure of their perceived relevance during learning. In general, although the heuristic search approach is natural when the result is to be understood by humans, the weighting approach is easier to implement in on-line incremental learning, and generally more purely motivated by performance consideration. Considering the lengthy process of GP, we prefer on-line and efficient methods for selecting relevant terminals. Thus we decided to adopt the weighting scheme for terminal selection in GP.

2.1 Terminal Weighting Method

In general feature weighting schemes, the relevant features get larger and larger weight incrementally over time. To find the relevant terminals in GP, terminal weights are recursively updated to give terminals of the fittest programs a larger weight.

In our terminal weighting method, the terminal weight is updated using the following formula:

$$w_n(g) = \sum_{i \in S}(fit_i(g) * freq_{i,n}(g)) + w_n(g-1)$$

where,

$w_n(g)$: weight of the terminal n in generation g.
$fit_i(g)$: fitness of the program i in generation g.
$freq_{i,n}(g)$: frequency of terminal n used in the program i in generation g.
S : the set of the top 10% of the fittest programs in the population.

Terminals included in programs with a high fitness value (i.e., top 10% of the entire population) get additional weight according to the quality of the programs and occurrence of the terminal in the programs. In this way, the relevancy of the terminal is estimated iteratively as it affects on the fitness of programs.

2.2 Adaptive Mutation

In general, the mutation operation in GP begins by selecting a point randomly within the S-expression in the tree. The mutation point can be either a function node or a terminal node in the tree. A random mutation operator then removes whatever is currently at the selected point and whatever is below that selected point, and then inserts a randomly generated subtree at that point. In traditional GP, normally all function nodes and terminal nodes have the same probability of being selected by the mutation operator. We use this mutation process for eliminating irrelevant terminals and call it *adaptive mutation*.

In adaptive mutation, a terminal node with a smaller weight has higher probability of being selected as a mutation point and removed from a tree. Thus, when the evolution process proceeds at a certain rate of mutation, irrelevant terminals have little chance of being included in the trees. An overview of adaptive mutation process is depicted in Fig. 1.

Adaptive mutation consists of 4 steps. The first two steps concern the selection of relevant terminals and remaining two steps are mutation process. The details of each step are as follows:

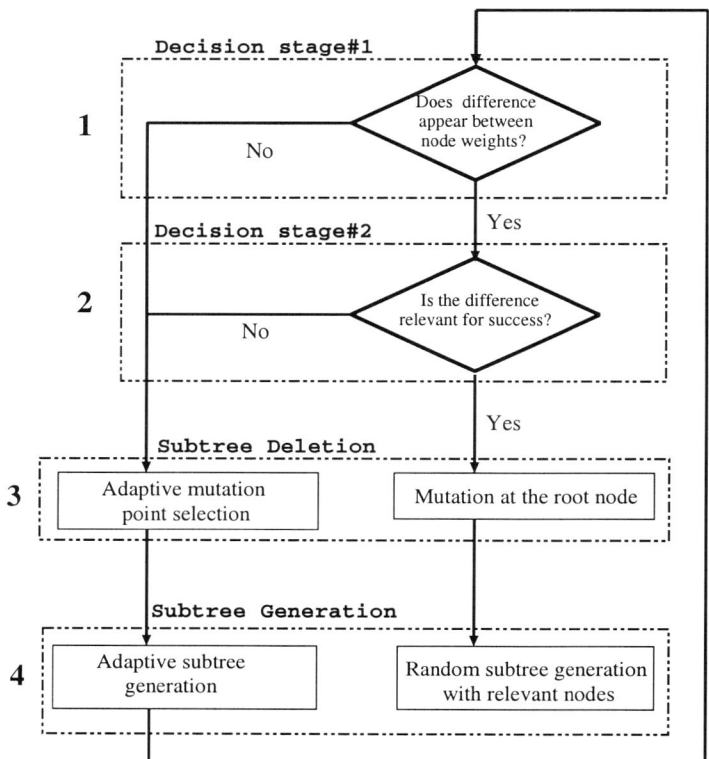

Fig. 1. Adaptive Mutation

1) To distinguish between relevant terminals and irrelevant terminals, there must be a *significant* difference in the terminal weights. This can be checked by clustering a terminal set into two categories based on the weight value of the terminal. Only if the average of the normalized terminal weights in the lower category is smaller than 0.05, the population is judged as having undergone sufficient evolution and the terminals have accumulated enough evidence for judging their relevancy. Terminals in the category of larger weights are selected as candidates for relevant terminals.

2) To decide whether terminals with a large weight are really relevant to the problem at hand, occurrence of the selected terminals in the fittest programs is examined. Only if those terminals contained in the top 1% of the fittest programs match to the terminals in the large weight category, they are judged to be relevant terminals. This is based upon our assumption that the fittest programs should contain only relevant terminals after a sufficient number of generations in the evolutionary process.

3) In the mutation operation, first a mutation point is determined and the corresponding subtree is removed. In adaptive mutation, one of the two types of mutation point selection is applied depending on whether relevant terminals are found or not.

- When relevant terminals are yet to be found:
  First, either function node or terminal node is selected at random as a target of mutation. Then, if mutation is to be made to the function node, a function node is selected randomly. If mutation is to occur in the terminal node, a terminal node is selected for mutation based on the inverse proportion to its weight.
- When relevant terminals are found (only once in the process):
  Mutation occurs at the root of every tree. This causes initialization of the entire population with only relevant terminals

4) After a mutation point is selected, a new subtree is generated and concatenated at the mutation point. In adaptive mutation, there are two types of subtree generation method.

- When relevant terminals are yet to be found:
  A subtree is generated with random functions and terminals drawn at random, in proportions to their weight. Terminals with higher weights have a higher probability to be included.
- When relevant terminals are found (only once in the process):
  A subtree is generated using only relevant terminals and functions.

Once relevant terminals are fixed, adaptive mutation is replaced with normal mutation in the traditional GP and the evolution process continues with the selected relevant terminals.

3 Experiments

In our experiments, we investigated the performance improvement of GP by selecting relevant terminals using adaptive mutation. Experiments were conducted on two symbolic regression problems. The goal was to evolve the programs that approximate the function (1) $F_1(x_1, \ldots, x_{33}) = x_1^3 + x_1^2 + x_1$ and (2) $F_2(x_1, \ldots, x_{33}) = \sin(x_4) + \sin(2*x_4) + \sin(3*x_4) + \sin(4*x_4) + \sin(x_5) + \sin(2*x_5) + \sin(3*x_5) + \sin(x_{13}) + \sin(2*x_{13})$, respectively, in 200 data points that were randomly selected in the [-1,1] interval. The GP parameter setting is shown in Table 1.

We have implemented our GP system by modifying lil-gp1-1 [5] that is a generic program for developing GP application.

3.1 Simple Symbolic Regression Problem

The first problem investigated was the simple regression function which is the same problem that Koza used to describe the effect of extraneous terminals in his book [3].

Table 1. GP parameter setting

Objective	Evolve a function that fits the data points of the fitness cases
Terminal set	$x_1 \ldots x_{33}$
Function set	$+, -, *, \%, \sin, \cos, \exp, rlog$
Fitness cases	The given sample of 200 data points $x_1(i), ..., x_{33}(i)$ in the interval $[-1, +1]$, (1) $y(i) = x_1^3(i) + x_1^2(i) + x_1(i)$ (2) $y(i) = \sin(x_4) + \sin(2*x_4) + \sin(3*x_4) + \sin(4*x_4) + \sin(x_5) + \sin(2*x_5) + \sin(3*x_5) + \sin(x_{13}) + \sin(2*x_{13})$
Raw fitness	The sum, taken over the 200 fitness cases, of the absolute value of difference between value of the dependent variable produced by the S-expression and the target value y_i of the dependent variable.
Hits	Number of fitness cases for which the value of the dependent variable produced by the S-expression comes within 0.01 of the target value y_i of the dependent variable.
Parameters	Population size = 2000, Generation = 200 for the function (1), Generation = 1000 for the function (2).
Crossover Probability	80%
Reproduction Probability	10%
Mutation Probability	10%
Success Predict	An S-expression scores 200 hits

The problem is the symbolic regression problem with $x_1^3 + x_1^2 + x_1$ as the target curve. In this problem, only one terminal is relevant (i.e., x_1) in the terminal set, which contains additional 32 extraneous terminals (i.e., $x_2, \ldots, x_{33}$). The value of the terminals were set independently and randomly in the range between -1.0 to 1.0. the other GP parameters used in this experiment are shown Table 1.

The experiment was made 100 times by changing a random seed value and the results shown in this paper is the average of the 100 experiment results. To examine the effectiveness of our terminal selection method in terms of GP performance, we conducted the following 3 types of experiments and compared the results:

1. Standard GP without extraneous terminals (Standard GP(1))
   Standard GP which uses random mutation is applied to the problem with the only relevant terminal x_1 in the terminal set.
2. Standard GP with extraneous terminals (Standard GP(2))
   Standard GP which uses random mutation is applied to the problem with the irrelevant terminals $x_2, \ldots, x_{33}$ in addition to the relevant terminal x_1.
3. Adaptive GP with extraneous terminals
   GP using the adaptive mutation method (*Adaptive GP*) is applied to the problem with the irrelevant terminals $x_2, \ldots, x_{33}$ in addition to the relevant terminal x_1.

Fig. 2 shows the change of terminal weights over generations in Adaptive GP. In the graph values of the terminal weight are normalized among 33 terminals so that sum of the weights is 1.0. From the graph, we find that by the 8th generation Adaptive GP has succeeded to find a relevant terminal from the other extraneous terminals.

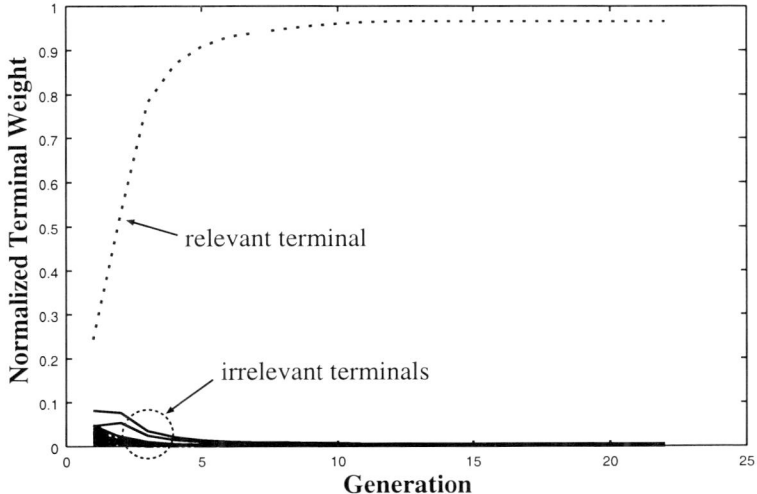

Fig. 2. Change of Terminal Weights in Simple Regression Problems

We think that the terminal selection pressure of adaptive mutation exerts the greatest and most important influence on the direction of evolution when many irrelevant terminals are included in the data.

Fig 3 shows the probability of success by the 3 types of GP runs explained above. From the graph, we find that Adaptive GP is slower to find a solution than Standard GP without extraneous terminals until it finds a relevant terminal, but after fixing the relevant terminal the performance of Adaptive GP becomes comparable with Standard GP without extraneous terminals. Compared with these 2 results, the result of Standard GP with extraneous terminals is worse.

From the experiments of the simple symbolic regression problem with 1 relevant terminal, it is clear that adaptive mutation is effective in selecting a relevant terminal and it contributes to improve the performance of GP. But when there are multiple relevant terminals, we are still not sure that adaptive mutation can find *all* of the relevant terminals and if so *how quickly*. In the next experiments, we made the experiments of symbolic regression with 3 variables included in the expression.

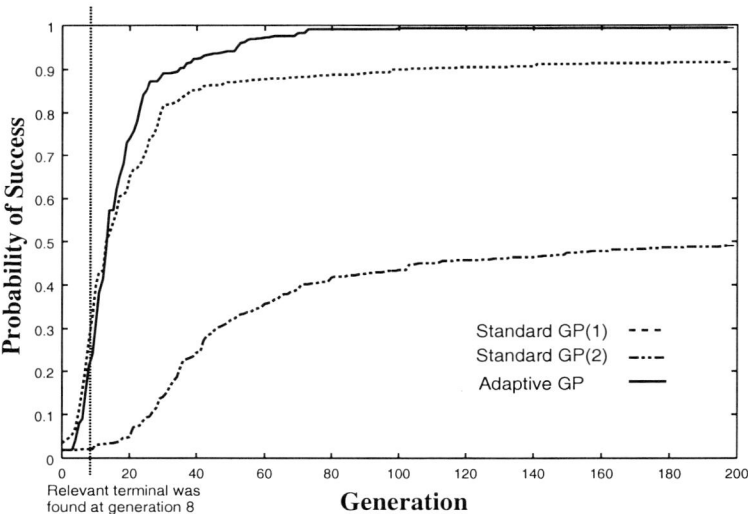

Fig. 3. Success Rate in Simple Regression Problems

3.2 Harder Symbolic Regression Problem

The second experiment uses more difficult symbolic regression problems with a target curve of the following expression:

$$y = \sin(x_4) + \sin(2*x_4) + \sin(3*x_4) + \sin(4*x_4) + \\ \sin(x_5) + \sin(2*x_5) + \sin(3*x_5) + \\ \sin(x_{13}) + \sin(2*x_{13})$$

This problem has 3 relevant terminals x_4, x_5, x_{13} in the terminal sets of 33 terminals. Setting of the terminal values and GP parameters are same as the previous experiments of the simple symbolic regression. To be noted is that among 3 relevant terminals relevance of each terminal in the expression is different from each other. Hence, it is difficult to distinguish relevant terminals from other irrelevant terminals.

In this experiments, we conducted 3 types of experiments 100 times using different random seed values as we did in the previous experiment of the simple symbolic regression problem. Fig. 4 shows the change of normalized terminal weights over generations in Adaptive GP. From the graph, difference of terminal weights among relevant terminals and irrelevant terminals becomes clear over the generations. In the experiment, we found that Adaptive GP succeeded to select all of the relevant terminals by th 90th generation.

Fig. 5 shows the probability of success among 3 types of GP runs. We can see that this problem is harder than the previous problem by comparing the success rate of Standard GP runs without extraneous terminals among 2 experiments. From the graph, we find that in the early generations Adaptive GP is comparable with Standard GP with extraneous terminals, but as generation proceeds,

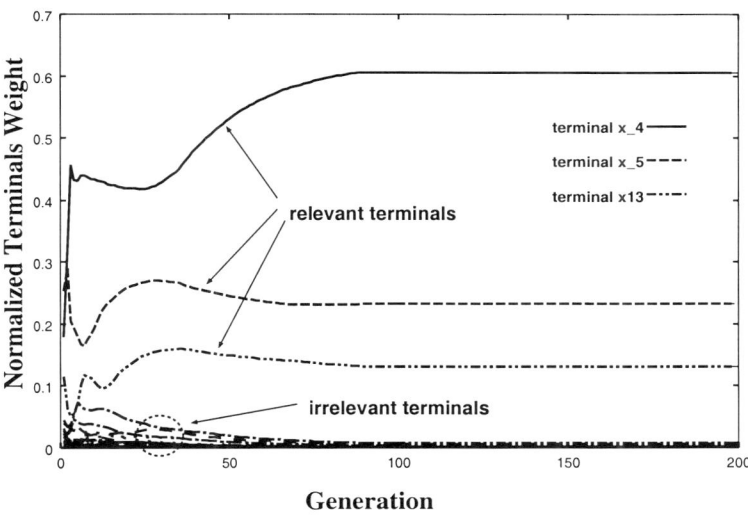

Fig. 4. Change of Terminal Weights in Harder Regression Problems

Adaptive GP outperforms it and approaches to the performance of Standard GP without extraneous terminals. From this result, we think that adaptive mutation method used in Adaptive GP is effective to find multiple relevant terminals among many redundant terminals.

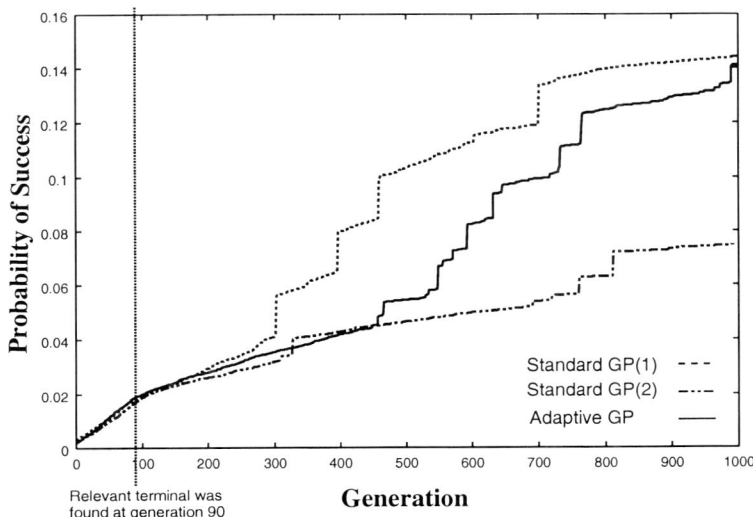

Fig. 5. Success Rate in Harder Regression Problems

Table 2. Irrelevant Terminals Overlooked by Standard GP(2)

	Simple symbolic regression problem	Harder symbolic regression problem
Ratio of best trees with irrelevant terminals	17.0 %	25.0 %
Average number of total terminals in the above trees	21.6	43.2
Average number of irrelevant terminals in the above trees	4.1	8.2

3.3 Discussion

In the above presented experiments, as Table 2 shows, among the best trees found by the standard GP with extraneous terminals in 100 random-seed experiments, about 17 to 25% of the trees include irrelevant terminals in their nodes. In those trees with irrelevant terminals, about 20% of the terminal nodes belong to the irrelevant terminals. This result shows that even when a perfect success is achieved in the fitness cases (i.e., 200 hits), the tree produced by the standard GP may still contain erroneous information. On the contrary, the best trees found by Adaptive GP never included irrelevant terminals. In the other words, Adaptive GP can find more correct answers than standard GP not just in terms of the number of hits in the fitness cases but in terms of the relevance of included terminals.

Table 3. Comparison of CPU time

	Standard GP(1)	Standard GP(2)	Adaptive GP
Evaluation CPU time (sec)	61.7	205.4	22.2
Breeding CPU time (sec)	2.2	6.0	11.4
Total CPU time (sec)	64.6	213.2	34.4

Table 3 shows the comparison result of CPU time among 3 types of GP's in the above experiments. We provide the CPU time on simple regression problems only, since in the harder regression problems any GP could not find a solution within the limited number of the generation (i.e., 1000 generations). From the table, Adaptive GP takes more time in breeding than the other GP's because of its extra computation in adaptive mutation process. But, since Adaptive GP could find a solution in less generation than Standard GP(1), the total computational time of Adaptive GP is actually smaller than the Standard GP's. The authors guess that Adaptive GP could find a solution faster than Standard GP(1) because it prevented the growth of bloat by re-initializing all the trees when fixing the relevant terminals. This idea is not yet fully analyzed. More thorough investigation is required for understanding the efficiency of Adaptive GP process.

4 Conclusion

One of main problems in GP is to determine the relevant terminals, from a large set of relevant, as well as redundant or irrelevant terminals. An optimal performance of GP depends crucially on the design of the set of primitive terminals. In this paper, we have presented an adaptive mutation method that selects relevant terminals with better success than the random mutation scheme of standard GP. The success of the presented adaptive mutation process approaches the performance of GP using *only* relevant terminals, within a limited number of generations. Adaptive mutation provides a means to avoid fruitless exploration in the invalid search space by providing more specific terminal set, which excludes both redundant terminals and redundant terminal combinations. From the empirical results shown in the paper, it is concluded that terminal selection by means of adaptive mutation is effective in improving efficiency of GP. Our next step is applying adaptive mutation to larger and more realistic problems whose relevant terminals are difficult to be found.

Acknowledgement

We thank Dr. Christer Johanson for his valuable comments and discussion.

References

1. Avrim L. Blum and Pat Langey.: Selection of relevant features and examples in machine learning. Artificial Intelligence, (1997) Vol 97, 245–271.
2. Daphne Koller and Mehran Sahami.: Toward optimal feature selection. Proc. 13th International Conference on Machine Learning. Morgan Kaufmann, (1996) 284–292.
3. Koza, John R. : Genetic Programming: On the Programming of Computers by Means of Natural Selection. Cambridge, MA: The MIT Press. (1992)
4. Liu, H. and Setiono, R.: A probabilistic approach to feature selection – A filter solution. In 13th International Conference on Machine Learning (ICML'96), (1996) 319–327.
5. Douglas Zongker and Bill Punch.: lil–gp 1.0 User's Manual. (1995)

Evolving Neural Networks for Decomposable Problems Using Genetic Programming

Brett Talko*, Linda Stern, and Les Kitchen

Department of Computer Science and Software Engineering,
The University of Melbourne,
221 Bouverie Street, Carlton, Victoria 3053, Australia.
{talko,linda,ljk}@cs.mu.oz.au

Abstract. Many traditional methods for training neural networks using genetic algorithms and genetic programming do not have any special provisions for taking advantage of decomposable problems which can be solved by combining solutions to each subproblem. This paper describes a new approach to neural network construction using genetic programming which is designed to rapidly construct networks composed of similar subnetworks. A system has been developed to produce trained weightless neural networks by using construction rules to build the networks. The network construction rules are evolved by the genetic programming system. The system has been applied to decomposable Boolean problems and the results were compared with a modified version of the system in which networks cannot be constructed modularly. The modular version of the system obtains significantly better results than the non-modular version of the program.

Keywords: Genetic Programming, Modular Neural Networks, Rule-Based Systems

1 Introduction

In image processing and in other areas, repeated evaluations of functions are typically carried out. In the case of image processing, the same local neighborhood function is applied to every pixel of the input image in order to obtain the corresponding pixel value of the processed image.

For this type of application, a neural network (NN) learns the function and is applied repeatedly in place of the function. This approach makes a number of assumptions when traditional learning methods such as backpropagation are used. These are that the number of input neurons of the function are known, the number of neurons that will implement the function is known, and that only one function is required to be learned. If some or all of these conditions cannot be assumed, then another learning method must be employed.

---

* Brett Talko is now with the Defence Science and Technology Organisation, 506 Lorimer Street, Fishermans Bend, Victoria 3207, Australia.

Another approach attempts to learn all of the functions at the same time in one combined neural network, even though in reality many of these functions are identical. Conventional learning algorithms such as backpropagation will not exploit the decomposability of the learning problem and will attempt to learn each of the identical functions independently of each other.

Genetic algorithms (GAs) have been used for NN learning [1–3, 6–12, 15–17]. GAs are able to automatically determine the number of neurons required in solution networks in addition to connection weights. Recurrent networks can be produced.

A problem with GA approaches for NN learning is the need for fixed-length GA chromosomes to encode variable-sized networks. The chromosome size is generally chosen to over-estimate the sufficient length for encoding a solution network, which leads to longer evolution durations.

Genetic programming (GP) is a form of evolutionary computation related to GAs which evolves variable-sized tree structures rather than fixed-length bit-strings. GP has also been applied to NN learning. The GP-based Cellular Encoding system of Gruau [4, 5] has shown the ability to exploit the decomposability of problems.

This paper presents the Genetically Programmed Neural Network (GPNN) system [13, 14] which is a novel GP-based system for evolving neural networks that implement functions and can take advantage of decomposable problems. The system evolves weightless neural networks and evolves the activation functions of each neuron. Results are presented which demonstrate the ability of the system to find solution networks to test problems and shows that decomposable problems are efficiently learned.

2 System Outline

The GP algorithm searches for a collection or population of individuals which solve a problem, and does so as follows. First, each individual is a tree and is assigned a number called its *fitness* which gives an indication as to how well the individual solves the problem. Next, a new empty population is filled by randomly selecting individuals from the current population such that individuals with high fitness are chosen more often than individuals of low fitness. These selected individuals are either *mutated* by changing a subtree within the tree, or *crossed over* by swapping two subtrees between two selected individuals. In either case, the resulting new individuals are placed in the new population, and the new population is made the current population. The process repeats until a solution is found or too many iterations have occurred.

In the GPNN system, GP individuals are trees of rules. Each tree of rules constructs a neural network. Hence the GP system must find a sequence of rules which when executed constructs a neural network that solves the specified problem.

2.1 Neural Network Model

The GPNN system evolves the activation functions of the network neurons itself, so the need for connection weights disappears. Consequently the GPNN system uses weightless networks. The operation of the network is determined solely by the activation functions of the neurons and the connections between the neurons. The evolved activation functions are subtrees representing arithmetic expressions.

2.2 Growing a Neural Network

Given a sequence of rules which are encoded in a GP individual, a neural network can be constructed from these rules. In order to do this, a two-dimensional grid is used which contains the input and output neurons for the complete network together with an initial neuron from which the rest of the network will be constructed. Figure 1 shows the initial network configuration which will be used for the experimentation in this paper. Neurons are located at grid vertices. Each neuron has a class number, allocated when the neuron is formed. Class numbers can be the same.

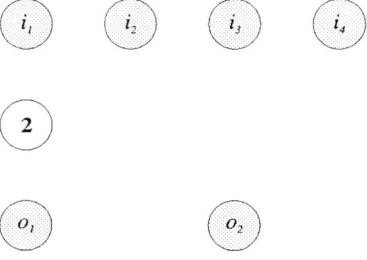

Fig. 1. The initial neuron configuration used for solving the modular Boolean functions. Neurons i_1 to i_4 are input neurons with class 0, and neurons o_1 and o_2 are output neurons with class 1. The neuron of class two is the initial neuron. The neurons are located on an invisible equally-spaced grid.

The rules specify an action and a set of classes that the action operates on, together with details particular to the action. Actions available include adding a neuron to the network, adding a connection between neurons, or changing the activation function of a neuron. There also exist actions which perform multiple simple actions because in previous studies it was found that this was beneficial.

To execute a rule, the partially-grown network is scanned to find all neurons whose class is a member of the set of classes specified by the rule. These neurons then apply the action of the rule at the same time.

It is important to notice that if multiple neurons have the same class, then they will always execute the same rules. In this way groups of identical subnetworks can be quickly produced.

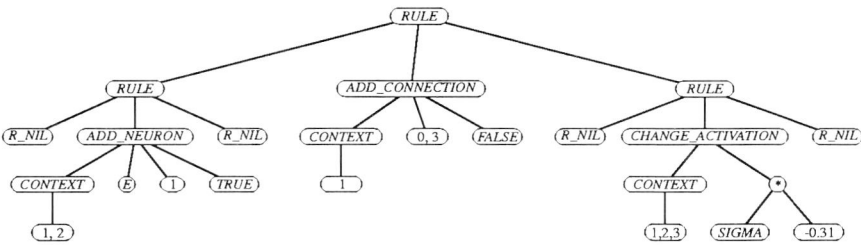

Fig. 2. An example rule tree.

2.3 GP Individual Structure

In the GPNN system, each GP individual consists of three trees instead of one: a rule tree, an initial neural activation function tree, and a processing cycles tree. All trees undergo evolution. The rule tree contains the construction rules that are applied to the initial neuron configuration to produce the final network. The processing cycles tree is a single root node that contains a bitstring encoding the number of times the activation values of the network neurons must be updated before reading the output neuron values, and is encoded as a binary number. This number is referred to as the number of *processing cycles* of the network. The initial neural activation function tree contains the activation function for the initial neuron (the neuron of class 2 in Figure 1).

The rule tree contains a number of dummy nodes whose children can be either more dummy nodes or actual construction rule nodes. During network construction, the construction rules are executed in a left-to-right order. The number of dummy nodes in a rule tree governs how many construction rules the tree has.

As an illustration, consider the rule tree shown in Figure 2. The dummy nodes contain the labels "RULE" and "R_NIL". The three rules in the tree are interpreted as follows. The ADD_NEURON rule will apply to neurons of classes 1 and 2 (specified below the "CONTEXT" node), will add the new neuron to the east ("E"), and will make the new neuron have class 1 (the "TRUE" node refers to how to move neurons to make room for the new neuron and will not be discussed here). The ADD_CONNECTION rule will be applied to neurons of class 1, will connect to the closest neuron(s) of class 0 or 3, and the connection(s) will point inwards rather than outwards (specified by the "FALSE" node). The CHANGE_ACTIVATION rule applies to neurons of classes 1, 2 and 3, and changes the activation function to -0.31Σ (Σ equals the sum of activation values of connecting neurons; another available symbol Π multiplies rather than adds).

If the rule tree shown in Figure 2 is applied to the example network shown in Figure 3(a), the resulting modified network is shown in Figure 3(b).

The evolution of each tree occurs using the GP operators outlined in the beginning of Section 2.

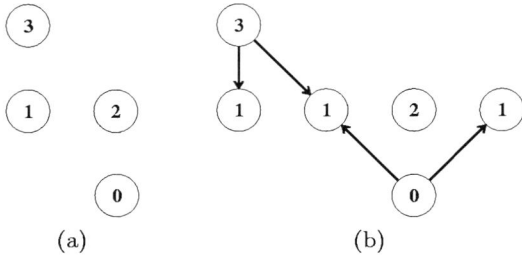

Fig. 3. Example application of construction rules. (a) Initial network. (b) Result of applying rules in the rule tree of Figure 2 to the initial network.

2.4 GP Fitness Function

In order to assign a fitness value to a GP individual, three steps are performed. First, the construction rules are executed to build the network. Second, training examples are presented to the network and the output compared to the desired responses in order to calculate an error measure E. Third, the fitness function for the individual is calculated based on the error E.

The error E is equal to

$$E = \sum_{p=1}^{P} \sum_{i=1}^{N} |d_{p,i} - o_{p,i}| \qquad (1)$$

where P is the number of input training patterns, $d_{p,i}$ denotes the desired output activation value of the ith output neuron and the pth input pattern, $o_{p,i}$ is the corresponding actual output activation from the network, and N is the number of output neurons in the network.

For a network containing n neurons with n_c being connected (a neuron is connected if it has at least one input connection, or if it is an input neuron and it has one output connection), the fitness value f is calculated as

$$f = \frac{1}{1 + E + n - n_c} \qquad (2)$$

The penalty $n - n_c$ is included in the fitness function to promote the formation of connections early in GP runs when networks do not make many connections between neurons.

2.5 A Non-modular System

There are two versions of the GPNN system: a *modular* version and a *non-modular* version.

The GPNN system as currently described is the modular version of the GPNN system. If a network contains subnetworks which have the same set of neuron classes then construction rules affecting one subnetwork also affect the other subnetworks. Hence networks containing multiple identical subnetworks can be quickly generated.

The non-modular system removes the modular construction ability of the GPNN system by keeping note of the most recently-added neuron of each class and limiting construction rules to affect only the most recently-added neuron of the class specified by the rule. In this way each rule may at most affect one network neuron.

3 Experimental Design

The aim of the experimentation in this paper is to determine whether there exist appreciable performance differences between the modular and non-modular GPNN systems when applied to decomposable problems.

Both the modular and non-modular GPNN systems were run on 16 decomposable Boolean functions each having four input variables and two output values. Boolean functions were used here, but real-valued functions can also be readily used with the system.

Each of the 16 functions to be learned is decomposable into two identical subfunctions having two inputs and one output value. In Fig. 1 the first subfunction uses input neurons i_1 and i_2 and output neuron o_1 whereas the second subfunction uses the remaining input and output neurons. The decomposable functions consist of the full 16 different 2-input subfunctions possible. Figure 4 details the construction of truth tables of the Boolean functions. Note in this figure how the subfunctions are identical because if in one training pattern $i_1 = \alpha$, $i_2 = \beta$ and $o_1 = \gamma$ (where $\alpha, \beta, \gamma \in \{0,1\}$), then for all other training patterns where $i_3 = \alpha$ and $i_4 = \beta$, $o_2 = \gamma$ also, and vice versa.

For each function both the modular and non-modular versions of the GPNN system are run 100 times using different initial random number seeds. The system runs until it finds a solution network in which each output neuron responds within 0.25 of the correct value for all the training patterns, or until a maximum number of generations have passed.

The performance measure used for rating the performance of the GPNN system on each function is the *success rate*, which equals the proportion of the 100 system runs which find a solution.

4 Experimental Results

A population size of 100 was used with the maximum number of generations per run equal to 1000. Table 1 presents the success rates for each decomposable function.

Excepting Boolean function 7, the success rates obtained by the modular version of the system are equal to or greater than the success rates obtained by the non-modular system. For Boolean functions 3, 5, and 12 the success rates between the two system versions are significantly different. From these results it

i_1	i_2	o
0	0	a
0	1	b
1	0	c
1	1	d

(a)

i_1	i_2	i_3	i_4	o_1	o_2
0	0	0	0	a	a
0	0	0	1	a	b
0	0	1	0	a	c
0	0	1	1	a	d
0	1	0	0	b	a
0	1	0	1	b	b
0	1	1	0	b	c
0	1	1	1	b	d
1	0	0	0	c	a
1	0	0	1	c	b
1	0	1	0	c	c
1	0	1	1	c	d
1	1	0	0	d	a
1	1	0	1	d	b
1	1	1	0	d	c
1	1	1	1	d	d

(b)

Fig. 4. The formation of each decomposable Boolean function. (a) The input and output patterns for one of the two identical subfunctions comprising the decomposable Boolean function. Each output value is either 0 or 1 and collectively satisfies $n = a + 2b + 4c + 8d$ where n is the Boolean function number and is between 0 and 15. (b) The input and output patterns for the decomposable Boolean function as formed from the subfunctions. Input variables i_1 and i_2 and output variable o_1 define one subfunction, whereas input variables i_3 and i_4 and output variable o_2 define the other.

can be concluded that the modular system performs significantly better in some cases than the non-modular system, and at least as well in the remaining cases.

Two solution networks obtained using the modular system are shown in Fig. 5 and a solution network produced by the non-modular system is shown in Fig. 6. Note in particular that in Fig. 5(a) there are two identical subnetworks which

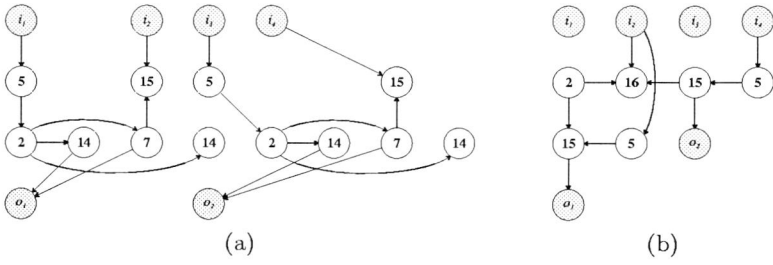

Fig. 5. Two solution networks found by the modular system. Figure (a) shows a solution to Boolean function 3 and (b) is a solution to Boolean function 10. Neuron classes are shown within the neurons except input neurons which are labeled with i_k and output neurons labeled with o_k.

Table 1. The success rates obtained by the modular and non-modular versions of the GPNN system applied to the sixteen decomposable Boolean problems. Each success rate is equal to the proportion of the 100 runs of the system that find a solution. When the p-value for the significance test that the success rate obtained by the modular system is the same as the success rate obtained using the non-modular system is significant (i.e. not greater than 0.05) then the p value is footnoted.

Boolean Function Number	Modular System	Non Modular System
0	100	100
1	4	1
2	2	0
3[a]	21	3
4	1	0
5[b]	16	1
6	4	0
7	0	1
8	17	9
9	1	0
10	49	37
11	1	0
12[c]	72	57
13	0	0
14	1	0
15	100	100

[a] $p = 0.0002$
[b] $p = 0.0003$
[c] $p = 0.0319$

perform each 2-input Boolean subfunction. This two-subnetwork partitioning is noted in some but not all solution networks obtained using the modular system.

5 Discussion

The success rates obtained are not approximately equivalent to each other and depend on the Boolean functions. This section discusses the differences between the modular and non-modular system results.

Both the modular and non-modular systems work well with functions 0 and 15 because all output neurons are a constant 0 or 1.

The modular system achieves clearly better success rates than the non-modular system for functions 3, 5, 10 and 12, and this is significantly so except for function 10. These functions are relatively simple to solve because the output of each subfunction depends on one of the two input values.

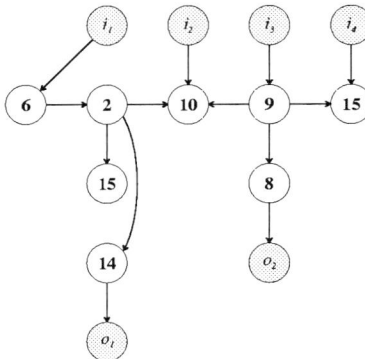

Fig. 6. A solution network found by the non-modular system which is a solution to Boolean function 12.

The modular system is able to out-perform the non-modular system for function 8, although by a lesser extent than for functions 3, 5, 10 and 12. Function 8 implements the logical AND function and can be solved by simply multiplying both input values of each subfunction together and sending the result to the output neurons.

For the remaining functions there is an indication that the modular system is able to out-perform the non-modular system. The success rates for functions 1, 2, 4, 6, 9, 11 and 14 show higher success rates for the modular system. These remaining functions are more difficult to solve because all input neurons are required to calculate the correct output values. Consequently the success rates are low for both the modular and non-modular systems.

In summary, the differences in success rates between functions are attributable to the number of input neurons that are needed in order to calculate the solution. For functions in which all input neurons are required to calculate the output, the success rates are lower than functions which require fewer input neurons in order to calculate the output.

6 Conclusion

This paper has shown the ability of the modular GPNN system to find solutions to decomposable Boolean functions. The GPNN system evolves the network architecture in addition to the neuron activation functions.

The results of this paper show that the system can take advantage of decomposable problems by achieving higher success rates than a non-modular version of the system which cannot take advantage of decomposable problems.

References

1. Richard K. Belew, John McInerney, and Nicol N. Schraudolph. Evolving networks: Using the genetic algorithm with connectionist learning. In Christopher G. Lang-

ton, Charles Taylor, J. Doyne Farmer, and Steen Rasmussen, editors, *Artificial Life II. Proceedings of the Workshop on Artificial Life*, pages 511–547, Santa Fe, New Mexico, 1991. Addison-Wesley.
2. Egbert J. W. Boers and Herman Kuiper. Biological metaphors and the design of modular artificial neural networks. Master's thesis, Departments of Computer Science and Experimental and Theoretical Psychology, Leiden University, The Netherlands, 1992.
3. Toshio Fukuda, Tadashi Kohno, and Takanori Shibata. Dynamic memory by recurrent neural network and its learning by genetic algorithm. In *Proceedings of the 32nd Conference on Decision and Control*, volume 3, pages 2815–2820, San Antonio, Texas, 15–17 December 1993. IEEE Press.
4. Frédéric Gruau. Cellular encoding of genetic neural networks. Technical Report RR92-21, Laboratoire de l'Informatique du Parallélisme, Ecole Normale Supérieure de Lyon, France, May 1992.
5. Frédéric Gruau. *Neural Network Synthesis Using Cellular Encoding and the Genetic Algorithm*. PhD thesis, Laboratoire de l'Informatique du Parallélisme, Ecole Normale Supérieure de Lyon, France, 4 January 1994.
6. Steven Alex Harp, Tariq Samad, and Aloke Guha. Towards the genetic synthesis of neural networks. In J. David Schaffer, editor, *Proceedings of the Third International Conference on Genetic Algorithms*, pages 360–369, George Mason University, Washington D.C., 4–7 June 1989. Morgan Kaufmann.
7. Hiroaki Kitano. Designing neural networks using genetic algorithms with graph generation system. *Complex Systems*, 4:461–476, August 1990.
8. Martin Mandischer. Representation and evolution of neural networks. In R. F. Albrecht, C. R. Reeves, and N. C. Steele, editors, *Artificial Neural Nets and Genetic Algorithms: Proceedings of the International Conference*, pages 643–649, Innsbruck, Austria, 1993. Springer-Verlag, Wien and New York.
9. Geoffrey F. Miller, Peter M. Todd, and Shailesh U. Hegde. Designing neural networks using genetic algorithms. In J. David Schaffer, editor, *Proceedings of the Third International Conference on Genetic Algorithms*, pages 379–384, George Mason University, Washington D.C., 4–7 June 1989. Morgan Kaufmann.
10. David J. Montana and Lawrence Davis. Training feedforward neural networks using genetic algorithms. In *Proceedings of the Eleventh International Joint Conference on Artificial Intelligence*, volume 1, pages 762–767, Detroit, Michigan, 20–25 August 1989.
11. Stefano Nolfi and Domenico Parisi. "Genotypes" for neural networks. In Michael A. Arbib, editor, *The Handbook of Brain Theory and Neural Networks*, pages 431–434. The MIT Press, 1995.
12. J. Santos and R. J. Duro. Evolutionary generation and training of recurrent artificial neural networks. In Zbigniew Michalewicz, editor, *Proceedings of the 1st IEEE Conference on Evolutionary Computation*, volume 2, pages 759–763, Orlando, Fla, 27–29 June 1994. IEEE Press.
13. Bret Talko. Evolving modular neural networks using rule-based genetic programming. In Norman Foo, editor, *12th Australian Joint Conference on Artificial Intelligence, AI'99*, volume 1747 of *Advanced Topics in Artificial Intelligence, Lecture Notes in Artificial Intelligence*, Sydney, Australia, 6–10 December 1999. Springer-Verlag.
14. Bret Talko. A rule-based approach for constructing neural networks using genetic programming. Master's thesis, Department of Computer Science and Software Engineering, The University of Melbourne, Australia, March 1999.

15. Jan Torreele. Temporal processing with recurrent networks: An evolutionary approach. In Richard K. Belew and Lashon B. Booker, editors, *Proceedings of the Fourth International Conference on Genetic Algorithms*, pages 555–561, University of California, San Diego, 14–17 July 1991. Morgan Kaufmann.
16. Darrell Whitley, Stephen Dominic, and Rajarshi Das. Genetic reinforcement learning with multilayer neural networks. In Richard K. Belew and Lashon B. Booker, editors, *Proceedings of the Fourth International Conference on Genetic Algorithms*, pages 562–570, University of California, San Diego, 14–17 July 1991. Morgan Kaufmann.
17. Xin Yao. Evolutionary artificial neural networks. *International Journal of Neural Systems*, 4(3):203–222, September 1993.

Dual Encoding Using Constraint Coverings

S. Nagarajan[1], S.D. Goodwin[1], and A. Sattar[2]

[1] Department of Computer Science, University of Regina,
Regina, Saskatchewan, Canada
[shiv, goodwin]@cs.uregina.ca

[2] School of Computing and Information Technology,
Griffith University, Nathan, Queensland, Australia
sattar@cit.gu.edu.au

Abstract. Constraint satisfaction problems (CSPs) involve finding an assignment of values to variables that satisfy a set of constraints between variables. Non-binary constraints have recently begun to attract more attention, since many real-life problems are naturally expressed as non-binary formulations. In order to solve a non-binary CSP, one either uses an algorithm that has been generalised for non-binary constraint satisfaction or one can convert the problem into an equivalent binary CSP. The dual encoding has been shown to be impractical in some cases where the constraints have very large domains, but need to be represented in extension. It is often the case that such constraints (e.g. **all-diff**) have compact intensional representations, and this is often the reason why algorithms based on the primal graph which can store them intensionally have an edge. In this paper we present a dual encoding that is based on the construction of constraint coverings from the original CSP. This allows us to benefit from the intensional representation of some constraints that are impractical to represent extensionally. We show how this covering based dual encoding can be used to address the space complexity issue of the dual encodings, while still retaining the soundness and completeness of the solution procedures.

1 Introduction

Two well known methods for the conversion of the non-binary CSPs into binary CSPs are the **dual graph method** and the **hidden variable method**. In [1], the dual encoding and hidden variable encodings are compared under backtracking algorithms like forward checking, as also compared against an algorithm, FC^+, that operates on the original non-binary formulation. The results indicate that in some cases the dual encoding can perform very well. In [15], the two different binary encodings for non-binary constraint satisfaction problems, the hidden variable and the dual encoding, are compared with respect to the levels of pruning achieved by enforcing arc consistency (AC) on each of them. It has been shown that the levels of pruning achieved by enforcing AC on the hidden variable encoding and enforcing GAC (generalised arc consistency) on the non-binary formulation are equivalent, while enforcing AC on the dual encoding is strictly stronger than AC on the hidden encoding (and therefore than GAC on the non-binary formulation). As mentioned in both [1,15], this additional pruning comes at some computational cost.

Algorithms for search in the dual or hidden encodings that are similar to forward checking (FC), use space that is proportional to the domains of the dual variables (constraints in this case), to order the search and to remember which values have been pruned from the search space. If $||C_i||$ is the size of a constraint, then the additional space required by the dual and hidden variable encodings to store all the constraints extensionally is $\sum_{i=1}^{m} ||C_i||$. As described in [1] this becomes a space time tradeoff only when the constraints in the original problem are given intensionally, and one is forced to construct the extensional representation from this. When the constraints are loose, or if the problem includes large arity **all-different** constraints, this additional space can become prohibitively large. (For all-different constraints of arity k the number of satisfying tuples could be as high as $k!$). This implies that the space required to store k-ary relations like the *all-different* constraint, could be as high as $k * k!$.

In this paper we present a dual encoding that is based on the construction of constraint coverings from the original CSP. This allows us to benefit from the intensional representation of some constraints that are impractical to represent extensionally. We show how this covering based dual encoding can be used to address the space complexity issue of the dual encodings, while still retaining the soundness and completeness of the solution procedures.

Precisely, the contributions of this paper are:

- a new encoding of constraint satisfaction problems, that is based on the construction of constraint coverings. The new encoding can take advantage of both intensional and extensional representations of constraints and also addresses the space complexity issue related to the existing dual encodings;
- we show the new encoding scheme is complete in the sense that all solutions to the CSP are preserved.
- we establish equivalence between the construction of minimal constraint coverings and the computing of a minimal cardinality set covering problem, and demonstrate that the greedy heuristics studied in the set covering can be efficiently used in the constraint coverings.
- we present preliminary experimental results on a large set of random non-binary problems including problems in the phase transition region.

2 Preliminary Definitions

Given below are a few definitions. Let $\langle V, D, C \rangle$ be a *CSP* where V is the set of variables, D are their domains, and C is the set of constraints. Furthermore, we can assume that each constraint $C_i = \langle V_i, S_i \rangle \in C$ consists of a list of variables $V_i = (v_{i1}, \ldots, v_{ik}) \subseteq V$ and a predicate on these variables, $S_i \subseteq D_{v_{i1}} \times \cdots \times D_{v_{ik}}$. A **binary** *CSP* is one in which all the constraints are defined over pairs of variables. Associated with every binary *CSP* is a constraint graph with a node for every variable and an edge between two nodes if their variables share a constraint.

Definition 1. *Given a binary* CSP, *the* **primal constraint graph** *associated with it is a labeled constraint graph, where* $N=V$, $(v_i, v_j) \in A$ *iff* $\exists C_{ij} \in C \mid V_{ij} = \{v_i, v_j\}$. *Also the label on arc* (v_i, v_j) *is* C_{ij}. *Given an arbitrary* CSP, *the* **dual constraint graph** *associated with it is a labeled graph, where* $N=C$, $(C_i, C_j) \in A \leftrightarrow V_i \cap V_j \neq \emptyset$. *Also the label on arc* (C_i, C_j) *is* $V_i \cap V_j$.

Dechter and Pearl [7] propose the transformation of any *CSP* P_1 into its dual form, i.e., a new *CSP* P_2 where constraints are now variables with structured domains and variables are now the constraints. The domain of each dual variable now is the set of tuples that satisfy the original constraint, and there is a binary constraint in the new CSP between two dual variables iff the original constraints shared some variables. These binary compatibility constraints ensure that the shared variables are assigned the same values by the satisfying tuples for each dual variable.

Although binary and non-binary constraint representations have been shown to have equivalence it is not necessarily the case that one must abandon the study of either of these. Many problems are expressed naturally in one of these forms and trying to represent them in the other will be unnatural [1].

Definition 2. *If* V_i *and* V_j *are sets of variables, let* S_i *be an instantiation of the variables in* V_i. $S_i[V_j]$ *is the tuple consisting of only the components of* S_i *that correspond to the variables in* V_j. *This is also called the* **projection** *of tuple* S_i *on the variables in* V_j. *Let* C_i, C_j *be two constraints* $\in C$. *The* **join** *of* C_i, C_j, *denoted by* $C_i \bowtie C_j = C_{ij}$, *is the set* $\{t \mid t \in S_{ij} \land (t[V_i] \in S_i) \land (t[V_j] \in S_j)\}$.

The set of all solutions of a constraint satisfaction problem, is equal to the join of the relational instances corresponding to the constraints [3]. An assignment of values to a subset of variables is called a *partial assignment* or a *tuple*.

Definition 3. *Consider a tuple* t_i *as a consistent instantiation of variables in* V_{t_i}. *An* **extension** *of* t_i *to variables in* $V_{t_i} \cup V_{t_j}$ *is a tuple* t_{ij} *where* t_{ij} *is an instantiation to variables in* $V_{t_i} \cup V_{t_j}$. *The two tuples* t_i *and* t_j *are* **compatible** *if* $t_i[V_{t_i} \cap V_{t_j}] = t_j[V_{t_i} \cap V_{t_j}]$, *i.e., the two tuples agree on values for all common variables.*[1] *The tuple* $t_{ij} = t_i \bowtie t_j$ *is a* **consistent extension** *of* t_i *iff* t_i *and* t_j *are* **compatible** *and* $\forall C_i$ *such that* $V_i \subseteq V_{t_{ij}}, t_{ij}[V_i] \in S_i$.

A tuple, t_i, is consistent if it satisfies all the constraints whose variables are completely instantiated by t_i. A complete solution is a consistent instantiation of all the variables. Arc consistency is a lower form of consistency defined for binary constraints defined using the notion of support and viability [2].

Definition 4. *Given a constraint* C_{ij}, *the value* b *in* D_j, *is called a* **support** *for value* a *in* D_j, *if the pair* $(a, b) \in S_{ij}$. *A value* a *for a variable* i *is* **viable**

---
[1] If $V_{t_i} \cap V_{t_j} = \emptyset$, t_i and t_j are automatically compatible.

iff for every variable j such that a constraint C_{ij} exists, a has a support in D_j. The domain D of a constraint network, is **arc consistent** if for every variable i in the network, all the values in d_i are viable.

Arc consistency is extended for non-binary constraints as generalised arc consistency (GAC). A non-binary CSP is GAC iff for any variable in a constraint and a value that is assigned to it there exist compatible values for all other variables in the constraint [14]. The notion of arc consistency can be defined for tuples and dual variables in the dual encoding as follows.

Definition 5. *Given two constraints C_i and C_j, the tuple $t_j \in S_j$ is called a* **support** *for tuple $t_i \in S_i$, if $t_i \bowtie t_j$ is a consistent extension. A tuple t_i in a constraint C_i is* **viable** *iff for every constraint C_j, tuple t_i has support in C_j. A constraint network is* **dual arc consistent***, if for every constraint C_i, all the tuples in S_i are viable.*

Many algorithms have been proposed for constructing an arc consistent domain in a constraint network. The best known AC algorithms are AC-6 [2] and AC-7 [4]. The worst case time complexity of both AC-6 and AC-7 are optimal at $O(ed^2)$, while the space complexity is $O(ed)$, where e is the number of arcs in the constraint graph, and d is the size of the largest domain.

3 Constraint Covering

As mentioned earlier, set of all solutions of a constraint satisfaction problem, is equal to the join of the relational instances corresponding to all the constraints. But from the definition of a consistent extension (Definition 3), it is clear that if tuple t_i and tuple t_j are compatible, **and** $t_i \bowtie t_j$ is a consistent extension, then all constraints $C_i \in C$ such that $V_i \cap V_{t_{ij}} \neq \emptyset$ are satisfied. The goal of CSP solving algorithms is to find one (or all) consistent extensions on n variables.

Definition 6. *Let $C_{cover} = \{C_1, C_2, \ldots, C_m\}$. Also $C_{cover} \subseteq C$. Each $C_i \in C_{cover}$ is given as $\langle V_i, S_i \rangle$, where $V_i \subseteq V$. C_{cover}* **covers** *V iff $\bigcup_{i=1}^{m} V_i = V$. C_{cover} is a* **constraint cover** *of V. As well, C_{cover} is a* **minimal constraint cover** *of V if it is a constraint cover of V and no proper subset of C_{cover} is a constraint cover of V.*

If C_{cover} is a minimal constraint cover, $|C_{cover}| \leq |V|$. This can be seen by the fact that while selecting constraints to form the minimal cover, each additional constraint, covers at least one new variable, and hence all that is required is a cover of size of at most $|V|$.

Lemma 1. *Given a constraint cover (minimal or otherwise), any consistent extension constructed by joining one tuple from each constraint in the cover is a solution on n variables.*

Proof. Let $C_{cover} = \{C_1, C_2, \ldots, C_m\}$. Consider tuples selected from each constraint in C_{cover}, $\{t_1, t_2, \ldots, t_m\}$. $t_{sol} = t_1 \bowtie t_2 \bowtie \ldots \bowtie t_m$ is a tuple on n

variables, since $\bigcup_{i=1}^{m} V_i = V$ (from definition 6). If t_{sol} is a consistent extension, then $\forall C_i$ such that $V_i \subseteq V_{t_{sol}}, t_{sol}[V_i] \in S_i$ (from definition 3). But since t_{sol} is a consistent tuple on n variables, it is a solution. □

Lemma 2. *For every solution* $\mathbf{t}_{sol}$ *of the CSP on n variables, given a constraint cover (minimal or otherwise), $C_{cover} = \{C_1, C_2, \ldots, C_m\}$, there exist tuples $\{t_1 \in S_1, t_2 \in S_2, \ldots, t_m \in S_m\}$, such that $t_1 \bowtie t_2 \bowtie \ldots \bowtie t_m = t_{sol}$.*

Proof. Let $C_{cover} = \{C_1, C_2, \ldots, C_m\}$. Let t_{sol} be a solution n variables. Since t_{sol} is a solution, $\forall C_i \in C, t_{sol}[V_i] \in Si$. But $C_{cover} \subseteq C$. Therefore $\forall C_c \in C_{cover}$, $t_{sol}[V_c] \in S_c$. Consider the set of tuples, $\{t_1, t_2, \ldots, t_m\}$, such that $t_i = t_{sol}[V_{t_i}]$. Then $t_1 \bowtie t_2 \bowtie \ldots \bowtie t_m = t_{sol}$. □

Consider a dual encoding of a CSP, where the nodes of the dual are the constraints in a constraint cover of the given CSP. From Lemmas 1 and 2, we can show the soundness and completeness of a search procedure that chronologically searches in this dual encoding of the CSP.

Theorem 1. *Backtracking in the constraint covering based dual encoding of a CSP, where the nodes of the dual encoding are the constraints in a covering $C_{cover} = \{C_1, C_2, \ldots, C_m\}$, is* **sound**.

Proof. From Lemma 1, any consistent extension from this dual encoding of the CSP is a solution. □

Theorem 2. *Backtracking in the constraint covering based dual encoding of a CSP, where the nodes of the dual encoding are the constraints in a covering $C_{cover} = \{C_1, C_2, \ldots, C_m\}$, is* **complete**.

Proof. From Lemma 2, for any solution to the CSP, there exists a consistent extension in this dual encoding of the CSP, that results in this solution. □

Given a constraint cover, $C_{cover} = \{C_1, C_2, \ldots, C_m\}$ if $m > |V|$, $\exists C_i \in C_{cover}$ such that $C_{cover} - C_i$ is still a constraint cover. Although the size of a minimal constraint cover is upper bounded by $|V|$,[2] in practice, in CSPs of higher arities, this number is even less. In fact, if C_{cover} is a minimal constraint cover of a *CSP* of arity k, $|C_{cover}| \leq n\text{-}k\text{+}1$, since a *CSP* of arity k has at least one constraint of arity k. Including this constraint in a minimal constraint cover C_{cover} covers k variables. This leaves $n\text{-}k$ variables to be covered. At most $n\text{-}k$ constraints are required to cover these variables. So the total number of constraints in a minimal constraint cover is $\leq n\text{-}k\text{+}1$.

In the previous section we mentioned that the additional space required by the dual encodings to store all the constraints extensionally is $\sum_{i=1}^{z} ||C_i||$ (where z is the number of constraints in the CSP). Using Theorems 1 and 2, we can now conclude that the only constraints that need to be represented in extension are the constraints in a cover. For all constraints in the CSP that are **not** in the cover, we can use an intensional representation if one exists. Therefore given

---
[2] This upper bound is attained, when the cover contains only unary constraints.

a constraint cover, $C_{cover} = \{C_1, C_2, \ldots, C_m\}$, the total space required to store these constraints in extension is $\sum_{i=1}^{m} ||C_{cover}||$. Since $m \leq n\text{-}k\text{+}1 \leq z$, the total space requirement for the constraint covering based dual encoding, is less than a standard dual encoding that involves all the constraints in the CSP with n variables, z constraints and arity k.

3.1 Example

Consider a very simple CSP, with 4 variables, a, b, c, d. The domain of each of the variables is $1, 2, 3$. Consider the following 4 constraints.
$C_{a,b}$ ← $a+b$=5, **$C_{b,d}$** ←**abs**$(b\text{-}d)$=2, **$C_{a,b,c}$** ←**alldiff**(a, b, c), **$C_{a,c}$** ← $a > c$
Clearly all the constraints can be represented in either intensional or extensional form. The extensional form is given below.
$C_{a,b}$=$\{(2,3),(3,2)\}$, $C_{b,d}$=$\{(1,3),(3,1)\}$, $C_{a,c}$=$\{(3,1),(3,2),(2,1)\}$
$C_{a,b,c}$=$\{(1,2,3),(1,3,2),(2,1,3),(2,3,1),(3,1,2),(3,2,1)\}$

A simple dual encoding would require space to store 13 tuples. If the size of a constraint is defined as the product of arity and the number of tuples in the relation, the total space required by the dual encoding is 32. Consider a constraint cover constructed using constraints $C_{a,b}, C_{b,d}, C_{a,b,c}$. This is not a minimal constraint cover. The total number of tuples required by a dual encoding using this constraint cover is 10 and the total space is 26. Similarly a cover $C_{b,d}, C_{a,b,c}$, would require 8 tuples and space of 22 for its dual encoding. This is a minimal constraint cover. Another possibility for a cover is $C_{a,b}, C_{b,d}, C_{a,c}$ with number of tuples 7 and total space 14. This is also a minimal constraint cover. With this constraint cover the savings in space are because we can represent the **all-diff** constraint intensionally.

When the CSP has higher arity constraints like **all-diff**, whose extensions are exponential in the size of the relation, the standard dual encoding is very impractical. On the other hand the **all-diff** constraint has a very compact intensional form. By constructing a cover that does not include such constraints, we can instead use intensional representations for the constraints that have expensive extensional representations. This idea can be extended to any constraint that has an impractical extensional form. In the following sections we present some algorithms for constructing constraint covers.

3.2 Set Covering

The problem of finding a minimum cardinality constraint covering is equivalent to that of finding a set covering. The set covering problem is defined below.

Definition 7. *Let S be a collection of n points, and $\mathcal{F} = \{S_1, S_2, \ldots, S_m\}$ a collection of subsets of S. The **minimum set cover problem**, is the problem of selecting as few as possible subsets from $\mathcal{F}$ such that every point in S is contained in at least one of the contained subsets.*

The set covering problem has been shown to be NP-hard [6, 8, 9]. All the same, it has been well studied, and approximation algorithms exist for the set cover problem that can approximate the set cover within a ratio of ln m, where m is the size of the largest set in the collection. The most popular algorithm for set cover is the greedy algorithm due to Johnson [8], Lovasz [10] and Chvatal [6]. Very tight approximation bounds exist for the performance of this greedy algorithm for the minimum set cover problem.

Greedy heuristic for set covering. The greedy algorithm for approximating minimum cover, at each step, simply chooses the covering set with the maximum elements left, deletes these elements from the remaining covering sets, and repeats this until the ground set U, is covered. Johnson and Lovasz([8, 10]) showed that the performance ratio of the greedy algorithm when compared to the optimal is between m and ln $m + 1$.

It is unlikely that there exists an efficient procedure to calculate a minimum cardinality constraint covering. But it is also clear that the greedy algorithm for minimum set covering can be appropriately modified to calculate a minimum cardinality constraint covering.

3.3 Greedy Heuristic for Minimum Cardinality Constraint Covering

In this section, we present an algorithm to compute a constraint covering using a greedy heuristic. The greedy heuristic is based on the similar heuristic for set covering, which has provable approximation bounds. Figure 1 gives the algorithm. In this algorithm the termination condition for the *while* loop reflects finding of the covering. Also $SET[i]$ initially corresponds to the variable set in

---

Input: CSP $\langle V, D, C \rangle$
Output: $C_{cover} \equiv \bigcup_{i=1}^{i=k} C_i \in C_{Cover}$=V

procedure greedy_cover
begin
1. C_{cover} := $\emptyset$;
2. $\forall C_i \in C, SET[i]$:= V_i;
3. Let $UNCOV$:= V;
4. while $UNCOV \neq \emptyset$ do
5.   select $C_I \in C$ such that $|SET[I]|$ is maximised;
6. C_{cover} := $C_{cover} \cup C_I$;
7. $UNCOV$:= $UNCOV$-$SET[I]$;
8. $\forall C_i \in C, SET[i]$:= $SET[i]$-$SET[I]$;
9. end while;
10. return C_{cover};
end

Fig. 1. Greedy heuristic for constraint covering

each constraint $C_i \in C$. At each step the algorithm selects that constraint that has the largest number of uncovered elements left. (i.e., $SET[i]$ is maximum). It adds this constraint to the cover and deletes all the elements from this variable set from all the $SET[i]$'s.

At each iteration of the algorithm, at least one variable in the base set is covered since at every stage the algorithm attempts to select a constraint that contains the maximum number of uncovered variables. If this number were zero, the algorithm would have terminated. So the greedy constraint covering algorithm, performs at most m iterations, where $m=|V|$.

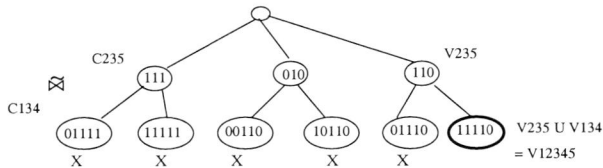

Fig. 2. CDBT with Greedy Heuristic on Example

3.4 Example

In [11] we presented an algorithm based on the dual encoding which was a revised version of constraint directed backtracking (CDBT) [13]. Here we present an example and illustrate the execution of the revised $CDBT$ procedure using a covering based dual encoding and the greedy heuristic in trying to solve this CSP. Consider a CSP with $V = \{V_1, V_2, V_3, V_4, V_5\}$, and with 6 constraints, which are given as, $C_{235}=\{(111),(010),(110)\}$, $C_{125}=\{(011),(110),(100)\}$, $C_{24}=\{(1,1)\}$, $C_{134}=\{(011),(101),(111)\}$, $C_{145}=\{(111),(110),(001)\}$, $C_{135}=\{(010),(001),(110)\}$.

The domains of all the variables are $\{0,1\}$. In figure 2, we show the execution of plain $CDBT$ on the example. The search tree associated with the execution of the algorithm with the greedy heuristic incorporated is given in the figure. The algorithm visits only 9 nodes, before finding the same solution. The constraint cover that is constructed has 2 constraints, $\{C_{235}, C_{134}\}$.

3.5 Greedy Feuristic for Weighted Minimal Constraint Ccovering

In the previous section we showed how the use of a greedy heuristic to select a constraint covering for the CSP can be used. It is often the case that although a certain covering has fewer constraints, the size of the individual tuple sets of the constraints in the cover, are larger. Intuitively the greedy heuristic selects constraints of higher arity earlier on, but it is also the case that higher arity constraints have more individual tuples than lower order constraints (since the product domain space is larger). In this section we present an extension of the

```
Input: CSP ⟨V, D, C⟩
Output: C_cover ≡ ⋃_{i=1}^{i=k} C_i ∈ C_Cover =V

procedure weighted_greedy_cover
begin
1.   C_cover := ∅;
2.   ∀C_i ∈ C, SET[i] := V_i;
3.   Let UNCOV := V;
4.   while UNCOV ≠ ∅ do
5.      select C_I ∈ C such that |SET[I]|/Cost_i is maximised;
6.      C_cover := C_cover ∪ C_I;
7.      UNCOV := UNCOV-SET[I];
8.      ∀C_i ∈ C, SET[i] := SET[i]-SET[I];
9.   end while;
10.  return C_cover;
end
```

Fig. 3. Greedy heuristic for weighted constraint covering

greedy heuristic which takes into account the size of the individual tuple sets of each of the constraints, and uses this information to construct a covering. There is a similar extension for the set covering problem where the the individual sets have costs associated with them, so that a covering is found that minimises the total cost of all the constraints in the covering. This gives us the *weighted set cover* problem, for which a simple variation to the set cover heuristic is sufficient. For the case of constraint covering, what we are trying to do is construct a constraint cover, such that the relational join of the constraints in the join gives an n-ary instantiation.

In figure 3, we present the revised *CDBT* algorithm using a covering based dual encoding with the weighted constraint covering heuristic incorporated. We associated with each constraint a weight (or cost) which is given by the product of the arity of the constraint and the number of tuples that are admissible by that constraint. The algorithm selects the constraint that maximises the ratio $\frac{|SET[I]|}{Cost_i}$. Intuitively the probability of including C_i in a constraint cover increases with the ratio $\frac{|SET[I]|}{Cost_i}$ which represents the new variables covered by the constraint per unit cost.

Example Revisited. In figure 4 we show the execution of the algorithm on the example. As seen the algorithm constructs a cover of size 2, including the constraints C_{24} and C_{135}. The algorithm visits just 4 nodes before finding the solution that violates no constraints.

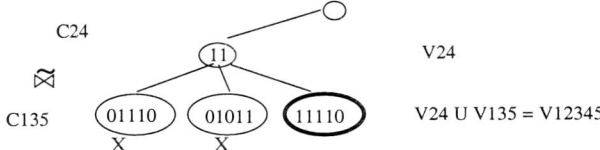

Fig. 4. CDBB with weighted greedy heuristic on Example

4 Results

We performed some experiments to empirically evaluate the dual encoding presented in this paper. Random problems were generated using an extension to the standard four parameter binary model. We generated non-binary constraint satisfaction problems using four parameters (n, m, p_1, p_2) [5], where n is the number of variables, m, the size of the indivdual domains, p_1, the probability of constraint inclusion and p_2, the probability of tuple exclusion. We generated problems with ternary constraints, using a normal distribution with the following parameters: 1) $(15, 5, 0.06, p_2)$ and 2) $(10, 5, 0.2, p_2)$. We generated 50 problems for each value of p_2 between 0.15 and 0.9 in increments of 0.05, to give a total of 800 problems in each class, and for a total of 1600 problems. For each problem class we executed backtracking algorithms that construct the dual encoding using the greedy covering algorithm, and the weighted covering algorithm. The parameters measured were *nodes visited* and *number of backtracks*. The results for a simple backtracking algorithm with a dual encoding based on coverings are given in the figures below. Each graph compares the *greedy* algorithm with the *weighted* algorithm. The results given are measured to find the first solution. The algorithms themselves are complete and can find all solutions if necessary. Results for the same problem classes using a forward checking algorithm are also given. We observe that the weighted covering based dual encoding, reduces the number of nodes visited, as also the number of backtracks. The empirical results also indicate that the weighted constraint covering based encoding also enhances the performance of the forward checking based algorithms too.

5 Conclusions and Future Directions

In this paper we showed how the space problem associated with standard dual encodings of CSPs can be addressed by a new dual encoding based con constraint coverings. Our empirical results indicate that this encoding is promising for a wide range of problems. Some interesting future directions, will be to theoretically study the amount of pruning achieved by algorithms like FC and AC on the covering based dual encoding scheme and compare them to the pruning achieved by AC and FC on the standard dual encoding and on the pruning achieved by GAC on the primal encoding [12].

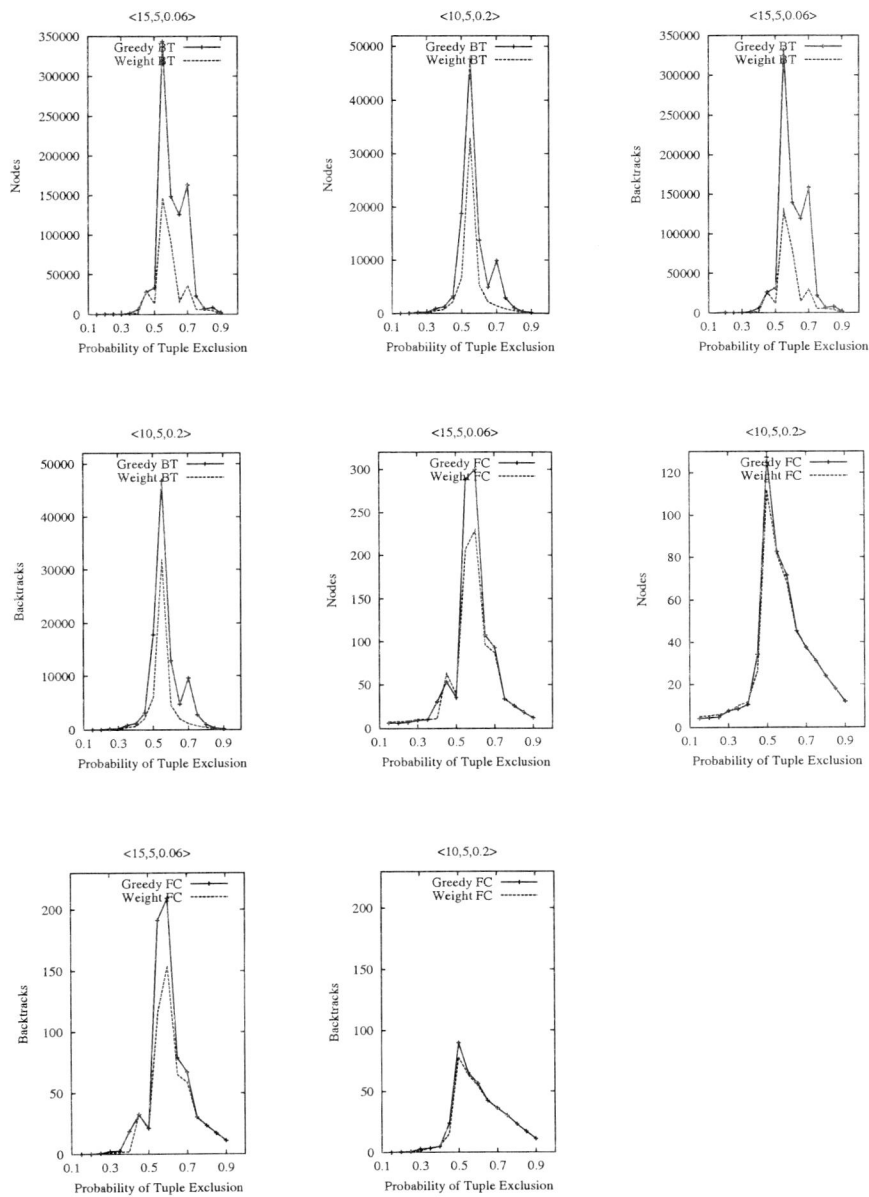

Acknowledgements

This research was supported by National Science and Engineering Research Council (NSERC), Canada and Australian Research Council (ARC) Large grant scheme.

References

1. Fahiem Bacchus and Peter van Beek. On the conversion between non-binary and binary constraint satisfaction problems. In *Proceedings of the 15th National Conference on Artificial Intelligence*, pages 311–318, 1998.
2. Christian Bessiere and Marie-Odile Cordier. Arc-consistency and arc-consistency again. In *Proceedings of the 11th National Conference on Artificial Intelligence*, pages 108–113, 1993.
3. W. Bibel. Constraint satisfaction from a deductive viewpoint. *Artificial Intelligence*, 35:401–413, 1988.
4. Bessiere C., Freuder E. C., and Regin J. C. Using inference to reduce arc consistency computation. In *Proceedings of IJCAI 95*, pages 592–598, 1995.
5. Bessiere C., Freuder E. C., Meseguer P., and Larrosa J. On forward checking for non-binary constraint satisfaction. In *Principles and Practice of Constraint Programming, CP-99*, volume 1713, pages 88–102. Springer Verlag, 1999.
6. V. Chvàtal. A greedy heuristic for the set covering problem. *Mathematics of Operations Research*, 4:233–235, 1979.
7. R. Dechter. Constraint networks. In Stuart C. Shapiro, editor, *Encyclopedia of Artificial Intelligence*, pages 276–285. Wiley, 1992. Volume 1, second edition.
8. D. S. Johnson. Approximation algorithms for combinatorial problems. *Journal of Computer and System Sciences*, 9:256–278, 1974.
9. R. M. Karp. Reducibility among combinatorial problems. In R. E. Miller and J. W. Thatcher, editors, *Complexity of computer communications*, pages 85–103. Plenum Press, New York, 1972.
10. L. Lovasz. On the ratio of optimal integral and fractional covers. *Discrete Mathematics*, 13:383–390, 1975.
11. S. Nagarajan, S. Goodwin, and A. Sattar. A constraint directed model for partial constraint satisfaction problems. In *Proceedings of AI'2000, the 13th Canadian Conference on Artificial Intelligence*, volume 1822, pages 26–39, 2000.
12. S. Nagarajan, S. Goodwin, A. Sattar, and J. Thornton. On dual encodings for non-binary constraint satisfaction problems. In *To Appear in Principles and Practice of Constraint Programming, CP-2000*. Springer Verlag, 2000.
13. W. Pang and S. Goodwin. Constraint directed backtracking. In A. Sattar, editor, *Advanced Topics in AI*, pages 47–56. Springer Verlag, 1997. Volume 1342, LNAI.
14. Mohr R. and Masini G. Good old discrete relaxation. In *Proceedings ECAI'88*, pages 651–656, 1988.
15. Kostas Stergiou and Toby Walsh. Encodings of non-binary constraint satisfaction problems. In *Proceedings of the 16th National Conference on Artificial Intelligence*, pages 163–168, 1999.

Consistency in General CSPs

Wanlin Pang[1] and Scott D. Goodwin[2]

[1] Institute for Information Technology, National Research Council of Canada,
Ottawa, Ontario, Canada K1A 0R6
[2] Department of Computer Science, University of Regina,
Regina, Saskatchewan, Canada S4S 0A2

Abstract. In this paper, we introduce a new form of consistency in general constraint satisfaction problems (CSPs), called ω-pairwise-consistency which can be applied to both binary and non-binary constraints. Enforcing ω-pairwise-consistency in a CSP simplifies the problem representation by removing those tuples from the given constraints that will not participate in any solution. Typical CSP solving algorithms can then solve the simplified CSP more efficiently. We show that ω-pairwise-consistency is stronger than some other forms of consistency reported in the literature. We also present an algorithm for achieving ω-pairwise-consistency.

1 Introduction

Solving a constraint satisfaction problem usually involves two steps: simplifying the problem representation by removing local inconsistencies and finding solutions by search. A local inconsistency is a consistent partial instantiation to a variable set that cannot be consistently extended to a proper superset of that variable set and, therefore, will not participate in any solution. Local inconsistencies are a major cause of *thrashing* in backtracking search. To improve efficiency of solving CSPs, several notions of consistency have been introduced and many consistency algorithms have been proposed and developed to remove local inconsistencies.

Much work has been done on consistency in binary CSPs [14, 10, 6, 13, 8, 3, 18, 2]. Several researchers have generalized consistency to apply to general CSPs [9, 5] but some functionality is lost in the generalization. Furthermore, enforcing these general consistencies is either too expensive (even intractable) or it does not remove local inconsistencies as expected.

In this paper, we define a new form of consistency, called *ω-pairwise-consistency* which can be applied to both binary and non-binary constraints. Unlike enforcing arc-consistency, which removes values from variable domains, enforcing ω-pairwise-consistency in a general CSP tightens original constraints by removing those tuples from constraints that cannot be part of any solution. This effectively reduces thrashing and is useful in solving both binary and non-binary CSPs. Rather than replace arc consistency, ω-pairwise-consistency complements it. Enforcing ω-pairwise-consistency in a binary CSP which is arc-consistent will (in general) result in a simplified CSP which is no longer arc-consistent.

Re-enforcing arc-consistency after enforcing ω-pairwise-consistency can result in the removal of additional values from the variable domains. An algorithm for enforcing ω-pairwise-consistency is presented later in this paper.

Another virtue of ω-pairwise-consistency is its power in characterizing tractable CSPs. By associating the structural properties of underlying constraint hypergraph with the level of ω-pairwise-consistency, we can identify a class of tractable CSPs that properly contains the class of tractable CSPs identified using other forms of consistency. Due to space limitation, the issue of characterizing tractable CSPs will not be discussed here but can be found in [15].

The paper is organized as follows. We first review related notions of consistency. We then define ω-pairwise-consistency and discuss its usefulness. We also present an algorithm for achieving ω-pairwise-consistency. Lastly, we generalize the notion of ω-pairwise-consistency to high level ω-consistencies and compare them with other forms of local consistency.

2 Preliminaries

2.1 Constraint Satisfaction Problems

A *constraint satisfaction problem (CSP)* is a structure (X, D, V, S). Here, $X = \{X_1, X_2, \ldots, X_n\}$ is a set of variables that may take on values from a set of domains $D = \{D_1, D_2, \ldots, D_n\}$, and $V = \{V_1, V_2, \ldots, V_m\}$ is a family of ordered subsets of X called *constraint* or *relation schemes*. Each $V_i = \{X_{i_1}, X_{i_2}, \ldots, X_{i_{r_i}}\}$ is associated with a set of tuples $S_i \subseteq D_{i_1} \times D_{i_2} \times \ldots \times D_{i_{r_i}}$ called *constraint* or *relation instance*, and $S = \{S_1, S_2, \ldots, S_m\}$ is a family of such constraint instances. Together, an ordered pair (V_i, S_i) is a *constraint* or *relation* which permits the variables in V_i to take only value combinations in S_i.

Let (X, D, V, S) be a CSP, $V_K = \{X_{k_1}, X_{k_2}, \ldots, X_{k_l}\}$ a subset of X. A tuple $(x_{k_1}, x_{k_2}, \ldots, x_{k_l})$ in $D_{k_1} \times D_{k_2} \times \ldots \times D_{k_l}$ is called an *instantiation* of variables in V_K. An instantiation is said to be *consistent* if it satisfies all constraints restricted in V_K. A consistent instantiation of all variables in X is a *solution to the CSP* (X, D, V, S). The task of solving a CSP is to find one or all solutions. The set of all solution is denoted by $\rho(X)$.

A *binary CSP* is a CSP with unary and binary constraints only, that is, every constraint scheme contains at most two variables. A CSP with constraints not limited to unary and binary is referred to as a *general CSP*.

Since constraints are defined as relations, we use some relational operators, specifically, *join* and *projection* [12]. Let $C_i = (V_i, S_i)$ and $C_j = (V_j, S_j)$ be two constraints, $t_i \in S_i$ and $t_j \in S_j$ two tuples, and V_h a subset of V_i. The *join* of C_i and C_j is a constraint denoted by $C_i \bowtie C_j$. The *projection* of $C_i = (V_i, S_i)$ on $V_h \subseteq V_i$ is a constraint denoted by $\Pi_{V_h}(C_i)$. The *projection* of t_i on V_h, denoted by $t_i[V_h]$, is a tuple consisting of only the components of t_i that correspond to variables in V_h. t_i and t_j are *compatible* if $t_i[V_i \cap V_j] = t_j[V_i \cap V_j]$. If t_i and t_j are compatible, the *join of t_i and t_j*, denoted by $t_i \bowtie t_j$, is a tuple such that $(t_i \bowtie t_j)[V_i] = t_i$ and $(t_i \bowtie t_j)[V_j] = t_j$.

2.2 Related Work

Mackworth [10] introduces *node, arc*, and *path consistency* to control pathological thrashing behavior of backtracking CSP solvers. The most useful of these is arc-consistency. When backtracking is used to solve a binary CSP (X, D, V, S), suppose the variables are instantiated in the order $X_1, X_2, \ldots, X_n$, and for $X_i = x$ and X_j where $j > i$, the pair (x, x') is not allowed by the constraints on (X_i, X_j) for any value x'. Backtracking will try all values of X_j, fail and try all values of X_{j-1} (and for each of these try all values of X_j) and so on until it tries all combinations of values for $X_{i+1}, X_{j+2}, \ldots, X_j$, before finally discovering that x is not a possible value for X_i. By enforcing arc-consistency, the value x will be deleted from the domain of variable X_i, and therefore, a substantial subspace will be eliminated from the backtracking search space. Node, arc, and path consistency are formally defined as follows:

Definition 1. *(Mackworth [10])* A node X_i is *node-consistent* if for any value $x \in D_i$, x is permitted by the unary constraint posed on X_i. An arc (X_i, X_j) is *arc-consistent* if for any value $x_i \in D_i$, there is a value $x_j \in D_j$ such that (x_i, x_j) is permitted by the binary constraint posed on (X_i, X_j). A path $(X_{k_1}, X_{k_2}, \ldots, X_{k_l})$ is *path-consistent* if for any value $x_{k_1} \in D_{k_1}$ and $x_{k_l} \in D_{k_l}$ such that (x_{k_1}, x_{k_l}) is permitted by the binary constraint posed on (X_{k_1}, X_{k_l}), there is a sequence of values $x_{k_2} \in D_{k_2}, \ldots, x_{k_{l-1}} \in D_{k_{l-1}}$, such that $(x_{k_1}, x_{k_2}), (x_{k_2}, x_{k_3}), \ldots, (x_{k_{l-1}}, x_{k_l})$ are permitted by binary constraints posed on $(X_{k_1}, X_{k_2}), (X_{k_2}, X_{k_3}), \ldots, (X_{k_{l-1}}, X_{k_l})$, respectively. A CSP is said to be node, arc or path consistent if every node, arc or path of its graph is consistent.

Freuder [6] generalizes node, arc, and path consistency into *k-consistency*, which is useful for identifying subclasses of tractable CSPs.

Definition 2. *(Freuder [6])* A binary CSP is *k-consistent* if for any set of $k-1$ variables, $X_{p_1}, X_{p_2}, \ldots, X_{p_{k-1}}$, any consistent instantiation of these variables, $x_{p_1}, x_{p_2}, \ldots, x_{p_{k-1}}$, and any choice of a k-th variable X_{p_k}, there exists an value x_{p_k} for X_{p_k} such that the combined k-tuple $x_{p_1}, x_{p_2}, \ldots, x_{p_{k-1}}, x_{p_k}$ is a consistent instantiation of these k variables. A binary CSP is *strongly k-consistent* if it is l-consistent for $1 \leq l \leq k$.

Node, arc, and path consistency can be achieved in polynomial time. Many competitive algorithms have been proposed to achieve arc and path consistency. Achieving k-consistency is exponential in k.

Arc, path, and k-consistency are defined on binary constraints. Dechter and van Beek [5] extend arc, path, and k-consistency to general constraints, which are called *relational arc, path*, and *k-consistency*. Relational arc, path, and k-consistency are identical to the ordinary arc, path, and k-consistency when they are applied to binary constraints.

Definition 3. *(Dechter and van Beek [5])* Let (X, D, V, S) be a CSP. A constraint (V_i, S_i) is *relational arc-consistent relative to variable X_l* if any consistent instantiation of the variables in $V_i - \{X_l\}$ has an extension to X_l that satisfies (V_i, S_i); that is, if $\rho(V_i - \{X_l\}) \subseteq \Pi_{V_i - \{X_l\}} S_i$. A constraint (V_i, S_i) is *relational arc-consistent* if it is relational arc-consistent relative to each variable in V_i. A CSP is relational arc-consistent if every constraint is arc-consistent.

Definition 4. *(Dechter and van Beek [5])* Let (X, D, V, S) be a CSP. A pair of constraints (V_i, S_i) and (V_j, S_j) is *relational path-consistent relative to variable* X_l if any consistent instantiation of the variables in $(V_i \cup V_j) - \{X_l\}$ has an extension to X_l that satisfies both constraints; that is, if $\rho((V_i \cup V_j) - \{X_l\}) \subseteq \Pi_{(V_i \cup V_j) - \{X_l\}}(S_i \bowtie S_j)$. A pair of constraints (V_i, S_i) and (V_j, S_j) is *relational path-consistent* if it is relational path-consistent relative to each variable in $V_i \cap V_j$. A CSP is relational path-consistent if every pair of constraints is relational path-consistent.

Definition 5. *(Dechter and van Beek [5])* Let (X, D, V, S) be a CSP. A set of constraints $(V_1, S_1), \ldots, (V_{k-1}, S_{k-1})$ is *relational k-consistent relative to variable* X_l if any consistent instantiation of the variables in $\cup_{i=1}^{k-1} V_i - \{X_l\}$ has an extension to X_l that satisfies this set of constraints; that is, $\rho(\cup_{i=1}^{k-1} V_i - \{X_l\}) \subseteq \Pi_{\cup_{i=1}^{k-1} V_i - \{X_l\}}(\bowtie_{i=1}^{k-1} S_i)$. A set of constraints $(V_1, S_1), \ldots, (V_{k-1}, S_{k-1})$ is *relational k-consistent* if it is relational k-consistent relative to each variable in $\cap_{i=1}^{k-1} V_i$. A CSP is relational k-consistent if every set of $(k-1)$ constraint is relational k-consistent.

Algorithms to achieve relational consistencies are given in [5]. Unfortunately, enforcing relational path-consistency is likely to be NP-complete in general [5].

Another well-known consistency in general CSPs was originally introduced in databases [1], called *pairwise consistency*. In CSP terms, pairwise consistency requires that a pair of constraints be compatible. More formally,

Definition 6. *(Beeri et al. [1])* A CSP (X, D, V, S) is *pairwise consistent* if for any $V_i, V_j \in V$, $\Pi_{V_i}(S_i \bowtie S_j) = S_i$ and $\Pi_{V_j}(S_i \bowtie S_j) = S_j$.

Gyssens [7] generalizes pairwise consistency into *k-wise consistency* (also called *inter-k-consistency*). Pairwise consistency is then identical to 2-wise consistency.

Definition 7. *(Gyssens [7])* A CSP (X, D, V, S) is *k-wise consistent* if for any $V_{p_1}, V_{p_2}, \ldots, V_{p_{k-1}}, V_{p_k} \in V$, $\Pi_{V_{p_k}}(\bowtie_{i=1}^{k} S_{p_i}) = S_{p_k}$.

In words, a set of k constraints is k-wise consistent if any tuple in any constraint has a consistent extension to all the variables involved in these k constraints. A CSP is k-wise consistent if every set of k constraints is k-wise consistent. Obviously, if a CSP is $|V|$-wise consistent then it is globally consistent.

Jegou introduces another notion of consistency called *hyper-k-consistency* [9]. Hyper-k-consistency is a generalization of pairwise consistency in a way similar to the way in which k-consistency is a generalization of arc consistency in binary CSPs. Pairwise consistency is identical to hyper-2-consistency.

Definition 8. *(Jegou [9])* A CSP (X, D, V, S) is *hyper-k-consistent* if for any $V_{p_1}, V_{p_2}, \ldots, V_{p_{k-1}}, V_{p_k} \in V$, $\Pi_{(\cup_{i=1}^{k-1} V_{p_i}) \cap V_{p_k}}(\bowtie_{i=1}^{k-1} S_{p_i}) \subseteq \Pi_{(\cup_{i=1}^{k-1} V_{p_i}) \cap V_{p_k}}(S_{p_k})$. A CSP is *strongly hyper-k-consistent* if it is hyper-l-consistent for all $1 \leq l \leq k$.

Pairwise consistency can be achieved in polynomial time. We are not aware of any algorithms for achieving k-wise consistency or hyper-k-consistency.

3 ω-Consistency

Consistency for binary CSPs has been extensively studied. Recently, more and more attention has been paid to general constraints because of real-world applications. To solve general CSPs directly, a constraint directed backtracking algorithm (CDBT) has been proposed in [17]. CDBT searches for instantiations of variables in a variable set from the given constraint posed on that variable set. Just as with standard backtracking applied to binary CSPs, CDBT applied to general CSPs suffers from the thrashing problem. Unfortunately, unlike standard backtracking applied to binary CSPs, the trashing behaviour of CDBT applied to general CSPs is not reduced by arc, path, or k-consistency. A new form of consistency, ω-*pairwise-consistency*, is needed.

3.1 ω-Pairwise-Consistency

If a binary CSP is arc-consistent then there is always a consistent instantiation of any pair of variables. However, pairwise consistency of a general CSP does not guarantee a consistent instantiation of the variables involved in a pair of the constraints. This is so because a consistent instantiation of the variables involved in a pair of constraints must also satisfy any other constraints posed on the variables involved. Pairwise consistency does not ensure that the instantiation of the variables involved satisfies the other constraints. For example, a CSP as shown in Figure 1 is pairwise consistent, but there is no consistent instantiation of the variables involved in any pair of constraints. This insight leads to the definition of ω-pairwise-consistency.

ω-pairwise-consistency requires that any tuple in any constraint can be extended to a consistent instantiation of the variables involved in another constraint. If a tuple in a constraint does not satisfy this condition then it can be safely removed without losing any solutions. Enforcing ω-pairwise-consistency in a CSP ensures that there is always a consistent instantiation of the variables involved in any pair of constraints.

Definition 9. Given a CSP (X, D, V, S). An ordered pair (V_i, V_j) is said to be ω-*pairwise-consistent* if for any $t_i \in S_i$ there is $t_j \in S_j$ such that $t_i[V_i \cup V_j] = t_j[V_i \cup V_j]$ and the joint tuple $t_i \bowtie t_j$ satisfies every constraint restricted to $V_i \cup V_j$; that is, for any constraint (V_h, S_h) such that $V_h \subset V_i \cup V_j$, $(t_i \bowtie t_j)[V_h] \in S_h$. A pair V_i and V_j is ω-*pairwise-consistent* if both ordered pairs (V_i, V_j) and (V_j, V_i) are ω-pairwise-consistent. The CSP is ω-*pairwise-consistent* if every pair V_i and V_j in W is ω-pairwise-consistent.

For example, given a CSP (X, D, V, S) as shown in Figure 1, where $X = \{X_1, X_2, X_3, X_4\}$, $D_1 = D_2 = D_3 = D_4 = \{a, b, c, d\}$, $V = \{V_{12}, V_{13}, V_{14}, V_{23}, V_{24}, V_{34}\}$, and $S = \{S_{12}, S_{13}, S_{14}, S_{23}, S_{24}, S_{34}\}$. For each i and j, $V_{ij} = \{X_i, X_j\}$, and $S_{ij} = \{(a, b), (a, c), (b, a), (b, c), (c, a), (c, b), (d, d)\}$. Obviously, the CSP has only one solution (d, d, d, d).

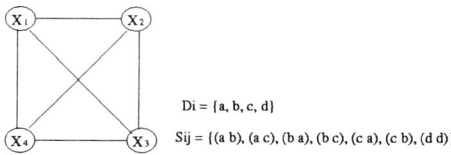

Fig. 1. An example of CSP

This CSP is arc-consistent, path-consistent, and pairwise-consistent. However, the CSP is not ω-pairwise-consistent, because, for example, the pair of constraints on V_{12} and V_{34} is not ω-pairwise-consistent. For a value pair $t = (a, b)$ in S_{12}, there is no value pair t' in S_{34} such that the joined tuple $t \bowtie t'$ satisfies the other constraints. For instance, if $t' = (a, b)$, then $t \bowtie t' = (a, b, a, b)$ does not satisfy constraint (V_{13}, S_{13}); that is, $(t \bowtie t')[V_{13}] = (a, a) \notin S_{13}$. If $t' = (b, a)$, then $t \bowtie t' = (a, b, b, a)$ does not satisfy constraints (V_{23}, S_{23}). Other value pairs can be similarly verified.

When a backtracking algorithm is used to solve this CSP, it will try values $\{a, b, c\}$ for all the variables and fail, again and again, before finally discovering that these values are not possible values for all the variables. If we enforce ω-pairwise-consistency first, all of these pairs (except (d, d)) will be removed from the given constraints. The resulting CSP is no longer arc-consistent. If we now enforce arc-consistency the values $\{a, b, c\}$ will be removed from each variable domain, which makes the problem easier to solve.

When we use CDBT to solve this CSP, we search instantiations of variables from the given constraints. The CDBT algorithm will thrash because it will try all those value pairs that cannot be extended to a solution. By enforcing ω-pairwise-consistency, all these value pairs other than (d, d) will be removed from the given constraints and, therefore, the thrashing behavior will be eliminated.

3.2 Achieving ω-Pairwise-Consistency

Let $\mathbb{P} = (X, D, V, S)$ be a CSP, (V_i, S_i) and (V_j, S_j) two constraints. For a tuple $t_i \in S_i$, if there is no tuple $t_j \in S_j$ such that $t_i[V_i \cap V_j] = t_j[V_i \cap V_j]$ and $t_i \bowtie t_j$ satisfies all the constraints restricted to $V_i \cup V_j$, then t_i can be deleted from S_i without losing any solution. When that has been done for each $t_i \in S_i$ then the ordered pair (V_i, V_j) (but not necessarily (V_j, V_i)) is ω-pairwise-consistent. Procedure *revise* deletes all those tuples in S_i that are not ω-pairwise-consistent with V_j. Function *test* returns *true* if tuple $t_i \bowtie t_j$ satisfies all the constraints involved and *false* otherwise.

$revise(V_i, V_j, I\!P)$

1. **begin**
2.   changed $\leftarrow$ false;
3.   **for** each $t_i \in S_i$ **do**
4.   **if** $\not\exists t_j \in S_j$ s.t. $(t_i[V_i \cap V_j] = t_j[V_i \cap V_j]$
            $\wedge\ test(t_i \bowtie t_j, V_i, V_j, I\!P))$
5.   **then** delete t_i from S_i; changed $\leftarrow$ true;
6.   **return** changed;
7. **end**

$test(tup_I, V_i, V_j, I\!P)$

1. **begin**
2.   **for** each $C_h = (V_h, S_h)$ s.t. $V_h \subset V_i \cup V_j$ **do**
3.   **if** $tup_I[V_h] \notin S_h$ **then return** *false*;
4.   **return** *true*;
5. **end**

An ordered pair (V_i, V_j) must be ω-pairwise-consistent after applying *revise* to it, but it might not remain consistent when *revise* is applied to other ordered pairs, for example, (V_j, V_k), because some tuples in S_j may subsequently be deleted. To achieve the ω-pairwise-consistency, algorithm *revise* should be applied to every ordered pair of constraints repeatedly until no tuples can be further deleted. An algorithm for achieving ω-pairwise-consistency is given below. Notice that this algorithm is similar to algorithm AC-3 in [10] which enforces arc-consistency in binary CSPs.

$\omega\text{-}pairwise\text{-}consistency(I\!P)$

1. **begin**
2. $F_d \leftarrow \{(V_i, V_j), (V_j, V_i) | V_i \in C, V_j \in V, i \neq j\}$;
3. $A \leftarrow F_d$;
4.   **while** $A \neq \emptyset$ **do**
5.   select and delete a pair (V_i, V_j) from A;
6.   **if** $revise(V_i, V_j, I\!P)$
7.   **then** $A \leftarrow A \cup \{(V_k, V_i) \in F_d | k \neq i, j\}$;
8.   **end while**
9. **end**

Let $I\!P = (X, D, V, S)$ be a CSP, n the numbers of variables, m the number of constraints, a the size of the largest domain, and r the arity of the CSP. Function $revise(V_i, V_j, I\!P)$ requires at most a^{2r} calls to $test(t_i \bowtie t_j, V_i, V_j, I\!P)$, which performs at most m consistency checks. It has been reported in [11] that algorithm

AC-3 makes at most $2m + a(2m - n) \approx 2am$ calls to *revise*. Similarly, algorithm ω-*pairwise-consistency*($I\!P$) requires at most $2|F|a^r$ calls to *revise*, where $|F| \leq m(m-1)/2$. The complexity of algorithm ω-*pairwise-consistency* can be written as $O(m^3 a^{3r})$.

The ω-pairwise-consistency algorithm is not optimal, and we intend to develop an improved version in the future. It is worth noting that if we enforce ω-pairwise-consistency prior to solving a CSP using solvers such as the search algorithm CDBT [17] or the synthesis algorithm CDGT [16], we only need to tighten the constraints in a selected constraint subset. The number of constraints in the selected constraint subset is usually much less than m and it is at most n. In this case, the complexity of enforcing ω-pairwise-consistency is $O(mn^2 a^{3r})$.

3.3 High Level ω-Consistency

In this subsection, we will generalize ω-pairwise-consistency into two different high level ω-consistencies which we call ω-*k-wise-consistency* and ω-*k-consistency* respectively. In the next section, we will compare them with other forms of consistency.

Definition 10. A CSP is ω-*k-wise-consistent* if for any $V_{p_1}, V_{p_2}, \ldots, V_{p_{k-1}}, V_{p_k} \in V$ and for any $V_h \subseteq \cup_{i=1}^{k} V_{p_i}$, $\Pi_{V_{p_k}}((\bowtie_{i=1}^{k} S_{p_i}) \bowtie S_h) = S_{p_k}$.

Definition 11. A CSP is ω-*k-consistent* if for any $V_{p_1}, V_{p_2}, \ldots, V_{p_{k-1}}, V_{p_k} \in V$, for any $V_l \subseteq \cup_{i=1}^{k-1} V_{p_i}$, and for any $V_h \subseteq V_{p_i} \cup V_{p_k}$ such that $i \neq k$, $\Pi_A((\bowtie_{i=1}^{k-1} S_{p_i}) \bowtie S_l) \subseteq \Pi_A(S_{p_k} \bowtie S_h)$, where $A = (\cup_{i=1}^{k-1} V_{p_i}) \cap (V_{p_k} \cup V_h)$. A CSP is *strongly ω-k-consistent* if it is ω-i-consistent for all $1 \leq i \leq k$.

Notice that ω-2-wise-consistency is identical to ω-2-consistency since they both are ω-pairwise-consistency. However, ω-k-wise-consistency does not equal ω-k-consistency when $k > 2$.

As with enforcing high level consistency in binary CSPs, enforcing high level ω-consistency in general CSPs entails global consistency under certain conditions.

4 Comparison

Relational k-consistency is identical to k-consistency when dealing with binary constraints. However, pairwise-consistency, ω-pairwise-consistency, and their generalizations are not identical to arc or k-consistency when they are applied to binary constraints. In other words, an (ω-)pairwise-consistent binary CSP may not be arc-consistent, and vice verse. A relationship between (ω-)pairwise-consistency and arc-consistency can be established through the underlying constraint graph; that is, if we convert a general CSP to a binary CSP according to the associated dual-graph [4], the original CSP is (ω-)pairwise-consistent if and only if the binary CSP obtained is arc-consistent. The original CSP is hyper-k-consistent (or ω-k-consistent) if and only if the binary CSP is k-consistent.

The diagram in Figure 2 illustrates the context position of different consistencies we have discussed so far. A solid arrow pointing from X to Y indicates that Y is a generalization of X. A dash line connecting X and Y indicates that X and Y are related through a dual-graph conversion.

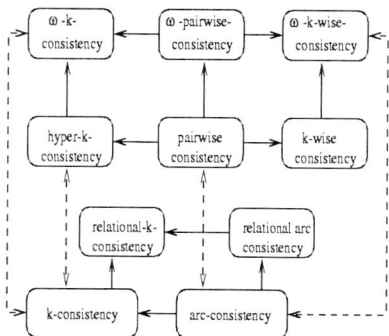

Fig. 2. Context position of different consistencies

The advantage of ω-consistency over other forms of consistency in characterizing tractable CSPs will not be discussed here. In the following, we give a detailed comparison in terms of removing local inconsistencies.

4.1 Arc-Consistency vs. ω-Pairwise-Consistency

Unlike relational arc consistency, ω-pairwiseconsis-tency is not an extension of arc-consistency, and therefore it is not identical to arc-consistency if it is applied to a binary CSP. A binary CSP that is arc-consistent might not be ω-pairwise-consistent since enforcing arc-consistency does not remove any pairs from given constraints. Similarly, a binary CSP that is ω-pairwise-consistent might not be arc-consistent since enforcing ω-pairwise-consistency does not remove any values from the given variable domains. For example, the CSP in Figure 1 is arc-consistent, but it is not ω-pairwise-consistent; and the CSP, where every $S_{ij} = \{(d,d)\}$, is ω-pairwise-consistent but it is not arc-consistent.

As discussed previously, a binary CSP which is arc-consistent might not remain arc-consistent after enforcing ω-pairwise-consistency. Subsequently, enforcing arc-consistency again may further remove those values from the variable domains that will not participate in any solution. In the example shown in Figure 1, enforcing ω-pairwise-consistency removes all value pairs except (d,d) from every constraint. Enforcing arc-consistency afterwards removes all values except d from every variable domain.

More interestingly, a binary CSP which is path-consistent might not be ω-pairwise-consistent since ω-pairwise-consistency might involve 4 variables, and a binary CSP which is ω-pairwise-consistent might not be path-consistent since enforcing path-consistency may add new constraints. For example, the CSP in Figure 1 is path-consistent but not ω-pairwise-consistent.

4.2 Pairwise-Consistency vs. ω-Pairwise-Consistency

It is not difficult to see that ω-pairwise-consistency is stronger than pairwise-consistency; that is, if a CSP is ω-pairwise-consistent then it is also pairwise-consistent; whereas the converse does not necessarily hold. Consequently, enforcing ω-pairwise-consistency in a CSP can (in general) eliminate many tuples that are not eliminated by enforcing pairwise-consistency, and therefore the simplified CSP can be solved more efficiently. For example, the CSP in Figure 1 is pairwise-consistent, but it is not ω-pairwise-consistent. If we use a search algorithm such as CDBT to solve this problem, and if we choose constraints V_{12} and V_{34} in the search process, the size of the search space is $7 + 7 \times 7$. By enforcing ω-pairwise-consistency, the search space is reduced to only 2 nodes.

ω-pairwise-consistency can also be considered to be an extension of pairwise-consistency. For a class of CSPs (X, D, V, S), where there are no V_i, V_j and V_k in V such that $V_k \subset V_i \cup V_j$, ω-pairwise-consistency and pairwise consistency are identical when they are applied to this class of CSPs. Similarly, ω-k-wise-consistency and ω-k-consistency are extensions of k-wise-consistency and hyper-k-consistency. As pointed out in [9], k-wise consistency is different from hyper-k-consistency when $k > 2$. Therefore, ω-k-wise-consistency does not equal ω-k-consistency when $k > 2$.

4.3 Relational Consistency vs. ω-Consistency

There is no direct link between relational consistency and any level of ω-consistency. A relational arc (or path) consistent CSP might not be ω-consistent, and vice verse. Let (X, D, V, S) be a CSP. A constraint (V_i, S_i) is *relational arc-consistent relative to variable* X_l if $\rho(V_i - \{X_l\}) \subseteq \Pi_{V_i - \{X_l\}} S_i$. If the constraint (V_i, S_i) is not relational arc consistent, by enforcing relational arc consistency, a new constraint (V_i', S_i') will be added, where $V_i' = V_i - \{X_l\}$ and $S_i' = \Pi_{V_i - \{X_l\}}(S_i)$. Adding new constraints has not effect on whether the CSP is ω-pairwise-consistent; that is, if the (V_i, S_i) contains a tuple that cannot be extended to a solution, it cannot be removed by enforcing relational consistency. Similarly, enforcing ω-pairwise-consistency has no effect on whether the CSP is relational consistent. Notice that by adding new constraints, the CSP becomes more explicit but not necessarily simpler.

5 Conclusion

Consistency in binary CSPs has been studied extensively, not only as a reduction technique to simplify a CSP so that it is easier to solve, but also as a critical property to characterize tractability of a problem. We presented a new definition of consistency, called ω-pairwise-consistency, which plays an important role in general CSPs similar to arc-consistency in binary CSPs. We generalized ω-pairwise-consistency to high level ω-consistency, which is stronger than some related forms of consistency, and therefore can be used to simplify CSP solving by enforcing a greater degree of consistency. We also provided a basic algorithm for achieving ω-pairwise-consistency, which can be used to simplify a given CSP prior to the solving process or to maintain consistency during the search process.

References

1. C. Beeri, R. Fagin, D. Maier, and M. Yannakakis. On the desirability of acyclic database schemes. *J. ACM*, 30(3):497–513, 1983.
2. C. Bessiere and M. Cordier. Arc-consistency and arc-consistency again. In *Proceedings of AAAI-93*, pages 108–113, 1993.
3. M. Cooper. An optimal k-consistency algorithm. *Artificial Intelligence*, 41:89–95, 1989.
4. R. Dechter and J. Pearl. Tree clustering for constraint networks. *Artificial Intelligence*, 38:353–366, 1989.
5. R. Dechter and P. van Beek. Local and global relational consistency. In *Proceedings of the 1st International Conference on Principles and Practices of Constraint Programming*, pages 240–257, Cassis, France, September 1995.
6. E. Freuder. Synthesizing constraint expressions. *Communications of the ACM*, 21(11):958–966, 1978.
7. M. Gyssens. On the complexity of join dependencies. *ACM Transactions on Database Systems*, 11(1):81–108, 1986.
8. C. Han and C. Lee. Comments on Mohr and Henderson's path consistency algorithm. *Artificial Intelligence*, 36:125–130, 1988.
9. P. Jegou. On the consistency of general constraint satisfaction problems. In *Proceedings of AAAI-93*, pages 114–119, 1993.
10. A. Mackworth. Consistency in networks of relations. *Artificial Intelligence*, 8(1):99–118, 1977.
11. A. Mackworth and E. Freuder. The complexity of some polynomial network consistency algorithms for constraint satisfaction problems. *Artificial Intelligence*, 25(1):65–74, 1985.
12. D. Maier. *The Theory of Relational Databases*. Computer Science Press, 1983.
13. R. Mohr and T. Henderson. Arc and path consistency revisited. *Artificial Intelligence*, 28:225–233, 1986.
14. U. Montanari. Networks of constraints: Fundamental properties and applications to picture processing. *Information Science*, 2:95–123, 1974.
15. W. Pang. *Constraint Structure in Constraint Satisfaction Problems*. PhD thesis, University of Regina, Canada, 1998.
16. W. Pang and S. D. Goodwin. A new synthesis algorithm for solving CSPs. In *Proceedings of the 2nd International Workshop on Constraint-Based Reasoning*, pages 1–10, Key West, FL, May 1996.
17. W. Pang and S. D. Goodwin. Constraint-directed backtracking. In *The 10th Australian Joint Conference on AI*, pages 47–56, Perth, Western Australia, December 1997.
18. P. Van Hentenryck, Y. Deville, and C. Teng. A generic arc-consistency algorithm and its specialization. *Artificial Intelligence*, 57:291–321, 1992.

Need for Optimisation Techniques to Select Neural Network Algorithms for Process Modelling of Reduction Cell

V. Karri[1] and F. Frost[2]

[1] School of Science and Engineering, University of Tasmania, GPO Box 252-65, Hobart, Tasmania, 7001, Australia.
Vishy.Karri@utas.edu.au

[2] Comalco Aluminium Limited, PO Box 290, George Town, Tasmania, 7253, Australia.
Fred.Frost@comalco.riotinto.com.au

Abstract. While there exists a broad range of neural networks for a particular task, different neural network architectures are selected depending upon the nature of application in industry. The range of applications covers anything from performance estimation and pattern recognition to process modelling and control. The network selection can be carried out based on economic considerations, such as cost associated with neural network computation time and obtaining data for required model variables. While each of the selected models can be a possible solution, depending upon the performance criteria, they all can be ranked from most suitable to least suitable for a particular application. In this paper, appraisal of neural networks for three industrial applications, involving process modelling of reduction cells for aluminium production, is discussed. Regression analysis techniques and six neural network models are assessed for their performance, using specific assessment criteria. It is shown that there is no single model that is most appropriate for each of the assessment criteria considered in each instance, hence, the decision of which neural network model is most suitable for a specific application is complex, particularly as the assessment criteria are not fundamentally of equal significance. It is shown that optimisation techniques are necessary to select an appropriate model for an application.

1. Introduction

It is useful to give a brief description of each of the three industrial applications studied in this paper. In particular, the applications are electrolyte additive prediction, cell failure prediction and electrolyte temperature prediction. The objective of the electrolyte additive prediction application is to accurately model the aluminium smelting process such that it is possible to correctly specify the quantity of electrolyte additives to schedule to the reduction cell to maintain process stability. It is necessary to add particular chemicals to the reduction cell periodically to compensate for those that are consumed during aluminium production. However, for maximum process efficiency it is critical to add only the minimum amount of chemicals required.

The cell failure prediction application incorporates a neural network model to identify potential failure candidates. It is important to identify reduction cells that are at high risk of failing, prior to the failure incident occurring. This allows sufficient scheduling of maintenance for reduction cell removal and replacement and minimises the damage caused to the surrounding area of the reduction cell. There are particular indicators in the reduction cell that can be incorporated into a neural network model to allow an accurate diagnosis of cell condition to be made.

Electrolyte temperature prediction involves the use of a neural network to periodically predict the temperature of the electrolyte in the aluminium reduction cell. This is necessary to eliminate the problems associated with the existing manual thermocouple temperature measurement technique. Due to the dynamics of the aluminium melting process the electrolyte temperature is constantly changing and needs to be maintained within specific control limits. The purpose of predicting electrolyte temperature is to assess whether corrective actions are required to return or maintain the temperature within the predetermined control limits.

In the following work, the applied regression analysis and neural network models are sorted from most suitable to least suitable for each of the studied industrial applications, based on the assessment criteria of RMS error, number of input variables required and computation time, as discussed below.

1.1 RMS Error

In order to determine the success and sufficiency of supervised training for backpropagation networks it is necessary to have a quantitative measure of learning. As the supervised training algorithm involves the reduction of an error value then it follows that an error value be used to evaluate network training. Hence, the root-mean-squared, RMS, error is an adequate and commonly used error measure and is computed using the following formula [1-4]:

$$\text{RMS error} = \sqrt{\frac{\sum_p \sum_k (t_{kp} - a_{kp})^2}{n_p n_k}} \quad (1)$$

where, t_{kp} = target output for output neuron k after presentation of pattern p,
a_{kp} = the output value produced by output neuron k after presentation of pattern p,
n_p = number of training patterns, and
n_k = number of neurons in the output layer

RMS error is a useful measure of how close a network is getting its predictions to its target output values. The applied models are sorted based on the RMS error achieved using the optimum model architecture and algorithms and further, when all non-contributing input variables are removed from the model. The model achieving minimum RMS error is ranked as most suitable for the application, while the model with the highest associated RMS error is the least suitable.

1.2 Number of Input Variables Required

Preliminary investigations [5-10] have shown that the number of input variables required by the neural networks to develop a process model is different in each instance. Further, the percentage contribution of each input parameter towards estimation of the performance feature can be determined using appropriate techniques [11]. It is important to note that the cause and effect are fixed in any physical process. Further, there may be multiple causes for the same effect. If several process parameters are correlated with some particular performance feature, then there will be some process parameters that have more influence than others on that performance feature. Although the physics and chemistry of the process is well understood, the degree of influence of each of such possible process parameters on the performance need not be well known. Depending upon the nature of the developed neural network models, the range and extent of input parameter influence on the network decision will change. While this does not change the physics of the problem, it gives a better understanding of which model and corresponding inputs to select as mere mathematical tools that best represent the process. Further, it is economically beneficial to minimise the number of input parameters used in a neural network model. In particular, the complexity of the neural network model reduces with reducing number of inputs, yielding lower computation time for model processing. Further, the cost associated with measuring the input variables is lower if less parameters are required to predict the performance feature, as there are less variables to measure. Hence, as it is economically beneficial to use the minimum number of parameters required to specify the process behaviour, the applied models are sorted for each application based on the number of input parameters required by each model. Further, the models are sorted in order of descending suitability, from minimum number of inputs required to maximum number required.

1.3 Computation Time

The time required by each of the neural networks to converge to a solution is an important consideration. Hence, the neural networks are ranked in order of ascending computation time, with the most suitable model in each instance being that with the lowest associated computation time. While the studied neural networks are ranked according to the specified assessment criteria, it is interesting to consider the regression analysis modelling results as a part of this investigation, to allow a comparison with the applied neural network models.

2. Applied Models and Data Acquisition

The models studied for each industrial application and ranked based on the specified assessment criteria are those listed below, with appropriate references noted for each model:
- Multi-Variable Regression Analysis (MVRA) [12]
- Widrow-Hoff (WH) Neural Network [13,14]

- Backpropagation – 1 hidden layer - (BP1) Neural Network [13]
- Backpropagation – 2 hidden layers - (BP2) Neural Network [13]
- Radial Basis Function (RBF) Neural Network [15-19]
- Radial Basis Function –Kohonen - (RBFKOH) Neural Network [11,20-23]
- General Regression Neural Network (GRNN) [24-27]

The general algorithms and architectures of these models are well established procedures and hence, are not discussed in the scope of this paper. There are twelve process parameters selected as potential neural network inputs for the above neural network models for the three industrial applications. In particular, these parameters are cell stability, cell efficiency, anode displacement, current flow, potential change, sludge level, volume indicator, amperage, surface roughness, surface displacement, sludge density and cell identification. For the electrolyte additive, cell failure and electrolyte temperature prediction applications, the output variables are electrolyte additive quantity (primary and secondary), cell life remaining and electrolyte temperature, respectively. In the recent past a number of manufacturing related applications [32] of neural networks have resulted in significant advances both in conceptual and application areas.

Data acquisition from the smelter knowledge base with subsequent data formatting and pre-processing produced 1,565 data patterns in total for each industrial application. Data preparation formed a complex stage of network modelling, including the elimination of corrupt information from the acquired data, ensuring sufficient data for each model variable was included in the data patterns, covering the entire operating range for each parameter, and scaling each variable between the minimum and maximum limits of its operating range. The processed data was then divided into 1,365 training data patterns, with the remaining 200 patterns used as test data. The train and test data sets were carefully selected to ensure the network output variables were well represented in each data set, covering the entire range of values for each parameter.

3. Ranking of Models Based on Specified Criteria

For each of the studied industrial applications, the regression analysis model and the applied neural network models are ranked in descending order of suitability based on the specified assessment criteria. While a model selection methodology is not discussed here, this analysis is necessary to highlight the complexities associated with selecting a particular phenomenological model for a specific application, when economic benefit is the driving force for model selection. Moreover, the model ranking completed here, using the given assessment criteria, is critical for developing a qualitative understanding for neural network selection.

3.1 Model Ranking Based on Assessment Criteria One – RMS Error

The RMS error used for the model ranking in this instance is the minimum RMS error achieved by each model. This is the RMS error achieved using the optimum model architecture with all non-contributing inputs removed. The optimum architecture is established in each instance by observing RMS error with changing neural network architecture. While a single training and test data set are used in each instance, for each model the neural network architecture is varied over a broad range of hidden layer neuron's and value of learning rate and receptive field width where appropriate. The error associated with each architecture and adjustable parameter value is recorded and consequently, the optimum model architecture is identified by selecting the architecture that yields minimum error. The process of removing non-contributing parameters is carried out by established methods and numerical investigation [33]. Hence, the model achieving minimum RMS error is ranked as the most appropriate model for this particular assessment criterion, while the highest RMS error model is ranked as most unsuitable. Table 1 documents the ranking from lowest RMS error through to highest for each of the applied models.

Table 1. Ranking of Models Applied to Industrial Applications Based on Assessment Criteria One – RMS Error

Ranking	Electrolyte Additive		Cell Failure		Electrolyte Temperature	
	Model	Error	**Model**	Error	Model	Error
1st	GRNN	0.0671	BP1	0.0451	BP2	0.0573
2nd	RBFKOH	0.0715	BP2	0.0580	BP1	0.0625
3rd	BP2	0.0719	WH	0.0761	WH	0.0626
4th	RBF	0.0729	RBFKOH	0.1074	RBFKOH	0.0640
5th	BP1	0.0774	RBF	0.1279	RBF	0.0665
6th	WH	0.1121	GRNN	0.1598	GRNN	0.0702
7th	MVRA	0.1129	MVRA	0.3264	MVRA	0.0714

It can be seen that while the GRNN model achieved minimum RMS error for the electrolyte additive application, the BP1 network has shown the lowest error for cell failure prediction and BP2 for temperature prediction. Moreover, the MVRA model has shown the highest RMS error of the applied models in each instance. The results documented here highlight the importance of applying and studying a range of different neural networks for each specific application, not selecting a particular model based solely on its success with previous applications.

3.2 Model Ranking Based on Assessment Criteria Two – Number of Input Variables

The model ranking from lowest number of input variables required through to highest number of input variables is documented in Table 2 for each application. While some input variables are shown to have a low percentage contribution in some instances, these input parameters are nevertheless included as contributing network inputs in the following ranking for this assessment criterion. It is shown that a low percentage contribution for a particular input parameter corresponds to a low change in RMS error if that particular input is omitted from the model. However, this change, while only small, is considered significant in this instance as it does indeed decrease model accuracy. Moreover, the removal of many parameters with a low percentage contribution has a cumulative effect on RMS error, decreasing model accuracy substantially if many low percentage contribution parameters are omitted from the model.

Table 2. Ranking of Models Applied to Industrial Applications Based on Assessment Criteria Two – Number of Input Variables

Ranking	Electrolyte Additive		Cell Failure		Electrolyte Temperature	
	Model	Inputs	Model	Inputs	Model	Inputs
1st	GRNN	5	MVRA	6	BP1	5
2nd	MVRA	6	GRNN	7	RBF	6
3rd	WH	7	RBFKOH	7	RBFKOH	6
4th	RBFKOH	8	RBF	8	GRNN	8
5th	BP1	9	WH	9	WH	9
6th	RBF	10	BP2	11	MVRA	10
7th	BP2	12	BP1	12	BP2	12

Similar to the model ranking based on RMS error, it can be seen that the model ranking for this assessment criterion is significantly different for each of the studied industrial applications. While it is shown that the GRNN model required the lowest number of parameters for the electrolyte additive prediction application, it is shown that the MVRA model required the minimum number of input variables for the cell failure prediction application and the BP1 network for the electrolyte temperature prediction application.

3.3 Model Ranking Based on Assessment Criteria Three – Computation Time

The computation time used to rank the applied models in this instance is the minimum time required by each model to achieve the minimum RMS error documented in Table 1, using the optimum model architecture and algorithms, with all non-contributing input variables removed from the model. Hence, the computation time used is the minimum achievable by each of the applied models to obtain the noted minimum RMS error. The ranking of the applied models for each of the industrial applications is shown in Table 3 in order of increasing computation time.

Table 3. Ranking of Models Applied to Industrial Applications Based on Assessment Criteria Two – Computation Time

Ranking	Electrolyte Additive		Cell Failure		Electrolyte Temperature	
	Model	Time (s)	Model	Time (s)	Model	Time (s)
1st	MVRA	4.5	MVRA	5.0	MVRA	4.2
2nd	GRNN	24.6	GRNN	24.8	GRNN	34.9
3rd	WH	281.0	WH	271.3	WH	166.9
4th	BP1	1,010.3	RBF	1,793.3	BP1	637.2
5th	RBF	1,319.4	BP2	2,871.1	RBF	897.7
6th	RBFKOH	2,711.1	BP1	4,438.2	BP2	2,480.2
7th	BP2	3,089.0	RBFKOH	4,547.4	RBFKOH	3,117.8

The ranking of the applied models based on computation time is consistent with model complexity and number of iterations required by each of the models to develop a suitable process model. Hence, the MVRA model, which is shown to have low complexity and requires no computational training iterations subsequently has a low computation time. Similarly, the GRNN model, although of higher complexity than the MVRA model, also requires no computational training iterations and therefore has a low associated computation time. However, the higher complexity models, such as BP2, RBF and RBFKOH, requiring a relatively large number of computational training iterations, have shown high computation time and therefore are ranked after the MVRA, GRNN and WH models in terms of suitability for this particular assessment criterion.

4. Comparison of Models Based on Industry Application

While the model ranking is completed on an individual basis for each of the specified assessment criteria, it is now useful to tabulate these results for each of the studied industrial applications, as shown in Table 4. The objective of this is to highlight for each application that a different model ranking is achieved for each of the assessment criteria used.

It can be seen from the analysis completed that the ranking of the developed neural network models for each of the studied industrial applications is different in each instance. Further, for each application there is no single model that is ranked first for each assessment criteria. Hence, for each industrial application there is no particular model that is an obvious choice as most suitable. Moreover, the decision of which neural network model to select for a specific application is complex as the assessment criteria are not fundamentally of equal significance in each instance. Rather, the influence of each assessment criteria is highly dependent on the application considered. For instance, RMS error maybe of high significance for a particular application where high prediction accuracy is critical, but of low significance for an application where high prediction accuracy is not essential. Hence, a decision model is required to analyse the decision problem using systematic identification and evaluation of all the available alternatives. The decision of the optimum model for each application is then reached by selecting the alternative that provides maximum economic benefit. Hence, it becomes necessary to complete the decision of neural network selection using appropriate operations research techniques.

5. Conclusions

In this work it is highlighted that several networks can be used as performance predictive tools in the smelting industry. The estimation of electrolyte additive, cell failure and electrolyte temperature are three industrial applications highlighted in this work. It is shown that established neural network models such as backpropagation, Widrow-Hoff, radial basis function and general regression networks can all be applied to each of the industrial applications. Three assessment criteria were selected, namely RMS error, number of input variables required and computation time, to assess and rank the applied models. For each application, the ranking of the models for the assessment criteria was different, which complicates the selection process for an optimum model. This suggests that although each of the models can be used as a tool for a given industrial application, the optimum model needs to be selected using extensive operations research techniques. Work in progress will establish a reliable optimum model by appropriate operations research techniques.

Table 4. Ranking of Models for Industrial Applications Based on Specified Assessment Criteria

Model Ranking	Assessment Criteria One	Assessment Criteria Two	Assessment Criteria Three
Electrolyte Additive Prediction Application			
1st	GRNN	GRNN	MVRA
2nd	RBFKOH	MVRA	GRNN
3rd	BP2	WH	WH
4th	RBF	RBFKOH	BP1
5th	BP1	BP1	RBF
6th	WH	RBF	RBFKOH
7th	MVRA	BP2	BP2
Cell Failure Prediction Application			
1st	BP1	MVRA	MVRA
2nd	BP2	GRNN	GRNN
3rd	WH	RBFKOH	WH
4th	RBFKOH	RBF	RBF
5th	RBF	WH	BP2
6th	GRNN	BP2	BP1
7th	MVRA	BP1	RBFKOH
Temperature Prediction Application			
1st	BP2	BP1	MVRA
2nd	BP1	RBF	GRNN
3rd	WH	RBFKOH	WH
4th	RBFKOH	GRNN	BP1
5th	RBF	WH	RBF
6th	GRNN	MVRA	BP2
7th	MVRA	BP2	RBFKOH

References

1. Caudill, M. and Butler, C., "Naturally Intelligent Systems", Massachusetts Institute of Technology, 1990.
2. Caudill, M. and Butler, C., "Understanding Neural Networks - Computer Explorations", vol. 1, Massachusetts Institute of Technology, 1992.
3. Hertz, J., Krogh, A. and Palmer, R. G., "Introduction to the Theory of Neural Computing", Addison-Wesley Publishing Company, 1991.
4. Zurada, J. M., "Introduction to Artificial Neural Systems", West Publishing Company, 1992.
5. Karri, V. and Frost, F., "Optimum Backpropagation Network Conditions with Respect to Computation Time and Output Accuracy", Proc. International Conference on Computational Intelligence and Multimedia Applications (ICCIMA), Sep. 1999, New Delhi, India, pp. 50-54.
6. Karri, V., "RBF Neural Networks For Thrust and Torque Predictions in Drilling Operations", Proc. International Conference on Computational Intelligence and Multimedia Applications (ICCIMA), Sep. 1999, New Delhi, India, pp. 55-60.
7. Frost, F. and Karri, V., "Performance Comparison of BP and GRNN Models of the Neural Network Paradigm Using a Practical Industrial Application", Proc. 6th International Conference on Neural Information Processing (ICONIP), Nov. 1999, Perth., pp 1069-1075.
8. Karri, V. and Frost, F., "Effect of Altering the Gaussian Function Receptive Field Width in RBF Neural Networks on Aluminium Fluoride Prediction in Industrial Reduction Cells", Proc. 6th International Conference on Neural Information Processing (ICONIP), Nov. 1999, Perth., pp 101-106.
9. Frost, F. and Karri, V., "Intelligent Control of Aluminium Reduction Cells Using Backpropagation Neural Networks", Proc. International Conference on Advances in Intelligent Systems: Theory and Applications (AISTA), Feb. 2000, Canberra, Australia, pp. 350-356.
10. Karri, V. and Frost, F., "Combined Kohonen and RBF Networks to Predict Electrolyte Additives in Hall-Heroult Cell", Proc. International Conference on Advances in Intelligent Systems: Theory and Applications (AISTA), Feb. 2000, Canberra, Australia, pp. 19-24.
11. Sarle, W., "How to Measure Importance of Inputs", ftp://ftp.sas.com/pub/neural/FAQ.html, Apr. 24, 1999.
12. Moore, D. S. and McCabe, G. P., "Introduction to the Practice of Statistics", W. H. Freeman and Company, 1989.
13. Rumelhart, D. E. and McClelland, J. L., "Parallel Distributed Processing: Explorations in the Microstructure of Cognition", vol. 1, Cambridge: The MIT Press, 1988.
14. Khanna, T., "Foundations of Neural Networks", Massachusetts: Addison-Wesley, 1990.
15. Song, X. M., "Radial Basis Function Networks", http://www.cs.helsinki.fi/~xianming/thesis/m_conten.html, 13th Oct. 1998.
16. Lowe, D., "Radial Basis Function Networks", Neural Computing Research Group, Aston University, Aston Triangle, Birmingham, 1988, pp. 1-14.
17. Lowe, D., "Radial Basis Function Networks and Statistics", Neural Computing Research Group, Aston University, Aston Triangle, Birmingham, 1988, pp. 1-32.

18. Broomhead, D. S. and Lowe, D., "Multi-Variable Functional Interpolation and Adaptive Networks", Complex Systems 2, 1988, pp. 321-355.
19. Kosko, B., "Neural Networks and Fuzzy Systems: A Dynamical Systems Approach to Machine Intelligence", Prentice-Hall, Inc., 1992.
20. Kohonen, T., "Self-Organisation and Associative Memory", Berlin, Springer-Verlag, 1984.
21. Kohonen, T., "Adaptive, Associative and Self-Organisation Functions in Neural Computing", Applied Optics, vol. 26, 1987, pp. 4910-4918.
22. Kohonen, T., "Self-Organised Formation of Topologically Correct Feature Maps", Biological Cybernetics, vol. 43, 1982, pp. 59-69.
23. Kohonen, T., "An Introduction to Neural Computing", Neural Networks, vol. 1, 1988, p. 4.
24. Specht, D. F., "General Regression Neural Networks", Institute of Electrical and Electronic Engineers Transactions on Neural Networks, vol. 2, no. 6, Nov. 1991, pp. 568-576.
25. Masters, T., "Advanced Algorithms for Neural Networks: A C++ Sourcebook", John Wiley and Sons, 1995.
26. Shaffer, R., "General Regression Neural Networks", http://cheml.nrl.navy/~shatter/grnn.html, 1998.
27. Sarle, W., "FAQ for comp.ai.neural-net, What is a GRNN?", part 2, ftp://ftp.sas.com/pub/neural/FAQ.html, 1997.
28. Grjotheim, K. and Kvande, H., "Understanding the Hall-Heroult Process for Production of Aluminium", Aluminium-Verlag, Dusseldorf, 1986.
29. Haupin, W. E., "Principles of Aluminium Electrolysis", Proc. 124th TMS Annual Meeting, Las Vegas, Feb. 12-16, 1995, pp. 195-203.
30. Grjotheim, K. and Welch, B. J., "Aluminium Smelter Technology", Aluminium-Verlag, 1988.
31. Matheou, N., "Electrolyte Control in Aluminium Cell", Proc. Al. Fund., 1994.
32. Huang, S. H. and Zhang, H. C., "Artificial Neural Networks in Manufacturing: Concepts, Applications and Perspectives", Institute of Electrical and Electronic Engineers Transactions on Components, Packaging and Manufacturing Technology, pt. A, vol. 17, no. 2, 1994, pp. 212-228.
33. Frost, F. and Karri, V., "Determining the Influence of Input Parameters on BP Neural Network Output Error Using Sensitivity Analysis", Proc. International Conference on Computational Intelligence and Multimedia Applications (ICCIMA), Sep. 1999, New Delhi, India, pp. 45-49.

Productivity Improvements through Prediction of Electrolyte Temperature in Aluminium Reduction Cell Using BP Neural Network

F. Frost[1] and V. Karri[2]

[1]Comalco Aluminium Limited, PO Box 290, George Town,
Tasmania, 7253, Australia. Fred.Frost@comalco.riotinto.com.au
[2]School of Science and Engineering, University of Tasmania, GPO Box 252-65, Hobart,
Tasmania, 7001, Australia. Vishy.Karri@utas.edu.au

Abstract. Primary aluminium is produced using a highly dynamic and unstable technique known as the Hall-Heroult process. An important consideration for aluminium smelting is minimisation of process variation, which is monitored by measuring particular parameters of the Hall-Heroult process and administering corrective action as appropriate to return or maintain the process within a predetermined control range. A critical parameter to be controlled is electrolyte temperature. Due to the high temperature and corrosive environment associated with the Hall-Heroult process it is beneficial to have some alternative methodology of electrolyte temperature measurement than the existing thermocouple technique. In this paper it is shown that a neural network is applied to predict electrolyte temperature in the Hall-Heroult cell, yielding significant productivity improvements. In particular, the backpropagation, BP, neural network is used to develop an appropriate process model. Moreover, it is shown that careful consideration given to the training data used to develop the neural network model has given an accurate electrolyte temperature prediction methodology.

1. Introduction

The Hall-Heroult process is an electrolysis process involving the conversion of bauxite ore to aluminium metal. Electrolysis is an electrochemical process by which electrical energy is used to promote chemical reactions that occur at electrodes. The anode involves the oxidation process where species lose electrons, which are deposited at the anode, while gaining of electrons occurs at the cathode [1]. Since its discovery, the Hall-Heroult process has remained virtually unchanged in principal. In this process pure alumina is dissolved in a electrolyte of molten cryolite in large electrolytic furnaces, called reduction cells. Molten cryolite, having a high solubility for aluminium oxide, is the major component of the Hall-Heroult electrolyte [2]. By means of a carbon anode suspended in the electrolyte, electric current is passed through the electrolyte mixture causing metallic aluminium to be deposited on the carbon cathode at the bottom of the cell, as shown in Figure 1. The heat generated by passage of this electric current keeps the electrolyte molten, so that alumina can be added as necessary to make the process continuous. At intervals, aluminium is siphoned from the reduction cells. Metal removal from the reduction cell is a routine procedure and is usually completed on a daily basis by syphoning the metal into a transportable vessel. For stable cell operation, it is important that the amount of metal removed balances the production in the time interval [3]. The aluminium metal removed from the reduction cell is in a molten state and is generally processed further into solid aluminium ingots or billet, packaged for shipping and sent to respective customers. The efficiency with which aluminium metal can be produced contributes significantly to the economic status and existence of the producer.

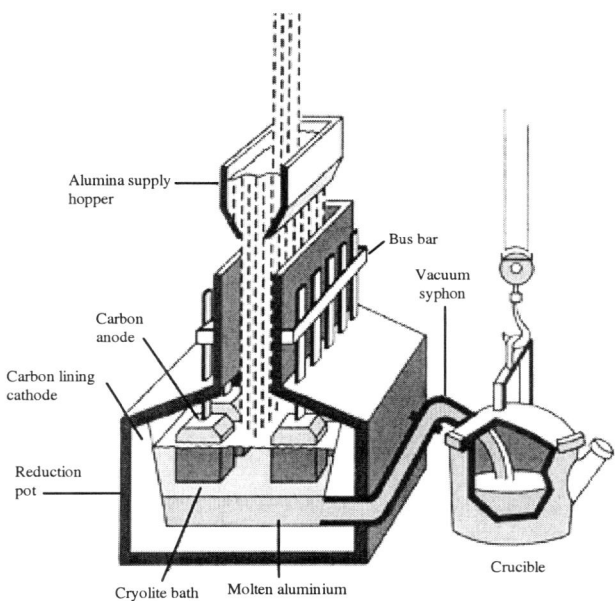

Fig. 1. Basic Components of the Hall-Heroult Reduction Cell Highlighting Removal of Molten Aluminium [4]

Electrolyte temperature is an important cell parameter in aluminium electrolysis, as it is a significant indicator of how stable and efficiently a reduction cell is operating. In electrolytic processes in molten salts, such as the production of aluminium, the corrosive nature of the electrolyte, due to high sodium content and high temperature, produces associated problems with electrolyte temperature measurements [5]. While temperature is one of the most important process control parameters, continuous measurements of electrolyte temperature have not proven to be technically or economically viable. Remote sensors, such as optical pyrometers and measurements of the intensity of infra-red radiation, are not practical or accurate enough [6]. While the most commonly used practical technique for measuring electrolyte temperature in industrial aluminium electrolysis cells is by use of type K mineral insulated metal sheathed thermocouples, such thermocouples only last for a very short period, deteriorating rapidly each time they are placed in the electrolyte, eventually being destroyed by this highly corrosive medium [7]. However, the thermocouple technique has an associated error of approximately 4.0 to 5.0°C for electrolyte temperature measurement, attributed to operator and equipment error. This error is relatively low considering the high temperatures and broad temperature range associated with aluminium smelting. Hence, it is important that a prediction technique, such as a neural network, if used to eliminate the problems associated with manual temperature measurements, does not compromise the low error achieved with the existing thermocouple technique. This is the major objective to be achieved by the neural network. In this instance, the backpropagation, BP, neural network is applied. BP is the most widely used model of the neural network paradigm and has been applied successfully in applications studies in a broad range of areas [8-11]. BP networks [12-14] are multi-layered feedforward neural networks that are trained using the error BP procedure [15], a supervised mode of training. The architecture of a BP network, as shown in Figure 2, consists of an input layer, one or more hidden layers and an output layer. There are i input nodes, j hidden nodes and k output nodes. All input nodes are connected to all hidden nodes through weighted connections, w_{ji}, and all hidden nodes are connected to all output nodes through weighted connections, w_{kj}. During supervised training, input patterns supplied to the BP network are processed in two stages. In the first stage, the training patterns are passed forward through the network architecture to provide a predicted value for each output variable of the BP model. Any error associated with the prediction is then passed back through the model to update the hidden and output layer weights, with the objective of reducing the associated prediction error. This network training procedure continues until the network weights are updated sufficiently so that further error reduction is not possible [16].

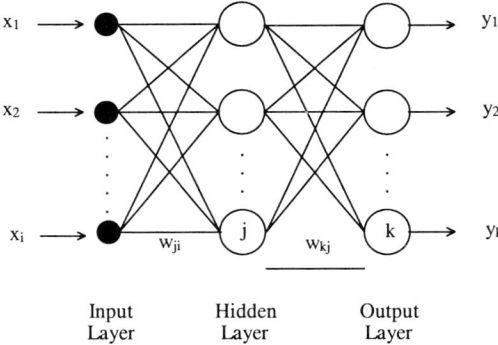

Fig. 2. Basic Structure of a Backpropagation Neural Network [16]

2. Development of Neural Network Training and Test Data for Electrolyte Temperature Prediction Application

In the first instance, process parameters that are shown to have at least some relationship with the output variable are selected as potential input variables for the neural network model. Observing, graphically, behaviour of the output variable with changes in the process parameters provides an indication of the existence of a relationship between a process parameter and the output variable. While many parameters may be selected in the first instance as potential input variables, only those that are shown to contribute towards the prediction of the output variable are maintained in the model. A technique known as predictive importance [17] is used to identify contributing and non-contributing process parameters. Consequently, those parameters that are identified as non-contributing are eliminated from the model. For this particular application there are ten process parameters selected in the first instance as potential neural network inputs, while electrolyte temperature is the single output of the model, as shown in Figure 3 using an arbitrary BP neural network architecture. A total of 1,444 data patterns were obtained from the smelter knowledge base for this application. Data preparation formed a complex stage of network modelling in this instance, including the elimination of corrupt information from the acquired data, ensuring sufficient data for each model variable was included in the data patterns, covering the entire operating range for each parameter, and scaling each variable between the minimum and maximum limits of its operating range. The processed data was divided into 1,244 training data patterns, with the remaining 200 patterns used as test data.

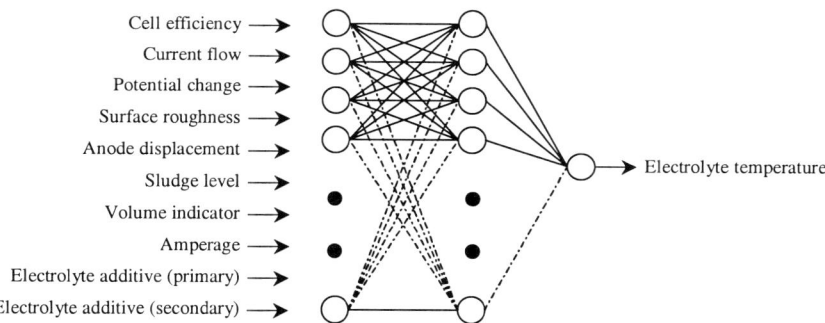

Fig. 3. Illustration of Neural Network Model Used for Electrolyte Temperature Prediction Application

Figure 4 shows an approximately uniform distribution of data for the network output variable for the train and test data sets, which is an important consideration for sufficient network training and testing.

It should be noted, however, that while a uniform distribution of data is achieved for the electrolyte temperature range of 956.0 to 985.0°C, temperatures outside this range are extremely rare and therefore difficult to obtain from the smelter knowledge base. Hence, while there is less representative data for the low and high electrolyte temperature values, all available data for these values is included in the training and test data patterns so that there are some train and test examples for the extremes of the operating range.

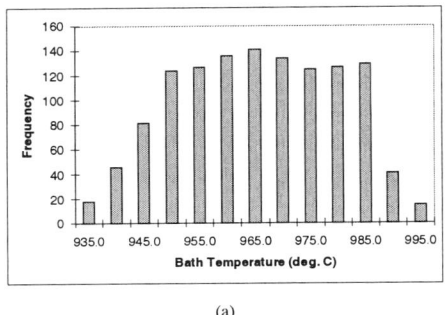 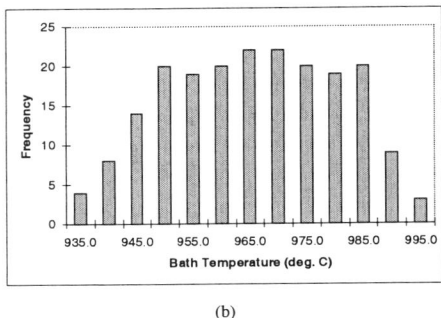

Fig. 4. Histogram Showing Distribution of the Network Output Variable in the Data Sets. (a) Training, and (b) Test

3. Neural Network Modelling Results for Electrolyte Temperature Prediction Application

The analysis completed here compares the RMS error behaviour of the BP network with increasing number of hidden layer nodes, using a single hidden layer, BP1, and two hidden layer, BP2, model. For BP networks, it has been shown in the literature [18] that there is no theoretical reason to ever use more than two hidden layers and for the vast majority of practical problems it is rarely necessary to use more than one hidden layer [19]. The use of two hidden layers is usually only necessary in practice when the network must learn a function that has discontinuities [18].

It is important to note that the learning rate, α, used in the delta rule for the weight update procedure in the BP network is an adjustable parameter, generally set to a value in the range 0.1 to 0.9 [18]. The convergence speed of the neural network is directly related to the value of α. In particular, if α is small then the search path will closely approximate the gradient path, but convergence will be very slow due to the large number of update steps required to reach a local minima [20]. On the other hand, if α is large then convergence will initially be very fast, but the algorithm will eventually oscillate and thus not reach a minimum [20]. However, the BP neural network in this instance incorporates a procedure to decrease a large initial value of α to a small value, not less that 0.1, as network iterations progress. This technique allows large weight changes to occur when the search point is far away from the minimum, decreasing to a smaller value as iterations progress and the search path approaches the minimum, optimising network convergence speed and consequently, minimising computation time.

RMS error behaviour with increasing number of hidden layer nodes in the BP1 network is shown in Figure 5, using the sigmoidal activation function in the hidden and output layer nodes. It is shown that 5 hidden layer nodes produced the lowest error, giving RMS error values of 0.0620 and 0.0632 for the train and test data sets, respectively. This is achieved using approximately 650 iterations, which has been found sufficient for weight convergence from a study of RMS error behaviour over a duration of 1,000 iterations. However, it is shown in Table 1 that 5 of the input variables, namely, potential change, surface roughness, anode displacement and primary and secondary additive, do not yield an increase in RMS error when omitted from the model. Hence, these inputs are permanently removed and the model retrained, giving a slightly improved RMS error of 0.0617 and 0.0625 for the train and test data sets, respectively. Consequently, the percentage contribution of the input variables can be determined by summing the total error increase when parameters are omitted from the model and dividing the individual error increase by the sum in each instance, highlighting the ranking of importance of the input variables for prediction of electrolyte temperature, as highlighted in Table 1.

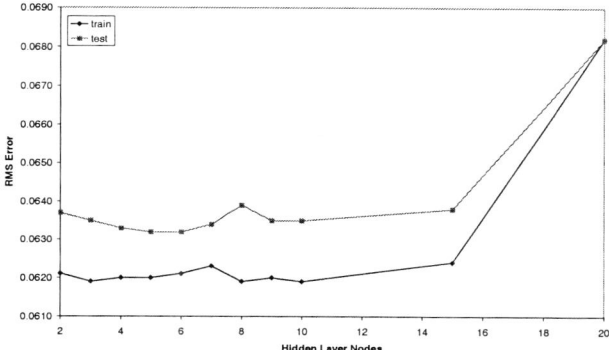

Fig. 5. BP1 Network RMS Error Behaviour with Changing Architecture

Table 1. RMS Error Behaviour with Omitted Input Variables and Percentage Contribution of Input Variables

Input Variable Omitted	RMS Error Train	Test	Per. Cont.	RMS Error Train	Test	Per. Cont.
no variables omitted	0.0620	0.0632	-	0.0553	0.0573	-
cell efficiency	0.0641	0.0682	31.1	0.0591	0.0646	13.6
current flow	0.0667	0.0708	47.2	0.0630	0.0695	22.8
Potential change	0.0620	0.0624	0.0	0.0616	0.0600	5.0
surface roughness	0.0619	0.0632	0.0	0.0578	0.0604	5.8
anode displacement	0.0620	0.0628	0.0	0.0596	0.0623	9.3
sludge level	0.0624	0.0655	14.3	0.0588	0.0649	14.2
volume indicator	0.0621	0.0640	3.5	0.0579	0.0623	9.3
Amperage	0.0625	0.0636	4.0	0.0579	0.0617	8.2
Primary additive	0.0618	0.0629	0.0	0.0567	0.0608	6.5
Secondary additive	0.0616	0.0623	0.0	0.0562	0.0601	5.2
non-cont. omitted	0.0617	0.0625	-	-	-	-

The BP2 network has shown lower RMS error than the BP1 model. It is shown in Figure 6 that the best network architecture for achieving minimum RMS error is 10 nodes in the first hidden layer and 3 nodes in the second hidden layer. The resulting RMS error using this particular architecture is shown to be 0.0553 and 0.0573 for the train and test data sets, respectively. It was found that approximately 800 iterations were required to allow convergence of the network weights, determined from a study of RMS error behaviour over a duration of 1,000 iterations. It is useful to note that the sigmoidal activation function was used in the hidden layer nodes of the BP2 network and also in the output layer nodes. A predictive importance analysis has shown that all of the input variables contribute towards the prediction of electrolyte temperature in the BP2 model. It is shown that there is an increase in RMS error when any of the input parameters are individually omitted from the model.

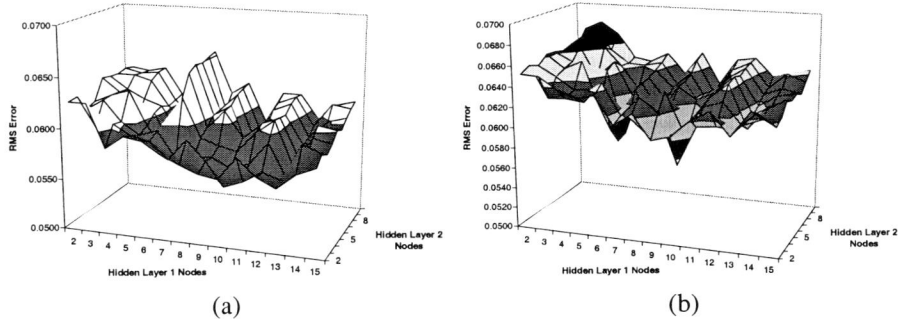

Fig. 6. BP2 Network RMS Error Behaviour with Changing Architecture. (a) Training, and (b) Test

In order to study the practical implications of the neural network modelling completed in this instance, it is useful to compare the actual and predicted values of electrolyte temperature, as shown in Figure 7, using the BP2 model, as it has shown the lowest RMS error of the applied networks for this application. It can be seen that while the predicted and actual values are similar over the temperature range 956.0 to 985.0°C, the prediction error is higher outside this range. This behaviour indicates a correlation between prediction error and number of training data patterns. It has been shown that while the temperature range of 956.0 to 985.0°C is well represented in the training data, temperatures outside this range are rare and therefore less data is available for the extremes of the operating range. Consequently, the error associated with temperature predictions at the extremes of the operating range have a higher associated error due to lack of sufficient training for these minority instances.

An approximately normal distribution of prediction error is shown to be associated with the neural network in this instance, as shown in Figure 8. It can be seen that a significant number of predictions of electrolyte temperature have approximately zero error, while there is an equal distribution of predictions that are higher and lower than the actual values. Moreover, the normal curve approximation of the histogram is shown to represent a normal distribution symmetrical about the mean, confirmed by a skewness value of -0.01°C. While it is shown that the maximum prediction error has a magnitude of 26.0°C, it is noted that the mean prediction error, or 50th percentile, is -0.03°C and that approximately 50.0% of the prediction error is lower than 0.0°C, ie. the neural network is not biased towards higher- or lower-than-actual predictions.

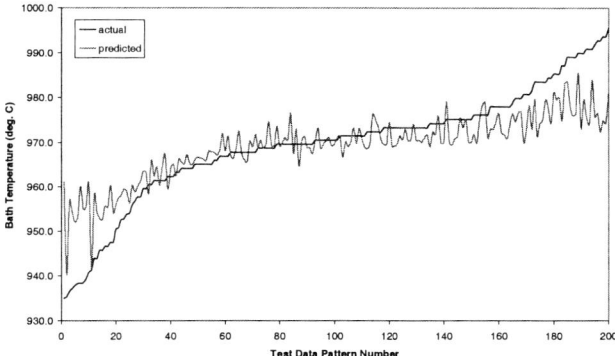

Fig. 7. Comparison of Actual and Neural Network Predicted Values for Electrolyte Temperature Prediction Application

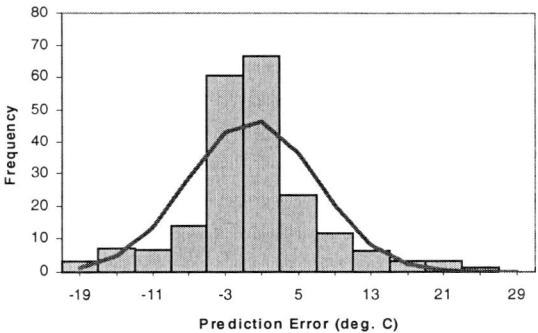

Fig. 8. Histogram Showing Prediction Error Distribution for Electrolyte Temperature Prediction Application

The average prediction error associated with the nominated ranges for electrolyte temperature, as shown in Table 2, confirms the existence of a correlation between prediction error and the number of training data patterns for a particular range of data.

Table 2. Prediction Error Associated with Specified Data Ranges for Electrolyte Temperature Prediction Application

Electrolyte Temperature Range (°C)	Average Prediction Error (°C)
935.0 to 945.0	15.1
946.0 to 955.0	6.9
956.0 to 965.0	2.7
966.0 to 975.0	2.1
976.0 to 985.0	4.9
986.0 to 995.0	11.9

4. Conclusions

The availability of adequate data from the smelter knowledge base, to use as training and test patterns, together with the supervised training algorithm used in the BP network has allowed the development of an accurate neural network model in this instance for the prediction of electrolyte temperature within a reduction cell for aluminium production. While it is shown that prediction error is high for electrolyte temperatures outside the typical operating range, it is shown that low error is associated with the majority of electrolyte temperatures encountered in the reduction cell. Further, it is important to note that the average error associated with the developed neural network model in this instance is comparable to the typical error associated with manual thermocouple measurements of electrolyte temperature in the aluminium smelting industry.

While the Hall-Heroult process is known to be highly dynamic, non-linear and unstable, it is shown in this paper that neural networks offer an accurate modelling methodology to improve process control while minimising labour costs associated with the measurement of process parameters. The results exhibited by the neural network modelling investigation in this instance have given confidence in implementing such a system for on-line predictions of electrolyte temperature. In fact, such a system has been implemented with comparable results as those documented in this paper. That is, for the usual operating range of electrolyte temperature, the prediction error is typically in the range 0.0 to 4.0°C.

References

1. Logan, R. H., "What is Electrolysis?", http://edie.cprost.stu.ca/~rhlogan/electrol.html, Oct. 13, 1998.
2. Haupin, W. E., "Principles of Aluminium Electrolysis", Proc. 124th TMS Annual Meeting, Las Vegas, Feb. 12-16, 1995, pp. 195-203.
3. Grjotheim, K. and Kvande, H., "Understanding the Hall-Heroult Process for Production of Aluminium", Aluminium-Verlag, Dusseldorf, 1986.
4. Tomago Aluminium, "The Aluminium Production Process", http://www.tomago.com.au/aluminium.html, Feb. 24, 1999.
5. Zhuxian, Q., Jingjiang, L., Xiaoli, C., Grjotheim, K., Kvande, H. and Oye, H., "Electrolyte Temperature Measurements in Aluminium Electrolysis Cells", Proc. 124th TMS Annual Meeting, Las Vegas, Feb. 12-16, 1995, p. 233
6. Grjotheim, K. and Welch, B. J., "Aluminium Smelter Technology", Second Edition, Aluminium-Verlag, Dusseldorf, 1988.
7. Madsen, D. J., "Temperature Measurement and Control in Reduction Cells", Proc. 121st TMS Annual Meeting, San Diego, California, Mar. 1-5, 1992, pp. 453-456.
8. Willis, M. J., Montague, G. A. and Peel, C., "On the Application of Artificial Neural Networks for Process Control", Kluwer Academic Publishers, London, 1995.

9. Sobajic, D. J., Lu, J. J. and Pao, Y. H., "Intelligent Control for the Intelledex 605 T Robot Manipulator", Proc. 1998 Institute of Electrical and Electronic Engineers Int. Neural Networks Conf., vol. 2, 1988, pp. 613-640.
10. Chryssolouris, G., Domroesse, M. and Beaullieu, P., "Sensor Synthesis for Control of Manufacturing Processes", Journ. Engineering for Industry, vol. 114, May, 1992, pp. 158-174.
11. Karri, V., "Performance Estimation in Wood Machining Using ANN", Proc. Advanced Manufacturing Processes, Systems and Technologies (AMPST), Bradford, England, Mar. 1996, pp. 271-276.
12. Zurada, J. M., "Introduction to Artificial Neural Systems", West Publishing Company, 1992.
13. Weijters, A. J. M. M. and Hoppenbrouwes, G. A. J., "Backpropagation Networks for Grapheme-Phoneme Conversion: A Non-Technical Introduction", Artificial Neural Networks, Springer-Verlag Berlin Heidelberg, 1995, pp. 13-36.
14. Freeman, J. A. and Skapura, D. M., "Neural Networks: Algorithms, Applications, and Programming Techniques", Addison-Wesley Publishing Company, Inc., 1992.
15. Huang, S. H. and Zhang, H. C., "Artificial Neural Networks in Manufacturing: Concepts, Applications and Perspectives", Institute of Electrical and Electronic Engineers Transactions on Components, Packaging and Manufacturing Technology, part A, vol. 17, no. 2, 1994, pp. 212-228.
16. Hertz, J., Krogh, A. and Palmer, R. G., "Introduction to the Theory of Neural Computing", Addison-Wesley Publishing Company, 1991.
17. Sarle, W., "How to Measure Importance of Inputs", ftp://ftp.sas.com/pub/neural/FAQ.html, Apr. 24, 1999.
18. Masters, T., "Practical Neural Network Recipes in C++", Academic Press Inc., 1993.
19. Wasserman, P. D., "Advanced Methods in Neural Computing", Van Nostrand Reinhold, 1993.
20. Hassoun, M. H., "Fundamentals of Artificial Neural Networks", Massachusetts Institute of Technology, 1995.

Pruned Neural Networks for Regression

Rudy Setiono and Wee Kheng Leow

School of Computing
National University of Singapore
Singapore 117543

Abstract. Neural networks have been widely used as a tool for regression. They are capable of approximating any function and they do not require any assumption about the distribution of the data. The most commonly used architectures for regression are the feedforward neural networks with one or more hidden layers. In this paper, we present a network pruning algorithm which determines the number of units in the input and hidden layers of the networks. We compare the performance of the pruned networks to four regression methods namely, linear regression (LR), Naive Bayes (NB), k-nearest-neighbor (kNN), and a decision tree predictor M5$'$. On 32 publicly available data sets tested, the neural network method outperforms NB and kNN if the prediction errors are computed in terms of the root mean squared errors. Under this measurement metric, it also performs as well as LR and M5$'$. On the other hand, using the mean absolute error as the measurement metric, the neural network method outperforms all four other regression methods.

1 Introduction

In addition to pattern classification problems, regression or function approximation is the predictive learning problem for which feedforward neural networks have been widely applied. Neural networks have several advantages over statistical regression techniques. First, no assumption about the distribution of the data is required. Second, there is no need to select the regression model *a priori*. And third, neural networks have been shown to be capable of approximating any continuous function with arbitrary precision [3, 7].

Different problems require different network architecture and selecting an appropriate network architecture is the most important step in obtaining an accurate model for regression. Since we restrict ourselves to networks with a single hidden layer, architecture selection boils down to finding appropriate numbers of units in the input and hidden layers. To find an appropriate number of hidden units, constructive algorithms start with a few hidden units and add more units as needed to improve network accuracy [1, 8, 14]. Destructive algorithms, on the other hand, start with a large number of hidden units and remove those that are found to be redundant [11]. The number of useful input units correspond to the number of relevant input attributes of the data. Typical algorithms usually start by assigning one input unit to each attribute, train the network with all input attributes and then remove network input units that correspond to irrelevant data attributes [15, 16]. Various measures of the contribution of an input attribute to the network predictive accuracy have been developed [2, 10, 13, 18].

The purpose of this paper is (1) to present an algorithm for removing redundant or irrelevant input and hidden units from feedforward neural networks for regression and (2) to compare the predictive accuracy of the neural networks with those of other methods for regression on publicly available data sets. Our proposed pruning algorithm removes units from the network by making use of a cross-validating data set. The weights of network connections from a unit that is considered for removal are set to zero and the network is retrained. If the accuracy of the network on the cross-validation set improves or deteriorates within an acceptable level, then the unit is pruned from the network. The same criteria for removal is applied to the input and hidden units. The pruning process is terminated when no unit can be removed without causing the network accuracy on the cross-validation set to drop below the prescribed level.

While there are several papers that propose algorithms for constructing and/or training neural network for regression [6, 8, 9], we have been unable to find a paper that compares the accuracy of neural networks for regression against those of other traditional methods such as statistical regression method. A recent study by Frank et al. [5] on the application of naive Bayes methodology for regression provides us with an excellent opportunity for making comparisons among the various regression methods. Test results from thirty-two problems, all but one are real-world problems, are reported in the study. The data sets are available from their website[1] as part of the WEKA project. The results from our network pruning algorithm show that neural networks perform as well as linear regression if the prediction errors are measured in terms of the root mean squared errors. However, using the mean absolute error as the measurement metric, neural networks outperform linear regression and three other regression methods.

The paper is organized as follows. Section 2 presents the neural network architecture, training and pruning for regression. Section 3 describes our pruning algorithm. Section 4 presents the results from our pruning algorithm and compares them to those of other methods reported in [5]. Finally, Section 5 discusses future works and concludes the paper.

2 Network Training and Pruning

In this section we describe our training and pruning algorithm. The available data samples $(\mathbf{x}^i, y^i), i = 1, 2, \ldots$, where $\mathbf{x}^i \in \mathbb{R}^N$ and $y^i \in \mathbb{R}$, are first randomly divided into 3 subsets: the training, the cross-validation and the test sets. Using the training data set, a network with H hidden units is trained, so as to minimize the sum of squared errors $E(\mathbf{w}, \mathbf{v})$ augmented with a penalty term $P(\mathbf{w}, \mathbf{v})$:

---

[1] http://www.cs.waikato.ac.nz/~ml/weka/index.html

$$E(\mathbf{w}, \mathbf{v}) = \sum_{i=1}^{K} \left(\tilde{y}^i - y^i\right)^2 + P(\mathbf{w}, \mathbf{v}) \qquad (1)$$

$$P(\mathbf{w}, \mathbf{v}) = \epsilon_1 \left(\sum_{m=1}^{H} \sum_{\ell=1}^{N} \frac{\beta w_{m\ell}^2}{1 + \beta w_{m\ell}^2} + \sum_{m=1}^{H} \frac{\beta v_m^2}{1 + \beta v_m^2} \right) +$$
$$\epsilon_2 \left(\sum_{m=1}^{H} \sum_{\ell=1}^{N} w_{m\ell}^2 + \sum_{m=1}^{H} v_m^2 \right) \qquad (2)$$

where K is the number of samples in the training data set, $\epsilon_1, \epsilon_2, \beta$ are positive penalty parameters, and $\tilde{y}^i$ is the predicted function value for input sample $\mathbf{x}^i$

$$\tilde{y}^i = \sum_{m=1}^{H} \delta\left((\mathbf{x}^i)^T \mathbf{w}_m\right) v_m,$$

$\mathbf{w}_m \in \mathbb{R}^N$ is the vector of network weights from the input units to hidden unit m, $v_m \in \mathbb{R}$ is the network weight from hidden unit m to the output unit, $\delta(\xi)$ is the hyperbolic tangent function $(e^\xi - e^{-\xi})/(e^\xi + e^{-\xi})$, and $(\mathbf{x}^i)^T \mathbf{w}_m$ is the scalar product of $\mathbf{x}^i$ and $\mathbf{w}_m$.

A local minimum of the error function $E(\mathbf{w}, \mathbf{v})$ can be obtained by applying any nonlinear optimization methods such as the gradient descent method or the quasi-Newton method. In our implementation, we have used a variant of the quasi-Newton method, namely the BFGS method [4] due to its faster convergence rate than the gradient descent method.

A new pruning algorithm called N2PFA (Neural Network Pruning for Function Approximation) is proposed. In the algorithm, the mean absolute error (MAD) of the network's prediction is used to measure the network's performance. In particular, MAD p on the training set $\mathcal{T}$ and MAD q on the cross-validation set $\mathcal{X}$ are used to determine when pruning should be terminated:

$$p = \frac{1}{|\mathcal{T}|} \sum_{y^i \in \mathcal{T}} |\tilde{y}_i - y^i| \qquad q = \frac{1}{|\mathcal{X}|} \sum_{y^i \in \mathcal{X}} |\tilde{y}_i - y^i| \qquad (3)$$

Algorithm N2PFA

Given: Data set $(\mathbf{x}^i, y^i), i = 1, 2, \ldots, K$.
Objective: Find a neural network that fits the data and generalizes well.

Step 1. Split the data into 3 subsets: training, cross-validation, and test sets.
Step 2. Train a network with a relatively large number of hidden units to minimize the error function (1).
Step 3. Compute p and q, and set $pbest=p$, $qbest=q$, $ermax=\max\{pbest, qbest\}$.
Step 4. Remove redundant hidden units:
  1. For each $m = 1, 2, \ldots, H$,
     set $v_m = 0$ and compute the prediction errors p_m and q_m.
  2. Retrain the network with $v_h = 0$ where $p_h = \min_m p_m$, and compute p and q of the retrained network.

3. If $p \leq (1+\alpha)ermax$ and $q \leq (1+\alpha)ermax$, then
   - Remove hidden unit h.
   - Set $pbest = \min\{p, pbest\}$, $qbest = \min\{q, qbest\}$ and $ermax = \max\{pbest, qbest\}$.
   - Set $H = H - 1$ and go to Step 4.1.

   Else use the previous setting of network weights.

Step 5. Remove irrelevant inputs:
1. For each $l = 1, 2, \ldots, N$,
   set $w_{ml} = 0$ for all m and compute the prediction errors p_l and q_l.
2. Retrain the network with $w_{mn} = 0$ for all m where $p_n = \min_l p_l$, and compute p and q of the retrained network.
3. If $p \leq (1+\alpha)ermax$ and $q \leq (1+\alpha)ermax$, then
   - Remove input unit n.
   - Set $pbest = \min\{p, pbest\}$, $qbest = \min\{q, qbest\}$ and $ermax = \max\{pbest, qbest\}$.
   - Set $N = N - 1$ and go to Step 5.1.

   Else use the previous setting of network weights.

Step 6. Report the accuracy of the network on the test data set.

The parameter $ermax$ is used to determine if a unit can be removed. Typically, at the beginning of the algorithm when there are many hidden units in the network, the training error p will be much smaller than the cross-validation error q. The value of p increases as more and more units are removed. As the network approaches its optimal structure, we expect q to decrease. As a result, if only *pbest* is used to determine if a unit can be removed, many redundant units can be expected to remain in the network when the algorithm terminates because *pbest* tends to be small at the beginning of the algorithm. On the other hand, if only *qbest* is used, then the network would perform well on the cross-validation set but may not necessarily generalizes well on the test set. This could be caused by the small number of samples available for cross-validation or the uneven distribution of the data in the training and cross-validation sets. Therefore, $ermax$ is assigned the larger of *pbest* and *qbest* so as to remove as many redundant units as possible without sacrificing generalization accuracy. The parameter α is introduced to control the chances that a unit will be removed. With a larger value of α, units are more likely to be removed. However, the accuracy of the resulting network on the test data set may deteriorate. We have conducted extensive experiments to find a value for this parameter that works well for all of our test problems. We report our experimental results in the next section.

3 Experimental Results

3.1 Experimental Methodology

The data sets used in the experiment and the summary of their attribute features are listed in Table 1. They are shown in increasing order of the number of samples. Most of the data sets consist of both numeric and discrete attributes. The total number of attributes ranges from 2 to 25. Except for problem no. 19 pwLinear, all of the problems are from real world domains.

Table 1. Characteristics of the datasets used for experiments.

No.	Dataset	Instances	Missing values (%)	Numeric attributes	Discrete attributes	Neural network inputs
1	schlvote	38	0.4	4	1	6
2	bolts	40	0.0	7	0	8
3	vineyard	52	0.0	3	0	4
4	elusage	55	0.0	1	1	14
5	pollution	60	0.0	15	0	16
6	mbagrade	61	0.0	1	1	3
7	sleep	62	2.4	7	0	8
8	auto93	93	0.7	16	6	62
9	baskball	96	0.0	4	0	5
10	cloud	108	0.0	4	2	10
11	fruitfly	125	0.0	2	2	9
12	echoMonths	131	7.5	6	3	11
13	veteran	137	0.0	3	4	11
14	fishcatch	158	6.9	5	2	15
15	autoPrice	159	0.0	15	0	16
16	servo	167	0.0	0	4	20
17	lowbwt	189	0.0	2	7	20
18	pharynx	195	1.1	1	10	37
19	pwLinear	200	0.0	10	0	11
20	autoHorse	205	1.1	17	8	69
21	cpu	209	0.0	6	1	37
22	bodyfat	252	0.0	14	0	15
23	breastTumor	286	0.3	1	8	37
24	hungarian	294	19.0	6	7	23
25	cholesterol	303	0.1	6	7	23
26	cleveland	303	0.1	6	7	23
27	autoMpg	398	0.2	4	3	26
28	pbc	418	15.6	10	8	30
29	housing	506	0.0	12	1	14
30	meta	528	4.3	19	2	66
31	sensory	576	0.0	0	11	33
32	strike	625	0.0	5	1	24

The following experimental setting were used to obtain the statistics from our network pruning algorithm:

- Ten-fold cross-validation scheme: We divided each data set randomly into 10 subsets of equal size. Eight subsets were used for training, one subset was used for cross validating, and one subset for measuring the predictive accuracy of the pruned network. This procedure was performed 10 times so that each subset was tested once. Test results were averaged over 20 ten-fold cross-validation runs.
- The same set of values for the penalty parameters in the penalty term (2) were used: $\epsilon_1 = 0.5, \epsilon_2 = 0.05$ and $\beta = 0.1$.

- During pruning, the value of α was set to 0.025.
- The starting number of hidden units for all problems was 8. The number of input units are shown in Table 1. The number of input units includes one unit with a constant input value of 1 to implement hidden unit bias.
- One input unit was assigned to each continuous attribute in the data set. Discrete attributes were binary coded. A discrete attribute with D possible values was assigned D network inputs.
- Continuous attribute values were scaled to range in the interval $[0, 1]$, while binary-encoded attribute values were either 0 or 0.2. We found that the 0/0.2 encoding produced better generalization than the usual 0/1 encoding.
- A missing continuous attribute value was replaced by the average of the non-missing values. A missing discrete attribute value was assigned the value "unknown" and the corresponding input **x** was set to the zero vector **0**.
- Target output values were linearly scaled to range in the interval $[0, U]$, where U was 32 for bolts; 16 for auto93, fishcatch, autoPrice, servo, autoHorse, cpu, bodyfat and housing; and 4 for all other problems.

3.2 Results and Comparison to Other Methods

The predictive accuracy of various regression methods have been measured in terms of the relative root mean squared error (RRMSE) and the relative mean absolute error (RMAE):

$$\text{RRMSE} = 100 \times \sqrt{\sum_i (\tilde{y}_i - y_i)^2 / \sum_i (\overline{y} - y_i)^2}$$

$$\text{RMAE} = 100 \times \sum_i |\tilde{y}_i - y_i| / \sum_i |\overline{y} - y_i|$$

where the summation is computed over the samples in the test set and $\overline{y}$ is the average value of y_i in the test set. These relative errors are preferred over the usual sum of squared errors because they normalize the differences in the output ranges of different data sets.

Our results are summarized in Tables 2 and 3. For comparison purpose, we also reproduce the statistics from Frank et al. [5] for four other regression methods. Naive Bayes (NB) method [5] applies Bayes' theorem to estimate the probability density function of the target value y given a sample **x**. A crucial assumption is that given the predicted value y, the attributes of **x** are independent of each other. LR is the standard linear regression method. Attribute selection was accomplished by backward elimination. The k-nearest-neighbor (kNN) is a distance-weighted k-nearest-neighbor method. The value of k varied from 1 to 20 and the optimal value of k was chosen using leave-one-out cross-validation on the training data. The model-tree predictor method M5$'$ generates binary decision trees with linear regression functions at the leaf nodes [17]. This method is an improved re-implementation of Quinlan's M5 [12].

To compare the neural network accuracy on a test problem with that of another method, we computed the estimated standard error of the difference

Table 2. Relative root mean square error ± the standard deviation from five regression methods.

No.	NN	NB	LR	kNN	M5′
1	193.42 ± 58.02	263.70 ± 87.2	233.31 ± 93.3	267.91 ± 97.1	164.24 ± 70.8
2	42.45 ± 20.41	57.61 ± 10.7	53.37 ± 10.6	77.95 ± 10.9 •	32.28 ± 7.6
3	80.65 ± 10.01	82.90 ± 9.6	77.37 ± 9.7	75.52 ± 8.1	77.21 ± 9.9
4	60.39 ± 8.18	65.51 ± 6.3	53.21 ± 5.9	70.94 ± 7.0 •	49.36 ± 3.9 ◇
5	73.50 ± 9.70	97.03 ± 11.1 •	98.86 ± 9.2 •	85.99 ± 8.4 •	79.09 ± 8.5
6	105.00 ± 10.21	103.84 ± 6.8	85.63 ± 4.0 ◇	118.54 ± 8.3 •	85.63 ± 4.0 ◇
7	89.87 ± 7.62	95.01 ± 10.5	82.08 ± 7.6	90.88 ± 8.5	92.48 ± 25.8
8	55.80 ± 5.67	66.62 ± 6.4 •	67.25 ± 5.7 •	71.77 ± 4.2 •	61.79 ± 4.8 •
9	86.94 ± 3.53	92.03 ± 4.0 •	80.11 ± 2.1 ◇	90.02 ± 3.6	81.35 ± 2.3 ◇
10	42.76 ± 2.58	56.55 ± 2.9 •	39.71 ± 2.2 ◇	75.46 ± 2.8 •	40.07 ± 2.0 ◇
11	106.57 ± 2.82	123.54 ± 4.6 •	100.16 ± 0.5 ◇	120.30 ± 4.2 •	100.38 ± 0.6 ◇
12	74.92 ± 3.55	81.63 ± 2.2 •	68.93 ± 1.2 ◇	72.61 ± 2.2	68.50 ± 1.4 ◇
13	97.80 ± 4.83	93.66 ± 5.7	97.39 ± 7.0	106.15 ± 8.5 •	93.70 ± 6.0
14	15.46 ± 0.84	32.14 ± 2.2 •	30.76 ± 2.3 •	34.82 ± 4.2 •	16.61 ± 0.7 •
15	44.85 ± 3.92	43.63 ± 1.6	49.28 ± 3.4 •	46.05 ± 2.2	37.95 ± 2.5 ◇
16	32.27 ± 6.18	75.07 ± 1.8 •	62.71 ± 9.6 •	57.21 ± 7.0 •	38.35 ± 2.2 •
17	66.64 ± 2.81	64.32 ± 1.3	62.77 ± 2.0 ◇	70.02 ± 1.8 •	62.27 ± 1.1 ◇
18	67.48 ± 3.29	87.38 ± 2.9 •	79.33 ± 2.6 •	80.23 ± 1.6 •	72.86 ± 2.1 •
19	37.99 ± 1.31	53.53 ± 1.1 •	51.08 ± 1.4 •	54.80 ± 1.6 •	33.19 ± 0.8 ◇
20	26.79 ± 2.43	39.11 ± 2.0 •	54.20 ± 5.4 •	44.81 ± 1.4 •	31.72 ± 2.5 •
21	13.99 ± 2.66	35.91 ± 4.4 •	52.17 ± 8.4 •	38.57 ± 5.9 •	18.99 ± 2.6 •
22	12.66 ± 1.17	26.73 ± 0.6 •	12.50 ± 0.7	36.72 ± 0.9 •	10.49 ± 0.9 ◇
23	99.61 ± 1.59	103.04 ± 1.5 •	97.23 ± 1.2 ◇	105.98 ± 1.2 •	97.03 ± 1.1 ◇
24	73.97 ± 2.06	73.04 ± 2.3	74.16 ± 0.7	72.67 ± 1.7	76.95 ± 2.1 •
25	100.78 ± 1.07	103.90 ± 1.5 •	99.68 ± 1.7	102.69 ± 1.1 •	103.54 ± 1.9 •
26	70.36 ± 1.83	76.00 ± 2.0 •	70.54 ± 1.0	73.49 ± 1.4 •	74.51 ± 2.1 •
27	34.92 ± 0.54	42.44 ± 0.7 •	38.43 ± 0.9 •	42.62 ± 1.1 •	36.37 ± 0.6 •
28	80.99 ± 0.95	87.33 ± 1.1 •	80.48 ± 0.7	87.73 ± 1.2 •	86.22 ± 1.4 •
29	36.96 ± 1.10	61.00 ± 1.6 •	52.78 ± 1.1 •	45.14 ± 1.5 •	39.20 ± 1.9 •
30	165.09 ± 34.30	238.24 ± 71.7 •	281.85 ± 51.1 •	240.99 ± 47.0 •	200.17 ± 75.3
31	88.86 ± 1.22	93.11 ± 0.9 •	94.58 ± 1.6 •	90.07 ± 0.7 •	86.10 ± 0.9 ◇
32	86.47 ± 1.38	162.37 ± 12.9 •	84.55 ± 1.7 ◇	86.59 ± 2.3	84.47 ± 1.2 ◇

between the two averages. The t statistic for testing the null hypothesis that the two means are equal was then obtained. We conducted a two-tailed test with significance level $\alpha = 0.01$. If the null hypothesis is rejected and the network's testing error is smaller than that of an existing method, the neural network wins; otherwise it loses. Neural network wins are marked by bullets (•), while losses are marked by diamonds (◇). Cases with no significant difference in the average accuracy (i.e., ties) are left unmarked.

Table 4 summarizes the wins and losses of the various methods. NN outperforms NB and kNN regardless of the performance measure. When measured using the relative root mean squared errors, NN is as accurate as or more accu-

Table 3. Relative mean absolute error ± the standard deviation from five regression methods.

No.	NN	NB	LR	kNN	M5'
1	180.44 ± 53.81	249.71 ± 88.6	347.09 ± 130.1 •	225.52 ± 83.4	223.48 ± 100.3
2	36.15 ± 17.42	53.63 ± 9.0 •	67.27 ± 16.7 •	67.80 ± 9.4 •	36.19 ± 10.0
3	78.52 ± 9.43	80.87 ± 8.7	89.15 ± 10.2 •	74.09 ± 7.4	86.47 ± 11.6
4	58.03 ± 7.54	63.57 ± 5.6	58.61 ± 6.6	66.00 ± 6.0 •	53.67 ± 3.4
5	69.58 ± 9.49	98.86 ± 14.0 •	110.73 ± 13.0 •	85.76 ± 13.6 •	85.40 ± 12.4 •
6	102.86 ± 11.84	101.90 ± 7.9	93.51 ± 8.3	112.10 ± 10.6	93.51 ± 8.3
7	92.82 ± 7.19	96.65 ± 12.3	92.83 ± 11.1	95.17 ± 14.1	104.61 ± 24.1
8	51.21 ± 4.86	61.15 ± 4.5 •	70.66 ± 5.8 •	65.08 ± 4.1 •	59.98 ± 4.2 •
9	86.82 ± 4.22	89.96 ± 3.3	83.27 ± 2.5	88.83 ± 2.5	84.50 ± 2.4
10	39.31 ± 2.42	49.60 ± 2.5 •	39.18 ± 2.4	68.10 ± 2.7 •	38.84 ± 2.2
11	104.97 ± 3.47	122.10 ± 4.4 •	105.39 ± 3.4	122.67 ± 4.1 •	105.90 ± 3.2
12	70.93 ± 3.96	75.04 ± 2.7 •	72.27 ± 2.1	68.97 ± 2.5	66.54 ± 2.3 ◇
13	89.34 ± 5.43	82.56 ± 3.7 ◇	99.02 ± 6.4	101.56 ± 6.5 •	93.13 ± 6.1
14	11.38 ± 0.60	23.28 ± 1.2 •	30.05 ± 2.6 •	21.31 ± 1.6 •	15.31 ± 0.6 •
15	39.54 ± 3.05	40.50 ± 2.4	46.04 ± 3.2 •	38.56 ± 2.2	34.30 ± 2.5 ◇
16	26.27 ± 3.40	55.77 ± 1.6 •	66.42 ± 8.2 •	53.40 ± 4.7 •	30.23 ± 1.6 •
17	66.15 ± 3.35	63.40 ± 1.4	65.31 ± 2.3	65.61 ± 1.7	63.88 ± 1.4
18	65.17 ± 2.73	80.05 ± 2.2 •	78.20 ± 2.6 •	74.76 ± 1.6 •	71.88 ± 2.2 •
19	37.72 ± 1.08	52.35 ± 0.9 •	52.38 ± 1.4	53.11 ± 1.4 •	34.03 ± 1.0 ◇
20	21.61 ± 1.64	29.37 ± 1.4 •	50.71 ± 6.2 •	29.53 ± 1.3 •	26.87 ± 1.6 •
21	10.25 ± 1.46	31.29 ± 3.0 •	56.63 ± 7.4 •	27.22 ± 2.5 •	17.34 ± 1.7 •
22	7.89 ± 0.46	21.92 ± 0.3 •	7.74 ± 0.1	34.95 ± 1.0 •	5.51 ± 0.1 ◇
23	100.17 ± 1.75	104.88 ± 1.2 •	99.61 ± 1.8	106.57 ± 1.6 •	100.13 ± 1.8
24	55.36 ± 3.09	39.81 ± 1.0 ◇	93.72 ± 3.2 •	49.22 ± 2.9 ◇	57.72 ± 3.2
25	99.92 ± 1.24	101.91 ± 0.9 •	101.83 ± 2.2 •	102.37 ± 1.4 •	105.57 ± 2.3 •
26	59.77 ± 1.47	59.37 ± 1.7	66.21 ± 1.1 •	62.91 ± 1.6 •	64.89 ± 1.2 •
27	30.89 ± 0.64	37.55 ± 0.6 •	35.64 ± 0.9 •	36.82 ± 0.8 •	32.07 ± 0.7 •
28	78.48 ± 0.92	81.55 ± 1.4 •	80.88 ± 1.1 •	86.22 ± 1.5 •	83.66 ± 1.3 •
29	34.94 ± 0.92	56.74 ± 0.7 •	51.76 ± 0.5 •	40.76 ± 1.0 •	36.43 ± 1.2 •
30	120.96 ± 19.12	134.28 ± 23.0	236.82 ± 35.2 •	163.12 ± 21.4 •	119.84 ± 20.4
31	89.64 ± 1.30	94.02 ± 1.0 •	96.25 ± 1.5 •	91.21 ± 0.8 •	88.24 ± 1.1 ◇
32	71.52 ± 1.49	93.63 ± 2.9 •	75.46 ± 1.6 •	68.42 ± 1.0 ◇	70.83 ± 1.5

rate than NB and kNN for all the problems tested. NN is more accurate than LR on 13 data sets and is less accurate on 8 data sets. NN's performance is comparable to that M5', winning and losing in about the same number of problems.

In terms of the relative mean absolute prediction errors, NN clearly outperforms the statistical methods in most of the problems tested. NN predictions are more accurate than those of NB, LR and kNN on 2 out of 3 problems tested. Only on 2 problems are the predictions of the neural networks significantly worse than those of NB and kNN. For all problems, the relative mean absolute errors of the neural networks are as good as or better than those of linear regression. Compared to M5', neural networks are more accurate on 12 problems and less ac-

Table 4. Summary of the results from neural networks compared to those from other methods.

NN versus	Relative RMSE			Relative MAE		
	Wins (•)	Ties	Losses (◇)	Wins (•)	Ties	Losses (◇)
Naive Bayes	22	10	0	20	10	2
LR	13	11	8	22	10	0
kNN-RMSE/MAE	24	8	0	22	8	2
M5$'$	12	7	13	12	15	5

curate only on 5 problems. For the remaining 15 problems, there is no significant difference in the performance of the two methods.

4 Conclusion and Future Work

A simple method for removing redundant hidden units and irrelevant input units from feedforward neural networks has been presented. We have shown the effectiveness of the proposed method on 32 publicly available data sets. With respect to the relative root mean squared errors, NN predicts as well as or better than Naive Bayes and k-nearest-neighbors on all the problems. Its performance is comparable to those of linear regression and M5$'$. Using the relative mean absolute error as the performance measure, NN outperforms all four regression methods.

Acknowledgments

This work was done while the first author was spending his sabbatical leave at the Computational Intelligence Lab, University of Louisville, Kentucky. He is grateful to Professor J. M. Zurada for providing him with office space and computing facilities.

References

1. Ash, T. (1989) Dynamic node creation in backpropagation networks. *Connection Science*, 1 (4), 365-375.
2. Belue, L.M. and Bauer, Jr. K.W. (1995) Determining input features for multilayer perceptrons. *Neurocomputing*, 7 (2) 111-121.
3. Cybenko, G. (1989) Approximation by superpositions of a sigmoidal function. *Mathematics of Control, Signals, and Systems*, 2, 303-314.
4. Dennis Jr. J.E. and Schnabel, R.E. (1983) Numerical methods for unconstrained optimization and nonlinear equations. Englewood Cliffs, New Jersey: Prentice Halls.
5. Frank, E., Trigg, L., Holmes, G. and Witten, I.H. (1998) Native Bayes for regression. Working Paper 98/15, Dept. of Computer Science, University of Waikato, New Zealand.

6. Gelenbe, E., Mao, Z.-H., Li. Y.-D. (1999) Function approximation with spike random networks. *IEEE Trans. on Neural Networks*, 10 (1), 3-9.
7. Hornik, K. (1991) Approximation capabilities of multilayer feedforward networks. *Neural Networks*, 4, 251-257.
8. Kwok, T.Y. and Yeung, D.Y. (1997) Constructive algorithms for structure learning in feedforward neural *IEEE Trans. on Neural Networks*, 8 (3),630-645, May 1997.
9. Kwok, T.Y. and Yeung, D.Y. (1997) Objective functions for training new hidden units in constructive neural networks. *IEEE Trans. on Neural Networks*, 8 (5) 1131-1148.
10. Mak, B. and Blanning, R.W. (1998) An empirical measure of element contribution in neural networks. *IEEE Trans. on Systems, Man, and Cybernetics - Part C*, 28 (4) 561-564.
11. Mozer, M.C. and Smolensky, P. (1989) Using relevance to reduce network size automatically. *Connection Science*, 1 (1), 3-16.
12. Quinlan, R. (1992) Learning with continuous classes. In *Proc. of the Australian Joint Conference on Artificial Intelligence*, 343-348, Singapore.
13. Steppe, J.M. and Bauer, Jr. K.W. (1996) Improved feature screening in feedforward neural networks. *Neurocomputing*, 13 (1) 47-58.
14. Setiono, R. and Hui, L.C.K. (1995) Use of a quasi-Newton method in a feedforward neural network construction algorithm. *IEEE Trans. on Neural Networks*, 6 (1), 273-277.
15. Setiono, R. and Liu, H. (1997) Neural network feature selector. *IEEE Trans. on Neural Networks*, 8 (3), 654-662.
16. Zurada, J.M., Malinowski A. and Usui, S. (1997) Perturbation method for deleting redundant inputs of perceptron networks. *Neurocomputing*, 14 (2) 177-193.
17. Wang, Y. and Witten, I.H. (1997) Induction of model trees for predicting continuous classes. In *Proc. of the Poster Papers of the European Conference on Machine Learning*. Prague: University of Economics, Faculty of Informatics and Statistics.
18. Yoon, Y., Guimaraes, T. and Swales, G. (1994) Integrating artificial neural networks with rule-based expert systems. *Decision Support Systems*, 11, 497-507.

Optimal Design of Neural Nets Using Hybrid Algorithms

Ajith Abraham and Baikunth Nath

Gippsland School of Computing & Information Technology
Monash University, Churchill 3842, Australia
Ajith.Abraham, Baikunth.Nath@infotech.monash.edu.au

Abstract. Selection of the topology of a network and correct parameters for the learning algorithm is a tedious task for designing an optimal Artificial Neural Network (ANN), which is smaller, faster and with a better generalization performance. Genetic algorithm (GA) is an adaptive search technique based on the principles and mechanisms of natural selection and survival of the fittest from natural evolution. Simulated annealing (SA) is a global optimization algorithm that can process cost functions possessing quite arbitrary degrees of nonlinearities, discontinuities and stochasticity but statistically assuring a optimal solution. In this paper we explain how a hybrid algorithm integrating the desirable aspects of GA and SA can be applied for the optimal design of an ANN. This paper is more concerned with the understanding of current theoretical developments of Evolutionary Artificial Neural Networks (EANNs) using GAs and other heuristic procedures and how the proposed hybrid and other heuristic procedures can be combined to produce an optimal ANN.

1 Introduction

Many of the conventional ANNs now being designed are statistically quite accurate but they still leave a bad taste with users who expect computers to solve their problems accurately. The important drawback is that the designer has to specify the number of neurons, their distribution over several layers and interconnection between them. The interest in evolutionary search procedures for designing ANN architecture has been growing in recent years as they can evolve towards the optimal architecture without outside interference, thus eliminating the tedious trial and error work of manually finding an optimal network [1]. Genetic Algorithms and Simulated Annealing which are the most general purpose optimization procedures are increasingly being applied independently to a diverse spectrum of problem areas. Relative performance of GA and SA have been primarily confined to empirical evaluations on test problems and previous works have clearly shown that both these techniques have got their own merits on different classes of problems. For a long time theoretical investigators of SA and GA have focused on developing a hybrid algorithm that employs the desirable properties and performance of both GA and SA [2]. In certain situations GA outperformed SA and vice versa. GA is not designed to be ergodic and cover the space in a maximally efficient way. But the prime benefit of GAs is the parallalization capability. In contrast SA is largely sequential in moving from one optimal value to the next. States must be sampled sequentially, for acceptability and to permit identification of current local minima about which new test parameters are chosen.

2 Genetic Algorithm (GA)

GAs are adaptive methods, which may be used to solve optimization problems, based on the genetic processes of biological organisms. Over many generations, natural populations evolve according to the principles of natural selection and "Survival of the Fittest", first clearly stated by Charles Darwin in "The Origin of Species". By mimicking this process, GAs are able to "evolve" solutions to real world problems, if they have been suitably encoded. The procedure may be written as the difference equation:

$$x[t+1] = s(v(x[t])) \qquad (1)$$

$x[t]$ is the population at time t under a representation x, v is a random variation operator, and s is the selection operator.

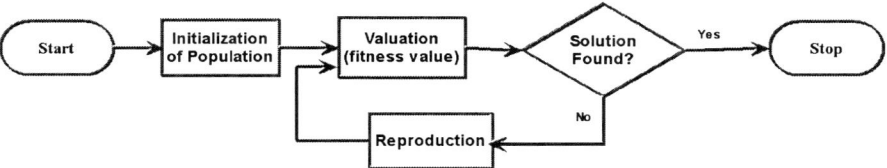

Fig. 1. Flowchart of GA iteration

GAs deal with parameters of finite length, which are coded using a finite alphabet, rather than directly manipulating the parameters themselves [20]. This means that the search is unconstrained neither by the continuity of the function under investigation, nor the existence of a derivative function. Figure 1 illustrates the functional block diagram of a GA. It is assumed that a potential solution to a problem may be represented as a set of parameters. These parameters (known as genes) are joined together to form a string of values (known as a chromosome). The particular values the genes can take are called its alleles. The position of the gene in the chromosome is its locus. Encoding issues deal with representing a solution in a chromosome and unfortunately, no one technique works best for all problems. A fitness function must be devised for each problem to be solved. Given a particular chromosome, the fitness function returns a single numerical fitness or figure of merit, which determines the ability of the individual that the chromosome represents. Reproduction is another critical attribute of GAs where two individuals selected from the population are allowed to produce offspring, which comprise the next generation. Having selected two parents, their chromosomes are recombined using the mechanisms of crossover and mutation.

Traditional view is that crossover is the more important of the two mechanisms for rapidly exploring a search space. Mutation provides a small amount of random search, and helps ensure that no point in the search space has a zero probability of being examined. If the GA has been correctly implemented, the population should evolve over successive generations so that the fitness of the best and the average individual in each generation moves towards the global optimum. Selection is the conservation of the fittest individuals for the next generation and is based on 3 parts. The first part involves determination of the individual's fitness by the fitness function. The second part involves converting the fitness function into an expected value followed by the last part where the expected value is then converted to a discrete number of offspring. To avoid premature convergence of GAs due to interference from mutation and genetic drift, sharing and crowding may be used to decrease the amount of duplicate schemata in the population. Elitism may be incorporated to keep the most superior individuals (and superior schemata) within the population. Parallel genetic algorithms use the convergence of its sub-populations to superior schemata(s) of low order and, then, propagation of individuals between sub-populations to achieve global optimization.

3   Simulated Annealing (SA)

SA exploits an analogy between the way in which a metal cools and freezes into a minimum energy crystalline structure (the annealing process) and the search for a minimum in a more general system. The algorithm can converge to global optimum theoretically, but usually finds a near optimum in practice. SA's major advantage over other methods is its ability to avoid becoming trapped at local minima. Figure 2 shows a flowchart of SA iteration. The annealing schedule, i.e., the temperature-decreasing rate used in SA is an important factor, which affects SA's rate of convergence.

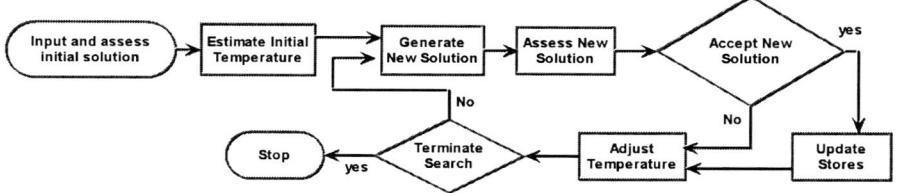

Fig. 2. Flow chart of SA iteration.

The algorithm employs a random search, which not only accepts changes that decrease objective function f, but also some changes that increase it. The latter are accepted with a probability $p = \exp\left(-\dfrac{\delta f}{T}\right)$, where δf is the increase in objective function, and f and T are control parameters. Several SAs have been developed with annealing schedule inversely linear in time (Fast SA), exponential function of time (Very Fast SA), etc. We explain an SA algorithm [5], which is exponentially faster than the Very Fast SA whose annealing schedule is given by $T(k) = \dfrac{T_0}{\exp(e^k)}$, where T_0 is the initial temperature, $T(k)$ is the temperature we wish to approach to zero for $k=1,2,......$

Representing the generation function of the simulated annealing algorithm as:

$$g_k(Z) = \prod_{i=1}^{D} g_k(z_i) = \prod_{i=1}^{D} \dfrac{1}{2(|z_i| + \dfrac{1}{\ln(1/T_i(k))})\ln(1 + \ln(1/T_i(k)))} \qquad (2)$$

where $T_i(k)$ is the temperature in dimension i at time k and D is the dimension of the state space.

The generation probability will be given by

$$G_k(Z) = \int_{-1}^{z_1}\int_{-1}^{z_2}.....\int_{-1}^{z_D} g_k(Z)dz_1 dz_2....dz_D = \prod_{i=1}^{D} G_{ki}(z_i) \qquad (3)$$

where $G_{ki}(z_i) = \dfrac{1}{2} + \dfrac{\text{sgn}(z_i)\ln(1 + |z_i|\ln(1/T_i(k)))}{2\ln(1 + \ln(1/T_i(k)))} \qquad (4)$

It is straightforward to prove that an annealing schedule for

$$T_i(k) = T_{0i}\exp(-\exp(b_i k^{1/D})) \qquad (5)$$

a global minimum (statistically) can be obtained. That is,

$$\sum_{k=k_o}^{\infty} g_k = \infty \qquad (6)$$

where $b_i > 0$ is a constant parameter and k_o is a sufficiently large constant to satisfy (6).

4 Genetic Annealing Algorithm (GAA)

Genetic annealing is a hybrid random searching technique fusing SA and GA methodologies into a more efficient algorithm. Such Hybrid algorithms can inherit the convergence property of simulated annealing and parallalization capability of GA. Each genotype is assigned an energy threshold, initially equal to the energy of the randomized bit string to which it is assigned. It is the genotype's threshold, not its energy that determines which trial mutations constitute acceptable improvements. If the energy of the mutant exceeds the threshold of the parent that spawned it, the mutant is rejected and a new genotype is considered. However if the energy of the new genotype is less than or equal to the energy of the parent, the mutant is accepted as a replacement for its progenitor. GAA uses an Energy Bank (EB) to keep track of the energy liberated by the successful mutants. Whenever a mutant passes the threshold test, the difference between the threshold and the mutant's energy is added to the EB for temporary storage. Once the quantum of energy is accounted, the threshold is reset so that it equals the energy of the accepted mutant and move on to next member of the population.

After each member has been subjected to a random mutation, the entire population is reheated by changing the threshold. The rate of reheating is directly proportional to the amount of energy accumulated in the EB (from each member of the population) as well as designer's choice of coolant rate (Section 3). Annealing results from repeated cycles of collecting energy from successful mutants and then redistributing nearly all of it by raising the threshold energy of each population member equally [14].

5   Back-Propagation (BP) Algorithm

BP is one of the most famous training algorithms for multilayer perceptrons [8]. Basically, BP is a gradient descent technique to minimize the error E for a particular training pattern. For adjusting the weight (w_{ij}) from the i-th input unit to the j-th output, in the batched mode variant the descent is based on the gradient ∇E ($\frac{\delta E}{\delta w_{ij}}$) for the total training set:

$$\Delta w_{ij}(n) = -\varepsilon^* \frac{\delta E}{\delta w_{ij}} + \alpha^* \Delta w_{ij}(n-1) \qquad (7)$$

The gradient gives the direction of error E. The parameters ε and α are the learning rate and momentum respectively. A good choice of both the parameters is required for training success and speed of the ANN. Empirical research has shown that the backpropagation algorithm used for training the ANN has the following problems:

- BP often gets trapped in a local minimum mainly because of the random initialization of weights.

- BP usually generalizes quite well to detect the global features of the input but after prolonged training the network will start to recognize individual input/output pair rather than settling for weights that generally describe the mapping for the whole training set.

Design of ANN by Global Optimization Algorithms (GOAs) is attractive because it can handle the above-mentioned problems more effectively. Moreover design using global search approach could be extended to a wide range of ANNs, not just feedforward ANNs.

6 A General Framework for Optimal Design of Neural Networks

An optimal design of an ANN can only be achieved by the adaptive evolution of connection weights, architecture and learning rules which progress on different time scales [1]. Figure 1 illustrates the general interaction mechanism with the architecture of the ANN evolving at the highest level on the slowest time scale.

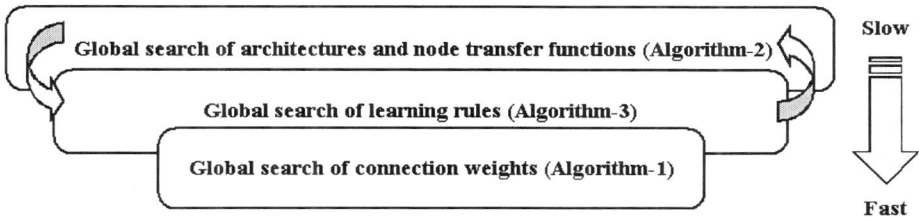

Fig. 3. Interaction of various search mechanisms in the design of optimal ANN

For every architecture, there is the evolution of learning rules that proceeds on a faster time scale in an environment decided by the architecture. For each learning rule, evolution of connection weights proceeds at a faster time scale in an environment decided by the problem, the learning rule and the architecture. Hierarchy of the architecture and learning rules rely on the prior knowledge. If there is more prior knowledge about the learning rules than the architecture then it is better to implement the learning rule at a higher level.

6.1 Hybrid Algorithm for Global Search of Connection Weights (*Algorithm 1*)

The shortcomings of the BP algorithm mentioned in Section 6 could be overcome if the training process is considered as a global search of connection weights towards an optimal set defined by the GA. Optimal connection weights can be formulated as a global search problem wherein the architecture and learning rules of the ANN are pre-defined and fixed during the evolution.

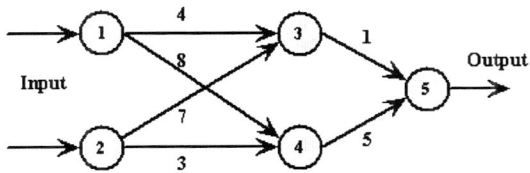

Genotype: 0100 1000 0111 0011 0001 0101

Figure 4. Genotype of binary representation of weights

Connection weights may be represented as binary strings of a certain length. The whole network is encoded by concatenation of all the connection weights of the network in the chromosome. A heuristic concerning the order of the concatenation is to put connection weights to the same node together. Fig 4 illustrates the binary representation of connection weights wherein each weight is represented by 4 bits.

Real numbers have been proposed to represent connection weights directly [10]. A representation of the ANN could be (4.0, 8.0, 7.0, 3.0, 1.0, 5.0). However proper genetic operators are to be chosen depending upon the representation used.

Global search of connection weights using the hybrid heuristic can be formulated as follows:

1) *Generate an initial population of N weight vectors and for i =1 to N, initialize the ith threshold, $T_h(i)$, with the energy of the ith configuration.*

2) *Begin the cooling loop*

   - *Energy bank (EB) is set to zero and for i = 1 to N randomly mutate the ith weight vector.*
   - *Compute the Energy (E) of the resulting mutant weight vector.*
     - *If $E > T_h(i)$, then the old configuration is restored.*
     - *If $E \leq T_h(i)$, then the energy difference $(T_h(i) - E)$ is incremented to the Energy Bank (EB) = EB+ $T_h(i)$ –E. Replace old configuration with the successful mutant*

   End cooling loop.

3) *Begin reheating loop.*

   - *Compute reheating increment $eb = \dfrac{EB * T_i(k)}{N}$, for i= 1 to N. ($T_i(k)$=cooling constant).*
   - *Add the computed increment to each threshold of the weight vector.*

   End reheating loop.

4) *Go to step 2 and continue the annealing and reheating process until an optimum weight vector is found (required min error is achieved).*

5) *Check whether the network has achieved the required error rate. If the required error rate is not achieved, skip steps 1 to 4, restore the weights and switch on to backpropagation algorithm for fine-tuning of the weights.*

6) *End*

While gradient based techniques are very much dependant on the initial setting of weights, the proposed algorithm can be considered generally much less sensitive to initial conditions. It is worthwhile to incorporate a gradient-based search (BP) during the final moments of the global search to enhance fine tune of local search and avoid the global search being trapped in some local minima [11].

6.2 Hybrid Algorithm for Global Search of Optimal Architecture (*Algorithm 2*)

Evolutionary architecture adaptation can be achieved by constructive and destructive algorithms. Constructive algorithms starting from a very simple architecture add complexity to the network until the entire network is able to learn the task [3-4, 9]. Destructive algorithms start with large architectures and remove nodes and interconnections until the ANN is no longer able to perform its task [15]. Then the last removal is undone. Figure 5 demonstrates how a typical neural network architecture could be directly encoded and how the genotype is represented.

We assume that the node transfer functions are fixed before the architecture is decided. For an optimal network, the required node transfer function (gaussian, sigmoidal, tangent et al) can be formulated as a global search problem, which runs at a faster time scale than the search for architectures.

From\To	1	2	3	4	5	Bias	Gene	Complete genotype
1	0	0	0	0	0	0	000000	000000000000110001110001001101
2	0	0	0	0	0	0	000000	
3	1	1	0	0	0	1	110001	
4	1	1	0	0	0	1	110001	
5	0	0	1	1	0	1	001101	

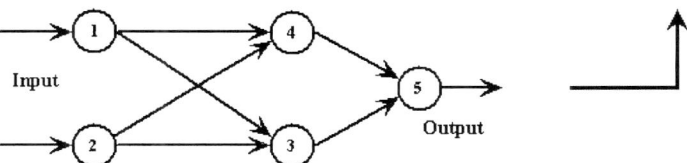

Fig. 5. Direct coding and genotype representation of neural network architecture

Scalability is often an issue when the direct coding (low level) scheme is used. The genotype string will be very large as the ANN size increases and thus increase the computation time of the evolution.

To minimize the size of the genotype string and improve scalability, when priori knowledge of the architecture is known it will be efficient to use some indirect coding (high level) schemes. For example, if two neighboring layers are fully connected then the architecture can be coded by simply using the number of layers and nodes. The blueprint representation is a popular indirect coding scheme where it assumes that architecture consists of various segments or areas. Each segment or area defines a set of neurons, their spatial arrangement and their efferent connectivity. Several high level coding schemes like graph generation system [13], Symbiotic Adaptive Neuro-Evolution (SANE) [12], Marker Based Genetic Coding [16], L-Systems [6], Cellular Encoding [17], Fractal Representation [18] and Evolutionary Network Optimizing System (ENZO) [7] are some of the rugged techniques.

Global search of transfer function and the connectivity of the ANN using the hybrid algorithm can be formulated as follows:

Generate an initial population of N architecture vectors and for $i =1$ to N, initialize the ith threshold, $T_h(i)$, with the energy of the ith configuration. Depending on the coding schemata used, each vector should represent the architecture and the node transfer function.

1) and 3) are same as in Algorithm 1. Replace weight vector by architecture vector

4) Go to step 2 and continue the annealing and reheating process until an optimum architecture vector is found.

5) End

6.3 Hybrid Algorithm for Global Search of Learning Rules (*Algorithm 3*)

For the neural network to be fully optimal the learning rules are to be adapted dynamically according to its architecture and the given problem. Deciding the learning rate and momentum can be considered as the first attempt of learning rules [19]. The basic learning rule can be generalized by the function [1]:

$$\Delta w(t) = \sum_{k=1}^{n} \sum_{i_1,i_2,\ldots,i_k=1}^{n} (\theta_{i_1,i_2,\ldots,i_k} \prod_{j=1}^{k} x_{ij}(t-1))$$

Where t is the time, Δw is the weight change, $x_1, x_2, \ldots x_n$ are local variables and the θ's are the real values coefficients which will be determined by the global search algorithm. In the above equation different values of θ's determine different learning rules. In deriving the above equation it is assumed that the same rule is applicable at every node of the network and the weight updating is only dependent on the input/output activations and the connection weights on a particular node.

Genotypes (θ's) can be encoded as real-valued coefficients and the global search for learning rules using the hybrid algorithm can be formulated as follows:

1) Generate an initial population of N θ vectors and for $i =1$ to N, initialize the ith threshold, $T_h(i)$, with the energy of the ith configuration.

2) and 3) are same as in Algorithm 1. Replace weight vector by θ vector.

4) Go to step 2 and continue the annealing and reheating process until an optimal θ vector is obtained.

5) End

It may be noted that a BP algorithm with an adaptive learning rate and momentum can be compared to a similar situation.

7 Conclusion

ANNs are no more a concept within the academic environment. It has become a part of the harsher world of users who simply want to get the tasks completed. Unfortunately, few applications tolerate the level of error produced mainly due to trial and error design of ANNs.

In this paper we have presented how the optimal design of an ANN could be achieved using a 3-tier global search process that is based on a meta-heuristic hybrid algorithm. When compared to the pure genetic evolutionary search, the proposed hybrid algorithm has a better convergence and moreover by incorporating other algorithms (BP for fine tuning of weights), optimality could be further ensured. However, the real success in modeling such systems will directly depend on the genotype representation of the connection weights, architecture and the learning rules. Depending on the priori information available about architecture and learning rules, the global search procedures are to be formulated accordingly.

GOAs attract considerable computational effort. Fortunately GAs work with a population of independent solutions, which makes it easy to distribute the computational load among several processors. As computers continue to deliver accelerated performance, global search of large ANNs become more easily feasible.

The authors are currently working on the implementation part of the proposed algorithm.

Acknowledgements

Authors wish to thank the three anonymous referees for their constructive comments that improved clarity of the paper.

References

1. Yao X.: *Evolving Artificial Neural Networks*, Proceedings of the IEEE, 87(9):1, 423-1447, (1999).
2. Hart W.E.: *A Theoretical Comparison of Evolutionary Algorithms and Simulated Annealing*, Proceedings of the Fifth Annual Conference on Evolutionary Programming. MIT press, (1996).
3. Frean M.: *The Upstart Algorithm: A Method for Constructing and Training Feed Forward Neural Networks*, Neural computations Volume 2, pp.198-209, (1990).
4. Mezard M., Nadal J.P.: *Learning in Feed Forward Layered Networks: The Tiling Algorithm*, Journal of Physics A, Vol 22, pp. 2191-2204, (1989).
5. Yao X.: *A New Simulated Annealing Algorithm*, International Journal of Computer Mathematics, 56:161-168, (1995).
6. Boers E.J.W., Kuiper H., Happel B.L.M., Sprinkhuizen-Kuyper I.G.: *Designing Modular Artificial Neural Networks,* In: H.A. Wijshoff (ed.); Proceedings of Computing Science in The Netherlands, pp. 87-96, (1993).

7. Gutjahr S., Ragg T.: *Automatic Determination of Optimal Network Topologies Based on Information Theory and Evolution,* IEEE Proceedings of the 23rd EUROMICRO Conference, (1997).

8. Schiffmann W., Joost M., Werner R.: *Comparison of Optimized Backpropagation Algorithms,* Proceedings. Of the European Symposium on Artificial Neural Networks, Brussels, pp. 97-104, (1993).

9. Mascioli F., Martinelli G.: *A Constructive Algorithm for Binary Neural Networks: The Oil Spot Algorithm,* IEEE Transaction on Neural Networks, 6(3), pp 794-797, (1995).

10. Porto V.W., Fogel D.B., Fogel L.J.: *Alternative Neural Network Training Methods,* IEEE Expert, volume 10, no.4, pp. 16-22, (1995).

11. Topchy A.P., Lebedko O.A.: *Neural Network Training by Means of Cooperative Evolutionary Search,* Nuclear Instruments & Methods In Physics Research, Section A: accelerators, Spectrometers, Detectors and Associated equipment, Volume 389, no. 1-2, pp. 240-241, (1997).

12. Polani D., Miikkulainen R.: *Fast Reinforcement Learning Through Eugenic Neuro-Evolution.* Technical Report AI99-277, Department of Computer Sciences, University of Texas at Austin, (1999).

13. Kitano H.: *Designing Neural Networks Using Genetic Algorithms with Graph Generation System,* Complex Systems, Volume 4, No.4, pp. 461-476, (1990).

14. Price K.V.: *Genetic Annealing,* Dr. Dobbs Journal, Vol.220, pp. 127-132, (1994).

15. Stepniewski S.W., Keane A.J.: *Pruning Back-propagation Neural Networks Using Modern Stochastic Optimization Techniques,* Neural Computing & Applications, Vol. 5, pp. 76-98, (1997).

16. Fullmer B., Miikkulainen R.: *Using Marker-Based Genetic Encoding of Neural Networks To Evolve Finite-State Behavior,* Proceedings of the First European Conference on Artificial Life, France), pp.255-262, (1992).

17. Gruau F.: *Genetic Synthesis of Modular Neural Networks,* In S Forrest (Ed.) Genetic Algorithms: Proceedings of the 5th International Conference, Morgan Kaufman, (1993).

18. Merril J.W.L., Port R.F.: *Fractally Configured Neural Networks,* Neural Networks, Vol 4, No.1, pp 53-60, (1991).

19. Kim H.B., Jung S.H., Kim T.G., Park K.H: *Fast Learning Method for Back-Propagation Neural Network by Evolutionary Adaptation of Learning Rates,* Neurocomputing, vol. 11, no.1, pp. 101-106, (1996).

20. Goldberg D.E.: *Genetic Algorithms in Search, Optimization and Machine Learning,* Addison-Wesley Publishing Company, Inc., (1989).

A POMDP Approximation Algorithm That Anticipates the Need to Observe

Valentina Bayer Zubek and Thomas Dietterich

Department of Computer Science, Oregon State University, Corvallis, OR 97331 USA
{bayer, tgd}@cs.orst.edu

Abstract. This paper introduces the *even-odd POMDP*, an approximation to POMDPs (Partially Observable Markov Decision Problems) in which the world is assumed to be fully observable every other time step. This approximation works well for problems with a *delayed need to observe*. The even-odd POMDP can be converted into an equivalent MDP, the 2MDP, whose value function, V^*_{2MDP}, can be combined online with a 2-step lookahead search to provide a good POMDP policy. We prove that this gives an approximation to the POMDP's optimal value function that is at least as good as methods based on the optimal value function of the underlying MDP. We present experimental evidence that the method finds a good policy for a POMDP with 10,000 states and observations.

1 Introduction

The Partially Observable Markov Decision Problem (POMDP) is a general model of a single agent interacting with a partially observable environment. POMDP applications include quality control, autonomous robots, weapon allocation and medical diagnosis. Consequently, solving POMDPs is a central goal of artificial intelligence. However, the great generality of the model means that no single method can be expected to solve all POMDPs effectively and efficiently. Indeed, the problem of finding optimal solutions for POMDPs is undecidable [9].

Researchers have explored three main approaches to POMDP approximation. Any POMDP can be converted into a Markov Decision Problem (MDP) in belief space (see below), and one approach is to approximate this belief space MDP via value function approximation, factored decomposition, discretization of the belief state, or a combination of these [8, 11, 12, 3]. The second approach is based on solving the underlying MDP (i.e., the same POMDP but with a fully-observable state). This approach computes the optimal value function V^*_{MDP} and then applies it online to construct approximately-optimal policies for the POMDP [4]. Our paper presents a new method related to this approach. The third approach attempts to directly construct a finite-state controller that implements a good POMDP policy [6, 10].

What makes POMDP's difficult? The fundamental problem is that the agent may become "lost"–that is, the agent may have a large amount of uncertainty about the current state of the environment. Consequently, the optimal policy may involve "avoiding getting lost" and also "acting when lost".

As an example of the need to avoid getting lost (avoiding states where actions become highly uncertain), consider a robot that has a choice of two different hallways to traverse. One hallway is completely dark and provides no visual landmarks. The other hallway is brightly-lit and has many visual landmarks. Even when the second hallway requires traveling a longer distance to reach the goal, it may still be the optimal choice, because the robot avoids getting lost in the dark hallway (and colliding with obstacles).

An example of the need to act when lost is the task of disease diagnosis. Given a patient's initial symptoms, a physician may be uncertain about the true state of the patient (i.e., the disease). The physician must have a policy for how to act (i.e., by performing tests and prescribing therapies) under this uncertainty.

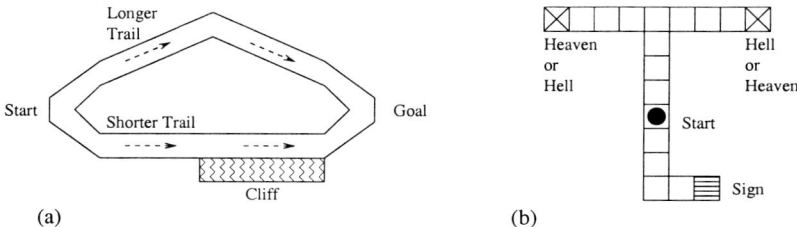

Fig. 1. POMDPs illustrating (a) delayed need to observe and (b) delayed opportunity to observe

Fortunately, in cases where the effects of actions are immediately apparent, both of these problems can be solved by performing a shallow lookahead search, evaluating the leaf nodes in this search tree using V^*_{MDP}, and backing-up these values to choose the best action to perform. For the robot, a shallow lookahead search reveals that the robot rapidly becomes uncertain of its position. The expected value of the resulting positions according to V^*_{MDP} is poor, so the robot prefers the well-lit hallway. In the medical diagnosis case, many successful diagnostic systems have been based on a one-step value-of-information (VOI) calculation [7]. The physician considers the expected utility of choosing a therapy immediately versus the expected utility of performing one test and then choosing the therapy after the test results are known. Greedy VOI often works extremely well, both for choosing the best test to perform and for deciding when to stop testing and recommend a therapy.

The most difficult POMDPs are those where the consequences of actions are not immediately apparent. Consider the "skier problem" in Figure 1(a). It involves a skiing robot that starts at a known location at the top of the mountain and must choose which trail to take. The upper trail is very safe—so safe that the robot can ski this route with its eyes closed, because the trail goes through a bowl-shape valley that naturally steers the robot down the center. The lower trail is initially just as safe as the upper one, but then it takes the skier along the side of a cliff. Here, the skiing robot must constantly observe its position to avoid falling off the cliff. Each time the robot uses its vision system, it consumes battery power, so the robot wants to minimize sensing. If this problem is solved while ignoring the costs of observation (i.e., computing V^*_{MDP}), the optimal policy will take the lower trail, because it is shorter. However, when the cost of observation is included, the upper policy is better. At the start state there is no apparent difference between the two paths, and a shallow lookahead search combined with V^*_{MDP} will choose the cliff trail. The key difficulty is that there is a *delayed need to observe* (or equivalently, a delayed risk of getting lost), and the shallow lookahead search cannot overcome this delay.

The problem in Figure 1(b), due to S. Thrun, is the "heaven and hell" domain, in which there are two terminal states, "heaven" and "hell", at the opposite ends of the top hallway. In the initial state, the robot knows its position, but it does not know which terminal state is heaven and which is hell, because the two possibilities are equally likely. There is one way of finding out this information: the robot can walk *down* the hallway, turn left, and read a sign that indicates where heaven is. So the optimal POMDP policy is to go down, read the sign, then go up and turn toward heaven. Now consider computing V^*_{MDP}. In the underlying MDP, there is no uncertainty about which terminal state is heaven, so the MDP optimal policy is to go up and turn appropriately. A shallow lookahead search using V^*_{MDP} will therefore go upwards and then turn arbitrarily either left or right. The difficulty here is that there is a *delayed opportunity to observe*.

Table 1. Taxonomy of difficult POMDPs

	Avoiding getting lost (need to observe)	Acting when lost (opportunity to observe)
Immediate	Two hallways	Disease diagnosis
Delayed	Skier	Heaven-hell

This paper presents a new approximate solution of POMDPs that works well when there is a delayed need to observe (lower left box, Table 1). The core idea is to define a new POMDP, the even-odd POMDP, in which the full state of the environment is observable at all times t where t is even. When t is odd, the environment returns the same information as in the original POMDP. Following an observation of Hansen [5], we show that the even-odd POMDP can be converted into an equivalent MDP (the 2MDP) with different actions and rewards. Let V^*_{2MDP} be the optimal value function for the 2MDP. Then we get an improved approximation to the optimal POMDP value function by performing a shallow lookahead search and evaluating the leaf states using V^*_{2MDP}.

The 2MDP will incorporate the costs of observation in cases where those costs become immediately apparent at some point in the future. For example, in the skier domain, as the skier approaches the cliff, it becomes immediately apparent (i.e., to a 2-step lookahead search) that there is a need to observe.

Hence, the V^*_{2MDP} will include those observations—but only at times when t is odd! As the 2MDP is solved, these underestimated observation costs will be propagated backwards along the temporal sequence so that in the starting state at the top of the mountain, the robot skier will be able to make the optimal decision to take the upper trail.

This paper is organized as follows. Section 2 introduces our notations. Section 3 introduces and theoretically justifies our approximation algorithm. Section 4 presents three experimental studies showing the strengths and weaknesses of the 2MDP approximation. Conclusions are presented in Section 5.

2 POMDP Notations

A POMDP is a tuple $\langle S, A, O, P_{tr}(S|S,A), P_{obs}(O|S,A), R(S|S,A), \gamma \rangle$ where S is the set of states in the world, A is the set of actions, $P_{tr}(s_{t+1}|s_t, a_t)$ is the probability of moving to state s_{t+1} at time $t+1$, after performing action a_t in state s_t at time t, $R(s_{t+1}|s_t, a_t)$ is the expected immediate reward for performing action a_t in s_t causing a transition to s_{t+1}, O is the set of observations, $P_{obs}(o_t|s_t, a_{t-1})$ is the probability of observing o_t in state s_t at time t, after executing a_{t-1}, and γ is the discount factor.

A Markov decision process (MDP) is a simplification of the POMDP where the agent can observe the true state s of the environment after each action. Any POMDP can be converted into a continuous-state MDP called the belief MDP. The states in this MDP, called belief states, are probability distributions b such that $b(s_t) = P(s_t|a_0, o_1, \ldots, a_{t-1}, o_t)$ is the agent's belief that the environment is in state s_t, given the entire action and observation history.

A policy π for an MDP is a mapping from states to actions. Hence, a policy for the belief MDP is a mapping from belief states to actions. The value function of a policy, $V^\pi(b) = E[\sum_{t=0}^{\infty} \gamma^t r_{t+1}]$, is the expected cumulative discounted reward of following policy π starting in belief state b. The optimal policy π^* maximizes $V^\pi(b)$ for all belief states. The value function of the optimal policy is denoted V^*. We will say that a belief state b is "pure" if $b(s) = 1$ for some state s, and instead of $V(b)$ we will write $V(s)$.

3 The Even-Odd Approximation

3.1 Even-Odd POMDP and Even MDP

Given a POMDP we can define a new POMDP, the even-odd POMDP, where everything is the same except that at even times t, the set of observations is the same as the set of states ($O = S$), and the observed state is the true underlying state ($P_{obs}(o|s,a) = 1$ iff $o = s$). Note that at even times, the belief state will be pure, but at odd times, the belief state may become "spread out." The optimal value function for the even-odd POMDP can be computed by converting it into an equivalent MDP, which we call the even MDP (abbreviated 2MDP).

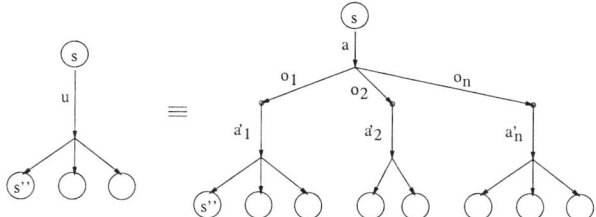

Fig. 2. 2MDP has actions of the form $\langle a, a'_1, a'_2, \ldots, a'_n \rangle$

The 2MDP is constructed as follows. The states are the same as the even-odd POMDP's (world) states. Each action u in the 2MDP (Figure 2) is a tuple $\langle a, a'_1, a'_2, \ldots, a'_n \rangle$, where $n = |O|$. We will write $u[0] = a$ and $u[o_i] = a'_i$. An action u is executed in state s by first performing $a = u[0]$ in the even-odd POMDP. The agent will move to state s' with probability $P_{tr}(s'|s, a)$, and an observation o will be received with probability $P_{obs}(o|s', a)$. The agent then executes action $a' = u[o]$, which will cause a transition to state s'' with probability $P_{tr}(s''|s', u[o])$. This is the fully observable result state in the 2MDP. The discount factor is γ^2. The probability transition function is $P_{tr}(s''|s, u) = \sum_{s'} P_{tr}(s'|s, u[0]) \cdot \sum_o P_{obs}(o|s', u[0]) \cdot P_{tr}(s''|s', u[o])$. The immediate reward of executing action u in state s is $R(s, u) = \sum_{s'} P_{tr}(s'|s, u[0]) \cdot [R(s'|s, u[0]) + \gamma \sum_o P_{obs}(o|s', u[0]) \cdot \sum_{s''} P_{tr}(s''|s', u[o]) \cdot R(s''|s', u[o])]$.

The "Bellman backup operator" for this 2MDP is

$$h_{2MDP} V(s) = \max_u \left(R(s, u) + \sum_{s''} P_{tr}(s''|s, u) \cdot \gamma^2 V(s'') \right) .$$

By expanding the definitions, this can be simplified to

$$h_{2MDP} V(s) = \max_a (R(s, a) + \sum_o \gamma \max_{a'} (\sum_{s'} P_{tr}(s'|s, a) \cdot P_{obs}(o|s', a) \cdot \sum_{s''} P_{tr}(s''|s', a') \cdot (R(s''|s', a') + \gamma V(s'')))) ,$$

where $R(s, a) = \sum_{s'} P_{tr}(s'|s, a) \cdot R(s'|s, a)$. Standard results tell us that h_{2MDP} is a max-norm contraction (under various conditions) and that it is monotonic (i.e., for any pair of value functions V_a and V_b, if for all s, $V_a(s) \leq V_b(s)$ then $h_{2MDP} V_a(s) \leq h_{2MDP} V_b(s)$). Furthermore, V^*_{2MDP} is the unique solution to the fixed-point equation $V = h_{2MDP} V$ [2].

3.2 Improved Approximation

Let V^*_{POMDP} be the optimal value function for the POMDP and V^*_{MDP} be the optimal value function for the underlying MDP. We show that V^*_{2MDP} is a better approximation to V^*_{POMDP} than is V^*_{MDP}. First we prove that $V^*_{2MDP}(s) \leq V^*_{MDP}(s)$ for all states s. This, of course, makes sense, because the MDP optimal value function has perfect information about all the states, while the 2MDP only has perfect information about every other state. Then we apply a similar argument to show that $V^*_{POMDP}(s) \leq V^*_{2MDP}(s)$ for all $s \in S$. This will show that on pure belief states, V^*_{2MDP} is a better approximation to V^*_{POMDP}.

Theorem 1. $V^*_{2MDP}(s) \leq V^*_{MDP}(s)$ for all $s \in S$.

Proof: We first show that $h_{2MDP}V^*_{MDP}(s) \leq V^*_{MDP}(s)$. Consider applying h_{2MDP} to V^*_{MDP}. If a^* is the action that achieves the maximum in $\max_a$, then
$$h_{2MDP}V^*_{MDP}(s) = R(s, a^*) + \sum_o \gamma \max_{a'} (\sum_{s'} P_{tr}(s'|s, a^*)P_{obs}(o|s', a^*) \cdot \sum_{s''} P_{tr}(s''|s', a')(R(s''|s', a') + \gamma V^*_{MDP}(s''))) \ .$$
By applying the inequality $\max_a \sum_s X(a, s) \leq \sum_s \max_a X(a, s)$ for a' and s', we can rewrite this as
$$h_{2MDP}V^*_{MDP}(s) \leq R(s, a^*) + \sum_o \gamma \sum_{s'} P_{tr}(s'|s, a^*)P_{obs}(o|s', a^*) \cdot \max_{a'} (\sum_{s''} P_{tr}(s''|s', a')(R(s''|s', a') + \gamma V^*_{MDP}(s''))) \ .$$
The last line is just the Bellman backup for the MDP, so it becomes $V^*_{MDP}(s')$:
$$h_{2MDP}V^*_{MDP}(s) \leq R(s, a^*) + \sum_o \gamma \sum_{s'} P_{tr}(s'|s, a^*)P_{obs}(o|s', a^*) \cdot V^*_{MDP}(s') \ .$$
$V^*_{MDP}(s')$ does not depend on o, so $\sum_o P_{obs}(o|s', a^*)$ becomes 1:
$$h_{2MDP}V^*_{MDP}(s) \leq R(s, a^*) + \sum_{s'} P_{tr}(s'|s, a^*)\gamma V^*_{MDP}(s') \ .$$
The right hand side is a Bellman backup for a particular action a^*, so it is less than or equal to $V^*_{MDP}(s)$, which would be obtained by backing up the best action for the MDP. Hence, we obtain $h_{2MDP}V^*_{MDP}(s) \leq V^*_{MDP}(s)$ for all s. Because h_{2MDP} is monotonic, the inequality is true when we apply h_{2MDP} to both sides: $h^2_{2MDP}V^*_{MDP}(s) \leq h_{2MDP}V^*_{MDP}(s)$. By induction, $h^k_{2MDP}V^*_{MDP}(s) \leq V^*_{MDP}(s)$ for all k. $\lim_{k \to \infty} h^k_{2MDP}V^*_{MDP} = V^*_{2MDP} \leq V^*_{MDP}$. **Q.E.D.**

Theorem 2. $V^*_{POMDP}(s) \leq V^*_{2MDP}(s)$ for all $s \in S$. (see [1] for proof.)

These two theorems establish that V^*_{2MDP} is a better approximation to V^*_{POMDP} than V^*_{MDP} on pure belief states. We extend this result to arbitrary belief states b by considering a 2-step lookahead process. Let $LA(n)$ be an operator defined such that "$LA(n)V(b)$" estimates the value of belief state b by performing an n-step lookahead search and evaluating the fully observable leaf states using V. For example, $LA(1)$ can be written
$$LA(1)V(b) = \max_a (\sum_s b(s) \sum_{s'} P_{tr}(s'|s, a)(R(s'|s, a) + \gamma V(s'))) \ .$$

Theorem 3. For all belief states b,
$$V^*_{POMDP}(b) \leq LA(2)V^*_{2MDP}(b) \leq LA(2)V^*_{MDP}(b) \leq LA(1)V^*_{MDP}(b) \ .$$
(see [1] for proof.)

Figure 3 depicts this relationship for a 2-state finite-horizon POMDP. All value functions are piecewise linear and convex.

3.3 Even MDP Approximation Algorithm

We can easily compute V^*_{2MDP} offline via value iteration. To generate a policy for the original POMDP, we maintain a belief state, and at each time t we perform a 2-step lookahead (evaluating the leaf states with V^*_{2MDP}), and choose the action with the best backed-up value. This policy is called the $LA(2)V^*_{2MDP}$ policy. If the leaf states are instead evaluated with V^*_{MDP}, we obtain the $LA(2)V^*_{MDP}$ policy.

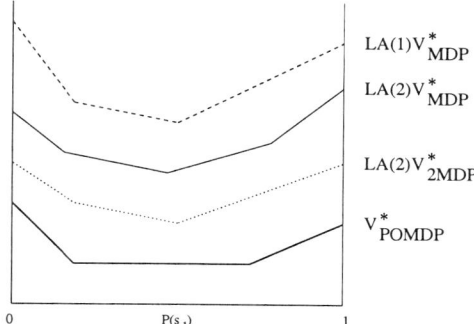

Fig. 3. Schematic diagram of the optimal POMDP value function and three approximations to it for a 2-state finite-horizon POMDP

4 Experimental Studies

4.1 Example with Delayed Need to Observe

In the first example (Figure 4, a), a skier is at the known start state on the left, and there are three trails leading down the mountain to circled absorbing states. The skier has four actions: SE, N, E, and EO. SE is only available in the start state, and it deterministically takes the agent to the start of Trail 3 (reward -1). N deterministically moves the agent north one square (reward -4). Bumping against a "wall" leaves the state unchanged. E normally moves east with probability 0.5 and southeast with probability 0.5. The reward of E is normally -1, but -100 if the skier goes over the cliff. E moves east with probability 1 in the start state and in all states where there is no choice. The SE, N and E actions provide no observation information. The EO (east, observe) action behaves like E and deterministically tells the skier's location (reward -2).

First consider what happens if Trail 2 is closed. In this case, the 2MDP approximation chooses the optimal policy. The $LA(1)V_{MDP}^*$ and $LA(2)V_{MDP}^*$ policies will take Trail 3, whereas the optimal POMDP policy and the $LA(2)V_{2MDP}^*$ policy will take Trail 1. The 2MDP value function, V_{2MDP}^*, detects 2.5 out of 4 observations needed along Trail 3, but this is enough to make it choose the optimal path. Interestingly, because of the lookahead search, none of the policies goes over the cliff. The $LA(1)V_{MDP}^*$ policy never chooses to observe. Instead it relies on the N action to move away from the cliff. The $LA(2)V_{MDP}^*$ policy will observe just as much on Trail 3 as the POMDP optimal policy and the $LA(2)V_{2MDP}^*$ policy would if they were to take Trail 3. This shows that 2-step VOI computations are enough to permit $LA(2)V_{MDP}^*$ to act sensibly in this case.

Now suppose we open Trail 2. In this case, the policies based on V_{MDP}^* still prefer Trail 3, and the optimal POMDP policy is still Trail 1. But the $LA(2)V_{2MDP}^*$ policy will choose Trail 2, because it detects too few of the necessary observations to prefer the optimal path (it only anticipates a need for 0.5 EO actions instead of the 2 EO actions that will actually be required). At run time, the policy does observe correctly.

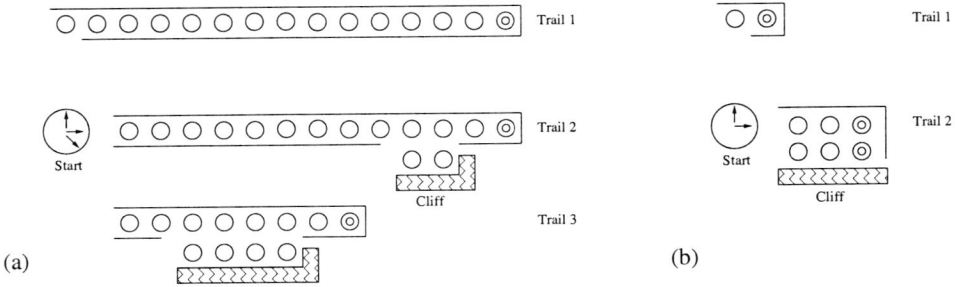

Fig. 4. (a) Three paths for skiing down a mountain. There is a delayed need to observe on Trails 2 and 3. (b) A second skier example

Because the even MDP only needs to observe every other time step, it underestimates the observation costs of both Trail 2 and Trail 3.

4.2 Example of Gradually Getting Lost

Figure 4 (b) shows a slightly different skiing problem. Here we have changed the dynamics so that the E action moves east with probability 0.9 and southeast with probability 0.1. The optimal POMDP policy is to take Trail 1, but all the approximations take Trail 2. The MDP approximations ($LA(1)V^*_{MDP}$ and $LA(2)V^*_{MDP}$) take Trail 2 for the same reasons as before: they cannot detect the need to observe. Unfortunately, the 2MDP approximation has the same problem: the probability 0.1 of moving southeast is not large enough to cause the 2MDP to choose an EO action during value iteration. So the 2MDP does not detect the need to observe. This illustrates a second weakness of the 2MDP approximation: the gradual accumulation of uncertainty. If uncertainty accumulates gradually, the 2MDP approximation will not detect the need to observe, and it will behave just like the MDP approximations. At execution time, the agent maintains a belief state, so it realizes when the uncertainty has accumulated, and it will choose to observe. So even in this case, it will usually avoid going over the cliff. The $LA(2)V^*_{MDP}$ and $LA(2)V^*_{2MDP}$ policies behave identically on this problem.

4.3 A Large Example

Figure 5 presents a large maze problem with delayed need to observe. The agent starts in the upper left corner of a 100 × 100 grid world, and it must reach an absorbing state in the lower right corner. Along the diagonal, there are several "hazard" states. Each time the agent enters a hazard state, it gets a reward of −1000, but the task does not terminate. There are 6 actions: E, S, SE, EO, SO, and SEO. The E, S, and SE actions do not return any observation information and have a reward of −1. The EO, SO, and SEO actions have the same dynamics as E, S, and SE, but they return the exact location of the agent as well, with a

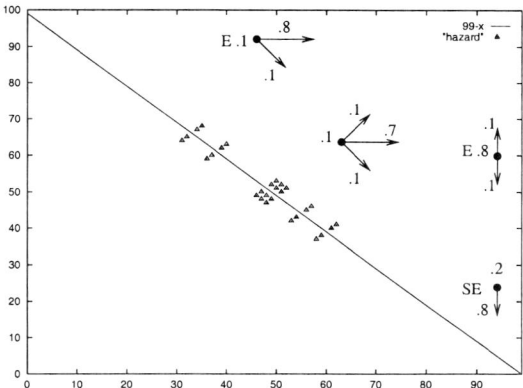

Fig. 5. POMDP with 10000 states, 10001 observations and 6 actions. Hazards are shown as triangles. The (.7,.1,.1,.1) transition probabilities of an action are shown schematically along with special cases for E and SE along the walls

reward of −10. We believe this problem is too large to be solved by any of the exact algorithms for POMDPs.

We implemented the $LA(2)V^*_{MDP}$ and $LA(2)V^*_{2MDP}$ approximations. Value iteration required 30s to compute V^*_{MDP} and 444s to compute V^*_{2MDP}. To test the resulting online policies, we ran both for 100 trials.

The MDP optimal policy follows the diagonal towards the goal—there is enough space between the hazards to ensure that in a fully-observable world, the agent can avoid hitting any hazards (with probability 1). When the $LA(2)V^*_{MDP}$ policy is executed online, it first performs a long series of SE actions (with no observation). This causes the belief state to spread out, and when the belief state starts to include some points near the hazards, it chooses to observe. It then exhibits two general behaviors. If it discovers that it is still near the diagonal, it continues to follow the diagonal, and it is forced to perform an average of 20 observations to avoid hitting the hazards. Otherwise, if it discovers that it has drifted away from the diagonal, then it follows a blind policy and goes "outside" the hazards. This actually leads to better performance, and online updating of V^*_{MDP} (e.g., linear Q-learning [8]) might yield improved performance in these cases. Over the 100 trials, the $LA(2)V^*_{MDP}$ policy never hit a hazard.

The even MDP determines that in states close to the hazards it is worth observing. V^*_{2MDP} includes these observation costs and propagates them back through the state space. Even if the true observation costs are underestimated, they are enough to make the 2MDP optimal policy go outside the hazards. When executed online, $LA(2)V^*_{2MDP}$ never performs any observations. It executes 30 SE steps, then it turns E for 15 steps, SE for 16 steps, then E, SE, E, SE, SE, E, followed by 40 SE actions, and finally it alternates single S actions with chains of SE actions. Over the 100 trials, this policy hit a hazard twice.

Figure 6 shows the steady state occupancy probabilities for the two policies. The MDP approximation stays primarily on the diagonal. The distributions

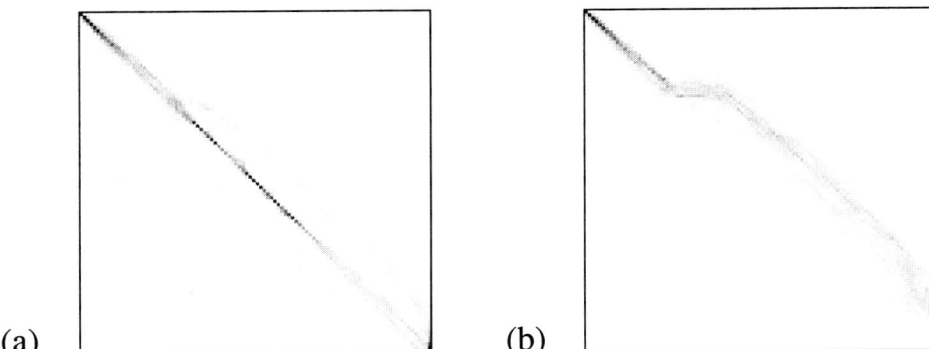

Fig. 6. Steady state occupation probabilities for (a) the MDP approximation $LA(2)V^*_{MDP}$ and (b) the 2MDP approximation $LA(2)V^*_{2MDP}$ over 100 trials

become concentrated near the hazards and near the start and end states. The 2MDP approximation follows the diagonal for a while and then moves E of it. The probabilities become concentrated along the east wall north of the terminal state as the agent relies on the walls to "funnel" it into the terminal state.

Table 2 summarizes the total cost (= −reward) per trial for the two methods. The MDP approximation's average cost was 239.52, whereas the 2MDP approximation's average cost was 160.34. The table reports a 95% bootstrap confidence interval, which shows that this difference is statistically significant. The $LA(2)V^*_{2MDP}$ policy correctly anticipated the need to observe along the diagonal, while $LA(2)V^*_{MDP}$ did not. The difference in performance is due to the extra cost of observing incurred by the $LA(2)V^*_{MDP}$ policy near the hazards.

Table 2. Cost (–reward) per trial, averaged over 100 trials

	min	max	mean	median	95%
MDP	136	398	239.52	271	[223,258.8]
2MDP	125	1136	160.34	140	[140.4,200.5]

How close does the 2MDP approximation come to the optimal POMDP policy? From Theorem 2, we know that $V^*_{2MDP}(s_0) \geq V^*_{POMDP}(s_0)$ is an upper bound on the value of the optimal policy, where s_0 is the start state. In terms of cost, this is a lower bound, and in this problem it is 131.38. Hence, we can infer that the cost of the optimal POMDP policy is between 131.38 and 160.34 (the average cost of the 2MDP approximation). This shows that the 2MDP approximation is a large improvement over the MDP approximation.

5 Conclusions

The even MDP approximation provides a partial solution to the problem of avoiding getting lost when there is a delayed need to observe. While solving the

2MDP, a 2-step lookahead search detects cases where there is an immediately obvious need to observe. Value iteration then propagates the associated observation costs backward through the state space so that earlier states can detect a delayed need to observe. This makes V^*_{2MDP} much more informed about future sensing in a POMDP framework than V^*_{MDP} is.

There are two limitations to the method which result in an underestimate of the true observation costs. First, if uncertainty accumulates gradually, the 2-step lookahead will not choose to observe, because the belief state after the first step will not be sufficiently diffused to make an observation worthwhile. One solution to this problem is to use a k-step lookahead, which will capture the costs of sensing that are apparent within k steps. But the computational cost of this solution grows exponentially with k.

The second limitation arises from the fact that the 2MDP only needs to observe at odd times t. This is because at the end of the 2-step lookahead the states are assumed to be fully observable, and this implies that the second actions $u[o]$ of the 2MDP will never be observation actions. We are exploring modifications to the 2MDP approximation that estimate observation costs at every step.

Despite these limitations, the 2MDP method performed well on the first skier example and on a large maze problem. In addition, the value function V^*_{2MDP} is an upper bound on the value of the optimal POMDP policy, which is useful for evaluating hand-derived policies.

Because the 2MDP method incorporates a 2-step value-of-information computation, it is also suitable for solving problems, such as medical diagnosis, where there is an immediate opportunity to observe, and the two hallways problem, where there is an immediate need to observe (see Table 1). However, the 2MDP method does not provide any solution to problems where there is a delayed opportunity to observe, such as the "heaven and hell" problem.

The 2MDP method can be applied to very large POMDPs because it only requires solving a Markov decision problem, and existing reinforcement learning algorithms can solve very large MDPs. This makes the 2MDP method the first scalable POMDP approximation that can anticipate the need to observe.

Acknowledgements

This research was supported by AFOSR F49620-9810375. We also thank Michael Littman and Tony Cassandra for helpful advice.

References

1. Bayer, V., Dietterich, T.: A POMDP Approximation Algorithm that Anticipates the Need to Observe. Technical Report 00-30-01, Oregon State University, Dept. of Computer Science (2000)
2. Bertsekas, D. P. ,Tsitsiklis, J. N.: Neuro-Dynamic Programming. Athena Sci. (1996)
3. Bonet, B., Geffner, H.: Planning with Incomplete Information as Heuristic Search in Belief Space. AIPS 2000. AAAI Press/MIT Press (2000) 52–61

4. Cassandra, A. R., Kaelbling, L.P., Kurien, J. A.: Acting under Uncertainty: Discrete Bayesian Models for Mobil-Robot Navigation. IROS-96. IEEE (1996)
5. Hansen, E. A.: Cost-Effective Sensing During Plan Execution. AAAI-94. AAAI Press/MIT Press (1994) 1029–1035
6. Hansen, E. A.: Solving POMDPs by Searching in Policy Space. UAI-14. Morgan Kaufmann (1998) 211–219
7. Howard, R. A.: Information Value Theory. IEEE Trans. Sys. Sci. and Cyber., Vol. SSC-2 (1966) 22–26
8. Littman, M. L., Cassandra, A. R., Kaelbling, L.P.: Learning Policies for Partially Observable Environments: Scaling Up. ICML-95. Morgan Kaufmann (1995) 362–370
9. Madani, O., Hanks, S., Condon, A.: On the Undecidability of Probabilistic Planning and Infinite-Horizon POMDPs. AAAI-99. AAAI Press/MIT Press (1999) 541–548
10. McCallum, R. A.: Instance-based Utile Distinctions for Reinforcement Learning with Hidden State. ICML-95. Morgan Kaufmann (1995) 387–396
11. Parr, R., Russell, S.: Approximating Optimal Policies for Partially Observable Stochastic Domains. IJCAI-95. Morgan Kaufmann (1995) 1088–1094
12. Rodríguez, A., Parr, R., Koller, D.: Reinforcement Learning Using Approximate Belief States. NIPS-12, MIT Press (2000)

Generating Hierarchical Structure in Reinforcement Learning from State Variables

Bernhard Hengst

School of Computer Science and Engineering
University of New South Wales, UNSW Sydney 2052 AUSTRALIA
bernhardh@cse.unsw.edu.au

Abstract. This paper presents the CQ algorithm which decomposes and solves a Markov Decision Process (MDP) by automatically generating a hierarchy of smaller MDPs using state variables. The CQ algorithm uses a heuristic which is applicable for problems that can be modelled by a set of state variables that conform to a special ordering, defined in this paper as a "nested Markov ordering". The benefits of this approach are: (1) the automatic generation of actions and termination conditions at all levels in the hierarchy, and (2) linear scaling with the number of variables under certain conditions. This approach draws heavily on Dietterich's MAXQ value function decomposition and Hauskrecht, Meuleau, Kaelbling, Dean, Boutilier's and others region based decomposition of MDPs. The CQ algorithm is described and its functionality illustrated using a four room example. Different solutions are generated with different numbers of hierarchical levels to solve Dietterich's taxi tasks.

1 Introduction

Reinforcement learning (RL) is known not to scale well as the number of state variables increases in the state description of a problem.

Many tasks tackled by agents involve repeatable sub-tasks. If a reinforcement learner could learn these sub-tasks separately and then invoke them at a higher level as a composite or abstract action, the learner could save itself the effort of relearning each sub-task for every situation in which it was required and help scale up RL problems.

An example will help to clarify the issue. Sutton, Precup and Singh [10] discuss a traveller journeying to a distant city who needs to decide whether to fly, drive or take a taxi. Each of these possible actions is a sub-task that requires still smaller steps for its execution. Calling a taxi may involve finding a telephone, dialling each digit, etc. Which city the traveller has in mind for the destination is generally not relevant for calling-a-taxi. In other words, the traveller must still find a telephone and dial the number, etc if the taxi action is chosen, no matter which destination city is in mind.

There are advantages in learning the calling-a-cab sub-task only once. A reinforcement learner that treats each city as a special case will relearn the calling-a-taxi sub-task for each city. By contrast a hierarchical learner need only learn the sub-task once and *reuse* it for each city.

Conceptually, this is much like a computer programmer calling the same subroutine many times throughout the main program, rather than repeating the same code over and over again throughout the program.

Several researchers have used a hierarchical approach in reinforcement learning to tackle related issues ([3],[4],[5],[6],[9],[10],[11]). More recently Dietterich [2] showed how some problems, decomposed by a MAXQ graph, benefit from sub-task reuse. Dietterich requires a designer to specify the hierarchical structure of the sub-tasks. For each sub-task, the designer is required to define (1) active and termination states, (2) allowable actions and (3) safe state abstractions, (4) pseudo-reward functions and (5) hierarchical credit assignment, to complete the specification of the hierarchical reinforcement learner. This process requires considerable effort and is error prone.

A hierarchical reinforcement learning algorithm called CQ will be presented which can, for a certain class of problems, *automatically* generate a hierarchy of sub-tasks. The designer is *only* required to provide an ordered set of state variables as discussed in section 5.

This paper will now introduce a simple four room example problem which will be used to help explain the operation of the CQ algorithm. The CQ algorithm will then be demonstrated with the taxi domain used by Dietterich [2] and results compared.

2 The Four Room Problem

Imagine a situation where a robot is started in one of three connected rooms and required to navigate to a fourth room. This example is similar to the one in Hauskrecht, et al. [4] and will be used here to help explain the operation of the CQ algorithm. The four room problem is shown diagrammatically in figure 1.

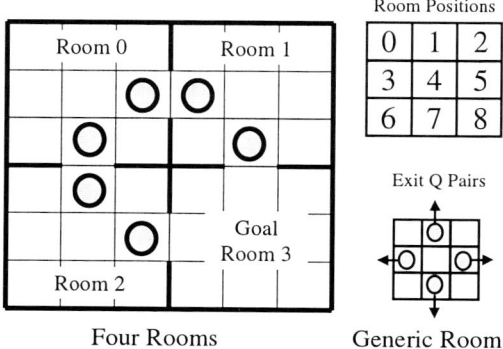

Fig. 1. Four Room Example

Each room is connected via a doorway to the adjacent room. The rooms are labelled 0,1,2 & 3. The nine internal room positions are labelled 0 to 8 as illustrated in figure 1. The robot is started at random in any position in any one of the rooms 0,1 or 2 and required to learn to move to the goal, which is room 3. The deterministic primitive actions available are moves one step in any of the compass directions. A reward of -1 is administered for each step the robot takes, except when entering the goal room 3, in which case the reward is 20.

The robot does not have a model of the rooms and must therefore learn by observing only its location and the reward after taking an action.

3 Reinforcement Learning

Reinforcement learning addresses situations, such as these, where an autonomous agent uses sensory information to learn to take appropriate actions in an environment in order to achieve its goal.

The reinforcement learning framework is usually modelled as a Markov Decision Process M: <S,A,P,R>, where: S is a set of finite states; A is a finite set of primitive actions; $P: S \times A \times S \rightarrow [0,1]$ is a probabilistic state transition function; and $R: S \times A \rightarrow \Re$ is a reward function. The agent's objective is to learn an action policy to maximise a measure of expected future reward.

In the four room example, the state is defined by the individual cells in the grid. There are 27 possible states in this problem, 3 rooms with 9 positions in each room. The state could be represented by one variable with 27 values.

This MDP is usually referred to as "flat" in comparison to one structured hierarchically.

4 Hierarchical Approach and Exit Q Pairs

Each of the rooms in the above example present a similar environment to the robot except that the doorways are located in different directions.

Nevertheless, if the reinforcement learner could learn the sub-tasks of exiting a room in any one of the four directions, this skill could be reused for each room and would not have to be re-learnt. For example, the skill of leaving room 0 to the east is the same as that required to leave room 2 to the east.

To achieve this, the problem is reformulated. The 27 states are partitioned into three regions. Each room becomes a region. The state is now defined by two state variables, instead of one with 27 values. The room number becomes one variable and the position in each room the second variable. Hence, the overall state is defined by the designer as $s = (s^0, s^1)$ where s^0 represents the room number and s^1 the location in each room. For example, the middle position in the top left room is (0,4).

In looking for reusable sub-tasks it can be seen that the skill required to navigate inside each room is not dependent on the room number. "Room Navigation" is therefore a good candidate for a reusable sub-task.

There is, however, one problem. The rooms differ in their doorway locations. It may seem that this would prevent reusable sub-tasks to be defined. The way around this difficulty is to identify all the potential ways to exit a room and model them explicitly. Exit information is extracted so that it can be used when navigating from room to room at a higher level and make the rest of the intra-room navigation common to all rooms. Internal room navigation can now be learnt as a common sub-task.

The exit conditions are identified by finding all potential boundary state/exit action pairs for a generic room. These are the states and actions in a generic room that can potentially lead the agent to leave that room. These boundary state/exit action pairs will be called *exit Q pairs* in this paper. The exit Q pairs for the generic room are shown in figure 1. The circles represent the boundary states for each of the rooms, the arrows the exit actions. The four exit Q pairs are: position1/move north; position 5/move east; position 7/move south; position 3/move west.

Four sub-MDPs are now created to learn the skill of leading the robot out of a generic room, one for each of the four exit Q pairs. This treatment differs from Hauskrecht et al. [4] in that, in this paper, similar regions (rooms) are treated as *generic* or *aliased*, considerably scaling down the state space.

These sub-MDPs have their state defined by just the position in a room. The room number is irrelevant because internally all rooms have similar reward and transition functions. The actions are the primitive actions and the reward and state transition functions at each step are those defined for the overall problem. The termination condition for each sub-MDP is defined by its associated exit Q pair.

To complete the hierarchical reformulation a higher level or abstract MDP is now defined, but this time using the room number as the state variable. The actions become the 4 sub-MDPs. These actions are called composite or abstract because they do not invoke primitive actions directly, but cause a more complex sequence of primitive actions to be performed as the sub-MDP executes its policy. A composite action works much like a subroutine in a program.

At the abstract level the reinforcement learner is therefore faced with the question of which composite action to use in which room. If the robot is in room 0 and explores the composite action represented by the sub-MDP with termination condition "position 1/move north", it will navigate successfully inside room 0 but hit the wall in the middle of the room on the north side while trying to exit the room. Eventually it will learn to take the composite action which leads it out of room 0 either to by the eastern or southern doorway.

The robot thus learns how to navigate at the higher room level to reach the goal by invoking composite "leaving room" actions.

5 Nested Markov Ordering of State Variables

If the state space of a larger MDP can be represented by two state variables it can be partitioned into regions by using the values of one of the variables to designate each region. In the four room example the room number is used to partition the state space into room regions.

For the following CQ algorithm to be applicable, a designer is required to specify the variable to use for the partitioning so that *all the regions have a similar reward and state transition function*. It is then possible to "navigate" within a region without reference to the value of the variable for that region. In other words the same action policy can be used inside each region knowing that similar state transition and

Generating Hierarchical Structure in Reinforcement Learning from State Variables

rewards will produce the same outcome. Regions are thus aliased and can be modelled generically.

This means that an ordering of the state variables is required (supplied by the designer) to exploit and define the reusable sub-tasks within the problem. The order of the two state variables specifies how the overall MDP is to be partitioned. In this paper, when the state is represented by $s = (s^0, s^1)$. The first variable, s^0, will be taken to be the variable whose value identifies the regions and s^1 will define the state inside a region.

This ordering of state variables will be referred to as nested Markov because all the regions are defined to have similar Markov properties internally (i.e. reward and state transition functions). s^1 is said to be nested within s^0. The higher level MDP associated with state variable s^0 will invoke composite actions made up of sub-MDPs associated with state variable s^1. An analogy is that the sub-MDPs are subroutines of the higher level MDP. They are *nested* in this sense.

This concept can be generalised to any number of levels by considering regions of regions, and so on. For example, if the four rooms were located in a building with multiple floors, where each floor had the same room layout, then a third variable could be introduced to represent the floor number. The floor number would now be chosen as the basis for the first partitioning. Next, the generic floor region is partitioned by the rooms. The overall state would be represented by an ordered Markov set of state variables $s = (s^0, s^1, s^2)$, where the variables are floor number, room number and room location respectively.

Given a nested Markov ordering of state variables, the CQ algorithm generates one hierarchical level per variable and attempts to solve the overall problem along the lines described in section 4 for the four room example.

Interestingly, any problem that can be modelled by n state variables with a nested Markov ordering can generate $2^{n-1}-1$ different hierarchical decompositions (excluding the flat formulation), simply by grouping and combining the variables into various ordered sets. Combining means making one variable out of several that are next to each other. For example the room and location variable can be combined into one variable with 27 values[1].

6 The CQ Algorithm

The CQ hierarchical reinforcement learning algorithm takes a nested Markov ordering of state variable as its input state and outputs primitive actions, as it learns a hierarchical policy. The current CQ algorithm proceeds through two phases, (1) hierarchy construction and (2) solving the total decomposed problem.

---

[1] States in the goal room need not be counted as the problem is restarted at random each time the robot enters the goal room.

6.1 Hierarchy Construction

A MDP with state $s = (s^0, s^1, \ldots, s^i, \ldots, s^n)$, where the state variables conform to the nested Markov ordering, will generate one hierarchical level per state variable. It is assumed that any grouping of original state variables has already taken place. The CQ algorithm iterates through all the state variables, starting with the inner most nested MDP corresponding to the variable s^n in s (level n) and concludes with variable s^1 (level 1). At the top level, 0, there is only one MDP to solve the overall task and hierarchy construction is not required.

The steps followed during construction at a level i are:

1. choose an action a at random at level i.
2. Execute(action a at level $i+1$). Note that action a is composite other than for level n and this function means execute the policy for MDP a at level $i+1$. The Execute function is outlined in the next section.
3. if any of the variables $s^0, s^1, \ldots, s^{i-1}$ has changed, add a new MDP at level i with termination condition (i.e. exit Q pair) a/value of s^i.
4. else update the CQ value function for all MDPs already created at level i.

These four steps are repeated for as many times it is estimated to take to discover all the exit Q pairs.

The CQ algorithm constructs sub-MDPs at each level by using the values of one state variable as the state space. At the lowest level it creates sub-MDPs which uses s" as the state space.

The algorithm executes a purely random exploration strategy searching for exit Q pairs that are recognised when any higher level variable changes value. Each of these exit Q pairs that can potentially create a region exit condition, generates a separate MDP with the exit Q pair as its termination condition. The number of MDPs generated at each level, therefore, depends on the number of exit Q pairs.

MDPs generated at one level become the available (composite) actions at the next level.

Having generated MDPs for all possible exit Q pairs at the lowest level n, the CQ algorithm repeats this procedure at the next level up, $n-1$, and so on. From now on only composite actions corresponding to the next level down MDPs are used in the random exploration of potential exit conditions for this level.

Learning the value function starts in the construction phase to save time during exploration at higher levels.

CQ employs off-policy [8] updating to learn the value functions for all the MDPs at a particular level simultaneously. This counterbalances, to some degree, the potentially large number of MDPs that may be generated. It should also be noted that solving MDPs during the construction phase will help substantially in speeding up the effort to learn the overall task in the next phase.

6.2 Solving the Hierarchical Problem

Once the hierarchy of MDPs has been constructed the MDP (there is only one) at level 0 is run to solve the overall task by simply calling Execute(MDP 0, level 0). The procedure to Execute MDP *m* at level *i* follows:

Execute(MDP *m* at level *i*)
1. if $i = n+1$ take primitive action *m* in the domain.
2. else repeat (until RETURN)
   - choose an action *a* according to the exploration policy for MDP *m* at level *i*.
   - Execute(*a* at level $i+1$) & observe state *s* and reward *r*.
   - if any of the variables $s^0, s^1, \ldots, s^{i-1}$ has changed or if MDP m has terminated, RETURN.
   - update CQ values for all MDPs at level *i*. Note that this update actually uses the number of steps taken by levels below to discount future value.

The CQ algorithm defines a CQ function along similar lines to Dietterich's [2] completion function but differs in one very important respect. The values stored to represent the value function are $CQ(i,m,s,a)$ and defined as the expected future reward at level *i* of executing the current MDP *m* after taking action *a* in state *s*, but *including* the *primitive reward* generated after completing the action. The inclusion of primitive reward automatically assigns credit hierarchically. The CQ algorithm is named after this function which is a type of hybrid completion and Q function. At the lowest level the CQ function is in fact the standard Q function, because the immediate reward for a primitive actions is included in the CQ value. The CQ function for an exit Q pair is zero.

In the four rooms, for example, after finding a hierarchical solution, the value of the middle position in room 0, that is s=(0,4), is 16. This is composed of a value of -1 representing the level-1 CQ value of position 4 for leaving the room either to the south our east and a level-0 CQ value of 17 for exiting from either boundary state. The CQ value of 17 represents a reward of -1 for exiting room 0, -2 for navigating to the entry of goal room 3 and 20 for entering room 3. (An episodic or undiscounted value function is used here)

7 Simple Taxi Task

Dietterich [2] used a simple taxi task to illustrate the MAXQ algorithm. The same example will be used here to demonstrate how the CQ algorithm generates hierarchical structure and then solves the overall task. The taxi domain description is reproduced here for the reader's convenience.

Figure 2 shows Dietterich's 5-by-5 grid in which a taxi can move in any one of the four compass directions at each step. The overall objective of the task is for the taxi to pick up a passenger from one of the four specially designated locations (Red, Green, Yellow or Blue) and drop the passenger off at one of these designated locations, at which point the task (or trial) terminates. The taxi starting position can be any one of the 25 grid locations.

The taxi starting position, passenger pick-up location and destination location are chosen at random for each trial. There are six deterministic primitive actions, namely, move north, move east, move south, move west, pick-up passenger and put-down passenger. Each action incurs a reward of -1. If the taxi moves into a wall at the boundary of the grid or at a barrier between the cells, its position remains the same, but it still receives a reward of -1. If it attempts a pick-up action anywhere other than with the passenger waiting at the pickup point or a put-down action without the passenger in the taxi and the taxi located at the destination point, it receives a reward of -10. If the taxi delivers the passenger successfully it receives a reward of 20 and this completes one trial.

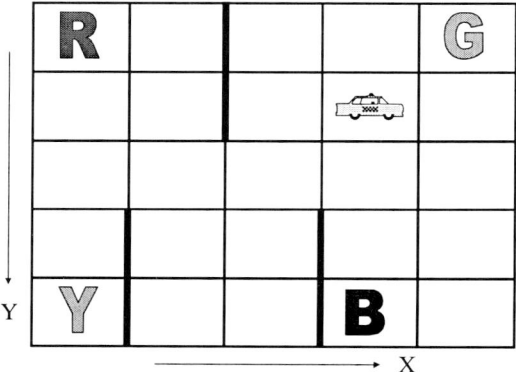

Fig. 2. The Taxi Domain

The state variables for this task are the co-ordinates of the taxi location in the grid, the location of the passenger and the location of the pickup point. The total number of states, |S|, is 500: 4 possible destinations, 5 possible passenger locations (4 for the designated locations and in the taxi itself), 5 for the x position and 5 for the y position.

8 CQ Hierarchical Decomposition

The 4 state variables can be arranged into a nested Markov order, namely: destination location, passenger location, x-grid position, y-grid position. The order of x and y is dictated by the fact that there are no barriers between cells moving north or south. The vertical regions, defined by x, have identical intra-region transition and reward functions. The four variables can generate $2^{4-1}-1 = 7$ different hierarchical decompositions by grouping and combining them as discussed. Three of these seven state representations were tried separately with the CQ algorithm and results compared to flat Q and MAXQ.

Three different state representations for the taxi task were:
Case 1: Two State Variables, S=(Destination & Passenger, XY Grid Position)
Case 2: Three state variables, S=(Destination, Passenger, XY Grid Position)
Case 3: Four state variables, S=(Destination, Passenger, X, Y)

In case 2, for example, the three variables generate a three level hierarchy, as shown in figure 3.

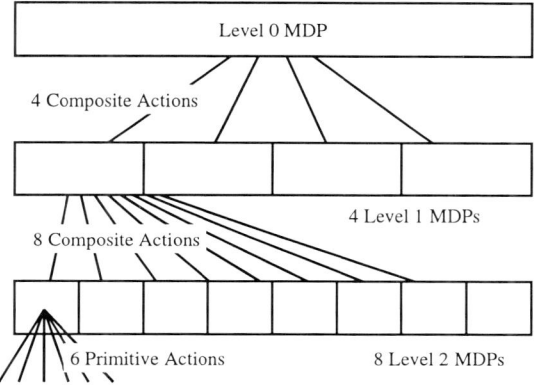

Fig. 3. Hierarchies of MDPs generated by the CQ algorithm for Case 2 in the simple taxi task

Eight exit Q pairs are generated by the CQ algorithm at the lowest level. These are the four specially designated locations together with a pick-up or put-down action. The middle level then uses these 8 composite actions to generate 4 possible exit Q pairs at this level. These are the boundary state where the passenger is in the taxi and the four composite actions that can navigate to a special location and perform a put-down action.

Results comparing the performance of the three different state value representations, MAXQ and flat learning are show in figure 4. In each case CQ learns in fewer trials than the flat Q reinforcement learner but not as well as MAXQ. Of course, handcrafting a MAXQ decomposition means that the designer has provided additional background knowledge which is not provided to CQ. For example, with MAXQ, the primitive actions to pick-up and put-down the passenger are not specified for the navigation task because the designer knows a priori they are not required. The CQ algorithm is not given this information and needs to learn this for itself.

CQ also solves the more complex "Fuel Taxi Problem" problem [2] with similar performance characteristics compared to MAXQ and flat Q reinforcement learning. In this problem the taxi uses 1 unit of fuel for each step taken and can decide to refuel at a filling station to complete its mission. If the taxi runs out of fuel it receives a reward of -20. An extra Fillup action is introduced which fills the fuel tank to 12 units of fuel at the filling station. The taxi is started with a random fuel level between 5 and 12. This problem is more complex with 7000 states and 7 actions.

Employing MAXQ requires the designer to assign credit hierarchically by decomposing the primitive reward function manually amongst the various sub-tasks. CQ's value function specification and nested Markov ordering of state variables ensures that credit is assigned automatically amongst the hierarchical levels.

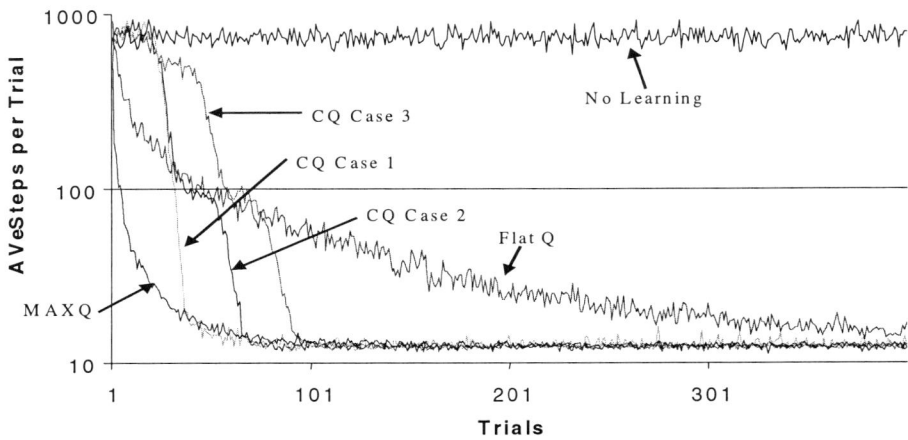

Fig. 4. Performance comparison between Flat RL, MAXQ and the three CQ Algorithm hierarchies for the simple taxi task

9 Limitations and Extensions

One limitation is the potentially large number of sub-task Markov decision problems that are generated, one for each exit Q pair of a region. In a stochastic situation or where there is a large interface between regions, this could become problematic. Further research will explore ways in which exit Q pairs can be grouped into common classes with only one sub-MPD for each class.

The application to continuous action and state spaces and to hidden state is left to further research.

A shortcoming of course is that the CQ algorithm cannot be said to *learn* the hierarchy, because a designer is still required to specify the special form of the state variables. Further research is intended to find ways of bridging the gap between an arbitrarily designated sensor and a nested Markov ordering of state variables.

10 Conclusion

For MDPs for which sub-tasks can be identified via a set of state variables, the CQ algorithm can solve the problem by automatically generating a set of sub-MDPs. The CQ algorithm does *not* require a designer to specify sub-task termination conditions, allowable actions, state abstractions, pseudo rewards or any hierarchical credit assignment.

References

1. Dean, T., Lin, S-H.: Decomposition Techniques for Planning in Stochastic Domains. (Technical Report CS-95-10). Department of Computer Science, Brown University, Providence, RI (1995)
2. Dietterich, T. G.: Hierarchical Reinforcement Learning with MAXQ Value Function Decomposition. Department of Computer Science, Oregon State University, Corvallis, OR (1999)
3. Digney, B. L.: Emergent Hierarchical Control Structures: Learning Reactive / Hierarchical Relationships in Reinforcement Environments. In: Maes, P., et al (eds.): From animals to animats 4: Proceedings of the fourth international conference on simulation of adaptive behaviour, MIT Press, Cambridge(MA) London (1996) 363-372
4. Hauskrecht, M., Meuleau, N., Kaelbling, L. P., Dean, T., Boutilier, C.: Hierarchical Solution of Markov Decision Processes using Macro-actions. (Technical Report). Department of Computer Science, Brown University, Providence, RI (1998)
5. Parr, R. E.: Hierarchical Control and Learning for Markov Decision Processes. Doctoral dissertation, Computer Science, University of California, Berkley (1998)
6. Parr, R, Russell, S.: Reinforcement Learning with Hierarchies of Machines, Advances in Neural Information Processing Systems 10. MIT Press (1998)
7. Singh S.: Reinforcement Learning with a Hierarchy of Abstract Models. Proceedings of the Tenth National Conference on Artificial Intelligence, Menlo Park: AAAI Press (1992)
8. Sutton, S., Barto, A. G.: Reinforcement Learning: An Introduction. MIT Press, Cambridge (1998)
9. Sutton, R. S., Singh, S., Precup, D., Ravindran, B.: Improved switching among temporally abstract actions. Advances in Neural Information Processing Systems 11 (Proceedings of the 1998 conference), MIT Press (1999) 1066-1072
10. Sutton, R. S., Precup, D., Singh, S.: Between MDPs and Semi-MDPs: Learning, Planning, and Representing Knowledge at Multiple Temporal Scales. (Technical Report) Department of Computer and Information Sciences, University of Massachusetts, Amherst, MA (1998)
11. Thrun, S., O'Sullivan, J.: Discovering Structure in Multiple Learning Tasks: The TC Algorithm. Proceedings of the Thirteenth International Conference on Machine Learning. Morgan Kaufmann, San Mateo (1996)
12. Thrun, S., Schwartz, A.: Finding Structure in Reinforcement Learning. Advances in Neural Information Processing Systems 7, Morgan Kaufmann, San Mateo (1995)

Humanoid Active Audition System Improved by the Cover Acoustics

Kazuhiro Nakadai[1] and Hiroshi G. Okuno[2] and Hiroaki Kitano[3]

[1] Kitano Symbiotic Systems Project ERATO, Japan Science and Technology Corp.
Mansion 31 Suite 6A, 6-31-15 Jingumae, Shibuya-ku, Tokyo 150-0001, Japan
Tel: +81-3-5468-1661, Fax: +81-3-5468-1664
[2] Department of Information Sciences, Science University of Tokyo
[3] Sony Computer Science Laboratories, Inc.

Abstract. Perception system for humanoid should be active, e.g., by moving its body or controlling parameters of sensors such as cameras or microphones, to perceive environments better. This paper focuses on active audition, whose main problem is to suppress internal sounds made by humanoid movements. Otherwise, such sounds would deteriorate the performance of auditory processing. Our 4-degree-of-freedom (DOF) humanoid, called *SIG*, has a cover to enclose internal sounds from the outside. *SIG* has a pair of left and right microphones to collect internal sounds and another pair to collect external sounds originating from the outside of *SIG*. A simple strategy of choosing a subband of external sounds if sounds from internal microphones in the same subband is weaker than those from external microphones sometimes fails in internal sound cancellation due to resonance within the cover. In this paper, we report the design of internal sound cancellation system to enhance external sounds. First, the acoustic characteristic of the humanoid cover is measured to make a model of each motor movement. Then, an adaptive filter is designed based on the model by taking movement commands into accounts. Experiments show that this cancellation system enhances external sounds and *SIG* can track and localize sound sources during its movement.

Keywords : robotics, cognitive modelling, active audition

1 Introduction

We have been studying humanoid to understand high-level perceptual functions and their multi-modal integration. We use an upper-torso humanoid called *SIG* as a platform of our research, because we believe that the integration of multi-modal sensory input and high degree-of-freedom (DOF) is essential for intelligence [10].

Recently active perception, i.e. the coupling of perception and behavior, has been studied using high DOF robots [3, 8, 9]. Most of such researches have been carried out as active vision [1]. Although it provides a framework for obtaining necessary information by controlling camera parameters, vision alone is not sufficient for some cases where occluded and/or out-of-sight objects exist.

On the other hand, in audition research, audition with behaviors, i.e. *active audition*, has not been studied yet even though people hear sounds while in motion. Indeed, some robotics researches notice the importance of auditory processing with motion, but they assume that the number of meaningful sound sources is at most 1 and the input sound is loud enough to ignore motor noises [19, 11]. These assumptions are too strong to understand high-level auditory functions. In addition, they also assume that auditory processing is done without motion. Therefore, active vision cannot be integrated with auditory processing.

As traditional auditory research attempts to understand psychological phenomenon such as the *cocktail party effect*[4], Computational Auditory Scene Analysis (CASA) studies a general framework of sound processing and understanding [4, 6, 16, 18]. Its goal is to understand an arbitrary sound mixture including speech, non-speech sounds, and music in various acoustic environment. However, most of these approaches still stay within the realm of audition research.

Therefore, active audition is expected to bring a major breakthrough One of main problems in active audition is to suppress internal sounds made by humanoid movements. Otherwise, such sounds would deteriorate the performance of auditory processing.

SIG is equipped with the cover to enclose internal sounds from the outside. However, a simple strategy of treating external sounds as internal noises if internal sounds are stronger than external sounds sometimes fails in internal sound cancellation due to resonance within the cover. Therefore, in this paper, internal noise cancellation system is designed by taking the acoustic characteristics of the cover into accounts.

The paper is organized as follows: Section 2 presents the active audition system. Section 3 presents acoustics of the humanoid cover. Section 4 proposes new sound source localization method by using acoustic measurements. Section 5 shows evaluation of our new localization method, and last two sections give discussion and conclusion.

2 Active Audition System

Fig. 1 shows the active audition system. The input of the system is assumed mixture sounds which come from different directional sound sources. The system consists of 5 modules; the humanoid *SIG* with 4 DOFs and 2 pairs of microphones, pre-processing, internal sound suppression, sound stream separation and motor control. The output is each separated sound source and tracking the specified sound source.

2.1 The Humanoid *SIG*

The mechanical structure of *SIG* is shown in Fig. 2(a). *SIG* has 4 DOFs of body driven by 4 DC motors, a pair of CCD cameras of Sony EVI-G20 as each eye, and

---
[4] A capability that people usually can separate sounds from the mixture and focus on a particular voice or sound even in a noisy environment.

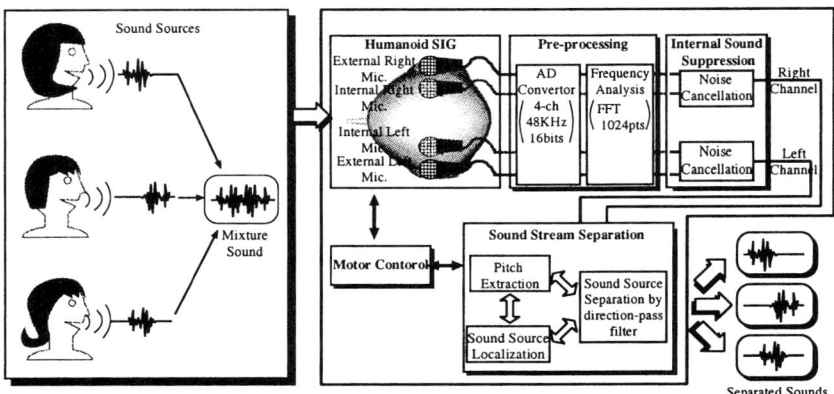

Fig. 1. Active Audition System

two pairs of omnidirectional microphones of Sony electret condenser microphone ECM-77S. Two pairs of microphones are used to separate the outer world from the inner world. One pair of microphones are installed at the ear position of the head to gather sounds from outer world. The other pair of microphones are installed very close to the corresponding microphones to gather sounds from inner world as shown in Fig. 2(b). And the cover is shown in Fig. 2(c). The cover not only separates the inner and outer world of *SIG* , but also has the beauty and functionality for humanoid exterior design [13].

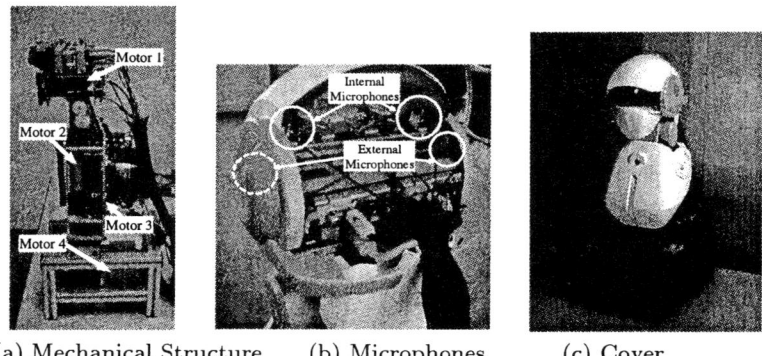

(a) Mechanical Structure   (b) Microphones   (c) Cover

Fig. 2. *SIG* the humanoid

2.2 Sound Pre-processing

The system carries out processing of AD conversion and frequency analysis against the input sounds in pre-processing module.

Sonorus AUDI/O is adopted as an AD converter in the system. It can process 48 KHz AD conversion of 4 channels (up to 8 channels) synchronously, i.e. mutual time differences between channels are kept. And it converts sampled 4-channel sound into ADAT[5] signal. ADAT signal is captured by Sonorus STUDI/O (PCI sound card) through a optical fiber. The card is installed in a PC which has a Pentium III 600MHz CPU and 512M byte memory.

Then, by each channel, frequency analysis transform captured digital sounds into sound spectrograms on the PC. Fast Fourier Transformation (FFT) for 1,024 points is used for frequency analysis.

2.3 Internal Sound Suppression

In this module, motor noises are cancelled by applying a kind of adaptive filter. Because burst noises among motor noises have worse influences on the system, the filter is designed to cut off mainly burst noises by comparing external sounds with the corresponding internal sounds on sound spectrograms. It uses *heuristics*, which orders that localization by sound or direction-pass filter ignore a subband if the following conditions hold:

1. The power of internal sounds is much stronger than that of external sounds.
2. Twenty adjacent subbands have strong power.
3. A motor command is being processed.

The output is two channel; right and left external sounds, which are cancelled burst noises using the corresponding internal sounds.

2.4 Sound Stream Separation

This module consists of three sub-modules; sound source localization, pitch extraction, and sound source separation by a direction-pass filter.

Sound Source Localization Direction information of sound sources is extracted using *auditory epipolar geometry* [12]. Epipolar geometry is a popular localization method for stereo vision [7]. *Auditory epipolar geometry* expands the epipolar geometry in vision to auditory field as shown in Fig 3. This method extracted direction information without using *Head Related Transfer Function (HRTF)*. It is useful to localize sound source without using $HRTF$ because $HRTF$ is easy to change even if surrounded environments are changed a little, in other words, $HRTF$ is hard to use for sound source localization in real environments.

It extracts peaks by using FFT for each subband, and calculates the *interaural phase difference (IPD)* as the difference between phases of right and left peaks. The bandwidth of each subband is 47Hz in our implementation. The sound source direction is estimated by Equation (1):

$$\cos\theta = \frac{v}{2\pi fb}\triangle\varphi \qquad (1)$$

---
[5] ADAT is a kind of digital format for multi-channel optical digital signals

where v is the velocity of sound, b is the distance (baseline) between left and right microphones, $\Delta\varphi$ is *IPD* and f is the frequency of sound. For the moment, the velocity of sound is fixed to 340m/sec and is invariant to the temperature and humidity. In *SIG* , the baselines for vision and audition are in parallel. Therefore, whenever sound source is localized by epipolar geometry in vision, it can be converted easily into the angle θ. This can apply to a method of integration visual and auditory information, and we reported the feasibility of such integration based on epipolar geometry [12].

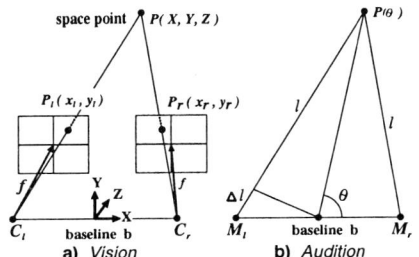 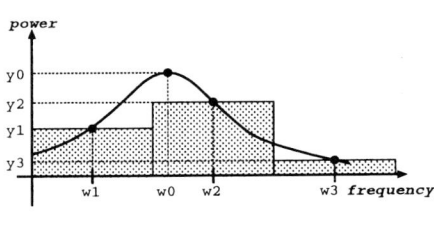

Fig. 3. Epipolar geometry for localization (C_l, C_r: camera center, M_l, M_r: microphone center)

Fig. 4. A spectral peak by Fourier Transformation

Pitch Extraction Pitches are extracted by a kind of spectral subtraction [2]. It uses peak approximation method based on characteristics of FFT and window function. Consider that the peak $[\omega_2, y_2]$ is detected, and the values of both neighbors are $[\omega_1, y_1]$ and $[\omega_3, y_3]$ as shown in Fig. 4. Then, the true peak $[\omega_0, y_0]$ is estimated as follows:

$$\omega_0 = \begin{cases} \omega_2 + \dfrac{2\pi\,(2|y_1| - |y_2|)}{T\,(|y_1| + |y_2|)} & (\omega_1 < \omega_0 \leq \omega_2) \\ \omega_2 - \dfrac{2\pi\,(-|y_2| + 2|y_3|)}{T\,(|y_2| + |y_3|)} & (\omega_2 < \omega_0 < \omega_3) \end{cases} \quad (2)$$

$$\begin{aligned} Arg(y_0) &= \tan^{-1}\left(\frac{\Im[y_0]}{\Re[y_0]}\right) \\ &= \tan^{-1}\left(\frac{\Im[y_2]}{\Re[y_2]}\right) + \frac{T}{2}(\omega_2 - \omega_0) \end{aligned} \quad (3)$$

$$|y_0| = \frac{\Delta\omega\,(-T^2\Delta\omega^2 + 4\pi^2)}{2\pi^2 \sin\frac{T}{2}\Delta\omega}\,|y_2|,$$
$$\Delta\omega = \omega_2 - \omega_0 \quad (4)$$

ω_0 is estimated as the following Equation (2). And the phase and amplitude of the true peak y_0 are estimated as Equations (3) and (4), respectively. $\Re[x]$ and $\Im[x]$ are the real and imaginary part of a complex number x.

Because the above equations require relatively the small number of calculation, our method can run faster and extract more accurate pitches. For example, in comparison with Bi-HBSS [17], which is known as a sound source separation system using a pitch extraction method by spectral subtraction, our method needs only 1/200 of amount of calculation per a peak [14].

Sound Source Separation by Direction-pass Filter The direction-pass filter selects subbands that satisfies the *IPD* of the specified direction. The detailed algorithm is describes as follows:

1. The specified direction θ is converted to $\Delta\varphi$ for each subband (47 Hz).
2. Extract peaks and calculate *IPD*, $\Delta\varphi'$.
3. If *IPD* satisfies the specified condition, namely, $\Delta\varphi' = \Delta\varphi$, then collect the subband.
4. Construct a wave consisting of collected subbands.

2.5 Problem in Active Audition System

The system, however, has a problem that noise cancellation can not be sufficient because the internal microphones can capture louder sounds originating from the outer world than the external microphones.

We considered that the problem was caused by resonance inside the cover. We needed to measure acoustics of the cover to confirm it and to improve noise cancellation. Acoustic measurement is described as the next section.

3 Acoustic Analysis of the Cover

The cover acoustics is measured in an anechoic room. The items of acoustic measurements are shown in the following.

1. Frequency response of each motor noise with both internal and external microphones (Figs. 5(a) and (b)). Each motor moves from $-45°$ to $45°$ ($0°$ is the center of *SIG*) at the constant velocity (14.9 degree/sec). The noises of each motor are captured three times, and the averages are calculated.
2. Intensity difference between internal and external microphones. Fig. 6(a) shows intensity difference of each motor noise. The conditions of motors are the same as 1. The graph is estimated by subtracting internal microphone's frequency response from external one. Fig. 6(b) shows intensity difference of the outer sounds. This is estimated by impulse responses. The impulse responses are measured at 12 points which are elements of a matrix of horizontal and vertical directions; horizontal directions (azimuths) are $0°$, $\pm 45°$, $\pm 90°$ and $180°$ from robot center and vertical directions (elevations) are $0°$ and $30°$.

From the figures, main observations are summarized as follows:

1. Motor noise is broadband and is captured less than 30 dB by internal microphones, is captured less than 20 dB by external ones as shown in Figs. 5(a) and (b).
2. Motor noise is captured louder by external microphones than by internal microphones for frequencies of more than 2.5 KHz as shown in Fig. 6(a). This shows that the cover makes it easier to capture motor noise by internal microphones, because sounds from outer world is cut off by the cover.

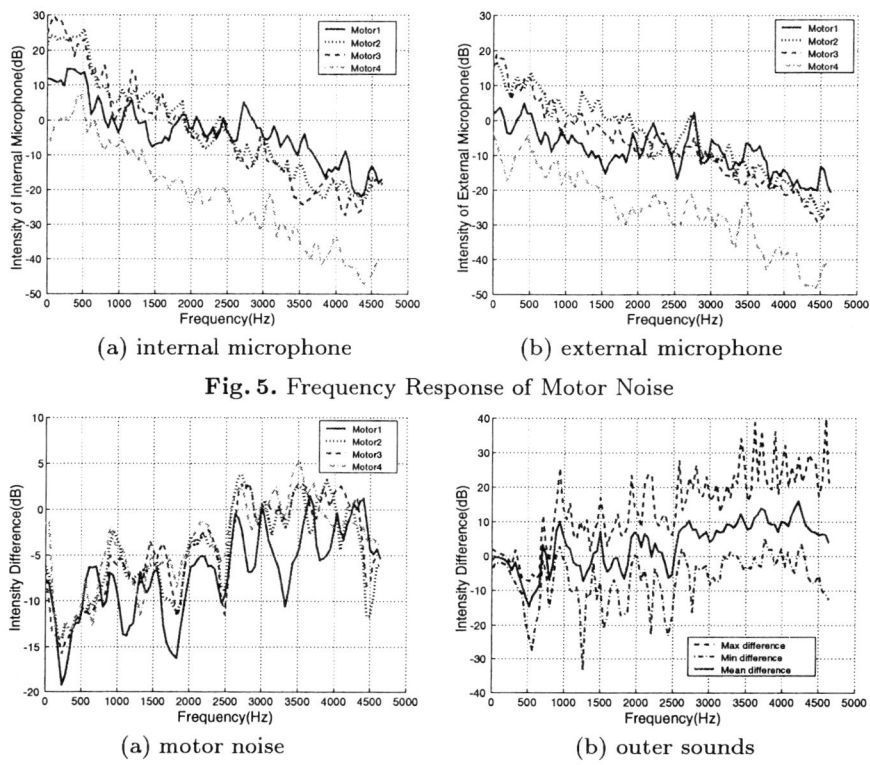

(a) internal microphone (b) external microphone

Fig. 5. Frequency Response of Motor Noise

(a) motor noise (b) outer sounds

Fig. 6. Intensity Difference

3. Acoustic signals are often captured louder by internal microphones than by external microphones for frequencies of less than 2 KHz. Especially, the tendency is more remarkable for frequencies of less than 700Hz as shown in Fig. 6(b). This shows resonance within the cover. The diameter of the cover is about 18 cm, which is corresponded to $\lambda/4$ at frequency of 500Hz. This causes resonance which has 500 Hz of center frequency. The similar resonance is occurred in Fig. 6(a).

4. Internal sound is captured about 10 dB louder than external sound on average by comparing Fig. 6(a) and Fig. 6(b). Therefore, the cover efficiency to separate the inner and outer sounds is about 10 dB.

4 New Noise Cancellation Method

We revise a noise canceling method using the acoustics. First, we store the data of the acoustic measurement in the system. The noise data of each motor is stored as a power spectrum of the averaged measured noises. Next, we use the stored data as templates to judge burst noises. When the motor makes a burst noise, the intensity of the noise is quite stronger because microphones location is relatively near the motor. Therefore if the spectrum and intensity of captured noise is similar to those of a noise template, the captured noise is regarded as a burst noise. Specifically, the subband is cancelled if the following conditions are satisfied:

1. Intensity difference between external and internal microphones is similar to measured motor noise intensity differences.
2. Intensity and pattern of the spectrum are similar to measured motor noise frequency responses
3. A motor command is being processed.

5 Experiments

In this section, we demonstrate the effectiveness of noise cancellation by the new method in sound source localization.

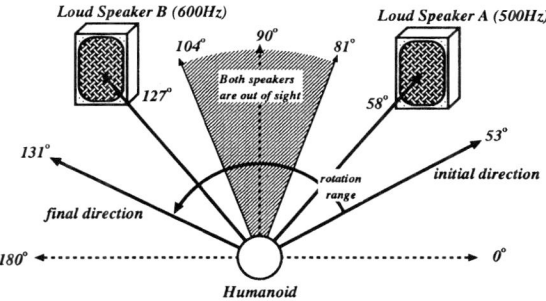

Fig. 7. Experiment: Sound source localization while SIG moves.

There are two sound sources: two B&W Noutilus 805 loud speakers located in a room of 12 square meters. The system is installed in a conventional residential apartment facing a road with busy traffic, and exposed to various daily life noise. Sound environment is not at controlled for experiment to ensure feasibility of the approach in daily life.

One sound source A (Loud Speaker A) plays a pure tone of 500 Hz. The other sound source B (Loud Speaker B) plays that of 600 Hz. A and B are located in front of SIG. SIG turns toward the direction of the sound source B at the velocity of 14.9 degree/sec using the direction obtained by audition under the condition that both A and B make sounds. Fig. 7 shows this situation.

Fig. 8(a) shows the captured sound spectrogram, Figs. 8(b), (c) and (d) show the localization results. The Y axis of each graph describes direction of A and B in humanoid coordinate system. Figs. 8(b), (c) and (d) show the results of sound source localization without noise cancellation, with noise cancellation by the previous method, and with our new noise cancellation, respectively.

Fig. 8(a) depicts 4 burst noises at 5.5, 7.0, 8.1 and 9.0 seconds. Fig. 8(b) also shows that sound source localization is badly impaired. Using our previous method, burst noises at 5.5 and 7.0 seconds are cancelled or weakened as shown

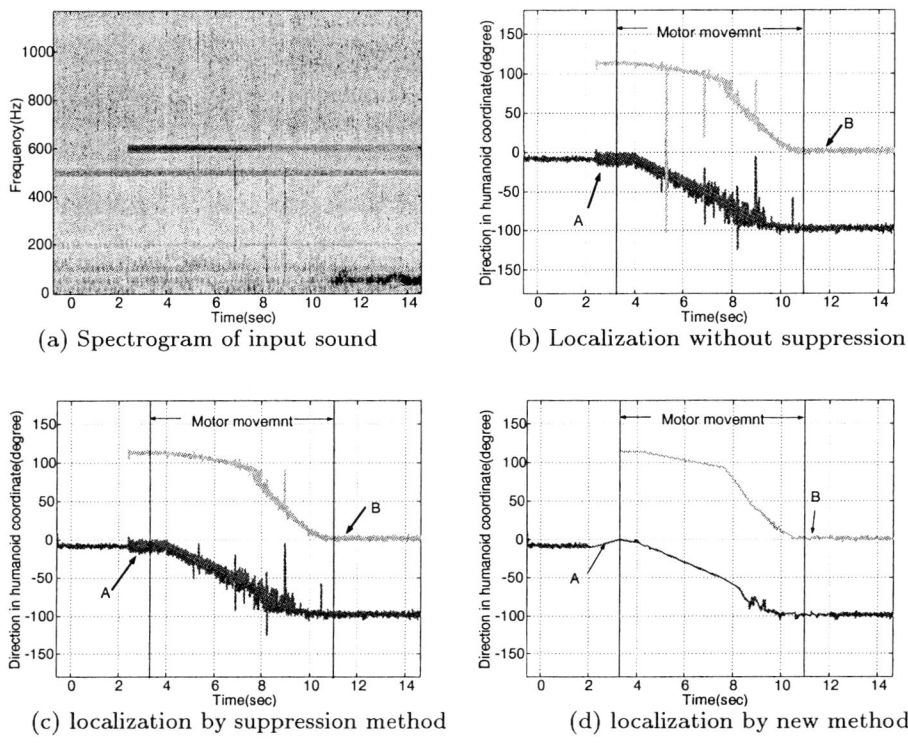

Fig. 8. Localization Experiments of sound sources

in Fig. 8(c), but other noises still remain. Fig. 8(d) shows that our new method cancels all burst noises and suppresses vibration.

However, location error of ±10° can be observed; when the robot has rotated by 80°, the actual sound source is located at the angle of 100°. This *IPD* error may be caused by the mismatch between FFT window length and wave length, and by ambiguity of peak position due to discretization of FFT. And we demonstrate the noise cancellation in case of using a motor and the constant velocity of the motor. Our noise cancellation method should be extended to the variable velocities of motors.

6 Discussion

We propose *auditory epipolar geometry*, which provides a sound source localization method without using *Head Related Transfer Function (HRTF)*. In real world, localization without using *HRTF* is needed because *HRTF* depends on environments. And the method can be easily used for integrating auditory and visual information as shown in section 2.4. Though the experiments demonstrate effective noise cancellation method using noise database in real-world environments, the system still has about ±10° error in sound source localization. It may be difficult to solve the problem only using auditory information because it is said that even human auditory capability has ±8° error in sound source localization [5].

Therefore, other sensory information such as vision and tactile information is required to compensate the error. The integration of vision and audition was done by Nakagawa et al [15]. However, their system fails in sound source localization and separation in real environments because it works only in simulated environments and using *HRTF*. We have already demonstrated the feasibility of the integration of audition, vision, and motor information in real-world environments [12]. This performance will be improved by incorporating the proposed method. Real time processing of active audition is critical in real world applications. To calculate *IPD* by *auditory epipolar geometry* is not difficult to speed up, but an *IPD* error described in Sec. 5 needs more sophisticated theoretical treatment. Other future work includes incorporating various acoustic features such as harmonics, onset, offset, common amplitude modulation, common frequency modulation, formants, timbre, and so on.

7 Conclusion

We discuss the importance of this research with respect to active audition since it has not been studied so far. We also discuss that the cover is important for active audition. By analyzing the acoustics of the cover, we demonstrate the effectiveness of noise cancellation method which improves sound source localization even while the humanoid is moving. In addition, we show that *auditory epipolar geometry* method without using *HRTF* plays an important role of sound source localization in real environments. Because this method can be easily expanded to combine visual information, it can be a useful method not only for active audition but also for active perception which integrates various sensory information. Active perception is important for the integration of perceptual information as well as to understand fundamental principles of intelligence.

Acknowledgments

We thank *NITTOBO Acoustic Engineering Co., Ltd.* for the acoustic measurements and offering the anechoic room. We thank our colleagues of Symbiotic Intelligence Group, Kitano Symbiotic Systems Project; Dr. Theo Sabish, Dr. Tino Lourence, Yukiko Nakagawa and Dr. Iris Fermin for their discussion.

References

1. Y. Aloimonos, I. Weiss, and A. Bandyopadhyay. Active vision. *International Journal of Computer Vision*, 1(4):333–356, 1987.
2. S. F. Boll. A spectral subtraction algorithm for suppression of acoustic noise in speech. In *Proceedings of 1979 International Conference on Acoustics, Speech, and Signal Processing (ICASSP-79)*, pages 200–203. IEEE, 1979.
3. R. Brooks, C. Breazeal, M. Marjanovie, B. Scassellati, and M. Williamson. The cog project: Building a humanoid robot. Technical report, MIT, 1999.

4. G. J. Brown. *Computational auditory scene analysis: A representational approach.* PhD thesis, Dept. of Computer Science, University of Sheffield, 1992.
5. J. Cavaco, S. ad Hallam. A biologically plausible acoustic azimuth estimation system. In *Proceedings of IJCAI-99 Workshop on Computational Auditory Scene Analysis (CASA'99)*, pages 78–87. IJCAI, Aug. 1999.
6. M. P. Cooke, G. J. Brown, M. Crawford, and P. Green. Computational auditory scene analysis: Listening to several things at once. *Endeavour*, 17(4):186–190, 1993.
7. O. D. Faugeras. *Three Dimensional Computer Vision: A Geometric Viewpoint.* The MIT Press, MA., 1993.
8. M. Kawato. Bi-directional theory approach to consciousness. In *Cognition, Computation, and Consciousness.* Oxford University Press, 1996.
9. N. Kita, S. Rougeaux, Y. Kuniyoshi, and S. Sakane. Real-time binocular tracking based on virtual horopter. *Journal of Robotics Society Japan*, 13(5):101–108, 1995.
10. H. Kitano, H. G. Okuno, K. Nakadai, I. Fermin, T. Sabish, Y. Nakagawa, and T. Matsui. Designing a humanoid head for robocup challenge. In *Proceedings of 4th Internatianal Conference on Autonomous Agents (Agents 2000).* ACM, 2000.
11. Y. Matsusaka, T. Tojo, S. Kuota, K. Furukawa, D. Tamiya, K. Hayata, Y. Nakano, and T. Kobayashi. Multi-person conversation via multi-modal interface – a robot who communicates with multi-user. In *Proceedings of Eurospeech*, pages 1723–1726. ESCA, 1999.
12. K. Nakadai, T. Lourens, H. G. Okuno, and H. Kitano. Active audition for humanoid. In *Proceedings of 17th National Conference on Artificial Intelligence (AAAI-2000).* AAAI, 2000. (*to appear*).
13. K. Nakadai, T. Matsui, H. G. Okuno, and H. Kitano. Active audition system and humanoid exterior design. In *Proceedings of International Conference on Intelligent Robots and Systems (IROS 2000).* IEEE, 2000. (*accepted*).
14. K. Nakadai, H. G. Okuno, and H. Kitano. A method of peak extraction and its evaluation for humanoid. In *SIG-Challenge-99-7*, pages 53–60. JSAI, 1999.
15. Y. Nakagawa, H. G. Okuno, and H. Kitano. Using vision to improve sound source separation. In *Proceedings of 16th National Conference on Artificial Intelligence (AAAI-99)*, pages 768–775. AAAI, 1999.
16. T. Nakatani, H. G. Okuno, and T. Kawabata. Auditory stream segregation in auditory scene analysis with a multi-agent system. In *Proceedings of 12th National Conference on Artificial Intelligence (AAAI-94)*, pages 100–107. AAAI, 1994.
17. T. Nakatani, H. G. Okuno, and T. Kawabata. Residue-driven architecture for computational auditory scene analysis. In *Proceedings of 14th International Joint Conference on Artificial Intelligence (IJCAI-95)*, volume 1, pages 165–172. AAAI, 1995.
18. D. Rosenthal and H. G. Okuno, editors. *Computational Auditory Scene Analysis.* Lawrence Erlbaum Associates, NJ., 1998.
19. A. Takanishi, S. Masukawa, Y. Mori, and T. Ogawa. Development of an anthropomorphic auditory robot that localizes a sound direction (*in japanese*). *Bulletin of the Centre for Informatics*, 20:24–32, 1995.

Overcoming the Effects of Sensory Delay by Using a Cerebellar Model

David Collins and Gordon Wyeth

Department of Computer Science and Electrical Engineering
University of Queensland
Brisbane, QLD Australia 4072

Abstract. Fast and accurate control of a system exhibiting significant feedback delay is traditionally a difficult problem to solve. In biological systems, it is thought that a part of the brain called the cerebellum overcomes such difficulties. This paper outlines the use of a cerebellar model in the control of a simulated mobile robot. The model is based around Albus's CMAC neural network, and uses the response of a non-delayed teaching module as a basis for learning. The model was able to produce results comparable to the teacher despite being subjected to severe sensory latency. After limited initial training the system can rapidly adapt to new situations and proved to have good generalisation between similar movements.

1 Introduction

Using traditional control techniques, applications that require fast and accurate movements are typically limited by the latency associated with sensory data acquisition. To successfully execute such movements the controller needs immediate state information to reliably ascertain the correct control signal for the next portion of the movement. If the sensor data is unavoidably delayed, the control loop will suffer with the effects of using old data as the basis of the next motor command. This situation usually presents the undesirable options of carrying out a fast but oscillatory trajectory or an accurate but slow response, depending on the system gains. Neither of the two alternatives will meet the necessary requirements of both speed and accuracy. This scenario is all too common in many modern robotic applications, particularly with respect to machine vision, with frame latency introducing a large and mostly insurmountable amount of uncertainty into the control loop. It is possible to improve the performance of such a system through the use of a model predictive controller. This technique often requires an accurate estimation of the system model, which in highly non-linear systems is difficult to ascertain. Advances in both sensor and computational technology are reducing the time between data sampling and usability, but as the need to make movements faster and more accurate increases, techniques that overcome the problem will be invaluable.

The human body as a system exhibits some striking similarities to the one described above. We have the ability to perform a stunning array of swift and precise movements, which for most of us occurs without so much as a conscious thought. But the attribute that makes our feats truly remarkable is the fact that nature has engrained in us some feedback latencies that theoretically should prevent successful execution of even the most basic human movements. Latency times in the human body range from 100ms for proprioception to 200ms for visual feedback [6]. With delays of this order how can the human body exhibit such accurate yet rapid voluntary movement? The answer lies in a part of the brain called the cerebellum.

The cerebellum is thought to be the mechanism that eliminates this apparent anomaly. Research suggests that the cerebellum learns to produce coordinated movements through exposure to previous attempted movements. In doing so it learns to implicitly predict actual state parameters when presented with obsolete state information. Learning occurs on a continual basis providing infinite adaptability throughout the life of the system. The cerebellum also eliminates the need for a complex mathematical model of the plant, instead learning system parameters with the aid of a crude teaching module [5]. Other theories of cerebellar function suggest that the cerebellum can build an inverse model of the controlled system, hence virtually eliminating the need for feedback [7].

Within the robotics domain it is clear that any such system would have many tangible benefits. This paper outlines a cerebellar modeling approach as applied to the mobile robot domain. The study is designed to explore the cerebellum's ability to overcome the effects of sensory latency. More specifically the study aims to:

1. Determine if a cerebellar module can perform as well in the delayed environment as its teaching module can in the non-delayed environment.
2. Explore the generalisation ability of the cerebellum between similar movements.
3. Examine the models ability to continually adapt to new and unexpected conditions.

2 System Architecture

The task chosen to explore the relative effectiveness of a cerebellar model is outlined in Figure 1.

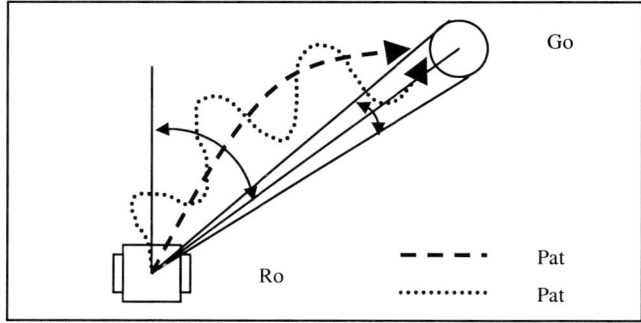

Fig. 1. The Robot Task. Angles Θ and Φ represent the robots angular offset and width to the target respectively. Paths 1 and 2 show the TM's response in a non-delayed and delayed environment respectively.

It consists of a mobile robot executing a goal approach trajectory. The simulated robot must approach the target quickly and smoothly, having time delayed sensor readings as its only source of input. The goal can be considered to be a spherical object or column. A movement is complete when the robot comes within a certain radius of the target. The sensors are designed to emulate on-board vision with two quantities, *angular offset* (Θ) and *angular width* (Φ) used to define the position and orientation of the robot with respect to the target. Path 1 shows the trajectory of the robot if no sensory delay is present, where path 2 displays the oscillatory effects of severe sensor latency when applied to the same simple control loop. This simple control loop, called *the Teaching Module (TM)*, can only provide a smooth trajectory to the target if the system gains are reduced, resulting in a much slower movement. The TM, which as the name suggests is used as a reference for cerebellar learning, will be discussed in more detail later.

2.1 Modular Architecture

The modular architecture of the system is illustrated in Figure 2. The structure of the system is inspired by a model developed by Fagg *et al.* [4]. The Fagg model was developed for a two-link arm in muscle space. It is trained using a crude corrective teacher, called an *extra-cerebellar* module, that assumes control of the arm when the cerebellar response is not yet capable of accurate control. In the model proposed in this paper the cerebellum is always the source of descending motor efferent commands, never allowing the teaching module to control the robot directly with obsolete motor commands.

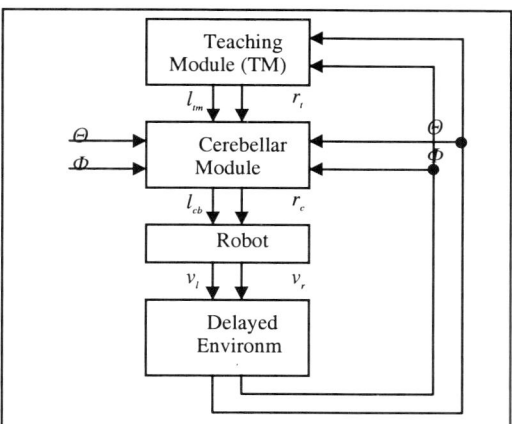

Fig. 2. Modular Architecture. l_{tm} and r_{tm} represent the Teaching Modules left and right motor commands. l_{cb} and r_{cb} represent the same quantities for the cerebellar module. v_l and v_r are the actual motor velocities. Θ_g and Φ_g are the initial angular offset and width quantities of the goal in local coordinates with respect to the robot, whereas Φ and Θ represent the current (delayed) state parameters.

The cerebellar module will view the TM's suggested output but use this information for future learning, instead of a guide for immediate action. The cerebellar module uses the least mean square (LMS) rule for weight modification.

2.2 Robot Model

The simulated robot is based on a conventional differential drive system. The motor responses for each wheel are modeled as 1st order systems:

$$\frac{dv(t)}{dt} = \frac{k}{\tau}c(t) - \frac{v(t)}{\tau}$$

where $v(t)$ is the wheel velocity, $c(t)$ is the wheel command, k is a constant and τ is the time constant.

2.3 The Teaching Module

The Teaching Module (TM) is based on a Braitenberg vehicle [3] as shown in Figure 3.

The two lateral sensors in the model respond to the angular offset (Θ) of the robot. If the goal is sensed as being offset to one side of the robot, the command to the wheel on the goal side will be inhibited proportionally with the magnitude of the offset. If the offset angle is greater than 90 degrees, the wheel command is maximally inhibited causing it to stop. The other wheel will continue to move at the maximum base velocity causing the robot to turn sharply towards the goal. With the offset angle between zero and 90 degrees the level of inhibition varies between zero and 100 percent respectively. This results in both wheels travelling at the maximum base velocity if the target is directly in front of the robot.

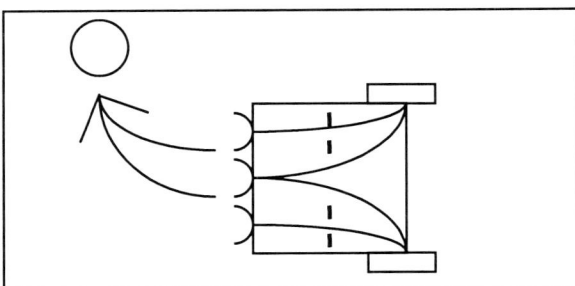

Fig. 3. The Teaching Module (Braitenberg Vehicle).

The centre sensor responds to the angular width (ϕ) parameter. It exhibits an inhibitory influence over both drive wheels equally. This sensor has no effect until the robot is close enough to the goal to trigger a threshold response. When this occurs it will progressively bring the robot to rest.

The simulator allows a fixed interval delay to be introduced between the sensors and the actuators. This leads to the situation where the motors could be trying to correct a left offset condition, based on the delayed data received, when the real time data indicates a right offset. The resulting movement will only serve to compound the problem leading to an undesirable oscillatory path.

It should be noted that the TM will not necessarily perfectly align the robot with the target, even with non-delayed input. The TM used was chosen for its simplicity and ability to produce smooth trajectories in the non-delayed environment and oscillatory trajectories in the delayed environment. The aim of the study is to see if the cerebellar module will replicate the non-delayed TM in the delayed domain, not perfectly align with the target.

2.4 The Cerebellar Module

The internal structure of the Cerebellar Module (CBM) is illustrated in Figure 4.

A CMAC (Cerebellar Model Articulation Controller) [2] neural network is the central feature of the cerebellar module. It was developed as result of Albus's theory of cerebellar function [1]. A CMAC exhibits the properties of an *expansive recoding network*, with inputs subjected to an expansive remapping in memory space such that similar input states share similar parts of memory, whereas significantly different input states are unlikely to share any common memory. The signals then undergo a convergent mapping to produce an output. This results in a network that has good local generalisation properties, due mainly to an overlapping receptive field arrangement at the inputs to the network.

The CMAC receives as input, the current (delayed) and initial angular widths and offsets, with the initial quantities held constant throughout the time course of the movement.

The CMAC produces left and right wheel commands as outputs which are passed through to both the motors and the output queue. The output queue stores past CMAC responses that will eventually be compared to the TM response during future learning.

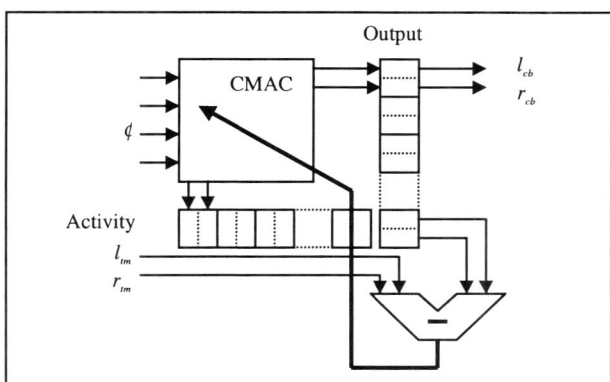

Fig. 4. The Cerebellar Module. All quantities are the same as those outlined in Figure 2. The Output and Activity Queues store past cerebellar outputs and weight activation patterns respectively.

Any connections in the network that are responsible for producing the current output have their indices recorded and stored in the activity queue. This structure acts as a register of past cerebellar activity, again to assist in future learning.

3   Learning

For the system to learn to perform as well as a non-delayed TM in the delayed environment, it must address the issues of structural and temporal credit assignment.

Structural credit assignment identifies which connections in the network contributed to the production of an undesirable response. Tagging the weights that are influenced by these connections enables the learning process to specifically modify only the weights that were involved in this response and not the weights that were dormant at the time and probably aligned with a different class of movement.

Temporal credit assignment is used to record the history of structural credit assignment. This is particularly important in the application under consideration, as a record of connection activity is required later to enable effective delayed learning. The activation queue is used to store a history of active synapses as a function of time. This is analogous to an *eligibility trace* [9].

By introducing a delay in the feedback pathway of the system, the current state parameters $\phi(t)$ and $\Theta(t)$ reach the controller in the form $\phi(t-N)$ and $\Theta(t-N)$, where N is the delay parameter in iterations. The CMAC will respond with the commands $l_{cb}(t)$ and $r_{cb}(t)$, but will have the past commands, $l_{cb}(t-N)$ and $r_{cb}(t-N)$, stored in the output queue. These variables correspond to the cerebellar response N iterations previously, when the supplied data was current. The TM produces the desired commands for the delayed state information, $l_{tm}(t)$ and $r_{tm}(t)$, which when compared with the retrieved cerebellar commands produce an error signal for supervised learning. The weights ($W(t-N)$) active N iterations earlier are fetched from the activation queue and modified during learning. This scheme should encourage the CMAC to predict the TM response to the current state parameters given only delayed information. The learning algorithm is in the form of the least mean square (LMS) rule:

$$\Delta w_i(t-N) = \frac{\alpha}{f}\left(c_{tm}(t) - c_{cb}(t-N)\right) \qquad (2)$$

where $w_i(t-N)$ is the active weight selected from the activity queue, f is the field width parameter for the CMAC inputs, α is the learning rate parameter, $c_{tm}(t)$ is the current teaching module motor command and $c_{cb}(t-N)$ is the cerebellar command selected from the output queue.

This paradigm requires learning to be started only when the queues have been filled and should continue after the movement has terminated, to empty the queues.

4 Results

4.1 Single Point Trajectory

The first experiment conducted on the system consists of repeated trials from the same starting point, to demonstrate the emerging learning pattern of the cerebellar module. The CMAC neural network is configured with 65 receptive fields for each input quantity. The network has a receptive field width (f) of 5, meaning 5 of the 65 input units will be excited for any given input value. This parameter relates to the local generalisation capability of the network, the larger the field width with respect to the field number, the greater the influence a given input state has on surrounding input states. Each input can be separated into 61 discrete states resulting in $(61)^4$ possible state combinations being separable into discrete state partitions. The learning parameter (α) is set to 0.5 and all the CMAC weights are initially set to zero. For all the experiments herein, the data sampling period is 100 ms and the sensory delay parameter is set to 700 ms.

In the first experiment the robot is placed at the position corresponding to (300cm, 100cm) in Cartesian co-ordinates, with its heading aligned with the negative x-axis. The target is placed at (300cm, 300cm), 200cm to the right of the robot, corresponding to an angular offset of 90° and an angular width of 8.58°. The robot is then made to execute a series of trials each replicating the same initial conditions described above. Figure 5 displays the evolving competence of the cerebellar module for trials 1,3 and 30 respectively. The average wheel velocity, otherwise known as the translational component of the motion, is plotted against time for both the cerebellar response in the delayed environment and the TM response in the non-delayed environment (desired response).

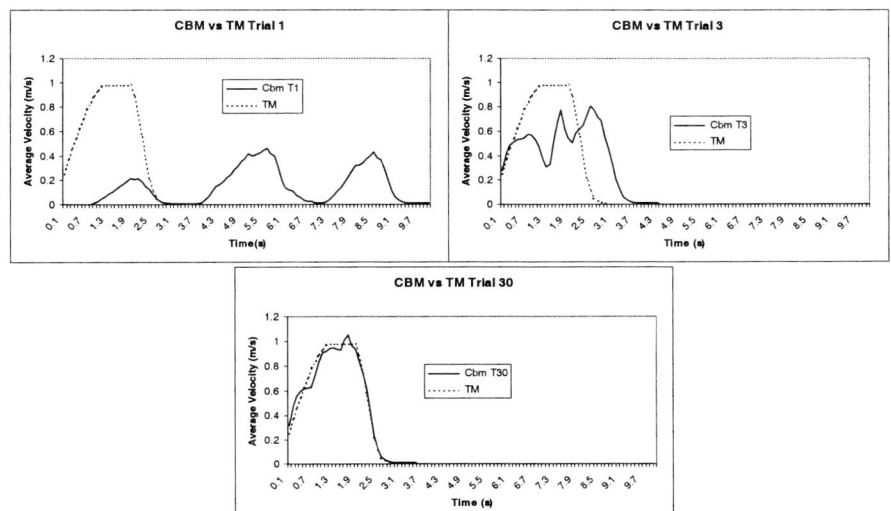

Fig. 5. Cerebellar Learning. CBM velocity response in the delayed environment versus the TM response in the non-delayed environment (desired response), for trials 1,3 and 30 respectively.

It can be seen that by trial 30, the cerebellum has learnt to closely replicate the response of the non-delayed TM, finishing with a relatively smooth motion in approximately 2.8 seconds. In trial 1 the cerebellar module can only manage to complete the movement in 9.7 seconds, utilising 3 distinct velocity peaks in the process.

Figure 6 displays the x-y trajectory plots of the experiment. It should be noted that the x-axis in Figure 6 has been expanded against the y-axis to separate the trajectory points in a 5 to 1 ratio. The pulsing velocities exhibited on trial 1 are evident by the clustering and expansion of trajectory points, each representing a 100 ms sample. The delayed TM response, not shown in figure 6, executed a terminally oscillatory trajectory. The movement could not reach the required proximity to the goal converging in an infinite "figure 8" loop.

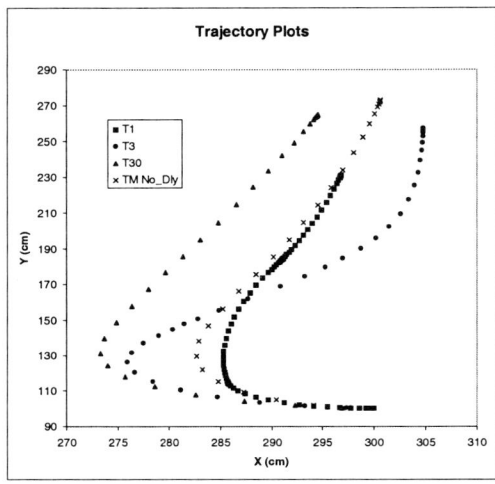

Fig. 6. X-Y Trajectory Plots. Paths executed for trials 1,3 and 30, as well as the course executed by a non-delayed TM. Note the expanded x-axis with respect to the y-axis.

4.2 Multiple Point Trajectory Generalisation

To examine the generalisation capabilities of the network, 150 random starting positions were generated for both a training and testing set. The random co-ordinates were limited to a square with borders 2 m above, below, left and right of the goal, with the region 0.5 m from the goal excluded. The robot heading was held aligned with the negative x-axis, with the position of the points with respect to the target producing angular widths and offsets of varying degrees. The network and delay parameters were the same as those selected for the first experiment.

The robot executed the first training set 10 times. In the first epoch, the average time of an approach was 4.56 seconds and the average distance from the goal centre was 58.2 cm. These figures improved to 2.26 seconds and 39.86 cm respectively by epoch 10. The non-delayed TM produced 2.26 seconds and 31.50 cm for these quantities respectively. The average starting distance between the centres of the robot and goal was 154.48 cm.

The system then navigated the testing set, recording 2.60 seconds for average execution time, corresponding to a 15% increase on the training set, and 48.73 cm for goal centre displacement. Exposure to a single epoch of the testing set quickly reduced the quantities to 2.30 seconds, (only 1.7% higher than the training set) and 44.61 cm respectively.

5 Discussion

In the single point trajectory experiment the system achieved a good match between the velocity profiles of the delayed cerebellar module and the non-delayed TM. The fact that a similarly delayed TM response failed to complete the task due to a lack of convergence highlights the significance of this result.

Perhaps the most interesting characteristic of the trial was the velocity profiles produced by the cerebellum during learning. Studies suggest that when an infant first learns to execute a reaching movement, the limb exhibits several peaks in its velocity profile [10]. This is in direct contrast to a similar adult attempt, which displays a single peaked, bell shaped profile. It has been argued [5] that the multi-peaked infant profile is due to a corrective mechanism external to the cerebellum producing pulsing trajectories in the direction of the goal. The authors hypothesize that there may be a simpler explanation that does not require an external mechanism to produce the pulsed behaviour.

With the CMAC weights initialised to zero, coupled with the fact that descending motor commands must come from the cerebellar module, the robot must first learn to respond to the current state parameters if it is to move. When sufficient time has passed to fill the queues, a learning operation will occur causing the cerebellar module to produce a small non-zero output on the subsequent iteration. This causes the robot to move into a different state space region. Due to the relatively small magnitude of the velocity command, the new region should significantly overlap with the first, resulting in it sharing a portion of the weight increase. After further learning the velocity command is larger than the last, displacing the robot into a progressively dissimilar region. This continues until the robot ventures into a region that has minimal learning overlap with the previous region, resulting in a near-zero velocity command, causing the process to repeat. As a consequence of this behaviour, more peaks will be visible in the initial trial if the width of local generalisation (f) is reduced.

The current model does have the disadvantage of being unable to respond to changing conditions until the initial latency period has elapsed. The velocity profile of trial 30 shows an initial 1st order step response converging to 0.6 ms^{-1} for the initial 700 ms of the trial. After this time, the cerebellar module attempts to track the desired response. Although the cerebellar module learns to respond to the initial state parameters, it cannot actively change its response in the initial latency period as the sensor data indicating movement has not yet reached the controller. This is evident in the trajectory plot of trial 30. It indicates a slower rate of turn in the initial stages of the movement, resulting in a slightly wider trajectory from the non-delayed TM trajectory. Despite this the system still manages to produce results comparable to the reference trajectory and significantly better than the non-delayed TM.

The generalisation experiment showed the system to be capable of rapidly adapting to new situations. After repeated exposure to the relatively sparse training set, one presentation of the test set was enough to bring execution time to within 1.7% of the training set.

The system appears to have evolved into a predictive controller that uses delayed state information to implicitly predict the current state parameters and generate the action corresponding to the current state. To do this effectively the system must have made previous attempts of the movement. The response of the teaching module must be consistent for a given set of state parameters. An erratic or random reference trajectory will cause the prediction mechanism of the cerebellar module to fail. This results in the CMAC network associating incorrect responses with a given set of input conditions.

6 Conclusions and Future Work

A cerebellar control architecture for a mobile robot in a sensory delayed environment has been presented. The system demonstrated the ability to perform as well in a time delayed environment as the teaching module did in the non-delayed environment. The system also exhibited impressive generalisation and adaptation qualities, being capable of rapidly learning new situations after prior exposure to similar situations.

The main issue brought to light by this study that will be the focus of immediate future work is a method to overcome the initial delayed reaction of the cerebellar module. Fast movements in humans can be completed in within 200-300ms, so requiring that a movement will not begin until the first reafference arrives (700ms) is not a desirable characteristic of the system.

Another possible avenue to explore with the current model is its ability to cope with varying sensory delays. The current system is able to operate with a known fixed delay period. If varying delays distributed about a fixed mean were introduced, they could be accommodated through the use of a temporally spread eligibility profile. This way instead of selecting only one entry in the activity queue, the model would also select adjacent members in the queue, but reduce their eligibility for weight change. The system could also be modified to deal with an unknown fixed delay by eliciting a discrete motor command [8] and then timing the period until a spike in reafference activity is received. This measured period could then be used to select the correct position in the activity queue for future weight modification. The models ability to deal with unknown variable delays would most likely be solved using a combination of the two techniques described above, but would require more complex analysis of reafference activity patterns. These suggested techniques will be examined in future studies.

Following these investigations the study will be introduced to the real domain of robot soccer. Instead of approaching a stationary target, the model will be adapted to strike a moving ball to a specified goal, using delayed feedback provided by a global vision system.

References

[1] J. S. Albus, "A Theory of Cerebellar Function," *Mathematical Biosciences*, 10, pp. 25-61, 1971.

[2] J. S. Albus, "A New Approach to Manipulator Control: The Cerebellar Model Articulation Controller (CMAC)," *Transactions of the ASME, Journal of Dynamic Systems, Measurement and Control*, pp. 220-227, September 1975.

[3] V. Braitenberg, *Vehicles: Experiments in Synthetic Psychology*, MIT Press, 1984

[4] A. H. Fagg, N. Sitkoff, A. G. Barto and J. C. Houk, "Cerebellar Learning for Control of a Two-Link Arm in Muscle Space," *Proceedings of the IEEE Conference on Robotics and Automation*, pp. 2638-2644, May 1997.

[5] A. H. Fagg, L. Zelevinsky, A. G. Barto and J. C. Houk, "Using Crude Corrective Movements to Learn Accurate Motor Programs for Reaching," *Extended Abstracts of the NIPS*97 Workshop, Can Artificial Cerebellar Models Compete to Control Robots?*, Chapter 6, pp. 20-24, 1997.

[6] M. Kawato, "Cerebellum and Motor Control," *The Handbook of Brain Theory and Neural Networks*, MIT Press, Cambridge, Massachusetts, pp. 172-178, 1995.

[7] M. Kawato and H. Gomi, "A Computational Model of Four Regions of the Cerebellum Based on Feedback-Error Learning," *Biological Cybernetics*, 68, pp. 95-103, 1992.

[8] R. C. Miall, D. J. Weir, D. M. Wolpert and J. F. Stein, "Is the Cerebellum a Smith Predictor ?," *Journal of Motor Behavior*, Vol. 25, No.3 pp. 203-216, 1993.

[9] R. S. Sutton and A. G. Barto, "Time-Derivative Models of Pavlovian Reinforcement," In M. Gabriel and J. Moore, editors, *Learning and Computational Neuroscience: Foundations of Adaptive Networks*, pp. 497-537. MIT Press, 1990.

[10] C. von Hofsten, "Development of Visually Directed Reaching: The Approach Phase," *Journal of Human Movement Studies*, 5:160-168, 1979.

Layered Specification of Intelligent Agents

Paul Scerri, Johan Ydrén, and Nancy Reed

Department of Computer and Information Science
Linköping University, SE-581 83 Linköping, Sweden
pausc@ida.liu.se johan.ydren@meridium.se nanre@ida.liu.se

Abstract. Interactive simulation environments with large numbers of intelligent agents are becoming increasingly common. In general, knowledge of precisely what agents should do in the environment is not an agent developer's area of expertise, rather it is a *domain expert's* expertise. In this paper we present an approach to specifying agents that takes advantage of the domain expert's knowledge where possible, but still allocates difficult programming tasks to expert programmers. In particular, the task of specifying agent behavior is layered and tasks are allocated according to the relative amounts of programming and domain expertise required for each one. Results are presented for an implementation of the technique for RoboCup players. An interesting benefit of the layered specification we observed was that an efficient, parallel development approach emerged.

1 Introduction

Interactive simulation environments with large numbers of intelligent agents are becoming increasingly common. Such simulation environments often have agents playing the roles of humans within the simulation [17]. Examples of this type of environment are military simulations [16,8], training [1], computer games [4] and RoboCup [10]. In general, knowledge of precisely what agents should do in such environments is not an agent developer's area of expertise, rather it is a *domain expert's* expertise. It follows that it is desirable to have domain experts as closely involved in the development of the agents as possible. Unfortunately in general, domain experts will not also be programming experts, rather they will be average computer users, i.e. they know *what* the agents should do but not necessarily *how* to get the agent to do the job. Easy-to-use specification tools are necessary for allowing domain experts to directly specify the behavior of the agents.

The ideal situation would be to have domain experts directly specifying all agent behavior using an off-the-shelf environment. Unfortunately that is a difficult, and perhaps unrealistic goal, take a smaller step we take an approach to agent specification which combines the desirability of non-expert agent specification with the practical limitation that programming agents is hard [3].

In particular we propose that the task of specifying an agent be broken into layers where the more difficult-to-program parts are assigned to expert programmers who are provided with appropriate expert programming tools, while the domain knowledge intensive aspects of specifying the agent are assigned to domain experts with easy to use tools. In particular, agent expertise is required for specifying low level *skills*, an intermediate level of agent programming experience is required for developing *individual strategies* and primarily domain experience is required for specifying *scenarios*. Figure 1 illustrates this idea.

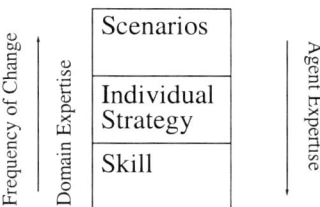

Fig. 1. The relative frequency of change and level of expertise needed in three abstract levels of the agent specification process.

At each layer of the design, a different tradeoff can be made in the specification tools between expressive power and ease of use. At the skill layer, expressive power is the major concern, at the individual strategy layer, both expressive power and ease of use have equal weight. Finally at the scenario specification level, ease of use takes precedence. Ideally no tradeoffs would be necessary but in reality they are required. Our approach is to acknowledge that tradeoffs will be made and to make them intelligently.

Many researchers have explored the idea of how to create agents composed of multiple layers. Usually the layers are selected to be appropriate to the kinds of agent reasoning required at different levels of abstraction (e.g. [7, 12]). In this paper we take a slightly different view on layering, i.e. we look at layering from the perspective of the specification tools a designer uses to specify agents. When separating an agent specification into layers, emphasis is on providing appropriate specification tools rather than on an appropriate runtime architecture (although clearly this cannot be ignored.)

Skill specifications need to be available to be used in the individual strategy layer and individual strategy specifications made available in the scenario specification. In effect, in the lower layers *building blocks* are specified which are used as the basis of specifications at the next layer. A critical aspect of making the layered approach work is that the building blocks exported from one layer support a good specification process at the next layer.

The precise types of tools required for each specification layer will vary depending on the agent's destination environment. For some environments the specification tools will need to support formal verification, while for other environments supporting rapid prototyping or enabling specification of physical distribution of the agents will be critical. The particular layering breakdown presented here is tailored to a specific type of domain with the following characteristics:

- There exists a large amount of expert domain knowledge that is not general knowledge, e.g. how to fly a combat aircraft or soccer strategies.
- At higher levels of abstraction the required agent behavior changes more often than at lower levels of abstraction.
- A relatively large number of similar agents are immersed in the same environment.
- Reasonably "intelligent" performance is expected of the actors. E.g. if the agents have only very simple strategies then the individual strategy layer may be superfluous.

Despite the apparently strong constraints listed above on the domains, a wide range of entertainment and training applications do meet these requirements. Furthermore, it should be straightforward to adapt the ideas to use with other types of applications.

For RoboCup 1999, we developed a layered specification system for a simulation team called the Headless Chickens III (HCIII) [14]. Low-level skills were written in Java, the individual strategies were created with a graphical system for developing behavior-based agents and the team strategies were built using a team-level strategy editor based on the idea of a coach's white board.

Three important observations were made while using this system. Firstly, after an initial start up time development was able to proceed at each layer almost completely in parallel. Secondly, the rapid scenario development system allowed extremely rapid, yet dramatic and effective, changing of team behavior. This enabled us to quickly adapt the HCIII strategy for different opponents during the 1999 World Cup. Finally, the runtime architecture layers were found to be relatively interchangeable. In fact for the 2000 RoboCup World Cup, the team scenario specification environment is being reused with two different individual strategy and skill runtime architectures (in different teams) and specification tools.

2 Layered Development Model

When beginning to develop agents for a new domain, appropriate development tools must first be designed/selected. Some analysis of the domain will need to be done to establish what properties the tools and resulting agents should have. The specific specification tools chosen for each development level depend on the requirements of the domain, e.g. reactive agent or formal verification. An important constraint is that the tools must export a specification in a form that the layer above can interpret. Once the tools are designed (or in practice probably simultaneously) a mapping to a runtime architecture needs to be developed. Next, skills, individual strategies and scenarios are developed and tested in parallel. There will be significant feedback between the specification layers, especially early on, but over time the bulk of the work will be centered in the

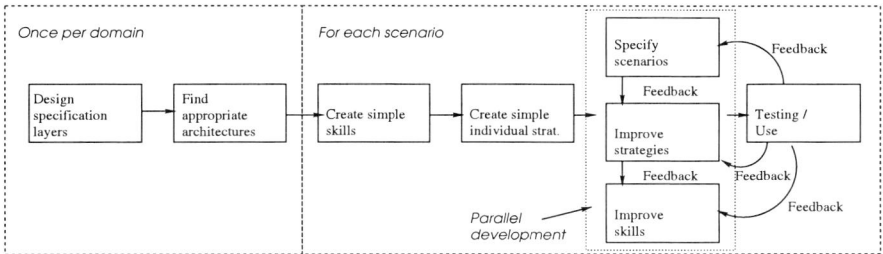

Fig. 2. The agent development process.

scenario specification tool. Ideally a stable set of skills and a library of individual strategies will be developed and most effort will go into creating and modifying scenarios, hence most work will become the domain expert's sole responsibility. See Figure 2 for an overview of the proposed development process.

At the skill layer the basic abilities of the agents are defined. For example in the air-combat domain skills would involve basic maneuvers such as landing and ground-avoidance. The individual strategies will be developed with a specification tool tailored to the type of agents required in the domain, e.g. a tool for specifying reactive rules or a tool for specifying sequences of actions. The individual strategies use the skills as their basic building blocks. For the air-combat domain individual strategies may include different flying formations and different opponent engagement strategies. Finally, at the top level, entire scenarios potentially consisting of many agents, or simply a particular "mission" for one agent, are defined. The scenario level strategies should be specified in an environment particularly suited to the domain and matching the domain expert's ways of explaining strategies.

Notice that the layering breakdown refers only to divisions in the tool support, not to where the layers in the runtime agent will be. The runtime architecture of the agent may not be layered in the same way as the tools (or not layered at all). The tools may simply be different ways of specifying things for the same runtime architecture or, map to possibly a seven layer architecture. The HCIII mapped the three specification layers to two runtime layers (see Figure 3) while Headless Chickens IV (HCIV – our RoboCup 2000 entry) maps to a single runtime layer. Although in the actual agent the same layered structure may not exist, it is important to preserve the illusion that it does for the benefit of the user of the specification tools. The usability of the tools will decrease if, for example, at the scenario specification level the designer needed to consider how the compilation process for the upper two layers works.

2.1 Skills

Skills are simple, self-contained pieces of agent functionality. Examples of skills include *landing* for aircraft simulation and *dribbling* for RoboCup players. From

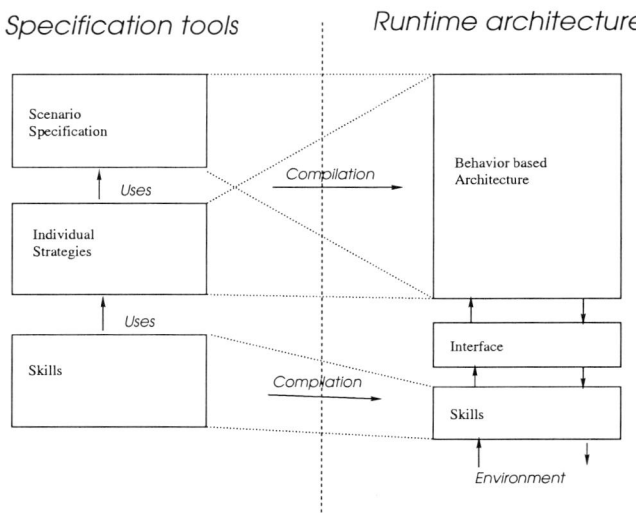

Fig. 3. An example mapping between specification tools and the agent architecture.

the perspective of the user of higher specification layers a skill is turned on and continuously attempts to achieve some simple task until being turned off.

The skills of agents are not expected to change much over the lifetime of the simulation or to vary from scenario to scenario. For example the way a pilot lands his aircraft is fairly independent of the mission in which he was involved. As the skills will often be fairly complex control routines, low level general purpose languages and associated general purpose programming environments will often be well suited. Furthermore in many simulation environments at low levels of abstraction a domain expert's knowledge may not be relevant due to the design of the agent to environment interface. For example the interface between a RoboCup player and the SoccerServer for a kick is a string "kick power direction" which makes the domain experts knowledge of muscle movements required to dribble quite irrelevant. Likewise, the particular movements of the control stick to land an aircraft are probably not relevant when specifying the skill for a simulated pilot to land a simulated aircraft.

Because of the relative infrequency of the required changes to the skills and the difficulty in encoding the knowledge it is reasonable that expert programmers be employed to create efficient, robust skills using languages and tools most appropriate for the task. The specification tools at the skill layer should support an expert programmer in efficiently defining skills. The emphasis in the tool should be on providing an effective means for specifying a low level skill in a machine interpretable format.

HCIII skills were written in Java, i.e. they were completely in the realm of an expert programmer. Most skills were parameterized by a field position, for example the position to kick to, dribble to or run toward.

2.2 Individual Strategies

The individual strategies are the abstract behaviors of a single agent. For example in air combat simulation an individual strategy may be a certain opponent engagement strategy. As a whole the individual strategies of the agent define a sort of agent "template" which will be instantiated for a particular scenario. From the perspective of the user of the scenario specification layer individual strategies are the abstract, parameterizable behaviors that the agent has at its disposal. Some mechanism needs to be developed that allows the team level strategy editor to use the individual strategy "templates" and to allow the individual strategy editor to use the skills.

For the purposes of the scenario specification layer the behaviors will be atomic. The individual strategies of an agent will change more often and more markedly over the lifetime of the simulation than will the agent's skills. On the other hand, for the targeted domains, the individual strategies will change less often than the scenarios. For example in RoboCup, an individual's strategy for marking another player will change infrequently, while the skill of dribbling will almost never change and the team formation (i.e. scenario) will change the most often. Because of the slightly higher rate of change, and more importantly because there is more domain knowledge relevant to individual strategies, domain experts need to be closely involved in specifying individual strategies. However because of the potential complexity of the strategies the problem of encoding the strategies will often not be possible by a domain expert alone (at least with the current state of the art). When designing tools for specifying individual strategies, a tradeoff between ease of use and expressive power should be made more towards the side of ease of use than for skills, though more towards expressive power than for scenarios.

For HCIII individual strategies are specified in a graphical editor – no code needs to be written. The tool allows relatively fast development of fairly complex behavior-based agents. However the complex concepts underlying these systems mean that the average end-user (i.e. domain expert) cannot do significant development work unassisted. To allow the team level specification system to "understand" individual strategies a simple "language" is embedded into the specification system (for HCIV this interface is in XML). When a team level strategy is created, the behavior specification is "compiled" into separate players, i.e the scenario and individual strategies are combined together into a single runtime layer (see [14] for details).

2.3 Scenario Specification

The scenario specification tool is the most important of the specification tools. Over the lifetime of the agents it is the scenario specification system that will be used the most often. The scenario specification is used to design the high level "organizations" or "missions" of the agents. For example in RoboCup it is used to specify team formations and tactics, in air-combat simulation it is used to specify missions and for computer games to specify the initial positions and movements of the "characters".

At the scenario specification system's high level of abstraction expert knowledge is crucial – even more so than for the lower levels. The scenario specification tool should support the expert in their job of developing appropriate behavior for the application. There is a subtle but important difference between the design emphasis for the scenario specification tool and the lower level tools. At lower levels the specification tools were chosen or designed to simplify the designers task of translating their knowledge into a computer understandable format. At the scenario level there is far more experimentation, iteration etc., so the emphasis moves from providing means to effectively encode well understood activities to creatively creating specialized scenarios. In particular it is desirable that a scenario specification system have the following characteristics:

- A specification method that allows domain experts, rather than system experts, to interact easily with the system.
- A specification method that is natural to the domain expert. Most desirable is to draw on explanation methods from the domain for inspiration.
- Very rapid development abilities.

To integrate with the rest of the system the scenario specification tool needs to be able to "understand" the templates provided by the individual strategy tool. Additionally it needs to instantiate the provided templates into specialized agents in some way.

The scenario specification system of HCIII is based on the idea of a coach's white board, as shown in Figure 4. In other words we took a medium for expressing strategies that a domain expert was used to using and attempted to reproduce that medium in the computer. The "white board" provides different panels for each of the modes of play that the agents know about. The known modes are determined by looking for a special keyword in the agent template (imported from the individual strategy specification tool). The domain expert (i.e. a soccer coach) places the players, represented by circles, on a diagram of the ground and then indicates directions they should dribble and pass in each of their modes. The tool allows coaches to express strategies in a way that they are used to as well as encouraging creativity and experimentation. For the RoboCup domain there was a clear real-world analogy between the white board and the specification system. For other domains the scenario specification method may appear much different. For example air-combat tactics may be written as a set of responses to possible situations, using a specification system styled after they way tactics are normally written down.

3 Discussion

Developing a layered model like the one described in this paper will often require significant development effort for a new domain. For example, the development of the team strategy editor for HCIII was far from a trivial exercise. However in the RoboCup case it was decided the complexity of designing team strategies and the advantages to be gained by being able to quickly change strategies outweighed the extra effort required. This will not always be the case for a domain.

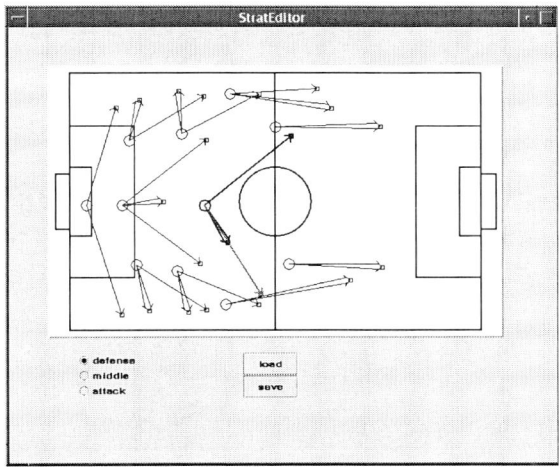

Fig. 4. A screen shot of a defensive team formation in the HCIII scenario editor.

Sometimes the relative simplicity or infrequency of creating scenarios will not justify the development time of a scenario editor. In all cases, the significant cost of creating domain specific, easy-to-use scenario specification environments can be largely offset by the removal of the expert programmer from the scenario design and testing loop.

A number of specification environments allow specification across a very broad range of abstraction levels, i.e. skill through scenario, e.g. [13, 5]. Such a specification means that the "artificial" breakdown into layers of our layered model need not be made. This in turn avoids some potentially inelegant designs forced by the layering. On the other hand using the one specification environment for all aspects of development means that the same tradeoffs between ease of use and expressive power exist at all levels. Layering allows tradeoffs to be made on the basis of the type of specification to be done at a particular specification level. For example more flexible and complex low level (and hence generally harder to use) tools are advocated for skills while easy-to-use (and hence less flexible) tools are used for scenario specification. If the same tool is used across all levels, the same tradeoff must be made across all levels perhaps resulting in lack of expressive power at the lower levels (e.g. AgentSheets [13]) and/or undesirably low usability at higher levels (e.g. dMars [5]).

Some development environments, such as JACK [9] and AgentBuilder [15], provide different mechanisms for specifying individual and team behavior. However, unlike in the tool specification editor presented here, the tools provided for specification of team behavior in both Jack and AgentBuilder require an solid understanding of programming and of agents. However for the types of domains and applications these tools target, e.g. integrating legacy systems in an intelligent way, this is a perfectly reasonable design decision as the *domain expert* in this case is a programmer! If the tools were targeted to domains where the domain experts were not computer experts a different approach would probably need to be taken.

In layered agent architectures, such as 3T [2] and Raps [6], agents usually have three or four architectural styles in different layers at runtime. The rationale is much the same as the rationale for layered specification tools, i.e. to provide appropriate tools for the job at different layers of abstraction. In the case of tools the job is specification, in the case of agent architectures the job is action selection. However specification layering is not simply a translation of the layered idea from the computational side of agent development to the specification tool side. Firstly most layered architectures predefine the structure of the layers before examining the domain, i.e. *general* layered architectures are developed then applied to a particular domain. On the other hand our model advocates selection/development of tools based on the requirements of the domain. By analyzing the domain before choosing the layers the appropriateness of the overall system to the domain is likely to be better. The improved suitability comes at the cost of having to build new tools for each domain. Secondly, the layers for layered agent architectures exist both at design time and at runtime, whereas for layered specification the layering may only exist at design time. For example in the RoboCup system presented here the scenario specification and individual strategies are compiled together so there exists only two layers at runtime.

The abstract model was used to develop a team that competed in the 1999 RoboCup World cup and finished 5th out of 35 teams. However it was not the quality of the agent behavior that was interesting rather the development process used to create the team. In the last weeks leading up to the competition there were three separate "groups" working almost completely in parallel to develop HCIII. One expert programmer worked at the lowest level of abstraction constantly trying to improve the skills of the team. Another programmer worked on the individual strategies of players. Finally, a group of students, who joined the project in the last months worked exclusively on the team strategies. Whenever significant improvements were made in either the skills or individual strategies the changes were passed to the team strategy group.

Feedback down levels of abstraction occurred frequently. Usually feedback from the team to individual player to the skill layer was in the form of comments like "Players need to be more keen to shoot when around the goal" or "They don't follow the ball far enough from their position". Feedback from the individual strategies to the skills was usually something like "Can we make them shoot harder" or "They should look in the area where we tell them to pass to make the pass hit, rather than just kicking to the exact point". The critically important factor of the development process was that all specification layers could work easily in parallel allowing a large team to work relatively independently yet still effectively.

Although the RoboCup implementation of the layered model was successful and useful it was at least partially due to the characteristics of the domain and the specifics of the architectures chosen, rather than just a good model.

All layers, both on the specification and runtime side, were very reactive. The reactiveness allowed layers to "make decisions" independently of previous actions drastically simplifying specification system design. Even more critically it made the interfaces between the tools, e.g. the way a skill specification was imported into the individual specification tool, simple to design and build. The reactive nature of the layers also meant that the only communication between layers was in the form of the upper laying setting the new group of behaviors or skill at the next layer down – the environment being used to provide feedback about the effects of that action. The design of scenarios which involve communication protocols may be fundamentally more difficult and not possible for genuine end users.

4 Conclusion and Future Work

Experience with RoboCup using an instantiation of the specification model presented here supports the idea that layering the specification task provides benefits with respect to other specification methods. In particular appropriate tools were available at the different levels to make the specification task as easy as possible. A further, somewhat surprising, result was that the layering led to a very efficient and practically desirable development process.

There seem to be a variety of other domains/environments where such an approach to designing specification tools would be appropriate. MissionLab [11], for example, successfully uses a similar layered structure for specifying multi-robot missions. Hopefully more agent designers will consider layered specification approaches when examining possibilities for deploying agents in new domains.

Acknowledgments

This work is supported by Saab Corporation, Operational Analysis Division, the Swedish National Board for Industrial and Technical Development (NUTEK) under grants IK1P-97-09677, IK1P-98-06280 and IKIP-99-6166, and the Center for Industrial Information Technology (CENIIT) under grant 99.7.

References

1. R. Bindiganavale, W. Schuller, J. Allbeck, N. Badler, A. Joshi, and M. Palmer. Dynamically altering agent behaviors using natural language instructions. In *Proceedings of Fourth International Conference on Autonomous Agents*, 2000.
2. R. Bonasso, R. Firby, E. Gat, D. Kortenkamp, D. Miller, and M. Slack. Experiences with an architecture for intelligent reactive agents. *Journal of Experimental and theorectical Artificial intelligence*, 9(1), 1997.
3. J. Bradshaw, M. Greaves, H. Holmback, T. Karygiannis, W. Jansen, B. Silverman, and Alex Wong. Agents for the masses. *IEEE Intelligent Systems and their applications*, 14(2):53–63, 1999.
4. Johanna Bryson. Creativity by design: A character based approach to creating creative play. In *AISB Symposium on AI and Creativity in Entertainment*, 1999.

5. M. d'Inveron, D. Kinny, M. Luck, and M. Wooldridge. A formal specification of dMars. Technical report, Australian Artificial Intelligence Institute, Melbourne, Australia, November 1997.
6. James Firby. Task networks for controlling continuous processes. In *Proceedings of the Second International Conference on AI Planning Systems*, June 1994.
7. Erann Gat. On three layered architectures. Online Publication, May 1997.
8. R. Hill, J. Gratch, and P. Rosenbloom. Flexible group behavior: Virtual commanders for synthetic battlespaces. In *Proceedings of Fourth International Conference on Autonomous Agents*, 2000.
9. A. Hodgson, R. Rönnquist, and P. Busetta. Specification of coordinated agent behavior (the SimpleTeam approach). Technical report, Agent Oriented Software, 2000. http://www.agent-software.com/.
10. Hiraoki Kitano, Minoru Asada, Yasuo Kuniyoshi, and et. al. RoboCup: A challenge problem for AI. *AI Magazine*, 18(1):73–85, Spring 1997.
11. Douglas MacKenzie. *A design methodology for the configuration of behavior-based mobile robots*. PhD thesis, Georgia Institute of Technology, 1996.
12. K. Pfleger and Barbara Hayes-Roth. Using abstract plans to guide behavior. Technical Report KSL-98-02, Knowledge Systems Laboratory, Stanford, Jan 1998.
13. Alexander Repenning and Andri Ioannidou. Behavior processors: Layers between end-users and java virtual machines. In *Proceedings of VL'97*, Capri, Italy, September 1997.
14. Paul Scerri and Johan Ydrén. *RoboCup-99: Robot Soccer World Cup III*, chapter End User Specification of RoboCup Teams. Springer, 1999.
15. Reticular Systems. Agent builder: An integrated toolkit for constructing intelligent software agents. Technical report, 2000. http://www.agentbuilder.com.
16. M. Tambe, K. Schwamb, and P. Rosenbloom. Constraints and design choices in building intelligent pilots for simulated aircraft. In *AAAI Spring symposium on "Lessons Learned from implemented software architectures for phyiscal agents"*, 1995.
17. Milind Tambe, W. Lewis Johnson, Randolph Jones, Frank Koss, John Laird, Paul Rosenbloom, and Karl Schwamb. Intelligent agents for interactive simulation environments. *AI Magazine*, 16(1):15–39, Spring 1995.

Sub-pixel Precise Edge Localization:
A ML Approach Based on Color Distributions

Robert Hanek

Forschungsgruppe Bildverstehen (FG BV)
Technische Universität München, Germany
http://www9.in.tum.de/people/hanek/

Abstract. We present a novel, sub-pixel precise approach for the localization of the most salient edge point in the vicinity of an initial point. The localization is done within a 1D array of color pixels. The approach consists of the iteration of two steps. In the distribution estimation step, the color distributions of the two regions separated by an edge are estimated or updated. In the edge fitting step, the edge position is estimated by maximizing the joint likelihood for the observed color values. The approach automatically adapts the smoothing to the progress of the edge estimation. Therefore, no critical parameters such as window sizes have to be chosen by the user. Due to the statistical modeling by distributions, the presented approach can separate regions with strong internal edges or texture. Experiments show that the achieved precision is higher than that of a multi-dimensional gradient method.

1 Introduction

Many computer vision problems, like 3D model reconstruction, pose estimation, tracking, and even object recognition can be regarded as the problem of fitting curves into images. Usually the curves, e.g. the contour of an object, are functions of a set of unknown parameters, e.g. the object's pose, structure or the parameters of the camera(s). The goal of our project is to estimate such unknown parameters in one single optimization using the sensor data directly. No intermediate discrete decisions should be made, such as "At position X is a feature of type Y, which corresponds to feature Z of the object model".

From a local observation of a smooth curve, the translation along the tangent on the curve cannot be obtained. Therefore, most approaches, e.g. [11, 2, 5], use relations between points of the curves and image measurements made on the perpendiculars of the curve passing through the curve points. Blake and Isard [2] scan the image samples along the perpendiculars using interpolation in order to obtain a 1D pixel array. Usually the initial estimates of the edge points and sometimes its standard deviation are used in order to determine a suitable search–region. Image features, e.g. edges, can be detected and localized by applying filtering to this search–region. However, in practice, where for example texture is given, the filter response has several local maxima which results in a set of surmised edges. The problem is to decide which point in the image corresponds to the point on the curve. Applying a threshhold to the filter response often does not yield the corresponding edge point.

The approach, presented here, estimates for a 1D array of color pixels the most salient edge point, within the vicinity of a given initial edge estimate. This approach can also be applied in order to fit a set of edge points $\{e_1(\mathbf{u}),..,e_M(\mathbf{u})\}$, all of which depend upon a common, unknown parameter vector $\mathbf{u}$, simultaneously into the image. In such a combined estimation, a non-salient edge has less impact than a salient edge, but it can still contribute to the estimation of $\mathbf{u}$. However, in this paper we focus on the localization of a single color edge. In the following we present a brief selection of previous work on edge detection, especially color edge detection. We would like to emphasize that no short bibliography represents the full range of work done in the area of edge detection. A more extensive review can be found in [7].

Some approaches, e.g. [6], first treat the channels of the image as independent measurements and then fuse the result. Since the image channels are usually highly correlated, such a separated treatment does not exploit the interdependence of the channels.

The basic assumption for most step edge detectors is that the regions on both sides of the edge have constant color or intensity, e.g. [3]. However, very often the regions have internal structure, e.g. due to texture. Canny's edge detector [3] can be generalized for multi-dimensional data, see e.g. [10]. Each channel is convolved with a Gaussian derivative and then the derivatives (in the 2D case the gradients) are combined to a single derivative. Most edge detectors assume a specific edge profile (shape) and a specific distribution of the noise. Usually neither the profile nor the noise distribution are known in advance.

The approaches [1, 12] can also be generalized for color images. These methods do not assume constant values for pixels of one side of the edge. However they require a model describing the pixel values in the vicinity of the edge. Deviations from this model are regarded as noise. In practice usually a model of the edge environment is not known in advance especially if the edge separates non-homogeneous regions.

In contrast to most other methods, Ruzon and Tomasi [10] do not explicitly model the pixels values of the regions adjacent to the edge. They divide a circular window into two halves and estimate the edge by maximizing the so called Earth Mover's Distance [9] between the two halves. The authors show that this approach performs better than multi-dimensional gradient methods when the adjacent regions of the edge have considerable internal edges.

From our point of view, published color edge detection approaches suffer from at least one of the following disadvantages. 1. Dependence on scale: the result of methods which optimize distances between windows, e.g. [3, 10], depends on the size of the windows. 2. Sub-pixel accuracy: edge detectors compute a response for a fixed number of points (usually for each pixel). By interpolation sub-pixel accuracy can be achieved. However, interpolation usually yields just an approximation. 3. No context sensitivity: in order to detect salient edges it seems to be desirable that the detector learns, e.g. from the environment of the surmised edge, what a frequently observable, non-salient variation of the signal is and what is not.

Cluster-based segmentation approaches, such as [8], yield edges too, but implicitly. Such methods show a lot of similarities to our approach. The often used EM-algorithm [4] maximizes the likelihood of the clusters by iterating two steps:

1. classification of the points by using probability distributions of the classes and
2. estimation of class distributions using classified points.

Since we want estimate a single edge, the main problem of clustering approaches is that the resulting regions are not necessarily coherent, which results in multiple edges. Therefore, we do not classify the pixels independently, but estimate instead a single edge by maximizing the joint likelihood of the pixels.

In the presented approach, we do not maximize the response of a filter. We regard an edge as a point which separates its vicinity into two regions with two different color distributions. We iteratively estimate the edge by maximizing the statistical significance of the color change in the surmised edge. In order to assess this statistical significance the context of the surmised edge is taken into account. The context knowledge can be obtained from the vicinity or the edge. The advantage of the resulting context sensitivity is that a color change, which often occurs (possibly with slight variations), is assessed as not significant, whereas a unique color change, even with a smaller gradient, is assessed as significant.

The rest of this paper is organized as follows: section 2 presents a ML approach for the localization of a single salient color edge. This approach can be used if the color distributions of the two regions adjacent to the edge are known in advance. In section 3 we describe how the color distributions of the two sides can iteratively be updated using the improving edge estimation. The results of our experiments and a discussion of the performance are presented in section 4. Finally this paper is summarized in section 5.

2 Edge Localization Based on Known Color Distributions

In paragraph 2.1 we develop a statistical model which specifies the probability density $p_i(\mathbf{Y})$ for observing the color vector $\mathbf{Y}$ at pixel i. This likelihood $p_i(\mathbf{Y})$ is a function of the edge. In paragraph 2.2 a maximum-likelihood approach is used to estimate the edge. The convergence of the numerical optimization is addressed in paragraph 2.3.

2.1 Statistical Modeling

We denote the edge which we want to estimate by e. The closest integer E is the index of the pixel which contains e. The edge point e splits its vicinity into two intervals with different color distributions. We assume that within the lower interval I_l all pixels i have the same Gaussian probability density for observing a color vector $\mathbf{Y}$:

$$\forall i \in I_l \quad p_i(\mathbf{Y}) = p(\mathbf{Y}|\mathbf{m}_l, \mathbf{C}_l) \tag{1}$$
$$= |2\pi \mathbf{C}_l|^{-1/2} \exp\left[-(\mathbf{Y} - \mathbf{m}_l)^T \mathbf{C}_l^{-1}(\mathbf{Y} - \mathbf{m}_l)/2\right]$$

The vector $\mathbf{m}_l$ and the matrix $\mathbf{C}_l$ are the mean and the covariance of the Gaussian probability density. For the upper interval I_u we analogously assume another Gaussian density which is given by the mean $\mathbf{m}_u$ and the covariance $\mathbf{C}_u$.

Note that this assumption, of two different Gaussian distributed sides with two means and two covariance matrixes, is different to assuming two sides with different means and a single covariance matrix $\mathbf{C}$. Usually a single covariance matrix is used in order to describe the distribution of noise. Here the covariances $\mathbf{C}_l$ and $\mathbf{C}_u$ describe specifically for each side which variations of the mean color vectors $\mathbf{m}_l$, $\mathbf{m}_u$ are likely and which are not. In general, $\mathbf{C}_u$ and $\mathbf{C}_u$ differ a lot, even if the two regions adjacent to the edge have the same distribution of noise. The problem of finding a salient edge is closely related to the problem of classifying pixels to the left side or to the right side. Such a classification may be done with a low error probability, even if the two classes differ only in their covariance matrixes. Hence, good estimates of this covariances are important.

In section 3 we describe how $\mathbf{m}_l$, $\mathbf{m}_u$, $\mathbf{C}_l$ and $\mathbf{C}_u$ can be estimated. We assume in the following that these distribution parameters are given.

In order to develop a sub-pixel precise edge localization we need to derive the probability density $p_E(\mathbf{Y})$ for observing the color vector $\mathbf{Y}$ at the edge pixel E. We define two functions $d_l(x,e)$ and $d_u(x,e)$ which indicate on which side of the edge e the parameter x lies:

$$d_l(x,e) = \begin{cases} 1 & : \quad x \leq e \\ 0 & : \quad x > e \end{cases} \quad (2)$$

$$d_u(x,e) = 1 - d_l(x,e) \quad (3)$$

We assume the area of sensitivity of pixel i reaches from $i-D$ to $i+D$. For our experiments we used $D = 0.5$. By integrating d_l and d_r we obtain which fraction of the area of sensitivity belongs to the lower and which to the upper side of the edge e:

$$a_{li}(e) = \int_{i-D}^{i+D} d_l(x,e)dx \quad (4)$$

$$a_{ui}(e) = \int_{i-D}^{i+D} d_u(x,e)dx = 1 - a_{li}(e) \quad (5)$$

We assume that the color vector $\mathbf{Y}_E$ of the edge pixel E is given by a linear mixture of the two adjacent regions. This assumption is suitable e.g. for the RGB color space. For non-linear color spaces such as the YUV space a nonlinear mixture has to be used in order to achieve optimal sub-pixel accuracy. If a linear mixture is given then the mean $\mathbf{m}_i$ and the covariance $\mathbf{C}_i$ for any pixel i, including the edge pixel ($i = E$), are given by

$$\mathbf{m}_i(e) = \mathbf{m}_l \cdot a_{li}(e) + \mathbf{m}_u \cdot a_{ui}(e) \quad (6)$$
$$\mathbf{C}_i(e) = \mathbf{C}_l \cdot a_{li}(e) + \mathbf{C}_u \cdot a_{ui}(e) \quad (7)$$

In equations (6) and (7) the means and the covariances of the two sides are weighted by $a_{li}(e)$ and $a_{ui}(e)$, which measure how much of the area of sensitivity of pixel i belongs to the lower side and how much to the upper side.

2.2 ML Estimation

From the discussion above follows that for any pixel i the probability density $p_i(\mathbf{Y}_i)$ for observing $\mathbf{Y}_i$ can be written as

$$p_i(\mathbf{Y}_i) = p(\mathbf{Y}_i | \mathbf{m}_i(e), \mathbf{C}_i(e)) \quad (8)$$

Due to statistical independence of the pixels, the probability density $p(\mathbf{S})$ for observing the sequence $\mathbf{S} = [\mathbf{Y}_{i_{\min}}, ..., \mathbf{Y}_{i_{\max}}]$ of color vectors is

$$p(\mathbf{S}) = \prod_{i=i_{\min}}^{i_{\max}} p(\mathbf{Y}_i | \mathbf{m}_i(e), \mathbf{C}_i(e)) \qquad (9)$$

Hence, the ML estimation $\hat{e}$ of the edge e is given by

$$\hat{e} = \operatorname*{argmax}_{e} \prod_{i=i_{\min}}^{i_{\max}} p(\mathbf{Y}_i | \mathbf{m}_i(e), \mathbf{C}_i(e)) \qquad (10)$$

By taking the negative logarithm, the maximization of the product in (10) can be transformed into a more convenient minimization of a sum:

$$\hat{e} = \operatorname*{argmin}_{e} \chi^2(e) \qquad \text{with} \qquad (11)$$

$$\chi^2(e) = - \sum_{i=i_{\min}}^{i_{\max}} ln\left[p(\mathbf{Y}_i | \mathbf{m}_i(e), \mathbf{C}_i(e))\right] \qquad (12)$$

In order to estimate the edge we have to minimize the objective function $\chi^2(e)$ with respect to e.

Often the given problem is not just to localize a single edge but to fit a number of edges $e_1(\mathbf{u}), e_2(\mathbf{u}), .., e_N(\mathbf{u})$ simultaneously into the image in order to estimate a common parameter vector $\mathbf{u}$, e.g. the pose of an object. In this case, the objective function we have to minimize, is the sum of the χ^2 functions for each edge. Such a simultaneous optimization is much more robust and precise than first localizing the edges and then combining the results into one estimation of $\mathbf{u}$.

2.3 Convergence through Smoothing

In many applications, e.g. object tracking, a rough initial estimate $\hat{e}_0$ of the edge e is given. However, if one tries to minimize χ^2 by an iterative optimization method started with $\hat{e}_0$, the algorithm usually converges towards a local minimum. This is due to the functions $d_l(x,e)$ and $d_u(x,e)$ being non-continuous. If we smooth $d_l(x,e)$ and $d_u(x,e)$, then the area of convergence increases. However, then the localization also becomes imprecise. Therefore, we start the iteration with a strong smoothing and adapt the smoothing iteratively to the progress of the edge estimation. We convolve the functions $d_l(x,e)$ and $d_u(x,e)$ defined in (2, 3) with a Gaussian kernel of standard deviation σ. The new, smoothed equivalents to (2, 3) are

$$d_l(x,e,\sigma) = \frac{1}{\sqrt{2 \cdot \pi}\sigma} \int_{-\infty}^{x} \exp\left[\frac{-(t-e)^2}{2\sigma^2}\right] dt \qquad (13)$$

$$d_u(x,e,\sigma) = 1 - d_l(x,e,\sigma) \qquad (14)$$

If σ approaches zero, then the equations (13, 14) become equivalent to (2,3). With the new definition of d_l and d_u the objective function χ^2 depends on e and σ. Hence, $\chi^2(e,\sigma)$ has to be minimized with respect to e and σ.

Due to several reasons, e.g. unsharp focusing, inaccuracy of sensors and transmission, real images are usually not perfectly sharp. An image can rather be regarded as a convolution product of an ideally sharp image and a Gaussian with standard deviation σ_c. Therefore, the minimization of $\chi^2(e,\sigma)$ with respect to e and σ leads usually not to $\widehat{\sigma} = 0$ but rather to $\widehat{\sigma} = \sigma_c$. This means $\widehat{\sigma}$ is an estimation of the image sharpness. This estimation is obtained in a single point and therefore very noisy.

On the other hand, one can use vague knowledge of σ_c in order to improve the precision of the edge estimation $\widehat{e}$. Let $\widehat{\sigma}_c$ be the estimation of σ_c and $\widehat{\tau}_c$ the estimated standard deviation of $\widehat{\sigma}_c - \sigma_c$. We incorporate vague knowledge of the image sharpness by minimizing the objective function $\psi(e,\sigma)$:

$$\psi(e,\sigma) = \chi^2(e,\sigma) + \left(\frac{\sigma - \widehat{\sigma}_c}{\widehat{\tau}_c}\right)^2 \tag{15}$$

$$(\widehat{e},\widehat{\sigma}) = \underset{(e,\sigma)}{\mathrm{argmin}}\, \psi(e,\sigma) \tag{16}$$

If no knowledge of σ_c is given, then $\widehat{\sigma}_c = 0$ and a high value for $\widehat{\tau}_c$ can be used. For experiments the values $\widehat{\sigma}_c = 0$ and $\widehat{\tau}_c = 4$ are chosen.

The minimization is done by Newton-iteration. In order to avoid local minima σ must not decline too fast. Therefore, we limit the change of σ such that in one iteration step σ can only change by P_σ % (in experiments $P_\sigma = 65$). This also ensures that σ does not change its sign.

3 Estimation of Color Distributions

In the previous section we regarded the means $\mathbf{m}_l$, $\mathbf{m}_u$ and the covariances $\mathbf{C}_l$, $\mathbf{C}_u$ which describe the color distributions of both sides of the edge as known. In many applications estimates $\widehat{\mathbf{m}}_l$, $\widehat{\mathbf{m}}_u$, $\widehat{\mathbf{C}}_l$ and $\widehat{\mathbf{C}}_u$ can be obtained in advance. However, often one needs to update these estimates, and sometimes one cannot rely at all on prior learned color information. This section describes how the distribution parameters $\widehat{\mathbf{m}}_l$, $\widehat{\mathbf{m}}_u$, $\widehat{\mathbf{C}}_l$ and $\widehat{\mathbf{C}}_u$ are obtained and incrementally updated using the improving estimation $\widehat{e}$ of the edge.

During the minimization of $\psi(e,\sigma)$ each iteration step yields a new edge estimation $\widehat{e}$ and an associated standard deviation $\widehat{\sigma}$. They are used to estimate the probabilities p_{li} and p_{ui} of a pixel i belonging to the lower or upper side of the edge e by

$$p_{li} = d_l(i,\widehat{e},\widehat{\sigma}) \tag{17}$$

$$p_{ui} = 1 - p_{li} = d_u(i,\widehat{e},\widehat{\sigma}) \tag{18}$$

The functions d_l and d_u are defined in (13,14) as the integral over a Gaussian density with mean $\widehat{e}$ and standard deviation $\widehat{\sigma}$.

The goal is to update the distribution parameters $\widehat{\mathbf{m}}_l$, $\widehat{\mathbf{m}}_u$, $\widehat{\mathbf{C}}_l$ and $\widehat{\mathbf{C}}_u$ such that for not yet clearly classified pixels (p_{li} not close to 0 or 1) the probability of a classification error declines. Therefore, pixels which are not clearly classified to one side should not be used to estimate $\widehat{\mathbf{m}}_l$, $\widehat{\mathbf{m}}_u$, $\widehat{\mathbf{C}}_l$ and $\widehat{\mathbf{C}}_u$. On the other hand, a sufficiently large number of samples is necessary for the estimation. If the color distribution does not change with the distance to the edge, then in general enough clearly classified pixels are given. Usually the probability density $p_i(\mathbf{Y}_i)$ to observe the color vector $\mathbf{Y}_i$ is not constant for all pixels i belonging to one side of the edge. There can be continuous changes caused e.g. by a gradually changing illumination angle. Often non-continuous changes are also given. For example, the position of the next edge could be known or could be estimated simultaneously in one combined optimization process. In this case, the set of pixels used to estimate $\widehat{\mathbf{m}}_l$, $\widehat{\mathbf{m}}_u$, $\widehat{\mathbf{C}}_l$ and $\widehat{\mathbf{C}}_u$ should be limited.

As a compromise between certainty of classification, number of pixels, and distance to the estimated edge $\widehat{e}$, we use for the side $s \in \{l, u\}$ the heuristically obtained weights

$$W_{si} = \max(0, p(i|\widehat{e}, \sigma_w^2) \cdot (p_{si} - B_w)^7) \qquad (19)$$

where $p(i|\widehat{e}, \sigma_w^2)$ is the density of a Gaussian distribution with mean $\widehat{e}$ and variance σ_w^2. Pixels which have a probability p_{si} lower than the parameter B_w have weights W_{si} equal to zero and are not taken into account. In experiments we used the values $\sigma_w^2 = 10$ and $B_w = 0.65$.

Contrary to methods like [3, 10], which maximize distances between two windows, the windows used here have a minor influence on the localization result. The windows might not be symmetric and they can have different shapes and sizes, which is a major advantage, for example at the border of the image.

The distribution parameters $\mathbf{m}_s$ and $\mathbf{C}_s$ for the side $s \in \{l, u\}$ are estimated by

$$\widehat{\mathbf{m}}_s = \frac{1}{G} \sum_{i=i_{\min}}^{i_{\max}} W_{si} \cdot \mathbf{Y}_i \qquad (20)$$

$$\widehat{\mathbf{C}}_s = \frac{1}{G} \sum_{i=i_{\min}}^{i_{\max}} W_{si} \cdot (\mathbf{Y}_i - \widehat{\mathbf{m}}_s)^T (\mathbf{Y}_i - \widehat{\mathbf{m}}_s) \qquad (21)$$

$$G = \sum_{i=i_{\min}}^{i_{\max}} W_{si} \qquad (22)$$

These estimations are based only on the actual image. In many applications, like tracking or object recognition, one might want to use prior obtained color information for one or both sides of the edge. For example, one could use a recursive filtering approach, which not only allows to track and predict the position of an object, but also its local color distributions. In the following experimental evaluation we examine the case where no a priori knowledge exists.

4 Experimental Evaluation

In order to evaluate our approach, we first use synthetic data with a well known ground truth. Then we present results on real images.

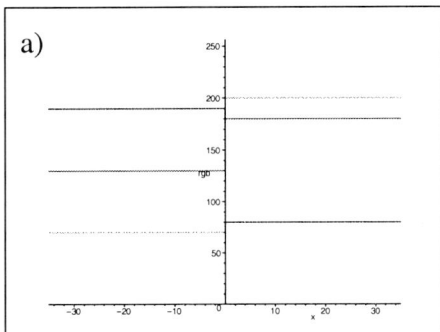
a) An ideal step edge: The RGB-values are constant on both sides of the edge.

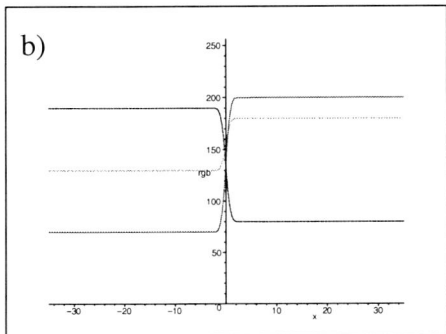
b) An step edge with a smooth change between two constant color vectors

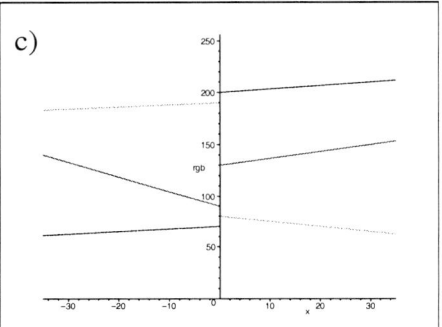
c) The RGB-color values of the two sides, separated by the edge, depend linearly on the position (abscissa).

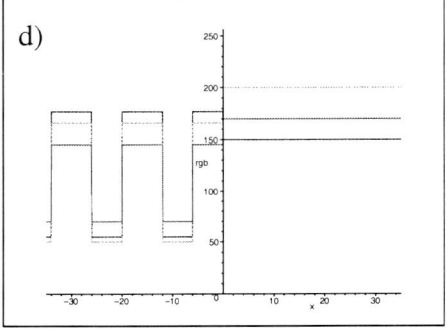
d) A constant side and a side with bimodal color distribution

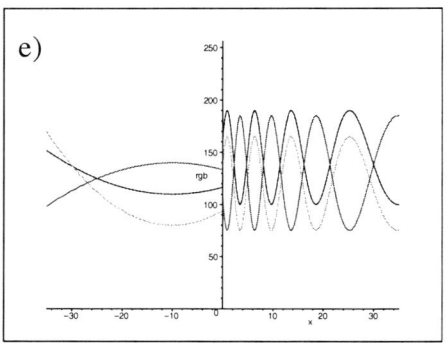
e) Two sides with similar means and high variances

Fig. 1. Five different edge profiles (ordinate: RGB-values; abscissa: position within the 1D array)

Table 1. Average error in pixels for different noise levels and different edge profiles in the following order: first our approach / followed by an approach based on the Canny detector with window sizes $\sigma \in \{1, 2, 4, 8\}$

edge profile	noise level $\tilde{n} \in [-1,..,1] \times [-2,..,2] \times [-4,..,4]$		
	$5^0 \cdot \tilde{n}$	$5^1 \cdot \tilde{n}$	$5^2 \cdot \tilde{n}$
a	.017 / .027 / .016 / .015 / .025	.058 / .050 / .057 / .082 / .12	.090 / .36/ .39 / .52 / .50
b	.018 / .031 / .017 / .018 / .024	.078 / .072 / .067 / .086 / .12	.25 / .68/ .48 / .55 / .51
c	.018 / .023 / .023 / .088 / .32	.055 / .057 / .082 / .16 / .36	.080 / .21/ .39 / .58 / .50
d	.064 / 3.6 / 3,8 / 4.0 / .74	.24 / 3.9 / 4.3 / 3.8 / .72	>5 / 5.0/ 3.9 / 4.4 / 1.2
e	.20 / 2.7 / 1.3 / 1.8 / 1.5	.79 / 4.0 / 2.8 / 1.4 / 1.2	>5 / 3.1/ 4.0 / 2.4 / 1.8

We use five different edge profiles, which are depicted in Figures 1. The abscissa x is the position within the 1D array of color pixels. In all these profiles the RGB–values show at position $x = 0$ a salient change in color distribution. In example a) the regions on either side of the edge have constant color values. Example b) is the same as example a) but smoothed with a Gaussian kernel. In example c) on both sides the color values are a linear function of the x–coordinate. The lower (left) side of example d) contains several points with stronger color discontinuities than in the edge point. This is often the case for regions with strong texture. The function in example e) consists of two continuous sides with similar means and high variances.

For each of these edge profiles, we generate 20 noisy 'images' as follows: first the functions are shifted along the x-axis by a randomly generated, uniformly distributed offset $e \in [-5, .., 5]$, which specifies the position of the edge. Then for each pixel i the noise free color vector is obtained by integrating the example functions from $i - 0.5$ to $i + 0.5$. In real images the different color channels show different noise distributions. We simulate for each pixel independent noise by a three-dimensional, uniform distributed random variable $\tilde{n} \in [-1, .., 1] \times [-2, .., 2] \times [-4, .., 4]$, which is scaled by a specific multiplier $\in \{5^0, 5^1, 5^2\}$ and added to the noise free color vector.

Note that the distribution of noise and the edge profiles are chosen such that the probability densities $p(\mathbf{Y})$ for observing a color vector $\mathbf{Y}$ do not meet our assumption of Gaussian distribution made in (1). For example, the left side of example d) does not result in a unimodal color distribution but in a bimodal color distribution.

For comparison, we use a multi–dimensional gradient method, a generalization of the Canny edge detector [3]. From all the edges, the one with the strongest response in the interval $[-5, ..5]$ is selected. Due to this interval, the possible errors are strongly confined. Sub-pixel values for the edge are obtained by quadratic interpolation of the gradient.

Table 1 summarizes the measured average errors. The results of the method based on the Canny edge detector vary strongly for different window sizes. For different edge profiles different window sizes achieve the best results. In the following we compare the results of our approach with the best results of the Canny edge detector.

For the examples a) and b) with low and middle noise our approach performs slightly worse than the Canny's approach, which is optimized for a ideal step edge. However for strong noise our approach achieves better results. For a step edge, we obtain covariance matrices $\mathbf{C}_l$ and $\mathbf{C}_l$, which describe the distribution of noise. In the edge fitting step our approach weights the three color channels according to the estimated noise. A multi-dimensional gradient method dose not adapt the influence of the three channels to the estimated noise distribution.

Usually an ideal step edge is not given. The color values are rather a function of the position. If the curvature within the two sides of an edge is small, then the function can be approximated by two linear sides, as done in example c). In this case our approach achieves a clearly higher accuracy. For a high noise level the error of Canny's method is almost three times higher.

In the first three examples the errors of both approaches are less than a pixel. The problem in examples d) and e) is not just to localize the edge precisely but to select the most salient color change. The maximum of the Canny filter response does often not correspond to the correct edge. In the examples d) and e) for a moderate noise level the error of the method based on Canny filter is several times higher than the error of our approach. For a Canny filter a big window size is necessary in order to reduce wrong maxima. In example d) the distances between the two colors adjacent to the edge is about 30 units for each channel. For the highest examined noise level the noise is within $[-25,..,25] \times [-50,..,50] \times [-100,..,100]$. With this noise level for the examples d) and e) our approach does not always converge to an edge in the vicinity of the correct edge.

but the presented approach can still separate both sides. The multi-dimensional gradient method yields usually edges within the right side, due to the high gradients.

Figure 2 shows a natural scene. The stars mark the initialization points for our approach. The search for the correct edge is done along the vertical image axis. The results of the presented method are marked by crosses. The estimated edges correctly separate the different regions, despite the strong gradients within the regions.

Since our method is a non-linear optimization the required computation time is clearly higher (in experiments about 70 times) than the computation time of the multi-dimensional gradient method which is based on a linear filter.

5 Summary

The presented approach estimates for a 1D array of color pixels the most salient edge point, within the vicinity of an initial edge estimate. This approach learns from the neighborhood of the surmised edge, by estimating two distributions, to distinguish between a non-salient variation of the color and a salient variation. With these two distributions the edge is estimated using a ML approach.

For the cases that are relevant in practice, where not an ideal step edge is given and the noise level is realistic, the achieved accuracy is clearly higher than for a multi-dimensional gradient method. If the regions adjacent to the edge have strong internal edges, then a multi-dimensional gradient method often results in a higher response for such internal edges than for the correct edge. In general, the presented approach assesses the correct edge as the salient edge, even when its gradient is much smaller. In future work we will generalize the presented 1D approach for the refinement of parametric contours in 2D images.

* Initialization
+ Estimated edge point

Fig. 2. Performance on an image of the Grand Canyon

References

1. BAKER, S., NAYAR, S., AND MURASE, H. Parametric feature detection. *IJCV 27*, 1 (March 1998), 27–50.
2. BLAKE, A., AND ISARD, M. *Active Contours.* Springer-Verlag, Berlin Heidelberg New York, 1998.
3. CANNY, J. A computational approach to edge detection. *PAMI 8*, 6 (November 1986), 679–698.
4. DEMPSTER, A., LAIRD, N., AND RUBIN, D. Maximum likelihood from incomplete data via the EM algorithm. *J. R. Statist. Soc. B 39* (1977), 1–38.
5. LOWE, D. G. Fitting parameterized 3-d models to images. *IEEE Transactions on Pattern Analysis and Machine Intelligence 13*, 5 (1991), 441–450.
6. NEVATIA, R. A color edge detector and its use in scene segmentation. *SMC 7*, 11 (November 1977), 820–826.
7. PAL, N., AND PAL, S. A review on image segmentation techniques. *PR 26*, 9 (September 1993), 1277–1294.
8. PAUWELS, E., AND FREDERIX, G. Cluster-based segmentation of natural scenes. In *ICCV99* (1999), pp. 997–1002.
9. RUBNER, Y., TOMASI, C., AND GUIBAS, L. A metric for distributions with applications to image databases. In *ICCV98* (1998), pp. 59–66.
10. RUZON, M., AND TOMASI, C. Color edge detection with the compass operator. In *CVPR* (1999), pp. II:160–166.
11. SULLIVAN, S., AND PONCE, J. Automatic model construction and pose estimation from photographs using triangular splines. *IEEE Transactions on Pattern Analysis and Machine Intelligence 20*, 10 (1998), 1091–1096.
12. WANG, S., AND BINFORD, T. Detection, estimation and aggregation of three major types of discontinuities in image surfaces. In *ARPA96* (1996), pp. 923–926.

Efficient Joint Detection Considering Complexity of Contours

Masayoshi Kanoh[1], Shohei Kato[2], and Hidenori Itoh[1]

[1] Nagoya Institute of Technology.
Gokiso-cho, Showa-ku, Nagoya 466-8555, Japan.
[2] Toyota National College of Technology.
2-1 Eisei-cho, Toyota 471-8525, Japan.
kanoh@juno.ics.nitech.ac.jp, shohey@toyota-ct.ac.jp, itoh@ics.nitech.ac.jp

Abstract. In the field of archaeology, reconstruction of earthenware imposes a heavy task on archaeologists. In order to reduce their task, we have developed a system, which can automatically reconstruct earthenware from given potsherds. The system is required to detect a pair of segments to join from potsherds correctly, by evaluation of salient values for shape of its contours. In existent method, the salient values are calculated with fixed precision. The calculation, thereby, makes the system computationally very expensive, when the number of potsherds increases. In this paper, we introduce search control, *iterative deepening*, into joint detection, and propose JDID (Joint Detection with Iterative Deepening), which can efficiently detect a pair of segments to join by dynamically changing its precision of salient value calculation; depending upon complexity of shape of potsherds. We have also implemented an earthenware reconstruction system and performed drastic speedup of the reconstruction.

1 Introduction

Recently, many potsherds of broken earthenware have been excavated from ruins (see Figure 1). Reconstruction of earthenware, however, is attended with difficulties, due to a numerous excavation of potsherds, weathering and lack of parts. The reconstruction, therefore, imposes a heavy task on archaeologists, and a numerous earthenware have not been reconstructed yet. The reconstruction offers significant knowledge of not only the era when it is used, but also ancestor's life style and cultural interchange. The reconstruction, accordingly, is very important in the field of archaeology.

In order to reduce the task of the reconstruction, we have developed a system, which can automatically reconstruct earthenware from given potsherds. In general, as potsherds have three dimensional shape, earthenware should be reconstructed in three dimensions. At the beginning of this research, in this paper, we consider reconstructing earthenware in two dimensions, such as plates, pot-lids and so on.

In solving jigsaw puzzles, one of the similar problems in two dimensions, some work has been reported by utilizing inherent properties of jigsaw puzzles

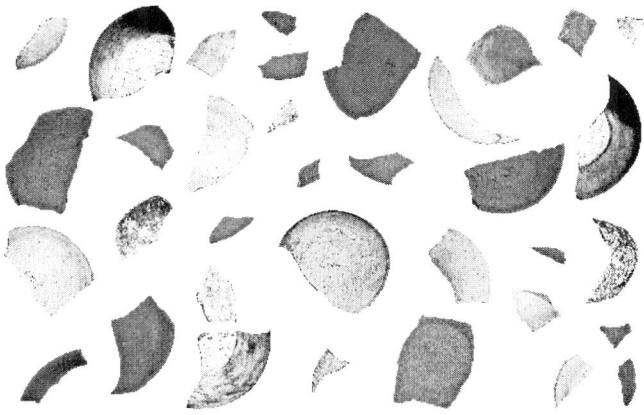

Fig. 1. Potsherds Excavated from Ruins.

(e.g., [1][2]); 1) all pieces consist of four contours and 2) each contour has simple and clear shape. Earthenware reconstruction, however, can not utilize these properties because potsherds have complex and irregular contours. This requires an efficient joint detection method independent upon shape of potsherds. Hori and et al. [3] have proposed a joint detection method independent upon shape of potsherds. The method, however, can detect joint only from two potsherds, and does not consider the case when the number of potsherds increases.

In this paper, we introduce a search control technique, *iterative deepening* [4][5], into joint detection and propose an efficient algorithm, Joint Detection with Iterative Deepening (JDID), which can automatically detect a joint from given potsherds. Taking into consideration of the complexity of contours, the algorithm avoids redundant computation by dynamically changing the precision. We have implemented an earthenware reconstruction system with proposed algorithm, and performed drastic speedup of the reconstruction when the number of potsherds increases.

The paper is laid out as follows. Section 2 gives an overview of an earthenware reconstruction system. Section 3 describes the algorithm JDID. Section 4 shows experimental results produced by our system with JDID.

2 System Overview

In order to reduce the task of reconstruction, we here implemented an earthenware reconstruction system on UNIX workstation. Figure 2 shows an overview of the system.

Firstly, the system detects contours from input images of potsherds. Secondly, salient points are detected, and each of contours is divided into some opened curves called *sub-contour* by the salient points. These sub-contours are candidates for joints. Thirdly, for each sub-contour, salient value is calculated,

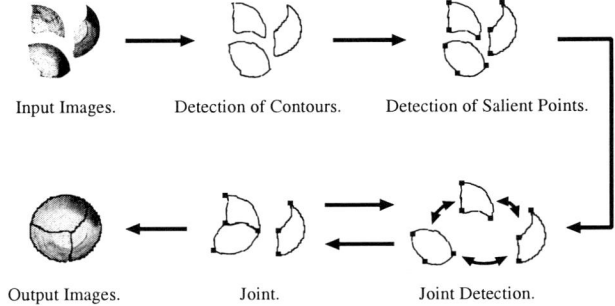

Fig. 2. An Overview of the Earthenware Reconstruction System.

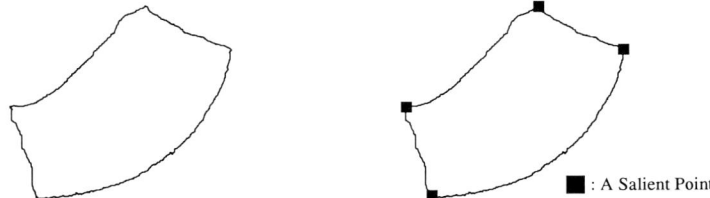

Fig. 3. A Contour Image.

Fig. 4. A Divided Contour by Salient Points.

and then, for all pairs of sub-contours, similarities are evaluated by the salient values. The most similar pair is selected after that. If the similarity of selected pair satisfies some condition, two potsherds having these sub-contours are joined. The above procedures are iterated, and finally, the system outputs images of some reconstructed earthenware. This process is repeated until there is no pair for joint, and then output reconstructed images.

2.1 Detection of Salient Points

Contours detected from given potsherds should be divided into sub-contours by salient points. In our system, the sub-contours are considered candidates for joint, and the shape of sub-contour is utilized as a criterion for joint detection. Accordingly, dividing contours is important in terms of performance of the system.

Paying attention to reconstructed earthenware, a contour of a potsherd is almost divided into joints by salient points such that the points become vertexes constructing a polygon which approximates the contour with as few vertexes as possible. We, therefore, adopt Rosenfeld and Johnston's method [6] for detecting salient points having above property.

Figure 4 shows the result of detecting salient points from a contour shown in Figure 3.

2.2 Joint Detection

In this paper, we propose an efficient joint detection algorithm considering complexity of contours. The algorithm reduces computational cost of joint detection drastically, therefore numerous potsherds can be reconstructed at once. Preliminary to our algorithm, we give brief description about salient value and similarity between two sub-contours, which are utilized as evaluation value for our algorithm.

Salient Value. We give the P-type Fourier descriptors proposed by Uesaka [7][8] to salient values for shape of sub-contours. Using the descriptors, we evaluate similarity between two sub-contours, and we refer to the similarity as *shape similarity*. The descriptors are represented by the Fourier transform of curves and characterized as follows:

- It is applicable to opened curves.
- Two endpoints of a reproduced curve always correspond to two endpoints of the original one, respectively.
- Information about a certain shape of an original curve is concentrated in low frequency range.
- A Curve is represented by only the angular function.

In earthenware reconstruction, the shape of a sub-contour is not completely equal to the shape of its joining pair because of weathering and so on. The P-type Fourier descriptors are, therefore, applicable to joint detection. A salient value $c_N(k)$ of a sub-contour c is calculated by low-pass spectrum with cut frequency N of Fourier transformation as follows:

$$c_N(k) = \frac{1}{n}\sum_{i=0}^{n-1} \omega(i) exp(-j2\pi ik/n) \quad (1)$$
$$(k = -N, \ldots, N),$$

where $\omega(i)$ is the P-type expression of c and n is an enough large natural number. For more precise, please refer to [7][8]. Using the salient value, similarity $\varepsilon_{a,b}(\phi)$ between sub-contour a and b can be evaluated by the following equation:

$$\varepsilon_{a,b}(\phi) = \sum_{k=-N}^{N} |a_N(k) - exp(j\phi)b_N(k)|^2 \quad (2)$$
$$(\phi = 0, \ldots, 2\pi),$$

where $a_N(k)$ and $b_N(k)$ denote the low-pass spectrums of P-type Fourier descriptors of a and b, respectively.

Shape Similarity. The P-type Fourier descriptors are invariant under translations, rotations, and changes of the scale. Rotations of an original curve are represented by the descriptors multiplied by $exp(j\phi)$. It follows from the equation (2) that b becomes more similar to a when $\varepsilon_{a,b}(\phi)$ gets nearer to zero. It also follows that $\varepsilon_{a,b}(\phi) = 0$ when the shape of b is completely equivalent to the shape of a.

In our system, we, therefore, define the shape similarity between a and b by the following equation:

$$ss(a,b) = \frac{1}{min_\phi \varepsilon_{a,b}(\phi)}. \qquad (3)$$

The above salient value and similarity are also adopted by the existent work in [3].

3 An Efficient Method for Joint Detection

When the number of potsherds increases, incurring combinational explosion of sub-contours, the computational cost of joint detection becomes very expensive, thereby requiring sophisticated techniques to reduce the cost. In the following section, let us discuss about precision, *shape-precision*, for calculating salient value of shape.

3.1 Computational Precision versus Complexity of Contours

For a sub-contour, from the viewpoint of detection of its joint pair, shape similarity requires adequate shape-precision to distinguishing the most similar pair to the sub-contour from the second best one. We call the shape-precision *selective precision*. It is obvious that a selective precision for a sub-contour is necessary to only comparison with its joint pair. This implies that lower shape-precision may be sufficient for the sub-contour to be compared with the other sub-contours except its joint pair. The above remarks suggest that highly fixed shape-precision, without considering selective precision, causes redundant computation to calculation of salient value. It should be also noticed that selective precision for a sub-contour varies with its shape. Selective precision should be assigned individually to sub-contours. It is, however, impossible to obtain selective precision in advance. We, therefore, attempt to reduce the computational cost of calculation of salient value, by dynamically changing the shape-precision, depending upon complexity of given sub-contours, thereby making joint detection much more efficient. In this research, shape-precision is, now, defined by the following definition.

Definition 1. Shape-precision
Let S be a set of sub-contours, and c be a sub-contour in S, and $s(c)$ be a sequential line composed of $2^i + 1$ ($i \geq 0$) points, which approximates c. Then, shape-precision sp_S for S is defined by the following equation:

$$sp_S = i. \qquad \square$$

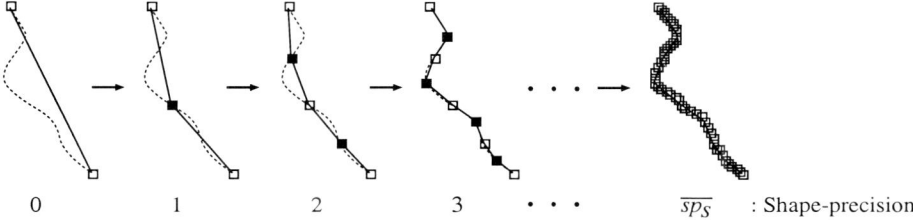

Fig. 5. Sequential lines with different shape-precisions.

Note 2. Upper bound of shape-precision exists, because sub-contour is composed of finite contour points. Let m be a maximum number of contour points composing any sub-contour in S. Then, upper bound $\overline{sp_S}$ of sp_S is derived as follows:
$$\overline{sp_S} = i, \text{ where } 2^i + 1 \leq m < 2^{i+1} + 1.$$
For each sub-contour c in S, we, therefore, consider sequential lines $s(c)$s with case that $sp_S = 0, \cdots, \overline{sp_S}$ (shown in Figure 5). It should be noticed that for all $c \in S$, $s(c)$, with case that sp_S is higher, can approximate c more accurately. In this paper, $s_i(c)$ denotes the sequential line of sub-contour c with its shape-precision $sp_S = i$. □

Note 3. Let a and b be sub-contours in S, and suppose that two sequential lines $s_{sp_S}(a)$ and $s_{sp_S}(b)$ are given. We, then, consider shape similarity between $s_{sp_S}(a)$ and $s_{sp_S}(b)$. It is also noticed that $ss(s_{sp_S}(a), s_{sp_S}(b))$ has the following relation to the variation of shape-precision:
$$ss(a,b) = ss(s_{\overline{sp_S}}(a), s_{\overline{sp_S}}(b)) \leq ss(s_i(a), s_i(b)) \leq ss(s_j(a), s_j(b)),$$
where i and j are values of sp_S satisfying the following inequality:
$$\overline{sp_S} \geq i \geq j.$$
□

3.2 Applying Iterative Deepening to Joint Detection

In this paper, we introduce a search control technique, Iterative Deepening, into joint detection and propose JDID (Joint Detection with Iterative Deepening).

Figure 6 shows an outline of search trees constructed by JDID. The search begins at the lowest shape-precision $sp_S = 0$. In the figure, the leftmost tree, for example, shows joint detection from two potsherds A and B. The leftmost branch in the tree, for example, shows a comparison of shape between two sub-contours a_1 and b_1 in A and B respectively. In the branch, a node at the depth of i ($i > 0$) has two sequential lines $s_{i-1}(a_1)$ and $s_{i-1}(b_2)$. A node at the deeper depth has sequential lines with their higher shape-precision. The search proceeds in the breadth-first manner with iterative deepening. Node expansion at the depth of i behaves intuitively as follows:

i) calculate shape similarity $ss(s_{i-1}(a), s_{i-1}(b))$, and then judge whether the pair is a joint or not,

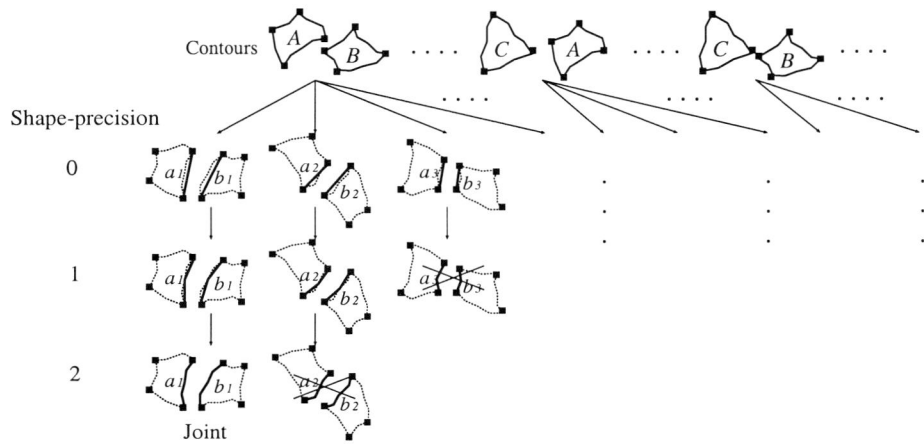

Fig. 6. An Outline of Search Trees Constructed by JDID.

ii) from the above judgment, delete nodes containing inconsistent pairs (see nodes marked with × in Figure 6),
iii) go on in either of following three ways according to the number of remaining nodes at the same depth:
   zero: terminate the search in failure.
   one: terminate the search in success, and detect the pair of sub-contours in the node as joint.
   more than one: generate a descendant node, which contains pair $(s_i(a), s_i(b))$ of sub-contours, with their shape-precision $sp_S = i$.

The search iterates the above node expansion in breadth-first manner with successively heightening shape-precision.

3.3 JDID Algorithm

Figure 7 shows the algorithm of JDID. In the figure, S denotes a given set of sub-contours, Q denotes a set of pairs of sub-contours, and $a, b, c1$, and $c2$ denote sub-contours in S. $|a|$ denotes the length of a, and i has a value of shape-precision sp_Q. $ss(a, b)$ returns the value of shape similarity between a and b. R indicates sets of sub-contours.

The algorithm detects the most similar pair $(c1, c2)$ from given set S of sub-contours by successively heightening shape-precision. Previous to the iteration, JDID, considering the lowest shape-precision $i = 0$, checks the length of all sub-contours in S, and generates set Q of pairs of sub-contours (a, b)s such that difference of length between a and b is within $\alpha\%$ (see *ll.* 4–9 in Figure 7). In the i-th iteration, for all pairs (a, b)s in Q, JDID executes the following procedures. It generates sequential lines $s_i(a)$ and $s_i(b)$, which approximate a and b with shape-precision i respectively, and calculates shape similarity $ss(s_i(a), s_i(b))$ between $s_i(a)$ and $s_i(b)$. Then, if $ss(s_i(a), s_i(b))$ is less than threshold β, it deletes

```
JDID: Joint Detection with Iterative Deepening
    Input:    S:        a set of sub-contours
    Output:   ANS: an answer   : (c1, c2)      (in success)
                                : false          (in failure)
 1 begin
 2    R := S;
 3    Q := φ;
 4    for each a ∈ S                         % pruning by the length of sub-contours
 5       begin
 6          R := R \ {a};
 7          for each b ∈ R
 8             if (−α ≤ (|b|−|a|)/|a| × 100 ≤ α) then Q := Q ∪ {(a, b)};
 9       end
10    i := 1;
11    escape := false;
12    repeat                                  % iteration begins at shape-precision i
13       for each (a, b) ∈ Q
14          begin
15             generate s_i(a) and s_i(b) from a and b with shape-precision i respectively;
16             if (ss(s_i(a), s_i(b)) < β) then Q := Q \ {(a, b)};
17          end
18       if ((s_i(a) = s_{i−1}(a)) and (s_i(b) = s_{i−1}(b))for all(a, b) ∈ Q) then escape := true;
19       i := i + 1;                          % heightening shape-precision i = i + 1
20    until (escape or |Q| ≤ 1)              % |Q| denotes the number of elements in Q
21    if (escape) then ANS := (c1, c2) | ss(c1, c2) ≥ ss(a, b) for all (a, b) ∈ Q;   % in success
22    if (|Q| = 1) then ANS := (c1, c2) ∈ Q;                                         % in success
23             else ANS := false;                                                    % in failure
24 end.
```

Fig. 7. The JDID Algorithm.

(a, b) from Q. The above series of procedures is repeated until i reaches the upper bound $\overline{sp_Q}$ of shape-precision, or until the number of elements in Q is not more than one (see $ll.$ 12–20 in Figure 7). In the former case, JDID selects one pair $(c1, c2)$ from Q such that $c1$ and $c2$ are the most similar each other, and terminates in success with $(c1, c2)$. In the latter case, if $|Q| = 1$, Q containing only one pair $(c1, c2)$, JDID terminates in success with $(c1, c2)$, otherwise if $|Q| = 0$, JDID terminates in failure (see $ll.$ 21–23 in Figure 7). In our eathenware reconstruction system, two potsherds, whose contours include sub-contours $c1$ and $c2$, are joined.

We, now, discuss related work and the problems. Hori and et al. [3] proposed a two dimentional array, called Matching Score Array, so as to detect a joint among two potsherds. In the method, a potsherd is divided into numerous segments, and, for two potsherds, two sequences of segments are assigned to columns and rows in the array. Shape similarities among two potsherds are checked in round-robbin fashion, that is, for all elements in the array, shape similarities among two segments assinged in the elements should be calculated. The method is to detect carefully one joint from only two potsherds, and suitable to reconstruction some earthenware from a few potsherds. The method, however, has no efficiency in calculation of shape similarity, thus, it results in computational explosion when the number of potsherds increases. On the other hand, JDID, taking the complexity of contours into consideration, is embedded with a search control mechanism so as to restrain computational explosion.

4 Experimental Results

We have implemented the JDID algorithm in our earthenware reconstruction system. We have also made some experiments of reconstruction of earthenware from excavated potsherds. In one of the experiments, we have given 35 potsherds shown in Figure 1 to our system. Figure 8 shows earthenware reconstructed by our system. In this particular example, the result indicates that our system can

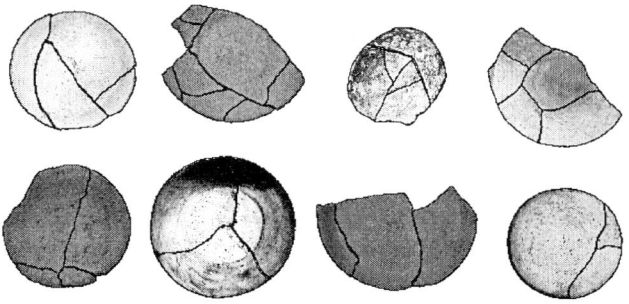

Fig. 8. Output Images.

correctly and completely reconstruct 8 pieces of earthenware from given potsherds. Our system takes 35.7 (sec.) to reconstruct all the pieces of earthenware from the 35 potsherds.

In order to verify effectiveness of JDID, we have compared execution time of our system with a naive system, in which joint detection is executed with shape-precision fixed on the upper bound, by changing the number of potsherds. The both systems are written in C++, and all runtime is CPU time on Intel PentiumIII/500MHz. In the experiments, parameters for the both systems, $n = 64 \times 2^i$, where i is a value of shape-precision, $N = 5$, $\alpha = 5$, and $\beta = 100$. Figure 9 shows the experimental results. The solid line in the figure shows the runtime by our system, while the broken line is those by the naive system. The results indicates that our system embedded with JDID is about $4.2 \sim 38.3$ times faster than the naive system as the number of potsherds increases.

5 Conclusion

We proposed an earthenware reconstruction system, which can automatically reconstruct earthenware from given potsherds. It this paper, we proposed an efficient joint detection algorithm JDID, which can efficiently detect a joint from numerous potsherds. Taking the complexity of contours into consideration, the algorithm can avoid redundant computation of shape similarity, by dynamically

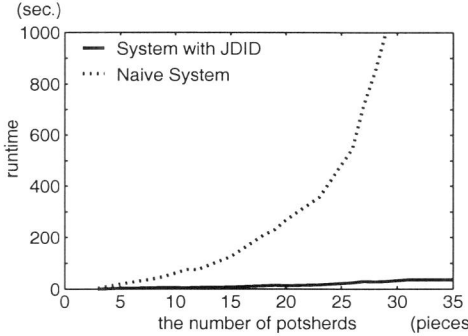

Fig. 9. Experimental Results.

changing shape-precision for representing the contours. We also made some experiments, and reported good performance results comparable to a system using naive joint detection.

Our proposed system can automatically reconstruct several pieces of earthenware from given numerous potsherds. In general, the process of identifying which potsherds belong to the same earthenware is the most difficult part. Our system does not, however, have the identification process, because the system utilizes only shape of contours of potsherds as a criterion of joint detection. For a potsherd, its joint pair is detected from all other potsherds. The above identification process requires more effective information about potsherds, such as surface pattern, color, three dimensional character, and so on.

As future work, a new joint detection method utilizing surface patterns on potsherds, and enhancement of our system so as to recognize three dimensional shape and utilize three dimensional character, will be discussed in forthcoming papers.

Acknowledgment

We are grateful to Nagoya City Miharashidai Archaeologocal Museum for excavated potsherds. This work was funded in part by Grant-in-Aid for Scientific Research Program of Japan Society for the Promotion of Science.

References

1. David A. Kosiba et al. An Automatic Jigsaw Puzzle Solver. *12th IAPR International Conference on Pattern Recognition*, Vol.I:616–618, 1994.
2. Kalvin Alan, Wolfson Haim, Schonberg Edith, and Lamdan Yehezkel. Solving Jigsaw Puzzles by Computer. *Annals of Operations Research(12)*, pages 51–64, 1988.
3. Kenta Hori, Masakazu Imai, and Tsukasa Ogasawara. Joint Detection for Potsherds of Broken Earthenware. *Proceedings of Computer Vision and Pattern Recognition '99*, Vol.2:440–445, June 1999.

4. Richard E. Korf. Depth-First Iterative-Deepening: An Optimal Admissible Tree Search. *Artif. Intell.*, Vol.27:97–109, 1985.
5. Richard E. Korf. Iterative-Deepening-A*: An Optimal Admissible Tree Search. *In Proc. of the 9th IJCAI*, pages 1034–1036, 1985.
6. Azriel Rosenfeld and Emily Johnston. Angle Detection on Digital Curves. *IEEE Transactions on Computers*, C-22:875–878, 1973.
7. Yoshinori Uesaka. Spectral Analysis and Complexity of Form. *Proceedings of the Eighth Symposium on Applied Functional Analysis*, pages 18–29, 1985.
8. Yoshinori Uesaka. Spectral analysis of form based on Fourier descriptors. *Science on Form, Proceedings of the First International Symposium for Science on Form*, pages 405–412, 1986.

Feature-Based Face Recognition:
Neural Network Using Recognition-by-Recall

Wenli Zhang[1] and Yan Guo[2]

[1] RWCP, Information-Base Functions KRDL* Lab
[2] RWCP, Multi-Modal Functions KRDL* Lab
*Kent Ridge Digital Labs,
21 Heng Mui Keng Terrace, Singapore 119613
yguo@krdl.org.sg

Abstract. Accurate face recognition is very hard to achieve but very important in practical applications. We propose a neural network, based on recognition-by-recall paradigm, to improve the performance. We observe that human has remarkable capability in verifying if two photographs are from the same person or not, thus we devise a neural network to simulate the capability. We use eigen-face features to train the network and adopt a training method of the neural network to tolerate the errors in eye locations. The result shows that the verification performance of the system is very promising.

1. Introduction

Automatic human face recognition is very useful in many applications, for example, office security, criminal identifications, etc. Two main approaches have been developed: recognition via neural networks and recognition based on detailed face features. Neural networks can provide satisfactory recognition through training and sometimes through developing features, and several neural network based face recognition systems have been proposed [7].

Neural network models proposed for face recognition so far include: multi-layer feed forward classification network, clustering network, SOM network, etc. The most popular one seems to be the simplest multi-layer feed forward network applying back propagation algorithm to training the system. In paper [3], it mentioned that recently several authors have tested neural network techniques on face identification tasks. Multi-layered perceptrons - MLPs perform well on noisy data and are able to encode geometrical transforms such as head rotations, smiles and funny faces. In an image analysis system, faces are often inaccurately segmented in the images. Bad segmentation usually results in size distortion and/or incomplete facial parts (such as hair and chin). Neural networks are known to be robust in such situations, being able to recover the whole from a partial part. It is said that fully connected MLPs with only one hidden layer are not robust to image translations or to lighting condition changes, though they are good classifiers most of time. Neural networks are not solutions to all the recognition challenges, but they are handy tools for the tasks they suit.

We observe that human has remarkable capability in verifying if two photographs are from the same person or not, thus we devise an artificial neural network to simulate the capability. Conventional applications of neural networks to face recognition are trying to train the neural networks to identify a person among a given database of people's face images. However, it is impractical to collect large amount of samples from each individual to sufficiently train the network. Our method requires only pairs of photos from either same persons (positive samples) or different persons (negative samples); it is easy to collect sufficient amount of image pairs to train the network.

Our approach is to adopt a neural network to do face verification under recognition-by-recall paradigm [1]. It is aimed at properly classify a pair of face images into two groups: same person or different person.

Performance of a biometrics based person authentication system is most commonly measured in two ways: *False Rejection Rate* (FRR), and *False Acceptance Rate* (FAR) [6]. FAR and FRR rates are generally expressed in terms of probability.

FAR: is the chance that someone other than you is granted access to your account, in other words, the probability that a non-mated comparison (i.e. two biometrics samples of different faces) match.

FRR: is the probability that you are not authenticated to access your account. A strict definition states that the FRR is the probability that a mated comparison (i.e. 2 biometrics samples of the same face) incorrectly determines that there is no match.

Both FAR and FRR are functions of threshold, we cannot reduce FAR and FRR at the same time. Applying different thresholds, we can get different FAR and FRR. At certain threshold, FAR and FRR can be equal, this rate is called *Equal Error Rate* (EER). Here we use the EER as the verification performance measure. EER is an important parameter to judge the overall system performance. Here our goal of improving performance is to reduce the EER.

2. System Overview and Our Approach

In our feature based recognition-by-recall system, the inputs to the neural network are eigen-face features processed from PCA (Principal Component Analysis) [2], [5], [15]. PCA based algorithm forms the basis of numerous algorithms and studies in the face recognition literature [15].

PCA is based on the following idea: The space of all images, whose dimension is w by h pixels, is the image space [5]. All the faces look like each other in the sense that they all have two eyes, a mouth, and a nose. Therefore, all the face vectors are located in a very narrow cluster in the image space. Hence, the full image space is not an optimal space for face description. The task for PCA aims to build a face space, which better describes the faces. The basis vectors of this face space are called the principal components. The goal of is to reduce the dimension of a set or space so that the new basis better describes the typical 'models' of the set.

We extract PCA features based on the system proposed by paper [2]. It will extract 32 features from a normalized face [2], [5], [15]. Our system works as follows: first we create the face database to store the images used for recall. We train a MLP classifier to do the verification task. Here the inputs of the MLP classifier are the features generated from the normalized face images using PCA [2]. After the network is trained, the system adopts recognition-by-recall approach. Given a person's face image, the system will compare through the face database and tell if the person is the same person or not with the person inside the database. The flowchart of the system is illustrated in Fig. 1.

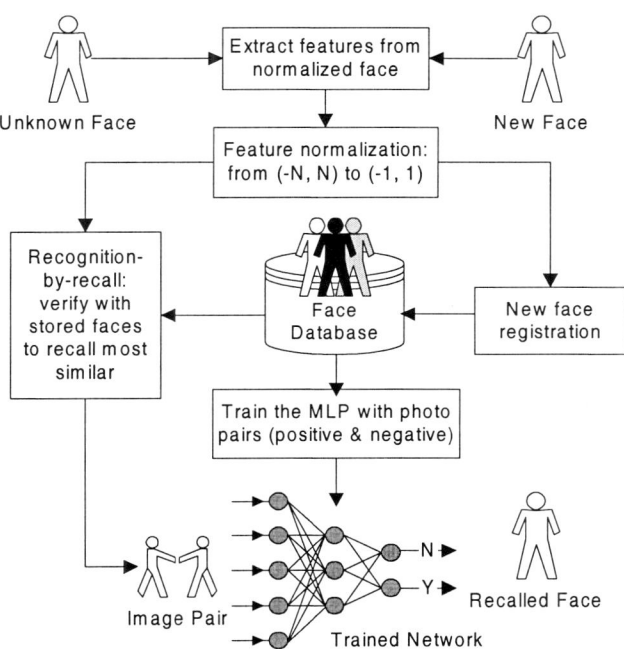

Fig. 1. Flowchart of the system depicting three working scenarios: 1) new face recognition; 2) neural network training; and 3) unknown face recognition by recall.

2.1 Recognition-by-Recall

Recognition-by-recall [1], [2] works as follows: For a given sequence of patterns generated by an unknown object, identify the object by recalling the memory where patterns or knowledge of patterns previously generated by various objects are stored. In the case of face recognition, the pattern is a function of time and space. Recognition-by-recall is based on the fact that when we recognized a familiar face, we do not match every single feature but rather recall the unique features of the face, that have been remembered in the memory for comparison. It means that we recognize them by recalling from our memory [1], [2]. In this case, the memory is the face database of pre-registered persons.

2.2 Preparing Training Data Set

One of the advantages of our approach is that it uses photo pairs from same persons (positive samples) or different persons (negative samples) to train the network. It does not need large amount of samples from the each person, as required by conventional neural networks trained to perform identification tasks. Of course, more photos from the same person will be better to train the network. In order to make the system more robust to tolerate minor eyes location errors, which cause significant EER surge with Euclidean distance based verification, we create eight extra sets of features from each image. We shift the eye locations up to (-3, +3) pixels, as shown in **Table 1**. So altogether we have 9 sets of training data from each image.

Table 1. Shifting eye locations before image normalization to generate more training data sets. The trained network is thus more robust to eye location errors. (Δl_x, Δl_y) and (Δr_x, Δr_y) are shifting from left and right eye positions respectively.

Δl_x	Δl_y	Δr_x	Δr_y
-3	0	3	0
-3	3	3	-3
0	3	0	-3
3	3	-3	-3
3	0	-3	0
0	-3	0	3
-3	-3	3	3
3	-3	-3	3

2.3 MLP Classifier

Choosing MLP with back propagation is because MLP is accurate for classification task and back propagation is the most popular learning algorithm for connectionist networks, which uses the steepest descent method to obtain the weight values that minimize an error mean [4]. Also, back propagation is robust and fast for classification task.

The task is to train a network to perform verification of face images pairs. The network consists of 64 input units, 129 hidden units and 2 output nodes corresponding to the two classification classes: justify as the same person class and justify as the different person class. The reason we choose two classes for output instead of one is purely for performance purpose. The reason for choosing 129 nodes for hidden units is based on the benchmark testing results. The result shows that if we choose for example 64 nodes, the EER will increase 2%. The learning rate and the momentum are both set to 0.15. The weights are initialized by random numbers between −1.0 to 1.0. The comparison threshold we choose is from 0.5 to 0.95 with 0.05 interval. The learning process is controlled by input parameter of epoch. The network is shown in Fig. 2.

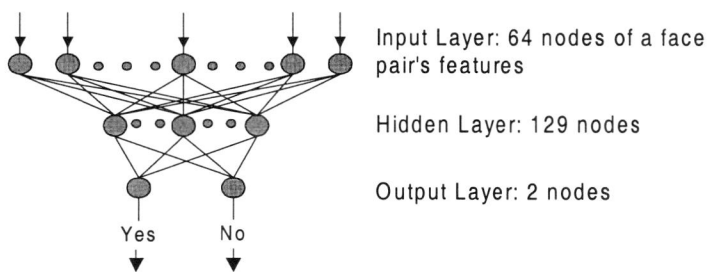

Fig. 2. Fully connected MLP neural network. Its input are two groups of features of two face images. Each group has 32 features. It has 129 hidden nodes and 2 output nodes.

2.4 Input Feature Normalization

The input units of the MLP network are the two normalized faces' eigen features. Each of the normalized faces has 32 features. The input normalization [4] is done to make the original feature value ranging from -N to N to range from -1 to 1. This is done by first calculating the mean value M of the features and then offsetting each feature's value by:

$$f^{off} = f^{original} - M$$

where f^{off} is the offset features value and $f^{orinigal}$ is the original value of the feature. The offset features are then divided by the vector length L_v, which is calculated as following:

$$L_v = \sqrt{\sum_i^N f^{off\,2}}$$

3. Benchmark Testing and Performance Analysis

3.1 The Databases for Experiments

The benchmark testing is based on two sets of very different types of databases. The first set is the XM2VTSDB (CDS001) face database from University of Surrey [8]. The XM2VTSDB contains four recordings of 295 subjects taken over a period of four months.

Each recording contains a speaking head shot and a rotating head shot. Most of them are frontal faces with similar lighting condition and slightly different facial expression and orientation. A few of them are in between of frontal face and side face. Each person has 4 different face images taken at around one-month time difference one after another. That is, each person's face image 1 is taken one month before image 2, image 2 is taken one month before image 3 and so on.

The second database sets (here we call it BDIS - Big Difference Image Set which is not for public use) contains 5734 face images. Among those 5734 face images, there are 1955 persons who have two different photos. We use these 1955 persons' photos as our second data set for further processing. Those persons' photos are taken around 10 to 20 years time difference. Some of the images have quite bad lighting conditions. Most of the faces are frontal faces with different orientation.

3.2 Verification Performance

The verification performance shown here is from testing set. We only use the testing set for the performance evaluation because the testing set reflects more real than training set to do the comparison. We use PCA with Euclidean distance as the comparison measure to compare with the neural network using recognition-by-recall. We tested on the XM2VTSDB images, the result is shown in Fig. 3. From Fig. 3, we can see that the EER of the neural network system is 7%.

On the same XM2VTSDB, PCA with Euclidean distance method gives the results as shown in Fig. 4. The EER is about 19%.

Comparing to PCA-Euclidean distance method, the performance of the neural network is 2.7 times better. It demonstrates that our neural network using recognition by recall approach is very encouraging in improving face recognition performance. It is much better than PCA using Euclidean distance in terms of verification performance, although the neural network using recognition-by-recall is data set training dependent. But it is still a method to improve the system performance. We can adopt incremental training strategy to solve this problem. That means when new face is coming, we can train the neural net incrementally based on the existing network.

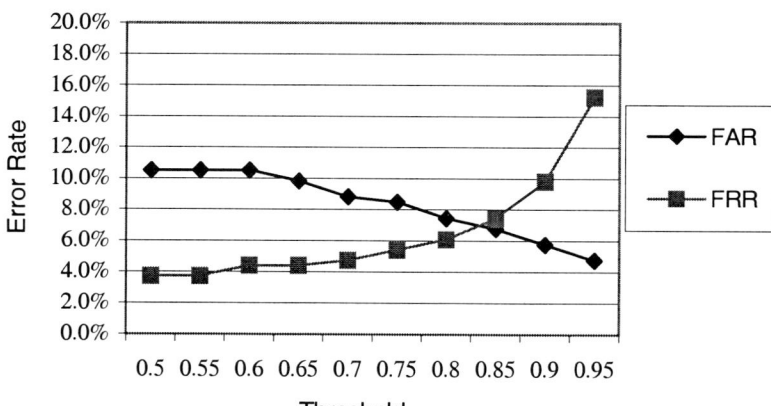

Fig. 3. Verification performance of the neural network system on XM2VTSDB. We use image sets 1,3 for training, and image sets 2,4 for testing.

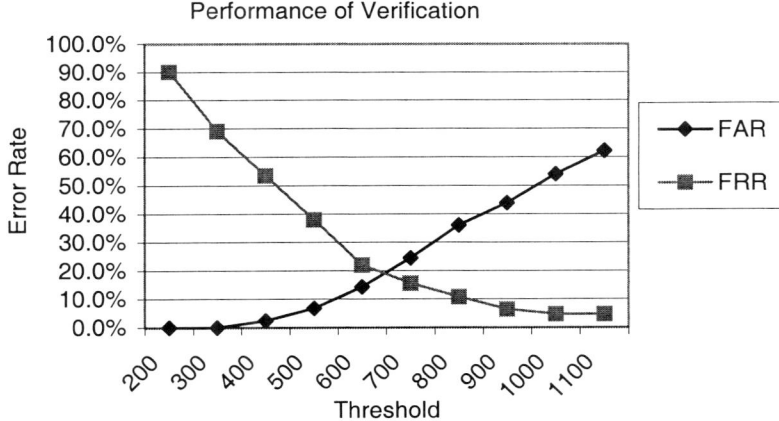

Fig. 4. Verification performance of the PCA-Euclidean distance method on XM2VTSDB.

We conducted the benchmark testing using data set BDIS. We trained the neural net using BDIS and tested it using subset of BDIS, the result shows that the EER is still very high: nearly 43% [9]. Which is almost the same as PCA with Euclidean distance [9]. That means even neural network can't solve the problem if the same person's photos have too much difference and /or the images' quality is too poor.

3.3 Robustness to Eye Location Errors

We also tested the robustness of this approach regarding to errors up to (-3,3) pixels in eye location on XM2VTSDB images. The results are shown in table 2. From the results we can see that it achieves an average EER 11%, which is 2.6 times better than PCA with Euclidean distance (The average EER is 29% [9]).

Table 2. The neural network system's EER results on XM2VTSDB images with eye location shifting up to ±3 pixels.

▲ lx	▲ ly	▲ rx	▲ ry	EER
-3	0	3	0	13%
-3	3	3	-3	13.7%
0	3	0	-3	9%
3	3	-3	-3	12%
3	0	-3	0	9%
0	-3	0	3	7%
-3	-3	3	3	15%
3	-3	-3	3	10%

4. Conclusion and Future Work

We proposed a neural network using recognition-by-recall approach to face recognition. Our effort here is to deploy a strategy integrating PCA, neural network, and recognition-by-recall to improve the system verification performance. From the benchmark results we can see that our approach proposed here demonstrates much better performance than the PCA-Euclidean method. The strategy of training the network using generated samples by eyes shifting is proven to be effective to tolerate minor eye location errors.

However, it is still an open problem to verify two photos taken many years apart. We did a test to recognize a person by human using data set BDIS, which are the persons' images with more than 10 years time difference. Human is capable to recognize 80% of the faces, which is much better than the state-of-the-art face recognition technology. That is the gap between human vision and computer vision. Although the neural network approach is more accurate, but one of the shortcomings is that the speed is not as faster as some other approach like PCA with Euclidean distance. Now we are working on the new strategy of combining different approach together to get better performance both in speed and accuracy. We will first use a fast algorithm like PCA with Euclidean distance to narrow down the data set to gain the speed, after that we use more accurate neural network system to verify the prescreened set to achieve higher accuracy.

References

1. Wu, J., K.: Recognition by recall. 1997 Real World Computing Symposium, pp. 142-147, Tokyo, Japan, (1997).
2. Sun, Q.-B., Lam, C-P., Wu, J., K.: A practical automatic face recognition system. In: Wechsler H, et al., (eds): Face recognition, from theory to applications. Springer-Verlag.
3. Boattour, H., Fogelman Soulie , F. & Viennet, E.: Solving the human face recognition task using neural nets. Proceedings of the ICANN-92, Brighton, England, Sept. (1992), pp. 1595-1598
4. Evans, D., J., Zainuddin Z.: Acceleration of the back propagation through dynamic adaptation of the momentum. Report No. 1029, PARC, Loughborough University of Tech., U.K., (1996).
5. Feraud, R.: PCA, Neural Networks and estimation for face detection. In: Wechsler H, et al., (eds): Face recognition, from theory to applications. Springer-Verlag.
6. American Biometric Company: What is Biometric Authentication? White paper: http://www.abio.com/whitepapers/biometric.htm.
7. Jia, X., Nixon, M., S.: On developing an extended feature set for automatic face recognition.
8. University of Surrey: The extended M2VTS database, http://www.ee.surrey.ac.uk/CVSSP/xm2vtsdb/
9. Zhang, W., and Guo, Y.: Benchmark testing and performance improving using neural network for face recognition. In the proceedings of the 2000 International conference on Artificial Intelligence (IC-AI'2000).
10. Crowley, J.: A local feature based human face recognition system, 0-7803-2404-8/94, IEEE pp. 32-36.
11. Fukuda, T., Itou, S., Arai, F.: Recognition of human face using fuzzy inference and neural network. IEEE International Workshop on Robot and human communication, pp. 375-380.

12. Ahmad Fadzil M. H., Abu Bakar H.: Human face recognition using neural networks. 0-8186-6950-0/94 IEEE pp. 936-939
13. Graham, D. B., Allinson, N., M.: Face recognition using virtual parametric eigenspace signatures. IPA97, 15-17 July 1997, Conference publication No. 443 IEE, 1997, pp. 106-110
14. Lawrence, S., Giles, C., L., Tsoi, A. C., Back, A. D.: Face recognition: A convolutional neural-network approach. IEEE Transactions on neural networks, Vol. 8, No. 1, January (1997).
15. Moon H, Phillips, P., J.: Analysis of PCA-based Face Recognition Algorithms. In: Bowyer, K.W., Phillips, P.J. (eds): Empirical Evaluation Techniques in Computer Vision. IEEE Computer Society Press.
16. Rowley, H., A., Baluja, S., Kanade T.: Human face detection in visual scenes. CMU-CS-95-158R
17. Sung, K.-K., Poggio, T.: Example-based learning for view-based human face detection. IEEE Transactions on PAMI, Vol. 20, No. 1, Jan., (1998)

Segmentation of Connected Handwritten Chinese Characters Based on Stroke Analysis and Background Thinning

Shuyan Zhao and Pengfei Shi

Institute of Image Processing & Pattern Recognition, Shanghai Jiao Tong University,
Shanghai, 200030, People's Republic of China
syzhao_99@yahoo.com, pfshi@ippr.sjtu.edu.cn

Abstract. Segmentation of connected handwritten Chinese characters is a very difficult task in document image analysis. In this paper, a novel algorithm based on stroke analysis and background thinning is proposed to segment connected handwritten Chinese characters. The feature points, viz. end points, fork points and corner points are detected in the thinned image. The segments between feature points are considered as substrokes and are extracted. Lengths of substrokes and the topological relations between them are employed to locate connected point. A new method based on background thinning is developed to decide a proper segmentation path. The experimental results show that satisfactory performance is achieved by the presented method for segmentation of connected handwritten Chinese characters.

1 Introduction

Off-line handwritten Chinese character recognition is always regarded as a difficult and challenging problem in pattern recognition field. The major difficulties encountered in solving this problem are the large number of characters, the high complexity, many mutually similar characters, and the large variations in writing from person to person. The ultimate goal of handwritten Chinese character recognition is high writing freedom and recognition rate, while connected handwritten characters have great negative effects on recognition [1-2]. Therefore, correct segmentation of the connected characters is the premise of correct recognition. Recently, some segmentation algorithms mainly aim at processing connected handwritten letters and digits, these methods usually make use of the inherent features in the image and locate the position of connected point [3-7]. However, there are few literatures on segmentation of connected handwritten Chinese characters.

In this paper, we directly take segmentation of connected handwritten Chinese characters as our goal and propose a new approach based on stroke analysis and background thinning. At first the feature points, viz. end points, fork points and corner points are detected and substrokes are extracted in the thinned image. The lengths of substrokes and the topological relations between them are employed to locate connected point. When determining the segmentation path, most approaches only utilize the foreground image, while we make full use of the information of thinned background and then obtain proper segmentation path. The experimental results show that the presented method is very effective for segmentation of connected handwritten Chinese characters.

2 Detection of Feature Points and Extraction of Substrokes

For convenience of further explanation, it is necessary to distinguish between "stroke" and "substroke". In this paper, "substroke" is defined as the segment between two feature points, while the term "stroke" is reserved for the truly primitive writing element for Chinese characters, i.e. the pen-movement trajectory. The existing methods for extraction of substrokes can be generally divided into two categories, i.e. with and without thinning processing, respectively. There are advantages and disadvantages for the methods of both categories. Compared to those belonging to the second category, the methods with thinning are much simpler and faster for implementation. However, an intrinsic problem in the methods of the first category is that they may produce spurious short branches or pattern distortion caused by splitting cross or touching points into two fork points. On the other hand, the methods without thinning have good performance in keeping the substroke shape at the expense of computation complexity and time consumption.

In this paper, the long substrokes in the particular region of the image are utilized to find out connected point while short ones are neglected, so the thinning method is employed [8].

2.1 End Points and Fork Points

Feature points in the thinned image must be detected, which include end points, fork points and corner points. Just as Fig.1 shows, A is a corner point, B is a 3-fork point, C is a 4-fork point and D is an end point.

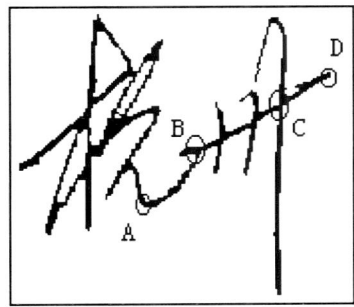

x_4	x_3	x_2
x_5	P	x_1
x_6	x_7	x_8

Fig. 1. Feature points

Fig. 2. Pixel P and its 8 neighbours

in the thinned character image, the crossing number $X(p)$ of a black pixel p is calculated as

$$X(p) = \sum_{i=1}^{8} |x_{i+1} - x_i| \quad (1)$$

Where $x_9 = x_1$, and x_i is the value of the pixel arranged in Fig.2, which is one or zero. Then according to the crossing number $X(p)$, the pixel p can be decided to be an end point, a 3-fork point or a 4-fork point, just as

$$X(p) = \begin{cases} 2 & p \text{ is an end point} \\ 6 & p \text{ is a } 3\text{-fork point} \\ 8 & p \text{ is a } 4\text{-fork point} \end{cases} \quad (2)$$

The detected points are put into the feature points set for extraction of substrokes. Then one of the points is taken out from the feature points set, from which tracing of the entire image begins. We search its 8 directions until reaching another feature point and end this search. We need to judge the attribute of the feature point which has just been found. If it is an end point, it can be deleted from the feature points set at once; if it is a 3-fork or 4-fork point, then it can only be removed until all of its directions have been searched. When the feature points set is empty, we can conclude that the complete image has been traced and all the substrokes have been found out.

We define a date structure sk[i] to save the information of beginning and ending positions and the length of stroke i, where i=1,.....StrokeNum, and StrokeNum is the total number of strokes. sk[i].x_0 and sk[i].y_0 are the coordinates of the beginning point $p_0(x_0,y_0)$•sk[i].x_1 and sk[i].y_1 are the coordinates of the ending point $p_1(x_1,y_1)$, and sk[i].SL is the length of stroke i. In addition, we presume $x_0 < x_1$.

2.2 Corner Points

By observing and analysing a lot of connected handwritten Chinese characters, we find that the connection of two characters often produces corner points. Therefore, corner points are also important feature points. As Fig.3 illustrates, the two connection characters should be separated at the location of the corner point.

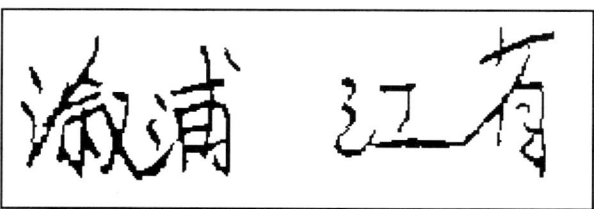

Fig. 3. Corner points at the location of connection

Usually, the pixel p(x,y) which satisfies one of the following two conditions is a corner point(Fig.4):
(1) The perpendicular distance from p to the straight line through two terminals p_0 and p_1 is maximum;
(2) The angle between the two vectors emitted from p to p_0 and p_1 is minimum.

The local angle is generally an important parameter to detect corner points. At first, three definitions are presented:

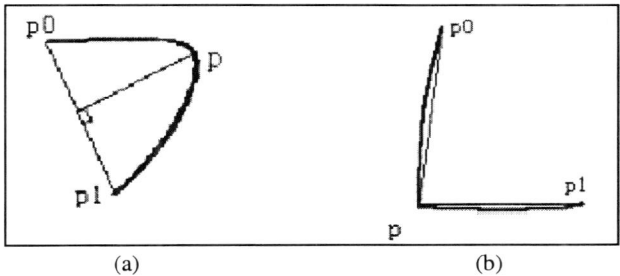

Fig. 4. Corner points

- Definition 1. The perpendicular distance D(x,y) of pixel p(x,y) to the line determined by the two terminals $p_0(x_0,y_0)$ and $p_1(x_1,y_1)$ is

$$D(x,y) = \frac{|a \cdot x + b \cdot y + c|}{\sqrt{a^2 + b^2}} \quad (3)$$

Where a= $y_1 - y_0$, b= $x_0 - x_1$, c= $x_1 y_0 - x_0 y_1$.

- Definition 2. The angle A(x,y) between the two vectors from p(x,y) to $p_0(x_0,y_0)$ and $p_1(x_1,y_1)$ is

$$A(x,y) = acos(\mathbf{u} \cdot \mathbf{v} / |\mathbf{u}| \cdot |\mathbf{v}|) \quad (4)$$

Where the two vectors are **u** and **v**, **u**=$(x_0 - x, y_0 - y)$, **v**=$(x_1 - x, y_1 - y)$.

- Definition 3. The local angle of p(x,y), Al(x,y), is defined as the angle between the two vectors with their end points k pixels away from their common point, p(x,y). k is an empirical value and can be adapted according to the character size. In our approach, k is 5.

The iterative detection of corner points is based on the above three definitions, which can be introduced as follows:

Step 1: For a stroke containing SL pixels, compute the D(x,y) and A(x,y) of each pixel in the interval[k, SL-k]. Presume the maximum D(x,y) is Dmax(x', y'),and the minimum A(x,y) is Amin(x'', y'');

Step 2: If $Dmax(x', y') < k$, then there are no corner points and exit; otherwise, go to the next step;

Step 3: Compute the local angle of (x', y'), $Al(x', y')$. If $Al(x', y') < T$, then go to step 5; otherwise, go to the next step;

Step 4: If $Amin(x'', y'') < T$, then go to the next step; otherwise, there are no corner points and exit;

Step 5: This point is regarded as a corner point.

Where T is another empirical value, here $T = 0.85\pi$.

The stroke, where a corner point has been found, is split from the corner point, and each of the two parts is taken as a substroke. "StrokeNum" and the corresponding "sk[i]" should be updated at the same time.

3 Location of Connected Point

In this section, we at first look for the substrokes perhaps with the connected point and then determine which point in them is the connected point. By observing a lot of handwritten Chinese characters, we find that connection often occurs in the long substrokes in the middle region of the image, e.g. if sk[i] satisfies the following two conditions:

(1) sk[i].x_0<Width/2 and sk[i].x_1> Width/2•

(2) sk[i].SL >Width/5.

Then in substroke i there may be connected point, where "Width" is the width of the image. If no such substroke is found in the middle region, then the search area should be moved to the left or the right.

The connected corner is usually corner point or fork point. In addition, the projection of the thinned image "proj" is also a main feature, for the feature point in the position where the distribution of substrokes is dense is not suitable to be regarded as the connected point.

The rules for determining the connected point are as follows:

Rule 1•If $p_0(x_0, y_0)$ is a corner point•while $p_1(x_1, y_1)$ is not a corner point, and Width*1/4<x_0<Width*3/4, and proj[x_0]•=2 or proj[x_0+1]•=2•then $p_0(x_0, y_0)$ is the connected point;

Rule 2: If $p_1(x_1, y_1)$ is a corner point, while $p_0(x_0, y_0)$ is not a corner point•and Width*1/4<x_1<Width*3/4, and proj[x_1]<=2 or proj[x_1-1]<=2•then $p_1(x_1, y_1)$ is the connected point;

Rule 3: If $p_0(x_0, y_0)$ and $p_1(x_1, y_1)$ are both corner points, then if proj[x_0]<=2 or proj[x_0+1]<=2•then $p_0(x_0, y_0)$ is the connected point•else if proj[x_1]<=2 or proj[x_1-1]<=2•then $p_1(x_1, y_1)$ is the connected point;

Rule 4•If $p_0(x_0, y_0)$ is an end point•while $p_1(x_1, y_1)$ is a fork point•then $p_1(x_1, y_1)$ is the connected point;

Rule 5•If $p_0(x_0, y_0)$ is a fork point, while $p_1(x_1, y_1)$ is an end point•then $p_0(x_0, y_0)$ is the connected points ;

Rule 6: If $p_0(x_0, y_0)$ and $p_1(x_1, y_1)$ are both fork points, then if proj[x_0]< =2 or proj[x_0+1]<=2•then $p_0(x_0, y_0)$ is the connected point•else if proj[x_1]<=2 or proj[x_1-1]<=2•then $p_1(x_1, y_1)$ is the connected point.

All substrokes possibly with connected point are tested, until the appropriate connected point has been found.

4 Segmentation

After locating the connected point, how to segment the two connected characters with a proper path is also a difficult task. Many connected characters overlap each other, so if they are separated with a straight-line path, some parts of one character are often split into the other (as showed by Fig.5). Therefore, the decision of a suitable segmentation path is a critical problem. Most segmentation methods only utilize foreground pixels, while in this paper we make full use of the background image. At first, the background of split character image is obtained, then in the thinned background image, the segmentation path is decided from the split point upward and downward, neglecting some short branches, until reaching the outmost of the thinned background. At that time, we have found a pretty good segmentation path.

The whole procedure of segmentation of two connected handwritten Chinese characters is illustrated by Fig.6. (a) is the original image, (b) is the thinned image. In the thinned image the feature points and substrokes are detected out and then the connected point is located, just as (c) shows. (d) is the split image, (e) is the thinned background with the original image and (f) shows the segmentation path.

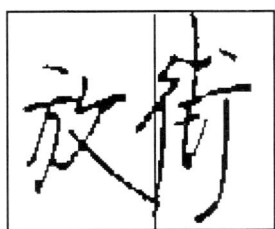

Fig. 5. Overlapping

5 Experimental Results

Testing images come from real mail addresses. At first, according to the estimated character width and aspect ratio of a character, we determine whether there exist connected characters in the string. Then the illustrated algorithm is applied to partition such connected characters. A series of experiments have been done as Fig. 7 shows. The results show the effectiveness of our algorithm.

Though the algorithm is employed to segment the connected character pairs, it can be easily extended to adapt to more than two characters. In such case, we at first estimate the character number the image contains, then use this segmentation method in the particular regions of the image. Repeat the segmentation procedure until each segmented part has acceptable width. However, when the characters connect in more than one position, the algorithm seems ineffective. In the meanwhile, the algorithm fails in some special cases. In Fig.8, we identify that connection occurs in B rather than A, but this algorithm will take B as the connected point. This problem can be solved by adding more structure information to the segmentation rules. If the connected characters shown in Fig.9 are manually collected, they can be correctly segmented by this method. Otherwise, they will separated by the dashed, and will not be considered as the connected characters in the preprocessing stage. This will only be overcome by combining the information of recognition.

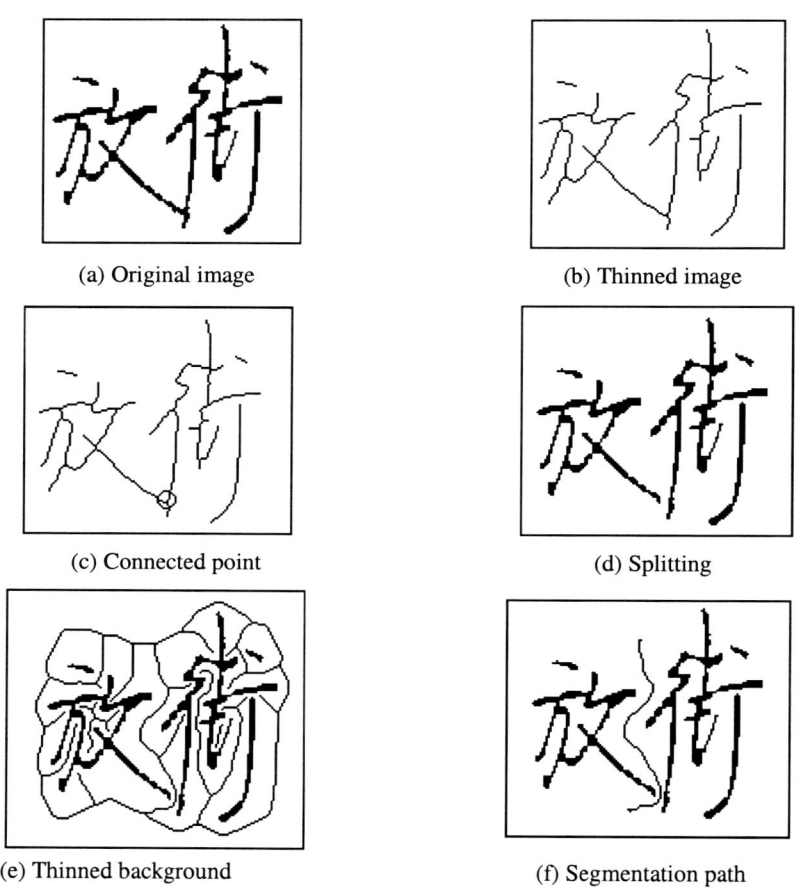

(a) Original image (b) Thinned image

(c) Connected point (d) Splitting

(e) Thinned background (f) Segmentation path

Fig. 6. Segmentation procedure

Fig. 7. Segmentation of connected handwritten Chinese characters: (a) Original Images; (b) Segmentation results

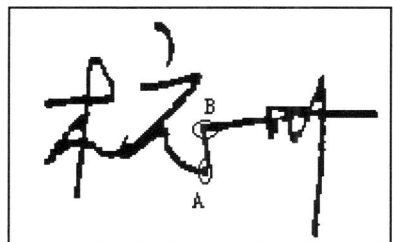

Fig. 8. Wrong connected point

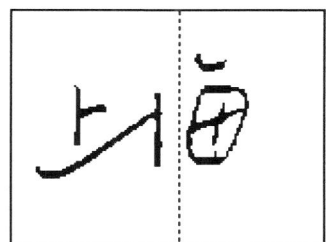

Fig. 10. Wrong segmentation path

6 Conclusion

In this paper, we propose a new approach based on stroke analysis and background thinning to segment connected handwritten Chinese characters. By introducing stroke analysis, we can obtain the feature of connected characters, then using particular rules, we can correctly locate the connected point. In order to find suitable segmentation path, we do not use foreground pixel analysis as others do, but develop a new method where the information of thinned background is employed. The experimental results show the effectiveness of our approach.

Acknowledgement

The authors would like to thank Dr.Lu Yue for his sincere help.

References

1. Casey R G and Lecolinent E. A survey of methods and strategies in character segmentation. IEEE trans. PAMI, 1996,18(7):690-709
2. Lu Y and Shridhar M. Character segmentation in handwritten words-an overview. Pattern Recognition, 1996,29(1):77-96
3. Yu D and Yan H. Separation of single-touching handwritten numeral strings based on structure features. Pattern Recognition,1998,31(12):1835-1847
4. Lu Z,Chi Z,Siu W C and Shi P. A background-thinning-based approach for separating and recognizing connected handwritten digit strings. Pattern Recognition ,1999,32(6):921-933
5. M.Shridhar and A.Vadreldin. Context-directed segmentation algorithm for handwritten numeral strings. Image Vision Computer,1987,5:3-8
6. M.Suters and H.Yan. Connected handwritten digit separation using external boundary curvature. J.Electron.Imaging,1994,3(3):251-256
7. J.M.Westall and M.S.Narasimha. Vertex directed segmentation of handwritten numerals. Pattern Recognition,1993,26(10):1473-1486
8. J.K.Lin and Z.Chen. A Chinese-character thinning algorithm based on global features and contour information. Pattern Recognition, 1995,28(4): 493-512

A Framework of Two-Stage Combination of Multiple Recognizers for Handwritten Numerals

K. Lee and Y. Lee

[1] Electronics and Telecommunications Research Institute, Taejon, Korea
    kylee@econos.etri.re.kr
[2] Dept. of Computer Science, Yonsei University, Seoul, Korea
    yblee@csai.yonsei.ac.kr

Abstract. In this paper, we propose a framework of two-stage combination method to recognize unconstrained handwritten numerals. It uses multiple combination methods simultaneously unlike the existing methods with only one combination algorithm. The recognizers are first combined by several combination methods at the same time, and the results of them are finally combined by a combination method to generate the final result of recognition. Five recognizers and eight combination methods are used to make a good framework of two-stage combination. The proposed framework was experimented and evaluated with CENPARMI and CEDAR databases. The results showed that we could get the best performance by exploiting the combination methods of different classes at the first stage and then by combining the results of the previous stage by means of Bayesian method.

1 Introduction

Current researches on making a recognition system with high performance is in progress with two different aspects. One is to build a recognizer using several different features at the same time, and the other is to use some recognizers. The fact that the recognition performance can be increased by using multi-features and multi-recognizers has been already proved by the character recognition competition [1] [2].

Many researchers have placed their attention to the multiple recognizer system which in general gives the final result by combining the results of recognizers, because the performance can be easily improved without much efforts on recognizers themselves. The multiple recognizer system can be classified into the serial combination type and the parallel combination type, according to the arrangement of recognizers. The serial combination type arranges the recognizers like a pipeline, so that simple patterns are recognized in the fore part of the system and more complicated patterns in the rear part. The parallel combination type, on the contrary, organizes the recognizers in parallel, recognizes a pattern with several recognizers simultaneously, and generates the final output by another module which combines the results of recognizers. Since the way of arranging the recognizers has a great influence on the performance in the serial combination, there is little flexibility in designing a system and no remarkable improvement in the performance after the combination. In the parallel combination, the system performance largely depends on the characteristics of the combination modules.

In this paper, we propose a framework of two-stage combination method for unconstrained handwritten numerals to get better performance under the limited performance of recognizers. The method basically extends the conventional methods with a single combination module so as to use several combination module at the same time. It is said in general that the choice of recognizers is the most important factor to get success of the multiple recognizer system, but we can see that the performance varies according to the combination methods although the same recognizers are used. This may indicate that every combination method has its own distinctive characteristics. To fully use the characteristics of every recognizer and every combination method, we use a two-stage method which first combines the results of recognizers by using several different combination methods and then re-combines the results of the combination methods. Five recognizers and eight combination methods are exploited to make a good framework of the two-stage combination system, and CENPARMI and CEDAR databases are used to evaluate the performance of the proposed system.

The organization of the paper is as follows. We briefly review the works on handwritten digit recognition and the combination method for multiple recognizers in Section 2. The five different recognizers and the proposed two-stage method for combining multiple recognizers are explained in Section 3 and Section 4, respectively. Section 5 shows the experimental results and evaluations. The conclusions are presented in Section 6.

2 Related Works

The choice of feature vectors and classifiers is the important problem in the digit recognition like any other character set recognition. The two factors, consequently, could be critical to characterize a system. In general, the feature vectors contain statistical features, global features, and geometrical features. The classifiers can be classified into three categories; structural classifier, statistical classifier, and artificial neural network classifier.

Most of the systems for digit recognition are built by combining the features vectors and classifiers mentioned above. It is frequent that these systems are apt simply to be evaluated only by the performance. It seems inadequate to evaluate the systems only by the performance in that the experimental data and even the qualities of the systems themselves are different, therefore we review the works for handwritten digit recognition in three aspects; the characteristics of features and classifiers, the kind of databases used in experiments, and the performance such as recognition rate, error rate, and rejection rate.

By these criteria, the results of digit recognition on CENPARMI and CEDAR are summarized in Table 1 and Table 2, respectively.

As the efforts to improve the recognition performance from the recognition system's viewpoint, not the individual recognizer's viewpoint, some works on making a recognition system with several recognizers have been done. When we apply several recognizers to a recognition system the most important thing to be considered is that how to effectively combine the results of recognizers. To organize several recognizers in an efficient and effective manner, several studies on combination of multiple recognizers and multi-level classifiers have been conducted [11] [12] [13] [14].

Table 1. Comparisons of the recognition systems on CENPARMI database

Authors	Method (features, classifier)	Data (learning : test)	Performance (%)		
			recognition	error	reject
Legault [3]	Structural features based on contours	4000 : 2000	93.90	1.60	4.50
Mai [4]	Knowledge base obtained from the process of structural features	4000 : 2000	92.95	2.15	4.90
Krzyzak [5]	Contours and topological features, NN(neural network)	4000 : 2000	94.85	5.15	0.00
S.-W.Lee [6]	Kirsch mask, NN	4000 : 2000	96.15	3.85	0.00
Paik [7]	Gradient features, NN	2000 : 2000	96.20	3.80	0.00

Table 2. Comparisons of the recognition systems on CEDAR database

Authors	Method (features, classifier)	Data (learning : test)	Performance (%)		
			recognition	error	reject
Paik [7]	Gradient features, NN	13923 : 2711	97.42	1.83	0.74
Cohen [8]	Decision tree	: 2711	95.54	1.99	2.47
		: 1762	97.10	0.96	1.94
Lee [9]	NN using multi-features	18468 : 2711	97.05	2.95	0.00
Choi [10]	Size-normalized image, Dual Cooperative NN	6000 : 2213	97.33	2.67	0.00

3 Recognizers for Handwritten Digits

Determining which recognizers we use is the most critical point in designing a system of multiple recognizers. The ideal case is to use several recognizers which have reciprocal complement. There, however, is little works on mutual complement of recognizers, unfortunately. It is generally known that the recognizers with different feature vectors show the different tendencies of recognition.

In this paper, we use five recognizers with different vectors each other to give the different tendencies of recognition to each recognizer. Every recognizer is based on the multilayer perceptron. That is not only because we can keep consistence in the type of results when combining the results, but also because we can easily use the learning mechanism of neural network. Each multilayer perceptron is consisted of three layers, including one hidden layer. Table 3 shows the characteristics and structure of 5 recognizers. In Table 3, a size x-y-z means that the number of input nodes, hidden nodes, and output nodes are x, y, and z, respectively.

Table 3. Characteristics of 5 recognizers

Recognizer	Feature Vector	Size
K-recognizer	four 4×4 directional features obtained by Kirsch operators on contours and a 4×4 global feature from an original image	80-45-10
G-recognizer	12 gradients for each region of 4×4 normalized image by Sobel operators on contours	192-77-10
C-recognizer	frequency of 8-directional chain codes for each region of 4×4 normalized image	128-71-10
D-recognizer	dynamic mesh	64-39-10
H-recognizer	30 features for hole histograms and 40 features for contour histograms	70-41-10

4 Two-Stage Combination Method

Most of the existing multiple recognizer systems use only a combination method to combine the results of recognizers. It is said that the characteristics of recognizers is the most important factor to affect the performance, while it is no doubt that the features of combination methods also have a great influence on the performance. We, therefore, propose a combination method in this paper to get better performance with the limited recognizers.

The two-stage combination method proposed first combines the results of recognizers by several combination methods with different characteristics, and then again combines the temporary results of the combination methods by another combination method to generate the final result. The recognition stage comprises the five recognizers to take into account of a variety of the types of feature vectors and the inclinations of recognizers. The first combination stage for combining the recognition results consists of the three methods with the best performance which are selected from each level through the experiments on all of the eight methods. Table 4 shows the representative methods according to each level. We have to select a method for the second combination stage from the abstract level so as to accommodate all the types of results generated by the three methods of the first combination stage. We, therefore, use the Bayesian method which has the best performance among the methods of the abstract level.

The recognition system with the proposed two-stage combination method has the structure as shown in Fig. 1.

Table 4. Methods used in the combination stages

Level	Methods
Abstract level	Majority voting
	Bayesian
	BKS
Rank level	Borda function
	Weighted Borda
	Condorect function
Measurement level	Sum of confidence values
	Neural network

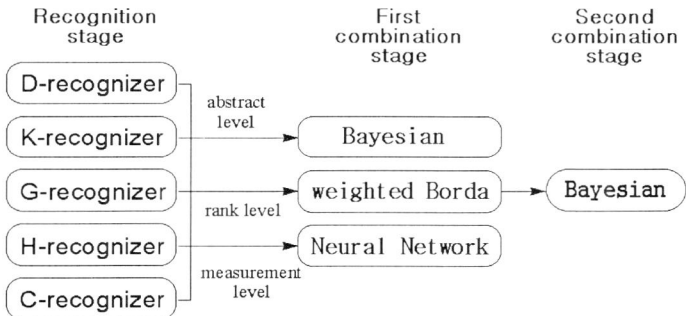

Fig. 1. The structure of the proposed two-stage combination method

5 Experimental Results

5.1 Experimental Environment

To evaluate the method, we used two different databases, CENPARMI and CEDAR databases. Table 5 shows the number of data and their use according to the database.

Table 5. Date used in the experiments

	CENPARM	CEDAR
Learning of recognizers	2000 (A)	13923 (br)
Learning of combination methods	2000 (B)	4545 (br)
Performance test	2000 (C)	2561 (bs)

5.2 Results on the Recognition Stage

The results of the five recognizers on the learning data of the two databases are summarized in Table 6 and Table 7. G-recognizer based on the gradient vector showed the best performance on both databases than any other recognizers.

On the other hand, we can see that D-recognizer has the lowest performance than others, especially, in the case of CENPARMI data, and the performance difference between D-recognizer and other recognizers is 3 to 5%, which is likely to lead the overall performance of the system to lower.

Table 6. Performance of recognizers on CENPARMI data (%)

	Threshold	Recog. rate	Error rate	Rejection rate	Reliability
D-recognizer	0.0	91.65	8.35	0.00	91.65
	0.4	89.25	5.20	5.55	94.80
	0.6	87.45	4.15	8.40	95.85
K-recognizer	0.0	95.85	4.15	0.00	95.85
	0.4	94.55	3.30	2.15	96.70
	0.6	93.60	2.45	3.95	97.55
G-recognizer	0.0	96.20	3.80	0.00	96.20
	0.4	94.00	2.35	3.65	97.65
	0.6	92.35	1.80	5.85	98.20
H-recognizer	0.0	94.10	5.90	0.00	94.10
	0.4	92.30	4.15	3.55	95.85
	0.6	91.05	3.40	5.55	96.60
C-recognizer	0.0	94.80	5.20	0.00	94.80
	0.4	92.70	3.35	3.95	96.65
	0.6	90.80	2.70	6.50	97.30

Table 7. Performance of recognizers on CEDAR data (%)

	Threshold	Recog. rate	Error rate	Rejection rate	Reliability
D-recognizer	0.0	95.43	4.57	0.00	95.43
	0.4	93.64	2.73	3.63	97.27
	0.8	91.72	1.60	6.68	98.40
K-recognizer	0.0	97.50	2.50	0.00	97.50
	0.4	96.84	1.80	1.36	98.20
	0.8	95.70	1.29	3.01	98.71
G-recognizer	0.0	97.89	2.11	0.00	97.89
	0.4	96.80	1.44	1.76	98.56
	0.8	94.81	0.78	4.41	99.22
H-recognizer	0.0	97.07	2.93	0.00	97.07
	0.4	96.37	2.23	1.40	97.77
	0.8	94.77	1.72	3.51	98.28
C-recognizer	0.0	97.34	2.66	0.00	97.34
	0.4	96.56	1.99	1.45	98.01
	0.8	94.73	1.41	3.86	98.59

Judging from the overall point of view, the recognizers using the contour features and the directional features at the same time have higher performance on the whole. We can see that the order with high performance is G, K, C, H, and D-recognizer. The performance on CEDAR data with relatively more learning data is higher than that on CENPARMI data.

5.3 Results on the Two-Stage Method

According to the level of the methods used in the first combination stage, the recognizers generate the different type of results. They give only one result for the abstract level, a list of rank on classes for the rank level, and the confidence values on each class for the measurement level. The results after the first combination by means of the eight methods are summarized in Table 8 and Table 9, respectively.

Table 8. Performance after the first combination on CENPARMI data (%)

Level	Method		Recog. rate	Error rate	Rejection rate
Abstract level	Majority voting	threshold 3	96.65	2.00	1.35
		0.5-1% error	93.90	0.90	5.20
	Bayesian	no rejection	97.55	2.45	0.00
		0.5-1% error	94.45	1.00	4.55
	BKS + Bayesian	no rejection	97.50	2.50	0.00
		0.5-1% error	94.40	1.25	4.35
Rank level	Nonweighted Borda	no reject	97.40	2.60	0.00
		0.5-1% error	94.30	0.75	4.95
	Weighted Borda	no rejection	97.40	2.60	0.00
		0.5-1% error	96.00	1.10	2.90
	Condorect	no rejection	97.40	2.60	0.00
		0.5-1% error	94.90	1.00	4.10
Measurement level	Sum of confidence value	no rejection	97.30	2.70	0.00
		0.5-1% error	94.35	0.90	4.75
	Neural network	no rejection	97.60	2.40	0.00
		0.5-1% error	94.35	0.90	4.75

Table 9. Performance after the first combination on CEDAR data (%)

Level	Method		Recog. rate	Error rate	Rejection rate
Abstract level	Majority voting	threshold 3	98.13	1.29	0.59
		0.5-1% error	95.98	0.66	3.36
	Bayesian	no rejection	98.36	1.64	0.00
		0.5-1% error	97.34	0.82	1.84
	BKS + Bayesian	no rejection	98.28	1.72	0.00
		0.5-1% error	96.68	0.98	2.34
Rank level	Nonweighted Borda	no reject	98.28	1.62	0.00
		0.5-1% error	96.88	0.86	2.26
	Weighted Borda	no rejection	98.40	1.60	0.00
		0.5-1% error	97.34	0.94	1.72
	Condorect	no rejection	98.32	1.68	0.00
		0.5-1% error	97.11	0.90	1.99
Measurement level	Sum of confidence value	no rejection	98.36	1.64	0.00
		0.5-1% error	97.19	0.82	1.99
	Neural network	no rejection	98.40	1.60	0.00
		0.5-1% error	97.54	0.62	2.97

As you can see the results of the first combination, the performance on CENPARMI and CEDAR data was increased to 97.6% and 98.4%, respectively. By comparing with the results of G-recognizer which has the highest performance among the recognizers, the performance after the first combination was 1.4% on CENPARMI and 0.6% on CEDAR high.

By looking into the results according to the combination methods, the majority voting has the lowest performance, while the Bayesian method, the weighted Borda function and the neural network, each of which considers the inclinations of recognizers, show high performance comparatively. It can be considered as a good result to show that the inclinations of recognizers are dealt enough to guarantee better performance when combining the results of recognizers.

The experiments for deciding the methods for the first combination stage were carried out in two aspects. One is to group the methods which belong to the same level, and the other is to group the methods which belong to different level. Only the methods which belong to the abstract level and the rank level can be used in the second combination stage. We cannot use a method of the measurement level because of the problem of the normalization of the results obtained from the first combination stage. The difficult and important problem when using a method of the measurement level is to keep consistency of the type of results. We, therefore, used the same classification method in the recognition stage. The details on this is behind the scope of this paper.

The methods used in the second combination stage are the majority voting and the Bayesian method from the abstract level, and the Borda function and the Condorect function from the rank level. Table 10 and Table 11 indicate the final combination results according to the combination method.

Table 10. Final results of the two-stage combination method on CENPARMI data (%)

	1st stage	2nd stage	Recog. rate	Error rate
Abstract level	Majority Voting, Bayesian, BKS+Bayesian	Majority Voting	97.55	2.45
		Bayesian	97.65	2.35
Rank level	Borda (nonweighted, weighted), Condorect	Majority Voting	97.55	2.45
		Bayesian	97.65	2.35
		Borda	97.60	2.40
		Condorect	97.60	2.40
Measurement level	Weighted Borda, Sum of confidence value, Neural network	Majority Voting	97.55	2.45
		Bayesian	97.75	2.25
		Borda	97.60	2.40
		Condorect	97.60	2.40
Mixture of level	Bayesian, Weighted Borda, Neural network	Majority Voting	97.65	2.35
		Bayesian	97.80	2.20

We can see that the performance is hardly improved or a little increased when the methods of the same level are used in the first combination stage. On the other hand, the increase of 0.2% is achieved when three different methods from each level are used. We can say from the results that the combination methods have their own characteristics and the methods which can well express the inclinations of recognizers show the best performance.

Table 11. Final results of the two-stage combination method on CEDAR data (%)

	1st stage	2nd stage	Recog. rate	Error rate
Abstract level	Majority Voting, Bayesian, BKS+Bayesian	Majority Voting	98.36	1.64
		Bayesian	98.48	1.52
Rank level	Borda (nonweighted, weighted), Condorect	Majority Voting	98.44	1.56
		Bayesian	98.50	1.50
		Borda	98.48	1.52
		Condorect	98.48	1.52
measurement level	Weighted Borda, Sum of confidence value, Neural network	Majority Voting	98.44	1.56
		Bayesian	98.52	1.48
		Borda	98.48	1.52
		Condorect	98.48	1.52
Mixture of level	Bayesian, Weighted Borda, Neural network	Majority Voting	98.50	1.50
		Bayesian	98.62	1.48

6 Conclusions

In this paper, we proposed the new combination method, what we called the two-stage combination method to get better performance in the multiple recognizer system. Unlike the existing systems which combine the recognition results just one time with a particular combination method to output the final result, the proposed method first combines the results of multiple recognizers by several combination methods that have different characteristics of combination and then combine their results again to generate the final recognition result.

We used five recognizers with the different feature vectors, eight representative combination methods and two different databases, CENPARMI and CEDAR for the experiments and evaluations. As the final results on the two-stage combination method, we got the recognition rates of 97.80% and 98.62% for CENPARMI and CEDAR data, respectively. The proposed method might be considered as an extended version of the existing combination methods.

References

1. T. Matsui, T. Noumi, I. Yamashita, T. Wakahara, M. Yoshimuro, "State of the Art of Handwritten Numeral Recognition in Japan - The Results of the First IPTP Character Recognition Competition," Proceedings of 2nd ICDAR, pp.391-396, 1993.
2. T. Noumi, T. Matsui, I. Yamashita, "Result of Second IPTP Character Recognition Competition and Studies on Multi-Expert Handwritten Numeral Recognition," Proceedings of 4th IWFHR, pp.338-346, 1994

3. R. Legault and C. Y. Suen, "Contour Tracing and Parametric Approximations for Digitized Patterns," Computer Vision and Shape Recognition, pp.225-240, 1989
4. T. Mai and C. Y. Suen, "A Generalized Knowledge-Based System for the Recognition of Unconstrained Handwritten Numerals," IEEE Trans. on System, Man and Cybernetics, vol.20, pp.835-848, 1990
5. A. Krzyzak, W. Dai and C. Y. Suen, "Unconstrained Handwritten Character Classification Using Modified Backpropagation Model," Proceedings of 1st IWFHR, pp.155-166, 1990
6. Seong-Whan Lee, "Off-Line Recognition of Totally Unconstrained Handwritten Numerals Using Multilayer Cluster Neural Network," IEEE Trans. on Pattern Recognition and Machine Intelligence, vol.18, no.6, pp.648-652, 1996
7. J. Paik, S.-B. Cho, K. Lee and Y. Lee, "Multiple Recognizers System using Two Stage Combination," Proceedings of 13th ICPR, vol.4, pp.581-584, 1996
8. E. Cohen, J. J. Hull and S. N. Srihari, "Understanding Handwritten Text in a Structured Environment: Determining ZIP Codes from Addresses," Int'l Journal of Pattern Recognition and Artificial Intelligence, vol.5, no.1/2, pp.221-264, 1994
9. D.-S. Lee. S. N. Srihari, "Handprinted Digit Recognition : A Comparison of Algorithms," Proceedings of 3rd IWFHR, pp.153-162, 1993
10. Y. Choi, "Recognition of Unconstrained Handwritten Numerals Based on Dual Cooperative Neural Network," Doctoral Dissertation, Department of Computer Engineering, University of Southern California, 1994
11. T. K. Ho, J. J. Hull and S. N. Srihari, "Decision Combination of Multiple Classifier Systems," IEEE Trans. on Pattern Analysis and Machine Intelligence, vol.16, no.1, pp.66-75, 1994
12. K. Woods, W.P. Jr. Kegelmeyer and K. Bowyer, "Combination of Multiple Classifiers Using Local Accuracy Estimates," IEEE Trans. on Pattern Analysis and Machine Intelligence, vol.19, no.4, pp.405-410, 1997
13. J. Kittler, M. Hatef, R. P. W. Duin, and J. Matas, "On Combining Classifier," IEEE Trans. on Pattern Analysis and Machine Intelligence, vol.20, no.3, pp.226-239, 1998
14. Sharkey, Combining Artificial Neural Nets, Springer, 1999 (recollection of special issues on connection Science Vol.8, No.3/4, 1996 and Vol.9, No.1, 1997)

Aligning Portuguese and Chinese Parallel Texts Using Confidence Bands

António Ribeiro[1], Gabriel Lopes[1], and João Mexia[2]

[1] Universidade Nova de Lisboa, Faculdade de Ciências e Tecnologia,
Departamento de Informática, Quinta da Torre,
P-2825-114 Monte da Caparica, Portugal
{ambar,gpl}@di.fct.unl.pt
[2] Universidade Nova de Lisboa, Faculdade de Ciências e Tecnologia,
Departamento de Matemática, Quinta da Torre,
P-2825-114 Monte da Caparica, Portugal

Abstract. This paper describes a language independent method that makes use of tokens which are homograph for a pair of languages, in order to align parallel texts. We will show that even for such different languages as Portuguese and Chinese it is possible to use homographs with great reliability. This work was originally inspired and extends work done by Pascale Fung & Kathleen McKeown, and Melamed. In order to filter out words that may cause misalignment, we use confidence bands of linear regression lines instead of statistically unsupported heuristics. This is a completely statistically supported alignment algorithm.

1 Introduction

"The College of St. Paul [in Macao], founded by Jesuits in 1594, deserves special mention. Portuguese, Latin and Chinese were taught here and the first translations of Chinese texts into Portuguese and European texts into Chinese were produced at this College. The first Sino-Portuguese [Chinese–Portuguese] dictionary was also prepared in Macau, in the late 16th century." [http://www.museuvirtualmacau.pt].

500 years ago the first contacts between the Portuguese and the Chinese communities in Macao pressed for a great domain of these quite disparate new languages. The need for an easy communication spurred the production of the first Chinese–Portuguese dictionary by the Jesuits. However, we are no longer at the time of the Discoveries and, presently, we can no longer afford to waste human time and effort building manually these ever changing databases or design language specific applications to solve this problem.

If we are aiming at building bilingual databases of equivalent expressions (typical translations) either for cross-language information retrieval (e.g. web applications, web search engines), machine translation, bilingual lexicography or terminology research, we should be able to make this an automatic language independent task.

Parallel texts (texts that are mutual translations) are valuable sources of information for these information extraction tasks as they provide the typical usage of equivalent expressions. However, they are not of much use unless a computational system may find which piece of text in one language corresponds to which piece in the other language. In order to achieve this goal, they must be *aligned* first, i.e. the various text pieces must be put into correspondence. This is usually done by finding *correspondence points* – sequences of characters with the same form (homographs, e.g. numbers, names, punctuation marks) or even known translations. The problem of building automatically these bilingual dictionaries becomes quite delicate and difficult when it comes to the non-Latin alphabet languages, as is the case of Portuguese – Chinese, where almost no orthographic hints are available in parallel texts to identify possible translations. It is true that if we are to build a large dictionary for these languages, we have to *discover* relations between words in some special way.

The alignment algorithm in [5] used term translations as correspondence points between English and Chinese texts. Two terms were identified as translations when they co-occurred with similar frequencies. In [8], texts were aligned using correspondence points taken either from orthographic cognates [12] or from a seed translation lexicon. This lexicon was used for alignment of English and Korean texts. However, both approaches used statistically unsupported heuristics to filter "bad" correspondence points (noisy points). The former approach considered a candidate correspondence point reliable as long as, among some other constraints, "[...] it is not too far away from the diagonal [...]" ([5], p.72) of a rectangle whose sides sizes are proportional to the lengths of the texts in each language (henceforth, the "golden translation diagonal"). The latter approach used various heuristic filtering parameters ([8], pp. 115–116): maximum point ambiguity level (measures how ambiguous a point is for alignment), point dispersion (measures how well the points fit to a linear interpolation) and angle deviation (measures how much the angle formed by a cluster of points deviates from the "golden translation diagonal" angle). Although the heuristics found in these previous researches may be intuitively quite acceptable and may significantly improve the results, they are just heuristics. We need a theoretically backed up method to filter candidate correspondence points.

A method to filter candidate correspondence points using confidence bands of linear regression lines is proposed in [9]. The points of this line were generated from homographs (words that look the same in two languages) which occur with the same frequency in parallel texts segments. These words are quite reliable and give strong hints of alignment of parallel texts. This work extends [10] where only *hapaxes* (single frequency words) were used as candidate correspondence points. Both approaches avoid heuristic filters and the authors claim alignment precisions close to 100%. Their approach reports more than 20 thousand points for large texts (600 pages), leading to segments ranging from four to 20 words, on average. In order to avoid heuristic parameters, they used confidence bands of linear regression lines [14]. Points that lie outside the confidence bands are filtered out. The method is recursive and uses repeatedly the confidence bands within each parallel text segment in order to identify further candidate correspondence points which satisfy the same initial conditions: homographs with equal frequencies.

In this paper we will extend their work for parallel Portuguese–Chinese texts, for the first time. We will show that we may use the few homographs existing in both languages with a high reliability using completely statistically based techniques. The homographs help to break the initial texts in smaller pieces and other methods are intended to be used in the future in order to extract translation equivalents.

The following section will discuss related work. The method is described in section 3 and evaluated in section 4. Finally, we present conclusions and future work.

2 Related Work

There have been two mainstreams to parallel text alignment. One assumes that translations have proportional sizes; the other tries to use lexical information in the parallel texts to generate candidate correspondence points. However, both use some notion of correspondence points.

In early work, [1] and [6], alignment was made at sentence level only, counting the number of words and characters in each sentence, respectively. The algorithms grouped sequences of sentences till they had proportional sizes. Pairs of sentence delimiters (full stops) were used as candidate correspondence points which ended up being selected while aligning. However, these algorithms tended to break down when sentence boundaries were not clearly marked. Full stops do not always mark sentence boundaries, they may not exist due to OCR noise and languages may not even share the same punctuation policies. Moreover, these sentence based alignment methods are unable to make correspondences between segments smaller than sentences (e.g. clauses, phrases or terms).

The research reported in [2] showed that *cheap* alignment of text segments was still possible exploiting lexical information, namely, orthographic cognates, instead of sentence delimiters. In order to avoid noisy points, an *empirically* estimated bounded search space was used to filter them out.

Clearly delimited sentences were also needed in [7]. The alignment algorithm aligned two sentences if the number of correspondence points associating them was greater than an *empirically* defined threshold. Those correspondence points were generated from words with similar distributions, i.e. words occurring in the same sentences. Correspondence points were generated in [3] from pairs of translations whose words frequencies were *neither high nor low*. Empirically, they found that these words "caused difficulties" and therefore they were filtered out. The most probable word translations were aligned based on translation probabilities estimated using a window 20 words long. About 55% of the words were correctly aligned.

The requirement for clear sentence boundaries was also dropped in [4] on a case-study for English–Chinese texts. This is one of the earliest experiments using languages with different alphabets. They used vectors that stored distances between consecutive occurrences of a word (DK-vec's) and candidate correspondence points were identified from words with similar distance vectors. Noisy points were filtered using some heuristics. Later, in [5], the algorithm used extracted terms, when possible, to compile a primary list of reliable pairs of translations. Those pairs whose distribution similarity was above a threshold became candidate correspondence points (named potential anchor points). Therefore, terms were selected based on similarity of the occurrence rate despite *looking different*. The borderline between alignment and identification of translation equivalents is blurred. Points were further constrained not to be "too far away" from the "golden translation diagonal".

[15] started by aligning English–Chinese parallel sentences using their length. Sentence alignment precision was reported to reach over 96% when the method incorporated a bilingual lexicon of words commonly found in the texts to be aligned (e.g. *December* and its equivalent 十二月). In [13], sentences were aligned using isolated cognates as candidate correspondence points, i.e. cognates that were not mistaken for others within a text window. Some were filtered if they either lied outside a search space, named a corridor, or were "not in line" with their neighbours.

Candidate correspondence points obtained from orthographic cognates also needed filtering in [8]. The following filters were used: a maximum point ambiguity level filtered points outside a search space, a maximum point dispersion filtered points too distant from a line formed by candidate correspondence points and a maximum angle deviation filters points that make this line slope too much. With these heuristic filters, the alignment precision could reach 98.7%. It is true that there are almost no cognates between Chinese and European languages, but even the few ones that exist may help to start the alignment task. Further cognates may be found if we use *phonetic cognates* [8], i.e. words which are almost homophone.

We all want to find reliable correspondence points for parallel texts alignment. They provide the basic means for extracting reliable information from parallel texts. However, as far as we have learned from the above papers, current methods have repeatedly used statistically unsupported heuristics in order to filter out noisy candidate correspondence points. For instance, all mention the "golden translation diagonal" to filter out noisy points, which follows the hypothesis that parallel texts have proportional lengths.

3 Correspondence Points Filters

3.1 Overview

The basic insight behind our approach is that not all candidate correspondence points are reliable. No matter how we filter candidate correspondence points, either using similar word distributions ([5], [7]), search corridors [13], point dispersion and angle deviation [8] or some other heuristic, candidate correspondence points must be filtered in order to ensure a correct text alignment. Our assumption is that reliable points have similar characteristics. For instance, they tend to gather somewhere near the "golden translation diagonal". In this paper, we will use tokens which are homograph for Portuguese and Chinese and which occur with the same frequency within a parallel text segment. They provide interesting clues for text alignment. If we find them in *similar* word positions, then they will turn out to be reliable correspondence points. We will now elaborate more on this. In contrast with [15] we decided not to use hand built bilingual lexicons in order to enrich the number of cues, i.e. the number of candidate correspondence points. Instead, we decided to confine ourselves to using the few homographs found in the texts. This also allows us to measure how much previous translations knowledge will improve the results.

3.2 Source Parallel Texts

We worked with a parallel corpus consisting of texts from the Basic Law of the Macao Special Administrative Region of China, in both Portuguese and Chinese (http://www.imprensa.macau.gov.mo/bo/i/1999/leibasica/). As a former Portuguese territory till 1999, this is one of the best places to find parallel Portuguese–Chinese texts much like Hong Kong with parallel English–Chinese texts. The corpus used contains about 200kB of raw data in a set of 10 parallel texts, comprising approximately 16k tokens in Portuguese and Chinese. At the moment, we are on the process of compiling a larger corpora. We counted each Chinese character as one token though some Chinese words may be more than one token long (e.g. *Macau* in Portuguese and its Chinese equivalent 澳門). To be fair both for Portuguese and Chinese, we identified and tokenised numbers (e.g., *1993* and 一九九三). Notice that, although we know what Chinese character corresponds to digit *1*, we decided not to use this information for alignment purposes since it would be considered as a seed translation lexicon.

3.3 Generating Candidate Correspondence Points

As previously mentioned, we generated candidate correspondence points from *homographs* (various punctuation marks and paragraph separators). These homographs accounted for an average of 5% of the total tokens. We should notice that we also found a few common English words in those texts, especially at the beginning and at the end. Html mark-ups were discarded for they would bias the results.

Table 1: Average number of homographs with equal frequencies between the Portuguese and Chinese parallel texts and corresponding percentages (html mark-ups discarded).

Text	pt Tokens	Homographs	Percentage
CH1.html	822	69	8,4%
CH2.html	1624	76	4,7%
CH3.html	1884	93	4,9%
CH4.html	6014	179	3,0%
CH5.html	1594	74	4,6%
CH6.html	1605	81	5,0%
CH7.html	1119	75	6,7%
CH8.html	617	72	11,7%
CH9.html	344	79	23,0%
MAIN.html	775	84	10,8%
Average	1640	88	5,4%

Each pair of texts gives a set of candidate correspondence points from which we draw a line based on linear regression. These points are defined using the co-ordinates of the token positions in each of the parallel texts. For example, if the first occurrence of the token ')' occurs at position 402 in the Portuguese segment and at token position 349 in the Chinese segment, then the point co-ordinates are (402, 349). Points may adjust themselves well to a linear regression line or may be dispersed around it. In order to filter out extreme points, we apply first a filter based on the histogram of the distances between the expected and real positions. Next, we remove other noisy points using a finer-grained filter based on the confidence bands of the linear regression line. We will elaborate on these statistical filters in the next subsections.

3.4 Eliminating Extreme Points

The points obtained initially from the positions of homographs are still prone to be noisy. Moreover, it may also be the case that there is no corresponding homograph token in one parallel segment. Here is one such example:

```
  522|Elaborar, mandar publicar e fazer cumprir os
regulamentos administrativos
  477|制 定 行 政 法 規 并 頒 布 執 行
  [...]
  2920|Examinar e aprovar a proposta de orçamento apresentada
pelo Governo, bem ¶ como apreciar o relatório sobre a execução
do ¶ orçamento apresentado pelo Governo ; ¶ ¶ ¶ ¶ 3
  2758|審 核 、通 過 政 府 提 出 的 財 政 預 算 案;審 議 政 府 提 出 的
預 算 執 行 情 況 報 告;¶¶¶ （三
```

Fig. 1: Unpaired homographs in parallel segments.

In this figure, the commas are unpaired in the Chinese parallel segment. In the first segment (522||477) there is no parallel comma at all. In the second segment, (2920||2758) the commas do not appear in *similar positions*. Quite on the contrary, they appear in positions quite apart, i.e. the comma was *expected somewhere much later* in the Chinese text segment and it appears almost at the beginning. We should feel reluctant to accept this pairing and this is what the first filter does. It filters out those points which are clearly quite far apart from their *expected* positions. *Expected* positions are computed from the linear regression line equation defined by a linear regression on all candidate correspondence points. In the previous case, the token at 2930 in the Portuguese segment was expected at position 2770 in the Chinese segment and the pairing was made with 2760, almost 10 tokens behind.

If we draw a histogram for all the distances between the expected and real positions, ranging from the smallest to the largest distance, we are able to identify extreme points. They appear in the end of the histogram. With the histogram technique, we are able to identify and filter out those tokens which are too distant from their expected positions.

3.5 Linear Regression Line Confidence Bands

Linear regression lines define confidence bands which help us to identify reliable points, i.e. points which belong to that linear regression line with a great confidence level (95%). The band is wider in the extremes of the linear regression line and narrower in the middle, where the confidence is lower.

We start from the linear regression line defined by the points filtered using the histogram technique described in the previous section. We compute the confidence bands of the linear regression line in order to filter out points lying outside the bands, since they are credited as too unreliable for alignment. Then, for each sub-segment defined by the remaining "well-behaved" correspondence points, we recursively re-apply the alignment algorithm. In this way, we are able to do a local identification of candidate correspondence points and to filter noisy points.

Here is a summary of the recursive alignment algorithm:

1. Take two parallel texts A and B;
2. Define the texts' beginnings – the point (0,0) – and the texts' ends – the point (length of text A, length of text B) – as the extremes of the initial parallel text segment;
3. Consider as candidate correspondence points those points defined by homograph tokens which occur with the same frequency within the parallel text segment;
4. Build a linear regression line with these points;
5. Filter out extreme points using the Histogram technique;
6. Rebuild the linear regression line with the filtered points;
7. Filter out those points which lie outside the confidence bands of the new linear regression line;
8. For each sub-segment defined by two consecutive points, repeat steps 3 to 8.

Although we initially require homographs to have the same frequency, the recursive nature of the algorithm allows it to select unnoticed homographs later: One word may not have the same frequency in the initial parallel text segment, but may turn out to have the same frequency within some parallel sub-segments.

4 Evaluation

We ran the previous algorithms on the parallel texts described in section 3.2. With the current implementation, which is not streamlined, and on a Pentium II 366 MHz with 64MB, the algorithm takes less than one minute for each of the texts. The following table gives a summary of the number of segments for each parallel Portuguese–Chinese text. For instance, 69 correspondence points split the CH1.html parallel text into 70 segments.

Table 2: Number of segments and average number of tokens per segment for each language.

Text	# Segments	Per Segment	
		pt Tokens	ch Tokens
CH1.html	70	12	13
CH2.html	77	21	23
CH3.html	94	20	20
CH4.html	180	33	32
CH5.html	75	21	22
CH6.html	82	20	18
CH7.html	76	15	17
CH8.html	73	8	10
CH9.html	80	4	5
MAIN.html	85	9	9
Average	89	23	23

Fig. 2, below, shows the correspondence points that were found in a Portuguese–Chinese parallel text.

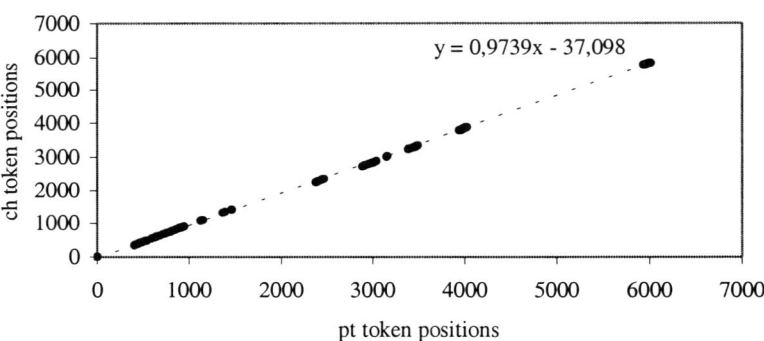

Fig. 2: Correspondence Points in a Portuguese Chinese parallel text. The linear regression line equation is on the top right corner of the graphic.

The sparse distribution of the points is due to the lack of homographs between Portuguese and Chinese. If we were to add a bilingual lexicon as in [15], then the number of candidate correspondence points would increase. However, we decided not to do so in order to evaluate the final alignment using such little knowledge and also to explore the automatic extraction of translation equivalents as future work.

The following text shows the alignment at text level:

```
2405|;  || 2271|;
2406|¶ ¶ ¶ ¶ 3
2272|¶ ¶ ¶ ( 三
2411|)  || 2277|)
2412|Tratar dos assuntos externos , quando autorizado pelo
Governo Popular ¶ Central , nos termos previstos nesta Lei
```

```
2278|辦理本法規定的中央人民政府授權的對外事務
2430|;  || 2298|;
2431|¶ ¶ ¶ ¶ 4
2299|¶ ¶ ¶ ( 四
2436|)  || 2304|)
2437|Organizar e apresentar o orçamento e as contas finais
2305|編制并提出財政預算、決算
2446|;  || 2317|;
2447|¶ ¶ ¶ ¶ 5
2318|¶ ¶ ¶ ( 五
2452|)  || 2323|)
2453|Apresentar propostas de lei e de resolução
2324|提出法案、議案
2460|,  || 2331|,
2461|e elaborar regulamentos ¶ administrativos
2332|草擬行政法規
2466|;  || 2338|;
2467|¶ ¶ ¶ ¶ 6
2339|¶ ¶ ¶ ( 六
2472|)  || 2344|)
```

Fig. 3: Aligned Portuguese–Chinese segments. Numbers show the word number.

In the end, we could even get the translation equivalents of the Chinese characters for numbers (e.g. *6* is written as 六) and parallel segments provide some translation equivalents. The final alignment we obtained is finer-grained than previous sentence based approaches ([1], [6], [7], [13] and [15]) since we were able to split and align segments smaller than sentences. In [5], a non-sentence based alignment algorithm, segments are reported to have an average of 253 and 150 words for 100k and 550k words texts, respectively. A bilingual primary lexicon was extracted from the first rough alignment in order to obtain the final alignment. Although the size of these segments may still look large, they allowed the compilation of a secondary bilingual English–Chinese lexicon with almost 90% precision. In our case, it should be easier to get a reliable bilingual lexicon for we obtained smaller segments.

5 Conclusions

In this paper we have presented a completely statistically backed up algorithm to select correspondence points for parallel texts alignment, that uses no heuristics in contrast with earlier research work. It is based on confidence bands of linear regression lines built from homographs which occur with equal frequencies in parallel texts segments. Since the algorithm is recursive, it explores reliable correspondence points within each aligned parallel sub-segment. Candidate correspondence points are selected as long as they are inside the linear regression lines confidence bands. As the alignment becomes finer-grained, since it is not restricted to sentences as in previous work ([1], [6], [7], [13] and [15]), the 100% precision may be degraded by ordering policies in small sub-segments. The smaller the segments, the more reliable are the extracted translation equivalents. We should note, however, that at this moment it is not clear how much smaller the segments should be. The method is language and character-set independent. It does not assume any a priori language knowledge, text tagging, well defined sentence or paragraph boundaries nor one-to-one translation of sentences. Moreover, it does not use any stop-list nor removes any words from the text except for mark-ups which might lead to biased results.

In contrast with [8] and [15] we use no previously built bilingual lexicon in order to increase the number of candidate points. At the moment, we cannot quantify how significant is the amount of information that a bilingual lexicon may provide. Still, we are sure that it will affect the results as previous work showed. All in all, it is clear that aligning languages with such different alphabets as Portuguese and Chinese requires an automatic method to identify some translation equivalents (e.g. [5]) in order to increase the number of candidate correspondence points.

6 Future Work

After compiling a larger parallel Portuguese–Chinese corpora, we wish to extract translation equivalents in a larger scale by comparing the similarity of co-occurrence of terms in the aligned segments [5]. This can be done using similarity and cohesion measures and taking special care with term inversions, where they may occur. We are also planning to extend our work to using words which occur with different frequencies within parallel text segments so as to define more candidate correspondence points. A method for extracting meaningful multiword units, string patterns and part of speech tags patterns is described in [11] which will help to extract both Portuguese and Chinese term translations.

Acknowledgements

This research was partially supported by a grant from Fundação para a Ciência e Tecnologia / Praxis XXI. We would like to thank the anonymous referees for their valuable comments on the paper.

References

1. Brown, P., Lai, J., Mercer, R.: Aligning Sentences in Parallel Corpora. In: Proceedings of the 29th Annual Meeting of the Association for Computational Linguistics, Berkeley, California, U.S.A. (1991) 169–176.
2. Church, K.: Char_align: A Program for Aligning Parallel Texts at the Character Level. In: Proceedings of the 31st Annual Meeting of the Association for Computational Linguistics, Columbus, Ohio, U.S.A. (1993) 1–8.
3. Dagan, I., Church, K., Gale, W.: Robust Bilingual Word Alignment for Machine Aided Translation. In: Proceedings of the Workshop on Very Large Corpora: Academic and Industrial Perspectives, Columbus, Ohio, U.S.A. (1993) 1–8.

4. Fung, P., McKeown, K.: Aligning Noisy Parallel Corpora across Language Groups: Word Pair Feature Matching by Dynamic Time Warping. In: Technology Partnerships for Crossing the Language Barrier: Proceedings of the First Conference of the Association for Machine Translation in the Americas, Columbia, Maryland, U.S.A. (1994) 81–88.
5. Fung, P., McKeown, K.: A Technical Word- and Term-Translation Aid Using Noisy Parallel Corpora across Language Groups. In: Machine Translation, Vol. 12, numbers 1–2 (Special issue) (1997) 53–87.
6. Gale, W., Church, K.: A Program for Aligning Sentences in Bilingual Corpora. In: Proceedings of the 29th Annual Meeting of the Association for Computational Linguistics, Berkeley, California, U.S.A. (1991) 177–184 (short version). Also in: Computational Linguistics, Vol. 19, number 1 (1993) 75–102 (long version).
7. Kay, M., Röscheisen, M.: Text-Translation Alignment. In: Computational Linguistics, Vol. 19, number 1 (1993) 121–142.
8. Melamed, I.: Bitext Maps and Alignment via Pattern Recognition. In: Computational Linguistics, Vol. 25, number 1 (1999) 107–130.
9. Ribeiro, A., Lopes, G., Mexia, J.: Linear Regression Based Alignment of Parallel Texts Using Homograph Words. In: Horn, W. (ed.): ECAI 2000. Proceedings of the 14th European Conference on Artificial Intelligence, Berlin, Germany. IOS Press, Amsterdam, Netherlands (2000).
10. Ribeiro, A., Lopes, G., Mexia, J.: Using Confidence Bands for Alignment with Hapaxes. In: Proceedings of the 2000 International Conference on Artificial Intelligence (IC-AI' 2000), Las Vegas, U.S.A.. CSREA Press, U.S.A. (2000).
11. da Silva, J., Dias, G., Guilloré, S., Lopes, J.: Using Localmaxs Algorithms for the Extraction of Contiguous and Non-contiguous Multiword Lexical Units. In: Barahona, P., Alferes, J. (eds.): Progress in Artificial Intelligence – Lecture Notes in Artificial Intelligence, Vol. 1695. Springer-Verlag, Berlin Heidelberg New York (1999) 113–132.
12. Simard, M., Foster, G., Isabelle, P.: Using Cognates to Align Sentences in Bilingual Corpora. In: Proceedings of the Fourth International Conference on Theoretical and Methodological Issues in Machine Translation TMI-92, Montreal, Canada (1992) 67–81.
13. Simard, M., Plamondon, P.: Bilingual Sentence Alignment: Balancing Robustness and Accuracy. In: Machine Translation, Vol. 13, number 1 (1998) 59–80.
14. Wonnacott, T., Wonnacott, R.: Introductory Statistics, 5th edition, John Wiley & Sons, New York Chichester Brisbane Toronto Singapore (1990).
15. Wu, D.: Aligning a Parallel English–Chinese Corpus Statistically with Lexical Criteria. In: Proceedings of the 32nd Annual Conference of the Association for Computational Linguistics, Las Cruces, New Mexico, U.S.A. (1994) 80–87.

Interactive Japanese-to-Braille Translation Using Case-Based Knowledge on the Web

Satoshi Ono, Yoshinobu Hamada, Yoshitsugu Takagi,
Seiichi Nishihara, and Kazunori Mizuno

Institute of Information Sciences and Electronics, University of Tsukuba
Tennoudai 1-1, Tsukuba, Ibaraki 305-8573, Japan
ono@algor.is.tsukuba.ac.jp

Abstract. We propose an interactive system for translating Japanese into Braille on the Web. Accurate automatic translation is difficult due to the ambiguous, complicated translation rules. Braille expressions must be made consistent throughout a text, even if a translation can be interpreted in more than one way. Braille translation productivity is slowed by the need for user intervention. Our system provides interactive Japanese-to-Braille translation and updates the knowledge base to keep results consistent and improve translation accuracy. Experimentals show that case acquisition reduces errors and that the user interface reduces output instability without requiring that the whole document be rechecked.

1 Introduction

A computer extends information resources for visually disabled people who have difficulty getting information[1] . As use of the Internet has become widespread, the need for computer skills has increased. Technical manuals take three to four months to translate into Braille, even by experts. Despite the existence of advisory resources on Japanese-to-Braille translation such as 'Ten-yaku no Tebiki', ("A Guide to Braille Translation") translators must often clarify ambiguous expressions caused both by ambiguous, complicated translation rules and the peculiarities of the Japanese language. Texts must be made consistent throughout, even if a translation can be interpreted in more than one way. In the final phase, translations must be completely checked manually to eliminate any remaining errors or doubtful meanings – a process that further compromises translation productivity.

Japanese-to-Braille translation using a computer is done using two types of software – an automatic translator to output Braille text, including errors, and a Braille editor for finding and correcting errors[2, 3, 4]. The editor is also used to input, edit, and output both Braille and kana sentences that are easily mutual converted. This presents users with two problems, however: (1) Users must correct the same or similar errors in both current and future documents. (2) Users must recheck entire texts each time a sentence occurs with more than one translation to make results consistent.

In this paper, we introduce interactive Japanese-to-Braille translation using case-based reasoning on the Web, maintaining an up-to-date knowledge base, enabling the system to keep results consistent and improve translation accuracy.

Developing the system on the Web enables to get large numbers of cases to be accumulated without restriction on the computer environment.

Section 2 gives an overview of Japanese-to-Braille translation. Section 3 describes our system's configuration and functions. Section 4 evaluates how the system improves translation accuracy by learning from user interaction and keeping results consistent.

2 Japanese-to-Braille Translation

We define both kana sentences obeying the translation rules and sentences written in Braille characters as Braille sentences; they can be converted each other without ambiguity. We also define Japanese sentences that uses several types of characters – kanji, hiragana, katakana, letters, numerals, and symbols – as mixed Japanese. The task for translating Japanese into Braille is thus defined as translation of mixed Japanese into Braille, and is done in two steps – sentence segmentation and kanji-to-kana conversion. A Japanese sentence is a string of characters concatenated without blanks, so spaces must be inserted between words to get a proper interpretation. Kanji must be converted to kana, because Braille characters expressing Japanese correspond only to kana.

The many translation rules that must be obeyed, are themselves ambiguous and full of exceptions. In sentence segmentation, for example, rules require that semantic and phonetic information be considered. The word 'コーシューヨクジョー (公衆浴場)' (a public bath, pronounced 'kōshū-yokujō') must be segmented as 'コーシュー＿ヨクジョー (公衆＿浴場)' to be easily understood ('ヨクジョー (浴場)' means a bath), but the word 'カイスイヨクジョー (海水浴場)' (a beach, pronounced 'kaisui-yokujō') must not be segmented as exceptions, because the segmented word 'カイスイ＿ヨクジョー (海水＿浴場)' has different meaning, a bath using seawater. In kanji-to-kana conversion, rules for distinguishing ordinary vowels are unclear, i.e., 'ア', 'イ', 'ウ', 'エ', and 'オ', and the symbol 'ー' , denoting a long vowel, are used in writing, whereas a long vowel in regular Japanese is only used to express words of foreign origin or imitation sounds. Basically in Braille, a long vowel 'ō' is written as 'ー', so the word 'ガッコー (学校)'(a school, pronounced 'gakkō') uses 'ー'. But the word 'コオリ (氷)' (an ice, pronounced 'kōri') uses 'オ', not the symbol, to express the long vowel as exceptions. It is thus very difficult to represent rules so that they are followed automatically by a computer.

In such work, it is important both to reduce errors and to make Braille expressions consistent throughout a text even when more than one translation is possible. Assuming, for example, that it cannot be judged whether '多い'(a lot of, pronounced 'ōi') should be converted to 'オオイ' or 'オーイ', all sentences in a document containing '多い' must be corrected either one way or the other.

3 Proposed System

3.1 Basic Concepts

Our system is based on three concepts.

1. **Both rule-based and case-based reasoning are used.**
   Using case-based reasoning[5, 6] in addition to rule-based reasoning enables the system can learn from user corrections and automatically improve the knowledge base. Translation is quick and accurate[7, 8] and no need exists to repeatedly correct same or similar errors.
2. **Translated text is checked and corrected incrementally and interactively.**
   Our system's user interface has two editing modes – basic editing and package correction. Basic editing enables users to check and correct the results of automatic translation easily by showing results in Braille and inputted corresponding sentences. Package correction enables users to make results using a list of all clauses having the same ambiguity in a text.
3. **The system is accessible via the Net sharing a huge knowledge base.**
   The interactive translator and editor are implemented on the Web as a client-server system, enabling the accumulation of large numbers of cases. Users can accees the system with any computer that can access the Internet, since processing capacity is mainly needed by the server.

3.2 System Configuration

Our system consists of a server and clients (Fig.1). Processes are distributed between the server and clients to reduce time spent sending and receiving data. The server mainly processes time-consuming tasks such as automatic translation and retrieval of similar clauses using modules written in C. Clients implemented by a Java applet provide a user interface that accepts document input, edits the document, and displays output.

Japanese-to-Braille translation is done in six steps (numbers correspond to those in Fig.1).

1. *The user supplies a source document, i.e., a set of sentences in mixed Japanese, and the client sends it to a server.*
2. *The server translates it using a rule base and a case base, sends a draft of Braille sentences to the client, and retains it for use in subsequent processes on the server.*
3. *The user edits the draft aided by interaction with the client. The client has two interface modes – basic editing (BE) mode and package correction (PC) mode.*
4. *When the user starts PC mode, the client requests from the server a list of sentence positions to be displayed.*

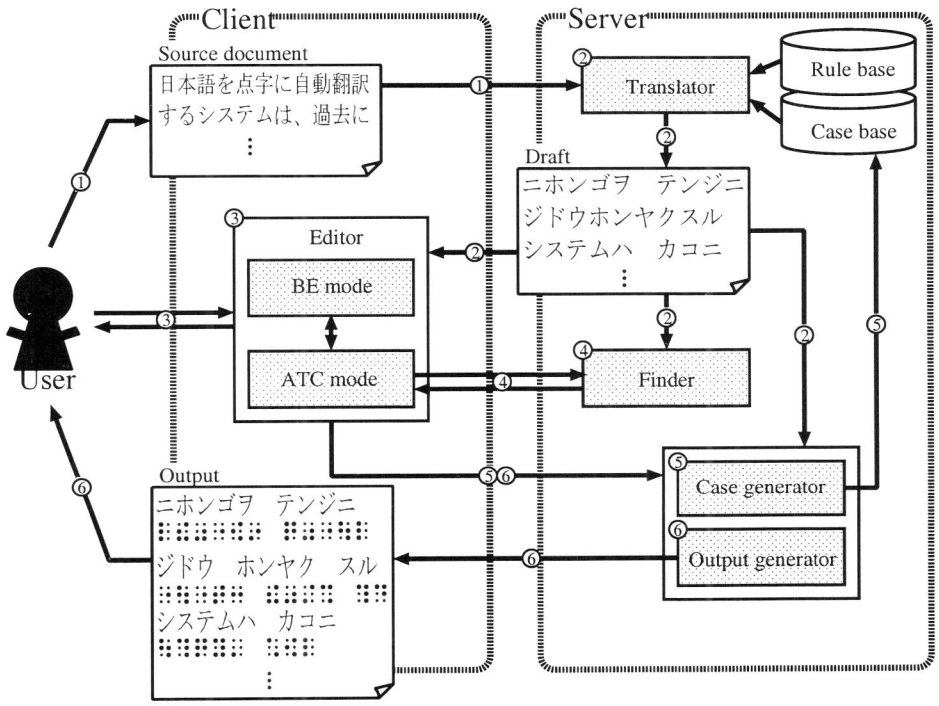

Fig. 1. System Configuration

5. As the user corrects the draft, the client sends a log of corrections, or correction data, to the server, which extracts cases from the log.
6. After editing is finished, the server generates an output, corrected Braille sentences.

The system uses two types of knowledge resources: a rule base and a case base. Rules are implemented from 'Ten-yaku no Tebiki'. Cases are exceptional knowledge that rules cannot handle. Cases are specific to individual rules, so the rule base indexes cases reducing search time. Cases are made from user revision and a collection of Braille-Japanese document pairs.

3.3 Translation Using Cases and Rules

!!
Cases and rules segment sentences and revise strings in a draft. A rule consists of an action (example: insert a space), conditions for applying the action, and a priority score to resolve rule conflicts. A condition is stated by checking the value of an attribute. Attributes are obtained by morphological analysis, e.g., parts

of speech, positions of accents, reading, i.e., a pronunciation written in kana, character type, and a mora, all of which are defined as symbolic attributes. The system uses a morphological analysis program for voice synthesis to get phonetic information and accurate readings. A case consists of an action, a set of attributes of morphemes to which the action of this case makes revision, and an identification number of a root rule, i.e., the rule for which the case is an exception. We define an object to which an action of a rule or a case makes revision, i.e. a string or an interval between characters, as a spot.

The server translates using the following steps.

1. Analyze the source document and make a first draft of readings given by the analysis.
2. For each spot in a source document:
   (a) Find the most appropriate rule R for the spot.
   (b) Search cases whose root rule corresponds to R and calculate the similarity between the spot and each of the applicable cases.
   (c) If similarity between the nearest case C and the spot is higher than the threshold, then apply C. Otherwise, apply R.

The similarity between a spot in a draft and a candidate case is calculated by dividing the number of corresponding attributes by the number of all attributes.

3.4 User Interface

!!
To enable users to edit a draft easily, the system provides two interface modes switchable at any point: basic edit (BE) mode and package correction (PC) mode. BE mode is used to check a draft from the beginning and correct any errors. If translation errors or instability occur, users start PC mode.

In BE mode(Fig.2(a)), the system displays the source document and its draft aligned on two consecutive lines, the source above and the draft below. Underlines on the lower line indicate segmentation that will be replaced with spaces in output. Users use BE mode to

1. add or remove a space for segmentation by clicking on the left mouse button (changing segmentation);
2. correct a string by editing it using a supporting dialog box displayed by dragging the string (editing string);
3. get PC mode started by clicking the right button at the bottom of the screen; or
4. get an output by clicking the left button at the bottom of the screen when finished checking.

In PC mode (Fig.2(b)), the system displays clauses having the same ambiguity as a base spot, i.e., the spot corrected most recently in BE mode. Users use PC mode to

1. correct clauses selected among candidates;

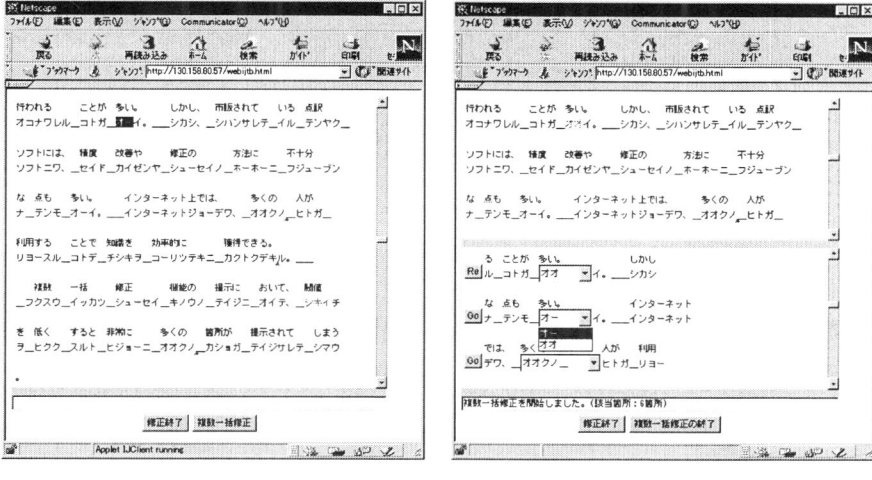

(a) BE mode (b) PC mode

Fig. 2. Sample interface mode screens.

2. adjust the upper part of the screen on the place where the provided clause is in the draft by clicking 'Go' button to grasp the context; or
3. return to BE mode by clicking the right button at the bottom of the screen.

When users start PC mode, the server searches the source document and its draft to list clauses having ambiguity similar to the base spot in one of two ways:

1. If segmentation of the base spot was changed, the system calculates the similarity of all intervals in the document and the base spot, then the server provides clauses involving spots with similarity higher than the threshold.
2. If the string of the base spot was edited, the system searches for clauses including the same string to the base spot in mixed Japanese, and has the same string to pre-edit or post-edit string of the base spot in Braille.

When users complete a revised document, the client sends revision data and the server acquires a case. Users need neither to specify a case nor wait until a case is created.

4 Evaluation

We evaluated system functions by studying the efficiency of case acquisition and the efficiency of PC mode.

4.1 Case Acquisition

To estimate the contribution of case acquisition, we varied the number of cases and observed the effects on system performance. The rule base contains 51 rules.

Table 1. Comparison of the number of cases

Number of cases	0	500	1,022
Number of string errors	166	143	126
Number of segmentation errors	584	453	410
Translation time (*sec.*)	117	146	171

Three case base sizes were studied: 0, 500, and 1,022. Cases were acquired using a text that is part of 'Chosakuken-Hou', the Copyright Act containing 25,749 characters. Translation was done with another text containing 17,001 characters. A document in Braille, translated by experts, is used as the standard to judge whether results of automatic translation are correct.

Table 1 shows numbers of errors and translation time. Errors are categorized into string and segmentation errors, both of which decreased monotonically as the number of cases increased. Acquiring cases thus contributes to improving accuracy. The more cases the system acquires, the fewer users have to correct. Translation time, however, increased in proportion to the number of cases. Indexing cases enabled limited the cost increase; in 1,022 cases, it takes 308 seconds to translate without indexing. Adding rules that divide cases equally to the rule base may reduce translation time.

4.2 PC Mode

We studied how appropriately PC mode produces clauses having the same ambiguity as a base spot using two measurements – recall rate and relevance ratio. The recall rate is equal to the number of clauses to be checked and provided by the system divided by the number of all clauses to be checked in the whole document. The relevance ratio is equal to the number of clauses to be checked and provided by the system divided by the number of the clauses the system provides. Experiments were conducted for each of the two revisions – changing segmentation and editing string. 10 base spots were used for each revision and clauses to be checked were selected per base spot assuming user demand in advance; e.g., in setting a base spot 'ショウ(しょう)'(let's, pronounced 'siyō') and correcting to 'ショー', clauses including 'ヨウナ(ような)'(as if, pronounced 'yōna') and 'ダロウ(だろう)'(I think, pronounced 'darō') having the same ambiguity as the base spot to be provided and clauses including 'トイウ(という)'(express, pronounced 'toiu') having another one not needed. We used 3,346 characters from 'Chosakuken-Hou' as the source document. The threshold for finding clauses to be provided in changing segmentation was set to 0.65.

In both cases(Table 2), the average recall rate exceeds 70% and in the 13 cases the recall rates are 100%, so using PC mode reduces output instability without making it necessary to recheck the whole document, thus increasing translation

Table 2. Experimental results on propriety of provided clauses.

(a) Changing segmentation.

Serial number of base spots	Recall rate(%)	Relevance ratio(%)
1	100.0	100.0
2	100.0	100.0
3	100.0	100.0
4	100.0	100.0
5	57.1	100.0
6	50.0	100.0
7	100.0	60.0
8	42.9	100.0
9	20.0	100.0
10	50.0	100.0
Average	72.7	96.0
Standard deviation	29.4	12.0

(b) Editing string.

Serial number of base spots	Recall rate(%)	Relevance ratio(%)
1	100.0	100.0
2	100.0	100.0
3	100.0	100.0
4	100.0	100.0
5	14.3	100.0
6	100.0	100.0
7	100.0	25.0
8	100.0	100.0
9	12.5	100.0
10	100.0	100.0
Average	82.6	92.5
Standard deviation	34.6	22.5

throughput. The average relevance ratio is nearly 100%, and in all 20 cases tested, the number of provided clauses was 16 at most, requiring very little workload to check and correct clauses. But the system is poor at some ambiguities, so the average recall rates did not reach 100%. It is therefore important to improve the algorithm for finding clauses to be provided so the average recall rate becomes nearly 100%, thus reducing output instability.

In changing segmentation, the most suitable threshold differs for each base spot. In the base spot of No. 5, for example, the recall rate increases to 71.4% and the relevance ratio remains 100% when the threshold is set to 0.60. In the base spot of No. 7, the relevance ratio increases to 100% and the recall rate remains 100% when the threshold is set to 0.70. The average recall and relevance are thus improved by automatically adjusting the threshold.

In editing string, the reason that recall rates of No. 5 and No. 9 in Table 2 (b) are low is because the system cannot set a correspondence between kanji and reading per character[1], whereas the system can set a correspondence per morpheme. When users revised a spot 'トウガイ(当該)' to 'ト—ガイ'(concerned, pronounced as 'tōgai'), the system cannot provide 'ソウトウ(相当)' (correspond, pronounced as 'sōtō') the user must check and correct. Because the system recognizes this correction as the edit of a string 'ト—ガイ(当該)', not a string 'ト—(当)'. If the system could do this, the recall rates of No. 5 and No. 9 would become 100%.

Adding a function in which users can control the condition for providing would enable the system to output more accurate results and be more useful since user requests must be managed based on circumstances.

---

[1] To enable this, morphological analysis must be modified. Since morphological analysis is done by a company-owned program, modification was not possible.

5 Conclusion

We proposed interactive Japanese-to-Braille translation on the Web that provides quick, accurate translation by combining rules and cases. The system learns user modifications incrementally. It helps check output consistency by providing a list of all clauses having the same ambiguity. Experiments showed that case acquisition reduces errors that users must correct and the system reduces output instability without necessitating a recheck of the whole document.

We expect to expand our system for multipurpose Braille translation. Inexperienced uses and beginners could use the system as an automatic translator and as an educational tool. Experts could use it as groupware enabling them to make consistent translations free of personal bias.

Acknowledgements

We thank Nippon Telegraph and Telephone Corporation for the use of JTAG, a morphological analyzer for voice synthesis, and Professor Yukio Fukui and Dr. Christer Johansson for providing invaluable advices.

References

1. Koide, A., Asakawa, C., Suzuki, N.: Research on Computer Aids for the Visually Disabled. World Scientific (1994) 66-69
2. Kawahara, M.: Yet Another Japanese Braille Translation Program. Technical report of IEICE HC94-49 (1994) 51-58.
3. Suzuki, E., Ono, S., Hiraoka, T., Kanoh, H.: Interactive Japanese Sentence Segmentation System for translating Japanese into Braille. Proceedings of the Natural Language Processing Pacific Rim Symposium (1997) 621-624.
4. Suzuki, E., Ono, S., Kanoh, H.: Japanese Sentence Segmentation System for Translating Japanese into Braille. Journal of Natural Language Processing, Vol. 5, No. 4 (1998) 95-110.
5. Cost, S., Salzberg, S.: A weighted nearest neighbor algorithm for learning with symbolic features. Machine Learning, Vol. 10 (1993) 57-78.
6. Kobayashi, S.: Present and Future of Case-Based Reasoning. Journal of Japanese Society for Artificial Intelligence Vol. 7, No. 4 (1992) 559-566.
7. Golding, A. R., Rosenbloom, P. S.: Improving accuracy by combining rule-based and case-based reasoning. Artificial Intelligence, Vol. 87 (1996) 215-254.
8. Takagi, Y., Ono, S., Miyashita, K., Nishihara, S.: A Japanese Sentence Segmentation Method for Braille Based on Surface Analysis and Case-Based Reasoning. IPSJ Natural Language, Vol. 99, No. 2 (1999) 79-86.

Psychological Effects Derived from Mimicry Voice Using Inarticulate Sounds

Noriko Suzuki, Yugo Takeuchi and Michio Okada

ATR Media Integration & Communications Research Laboratories,
2-2-2 Hikaridai, Seika-cho, Soraku-gun, Kyoto JAPAN 619-0288

Abstract. In this paper, we describe results from an experiment on interaction with artificial creatures that mimic the human voice echoicly using inarticulate sounds. We consider that humans are apt to find a partner's intention or emotion towards themselves, when the partner mimics their utterances echoicly at the prosodic level. As a result, we regard that empathic interaction emerges between them. We test this hypothesis by having subjects interact with five artificial creatures that give different rates of their respective response as mimicked voice at the prosodic level: (a) 100%, (b) 80%, (c) 50%, (d) 20%, and (e) 0%. For the remaining voice probability expressing non-mimicry voice, we have constant prosody voice like a back-channel response. The subjects' evaluations of the creatures were collected with a questionnaire according to their impressions on their interaction with the creatures: *cooperation, friendliness, memory retention, sympathy, and verbal understanding*. We consider that the results support our hypothesis that echoic mimicry is key for the emergence of empathic interaction between humans and computers.

1 Introduction

Does mimicry voice which traces the prosody-only aspect of human voice work positively or negatively in human-computer interaction? Almost all designers and programmers of interactive systems using speech have dismissed the power of mimicry voice at the prosodic level, because of their focus on the efficiency and accuracy of task-achievement [1, etc.]. This conventional view argues that computers are tools or assistants that should be designed to show the most suitable answers for the completion of tasks using the function of problem solving.

However, people generally use mimicry voice at the prosodic level using inarticulate sounds, e.g., the call of an animal or the babbling of a baby, in their interpersonal interaction, especially in human-pet interaction or in mother-infant interaction. In addition, research has shown that users interact with computers in the same way as they interact with other people [2, 3, 4]. These findings suggest that mimicry voice at the prosodic level may be welcomed in human-computer interaction, just as it is in interpersonal interaction.

From the above viewpoint, we have constructed an interactive system with an artificial creature that detects prosodic patterns in the human voice, i.e., power, f_0, and rhythm patterns, and expresses a synthesis voice by tracing these prosodic patterns as mimicry voice, or expresses a type of templates voice with constant prosody using inarticulate sounds as non-mimicry voice. The mimicry voice of inarticulate sounds is synthesized by combining sine waves based on the power and f_0 patterns.

We performed a psychological experiment to evaluate the effect of mimicry voice using inarticulate sounds by having subjects interact with five kinds of artificial creatures each giving a different output probability of mimicry voice: (a) 100%, (b) 80%, (c) 50%, (d) 20%, and (e) 0%. The subjects' evaluations of the creatures were collected through a questionnaire according to their impressions on their interaction with the creature: *cooperation, friendliness, memory retention, sympathy,* and *verbal understanding.*

First, we explain the factors deriving the intentional stance of humans. Second, we describe a psychological experiment on the mimicry voice using inarticulate sounds. Finally, we discuss the results of the experiment.

2 Factors Deriving of the Intentional Stance

We can interact with a variety of partners including humans, animals, and objects to understand their features through their behaviors. Dennett has proposed three kinds of stances, i.e., *physical stance, design stance,* and *intentional stance,* as ways of understanding our partner's features [5]. *Physical stance* is a way of explaining objects according to physical principals. *Design stance* is a way of explaining objects by designed mechanisms. *Intentional stance* is a way of explaining objects by autonomous functions with either intention or emotion.

For example, after one shouts "Yoo-hoo!" to a wall before her/his eyes, the same "Yoo-hoo!" sound returns. From the viewpoint of *physical stance*, it is considered that the sound echoed off the wall according to physical principals. From the viewpoint of *design stance*, it is considered that a recorded sound was played because the wall has equipment to record and play sounds. From the viewpoint of *intentional stance*, it is considered that the wall intended to mimic the person.

Recently, a lot of research has been done to develop robots and interface agents not only to be useful for humans but also to live symbiotically with humans [6, 7, etc.]. Such research is apt to derive the intentional stance of humans from its life-like designs, e.g., appearance of existing humans and animals, and behaviors based on emotion or intention.

It has been suggested that humans are apt to interact with their partners from the viewpoint of intentional stance [2, 3]. These works have stated that the intentional stance of humans can be derived by having them interact with computers under certain conditions. The results of these works have suggested that anthropomorphic behaviors of humans are facilitated not by the appearance of but by the behavior of computers, through interaction without the element of intention or emotion. These studies, however, have not really considered the link that this intentional stance derives from phatic interaction. Our focus is

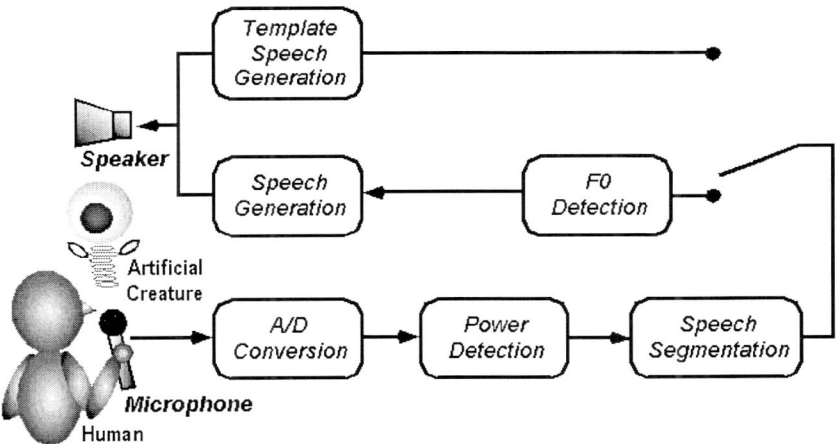

Fig. 1. Example of a system implementation for an experiment

the psychological effect of "echoic mimicry using inarticulate sounds" as a key towards examining this link.

3 Psychological Experiment

3.1 Experimental Environment

An experiment was performed to examine psychological effects when a subject's speech voice was mimicked using inarticulate sounds, e.g., a prosody-only voice, by computer. In this experiment, we used an artificial creature on a computer as the interface for interaction. The creature has the ability to produce inarticulate sounds according to the system in Fig. 1. The subjects' can interact with the creature without any bias because the creature has an abstract appearance and voice (Fig. 2). The subjects interact with the creature displayed on a 17-inch screen via a headset.

The system works as follows: an audio signal from a microphone is sampled at 16 (kHz) (A/D Conversion). The time sequence of the power pattern, e.g., the loudness of the human voice, is calculated for each frame of the audio (Power Detection). The segmentation of the speech is determined by the threshold energy based on the result of the power calculation (Speech Segmentation). The time sequence of an f_0 pattern, e.g., the pitch of the human voice, is calculated for each segment (F_0 Detection). For the experiment, f_0 patterns are detected by the AMDF (Average Magnitude Differential Function) method. Inarticulate sounds are synthesized by combining sine waves based on the power calculation and f_0 pattern (Speech Generation). For the purpose of experimental control, we prepared templates as non-mimicry voice using inarticulate sounds that include

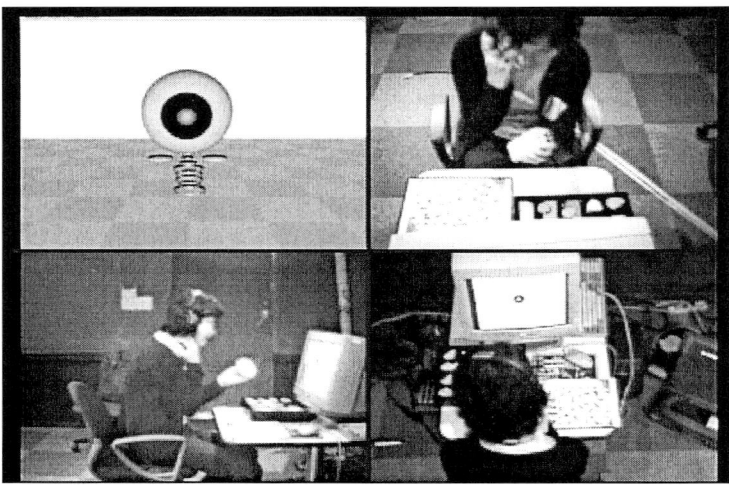

Fig. 2. Example of an interactive session between a human and an artificial creature

one to four syllables synthesized by a combination of sine waves or triangular waves. These templates use constant prosody like a back-channel response of humans (Template Speech Generation). These sounds are output through speakers. A human can interact with the system independently of her/his language.

Figure 3 shows two examples of time sequences of sound waves and f_0 patterns on the interaction between a subject (right channel) and an artificial creature (left channel): Fig. 3 upper shows the artificial creature expressing mimicking voice against the subject's voice (*Torisan* (This is a bird.)), and Fig. 3 lower shows the artificial creature expressing non-mimicking voice using inarticulate sounds based on templates against the same subject's voice (*Torisan* (This is a bird.)). The upper part shows that the loudness, pitch, and rhythm patterns of the creature's voice are similar to the features of the human voice. By contrast, the lower part shows that the loudness, pitch, and rhythm patterns of the creature's voice is constant and independent of the human voice.

3.2 Hypothesis

We assume that the subject can find an intention or emotion towards herself/himself in the behavior of the creature, even though the creature only has a function to mimic the input voice of the subject echoicly at the prosodic level. As a result of deriving the intentional stance, the subject receives a psychological effect from the creature. In this experiment, we prepare five kinds of creatures with different output probabilities of mimicry voice to examine the effects of mimicry voice.

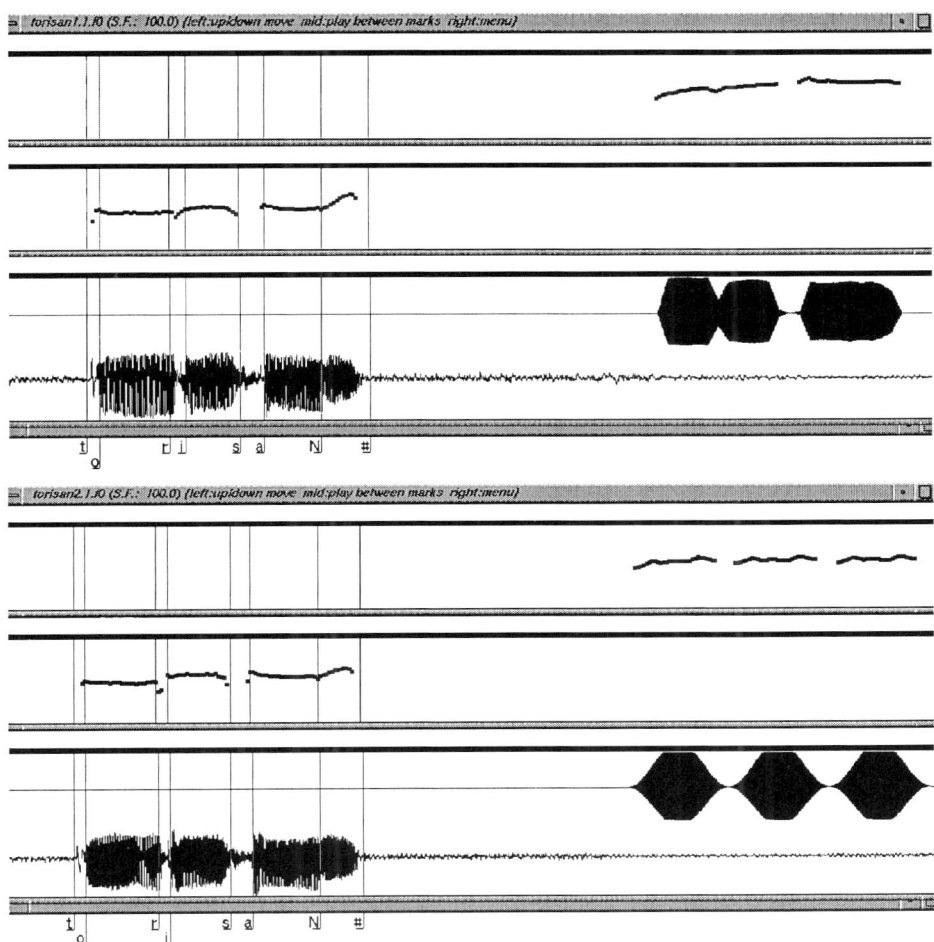

Fig. 3. Examples of time sequences of sound waves and f_0 patterns on the interaction between a subject and an artificial creature: (a) the system expresses mimicking voice against the subject's utterance (upper), and (b) the system expresses non-mimicking voice of three syllables with constant prosody against the subject's utterance (lower)

Our experimental hypothesis is that with a high output probability of mimicry voice the subject will have a more positive impression of the creature even the creature lacks a function for expression based on intention or emotion. The subject will be able to empathically recognize the creature's behavior towards herself/himself, because she/he will be made to believe that the creature can distinguish her/him from other subjects.

3.3 Conditions

There are five conditions for the *voice* of the creature as follows:

(a) The creature produces a 100% output probability of mimicry voice of all voices and a 0% output probability of non-mimicry voice.
(b) The creature produces an 80% output probability of mimicry voice of all voices and a 20% output probability of non-mimicry voice.
(c) The creature produces a 50% output probability of mimicry voice of all voices and a 50% output probability of non-mimicry voice.
(d) The creature produces a 20% output probability of mimicry voice of all voices and a 80% output probability of non-mimicry voice.
(e) The creature produces a 0% output probability of mimicry voice of all voices and a 100% output probability of non-mimicry voice.

For the *glance* and *motion* conditions, however, the creature is set to perform the same expression under all voice conditions. For the glance condition, it always turns its head to the front. For the motion condition, it rolls from side to side by default. When it detects the voice of a human, it stops rolling. Then, when it starts to talk to the subject, it becomes larger than its default size. The creature responds after an 800 (msec) delay for both mimicry voice and non-mimicry voice when the subject talks to it.

3.4 Method

Subjects: 40 university students (from 18 to 22 years old). 40 subjects, however, were divided in the following two groups; i) the former 20 subjects interacted with the creatures under (a), (c), and (e) conditions, and ii) the latter 20 interacted with the creatures under (b), (c), and (d).
Sequence: The experiment was carried out in the following sequence.

(1) Subjects watch a sample interaction video for about two minutes.
(2) They listen to the instructions written below.
(3) They interact with the creature using blocks for infants (Fig. 4) for a period of four minutes.
(4) They answer a questionnaire about their impression of interaction with the creature.
(5) They repeat steps 1 - 4 four more times under different conditions.

3.5 Instructions and Evaluations

The experimenter explains that the creature on the computer screen in front of subject has the same intelligence level as a one-year-old child and it is not so smart. The subject is told to teach the creature the names of objects while assembling the objects with building blocks. While giving the instructions, the experimenter shows the subject samples of animals or cars for the building blocks.

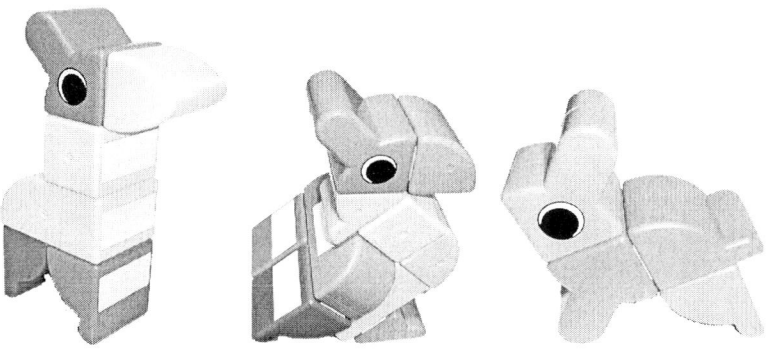

Fig. 4. Examples of building blocks used by a subject (giraffe (left), parrot (middle), rabbit (right))

The subject can start to interact with the creature easily because the subject has been given the above instructions. In a psychological evaluation after the interactive session, the experimenter asks the subject to answer a questionnaire including the following evaluation items which are prepared based on a pilot study on psychological evaluations of interaction between humans and robots [8], or anthropomorphic agents [9].

Cooperation: Degree of cooperation that the subject feels towards the creature when the subject interacts with the creature
Friendliness: Degree of friendliness that the subject feels towards the creature when the subject interacts with the creature
Memory Retention: Degree of memory retention that the subject feels towards the creature when the subject interacts with the creature
Sympathy: Degree of sympathy that the subject feels towards the creature when the subject interacts with the creature
Verbal Understanding: Degree of verbal understanding that the subject feels towards the creature when the subject interacts with the creature

All of these items were evaluated based on a 7-point scale by the subjects.

3.6 Results and Discussion

Figure 5 shows the average MOS (mean opinion score) value of the subjects on each of the above evaluation items related to the subjects' impressions of their interactions with the artificial creatures. The horizontal axis shows the output probability of mimicry voice of the creature and the vertical axis shows the average evaluation MOS value for 20 subjects except condition (c). A score greater than four for the MOS value shows a positive impression and a score lower than four means a negative impression.

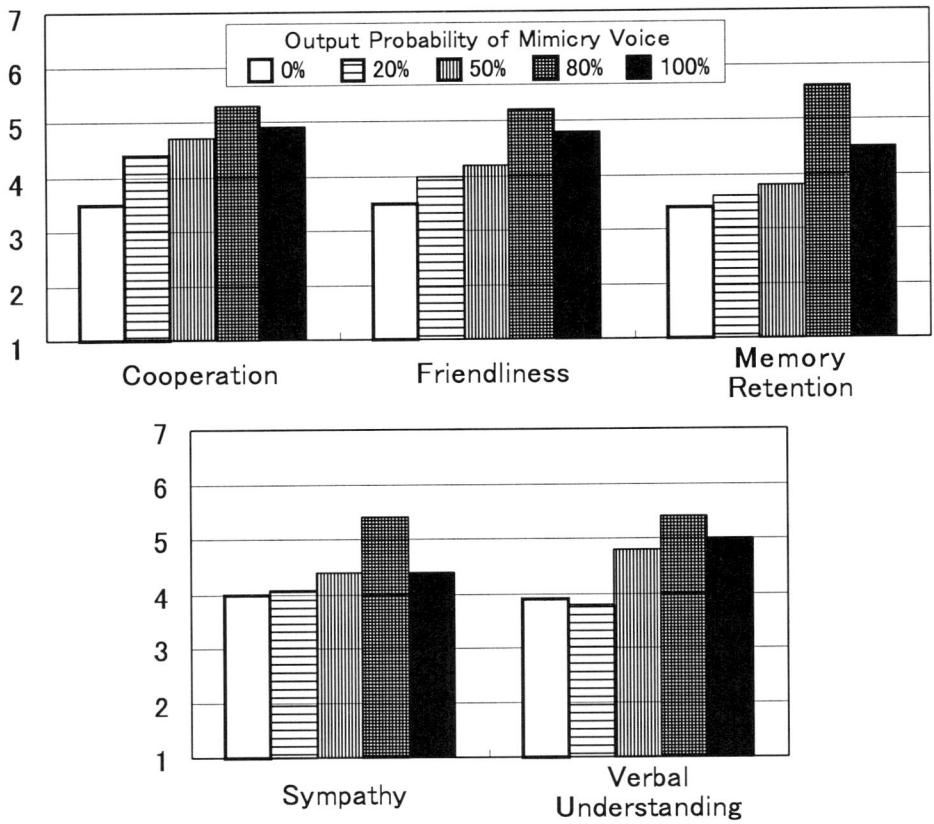

Fig. 5. Results of evaluation: impression of interaction with artificial creature

These results are integrated the MOS values of two groups and are put them in order, because the MOS values of each group under condition (c) are almost all the same.

All of the evaluation items in Fig. 5 show that the total tendencies of the MOS values were almost all the same, and the subjects evaluated the creatures positively according to the following order of output probabilities of mimicry voice: 80% > 100% > 50% > 20% > 0%. This result indicates that the creature with a 100% output probability of mimicry voice gave the subject a more negative impression than the creature with an 80% probability. We assume the following two reasons for this:

- The subjects had a mechanical impression of this creature, because the creature always returned responses with mimicry of the human voice. Namely,

the subjects derived a design stance by interaction with the creature having a 100% output probability of mimicry voice rather than an intentional stance.
– The subjects found negative behavior, i.e., impertinent behavior, in the creature with a 100% output probability of mimicry voice because the creature always repeated the human voice using inarticulate sounds.

Moreover, Fig. 5 also shows that the creature with a 0% output probability of mimicry voice did not give the subjects such a negative impression. We assume the following reasons for this:

– The subjects did not have a very negative impression of the creature that always returned non-mimicry voice because the creature at least returned some response with even constant prosody against human utterances.
– The subjects found non-linear, unpredictable behaviors towards the creature that always returned non-mimicry voice because the creature had seven kinds of response patterns, e.g., one to four syllables' voice with constant prosody like a back-channel response.

4 Conclusions

These results suggest that computers can derive the intentional stance of humans when they have a function that expresses an approximately 80% output probability of mimicry voice and an approximately 20% output probability of non-mimicry voice using inarticulate sounds, and can provide facilitation about social relationship with humans.

These results also support the idea that mimicry voice at the prosodic level using inarticulate sounds still has such a basic, inherent, and robust element of social facilitation in human-computer interaction, even when computers do not include a function based on intention or emotion.

Perhaps the most important implication for designers and programmers of interactive systems using speech is that mimicry voice at the prosodic level can provide effects in human-computer interaction similar to those interpersonal interaction. Therefore, as in interpersonal interaction, especially in mother-infant interaction, an adult can consider the voice of an infant positively, even if the infant mimics the voice of the adult echoicly without any intention. However, people sometimes treat the behavior of mimicking an adult negatively. Consequently, mimicry voice can have a positive or negative effect depending on the situation of interaction.

These results also suggest an important open question: How many output probabilities of mimicry voice at the prosodic level using inarticulate sounds can be considered likable and empathetic for humans? In addition, how do people feel about mimicry voice at the word or language level? Our study will continue to seek answers to these questions.

Another important implication of this study is that the mimicry voice at the prosodic level is a key to empathic interaction in human-computer interaction.

A function for expressing intentional behavior is not always required. The echoic mimicry at the prosodic level of the human voice, as used in this study, can be an inexpensive, high-impact method for increasing the likability of an interface. For example, the function of echoic mimicry at the prosodic level of the human voice might be used in CAI (computer aided instruction) systems, communication robots [6, 7, etc.] and toy interfaces [10, 11, 12, etc.].

Acknowledgment

We would like to thank President Ryohei Nakatsu, Dr. Yasuhiro Katagiri, and each member of Department 4, for their continuous support in this work. We also thank Mr. Takashi Furuya and Mr. Shigeo Nishigaki for their technical support in the implementation of the system.

References

1. Zue, V., et al. "PEGASUS: A spoken language interface for on-line air travel planning", *ARPA Workshop on Human Language Technology*, pp. 196 – 201 (1994).
2. Nass, C., Steuer, J., Henriksen, L., and Dryer, D.C. "Machines, social attributions, and ethopoeia: performance assessments of computers subsequence to "self-" or "other-" evaluations", *Human-Computer Studies*, Vol. 40, pp. 543 – 559 (1994).
3. Takeuchi, Y., Katagiri, Y., Nass., C., and Fogg., B.J. "Social response and cultural dependency in human-computer interaction", *joint workshop on cross-cultural communication – towards culturally situated agents – on PRICAI'98*, pp. 114 – 123 (1998).
4. Suzuki, N., Takeuchi, Y., Ishii, K., and Okada, M. "Talking Eye: Autonomous Creatures for Augmented Chatting", *Robotics and Autonomous Systems*, Vol. 31, No. 3, pp. 171 – 184 (2000).
5. Dennett, D.C. The Intentional Stance. MIT Press, (1987)
6. Fujita, F. and Kageyama, K. "An open architecture for robot entertainment", *Autonomous Agents*, pp. 435 – 442 (1997).
7. Ushida, H., Hirayama, Y., and Nakajima, H. "Emotional model for life-like agent and its evaluation", *American Association for Artificial Intelligence*, pp. 62 – 69 (1998)
8. Nakata, T., Sato, T., Mori, T., and Mizoguchi, H. "Expression of emotion and intention by robot body movement", *Intelligent autonomous systems 5 (IAS-5)*, pp. 352 – 359 (1998)
9. Cassel, J. and Thrisson, K. R. "The power of a nod and a glance: envelope vs. emotional feedback in animated conversational agents", *Applied Artificial Intelligence*, Vol. 13, pp. 519 – 538 (1999)
10. Strommen, E. "When the interface is a talking dinosaur: learning across media with ActiMates Barney", *CHI98*, pp. 288 – 295 (1998)
11. Druin, A., et al. "Designing PETS: a personal electronic teller of stories", *CHI99*, pp. 326 – 329 (1999)
12. Johnson, M. P., et al. "Sympathetic interfaces: using a plush toy to direct synthetic characters", *CHI99*, pp. 152 – 158 (1999)

Statistical Model Based Approach to Spoken Language Acquisition

Naoto Iwahashi

Sony Computer Science Labs Inc., Takanawa Muse Bldg. 3-14-13 Higashi-Gotanda Shinagawa-ku, Tokyo 141-0022, Japan, iwahashi@csl.sony.co.jp,

Abstract. This paper describes an algorithm for spoken language acquisition through natural interface based on the perception of speech and other information conveyed in continuous signal spaces. In this algorithm the grounded language knowledge is represented by statistical model consisting of hidden Markov models and stochastic context-free grammar. The syntactic structure in each spoken utterance is inferred from the conceptual structure extracted from the perceptual information in the learning process. The algorithm is robust against ambiguity and sparseness of learning data because it uses statistical learning methods, such as Bayesian learning. Experimental results show that spoken language is learned robustly from a small amount of learning data.

1 Introduction

The study of language acquisition by machines has been attracting interest in various research areas, and the recent progress in both linguistics and machine learning theory has made it a very fruitful field of study (Brent 1996). On the other hand, the recent progress of such application technologies as computation, telecommunications, sensing, and robotics has made the development of natural-language interfaces with machines more important because it has increased the demand for easy and comfortable relationships with machines. The use of language acquisition schemes in interactive machines has been studied in attempts to increase the flexibility of the language interface, and one of the practical applications investigated was an automatic call-routing system using speech recognition (Gorin, Levinson and Sanker, 1994). The language acquisition techniques used in these interfaces must be able to cope with the following two major problems faced by intelligent systems dealing with spoken language:

1. Various aspects of spoken language are *open* – vocabulary, sentence expression, meaning, speaking style, speaker's voice characteristics, and so on – and are hard to restrict even when the functions of the systems are limited.
2. Spoken language should be *grounded* in the real world or in the process dealt with by the systems.

Several pioneering studies have developed language acquisition algorithms based on inductive learning using a set of pairs each consisting of a word sequence and either its nonlinguistic information or its semantic information. For example algorithms for learning the meanings of English prepositions with surrounding words by using the symbolic attributes for spatial relationship, were presented in (Harris 1989, Munro, Cosic and Tabasko 1991). And (Siskind 1996) described a word-to-meaning mapping algorithm using a set of pairs each consisting of a sentence and a collection of its possible meanings represented symbolically with Jackendoff-style expression. It was based on cross-situational learning (Pinker 1989) and successfully addressed the problems due to homonyms and to noisy learning data. Visual rather than symbolic information has been used in word-to-meaning learning tasks (Dyer and Nenov 1993, Nakagawa and Masukata 1995, Regier 1997, Roy and Pentland 1998), and the judgement of whether or not the system's response is appropriate has also been used as nonlinguistic information (Gorin et al. 1991, Fujie and Kobayashi 1999). And spoken-word acquisition algorithm based on unsupervised clustering of speech tokens, without the learning data being divided into any clusters beforehand, was presented in (Gorin, Levinson, and Sanker 1994). This algorithm used template-pattern-matching method. There have also been some studies on the use of semantic information in the learning of syntactic rules (Langley 1982, Berwick 1985). An algorithm for the learning of stochastic regular grammar in a visually grounded way was presented in (Nakagawa and Masukata 1995), in which the order of words in utterances was dealt with. In all these algorithms, however, some categories of the observed linguistic and nonlinguistic information were specified beforehand, and these categories were not expandable. Because of this, the learning algorithms were based mainly on symbolic or discrete information, although continuous information was also used. The learnability was restricted by such unnatural setup.

This paper therefore describes an algorithm in which the grounded language knowledge can be expansively acquired through natural interface based on speech and the perception of other information conveyed in continuous signal spaces. To process the information in the continuous space robustly, the algorithm must include a suitable pattern recognition mechanism. In the algorithm described here the semantic bootstrapping scheme in grammar acquisition (Pinker 1984), which appears to be natural and effective scheme even in a machine learning, is implemented based on associating speech with the other perceptual information through conceptual structures.

2 Learning Task

We set up the following spoken language acquisition task. A person and the system "see" the same scenes on a system display, showing graphical objects, each of which may be stationary or moving. Each scene is made by the person by using a pointing device. The person making a scene chooses colors for the objects from a color map, puts the objects into the scene, and makes them move there. The system initially does not have any individual graphical concepts and does not know any words. To teach the system, the person speaks about the scene into a microphone while using a pointing device to point to and move one

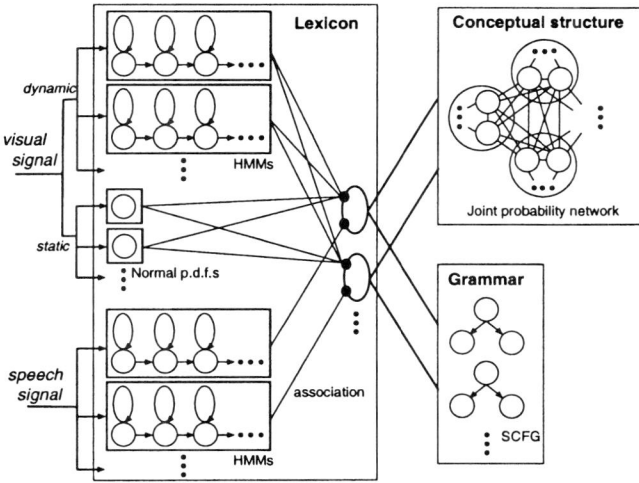

Fig. 1. Statistical models for knowledge representation

of the graphical objects in the scene. The person speaks slowly pausing briefly between words. The person can also move one of the objects without speaking. The system learns language through a sequence of such learning strokes, which provides the set of the scenes with the operations and the speech describing them. During the course of the task, the person can see how well the system has learned by asking the system to speak about a given scene and or by asking the system to move objects.

3 Algorithm

3.1 Outline

The system initially has no lexicon. It acquires linguistic and nonlinguistic knowledge, and the knowledge it obtains is represented by graphical statistic models consisting of normal probability density functions ($p.d.f.$s), hidden Markov models (HMMs), stochastic context-free grammar (SCFG), and joint probability network (Fig. 1). These statistical models are learned inductively by using the set of the episodes (the set of scenes and the speech describing them). When the operation is accompanied by the speech describing it, the sequences of spoken words in the speech are recognized. Possible concepts corresponding to recognized words are extracted from the scene during each operation, and then a possible structural relation among them as a whole is constructed by scene analysis. This conceptual structure is the candidate meaning of the given speech, and possible associations between the recognized spoken words and the individual concepts extracted are obtained. The learning of the grammar is based on this association. Speech recognition is carried out as a part of the unsupervised incremental clustering process for lexicon acquisition. The conceptual structure model is learned as the memory of perceptual experience and represents the information of the co-occurrence of individual concepts in conceptual structures. The complexity of the statistical models grows automatically according to given learning data. The input speech is understood by using the lexicon, the grammar and the conceptual structure model according to the given scene. The way in which the system generates action in the scene is based on maximum likelihood criteria. No text is dealt with in either the input or output of the system.

3.2 Membership Representation of Graphical Concepts and Spoken Words

The raw speech signal and graphical information are mapped into the perceptually appropriate feature spaces. The features of the speech and the scene are respectively decided by the requirements derived from speech recognition and by the requirements derived from conceptual scene analysis. Speech and the movement of the graphical objects are represented by the time sequence of these feature vectors.

The concepts of graphical objects and spoken words are acquired as membership functions represented by statistical models in the respective feature spaces. These membership functions are used as discriminant functions in speech recognition and scene analysis. HMMs, each of which has left-to-right state structure, are used to represent the membership function of the dynamic characteristics of graphical objects and speech sounds. The number of states in each HMM is determined by cross validation among learning samples, and the output *p.d.f.* at each state is represented by a multivariate normal distribution. Multivariate normal *p.d.f.*s are used to represent the membership functions of the static characteristics of graphical objects. To reduce the severity of the problem of data sparseness and the so-called *curse of dimensionality* and to make it easy to use high-dimensional features, the Bayesian learning method (DeGroot 1970) is used for the learning of the *p.d.f.*s characterizing static graphical characteristics.

3.3 Lexicon Acquisition

Each item in the lexicon includes concept and spoken-word membership functions. The set of pairs of the features of the spoken word and graphical scene is divided into clusters, the membership functions that are the lexical items are estimated using tokens in each cluster. The clusters for the lexicon are built up by using an unsupervised clustering algorithm in an incremental manner with regard to token input (Iwahashi 2000). When a new word (one not in the lexicon) is spoken, a new cluster should be generated. The algorithm adds each input spoken word to the nearest cluster, and checks whether the cluster should be split or not by using the verification score

$$R = \max_{o_i \in c} |L(o_i, h_{c,l}) - L(o_i, h_{c,r})|,$$

where c and o_i respectively denote the cluster considered to be split and the ith token. The HMMs $h_{c,l}$ and $h_{c,r}$ are the HMMs split from HMM h_c for cluster c by using the expectation-maximization algorithm (Dempster, Laird, and Rubin 1977), and $L(\cdot,\cdot)$ denotes a likelihood function. In the present algorithm the clustering is based only on speech information, but the algorithm can be extended to also use perceptual information. Language dependence is avoided by not assuming any phonemic units as prior knowledge.

3.4 Conceptual Scene Analysis

Each scene is analyzed in order to obtain its conceptual structure, which is represented by a conceptual expression (CE) consisting of some of the lexical items and their semantic attributes[1], such as [object], [action], and [to]. The scene analysis assigns the semantic attributes to each extracted graphical concept. In this process the system judges by checking the pointer movement whether the object movement is spontaneous or forced by the person. For instance, if the concept *rotate* is extracted as the spontaneous state of an object, the attribute [object] is assigned. And if it is extracted as the action to an object, the attribute [action] is assigned. When the operation is

to put a rotating red ball on the blue block on the right-hand side,

the CE might be

$$\begin{bmatrix} [\text{action}] : put \\ [\text{object}] : rotate, red, ball \\ [\text{to}] \quad\;\, : blue, block, right \end{bmatrix}$$

where the items in the right-hand column are concepts in the lexicon. Note that although the concepts are denoted by text here for convenience, in the algorithm they are identified by the indices assigned by the system. The CE is constructed using the individual concepts of possible words in a speech such that the likelihood of the membership function made by the composition of the individual concept membership functions is maximized for the operation in the scene.

3.5 Grammar Learning

Grammar is learned through adaptation of the initial neutral grammar. Learnable grammar is rather restricted so far: functional words such as prepositions and articles, for example, are not treated. Let a constituent of a sentence be defined as a word group that describes a concept, which could be a structural combination of multiple concepts. Each constituent is characterized by the semantic attribute assigned to the concept that the constituent describes. The set

---

[1] These can be defined task-dependently. We may be able to use the semantic primitives described in Schank 1972 and Jackendoff 1990, although the extraction of such semantic primitives from a scene is a problem.

A of semantic attributes a_i ($i = 1, 2, ...$) is initially given and fixed. The stochastic grammar SG consisting of probabilities $P(a_i \to a_j a_k)$ that the constituent with semantic attribute a_i consists of two constituents each with semantic attribute a_j and a_k in this order and probabilities $P(a_i \to c_j c_k \cdots)$ that the constituent with semantic attribute a_i consists of word sequence '$c_j c_k \cdots$'. The adaptation is based on the association between the speech and the scene. The following is an example of the procedure of determining such an association. Ideally, the speech recognizer recognizes the word sequence *"put rotate ball blue block"* perfectly. Then the scene analyzer produces a CE by using the concepts of these words. The comparison of the recognized word sequence with the CE results in the sentence being divided into the following three constituents:

(([action], *put*), ([object], (*rotate, ball*)),
([to], (*blue, block*))).

The SG is adapted using the information of the order ([action], [object], [to]) of the constituents' attributes.

Because the input utterance itself could be ungrammatical or not describe the scene correctly, the algorithm utilizes Bayesian learning so that the values of SG probabilities are adapted robustly, that is, a small number of improper samples do not much influence the grammar adaptation.

3.6 Learning of Conceptual Structure

The statistical model of the conceptual structure is represented by the probabilities of the co-occurrence of the concepts in the conceptual structure extracted from the scene. The probability that concept c_i and c_j respectively occur with semantic attributes a_k and a_l simultaneously is calculated by using *a posteriori* probabilities as

$$P(Concept(c_i, a_k), Concept(c_j, a_l)) = \frac{1}{M} \sum_{m=1}^{M} (P(Concept(c_i, a_k)|o_m) P(Concept(c_j, a_l)|o_m))$$

where o_m denotes the mth graphical episode. The *a posteriori* probabilities are calculated by using the likelihood values of possible concepts with regard to each graphic episode.

3.7 Speech Understanding and Action Generation

The meaning of an utterance asking the system to move a object is inferred by using linguistic knowledge and nonlinguistic knowledge. According to the meaning obtained, one of objects in the scene is selected and moved. The calculation of the trajectory of the movement is based on the maximum likelihood criterion with regard to HMMs (Tokuda, Kobayashi and Imai 1995), with the constraint on current object position. If the utterance includes the dynamic concept c_d

for action but does not include enough information to identify the object to be moved, the selection of an appropriate object is based on the following two principles:

1. An object that has a concept c_i such that the value of $P(Concept(c_i, [object])$, $Concept(c_d, [action])$ is high should be selected.
2. The object whose movement would be typical of concept c_d should be selected. Typicality is evaluated by rehearsing in the internal process of the system the movement of each possible candidate object, without moving the actual graphical object, and calculating the likelihood of the HMM for c_d with regard to the trajectory generated in the rehearsal process is calculated.

The judgement is done by integrating the above two values with the likelihood values obtained in the conceptual scene analysis.

4 Experiments

The algorithm was tested using a setup, in which the position on the display (two-dimensional: horizontal and vertical coordinates), the velocity (two-dimensional), and the color information (three-dimensional: L*a*b* parameters) were used as the features of the concept representations of graphical objects. Mel-scale cepstrum coefficients and their delta parameters (thirty-two dimensional) were used as the features of speech. A normal-Wishart *p.d.f.* was used as the *a priori p.d.f.* of the parameters in the normal *p.d.f.* for each concept representation. A rectangular block was put at the bottom on the right-hand side of the scene, and was fixed there. Each object was drawn as a circle, the color of which was chosen from a continuous color map.

A male participant taught language to the system under acoustic conditions typical of an office environment. In the first step, seventeen lexical items consisting of concepts in terms of position, color, and movement were taught (Table 1). These lexical items were taught in seventy learning strokes. In each stroke, either concepts about the static characteristics of objects (static position and color) were taught by uttering word sequence and pointing to a stationary object, or else concepts about dynamic characteristics (movement) were taught by uttering a word and moving an object.

Table 1. The concepts taught in the experiments

attribute	concept			
static	right	left	top	bottom
	middle	red	blue	yellow
	green	gray	red-on-the-block	
dynamic	up	down	rotate	put-on-the-block
	slide	write-a-star		

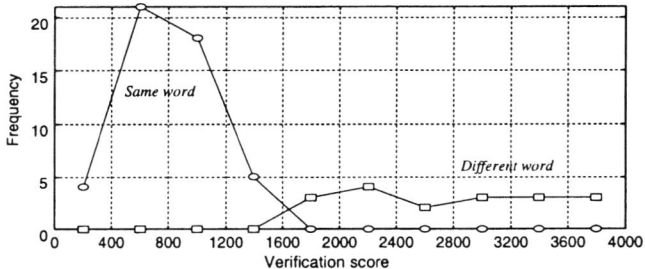

Fig. 2. The distributions of the verification score obtained in the cases that each new input speech sample and the speech samples in the selected cluster are same word (*Same word*) and different word (*Different word*)

In the next step, grammar was taught by uttering multiple words as a sentence while pointing to or moving a stationary or moving object. The utterances in the experiments were rather simple. When, for example, the operation was *to lift a red rotating object at the bottom* and the utterance was "*rotate red bottom up*", only by which the system could not know without the grammar whether "*rotate*" meant action or spontaneous state of the object, the extracted CE was

$$\begin{bmatrix} [\text{action}] : up \\ [\text{object}] : rotate,\ red,\ bottom \end{bmatrix}$$

The following probability was learned:

$$P([\text{S}] \to [\text{object}]\ [\text{action}]) = 1 - P([\text{S}] \to [\text{action}]\ [\text{object}])$$

In Bayesian leaning, a beta distribution ($\alpha = \beta = 5.$) was used as the *a priori* distribution of the values of this probability.

The lexicon was learned after seventy strokes, and the distribution of the verification score R calculated in the learning process is shown in Fig. 2. We can see that the verification score R clearly separated new words from the clusters of different words.

The concepts could be acquired suitably with such a small number of learning samples because the algorithm is based on Bayesian learning. The learned values of the parameters in gaussian *p.d.f.*s for static concepts are listed in Table 2. We can see that the values of σ^2 were small for the components which are important to represent each concept.

The values of the parameters in HMMs for dynamic concepts *put-on-the-block* and *write-a-star* are listed in Table 3. In the HMM for *put-on-the-block*, the final state can be considered to represent the location on the block. The σ^2 values for the position components in the final state were small desirebly. In the HMM for *write-a-star*, the σ^2 values in the velocity components of each of the states were small. Each state can be considered to represent a stroke during the drawing of a star.

Table 2. The values of the gaussian density parameters for the static concepts

concept	x		y		L		a		b	
	μ	σ^2	μ	σ^2	μ	σ^2	μ	σ^2	μ	σ^2
red	242,	38436	230,	33946	71,	34	42,	314	16,	255
blue	253,	39816	224,	33488	53,	10	46,	65	−70,	39
yellow	244,	42558	224,	36028	97,	10	−19,	10	66,	185
green	242,	37111	228,	33609	90,	10	−56,	75	50,	118
gray	250,	36976	232,	32026	93,	10	−2,	10	−0,	4
right	434,	2385	246,	27073	75,	298	3,	2099	19,	2553
left	44,	11	248,	24998	84,	240	−6,	970	8,	2157
top	246,	24603	39,	10	76,	302	10,	2377	12,	2233
bottom	199,	12103	459,	10	78,	267	2,	1774	17,	2394
middle	229,	1	244,	10	84,	95	1,	1494	19,	1500
red-on-the-block	441,	96	346,	242	72,	10	41,	122	18,	242

Table 3. The values of the output probability density parameters of the HMM for dynamic concepts

concept	state No.	position x		position y		velocity x		velocity y	
		μ	σ^2	μ	σ^2	μ	σ^2	μ	σ^2
put-on-the-block	1	144	8851	363	24087	3	30	−19	76
	2	198	5913	279	13529	153	144	−81	384
	3	344	2026	243	4029	195	180	109	453
	4	433	158	332	746	62	37	120	47
	5	449	17	374	1	3	30	9	30
write-a-star	1	240	12629	213	8566	−187	992	−5	30
	2	235	8467	279	11248	210	906	174	677
	3	295	7278	200	11420	−71	123	−199	1497
	4	189	5648	252	9414	−93	127	160	407
	5	282	10155	248	9286	176	830	−100	251

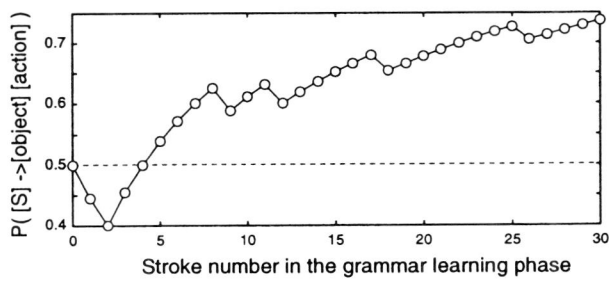

Fig. 3. The change of probability in the SG during the course of learning

The stochastic grammar was also learned robustly. The change of the value of probability $P([S] \rightarrow [object][action])$ is shown in Fig. 3, where it is obvious that the learning was robust against early errors in the learning process.

The speech understanding function was also tested. When the participant was shown a scene with red and blue objects on the bottom, he uttered *"put-on-the-block"*. Then the system selected the red object and put it on the block because $P(Concept(red, [object]), Concept(put\text{-}on\text{-}the\text{-}block, [action])) = 0.04$ was larger than $P(Concept(blue, [object]), Concept(put\text{-}on\text{-}the\text{-}block, [action])) = 0.02$. And when shown a scene with one red object at the bottom and another red object on the block, he uttered *"put-on-the-block red"*. Then the system selected the red object at the bottom and put it on the block because the log likelihood -15.2 of the *put-on-the-block* HMM with regard to the rehearsed trajectory was larger for the red object at the bottom than -18.9 for the red object on the block.

5 Discussion

Although the algorithm tested was a preliminary version and the spoken language used was not natural, the experimental results are promising. They showed that the speech understanding and the action generation could be implemented by using the knowledge obtained by a simple learning mechanism unified in a probabilistic framework.

During the experiments, it was found that statistically robust learning provides human participants with an intuitive understanding of how well the machine is learning. Only a small sample of the results obtained were presented in this paper, but analysis of the other results revealed that the learning performance was influenced by, for example, the distribution of learning samples the participants showed. The performance of the algorithm needs to be evaluated statistically.

Finally, the following is a list of some of the limitations of the described algorithm:

1. Lexicon and grammar cannot be learned simultaneously.
2. Continuous speech cannot be treated.
3. Functional words cannot be treated.
4. Speech which does not describe the current scene cannot be treated.

6 Conclusion

An algorithm based on the association between speech and other perceptual information through the conceptual structure was presented. Lexicon, grammar, and conceptual structure model could be used effectively to understand the meaning of speech in the given situations. Experiments with a simple task show that using a statistical-model approach is a useful to cope with the ambiguity of information in the continuous signal space and with the sparseness of learning data. Future work will include the expansion of the algorithm and statistical evaluation of the performance.

References

Berwick, R. C.: The acquisition of syntactic knowledge. MIT Press (1985).
Brent, M. R.: Advances in the computational study of language acquisition. Cognition 61 (1996) 1–61
DeGroot, M. H.: Optimal statistical decisions. McGraw-Hill (1970)
Dempster, A. P., Laird, N. M., and Rubin, D. B.: Maximum likelihood from incomplete data vie the EM algorithm. Jornal of Royal Statistocal Society B **39** (1977) 1–38
Dyer, M. G. and Nenov, V. I.: Learning Language via Perceptual/Motor Experiences, Proc. of 15th Annual Conf. of the Congnitive Science Society (1993) 400–405
Fujie, S. and Kobayashi, T.: Language acquisition of autonomous robot with action (in Japanese). Proc. of 13th Annual Conf. of Japanese Society of Artificial Intelligence (1999) 223–224
Gorin, A. L., Levinson, S. E., and Gertner, A. N. and Goldman, E.: Adaptive acquisition of language. Computer Speech and Language **5** (1991) 101–132
Gorin, A. L., Levinson,S. E., and Sanker, A.: An experiment in spoken language acquisition, *IEEE Trans. on speech and audio processing*, **2-1** (1994) 224–240
Harris, C.: A connectionist approach to the story of 'over'. Berkeley Linguistic Society. **15** (1989) 126–138
Iwahashi, N.: Spoken language acquisition algorithm with the conceptual analysis of nonlinguistic perceptual information. Proc. Joint Conf. on Information Science. Vol.2 (2000) 852–857
Jackendoff, R.: Semantics Structures. MIT Press (1990)
Langley, P.: Language acquisition through error recovery. Cognition and Brain Theory. **5**)1982) 221–225
Munro, P., Cosic, C. and Tabasko, M.: A network for encoding, decoding and translating locative prepositions. Connection Science. 3 (1991) 225–240
Nakagawa, S. and Masukata, M.: An acquisition system of concept and grammar based on combining with visual and auditory information (in Japanese). Trans. of Information Society of Japan. **10-4** (1995) 129–137
Pinker, S.: Language Learnability and Language Development. Harvard University Press (1984)
Pinker, S.: Learnability and cognition. Harvard University Press (1989)
Regier, T.: The Human Semantic Potential. MIT Press (1997)
Rose, R. C.: Word spotting from continuous speech utterances. In Lee, C-H., Soong, F. K., and Paliwal, K. K. eds. Automatic speech and speaker recognition advanced topics. Kluwer Academic Publisher (1996)
Roy, D. and Pentland, A.: Word Learning in a multimodal environment. Proceedings of International Conference on Acoustics, Speech and Signal Processing. (1998) 3761–3764
Shank, R. C.: Conceptual Dependency: The theory of Natural Language Understanding. Cognitive Psychology **3-4** (1972) 552–631
Siskind, J. M. Grounding Language in Perception. Artificial Intelligence Review. **8** (1994) 371–391
Siskind, J. M.: A computational study of cross-situational techniques for learning word-to-meaning mappings. Cognition **61** (1996) 39–91
Tokuda, K., Kobayashi, T., and Imai, S.: Speech paramter generation from HMM using dynamic features. Proc. of International Conference on Acoustics, Speech and Signal Processing (1995) 660–663

Discovery of Shared Topics Networks among People
— A Simple Approach to Find Community Knowledge from WWW Bookmarks —

Hideaki Takeda[1,2], Takeshi Matsuzuka[2]* and Yuichiro Taniguchi[2]

[1] National Institute of Informatics,
2-1-2, Hitotsubashi, Chiyoda-ku, Tokyo 101-8430, Japan
takeda@nii.ac.jp
[2] Graduate School of Information Science,
Nara Institute of Science and Technology
8916-5, Takayama, Ikoma, Nara 630-01, Japan
yuichi-t@is.aist-nara.ac.jp

Abstract. In this paper, we propose a system called *kMedia* that can assist users to form knowledge for community by showing shared topics networks (STN) among them. One of the important aspects to know each other is to know topics interested by others and relationship between her/his and others' topics. kMedia can use a simple but effective way to find them. It uses folders in WWW bookmarks as interested topics and can calculate their relations by evaluating similarity of WWW pages under folders. The results are displayed in two ways. One is to show relationship among users by shared topics networks, i.e., a user is connected to the other through both her/his topics and the other's topics that are related to her/his ones. A user can know what kind of relations to others s/he can have, and more precisely know what are counterpart of her/his topics for others. The other way is to show recommended pages for pages in users' bookmarks. Recommended pages are selected from others' bookmarks, and it is the primary result of similarity evaluation among pages by contents. A user can use this result just as recommendation for her/his bookmarked pages or use checking how her/his bookmarked pages are related to others. We tested this system in an experiment with actual bookmark data. Discovery of related topics among users are evaluated as good enough in spite of bad results for recommendation of pages. This result tells that our approach to find common topics among users is effective and practical.

1 Introduction

Although the number of the World Wide Web users is increasing every year and available information is also increasing so rapidly, we are getting frustrated to join WWW networks. Compared to rapid growth of users and contents, our

---
* Currently Toppan Printing Co.,Ltd.

capacity to access them is almost invariable. We seek better ways to improve our capacity for it. We focus on relationship among people to solve this problem.

Even in the actual society, we already have problems of information flood. Then how can we solve them? One of the key issue to solve them is usage of relationship among people. For example, if one of your friends recommends some TV program to you, you may watch it. Of course just "friend" may not be enough. It depends on what relationship between her/him and you, e.g., a close friend or not, a trustful friend or not, and so on. The most important aspect for relationship for information selection is what and how much they can share interest. We have such knowledge when we are joining a community, e.g., who is the appropriate person to ask this question and how much other members would be interested in a specific topic. This community knowledge can save people from information flood and guide them to access appropriate information in appropriate amount.

In this paper, we propose a system called **kMedia** that can support users to form community knowledge by showing shared topics networks (STN) among them. A shared topics network is a network where each user can be associated to other user via topics owned by both users. A node represents a user or a topic, and a link represents either a relation between a topic and its owner or a similarity relation between topics of different users. Existence of a path from a user to the other shows that there is a shared topic between them. A shared topic is represented by a pair of topics that are provided by two users. Each path shows how topics of a user can be shared with others, and what are counterpart of her/his topics for others. There can be multiple paths each of which denotes independent shared topic. By viewing this network, a user can know how her/his topics are interested by others and how is relationship between her/him and others as a result.

In this paper, we firstly discuss requirements for community knowledge for information management and propose our method that is to find shared topics networks among people from bookmark data in Section 2. Then we describe our system called **kMedia** that is implementation of our method in Section 3 and show examples in Section 4. We show results of an experiment to evaluate how this system is suitable for community understanding. We compare our system with other systems in Section 6, and conclude the paper in Section 7.

2 Community Knowledge for Information Management

As we mentioned, relationship among people is one of the important resources for information management. But what relationship is needed for this purpose?

Relations among users should be described in some appropriate level, i.e., not too abstract and not too specific. Most of recommender systems use information objects themselves as shared information among users, e.g., netnews items [12], music[19], WWW pages[1][21], but they are too specific. This approach is desirable to know whether each object is good to share or no, but it is too intricate to understand what is relationship among people. On the other hand, community support systems like Beehive[7], Babble[5], and Visual Who[4] use more simple relationship. For example, Beehive just calculates active members or not by observing email communication, and Babble shows relations among users in two-dimensional space. Visual Who also use two-dimensional space but show them more dynamically. Such visualization is intuitively easy to understand but it is too abstract to know what kind of relations can be found. In our approach, it is realized as relations between topics of different users. Topics are also intuitively easy to understand and furthermore informative enough to know types or aspects of relations.

Then difficulty lies on how we can identify users' topics. There are many proposals to track users' interest in information filtering field, e.g., WebWatcher[8] and Letizia[14] for WWW browsing, but they are not successful to identify users' interest as topics. There are two methods to capture users' interest on WWW. One is to use machine learning techniques like reinforcement learning and Bayesian network to detect it. The advantage and also disadvantage of this approach stem from assuming "persistence of interest". It is possible to track users' behavior but it is easily confused with big changes or branching of users' interest. Furthermore it is difficult to identify what they are interested because the learned data is just for programs not for users. The other method is to use classification techniques like hierarchical classification., e.g., Scatter/Gather[3] and Webmate[2]. It can show what users are interested more specifically, but its specification is ambiguous and needs efforts to understand because it often shows a (weighted) list of keywords.

We are skeptical about detecting users' interest by text analysis because of a more primitive reason. Most of systems above analyze texts by statistical information and some techniques to highlight importance like TF/IDF method [18]. There is a pit hole to apply these methods to detect users' interest, i.e., it is lack of background knowledge. Important words are often missing or appears very few times in text. For example, suppose that you are collecting pages on animals like pages for elephants, monkeys and so on. But there are probably a few occurrences of word "animal" because a sentence like "elephants are animals" is too common knowledge to describe in text. Applying statistical methods to those pages may produce some other words like "life" and "food" as important words instead.

We here abandon to detect users' interest by computation, but adopt users' own knowledge instead. In our case, it is the folder structure of WWW bookmarks. Names and contents of folders are results of efforts by users to explicate their intension, i.e., a folder name shows what kind of aspect the user are interested in, and contents of the folder show examples what s/he thinks within this category. Although it is restricted to a single hierarchical structure[3], it provides a basic knowledge of each user to use WWW.

Then the left problem is to find relationship among such topics. We regard a relation between topics as having some similarity relation between pages con-

---

[3] There are some proposals to extend more free structures like lattice structure[11] and bookmarks with comments[13].

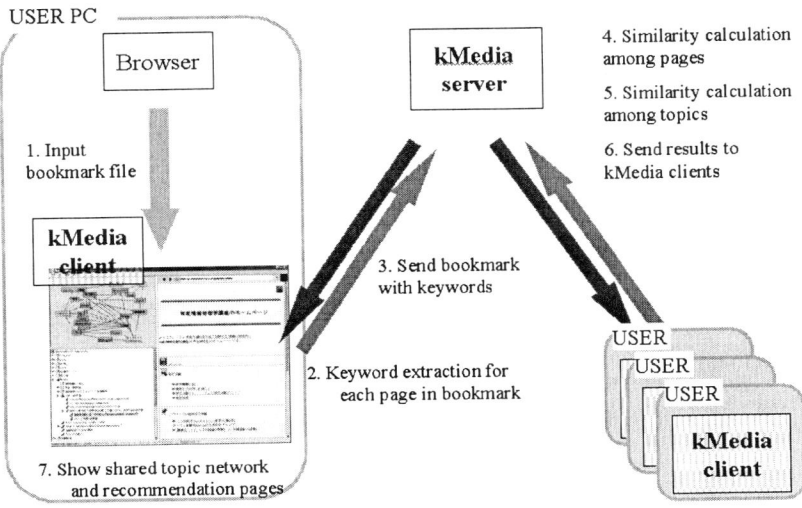

Fig. 1. System Architecture of kMedia

tained by both topics. At this process, we use traditional methods to calculate similarity among texts. The current implemented system just extracts some of most frequent words in each text and determines pairs of similar pages by checking how much such words are shared. As we mentioned above, we do not rely on text analysis so much, i.e., we do not expect high quality of similarity among texts. This similarity just tells that two pages are similar in comparison with other pages. But we expect that the amount of such similarity relations between two topics should suggest some relation between these topics. This expectation is proved by our experiment explained in Section 5.

3 System Overview

kMedia is a client-server system where each client system is provided for a user and a server system is provided for a community. A client works to process a user's bookmark files to extract keywords and show results to the user, and the server to calculate page similarity and determine topic relations (see Figure 1). The client system is implemented for Windows 95/98 with Sun Java2 and IBM XML parser[4], and the server system for FreeBSD/Linux with CGI and Perl 5.005.

There are two reasons that the client system performs keyword extraction instead of the server systems. One is to avoid heavy burden on the server system. The other is to make it to personalize the client system. We are planning

---

[4] We defined syntax by XML for communication between the client and server.

to have favorite lists of words or personalized ontology[20] to reflect personal activities of information management for keyword extraction, and use local files as information sources.

kMedia works as follows; first a user invokes a kMedia client system on her/his personal computer. The client system requires a location of her/his bookmark file if its execution of the client system is the first time for her/him. The client system reads her/his bookmark file and extract keywords for each URL in the bookmark file by fetching pages for these URLs and analyzing their texts. It extracts words from texts except stop words and some common words, then selects some of the most occurred words in them. It composes a bookmark data in which each URL is followed by keywords with occurrence numbers, and sends it to the server system.

The server system first calculates similarity between every pair of pages in the collected bookmark files. Similarity is measured by sums of occurrence of keywords that appeared in the both pages. Pairs of pages of which similarity measurement exceeds a threshold are marked as similarity pairs except pairs of pages from the same users. Then the system calculated similarity between folders. It counts numbers of marked pairs for every pair of folders, i.e., if there is a marked pair of pages and one page belongs to one of the folders and the other page to the other folder, then the pair of folders has one marked pairs of pages. Pairs of folders are marked "found" if the number of marked pairs of pages for them exceeds the threshold. The shared topics network is composed with these marked pairs of folders and folder structures of all users' bookmarks. Finally the server systems returns to client systems the shared topics network and similarity pages concerning to the bookmark of its owner.

4 An Example

Figure 2 shows a snapshot of the client system. The top-left windows shows a shared topics network, the bottom-left window her/his bookmark with recommended pages, and the right window a WWW page specified by the user with the bottom-left window.

Figure 3 shows an example of shared topics networks obtained with the actual bookmarks. These bookmarks are brought by members of the artificial intelligence lab. There are three users that are represented as light gray boxes labeled A, B, and C[5]. Each user has several topics represented as dark gray boxes[6]. We can find nine inter-topic relations except root(/) folders, i.e., three relations between A and B: ("computer-related", "free soft"), ("research-related", "Study"), and ("search", "Sarch")[7], five relations between A and C: ("research-related", "Academia"), ("search", "information retrieval"), ("UNIX",

---

[5] We substituted user names by Alphabets like A, B, and C for privacy.
[6] In this example, we use only the first level of folder structures to simplify the network. And we translated topics' names in Japanese to those in English that are indicated with white boxes in Figure 3.
[7] "Sarch" is a typographical error by User B.

Fig. 2. User Interface of kMedia Client

("Academia"), ("UNIX", "CGI, perl"), and ("UNIX", "Linux"), and one relation between B and C: ("Sarch", "information retrieval").

Some pairs of topics are very common like ("UNIX", "LINUX") and ("UNIX", "CGI, perl"), but some pairs are not. For examples, The combination of ("research-related", "Academia") and ("UNIX", "Academia") is meaningful for a community for computer science research but not for everyone. In other words, users can understand that they are belonging to such community by viewing this relation.

Viewing this network as relationship among users, we can find that A and B have the same interest on computer science research, while A and C have the same interest on UNIX matters. Furthermore three users have a common interest on search. From this result, they may think that A has more knowledge on computer than others because both B and C are links to A with computer-related topics.

Figure 4 shows recommendation of URLs based on the shared topics network. Recommendation is done for marked pairs of pages. In this figure, two pages are recommended to a single page[8]. Pages for "what is reinforcement Learning" and "AI meeting room" are recommended to the originally bookmarked page "Yamada Lab., TITECH"[9].

5 An Experiment

We tested our system by a simple experiment to evaluate its performance. The main objective of the experiment is how our proposed method is useful to identify users' relations. We asked three persons to submit their bookmark files to

---

[8] bookmarked and recommended pages are represented with different colors, i.e., green and red respectively.

[9] http://www.ymd.dis.titech.ac.jp/ where Ref. [16] is developed.

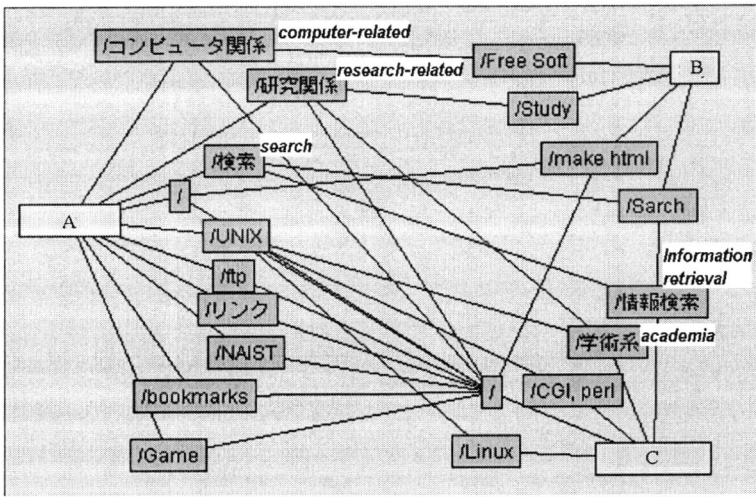

Fig. 3. Window for Shared Topics Network

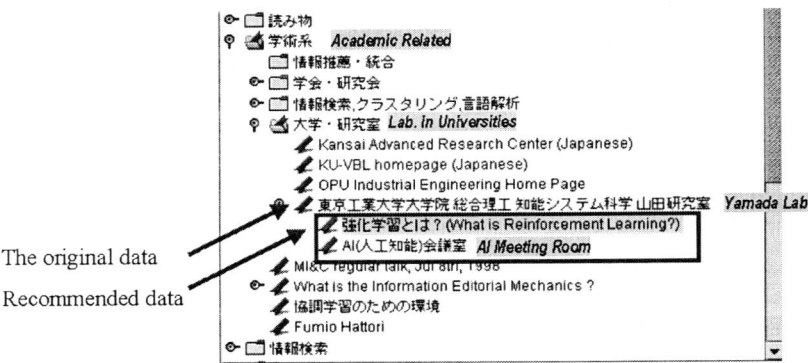

Fig. 4. Windows for Recommendation

the system, and asked subjective evaluation to each recommended page and each generated inter-topic relation by ranking 5 to 1 (5 is the best, and 1 is the worst). Criteria for evaluation is how suggested pages and inter-topic relations are acceptable according to their own bookmark. Table 1 shows data for submitted bookmark files and results generated by the system.

Evaluation for recommended pages is shown in Table 2(a) and evaluation for inter-topic relations is shown in Table 2(b). These tables show clearly different results. The highest scored rank for page recommendation is Rank 1 (the worst),

	User A	User B	User C
No. of Bookmarked Pages	376	278	297
No. of Analyzed Pages	263	185	240
No. of Topics	13	17	5
No. of Recommended Pages	345	513	454
No. of Shared Topics	10	10	3
Rate of Shared Topics/Total Topics	0.77	0.58	0.6

Table 1. Bookmark Data and Generated Results

	Good		Average		Bad
	Rank 5	Rank 4	Rank 3	Rank 2	Rank 1
User A	29	30	27	77	182
User B	94	86	73	185	75
User C	66	90	88	88	122
Total	189	206	186	350	379

(a) Subjective Evaluation for Recommended Pages

	Good		Average		Bad
	Rank 5	Rank 4	Rank 3	Rank 2	Rank 1
User A	3	3	2	0	2
User B	3	3	2	2	0
User C	2	0	1	0	0
Total	8	6	5	2	2

(b) Subjective Evaluation for Inter-Topic Relations

Table 2. Results of Evaluation

and the average is 2.6. The highest scored rank for inter-topic relations is Rank 5 (the best), and the average is 3.7. Discovery of related topics among users are evaluated as good enough in spite of bad results for recommendation of pages.

This result tells that our approach to find common topics among users is useful and practical. High average of evaluation for inter-topic relations means that it is useful to identify shared topics, and difference between page recommendation and inter-relation averages indicates that it can work even though text analysis methods are not sufficient.

6 Discussion

As we mentioned, the result of the experiment is interesting because two types of information generated from the same data shows different effects for users. The reason seems to lie on concept formation process of users. There can be three

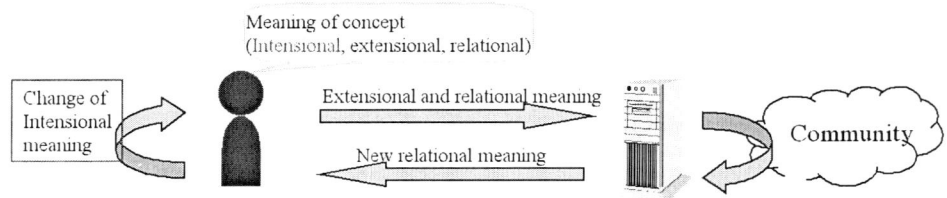

Fig. 5. Cycle of Concept Formation

types of meaning of concepts, i,e., *intensional* meaning that shows essential attributes, *extensional* meaning that shows the domain of objects, and *relational* meaning that describes relations to other concepts. Providing a folder and pages belonging to it is to define extensional meaning by its belonging pages and relational meaning by the folder structure whereas intensional meaning remains implicit. Page recommendation is then a question whether the recommended page can be within the extension of the concept or not. It is usually the severe question. On the other hand, proposal of inter-topic relations is a question whether addition of relational meaning of the concept is acceptable or not, which is more moderate question. Accept of the proposal in turn should cause modification of its intensional meaning that is kept in mind all the times. Considering that we need better understanding of each other in community, this change is preferable because they can integrate their knowledge more. We believe that supporting of such cycle of concept formation is the essential function of "intelligent" community support systems (see Figure 5).

7 Related Work

Kautz et al.[10] emphasized importance of people relations for WWW and have done primary work for finding people relations, i.e., their system called *Referral Web* can find people by analyzing bibliography database. Our aim is very similar to them, but we realized it differently. The benefit of our approach is to identify topics shared by users.

CommunityBoard[6][15] is another way to explicate users' relations by using topics. This system can show dynamics of interest on topics, i.e., who and when initiates and participates discussion for topics. But no discovery of topics are supported because topics themselves in this study are already shared by participants.

There are many bookmark-based WWW systems, e.g., bookmark-agent[16] and Webtagger[11]. Siteseer[17] also uses folder structures in bookmarks, but aims are different from us. It seems to aim large-scale social filtering, i.e., it uses folder information to decide recommended pages not either folders themselves nor people themselves. LOUIS[22] is another recommender system based on not "folder" but "label" that is extension of "folder" idea, but it still remains URL recommender. There are the other types of usage of bookmarks, e.g., direct integration of bookmark files of multiple users by multi-tree[23] and integration by comments[13], but they do not care relations among people directly.

Grassroots[9] proposed to use "folder structure" as a basic structure to organize information and people. Grassroots approach is excellent but imposes a heavy charge to every user because it requires to unify a folder structure of various activities from information storing to information and even folders for other users. Our system can ease this problem by finding topic relations among users automatically.

8 Conclusion

In this paper, we discuss how relation among people should be explicated to facilitate information exchanging and proposed a system called **kMedia** that can show shared topics networks for this purpose. Our method to identify shared topics networks is simple and effective. We use folder structures as topics and identify inter-topic relations by analyzing texts associated to the folders. This combination of human knowledge and automatic discovery of relations works well. Even discovered relations between pages are not sufficient, discovered relations between topics can be acceptable. It seems that people can re-define or extend meaning of their own categorization represented as folders, on the other hand they cannot change meaning of pages. In this sense, our method is appropriate to find relation among people, because finding relations among people is not finding exactly shared information or interest but finding possibility of sharing of information or interest.

References

1. Marko Balabanovic and Yoav Shoham. Fab: Content-based, collaborative recommendation. *Communications of the ACM*, 40(3):66–72, 1997.
2. L. Chen and K. Sycara. Webmate: A personal agent for browsing and searching. In *Proceedings of the 2nd International Conference on Autonomous Agents and Multi Agent Systems, AGENTS '98*, pages 132 – 139, 1998.
3. Douglass R. Cutting, David R. Karger, Jan O. Pederson, and John W. Tukey. Scatter/Gather: A cluster-based approach to browwing large document collections. In *15th Annual International ACM/SIGIR Conference*, pages 318–329, 1992.
4. Judith S. Donath. Visual who: Animating the affinities and activities of an electronic community. In *ACM Multimedia 95*, 1995.
5. Thomas Erickson, David N. Smith, Wendy A. Kellogg, Mark Laff, John T. Richards, and Erin Bradner. Socially translucent systems: Social proxies, persistent conversation, and the design of "babble". In *CHI*, pages 72–79, 1999.
6. F. Hattori, T. Ohguro, M. Yokoo, S. Matsubara, and S. Yoshida. Socialware: Multiagent systems for supporting network communities. *Communications of ACM*, 42(3):55 – 61, 1999.

7. B. A. Huberman and M. Kaminsky. Beehive: A system for cooperative filtering and sharing of information, 1996. ftp://parcftp.xerox.com/pub/dynamics/beehive.html.
8. T. Joachims, D. Freitag, and T. Mitchell. Webwatcher: A tour guide for the world wide web. In *IJCAI-97*, 1997.
9. Kenichi Kamiya, Martin R'oscheisen, and Terry Winograd. Grassroots: A system providing a uniform framework for communicating, structuring, sharing information, and organizing people. In *Proceedings of The 6th International World Wide Web Conference (WWW-6)*, 1997.
10. Henry Kautz, Bart Selman, and Mehul Shah. Referral web: Combining social networks and collaborative filtering. *Communications of the ACM*, 40(3):63–65, 1997.
11. Richard M. Keller, Shawn Wolfe, James R. Chen, Joshua L. Rabinowitz, and Nathalie Mathe. A bookmarking service for organizing and sharing urls. In *Proceedings of The 6th International World Wide Web Conference (WWW-6)*, 1997.
12. Joseph A. Konstan, Bradley N. Miller, David Maltz, Jonathan L. Herlocker, Lee R. Gordon, and John Riedl. GroupLens: Applying collaborative filtering to usenet news. *Communications of the ACM*, 40(3):76–87, 1997.
13. Wen-Syan Li, Quoc Vu, Divyakant Agrawal, Yoshinori Hara, and Hajime Takano. Powerbookmarks: A system for personalizable web information organization, sharing, and management. In *Proceedings of The 8th International World Wide Web Conference (WWW-8)*, 1999.
14. Henry Lieberman. Letizia: An agent that assists web browsing. In *Proceedings of IJCAI-95*, pages 924–929, 1995.
15. S. Matsubara, T. Ohguro, and F. Hattori. Communityboard: Social meeting system able to visualize the structure of discussions. In *Proceedings of the 2nd International Conference on Knowledge-based Intelligent Electronic Systems (KES'98)*, pages 423–428, 1998.
16. M. Mori and S. Yamada. Bookmark-agent: Information sharing of urls. In *Poster Proceedings of The 8th International World Wide Web Conference (WWW-8)*, 1999.
17. James Rucker and Marcos J. Polanco. Siteseer: Personalized navigation for the web. *Communications of the ACM*, 40(3):73–75, 1997.
18. G. Salton and M. McGill. *Introduction to Modern Information Retrieval*. McGraw-Hill, Inc., 1983.
19. Upendra Shardanand and Patti Maes. Social information filtering: Algorithms for automating "word of mouth". In *CHI*, pages 210–217, 1995.
20. Motoyuki Takaai, Hideaki Takeda, and Toyoaki Nishida. Knowledge sharing and organization by multiple ontologies. In *Proceedings First International Workshop on Strategic Knowledge and Concept Formation*, pages 73–84, 1997.
21. Loren Terveen, Will Hill, Brian Amento, David McDonald, and Josh Creter. PHOAKS: A system for sharing recommendations. *Communications of the ACM*, 40(3):59–62, 1997.
22. Hideo Umeki and Takehiko Yokota. Louis - a labeling-based recommender system for web resources and communities of interest. In *Poster Proceedings of The 8th International World Wide Web Conference (WWW-8)*, 1999.
23. Kent Wittenburg, Duco Das, Will Hill, and Larry Stead. Group asynchronous browsing on the world wide web. In *Proceedings of The 4th International World Wide Web Conference (WWW-4)*, 1995.

Collaborative Filtering with the Simple Bayesian Classifier

Koji Miyahara[1] and Michael J. Pazzani[2]

[1]Information Technology R&D Center
Mitsubishi Electric Corporation
5-1-1 Ofuna, Kamakura, Kanagawa 247-8501, JAPAN
miya@isl.melco.co.jp
[2]Department of Information and Computer Science
University of California, Irvine
Irvine, CA 92697-3425, USA
pazzani@ics.uci.edu

Abstract. Many collaborative filtering enabled Web sites that recommend books, CDs, movies, and so on, have become very popular on the Internet. They recommend items to a user based on the opinions of other users with similar tastes. In this paper, we discuss an approach to collaborative filtering based on the Simple Bayesian Classifier. We define two variants of the recommendation problem for the Simple Bayesian Classifier. In our approach, we calculate the similarity between users from negative ratings and positive ratings separately. We evaluated these algorithms using databases of movie recommendations and joke recommendations. Our empirical results show that one of our proposed Bayesian approaches significantly outperforms a correlation-based collaborative filtering algorithm. The other model outperforms as well although it shows similar performance to the correlation-based approach in some parts of our experiments.

1. Introduction

The growth of the Internet has resulted in a tremendous amount of information available and a vast array of choices for consumers. Recommender systems are designed to help a user cope with this situation by selecting a small number of options to present to the user [14]. They filter and recommend items based on a user's preference model. Various types of recommender systems have been proposed so far, their filtering techniques fall into two categories. One is content-based filtering (e.g. [12]) and the other is collaborative filtering or social filtering (e.g. [16]).

In content-based filtering, a user's preference model is constructed for the individual based upon the user's ratings and descriptions (usually, textual expression) of the rated items. Such systems try to find regularities in the descriptions that can be used to distinguish highly rated items from others. On the other hand, collaborative filtering tries to find desired items based on the preference of a set of similar users. In order to find out like-minded users, it compares other users' ratings with the target user's ratings. It is not necessary to analyze the contents of items, therefore it can be applied to many kinds of domains where a textual description is not available or regularities in the words used in the textual description are not informative (e.g. [4]). One of the most popular algorithms in collaborative filtering is a correlation-based approach. In this paper, we report experimental results comparing collaborating filtering with the Simple Bayesian Classifier as an alternative approach.

This paper is organized as follows. We present the central ideas of a current typical collaborative filtering algorithm. We define two alternative formulations of the Simple Bayesian Classifier for collaborative filtering. Then, we evaluate our algorithms on databases of user ratings for movies and jokes, and show that our approach outperforms the correlation-based collaborative filtering algorithm. Finally, we discuss the results and summarize this paper.

2. Collaborative Filtering

The main idea of collaborative filtering is to recommend new items of interest for a particular user based on other users' opinions. A variety of collaborative filtering algorithms have been reported and their performance has been evaluated empirically ([2], [15], [16]). These algorithms are based on a simple intuition: predictions for a user should be based on the preference patterns of other people who have similar interests. Therefore, the first step of these algorithms is to find similarities between user ratings. Suppose we have a database of user ratings for items, where users indicate their interest in an item on a numeric scale. Resnick et al. [15] use the *Pearson correlation coefficient* as a measure of preference similarity. The correlation between user j and k is:

$$w_{jk} = \frac{\sum_i (R_{ij} - \overline{R}_j)(R_{ik} - \overline{R}_k)}{\sqrt{\sum_i (R_{ij} - \overline{R}_j)^2 \sum_i (R_{ik} - \overline{R}_k)^2}}$$

where all summations over i are over the items which have been rated by both j and k. The predicted value of user j for item i is computed as a weighted sum of other users' ratings:

$$\hat{R}_{ij} = \overline{R}_j + \frac{\sum_k (R_{ik} - \overline{R}_k) w_{jk}}{\sum_k |w_{jk}|}$$

This correlation-based prediction scheme was shown to perform well. However, it should be valuable to think of other approaches. Breese et al. [2] report a variety of modifications to the above typical collaborative filtering technique and the use of Bayesian clustering and a Bayesian network. A primary difference between what we propose below and the work of Breese et al. is that we construct a separate Bayesian model for each user. This is practical only for the Simple Bayesian Classifier that is linear in the number of examples and the number of features.

3. Simple Bayesian Model

3.1 Rating Matrix

Most of collaborating filtering systems adopt numerical ratings and try to predict the exact numerical ratings. However, we are not interested in the prediction of the exact rating a user would have given to a target item. We would much rather like to have a system that can accurately distinguish between items to recommend and others. Therefore, we defined two classes, *like* and *dislike,* that were used as class labels.

Table 1 is an example of a rating matrix in which three users have reported ratings on five different items. Some entries in the matrix are empty because users do not rate every item. The last row represents the ratings of a user for which the system will make a prediction. Typically, the rating matrix is *sparse* because most users do not rate most items.

Table 1. Example of user ratings in a sparse matrix

	I_1	I_2	I_3	I_4	I_5
U_1	Like	Dislike	Dislike		Like
U_2	Dislike			Dislike	Dislike
U_3		Like	Like		Like
Class Label	Like	Dislike	Like	Like	?

Billsus and Pazzani [1] proposed transforming the format of a rating matrix so that every cell has an entry. In their format, each user's ratings are divided into two features, each of which has a Boolean value indicating whether the user reported liking the item or whether the user reported not liking the item. Table 2 shows the resulting Boolean feature matrix based on the original rating matrix. If $U_i like = 0$ and $U_i dislike = 0$ for an item I_m, it means the user U_i has not rated the item I_m yet. All of the features have a binary value in this format. Therefore, we can apply any supervised machine learning algorithms to the collaborative filtering tasks easily.

Table 2. Boolean feature transformation of a ratings matrix

	I_1	I_2	I_3	I_4	I_5
U_1like	1	0	0	0	1
U_1dislike	0	1	1	0	0
U_2like	0	0	0	0	0
U_2dislike	1	0	0	1	1
U_3like	0	1	1	0	1
U_3disike	0	0	0	0	0
Class Label	Like	Dislike	Like	Like	?

3.2 Simple Bayesian Classifier

The Simple Bayesian Classifier is one of the most successful machine learning algorithms on many classification domains. Despite its simplicity, it is shown to be competitive with other complex approaches especially in text categorization tasks. Making the "naive" assumption that features are independent given the class label, the probability of an item belonging to class j given its n feature values, $p(class_j | f_1, f_2, \ldots f_n)$ is proportional to:

$$p(class_j) \prod_i^n p(f_i | class_j)$$

where both $p(class_j)$ and $p(f_i | class_j)$ can be estimated from training data. To determine the most likely class of an example, the probability of each class is computed, and the example is assigned to the class with the highest probability. Although the assumption that features are independent once we know the class label of an item is not realistic in this domain, the Simple Bayesian Classifier has been shown to be optimal in many situations where this assumptions does not hold [3] and has been empirically shown to be competitive with more complex approaches in many others (e.g. [9]).

Here, we define two variants of the Simple Bayesian Classifier for collaborative filtering.

(1) Transformed Data Model
This model is identical to the multi-variate Bernoulli model applied to the transformed data such as that in Table 2. This model assumes that all the features, even dual features ($U_i like$ and $U_i dislike$), are completely independent. After selecting a certain number of features, absent or present information of the selected features is used for predictions. That is:

$$p(class_j | f_1=1, f_2=0, f_3=1 \ldots f_{n-1}=1, f_n=0)$$

where $f_i=1$ means that f_i is present on the target item and $f_i=0$ means that f_i is absent on the target item. When estimating conditional probabilities, e.g. $p(f_i =1| class_j)$, it is calculated over all items belonging to class j. The following conditions hold for this model:

$p(U_i like = 1 | class_j) + p(U_i like = 0 | class_j) = 1.$
$p(U_i dislike = 1 | class_j) + p(U_i dislike = 0 | class_j) = 1.$

However, $p(U_i like = 1 | class_j) + p(U_i dislike = 1 | class_j)$ and $p(U_i like = 0 | class_j) + p(U_i dislike = 0 | class_j)$ do not necessarily equal 1 because some users may have not indicated whether they like or dislike a particular item.

(2) Sparse Data Model
In this model, it is assumed that only present features are informative for classification. This assumption affects the calculation of the probability of each class and the estimates of conditional probabilities. When calculating the probability of an item belonging to class j, the following formula is considered:

$$p(class_j | f_1=1, f_3=1, \ldots f_{n-1}=1)$$

Moreover, we make an only use of the data which both users in common rated when estimating conditional probabilities. In this representation, the following condition holds:

$$p(U_i like = 1 \mid class_j) + p(U_i dislike = 1 \mid class_j) = 1$$

For example, in the rating matrix of Table 2, the estimated conditional probability of $p(U_i like \mid like) = 0.33$ in the Transformed Data Model and $p(U_i like \mid like) = 0.5$ in the Sparse Data Model[1] respectively.

By using the Simple Bayesian Classifier to make predictions, we expect to avoid a problem with typical correlation-based collaborative filtering algorithms. The correlation-based algorithms make a global similarity model between users, rather than separate models for classes of ratings (e.g. positive rating vs. negative rating). It might happen that a set of one user's positive ratings is a good predictor for other users' positive ratings but the negative ratings of one user may not be useful in making predictions. Since the proposed models treat each class of ratings separately, we expect that the Bayesian model will capture predictiveness between users more precisely.

3. 3 Feature Selection

Feature selection is a common preprocessing technique in many supervised learning algorithms. By restricting the number of features, it might be expected that it would increase the accuracy of the learner by ignoring irrelevant features or reduce the computation time. We apply a feature selection method to find a set of the n most informative features. Since our goal is to discriminate between classes, we define *informative* as being equivalent with *providing the most information* about an item's class membership. Intuitively, we would like to select features that appear more frequently in one class than in others. We use an information theory based approach to determine n most informative features. This is accomplished by computing the expected information gain[13] that the presence or absence of a feature F gives toward the classification of a set of labeled items S:

$$E(F, S) = I(S) - [p(F = 1) I(S_{F=1}) + p(F = 0) I(S_{F=0})]$$

where $p(F =1)$ is the probability that feature F is present on an item, and $S_{F=1}$ is the set of items for which $F = 1$ holds, and $I(x)$ is the entropy of a set of labeled items, defined as:

$$I(S) = \sum_{c \in classes} -p(S_c) \log_2(p(S_c))$$

where S_c is the set of all rated items that belongs to class c (In our case, $c = \{like, dislike\}$) by the target user. This formula is suitable for the *Transformed Data Model*, because it can calculate information gain of all the features independently even dual features such as $U_i like$ and $U_i dislike$. However the above formula doesn't guarantee that selected feature is informative in the *Sparse Data Model*, because the conditional probability is estimated from the common items rated by both users. For the *Sparse Data Model*, we extend the above formula as follows:

$$E_{sparse}(F, S) = E(F, S_{common}) * E(F,S) * E(\neg F,S)$$

---

[1] We use Laplacian prior in the actual calculation of conditional probabilities to smooth the probability estimates with few ratings and to avoid estimating a probability to be 0. Therefore, the value of $p(U_i like \mid like)$ is $(1+1)/(3+2) = 0.4$ in the Transformed Data Model and $(1+1)/(2+2) = 0.5$ in the Sparse Data Model respectively.

where S_{common} is the set of the common rated items by both users and $\neg F$ is the dual feature of F, that is $\neg U_i like = U_i dislike$ and $\neg U_i dislike = U_i like$. Note that since $E(U_i like, S_{common})$ is equal to $E(U_i dislike, S_{common})$, the value of $E_{sparse}(U_i like, S)$ is equivalent to the value of $E_{sparse}(U_i dislike, S)$ in the above formula. Accordingly, selecting features is identical to selecting users in the *Sparse Data Model*.

4. Experiments

4.1 Dataset

We used two datasets as test data. One is related to a movie recommendation task. The other is related to a joke recommendation task.

(1) EachMovie dataset
   The *EachMovie* service was part of a research project at the DEC Systems Research Center [10]. The service was available for an 18-months period and was shut down in September 1997. During that time 72,916 users entered numeric ratings for 1,628 movies. User ratings were recorded on a numeric six-point scale, ranging from 0 to 1 (0, 0.2, 0.4, 0.6, 0.8, 1.0). In our experiment, we use an experimental protocol similar to the one first used in [1]. We restricted the number of users to first 2,000 users in the database. These 2,000 users provided ratings for 1,410 different movies.

(2) Jester dataset
   Jester is a WWW-based joke recommendation system, which has been developed at University of California, Berkeley [4]. This dataset has 21,800 users entered numeric ratings for 100 jokes. User ratings were recorded on a real value, ranging from -10 to +10. Like the EachMovie dataset, we restricted the number of users to first 3,000 users in the database. These 3000 users provided rating for 100 different jokes.

4.2 Evaluation Criteria

As we have described in section 2, we are interested in discriminating between liked items and disliked items. To distinguish items, we transformed numerical ratings into two labels. We labeled items as *like* if the numerical rating for the item was above 0.7 (midpoint between the two possible user ratings *0.6* and *0.8*), or *dislike* otherwise in the EachMovie dataset. And, we labeled items as *like* if the numerical rating for the item was above 2.0, or *dislike* otherwise in the Jester dataset.

Not only does assigning class labels allow us to measure classification accuracy, we can also apply additional performance measures, *precision* and *recall,* commonly used for information retrieval tasks. However, it might be easy to optimize each of these measurements. To avoid this problem, we use F-Measure [7], which combines *precision* and *recall*:

$$F - Measure = \frac{2 \cdot precision \cdot recall}{precison + recall}$$

4.3 Experimental Methodology

In our first experiment, we have evaluated the effectiveness of feature selection for our proposed two alternative representations. We also have evaluated a typical correlation-based approach, which is described in [15]. We selected 20 test users who have rated at least 80 movies from the EachMovie dataset and 20 test users who have rated at least 60 jokes from the Jester dataset respectively. In the correlation-based approach, after calculating the predicted score, we labeled *like* or *dislike* according to the thresholds (0.7 in EachMovie and 2.0 in Jester). For each test user we ran a total of 20 paired trials for each algorithm, where we varied the number of features. For an each trial in an experiment, we randomly selected 50 rated items for the EachMovie dataset and 40 for the Jester dataset as a training set, and 30 items for the EachMovie dataset and 20 for the Jester dataset as a test set. The final results for one user are then averaged over all 20 trials, and we report the average value over 20 test users. In the *Transformed Model*, we selected n most informative features from all of the features. Predictions are made using all of these selected features. However, since the *Sparse Model* uses only present features, it would happen that no selected feature is present for the target items. To avoid this problem, we selected n most informative users (features) among users who had already rated the target item. We applied similar method to the correlation-based approach, except we selected n users based on an absolute value of correlation coefficient instead of the expected information gain.

In our second experiment, we have evaluated performance when we change the number of rated items in training data. We started training with 10 rated items and increased the training set incrementally in steps of 10 up to 50 items for the EachMovie dataset and up to 40 items for the Jester dataset, measuring the algorithms' performance on the test set for each training set size. For each algorithm, we set the number of features, which performed best at the first experiment. Like the first experiment, for each test user, we ran a total of 20 paired trials for each algorithm. We repeated this for all test users and the final results reported here are averaged over 20 test users.

5. Results

Figure 1 shows the classification accuracy of our first experiment with the EachMovie dataset. Note that since there are 4,000 (2000 users × 2 features per user) features at most in the EachMovie dataset, maximum number of features is 3,998 (4,000 features − 2 features) in the *Transformed Model*. The results show that the *Transformed Model* reaches a maximum accuracy of 67.3% at 100 features. It seems to be sensitive to the number of selected features and it is getting worse in proportion to the number of features significantly. The *Sparse Model* reaches a maximum classification accuracy of 71.6% at 200 users. However, there are no significant differences among the performance with 30 users or more. The *Correlation* reaches a maximum accuracy of

66.4% at 30 users. Its performance seems to be stable at 30 users or more like the *Sparse Model*.

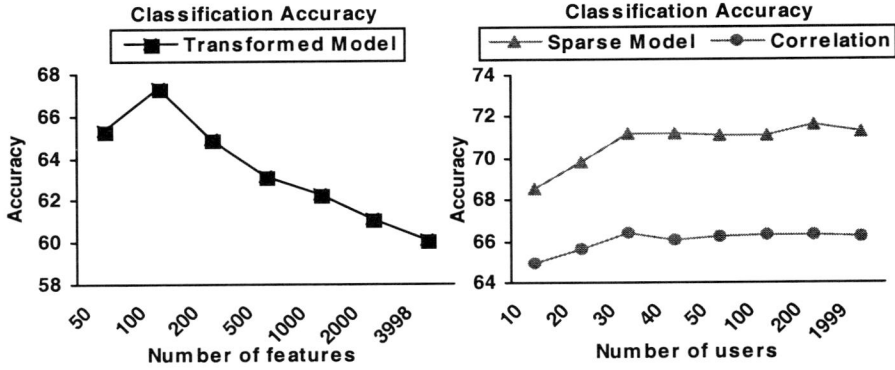

Fig. 1. Effects of feature selection (EachMovie dataset)

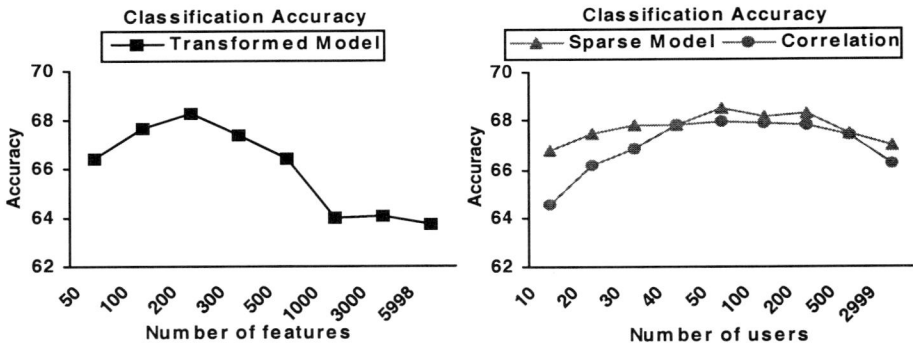

Fig. 2. Effects of feature selection (Jester dataset)

Figure 2 shows the classification accuracy with the Jester dataset. The *Transformed Model* reaches a maximum classification accuracy of 68.3% at 200 features, *Sparse Model* is 68.5% at 50 users and *Correlation* is 68.0% at 50 users. Like the EachMovie dataset, *Transformed Model* clearly has an optimal number of features. The performance of *Sparse Model* and *Correlation* is getting worse when selecting a larger number of users.

Figure 3 shows learning curves in our second experiment with the EachMovie dataset, and Figure 4 shows learning curves with the Jester dataset. For each model, we set the number of features which performed best in our first experiment. These results show that the *Sparse Model* performs best among three models. Especially, with the EachMovie dataset, it significantly outperforms other two models (as for accuracy, at 50 training examples, 71.6% for *Sparse Model* vs. 67.3% for *Transformed Model* and 66.4% for *Correlation*. As for F-Measure, 70.2% for *Sparse Model* vs. 64.4% for *Transformed Model* and 58.4% for *Correlation*). The *Transformed Model* almost performs better than the *Correlation* except the accuracy at 30 or less training examples. With Jester dataset, the *Sparse Model* performs slightly better than the *Transformed Model* and both models outperform the *Correlation*. At 40 training examples, *Transformed Model* reaches F-Measure of 66.3%, *Sparse Model* is 65.9% and *Correlation* is 60.1%. The accuracy of *Sparse Model* is 64.2%, *Transformed Model* is 62.7% and *Correlation* is 61.7% at 10 training examples. As for the F-Measure, *Sparse Model* is 62.8%, *Transformed Model* is 60.0%, and *Correlation* is 45.6%.

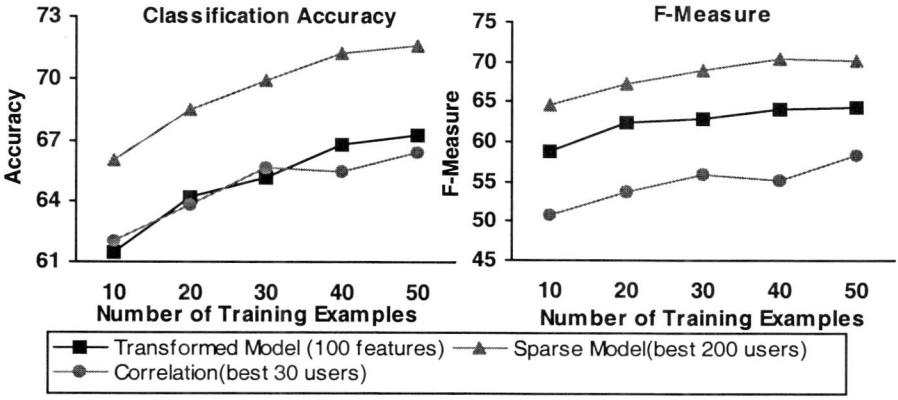

Fig. 3. Learning Curves (EachMovie dataset)

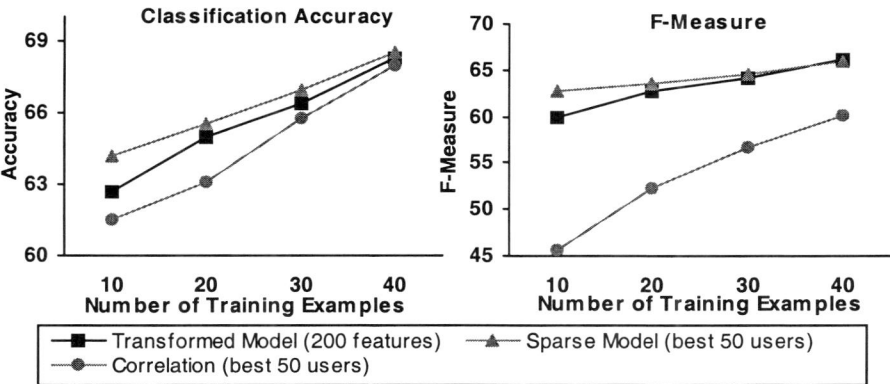

Fig. 4. Learning Curves (Jester dataset)

6. Discussion

Our experimental results show that our proposed collaborative filtering with the Simple Bayesian Model performs well. The *Sparse Model* significantly outperforms over the correlation-based algorithm. We think that the probability calculation by dividing positive ratings and negative ratings captures more precise similarity between users and it causes the better predictions. We also think that the probability smoothing by Laplacian prior in the *Sparse Model* might be effective especially in the case that the number of commonly rated items is small.

Feature selection is valuable in the *Transformed Model*. It has an optimum number of features which can work best. Similar results are reported in text classification tasks using the multi-variate Bernoulli model of the Simple Bayesian Classifier ([9], [12]). Although the *Sparse Model* has an optimum number of features with the Jester dataset, the effect of feature selection is not clearly shown with the EachMovie dataset.

It is interesting that the *Transformed Model* works well. This model treats even missing ratings as informative. This treatment may distort the similarity between users, because it would happen that a user doesn't rate items by chance. In text classification tasks, it is reasonable that an absent word is informative, because people tend to use suitable words for its domain of the text. Therefore, absence of the word can be thought a good predictor for its negative class. However, our empirical results show that the *Transformed Model* performs well in spite of this intuitive thought. One advantage of the *Transformed Model* is that it greatly reduces computational complexity. Once the model selects a set of features, it can make predictions using the selected features.

7. Conclusions and Future Work

In this paper, we reported on collaborative filtering with the Simple Bayesian Classifier. We proposed two representations for the Simple Bayesian Classifier. We found that the Sparse Data Model performs better than the Transformed Data Model and the typical correlation-based approach. This shows that the transformation proposed by Billsus and Pazzani [1] to use any machine learning algorithms for collaborative filtering may be improved upon by algorithms which handle missing data well. The Transformed Data Model also outperforms the correlation-based approach although it shows similar accuracy to the correlation approach in some parts of our experiments with the EachMovie dataset. Since our experiments used only two datasets, it is important to adopt other types of datasets to verify our methodology.

In future work, we will investigate to combine content based filtering and collaborative filtering. As a first step, we plan to integrate keyword features and user features within one framework using the Simple Bayesian Classifier.

References

[1] Billsus, D. & Pazzani, M. (1998). Learning Collaborative Filters. In *Proceedings of the 15th International Conference on Machine Learning*, San Francisco, CA., Morgan Kaufmann Publishers.
[2] Breese, J., Heckerman, D., Kadie, C. (1998). Empirical Analysis of Predictive Algorithms for Collaborative Filtering. In *Proceedings of the 14th Conference on Uncertainty in Artificial Intelligence*, Madison, WI., Morgan Kaufmann Publisher.
[3] Domingos, P. & Pazzani M. (1997). On the Optimality of the Simple Bayesian Classifier under Zero-One Loss. *Machine Learning*, 29, 103-130.
[4] Gupta, D., Digiovanni, M., Narita, H., Goldberg, K. (1999). Jester 2.0: A New Linear-Time Collaborative Filtering Algorithm Applied to Jokes. *Workshop on Recommender Systems Algorithms and Evaluation, 22nd International Conference on Research and Development in Information Retrieval*, Berkeley, CA.
[5] Herlocker, J., Konstan, J., Borchers, A., Riedl, J. (1999). An Algorithmic Framework for Performing Collaborative Filtering. In *proceedings of 22nd International Conference on Research and Development in Information Retrieval* 230-237, Berkley, CA., ACM Press.
[6] Hill, W., Stead, L., Rosenstein, M., Furnas, G. (1995). Recommending and Evaluating Choices in a Virtual Community of Use. In *Proceedings of the Conference on Human Factors in Computing Systems*, 194-201, Denver, CO., ACM Press.
[7] Lewis, D. & Gale, W. A. (1994). A sequential algorithm for training text classifiers. In *Proceedings of 17th International Conference on Research and Development in Information Retrieval*, 3-12, London, Springer-Verlag.
[8] Lewis, D. (1998). Naïve (Bayes) at forty: The independence assumption in information retrieval. In *Proceedings of the Tenth European Conference on Machine Learning*.
[9] McCallum, A. & Nigam, K. (1998). A Comparison of Event Models for Naïve Bayes Text Classification. *American Association for Artificial Intelligence (AAAI) Workshop on Learning for Text Categorization*.
[10] McJonese, P. (1997). EachMovie collaborative filtering data set. DEC Systems Research Center.
[11] Mitchell, T. (1997). *Machine Learning*. MacGraw-Hill, New York.
[12] Pazzani, M. & Billsus, D. (1997). Learning and Revising User Profiles: The identification of interesting web sites. *Machine Learning* 27, 313-331.
[13] Quinlan, J.R. (1986). Induction of decision trees. *Machine Learning* 1, 81-106.
[14] Resnick, P. & Varian, H. (1997). Recommender systems. *Communications of the ACM*, 40(3) 56-58.
[15] Resnick, P., Neophytos, I., Mitesh, S., Bergstrom, P., Riedl, J. (1994). GroupLens: An Open Architecture for Collaborative Filtering of Netnews. In *Proceedings of CSCW94: Conference on Computer Supported Cooperative Work*, 175-186, Chapel Hill, Addison-Wesley.
[16] Shardanand, U. & Maes, P. (1995). Social Information Filtering: Algorithms for Automating 'Word of Mouth'. In *Proceedings of the Conference on Human Factors in Computing Systems*, 210-217, Denver, CO., ACM Press.

Supervised and Unsupervised Learning Algorithms for Thai Web Pages Identification

Boonserm Kijsirikul[1], Puay Sasiphongpairoege[1], Nuanwan Soonthornphisaj[1], and Surapant Meknavin[2]

[1] Department of Computer Engineering, Chulalongkorn University, Phathumwan, Bangkok, 10330, Thailand.
{boonserm,puay,nuanwan}@mind.cp.eng.chula.ac.th
[2] Siamguru Co.,Ltd. 2922/103 Charn Issara Tower II, 126-7 New Petchburi Rd., Bangkapi, Huay Kwang, Bangkok 10310, Thailand.
surapan@siamguru.com

Abstract. The paper presents a learning method, called *iterative cross-training (ICT)* for identifying Thai Web pages. Our method combines two classifiers, i.e. a word segmentation classifier and a naive Bayes classifier, that use unlabeled examples to train each other. We compare ICT against other supervised and unsupervised learning methods: a supervised word segmentation classifier *(S-Word)*, a supervised naive Bayes classifier *(S-Bayes)*, an unsupervised naive Bayes classifier using the EM algorithm *(U-Bayes-EM)*, and a co-training-style classifier *(CoTraining)*. The experimental results show that ICT gives the best performance, followed by S-Bayes, CoTraining U-Bayes-EM and S-Word.

1 Introduction

Given pre-labeled training data, supervised learning has been successfully applied to text classification [1, 5, 6, 3, 10] However, one of the difficulties of using supervised learning is that we have to hand-label data for constructing training sets. Though it is costly to construct hand-labeled data, in some domains it is easy to obtain unlabeled ones, such as data in the World Wide Web. Thus, if we are able to effectively utilize the available unlabeled data, we will simplify the task of building text classifiers. Various methods have been proposed to use unlabeled data together with pre-labeled data for text classification, such as text classification using the EM algorithm [9], the co-training algorithm [2].

This paper describes our work that is a part of our project on building a system which retrieves information from the Web. The goal of our project is to build a Web robot that crawls the Web and determines if a page is of interest. In this paper, we focus on a method for classifying Web pages into the set of Thai pages and the set of non-Thai pages. In fact, we want our Web robot to retrieve only Thai pages. By a Thai page, we refer to the page that is intended to be read by Thai people and contains Thai texts and may contain texts in other languages.

We propose a method, called *iterative cross-training (ICT)*, for identifying Thai Web pages. Our method is an unsupervised learning in the sense that it needs no pre-labeled examples and thus is suitable for this domain where unlabeled data is plentiful and easy to obtain. The method combines two classifiers which iteratively train each other for improving the performance of the classifiers. Given two sets of unlabeled data, each of which is for each classifier, the classifiers label the data for the other. The first classifier is given some knowledge about the domain, and uses the knowledge to estimate labels of the pages for the second classifier. The first classifier may require expensive computation. The second classifier has no domain knowledge and requires inexpensive computation. It learns its model from pages labeled by the first, and uses the current model to label training data for the first. This cross-training process is iterated. The expensive classifier used in our task is a word segmentation classifier that is given knowledge in a form of dictionary. The inexpensive one is a naive Bayes classifier. With good interaction between two classifiers, the performance of the whole system is increasingly improved. After the classifiers are trained, only one classifier will be used by the Web robot. It is desirable to use the inexpensive one for fast retrieval of Thai Web pages. In case that the accuracy, not classification time, is the main concern, the expensive one can be used as well. One of the advantages of our method is that, as the method does not require human to label the Web pages, it can be trained with a lot of unlabeled pages and can be easily changed for identifying other languages.

To evaluate the effectiveness of our method, we implement other four classifiers to compare empirically with our method. The implementation is designed to explain, or at least give some answers to questions: "is iterative cross-training (ICT) which combines two classifiers an effective method?", "does this kind of combination of two classifiers perform better than only one?", and "can the method successfully use unlabeled data?". The other four classifiers are: (1) a supervised word segmentation classifier (S-Word), (2) a supervised naive Bayes classifier (S-Bayes), (3) a co-training-style classifier (CoTraining), and (4) an unsupervised naive Bayes classifier using the EM algorithm (U-Bayes-EM).

The experimental results show that ICT successfully and efficiently identifies Thai Web pages. The overall performance, evaluated by F_1-measure, of ICT is the best. The better performance of ICT over U-Bayes-EM, which uses single classifier, shows the effectiveness of the combination of two classifiers. The comparable performance of our method to supervised ones (S-Bayes and S-Word) demonstrates the successful use of unlabeled data.

2 Iterative Cross-Training

This section presents the iterative cross-training. First we describe the architecture of our learning system, and then give the details of two classifiers used in the system. Figure 1 shows our learning system which learns to classify Web pages. The system is composed of two classifiers: (1) a word segmentation classifier and (2) a naive Bayes classifier. These two classifiers estimate their parameters from unlabeled data by receiving training from each other. Two training data sets, called $TrainingData1$ and $TrainingData2$ are selected from the training data provided by user. These two training sets may overlap, be identical or different. Let θ_w and θ_n be sets of parameters of the word segmentation classifier and of the

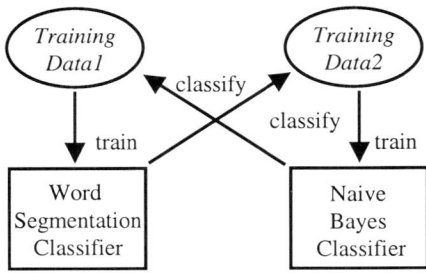

Fig. 1. The architecture of iterative cross-training. It is composed of two classifiers which use unlabeled data to train each other.

Table 1. The training algorithm of iterative cross-training.

Given:
- two sets $TrainingData1$ and $TrainingData2$ of unlabeled training examples

Initialize the parameter set of the word segmentation classifier to θ_{w0} ($\theta_w \leftarrow \theta_{w0}$).
Loop until θ_w does not change or the number of iterations exceeds a predefined value:
  − Use the word segmentation classifier with the current parameter set θ_w to classify $TrainingData2$ into positive examples and negative examples.
  − Train the naive Bayes classifier by the previously labeled $TrainingData2$ to estimate the parameter set θ_n of the classifier.
  − Use the naive Bayes classifier with the current θ_n to classify $TrainingData1$ into positive examples and negative examples.
  − Use the previously labeled $TraingingData1$ to determine the parameter set θ_w of the word segmentation classifier.

---

naive Bayes classifier, respectively. $TrainingData1$ is used for training the word segmentation classifier to estimate its parameter set, and the $TrainingData2$ is used for estimating the parameter set of the naive Bayes classifier. The algorithm for training the classifiers is shown in Table 1.

The idea behind our algorithm is that if we can obtain reliable statistical information contained in $TrainingData2$, it should be useful in classifying $TrainingData1$. If the starting θ_{w0} has property that it produces more true positive than wrong positive examples and more true negative than wrong negative examples for $TrainingData2$, the statistical information in correctly classified examples will be obtained. Using this information the naive Bayes classifier should classify more correct examples in $TrainingData1$ that have similar characteristics. If the newly labeled $TrainingData1$ can produce θ_w better than θ_{w0}, more reliable parameters of the whole system should be obtained after each iteration. We will discuss the property of θ_{w0} that produces more correct examples in Section 2.1. The following subsections describe the details of the classifiers.

2.1 Word Segmentation Classifier

One straightforward way to determine whether a Web page is in a specific language is to check the words in the page with a dictionary. If many words appear in the dictionary, it is likely that the page is in that language. We cannot expect that all words in the page appear in dictionary as the Web page usually contains names of persons, organizations, etc. not occurring in the dictionary and may contain words written in foreign languages. Therefore, it is necessary to determine how many words should be contained. This task is more difficult when it is considered in a language that has no word boundary delimiters, such as Thai, Japanese, etc. [7]. Below we describe our method for word segmentation.

Given a dictionary and a document d of n characters $(c_1, c_2, \ldots, c_n)$, the word segmentation classifier generates all possible segmentations and finds the best segmentation $(w_1, w_2, \ldots, w_m)$ that minimizes the cost function in Equation 1.

$$\operatorname{argmin}_{w_1,\ldots,w_m} \sum_{i=1}^{m} cost(w_i) \qquad (1)$$

where $cost(w_i) = \begin{cases} \eta_1 & \text{if } w_i \text{ is a word in the dictionary} \\ \eta_2 & \text{if } w_i \text{ is a string not found in the dictionary} \end{cases}$

In our experiments, η_1 and η_2 are set to 1 and 2, respectively. Any sequence of characters, $c_i, \ldots, c_j$, found in the dictionary must be considered as a word, and must not be grouped with nearby characters to form a long unknown string.

After the best segmentation is determined, the document is composed of (1) words appeared in the dictionary, and (2) unknown strings not found in the dictionary. A Thai Web page should be the page that contains many words and few unknown strings. We then define $WordRatio$ of a page as:

$$\frac{\text{the number of characters in all words}}{\text{the number of all characters in the document}}$$

Given sets of positive and negative examples, the classifier finds the threshold of $WordRatio$ that maximizes the number of correctly classified positive and negative examples. If $WordRatio$ of a page is greater than the threshold, we will classify the page as positive (Thai page). Otherwise, we will classify it as negative (non-Thai page). For simplicity, let us use only the threshold of $WordRatio$ as the parameter of the word segmentation classifier (θ_w). Having only the threshold of $WordRatio$ (θ_w) as the parameter, we can find θ_{w0} which produces more true positive and true negative examples for $TrainingData2$. As described above, most of Thai pages should have a high value of $WordRatio$, whereas non-Thai pages should have a low value one. If the numbers of Thai and non-Thai pages in $TrainingData2$ are the same, it is easily seen that any value of θ_{w0} will give more correctly classified pages than incorrect ones (except for $\theta_{w0}=0.0$ or $\theta_{w0}=1.0$, that gives the same number of correctly and incorrectly classified pages). In case that the number of Thai pages is lower than the number of non-Thai pages, a high value of θ_{w0}, (e.g. 0.7, 0.8, 0.9) will produce more correctly classified pages. A low value of θ_{w0} is for the case that the number of Thai pages is larger than non-Thai pages.

A new θ_w can be estimated, after the naive Bayes classifier labels data in $TrainingData1$. Let SP be the smallest value of $WordRatio$'s from all labeled positive examples, and LN be the largest value from all labeled negative examples. The new θ_w is estimated as:

$$\theta_w = (SP + LN)/2 \qquad (2)$$

2.2 The Naive Bayes Classifier

For text classification, naive Bayes is among the most commonly used and the most effective methods [8]. To represent text documents, the method usually employs *bag-of-words* representation. Instead of bag-of-words, we use the simpler *bag-of-characters* representation. This representation is suitable for a Web robot to identify Thai Web pages, because it requires no word segmentation and thus it is very fast. In spite of its simplicity, our results show the effectiveness of bag-of-characters representation in classifying Web pages, as shown later in Section 4.

Given a set of class labels $L = \{l_1, l_2, \ldots, l_m\}$ and a document d of n characters $(c_1, c_2, \ldots, c_n)$, the most likely class label l^* estimated by naive Bayes is the one that maximizes $Pr(l_j|c_1, \ldots, c_n)$:

$$l^* = \mathrm{argmax}_{l_j} Pr(l_j|c_1, \ldots, c_n) \qquad (3)$$

$$= \mathrm{argmax}_{l_j} \frac{Pr(l_j)Pr(c_1, \ldots, c_n|l_j)}{Pr(c_1, \ldots, c_n)} \qquad (4)$$

$$= \mathrm{argmax}_{l_j} Pr(l_j)Pr(c_1, \ldots, c_n|l_j) \qquad (5)$$

In our case, L is the set of positive and negative class labels. $Pr(c_1, \ldots, c_n)$ in Equation 4 can be ignored, as we are interested in finding the most likely class label. As there are usually an extremely large number of possible values for $d = (c_1, c_2, \ldots, c_n)$, calculating the term $Pr(c_1, c_2, \ldots, c_n|l_j)$ requires a huge number of examples to obtain reliable estimation. Therefore, to reduce the number of required examples and improve reliability of the estimation, assumptions of naive Bayes are made [8]. These assumptions are (1) the conditional independent assumption, i.e. the presence of each character is conditionally independent of all other characters in the document given the class label, and (2) an assumption that the position of a character is unimportant, e.g. encountering the character "a" at the beginning of a document is the same as encountering it at the end. Using the above assumptions, Equation 5 can be rewritten as:

$$l^* = \mathrm{argmax}_{l_j} Pr(l_j) \prod_{i=1}^{n} Pr(c_i|l_j, c_1, \ldots, c_{i-1}) \qquad (6)$$

$$= \mathrm{argmax}_{l_j} Pr(l_j) \prod_{i=1}^{n} Pr(c_i|l_j) \qquad (7)$$

This model is also called unigram model because it is based on statistics about single character in isolation. The probabilities $Pr(l_j)$ and $Pr(c_i|l_j)$ are used as the parameter set θ_n of our naive Bayes classifier, and are estimated from the

Table 2. The co-training-style algorithm.

Given:
- a set LE of labeled training examples
- a set UE of unlabeled examples

Create a pool UE' of examples by choosing u examples at random from UE.
Loop until no examples left in UE:
- Use LE to estimate θ_w of the word segmentation classifier.
- Use LE to estimate θ_n of the naive Bayes classifier.
- Allow the word segmentation classifier with θ_w to label p positive and n negative examples from UE'.
- Allow the naive Bayes classifier with θ_n to label p positive and n negative examples from UE'.
- Add these self-labeled examples to LE.
- Randomly choose $2p + 2n$ examples from UE to replenish UE'.
---

training data. The prior probability $Pr(l_j)$ is estimated as the ratio between the number of examples belonging to the class l_j and the number of all examples. The conditional probability $Pr(c_i|l_j)$, of seeing character c_i given class label l_j, is estimated by the following equation:

$$Pr(c_i|l_j) = \frac{1 + N(c_i, l_j)}{T + N(l_j)} \qquad (8)$$

Where $N(c_i, l_j)$ is the number of times character c_i appears in the training examples from class label l_j, $N(l_j)$ is the total number of characters in the training set for class label l_j, and T is the total number of unique characters in the training set. Equation 8 employs Laplace smoothing (adding one to all the character counts), to avoid assigning probability values of zero to characters that do not occur in the training examples for a particular class.

3 Other Classifiers Used in Comparison

3.1 Co-training-style Classifier

The co-training algorithm is described in [2]. The idea of the algorithm is that an example can be considered in two different views, and either view is assumed to be sufficient for learning. Based on this idea, we construct a co-training-style algorithm for our task. The algorithm is shown in Table 2. To apply this idea to our problem, we view each Web page as (1) a set of characters occurring in the page, and (2) a set of words occurring in that page. A naive Bayes classifier is employed to learn from the view of the character representation, and a word segmentation classifier is used for the word representation. The parameters θ_w and θ_n are estimated in the same way as described in Section 2. The algorithm requires a small set of hand-labeled data for beginning the training process. Therefore, we can think of this algorithm as semi-supervised one.

Table 3. Training algorithm for the naive Bayes classifier using the EM algorithm.

Given:

- a set UE of unlabeled examples

Use the word segmentation classifier with initial θ_{w0} to label UE.
Use the labeled examples in UE to estimate the parameters $Pr(c_i|l_j)$ and $Pr(l_j)$ of the naive Bayes classifier with $Pr(l_j|d) \in \{0,1\}$.
Loop until the parameters of Bayes do not change or the number of iterations exceeds a predefined value:
  – (E-step) Estimate the probabilistically-weighted class labels, $Pr(l_j|d)$, for every document using Equation 11.
  – (M-step) Use the estimated class labels, $Pr(l_j|d)$, to calculate new paramenters using all documents, by Equation 9 and 10.

3.2 Unsupervised Naive Bayes Classifier Using the EM Algorithm

This subsection describes an unsupervised naive Bayes classifier which uses Expectation-Maximization(EM) algorithm [4] for filling the missing class labels in training examples. Our method for training naive Bayes with the EM algorithm is the same as one described in [9], and is shown below.

Let $L = \{l_1, l_2, \ldots, l_m\}$ be a set of class labels, d be a document of n characters $(c_1, c_2, \ldots, c_n)$ from a data set D, $Pr(l_j|d) \in \{0,1\}$ be the class label of the document d. The estimate of the probability of character c_i in class label l_j is:

$$Pr(c_i|l_j) = \frac{1 + \sum_{d \in D} N(c_i, d) Pr(l_j|d)}{T + \sum_{k=1}^{T} \sum_{d \in D} N(c_k, d) Pr(l_j|d)} \quad (9)$$

Where T is the total number of unique characters in the training set, $N(c_i, d)$ is the number of times character c_i occurs in document d. The probability of a class label is given by Equation 10:

$$Pr(l_j) = \frac{1 + \sum_{d \in D} Pr(l_j|d)}{|L| + |D|} \quad (10)$$

Where $|L|, |D|$ are the number of class labels, and the number of documents in the training set. Given an unlabeled document d, of n character $(c_1, c_2, \ldots, c_n)$, the naive Bayes classifier estimates the probability that the document belongs to the class label l_j by using Equation 11 below.

$$Pr(l_j|d) = \frac{Pr(l_j)Pr(d|l_j)}{Pr(d)} = \frac{Pr(l_j) \prod_{i=1}^{n} Pr(c_i|l_j)}{\sum_{k=1}^{|L|} Pr(l_k) \prod_{i=1}^{n} Pr(c_i|l_k)} \quad (11)$$

Note that now $Pr(l_j|d)$ is a probabilistically-weighted value; each document d is considered to be of class label l_j with probability equal to the estimated $Pr(l_j|d)$. The algorithm for training the naive Bayes classifier using the EM algorithm is shown in Table 3. The algorithm uses the word segmentation classifier once for determining the initial labels for the training data.

4 Experimental Results

We conducted experiments to compare iterative cross-training (ICT) with the other four classifiers described in the previous section: the supervised word segmentation classifier (S-Word), the supervised naive Bayes classifier (S-Bayes), the co-training-style classifier (CoTraining), and the unsupervised naive Bayes classifier using the EM algorithm (U-Bayes-EM). S-Word and S-Bayes used in our comparison are the same as ones described in Section 2.1 and 2.2, except that they are trained by hand-labeled data.

4.1 Data Set and Experimental Setting

We collected the data set for our experiments by starting from four Web pages: a Japanese Web page, two Thai Web pages, and an English web page. From each of these four pages, a Web robot is used to recursively follow the links within the page until it retrieves 450 pages. Therefore, we have approximately 900 Thai pages as Thai pages may link to ones which are in English or other languages. We also have approximately 450 Japanese and 450 English pages. All of these pages were divided into three sets, denoted as A, B and C, each of which contains 600 pages (about 300 Thai, 150 Japanese and 150 English pages). We used 3-fold cross validation in all experiments below for averaging the results. The following are the parameter settings for the classifiers when C was used as the test set.

(1) For ICT, $A+B$ was used as both $TrainingData1$ and $TrainingData2$. The initial θ_{w0} was set to 0.7.

(2) For each of S-Word and S-Bayes classifiers, the pages in sets A and B were manually labeled and the experiment was run for two times; the first run with the labeled A and the second run with the labeled B as the training set. The results on classifying C were averaged.

(3) For CoTraining, $A+B$ was used as the training set. The values of the parameters of the classifier (in Table 2) were set in a similar way as in [2]. As CoTraining requires a small set of correctly pre-classified training data, we gave the algorithm with 18 hand-labeled pages. In our experiment, we set the values of $|LE|$, $|UE|$, p, n and u to 18, 1182, 3, 3 and 115, respectively.

(4) For U-Bayes-EM, $A+B$ was used as the training set. The initial θ_{w0} for the algorithm (in Table 3) was set to 0.7.

4.2 The Results

To evaluate the performance of the classifiers, we use standard precision(P), recall(R) and F_1-measure(F_1) defined as follows:

$$P = \frac{\text{no. of correctly predicted positive examples}}{\text{no. of predicted positive examples}}$$

$$R = \frac{\text{no. of correctly predicted positive examples}}{\text{no. of all positive examples}}$$

Table 4. The precision(P), recall(R) and F_1-measure(F_1) of the classifiers.

Classifier	P	R	F_1
ICT(Word)	99.78	100.00	99.89
S-Bayes	100.00	99.00	99.50
ICT(Bayes)	100.00	98.89	99.44
CoTraining(Bayes)	100.00	98.89	99.44
U-Bayes-EM	100.00	98.78	99.39
S-Word	99.08	99.61	99.34
CoTraining(Word)	100.00	98.66	99.33

$$F_1 = \frac{2PR}{P+R}$$

The results are shown in Table 4. In the table, "CoTraining(Bayes)" and "CoTraining(Word)" are the results of the naive Bayes and the word segmentation classifiers of CoTraining, respectively. "ICT(Bayes)" and "ICT(Word)" are for the naive Bayes and the word segmentation classifiers of ICT.

As shown in the table, ICT(Word) gives the best performance. S-Bayes is the second best classifier, followed by ICT(Bayes) and CoTraining(Bayes) according to F_1-measure. Among the classifiers tested in the experiments, ICT and U-Bayes-EM are unsupervised classifiers. The reason for better performance of ICT over U-Bayes-EM may be because ICT employs two sub-classifiers which help each other in learning while U-Bayes-EM uses only single classifier. Compared to supervised classifiers, the performance of ICT is comparable to that of S-Bayes and better than that of S-Word. The results demonstrate that our system can effectively use unlabeled examples and the two classifiers succeed in training each other. The training technique of ICT is also an effective one as its performance is better than that of CoTraining which uses a different training technique.

4.3 The Effect of Parameter Settings on the Performances of the Classifiers

This subsection shows additional experiments that were conducted to see the effect of parameter settings on ICT, U-Bayes-EM and CoTraining. For ICT and U-Bayes-EM, θ_{w0} is only the initial parameter that may effect the performance of the classifiers. We run experiments with different θ_{w0} varying from 0.0, 0.1, 0.2,..., 1.0. The results, when C was used as the test set, are shown in Table 5. When A or B was used as the test set, the similar results were obtained.

The results in the table show that each of θ_{w0} varying from 0.0 to 1.0 did not effect the precision and recall of ICT; with all of them the precision and recall were 100% and 98.33%, respectively. Each of these initial settings converged to the same final θ_w (0.301) The θ_{w0}'s which quickly converged were 0.2, 0.3, 0.4 and 0.5; each of them was close to the final θ_w. U-Bayes-EM is more sensitive to initial θ_{w0}. In case of θ_{w0} equal to 0.9 or 1.0, the algorithm converged to a local maximum which gave the precision and recall of 0%. When θ_{w0} was set to 0.0 or 0.1, U-Bayes-EM increased recall to 99.33% but decreased precision to

Table 5. The precision(P), recall(R), and number of iterations(I) before the convergence of ICT (Bayes) and U-Bayes-EM using different θ_{w0}.

θ_{w0}	ICT(Bayes)			U-Bayes-EM		
	P(%)	R(%)	I	P(%)	R(%)	I
0.0	100.00	98.33	5	66.08	99.33	3
0.1	100.00	98.33	3	66.08	99.33	4
0.2	100.00	98.33	2	100.00	98.33	3
0.3	100.00	98.33	2	100.00	98.33	3
0.4	100.00	98.33	2	100.00	98.33	4
0.5	100.00	98.33	2	100.00	98.00	5
0.6	100.00	98.33	3	100.00	98.00	6
0.7	100.00	98.33	4	100.00	98.00	7
0.8	100.00	98.33	5	100.00	98.00	11
0.9	100.00	98.33	3	0.00	0.00	6
1.0	100.00	98.33	3	0.00	0.00	9

66.08%. The reason for the better performance of ICT(Bayes) is because of the good interaction between the naive Bayes and the word segmentation classifiers of ICT.

We also run experiments to see the effect of parameter settings for CoTraining. As shown in Table 2, there are several parameters to be set, i.e., $|LE|$, p, n and u. To restrict the number of experiments, we varied only p and n, and left the other unchanged. The parameters p and n control the amount of self-labeled examples which will be added into the labeled training set. If the values of the parameters are large, the algorithm will rapidly add many self-labeled examples into the training set. We expected that the performance of CoTraining would decrease with increasing p and n. However, the results were not as expected as shown in Table 6.

Table 6. The precision(P), recall(R) and F_1-measure(F_1) of CoTraining as we vary p and n. All experiments used 3-fold cross validation.

Parameter setting	CoTraining(Word)			CoTraining(Bayes)		
	P(%)	R(%)	F_1	P(%)	R(%)	F_1
$p = n = 3$	100.00	98.66	99.33	100.00	98.89	99.44
$p = n = 6$	100.00	99.00	99.50	100.00	98.88	99.44
$p = n = 12$	100.00	98.77	99.38	100.00	98.88	99.44
$p = n = 24$	93.73	99.22	96.40	95.92	98.88	97.38
$p = n = 48$	100.00	98.55	99.27	100.00	98.88	99.44

The results show that CoTraining, especially CoTraining(Word), is sensitive to the parameter settings. Comparing the results in Table 5 and Table 6, we can see that ICT is more robust to the parameter settings and this is an advantage of ICT over U-Bayes-EM and CoTraining.

5 Conclusion

We have presented a method that effectively uses unlabeled examples to estimate the parameters of the system for classifying Web pages. The method is based on two components, i.e. the word segmentation classifier and the naive Bayes classifier, that train each other. Without the help of human in labeling the examples, the naive Bayes classifier of our system gives 100% precision and 98.89% recall of Thai Web pages tested in our experiments. This performance is competitive with those of supervised ones (S-Bayes and S-Word), which demonstrates the successful use of unlabeled data of our method. The performance is also better than that of U-Bayes-EM, which uses single classifier. The better performance of our method than U-Bayes-EM shows the effectiveness of interaction between two classifiers. Another advantage of our method over CoTraining and U-Bayes-EM is the ease of the initial parameter setting because our method is robust to the setting whereas CoTraining and U-Bayes-EM are more sensitive to the setting.

Despite simple model which uses only the threshold (θ_w) of $WordRatio$ for the word segmentation classifier and the character-unigram for the naive Bayes classifer, the high precision and recall are obtained. However, some Thai pages cannot be detected by this model. This is a limitation of the naive Bayes classifier of our current system. To improve the system, we are exploring more sophisticated models, e.g. a character or word n-gram model.

References

1. Apte, C., and Damerau, F. (1994) Automated learning of decision rules for text categorization. ACM TOIS 12(2):233-251.
2. Blum, A. and Mitchell, T. (1998) Combining labeled and unlabeled data with co-training. Proceeding of the Eleventh Annual Conference on Computational Learning Theory.
3. Cohen, W. W. and Singer, Y. (1999) Context-sensitive learning methods for text categorization. ACM Transactions on Information Systems, Vol. 17, No. 2, 141-173.
4. Dempster, A. P., Laird, N. M., and Rubin D. B. (1977) Maximum likelihood from incomplete data via the EM algorithm. Journal of the Royal Statistical Society, Series B, 39 (1), 1-38.
5. Joachims, T. (1998) Text categorization with support vector machines: Learning with many relevant features. Proceedings Tenth European Conference on Machine Learning, Springer Verlag.
6. Lewis, D. (1998) Naive (Bayes) at forty: The independence assumption in information retrieval. Proceedings of the Tenth European Conference on Machine Learning.
7. Meknavin, S., Charoenpornsawat, P. and Kijsirikul, B. (1997) Feature-based Thai word segmentation. Proceeding of Natural Language Processing Pacific Rim Symposium '97.
8. Mitchell, T. (1997) Machine Learning. pp. 180-184, McGraw-Hill. New York.
9. Nigam, K., McCallum, A., Thrun, S., and Mitchell, T. (2000) Text classification from labeled and unlabeled documents using EM. Machine Learning 39(2/3):103-134.
10. Yang, Y. (1999) An evaluation of statistical approaches to text categorization, Information Retrieval Journal.

Solving the Personal Computer Configuration Problems as Discrete Optimization Problems : A Preliminary Report

Vincent Tam and K.T. Ma

Department of Computer Science,
School of Computing, National University of Singapore,
Lower Kent Ridge Road, Singapore 119260
{vtam, makengte}@comp.nus.edu.sg

Abstract. Configuring personal computers (PCs) in a careful manner definitely represent difficult decision problems in which given the diversity of hardware components possible for each PC nowadays, and the limited compatibility between some hardware components, we are interested to obtain an (sub-)optimal configuration for each specific usage restricted to a budget limit and other possible criteria. In this paper, we firstly gave a formal definition of these PC configuration problems as discrete optimization problems. More importantly, we proposed a systematic and flexible framework for solving these difficult real-world discrete optimization problems. The major advantage of our proposed framework is that users can flexibly add in or modify their specific requirements at any time. To demonstrate the feasibility of our proposal, we built a prototype of an intelligent Personal Computer Configuration Advisor available on the Web to assist the general users in configuring their own PCs. Interestingly, our work opens up many new directions for future investigation including the improvement of our optimizer to handle more complicated users' requirements and the integration of other optimizers like the branch-and-bound method for comparison.

1 Introduction

Similar to many well-developed Asian countries like Hong Kong or Japan, Singapore, being a small country hardly with any natural resource, is moving very fast in the uses of Information Technology (IT) in many different sectors such as Education, Commerce, Government and Tourism for competitiveness. For example, there are many networked and touch-screen based workstations, namely the Kiosk Stations, providing on-line facilities to access the Singapore maps and some useful tourists' information, which are widely available on the major streets of tourists' spots in Singapore to promote Tourism. Accordingly, many people, due to the influence of the popular "Do-It-Yourself" (DIY) philosophy from western society, are keen in configuring and building their own personal computers (PC) to suit their own requirements, often as the first step to learn to use certain software or more importantly access the Internet.

Clearly, the PC configuration problems are world-wide decision problems faced by many people in which people are always interested to know the optimal, or possibly sub-optimal, PC configuration within their limited budget. However, since the PC technology nowadays are changing very quickly, the diversity of PC hardware components, such as the different types of processors, random-access memory (RAM) and the motherboards, and their limited compatibility between certain components due to the underlying proprietary manufacturers often complicates the whole decision problem, thus making it difficult to handle by the general public.

In fact, many configuration problems [2] as in the area of computer-aided design or manufacturing (CAD/CAM) [5] are well studied. In particular, there were some interesting research work [5] on formulating the machine configuration problems formally as discrete optimization problems, and then applying local search methods such as genetic algorithms [10,11] or simulated annealing [8,9] to handle these configuration problems successfully. The previous research experience reported in [5] already revealed that formulating the machine, or any general, configuration problems as constrained optimization problems (COPs) will definitely result in systematic handling of users' requirements as constraints or optimization criteria. At the same time, the users can flexibly add in or modify their requirements at any time to see the resulting configurations for planning or control [4].

Basically, a discrete constrained optimization problem involves a set Z of variables, each variable V_i ($\in Z$) with a finite domain D_i of discrete values, a set C of constraints on some subsets of variables limiting the combination of values assigned to those involved variables, and a set of objective functions f_j for minimization/maximization. The challenge is to find a globally optimal solution which minimizes/maximizes all the objective functions f_j while satisfying all the constraints in C. The discrete minimization problem can be formally specified as follow.

$$\min \sum_{j=1}^{m} f_j \quad \text{subject to} \quad \forall c \in C \quad cf(c) = 0$$

where m denotes the total number of objective functions in the problem, and $cf(c)$ is an arbitrary function which returns 0 when the specific constraint c is satisfied. Otherwise, it returns 1. Clearly, to solve maximization problems, we can simply negate all objective function f_j in the above formulation as $\min \sum_{j=1}^{m} -f_j$. In handling these optimization problems, which are always *NP-complete* [3], one of the frequently used heuristics is the branch-and-bound (B&B) heuristic [1,2] in which the exploration of any partial solution in a search tree will be abandoned immediately whenever the search cost of that partial solution, as represented by an arbitrary objective function, already exceeds the minimal cost for the optimal solution found so far. For instance, the B&B heuristic has been successfully applied to handle the famous traveling salesman problems [2,3] to guarantee the finding of the shortest path to transverse all the required cities in one round trip. However, in the worst cases, the B&B search method may still require exponential time to find out the optimal solution for any general COP. In general, many real-life PC configuration problems belong to those discrete COPs in which given the diversity of possible PC configurations as feasible solutions, the users will often accept a sub-optimal solution when the resulting configuration can be returned quickly from the optimizer.

Therefore, based on the discrete COP formulation, we proposed a flexible and systematic framework to handle the PC configuration problems in which most of the useful information about the PC hardware components is often stored in some database files locally in different computer companies. To demonstrate the feasibility of our proposed systematic framework, we firstly collected the actual data from some major computer shopping centers in Singapore to build our own centralized and local databases of PC components for investigation, and then used the widely available Practical Extraction and Report Language (PERL) [6, 7] Version 5.0 to implement the afore-mentioned preliminary search strategies to handle these practical PC configuration problems. The empirical experience of using our proposed approach to handle the PC configuration problems is fairly encouraging. Furthermore, the resulting optimizer is used to build a platform-independent prototype of the useful Web-based Personal Computer Configuration Advisor so as to facilitate the general users to quickly set up their required PC configurations. Obviously, our work opens up many new directions for future investigation such as improving our current optimizer to handle more complicated users' requirements, the integration of other optimizers such as the branch-and-bound heuristic search method [1,2] for evaluating the performance, and the possible uses of efficient learning algorithms such as the ID3 algorithm [1,2] to classify different user-defined configurations into useful examples to guide the search during optimization.

This paper is organised as follows. Section 2 describes the PC configuration problems as specific instances of discrete COPs, thus forming a systematic framework for optimizing choices of PC components to satisfy the users' requirement. In Section 3, we detail and justify our proposed search strategies to handle these specific COPs according to their unique problem structures. Section 4 provides the empirical evaluation of our cross-platform prototype implementation of the proposed optimizer in terms of efficiency and costs of the resulting configurations, with an example application of our optimizer to build a Web-based PC Configuration Advisor. Lastly, we conclude our work in Section 5.

2 PC Configuration Problems

Basically, the PC configuration problem is to select a configuration of personal computer hardware parts to build a complete system, taking into account the *compatibility* issues between the different hardware components. For instance, Intel Pentium II CPU should be attached to a Slot-1 Motherboard. Definitely, one of the most important optimization criteria in many real-life situation is *price*. Thus, a general formulation of the PC configuration problems as discrete COPs can be as follows.

$$\min \sum_{j=1}^{m} \text{cost}(Pj) \qquad \text{subject to} \qquad \forall comp(Pi, Pj) \in C$$

$$cf(comp(Pi, Pj)) = 0$$

in which cost(Pj) denotes the cost for the component Pj, C specifies all the compatible relations (constraints) between the components Pi and Pj, and the arbitrary function cf returns 0 when $comp(Pi, Pj)$ is evaluated as true. For example, when the variables for the CPU and motherboards are : P_{CPU} = "Intel PII CPU" and P_{MB} = "Slot-1 Motherboard" respectively, $comp(P_{CPU}, P_{MB})$ = true, then $cf(comp(P_{CPU}, P_{MB}))$ = 0. Clearly, given the above general COP formulation, it is flexible to add in or modify the users' requirements specified as constraints or optimization criteria. For instance, when new components P_X and P_Y are added into the PC market, it is easy to simply add a new constraint $comp(P_X, P_Y)$ into C to store their compatibility information.[1] Besides, for more complicated real-life cases, we can simply extend the minimization function to consider other important factors such as a weighting value for each component to reflect the users' preference.

2.1 Variables

The variables Pi's of interest for the PC configuration problem is the set of hardware components which will be assembled to build a working personal computer system. There are about 12 common variables usually involved in configuring a PC nowadays. The first three variables, namely CPU, Memory and MainBoard, of the table represent the most important variables which are often highly constrained. The remaining nine variables are totally un-constrained. Thus, this special relationship between the PC components depicts the unique problem structure of the PC configuration problem : the constraints between the first 3 variables will leave very few combinations of options to be matched against a possibly large number of possible choices in a later stage of the search. It should be noted that this large possibility occurred in the later search stage may pose major difficulty to most optimizers such the branch-and-bound techniques since no other available information can be used to prune off any value during the search.

---

[1] Clearly, some readers may argue that these compatibility constraints are in fact no different from the logical relations like "father(john, mary)" to specify "john" is the father of "mary" in some logic programs. Of course, we would agree on that since it is generally true for most constraints. However, the "encapsulation" of these general relations between objects as a specific constraint will in general provide *a more systematic way* to handle that particular kind of constraints. As a result, we will discuss how a special-purpose search algorithm (as constraint solver) can be designed to handle those compatibility constraints *more efficiently* for our PC configuration problems in the next section.

2.2 Domain

The average domain size for the first three highly constrained variables is about 52 while the average domain size for the remaining un-constrained variables is also 52, thus making the average domain size for all the variables is definitely 52. The size of the search space for all possible combinations of PC components is roughly of the order of 52^{12}. More importantly, this huge search space has lots of possible sub-trees which cannot be further pruned off by any heuristic. Accordingly, the conventional enumerative search [4] may simply give unsatisfactory performance to return the globally optimal PC configuration. Therefore, in the next section, we will discuss our proposed search strategy which sacrifices global optimality for efficiency to tackle these real-life COPs.

It should be noted that these PC, or possibly other, configuration problems are very much different from some famous routing problems such as the traveling salesman problem, on which the branch-and-bound (B&B) strategy performs reasonably well, in terms of the underlying domains for each variable. For a traveling salesman problem with *12* cities, the underlying domains for all the variables $V_1..V_{12}$, denoting the first to the last city to be visited on a trip, are the same. That is the range [1..12] to represent the **same** *12* cities. Thus, at each search step, we can use the B&B heuristic to prune off any alternative route starting and ending with the same cities, say "city 1 - .....- city 9", but with a higher total distance covered. However, in our PC configuration problems, the possible choices at each search step will be totally different from the previous choices already occurred in the previous search steps. Thus, the B&B heuristic may not necessarily be a useful heuristic in solving the PC configuration problems.

2.3 Constraints

The following list shows some example of the constraints frequently occurred in the PC configuration problems. The first one specifies that the total cost of the configuration must be less than or equal to the budget predefined by the user. The second and third constraints are obviously about the *CPU, Memory* and *MainBoard*. The second one states that the type of the *CPU* must match with the type of the *MainBoard* while the last one specifies that the speed of the *MainBoard* and the *Memory* must be the same.

- TotalPrice <= Budget
- CPU.Type = Mainboard.Type
- Mainboard.Bus_Speed = Memory.Bus_Speed

Clearly, it is straightforward to add in more constraints as users' new requirements. As in most PC configurations, the cost and performance are definitely two major factors for consideration. However, depending on the different types of computer programs to be used by individuals, the machine performance requirement for different users are relative and often subjective measures although there are lots of performance measurement figures published by various PC vendors for advertisement.

For instance, a general user who needs only word-processor to be run on his/her PC tends to consider a PC configuration with 'average' performance. But defining 'average' performance as a hard constraint for a particular application can readily be a tough question. Thus, to have more flexibility, we simply allow the users to express their performance requirements on the ultimate PC configurations possibly as some combined factors of users' preference or rating in the optimisation criteria rather than as hard constraints.

3 Our Proposed Framework and Search Strategies

In this section, we will firstly look into a systematic framework for integrating different optimizers to handle the PC configuration problems based on the formulation of discrete optimization problems which we discussed in the previous section. Figure 1 shows our proposed systematic framework for integration of different optimizers.

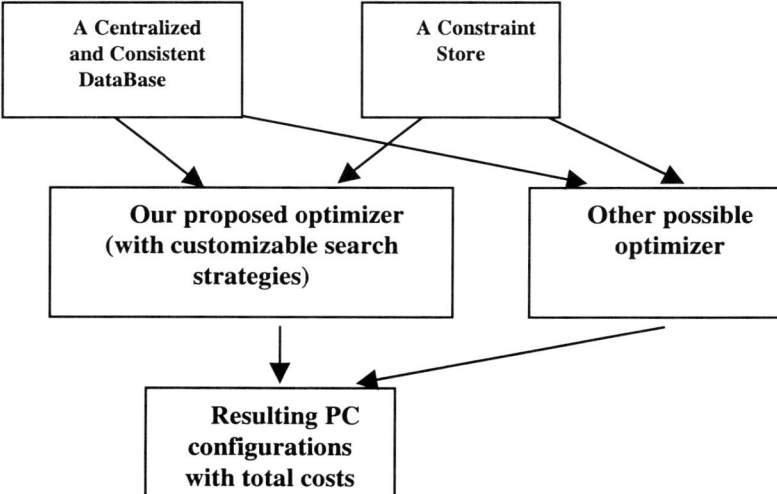

Fig. 1. Our Proposed Systematic Framework for Optimizing PC Configurations

It should be noted that in our systematic framework for constrained optimization to handle the PC configuration problems, we assume our search and optimization process have to performed on a set of consistent data from a centralized database system. In addition, there is a constraint store to provide useful information about the users' requirements as a collection of constraints. Based on these useful information, our optimizer with customizable search strategies will return a set of (sub-)optimal PC configurations with their total costs to the users according to the predefined optimization criteria. Clearly, other possible optimizers can also be added into our framework as some intelligent plug-in components for better efficiency or handling more complicated optimization criteria.

In the following, we will discuss our proposed optimizer with customizable search strategies which may not guarantee to always return the PC configuration with the globally minimal cost. However, as opposed to enumerative search, our proposal will definitely be more efficient. Table 3 shows the two main factors we used to control the search, together short descriptions to explain their roles. Both control parameters are predefined by the user of the search strategies.

Table 1. Our Control Factors to Search for (Sub-)Optimal PC Configuration

Control	*Short Descriptions*
Budget	The budget for the whole personal computer system. Total prices of the components are not allowed to exceed the budget.
Threshold	Number of the best partial solutions to be considered in each search step

Similar to the B&B heuristic, the predefined control parameter *Budget* will be used to filter out any partial configuration which already exceeds its allowed value. In addition, the *Threshold* value n will help to ensure the search will always return the best n partial configurations after sorting all possible partial configurations against their total prices at each search step. Based on these two strategies, we designed an optimizer to solve these PC configuration problems as follows.

1. Retrieve and sort the values for the current variable by price.

2. Find the next **matching** value of the variable in the sorted value queue. Check that all the constraints are satisfied for this value. This includes the budget constraint (that is *Total_price* <= *Budget*).

3. If no constraint is violated, goto 6.

4. Else if queue is not empty, repeat 2. Else Fail.

5. Set the current solution set to include this value.

6. If number of partial solutions < threshold, repeat 2. Else 7

7. If variable queue is not empty, proceed to set current variable to next variable in the queue. Repeat 1.

8. If number of solutions > 0 then report Solved. Else report Failure.

It should be noted that our work is related to the 'beam search' method. In Section 4, we will give an empirical evaluation of the above proposed optimizer to solve the actual PC configuration problems with different control parameter settings for experimentation.

4 Empirical Evaluation

Based on the above algorithm for our proposed optimizer, we built a prototype in PERL Version 5.0 since we planed to integrate our optimizer to build a Web-based PC Configuration Advisor to facilitate the general users to configure their own PC. To evaluate the performance of our prototype for the proposed optimizer to handle the PC configuration problems, we focused on two main aspects of the computational results returned by our optimizer in the following analysis. The first important factor to consider is the quality of the solution in term of the total costs of the PC configurations for minimization. The second factor of interest is the efficiency of our optimizer as reflected by the timings in CPU seconds. Accordingly, we run our prototype 10 times for different settings of threshold values on a DEC-Alpha workstation running Digital Unix Version 4.0.8.

The table below shows a sorted listing of the total costs of the different PC configurations, labeled from 01 to 30, returned by our optimizer for *Budget <= $3000* and *Threshold = 30*.

Cfg	Cost	Cfg	Cost	Cfg	Cost	Cfg	Cost	Cfg	Cost
01	753	07	757	13	763	19	765	25	766
02	755	08	759	14	763	20	765	26	767
03	755	09	760	15	763	21	765	27	767
04	755	10	762	16	764	22	765	28	768
05	757	11	762	17	764	23	765	29	769
06	757	12	763	18	764	24	766	30	769

Clearly, there is a fair difference of SG $16 between the first minimal total cost and the last total cost of the configuration 30 as shown in the above table. In addition, it should be noted that from our initial experiments, the top 10 configuration-cost pairs usually remain unchanged for the same budget limit even though we changed the threshold value from 30 to 20 and then to 10. This demonstrated the stable performance of our optimizer in handling these PC configuration problems.

Table 4 shows the performance of our optimizer for handling the PC configuration problems with *Budget <= $3000* and varying the *Threshold* value at *1, 5, 10, 20* and *30*. For each case, the reported data is the average CPU time in seconds over *10* runs.

Table 2. Performance of our Optimizer for Different Threshold Values

Threshold	Average CPU time in seconds (10 runs)
1	3.18
5	3.19
10	3.32
20	3.40
30	3.51

The above table clearly showed that our optimizer is fairly efficient in handling a typical PC configuration problem with different threshold values to control the search. Also, the performance of our optimizer is compact and stable since there is only slight increase in the average CPU time from 3.18 to 3.51 seconds when the corresponding threshold value is changed from *1* to *30*.

Since the performance of our proposed optimizer from the initial experiments is satisfactory, we integrated our optimizer as a plug-in component into our targeted Web-based PC Configuration Advisor for optimizing different PC configurations according to users' budget as shown in Figure 2.

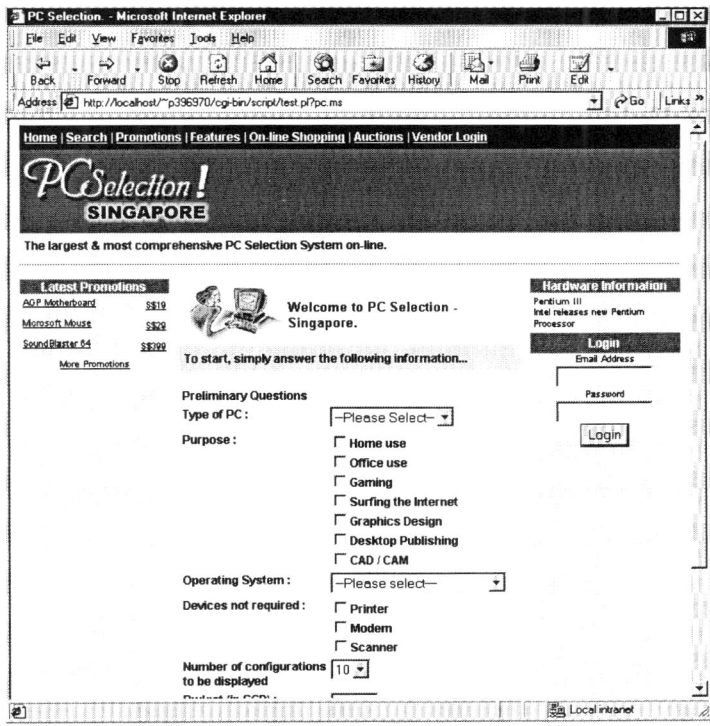

Fig. 2. Our PC Configuration Advisor

Firstly, our Web-based PC Configuration Advisor supports rule-based information processing to actively anticipate or validate users' inputs, and also analyze hardware information stored in databases to provide useful advice on the best PC configurations for certain usage subject to a user-defined budget limit, and a pre-defined threshold limit used during the search. Specially, we allow the active uses of rules, as stated in the rule script to represent some domain experts' knowledge, to "dynamically" prune off options within the same page (intra-page) or between the pages (inter-page). For example, when the user selects the "Type of PC" to be configured is "Server" on the first page, the option of "17-inch monitor" will be automatically removed in the last page[2] with the active use of the domain experts' rules. Besides ensuring valid inputs from the users, it is mainly used to remove irrelevant choices so as to facilitate the search efficiency. After all possible pruning, our proposed optimizer, implemented as a easy-to-modify plug-in component inside our PC Configuration Advisor, then performs the controlled (*best-n*) search according to the predefined budget limit and threshold values during optimization of PC configurations. Thus, for a user's requirement like *budget ≤ 3000 and threshold = 20,* our Web-based PC Configuration Advisor will definitely return only the first *20* optimal PC configurations with the total cost less than $*3000*. In case where no PC configuration can meet the specified budget, an error message will be printed on the resulting Web page.

5 Conclusion

It is undeniable that the PC configuration problems are both practical and interesting optimization problems widely occurring in many well-developed countries of the world. However, specific configuration problems are interesting since they have the unique problem structures that some components are highly constrained while the rest are totally unconstrained. This may pose challenge to some conventional enumerative search methods. As the PC technology is likely to be more complicated in the future, it will definitely become more difficult to handle these specific configuration problems. In this paper, we gave a formal definition of the PC configuration problems as discrete optimization problems. Based on this problem formulation, we proposed a systematic framework which allows the integration of different optimizers for optimizing the PC configurations according to the useful information stored in a centralized database and constraint store. More importantly, after analyzing the unique features of the PC configuration problems which may possibly lead to combinatorial explosion during the search, we proposed two useful search strategies to control the search and optimization process in our optimizer. To demonstrate the feasibility of our proposal, we implemented a prototype of our proposed optimizer for some empirical evaluation, and later integrated it into a Web-based PC Configuration Advisor to facilitate the general public in configuring their own PCs.

---

[2] Technically, this special feature is achieved with JavaScript through the uses of cookies to remember some important values for each page.

Clearly, there are several interesting directions for our future investigation. One obvious direction is to try our optimizer on many different cases, and also include other optimizers such as the B&B method for a complete comparison. Second, it would be interesting to improve our optimizer to handle more complicated constraints and optimization criteria to handle more complex real-life PC, or other general, configuration problems. Lastly, we are currently studying the possible uses of efficient learning algorithms such as the ID3 algorithm [2] to classify different user-defined configurations into useful examples so as to guide the search during the optimization process.

Acknowledgement

We are grateful to Mr. W.K. Foo for fruitful discussion and help in implementing the optimizer. Also, we would like to acknowledge the ARF grant (ref. no. RP3991612) supported by the National University of Singapore.

References

[1] "Artificial Intelligence : A Knowledge-Based Approach" by Morris W. Firebaugh, PWS-Kent Publishing Company, Boston, 1988.
[2] "Artificial Intelligence" by Elaine Rich and Kevin Knight, McGraw-Hill International Edition, 1991.
[3] "Discrete Mathematics – A Unified Approach" by Stephen A. Wiitala, McGraw-Hill International Edition, 1987.
[4] "Foundations of Constraint Satisfaction" by Edward Tsang, Academic Press, 1993.
[5] "Genetic algorithms versus simulated annealing : Satisfaction of large sets of algebraic mechanical design constraints" by A.C. Thornton, in *Proceedings of Artificial Intelligence in Design,* pp. 381-398, 1994.
[6] "Discover PERL 5" by Naba Barkakati, IDG Books WorldWide Inc., 1997.
[7] "Programming in PERL" by Larry Wall, O'Reilly, 1995.
[8] "Boltzmann machines for traveling salesman problems" by E. Aarts and J. Korst, *European Journal of Operational Research*, 39:79-95, 1989.
[9] "Optimization by simulated annealing : an experimental evaluation; Part II, graph coloring and number partitioning" by D. Johnson, C. Aragon, L. McGeoch, and C. Schevon. Operations Research, 39(3)378-406, 1991.
[10] "Solving small and large scale constraint satisfaction problems using a heuristic-based microgenetic algorithm" by G.Dozier, J. Bowen and D. Bahler. *In Proceedings of the IEEE International Conference on Evolutionary Computation,* 1994.
[11] "Improving Evolutionary Algorithms for Efficient Constraint Satisfaction" by Vincent Tam and Peter Stuckey, *International Journal on Artificial Intelligence Tools*, Vol. 8, No. 2, World Scientific Publishers, December 1999.

Improved Efficiency of Oil Well Drilling through Case Based Reasoning

Paal Skalle[1], Jostein Sveen[2], and Agnar Aamodt[3],

[1] Norwegian University of Science and Technology, Dept. of Petroleum Technology,
N-7491, Trondheim, Norway
pskalle@ipt.ntnu.no

[2] SINTEF, Dept. of Safety and Reliability
N-7465, Trondheim, Norway
jsveen@indman.sintef.no

[3] Norwegian University of Science and Technology, Dept. of Computer and Information Science
N-7491, Trondheim, Norway
agnar.aamodt@idt.ntnu.no

Abstract. A system that applies a method of knowledge-intensive case-based reasoning, for repair and prevention of unwanted events in the domain of offshore oil well drilling, has been developed in cooperation with an oil company. From several reoccurring problems during oil well drilling the problem of "lost circulation", i.e. loss of circulating drilling fluid into the geological formation was picked out as a pilot problem. An extensive general knowledge model was developed for the domain of oil well drilling. About fifty different cases were created on the basis of information from one North Sea operator. When the completed CBR-system was tested against a new case, five cases with descending similarity were selected by the tool. In an informal evaluation, the two best fitting cases proved to give the operator valuable advise on how to go about solving the new case.

1 Introduction

Drilling of oil wells is an expensive operation, costing around 150 000 US $ pr. day, and any loss of time caused by unwanted events is costly. Some unwanted events are repeatedly occurring but still so complex that they are not easily solved. The necessary experience obtained by individuals or by the organization is difficult to transfer efficiently to those that need it. Lost circulation during oil well drilling is an unwanted event characterized by not obtaining any or part of the drilling fluid (also called mud) back to the rig in spite of a running mud pump.

The failure type may be sub-divided into four categories, related to possible fractures or other undesired properties of the geological formation: Induced fractures; natural fractures, cavernous formation and permeable formation. The strengthe of the sedimentary formation is surpassed due to an unfortunate combination of operational events. The problem occurs on an average base once every well drilled, and may last for less than an hour, but sometimes it takes 14 days to solve it. It is too complex a problem to predict or solve by means of a mathematical simulator. The many necessary simplifying constraints would make the simulator unrealistic.

The necessary experience to deal with the problem may not be available at the time of occurrence; the "expert" may not be available, written experience is usually partial or scattered, or the problem is too delicate to select the optimal procedure based on on-site available experience. A promising approach in such situations is case based reasoning, an approach which is designed to mime a human being's typical way of reasoning when solving a new problem; searching through a "bank" of previous experience. A similar, previous experiences is a good initial approach to solving the problem.

The trend in case-based reasoning methods for complex decision support is currently towards data-centered approaches, in which a case often is viewed as a data base record (or data table). Case matching is based on a rather simple, syntax-based similarity metric – typically combining the number of common attributes with attribute weights. In contrast, we advocate a more knowledge-intensive and user-centered CBR approach, in which a case is a user experience, and where case matching is based on semantic criteria by using a body of general domain knowledge as explanatory support in the matching process. Different attributes may then match by being related in the general model.

2 State of the Art

2.1 CBR-Application on Diagnosis and Repair

Case-based approaches to problem solving and learning have been taken in a variety of diagnosis and repair applications. Along with help desk applications, successful fielded applications of this kind have been extensively reported over the last years [1, 2, 3]. However, the CBR approach has still to be seriously applied in the petroleum engineering field. A first approach has been observed in the field of drilling [4], but only at the conceptual and design levels. The current system is a continuation of that research into an implemented experimental system.

2.2 Data Support Methods During Oil Well Drilling

Several oil companies (Milheim-99) recognize the need to retain and centralize the knowledge and experience of the organization, often as a reaction against outsourcing and spreading of knowledge during the early 1990's. Milheim [5] presentes a heuristic simulation approach to the domain Drilling of Oil Wells, developed around data sets of 22 actual wells. The accumulated data are treated statistically and fitted to a model based on combining human thought, artificial intelligence and heuristic problem solving. The model will adopt to a specific geological area, and capture experience, reuse it and gradually improve and learn. They encompass and model the complete process, not primarily repetitive cases. Their approach is more ambisious but less focused than ours.

The Well Learning System (WLS) [6] is a simple, yet very efficient mechanism for organizational learning. A multi-diciplined team involved in planning or execution of the drilling plan is lead through a process including exposure to 30 templates, a process which manage company policies, standards, up-to-date engineering software finally ending up with all the necessary final reports. This system has been successfully tested by several oil companies. We are now discussing an extension of WLS by including CBR capabilities to provide more active advice and guidance.

The GeoFrame database built in a POSC standard data format or data model allows information to be shared between applications from many disciplines. Drilling engineers and geologists can share critical information while planning and monitoring a well. A data browser filters the information so that only data relevant to the e.g. drilling engineer is presented by default, and made suitable for different applications. The work of McCann [7] is thus limited to databases and their logistics

2.3 Engineering Solution to Lost Circulation

Different types of formation fractures are treated differently. A recent advancement [8] involves utilization of the combined knowledge of fracture size (obtained through downhole pressure recorder) and maintenance of the desired sealing material particle-size-distribution (special equipment is necessary).

Other advancements include fracture width determination on the basis of mud loss history [9], liner drilling through different zones [10], new mud and cement technology for drilling through salt domes [11].

New engineering technology will gradually expand and improve methods of solving the problem. This is implicitly taken into account in our system, described below, through retaining new cases as they are (attempted to) being solved.

3 Knowledge-Intensive Case Based Reasoning

The objective of this paper is to describe the two important aspects our knowledge-intensive CBR process, and described how they are combined in our system for drilling operations assistance. The CBR-method applied is properly documented elsewhere [12], [13] and summarized below through the following steps;
  a) Gather data
  b) Detect a possibly approaching problem
  c) Decide if gathered data are sufficient to define the situation as a new problem. If not;
  d) Perform additional examinations (i.e. check loss rate, check circ. pressure etc.).
  e) Search the case base for similar past cases.
  f) Generate a set of the most likely hypothesis and present a set of possible solutions in descending order to the current problem.
  g) Use general domain knowledge to provide explanatory support for each plausible hypothesis, and refine the hypothesis list.
  h) Interact with user to select the best hypothesis. Generate a detailed "to-do" list.
  i) After the case has been solved, the case base can be updated based on the situation just experienced.

The two aspects we will focus on in the following are the two core components of knowledge-intensive CBR:
- The general domain knowledge model
- The case model

3.1 General Domain Knowledge

The role of the general domain knowledge is to provide explanations for supporting the CBR process. The support is threefold: First, it enables the searching for past cases to be based on semantic rather than pure syntactic criteria, by using general knowledge to explain the similarity of two apparently different parameters. Second, its4 can explain how a past solution can be adapted to solve a new problem, and third, it can be used to explain what to retain in the case base from a case just solved (i.e. the machine learning part of the CBR process).

The domain knowledge describing the oil well drilling domain is organized in a general model containing concepts interrelated by a set of different relations, and situation-specific case knowledge. Below, the four main components knowledge of general knowledge are summarized: Domain objects, Relations, Tasks, and Cases.

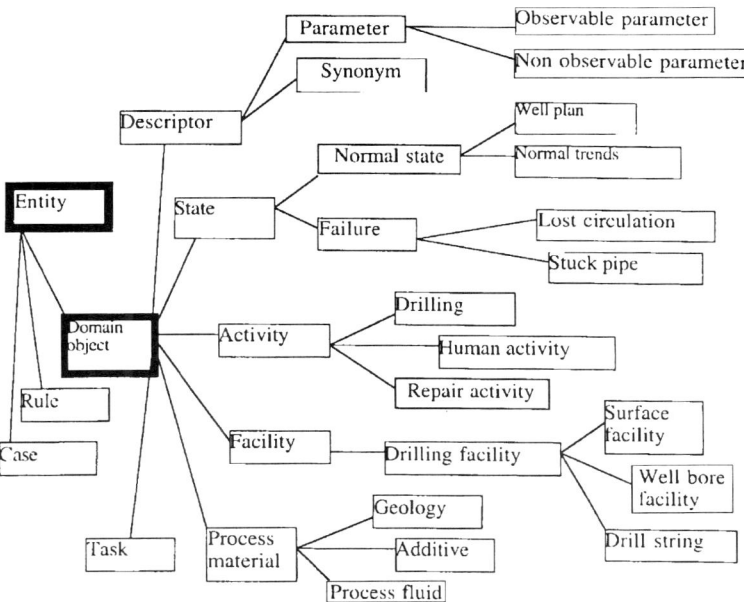

Fig. 1. Upper level structural model of the drilling domain. Cases and the drilling domain object are subclasses of Entity:

3.2 Domain Objects

All domain concepts are defined in a frame-based representation formalism. Each domain term is defined in its own frame. The representation may equally well be viewed as a densely linked semantic network, where a node represents a frame and the links represents slots. One of the relations is the "has-subclass" relation, and the upper level of the subclass hierarchy is shown in Figure 1.

As seen in the figure, a domain object can be described by one or more of six object types;
- Descriptor (recordable and non observable variables)
- State (the state at time of failure)
- Activity (within the drilling domain)
- Facility (equipment necessary to perform activity)
- Process material (involved in activity)
- Tasks (of operational problem solving and human learning)

In Figure 2 "Operation parameter", a subclass of "Observable parameter" is selected to exemplify further sub-classification. The knowledge base contain about 1500concepts interlinked by approximately 40 different relation types.

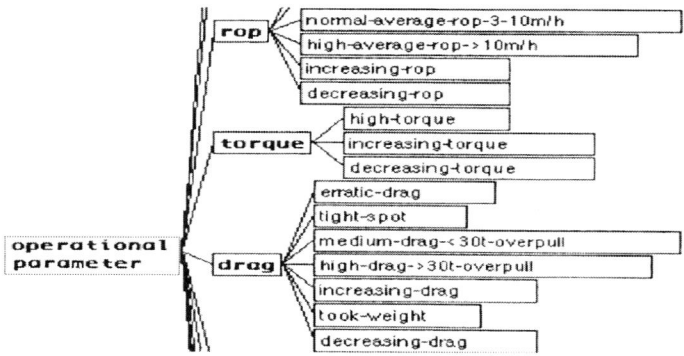

Fig. 2. Sub classification of operational parameter. Transformation from qualitative (high-drag) to quantitative value (>30t-overpull) is shown.

3.3 Relations

Attributes or parameters in the knowledge model are interconnected through structural relationships (has subclass, has part, has instance, has value), causal and other kinds of influence relations. Properties are inherited along the relation lines. The parameters, i.e. the outmost "leaves" on all "branches" in the class hierarchy, are inter-linked through the following relationships (where a relation's explanatory strength is shown in parenthesis):

Structural (1.00)
Causes (0.90)
Leads to (0.85
Enables (0.80)

Implies (0.70)
Involves (0.65)
Indicate (0.60)
Describes (0.55)

Influences (0.75) Occurs-in (0.50) Relations always have an inverse relation, e.g. "caused-by". In addition to numerical values a quantifier/modifier can be introduced to each relation (multiplication weight shown in parenthesis): always/strongly (1.1), typically (0.95=default), sometimes/moderately (0.7), or seldom/weakly (0.3).

A few examples from the Relationship list are:

```
HIGH-MUD-FILTER-LOSS INSTANCE-OF MUD-FILTER-LOSS
HIGH-MUD-FILTER-LOSS ENABLES CLOGGED-BHA
HIGH-MUD-GAS-CONTENT CAUSES LOW-DOWNHOLE-MUD-VISCOSITY
HIGH-PUMP-RATE CAUSES HIGH-PUMP-PRESSURE
```

An important notion in identifying a failure mode is the notion of an non-observable parameter state, i.e. a system condition that is not directly describable by measured parameters (or findings) at the surface, but usually related to other conditions in the open hole. The model links non-observable parameters (like "clogged-bha", "sagging-tendency", and "turbulent-flow-regime") to observable ones.

3.4 Tasks

In order to reach a goal the task has to be specified. Such tasks may be:
- Solve problem (stuck pipe, lost circulation, tool failure etc.)
- Plan drilling operation (in such a way that problems are avoided or minimized)
- Learn (learn from previous mistakes, learn about the knowledge model etc.)

The challenge is first of all to solve the problem. To enable solving by means of Case Based Reasoning the following task breakdown for lost circulation has been defined, partly based on Darley & Gray & Roger [14] and shown in Figure 3.

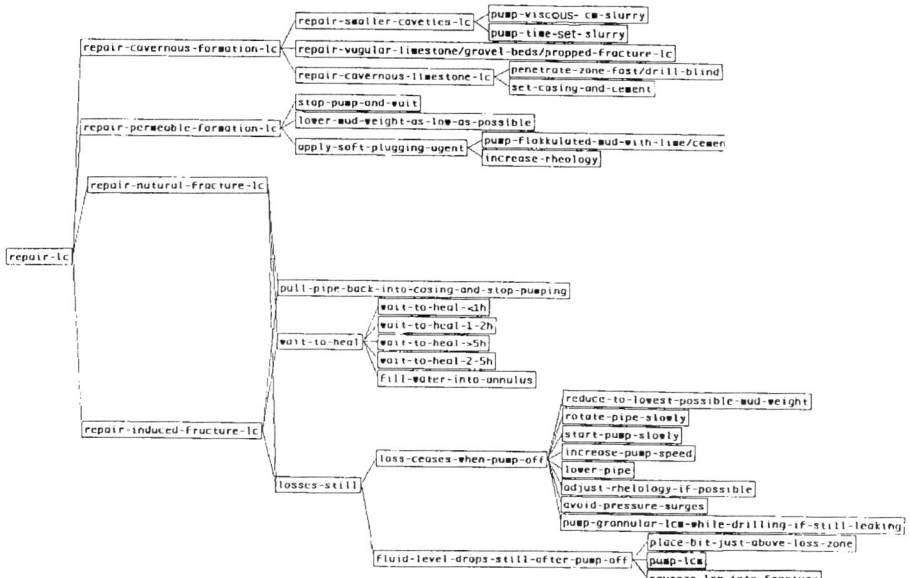

Fig. 3. The task "Repair Lost Circulation".

3.5 Cases

The case base contains all the problems of "lost circulation" experienced by a major North Sea drilling operator, a total of 43 cases. In Table 1 the structure of a new and its completed case is presented.

4 Case Matching Routine

Within a completed case an expert will evaluate the importance of each attribute in case substructure 2 and 3 (see Table 1), and esignate a proper level of relevance. Four levels were chosen;
 1; Sufficient, 2; Strongly indicative, 3; Indicative, 4; Spurious

Table 1. Case structure with a simplified content. Above the dashed line is an example of a new, unsolved case. The case information below the line, where the final result (outcome) of the solution path has been verified complete the case.

		Case structure	Case example
New case	1.	**Characteristics:** Place/date/Owner	34/07-P22/11.07.1994, 2203/ Saga Petroleum
	2.	**Observed parameters:** Activity Drilling fluid Leak off margin Initial loss	drilling Novaplus small (0.02 – 0.05 kg/l) complete
	3.	**Solution path:**	Pooh some stands ran pump at low rate small losses
Solved case			pooh-to-casing-shoe waited>2h increases-pump-rate-stepwise
	4.	**Outcome:** (Success ratio)	New lost.circ. incident after 500m drilling. (0.5)
	5.	**Explanation**	Since induced fracture may be caused by ECD, enabled by narrow ann. and very high YP which..
	6.	**Operators experience and lessons learned:**	Upper section was drilled with average. In WBM losses are cured fast and we know intuitively .....

4.1 Results and Example Run

As a part of the evaluation of the system it was decided to enter a new completely case (referred to as case 50), a lost circulation incident which occurred on April 1999 in well 34/7-P-20. Hence, this case had already been solved and was used as a test case against the system. The result of this test was analyzed and discussed with the user. By showing this example only, we also indicate that our evaluation regime has been of a qualitative rather than quantitative nature.

We entered a set of attributes describing the new lost circulation situation of case 50. Parts of the input window are shown in Figure 4.

Entering the attributes of case 50 was straight forward since acceptable attribute values are obtainable from drop down menus in the user interface for every new relation. After entering case 50 and pressing the "Return Cases" button, the CBR-tool returned the following list of similar cases, provided with matching degree as shown below.

Case number:	Matching degree:
16	0.70
21	0.43
12	0.38
06	0.27
02	0.22

Fig. 4. Entering lost circulation attributes of well 34/7-P-20, case 50

The content of the best matching case (case 16) is presented in Figure 5.

The suggestions presented in Figure 5 on why the problem occurred (has-operators-explanation, has-lessons-learned) and what solution were applied (has-repair-activity, has-outcome) in those two previous cases are highly relevant and indicative for the new case 50. In the actual situation the operator treated case 50 as follows:
- Numerous-lcm-pills-pumped and squeezed. Resulting in:
- Long-lc-repair-time (15 h)
- Very-large-final-pit-loss (100 m^3)

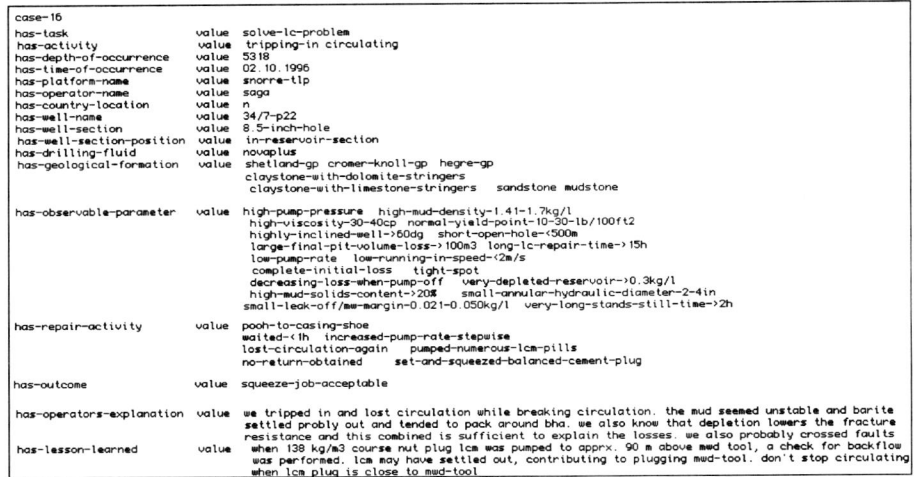

Fig. 5. The best matching case(case 16) of a new case (case 50)

Not surprisingly this is actually what happened in case 16 also. From the Has-repair-activity and Has-outcome in Figure 5 we see that the operator struggled at length and finally had to set a balanced cement plug and squeeze in order to stabilize the well. If given access to this CBR-tool and the findings in case 16, 21 and 12, case 50 could have been handled much better. In all three cases pseudo oil based mud were applied and the repair time was extensively long (> 15 h). In case 16 and 21 a lot of specifics on how to or especially not how to cure this very specific type of losses are stored. Both these experiences could have been applied to solve the losses in case 50 more efficiently.

4.2 Discussion

In this first version of a CBR-tool for support in the drilling operation, it is room for many improvements;
  The domain model and the cases are only as good as the data allow. An important improvement is to expand the basis for data input to the model and the cases by adding time-based mud logging data (today the tool only supports depth-based mud logging data). Time-based mud logging data is an integral part when trying to diagnose a lost circulation case.
  Three-parameter relationships are not included in the tool, an approach that will enhance the explanatory capability.
  Retrieved cases are lacking several qualities;

- Specify in detail type of fault (from sub class tree)
- Specify the relationship sequences applied in the matching process. This information which also includes non-observable-parameter will help explain and reveal the causes of the problem.

The present tool has the ability to suggest optimal solutions to occurred problems. The ability to predict and thus suggest preventive measures is more challenging and potentially more prosperous. It will require a "dynamic" CBR tool, where time dependent data and trend analysis must be combined with experience on dynamic changes.

Although the case base contains 43 cases, this is relatively small amount. Few successful cases are yet available. As more cases are stored, improved matching will be achieved, the tool's capability will improve with time.

5 Conclusion

1. Lost circulation is one example out of many of repetitive problems during oil well drilling. The time loss in handling lost circulation problems are costly (offshore operation costs world wide are around 150 000 US$ pr. day).
2. A CBR-tool has been developed with the aim of incorporating the ability to evaluate complex and ever repeating problems. As an integrated part of the tool a comprehensive model of the drilling domain has been designed and all attributes have been inter-related with relations of varying strength.
3. A pilot version of the tool has been tested on a new problem (a problem not previously shored in the case base) and provided useful knowledge such as cause factors and remedial actions.
4. The CBR-tool is in its "childhood", and its potential as a supporting tool is large.

Acknowledgement

The authors would like to thank Jon Carlsen, Trond Gravem and Jan Ledsaak, at that time in the Norwegian oil company Saga Petroleum, Stavanger, for their support and contribution.

References

1. Allen, B.R.: Case-based reasoning: Business applications. Communication of the ACM, 37 (3) (1994) 40-44
2. Auriol, 1999
3. Manago, 1998
4. Skalle, P., Aamodt, A. and Sveen, J.: Case-based reasoning, a method for gaining experience and giving advice on how to avoid and how to free stuck drill strings. Proc.., IADC Middle East Drilling Conference, Dubai (3. & 4. of Nov. 1998) 13 pp
5. Milheim, K.K. and Gaebler, T.: Virtual experience simulation for drilling – the concept. Paper SPE 52803 presented at SPE/IADC Drilling Conf., Amsterdam (9-11 March, 1999) 317-328

6. Minton, Jr. R.C. and Vik, R.: The Well Learning System – The evolution of a tool into a modern management system for drilling operations. Paper SPE 49112 presented at the 1998 SPE Ann. Tech. Conf. and Exhib., New Orleans (27-30 Sept., 1998) 525-534
7. McCann, 1998
8. Rojas, C.C., Fitzgerald, B.L., Modi, S. And Bzant, P.N.: Minimizing downhole mud losses. Paper SPE 39398 presented at the IADC/SPE Drilling Conf., Dallas (03-06 March, 1998) 871-877
9. Lietard, O., Ulvin, T., Guillot, D.J. and Hodder, M.H.: Fracture with logging while drilling and drilling mud/loss-circulation-material selection guidelines in naturally fractured reservoirs. SPE Drilling & Completion, 14(3), (Sept., 1999) 168-177
10. Sinor, L.A., Tyberø, P. and Eide,O.: Rotary liner drilling for depleted reservoirs. Paper SPE 39399, presented at the 1998 IADC/SPE Drilling Conf., Dallas (03-06-March, 1998) 879-890
11. Sweatman, R., Faul, R. and Ballow, C.: New solutions for subsalt-well lost circulation and optimized primary cementing. Paper SPE 56499, presented at the 1999 SPE Ann Tech. Conf. and Exhib., Houston (03-06 Oct., 1999) 157-167
12. Aamodt, A.: Explanation – driven-case-based reasoning. Published in Topics in case-based reasoning, edited by S. Wess et al., Springer Verlag, Berlin Heidelberg New York (1994) 274-288
13. Aamodt, A and Plaza, E.: Case-based reasoning: Foundation issues, methodological variation, and system approaches. AICOM, Vol. 7, no. 1 (Mar. 1994) 39-59
14. Darley, C.C., Rogers, A.F. and Gray, C.C.: Composition and function of drilling fluids. 4 the ed. Gulf Publishing Co., 4 th edition, Houston (1988)

Functional Understanding
Based on an Ontology of Functional Concepts

Yoshinobu Kitamura, Toshinobu Sano and Riichiro Mizoguchi

The Institute of Scientific and Industrial Research, Osaka University,
8-1, Mihogaoka, Ibaraki, Osaka 567-0047, Japan
{kita,sanop,miz}@ei.sanken.osaka-u.ac.jp

Abstract. This article discusses automatic identifications of functional structures of artifacts from given behavioral models of components and their connection information (called functional understanding). We propose an ontology of functional concepts which provides a rich vocabulary representing functions together with clear definitions grounded on behavior. The ontology enables the understanding system to limit the search space at functional level and to screen out meaningless interpretations. Furthermore, the ontology includes a new category of functional concepts named meta-function representing conceptual categories of relationship between functions. It plays a crucial role in consolidation of functions to give criteria of grouping functions, that is, identity of consolidated functions. It enables the understanding system to generate such functional hierarchies that do not correspond to physical structure.

1. Introduction

Functionality of artifacts represents a part of the design rationale, while structure and behavior do not show it [1,2]. Thus, a lot of research has been carried out on functional representation of artifacts such as [3,4,5,6,7,8]. A functional structure of an artifact generally consists of functions of components and a whole-part (aggregation) hierarchy of functions which correspond to a function of the whole system or those of subsystems [5,9]. It is essential for redesign of an existing artifact to understand its functional structure in order to consider the intention of the original design [9,10]. Moreover, the functional hierarchy is useful to diagnose artifacts efficiently [11,12].

Our goal here is to identify functional structures automatically from given behavioral models of components and their connection information, called *functional understanding task*. We focus on two problems here. One is how to limit the search space at the functional level, because human uses a large number of verbs representing functions (we call them *functional concepts*) without their operational definitions as discussed in Value Engineering research [13,14]. Nevertheless, almost all of functional models such as those in [1,4,6] are specific to the target system, and thus only a few generic functional concepts have been proposed [5,7,9]. We need a rich vocabulary of functional concepts with operational definitions in order to limit the search space and give constraints on the functional structures.

The other problem is identity of functions in the functional hierarchy. As pointed out in [5,15], the identity of the component from the viewpoint of function in the functional hierarchies is different from that from the structural (or topological) viewpoint. Then, when the understanding system consolidates (aggregates) functions of components into a super-function and then generates a functional hierarchy, the identification of functional groups of the given structural components is one of the crucial issues. Nevertheless, although functions of components [3,4,5,7] and causal relations among components at behavioral level [6,7] have been investigated, little is known concerning the relationship between functions. This is one of the reasons why the conventional functional understanding systems [3,12,15,16] generate such functional hierarchies that correspond to structure and topology. We need sophisticated conceptualization (categories) at the functional level of causal relations in order to give criteria for grouping functions and identity of consolidated functions in functional hierarchy.

We have been tackling these issues on the basis of Ontological Engineering [17], aiming at explicit specification of conceptualization of functional concepts. We identify an ontology of functional concepts of artifacts, which provides a rich vocabulary for functional representation. The ontology plays a role to limit the search space in functional understanding and to screen out meaningless functional interpretations. The ontology includes a new category of functional concepts named meta-function in order to represent conceptual categories of relationship (interdependence) between functions of components. It plays a crucial role in consolidation of functions to give criteria of grouping functions.

In this article we firstly overview the ontology of functional concepts. Section 3 describes the process of functional understanding. The contribution of this work by comparison with the related work is also discussed.

2. Ontology of Functional Concepts

The ontology of the functional concepts is designed to provide a rich and comprehensive vocabulary for both human and knowledge-based systems. It consists of the four spaces as shown in Fig. 1.

2.1 Base-Functions

A base-function of a component is defined as a result of interpretation of a behavior of the component under an intended goal [8]. Fig. 1a shows the energy-related base-functions organized in an is-a hierarchy with clues of classification. A base function is defined by conditions of behavior and the information for its interpretation called Functional Toppings (FTs) of the functional modeling language FBRL (abbreviation of a Function and Behavior Representation Language) [8]. There are three types of the functional toppings; (1)O-Focus representing focus on attributes of objects, (2)P-Focus representing focus on ports (interaction to neighboring components), and (3)Necessity of objects. For example, a base-function "to take energy" is defined as "an energy flow between two mediums" (a behavioral condition), and "focus on the

Functional Understanding Based on Ontology of Functional Concepts   725

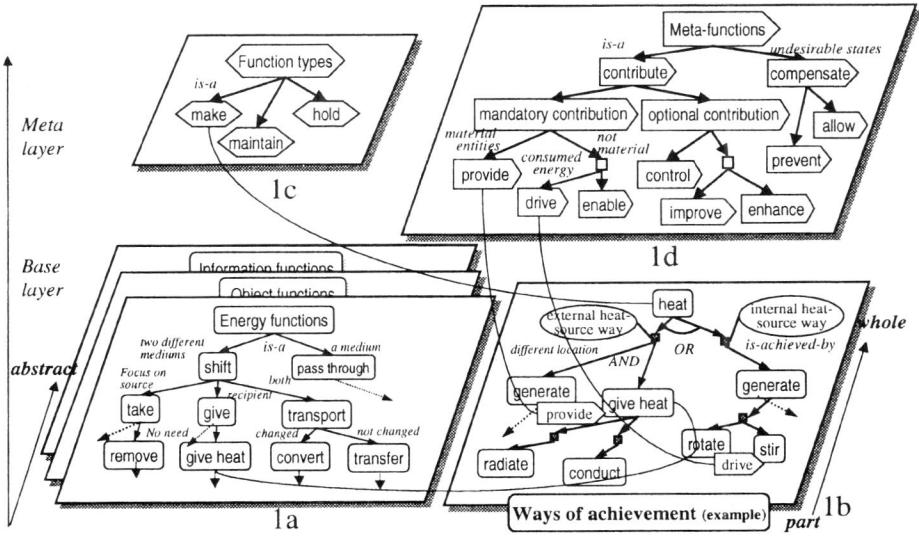

Fig. 1. The ontology of functional concepts (part)

source medium of the transfer" (functional toppings). The definition of "to remove" as a its specialized function is that of "to take" plus "the heat is unnecessary". Note that such definition using FTs is highly independent of its realization, that is, the details of behavior and internal structure of the component.

The ways of achievement represent such realization at the functional level, that is, "is-achieved-by" (whole-part) relation between the base-functions so-called functional decomposition [4,9,18]. We also explicated the background knowledge of the functional decomposition such as the physical law and the intended phenomena (we call it *a way of achievement*). Fig. 1b shows some ways of achievement of "to heat an object" in OR relationship, which are described in terms of concepts in other three spaces. For example, the external heat-source way implies a feature of structure; the location of heat generation is different from the target object.

2.2 Function Types and Meta-functions

The function types represent the types of goal achieved by the function [5]. Keuneke proposes some function types including "ToPrevent" which represents to "keep a system out of an undesirable state of objects" [5]. However, because it focuses on changes of objects associated with the component, the objective of the function is implicit, that is, another function would be affected by the state. Therefore, we redefined the function type as "ToMake", "ToMaintain", and "ToHold"[19] and redefined "ToPrevent" as a kind of a meta-function as below.

The meta-functions (denoted by *mf*) represent a role of a base function called an *agent function* (f_a) for another base function called a *target function* (f_t) [20]. A meta-function is concerned not with changes of objects of these components but with functions of the components, while other two kinds of functional concepts are concerned with existence or changes of objects. We have defined the eight types of meta-functions as shown in Fig. 1d (an is-a hierarchy). We begin definition of meta-functions with the condition where there is a causal relation from the focused parameter of f_a to that of f_t. If the goal of f_t is not satisfied when f_a is not achieved, the f_a is said to have a *mandatory contribution* for the f_t. Although we can intuitively say that f_a has a ToEnable meta-function for f_t in such a case, the authors define a narrower meaning of ToEnable by excepting the cases of ToProvide and ToDrive as follows.

Firstly, when a function f_a generates such an object (or energy) that will be a part of the focused entity of f_t (called *material*), the function is said to perform a meta-function "to provide material" for f_t. When a function f_a generates or transfers such an energy that intentionally consumed by f_t (called *driving energy*), the function is said to have the meta-function "to drive f_t". Lastly, ToEnable meta-function is used for changing a necessary condition for f_t excepting the cases of ToProvide and ToDrive. What we mean by this weak definition is that the conditions such as the existence of the material and that of the driving energy are too obvious to be said to enable a function.

Furthermore, a function f_a having positive effects on the undesirable side effect of a function f_{t1} is said to have a meta-function "to allow the side-effects of f_{t1}". On the other hand, if a serious trouble (e.g., faults) is caused in a function f_{t2} when a function f_a is not achieved, the function f_a is said to have a meta-function "to prevent malfunction of f_{t2}". The details of definitions and examples are shown in [20].

2.3 Application Domains and Assumptions of the Ontology

Up to now we have defined about one hundred and ten base-functions, three function types, eight meta-functions, and about one hundred ways of thirty base-functions. We do not claim completeness of the set of concepts. Note that we define precisely the meaning of concepts for discrimination. The definitions may be narrower than those we use in natural language, because we tend to use them confusingly. The ontology is applied to modeling of a power plant, an oil refinery, a chemical plant, and manufacturing processes [20]. The models in the all applications share many functional concepts except those specific to the chemical domain such as "react". Currently, our ontology assumes the existence of something flowing (or transferred) among components which carries energy (called objects) on the basis of the device ontology. Then, it covers functions in fluid-related plants and does not cover mechanical phenomena. An investigation on functional concepts in different domains is in progress.

3. Functional Understanding

The functional understanding problem is to identify functional structures of an artifact from the given behavioral models of components and connection information. The process of understanding shown in Fig. 2 consists of the following three steps; behavior-function mapping, identification of meta-functions among base-functions, and consolidation of functions to build functional hierarchies as discussed below.

Functional Understanding Based on Ontology of Functional Concepts

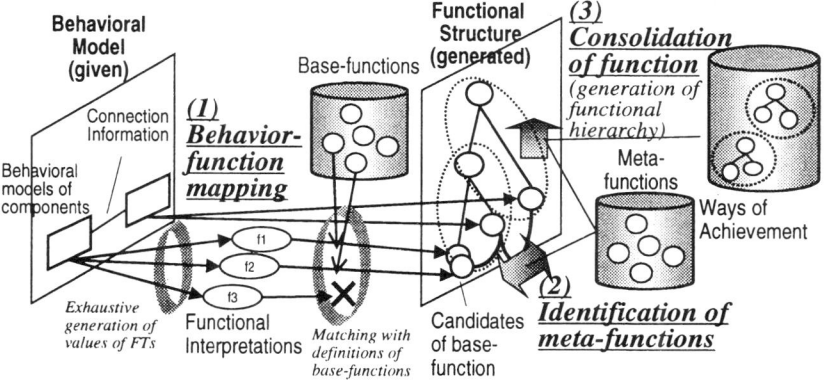

Fig. 2. Three steps of functional understanding

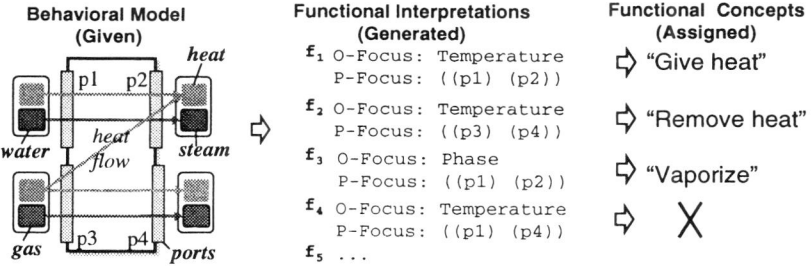

Fig. 3. Behavior-function mapping of a boiler

3.1 Behavior-Function Mapping

Firstly, the understanding system exhaustively generates candidates of base-functions to be performed by each component context-independently. It is enabled by FTs, because FTs can specify mapping from behavior to function and possible values of each FT for a behavioral model are limited. For example, in the case of the boiler shown in Fig. 3, the system generates a functional interpretation f_3 which consists of O-Focus on the "phase" parameter and P-Focus on the inlet water and the outlet steam.

Then, the understanding system screens out meaningless ones by matching them with the base-functions in the ontology. Such functional interpretations that match with no concept in the ontology are screened out as a meaningless interpretation assuming the completeness of the ontology in the functional space. In Fig. 3, the functional interpretation f_3 is successfully matched with a functional concept "vaporize". In contrast, f_4 is screened out as a meaningless interpretation. Although many candidates of the functional interpretations remain, plausible functional interpretations are identified by the following steps.

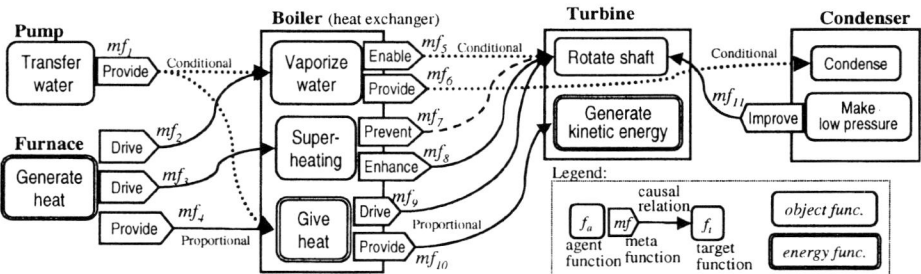

Fig. 4. Identified meta-functions in a power plant (part)

3.2 Identifying Meta-functions

Secondly, the understanding system identifies meta-functions between a pair of generated base-functions using a qualitative reasoning engine for checking causal relations and a diagnostic engine for predicting unintended phenomena. The identification algorithm is described in [20]. For example, imagine that we are given "to generate heat" function of the furnace and "to vaporize water" function of the boiler in Fig. 4. Firstly, causal relations between the functions are checked. Because there is a mandatory causal relation from the focused parameter of the heat generation (the amount of the heat energy of the combustion gas) to the focused parameter of the vaporization (the amount of the steam), then the heat generation is the agent function and the vaporization is the target function. Next, the conditions of meta-functions are checked. Because the heat energy generated by the furnace is not material (part of) the steam but is consumed by the boiler (i.e., the amount of the energy is reduced) for generating the steam, the meta-function between them is ToDrive (mf_2 in Fig. 4).

On the other hand, because the steam of which phase is gas is a necessary condition of the "to rotate" function of the turbine and the phase is neither material of rotation nor the consumed energy, the "to vaporize" function of the boiler is said to have a meta-function ToEnable (see mf_5).

According to identified meta-functions, the understanding system deletes such meaningless functional interpretations that do not contribute to any others. In the example, the functional interpretation f_2 "remove heat" of the boiler shown in Fig.3 is deleted. It represents reduction of heat energy of the combustion gas, which is meaningless in the power plant.

3.3 Consolidation of Base-Functions

Lastly, the base-functions generated in the behavior-function mapping are consolidated (aggregated) into super-functions (as a function of a subsystem or the whole system). Then, functional hierarchies are generated basically in a bottom-up manner. If the function of the whole system is not given, some whole functions could be inferred. Such top-most functions that do not have effects to the outside of the system, however, can be rejected according to the assumption of goals of artifacts.

Table 1. Heuristics for generating functional hierarchies

A: Functional concepts heuristics (mandatory)
- *A1:Super-function heuristic.* Given a viewpoint for recognition, there always exists a super-function for a functional group.
- *A2:Causal relation conservation heuristic.* The causal relations among parameters are conserved in generating functional hierarchies.

B: Preference heuristics (mandatory)
- *B1:Serial heuristic.* In serial functions, the system can consolidate functions in the head of chains.
- *B2:Simultaneous heuristic.* In functional groups which have parallel-type relations, the system can firstly consolidate simultaneous functions.
- *B3:Causal relations heuristic.* The super-function made from sub-functions which have many causal relations is preferred.
- *B4: Meta-function preference heuristics. (B4a)* ToDrive represents more cohesive relation than that of ToProvide to any f_t. *(B4b)*ToEnable and ToPrevent are preferred because they are more specific than others.

H: Hierarchical knowledge heuristics (alternative)
- *H1: Ways of achievement heuristic.* Functional hierarchies are generated according to the predefined knowledge of ways of achievement.
- *H2: Meta-functions heuristic.* Functional hierarchies are generated according to the meta-functions among base-functions. The main function according to meta-functions is interpreted as a super-function.

X: Preference heuristics (optional)
- *X1:Parallel-first heuristic.* Such functional groups that have parallel-type relations are preferred.
- *X2:Causal-relations-first heuristic.* Such functional groups that have causal relations are preferred.
- *X3:Coverage-first heuristic.* Such functional groups that have many functions are preferred.

Y: Grouping heuristics (optional)
- *Y1:Structural groups heuristic.* The component of the functions in a functional group should be the same.
- *Y2:Energy-groups heuristic.* The energy which the function focuses on should be the same.
- *Y3:Medium-groups heuristic.* The medium which the function focuses on should be the same.
- *Y4:Attribute-groups heuristic.* The type of functional parameters should be the same.
- *Y5:Meta-function-groups heuristic.* The groups are made according to meta-functions.

As discussed in the introduction, the crucial issues are the grouping of the base-functions and selecting super-functions from the candidates. Our approach is based on heuristics and meta-functions. We have identified 16 heuristics shown in Table 1 for grouping of functions (category Y. We call them *grouping heuristics*), knowledge source of super-functions (category H. *hierarchical knowledge heuristics*) and selecting a super-function from candidates (category A, B and X. *preference heuristics*).

Application of the heuristics in category H, X and Y can be specified by users, which enables the system to generate various functional hierarchies. The heuristics in the category H specify the knowledge for generating super-functions, that is, either the ways of achievement shown in Fig. 1b (*H1*) or the meta-functions among base-functions as discussed later (*H2*). The user can select a kind of knowledge alternatively. The heuristics in the category X determine preferences of groups of functions, that is, which groups of functions should be firstly consolidated into a super-function. The users can specify the order of applying the heuristics (or not apply the heuristics). For example, when a user specifies that the *X1*:parallel-first heuristic are preferred than the *X2*:causal-relations-first heuristic (denoted by *X1>X2*), functions in parallel-type relations are firstly consolidated, and then those in causal-type relations are consolidated. It means that additional functions will be integrated into the hierarchy.

The heuristics in the category Y specify the condition for grouping the functions. The users can specify the order of relaxing them (or not apply the heuristics). The understanding system firstly makes the groups of given base-functions according to the all criteria of the category Y specified by users, and then consolidates them into

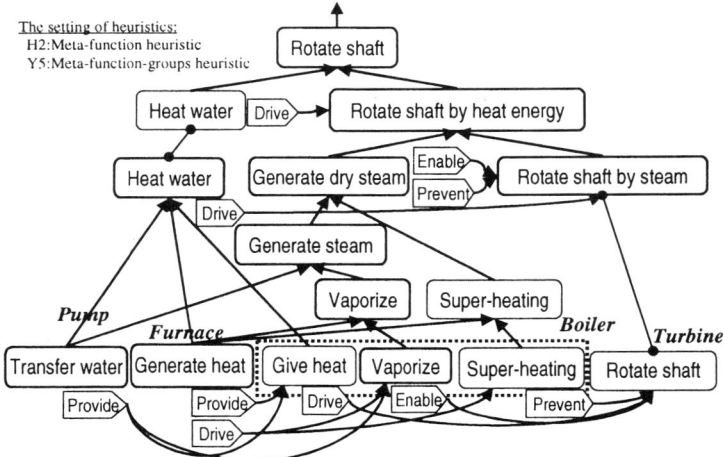

Fig. 5. A functional hierarchy generated according to meta-functions

super-functions according to the user-specified heuristics in H and X and all heuristics in A and B. When there is no functional group to be interpreted, one of the heuristics in the category Y is relaxed according to the specified order. Then new functional groups are made, and then functions in them are consolidated.

On the other hand, those in category A and B represent working assumptions of the system and thus are always applied. For example, *B1*:serial heuristic reflects humans understanding way based on the temporal order. *B3*:causal relations heuristic represents a preference of super-functions supported by many causal relations.

Meta-functions play a crucial role in consolidation. Firstly, because each type of meta-functions has own *strength* to make the functional groups, the grouping and selecting can be done according to the types of the meta-functions among them as well as causal relations and structural relations (e.g., serial, parallel, and simultaneous). It is implemented as *Y5* heuristic in Table 1 for generating groups according to meta-functions and *B4* heuristic for giving strength (i.e., preference) of each meta-functions for the case that some meta-functions contribute to the same target function.

Meta-functions also indicate a main function in the functional group which other functions contribute to. Because the whole function of a functional group can be equal to such a main function, the understanding system can generate a super-function which is equal to the main function (although the target objects of functions are different). According to *H2* heuristic representing this, the super-functions can be generated without the predefined aggregation patterns of functions such as [3,16,18] and our ways of achievements shown in Fig. 1b in the case of *H1* heuristic.

3.4 Examples of the Consolidation

Fig. 5 shows an example of the functional hierarchy of the power plant shown in Fig. 4, which is generated according to meta-functions among base-functions (the heuristics setting is *H2* and *Y5*). Firstly, "to generate heat" and "to vaporize" having To-Drive meta-function are consolidated into a super-function "to vaporize water", before

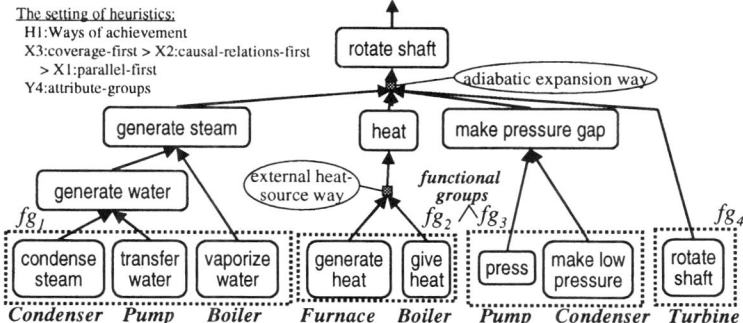

Fig. 6. Another functional hierarchy generated using ways of achievement

the pair of "transfer water" and "to vaporize" having ToProvide is consolidated according to *B4a* heuristic. In the case of "to rotate shaft" which is the target function of three meta-functions, "to generate dry steam" is interpreted earlier than "to heat water" because ToEnable and ToPrevent are more specific than others (*B4b* heuristic).

Fig. 6 shows another example according to another heuristics setting without using meta-functions. In this case, the super-functions are generated according to the knowledge base of ways of achievement of function shown in Fig. 1b. Firstly, the system makes the functional groups such as the functions changing pressure-type parameters (*fg₃* in Fig. 6) according to the specified grouping heuristics *Y4*, that is, groups made by kinds of parameters. Next, in the functional group *fg₂*, the external heat-source way of "to heat" in Fig. 1b matches "to generate heat" and "to give heat", then they are consolidated into a super-function "to heat". After functions in other functional groups are consolidated into each super-function, the groups are relaxed and then these consolidated functions are consolidated into a super-function "to rotate shaft" according to the adiabatic expansion way.

When the user changes the order of applying the heuristics or relaxing, the different functional hierarchies are generated. The user's specification of heuristics can be viewed as a viewpoint for recognition of the target system, and the generated hierarchy reflects the viewpoint. These functional hierarchies are very different from each other. While the first one (Fig. 5) represents how to obtain the driving energy and how to convert the heat energy to kinetic energy, the second one (Fig. 6) represents conditions for kinds of parameters. Some other hierarchies are shown in [19].

4. Related Work and Discussion

Ontology of Functional Concepts
Some sets of "primitives of behavior" are proposed in [7,9,12,21]. We added more intention-rich concepts such as "remove" with unnecessary intention and organized in is-a and part-of hierarchy. In Value Engineering research [13], standard sets of verbs (i.e., functional concepts) for value analysis of artifacts are proposed [14]. There is, however, no machine understandable definition of concepts.

We also identify a new category called a meta-function. The CPD in CFRL [6] represents causal relations among functions. Lind categorizes such relations into Connection, Condition and Achieve [7]. The meta-functions are results of interpretation of such causal relations between functions under the role of the agent function for the target functions without mention of the objects associated with components.

Functional Understanding

The teleological analysis in the de Kleer's work [3] identifies "function" of devices from results of qualitative simulation (i.e., behavior), which is a pioneer work of functional understanding task. Function is, however, defined (and identified) as a causal direction of parameters in his work, while our functional understanding can identify intention-rich concepts in the is-a hierarchy. Moreover, his process of aggregation (called "parsing") is done by some substitution rules according to the topology of the circuits. We decompose it into two phases, that is, identification of meta-functions and consolidation of functions according to them. Meta-functions are detached from the topology and then functional hierarchies which do not correspond to the structure can be generated. In summary, ontological consideration is premature in this work.

The functional understanding based on FR [16] uses templates of CPDs representing functional hierarchies as behavioral causal relations. Thus, functional hierarchies are directly generated from the behavioral model without the functional concepts. They are also limited to those associated with structure. We detached interpretation of function of components from the hierarchical (aggregate) abstraction. Price et al. discuss the interpretation of behavior with functional labels [15]. It corresponds only to the behavior-function mapping.

Furthermore, without the predefined aggregate patterns such as the substitution rules [3] and templates of CPDs [16], our system can generate functional hierarchies according to meta-functions among functions (see Fig. 5) as well as using the predefined general pattern knowledge called the ways of achievements (Fig. 6).

The consolidation theory [22] tries to capture the general rationales of consolidation of components. While we share the goal, its consolidation rules are simple and based on topological relations (e.g., series and parallel) between the limited behavioral primitives. Automatic aggregation in [12] also treats such topological aggregation. We try to explicate the identity of consolidated (aggregated) function as not only such topological relations but also interdependency between functions as meta-functions.

5. Summary

We proposed an ontology of functional concepts including the meta-functions, which contributes to solving the issues of functional understanding task mentioned in Introduction, that is, how to limit the reasoning space and how to identify functions in functional hierarchies. For the first issue, the ontology provides such primitives that are targets in the behavior-function mapping and screens out meaningless interpretations. For the second issue, the meta-function gives identity of functions in the hierarchies and then it enables the system to consolidate (sub-)functions into super-functions as functional hierarchies based on heuristics and meta-functions without the predefined patterns for aggregation. Furthermore, application of the heuristics can be specified by users, which enables the system to generate various functional hierarchies. An investigation on limitation of the ontology mentioned in Section 2.3 is in progress.

Acknowledgments. The authors are grateful to Mitsuru Ikeda for his valuable comments. This research is supported in part by the Japan Society for the Promotion of Science (JSPS-RFTF97P00701).

References

1. Chandrasekaran, B.; Goel, A. K.; and Iwasaki, Y. 1993. Functional representation as design rationale. *COMPUTER*, 48-56.
2. Lee, J. 1997. Design rationale systems: understanding the issues. *IEEE Expert*, 12(3):78-85.
3. de Kleer, J. 1984. How circuits work, *Artificial Intelligence* 24:205-280.
4. Umeda, Y. *et al.*, 1990. Function, behavior, and structure. *AI in Engineering*, 177-193, 1990.
5. Keuneke, A. M. 1991. A. device representation: the significance of functional knowledge. *IEEE Expert*, 24:22-25.
6. Vescovi, M.; Iwasaki, Y.; Fikes, R.; and Chandrasekaran, B. 1993. CFRL: A language for specifying the causal functionality of engineered devices. In *Proc. of AAAI-93*, 626-633.
7. Lind, M. 1994. Modeling goals and functions of complex industrial plants. *Applied Artificial Intelligence*, 8:259-283.
8. Sasajima, M.; Kitamura, Y.; Ikeda, M.; and Mizoguchi, R. 1995. FBRL: A Function and Behavior Representation Language. In *Proc. of IJCAI-95*, 1830-1836.
9. Pahl, G. and Beitz, W. 1998. "Engineering design - a systematic approach", The design council.
10. Goel, A., and Chandrasekaran, B. 1989. Functional Representation of Designs and Redesign Problem Solving. *Proc. of IJCAI-89*, 1388-1394
11. Larsoon, J. E.1996. Diagnosis based on Explicit Means-ends Models, *Artificial Intelligence*, Vol.80, pp.29-93.
12. Chittaro, L., Ranon, R., 1999. Automatic derivation of hierarchical representation for flow-based functional models, *Proc. of Tenth International Workshop on Principles of Diagnosis (DX-99)*, pp.45-50.
13. Miles, L. D. 1961. *Techniques of value analysis and engineering*. McGraw-hill.
14. Tejima, N. *et al.* eds. 1981. *Selection of functional terms and categorization*. Report 49, Soc. of Japanese Value Engineering (In Japanese).
15. Snooke, N. and Price, C. 1997, Hierarchical Functional Reasoning. In *Proc. of IJCAI-97 Workshop on Modeling and Reasoning about Function*, 11-22.
16. Thadani, S. and Chandrasekaran, B. 1994, Constructing Functional Models of a Device from its Structural Description. In *Working papers of QR-94*, 276-285.
17. Mizoguchi, R., and Ikeda, M. 1997. Towards ontology engineering. In *Proc. of PACES/SPICIS '97*, 259-266.
18. Bhatta, S. R., and Goel, A. K. 1997. A functional theory of design patterns. In *Proc. of IJCAI-97*, 294-300.
19. Kitamura, Y., and Mizoguchi, R. 1998. Functional ontology for functional understanding, Papers of *Twelfth International Workshop on Qualitative Reasoning (QR-98)*, 77-87.
20. Kitamura, Y., and Mizoguchi, R. 1999. Meta-functions of artifacts, Papers of *13th International Workshop on Qualitative Reasoning (QR-99)*, 136-145.
21. Hodges, J. 1992. Naive mechanics - a computational model of device use and function in design improvisation. *IEEE Expert* 7(1):14-27.
22. Bylander, T., and Chandrasekaran, B. 1985. Understanding behavior using consolidation, *Proc. of IJCAI-85*, 450-454.

Probabilistic Modeling of Alarm Observation Delay in Network Diagnosis

Kazuo HASHIMOTO[1], Kazunori MATSUMOTO[1] and Norio SHIRATORI[2]

[1] KDD R&D Laboratories Inc., 2-1-15 Ohara Kamifukuoka-Shi, Saitama 356-8502, Japan
[2] Tohoku University, 2-1-1 Katahira, Aobaku-ku, Sendai 980-8577, Japan

Abstract. This paper introduces a probabilistic modeling of alarm observation delay, and shows a novel method of model-based diagnosis for time series observation. Firstly, a fault model is defined by associating an event tree rooted by each fault hypothesis with probabilistic variables representing temporal delay. The most probable hypothesis is obtained by selecting one whose AIC (Akaike information criterion) is minimal. It is proved that by simulation that the AIC based hypothesis selection achieves the high precision in diagnosis.

1 Introduction

In the fault management of the network, when a fault occurs at one point of the network, all the apparatuses that detect the communication interruption generate alarms, and the alarms are transmitted to a monitor system.

A set of observable alarms caused by a fault is determined by the logical structure of the network. However, it is not easy to identify the fault due to the following uncertain factors:

- The order of alarm arrivals to a monitor system for each fault is not consistent because the delay of alarm observation is random rather than constant.
- Whether it should be attributed to ripple effect of a single fault or simultaneous occurrence of multiple faults cannot be determined based on the observed alarms.
- Alarms may not be observed due to the overload of the network and malfunction of the observation apparatus.

It is therefore one of the most important problems in network management to identify the true fault out of many alarms. The technology for identifying the fault from the observed alarms is called as alarm correlation[1], and various approaches have been proposed for fault management of networks.

The rule-based approach is the most common in developing expert systems. Brugnoni [2] investigates the fault diagnosis using the rule-based expert system. There are many cases that the once selected fault hypothesis is contradicted by the delayed arrival of an alarm, it is necessary to ensure the consistency of diagnosis whenever a new alarm is obtained. ATMS[3] is a well known mechanism to update the truth value of hypotheses, however, the computational time of

ATMS is known to increase exponentially as the number of managed hypothesis increases. It is therefore difficult to apply for a large scale application.

Yemini et al.[4] proposes a code book approach in which an observable alarm set is compared with fault hypotheses, and the hypothesis with the minimum hamming distance from the observed alarm set is selected. It is reported that the algorithm runs much faster than the rule-based approach. But the code book approach is suited for single fault diagnosis as well as the rule-based approach. Multiple faults cannot be treated well.

Reiter[5] gives the theoretical definition of diagnosis, which is applicable for both single fault and multiple faults. de Kleer and Williams [6] investigates diagnosis of multiple faults using circuit examples, and proposes[7] to introduce roughly estimated failure probability to localize the diagnosis in the smallest number of measurements.

Alarm correlation is different from the diagnosis of circuits in the followings:

- Alarm correlation is the problem to identify the fault in the smallest number of observation, which is given as a sequence of alarm notification events.
- As the number of the network components is relatively large, stronger constraint should be introduced.

2 Probabilistic Modeling of Alarm Observation Delay

Given the network topology, we can construct an event tree rooted by each fault hypothesis. Event tree is a path along which the effect of a fault propagates. However, any simple event tree is not possible to give a reasonable account for the order of observed alarms for network faults.

In order to explain the uncertainty of alarm arrival time, we will introduce two types of probabilistic variables, detection delay and propagation delay. The alarm detection delay is the required time to send an alarm notification event from a node to a monitor. The alarm propagation delay is the required time for the effect of a fault to propagate from one node to another along the link.

We call this model as a Probabilistic Temporal Fault Model (PTFM). Figure 1 shows a small example of PTFM.

For explanation of PTFM, the symbols defined in Table 1 are introduced. In a PTFM illustrated by Figure 1, the following equations hold, where t_0 is an occurrence time of l_{01}.

$$T_1 - t_0 = X_{01} + Y_1$$
$$T_2 - t_0 = X_{01} + X_{12} + Y_2$$
$$T_3 - t_0 = X_{01} + X_{12} + X_{23} + Y_3$$
$$\cdots \quad \cdots$$

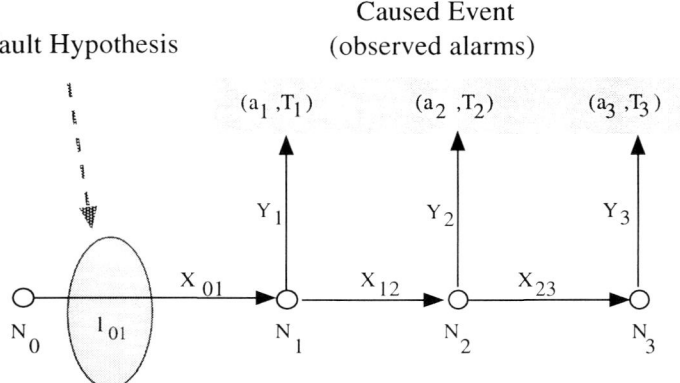

Fig. 1. A PTFM rooted by l_{01}

N_i	: the ith node
l_{ij}	: a link from N_i to N_j
$path(i,k)$	: a sequence of links from N_i to N_k
$X_{i,j}$	: an alarm propagation delay along l_{ij}
Y_j	: an alarm detection delay from N_j
T_j	: an alarm observation time for a_j
$\mathbf{pa}(T_j)$	: a set of variables which T_j depends on
a_j	: an alarm notified from node N_j
$\mathcal{A}$	: a set of alarms
A_{ij}	: a set of observable alarms under H_{ij} ($A_{ij} \subset \mathcal{A}$)
$H_{\alpha\beta}$	: a fault hypothesis of $l_{\alpha\beta}$
$\mathcal{H}$	: a set of fault hypotheses
$ET_{\alpha\beta}$	: an event tree associated with $H_{\alpha\beta}$
$\mathcal{ET}$	: a set of event trees

Table 1. Symbol definition

$$T_k - t_0 = \sum_{i=1}^{k} X_{(i-1)i} + Y_k$$

Let alarm propagation delay X_{ij} be a random variable of probability density function $p_{X_{ij}}(t)$, and alarm detection delay Y_j be a random variable of probability density function $p_{Y_j}(t)$, where $p_Z(t)$ is an abbreviation for $p(Z = t)$. $p_{T_j}(t|H_{\alpha\beta}, t_0)$ is the probability density function such that a_j is to be observed at time t under fault hypothesis $H_{\alpha\beta}$.

Then $p_{T_j}(t|H_{\alpha\beta}, t_0)$ is obtained by convoluting all the probability density functions of constituent random variables. For example, the probability density function for each alarm observation time in Figure 1 is given as follows, where $\otimes$ is a convolution operator.

$$p_{T_1}(t|H_{01},t_0) = p_{X_{01}+Y_1}(t|H_{01},t_0)$$
$$= p_{X_{01}} \otimes p_{Y_1}(t|H_{01},t_0) \qquad (1)$$
$$p_{T_2}(t|H_{01},t_0) = p_{X_{01}+X_{12}+Y_2}(t|H_{01},t_0)$$
$$= p_{X_{01}} \otimes p_{X_{12}} \otimes p_{Y_2}(t|H_{01},t_0) \qquad (2)$$
$$p_{T_3}(t|H_{01},t_0) = p_{X_{01}+X_{12}+X_{23}+Y_3}(t|H_{01},t_0)$$
$$= p_{X_{01}} \otimes p_{X_{12}} \otimes p_{X_{23}} \otimes p_{Y_3}(t|H_{01},t_0) \qquad (3)$$

Now, let us consider the joint probability of all the random variables contained in the set of observable alarms A_{ij}, $\{T_k|a_k \in A_{ij}\}$.

$$p(T_1, T_2, \ldots, T_k|H_{ij}, t_0) = \prod_i^k p(T_i|T_1, \ldots, T_{i-1}, H_{ij}, t_0) \qquad (4)$$
$$= \prod_i^k p(T_i|\mathbf{pa}(T_i), H_{ij}, t_0)$$
$$\approx \prod_i^k p(T_i|H_{ij}, t_0) \qquad (5)$$

It should be clear from the example of Figure 1 that the random variable T_k is dependent on a set of parent variables $\mathbf{pa}(T_k)$, because T_k shares all the propagation delay variables which $\mathbf{pa}(T_k)$ contains.

For example, $\mathbf{pa}(T_3)$ is $\{T_1, T_2\}$. As $T_3 - t_0$ is given by $X_{01} + X_{12} + X_{23} + Y_3$, T_3 depends on X_{01}, X_{12}, X_{23} and Y_3. In the same way, T_2 depends on X_{01}, X_{12} and Y_2, T_1 depends on X_{01} and Y_1. Therefore, T_3 depends on T_2 in terms of X_{01} and X_{12}, and T_1 in terms of X_{01}.

In general, the joint probability should be calculated as in Equation (4) by considering the dependence of variables. However, the dependence of variables can be safely neglected when $X_{max} = \max_{i,j}\langle X_{ij}\rangle$, $Y_{max} = \max_j\langle Y_j\rangle$, and $X_{max} \ll Y_{max}$, where $\langle Z \rangle$ is the mean value of Z. In that case, the joint probability is obtained by Equation (5).

3 Diagnosis as Model Selection

3.1 Measures for Model Comparison

Entropy is a known measure for comparison of probabilistic models. It is not appropriate, however, to use entropy when the number of model parameters differs, because the most complex model is likely to be chosen.

Akaike[8] introduces a measure, called Akaike information criterion (AIC). Let $|H_{ij}|$ be the number of parameters in H_{ij}. AIC for $p(T_1, T_2, \ldots, T_k|H_{ij}, t_0)$ is obtained as follows:

$$AIC(T_1, T_2, \ldots, T_k | H_{ij}, t_0) \equiv -2 \times \log p(T_1, T_2, \ldots, T_k | H_{ij}, t_0) + 2 \times |H_{ij}|$$

$$\approx -2 \times (\sum_i^k \log p(T_i | H_{ij}, t_0)) + 2 \times |H_{ij}|$$

Schwarz[9] introduces a similar measure, called Bayesian information criterion (BIC), with the second term given by $\frac{1}{2}|H_{ij}|\log(m)$, where m is a cases in the database. BIC is exactly minus the minimum description length (MDL) criterion described by Rissanen[11]. See Heckerman[10] for more detailed survey.

The comparison with these measures is outside of this paper. We will use AIC as the measure for model comparison in the rest of this paper.

3.2 Diagnosis Based on the Minimum AIC

This section defines the diagnosis based on the minimum AIC principle. Suppose that observation is given by $S = \{\langle a_k, t_k \rangle | a_k \in \mathcal{A}\}$, where $\langle a_k, t_k \rangle$ means that a_k is observed at time t_k. $p_{T_k}(t|H_{ij}, t_0)$ is the probability density function such that a_k is to be observed at time t under fault hypothesis H_{ij}. The likelihood of H_{ij} $h(t|H_{ij}, t_0)$, the log-likelihood $LL(t|H_{ij}, t_0)$, and AIC $AIC(t|H_{ij}, t_0)$ are defined by equation (7) (8) (9) respectively.

$$h_{a_k}(t|H_{ij}, t_0) \equiv \begin{cases} p_{T_k}(t|H_{ij}, t_0) & (t_0 < t < t_k) \\ p_{T_k}(t_k|H_{ij}, t_0) & (t_k \leq t) \end{cases} \qquad (6)$$

$$h(t|H_{ij}, t_0) \equiv \prod_{a_k \in A_{ij}} h_{a_k}(t|H_{ij}, t_0) \qquad (7)$$

$$LL(t|H_{ij}, t_0) \equiv \log h(t|H_{ij}, t_0) \qquad (8)$$

$$AIC(t|H_{ij}, t_0) \equiv -2 \times LL(t|H_{ij}, t_0) + 2 \times |H_{ij}| \qquad (9)$$

$$|H_{ij}| : number\ of\ parameters\ in\ H_{ij}$$

$|H_{ij}|$ is not the number of observable alarms or that of random variables, but the number of parameters to describe the probability $h(t|H_{ij}, t_0)$.

The number of parameters to describe a random variable X differs depending on the probabilistic model. For example, an exponential distribution, $p(X) = \delta e^{-\delta X}$, is characterized by one parameter, δ. A normal distribution, $p(X) = \frac{1}{\sqrt{2\pi\sigma^2}} e^{-\frac{(X-\mu)^2}{2\sigma^2}}$, is characterized by two parameters, μ and σ. $|H_{ij}|$ is the total summation of the number of parameters for all the random variables contained in $h(t|H_{ij}, t_0)$.

By definition, the number of parameters differs hypothesis to hypothesis, hypotheses cannot be compared in terms of log-likelihood. We will introduce AIC to compare hypotheses with different number of parameters. The most probable hypothesis is obtained by selecting one whose AIC is minimal.

$$H_{min} = \arg \min_{H_{ij} \in \mathcal{H}} AIC(t|H_{ij}, t_0) \tag{10}$$

As equation (7), (8) and (9) contain an event occurrence time t_0 as a variable, it is necessary to estimate it first. The event occurrence time $t_0(t|H_{ij})$ is given by (11).

$$t_0(t|H_{ij}) = \arg \max_{t_0} LL(t|H_{ij}, t_0) \tag{11}$$

4 Empirical Evaluation

4.1 Simulation

Figure 2 defines a topology of the network under consideration. The network is defined as a pair $\langle \mathcal{N}, \mathcal{L} \rangle$, where $\mathcal{N}$ is a set of nodes, and $\mathcal{L}$ is a set of links connecting neighboring nodes in the network. Let R be a set of receiving equipments, S a set of sending equipments, C a set of Cross Connect Equipment (CCE). $\mathcal{N}$ and $\mathcal{L}$ are given by $(R \cup S \cup C)$ and $\{L_{\alpha,\beta}|\alpha, \beta \in \mathcal{N}\}$, respectively.

In the network illustrated by Figure 2, R is a set, $\{a, b, c, d, e, f, g, h\}$, S is a set, $\{a', b', c', d', e', f', g', h'\}$, C is a set, $\{N_1, N_2, \ldots, N_{14}\}$, and $\{(a, a'), (b, b'),$ $\ldots, (h, h')\}$ is a set of connection relations.

When an alarm is observed at each node, it is reported to the monitoring process. We model this network by PTFM described in section 2. In the model proposed, two types of delay, propagation delay and detection delay are introduced to explain the difference of the ordering of effect propagation and that of observation. By setting detection delays much bigger than propagation delays, the ordering of observed events becomes very different from that of propagation.

For simplicity, we will consider only the link troubles in the rest of this paper, and the following tree assumptions are introduced.

assumption 1 *Probability density function of alarm propagation delay and alarm detection delay is exponential.*

$$p_{X_{i,j}}(t) = \delta_{ij} e^{-\delta_{i,j}t} \tag{12}$$
$$p_{Y_j}(t) = \lambda_j e^{-\lambda_j t} \tag{13}$$

assumption 2 *The parameters for propagation delay, and that for detection delay are equal respectively.*

$$\forall \delta_i = \delta \tag{14}$$
$$\forall \lambda_i = \lambda \tag{15}$$

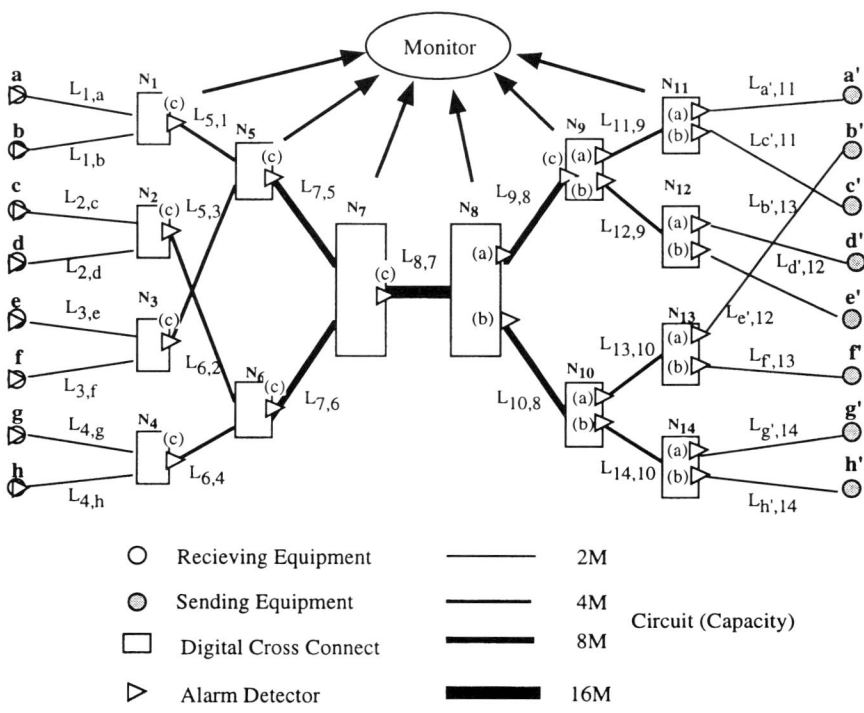

Fig. 2. Network Topology

assumption 3 *The mean propagation delay is much smaller than the mean detection delay.*

$$\frac{1}{\delta} \ll \frac{1}{\lambda} \tag{16}$$

In order to obtain a time series of alarm observation for a PTFM by simulation, necessary temporal delays are generated as random variables according to the PTFM.

4.2 Calculation of AIC

With the above mentioned assumptions, AIC for PTFM illustrated in Figure 1 is calculated as follows:

1. - H_{01} is a fualt hypothesis of l_{01}.
   - A_{01} is a set of observable alarms $\{a_1, a_2, a_3\}$.
2. - $h_{a_1}(t|H_{01},t_0)$, $h_{a_2}(t|H_{01},t_0)$, $h_{a_3}(t|H_{01},t_0)$ is respectively obtained by $p_{T_1}(t|H_{01},t_0)$, $p_{T_2}(t|H_{01},t_0)$, $p_{T_3}(t|H_{01},t_0)$.
   - $p_{T_1}(t|H_{01},t_0)$, $p_{T_2}(t|H_{01},t_0)$, and $p_{T_3}(t|H_{01},t_0)$ are given by equation (1), (2), (3), respectively.

3. – By equation (7), the likelihood $h(t|H_{01}, t_0)$ is given by $h_{a_1}(t|H_{01}, t_0)$, $h_{a_2}(t|H_{01}, t_0)$, and $h_{a_3}(t|H_{01}, t_0)$.
   – The log-likelihood $LL(t|H_{01}, t_0)$ is the logarithm of $h(t|H_{01}, t_0)$.
4. – The variables are $\{X_{01}, Y_1, X_{12}, Y_2, X_{23}, Y_3\}$. As an exponential distribution is assumed for each variable, $|H_{01}| = 6$.
   – $AIC(t|H_{01}, t_0)$ is obtained by equation (9).

4.3 Example: Model Selection Based on AIC

Let faulty parts be limited to $L_{10,8}$, $L_{13,10}$ and $L_{14,10}$ in Figure 2 network. Fault hypotheses considered are $H_{10,8}$, $H_{13,10}$, $H_{14,10}$, $H_{10,8} \cap H_{13,10}$, $H_{10,8} \cap H_{14,10}$, $H_{13,10} \cap H_{14,10}$, and $H_{10,8} \cap H_{13,10} \cap H_{14,10}$.

Figure 3 shows a simulation of $H_{10,8}$ fault, where AICs are calculated every 200 [msec] since the first event arrival. The decision suspension period is the period from the time of fault occurrence to the time of observation. We will use this term in the rest of the paper. The observations are as follows:

– In the range where the decision suspension period $\in [0, 0.2]$, $H_{14,10}$ is dominant because the number of necessary parameters is smallest. The ordering of dominance is as follows:

$$AIC(H_{14,10}) < AIC(H_{13,10}) < AIC(H_{10,8} \cap H_{13,10} \cap H_{14,10})$$
$$< AIC(H_{10,8} \cap H_{13,10}) < AIC(H_{10,8} \cap H_{14,10})$$
$$< AIC(H_{10,8}) < AIC(H_{13,10} \cap H_{14,10})$$

But hypotheses, $H_{14,10}$ and $H_{13,10}$, will soon meet events which are not explainable.
– In the range $[0.3, 0.7]$, the dominance of hypotheses changes over time, and the ordering of dominance is unstable.
– In the range > 0.7, the hypothesis $AIC(H_{10,8})$ becomes dominant, and the ordering of dominance is stable.

4.4 Precision of Diagnosis

The precision of diagnosis is observed for $H_{10,8}$ fault simulation. For each fault occurrence, AICs for possible hyphtheses are calculated every 200 [msec]. One session is the collection of 1,000 times faults occurrences for each parameter set $\{T_\lambda, T_\delta\}$, where $T_\lambda = \frac{1}{\lambda}$ and $T_\delta = \frac{1}{\delta}$. The range of T_λ and T_δ are $T_\lambda = 1,000$[msec] and $T_\delta = 20, 100, 500$ [msec] respectively.

In the experiment, the most probable hypothesis is selected based on the minimum AIC principle. The correctness of decision is evaluated in terms of precision. The precision for $L_{\alpha\beta}$ fault is defined as follows:

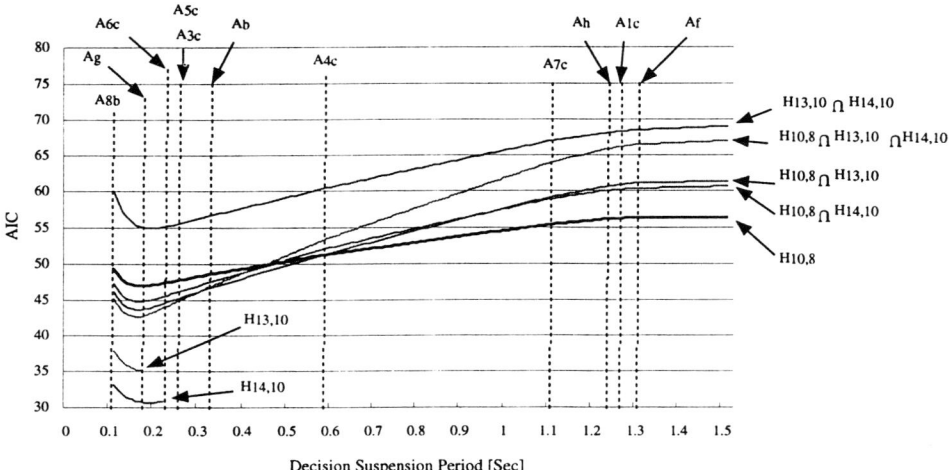

Fig. 3. AIC vs. decision suspension period

$H_{\alpha\beta}$	a hypothesis of $L_{\alpha\beta}$ fault
Num	the number of faults appeared in simulation
$R_{\alpha\beta}(t)$	the number of decision result identical to H_i at decision suspension period t
$W_{\alpha\beta}(t)$	the number of decision result not identical to H_i at decision suspension period t

$$Num = R_{\alpha\beta}(t) + W_{\alpha\beta}(t)$$
$$Precision(t) \equiv \frac{R_{\alpha\beta}(t)}{Num} \qquad (17)$$

The precision rate at decision suspension period t is plotted in Figure 4. The achieved precision is quite high, and it is observed that the precision is improved as the propagation delay T_δ decreases.

5 Conclusions

This paper introduced a probabilistic modeling of alarm observation delay. The proposed model, called PTFM, is featured by an event tree, where each edge is associated with probabilic variable of the alarm propagation delay and each node is associated with probabilic variable of the alarm detection delay. By PTFM, the probability density function for each alarm is obtained by convoluting a

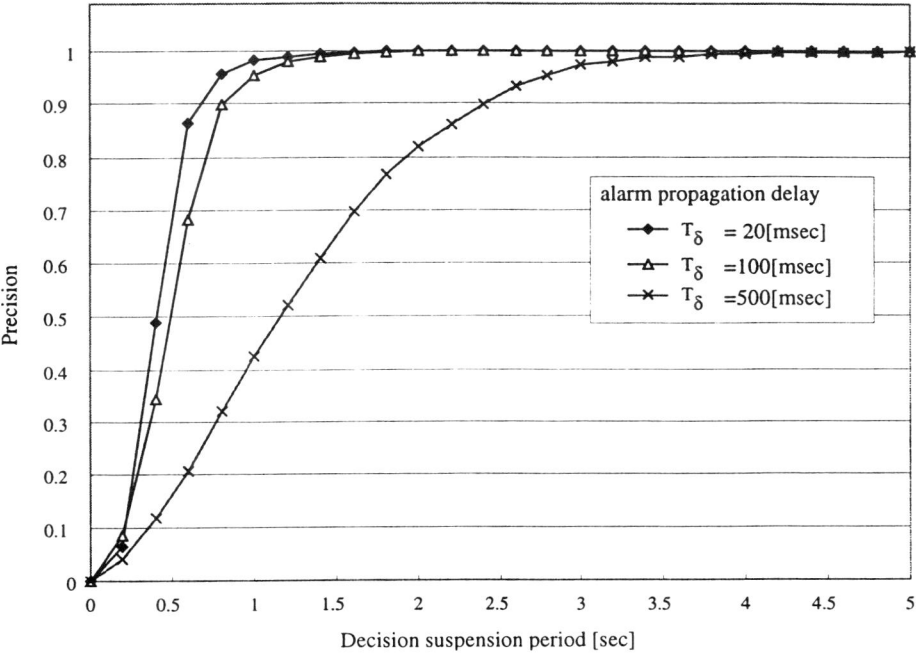

Fig. 4. Precision vs. decision suspension period

sequence of probability density functions along the path on the event tree. PTFM is capable of representing the probabilistic temporal nature of event causality, preserving the compactness of representation.

The paper gave a theoretical foundation of model selection based on the minimum AIC principle. By definition given here, AIC is a time-varying function. Therefore, the model selection based on the comparison of AICs are not event-driven. Even if no event occurrence is reported, the diagnosis will change in the course of time. It is proved that the minimum AIC principle achieves high precision in diagnosis.

References

1. Jacobson, G., Weissman, M. D.: Alarm Correlation. IEEE Network **Nov.** (1993) 52–59
2. Brugnoni, S., Bruno, G., Manione, R., Montariolo, E., Paschetta, E., Sisto, L.: An Expert System for Real Time Fault Diagnosis of the Italian Telecommunications Network. Integrated Network Management **III**(C-12), IFIP Transactions (1993) 617–628
3. de Kleer, J.: An assumption-based truth maintenance system. Artificial intelligence Vol.**28** (1986) 127–162

4. Yemini, S. A., Klinger, S., Mozes, E., Yemini, Y., Ohsie, D.: High Speed and Robust Event Correlation. IEEE Communications Magazine **May** (1996) 82–90
5. Reiter, R.: A Theory of Diagnosis from First Principles. Artificial intelligence Vol.**32** (1987) 57–95
6. de Kleer, J., Williams, B. C.: Diagnosing multiple faults Artificial intelligence Vol.**32** (1987) 97–130
7. de Kleer, J.: Using Crude probability estimates to guide diagnosis. Artificial intelligence Vol.**45** (1990) 381–392
8. Akaike, H.: Information theory and an extension of the maximum likelihood principle. 2nd International Symposium on Information Theory, Akademiai Kiado, Budapest (1973) 267–281
9. Schwarz, G.: Estimating the Dimension of a Model. Annals of Statistics **6** (1978) 461–464
10. Heckerman, D.: A Tutorial on Learning with Bayesian Networks. Learning in Graphical Models, MIT Press (1999) 301–354
11. Rissanen, J.: Stochastic Complexity. Journal of the Royal Statistical Society, Series B **49** 223–239 and 253–265

A Diagnosis Function of Arithmetical Word Problems for Learning by Problem Posing

Tsukasa Hirashima, Akira Nakano, and Akira Takeuchi

Kyushu Institute of Technology, Department of Artificial Intelligence
680-4, Kawazu, Iizuka, Fukuoka, 820-8502, JAPAN
tsukasa@ai.kyutech.ac.jp

Abstract. In this paper, we describe a problem diagnosis function for an ILE (Intelligent Learning Environment) that supports solution-based problem posing. In solution-based problem posing, learners must make a problem that can be solved by the solution-method specified beforehand. This problem posing is effective to master the use of the solution-method. By targeting solution-methods of arithmetical word problems, we are developing a problem diagnosis function and an ILE for solution-based problem posing. The diagnosis function first examines whether or not the problem can be solved by the target solution-method. When it can be solved, the problem is adequate. Then, the degree of difficulty of the problem is assessed to estimate the learner's progress. When the problem cannot be solved by the solution-method, the diagnosis function examines which information is lacking or wrong. A prototype of the ILE with the diagnosis function is already implemented. Interface of the ILE is implemented by Java, and the diagnosis function is implemented by Prolog. Therefore, the ILE can be used with a Web browser.

1. Introduction

Learning by problem posing is well recognized as an important way to learn mathematics. For example, in the USA, documents promoting curricular and pedagogical innovation in mathematics education [1][2] have called for an increased emphasis on problem posing activities in the mathematics classroom. Several investigations have also suggested that mathematical problem posing had a positive influence on the learners' problem-solving abilities or their attitude toward mathematics [3][4][5][6][7].

However, despite the importance of problem posing, it is not popular as a learning method in reality. This is due to a few factors. First, learners can make various kinds of problems, but some of the problems may be wrong. In addition, some of the learners might repeatedly make similar problems, or make problems that are too simple to be useful for learning. In such cases, adequate feedback for each problem is required. However, because learners can make a large range of problems, it is difficult to prepare adequate feedback for every problem that learners might make. In problem posing, assessment of each posed problem and assistance based on the assessment is necessary. Because the above task puts a heavy burden on teachers, it is very difficult for teachers to use problem posing as a learning method. From this point of view, if a diagnosis function of problems posed by learners is realized, learning by problem posing will come to be used more. Based on this consideration we are developing a function to diagnose problem made by learners. Our goal is to realize an ILE (Intelligent Learning Environment) that assists learners in problem posing based on the results of the diagnosis.

In this paper, we describe a problem diagnosis function for an intelligent learning environment that supports solution-based problem posing. In solution-based problem posing, learners must make a problem that can be solved by the solution-method specified beforehand. A learner who has already acquired a solution-method cannot always use it adequately. This problem posing is effective to master the use of the solution-method. By targeting solution-methods of arithmetical word problems, we are developing a problem diagnosis function and an ILE for solution-based problem posing.

The diagnosis function first examines whether or not the problem can be solved by the target solution-method. When it can be solved, the problem is adequate. Then, the degree of difficulty of the problem is assessed to estimate the learner's progress. When the problem cannot be solved by the solution-method, the diagnosis function examines which information is lacking or wrong. These results are necessary to help the learner in problem posing. A prototype of the ILE with the diagnosis function is already implemented.

In this paper, we introduce the outline of the ILE for solution-based problem posing of arithmetical word problems. Then, the diagnosis function of the problem is described. The results of the preliminary evaluation of the prototype are also reported. Interface of the ILE was implemented by Java, and the diagnosis function was implemented by Prolog. Therefore, the ILE can be used by a Web browser.

2. Framework of the ILE

Fig. 1 shows the architecture of the ILE. It is composed of three major components, the problem posing interface, the diagnosis module and the support module. To make the ILE available through a Web browser, the problem posing interface is implemented by Java as client. Then, the diagnosis and support modules are implemented by Prolog as server. The process of problem posing with the interface is introduced in Section 2.1. The diagnosis module, the main topic of this paper, is described in Section 3.

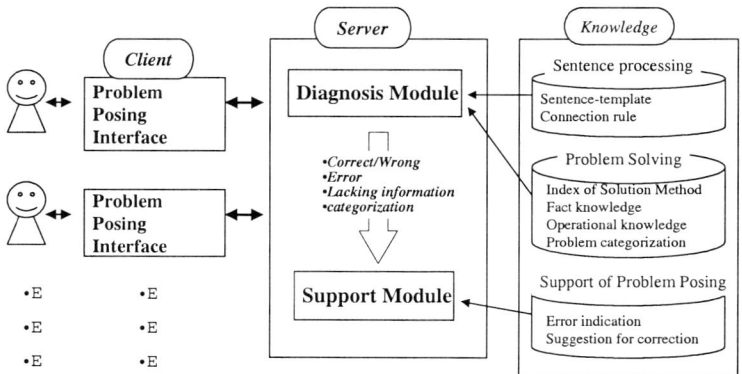

Fig.1. Architecture of the ILE.

2.1 Problem Posing in the ILE

Flow of Problem Posing
The problem posing interface is shown in Fig. 2 (at present, only in Japanese). The interface provides a learner with sentence-templates and concepts. To make a sentence, the learner selects a sentence-template from the sentence-template panel. The selected sentence-template appears in the problem-making panel. Then, the learner fills in the blanks of the template by selecting concepts from the concept panel or by inputting a number using the number keys. By making several sentences, a problem is completed. When the learner pushes the diagnosis button, the sentences are sent to the diagnosis module as a problem. The module diagnoses whether or not the problem can be solved by the solution-method specified in the subject panel. The solution-method should be specified before starting the problem posing. Based on the diagnosis, the support module gives messages about the problem. When the problem is correct, a praising message, the answer of the problem and the class of the problem are provided in the comment panel. In addition, the support module gives more difficult issue by changing the concepts in the concept panel, or by specifying the concepts used in the next problem.

Template Panel and Concepts
The sentence-templates and concepts are used to describe the value of an attribute of an object in one sentence. We call the relationship of the three the "basic relation." For example, "X of Y is Z" is a sentence-template. When a learner applies "legs" to X, "a crane" to Y, and "2" to Z, "legs of a crane are 2" is generated as a sentence. It means that the value of the attribute "legs" of the object "a crane" is "2." The concept

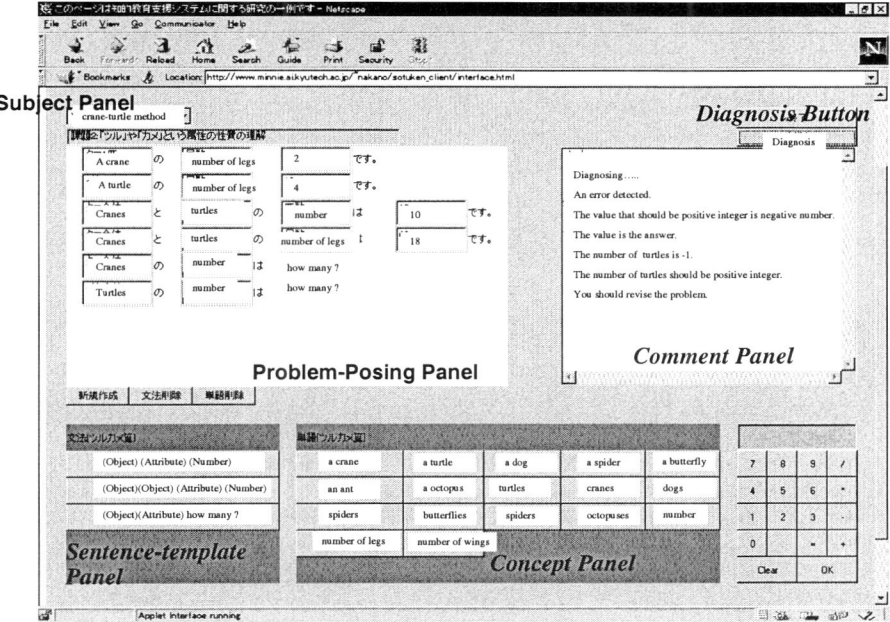

Fig.2. Interface for Problem Posing. Currently, the ILE can deal with only Japanese. Several words in this figure are translated into English from Japanese. Because of the differences in grammar of them, several sentences are not completed.

panel provides concepts by which more than one problem can be generated. Therefore, a learner is required to select and combine concepts competently. The process of problem posing is roughly divided into two: the combination of concepts and the generation of natural language. Because this interface avoids dealing with natural language, it's not complete problem posing. However, from the viewpoint of mastering the solution-method, it is sufficient.

2.2 Crane-Turtle Solution-Method

Currently, our prototype system can diagnose several kinds of arithmetical word problems. In this paper, we use the "crane-turtle problem" as an example. Fig. 3 shows a basic crane-turtle problem. This problem is solved by the solution-method shown in Fig. 4. This solution-method solves the problem without equations. We call the solution-method the "crane-turtle method." There are many problems that are composed of different concepts, but are solved by the crane-turtle method. In Japan, there are several solution-methods, like the crane-turtle method, taught when learning arithmetical word problems.

(1) A crane has 2 legs.
(2) A turtle has 4 legs.
(3) There are cranes and turtles, 20 in total.
(4) The total number of legs of cranes and turtles is 48.
(5) How many cranes are there?
(6) How many turtles are there?

Fig. 3. Problem-1: a basic crane-turtle problem.

{the total number of cranes and turtles} * {the number of a crane's(turtle's) legs} = X
|{the total number o their legs} − X| = Y
|{ the number of a turtle's legs} − { the number of a crane's legs}| = Z
Y / Z ={the number of turtles(cranes)}
{the total number of cranes and turtles} − {the number of turtles} = {the number of

Fig. 4. Crane-turtle method.

2.3 Solution-Based Problem Posing

In our researches of problem posing, we have classified problem posing in three: (1) solution-based problem posing, (2) problem-based problem posing and (3) story-based problem posing. The criteria that we used for the classification of the problem posing are that what is given to a learner in advance. In the solution-based problem posing, a solution is given to a learner and the leaner is required to pose the problem that can be solved by the solution. In problem-based problem posing, a problem is given and leaner is required to make problem by modifying the given problem, for example, by changing the state of values (that is, changing a given value to an answer value, and so on). In story-based problem posing, a story is given to a leaner and the learner makes a problem from the story. This classification corresponds to the classification by Silver.

The solution-based problem posing is also classified in three: (1a) law level, (1b) formula level, and (1c) equation level. Momentum preservation law is an example of the law. The law doesn't specify a formula. To pose problem that can be solved by using the law is an example of the law level problem posing. An example of the formula is (velocity) * (time) = (distance). The formula doesn't specify the calculation process. To pose problem that can be solved by using the formula is an example of formula level problem posing. When given and required values are decided in a formula, an equation is completed and calculation process is decided. The crane-turtle method specified calculation process. So, to pose problem that can be solved by the crane-turtle problem is equation level problem posing. In this paper, we deal with this type of problem posing.

The solution-based problem posing is effective in making learners recognize applicable conditions of solution methods. In problem solving practice, every problem that learners solve is solvable. Therefore, the task of the learners is to categorize the problems according to solution methods. Then the learners usually don't know the problems that cannot solve. Generally, in order to learn the applicable range of a concept, to know negative examples of the concept is useful. Problem posing provides the learners with rich negative examples according to application of solution methods. The negative examples are useful to make clear the applicable condition of solution methods.

3. Diagnosis Module

The diagnosis module is designed based on a model of problem solving for arithmetical word problems. The model is called MIPS (Model of Indexing for Problem Solving)[8]. In MIPS, the applicable condition of a solution-method is represented as a semantic network. The semantic network is called ISM (Index of Solution-Method). To apply a solution-method to a problem, a semantic network corresponding to the ISM has to be generated from the problem. The network generated from the problem is called PUN (Problem Understanding Network). A PUN directly generated from a problem is specifically called raw-PUN. The diagnosis module, first, examines whether or not a PUN corresponding to the ISM can be generated. A PUN that can satisfy the ISM is called a final-PUN. If such a PUN cannot be generated, the module examines which information is required to complete the PUN. Therefore, it is possible not only to judge whether the problem made by the learner is correct or not, but also to detect errors in the problem and to find a way to complete the problem.

The diagnosis process is divided into five steps: (1) generation of basic relations from sentences, (2) generation of a raw-PUN by connecting of the basic relations, (3) generation of a final-PUN by checking and refining the PUN with the generic ISM, (4) working out the answer by calculation with the solution-method, and (5) categorization of the problem. In steps (1)-(4), errors in the problem are detected. When the problem is correct, the degree of the problem is assessed in step (5). In this section, the problem diagnosis is describes step by step. The way to support problem posing is also described step by step.

3.1 Generation of Basic Relations

Process of Generation of Basic Relations
A basic relation is composed of the object, attribute and value. One basic relation is generated from one sentence made in the interface. Fig. 5 shows the basic relations

included in Problem-1 shown in Fig. 3. In this step, generated basic relations are checked with fact knowledge prepared in the system. The fact knowledge is also composed of the object, attribute and value. For example, the system has knowledge of the number of legs of a crane, that is, ft(crane, leg, 2) that means, "a crane has two legs". When there is no fact knowledge that matches with a basic relation, the basic relation is judged as an error.

> (1) atr(crane, leg, 2)
> (2) atr(turtle, leg, 4)
> (3) atr(set([crane, turtle]), [crane, turtle], 20)
> (4) atr(set([crane, turtle]), leg, 48)
> (5) atr(set(crane), crane, Answer)
> (6) atr(set(turtle), turtle, Answer)

Fig. 5. Basic relations generated from Problem-1.

Detected Errors in Generation of Basic Relations
The errors diagnosed in the generation of basic relations are categorized on two levels: (a) errors in value and (b) errors in attribute. Furthermore the errors in value are classified (a1) errors in specific value and (a2) errors in range of value. The basic relation of "a crane has four legs" is diagnosed as an error in specific value. In this error case, the support module indicates the correct basic relation, that is, "a crane has two legs, not four legs." When the range of the value is limited, like "the total number of crane and turtle is a positive integer," "the total number of cranes and turtles is − 10" is an error in range of value. In this case, the support module indicates the correct range. If a learner makes a sentence about the "number of horns of a crane", there is no fact knowledge about a crane's horns, so it is diagnosed as an error in attribute, like "a crane has no horns". In this error case, the support module indicates that the meaning of the sentence cannot be understood.

Currently, because the concepts learners are allowed to use are restricted, the system can diagnose basic relations sufficiently.

3.2 Generation of Raw-PUN

Process of Generation of Raw-PUN
When all sentences are changed to basic relations and they are correct, they are connected to each other. Usually, all basic relations are connected with one network that describes the whole meaning of the problem. A network that is generated by connecting all basic relations, is called a raw-PUN. In the process of the generation of a raw-PUN, the following three rules are used to connect the basic relations.

Connection rule-1: In two basic relations, when the concept corresponding to the object on the one is the same as the concept corresponding to the attribute on the other, it is decided that those two basic relations are connected through the common concept.

Connection rule-2: In two basic relations, when the concepts corresponding to the objects are the same, it is decided that the two basic relations are connected through the common concept.

Connection rule-3: When there is a relation of the set-operation among the concepts of the set, they are connected by the set-operation.

When all basic relations are combined into a network, it is decided that a raw-PUN is generated. For example, the basic relations shown in Fig. 5 are connected as a raw-PUN shown in Fig. 6.

Detected Errors in Generation of Raw-PUN
When all basic relations cannot be connected as one network, there are two possibilities of errors: (c) redundant information and (d) lacking of unity. If the diagnosis module can find several networks, the biggest network is used as a raw-PUN. When the solution-method can be applied to the raw-PUN, the rest of basic relations are redundant. For example, when a sentence "a dog has four legs" is added to Problem-1, it is redundant sentence. In this case, the support module indicates the redundant sentences, like ""a dogs has four legs" is not used to solve the problem. It is redundant". When the solution-method cannot be applied to the raw-PUN, unity of sentences is lacking. In this case, the support module indicates that the sentences cannot be interpreted as one problem.

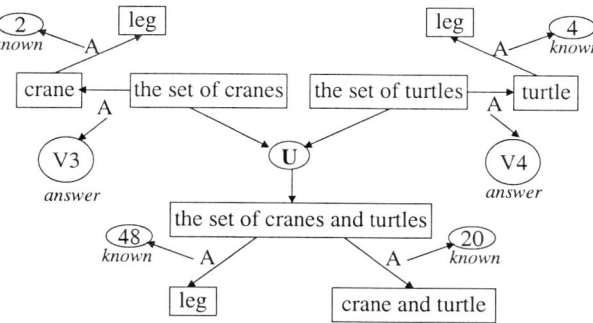

Fig. 6. Raw-PUN of Problem-1.

3.3 Generation of Final-PUN

Process of Generation of Final-PUN
The generic ISM is an index of the solution-method, which describes the numerical relations that are necessary to use the solution-method. Fig. 7 shows the generic ISM of the crane-turtle method. The calculation procedure of the crane-turtle method is shown in Fig. 8. Here, "known," "answer" and "unknown" are tags that specify the state of the values. If the generic ISM can be satisfied by using basic relations in a PUN, the solution method can be applied to the problem. A PUN that satisfies the generic ISM is called a final-PUN. In the process of the generation of final-PUN, when a PUN cannot satisfy the generic ISM, the lacking basic relations are detected and the ways to realize them. The concrete procedure of the above process is described below.

The process of generation of a final-PUN is divided into two steps: (1) assignment and (2) complement. In the assignment step, first, the basic relations in a PUN are assigned to the variables in the numerical relations in the generic ISM. In the assignment, the state of values between the basic relations and the variables must correspond. Fig. 9 is an assignment where the basic relations composing the PUN of Fig. 6 are assigned to the generic ISM of the crane-turtle method. Next, the assignment is examined by matching it with knowledge about binomial operations that are provided as system knowledge. We call the knowledge "operational knowledge". The first operational relation in Fig. 9, for example, matches with the operational knowledge "(number of legs of an animal A" * "number of animal A" = "total number of legs of animal A." Then, the "total number of legs of cranes" is substituted into V7. In this way, variables in the generic ISM are replaced by the basic relations. When it is impossible to replace all variables by basic relations, the assignment is carried out again. If the assignment in which all variables can be replaced by basic relations cannot be found, the system judges that the solution-method cannot be applied to the PUN. This is the assignment step.

After all the variables are replaced by basic relations as shown in Fig. 10, the states of numerical values are examined. When all states correspond to the states in the generic ISM, the solution method can be applied to the PUN. For example, V7 is substituted into the "total number of cranes" in Fig. 10 and its numerical value is "unknown." The state corresponds to the state of V7 in the generic ISM.

When "known" value in the generic ISM is "unknown" in the assignment, finding the value is required. We call this state "incomplete." For example, in Fig. 3, if the sentences of the number of a crane and turtle's legs are omitted, the replacement of variables shown in Fig. 10 is possible but the state of "number of legs of a crane" and "number of legs of a turtle" are incomplete. To dissolve the incomplete states, fact-knowledge and operational knowledge are used. When there is fact-knowledge, the "number of legs of a crane are two," the value can be added to the basic relation and the incomplete state is dissolved. If this trail fails, operational knowledge is used to complement a necessary value. Fig. 11 shows a problem that can be solved by the crane-turtle method. An assignment by using the PUN and operational knowledge is shown in Fig. 12. In the assignment, the "total score of students" is incomplete. There is no fact-knowledge to complement the value. If there is operational-knowledge, "(total score of students) = (average score of students) * (number of students)," the value can be deduced. When all incomplete states are dissolved, the PUN is a final-PUN that can be solved by the solution-method. When a final-PUN cannot be generated, the solution-method cannot be applied. But, it doesn't mean that the problem cannot be solved by any solution-methods.

Detected Errors in Generation of final-PUN
Detected errors in this step are categorized as follows: (e) errors in the assignment step, (f) errors in the complement step. When the assignment of variables fails, the solution method cannot be applied. In this case, the support module indicates the problem cannot be solved by the solution-method. For example, Fig. 13 shows an example of a problem. For this problem, the diagnosis module cannot find an adequate assignment. So the ILE gives the learner a message "this problem cannot be solved by the crane-turtle method".

[V5, known] × [V3, answer] = [V7, unknown]
[V6, known] × [V4, answer] = [V8, unknown]
[V7, unknown]+[V8, unknown]=[V2, known]
[V3, answer]+[V4, answer]=[V1, known]

Fig. 7. The generic ISM.

$V1 * V5 = X$, $|V2 - X| = Y$
$|V5 - V6| = Z$, $Y / Z = V4$
$V1 - V4 = V3$

Fig. 8. Calculation procedure of the crane-turtle method.

```
[number of legs of a crane, known] * [number of cranes, answer] = [V7, unknown]
[number of lens of a turtle, known] * [number of turtles, answer] = [V8, unknown]
[V7, unknown]+[V8, unknown]=[total number of legs of cranes, known]
[number of cranes, answer]+[number of turtles, answer]=[total number of cranes and turtles, known]
```

Fig. 9. Assignment by basic relations.

```
[number of legs of a crane, known] * [number of cranes, answer] = [total number of legs of cranes, unknown]
[number of legs of a turtle, known] * [number of turtles, answer] = [total number of legs of turtles, unknown]
[total number of legs of cranes, unknown]+[total number of legs of turtles, unknown]=[total number of legs, known]
```

Fig. 10. Replacement by operational knowledge.

```
(1) There are forty students in the class.
(2) The average score of the test of the students is 69.
(3) The average score of the test of boys is 65.
(4) The average score of the test of girls is 75.
(5) How many boys are there?
(6) How many girls are there?
```

Fig. 11. Problem-2: a crane-turtle problem.

```
[average score of boys, known] * [number of boys, answer] = [total score of boys, unknown]
[average score of girls, known] * [number of girls, answer] = [total score of girls, unknown]
[total score of boys, unknown]+ [total score of girls, unknown]=[total score of students, *incomplete*]
[number of boys, answer]+[number of girls, answer]=[total number of students, known]
```

Fig. 12. Replacement by operational knowledge.

```
There are cranes, 4 in total.
There are cranes and turtles, 20 in total.
How many turtles are there?
```

```
There are cranes and turtles, 20 in total.
How many cranes are there?
How many turtles are there?
```

Fig. 13. An example of problem (3).

Fig. 14. An example of problem (4).

When the complement step fails, the diagnosis module detects the lacking information. Therefore, the support module can indicate the lacking information. For example, the problem shown in Fig. 14 does not have a sentence that gives "the number of total legs of cranes and turtles." The diagnosis module can find that the value is incomplete, but cannot complement it. As a result, the module detects "the number of total legs of cranes and turtles" as information that is lacking. Then, the support module requires the learner add the information. First, the ILE gives a message "the number of total legs of cranes and turtles is necessary to solve this problem by the crane-turtle method".

3.4 Working Out the Answers

When a final-PUN of the crane-turtle method is generated, the answers are worked out by using the calculation procedure shown in Fig. 8. However, because the domain is the arithmetical word problem, the numerical values appearing in the solution are limited. Therefore, the diagnosis module checks them with fact-knowledge. For example, the total number of cranes and turtles must be a natural number. If it is a negative number or a decimal, the problem is inadequate. In this error case, the support module indicates that the value is inadequate. Then, it points out the proper range of the value.

3.5 Categorization of Problems

Learners can make large range of correct problems. Some of them are complex ones and some of them are simple ones. Assessing the difficulty of the problems is important to assist in adequate problem posing. We categorize problems with the following two factors: (1) the complement operations that are used to generate a final-PUN, and (2) the concepts that compose a problem. From the viewpoint of the complement operations, problems are divided into the following three categories: (I) none used, (II) fact knowledge is used, (III) operational knowledge is used. As for the complement operations, problems that do not require using complement operation are the simplest. Then, problems that require using operational knowledge are the most complex.

The difficulty of concepts is measured by the difference from the concepts included in the basic problem shown in Fig. 3. The basic problem is composed of cranes, turtles and legs. The values in the problem are discrete values. A problem that is composed of dogs, spiders and legs, is closer to the basic problem than a problem that is composed of apples, oranges and prices. From the viewpoint of the concepts, we think a problem that is closer to the basic problem in concepts is easier. By using the two factors, we prepared several categories of problems, which differ in difficulty. When a learner can pose problems that belong to a category, the support module facilitates posing of the problems that are included in more difficult category. Currently, the prototype of the ILE described in Section 4 has five categories of problems. By using the categories, the ILE changes concepts provided in the concept panel in the problem posing interface.

3.6 Preliminary Evaluation of the ILE

A prototype of the ILE has been developed. As a preliminary evaluation of the prototype, we asked several college students to use the prototype. They are experiences of tutoring and master the crane-turtle method. So, they evaluated the ILE from a position to teach the crane-turtle method. Questions and results are as follows: (question-1) the effect of problem posing to master the solution-method {Good:9, Bad: 0, So-so: 0}, (question-2) the effect of the ILE to master the solution-method {Good:8, Bad:0, So-so:1}, and (question-3) the convenience of the ILE {Good:8, Bad:0, So-so:1}. These results suggest that the ILE is a promising way to realize problem posing.

The prototype is available with Internet browser (at present, only in Japanese). Its URL is as follows.

(http://www.minnie.ai.kyutech.ac.jp/~nakano/problem-making.html)

4. Conclusion Remarks

In this paper, we described a problem diagnosis function for an intelligent learning environment that supports solution-based problem posing. The diagnosis function can examine not only whether or not the problem can be solved by the target solution-method, but also which information is lacking or wrong. Besides, the degree of difficulty of the problem is assessed to estimate the learner's progress. A prototype of the ILE with the diagnosis function is already implemented. The preliminary evaluation of the ILE was also reported. Interface of the ILE was implemented by Java, and the diagnosis function was implemented by Prolog. Therefore, the ILE can be used with a Web browser.

References

1. National Council of Teachers of Mathematics, *Curriculum and evaluation standards for school mathematics*. Reston, VA: Author, 1989.
2. National Council of Teachers of Mathematics, *Professional standards for teaching mathematics*, Reston, VA: Author, 1991.
3. Ellerton, N.F.: Children's Made Up Mathematics Problems: A New Perspective on Talented Mathematicians. *Educational Studies in Mathematics*, Vol.17, pp.261-271 (1986).
4. Brown, S.I., Walter, M.I.: *Problem Posing: Reflections and Applications*, Lawrence Erlbaum Associates, 1993
5. Silver, E.A., CAI, J.: An Analysis of Arithmetic Problem Posing by Middle School Students, *Journal for Research in Mathematics Education*, Vol.27, No.5, pp.521-539, 1996.
6. Silver, E.A, Mamona, J., Leung, S.S., Kenney, P.A.: Posing Mathematical Problems: An Exploratory Study, *Journal for Research in Mathematics Education*, Vol.27, No.3, pp.293-309, 1996.
7. English, L.D.: Children's Problem Posing Within Formal and Informal Contexts, *Journal for Research in Mathematics Education*, Vol.29, No.1, pp.83-106, 1998.
8. Hirashima, T. Kashihara, A. Toyoda, J: Providing Problem Explanation for ITS, Proc. of ITS'92 (Lecture Notes in Computer Science 608), pp.76-83, 1992.

Combining Kalman Filtering and Markov Localization in Network-Like Environments

Sylvie Thiébaux and Peter Lamb

CSIRO Mathematical & Information Sciences
PO Box 664, Canberra 2601, Australia
First.Last@cmis.csiro.au

Abstract. This paper presents a hybrid localization method designed for environments having the structure of a network (road networks, sewerage networks, underground mines, *etc*...). The method, which views localization as a problem of state estimation in a switching environment, combines the flexibility and robustness of Markov localization with the accuracy and efficiency of Kalman filtering. This is achieved by letting Markov localization handle the topological aspects of the problem, and Kalman filtering the metric aspects. The two techniques are closely coupled: the Markov model determines the Kalman filters to be initiated, and statistics computed by the Kalman filters are used to define the transition and observation probabilities in the Markov model. This approach has been applied to the problem of localizing a motor vehicle traveling on an urban road network, providing robust and accurate localization at low cost.

1 Introduction

A recent comparison of localization methods [9] indicates that Kalman filtering based techniques [12, 10, 3] and Markov localization [13, 6, 8] have complementary advantages. Kalman filtering is efficient and accurate, but is confined to small Gaussian sensor perturbations. Markov localization is robust to a larger amount and a wider range of uncertainty, but is computationally much more demanding while comparatively less accurate. As suggested in [9], judiciously combining these techniques could therefore result in hybrid methods that are efficient, accurate, flexible and robust.

The present paper describes such a hybrid localization method, designed for environments having a network structure. By network, we mean a set of straight line segments connected at their extremities. The segments are to be treated as one-dimensional (lateral or vertical displacement is irrelevant), so by localizing, we mean determining the current segment and the current coordinate from the origin of this segment. An application example, used in this paper, is localizing a motor vehicle traveling on an urban road network. This is a prerequisite to a number of tasks in the field of Intelligent Transport Systems, such as on-board vehicle navigation [16]. Another example is localizing robots navigating in, inspecting and repairing a network of sewerage pipes [11].

To achieve effective localization in these environments, we propose to view localization as a problem of state estimation in a switching environment (see [2] for the seminal paper), and to approach it using methods for multiple hypothesis tracking (see [4, pp. 450-483] for a survey). This amounts to letting Markov localization handle the topological aspects of the problem and Kalman filtering the metric aspects. At the topological level, a Markov model accounts for the progression from segment to segment, and maintains a probability distribution about the path (history of segments) followed. This permits a number of concurrent hypotheses to be considered about the current segment. At the metric level, a distinct Kalman filter is assigned to each of the most likely paths, and tracks the distance traveled along the current segment of this path. The two levels are closely coupled: the Markov model determines the Kalman filters to be initiated, and statistics computed by the Kalman filters are used to define the transition and observation probabilities in the Markov model.

This combination offers the best of both underlying techniques for the type of environment considered. While delivering the required accuracy, it reduces the complexity of Markov localization if it were used alone, yet inherits its flexibility and robustness (in particular the ability to operate with little *a priori* information on the starting location). It also avoids the need for explicit map-matching which usually accompanies Kalman filtering based techniques: since each Kalman filter operates only in one spatial dimension (the dimension of a segment), the location it produces is already constrained to lie on the network.

The method is particularly well-suited to applications for which (1) Kalman filtering techniques alone are inadequate because reliable sensory information is too expensive or unavailable, and (2) pure Markov localization is also unsatisfactory because landmarks are too rare to allow for quantization up to the required accuracy. The sewerage robot and motor vehicle localization problems share these properties. For instance, GPS signals are inaccessible in sewerage pipes which are installed meters below street level, and the high slip in these pipes makes reliable odometry difficult. Although GPS receivers are available to motor vehicles, their cost contributes to making navigation systems too expensive for the non-luxury car market. In both domains, natural landmarks are only present at the extremities of the network's segments (junctions between pipes, road intersections), and not inbetween.

In this paper, we shall present the principles of our hybrid method, using a motor vehicle localization problem for illustration. The example is chosen so as to expose the key features of the method and facilitate understanding of how this latter can address other application domains and more complex situations. The next section presents a Kalman filter operating in a single spatial dimension to estimate the distance traveled on a given segment. Then, we describe the use of Markov localization to determine the current path, and explain how the two techniques are coupled. The presentation in these sections does not assume familiarity with the respective techniques. We go on to give experimental results on field and simulated data, before concluding with some notes on related work.

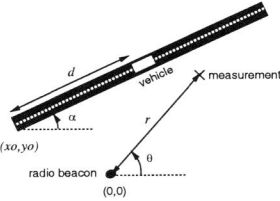

Fig. 1. Vehicle traveling on a road segment

2 One-Dimensional Kalman Filter

The purpose of a discrete-time Kalman filter is to give an optimal estimate of the state of a system at discrete points of time, taking into account the dynamics of this system, the available sensor information, and the uncertainty on these which is assumed to be Gaussian.[1] The basic type of Kalman filter handles *linear* systems, that is systems for which observations and dynamics can be expressed as linear systems of equations:

$$z(t) = C(t)x(t) + w(t) \qquad (1)$$
$$x(t+1) = A(t)x(t) + B(t)u(t) + v(t) \qquad (2)$$

Let us detail the functions involved in turn, using concrete examples from a vehicle localization application.

$x(t)$, the *state vector*, is a vector of n variables representing the state of the system at time t. Here in order to track a vehicle traveling on a single road segment (as in Figure 1), we model one spatial dimension, namely the distance d separating the vehicle from the segment's origin (x_0, y_0). We choose to represent the state of the vehicle by a third-order model comprising the distance d, the vehicle's speed $\dot{d}$, and its acceleration $\ddot{d}$. So $x(t) = [d, \dot{d}, \ddot{d}]'_t$.

$z(t)$, the *measurement vector*, is a vector of p variables representing the observations made at time t, if any. In our trials below, observations come from an experimental beacon-based positioning system[2] which measures the angle θ

---

[1] Let us recall that an n-dimensional Gaussian variable x (i.e. a vector of n Gaussian variables) is characterized by two quantities: its mean m, an n-dimensional vector, and its covariance C, a symmetric $n \times n$ matrix. This is written $x \sim N(m, C)$. $C_{i,i}$ is the variance of x_i and $C_{i,j}$ ($i \neq j$) indicates the extent to which x_i and x_j are correlated. The probability density at x is:

$$\Pr(x) = \frac{\exp\left[-0.5(x - m)' C^{-1}(x - m)\right]}{\sqrt{\det[2\pi C]}}$$

Note that the exponent indeed evaluates to a scalar, and that ′ refers to the transpose of a vector or a matrix.

[2] Without loss of generality, we use this positioning system which is much less reliable than GPS but also less expensive, to show that our method can cope with a large amount of noise and yield an affordable localization system.

and range r between a radio beacon and the vehicle (see Figure 1). From this, we can easily derive the x-y coordinates[3] of the vehicle relative to the segment's origin as $x = r\cos\theta - x_0$ and $y = r\sin\theta - y_0$, and take $\mathsf{z}(t) = [x, y]'_t$.

$\mathsf{C}(t)$, the *state to measurement matrix*, is a $p \times n$ matrix mapping the state vector into the measurement vector that would be obtained at time t in the absence of sensor uncertainty. Obviously here, if α is the angle between the horizontal axis and the segment, then:

$$\mathsf{C}(t) = \begin{bmatrix} \cos\alpha & 0 & 0 \\ \sin\alpha & 0 & 0 \end{bmatrix} \text{ for all } t$$

$\mathsf{w}(t)$, the *measurement noise vector*, is a p-dimensional Gaussian variable with mean zero and covariance matrix $\mathsf{R}(t)$, representing the uncertainty affecting the observations. For our vehicle localization example, it can be shown that if σ_r^2 and σ_θ^2 are the respective variances for the r and θ measured at time t, then (provided that σ_θ is small):[4]

$$\mathsf{R}(t) = \begin{bmatrix} r^2\sigma_\theta^2 \sin^2\theta + \sigma_r^2 \cos^2\theta & \cos\theta \sin\theta (\sigma_r^2 - r^2\sigma_\theta^2) \\ \cos\theta \sin\theta (\sigma_r^2 - r^2\sigma_\theta^2) & r^2\sigma_\theta^2 \cos^2\theta + \sigma_r^2 \sin^2\theta \end{bmatrix}_t$$

$\mathsf{A}(t)$, the *state transition matrix*, is an $n \times n$ matrix mapping the state vector at time t into the successor state vector that would be obtained at time $t+1$ in the absence of external action (or *input*) intending to control the system. Let T be the sampling interval separating two consecutive time steps t and $t+1$, then elementary kinematics yields the following transition matrix for the vehicle localization example:

$$\mathsf{A}(t) = \begin{bmatrix} 1 & T & T^2/2 \\ 0 & 1 & T \\ 0 & 0 & 1 \end{bmatrix} \text{ for all } t$$

$\mathsf{u}(t)$, the *input vector*, is a q-dimensional vector representing the input applied to the system at time t, and $\mathsf{B}(t)$, the *input gain*, is the $n \times q$ matrix translating the input into the corresponding modifications in the state vector. For a motor vehicle, the input typically corresponds to the rate of change in acceleration ($\dddot{d}$ or *jerk*) initiated by the driver, but unfortunately, this quantity is unknown to us. Another alternative which is commonly chosen when tracking robots is to use odometry information as (part of) the input. However, in the experiments below this possibility was not available to us either, since our vehicle had no interface to the odometer.[5] So for this particular application we are forced to ignore the

---

[3] A two dimensional space is sufficient for our application, however adding a third dimension is straightforward.

[4] Note that measurements (r, θ) are a *non-linear* function of the state, so we should in principle use an Extended Kalman Filter (EKF) [4, ch. 10]. Our way of computing $\mathsf{R}(t)$ is effectively an EKF approach, but which we found more stable.

[5] Odometry information would certainly improve the performance of the system. We are able to show that our method operates reliably even when such information is lacking.

input term in equation (2) and treat the jerk as the uncertainty affecting the dynamics of a vehicle operating otherwise at constant acceleration.

This leads us to $\mathsf{v}(t)$, the *process noise vector*, an n-dimensional Gaussian variable with mean zero and covariance matrix $\mathsf{Q}(t)$, which represents the uncertainty on the system's dynamics. Here $\mathsf{v}(t) = [0, 0, T\,\dddot{d}]'_t$, where $\dddot{d} \sim N(0, \sigma_j)$. For our experiments, we took σ_j to be the average of the second derivative of a speed profile (speed vs time) used for fuel consumption testing [1, p.19]. Using basic kinematics, we derived the following covariance matrix for $\mathsf{v}(t)$:

$$\mathsf{Q}(t) = \sigma_j^2 \begin{bmatrix} T^6/36 & T^5/12 & T^4/6 \\ T^5/12 & T^4/4 & T^3/2 \\ T^4/6 & T^3/2 & T^2 \end{bmatrix} \quad \text{for all } t$$

How does the Kalman filter work? For a formal treatment we refer to a standard textbook, e.g. [4]. Briefly, the Kalman filter starts with an initial estimate of $\mathsf{x}(1)$ characterized by its mean $\hat{\mathsf{x}}(1)$ and its covariance matrix $\mathsf{P}(1)$. At each step, equations (1) and (2) and the previous state estimate $\hat{\mathsf{x}}(t)$ are used to calculate a prior estimate $\hat{\mathsf{x}}^-(t+1)$ of the new state, the observations $\hat{\mathsf{z}}(t+1)$ that should result, and the respective covariance matrices. When measurement $\mathsf{z}(t+1)$ is made, the filter *innovation*, i.e., the difference $\mathsf{i}(t+1) = \mathsf{z}(t+1) - \hat{\mathsf{z}}(t+1)$ between the actual and predicted observations is computed, and the prior state estimate is revised using Bayes' rule to optimally account for the discrepancy. The assumptions of linearity and Gaussian uncertainty together guarantee that the state estimate at each time step is Gaussian. This give rise to a very economical update procedure, which consists of a few elementary matrix operations.

A well known result (see [4]) is that the innovation is also a zero-mean Gaussian variable with the useful property that the probability of the observations at time $t+1$ given the past history – i.e., the observation history $Z(t) = \mathsf{z}(1)\dots\mathsf{z}(t)$ combined with equations (1) and (2) – equals the probability density of the innovation:

$$\Pr(\mathsf{z}(t+1) \mid Z(t)) = \Pr(\mathsf{i}(t+1))$$

As the Kalman filter procedure also involves computing the covariance matrix of the innovation, the above probability, which we will need in the next section, is readily available.

3 The Markov Model

The one-dimensional Kalman filter will correctly track the distance traveled on a single segment. To handle the whole network[6] however, we need a further mechanism enabling us (a) to maintain multiple hypotheses about the current segment, (b) to initiate new filters to operate on new hypothesized segments when approaching a junction, and (c) to compute the most likely location overall. To this end, we model segment change as an abrupt change of linear system,

---
[6] Curved roads can easily be accommodated as piecewise linear approximations and handled as a special case of the operations on junctions presented here.

which we handle using methods for multiple hypothesis tracking [2,14,15,4]. This amounts to the embedding of one-dimensional Kalman filters in a Markov model of the path (segment history) taken through the network, and to viewing segment change as a change of state in this Markov model.

Like Kalman filters, discrete Markov models are designed to give a Bayesian estimate of the current state of a system, given information about the dynamics of this system, and about the way it can be observed. Markov models are however much more generally applicable than Kalman filters and in return much more computationally demanding. In particular they are not limited to Gaussian noise. The uncertainty on the current state is represented by an arbitrary probability distribution on the set of states, often called the *belief state*. In lieu of the observation equation of the Kalman filter, an arbitrary *observation probability* distribution specifies the probability of making some observation given the current state, and in lieu of the the dynamics equation of the filter, an arbitrary *transition probability* distribution specifies the probability of the next state given the current one.

Here, the *states* of the Markov model at time t are the segment histories $S(t) = s(1)\ldots s(t)$, a subset of which represent possible paths through the network. We denote the probability of segment history $S(t)$ in the belief state at time t as $b(S(t))$. To each segment history $S(t)$ is assigned a Kalman filter which tracks the distance traveled on the current segment $s(t)$ of this history. Naturally, the state to measurement matrix of this filter is parametrized by the angle $\alpha_{s(t)}$ of that segment. So the observation equation for that filter is:

$$\mathsf{z}(t) = \mathsf{C}_{s(t)}(t)\mathsf{x}(t) + \mathsf{w}(t)$$

The *transition probabilities* $\mathrm{Tr}(S(t), S(t+1))$ for the Markov model are defined by examining the events that may affect the path: at time $t+1$ we may stay on the current segment $s(t)$, or we may have turned onto a connected segment. The first type of event does not require initiating a new Kalman filter, while the second type does. What is the probability of each of these events? If d is the distance component of the state estimate $\hat{\mathsf{x}}(t)$ tracked by the filter assigned to history $S(t)$, and l is the length of segment $s(t)$, then the probability of remaining on $s(t)$ is $\Pr(0 \leq d \leq l)$. Everything being equal, the probability of turning on any of the n_1 segments connected to the origin of $s(t)$ is $\Pr(d < 0)/n_1$, and similarly the probability of turning on any of the n_2 segments at the other extremity is $\Pr(d > l)/n_2$ (see Figure 2). d being Gaussian, these probabilities are easily calculated. Naturally, this simple scheme can be elaborated to handle more complicated situations, as required. For instance, advice to make a certain turn given by a vehicle navigation system or by a robot navigation policy should result in that turn being assigned a higher probability than others.

As for the *observation probabilities* of the Markov model, they can be easily computed by noting that the probability of observing $\mathsf{z}(t)$ when traveling along segment history $S(t)$ is simply the probability $\Pr(\mathsf{i}_S(t))$ of the innovation in the filter assigned to that history. Again, this is the default: depending on the application, we may want to incorporate here observations of a topological nature

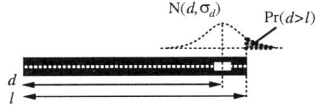

Fig. 2. Probability of exiting a segment

that were irrelevant at the Kalman filter level. For example, sewer robots are able to distinguish (with some probability of error) between several types of junctions connecting sewerage pipes, and can use this information for self-localization [11].

At each time step the belief state of the Markov model is updated using a straightforward application of Bayes' rule. So when at time $t + 1$ we extend segment history $S(t)$ by appending segment $s(t+1)$, then following measurement $\mathsf{z}(t + 1)$, the probability $\mathsf{b}(S(t + 1))$ of the resulting history is:

$$\mathsf{b}(S(t+1)) = \lambda \Pr(\mathsf{i}_S(t+1)) \mathrm{Tr}(S(t), S(t+1)) \mathsf{b}(S(t))$$

where λ is the normalizing factor.

At any time, the location returned by the system is that indicated by the Kalman filter assigned to the most probable segment history. Alternatively, we could use the expectation of the locations indicated by all the Kalman filters operating on the most probable segment. The more usual approach of using the expectation of the location estimates over all segment histories is not used here, because the resulting location will typically not lie on the network.

Even if the number of possible paths through the network is significantly lower than the total number of segment histories, the number of filters involved in the above estimation process grows exponentially with time. Since most segment histories have extremely low probabilities, it therefore makes sense to keep the computational cost bounded by pruning a large number of them. To this end, we act on two parameters. Firstly, we set a threshold p_{thresh} on the transition probabilities such that if $\mathrm{Tr}(S(t), S(t+1)) < p_{thresh}$ then the transition is simply ignored. Secondly, we follow [14] in only keeping the N most probable histories at each time step.[7] The robustness and accuracy of the localization process will depend on the settings for these two parameters, but we have observed that the algorithm operates satisfactorily over a wide range of settings. At present, we do not vary these parameters during a run, but it would be interesting to investigate ways of selecting their value according to the topology of the current junction (angle between the segments involved, connectivity).

---

[7] Further reduction of the tree size can be achieved using techniques from the field of multiple hypothesis tracking, e.g. merging histories having the same current segment and close distance estimate and pruning unlikely histories according to validation gates for the corresponding filters (see e.g. [14]). On the other hand, other well-known heuristics such as Generalised Pseudo Bayes (GPB) or Interacting Multiple Model (IMM) [4, ch. 11] do not seem to be as relevant here, as they deny the assumption that past locations are constrained to lie on the network.

4 Experiments

To validate our approach, we conducted a series of field trials and simulations with the motor vehicle localization system outlined in this paper. Our C++ implementation running under Windows 98 on a 133 Mhz Pentium with 24 Mb of memory proved sufficient to achieve real-time performance on field trials.

As our approach inherits Markov localization's ability to globally (re-)localize the vehicle, the starting location does not need to be known. At the start of each experiment and following a loss of the vehicle location,[8] the belief state was initialized by taking the projection of the first available measurement onto a large number of segments in the area, assigning to each of these segments a probability inversely proportional to the Euclidian distance between the measurement and the nearest point on the segment, and taking the projections to be the initial estimates for the respective filters. We observed that the localization system successfully resolved the ambiguity between the segments within a few seconds after the vehicle started moving.

An example of the localization system operating in the center of Canberra is shown in Figure 3(a). The successive measurements are represented by crosses and joined by gray lines. Location estimates returned by the system are represented by boxes and are joined to the corresponding measurements (when available) by dark gray lines.

The beacon is located at the respective origins of the axes. Measurements are made at the rate of one per second. The standard deviation of the measurement is around 5.9 m for r and 11.9° for θ. If the direct path to the vehicle is blocked, the measurement may indicate the distance and angle of a reflected path. This can introduce short term bias into the measurements, e.g. see the right hand end of Ainslie. Sometimes, measurements are completely missing due to interference, see e.g. the top of Bunda and the left half of Ainslie where many locations lack corresponding measurements. The Kalman filter is particularly useful in such cases, since it still exploits the vehicle's dynamics to return an estimate in the absence of observation. At each step however, the uncertainty about the location increases. For example, this keeps the probability that the vehicle has turned from Bunda to Ainslie below that of the vehicle maintaining its track along Bunda, until a measurement takes place which forces the transition.

An additional difficulty is caused by traffic lights and pedestrian crossings placed around intersections. When the vehicle is queuing near an intersection, the lateral error of the measurement makes it quite plausible that it has turned on a perpendicular street. This happens for instance at the traffic light at the intersection between Bunda and Akuna. However, provided the transition probability threshold is set to a reasonable value (e.g. $p_{thresh} = 0.01$), good track of the vehicle is kept, even if we only maintain a few filters (e.g. $N = 3$). Figure 3(a) has been produced with these settings. Recovery following a wrong segment selection only takes a few seconds even with sparse measurements, see e.g. the

---

[8] The system considers the vehicle location to be lost when the variance of the distance estimate returned by the most probable Kalman filter exceeds a certain threshold.

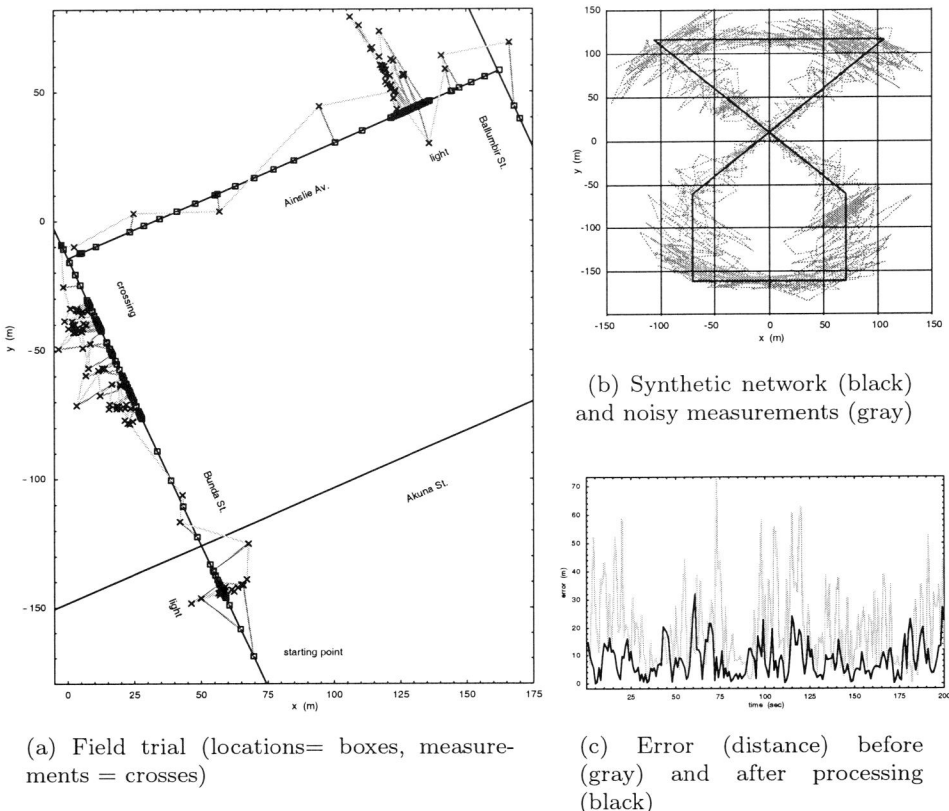

(a) Field trial (locations= boxes, measurements = crosses)

(b) Synthetic network (black) and noisy measurements (gray)

(c) Error (distance) before (gray) and after processing (black)

Fig. 3. Experiments

intersection between Bunda and Ainslie. We observed that maintaining a larger number of filters improves the accuracy of the location.

The 8 segment synthetic network shown in Figure 3(b) permits an accurate comparison of the raw positioning information with the estimated vehicle location. The simulation experiment we report here is based on a 12 km long car trajectory generated with the speed of the vehicle controlled by the same drive cycle data used to estimate the variance σ_j^2 of the jerk for the Kalman filters. At the middle of the network, the vehicle makes a random turn choice. The beacon is located near this intersection. Measurements following Gaussian distributions with standard deviation 5.9 m for r and 11.9° for θ (i.e., the same as for the above field test) are generated every second. As shown by the dotted lines in Figure 3(b), this leads to a large lateral error for large r.

Because of the large lateral noise, the length of the trajectory, and especially the top acute corners, the network is quite demanding of the algorithm – note that the total number of segments is of minor importance to this algorithm; more relevant is the local connectivity of the network. In order not to lose track of the vehicle at one point or another we find that a minimum of 10 filters must be maintained, and that the transition probability threshold needs to be set to a low value ($p_{thresh} = 10^{-6}$) to ensure that transitions are generated for locations "around the corner".

Figure 3(c) shows the error (distance) between the real vehicle position and the raw positioning information (gray), resp. the estimated location (black), as a function of time for a representative subset (about 1/5) of the trajectory. The localization process improves the average error from 21m to 8m. Occasionally an incorrect segment choice is made as a corner is approached, but the choice is corrected within a few (2-3) seconds of the turn being made. Conventional approaches to motor vehicle location achieve comparable figures only by using much more accurate positioning information integrating GPS and odometry.

5 Conclusion and Related Work

This paper describes a hybrid approach to localization in network-like environments. This approach inherits the accuracy and efficiency of Kalman filtering based techniques, as well as the robustness, generality and globality of Markov localization.

As mentioned above, our way of embedding Kalman filters in a Markov model follows the principles underlying multiple hypothesis tracking for state estimation in switching environments. Other related work includes approaches improving the efficiency and accuracy of Markov localization. For instance dynamic Markov localization [5] is a fine-grained grid-based Markov localization method which selectively updates the likely parts of the belief state, and dynamically modifies the grain of the quantization to adjust to the certainty of the current location. This technique is more general and uniform than ours. However, our method is very likely to prove more efficient for the type of applications considered in this paper, because as evidenced by the vehicle localization problem, acceptable accuracy cannot be delivered by a method based solely on Markov localization without excessive quantization within a segment. Monte Carlo localization [7] is another Markov localization technique which achieves impressive performance by judiciously sampling the belief state. We believe that Monte Carlo localization could profitably be incorporated to our framework to cope with highly connected networks.

Our method has successfully been applied to motor vehicle localization in urban road networks. In this context, it avoids the error-prone map-matching step which underlies most conventional approaches to motor vehicle localization [16], and is able to produce results with comparable accuracy without requiring high performance positioning systems. Our approach is particularly attractive in that respect, since reducing the cost of localization is an important step towards making navigation systems affordable for non-luxury vehicles. We are confident that this approach will prove useful in environments sharing similar properties, for instance in sewerage or underground mine networks to provide an accurate metric localization in real-time. It remains to be seen whether our method can easily be extended to environments having a different structure while still retaining most of its benefits.

Acknowledgements

We thank Jens-Steffen Gutmann, Joachim Hertzberg, Phil Kilby, John Slaney, and a number of anonymous reviewers for their valuable comments on earlier drafts of this paper.

References

1. Methods of test for fuel consumption of motor vehicles designed to comply with Australian Design Rules 37 and 40. Publication AS 2877-1986, Standards Association of Australia, 1986.
2. G. Ackerson and K.S. Fu. On State Estimation in Switching Environments. *IEEE Trans. Aut. Control*, 15(1), 1970.
3. K. Arras and S. Vestli. Hybrid, High-Precision Localisation for the Mail Distributing Mobile Robot System MOPS. In *Proc. ICRA-98*, 1998.
4. Y. Bar-Shalom and X.-R. Li. *Estimation and Tracking: Principles, Techniques and Software*. Artech House, 1993.
5. W. Burgard, A. Derr, D. Fox, and A.B. Cremers. Integrating Global Position Estimation and Position Tracking for Mobile Robots: The Dynamic Markov Localization Approach. In *Proc. IROS-98*, 1998.
6. A.R. Cassandra, L. Kaelbling, and J.A Kurien. Acting under Uncertainty: Discrete Bayesian Models for Mobile-Robot Navigation. In *Proc. IROS-96*, 1996.
7. D. Fox, W. Burgard, F. Dellaert, and S. Thrun. Monte Carlo Localization: Efficient Position Estimation for Mobile Robots. In *Proc. AAAI-99*, pages 343–349, 1999.
8. D. Fox, W. Burgard, S. Thrun, and A.B Cremers. Position Estimation for Mobile Robots in Dynamic Environments. In *Proc. AAAI-98*, pages 983–988, 1998.
9. J.-S. Gutmann, W. Burgard, D. Fox, and K. Konolige. An Experimental Comparison of Localization Methods. In *Proc. IROS-98*, 1998.
10. J.-S. Gutmann and C. Schlegel. AMOS: Comparison of Scan Matching Approaches for Self-Localization in Indoor Environments. In *Proc. EUROBOTS-96*. IEEE Computer Society Press, 1996.
11. J. Hertzberg and F. Kirchner. Landmark-Based Autonomous Navigation in Sewerage Pipes. In *Proc. EUROBOTS-96*, pages 68–73. IEEE Computer Society Press, 1996.
12. P.S. Maybeck. The Kalman Filter: An Introduction to Concepts. In I. Cox and G. Wilfong, editors, *Autonomous Robot Vehicles*. Springer Verlag, 1990.
13. R. Simmons and S. Koenig. Probabilistic Robot Navigation in Partially Observable Environments. In *Proc. IJCAI-95*, pages 1080–1087, 1995.
14. J.K. Tugnait and A.H. Haddad. Detection and estimation scheme for state estimation in switching environements. *Automatica*, 15:477–481, 1982.
15. K. Watanabe and S.G. Tzafestas. Generalised pseudo-bayes estimation and detection for abruptly changing systems. *Journal of Intelligent and Robotic Systems*, 7:95–112, 1993.
16. Y. Zhao. *Vehicle Location and Navigation Systems*. Artech House, 1997.

Microbes and Music

Fran Soddell[1] and Jacques Soddell[2]

[1] La Trobe University, Bendigo, Australia
F.Soddell@bendigo.latrobe.edu.au
http://ironbark.bendigo.latrobe.edu.au/~fran/
[2] Biotechnology Research Centre, La Trobe University, Bendigo, Australia
J.Soddell@bendigo.latrobe.edu.au
http://ironbark.bendigo.latrobe.edu.au/~soddell/

Abstract. L-systems are string rewriting mechanisms used to create images of complex organisms from a simple set of an axiom and production rules. They have also been used to create music. This study developed a Musical Instrument Digital Interface interpretation suitable for applying to strings generated by L-systems that had been previously developed to model the growth of filamentous microbes (fungi and bacteria). The resulting sound files helped distinguish between organisms with different growth rates, provided some insight into the temporal differences among stages of growth, and also resulted in interesting musical pieces.

1 Introduction

In the last decade, there has been an increasing interest in the us of sonification to assist our understanding of scientific data in the way that visualisation does [11, 27, 1, 12, 25, 4, 26, 5, 2, 3]. However, although the sonification of protein data has been used to create music [3], sonification has not been applied to modelling the growth and development of biological organisms. Building on our interest in modelling filamentous microbes using Lindenmayer systems (L-systems), we used L-systems that generate realistic images of growing fungal colonies, to generate Musical Instrument Digital Interface (MIDI) files. The resulting sound files, which we played using freely available software, provided some insight into the temporal differences among stages of growth. Furthermore the sound interpretation developed for modelling such differences resulted in interesting musical pieces not only from systems modelling fungi, but also from those developed by Prusinkiewicz and Lindenmayer [19] for producing realistic images of bushes.

1.1 L-Systems

L-systems are string rewriting mechanisms introduced to model the growth and development of multicellular organisms [7, 8]. Computer scientists investigated them through formal language theory [18], Smith [22] proposed using them to create computer generated images of plants, and Prusinkiewicz and Lindenmayer [19] created systems that produce realistic images of trees, bushes and flowers.

Although not applied as widely in biology as in computer graphics, they have been investigated as a way of specifying the spatial arrangement of plant components and their development over time [17].

Each L-system has a finite set of symbols, an *alphabet*, a start symbol or string of symbols, an *axiom*, and a finite set of rules, *productions*. Productions are applied in parallel to a given string, simultaneously replacing all symbols. They are applied first to the axiom, then to the resulting string (first generation), then to the first generation and so on. We used deterministic, stochastic, context-sensitive, context-free and parametric systems.

```
#define maxgen 4

START : F-F-F-F-

p1 : F -> FF-F-F-F-F-F+F
```

Fig. 1. L system for *lsys* to generate Koch curve from *The Algorithmic Beauty of Plants* [19] and Turtle Graphics Interpretation.

In deterministic systems, only one production applies to any one symbol at a given time, so they produce a single infinite derivation sequence [10]. Stochastic systems apply productions stochastically, so different strings can be derived from the same string at any step, and they may produce many derivation sequences. In context-free 0L-systems, productions rewrite a symbol without considering adjacent symbols. Fig. 1 gives an example of a deterministic, context-free DOL-system, taken from *The Algorithmic Beauty of Plants* [19].

The axiom for the DOL-system in Fig. 1 is F-F-F-F- and the single production specifies the replacement of every occurrence of F with FF-F-F-F-F-F+F. The first generation string from this system is FF-F-F-F-F-F+F-FF-F-F-F-F-F+F-FF-F-F-F-F-F+F-FF-F-F-F-F-F+F-. For the second generation, replace every F in the first generation as specified by the production, and so on for successive generations. Although the DOL-system in Fig. 1 has symbols to model the forward growth of fungal filaments, it has none to model branching structures. We found that bracketed L-systems (see [8] and [9]) are useful for modelling filamentous microbes (fungi and bacteria), which are simple life forms that develop by extending hyphae across a surface and by branching. Fungal colonies can be described in a string in which a left bracket delimiter, [, signals the beginning of a branch, and a right delimiter,], signals a return to the branching filament. This can be seen in Fig. 2, which also demonstrates how parameters may be associated with symbols so that the system controls the size of branching angles and step lengths.

```
#define maxgen 7
#define step 0.25
#define delta 25

START : F(step)b

p1: b -> [+(delta)F(step)b]F(step)a
p2: a -> [-(delta)F(step)b]F(step)b
```

Fig. 2. Parametric deterministic L system for lateral branching. The image on the right is a turtle graphics interpretation of the 7th (rewrite) generation.

L-system strings must be interpreted in a meaningful way. For example, the image of a Koch curve in Fig. 1 is the turtle graphics interpretation of the string produced as generation four by the accompanying L-system. F and f are interpreted as an instruction to move forward by one step, pen down for F and pen up for f. The symbol + means turn left and - turn right by a given angle.

1.2 Sonification and Mapping Data

L-systems have also been used to create music. Prusinkiewicz and Hanan [18] described how an L-system used to generate a fractal curve can be interpreted as a sequence of notes. For example, to interpret a Hilbert curve, with 90^0 turning angles, the pitch of each note maps to the y-coordinate of a line segment and duration is proportional to segment length [18]. Nelson extended this idea to compose "Summer Song" [15], as did Mason and Saffle to produce relatively complex musical scores [13]. The program LMUSe [20] provides a way of creating MIDI files using this mapping. McCormack [14] proposed L-system grammars as a basis for music composition and Mucherino [16] proposed a way of writing L-systems to be interpreted as music. These different approaches show that, although the turtle interpretation of strings generated by L-systems is widely accepted for producing images, there is no one apparent interpretation for producing sounds.

Parameter mapping is the usual approach to sonifying scientific data [2] and data characteristics have been mapped to pitch, duration, volume, loudness, and brightness[11, 2]. Mapping visual to audio is not always intuitive [1], some mappings are more pleasing and easier to understand [25] and some result in unpleasant sounds [2]. So the question of how best to map data to sound still remains [26]. We mapped changes in direction of growth (branching angles) to changes in pitch, and inter-branch distances to duration. Like Mason and Saffle [13], we found that the pitch went out of range - MIDI, hearing, and instrument range. Unlike them, we could not restrict our interpretation to images within audible range because we wished to explore the usefulness of sonifying them. Therefore, we adopted the idea of a circular keyboard as described below.

2 Using L-Systems to Model Microbial Growth

Although L-systems have been used to investigate simple branching organisms, for example Schneider and Walde generated computer simulations of branching in algae [21], they have not often been used to investigate fungi. Liddell and Hansen [6] created realistic images but were not concerned with the biological correctness of productions. We used L-systems to investigate how filamentous fungi may produce round colonies [23] and wished to apply a sound interpretation to our existing systems and so have corresponding visual and sound representations. In this preliminary investigation, we aimed at sonifying our visual models, and one of us (J. Soddell) aimed at exploring whether this may be a useful method for generating sound fragments to be used in experimental music.

2.1 MIDI Interpretation

To generate strings and create images (in PostScript), we used Lsys, released March 1991 by Jonathan Leech (leech@cs.unc.edu). To interpret strings as MIDI files, we used Lsys2midi written by students (Goodall, L. and Watson, M.) and staff (Soddell, F., Soddell, J., and Staehr, L.) at La Trobe University, Bendigo. Finally, we used various software packages to listen to the files and select different MIDI instruments.

Table 1. We used *lsys* to generate strings and images and *Lsys2midi* to generate MIDI files from strings.

Parametric Symbols and Interpretations

Symbol	Interpretation	
	lsys turtle graphics	*Lsys2midi* turtle sonics
F(x)	pen down move forward x	note down hold for time x (play)
f(x)	pen up move forward x	note up hold for time x (rest)
+(x)	change direction by angle of x^0 left	increase pitch by x
-(x)	change direction by angle of x^0 right	decrease pitch by x

Note: Angles of 360^0 and 0^0 are equivalent. Similarly, maximum and minimum pitches are equivalent. Maximum and minimum and start pitch (default=MIDI 60, middle C) may be specified by the user.

    Lsys2midi interprets parametric symbols as shown in Table 1. For MIDI files, available pitches range from 0 to 127, where the interval between each pitch is a semitone. At first, like McCormack [14], we interpreted + and - as instructions to increment and decrement pitch by one semitone. Further, if the pitch is at 127, an instruction to increment sets it back to 0, and if the pitch is at 0, decrementing sets it to 127. So we can consider a pitch of 0 equivalent to that of 128 and picture this interpretation in terms of a circular keyboard. This resembles the turtle interpretation of size of a turning or branching angle, where 360^0 coincides with 0^0.

We found two problems with this interpretation. First, MIDI 127 corresponds to a note of G and 0 to a note of C. Although this can be interesting, it seems more appropriate to move from B to C. That is, to specify a pitch range of 0 to 119 (the B before the C of the 10th octave) and regard a pitch of 120 (C) equivalent to that of 0 (C). Second, the range from 0 to 119 may not always be appropriate since it is too big a range for most instruments. So we enhanced Lsys2midi to allow users to specify the lowest pitch, the highest pitch, and the starting pitch. This means that the same string can be interpreted over different ranges with starting notes of different pitches.

```
#define maxgen 4
#define delta 90
#define step 0.75

START : F(step)-(delta)F(step)-(delta)F(step)-(delta)F(step)-(delta)

p1:F(x):x=step->F(step*2)-(delta)F(step)-(delta)F(step)-(delta)F(step)
            -(delta)F(step)-(delta)F(step)+(delta)F(step)
p2:F(x)->F(step*2)-(delta)F(step)-(delta)F(step)-(delta)F(step)-(delta)
        F(step)-(delta)F(step)+(delta)F(step)F(step*2)-(delta)F(step)
        -(delta)F(step)-(delta)F(step)-(delta)F(step)-(delta)F(step)
        +(delta)F(step)
```

Fig. 3. L system suitable for *lsys* to generate Koch curve from *The Algorithmic Beauty of Plants* [19] and for Lsys2midi to generate appropriate MIDI file.

Our L-systems for filamentous microbes specified branching angles, and sometimes turning angles, of particular sizes from $0°$ to $360°$. Lsys2midi converts these to pitch changes by regarding angles as proportionate to changes of pitch. So an angle of $90°$ is equivalent to a pitch change of 30 when the pitch ranges from 0 to 119, and to a pitch change of 3, when the pitch ranges from 60 to 71.

As shown in Table 1, we interpreted the parameter associated with F as the duration of a note. This resembles Prusinkiewicz and Hanan's suggestion that the length of a line segment may represent the duration of a note [18], but there is an important difference. Turtle graphics interpretations of FFF and F(3) appear the same, but MIDI interpretations sound very different. In the turtle interpretation, the first string is rendered with three down and three up pen events, the second with one up and one down, but the resulting images appear as the same straight line three steps long. In the MIDI interpretation, the first string is played as three notes of the same duration and the second as one longer note. It is important to hear this difference because differing durations symbolise differing inter-branch distances. Therefore our interpreter uses the duration specified by parametric strings, and our L-systems must contain duration information. So we redesigned existing systems [23], including simple D0L-systems, making them parametric. For example, the system shown in Fig. 3 generates the same image as that in

Fig. 1 but different sounds. To handle parameters of different value, the new system requires an extra production.

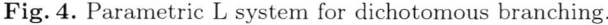

```
#define maxgen 11
#define step 0.25
#define delta 25

START : F(step)b

p1: b -> [+(delta)F(step)b][-(delta)F(step)b]
```

Fig. 4. Parametric L system for dichotomous branching.

2.2 Branching Patterns

We converted DOL-systems, designed to investigate the effect of branching patterns on the shape of growing colonies of filamentous microbes [23], to parametric systems. The system shown in Fig. 2 models lateral branching while that in Fig. 4 shows dichotomous branching. The step size is explicitly defined and can be easily redefined before running Lsys. The setting of 0.25 corresponds to a quarter-note duration (a whole note is 1). The difference between runs with different step sizes is obvious when listening to the organism but cannot be visualised. So we found that sonic visualisation helps distinguish between organisms with different growth rates. (Growth rate is important in describing the growth of microbes.)

We compared lateral with dichotomous branching by setting the same branching angles and step sizes for both systems and interpreting the same generation using the same pitch range and starting pitch. The resulting MIDI fragments sound melodious in a "conventional" sense, though very regular, and have some similarity (for example, the first bar is the same). Playing the fragments together emphasised the differences, which are easily seen by comparing the images in Fig. 2 and Fig. 4.

We also adapted two stochastic systems. The first, shown in Fig. 5, exhibits dichotomous branching and was designed to investigate the effect of a range of branching angles on the shape of a growing colony. For each generation, the stochastic production offers a choice of a branching angle of 10^0, 20^0, or 30^0. This system generates a variety of interesting melodies just as it provides a variety of images, some of which are displayed in Fig. 5.

The stochastic system in Fig. 6 generates realistic images that resemble filamentous bacteria found in wastewater treatment plants [24]. The filaments exhibit sub-apical branching, but we were unable to easily visualise this. So, to make the distinction between segments of hyphal growth visually clearer, production p3 specifies that a short space (heard as a rest) be left between segments.

```
#define maxgen 9
#define step 0.25
#define delta 10

START : F(step)b

p1: b -> (0.334)[+(delta)F(step)b][-(delta)F(step)b]
       -> (0.333)[+(delta*2)F(step)b][-(delta*2)F(step)b]
       -> (0.333)[+(delta*3)F(step)b][-(delta*3)F(step)b]
```

Fig. 5. Stochastic L-system with images of the 9th generation (three runs).

It seemed easier to detect the rests in the sound fragments than the spaces in the images, and the rests added interest to the sound.

The L-systems described in this section are theoretical models designed to visualise the effects that different growth variables may have on the shape of a growing colony. The next section is concerned with a model designed using data from growth experiments.

2.3 Mucor M41

To investigate whether characteristics exhibited in the early stages of growth may explain how filamentous organisms form circular colonies, we collected data from experiments with the fungus *Mucor* M41 [23], and visualised how colonies may develop by designing an L-system that summarises the data (see Fig. 7). The images in Fig. 8 show colonies developing a circular appearance. The stochastic production p43 stores observed branching angles and probabilities, while p44 stores observed angles of changes of direction and probabilities. The parametric productions p6 to p42 reproduce observed inter-branch distances and distances between changes of direction in the growing hyphae. Productions p1 to p5 were added to ensure that note durations correspond to the length of straight line segments. Step lengths and a variable controlling maximum duration are predefined. The values for the run shown in Fig. 7 ensure that the shortest duration is equivalent to a half-note and the longest to 4 whole notes. Fig. 8 shows a musical fragment that exhibits these features and was generated from one run. Every run generates different sound fragments some of which sound more melodious than others, that in Fig. 8 being one of the less musical. They sounded more random with development, so the MIDI interpretation appears to provide a good means for investigating temporal differences between stages of growth in *Mucor* M41.

```
#define maxgen 9
#define step 0.125
#define delta 10

START : gn

p1: n -> (0.5)+(delta)gn
       -> (0.5)-(delta)gn
p2: b -> (0.25)[+(delta*2)gn]
       -> (0.25)[-(delta*2)gn]
       -> (0.25)[+(delta*3)gn]
       -> (0.25)[-(delta*3)gn]
p3: g -> f(step)F(step*7)bF(2)
```

Fig. 6. Stochastic L-system that generates realistic images of microbes. Images represent the 9th generation of two runs.

3 Conclusion and Further Work

We developed a MIDI interpretation of strings generated by L-systems that is suitable for a sonic visualisation of growing colonies of filamentous microbes. We applied this interpretation to theoretical L-system models, and to a model that uses experimental data. We concluded that sound communicated more information about growth rates than images and that note duration emphasises different inter-branch distances. Once the pitch cues have been learned, it is as easy to distinguish between left and right branching using sound as it is using images. Other aspects, including the observation that the fungal colonies become round with time, are better determined by viewing images but it is also interesting to listen to them while viewing. This appears to be the first attempt at applying sonic visualisation to the grwoth of biological organisms.

Strings generated by L-systems are linear arrays of symbols with branches nested in brackets. Interpreters scan the symbols from left to right and each branch with its sub-branches is fully rendered before the next branch is encountered, which puts them out of growth order when used to model natural objects like trees and fungi. This does not affect the final image produced by the turtle graphics interpretation, but the sound interpretation has temporal significance, so we would like to have a method that traverses strings in temporal growth order.

During development, we tested five systems which create realistic images of bushes [19] and found they generated characteristic, attractive melodies suggesting there may be other musical opportunities. Although not as elegant as the

```
#define maxLength 4   #define step 0.5   #define maxgen 200
START : H(1,1,1,0)
p1:A(x,b,c,y)->F(step*x) BC H(1,1,1,0)
p2:B(x,b,c,y)->F(step*x) B H(1,1,1,0)
p3:C(x,b,c,y)->F(step*x) C H(1,1,1,0)
p4:D(x,b,c,y):x=maxLength
            ->F(step*x) H(1,b+1,c+1,0)
p5:D(x,b,c,y)->H(x+1,b+1,c+1,0)
p6:H(x,b,c,y):c=1 ->(0.33) Y(x,b,c,1)
                  ->(0.67) Y(x,b,c,0)
p7:H(x,b,c,y):c=2 ->(0.52239) Y(x,b,c,1)
                  ->(0.47761) Y(x,b,c,0)
p8:H(x,b,c,y):c=3 ->(0.40625) Y(x,b,c,1)
                  ->(0.59375) Y(x,b,c,0)
p9:H(x,b,c,y):c=4 ->(0.68421) Y(x,b,c,1)
                  ->(0.31579) Y(x,b,c,0)
p10:H(x,b,c,y):c=5->(0.5) Y(x,b,c,1)
                  ->(0.5) Y(x,b,c,0)
p11:H(x,b,c,y):c=6->(0.66667) Y(x,b,c,1)
                  ->(0.33333) Y(x,b,c,0)
p12:H(x,b,c,y):c=7->Y(x,b,c,1)
p13:Y(x,b,c,y):b=1&y=1->(0.07407) A(x,b,c,y)
                      ->(0.92593) C(x,b,c,y)
p14:Y(x,b,c,y):b=1->(0.07407) B(x,b,c,y)
                  ->(0.92593) D(x,b,c,y)
p15:Y(x,b,c,y):b=2&y=1->(0.04) A(x,b,c,y)
                      ->(0.96) C(x,b,c,y)
p16:Y(x,b,c,y):b=2->(0.04) B(x,b,c,y)
                  ->(0.96) D(x,b,c,y)
p17:Y(x,b,c,y):b=3&y=1->(0.16667) A(x,b,c,y)
                      ->(0.83333) C(x,b,c,y)
p18:Y(x,b,c,y):b=3->(0.16667) B(x,b,c,y)
                  ->(0.83333) D(x,b,c,y)
p19:Y(x,b,c,y):b=4&y=1->(0.15) A(x,b,c,y)
                      ->(0.85) C(x,b,c,y)
p20:Y(x,b,c,y):b=4->(0.15) B(x,b,c,y)
                  ->(0.85) D(x,b,c,y)
p21:Y(x,b,c,y):b=5&y=1->(0.35) A(x,b,c,y)
                      ->(0.65) C(x,b,c,y)
p22:Y(x,b,c,y):b=5->(0.35) B(x,b,c,y)
                  ->(0.65) D(x,b,c,y)
p23:Y(x,b,c,y):b=9&y=1->(0.09091) A(x,b,c,y)
                      ->(0.90909) C(x,b,c,y)
p24:Y(x,b,c,y):b=9->(0.09091) B(x,b,c,y)
                  ->(0.90909) D(x,b,c,y)
p25:Y(x,b,c,y):b=16&y=1->(0.1) A(x,b,c,y)
                       ->(0.9) C(x,b,c,y)
p26:Y(x,b,c,y):b=16->(0.01) B(x,b,c,y)
                   ->(0.9) D(x,b,c,y)
p27:Y(x,b,c,y):b=17&y=1->(0.22222) A(x,b,c,y)
                       ->(0.77778) C(x,b,c,y)
p28:Y(x,b,c,y):b=17->(0.22222) B(x,b,c,y)
                   ->(0.77778) D(x,b,c,y)
p29:Y(x,b,c,y):b=20&y=1->(0.14286) A(x,b,c,y)
                       ->(0.85714) C(x,b,c,y)
p30:Y(x,b,c,y):b=20->(0.14286) B(x,b,c,y)
                   ->(0.85714) D(x,b,c,y)
p31:Y(x,b,c,y):b=22&y=1->(0.16667) A(x,b,c,y)
                       ->(0.83333) C(x,b,c,y)
p32:Y(x,b,c,y):b=22->(0.16667) B(x,b,c,y)
                   ->(0.83333) D(x,b,c,y)
p33:Y(x,b,c,y):b=23&y=1->(0.2) A(x,b,c,y)
                       ->(0.8) C(x,b,c,y)
                       ->(0.005)-(60)
p34:Y(x,b,c,y):b=23
               ->(0.2) B(x,b,c,y)
               ->(0.8) D(x,b,c,y)
p35:Y(x,b,c,y):b=24&y=1
               ->(0.25) A(x,b,c,y)
               ->(0.75) C(x,b,c,y)
p36:Y(x,b,c,y):b=24
               ->(0.25) B(x,b,c,y)
               ->(0.75) D(x,b,c,y)
p37:Y(x,b,c,y):b=28&y=1
               ->(0.25) A(x,b,c,y)
               ->(0.75) C(x,b,c,y)
p38:Y(x,b,c,y):b=28
               ->(0.33333) B(x,b,c,y)
               ->(0.66667) D(x,b,c,y)
p39:Y(x,b,c,y):b=60&y=1
               ->A(x,b,c,y)
p40:Y(x,b,c,y):b=60->B(x,b,c,y)
p41:Y(x,b,c,y):y=1->C(x,b,c,y)
p42:Y(x,b,c,y)->D(x,b,c,y)
/* branching angles */
p43:B ->(0.01851)[+(70)H(1,1,1,0)]
      ->(0.01851)[-(70)H(1,1,1,0)]
      ->(0.05556)[+(85)H(1,1,1,0)]
      ->(0.05556)[-(85)H(1,1,1,0)]
      ->(0.14815)[+(90)H(1,1,1,0)]
      ->(0.14815)[-(90)H(1,1,1,0)]
      ->(0.07408)[+(95)H(1,1,1,0)]
      ->(0.07408)[-(95)H(1,1,1,0)]
      ->(0.11111)[+(100)H(1,1,1,0)]
      ->(0.11111)[-(100)H(1,1,1,0)]
      ->(0.03704)[+(110)H(1,1,1,0)]
      ->(0.03704)[-(110)H(1,1,1,0)]
      ->(0.01851)[+(115)H(1,1,1,0)]
      ->(0.01851)[-(115)H(1,1,1,0)]
      ->(0.03704)[+(120)H(1,1,1,0)]
      ->(0.03704)[-(120)H(1,1,1,0)]

/* observed angles of changes of
   direction and frequencies */
p44:C->(0.015)+(5)
     ->(0.015)-(5)
     ->(0.08)+(10)
     ->(0.08)-(10)
     ->(0.04)+(15)
     ->(0.04)-(15)
     ->(0.095)+(20)
     ->(0.095)-(20)
     ->(0.065)+(25)
     ->(0.065)-(25)
     ->(0.055)+(30)
     ->(0.055)-(30)
     ->(0.075)+(35)
     ->(0.075)-(35)
     ->(0.015)+(40)
     ->(0.015)-(40)
     ->(0.015)+(45)
     ->(0.015)-(45)
     ->(0.04)+(50)
     ->(0.04)-(50)
     ->(0.005)+(60)
```

Fig. 7. Stochastic parametric L system for *Mucor* M41. Production rule p33 specifies the observed branching angles and p44 specifies the observed angles of change in direction of hyphae. There is an equal probability that the angles occur to left and right.

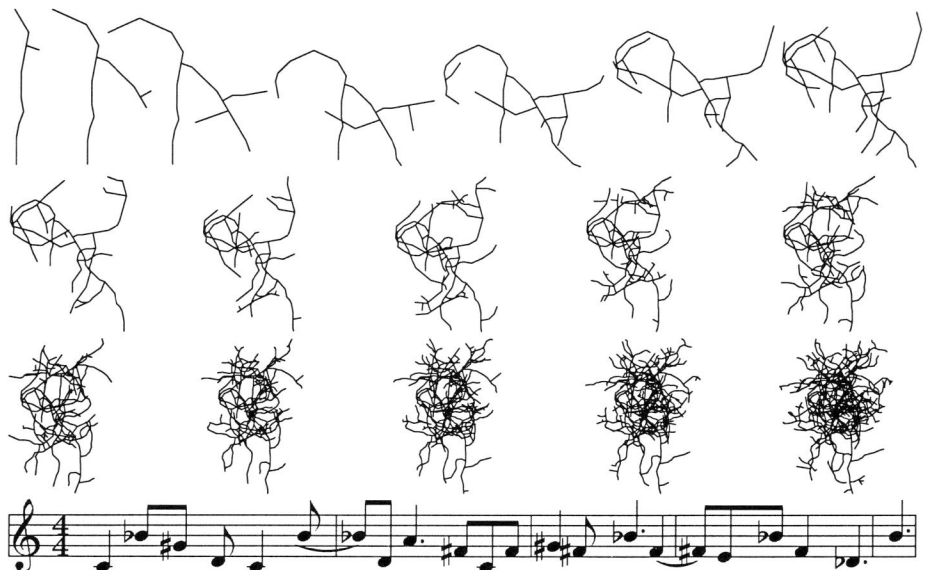

Fig. 8. Images and music generated by L system for *Mucor* M41 shown in Fig. 7. The images are from generation 39 to generation 199 at intervals of 10 generations. The music fragment corresponds to generation 59, the third image.

turtle graphics interpretation of L-systems, the MIDI interpretation proved to be very exciting.

References

1. Axen, U., Choi, I.: Investigating geometric data with sound. Proceedings of ICAD (1996) http://www.santafe.edu/~icad/ICAD96/proc96/axen.htm [accessed June 2000]
2. Barrass, S., Kramer, G.: Using sonification. Multimedia Systems **7** (1999) 23–31
3. Dunn, J., Clark, M.: Life Music: The sonification of proteins. Leonardo On-Line (2000) http://mitpress.mit.edu/e-journals/Leonardo/isast/articles/lifemusic.htm [accessed June 2000]
4. Flowers, J., Buhman, C., Turnage, K.:Data sonification from the desktop: Should sound be part of standard data analysis software? Proceedings of ICAD (1996) http://www.santafe.edu/~icad/ICAD96/proc96/flowers.htm [accessed June 2000]
5. Kaper, H., Wiebel, E.:Data sonification and sound visualization. Computing in Science & Engineering **1(4)** (1999) 48–58
6. Liddell, C., Hansen, D.: Visualizing Complex Biological Interactions in the Soil Ecosystem. The Journal of Visualization and Computer Animation **4** (1993) 3–12
7. Lindenmayer, A.: Mathematical models for cellular interactions in development I. Filaments with one-sided inputs. J. Theoret. Biol. **18** (1968) 280–299
8. Lindenmayer, A.: Mathematical models for cellular interactions in development II. Simple and branching filaments with two-sided inputs. J. Theoret. Biol. **18** (1968) 300–315

9. Lindenmayer, A.: Developmental systems and languages in their biological context. In: Developmental Systems and Languages. eds. Herman, G.T., Rozenberg, G. North-Holland Publ. Co., Amsterdam (1975) 1–40
10. Lindenmayer, A., Jurgensen, H.: Grammars of Development: Discrete state models for growth, differentiation, and gene expression in modular organisms. Report No. 285 Dept. of Computer Science, University of Western Ontario, Canada
11. Madhyastha, T., Reed, D.:Data sonification:Do you see what I hear? IEEE Software **12(2)** (1995) 45–56
12. Martins, A., Rangayyan, R., Portela, L., Amaro, E., Ruschioni, R.: Auditory display and sonification of textured image. Proceedings of ICAD (1996) http://www.santafe.edu/~icad/ICAD96/proc96/martins.htm [accessed June 2000]
13. Mason, S., Saffle, M.: L-Systems, Melodies and Musical Structure. Leonardo Music Journal **4** (1994) 31–38
14. McCormack, J.: Grammar-Based Music Composition. Complexity International **3** (1996) http://www.csu.edu.au/ci/vol3/mccorm/mccorm.html [accessed March 2000]
15. Nelson, G.: Real Time Transformation of Musical Material with Fractal Algorithms. Computers Math. Applic. **32,1** (1996) 109–116
16. Mucherino, N.: A Paradigm For Future Music? WWW. http://www-ks.rus.uni-stuttgart.de/people/schulz/fmusic/recursion.html, March (1998)
17. Prusinkiewicz, P.: Modeling of spatial structure and development of plants: a review. Scientia Horticulturae **74**, (1998) 113–149
18. Prusinkiewicz, P., Hanan, J.: Lindenmayer systems, fractals, and plants. Lecture Notes in Biomathematics, Springer-Verlag, Berlin (1989)
19. Prusinkiewicz, P., Lindenmayer, A.: The Algorithmic Beauty of Plants. Springer-Verlag, New York (1990)
20. Sharp, D.:LMUSe. Software. WWW. http://www.users.interport.net/~dsharp/readme.html (1998) [accessed June 2000]
21. Schneider, C., Walde, R.: L-system computer simulations of branching divergence in some dorsiventral members of the tribe Polysiphonieae (Rhodomelaceae, Rhodophyta). Phycologia **31**, (1992) 581–590
22. Smith, A.: Plant, fractals and formal languages. Comp. Graph. **18**,July (1984) 1–10
23. Soddell, F., Seviour, R., Soddell J.: Using Lindenmayer systems to investigate how filamentous fungi may produce round colonies. In: Complex Systems: Mechanisms of Adaptation. eds. Stonier, R.J., Xing Huo Yu. IOS Press, Amsterdam (1994) 61–68
24. Soddell, J., Seviour, R.: Incidence and morphological variability of *Nocardia pinensis* in Australian activated sludge plants. Water Research (1994) **28** 2343–2351
25. Walker, B., Kramer, G.: Mappings and metaphors in auditory displays: An experimental assessment. Proceedings of ICAD (1996) http://www.santafe.edu/~icad/ICAD96/proc96/walker5.htm [accessed June 2000]
26. Wilson, C., Lodha, S.: Listen: A data sonification toolkit. Proceedings of ICAD (1996) http://www.santafe.edu/~icad/ICAD96/proc96/lodha.htm [accessed June 2000]
27. Witten, M.: The Sounds of Science: II. Listening to dynamical systems–Towards a musical exploration of complexity. Computers Math. Applc. **32**, No. 1 (1996) 145–173

A Lightweight Multi-agent Musical Beat Tracking System

Simon Dixon

Austrian Research Institute for Artificial Intelligence,
Schottengasse 3, A-1010 Vienna, Austria.
simon@ai.univie.ac.at

Abstract. Beat tracking is what people do when they tap their feet in time to music. We present a software system which performs this task, processing music in a standard digital audio format and estimating the locations of musical beats. A time-domain algorithm detects salient acoustic events, and then a clustering algorithm groups the time intervals between events to obtain hypotheses about the current tempo. Multiple competing agents track these hypotheses throughout the music, with further agents being created at decision points. The output for each agent is a sequence of beat locations, which is evaluated for its closeness of fit to the data. This approach to beat tracking assumes no previous knowledge of the music such as the style, time signature or approximate tempo; all required information is derived from the audio data. The system has been tested with various styles of music (popular, jazz, and classical) and performs robustly, rarely making errors in popular music, and recovering quickly from errors in more complex styles of music, despite the fact that no high level musical knowledge is encoded in the system.

1 Introduction

Although most people can tap their feet in time with music, equivalent performance on a computer has proved remarkably difficult to achieve. One reason for this is that these systems have been based only on the codification of high level metrical knowledge. We show that such knowledge is secondary to the beat tracking task. Just as people can follow the beat of music without musical training and without previous knowledge of the particular piece of music, so can a computer program.

In this paper, we present a system which processes musical audio signals, estimating the tempo and determining the locations of musical beats. No specific assumptions are made about the music being analyzed, but the system performs robustly on various types of popular, jazz and classical music. We do not attempt to model or describe the cognitive mechanisms involved in human rhythm perception. However we do note certain features of human perception which motivate an ambitious unsupervised approach to the beat tracking problem, namely, that human rhythm perception is self-calibrating and copes well with both syncopation and noise in the input.

The subsequent sections of the paper contain a review of related work, then a description of the musical assumptions made in this work. The next sections present the algorithm for onset detection from raw audio data, followed by the algorithm for *tempo induction*, defined as the estimation of the time interval between successive occurrences of the main rhythmic pulse of the music. We then describe the multi-agent approach to *beat tracking*, which is the determination of beat locations (and therefore tempo fluctuations) in the light of the previous tempo estimations. The results from testing the system with various types of music are then presented and discussed, and the paper concludes with a description of applications of the beat tracking system.

2 Related Work

A substantial amount of research has been performed in the area of rhythm recognition by computer, including a demonstration of various beat tracking methods using a computer to control a shoe which tapped in time with the calculated beat of the music [5]. These systems are difficult to compare directly, as they make different assumptions about the input format, style and complexity of the music.

Much of the work in machine perception of rhythm has used MIDI files as input [18, 2, 14], which contain control information for a synthesizer rather than audio data. MIDI files consist of sequences of events, usually corresponding to pressing and releasing keys on a piano-style keyboard, plus an encoding of the time duration between successive events. Structural information such as the time signature and tempo can also be stored in MIDI files, but it is usually assumed that such information is not available to rhythm recognition programs.

Using MIDI files, the input is usually interpreted as a series of event times, ignoring the event duration, pitch, amplitude and chosen synthesizer voice. That is, each note is treated purely as an uninterpreted event. It is assumed that the other parameters do not provide *essential* rhythmic information, which in many circumstances is true. However, there is no doubt that these factors provide useful rhythmic cues; for example, more salient events tend to occur on stronger beats.

Notable work using MIDI file input is an emulation of human rhythm perception [18], which produces multiple hypotheses of possible hierarchical structures in the timing, assigning a score to each hypothesis, corresponding to the likelihood that a human listener would choose that interpretation of the rhythm. This technique gives the system the ability to adjust to changes in tempo and meter, as well as avoiding many of the implausible rhythmic interpretations produced by commercial systems.

Desain [2] compares two different approaches to modeling rhythm perception, the symbolic approach of Longuet-Higgins [16] and the connectionist approach of Desain and Honing [3]. Although this work only models one aspect of rhythm perception, the issue of quantization, and the results of the comparison are inconclusive, it does highlight the need to model expectancy, either explicitly or implicitly. Expectancy is a type of predictive modeling, particularly relevant to real time processing, as it provides a contextual framework in which subsequent rhythmic patterns can be interpreted with less ambiguity.

Allen and Dannenburg [1] describe a beat tracking system that uses beam search to consider multiple hypotheses of beat timing and placement. A heuristic evaluation function directs the search, preferring interpretations that have a "simple" musical structure and make "musical sense", although they do not define what they mean by these terms. They also do not describe the input format or any specific results.

An alternative approach uses a nonlinear oscillator to model the expectation created by detecting a regular pulse in the music [14]. A feedback loop controls the frequency of the oscillator so that it can track variations in the rhythm. This system performs quite robustly, but, like connectionist approaches, does not provide any intuition about the beat tracking process, and therefore would be difficult to extend using high level knowledge.

There has been only a small amount of rhythm research using audio input, beginning with the percussion transcription system of Schloss [19]. Onsets were detected as peaks in the slope of the amplitude envelope, where the envelope was defined to be equal to the maximum amplitude in each period of the high-pass filtered signal, and the period defined as the inverse of the lowest frequency expected to be present in the signal. The system was limited in that it required parameters to be set interactively, and it was evaluated only by resynthesis of the signal.

A more complete approach to beat tracking of acoustic signals was developed by Goto and Muraoka [10, 12, 13]. They developed two systems for following the beat of popular music in real time. The earlier system (BTS) used frequency histograms to find significant peaks in the low frequency regions, corresponding to the frequencies of the bass and snare drums, and then tracked these low frequency signals by matching patterns of onset times to a set of pre-stored drum beat patterns. This method was successful in tracking the beat of most of the popular songs on which it was tested. A later system allowed music without drums to be tracked by recognizing chord changes, assuming that significant harmonic changes occur at strong rhythmic positions. These systems required a powerful parallel computer in order to run in real time.

Commercial transcription and sequencing programs do not address the issues covered by these research systems. They generally require that the tempo and time signature are specified before the music is played, and the system then aligns each note with the nearest position on a metrical grid. Recent systems allow parameterization of this grid in terms of its resolution (the shortest allowed note length), and adjustment of restrictions on the complexity of rhythm that can be produced by the system. These systems often produce implausible rhythmic interpretations, and cannot be used in an unsupervised manner for anything but simple rhythms.

3 Musical Assumptions

Despite the large amount of research in time and rhythm in music, the beat tracking problem remains poorly defined. The reason is that the beat is a subjective property of performed music. Formal musical models tend to be based on the notational representation rather than performance [15, 17], and those which address performance timing do so from the point of view of generation and/or transformation of timing rather than extraction or explanation of performance data [4]. We follow [11] in evaluating the correctness of the beat tracking system relative to a subjective labelling of beat positions.

A theoretical definition of *beat* is "a perceived pulse marking off equal durational units" [9]; in practice, the durational units marked off by the onsets of notes on successive beats are only approximately equal. However, for a large amount of music, the subjective differences in perceived beat are minor, otherwise human activities such as ensemble playing and dancing would not be possible. In this study we restrict our attention to music which has such an agreed beat, and rely on the onset detection algorithm to choose the more salient events as possible beat locations.

4 Audio Processing

In this and the following sections, we describe the stages of processing performed by the beat tracking system. All of the software is written in C++ and runs on a Unix platform (Linux or Solaris). The complete processing of a song takes about 10 seconds on a current PC, making it viable for use in real time audio applications, although the software is not currently designed for real time use. The input to the system is a digitally sampled acoustic signal, such as is found on audio compact discs. The stereo compact disc data is converted to a single channel format by averaging the left and right channels, resulting in a single channel 16 bit linear pulse code modulated (PCM) format, with a sampling rate of 44.1kHz.

The aim of the initial signal processing stage is to detect *events* in the audio data, from which rhythmic information can be derived. For the purposes of this work, events correspond to note onsets, that is, the beginnings of musical notes, including percussive sounds. By ignoring note durations and offset times, we discard valuable information, but our results justify the present assumption, that there is sufficient information in note onsets to perform beat tracking.

A time-domain method similar to that of Schloss [19] is employed for onset detection. This method involves passing the signal through a simple high-pass filter, calculating the absolute sum of small overlapping windows of the signal, and then finding peaks in the slope of these window sums using a 4 point linear regression. Only the more salient event onsets are detected with the method, which is ideal for the subsequent task of tempo induction.

5 Tempo Induction

The tempo induction section of the system determines a set of hypotheses about the tempo of a given section of music, which may be expressed in beats per minute (BPM) or in seconds, as the *inter-beat interval* (IBI). The algorithm, described further in [6, 7], is based on clustering of *inter-onset intervals* (IOI's). In the literature, an IOI is defined as the time between the onsets of two successive events, but we extend the definition to include times between onsets of pairs of events that are separated by intervening event onsets. All possible pairs of onsets that occur within 2.5 seconds of each other are grouped by the clustering algorithm. Figure 1 shows clustering for five events (A, B, C, D, E) into intervals of similar size. For example, cluster C1 contains the intervals AB, BC and DE, while cluster C2 contains AC and CD. Each cluster is identified by its average interval size.

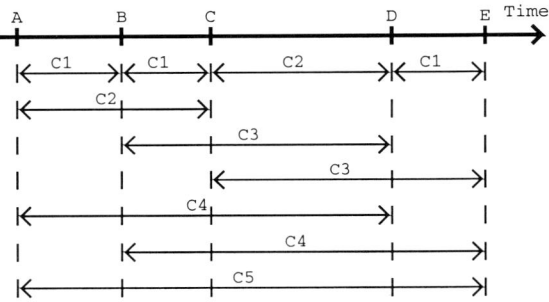

Fig. 1. Clustering of inter-onset intervals

After grouping IOI's into clusters, a score is calculated for each cluster, based on the number of IOI's in the cluster. The highly ranked clusters usually correspond to the beat or small integer multiples or fractions of the beat. For example, supposing that C2 represents the IBI, then C1 represents half of the IBI and C4 represents double the IBI. Each cluster's score is increased for each other cluster to which it is related by a small integer ratio, and a final ranking of the inter-beat interval hypotheses is determined.

In previous work [7], it was found that the correct tempo can be induced from a 5-10 second excerpt of the music with 90% reliability, and by using multiple (or longer) excerpts, the reliability quickly approaches 100%. In this work, it does not matter if the initial estimate is correct, as multiple hypotheses are checked in the beat tracking stage, so that an error in tempo induction can be corrected at a later time.

6 Beat Tracking Agents

The tempo induction algorithm computes the inter-beat interval, that is, the time between successive beats, but does not calculate the location of the beat. In Figure 1, the clustering might determine that C2 represents the inter-beat interval, but it does not reveal whether events A, C and D are beat locations or whether B and E are beat locations. By analogy with wave theory, we could say that it calculates the *frequency* but not the *phase* of the beat.

The phase is calculated by employing an agent-based architecture to examine multiple hypotheses simultaneously throughout the music. The agents are characterized by their *state* and *history*. The state is the agent's current hypothesis of the beat frequency and phase, and the history is the sequence of beat locations selected so far by the agent. Each agent is evaluated on the basis of its history, with higher scores being awarded for greater regularity in the spacing between events, greater salience of chosen events, and fewer gaps in the sequence.

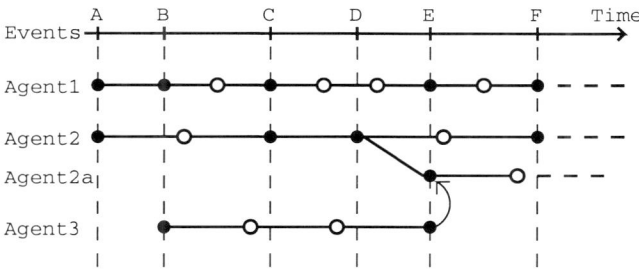

Fig. 2. Beat tracking agents (see text for details)

Initially, a number of agents are created for each of the tempo hypotheses from the tempo induction stage; for each tempo, one agent is created for each of the first few events in the piece, with its phase set to 0 at the time of the event onset. A simplified example is shown in Figure 2, where there are 2 tempo hypotheses, and two starting locations, events A and B. Agents 1 and 2 start with the same phase, but different tempo, while Agent 3 starts with a different phase, but the same initial tempo as Agent 2. Note there is no need to start an agent with the tempo of Agent 1 and phase of Agent 3, since Agent 1 covers event B itself.

The main loop of the beat tracking section passes each event to each agent, which compares the event's onset time with the predicted beat location. The agents have two windows of tolerance, an inner window, within which the agent is sure that the event corresponds to the predicted beat location, and an outer window, within which the agent is unsure if the event should be accepted as a beat location. If the event falls in the inner window, it is added to the agent's history, and the agent's tempo and phase hypotheses are updated. In the case that the event falls in the outer window around the predicted location, the agent creates a clone which accepts the event as a beat location, while the current agent rejects the event. In Figure 2, Agent 2 creates Agent 2a when event E falls in its outer window of expected beat locations. This guards against the current beat location being lost due to a rogue event, whilst also allowing for moderate deviations in tempo and phase to occur. When an accepted event is more than one beat from the previous beat location determined by the agent, the missing beats are filled in by interpolation (shown by hollow circles in the figure).

As the agents track the beats, a confidence value is maintained for each agent. This value is increased each time an event is accepted as a beat location. The amount of increase depends on the salience of the event and its proximity to the predicted beat location. The salience is measured in terms of the amplitude of the event onset, calculated on a logarithmic scale. The value is then reduced according to the difference between the predicted and actual beat locations, and then added to the agent's confidence value. The final confidence value for an agent is calculated by reducing the confidence for each beat which had to be interpolated, and normalizing the result so that the agents with a faster tempo are not advantaged by their greater number of beats.

It often occurs that two or more agents come to the same conclusion about the current tempo and beat phase. Since these are the only variables that determine the agent's state (and therefore its future behavior), it is computationally advantageous to remove all but one of these agreeing agents, retaining only the agent with the highest confidence (that is, with the best scoring history). In Figure 2, Agent 3 is terminated when its state coincides with that of Agent 2a, as indicated by the arrow at event E. Removal of duplicate agents is performed after each event is processed. Agents are also checked for currentness, and are removed if they are unable to find any event corresponding to a predicted beat for some fixed length of time.

After the last event is processed, the highest scoring current agent is selected, and its history is output as the beat tracking "solution". It is also possible to view a trace of the agents and their scores at each event during processing. For aural testing (and demonstrations) of the system, the music can also be played back or saved to file with a click track added to it, that is, a percussion track indicating the positions of beats as detected by the system. In the following section, testing methodology is discussed, and the results of beat tracking with various styles of music are presented.

7 Results and Discussion

Informal testing was performed by listening to the music with synthesized percussion strokes (e.g. cow-bell) played at the beat locations computed by the system. With this method, it is easy to check that the tempo estimation and tracking are approximately correct, but it is not a very precise form of testing. It is also very time-consuming if used repeatedly to test the effects of small adjustments to the system. However, aural testing provides intuition about the situations in which the beat tracker fails, which is useful for determining which aspects of the system require further work.

Song Title	Artist	Style	Date	Tempo range	Time sign.	Tracking Results
I Don't Remember A Thing	Paul Kelly and the Coloured Girls	Pop/rock	1987	139-142	4/4	100%
Dumb Things	" "	Pop/rock	1987	151-154	4/4	100%
Untouchable	" "	Pop/rock	1987	145-146	4/4	100%
Superstition	Stevie Wonder	Motown	1972	96-104	4/4	96%
You Are The Sunshine of My Life	Stevie Wonder	Motown	1972	127-136	4/4	92%
On A Night Like This	Bob Dylan	Country	1974	136-140	4/4	79%
Rosa Moreña	João Gilberto Trio	Bossa nova	1964	128-134	4/4	95%
Michelle	Béla Fleck and the Flecktones	Jazz swing	1991	180-193	3/4	92%
Jitterbug Waltz	James Morrison	Jazz waltz	1990	155-175	3/4	77%
Piano Sonata in C 3rd movt. 1st sect.	Wolfgang Mozart	Classical	1775	120-150	2/4	90%

Fig. 3. Beat tracking test details and results

In Figure 3, we present the results for beat tracking of songs representing various styles of music. The rightmost column of the table indicates the percentage of beat positions which were calculated correctly by the beat tracking system, a measure of the performance of the system. This does not indicate the nature of the errors made during beat tracking. For each of the songs listed, the tempo was estimated correctly. Therefore the results column can be considered to be the percentage of the song for which the phase was tracked correctly.

More precise testing was performed by comparison of results with manually calculated beat positions. The audio files were examined with standard digital audio editing software (GoldWave), and beat locations were determined for a number of beats on which clear percussive events occurred. These locations were then used to interpolate the locations of the intervening beats.

The first 3 songs are standard modern pop/rock, characterized by a very steady tempo, which is clearly defined by simple and salient drum patterns, similar to the data used in the early audio beat tracking work of Goto [10]. In the production of this style of music, it is common practice for each instrument to be recorded separately, using a metronome track for synchronization. In this case one expects the performed beat to be very regular, with only small deviations from mechanical regularity. The beat tracking system made no errors on these songs.

The next style examined was Motown/Soul, characterized by more syncopation, greater tempo fluctuations (5-10% in these examples), and more freedom to anticipate or lag behind the beat. This created a greater difficulty for the beat tracking system, which made errors of phase several times, but recovered quickly to track almost all of each song correctly.

The Bob Dylan song was more difficult again, because of his idiosyncratic style of singing and playing against the rhythmic context. Although the beat is reasonably clear to a human listener, the drums are not prominent, and there is a much lower correlation between the conceptual beat and the actual musical events than in the other styles. There were two main sections in which the beat tracking system lost synchronization and tracked the off-beats (i.e., it continued at the correct tempo but half a beat out of phase), but again the system recovered to the correct phase.

The next test involved a live bossa nova performance with syncopated guitar and vocals, and very little percussion to indicate beat positions. The song was tracked correctly except in few passages where it went out of phase, but the error was corrected within a few beats.

The two jazz pieces were chosen for their particularly complex, syncopated rhythms, which are difficult for humans to follow. These pieces also provided examples of a different time signature, swing eighth notes, and greater tempo variation. In both cases, the highest scoring agent was able to track the majority of the piece correctly, but encountered phase errors in some parts.

Finally, a classical piece was tested, the first section of the third movement of Mozart's Piano Sonata in C major (KV279). The system lost synchronization several times, tracking the off-beats rather than the beats, due to large tempo variations and the system's lack of musical knowledge for distinguishing between beats and off-beats.

It is interesting to note that phase errors were also encountered for simple pop music in an earlier version of the system. With the salience calculation removed, the system tracks the whole of *I Don't Remember A Thing* at half a beat out of phase. For pop music, the salience of events differentiates the beat from the offbeat at most points in the music. This may not be true in jazz, where the offbeat is often accentuated for long periods of time, so the system requires an alternative way of choosing the correct path through the data.

Note that the beat tracking system is not equipped with musical knowledge — no notion of off-beats or expected rhythmic patterns has been programmed into it. Its apparent musical intelligence comes from patterns *in the data*, without any high-level knowledge or reasoning. Apart from the advantage of simplicity, a further advantage is that the system is quite robust, and generalizes well to different styles of music, as long as there is a salient beat. In order to disambiguate complex or ambiguous rhythmic patterns, the system will need sources of musical knowledge other than timing of events; these are not presently available to it. In current work [8], we are examining a specialization of the system for solo piano music which incorporates a level of musical and stylistic knowledge with the aim of extracting the score from performance data.

8 Conclusion

We have described a beat tracking system which analyses acoustic data, detects the salient note onsets, determines possible inter-beat intervals and then employs multiple agents to find a sequence of events which represents the beat of the music. The system successfully tracks the beat in most popular music, but makes some phase errors, mainly when presented with extremely complex rhythms or music with large tempo deviations. Even in these situations, the performance is quite robust, with the system recovering from its errors and resuming correct tracking after a short period.

Unlike previous audio beat tracking systems which required a large parallel computer [13], our system has modest requirements, processing an average length song in about 10 seconds on a current personal computer, leaving sufficient resources for real time applications based on the beat tracking system.

One such application is an automatic disc jockey (DJ), which plays a list of songs, cross-fading between the songs so that the beats of successive songs are synchronized (beat-mixing). This has been implemented as part of the beat tracking system. Another application is that of a score extraction system. This application uses MIDI input rather than audio, and the system's job is to make "musical sense" of the performed rhythm. The nature of this problem is different, in that we seek a musical explanation for every event, whereas the current system ignores events which are determined not to lie on the beat. MIDI input also facilitates the use of other knowledge from the data, such as duration, pitch, repeated melodic patterns and musical voice. In recent work, such information has proved useful in calculating a more detailed salience value for musical events [8]. It is still an open problem how such details can be extracted reliably directly from audio data. A further application of beat tracking, and one which requires reliable recognition of pitch and duration of notes, is an automatic music transcription system, that is, a system which produces musical scores directly from audio data. Such a system requires a beat tracker as one component.

The use of manual beat tracking for evaluation of the system limits the amount of testing that can be performed, but is necessary when analyzing performed music. Unlike speech-related research, music recognition research currently has no large corpora of tagged data for thorough testing and comparison of results (or, for that matter, the use of probabilistic search techniques). In further work we plan to perform a study of beat tracking in synthetically generated music, where the variations in tempo and onset times can be controlled precisely, and performance can be evaluated automatically.

Acknowledgements

This research is part of the project Y99-INF, sponsored by the Austrian Federal Ministry of Education, Science and Culture in the form of a START Research Prize and support to the Austrian Research Institute for Artificial Intelligence. The author wishes to thank Emilios Cambouropoulos and Gerhard Widmer for suggestions and comments on an earlier version of this paper.

References

1. P.E. Allen and R.B. Dannenburg. Tracking musical beats in real time. In *Proceedings of the International Computer Music Conference*, pages 140–143. International Computer Music Association, San Francisco CA, 1990.
2. P. Desain. A connectionist and a traditional AI quantizer, symbolic versus subsymbolic models of rhythm perception. *Contemporary Music Review*, 9:239–254, 1993.
3. P. Desain and H. Honing. Quantization of musical time: A connectionist approach. *Computer Music Journal*, 13(3), 1989.
4. P. Desain and H. Honing. Towards a calculus for expressive timing in music. *Computers in Music Research*, 3:43–120, 1991.
5. P. Desain and H. Honing. Foot-tapping: a brief introduction to beat induction. In *Proceedings of the International Computer Music Conference*, pages 78–79. Computer Music Association, San Francisco CA, 1994.
6. S. Dixon. Beat induction and rhythm recognition. In *Proceedings of the Australian Joint Conference on Artificial Intelligence*, pages 311–320, 1997.
7. S. Dixon. A beat tracking system for audio signals. In *Proceedings of the Diderot Forum on Mathematics and Music*, pages 101–110. Austrian Computer Society, 1999.
8. S. Dixon and E. Cambouropoulos. Beat tracking with musical knowledge. In *ECAI 2000: Proceedings of the 14th European Conference on Artificial Intelligence*. IOS Press, 2000. To appear.
9. W.J. Dowling and D.L. Harwood. *Music Cognition*. Academic Press, 1986.
10. M. Goto and Y. Muraoka. A real-time beat tracking system for audio signals. In *Proceedings of the International Computer Music Conference*. Computer Music Association, San Francisco CA, 1995.
11. M. Goto and Y. Muraoka. Issues in evaluating beat tracking systems. In *Issues in AI and Music – Evaluation and Assessment: Proceedings of the IJCAI'97 Workshop on AI and Music*. International Joint Conference on Artificial Intelligence, 1997.
12. M. Goto and Y. Muraoka. Real-time rhythm tracking for drumless audio signals – chord change detection for musical decisions. In *Proceedings of the IJCAI'97 Workshop on Computational Auditory Scene Analysis*. International Joint Conference on Artificial Intelligence, 1997.
13. M. Goto and Y. Muraoka. An audio-based real-time beat tracking system and its applications. In *Proceedings of the International Computer Music Conference*. Computer Music Association, San Francisco CA, 1998.
14. E.W. Large. Beat tracking with a nonlinear oscillator. In *Proceedings of the IJCAI'95 Workshop on Artificial Intelligence and Music*. International Joint Conference on Artificial Intelligence, 1995.
15. F. Lerdahl and R. Jackendoff. *A Generative Theory of Tonal Music*. MIT Press, 1983.
16. H.C. Longuet-Higgins. *Mental Processes*. MIT Press, 1987.
17. H.C. Longuet-Higgins and C.S. Lee. The perception of musical rhythms. *Perception*, 11:115–128, 1982.
18. D. Rosenthal. Emulation of human rhythm perception. *Computer Music Journal*, 16(1):64–76, 1992.
19. W.A. Schloss. *On the Automatic Transcription of Percussive Music: From Acoustic Signal to High Level Analysis*. PhD thesis, Stanford University, CCRMA, 1985.

Frame-Structure Logic with Extended Attribute Relations

Koji Komatsu, Noritaka Nishihara, and Shoichi Yokoyama

Department of Informatics, Yamagata University, 4-3-16 Jonan, Yonezawa, Yamagata 992-0038, Japan

Abstract. Most logical approaches to knowledge representation and reasoning are based on predicate logic. In predicate logic, a proposition is constructed from predicates, functions, individual variables and quantifiers. Although predicate logic is highly expressive, the structure of the formulas that are produced is different to that of natural language. This difference is a result of the constructors that are used, particularly individual variables. In an effort to rectify this situation, the authors have proposed Frame-Structure Logic (FSL), in which propositions have a structure that resembles that of natural language. In FSL, objects that correspond to a noun phrase are constructed from basic objects and attribute pairs. For example, "students who like certain fruits" is described in FSL by "student[Favorite $\to$ {fruit}]". In predicate logic, the same object is described by "$\lambda x \exists y(\text{student}(x) \land \text{Favorite}(x,y) \land \text{fruit}(y))$". Certainly, the structure of modification in natural language can be explicitly reflected in FSL. In this paper, in order to enrich the expressive power of basic FSL, new attribute relations are proposed. And an axiomatic system of extended logic is constructed as FS1. For example, "students who like all kinds of fruits" is described by "student[Favorite $\leftarrow$ {fruit}]", and the following relations holds.

$$\text{student}[\text{Favorite} \leftarrow \{\text{fruit}\}] \models \text{student}[\text{Favorite} \to \{\text{fruit}\}]$$

Furthermore, an attribute function is introduced into FS1. For example, "objects that are kept as pets by students" is described as "Pet(student)" and a compound notion "black dogs that are kept as pets by students" can be constructed using an object operator "·" as "Pet(student)· dog [Color$\to$ black]". The notation of Frame-Structure Logic is based on that of F-logic and Quixote. In contrast to these similar logic systems, FS1 has the following features.
1. There are no individual variables in logical formulas
2. Attribute relations can be treated as objects
3. FS1 has mathematical semantics that are different from that in predicate logic and an axiomatic system complete under the semantics

Knowledge representation that is similar to the structure of natural language is possible as a result of Feature 1. Feature 2 allows various compound objects to be synthesized structurally by object operators. Feature 3 shows that the relations of attribute pairs, class hierarchy and attribute inheritance can be simulated without the need for individual variables.

Fast Hypothetical Reasoning by Parallel Processing

Yutaka Matsuo and Mitsuru Ishizuka

University of Tokyo, 7-3-1, Hongo, Bunkyo-ku, Tokyo, Japan
{matsuo,ishizuka}@miv.t.u-tokyo.ac.jp

Abstract

Cost-based hypothetical reasoning is an important framework for knowledge-based systems because it is theoretically founded and useful for many practical problems. Basically, it tries to find the minimum-cost set of hypotheses that is sufficient for proving a given goal. However, since the inference time of hypothetical reasoning grows exponentially with respect to problem size, slow inference speed often becomes the most crucial problem in practice.

We have developed a new method to efficiently find a near-optimal solution, i.e., a solution whose cost is nearly minimal. This method uses parallel software processors to search for a solution. In order to grasp the search intuitively, we emulate parallel processing on a single processor and develop efficient algorithms. We assume that each variable and each Horn-rule (constraint) is a processor and behaves as follows: a Variable processor sends a message to lower the cost of a solution and a Constraint processor sends a message to satisfy itself.

Our approach is realized mathematically by the augmented Lagrangian method, an efficient parallel computation method. A Variable processor has a (prime) variable which takes the value [0,1]. A Constraint processor has also a (dual) variable which represents how strongly the constraint should be considered. The messages and updating procedures are defined by mathematical formulae.

This approach has two major advantages. First, we can generalize related methods such as our earlier SL method[1], the breakout method or Gu's nonlinear optimization method for SAT problems. They are all variants of our approach, obtained by modifying a part of the message to be sent.

Second, we can design new algorithms superior to previous algorithms such as SL method. We currently experiment with seven different algorithms of the parallel processor model, and find two algorithms are prominent as to inference time and solution cost. One algorithm is similar to the breakout method except that it considers the cost of the solution. The other is an entirely new algorithm, which adds one new processor to a problematic Horn-rule if search gets stuck in a local minimum. Using this algorithm, we can obtain solutions whose cost on average is lower than that of any other algorithm compared in our experiment.

---

[1] Y. Matsuo and M. Ishizuka: SL Method for Computing a Near-optimal Solution using Linear and Non-linear Programming in Cost-based Hypothetical Reasoning, Proc. PRICAI-98, pp.611-625, 1998.

TURAS: A Personalised Route Planning System

Lorraine McGinty and Barry Smyth

Smart Media Institute, Department of Computer Science, University College Dublin,
Belfield, Dublin 4, IRELAND.
{Lorraine.McGinty, Barry.Smyth}@ucd.ie
http://www.cs.ucd.ie/projects/Turas/default.html

Route planning has always provided a rich vein of research for the artificial intelligence community. However, to date the majority of this research has focused on the generation of optimal routes using shortest path algorithms to minimise distance traveled. The problem of planning high quality realistic routes is difficult for several reasons. Firstly, real maps rarely contain the sort of information that is useful for constructing realistic, high quality routes (real-time traffic information or road quality data). Secondly, the notion of "route quality" is notoriously difficult to define and is likely to change from person to person. Consequently, in real-world route planning situations, the shortest route is rarely the best route for a given user.

We argue that many traditional approaches to route planning fail to generate high quality routes for real users in realistic route planning scenarios because they tend to plan according to complex, ill-defined preference models. Recent research has attempted to address this issue by proposing route planning algorithms that learn and use implicit user preference models. However, these approaches make strong assumptions about the general characteristics of a given user preference model. We feel that such assumptions are unrealistic because the factors that are important to users may not be known explicitly, and vary from user to user.

Turas[1] is a Web-based, personalised route planner that is capable of learning about the route planning preferences of individual users and of generating routes that reflect these preferences. It employs a novel case-based route planning technique that makes no strong assumptions about the preference models employed by users, but that nonetheless is capable of generating high quality user-specific routes. Each user's route planning preferences are represented as a collection of previous route cases liked by the user, and new routes are generated by reusing and combining relevant sections of multiple cases. Recent evaluations suggest that our planner is capable of generating superior quality routes in a fraction of the time required by traditional planning algorithms.

References

1. McGinty, L. and Smyth, B.: *Personalised Route Planning: A Case-Based Approach*, Proceedings of Fifth European Workshop on Case-Based Reasoning, 2000.

---

[1] Turas is a gaelic word meaning journey or trip.

Analysis of Phase Transitions in Graph-Coloring Problems Based on Constraint Structures

Kazunori Mizuno, Atsuki Hayashimoto, and Seiichi Nishihara

Institute of Information Sciences and Electronics, University of Tsukuba
Tsukuba, Ibaraki 305-8573, Japan {mizuno, atsuki}@algor.is.tsukuba.ac.jp,
nishihar@is.tsukuba.ac.jp

Situations very similar to phase transitions (PTs) have been observed in constraint satisfaction problems. In our analysis, applying the backtracking-based tree search algorithm with Brélaz heuristic to the graph-coloring problems with three colors (3GCPs), we first reconfirmed PT phenomena. We then traced the backtracking history for variables for which thrashing appears to occur in the hardest problems. As a result, we found a local key structure of a graph, or a rigid pair, which is a pair of nodes to each of which the same color must be assigned, and is included in a subgraph such as Fig. 1(a) in 3GCPs. We found many rigid pairs in extraordinarily hard problems, in which very heavy trial-and-error repetitions of coloring are performed until the same color is assigned to rigid pairs.

To ascertain that the rigid pairs is the major reason for inefficiency, we introduced a reduction operation that eliminates rigid subgraphs, where all edges incident to node B of the rigid pair are reconnected to the other node, A. Fig. 1(c) shows the maximum search cost for solvable 3GCPs with 100 nodes. Interestingly, the secondary PT disappears completely in the region from $d = 1.7$ to $d = 1.9$. As for the unsolvable 3GCPs, the key structure causing inefficiency is expected to be the clique K_4(Fig. 1(b)) rather than the rigid subgraphs.

References

1. Hogg, T. and Williams, C. P.: The hardest constraint problems: a double phase transition, *Artificial Intelligence*, 69, pp. 359-377 (1994).
2. Mammen, D. L. and Hogg, T.: A New Look at the Easy-Hard-Easy Pattern of Combinatorial Search Difficulty, *J. Artif. Intell. Res.*, 7, pp. 47-66 (1997).

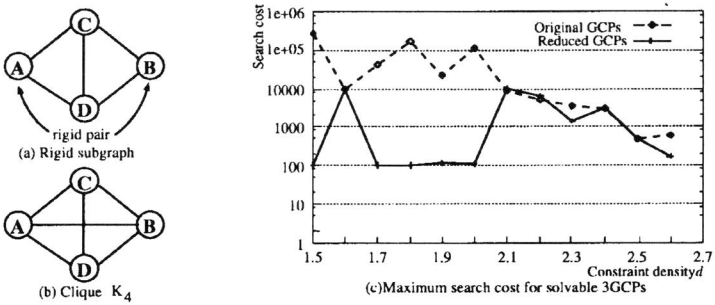

Fig. 1. Key substructures and search cost.

Minimal Model Generation with Factorization and Constrained Search

Miyuki Koshimura, Megumi Kita, and Ryuzo Hasegawa

Graduate School of Information Science and Electrical Engineering,
Kyushu University, Fukuoka 816-8580, Japan
{koshi, kita, hasegawa}@ar.is.kyushu-u.ac.jp

The notion of minimal models is important in a wide range of areas such as logic programming, deductive databases, software verification, and hypothetical reasoning. Some applications in such areas would actually need to generate Herbrand minimal models of a given set of first-order clauses.

A model generation algorithm can generate all minimal Herbrand models if they are finite, though it may generate non-minimal models[1]. Bry and Yahya propose a sound (in the sense that it generates only minimal models) and complete (in the sense that it generates all minimal models) minimal model generation algorithm [1]. The algorithm uses *complement splitting* (which is called *folding-down* in [2]) for pruning redundant proof and *constrained search* for eliminating non-minimal models.

We present another sound and complete minimal model generation algorithm which uses *tableau factorization* [2] and constrained search. It is known that factorization is more flexible than complement splitting for pruning the redundant search spaces [2]. This implies that our implementation obtains better performance than Bry and Yahya's when factorization performs well.

We give a short Prolog implementation FMM-SATCHMO obtained by modifying Bry and Yahya's implementation called MM-SATCHMO [1] and another short Prolog implementation FMMR-SATCHMO obtained by modifying FMM-SATCHMO. FMMR-SATCHMO omits unnecessary minimality tests, which are performed by MM- and FMM-SATCHMO, for constrained search.

We have proven that a model eliminated by factorization in the model generation process is not minimal. This implies that model generation with factorization is complete for generating minimal models. We have also shown a necessary condition for a generated model to be nonminimal.

Experimental results show that factorization can prune nonminimal models which are not pruned by complement splitting, and examining the necessary condition eliminates unnecessary minimality tests. Therefore, FMMR-SATCHMO often obtains better performance than MM-SATCHMO and FMM-SATCHMO.

References

1. F. Bry and A. Yahya. Minimal Model Generation with Positive Unit Hyper-Resolution Tableaux. In *Proc. of TABLEAUX'96*, LNAI 1071, pp. 143–159, 1996.
2. R. Letz, K. Mayr, and C. Goller. Controlled Integration of the Cut Rule into Connection Tableau Calculi. *Journal of Automated Reasoning*, 13:297-337, 1994.

Method of Ideal Solution in Fuzzy Set Theory and Multicriteria Decision Making

Gleb Beliakov

School of Computing and Mathematics, Deakin University,
Rusden campus, 662 Blackburn Rd., Clayton 3168, Australia
gleb@deakin.edu.au

Abstract. Multicriteria decision-making (MCDM) refers to making selections among some courses of action in the presence of multiple, usually conflicting criteria. In a large class of methods of MCDM, one can represent the preference relation $\succeq$ on a set of alternatives X with a single-valued function $u(x)$ on X, called utility, such that for any $x,y \in X$ $x \succeq y \Leftrightarrow u(x) \geq u(y)$. Utility is defined up to an increasing monotone transform, and consequently, it can always be normalised to the unit interval. In multiattribute utility theory the multicriteria problem is essentially substituted with a vector maximisation problem, *maximise* $u(\mathbf{x})=u(u_1(x_1),u_2(x_2),\ldots,u_n(x_n))$. Utility is equivalent to membership functions employed in Fuzzy Set Theory (FST) [3] and methods of combining individual utility values into the overall utility $u(\mathbf{x})$ correspond to aggregation operators in FST. A general aggregation operator is a monotone function f: $[0,1]^n \to [0,1]$, $f(\mathbf{0})=0$, $f(\mathbf{1})=1$. Triangular norms, averaging operators and ordered weighted aggregation are examples of aggregation operators.

Method of Ideal solution, in which the alternatives are ranked according to their distances (similarities) to the Ideal or nadir points, is also well known in the literature [4]. *L-p* metrics are commonly used in this context, and they correspond to the traditional methods in MCDM (additive and multiplicative utility, maximin) and FST (averaging operators, *max, min*). There is a semantic equivalence between the three concepts: utility, similarity and aggregation [3]. What was missing, however, is the equivalence at the syntactical level, which means that every method of utility combination has its mathematical counterparts among aggregation operators and similarity relations.

This work establishes this syntactical equivalence and demonstrates that every aggregation operator can be put into correspondence to a monotone pseudometric, in which the distance to the Ideal (nadir) is measured. It provides methods to build new aggregation operators based on metrics, and to incorporate criteria importance into the metric. It extends the results to fuzzy MCDM via aggregation of fuzzy sets of type II. Various examples are provided, but for more detailed discussion the reader is referred to [1]. Paper [2] provides details of construction of aggregation operators based on empirical data.

1. Beliakov, G.: Definition of general aggregation operators through similarity relations. Fuzzy Sets Systems 114 (2000) 437-453.
2. Beliakov, G.: Approximation of aggregation operators using splines, Proc. IPMU 2000 conference, Madrid, 3-7 July 2000.
3. Dubois, D., Prade, H.: The three semantics of fuzzy sets. Fuzzy Sets Systems 90 (1997) 141-150.
4. Zeleny, M., Multiple criteria decision making. McGraw-Hill, NewYork (1982).

A New Axiomatic Framework for Prioritized Fuzzy Constraint Satisfaction Problems*

Xudong Luo, Ho-fung Leung, and Jimmy Ho-man Lee

Department of Computer Science and Engineering
The Chinese University of Hong Kong
Shatin, Hong Kong SAR, P.R. China
{xluo,lhf,jlee}@cse.cuhk.edu.hk

Abstract. The paper introduces an axiomatic framework for prioritized fuzzy constraint satisfaction problems (PFCSPs), in which the notion of global satisfaction degree is based on three intuitive axioms. First, if a constraint with the highest priority in a PFCSP is completely violated by a variable assignment, the variable assignment cannot be a solution to the PFCSP. Second, a PFCSP with all constraints having the same priority should degenerate into a non-prioritized FCSP. Third, the global satisfaction degree of a PFCSP must be monotonic with respect to that of the corresponding FCSP. However, the precedent scheme for PFCSPs in [2, 1] satisfies only our last axiom but not the first two directly, especially in the case where the priorities of constraints are determined by voting. Also, our framework improves the precedent scheme on the scale for priorities. Thus, some issues in the precedent scheme can easily been handled in our framework. Besides, we discuss methods to construct various global satisfaction degrees that satisfy our axioms. In [2, 1], there is no similar discussion. Actually, the global satisfaction degree in [2, 1] is given by a special formula, while ours by a sort of more general formulas. Moreover, by our methods some new formulas for global satisfaction degree different from that in [2, 1] have been constructed. In addition, our results show that a PFCSP can be transformed equivalently into an FCSP, and so techniques developed for solving FCSPs can be adopted for solving PFCSPs. The idea behind our framework could be used to prioritize some other fuzzy problems.

References

1. D. Dubois and H. Prade, "Qualitative Possibility Theory and Its Applications to Constraint Satisfaction and Decision under Uncertainty", International Journal of Intelligent Systems, **14**, pp45-61, 1999.
2. R. Sabbadin, D. Dubois and H. Prade, "A Fuzzy Constraint Satisfaction Problem in the Wine Industry", Journal of Intelligent and Fuzzy Systems, **6**, pp.361-374, 1998.

---

* The work described in this paper was supported by a grant from the Research Grants Council of the Hong Kong Special Administrative Region, China (RGC Ref. No. CUHK4304/98E). The work is also partially supported by the Postdoctoral Fellowship Scheme of the Chinese University of Hong Kong.

Constraint Satisfaction over Shared Multi-set Value Domains

Michael J. Sanders

CSSE, Monash University, Clayton, Australia
msanders@csse.monash.edu.au

Conventional finite-domain constraint satisfaction problems (CSPs), and the algorithms that solve them, assume that: value domains are sets, variable instantiation is constrained only by value, and each variable, or node, has its own value domain. We extend the CSP definition to allow both domains and variable nodes to be multi-sets. By so doing we introduce a type of constraint we call *instance-* or *resource constraints*, which are orthogonal to (and may coexist with) conventional *value* constraints. Our definition further allows for the sharing of domains by multiple nodes, which effectively compete for resources. By allowing multi-sets in domains and in nodes we introduce the following problem: assigning a multi-set of variables $\delta_1\grave{}v_1 + \cdots + \delta_n\grave{}v_n$ from a multi-set domain $\sigma_1\grave{}e_1 + \cdots + \sigma_m\grave{}e_m$. This is a permutational search problem.

Our approach is to split each node multi-set into a set N of *elementary* multi-sets $\{\delta_1\grave{}v_1, \ldots, \delta_n\grave{}v_n\}$ such that variables $v_1, \ldots, v_n$ must all be assigned appropriate quantities of values from the same domain. For an elementary node $\delta_i\grave{}v_i \in N$ we call δ_i the *demand* of variable v_i. For a multi-set value domain $M = \sigma_1\grave{}e_1 + \cdots + \sigma_m\grave{}e_m$ and an element $\sigma_j\grave{}e_j$ of M, we call σ_j the *supply* of e_j in M. An implicit *unary resource* constraint exists for each elementary multi-set node, where value supply must be at least equal to node demand. As with unary value constraints, preprocessing can "remove" inconsistent values (those with inadequate supply). Where multiple nodes share a domain, a set of implicit *binary resource* constraints exists. This is because, given some arbitrary instantiation order, the assignment of a value to a variable depletes the remaining supply of that value, and potentially "starves" uninstantiated variables. For the set N of elementary multi-set nodes $\{\delta_1\grave{}v_1, \ldots, \delta_n\grave{}v_n\}$ sharing a domain, and a static order of instantiation $v_1, \ldots, v_n$, each variable v_i resource-constrains all subsequently instantiated variables $v_{i+1}, \ldots, v_n$. Resource binary constraints may be processed similarly to value constraints, using for example Forward Checking[1].

Conventional CSPs are a subset of our definition, which we call a *generalised* CSP. We have enhanced existing CSP techniques to produce an algorithm FC-CBJ-M which efficiently solves both value and resource constraints. We are investigating the use of generalised CSPs in resource-based constraint problem areas such as work-flow and scheduling.

References

1. R. Haralick and G. Elliott. Increasing Tree Search Efficiency for Constraint Satisfaction Problems. *Artificial Intelligence*, 14:263–314, 1980.

Algorithms for Solving the Ship Berthing Problem

Kai Song Goh, Andrew Lim

Department of Computer Science, National University of Singapore
3 Science Drive 2, Singapore 117543
gohkaiso@comp.nus.edu.sg, alim@comp.nus.edu.sg

Abstract. The Ship Berthing Problem (SBP) is one of the many problems faced by a port in its daily execution. Ships arriving at the port will have to be assigned specific berthing location based on certain constraints arising from the ship's cargo or physical characteristics. SBP can be solved as a minimization problem, in which the aim is to assign all ships in an arrangement that would result a minimum wharf length.

The SBP can be represented using a Directed Acyclic Graph (DAG) where vertices represents ships and edges represent the contemporary relationship between ships. Two ships are contemporary if they are both required to be berthed at a particular instance. The direction of the edges determines the relative positions of the ships and hence the resulting required wharf length. For the ease of manipulation, the DAG is represented by an acyclic list where each node in the list represents a vertex and the relative positions of the nodes reflects the direction of edges in the DAG.

A Greedy Local Search (GLS) algorithm is proposed to solve the SBP. The idea is to constantly displace nodes in the acyclic list as long as the resulting required berth length is reduced. A Tabu-Search (TS) post-optimization technique is proposed to improve the result of the GLS, here, a potentially 'bad' displacement is allowed in hope that the move would result in an escape from the local optimal, the performance of the TS can be varied by specifying the maximum number of consecutive 'bad' displacement allowed. Two displacement techniques with different local search neighbourhood were proposed. The initial solution in which the GLS is performed can be obtained by using a Greedy Heuristic, alternatively, a randomly generated initial solution can be used.

A different approach in solving the SBP is the use of Genetic Algorithm (GA). Due to the unique nature of the acyclic list, common crossover reproductive methods cannot be used, instead three reproductive methods that would not corrupt the acyclic list were proposed. The performance of the GA can be configured by using a decline factor on the fitness measure, a high decline factor would give rise to a more stringent natural selection by modifing the fitness measure as the generation progresses. The roulette selection method is used to ensure that the solution would not be moving towards the local optimal all the time.

We have experimented with a total of 22 different variants of the GLS, TS and GA and found that all techniques possess variants that produces good results for solving the SBP.

Temporal Interval Logic in Data Mining

Chris P. Rainsford[1] and John F. Roddick[2]

[1] Defence Science and Technology Organisation, DSTO C3 Research Centre
Fernhill Park, Canberra, 2600, Australia.
chris.rainsford@dsto.defence.gov.au
[2] School of Informatics and Engineering, Flinders University of South Australia
GPO Box 2100, Adelaide 5001, Australia.
roddick@cs.flinders.edu.au

Abstract. The last decade has seen the emergence of data mining as a significant field of research. Whilst the exploitation of time series data has been widely examined in this context, the accommodation of temporal interval semantics has not been widely investigated. Temporal intervals and the interaction of interval-based events are fundamental in many domains including commerce, medicine, computer security and various types of normalcy analysis. We have developed an algorithm for integrating temporal interval semantics into association rules, a form of rule that has become widely used in data mining. We have also developed a visualisation technique to view the discovered rules. The model of temporal reasoning that has been adopted accommodates both point-based and interval-based models of time simultaneously. In addition, the use of a generalized taxonomy of temporal relationships supports the generalization of temporal relationships and their specification at different levels of abstraction. This approach also facilitates the possibility of reasoning with incomplete or missing information.

1. Introduction

We have developed an algorithm to find temporal relationships between associated items in discovered association rules. Rules take the form of the following example:

policyZ $\Rightarrow$ investX, productY $\wedge$ *during*(investX, policyZ)
$\wedge$ *before*(productY, investX).

The rule can be read as follows: *The purchase of investment X and product Y are associated with insurance policy Z. The investment in X occurs during the period of policy Z and the purchase of product Y occurs before investment X.* Further details of the algorithm and its experimental testing can be found in [1,2].

1. Rainsford, C.P., Accommodating Temporal Semantics in Knowledge Discovery and Data Mining, PhD Thesis, University of South Australia, (1999).
2. Rainsford, C.P., Roddick, J.F. Adding Temporal Semantics to Association Rules. in The 3rd European Conference on Principles and Practice of Knowledge Discovery in Databases, (PKDD-99). Prague, Czech Republic, September 15-18, (1999).

Data Mining in Disease Management – A Diabetes Case Study

Hongxing He[1], Hari Koesmarno[1], Thach Van[1], and Zhexue Huang[2]

[1] Research and Analysis Section, Health Informatics Branch, Health Insurance Commission,
PO Box 1001 Tuggeranong ACT 2900, Australia
{hongxing.he, hari.koesmarno, thach.van} @hic.gov.au
[2] E-Business Technology Institute, The University of Hong Kong, Pokfulam Road,
Hong Kong, China
jhuang@eti.hku.hk

Recently, HIC has formulated its strategic direction for the 21st century. In the new direction, HIC will not only serve as a payment agency but also become a health information provider to the public. Following the new strategic direction, HIC has set up a new Information Management Division to fulfil its goals. The research section within the new division has entered a new research area for data mining applications to the management of diseases. This is an attempt to apply data mining techniques to analyze the medical service transaction data for disease management rather than the data used in the well-studied applications to medical diagnosis. The disease management project undergoing at The Health Insurance Commission of Australia is aimed at identifying good or not so good medical service practice from a large transaction database. In this paper, we present a case study on our application to diabetes management. In this case study, we selected 7443 diabetes patients living in Fairfeld and extracted their Medicare service data in 1998 from the Medicare transactional database item sequences. After selecting the 26 most frequently used items, we further transferred the patients' item sequences into a set of vectors, each components of which represent a group of services. The choose four service groups which are identified by the Clinic Advisory Group (CAG) of Diabetes to be the most essential tests for diabetic patients.

We use the cost function and total mutual information to select the best clustering results by Kmean and Self Organising Map. After selecting the best clustering from the two algorithms, we used both statistical methods and medical knowledge to identify interesting clusters. We are able to identify from the Medicare data, some clusters, in which the medical services of diabetes patients deviated from the guideline suggested by The Clinic Advisory Group. This discovery can be used to educate medical practitioners to improve their practice to achieve the best outcome of the medical treatment with minimal cost of the public health system.

Reference

1 Haykin, S. 1994 *Neural Networks: A Comprehensive Foundation*, New York, MacMillan

A Limited Lattice Structure for Incremental Association Mining

Yi Zhao[1], Jianliang Shi[2], and Pengfei Shi[1]

[1] Institute of Image Processing & Pattern Recognition, Shanghai Jiaotong University,
Shanghai 200030, China
zy80913@mail1.sjtu.edu.cn, pfshi@ippr.sjtu.edu.cn

[2] Guoxin Lucent Technologies Network Technologies Co., Ltd., Pudong,
Shanghai 200122, China
jlshi@gxlu.com.cn

Abstract. An association rule typically strives for discovering a dependency among attributes with respect to the externally defined parameters like support threshold and confidence threshold. As an important database discovery method, the kernel of association rule mining is the acquisition of large itemsets. It is an important field of data mining to represent the support and confidence of items that are purchased together in supermarket domain. In this paper, a novel limited concept lattice is first proposed for the transaction data itemsets modeling. Concept lattice is a form of a concept hierarchy in which each node represents a subset of objects (extent) with their common properties (intent). The Hasse diagram of the lattice represents a generalization / specialization relationship between the concepts. Therefore, the lattice and Hasse diagram corresponding to a set of objects described by some properties can be used as an effective tool for symbolic data analysis and knowledge acquisition. Based on this lattice structure, an algorithm, LCLL, is presented to incrementally generate large itemsets visually. The algorithm works by means of attaching frequency information to each lattice node, the corresponding support measure can be obtained with the limited lattice. Besides, the edges in the Hasse diagram of the new lattice must be modified: the generator of a new node is always its child, and original parent of the generator is updated. When a node is deleted till the frequency value turns to zero, the node and the edges between its parents and children are not deleted, but tagged. The key point lies in adding edges when searching for the new node's parents, the large itemsets can be obtained by judging whether the cardinal and frequency value of the node exceeds the threshold or not. And accordingly, association rules can be identified. The approach is especially efficient when the database is dynamically updated (insertion, deletion or simultaneous insertion and deletion). Compared with K. Hu's approach [5], our algorithm generates all the association rules with much less time complexity. The time complexity of the proposed algorithm has a relationship of inverse proportion with the cardinal of the transactions, which means the applicability of the approach to the supermarket.

Markov Modelling of Simple Directional Features for Effective and Efficient Handwriting Verification

Alan McCabe

School of Information Technology
James Cook University
alan@cs.jcu.edu.au

Abstract

Signature verification has long been a traditional means of authenticating an individual, with this process now being automated via a number of research activities. The problem with automated signature verification systems is that they can be susceptible to forgery as it is often possible to obtain a copy of an individual's signature. The work described here alleviates this problem to some degree in that a signature is not used but rather a user-determined "password".

This approach is centred on the fact that people don't write according to a standard penmanship and deviation from the norm is dependent on the individual. Additionally, individuals tend to deviate in a *similar way* from one instance to the next. This similarity of deviation can be exploited to allow identification of the author by analysing a small sample of handwriting.

The handwriting is captured and digitized in real-time using a graphics tablet, so no physical evidence of the handwriting sample is ever recorded (eliminating the possibility of the password being stolen). The samples are modelled in the system using a Markov model with five states. The state transitions of the model are determined by first segmenting the handwriting sample into a series of "strokes" (pen path between consecutive minima in the pen-tip velocity). The next step involves obtaining the "net direction" for each stroke by positioning the beginning of the stroke at the origin. The current state is then assigned a value corresponding to the quadrant in which the stroke end-point lies (or a fifth state representing a "pen-up" occurrence).

This system takes advantage of multiple security schemes in that users would benefit from the protection of password defenses as well as aspects of signature verification. A potential forger does not automatically gain access to a resource simply by finding out (or guessing) the user's password, they also need to be able to forge the writing style of that user. The opposite is also true - if a forger is familiar with the user's writing, that forger must also know the user's password if they are to break into the system.

The results obtained from a database of almost 1000 handwriting samples from 47 writers include an error rate of 0.64% when the potential forger does not know the genuine user's "password".

Texture Analysis and Classification Using Bottom-Up Tree-Structured Wavelet Transform

Yukinobu Miyamoto[1], Mahdad Nouri Shirazi[2], and Kuniaki Uehara[3]

[1] Department of Computer and Systems Engineering, Kobe University
miyamo@ai.cs.kobe-u.ac.jp
[2] Kansai Advanced Research Center, Communications Research Laboratory
mahdad@crl.go.jp
[3] Research Center for Urban Safety and Security, Kobe University
uehara@kobe-u.ac.jp

One difficulty in texture analysis was the lack of adequate tools for characterizing textures. Recent developments in multiresolution analysis, such as the wavelet transform, attempt to overcome this difficulty. The tree-structured wavelet transform (TSWT), which affords for an analysis in terms of the texture's decomposition structure and the corresponding spectrum in the space-frequency domain, has received a lot of attention. Recently, Chang [1] proposed a texture classification algorithm based on a top-down TSWT ($TSWT_{TD}$). Although high classification rates were reported, its performance is highly dependent on a set of parameters which have to be determined through elaborate tuning. We propose a texture classification algorithm based on a bottom-up TSWT ($TSWT_{BU}$), which is not dependent on ad-hoc parameters and shows also superior performance. We also provide an analysis of the structural stability of TSWT.

The proposed algorithm consists of the following steps: 1) decompose a given texture fully by using TSWT; 2) calculate the energy of each decomposed node; 3) if the energy of a parent node is larger than the average of its children's energies, prune the children; 4) repeat step 3 from the bottom to the top level. In the algorithm, since pruning proceeds from the bottom to the top, all nodes will be visited and there is no danger of missing a significant node, which was not the case with $TSWT_{TD}$. Furthermore, the algorithm is free from the ad-hoc and heavily data dependent parameters, which are needed for making a trade-off between the structural stability and the classification accuracy in $TSWT_{TD}$.

Experimental results shows that $TSWT_{BU}$ exhibits relatively higher classification accuracy (99.8%) than $TSWT_{TD}$ (99.1%), especially in the case of no overlapping between the training and test sets (94.8% and 82.5%, respectively). Moreover, the $TSWT_{BU}$ showed larger structural diversity, as compared to $TSWT_{TD}$, in terms of both the average number of tree-structures and the average structural entropy. Noting that the former scheme shows higher classification accuracy, the aforementioned fact points out the superiority of the $TSWT_{BU}$ scheme in generating relatively more representative and hence discriminative tree-structures of textures.

References

1. T. Chang and C.-C. J. Kuo, "Texture analysis and classification with tree-structured wavelet transform," *IEEE Trans. Image Processing*, vol. 2, no. 40, pp. 429–441, 1993.

A Stereo Matching Algorithm Using Adaptive Window and Search Range

Han-Suh Koo and Chang-Sung Jeong[1]

Department of Electronics Engineering, Korea University
1-5ka, Anam-dong, Sungbuk-ku, Seoul 136-701, Korea
csjeong@chalie.korea.ac.kr

Abstract

The stereo matching algorithm is a technique that analyses two or more images captured at diverse view points in order to find positions in real 3D space for the pixels of 2D image. The stereo matching methods have been used in various fields such as drawing the topographical map from aerial photograph and finding the depth information of objects in machine vision system. Nowdays, optical motion capture techniques using stereo matching algorithms are being developed for visual applications such as virtual reality or 3D graphics.

Stereo matching algorithms can be generally classified into two methods: feature-based and area-based ones. The feature-based method matches the feature elements between two images, and uses the interpolation to obtain the disparity information for the pixels other than the feature elements, while the area-based method performs matching between pixels in two images by calculating the correlations of the pixels residing in the search window. Area-based method cannot match feature element with more accuracy than feature-based method even though it can make more dense disparity map. Moreover, it has more possibility of error in the area of insufficient texture information or depth discontinuities.

In this paper we present a novel technique for area-based stereo matching algorithm which provides more accurate and error-prone matching capabilities by using adaptive search range and window size. We propose two new strategies (1) for determining search range adaptively from the disparity map and multiresolutional images of region segments obtained by applying feature-based algorithm, and (2) for changing the window size adaptively according to the edge information derived from the wavelet transform such that the combination of two adaptive methods in search range and window size greatly enhance accuracy while reducing errors. We test our matching algorithms for various types of images, and shall show the outperformance of our stereo matching algorithm.

---

[1] This work has been supported by KISTEP and BK21 Project.

A Design of Rescue Agents for RoboCup-Rescue

Masayuki Ohta[1,4], Nobuhiro Ito[2], Satoshi Tadokoro[3], and Hiroaki Kitano[4]

[1] Tokyo Institute of Technology [2] Nagoya Institute of Technology
[3] Kobe University [4] Kitano Symbiotic System Project,ERATO,JST

The RoboCup-Rescue project[1] was proposed, that aims at disaster mitigation, and we implemented a simulation system for it. The image of the system is shown in Figure:1. Making agents that maximize the rescue activity in this simulation system provides new problem domains compare to the Soccer Server[2], such as, cooperation between heterogeneous agent, dynamic planning reorganization and more strict limitation of sensor information.

The RoboCup-Rescue Simulation System consists of a Kernel which is the central module of this system and some modules which plug into the Kernel as shown in Figure:2. The simulation world is described as a set of objects, and the protocol between the Kernel and the other modules is realized by passing information of only necessary properties of the objects. This implementation makes it possible to plug-in the modules, and enables us to evaluate not only the performance of cooperative agents, but also the performance of each plug-in module, i.e, various disaster simulators and viewers. More details about this simulation system are shown in the "RoboCup-Rescue Simulator Manual"[3].

We made a simulation to decide the optimal distribution of rescue agents to fire sites. For each fire site, agents obtain the efficiency function of their rescue activity, and select the distribution which maximizes the total efficiency. We found concentrate policy minimizes the total damage in the simulation. One of the future works will be a learning method to predict the efficiency function from the map data.

Fig. 1. Image of the System

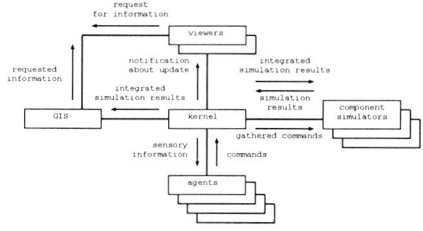

Fig. 2. Structure of the System

References

1. H.Kitano, S.Tadokoro et al. RoboCup-Rescue: search and rescue in large-scale disasters as a domain for autonomous agents research, Proc. of IEEE SMC, 1999.
2. I.Noda, H.Matsubara, K.Hiraki and I.Frank. Soccer Server: A Tool for Research on Multiagent Systems. Applied Artificial Intelligence, Vol.12, pages 233-250, 1998.
3. http://kiyosu.isc.chubu.ac.jp/robocup/Rescue/manual-English-v0r3/

A Cooperative Architecture to Control Multi-agent Based Robots

M. Becht, R. Lafrenz, N. Oswald, M. Schulé, and P. Levi

University of Stuttgart, IPVR
Breitwiesenstr. 20-22, D-70565 Stuttgart, Germany
robocup@informatik.uni-stuttgart.de
www.informatik.uni-stuttgart.de/ipvr/bv/projekte/comros/pricai2000.html

Internal Structure of a Robot. To control a group of cooperating autonomous mobile robots, we use a multi-agent architecture as introduced in [LBLM98]. The structure of a single robot consists of a set of concurrent Elementary Agents situated on different levels of abstraction. The levels are defined by different response time and are structured as reflexive, tactical, and strategical layer. E.g. in the reflexive layer tasks like object recognition and self-localization are processed.

Structure of Elementary Agents. The structure of the Elementary Agent leads back to [Lev92] and consists of react, adapt, behave, and plan cycles. These cyles are controlled by the decision unit. Another task of the decision unit is the cooperation with other Elementary Agents.

Behavior Patterns for Soccer Playing Robots. Each robot is able to take over roles based on behaviors. We call a set of behaviors for one type of a player (e.g. goalkeeper, forward, and defender) a role. A behavior requires a set of skills. In principle, a behavior or skill may be part of several roles.

Experiments. In the past, we had successfully shown that the presented architecture is suitable to control a team of autonomous robots. The CoPS Stuttgart team competed successfully at the *RoboCup 1999* [OBB+99] in Stockholm and became Vice Champion at the *German Open Championship 1999* in Stuttgart, where six German teams competed.

Conclusion. As an application of this architecture we chose soccer playing, because it is a well-defined scenario with suitable complexity. Nevertheless, this architecture can also be applied to other scenarios like cooperative vision and cooperative crossing of traffic intersections in a distributed robot system.

References

[LBLM98] P. Levi, M. Becht, R. Lafrenz, and M. Muscholl. COMROS - A Multi-Agent Robot Architecture. In *DARS 3*, 1998.

[Lev92] P. Levi. Architecture and restriction-based planning of autonomous traffic agents. *Journal for the Integrated Study of Artificial Intelligence Cognitive Science and Applied Epistemology (CC AI)*, 9(1):43–64, 1992.

[OBB+99] N. Oswald, M. Becht, T. Buchheim, G. Hetzel, G. Kindermann, R. Lafrenz, P. Levi, M. Muscholl, M. Schanz, and M. Schulé. CoPS-Team Description. In *RoboCup 99 Stockholm*, 1999.

Automatic Development of Robot Behaviour Using Monte Carlo Methods

James Brusey

Department of Computer Science, RMIT University,
P.O. Box 2476V, Melbourne 3001, Australia
brusey@cs.rmit.edu.au

Abstract. Control systems for autonomous robots often use an architecture known as *behaviour-based* [1], which means that the problem of defining what the robot does is broken down into a number of competing or cooperating modules, or *behaviours*. Although a single behaviour might have access to all sensory information and might be able to control all effectors, it doesn't necessarily do so all of the time, or may have its control outputs adjusted by other behaviours. The behaviour-based approach has been remarkably successful because the resulting control systems are fast and robust, in comparison with deliberative approaches used in the past, which tended to yield robots that were slow and sensitive to changes in the environment.

Our experience has been that, although it is often easy to develop behaviours that work, they tend to be inefficient. They are inefficient in the sense that the robot takes more sense-decide-act cycles than necessary. We address this problem by developing a general method for generating near optimal behaviours based on a reward function.

The approach is based on using a Monte Carlo algorithm [2] for solving Markov Decision Processes to learn the behaviour. Monte Carlo algorithms are a subclass of Reinforcement Learning algorithms and bears similarities to Q-learning or TD(λ). This algorithm is slow to converge and so we found it necessary to train using a simulator. The level of realism in the simulator is therefore quite important. We found that we were able to improve over hand-coded behaviours and that the improvement carried over to tests on the physical robot.

References

1. Ronald C. Arkin. *Behavior-Based Robotics*. MIT Press, 1998.
2. Richard S. Sutton and Andrew G. Barto. *Reinforcement Learning: An Introduction*. MIT Press, Cambridge, Massachusetts, 1998.

Adapting Behavior by Inductive Prediction in Soccer Agents

Tohgoroh Matsui, Nobuhiro Inuzuka, and Hirohisa Seki

Nagoya Institute of Technology, Gokiso-cho, Showa-ku, 466-8555 Nagoya, Japan
{tohgoroh, inuzuka, seki}@ics.nitech.ac.jp

This paper proposes new architecture of agent which adapts its behavior by predicting the results of actions and avoiding taking ones predicted to be failures shown in Fig. 1. Our agent consists of five parts: Observer, Planner, Actor which are same as those of basic agent and write perceiving information in the first-order formalism, Learner which acquires prediction rules using inductive logic programming (ILP), and Checker which predicts the result of an action selected by Planner and changes action if it seems to be failure. The agent classifies past actions into successes and failures, then it learns rules from them to assort the current action without information after taking it.

We implemented soccer agent using the RoboCup champion CMUnited-99 and an ILP system Progol to verify our agent. The experimental result in case of learning to kick the ball from some places into the goal is shown in Fig. 2. The agent learned prediction rules from 221 kicks (80 goals and 141 fails) and then the rate of successful kicks rose from 36.2% to 90.3% by using the rules.

ILP is also used in a reactive agent TRAIL [1] which learns action models called teleo-operator. Our agent acquires knowledge on action selection which is higher level than action models and adapts behavior using the knowledge.

References

1. Benson: Inductive learning reactive action models, *Machine Learning: Proc. of the 12th International Conference*, 1995.

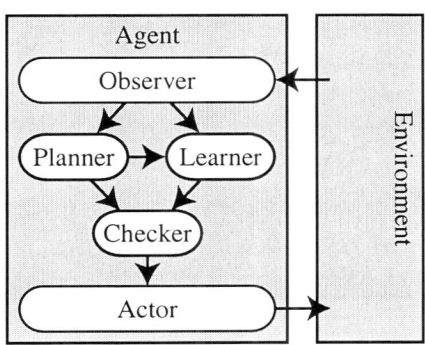

Fig. 1. Architecture of agent.

	$S(x)$	$\neg S(x)$	total
$P(x)$	62.5 ± 10.4	6.7 ± 2.0	69.2 ± 11.3
$\neg P(x)$	18.5 ± 10.3	143.4 ± 5.7	161.9 ± 12.8
total	81.0 ± 1.3	150.1 ± 5.8	231.1 ± 6.7

Accuracy of rules: 89.1 ± 4.2%

Success rate before learning: 36.2%
Success rate after learning: 90.3 ± 2.4%

Fig. 2. The contingency table of 10 fold cross validation in case of learning to kick the ball from some places into the goal. $S(x), P(x)$ represents x was success and had been predicted to be success, respectively.

Computing the Local Space of a Mobile Robot

Margaret E. Jefferies[1], Wai-Kiang Yeap[2], and Lyndsay I. Smith[1]

[1]Artificial Intelligence Laboratory, Computer Science Department,
University of Otago, Dunedin, New Zealand
megan@cs.otago.ac.nz
[2]Auckland University of Technology, Auckland, New Zealand

A popular approach to describing the environment of an autonomous system is to compute a representation for the space surrounding the robot, termed the local space. Recently the focus of much of the work in this area in robotics has been on acquiring a usable representation. To this end many computationally demanding algorithms have been devised in the hope that accurate representations which more closely match the real world will be computed. However this is very difficult to achieve from the robot's initial experience of its environment. We argue that an inaccurate but useful representation can be computed from the robot's initial view of the local space. We present an algorithm for computing this initial representation and show its implementation on a robot with sonar sensors.

In devising this algorithm the important issue is: "What can feasibly be computed from the input?". In addressing this issue we argue that much can be learned from the way in which humans solve similar problems. Humans rarely compute a representation of reasonable detail from a single experience of the environment. For them an immediate concern is how to get out of the space they are currently in. They tend to explore unfamiliar territory tentatively ever mindful of the way out. It is this idea of identifying exits first which gives us a clue as to how the boundary for the local space should be computed. Our algorithm identifies the exits first. It is then a simple problem to work out the rough extent of the local space from exit information.

Exits are found at occlusions. These are the points of discontinuity detected from adjacent sonar beams. The "true" edge of an exit could lie anywhere within the cones of reflection of the two sonar beams. Thus we use the points of discontinuity as a starting point to search for the "true" edges of the exit. Specular reflection initially causes the construction of false exits. However the robot will never be able to cross a false exit. Exits are validated as the robot moves around and sensor readings are collected from different locations.

With such a representation the robot has a rough idea of the extent of the local space. If the robot decides to leave the current space immediately on entering it, it can do so easily. The exits are not exact but they do not need to be. When the robot initially heads towards an exit, it need only be pointing in roughly the right direction. As it gets closer to the exit and receives feedback from its sensors it can make adjustments for any discrepancies it detects. If the robot decides to stay in the current space then the representation can become the basis for further exploration.

Learning Situation Dependent Success Rates of Actions in a RoboCup Scenario

Sebastian Buck[1] and Martin Riedmiller[2]

[1] Munich University of Technology
Computer Science Department IX
Orleansstr. 34
D - 81667 München, FRG
buck@in.tum.de

[2] University of Karlsruhe
Institute for Logic, Complexity
and Deductive Systems
D - 76128 Karlsruhe, FRG
riedml@ira.uka.de

Abstract. A quickly changing, not predictable environment complicates autonomous decision making in a system of mobile robots. To simplify action selection we suggest a suitable reduction of decision space by restricting the number of executable actions the agent can choose from. We use supervised neural learning to automaticly learn success rates of actions to facilitate decision making. To determine probabilities of success each agent relies on its sensory data. We show that using our approach it is possible to compute probabilities of success close to the real success rates of actions and further we give a few results of games of a RoboCup simulation team based on this approach.

The RoboCup soccer server offers a couple of low level commands for soccer agents to choose from each 100 ms. Mainly they have the following options: turn (*angle*), dash (*power*), kick (*power*) (*angle*). If we treat the task of playing soccer as an optimization problem the aim is to control our agents in the given environment such that they score more goals than the opponent team does. We can estimate the number of possible policies by discretising the angle and the power value of the low level commands: Assuming 72 possible angles (5 degree steps) to turn to or to kick to and 10 power levels to dash with or to kick with we get 802 different commands to choose from for a player possessing the ball at **one** time step. This means we have up to 802^{3000} different policies over a period of five minutes for only **one** agent. This forces us to reduce the number of possible choices per time step. To do this we introduce a number of actions such as pass, shoot2goal or go2ball from which the agent can choose. We compute explicit situation dependent success rates for these actions using neural networks (one for each action). From all promising actions (estimated success rate exceeds threshold) the one ranked highest in a priority list (shoot2goal is ranked higher than pass...) is chosen to be executed. In order to evaluate our concept we compared estimated success rates with real success rates and played simulation games against different teams. In addition to our statistics our concept was quite successful in official games of our team *Karlsruhe Brainstormers* against some simulator league teams of 1999. For further information please contact Sebastian Buck.

Cooperative Bidding Mechanisms among Agents in Multiple Online Auctions

Takayuki ITO[1], Naoki FUKUTA[1], Ryota YAMADA[1],
Toramatsu SHINTANI[1], and Katia SYCARA[2]

[1] Department of Intelligence and Computer Science, Nagoya Institute of Technology,
Gokiso, Showa-ku, Nagoya, 466-8555, JAPAN
[2] The Robotics Institute, Carnegie Mellon University,
5000 Forbes Ave., Pittsburgh, PA 15213-3890, USA

Increasingly, there have been growing interest on online auctions for electronic commerce. Currently, more than 150 online auction sites exist on the Internet. Agent-mediated electronic commerce has recently commanded much attention. Agents can act autonomously and cooperatively in a network environment on behalf of their users. It is hard for users to attend, monitor, and bid at the multiple auctions sites simultaneously. Therefore, we have proposed *BiddingBot* (Fig.1), a system which can support bidding to several auction sites simultaneously[1].

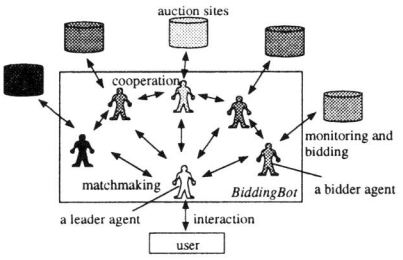

Fig. 1 The architecture of *BiddingBot*

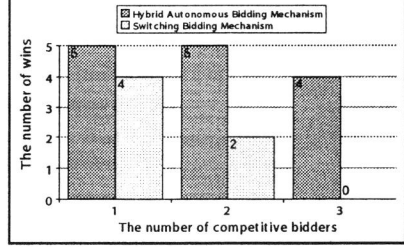

Fig. 2 Experimental Result

In this paper, we proposed new cooperative bidding mechanisms for *BiddingBot*: the Switching Bidding Mechanism, the Full Autonomous Bidding Mechanism, and the Hybrid Autonomous Bidding Mechanism. In order to compare the above bidding mechanisms, we conducted several experiments. The results (Fig.2) of our current experiments demonstrate the following two claims. (1) The Hybrid Autonomous Bidding Mechanism is an effective cooperative mechanism among several bidding agents. (2)When *BiddingBot* wins an item, the cost for money is lower if we employ the Switching Bidding Mechanism rather than the Hybrid Autonomous Bidding Mechanism.

References

1. T. ITO, N. FUKUTA, T. SHINTANI, K. SYCARA, "*BiddingBot* : A Multiagent Support System for Cooperative Bidding in Multiple Auctions," In *Proceedings of ICMAS2000*, 2000 (to appear).

This article was processed using the LaTeX macro package with LLNCS style

Framework of Distributed Simulation System for Multi-agent Environment

Itsuki Noda

Electrotechnical Laboratory, Tsukuba 305, Japan
noda@etl.go.jp

"Simulation" is an important research tool on multi-agent systems [1]. I investigate experience of development of Soccer Server, the official soccer simulator used in RoboCup Simulation League. It satisfies five conditions listed by Casti[1], that is, *fidelity*, *simplicity*, *clarity*, *bias-free*, and *tractability* [2].

Building on the lessons learned via the Soccer Server, I propose a new framework for distributed simulation system, calles *FUSS (Framework for Universal Simulation System)*, for general purpose of multi-agent researches. FUSS will provide a utility for creating simulations in a wide variety of multiagent domains. A simulation system built on FUSS consists of a `fskernel`, which provides shared memory management and synchronization control services, and a number of simulation modules, each of which calculate a part of a simulated world (see Figure 1). Its modular facilities enable incremental and distributed development of large simulation systems. By using FUSS, Soccer Server's problems are solved as follows:

- Generality: Actually, FUSS provides facilities for distributed modular simulation system. We can develop other kind of simulation system like rescue simulators using FUSS.
- Huge Traffic: Compared to Soccer Server, communications with clients are dealt with three modules, a monitor proxy and two player simulator/proxies, separately. Therefore, we can distribute the network traffic by invoking these modules on different machines in different network segments.
- Legacy: Communication with player clients is localized into by player proxies. This means that we can handle multiple protocol by providing multiple player proxies for each protocol. It makes easy to maintain legacy features.

Further information about FUSS is available from http://ci.etl.go.jp/noda/soccer/fuss/.

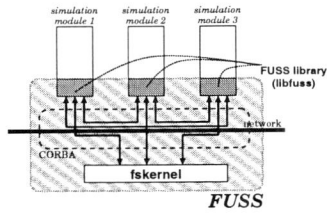

Fig. 1. A Simulation System Built on FUSS

References

1. J. L. Casti. *Would-be Worlds: how simulation is changing the frontiers of science.* John Wiley and Sons, Inc., 1997a.
2. Itsuki NODA and Ian FRANK. *Virtual Worlds : Synthetic Universes, Digital Life, and Complexity*, chapter Investigating the Complex with Virtual Soccer, pages 189–209. Perseus Books, Jan. 1999.

Dependence Based Coalitions and Contract Net: A Comparative Analysis (Extended Abstract)

Márcia Ito and Jaime Simão Sichman

Intelligent Techniques Laboratory, University of São Paulo
av. Prof. Luciano Gualberto, 158, tv. 3, 05508-900, São Paulo, SP, Brazil
{ito,jaime}@pcs.usp.br

Among several models of dynamic organizations, one can find *Contract Net* [4] and *Dependence Based Coalitions* [3] models. In this work [2], we present a comparative analysis of these models. More precisely, we compare their global communication flow, by changing some parameters that have influence on the total number of exchanged messages. Our main goal is to be able to detect under which conditions one of the models is better than the other, concerning the parameters values.

The Dependence Based Coalitions model (DBC) [3] is based on Social Power Theory, using the core notion of *dependence relation* [1]. In this model, information about the others is acquired during an initial *presentation phase*, which is followed by several *resolution cycles*, when an *active agent* tries to achieve one of his goals. The Contract Net model (CN) [4] is based on the notion of *economic market*. We suppose that agents do not have any information about others (CN*). Therefore, unlike the DBC model, there is no presentation phase.

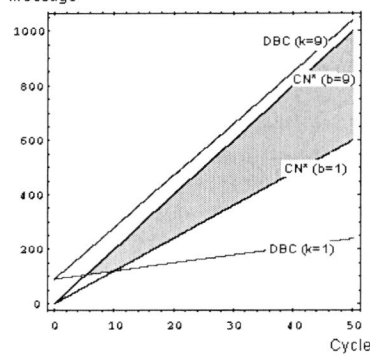

The main parameters that take part into the global communication flow in both models are the following: the total number of agents in the society (n), the total number of resolution cycles, i.e., the total number of goals to be achieved (g) and the number of possible partners (m). Considering the DBC model, another relevant parameter is the number of agents to whom coalition proposals are sent (k). As for the CN* model, a relevant parameter is the total number of agents that send proposals (b). Considering some simplifying hypothesis, the global communication flow of both models are respectively $S_{DBC} = n(n-1) + g(2k+1)$, where $0 < k \leq m$ and $S_{CN*} = g(n+b)$, where $0 < b \leq m$.

Generally speaking, we can conclude that given a number of agents n, there will always be a range for the values of k and b (dark area in the figure) where from some *critical cycle* on (i.e., intersection of the lines in the figure), the DBC model will have a smaller communication flow than the CN* model. The better situations correspond to those where the active agent's social reasoning mechanism is more accurate ($k \approx 1$).

1. CASTELFRANCHI, C.; MICELI, M.; CESTA, A. Dependence relations among autonomous agents. In: *Decentralized A.I. 3* Netherlands, Elsevier Science Publishers B.V., 1992, v.1, p. 215–227.
2. ITO, M. *Uma análise do fluxo de comunicação em organizações dinâmicas de agentes.* São Paulo, 1999. 141 p. MsC Disseratation — Escola Politécnica da Universidade de São Paulo.
3. SICHMAN, J. S. DEPINT: Dependence-based coalition formation in an open multi-agent scenario. *Journal of Artificial Societies and Social Simulation*, 1(2), 1998. <http://www.soc.surrey.ac.uk/JASSS/1/2/3.html>.
4. SMITH, R.G. The Contract Net Protocol: high-level communication and control in a distributed problem solver. *IEEE Transactions on Computers*, v.29, n.12, p. 1104–1113, 1980.

A Tracer for Debugging Multi-agent System Based on P-Q Signal Method

Tadachika Ozono[1] and Toramatsu Shintani[1]

Dept. of Intelligence and Computer Science, Nagoya Institute of Technology
Gokiso, Showaku, Nogoya, 466-8555, Japan
{chika, tora}@ics.nitech.ac.jp

We have developed RXF (Reflective Familiar) [1], a new programming environment for building a multi-agent system (MAS). We are interested in what types of functions are required when building MASs. An MAS in RXF consists of reflective agents, which are intelligent and autonomous agents based on reflection. RXF employs the constraint-logic programming for rapid prototyping, the multi-thread programming for concurrent programming, and the reflections for meta-level programming. On developing RXF we recognized the necessity of a new debugger for MASs because problems debugging concurrent processes makes debugging MASs more difficult. For example, a traditional tracer slows down only an agent debugged. As a result, a speed ratio of agents in an MAS becomes different from a speed ratio of agents without such a debugger. We proposed a multi-agent tracer that allows programmers to effectively debug MASs [2]. The tracer attempts to keep the speed ratio of agents in an MAS to solve the problem. The tracer is not enough robust against packet loss or network latency. We believe debugging MASs in unstable network environment. In this paper, we propose the P-Q signal method to improve the tracer in unstable network environment. The new method utilizes a P signal and a Q signal to inform non-debugged agents that the debugger suspends and resumes a debugged agent, respectively. The P and Q signals include suspend time and total suspend time to adjust the speed ratio. The new tracer can adjust a speed ratio of agents in an MAS more precisely by using P-Q signals.

Our new tracer has five advantages. (1) It can apply debugging heterogeneous multi-agent systems. (2) It does not require information about the execution speeds of agents before debugging. (3) It is tolerable against communication delay. (4) It does not need global clock. (5) It is very simple to implement and understand. We did an experiment to measure how precisely our new tracer can keep a speed ratio of agents in a MAS in unstable network environment and we can conclude that our tracer is effective to debug MASs.

References

1. Tadachika Ozono and Toramatsu Shintani, On Constraint Logic Programming Language RXF for Implementing Multiagent Systems, Trans.IPS.Japan, 37(10), 1996, 1765–1772.
2. Tadachika Ozono and Toramatsu Shintani: Implementing a Tracer for Debugging Concurrent Processes of a Multi-Agent System. Trans. of the Institute of Electoronics, Information and Communication engineers, 2000 (to appear).

A Multi-agent Approach for Simulating Bushfire Spread

William Magill and Xiaodong Li

Gippsland School of Computing and Information Technology
Monash University
Churchill, VIC 3840, Australia
{wgmag1, xil}@mugc.cc.monash.edu.au

Bushfires destroy vast areas of land every year and take many lives because we are unable to contain them in time. Without a clear idea of how fires spread, we can do little to combat them. Current efforts on simulating bushfire spread are often found to be focusing on modeling the system as a whole using system-level variables [1]. This kind of top-down approach generally requires finding mathematical expressions that summarise various aspects of the system to fit what has been observed [2]. In this research we have developed a model for simulating bushfire spread by using a multi-agent approach (i.e., bottom-up). The simulation is implemented by using SWARM, a multi-agent simulation framework developed at Santa Fe institute. This type of micro-simulation involves describing the variables that define how the individuals act. The main benefit of this form of simulation is that once a facet of an individual's interactions has been observed then this facet can be incorporated into the simulation without the necessity of finding a complex mathematical expression that adequately describes how it relates to the system. To produce the simulation of the whole system, only the interactions of the individuals with each other and the environment need to be modeled. In this research we simulate an artificial environment (2-dimensional grid) where bushes are randomly generated at various locations; and fire can be ignited from a certain spot or one side of the artificial world, then spread across the world according to some "interaction rules". The simulation allows for interaction between the fire and the environment, taking into account a number of environmental factors that contribute to the spread of bushfires such as *bush density*, *land height*, *flammability*, and *wind conditions*. These factors have undergone testing under some initial conditions, and as a consequence of their combined effect, the bushfire spread behavior at the landscape level can be observed to mimic the phenomena of bushfire spread in nature. In future, more experiments will be conducted to investigate how these factors can be used to predict and control fire behaviour.

References

1. Resnick, M. (1994), *Turtles, Termites and Traffic jams*, The MIT press, Cambridge, Massachusetts.
2. Beer, T. (1991), "Bushfire rate-of-spread forecasting: deterministic and statistical approaches to fire modeling", *Journal of Forecasting*, **10**, p.301-17.

Multi-agent Cooperative Reasoning Using Common Knowledge and Implicit Knowledge*

Lifeng He[1], Yuyan Chao[2], Koji Yamada[2], Tsuyoshi Nakamura[2] and Hidenori Itoh[2]

[1] Faculty of Information Science and Technology
Aichi Prefectural University, Aichi, 480-1198 Japan
[2] Department of Artificial Intelligence and Computer Science
Nagoya Institute of Technology, Nagoya, 466-8555 Japan

Abstract. This paper presents a method for multi-agent cooperative reasoning using common knowledge and implicit knowledge.

In multi-agent cooperation environments, it is often necessary to reason about the state of knowledge of all agents being considered, not simply the state of knowledge of each individual agent. Therefore, *common knowledge* and *implicit knowledge* [2] are necessary for multi-agent cooperative reasoning.

Common knowledge ϕ is such knowledge that not only everyone knows ϕ, but everyone knows that everyone knows ϕ, and everyone knows that everyone knows that everyone knows ϕ, and so on. For example, any game rule in a robot football game is common knowledge for all robots. On the other hand, ψ is an implicit knowledge for a group of agents if and only if it can be deduced from the combination of knowledge of all agents in the group. For example, suppose that agent a and agent b are two cooperating agents, and agent a knows p, agent b knows $p \rightarrow r$, then r is implicit knowledge, since r can be derived by the combination of the knowledge of agent a and agent b.

In this paper, we extend our automated reasoning system for Multi-Agent Knowledge and Time, presented in [1], with incorporating common knowledge and implicit knowledge under the conditions of linear, discrete and synchronous time and unbounded memory. We introduce how to use the possible-world semantics to explain the concepts of common knowledge and implicit knowledge, and consider how to translate them into their corresponding first-order formulas. A simple communication protocol is also discussed.

References

1. L. He, Y. Chao, S. Kato and H. Itoh, 'Implementing an Automated Reasoning System for Multi-Agent Knowledge and Time', LNAI 1286, pp.152-165, 1997.
2. J.Y. Halpern and Y. Moses, 'A Guide to the Modal Logics of Knowledge and Belief: Preliminary Draft', *IJCAI*, pp.480-490, 1985.

---

* This work is partially supported by the Japanese Ministry of Education, Science, Sports and Culture under Grand-in-aid for Encouragement of Young Scientist.

Life-Like Agent Design Based on Social Interaction

Yugo Takeuchi[1], Tooru Takahashi[1,2], and Yasuhiro Katagiri[1]

[1] ATR Media Integration & Communications Research Laboratories, Kyoto 6190288, Japan
[2] Nara Advanced Institute of Science and Technology, Nara 6300101, Japan
{yugo, tooru-t, katagiri}@mic.atr.co.jp

Abstract. This study focuses on the design of a life-like agent interface that considers the social aspects in human-agent interaction. We have designed and incorporated life-like guide agents into an exhibition guide system on the hypothesis that a user of the system establishes a social relationship with a life-like interface agent similar to a relationship with another human.

We studied the effect of inducing the users' affiliation need by incorporating life-like guide agents in the C-MAP (Context-aware Mobile Assistant Project) Exhibition Guidance System. This system features a personal mobile assistant that provides visitors touring exhibitions with information based on contexts (spatial/temporal locations and individual interests). The user of this system carries a hand-held guidance system called PalmGuide while touring an exhibition. PalmGuide maintains user contexts. A life-like personal guide agent runs on the user's PalmGuide and provides tour navigation information such as introduction of exhibit articles and recommendations of what to visit next. Information terminals called Information Kiosks are installed at each exhibit. Information Kiosks usually provide general information about the exhibit. When a user with a PalmGuide comes to an Information Kiosk, the user can connect her PalmGuide to the Information Kiosk by infrared communication. Then, the user's guide agent migrates to the Information Kiosk and personalizes it for her personal interests and needs.

We designed the behaviors of the guide agents as follows: Until the fourth access to an Information Kiosk, the user's guide agent returns to the original PalmGuide, after it provides relevant information of the exhibit and the recommendation for the next visit. However, at the end of the user's fourth access, the guide agent does not return to the original PalmGuide. Instead, the agent disappears from the current Information Kiosk by saying that it will go to an Information Kiosk and will be waiting for the user there. The user is expected to chase her agent by herself. When the user follows the agent to the recommended Kiosk, the agent thanks the user. When, on the other hand, the user comes to a different Kiosk, the agent reappears and gives a complaint to her. In either case, we expect that the agent's reaction induces its user's affiliation need and has an effect on the user's subsequent behaviors. We deployed our guide agent system at our annual Open House exhibition, and observed visitors behaviors toward the agents.

We compared acceptance rates of recommendations before and after each user obtained feedback from her agent to her reactions toward the agent's recommendation at the fifth access. We found that people, who did not follow her agent's recommendation at the fifth access, tend to behave differently toward the guide agents' recommendations before and after the fifth access, when the agents simply went ahead and waited for their users at the recommended Information Kiosk. We believe that the guide agents' action enhanced the users' affiliation needs toward the agent. The users try to recover the affinitive relationship with the agent when they did not access the recommended Kiosk and obtained a complaint from the agent in the fifth access. The changes in user behaviors are controlled by the enhancement of affiliation needs, which are effected by social interactions between the users and their agents.

Agent-Oriented Programming in Linear Logic: An Example

Abdullah-Al Amin   Michael Winikoff   James Harland

Department of Computer Science, RMIT University
GPO Box 2476V, Melbourne, 3001, AUSTRALIA
`{amin, winikoff, jah}@cs.rmit.edu.au`

Agent-oriented programming (AOP) represents a new way of analysing, designing, and implementing complex software applications. This approach has been successfully used in complex applications with distributed components, which require concurrent behaviour, efficient reasoning, dependable communication, sharing and integration of knowledge. Such applications range from from comparatively small systems such as personalised email filters to large, complex, mission critical systems such as air traffic control. Since its introduction, various approaches have been proposed to determine a suitable architecture for agent-based systems. There have been a number of attempts to model AOP, some of which also involve an implemented development environment (such as JACK [1], or dMARS) whilst others are an abstract specification of necessary constructs such as Agent0 [4].

In order to develop and reason about such programs, an ability to take into account concurrency and dynamic state is required. *Linear logic*, introduced by Girard in 1987 [2] has such properties, and has been successfully applied to modelling updates, reasoning about the environment, and implementing concurrent behaviour. Linear logic is often described as *resource-sensitive*, and has been the basis for a number of programming languages including Lygon [3], Lolli, Forum, ACL, $\mathcal{LC}$, and LO.

In this paper we investigate the advantages and disadvantages of developing agent-oriented programs in Lygon, a programming language based on linear logic. In particular, we develop a bank deposit example which serves as an illustration of the advantages and disadvantages of this approach. Due to its basis in linear logic, Lygon can easily and naturally model states, express concurrency, and describe actions. These are the primitive building blocks of agents and hence Lygon appears promising as an agent-oriented programming language.

References

1. Paolo Busetta, Ralph Ronnquist, Andrew Hodgson, and Andrew Lucas. JACK Intelligent Agents - Components for Intelligent Agents in Java. Technical report, Agent Oriented Software Pty. Ltd, Melbourne, Australia, 1998.
2. Jean-Yves Girard. Linear Logic. *Theoretical Computer Science*, 50:1–102, 1987.
3. James Harland, David Pym, and Michael Winikoff. Programming in Lygon: An overview. In Martin Wirsing and Maurice Nivat, editors, *Algebraic Methodology and Software Technology*, LNCS 1101, pages 391–405. Springer, July 1996.
4. Yoav Shoham. Agent-oriented Programming. *Artificial Intelligence 60*, 60(1):51–92, 1993.

---

[0] This paper is based on the first author's Honours thesis.

Emotional Intelligence for Intuitive Agents

Penny Ray[1], Mark Toleman[2], and Dickson Lukose[3]

[1,2]Department of Mathematics and Computing, University of Southern Qld, Toowoomba, Qld 4350, AUSTRALIA.
{ray, toleman}@usq.edu.au

[3]Brightware Inc., 90 Park Avenue, Suite 1600, New York, NY, 10016, USA.
dickson.lukose@brightware.com

Abstract. Currently, there are no machines with emotions that influence their reasoning, perception and decision-making abilities to the degree that emotions affect human behaviour in these areas. This could be for two reasons. Firstly, emotions have traditionally been broadly defined and no discrete categorization had been formulated, and secondly, emotions have been viewed as opposing logic, the very basis for computational machines, and as a disruption to rational reasoning and function. It is the very contrasting evidence in recent research that has seen a renewed enthusiasm into emotional research. The role of emotion in rational human behaviour may have a larger impact on cognitive processes than first thought. In this paper, we define emotions and discuss the importance that they will have on artificial intelligences of the future.

Dawkins, in *"The Selfish Gene"* (1976) wrote, *"A duck is a robot vehicle for the propagation of duck genes."* This sentence could be construed somewhat controversial when viewed in context for AI researchers. When he wrote this, Dawkins was commenting on evolutionary and survival instincts in line with Charles Darwin's view that emotions being prevalent in both humans and other animals are crucial to the survival of the species.

If AI researches were to build an artificial robot duck, the least use they would have in mind for it would be the parenting of baby robot ducks. This broaches a fundamental question in the AI domain. *Do emotions have any significant contributions to make to the area?*

Our research seeks to answer this question and concentrates on the emotional assessment of atomic elements within the virtual world of an artificial agent. We envisages a meshing of several psychological theories on emotion generation with agent technology, in order to produce an intuitively rational reasoning and decision making artificial being.

To these ends, our continuing research endeavours to expand our understanding of cognitive emotion theories and their influence on affective reasoning in humans and the translation of these models into an affective agent architecture.

Formalization for the Agent Method by Using π-Calculus

Kazunori Iwata[1], Nobuhiro Ito[2] and Naohiro Ishii[1]

[1] Dept. of Intelligence and Computer Science, Nagoya Institute of Technology,
Gokiso-cho, Showa-ku, Nagoya, 466-8555, Japan
{kazunori, ishii}@egg.ics.nitech.ac.jp

[2] Dept. of Electrical and Computer Engneering, Nagoya Institute of Technology,
Gokiso-cho, Showa-ku, Nagoya, 466-8555, Japan
bobson@phaser.elcom.nitech.ac.jp

Abstract. In a real-time, dynamically-changing environment, software agents have the following big two problems in executing their methods. If the environment is the real-time world, then the delay to calculate the parameters, which are referred to by a method, causes the delay to execute the method. In the second case, if the environment is the dynamic world, then the agents need special functions to change the reference to parameters that comes with the method.

In order to overcome these problems, we have proposed a new description for the method of agents by using π-calculus[1] and an agent model(cf. Fig.1) to operate this description. π-calculus is a process calculus which is able to describe dynamically-changing networks of concurrent processes.

In the proposed description, the parameters and the methods are regarded as processes in π-calculus. The reference from the method to the parameters is regarded as the network in π-calculus and hence the reference can be changed dynamically.

Further on, we have executed the experiments using fire-world as the environment on which the agents execute. In the fire-world, a dynamically-changing environment, agents can not predict how the environment will change, because the fire randomly moves and spreads. Finally, we have shown that the result obtained by executing the methods on this environment using the description given in this paper is useful in a dynamically-changing environment by overcoming the two above-mentioned problems.

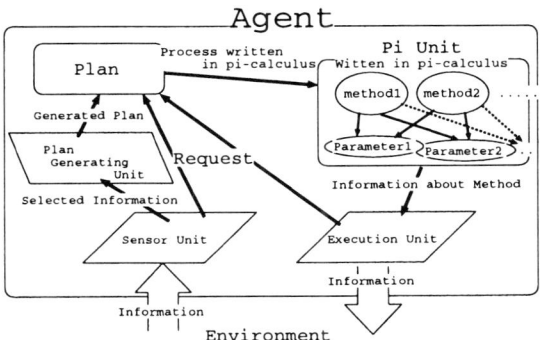

Fig.1. Agent Model

References

1. R. Milner. Polyadic π-calculus:a Tutorial. LFCS Report Series ECS-LFCS-91-180, Laboratory for Foundation of Computer Science, 1991.

Utilization of Coreferences for the Translation of Utterances Containing Anaphoric Expressions

Michael Paul and Eiichiro Sumita

ATR Spoken Language Translation Research Laboratories
{michael.paul, eiichiro.sumita}@slt.atr.co.jp

One of the major problems of current machine translation systems is the lack of contextual knowledge which might result in misinterpretations of the translation. Especially, short sentences frequently do not contain enough information to achieve an adequate translation in the context of previous utterances. Contextual information can be achieved through the analysis of coreferential relationships of anaphoric constituents. The utilization of coreferences, however, is not restricted to the word selection of the anaphor itself. We propose a *word selection* method which analyzes coreferences and uses the semantic features of the antecedent for the translation of the sentence predicate.

We are using a corpus-based anaphora resolution mechanism that combines a machine learning algorithm with a statistical preference scheme for the identification of reference objects [1]. First, a decision tree trained on an annotated corpus determines the coreference relation of a given anaphor and antecedent candidates. In the second step, the most salient antecedent is selected by taking into account the frequency information of non-/coreferential pairs tagged in the training corpus as well as distance features within the current discourse.

For the context-adopted target selection we collected samples of predicate translations from our corpus consisting of the source predicate and its corresponding translation in the context of the respective case-filler elements. Similarity between the input sentence and entries in the dictionary are calculated according to the semantic distance of the source constituents [2]. The distance is calculated for all entries and the determination of the sample with the minimal distance results in the selection of the most appropriate target predicate in the context of the source expressions. In the case of patterns with the same minimal distance we utilize the one most frequently occurring in our data corpus.

Given an utterance containing an anaphoric expression the word selection algorithm applies the resolution module in order to determine the most salient reference object. The semantic features of the antecedent in combination with those of the source predicate are then utilized to select the target predicate resulting in a context-adopted translation of the source utterance.

References

[1] Paul, M., Sumita, E.: Corpus-Based Anaphora Resolution Towards Antecedent Preference. In *37th ACL workshop "Coreference and It's Applications"*, p.47-52. 1999.
[2] Sumita, E., Iida, H.: Experiments and Prospects of Example-based Machine Translation. In *29th ACL*, p.185-192. 1991.

Word Alignment Using a Matrix

Eiichiro Sumita

ATR Spoken Language Translation Research Laboratories
eiichiro.sumita@slt.atr.co.jp

We propose a new method for aligning source words and target words in parallel corpora. Our proposal does not depend on syntactic parsing like [1] but on sentence alignment and morphological analysis like [2].

First, all possible alignments are hypothesized as a matrix filled with occurrence similarities between source words and target words. Here, we use *cosine* [3] as the occurrence similarity. Suppose that a corpus consists of N numbered sentence pairs. Each word is associated with an N-dimensional vector consisting of the sentence pair IDs in which the words occur. The occurrence similarity of a source word s and a target word t is computed as the *cosine* of the angle between their associated vectors. We propose using a matrix of *cosine* to represent all possible combinations of correspondences between source content words and target content words.

In order to find the most plausible combination of correspondences between words as a whole, we consider the following conditions: (1) The higher the occurrence similarities, the more plausible the correspondence; (2) There is at most one correspondent for each word.

For each sentence pair, the highest similarity in the matrix is selected and conflicting correspondences are eliminated, and then the next highest one is investigated. This process is repeated until no more words is aligned.

We propose *coverage*, i.e., *how many words are aligned of the total number of words* as the primary criterion for ranking alignments. Because a source sentence is equivalent to a target sentence, all source words correspond to one of target words in principle; this holds for the reverse direction. Although there are exceptions, we can suppose that the more aligned words there are on source and target sides, the better the alignment is. All alignments are sorted primarily by coverage and secondaril y by the total of the occurrence similarities. The top-ranked one is returned.

References

[1] Kitamura, M. and Matsumoto, Y.: Automatic Extraction of Translation Patterns in Parallel Corpora. In *Transactions of IPSJ*, Vol. 38, No. 4, p. 727-735. 1997.
[2] Haruno, M. and Ikehara, S.: Two-step extraction of bilingual collocations by using word-level sorting. In *IEICE Trans. of INF. & SYST.*, Vol. E81-D, No. 10, p. 1103-1110, 1998.
[3] Schutze, H. : Automatic Word Sense Discrimination. In *Computational Linguistics*, Vol. 24, No. 1, p. 97-123, 1998.

Deterministic Japanese Word Segmentation by Decision List Method

Hiroyuki Shinnou

Ibaraki University, 4-12-1 Nakanarusawa Hitachi Ibaraki 316-8511, Japan,
shinnou@dse.ibaraki.ac.jp

In Japanese natural language processing, morphological analysis is a very important technique, and many methods for it have been proposed. The task of Japanese morphological analysis is essentially word segmentation. In this study, we propose a new method of Japanese word segmentation. Our method regards word segmentation as the classification problem and solves it by the decision list method. The advantage of our method is that it avoids the unknown word problem because it is a kind of character based method. Another advantage is that it is deterministic, and the time taken for deterministic analysis is proportional to the length of the sentence. Moreover, our approach can use various features to solve the classification problem, and various machine learning methods.

The biggest problem of Japanese word segmentation is to cope with unknown words. To overcome this problem, character-based Hidden Markov Model (HMM) has been proposed. In HMM, the state transfer probabilities and the output symbol probabilities judge whether a word boundary exists between two characters or not. These probabilities are learned from bi-gram and tri-gram of the training corpus. However, character-based HMM needs further resources because n-gram alone cannot give high precision. In this study, we regard word segmentation as the problem judging whether a word boundary exists between two characters or not, that is, the classification problem. Therefore, we can conduct word segmentation by various machine learning methods for the classification problem. Moreover, we can use various resources besides n-gram as features to achieve the high precision.

In this study, we used the decision list method[1] as the machine learning method. Moreover, we used the kinds of Japanese character and the information of parentheses besides n-gram resources as features of the decision list.

In experiments, we constructed the decision list by using training data of one year of newspaper articles. With the constructed decision list, we conducted word segmentation for 1,000 sentences and compared our results with those of Chasen, which is the de facto standard system of Japanese morphological analysis. As a result, our method was slightly superior to the Chasen system.

References

1. Yarowsky, D. : "Decision Lists for Lexical Ambiguity Resolution: Application to Accent Restoration in Spanish and French", 32th Annual Meeting of the Association for Computational Linguistics, pp. 88–95 (1994).

Criteria to Choose Appropriate Graph-Types

Hayato Yonezawa, Mitsunori Matsushita, and Tsuneaki Kato

NTT Communication Science Labs.
2-4, Hikaridai, Seika-cho, Soraku-gun, Kyoto 619-0237, Japan
{hayatoyo, mat, kato}@cslab.kecl.ntt.co.jp

Abstract. Results from empirical studies on automatic visualization systems for statistical data are reported. These studies especially focused on a mechanism for choosing an appropriate graph type. Two experiments were conducted as a first step fowards proposing a mechanism with objective bases.

The first experiment employed a machine learning technique. Five data characteristics including categories of variables corresponding to graph axes and number of variables were taken as features. The relationships between graph types and these features were learned by using ID3. As 2D graphs including stacked bar charts and doughnuts charts were our concern, up to three axes and variables were taken into consideration.

265 graphs of seven graph types collected from newspapers were used, and the result was the average of 200 times of two-fold cross validations. 20% to 30% of the leaf nodes of the obtained decision trees contained more than one candidate. That is, the feature set used was insufficient to uniquely determine the graph type. The rate that a given learning sample was uniquely classified correctly was 79.8%. The rate that it was classified into a leaf node containing more than one candidate including the correct one was 96.6%. The data characteristics chosen were sufficient for selecting graph type candidates.

Another possible factor for determining the graph type is what a graph drawer intends to emphasize in a graph, i.e., aspects, such as precise values, tendency of transition, and mutual comparison. In the second experiment, impressive aspects to readers were collected and analyzed, as it is difficult to collect drawers' intentions behind drawn graphs.

75 graphs (25 graphs each for bar, line and pie charts) collected from newspapers were used. Three subjects were asked in questionnaires to state what information could be noticed easily on each graph and identify the data aspect related to that information. As a result, data aspects apt to be noticed differed between graph types. For example, mutual comparison was apt to be noticed on pie charts, while tendency of transition was found on line charts and bar charts.

The decision process for graph type suggested by these results is that first, candidates are determined by constraints from the data characteristics, and then the best one is chosen through consideration on the data aspect to be emphasized. The latter is needed because what aspect is apt to be noticed depends on the graph type.

A Document Classifier Based on Word Semantic Association

Li Xiaoli, Liu Jimin, Shi Zhongzhi

Institute of Computing Technology, Chinese Academy of Sciences, Beijing, China 100080
xminer@asia.com

Most of text classification methods are based on Vector Space Model (VSM). In the model, each document is mapped to a point (represented by a vector) in Vector Space. A metric measuring the distance of two vectors is then designed to decide the category of any new vector. If the distance is less than some threshold or satisfies some other criterion, the category is assigned to the new vector.

The disadvantage of these methods is that they don't concern the relation among features in vectors, which makes the computation of the distance inexact and results in low classification precision.

We process features according to the following ways. First, since a vector in text classification problem usually has tens of thousands of features, we reduce the dimension of feature space through feature selection. Second, those features that have a higher semantic coherence should occur together more often, so Association Rules Mining are applied to discover the association between features. Meanwhile it also defines the connecting strength between different features. The support degree of rules is recognized as a threshold to filter out noisy feature associations. If support degree is greater than the threshold, then the bigger the confidence degree of rules is, the more coherent the features in the rules are. In the end, in computation of distance between two documents belonging to one category, a new formula is defined to consider the association between features. Even if a feature doesn't occur, other features that have semantic association with can replace it in some degree. So it makes distance computation more accurate.

We construct an experimental classifier CTCSA to test the effectiveness of this method. After segmenting and tagging 13548 Chinese text in People's Daily, we classify them by human into 13 categories. They are Politics, military, economy, police and law, agriculture, physical education, medicine and sanitation, industry, science and technology, tour and traffic, culture and life, religion and race, astronomy and geography. The result of experiment expresses that our method can greatly improve the classification performance for either precision or recall.

Based on analysis of defect of traditional VSM, we develop a new classification approach. By selecting feature subset, it filters out unnecessary features. Data mining technique provides us a means to find semantic coherence between features. In addition, that other associated feature can replace a feature in some degree results in accurate distance computation. This method will undoubtedly improve the classification precision.

Incorporation of Japanese Information Retrieval Method Using Dependency Relationship into Probabilistic Retrieval

Hiroki Fujitani, Tsunenori Mine, and Makoto Amamiya

Department of Intelligent Systems, Kyushu University
{fujitani,mine,amamiya}@al.is.kyushu-u.ac.jp

Our Japanese information retrieval method using both dependency relationship between words and their semantic information, which we call DRB method, handles a frame that consists of a noun and a verb governing the noun as a key to judge whether or not a document is relevant to a query. This method proved that using dependency relationship in information retrieval is highly effective in terms of Precision. On the other hand, it is often too exacting to retrieve an appropriate number of documents, making Recall plunge. In order to solve this problem, we incorporate DRB method into a probabilistic method so that it scores and ranks documents with statistical information. In the experiments we compare performance of the incorporated methods, (A) Respective Frame matching with 2-Poisson Model and (B) Frame matching with 2-Poisson Model, with other four information retrieval methods, (C) 2-Poisson Model, (D) NEAR matching, (E) AND matching and (F) Frame matching, by utilizing BMIR-J2[1]. Respective Frame matching retrieves every document that has an identical frame with at least one of a query's frames while Frame matching retrieves documents that have the identical frames with the query's frames.

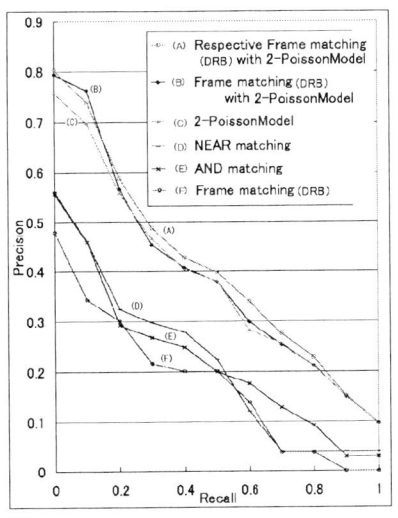

As Figure shows, Method (A) and (B) are more effective than Method (C) due to strong constraint of DRB method. They are also more effective than DRB method (F) because they can retrieve documents by totally depending on Robertson's 2-Poisson Model even though Method (F) retrieves nothing when relevant documents exist. For these reasons, we conclude that combining those two methods is effective. Furthermore, being still exacting, Method (B)'s Precision is higher only at lower Recall while that of Method (A) is higher over all. Therefore we conclude that Method (A) is the most effective.

---

[1] Tsuyoshi Kitani, "BMIR-J2 test collection for evaluating Japanese information retrieval system", Proc.of Information Processing Society of Japan 98-DBS-1143, 1998

A Step Towards Integration of Learning Theories to Form an Effective Collaborative Learning Group

Akiko Inaba, Thepchai Supnithi, Mitsuru Ikeda,
Riichiro Mizoguchi, and Jun'ichi Toyoda

I.S.I.R., Osaka University, 8-1 Mihogaoka, Ibaraki, Osaka, 567-0047 Japan
inaba@ai.sanken.osaka-u.ac.jp

We are aiming at building a sophisticated ontology through a survey of existing learning theories. On top of that, our research objectives include constructing a collaborative learning (*CL*) support system that detects appropriate situation for a learner to join in a CL session, and forms a CL group appropriate for the situation dynamically. To fulfill these objectives, we have to consider the following:
1. How to detect the appropriate situation to start a CL session and to set up the learning goal,
2. How to form an effective group which ensures educational benefits to the members of the group, and
3. How to facilitate desired interaction among learners in the learning group.

We have discussed item 1 in our previous papers, and now focus on item 2.

There are many learning theories to support the advantage of CL. A designer should construct CL-support systems taking the theories into consideration and represent what he/she intended as an explicit model of design with justification by the theories. The system designed, on the other hand, needs to understand the model and yields reasonable supporting behavior for CL based on the understanding. The understanding of learning theories used for justification is, needless to say, partial as compared with what the human expert of learning theories knows. However, we believe the learning theories, even partial, should be modeled as a basis of system design. The problem the system designer faces is caused by difficulty in understanding the learning theories due to the lack of common and solid background concepts for CL. An ontology represents common concepts of the learning theories as a solid system of concepts. It establishes the shared understanding among designers and systems about the model of CL which is justified with the learning theories.

We have been constructing a system of concepts, we call "Collaborative Learning Ontology", to represent CL sessions supported by these learning theories. Now, we focus on "Learning Goal Ontology" which is a part of the Collaborative Learning Otology. The ontology will ease the difficulty for the system designers in understanding the learning theories. Based on the ontology, we are probing into a possibility that theory-based learning groups can be combined into one in order to help a learner attain his/her learning goals.

Further information on our ontology is available at:
http://www.ai.sanken.osaka-u.ac.jp/~inaba/LGOntology/

Model-Based Software Requirements Design

Takumi Aida[1] and Setsuo Ohsuga[2]

[1] Graduate School of Science and Engineering, Waseda University
   takumi@ohsuga.info.waseda.ac.jp
[2] Department of Information and Computer Science, Waseda University
   ohsuga@ohsuga.info.waseda.ac.jp

Abstract. Software requirement design is the first phase of software development. A requirement must be correct and clear because it mediates between programmers and clients who require the software. Although a requirement is designed by clients, they can not easily complete it without enough knowledge about the object which integrates the software with itself. Not all clients are experts, and most clients have no time and no training for acquiring enough knowledge. If clients can design a requirement rapidly, correctly, and clearly. the cost of early stage software development must be reduced.

Computer aided requirement design systems using past design cases are needed. In many cases, a new object is designed by reference to existing designs facilitating rapid software development. However, they are not widely considered by clients, requirement designers, because their past design cases are written in a natural language that cannot be processed by computers. Past requirements should be represent by knowledge language so that they can be legible by both computers and human beings. Furthermore, model management systems are needed because a set of requirement knowledge to reproduce a past design becomes a past model. Each of past models in an individual field includes a common basic model and a characteristic part that can be used as a constant part and a variable part in design time respectively. And then sharing a common model can reduce a model-base size.

Past design cases should be represented as requirement models. Through storing design knowledge in computer systems, requirement designers can cope with requests for softwares to be larger and more complicated.

Acquiring Factual Knowledge through Ontological Instantiation

Hyopil Shin and Spencer Koehler

Computing Research Laboratory, New Mexico State University
Las Cruces, NM, 88003, USA
{hshin, sbk}@crl.nmsu.edu

We propose a method of acquiring factual knowledge using the Knowledge Base Acquisition Environment (KBAE) of CRL (Computing Research Laboratory). We observed that a Fact Database that is generated by instantiating ontological concepts takes advantage of the full expressive power of ontological structures for use in NLP systems, including machine translation, information retrieval and question-answering systems. We argue that both the construction of the Fact Database and the quality of applications that use it can be enhanced by ontological inferences that are available from the connected resources.

With hierarchical structures and interconnections, the ontology-based factual data can be expanded to other concepts, enabling us to generate more sophisticated inferences over the information. For instance, a typical information retrieval system might request that a user modify or further constrain the original query when the retrieved documents are marginally related. Through an ontological model, however, an application can automatically manipulate the grain size of the query response and the scope of documents returned by shifting its focus according to related concepts. We assume that this method will enhance the quality of relevance feed back in information retrieval.

Under this theoretical premise, we built a Fact Database Containing 260 world nations and incorporated it into the KBAE. The process of creating the Fact Database consisted of three stages. At the first stage knowledge is extracted from HTML sources using a resource-specific parser. At the second stage, the output from the parser is fully-automatically refined to conform to ontological formats. Lastly, refined resources are incorporated into the KBAE which has the Ontology as its conceptual basis for all knowledge resources.

This Fact Database is currently connected to lexicon entries through ontological mappings, which are used to generate text meaning representations (TMR) from the text. The monetary units for the nations are mapped to Chinese, Spanish and English lexical items. These resources are being incorporated into a knowledge-based cross language information retrieval system that exploits these connections in its inferencing.

There is still a significant amount of work required to build a useful, large-scale Fact Database. The current scope of this resource is not yet sufficient for handling diverse factual inferencing and we currently do not have a way to test the accuracy or benefit of this resource in NLP applications. Nonetheless we feel that this approach has the potential to improve the quality of NLP Systems through exploitations of the connected knowledge resources that we have described.

Intrusion Detection by Combining Multiple Hidden Markov Models

Jongho Choy and Sung-Bae Cho

Department of Computer Science, Yonsei University
134 Shinchon-dong, Sudaemun-ku, Seoul 120-749, Korea
{hosoft,sbcho}@candy.yonsei.ac.kr

Abstract. Intrusion detection techniques can be divided into two groups according to the type of information they use: misuse detection and anomaly detection. Anomaly detection models normal behaviors and attempts to detect intrusions by noting significant deviations from normal behavior. By constructing models using multiple measures and combining them, we can expect an enhanced reliability in intrusion detection. In this paper, we propose a technique that combine multiple models using voting technique to improve the detection rate of intrusion detection system.

The intrusion detection system is based on anomaly detection technique using hidden Markov model (HMM). Each HMM models and evaluates one aspect of events, which are collected by Sun Microsystem's Basic Security Module (BSM) auditing facility. Usually each event, such as a BSM event, consists of several measures. When one event is evaluated through each model, a vector of evaluation values is generated. A system call, one of the measures from BSM, can be either perfectly normal or very dangerous according to the situation. For example, a write() system call to an ordinary user file is normal, whereas it is suspiciously dangerous if done to a system file by an unprivileged user. Thus, a framework that can effectively combine various measures is needed.

In HMM, the probability with which a given sequence is generated from a model can be calculated using forward-backward procedure and an optimal model can also be built from a collection of sequences using Baum-Welch reestimation formulas. If normal behavior is modeled into an HMM, we can determine whether current behavior is normal or not by comparing the evaluation value of current behavior sequence against the model's threshold for normal behavior. Each HMM determines whether current sequence is abnormal from the measure's point of view it is responsible for and participates in final anomaly decision with a weight W_m according to its confidence. Voting is to determine whether or not the total result $R = \sum W_m * V_m$, where V_m representing a model's voting value, is greater than or equal to the threshold T.

In the experiment, a model based on system call measure and one on measure reduced by Self Organizing Map (SOM) are combined with voting. Each model is given the same voting weight. With unanimity voting, the overall false-positive error rate, a pivotal anomaly detection technique evaluation criterion, has been enhanced to 1.18% in contrast to those of previous models' 5.33% and 23.53%, respectively.

Conceptual Classification and Browsing of Internet FAQs Using Self-Organizing Neural Networks *

Hyun-Don Kim, Joon-Hyun Ahn, and Sung-Bae Cho

Department of Computer Science, Yonsei University
134 Shinchon-dong, Sudaemoon-ku, Seoul 120-749, Korea
{neoace, jhahn, sbcho}@candy.yonsei.ac.kr

Abstract. Widespread use of computer and internet leads to an abundant supply of information, so that many services for facilitating fluent utilization of the information have appeared. However, many computer users are not so familiar with such services that they need assistant systems to use the services effectively. In case of the internet portal services, users' e-mail questions are answered by operator, but the increasing number of users brings plenty of burdens. At the time of writing this paper, more than 5 million people use the Hanmail net that is the biggest portal service in Korea and users' questions per day come to about 200 cases. It is redundant and time-consuming to respond to duplicated questions by hand, and even worse user may not satisfy with the response time. Automatic processing of users' questions might be not only efficient for operators who can avoid redundant task but also satisfiable for users.

In this paper, we propose a two-level self-organizing map (SOM) which automatically responds to the users' questions on internet, and helps them to find their answer for themselves by browsing the map hierarchically. The system consists of two parts: classification and browsing subsystems. The classification system also consists of two parts. The first part is preprocessing and keyword clustering which help to encode the input vector for the next classification module. In case of keyword clustering, SOM reduces a variable length question to a normalized vector. Keyword clustering SOM plays the similar role of the thesaurus which discriminates the synonyms. The second part is classifying the queries and matching them with the corresponding answers by another SOM called document classification SOM. The browsing system is based on the completely learned document classification SOM. It helps users to search their answer conceptually by developing the system hierarchically with topology-preserving property of SOM.

Experiments with real world data from Hanmail net show the usefulness of the proposed method. The size of keyword clustring SOM is fexed as 10×10 and the size of document classification SOM is fixed as 150×150. The accuracy is 95.01% for training data and 82.7% for test data with 4.7% error rate.

---

* This research was supported by Brain Science and Engineering Research Program sponsored by Korean Ministry of Science and Technology.

The Role of Abduction in Internet-Based Applications

Akinori Abe

NTT Communication Science Laboratories

The Internet is a jewel box of information. Accordingly, research on an inference system interacting with information on the Internet is quite important to building an intelligent inference system. The main reason for this is that if we use information on the WWW, it is not necessary to build a large knowledge base by ourselves. Instead, missing or brand-new information can be searched in the Internet and then added when it is necessary. From this viewpoint, we are now doing research on an integrated reasoning system (Decision Support system for the Internet Users (DSIU)) involving knowledge acquisition from the Internet, knowledge selection, knowledge formation (integration), reasoning, and evaluation of the results of the reasoning [2]. The Internet includes a huge amount of knowledge and likely includes inconsistent information and errors. Moreover, some information sets may be missing. As a result, it becomes necessary to deal with an incomplete knowledge base.

This poster shows the role of abduction that can deal with an incomplete knowledge base as follows:

1. Explanation of an observation (specification).
   The proposed Internet-based application, DSIU, offers appropriate suggestions to the users according to their demands or preferences. Actually, it is a decision support system that operates according to the specification (observation). This type of reasoning is done by abduction or hypothetical reasoning.
2. Creation of missing knowledge.
   DSIU uses a knowledge base automatically retrieved from the Internet. Unfortunately, it may be incomplete, so a certain technique that can create missing knowledge is required. Therefore, abductive methods that can generate necessary knowledge are used for Internet-based applications.

In fact, in order to play the second role, Abductive Analogical Reasoning (AAR) [1] that can create missing knowledge is adopted. AAR can create necessary knowledge by referring to the existing knowledge to explain the observation.

References

1. Abe A.: *Abductive Analogical Reasoning, Systems and Computers in Japan, Vol. 31, No. 1, pp. 11–19* (2000)
2. Fujimoto K. and Matsuzawa K.: *Intelligent systems using web-pages as knowledge base for statistical decision making, New Generation Computing, Vol. 17, No. 4, pp. 349–358* (1999)

FERRET: An Intelligent Assistant for Internet Searching

Juhua Zhou and Jacky Baltes[1]

University of Auckland, Auckland, New Zealand,
j.baltes@auckland.ac.nz,
http://www.citr.auckland.ac.nz/ jacky

This paper describes the design and implementation of Ferret, an information-seeking assistant that helps a user find information on the World Wide Web. It analyzes and automatically clusters the returned pages from a search engine.

The Internet today contains millions of WWW pages containing a huge amount of information. In theory, this information is only a few keystrokes away. Automatic search engines are the most popular method for finding information. However, these search engines often return thousands of results even for specific queries. A lot of the returned pages are not relevant.

One reason for the large number of returned pages is that keywords often refer to different concepts. For example, cookies can refer to a method for maintaining state information on a WWW browser or oven-baked goodies.

The goal of FERRET is to automatically determine different concepts for the returned WWW pages and to cluster the pages into different groups. FERRET completes these tasks in several steps. Firstly, it lets users submit their search query and the desired page type and fetches the result pages from the search engine. Secondly, it filters the returned results according to the selected type. Then it extracts keyphrases from the pages and represents them with generated attributes. Finally it clusters the pages and presents the results in dynamic web pages where users can browse the results.

The paper primarily investigates three issues: (1) extracting keyphrases from web pages, (2) extracting features and creating a representation of web pages, and (3) clustering web pages. The paper contrasts the related machine learning techniques and selects KEA to extract keyphrases from pages and AutoClass to cluster pages. The representation of pages has been the main focus of the thesis. To build the representation for pages, the paper examines the possible resources of extracting features from text content and HTML components of web pages and selects extracted keyphrases and links.

The evaluation shows that FERRET is able to cluster web pages with high accuracy on both correctly clustered page numbers and class number and significantly outperforms random clustering.

Based on initial exploration, the authors are optimistic that FERRET sets up a mechanism by which the software agent can analyze the web pages and cluster them. FERRET can guide search engine users to access relevant pages and to avoid reading irrelevant pages and thus lead users to efficient searching. The clustering can provide users with a concept map of knowledge areas.

Author Index

Aamodt, A. 712
Abe, A. 831
Abraham, A. 510
Ahn, J.-H. 830
Aida, T. 827
Al Amin, A. 817
Albrecht, D.W. 241
Amamiya, M. 825
Amari, S.-i. 2, 199
Antoniou, G. 27
Arai, S. 125
Asaka, M. 373

Babaguchi, N. 104
Baltes, J. 832
Bayer Zubeck, V. 521
Becht, M. 805
Beliakov, G. 794
Billington, D. 27
Brusey, J. 806
Buchheim, T. 362
Buck, S. 809
Burger, I.C. 275
Byeon, O. 167

Chao, Y. 815
Cho, S.-B. 404, 829, 830
Choy, J. 829
Collins, D. 555

Dietterich, T. 521
Dixon, S. 778
Doktor, K. 241
Dowe, D.L. 61

Elio, R. 394
Estivill-Castro, V. 208, 424

Farr, G.E. 61
Foo, N. 318
Frost, F. 480, 490
Fujitani, H. 825
Fukumizu, K. 199
Fukuta, N. 810

George, S. 252
Goebel, R. 3

Goh, K.S. 797
Goodwin, S.D. 457, 469
Goto, S. 373
Governatori, G. 27
Guo, Y. 599

Haddadi, A. 394
Hamada, Y. 638
Hanaoka, M. 146
Hanek, R. 577
Harland, J. 817
Hasegawa, R. 793
Hashimoto, K. 734
Hayashimoto, A. 792
He, H. 799
He, L. 815
Heidema, J. 275
Hengst, B. 533
Hetzel, G. 362
Hirashima, T. 745
Hori, K. 340
Huang, Z. 799

Ikeda, M. 826
Inaba, A. 826
Inoue, T. 373
Inuzuka, N. 807
Ishii, N. 819
Ishikawa, T. 83
Ishizuka, M. 93, 790
Ito, M. 812
Ito, N. 804, 819
Ito, T. 810
Itoh, H. 588, 815
Iwahashi, N. 657
Iwata, A. 136
Iwata, K. 819

Jansen, A.R. 61
Jefferies, M.E. 808
Jennings, N. 1
Jeong, C.-S. 803
Jitnah, N. 252

Kaneko, T. 72
Kanoh, M. 588

Karri, V. 480, 490
Katagiri, Y. 816
Kato, S. 115, 588
Kato, T. 823
Kawai, S. 72
Kijsirikul, B. 690
Kim, H.-D. 830
Kim, H.-S. 404
Kim, T. 167
Kindermann, G. 362
Kita, M. 793
Kitahashi, T. 104
Kitamura, Y. 723
Kitano, H. 544, 804
Kitchen, L. 446
Kobayashi, M. 146
Koehler, S. 828
Koesmarno, H. 799
Komatsu, K. 789
Koo, H.-S. 803
Koshimura, M. 793

Lafrenz, R. 805
Lamb, P. 756
Lee, J.H.-m. 795
Lee, J.K. 4
Lee, K. 167, 617
Lee, K.-F. 5
Lee, Y. 199, 617
Leow, W.K. 500
Leung, H.-f. 795
Levi, P. 362, 805
Li, Xiaodong 814
Li, Xiaoli 824
Li, Y. 297
Liang, L.Y. 415
Lim, A. 797
Lim, S. 167
Liu, J. 824
Lopes, G. 627
Lu, Y. 5
Lukose, D. 818
Luo, X. 795

Ma, K.T. 701
Maeder, A. 177
Magill, W. 814
Maher, M.J. 27
Marcenac, P. 383
Matsui, T. 136, 807

Matsumoto, K. 734
Matsuo, H. 115, 136
Matsuo, Y. 790
Matsushita, M. 823
Matsuzuka, T. 668
McCabe, A. 801
McConachy, R. 252
McGinty, L. 791
Meknavin, S. 690
Mexia, J. 627
Meyer, T. 286
Mine, T. 825
Miyahara, K. 679
Miyamoto, Y. 802
Miyashita, K. 435
Mizoguchi, R. 723, 826
Mizuno, K. 638, 792
Moriyama, K. 329

Nagarajan, S. 457
Nakadai, K. 544
Nakamura, T. 815
Nakano, A. 745
Nakasuka, S. 340
Nath, B. 510
Nayak, A. 38
Nicholson, A.E. 241, 264
Nishihara, N. 789
Nishihara, S. 435, 638, 792
Noda, I. 811
Numao, M. 83, 329

Ohara, K. 104
Ohsuga, S. 16, 827
Ohta, M. 804
Ok, S. 435
Okada, M. 647
Okuma, A. 219
Okuno, H.G. 544
Onabuta, T. 373
Ono, S. 638
Oswald, N. 805
Ozono, T. 813

Pagnucco, M. 38
Pang, W. 469
Park, H. 199
Paul, M. 820
Payne, T.R. 125
Pazzani, M.J. 679

Peppas, P. 38
Pham, B. 177
Prendinger, H. 93
Prokopenko, M. 38

Rainsford, C.P. 798
Ray, P. 818
Reed, N. 566
Ribeiro, A. 627
Riedmiller, M. 809
Roddick, J.F. 798
Rumantir, G.W. 230

Sakai, H. 219
Sanders, M.J. 796
Sano, T. 723
Sasiphongpairoege, P. 690
Sattar, A. 457
Scerri, P. 566
Schulé, M. 805
Seki, H. 807
Setiono, R. 500
Shi, J. 800
Shi, P. 608, 800
Shi, Z. 824
Shin, H. 828
Shinnou, H. 822
Shintani, T. 810, 813
Shiratori, N. 734
Shirazi, M.N. 802
Sichman, J.S. 812
Singh, A. 394
Skabar, A. 177
Skalle, P. 712
Smith, L.I. 808
Smyth, B. 791
Soddell, F. 767
Soddell, J. 767
Soonthornphisaj, N. 690
Soulié, J.-C. 383
Stern, L. 446
Sugimoto, T. 308
Sumita, E. 820, 821
Supnithi, T. 826
Suzuki, N. 647
Sveen, J. 712
Sycara, K. 125, 810

Tadokoro, S. 804
Taka, H. 104
Takagi, Y. 638

Takahashi, T. 816
Takeda, H. 668
Takeuchi, A. 745
Takeuchi, Y. 647, 816
Talko, B. 446
Tam, V. 701
Taniguchi, Y. 668
Teng, C.M. 188
Terano, T. 83
Thiébaux, S. 756
Thompson, R.G. 415
Toleman, M. 818
Toyoda, J. 826

Uehara, K. 802
Uther, W.T.B. 156

Van, T. 799
Veloso, M.M. 156

Wang, H.-F. 5
Weitzenfeld, A. 351
Wen, J.-R. 5
Wilkin, T.A. 264
Winikoff, M. 817
Wong, P. 50
Wyeth, G. 555

Yairi, T. 340
Yamada, K. 815
Yamada, R. 810
Yamaguchi, K. 72
Yamamoto, T. 93
Yamazaki, H. 146
Yang, J. 208
Yang, Q. 5
Ydrén, J. 566
Yeap, W.-K. 808
Yokoyama, S. 789
Yonezawa, H. 823
Young, D.M. 415

Zhang, C. 297
Zhang, D. 318
Zhang, G. 5
Zhang, H.-J. 5
Zhang, W. 599
Zhao, S. 608
Zhao, Y. 800
Zhou, J. 832
Zukerman, I. 241, 252

Lecture Notes in Artificial Intelligence (LNAI)

Vol. 1735: J.W. Amtrup, Incremental Speech Translation. XV, 200 pages. 1999.

Vol. 1739: A. Braffort, R. Gherbi, S. Gibet, J. Richardson, D. Teil (Eds.), Gesture-Based Communication in Human-Computer Interaction. Proceedings, 1999. XI, 333 pages. 1999.

Vol. 1744: S. Staab, Grading Knowledge: Extracting Degree Information from Texts. X, 187 pages. 1999.

Vol. 1747: N. Foo (Ed.), Adavanced Topics in Artificial Intelligence. Proceedings, 1999. XV, 500 pages. 1999.

Vol. 1757: N.R. Jennings, Y. Lespérance (Eds.), Intelligent Agents VI. Proceedings, 1999. XII, 380 pages. 2000.

Vol. 1759: M.J. Zaki, C.-T. Ho (Eds.), Large-Scale Parallel Data Mining. VIII, 261 pages. 2000.

Vol. 1760: J.-J. Ch. Meyer, P.-Y. Schobbens (Eds.), Formal Models of Agents. Poceedings. VIII, 253 pages. 1999.

Vol. 1761: R. Caferra, G. Salzer (Eds.), Automated Deduction in Classical and Non-Classical Logics. Proceedings. VIII, 299 pages. 2000.

Vol. 1771: P. Lambrix, Part-Whole Reasoning in an Object-Centered Framework. XII, 195 pages. 2000.

Vol. 1772: M. Beetz, Concurrent Reactive Plans. XVI, 213 pages. 2000.

Vol. 1775: M. Thielscher, Challenges for Action Theories. XIII, 138 pages. 2000.

Vol. 1778: S. Wermter, R. Sun (Eds.), Hybrid Neural Systems. IX, 403 pages. 2000.

Vol. 1788: A. Moukas, C. Sierra, F. Ygge (Eds.), Agent Mediated Electronic Commerce II. IX, 239 pages. 2000.

Vol. 1792: E. Lamma, P. Mello (Eds.), AI*IA 99: Advances in Artificial Intelligence. Proceedings, 1999. XI, 392 pages. 2000.

Vol. 1793: O. Cairo, L.E. Sucar, F.J. Cantu (Eds.), MICAI 2000: Advances in Artificial Intelligence. Proceedings, 2000. XIV, 750 pages. 2000.

Vol. 1794: H. Kirchner, C. Ringeissen (Eds.), Frontiers of Combining Systems. Proceedings, 2000. X, 291 pages. 2000.

Vol. 1804: B. Azvine, N. Azarmi, D.D. Nauck (Eds.), Intelligent Systems and Soft Computing. XVII, 359 pages. 2000.

Vol. 1805: T. Terano, H. Liu, A.L.P. Chen (Eds.), Knowledge Discovery and Data Mining. Proceedings, 2000. XIV, 460 pages. 2000.

Vol. 1809: S. Biundo, M. Fox (Eds.), Recent Advances in AI Planning. Proceedings, 1999. VIII, 373 pages. 2000.

Vol. 1810: R. López de Mántaras, E. Plaza (Eds.), Machine Learning: ECML 2000. Proceedings, 2000. XII, 460 pages. 2000.

Vol. 1813: P.L. Lanzi, W. Stolzmann, S.W. Wilson (Eds.), Learning Classifier Systems. X, 349 pages. 2000.

Vol. 1821: R. Loganantharaj, G. Palm, M. Ali (Eds.), Intelligent Problem Solving. Proceedings, 2000. XVII, 751 pages. 2000.

Vol. 1822: H.H. Hamilton, Advances in Artificial Intelligence. Proceedings, 2000. XII, 450 pages. 2000.

Vol. 1831: D. McAllester (Ed.), Automated Deduction – CADE-17. Proceedings, 2000. XIII, 519 pages. 2000.

Vol. 1834: J.-C. Heudin (Ed.), Virtual Worlds. Proceedings, 2000. XI, 314 pages. 2000.

Vol. 1835: D. N. Christodoulakis (Ed.), Natural Language Processing – NLP 2000. Proceedings, 2000. XII, 438 pages. 2000.

Vol. 1836: B. Masand, M. Spiliopoulou (Eds.), Web Usage Analysis and User Profiling. Proceedings, 2000. V, 183 pages. 2000.

Vol. 1847: R. Dyckhoff (Ed.), Automated Reasoning with Analytic Tableaux and Related Methods. Proceedings, 2000. X, 441 pages. 2000.

Vol. 1849: C. Freksa, W. Brauer, C. Habel, K.F. Wender (Eds.), Spatial Cognition II. XI, 420 pages. 2000.

Vol. 1860: M. Klusch, L. Kerschberg (Eds.), Cooperative Information Agents IV. Proceedings, 2000. XI, 285 pages. 2000.

Vol. 1861: J. Lloyd, V. Dahl, U. Furbach, M. Kerber, K.-K. Lau, C. Palamidessi, L. Moniz Pereira, Y. Sagiv, P.J. Stuckey (Eds.), Computational Logic – CL 2000. Proceedings, 2000. XIX, 1379 pages.

Vol. 1864: B. Y. Choueiry, T. Walsh (Eds.), Abstraction, Reformulation, and Approximation. Proceedings, 2000. XI, 333 pages. 2000.

Vol. 1865: K.R. Apt, A.C. Kakas, E. Monfroy, F. Rossi (Eds.), New Trends Constraints. Proceedings, 1999. X, 339 pages. 2000.

Vol. 1866: J. Cussens, A. Frisch (Eds.), Inductive Logic Programming. Proceedings, 2000. X, 265 pages. 2000.

Vol. 1867: B. Ganter, G.W. Mineau (Eds.), Conceptual Structures: Logical, Linguistic, and Computational Issues. Proceedings, 2000. XI, 569 pages. 2000.

Vol. 1881: C. Zhang, V.-W. Soo (Eds.), Design and Applications of Intelligent Agents. Proceedings, 2000. X, 183 pages. 2000.

Vol. 1886: R. Mizoguchi, J. Slaney (Eds.), PRICAI 2000: Topics in Artificial Intelligence. Proceedings, 2000. XX, 835 pages. 2000.

Vol. 1889: M. Anderson, P. Cheng, V. Haarslev (Eds.), Theory and Application of Diagrams. Proceedings, 2000. XII, 504 pages. 2000.

Lecture Notes in Computer Science

Vol. 1851: M.M. Halldórsson (Ed.), Algorithm Theory – SWAT 2000. Proceedings, 2000. XI, 564 pages. 2000.

Vol. 1852: T. Thierauf: The Computational Complexity of Equivalence and Isomorphism Problems. VIII, 135 pages. 2000.

Vol. 1853: U. Montanari, J.D.P. Rolim, E. Welzl (Eds.), Automata, Languages and Programming. Proceedings, 2000. XVI, 941 pages. 2000.

Vol. 1854: G. Lacoste, B. Pfitzmann, M. Steiner, M. Waidner (Eds.), SEMPER — Secure Electronic Marketplace for Europe. XVIII, 350 pages. 2000.

Vol. 1855: E.A. Emerson, A.P. Sistla (Eds.), Computer Aided Verification. Proceedings, 2000. X, 582 pages. 2000.

Vol. 1857: J. Kittler, F. Roli (Eds.), Multiple Classifier Systems. Proceedings, 2000. XII, 404 pages. 2000.

Vol. 1858: D.-Z. Du, P. Eades, V. Estivill-Castro, X. Lin, A. Sharma (Eds.), Computing and Combinatorics. Proceedings, 2000. XII, 478 pages. 2000.

Vol. 1860: M. Klusch, L. Kerschberg (Eds.), Cooperative Information Agents IV. Proceedings, 2000. XI, 285 pages. 2000. (Subseries LNAI).

Vol. 1861: J. Lloyd, V. Dahl, U. Furbach, M. Kerber, K.-K. Lau, C. Palamidessi, L. Moniz Pereira, Y. Sagiv, P.J. Stuckey (Eds.), Computational Logic – CL 2000. Proceedings, 2000. XIX, 1379 pages. (Subseries LNAI).

Vol. 1862: P.G. Clote, H. Schwichtenberg (Eds.), Computer Science Logic. Proceedings, 2000. XIII, 543 pages. 2000.

Vol. 1863: L. Carter, J. Ferrante (Eds.), Languages and Compilers for Parallel Computing. Proceedings, 1999. XII, 500 pages. 2000.

Vol. 1864: B. Y. Choueiry, T. Walsh (Eds.), Abstraction, Reformulation, and Approximation. Proceedings, 2000. XI, 333 pages. 2000. (Subseries LNAI).

Vol. 1865: K.R. Apt, A.C. Kakas, E. Monfroy, F. Rossi (Eds.), New Trends Constraints. Proceedings, 1999. X, 339 pages. 2000. (Subseries LNAI).

Vol. 1866: J. Cussens, A. Frisch (Eds.), Inductive Logic Programming. Proceedings, 2000. X, 265 pages. 2000. (Subseries LNAI).

Vol. 1867: B. Ganter, G.W. Mineau (Eds.), Conceptual Structures: Logical, Linguistic, and Computational Issues. Proceedings, 2000. XI, 569 pages. 2000. (Subseries LNAI).

Vol. 1868: P. Koopman, C. Clack (Eds.), Implementations of Functional Languages. Proceedings, 1999. IX, 199 pages. 2000.

Vol. 1869: M. Aagaard, J. Harrison (Eds.), Theorem Proving in Higher Order Logics. Proceedings, 2000. IX, 535 pages. 2000.

Vol. 1872: J. van Leeuwen, O. Watanabe, M. Hagiya, P.D. Mosses, T. Ito (Eds.), Theoretical Computer Science. Proceedings, 2000. XV, 630 pages. 2000.

Vol. 1876: F. J. Ferri, J. Iñesta, A. Amin, P. Pudil (Eds.), Advances in Pattern Recognition. Proceedings, 2000. XVIII, 901 pages. 2000.

Vol. 1877: C. Palamidessi (Ed.), CONCUR 2000 – Concurrency Theory. Proceedings, 2000. XI, 612 pages. 2000.

Vol. 1878: J.P. Bowen, S. Dunne, A. Galloway, S. King (Eds.), ZB 2000: Formal Specification and Development in Z and B. Proceedings, 2000. XIV, 511 pages. 2000.

Vol. 1879: M. Paterson (Ed.), Algorithms – ESA 2000. Proceedings, 2000. IX, 450 pages. 2000.

Vol. 1880: M. Bellare (Ed.), Advances in Cryptology – CRYPTO 2000. Proceedings, 2000. XI, 545 pages. 2000.

Vol. 1881: C. Zhang, V.-W. Soo (Eds.), Design and Applications of Intelligent Agents. Proceedings, 2000. X, 183 pages. 2000. (Subseries LNAI).

Vol. 1883: B. Triggs, A. Zisserman, R. Szeliski (Eds.), Vision Algorithms: Theory and Practice. Proceedings, 1999. X, 383 pages. 2000.

Vol. 1886: R. Mizoguchi, J. Slaney (Eds.), PRICAI 2000: Topics in Artificial Intelligence. Proceedings, 2000. XX, 835 pages. 2000. (Subseries LNAI).

Vol. 1889: M. Anderson, P. Cheng, V. Haarslev (Eds.), Theory and Application of Diagrams. Proceedings, 2000. XII, 504 pages. 2000. (Subseries LNAI).

Vol. 1892: P. Brusilovsky, O. Stock, C. Strapparava (Eds.), Adaptive Hypermedia and Adaptive Web-Based Systems. Proceedings, 2000. XIII, 422 pages. 2000.

Vol. 1893: M. Nielsen, B. Rovan (Eds.), Mathematical Foundations of Computer Science 2000. Proceedings, 2000. XIII, 710 pages. 2000.

Vol. 1896: R. W. Hartenstein, H. Grünbacher (Eds.), Field-Programmable Logic and Applications. Proceedings, 2000. XVII, 856 pages. 2000.

Vol. 1897: J. Gutknecht, W. Weck (Eds.), Modular Programming Languages. Proceedings, 2000. XII, 299 pages. 2000.

Vol. 1899: H.-H. Nagel, F.J. Perales López (Eds.), Articulated Motion and Deformable Objects. Proceedings, 2000. X, 183 pages. 2000.

Vol. 1900: A. Bode, T. Ludwig, W. Karl, R. Wismüller (Eds.), Euro-Par 2000 Parallel Processing. Proceedings, 2000. XXXV, 1368 pages. 2000.

Vol. 1912: Y. Gurevich, P.W. Kutter, M. Odersky, L. Thiele (Eds.), Abstract State Machines. Proceedings, 2000. X, 381 pages. 2000.

Vol. 1913: K. Jansen, S. Khuller (Eds.), Approximation Algorithms for Combinatorial Optimization. Proceedings, 2000. IX, 275 pages. 2000.